Basic Marketing

A Global-Managerial Approach

NINTH CANADIAN EDITION

Basic Marketing

A Global-Managerial Approach

NINTH CANADIAN EDITION

STANLEY J. SHAPIRO, PhD

Simon Fraser University

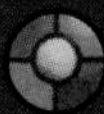

WILLIAM D. PERREAULT, JR. PhD

University of North Carolina

E. JEROME McCARTHY, PhD

Michigan State University

Toronto Montreal New York Burr Ridge Bangkok Bogotá
Caracas Lisbon London Madrid Mexico City Milan
New Delhi Seoul Singapore Sydney Taipei

McGraw-Hill
Ryerson Limited

A Subsidiary of The ***McGraw·Hill*** *Companies*

Basic Marketing
A Global–Managerial Approach
Ninth Canadian Edition

ISBN: 0-07-560536-8

1 2 3 4 5 6 7 8 9 10 GTC 8 7 6 5 4 3 2 1 9

Printed and bound in Canada

Sponsoring Editors: Evelyn Veitch/Paul Hutton
Associate Editor: Lenore Gray Spence
Manager, Editorial Services: Susan Calvert
Supervising Editor: Margaret Henderson
Production Co-ordinator: Nicla Dattolico
Cover Illustration: Bob Kebic
Typesetter: Carlisle Communication, Ltd.
Printer: Transcontinental Printing

Canadian Cataloguing in Publication Data

Shapiro, Stanley J
Basic marketing: a global-managerial approach

9th Canadian ed.
E. Jerome McCarthy listed first on 1st–7th Canadian eds.
Includes bibliographical references and index.
ISBN 0-07-560536-8

1. Marketing – Management. I. Perreault, William D. II. McCarthy, E. Jerome (Edmund Jerome). III. Title.

HF5415.13.M31 1999 658.8 C99-930110-1

To Roberta

Partner "par excellence" in all the joint ventures of a lifetime

SJS

Contents

Chapter Three
The Changing Marketing Environment 58

Chapter Four
Using Marketing Information to Make Better Decisions 86

Chapter Five
The Canadian Consumer Market: Demographic and Economic Dimensions 120

Chapter Six
Behavioural Dimensions of the Consumer Market 148

Chapter Seven
The Buying Behaviour of Business and Organizational Customers 172

Chapter Eight
Finding Target Markets Through Segmentation 204

Chapter Nine
Product Planning for Goods and Services 230

Chapter Thirteen

Chapter Fourteen

Chapter Fifteen

Chapter Nineteen
Developing Innovative Marketing Plans 508

Chapter Twenty
Implementing and Controlling Marketing Plans 534

Chapter Twenty-One
Managing Marketing's Link with Other Functional Areas 564

Preface

Can a textbook be a "contemporary classic"? We'd like to think that *Basic Marketing* qualifies as such. We consider it a classic text because its approach to the study of marketing continues to be as relevant today as when it was first developed. At the same time, this text is as contemporary as we could possibly make it. Both the most recent developments in marketing thought and the most important changes in current marketing practices are presented. In designing the product known as *Basic Marketing*, Ninth Canadian Edition, we have practised what we insist all successful marketers must do. The importance of being market driven and exceeding the expectations of our customers, instructors, and students alike, has been first and foremost in our minds throughout the entire process.

This edition introduces a number of important innovations, while simultaneously building on the traditional strengths of the text and all of the supporting materials that accompany it. We planned this revision based on extensive and detailed user feedback. That feedback gave us hundreds of ideas for additions, changes, and improvements. We'll highlight some of those changes in this Preface, but first it's useful to put this newest edition in a longer-term perspective.

The first American edition of *Basic Marketing* pioneered an innovative structure—using the four Ps with a managerial approach—for the introductory marketing course. Since publication of that first edition, there have been constant changes in marketing management. Some of the changes have been dramatic, and others have been subtle. Throughout all of these changes, *Basic Marketing*—and the supporting materials to accompany it—have been more widely used than any other teaching package for introductory marketing. It is gratifying that the four Ps concept has proved to be an organizing structure that has worked well and stood the test of time.

Of course, this position of leadership is not the result of a single strength or of one long-lasting innovation. With each new edition of *Basic Marketing*, we have strived to meet the needs of students and faculty. We believe that attention to quality in every aspect of the text and support materials does make a difference—a belief consistently reaffirmed by the enthusiastic response of students and teachers alike.

We believe that the Ninth Canadian Edition of *Basic Marketing* is the highest-quality teaching and learning resource available for the introductory course. The whole text and all the supporting materials have been critically revised, updated, and rewritten. As in past editions, clear and interesting communication has been a priority. Careful explanations provide a crisp focus on the important basics of strategic market planning. At the same time, we have researched and introduced new concepts and integrated new examples that bring the concepts alive. Some of the most significant of the many changes in this text are highlighted in Exhibit P–1.

The aim of all this revising, refining, editing, and illustrating is to make sure that each student really does get a good feel for a market-directed system and how he or she can help it—and some company—run better. We believe marketing is important and exciting, and we want every student who reads *Basic Marketing* to share our enthusiasm.

The Ninth Canadian Edition of *Basic Marketing* continues to emphasize strategic market planning. The important concepts in marketing management are introduced in a sequence designed to facilitate student understanding. This is achieved in part by the effort made to encourage readers to view the marketing process through the eyes of marketing managers. Using feedback from reviewers, the organization and sequencing of chapters have been somewhat revised. However, this has been done in a way that still makes it possible for professors to sequence the chapters in different ways to meet different needs.

The first chapter deals with the nature of marketing—touching upon its macro role (a topic revisited in greater detail in Chapters 11 and 22) but emphasizing its micro aspects both in business and in not-for-profit organizations. That chapter now ends with a detailed discussion of the marketing concept. This sets the stage for the second chapter—and the rest of the book—which focuses on how marketing managers respond to the opportunities they have identified by developing marketing strategies that satisfy specific target markets.

Exhibit P-1 What's New In This Edition?

1. A set of Internet Insites, prepared by Dr. Ramesh Venkat of Saint Mary's University, appear throughout the text. They go beyond the text's already extensive treatment of the Internet and explore in greater detail the current and potential impact of the Web on the practice of marketing management. The first of these Insites appears in this Preface. Additional text and illustrative material further highlight the impact of the Internet on such areas as retailing, business-to-business marketing, and marketing research. The marketing strategy followed in the launch of Sympatico, Canada's premier Internet service provider, is also presented in detail. A listing of the Internet addresses of all organizations mentioned in this text is provided in the Internet Index at the end of the text.

2. Each of the 22 chapters has a new opening vignette featuring Canadian organizations and their current marketing practices. We are particularly proud of the opening vignette for Chapter 4, which describes the marketing research strategy used for Health Canada's Challenge to Youth anti-tobacco campaign. This vignette was written for the Ninth Canadian Edition by Health Canada's social marketing team. As well, forty new Marketing Demos illustrating Canadian companies and current marketing practices appear throughout the text.

3. An exciting new Appendix C, "Marketing YOU INC.—Preparing a Personal Marketing Plan," written by Professor Deborah Lawton of the University College of the Cariboo for the Ninth Canadian Edition, shows students how to use the concepts introduced in this text to market themselves to prospective employers—both initially and throughout their careers.

4. The overall length of the text has been reduced by almost 15 percent. This was done at the request of reviewers of the Eighth Canadian Edition. These colleagues argued that a comprehensive coverage of all relevant topics could still be achieved if the amount of detail presented was reduced. In this matter, as in so many others, we took our marching orders from the market. The book appears all the stronger for our having done so.

5. Considerable effort was made to make the text more user friendly and to speak directly to the students. As well, students are frequently reminded of their responsibilities not only as future managers but also as consumers and ecologically concerned citizens.

6. The opening chapters of the text have been revised so that the initial focus is now almost entirely on marketing management. The macro-marketing material previously found in Chapter 1 has been moved to Chapters 4, 11, and 22. Experience suggests such issues are better considered after students have obtained a basic understanding of the marketing process.

7. Market segmentation is discussed after, rather than before, the student's consideration of the demographic, economic, and behavioural dimensions of consumer and organizational markets. This is but one, but perhaps the most significant, of the many changes made at the request of academic colleagues who reviewed the Eighth Canadian Edition.

8. The text incorporates the most up-to-date Canadian statistics available at the time of publication. Much of this information was drawn from 1996 Census Data released, in some cases, just days before the manuscript was sent to the publisher. The ethnic, mother tongue, and visible minority dimensions of the Canadian marketplace are highlighted in a manner reflecting the increasing importance of these factors.

9. Increased attention is paid to the role and impact of computerization in such areas as management information systems, data warehousing, electronic data interchange, point-of-purchase scanners, sales forecasting, physical distribution, and supply chain management.

10. Out of a total of 38 cases, 19 are new and 3 have been revised. Twenty-six Canadian marketing professors and four Canadian marketing practitioners contributed either one or more cases or originally commissioned material to this edition of *Basic Marketing*.

Chapter 3 alerts students to the importance of evaluating opportunities in the various external environments affecting marketing. Chapter 4 provides a contemporary view of how information—from marketing information systems and marketing research—can be used to improve each aspect of strategic market planning.

The next four chapters take a closer look at customers so that students will better understand how to segment markets and target market needs. Chapter 5 introduces the demographic and economic dimensions of the Canadian consumer market. The following two chapters focus on the behavioural features of that consumer market and on the ways that business and organizational customers such as manufacturers, market intermediaries, farmers, and government purchasers both resemble and differ from final customers. Only then is market segmentation discussed.

The next group of chapters—9 through 18—is concerned with developing an appropriate marketing mix using the four Ps: Product, Place (involving channels of distribution, logistics, and customer service), Promotion, and Price. These chapters are concerned with developing the "right" Product and making it available at the "right" Place with the "right" Promotion and the "right" Price—to satisfy target customers and still meet the objectives of the business. The key concepts related to each of the "4 Ps" are discussed in a manner that allows student thinking about strategic market planning to develop logically and systematically.

Chapter 19 reinforces the integrative nature of marketing management and offers a specific framework for creating innovative marketing plans. Chapter 20 offers updated coverage of marketing implementation and control and provides perspective on how new, computer-based approaches are reshaping these areas. The chapter also details how total quality management approaches can improve implementation and lead to better customer service.

Chapter 21 highlights the link between marketing and the company's other functional specialists. The marketing concept stresses the importance of people throughout the organization working together to satisfy customer needs at a profit. *Basic Marketing* is the only marketing text with a chapter that focuses on how to accomplish the "working together" aspect of that increasingly important idea.

The final chapter encourages the student to evaluate our marketing system. After important "macro" concepts are introduced, the effectiveness of both micro and macro marketing is explored. The competitive, ethical, social, and ecological challenges facing marketing managers, now and in the future, are also considered. Upon completing this chapter, students should review an entirely new Appendix C, which shows how they can use the marketing concepts discussed in the text to market themselves to prospective employers.

Some textbooks treat special topics—like international marketing, marketing ethics, environmental concerns, services marketing, marketing for not-for-profit organizations, and business-to-business marketing—in separate chapters. We have not done that because we are convinced that treating such topics separately leads to an unfortunate compartmentalization of ideas. We think they are too important to be isolated that way. Instead, they are interwoven and illustrated throughout the text to emphasize that marketing thinking is crucial in all aspects of our society and economy.

Understanding marketing and how to plan marketing strategies can build self-confidence—and it can help prepare students to take an active part in the business world. To move students in this direction, we deliberately include a variety of frameworks, models, classification systems, and how-to-do-it techniques that should speed the development of "marketing sense"—and enable students to analyze marketing situations in a confident and meaningful way. Taken seriously, they are practical and they work. In addition, because they are interesting and understandable, they equip students to see marketing as the challenging and rewarding area it is.

To orient students to each *Basic Marketing* chapter, objectives are included on the first page of each chapter and, to speed student understanding, important new terms are shown in orange and defined immediately. A glossary of these terms is also presented at the end of the text. Within chapters, major section headings and second-level headings immediately show how the material is organized *and* summarize key points in the text. Further, we have placed annotated photos and advertisements near the concepts they illustrate to provide a visual reminder of the ideas. All of these aids help the student to understand important concepts and to speed review before exams. End-of-chapter questions and problems offer additional opportunities. They encourage students to investigate the marketing process and develop their own ways of thinking about it. They can be used for independent study or as a basis for written assignments or class discussion.

Understanding of the text material can be deepened by analysis and discussion of specific examples. *Basic Marketing* features several different types of illustrations. Each chapter starts with an in-depth vignette chosen specifically to highlight that chapter's teaching objectives. In addition, every chapter contains Canadian marketing demos. Each demo illustrates how a particular company has developed its marketing strategy, with emphasis on a topic covered in that chapter. Because all of these demos provide an excellent basis for critical evaluation and discussion, they should be considered an essential part of the chapter.

All but three chapters end with the presentation of a computer-aided problem relevant to that chapter. These assignments also stimulate a problem-solving approach to strategic market planning and give students hands-on experience that shows how logical analysis of alternative strategies can lead to improved decision making. The award-winning software we developed specifically for use with these problems is provided free to instructors.

Once again, we've also custom developed an exciting set of video cases. Each of these combines a written case with an accompanying video. These cases provide the opportunity for students to analyze an organization's whole marketing program in more depth and with even greater integration. Marketing professors wrote the scripts for both the video and text portions of the cases—so that the videos reinforce real content while bringing a high-involvement multimedia dimension to the learning experience. And to ensure consistency with all of the other *Basic Marketing* materials, we've carefully edited and coordinated the whole effort.

We designed these cases so that students can analyze them before or after seeing the video, or even without seeing the video at all. They can be used in a variety of ways, either for class discussion or for individual assignments. We're proud of these video cases, and we're sure that they provide you with a valuable new way to learn about marketing.

The Ninth Canadian Edition of *Basic Marketing* is the centrepiece but nevertheless still only a piece of the entire *Basic Marketing* learning package. A complete listing of the components of that package is found in Exhibit P–2. However, those materials of particular interest to students are discussed below.

The most important new component of the learning package is the *Basic Marketing* home page (www.mcgrawhill.ca/college/shapiro) available to students and professors using this text. Accessing our home page will allow students to use the McGraw-Hill Learning Architecture approach to obtain a better understanding of what's in the text. "Hotlinks" to innumerable corporate, government, and media sites will also be provided. This *Basic Marketing* home page will, in addition, allow access to all sorts of relevant, up-to-the-minute material that did not become available until long after the text itself went to print. Our home page, especially if used along with Professor Venkat's Internet Insites, will provide students with an unparalleled opportunity to learn both how and to what extent this new technology is altering the way goods and services are marketed.

Also available is a new edition of *Applications in Basic Marketing*. This annually updated collection of marketing clippings—from publications such as *The Wall Street Journal, Fortune,* and *Business Week*—provides convenient access to short, interesting, and current discussions of marketing issues. There are a variety of short clippings related to each chapter in *Basic Marketing*. In addition, because we revise this collection *each year,* it can include timely material that is available in no other text.

A separate *Learning Aid* offers further opportunities to obtain a deeper understanding of the material. The *Learning Aid* can be used by the student alone or with teacher direction. Portions of the *Learning Aid* help students review what they have studied. For example, there is a list of the important new terms, true-false questions (with answers) that cover *all* the important terms and concepts, and multiple-choice questions (with answers) illustrating the kinds of questions that may appear in examinations. In addition, the *Learning Aid* has cases, exercises, and problems—

Introduction to Internet Insites

In almost every chapter of this text you will find an Internet Insite. The Insites will be related to the chapter topic. Each Insite will explore current marketing issues on the Internet and will present examples as well as Web site links. The objectives of the Internet Insites are as follows:

- To give you an understanding of how marketing concepts are being applied on the Internet.
- To highlight differences between Internet marketing and conventional marketing.
- To provide examples, and where applicable, short exercises or questions that will further your understanding of marketing on the Internet.

The terms Internet Marketing, Web-based Marketing and Electronic Commerce are used interchangeably in the Insites. The phrase virtual or electronic "marketspace" is sometimes used in the Insites because the Internet is a virtual space and not a physical space.

Internet marketing is in a state of continuous flux. Hence the ideas expressed in the Insites may have a limited life expectancy. In addition, there are many areas (such as copyright and intellectual property) where the application of laws and regulations is not yet clear.

After you read each Insite, take the time to browse through some of the Internet links provided in the text. While the Insites attempt to present diverse opinions, they do not include all points of view. Concepts are often explained with examples to trigger class discussion but are not explored in depth. Challenge the ideas expressed in the Insites. You will learn more by doing so. We hope you will find the Internet Insites to be both educational and fun.

Exhibit P-2 The Ninth Canadian Learning Package

Directly available to students
1. The *Basic Marketing* text (with cases and computer-aided problems)
2. The *Basic Marketing* home page (www.mcgrawhill.ca/college/shapiro)
3. The *Applications in Basic Marketing* readings book
4. The *Learning Aid* designed to accompany the text
5. *The Marketing Game*
Resource material for instructors
1. Instructor's Manual to accompany *Basic Marketing* (covers the text and *Learning Aid*)
2. Videotaped cases (with accompanying Instructor's Manual)
3. Teaching videos (with accompanying Instructor's Manual)
4. Instructor's Manual for *The Marketing Game*
5. Windows software for computer-aided problems
6. PowerPoint slides (with accompanying script)
7. Over 200 colour acetates supplementing the text
8. Over 200 transparency masters
9. Author prepared Manual of Tests
10. Brownstone Test generator system
11. *Instructor's CD-ROM* (multimedia teaching support system)

with clear instructions and worksheets for the student to complete. The *Learning Aid* exercises can be used as classwork or homework—to drill on certain topics and to deepen understanding of others by motivating application and then discussion. In fact, reading *Basic Marketing* and working with the *Learning Aid* can be the basic activity of the course.

Another element is *The Marketing Game!,* a microcomputer-based competitive simulation. It was developed specifically to reinforce the target marketing and strategic market planning ideas discussed in *Basic Marketing.* Students make marketing management decisions, blending the four Ps to compete for the business of different possible target markets. The innovative design of *The Marketing Game!* allows the instructor to increase the number of decision areas involved as students learn more about marketing. In fact, many instructors use the advanced levels of the game as the basis for a second course.

In closing, we return to a point raised at the beginning of this preface: *Basic Marketing* has been a leading Canadian textbook in marketing for close to twenty-five years. We take the responsibilities of that leadership seriously. We know that you want and deserve the very best teaching and learning materials possible. It is our commitment to bring you those materials—today with this edition and in the future with subsequent editions. We recognize that fulfilling this commitment requires a process of continuous improvement. Improvements, changes, and development of new elements must be ongoing—because needs change. You are an important part of this evolution, of this leadership. We encourage your feedback. Thoughtful criticisms and suggestions from students and teachers alike have helped to make *Basic Marketing* what it is. We hope that you will help make it what it will be in the future.

Stanley J. Shapiro
Simon Fraser University and
Stanley J. Shapiro Ltd.

Acknowledgments

The Ninth Canadian Edition of *Basic Marketing* could not have been prepared without many different types of support from many different people. I am most grateful to all of these individuals—not only those identified below but also anyone who, because of an error or oversight on my part, may not be adequately acknowledged in the paragraphs that follow.

How this Canadian edition differs from its predecessors is discussed in the accompanying Preface. However, each succeeding edition of any text builds on and refines what has preceded it. Consequently, all those who assisted in the preparation of previous Canadian editions are again deserving of thanks, for they have contributed as well to this latest effort. A complete listing of those individuals is found in preceding acknowledgment sections.

Contributions by professional colleagues took two forms—preparing material that was included in the text and critically evaluating both this volume and its immediate predecessor. Both types of contribution were essential to the preparation of this text. However, it was not until I was completing the accompanying Exhibit A–1 that I realized just how many others had graciously given of their time and effort.

The list appearing in Exhibit A–1 is a long one but in no way does it exhaust the honour role of individuals who provided invaluable assistance. These additional contributors include one of my former Simon Fraser students, Ms. Celina Benndorf of BC Tel Interactive, who played a key role in seeing that we received appropriate material on Sympatico. Ms. Nicole Brown, another outstanding SFU graduate now with the Open Learning Agency of British Columbia, relentlessly tracked down the Statistics Canada material required to update the text. Nicole also forwarded, from the wilds of Vancouver to the sylvan splendor of Salt Spring Island, articles which, electronic age or not, I could not access directly from Salt Spring. Ms. Eileen Fairey, Librarian for Business and Economics at Simon Fraser University, electronically provided instruction on how both the authors and the readers of this text could best access the new and exciting world of electronically based information sources. Then, of course, there was Tim Collins of Tribal Drum Computers Ltd., who painstakingly—and with a degree of patience matched only by that of a day care teacher—taught both Stan and Roberta Shapiro what they needed to know about computers and word processing in order to complete their assigned tasks.

This Canadian edition was the first prepared after McGraw-Hill purchased Times Mirror, thereby acquiring the publishing rights to this text. As might be expected, this takeover has led to some significant changes in publishing policy and procedures. Fortunately, Evelyn Veitch, our long-time Sponsoring Editor at Times Mirror, joined McGraw-Hill Ryerson after the merger and continued both to expedite matters and to provide boundless enthusiasm for the Ninth Canadian Edition. However, much of our day-to-day contact, and often it was daily contact, has been with Lenore Gray Spence, the Associate Editor for this project. I am most grateful for Lenore's patience, understanding and good humour throughout the entire process. Her colleagues at McGraw-Hill Ryerson, Margaret Henderson, Susan Calvert, and our new Sponsoring Editor Paul Hutton, who were involved in subsequent stages in the production process, also performed in an exemplary fashion.

We are grateful as well to all the many individuals and organizations that provided copyright clearance and art work for this text. Without that assistance, this edition would be lacking many of its Canadian illustrations. We are especially grateful to *Marketing Magazine* and its Editor, Stan Sutter, for granting permissions to use the many articles from that publication either as chapter opening vignettes or as Marketing Demos. Statistics Canada information is used with the permission of the Minister of Industry, as Minister responsible for Statistics Canada. Information on the availability of the wide range of data from Statistics Canada can be obtained from Statistics Canada's Regional Offices, its World Wide Web site at http://www.statcan.ca, and its toll-free access number 1-800-263-1136.

Exhibit A-1 Academic Colleagues and Marketing Practitioners Making Significant Contributions

Authors of Specially Commissioned Text Material	
1. Ramesh Venkat	Saint Mary's University
Author of the Internet Insites found throughout the text.	
2. Deborah Lawton	University College of the Cariboo
Author of Appendix C, "Marketing YOU INC.—Preparing a Personal Marketing Plan."	
3. Paulette Padanyi & Margaret Sutcliffe	Ryerson Polytechnic University
Original authors of much of the retailing material found in Chapter 13.	
4. Robert Tamilia	University of Quebec at Montreal
Author of material on Category Management and Efficient Consumer Response.	
5. Bryan Barbieri	Concordia University
Author of "A Marketing Approach for the 21st Century."	
6. James Mintz, Jane Hazel, and Tracy Schoales	Health Canada
Authors of "Challenge to Youth—*a Health Canada Anti-tobacco Campaign.*"	
7. Debra Hamilton	BC TEL Interactive
Author of "Introducing the Internet as a New Consumer Product."	
Case authors or supervisors (with affiliation at the time of case preparation)	
1. D. Aronchik	Ryerson Polytechnic University
2. Peter Banting	McMaster University
3. Ken Blawatt (3 cases)	Adjunct Professor SFU at the University College of the Cariboo
4. Maurice Borts (3 cases)	McGill University
5. Brahm Canzer (2 cases)	John Abbott College and Concordia University
6. Judith Cumby	Memorial University of Newfoundland
7. Jane Funk	Ontario Agricultural College, University of Guelph
8. Thomas Funk (3 cases)	Ontario Agricultural College, University of Guelph
9. Walter Good	University of Manitoba
10. Ken Hardy	University of Western Ontario
11. Mark Henderson (2 cases)	University of New Brunswick at Saint John
12. George Jacob	BCIT
13. David Litvack (3 cases)	University of Ottawa
14. Lindsay Meredith	Simon Fraser University
15. James Mintz	Health Canada
16. Philip Rosson	Dalhousie University
17. Julia Sagebian	Saint Mary's University
18. Robert Tamilia	University of Quebec at Montreal
19. Chris Vaughan	Saint Mary's University
20. Ramesh Venkat	Saint Mary's University
21. Chuck Weinberg	University of British Columbia
Academic Reviewers of the Eighth Canadian Edition	
1. Alex Boultbee	Seneca College
2. J. Neil Beattie	Sheridan College
3. Robert Isotalo	Lakehead University
Academic Reviewers of Selected Chapters of the Ninth Canadian Edition	
1. Alex Boultbee	Seneca College
2. Stanley J. Paliwoda	University of Calgary
SFU Colleagues Providing Valuable Input as to Content and Sequencing	
Colleen Collins-Dodd, June Francis, Lindsay Meredith, D.J. Sandhu, and Robert Wyckham	

My sincerest and most heartfelt thanks are due to my wife of 38 years and my research associate on this text for the very first time, Roberta Shapiro. Editing text, choosing visuals, searching for Marketing Demos, obtaining permissions and art work—all these tasks and many more were carried out by Roberta with the same degree of professionalism that characterized her former career as corporate counsel and a tax lawyer in private practice. I have been fortunate over the years to have had a number of extraordinary individuals working with me on this text. No one else, however, has carried out the varied mix of tasks the job requires with anything near the same relentless pursuit of excellence that characterized Roberta's involvement. If anyone ever paid homage to the old maxim "God is in the detail," it was Roberta in her commitment to this new edition. "Satisficing" has never been in her vocabulary, and on this project "good enough" never was. The end result was an incomparable performance by an editorial associate on what, in very large part because of Roberta's efforts, is the finest of the nine Canadian editions with which I have been associated. Would that Tessa, our bearded lady, could have done more than merely provide canine comic relief!

SJS

J. RICHARD BLICKSTEAD

PUBLISHER - MAGAZINE DIVISION
SENIOR VICE PRESIDENT
MARKETING & STRATEGIC PLANNING

Dear Student,

I first used this textbook during my undergraduate years. It then formed the basis for part of my graduate work. I thumbed through it again during my management consulting years and gave it to aspiring young marketers whilst managing marketing divisions or companies. Bottom line, I believe this is a very good textbook!

Marketing however, is more than just text. While this course will provide you with the fundamental principles regarding the 4 P's, customer research and brand management, successful marketers take learning to a higher level. Therefore, I would like to share my experience on what makes a great marketer.

First, always listen to the consumer. Great marketers are able to shift through reams of data to truly understand what the customer needs. Internal input is important (i.e., executive input, other departmental issues, etc.), but what really counts is how the customer feels.

Second, be on the vanguard of change. Anticipate how the market is evolving and what that means to the consumer. Marketing is all about managing transitions, but be careful, if you are too far ahead of the customer your "unbelievable" strategy may crash. Know when the second best idea is the one to choose because the customer will adopt it.

Third, take calculated risks. While the cost of failure can be high in both financial and market share terms, marketing needs visionary leaders. Ensure that your team feels empowered to try new concepts.

Fourth, know your competition. Always think of what they could do to your business and do it first. Never underestimate your competition. Think of your company as always striving to be number one, even if you are already there.

Finally, be passionate. If you dream it, you can believe it. If you can believe it, you can do it. Passion drives great ideas; that is why companies like Holt Renfrew become world class retailers!

Best wishes in your studies,

J. Richard Blickstead

When you finish this chapter, you should:

- Know what marketing is—and why you should study it.
- Understand the difference between micro-marketing and macro-marketing.
- Know what the marketing concept is—and how it should affect strategic planning in a firm or nonprofit organization.
- Understand how the marketing concept relates to customer value.
- Understand the important new terms (shown in orange).

Chap one

Marketing's Role Within the Firm or Nonprofit Organization

LIMITED®
snowboards
100 Broadview Avenue, Suite 422, Toronto, Ontario, Canada M4M 2E8
Tel 416.465.6513 Fax 416.465.0650 Visit us at www.limitedsnow.com

Limited Snowboards Inc. burst on the scene in 1993 as a Canadian design, marketing, sales, and distribution company for high-performance snowboards and related on-snow products. It supplies high-quality products designed by people who love to snowboard. The sport of snowboarding has experienced phenomenal growth and increased popularity, and so has Limited. With its strong niche-market position and its reputation as Canada's leading snowboard brand, Limited has gained strong consumer acceptance and is poised for continued success.

All of Limited's snowboards are designed and proudly manufactured in Canada. Utilizing extensive team rider product testing and feedback, Limited designs snowboards with original and innovative, terrain-specific shapes.

Limited has a worldwide distribution network covering North America, Europe, Japan, Australia, and New Zealand. North American sales are handled by independent sales representatives across Canada and the United States. International sales are handled by exclusive-territory distributors. Sales management and coordination takes place at Limited's head office in Toronto.

Limited's mission is to build the best-riding snowboards and to provide excellent customer service. High-performance snowboards, aggressive advertising in snowboard magazines, and grassroots-level promotions have allowed Limited to build brand awareness and to maintain credibility. Limited plans to continue increasing its sales and profits by strengthening its already excellent communications with team riders, customers, territory representatives, and distributors. The company's goal is to be the premier supplier of high-performance snowboards.

The major marketing issues facing Limited relate to brand identity and market niche. The snowboard industry grew phenomenally from 1993 to 1998: the market diversified and expanded, and core snowboard consumers grew more brand conscious. For these reasons, Limited is focusing on building brand awareness and customer loyalty through selling high-performance, high-quality products and promoting the company's Canadian roots. It continues to build on its market niche as a Canadian company with a reputation for excellent snowboard products. It has had stronger brand positioning in Canada than internationally, but it is increasing its brand positioning in the United States and other foreign markets as it grows at home.

Limited's marketing savvy seems to be working just fine. A retailer survey published by *Snowboard Canada* in February 1998 ranked Limited as the Canadian snowboard brand that will be stocked next season by the largest number of snowboard specialty shops in Canada.

Source: Courtesy of Limited Snowboards Inc. Used with permission.

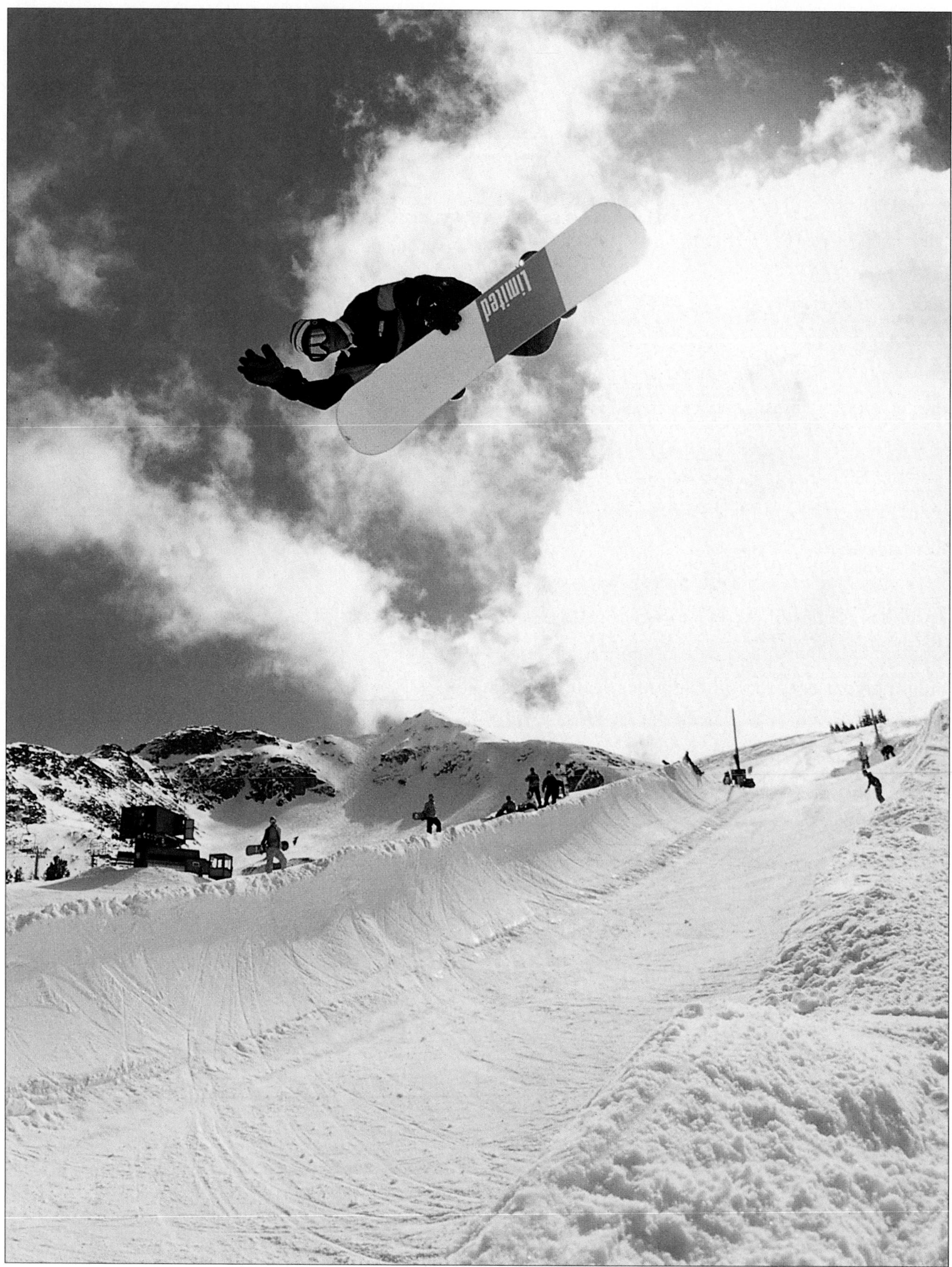

Photography by Scott Serfas ©1997. Rider: Etienne Tremblay, Limited Team Rider, at Blackcomb, B.C.

It should be obvious from this brief description of Limited's successful marketing activities that producing a good product will not produce sales and profits for a company unless there is a specific commitment and marketing plan to market that product. This chapter will introduce you to marketing, and tell you what it's all about and how it relates to the production of goods and services. This chapter will also tell you why you should study marketing, provide you with marketing definitions, and, hopefully, make you a believer in the marketing concept.

Marketing: What's it all about?

When forced to define marketing, most people, including some business managers, say that marketing means "selling" or "advertising." It's true that these are parts of marketing. But *marketing is much more than selling and advertising.*

To illustrate some of the other important things that are included in marketing, think about all the different types of snowboards that are available to snowboarders—both beginners and pros. Most snowboards are intended to do the same thing—get the snowboarder down the mountain. But a snowboarder can choose from a wide assortment of snowboards. There are different shapes, materials, weights, and lengths. You can buy a snowboard for as low as $350 or spend over $550.

The fact that the variety of snowboards is increasing complicates their production and sale. Below are listed a few of the many things a firm should do before and after it decides to produce snowboards.

1. Analyze the needs of snowboarders and determine what features appeal to these consumers.
2. Predict what types of snowboards—shapes, materials, weights, and lengths—different snowboarders will want, and decide which of these consumers the firm will try to satisfy.
3. Estimate how many of these consumers will be snowboarding over the next several years and how many snowboards they'll buy.
4. Predict approximately when these snowboarders will want to buy snowboards.
5. Determine the geographic locations of these snowboarders and how to get the firm's snowboards to them.
6. Estimate what price these snowboarders are willing to pay for their snowboards, and judge whether the firm can make a profit selling at that price.
7. Decide which kinds of promotion should be used to tell potential customers about the firm's snowboards.
8. Estimate how many competing companies will be making snowboards, how many they'll produce, what kinds, and at what prices.

The above activities are not part of **production**—actually making goods or performing services. Rather, they are part of a larger process, called **marketing,** that provides needed direction for production and helps ensure that the right goods and services are produced and find their way to consumers.

Our snowboard example shows that marketing involves much more than selling or advertising. We'll describe marketing activities throughout this book. For now, it's enough that you realize that marketing plays an essential role in providing consumers with need-satisfying goods and services.

How marketing relates to the production of goods and services

Production is a very important economic activity. Whether for lack of skill and resources or just lack of time, most people don't make most of the products they use. Picture yourself, for example, building a mountain bike, a compact disc player, or a digital watch—starting from scratch! We also turn to others to produce services such as health care, air transportation, and entertainment. Clearly, the high standard of living that most people in advanced economies enjoy is made possible by specialized production.

Products don't sell themselves

Although production is a necessary economic activity, some people overrate its importance in relation to marketing. Their attitude is reflected in the *Field of Dreams* idea that "if you build it, they will come." In other words, they think that if you just have a good product, your business will be a success. However, we have already seen that there's a lot more to marketing snowboards than just making them. The same is true for most goods and services.

The point is that production and marketing are both important parts of a total business system aimed at providing consumers with need-satisfying goods and services. Together, production and marketing supply five kinds of economic utility—form, task, time, place, and possession utility—that are needed to provide consumer satisfaction. Here, **utility** means the power to satisfy human needs. See Exhibit 1–1.

Products do not automatically provide utility

Form utility is provided when someone produces something tangible—for instance, a snowboard. **Task utility** is provided when someone performs a task for someone else—for instance, when a bank handles financial transactions. But just producing snowboards or handling bank accounts doesn't result in consumer satisfaction. Unless the product is something that consumers want, there is no need to be satisfied—and no utility.

Marketing decisions focus on the customer and include decisions about what goods and services to produce. It doesn't make sense to provide goods and services consumers don't want when there are so many things they do want or need. Marketing is concerned with what customers want—and it should guide what is produced and offered. This is an important idea, which we will develop more completely later.

Exhibit 1–1 Types of Utility and How They Are Provided

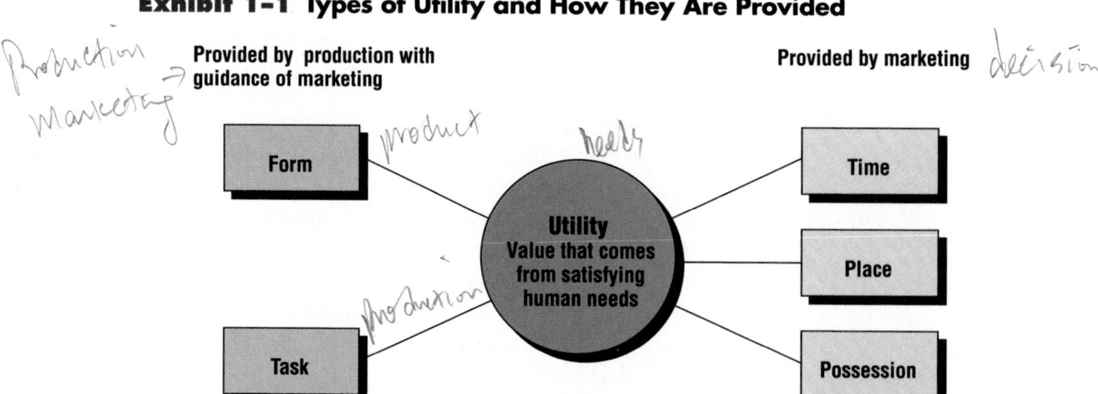

Even when marketing and production combine to provide form or task utility, consumers won't be satisfied until possession, time, and place utility are also provided. **Possession utility** means obtaining a good or service and having the right to use or consume it. Customers usually exchange money or something else of value for possession utility.

Time utility means having the product available *when* the customer wants it. And **place utility** means having the product available *where* the customer wants it. Snowboards that stay at a factory don't do anyone any good. Time and place utility are very important for services, too. For example, neighbourhood emergency care health clinics have become very popular. People just walk in as soon as they feel sick, not a day later when their doctor can schedule an appointment.

Stated simply, marketing provides time, place, and possession utility. It should also guide decisions about what goods and services should be produced to provide form utility and task utility. We'll look at how marketing does this later in Chapter 11. First, we want to discuss why you should study marketing; after that, we'll define marketing.

Why study marketing?

Marketing affects almost every aspect of daily life. All the goods and services you buy, the stores where you shop, and the radio and TV programs paid for by advertising are there because of marketing. This process doesn't come cheap. In advanced economies, marketing costs about 50 cents of each consumer's dollar. For some goods and services, the percentage is much higher.

Marketing is something you are exposed to all the time. Even your job résumé is part of a marketing campaign to sell yourself to some employer! Some courses are interesting when you take them but never relevant again once they're over. Not so with marketing—you'll be a consumer dealing with marketing for the rest of your life.

MARKETING COORDINATOR

Basketball Ontario is the provincial sport governing body for amateur basketball in the Province of Ontario. Basketball Ontario seeks an innovative, highly creative individual to manage all aspects of marketing, promotion and communications activities in conjunction with the sponsorship of Basketball Ontario programming.

Reporting to the Executive Director, you will write the template for the successful fulfillment of our contracts. A degree or a diploma in a related field is a must and excellent verbal and written communications skills are imperative. You are a good organizer with impressive strengths in creative thinking and interpersonal communications. You know what public relations is about and have produced positive media results. Your signature is a professional, mature manner in dealing with members, sponsors, the media and the public and you are skilled at managing people to satisfactorily execute program requirements. You are a self-starter; you excel at handling and prioritizing tasks in a fast-paced environment; and you work harmoniously with your colleagues, maintaining tight schedules in a dynamic, service-oriented team approach.

If this is you, forward your resume in confidence, including salary expectations, by January 23, 1998 to: Search Committee, Basketball Ontario, 1185 Eglinton Ave. E., Ste. 409, North York, ON M3C 3C6. We thank all applicants in advance, however, only those being considered will be contacted.

Basketball Ontario is an equal opportunity employer.

Marketing provides many interesting career opportunities.

Marketing will be important to your job

Another reason for studying marketing is that there are many exciting and rewarding career opportunities in marketing. Marketing is often the route to the top. Throughout this book you will find information about opportunities in different areas of marketing—in sales, advertising, product management, marketing research, distribution, and other areas. And Appendix C, which focuses on how you can use a marketing approach to plan your own future, is all about career planning, whether in marketing or other fields.

Even if you're aiming for a job that is not in marketing, you'll be working with marketing people. Knowing something about marketing will help you understand them better. It will also help you do your own job better. Marketing is important to the success of every organization. Remember, a company that can't successfully sell its products doesn't need accountants, financial managers, production managers, personnel managers, computer programmers, or credit managers.

Marketing concepts and techniques apply to nonprofit organizations, too. Many nonprofit organizations have a marketing manager. And the same basic principles used to sell soap are also used to "sell" ideas, politicians, mass transportation, health care services, conservation, museums, and even colleges and universities. Think about the school where you take this course. If you didn't know about its offerings—or if they didn't interest you—you probably would have picked some other school.[1]

Marketing affects economic growth

An even more basic reason for studying marketing is that marketing plays a big part in economic growth and development. Marketing stimulates research and new ideas—resulting in new goods and services. Marketing gives customers a choice among products. If these products satisfy customers, fuller employment, higher incomes, and a higher standard of living can result. An effective marketing system is important to the future of all nations.[2]

How should we define marketing?

The American Marketing Association defines "marketing" to mean "the process of planning and executing the conception, pricing, promotion and distribution of ideas, goods and services to create exchanges that satisfy individual and organizational objectives."[3]

But as we said earlier, some people think of marketing too narrowly as "selling and advertising." On the other hand, one authority defined marketing as the "creation and delivery of a standard of living."[4] That definition is too broad.

An important difference between the two definitions may be less obvious. The first definition is a *micro*-level definition. It focuses on activities performed by an individual organization. The second is a *macro*-level definition. It focuses on the economic welfare of a whole society.

Micro- or macro-marketing?

Which view is correct? Is marketing a set of activities done by individual firms or organizations? Or is it a social process?

To answer this question, let's go back to our snowboard example. We saw that a producer of snowboards has to perform many customer-related activities besides just making snowboards. The same is true for an insurance company, an art museum, or a family service agency. This supports the idea of marketing as a set of activities done by individual organizations.

On the other hand, people can't live on snowboards and art museums alone! In advanced economies, it takes thousands of goods and services to satisfy the many needs of society. For example, a typical Eaton's department store carries 200,000 different items. A society needs some sort of marketing system to organize the efforts of all the producers and intermediaries needed to satisfy the varied needs of all its citizens. So marketing is also an important social process.

The answer to our question is that *marketing is both a set of activities performed by organizations and a social process.* In other words, marketing exists at both the micro and macro levels. Therefore, we will use two definitions of marketing—one for micro-marketing and another for macro-marketing. The first looks at customers and the organizations that serve them. The second takes a broad view of our whole production–distribution system.

Micro-marketing defined

Micro-marketing is the performance of activities that seek to accomplish an organization's objectives by anticipating customer or client needs and directing a flow of need-satisfying goods and services from producer to customer or client.

Let's look at this definition.

Applies to profit and nonprofit organizations

To begin with, this definition applies to both profit and nonprofit organizations. Profit is the objective for most business firms. But other types of organizations may seek more members—or acceptance of an idea. Customers or clients may be individual consumers, business firms, nonprofit organizations, government agencies, or even foreign nations. While most customers and clients pay for the goods and services they receive, others may receive them free of charge or at a reduced cost through private or government support.

More than just persuading customers

You already know that micro-marketing isn't just selling and advertising. Unfortunately, many executives still think it is. They feel that the job of marketing is to "get rid of" whatever the company happens to produce. In fact, the aim of marketing is to identify customers' needs—and then meet those needs so well that the product almost "sells itself." This is true whether the product is a physical good, a service, or even an idea. If the whole marketing job has been done well, customers don't need much persuading. They should be ready to buy. Nortel understands this and has moved its people from thinking of sales as marketing to thinking of marketing as meeting customer needs. As a result, it understands its competition better. It also understands its customer requirements better and can translate them into functions and features in its products. It realizes that this is a necessary step to achieving the goal of becoming the preferred telecommunications equipment company of customers, suppliers, and professional talent around the world.[5]

Begin with customer needs

Nortel knows that *marketing should begin with potential customer needs*—not with the production process. Marketing should try to anticipate needs. And then marketing, rather than production, should determine what goods and services are to be developed—and this includes making decisions about product design and packaging; prices or fees; credit and collection policies; use of intermediaries; transporting and storing policies; advertising and sales policies; and, after the sale, installation, customer service, warranty, and perhaps even disposal policies.

Marketing does not do it alone

This does not mean that marketing should try to take over production, accounting, and financial activities. Rather, it means that marketing—by interpreting customers' needs—should provide direction for these activities and try to coordinate them.

After all, the purpose of a business or nonprofit organization is to satisfy customer or client needs. It is not to supply goods and services that are convenient to produce and that *might* sell or be accepted free.

Builds an ongoing relationship with the customer

When marketing helps everyone in a firm really meet the needs of a customer both before and after a purchase, the firm doesn't just get a single sale. Rather, it has a sale and an ongoing *relationship* with the customer. Then, in the future, when the customer has the same need again—or some other need that the firm can meet—other sales will follow. That's why we emphasize that marketing concerns a *flow* of need-satisfying goods and services to the customer. Often, that flow is not just for a single transaction; rather, it is part of building a long-lasting relationship that is beneficial to both the firm and the customer.

Macro-marketing defined

Macro-marketing is a social process that directs an economy's flow of goods and services from producers to consumers in a way that effectively matches supply and demand and accomplishes the objectives of society.[6]

Emphasis is on whole system

Like micro-marketing, macro-marketing is concerned with the flow of need-satisfying goods and services from producer to consumer. However, the emphasis with macro-marketing is not on the activities of individual organizations. Instead, the emphasis is on *how the whole marketing system works.* This involves looking at how marketing affects society, and vice versa.

Every society needs a macro-marketing system to help match supply and demand. Different producers in a society have different objectives, resources, and skills. Likewise, not all consumers share the same needs, preferences, and wealth. In other words, within every society there are both heterogeneous supply capabilities and heterogeneous demands for goods and services. The role of a macro-marketing system is to effectively match this heterogeneous supply and demand *and* at the same time accomplish society's objectives.

Is it effective and fair?

The effectiveness and fairness of a particular macro-marketing system must be evaluated in terms of that society's objectives. Obviously, all nations don't share the same objectives. For example, Swedish citizens receive many "free" services—such as health care and retirement benefits. Goods and services are fairly evenly distributed among the Swedish population. In India, the distribution of goods and services is very uneven, with a big gap between the "have nots" and the elite "haves." Whether each of these systems is fair or effective depends on the objectives of the society.

The focus of this text—management-oriented micro-marketing

Since most of you are preparing for a career in management, the main focus of this text will be on micro-marketing. We will see marketing through the eyes of the marketing manager. However, macro-marketing issues are discussed in Chapter 3, Chapter 11, and, most extensively, in Chapter 22 of this text.

It is important to keep in mind that the micro-marketing ideas and decision areas we will be discussing throughout this text apply to a wide variety of marketing management situations. They are important not only for large and small business firms but also for all types of public sector and nonprofit organizations. They are useful in domestic markets and international markets, and regardless of whether the organization focuses on marketing physical goods, services, or an idea or cause. They are equally critical whether the relevant customers or clients are individual consumers, businesses, or some other type of organization. In short, every organization needs to think about its markets and how effectively it meets its customers' and clients' needs. **For editorial convenience, and to reflect the fact that most of you will work in business settings, when we discuss marketing concepts, we will sometimes use the term *firm* as a shorthand way of referring to any type of organization, whether it is a corporation, a political party, a religious organization, or a government agency.** However, to reinforce the point that the ideas apply to all types of organizations, throughout the book we will be illustrating marketing management concepts with examples that represent a wide variety of marketing situations. Starting with Internet Insite 1–1, we will also be highlighting the many different ways the Internet is revolutionizing marketing management.

Marketing's role has changed over the years

From our Limited Snowboards example, it's clear that marketing decisions are very important to a firm's success. But marketing hasn't always been so complicated. In fact, it's only in the last 40 years or so that an increasing number of producers, wholesalers, retailers, and nonprofit organizations have adopted modern marketing thinking. Instead of just focusing on producing or selling *products,* these organizations focus on *customers*—and try to integrate an organizationwide effort to satisfy them.

Five stages of marketing evolution

We will discuss five stages in the evolution of marketing: (1) the simple trade era, (2) the production era, (3) the sales era, (4) the marketing department era, and (5) the marketing company era. We'll talk about these eras as if they applied generally to all firms—but keep in mind that *some managers still have not made it to the final stages.* They are stuck in the past with old ways of thinking.

The simple trade era

When societies first moved toward some specialization of production and away from a subsistence economy where each family raised and consumed everything it produced, traders played an important role. Early "producers for the market" made products that were needed by themselves and their neighbours. As bartering became more difficult, societies moved into the **simple trade era**—a time when families traded or sold their "surplus" output to local intermediaries. These specialists resold the goods to other consumers or distant intermediaries. This was the early role of marketing, and it is still the focus of marketing in many of the less-developed areas of the world. In fact, even in North America, the United Kingdom, and other more advanced economies, marketing didn't change much until the nineteenth century, when the Industrial Revolution brought larger factories.

From the production to the sales era

From the Industrial Revolution until the 1920s, most companies were in the production era. The **production era** is a time when a company focuses on producing a few specific products—perhaps because few of these products are available in the market. "If we can make it, it will sell" is management thinking characteristic of the

Internet Insite 1–1

Doing Business on the Internet: An Overview

Donna Hoffman and Tom Novak of the School of Management, Vanderbilt University, are coordinating Project 2000, which studies the marketing implications of commercializing the World Wide Web. They categorize Web-based businesses into two types: the integrated destination site, and the web traffic control site.[1]

Destination sites consist of:

1. online storefronts, which offer direct online sales through electronic catalogues;
2. Internet presence sites, which serve as online advertisements or information sites, but do not engage in online sales; and,
3. content sites, which can be free or fee-based. Most content sites, such as Time/Pathfinder (www.pathfinder.com) and CNN (www.cnn.com), are free because they get their revenues from advertisers.

Traffic sites consist of:

1. online malls, which consist of a collection of online storefronts (e.g., Internet Mall at www.internetmall.com);
2. incentive sites, which may have transitory content with the objective of "pulling" the user to a commercial site behind it (example: As the Web Turns carries an online soap opera, with innovative "product placement" links) (see www.metzger.com/soap/); and,
3. search agents. (examples: Yahoo!, WebCrawler, Infoseek).

Evan Schwartz, the author of *Webonomics*[2], points out that consumers are quite unwilling to pay for content online. Many publishers who went online found that out the hard way. *USA Today,* a newspaper with over 2 million daily circulation, went online in April 1995 but could barely attract 1,000 subscribers to its online edition. Now the site is free (www.usatoday.com).[3] Publishers such as *Time* (www.pathfinder.com) have also realized the futility of charging for online publications. But such online publications generate a lot of traffic, which in turn makes them attractive for advertisers. By charging advertisers on their sites, these publishers are able to generate significant revenues, while offering the product free of charge to consumers. On some of these sites, advertising costs between $30,000 and $100,000 for three months depending on the size of the ad.[4] Some would argue that such advertiser-supported products—which can be offered free or at a subsidized price—are nothing new. Isn't that the way newspapers, magazines, radio, and television have always been supported?

And speaking of advertising, a growing trend on the Web is to pay for advertising only if the consumer responds to the online advertisement (a response may include a click on the advertisement, which takes the consumer to the advertiser's Web site; or it may include an actual purchase). Thus, media owners (or Web sites) that offer advertising space cannot charge for that space up front. They get paid only if the advertising works! This concept is explored further in Internet Insite 16–1.

The Internet also allows some manufacturers to distribute their products at almost no additional cost! Software companies like Microsoft (www.microsoft.com), Netscape (www.netscape.com), and Adobe (www.adobe.com) allow consumers to download copies of software through the Internet, using FTP or File Transfer Protocol. The costs of loading the software on diskettes, packaging the diskettes, shrink-wrapping the manual, and shipping to retailers have now been eliminated! Most products that can be digitized (e.g., books and magazines, audio and video material) can benefit from a significant lowering of distribution costs. Notice that there is very little labour cost in the online distribution of such products.

The Internet, as a result of newly developing technology, allows marketers to price some products at a few cents, which would have been uneconomical before. For instance, it may soon be possible to charge someone a very low price for access to one article in an online database. This concept, called *Micropayments,* is still new.

Lastly, size and economies of scale are not that important in the online marketspace. Smaller firms and start-ups have upstaged established big firms online, by offering superior value to consumers, along with innovative products and services. Small firms that otherwise would have had access only to a limited local market, can now become global players. For example, Roswell's Cyberspace Computer Bookstore (www.roswell.com), a small Halifax-based firm, supplies books to customers around the world, thanks to the Internet.

These are but some of the differences between conventional and online markets. These concepts will be explored further in other Internet Insites. However, it should already be evident that what works in the traditional marketplace may not work, or even make sense, in the online marketspace.

[1]Donna L. Hoffman, Thomas P. Novak, and Patrali Chatterjee, "Commercial Scenarios for the Web: Opportunities and Challenges," *Journal of Computer Mediated Communication,* Vol. 1., No. 3 (shum.huji.ac.il/jcmc/vol1/issues3/vol1no3.html).

[2]Evan L. Schwartz, *Webonomics,* Bantam Doubleday, 1997 (www.webonomics.com).

[3]Evan L. Schwartz, "Advertising Webonomics 101," in *Wired* (www.wired.com/wired/4.02/webonomics.html).

[4]Ibid.

Source: This is one of a series of Internet Insites prepared in April 1998 by Dr. Ramesh Venkat of Saint Mary's University for *Basic Marketing,* Ninth Canadian Edition.

production era. Because of product shortages, many nations, including many of the newly independent republics of Eastern Europe, continue to operate with production era approaches.

By about 1930, most companies in the industrialized Western nations had more production capability than ever before. Now the problem wasn't just to produce, but to beat the competition and win customers. This led many firms to enter the sales era. The **sales era** is a time when a company emphasizes selling because of increased competition.

To the marketing department era

For most firms in advanced economies, the sales era continued until at least 1950. By then, sales were growing rapidly in most areas of the economy. The problem was deciding where to put the company's effort. Someone was needed to tie together the efforts of research, purchasing, production, shipping, and sales. As this situation became more common, the sales era was replaced by the marketing department era. The **marketing department era** is a time when all marketing activities are brought under the control of one department to improve short-run policy planning and to try to integrate the firm's activities.

To the marketing company era

Since 1960, most firms have developed at least some staff with a marketing management outlook. Many of these firms have even graduated from the marketing department era into the marketing company era. The **marketing company era** is a time when, in addition to short-run marketing planning, marketing people develop long-range plans—sometimes ten or more years ahead—and the whole-company effort is guided by the marketing concept.

What does the marketing concept mean?

The **marketing concept** means that an organization aims *all* its efforts at satisfying its *customers*—at a profit. The marketing concept is a simple but very important idea. See Exhibit 1–2.

It is not really a new idea—it's been around for a long time. But some managers act as if they are stuck at the beginning of the production era, when there were shortages of most products. They show little interest in customers' needs. These managers still have a **production orientation,** making whatever products are easy to produce and *then* trying to sell them. They think of customers existing to buy the firm's output rather than of firms existing to serve customers and—more broadly—the needs of society.

Exhibit 1-2 Organizations with a Marketing Orientation Carry Out the Marketing Concept

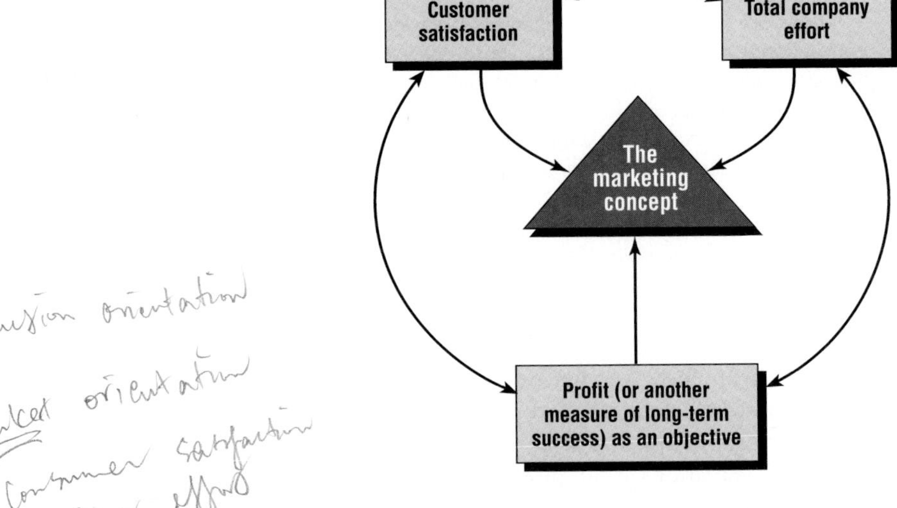

Well-managed firms have replaced this production orientation with a marketing orientation. A **marketing orientation** means trying to carry out the marketing concept. Instead of just trying to get customers to buy what the firm has produced, a marketing-oriented firm tries to produce what customers need.

Three basic ideas are included in the definition of the marketing concept: (1) customer satisfaction, (2) a total company effort, and (3) profit—not just sales—as an objective. These ideas deserve more discussion.

Customer satisfaction guides the whole system

"Give the customers what they need" seems so obvious that it may be hard for you to see why the marketing concept requires special attention. However, people don't always do the logical and obvious—especially when it means changing what they've done in the past. In a typical company 40 years ago, production managers thought mainly about getting out the product. Accountants were interested only in balancing the books. Financial people looked after the company's cash position. And salespeople were mainly concerned with getting orders. Each department thought of its own activity as the centre of the business, with others working around "the edges." No one was concerned with the whole system. As long as the company made a profit, each department went merrily on, doing its own thing. Unfortunately, this is still true in many companies today.

Work together to do a better job

Ideally, all managers should work together because the output from one department may be the input to another. But some managers tend to build "fences" around their own departments, as seen in Exhibit 1–3A. There may be meetings to try to get them to work together, but they come and go from the meetings worried only about protecting their own turf.

We use the term *production orientation* as a shorthand way to refer to this kind of narrow thinking—and lack of a central focus—in a business firm. But keep in mind that this problem may be seen in sales-oriented sales representatives, advertising-oriented agency people, finance-oriented finance people, directors of nonprofit organizations, and so on. It is not just a criticism of people who manage production. They aren't necessarily any more guilty of narrow thinking than anyone else.

The "fences" come down in an organization that has accepted the marketing concept. There are still departments, of course, because specialization makes sense. But the total system's effort is guided by what customers want, instead of what each department would like to do.

Exhibit 1-3 Contrasting Views of a Business

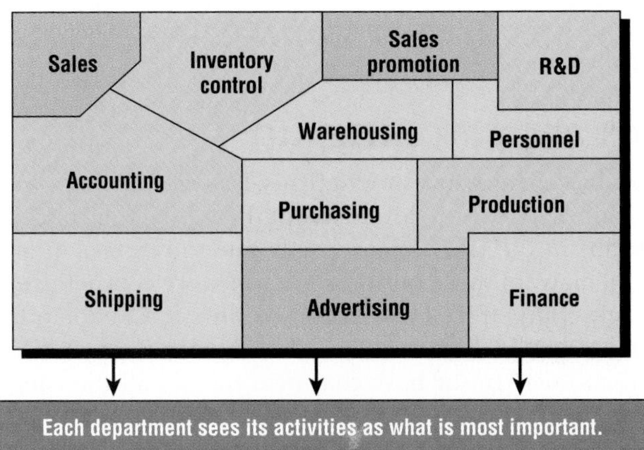

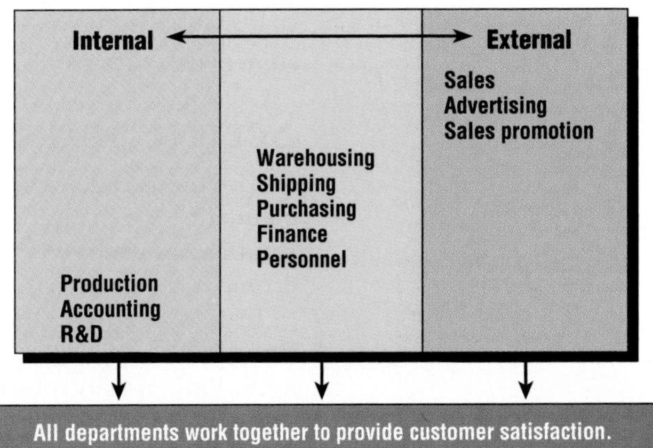

In such a firm, it is more realistic to view the business as a box with both internal and external activities, as shown in Exhibit 1–3B. Some internal departments—production, accounting, and research and development (R&D)—are mainly concerned with affairs inside the firm. The external departments—sales, advertising, and sales promotion—are concerned with outsiders. Finally, some departments—warehousing, shipping, purchasing, finance, and personnel—work with both insiders and outsiders.

In Chapter 21, we'll go into more detail about the relationship between marketing and other functions. Here, however, you should see that the marketing concept provides a guiding focus that *all* departments adopt. It should be a philosophy of the whole organization, not just an idea that applies to the marketing department. It helps the organization work as a total "system" rather than a lot of separate parts. The marketing concept, however, is more complete than many systems-oriented ideas. It actually specifies a high-level objective—customer satisfaction—that is logical for each and every part of the system. It also specifies a profit objective, which is necessary for the system's survival.

Survival and success require a profit

Firms must satisfy customers, or the customers won't continue to "vote" for the firm's survival and success with their money. But firms must also keep in mind that sales revenue from customers comes at a cost. It may cost more to satisfy some needs than any customers are willing to pay. So profit—the difference between a firm's revenue and its total costs—is the bottom-line measure of the firm's success and ability to survive. It is the balancing point that helps the firm determine what needs it will try to satisfy with its total (sometimes costly!) effort.

Adoption of the marketing concept has not been easy or universal

The marketing concept seems so logical that you would think most firms would quickly adopt it. But this isn't the case. Most firms are still production-oriented. In fact, the majority are either production-oriented, or regularly slip back that way, and must consciously refocus their planning on customers' interests.

The marketing concept was first accepted by consumer products companies such as General Electric and Procter & Gamble. Competition was intense in some of their markets, and trying to satisfy customers' needs more fully was a way to win in this competition. Widespread publicity about the success of the marketing concept at companies like General Electric and Procter & Gamble helped spread the message to other firms.[7]

Producers of industrial commodities—steel, coal, paper, glass, chemicals—have accepted the marketing concept slowly if at all. Similarly, many retailers have been slow to accept the marketing concept, in part because they are so close to final consumers that they think they really know their customers.

Service industries are catching up

Service industries, including airlines, banks, investment firms, lawyers, physicians, accountants, and insurance companies, were also slow to adopt the marketing concept. But this has changed dramatically in the last decade, partly due to changes in government regulations that forced many of these businesses to be more competitive.[8]

In response to an increasingly competitive business environment, Canadian law firms are beginning to hire marketers! Clients are becoming more savvy and less loyal. Rather than return to the same firm or have that firm handle all their legal business, they are more likely to shop around for a better price and the best service. Law firms are finding that they need to develop a marketing orientation in order to keep clients and attract new ones.[9]

It's easy to slip into a production orientation

The marketing concept may seem obvious, but it's very easy to slip into a production-oriented way of thinking. For example, a retailer might prefer only weekday hours, avoiding nights, Saturdays, and Sundays, when many customers would prefer to shop. Or a company might rush to produce a clever new product developed in its lab, rather than first finding out if it will fill an unsatisfied need. Many firms in high-technology businesses fall into this trap. They think that technology is the source of their success, rather than realizing that technology is only a means to meet customer needs.

Take a look at Exhibit 1–4. It shows some differences in outlook between adopters of the marketing concept and typical production-oriented managers. As the exhibit suggests, the marketing concept—if taken seriously—is really very powerful. It forces the company to think through *what* it is doing, and *why*. And it motivates the company to develop plans for accomplishing its objectives. Marketing Demo 1–1 carries this theme considerably further and argues for a whole new approach to marketing. This approach incorporates a renewed commitment to customers, improved information systems, and recognition of the importance of continuing relationships.

The marketing concept and customer value

A manager who adopts the marketing concept sees customer satisfaction as the path to profits. And to better understand what it takes to satisfy a customer, it's useful to take the customer's point of view.

A customer may look at a market offering from two perspectives: one deals with the potential benefits of that offering; the other concerns what the customer has to give up to get those benefits. For example, consider a student who has just finished an exam and is thinking about getting a cup of mocha latte from Starbucks. Our coffee lover may see this as a great-tasting snack, a personal reward, or a quick pick-me-up, or even as a way to break the ice and get to know an attractive classmate. Clearly, there are different needs associated with these different benefits. The cost of getting these benefits will include the price of the coffee and any tip, but there may be other, non-dollar costs as well: for example, how far it is to the Starbucks and how difficult it may be to park will be costs in terms of convenience. Slow service would be an aggravation. And you may worry about another kind of cost if the professor whose exam you have the next day sees you "wasting time" at Starbucks.

Exhibit 1-4 Some Differences in Outlook Between Adopters of the Marketing Concept and Typical Production-Oriented Managers

TOPIC	MARKETING ORIENTATION	PRODUCTION ORIENTATION
Attitudes toward customers	Customer needs determine company plans	They should be glad we exist, trying to cut costs and bringing out better products
Product offering	Company makes what it can sell	Company sells what is can make
Role of marketing research	To determine customer needs and how well company is satisfying them	To determine customer reaction, if used at all
Interest in innovation	Focus is on locating new opportunities	Focus is on technology and cost-cutting
Importance of profit	A critical objective	A residual, what's left after all costs are covered
Role of customer credit	Seen as a customer service	Seen as a necessary evil
Role of packaging	Designed for customer convenience and as a selling tool	Seen merely as protection for the product
Inventory levels	Set with customer requirements and costs in mind	Set to make production more convenient
Transportation arrangements	Seen as a customer service	Seen as an extension of production and storage activities, with emphasis on cost minimization
Focus of advertising	Need-satisfying benefits of products and services	Product features and how products are made
Role of sales force	Help the customer to buy if the product fits his or her needs, while coordinating with rest of firm	Sell the customer, don't worry about coordination with other promotion efforts or rest of firm
Relationship with customer	Customer satisfaction before and after sale leads to a profitable long-run relationship	Relationship is seen as short term—ends when a sale is made

Customer value reflects benefits and costs

As this example suggests, benefits and costs can take many different forms, ranging from economic to emotional. Also, they may vary depending on the situation. That being said, it is the customer's view of the various benefits and costs that is important. And combining these two perspectives leads us to the concept of **customer value,** which is the difference between the benefits a customer sees from a market offering and the costs of obtaining those benefits. A consumer is likely to be more satisfied when the customer value is higher—when benefits exceed costs by a larger margin. On the other hand, a consumer who sees the costs as greater than the benefits isn't likely to become a customer.

Some people think that low price and high customer value are the same thing. But, as you can see, that may not be the case at all. On the contrary—a good or service that doesn't meet a consumer's needs results in low customer value, even if the price is very low. Yet a high price may be more than acceptable when it obtains the desired benefits. Think again about our Starbucks example. You can get a cup of coffee for a much lower price, but Starbucks offers more than *just* a cup of coffee.

Customer may not think about it very much

It's useful for a manager to seek out ways to improve the benefits, or reduce the costs, of what the firm offers customers. However, this doesn't mean that customers stop and compute some sort of customer value score before making each purchase. If they did, there wouldn't be much time in life for anything else. So a manager's objective and thorough analysis may not accurately reflect the customer's impressions. Yet it is the customer's view that matters—even when the customer has not thought about it.

Marketing Demo 1-1

A Marketing Approach for the 21st Century

Marketing is more than a set of concepts and tools to be applied to the firm's efforts in the marketplace. In fact, marketing must be viewed from a holistic perspective as the energizing core of the firm's overall marketplace approach. Such a perspective reflects a true appreciation of the firm's dynamic interaction with and dependency on the macro-environment.

The following ideas and precepts are presented as major components of this new approach:

1. *Marketing is not a function—it is a way of doing business. Marketing is an attitude.* Traditionally, marketing has been viewed as a function analogous to production, finance, or human resources. In fact, marketing today incorporates an all-pervasive business philosophy. It is a way of thinking that reflects a deeply imbedded appreciation of and commitment to the most important corporate result that can be achieved: customer satisfaction. Profits will then logically follow. This way of doing business requires an ongoing openness to and focus on the customer and the external environment. All resources (including human resources) are ultimately directed to service excellence and customer satisfaction.

2. *Marketing requires vision, creativity, imagination, and anticipation.* These elements are absolutely essential keys to success in our constantly changing business environment with its unlimited potential for opportunity. The *vision* component requires a breaking away from the traditionally narrow definition of markets, products, and services and from the conventional boundaries of place, time, and technology to anticipate entirely new markets and needs.

   Creativity must characterize the approach that marketers adopt to recognize the unlimited possibilities for improving and delivering their offer more effectively and efficiently. *Imagination* is required to venture into the unknown and search for innovative concepts, leaving behind traditional approaches. The firm must look beyond the horizon of all products available today to all the possibilities that lie ahead. No constraints should exist in our conceptualization of the opportunities in this era of the information revolution. In order to identify and fully capitalize on these opportunities, *anticipation* is needed in the form of efforts to forecast macro-environmental trends, competitive strategies, and the evolution of technology.

3. *Good marketing planning makes things happen as opposed to waiting for them to happen.* This precept exemplifies the power and dynamism of marketing wherein today's leading companies strive constantly to generate new ideas and build competitive advantage in the marketplace. These efforts at continuous innovation take many different forms: predicting the evolution of the macro-environment and allocating resources accordingly; creating new products, new markets, and new uses for old products; generating new segmentation bases and new sources of value; inventing new distribution channels; and creatively approaching the development of media mixes and positioning options. Full advantage must be taken of the power to influence what consumers value most.

4. *Marketing is an investment.* While customarily treated as a current expense, marketing expenditures must be recognized for what they really are: investments that build long-term value in terms of customer satisfaction and loyalty. Maximizing customer satisfaction leads to long-term profitability. Maximization of the *lifetime* earning stream to be derived from each customer should constitute the primary focus of the firm's planned evolution. It costs five times as much to find a new customer as it does to retain an old one.

5. *Marketing involves creating maximum value for the customer.* Customers are not offered a product—they are offered a "bundle of benefits." The more a customer values and appreciates the "bundle," the more satisfaction is generated from the exchange. The objective is really to generate the maximum amount of benefit per dollar expended, to effectively communicate this value, and to make it accessible to the consumer. Direct, uninformed price comparisons per se will assume less prominence in purchase decisions. The successful firm must be dominated by a pervasive value-creating philosophy. All of the firm's employees should constantly be seeking ways to create, transform, and add value to the "bundle of benefits."

6. *Get close to the customer . . . and suppliers . . . and distributors . . . and stay there!* Relationship building is an important key to marketplace success. Consumer needs, wants, desires, and behaviour are constantly changing. In order to take full advantage of this relentless evolution of markets and opportunities, an ongoing relationship with consumers must be cultivated. What is required in fact is an ongoing dialogue with the firm's customers (as opposed to the traditional monologue), as well as a high degree of adaptability and responsiveness. Companies must constantly interact with their customers to find out what matters most.

   This relationship-building requirement is not restricted to customers. Companies must develop partnerships with their distributors and suppliers. Companies do not sell *to* their distributors but *through* them. They must thus develop value-laden programs to secure the cooperation of their distributors in ways that will enhance overall distributor effectiveness. Continuous dialogue here also plays an important role. Additionally, companies must cultivate relationships with their suppliers to ensure timeliness and efficiency of supply.

7 *A firm cannot be all things to all people. Generating possibilities and making choices are keys to strategic marketing success.* No two customers are alike in terms of their wants, desires, and expectations. This gives rise to innumerable possibilities in terms of potential benefit bundles that may be provided to the marketplace. No company could ever hope to satisfy every potential need–satisfaction combination. Attention must be focused on those customers that can best be served. This is the essence of strategic marketing: identifying possible segments, pursuing the segment(s) that the company can best serve, and proceeding to dominate that segment by successfully positioning the product and/or service in the minds of the targeted group of consumers.

Every company makes choices about which segments to pursue with which products at what price. The promotion campaigns and distribution systems to be utilized must also be chosen. Furthermore, companies must adopt a *worldwide* perspective, first in identifying segments that might be most effectively served and then in taking advantage of such international opportunities.

8 *The customer is number one!* A company is, in fact, a need-satisfying entity. These needs are manifested in the real (and subconscious) expectations and aspirations of customers. Without customers, a company is nothing. Customers must be the firm's number one priority, and the customer's point of view must guide every decision. Profitability is achieved through incessant companywide attention to delighting the customer. This can only be accomplished by constantly listening to the customer. An unyielding commitment to customer satisfaction from each employee must also be commanded.

Successful corporations are proving that dedication to the customer really is the key to marketplace success. Companies are finally realizing that delighted customers are their greatest assets. Such assets are much more important than those traditionally reflected on the firm's balance sheet.

9 *Marketing is about improving the firm's bottom line by satisfying customers better than competitors do.* Bottom-line results are the scoresheet that can be compared to the company's planned financial performance objectives. It is continuous improvement in customer satisfaction that perpetuates marketplace success and guarantees continued financial solvency.

The corporation's primary focus must always be the customer. Competitors (those seeking to satisfy the same customer needs) provide a reference point for benchmarking the firm's customer satisfaction performance. This broad view of competition (i.e., needs-oriented versus product-oriented) will facilitate the identification of additional market opportunities. It will also ensure that the corporation is not blindsided as a result of too narrowly defining the competition.

10 *Information is crucial in making the right marketing decisions.* The gathering, circulation, and use of appropriate information is required for successful implementation of this new approach. Environmental scanning, consumer surveys, and customer satisfaction measures are particularly important for future marketplace success. The latest technology must be utilized to optimize the potential benefits of the firm's marketing information system. The strategies adopted and action plans developed must be grounded in relevant and up-to-date information.

Source: Marketing Demo 1–1 was written by Professor Bryan Barbieri of Concordia University.

Where does competition fit?

You can't afford to ignore competition. Consumers usually have choices about how they will meet their needs. So a firm that offers superior customer value is likely to win and keep customers. This may be crucial when what firms have to offer is very similar.

Some critics say that the marketing concept does not go far enough in today's highly competitive markets. They think of marketing as "warfare" for customers, and argue that a marketing manager should focus on competitors, not customers. That view, however, misses the point. Often the best way to improve customer value, and beat the competition, is to be first to find and satisfy a need that others have not even considered.

The competition between Pepsi and Coke illustrates this. Coke and Pepsi were spending millions of dollars on promotion, fighting head to head for the same cola customers. They put so much emphasis on the cola competition that they missed other opportunities. That gave firms like Snapple the chance to enter the market and steal away customers. For these customers, the desired benefits—and the greatest customer value—came from the variety of a fruit-flavoured drink, not from one more cola.

Build relationships with customer value

Firms that embrace the marketing concept seek ways to build a long-term relationship with each customer. This is an important idea. Even the most innovative firm faces competition sooner or later. And trying to get new customers by taking them

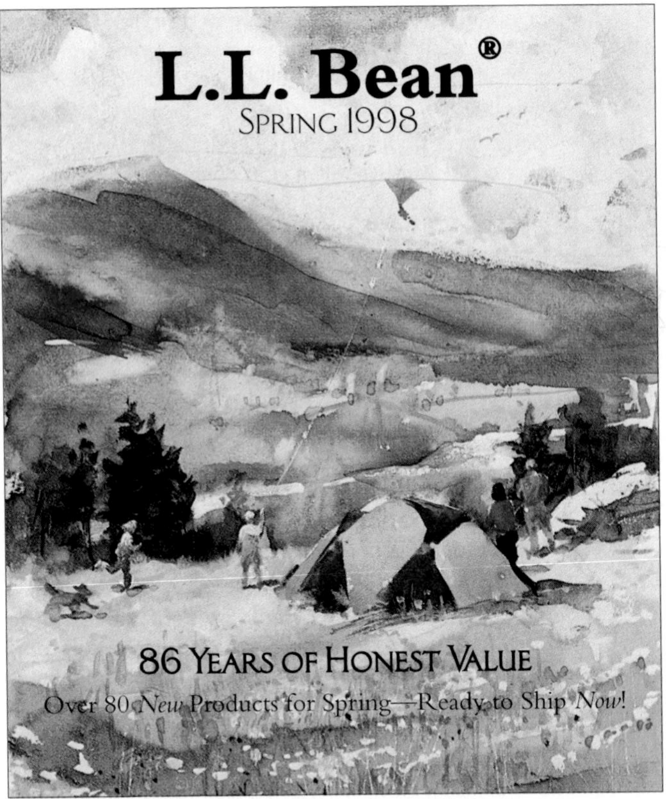

Everyone who works at L.L. Bean is part of a team effort to satisfy customers' needs before and after each sale, and that has helped it build profitable long-run relationships with its loyal customers.

away from a competitor is usually more costly than retaining current customers by really satisfying their needs. Satisfied customers buy again and again. This makes their buying job easier, and it also increases the selling firm's profits.

Building mutually beneficial relationships with customers requires that everyone in an organization work together to provide customer value before *and after* each purchase. If there is a problem with a customer's bill, the accounting people can't just leave it to the salesperson to straighten it out or, even worse, act like it's "the customer's problem." Rather, it's the firm's problem. The long-term relationship with the customer—and the lifetime value of the customer's future purchases—is threatened if the accountant, the salesperson, and anyone else who may be involved don't work together quickly to make things right for the customer. Similarly, the firm's advertising people can't simply develop ads that try to convince a customer to buy once. If the firm doesn't deliver on the benefits promised in its ads, the customer is likely to go elsewhere the next time the need arises. And the same ideas apply whether the issue is meeting promised delivery dates, or resolving warranty problems, or giving a customer help on how to use a product, or even making it easy for the customer to return a purchase made in error.

L.L. Bean is a firm that builds enduring relationships with its customers. It offers good customer value to consumers who are interested in enjoying the outdoors. Bean's quality products are well suited to a wide variety of outdoor needs, whether it's clothing for hikers or equipment for campers. The firm field-tests all its products to be certain they live up to the firm's "100% satisfaction" guarantee. Although L.L. Bean operates a retail store in Freeport, Maine, its Internet Web site and catalogues reach customers all over the world. Bean's computers track what each customer is buying, so new catalogues are mailed directly to the people who are most interested. To make ordering convenient, customers can call toll-free 24 hours a day—and they get whatever advice they need because the salespeople are real experts on what they sell. Bean also makes it easy for consumers to return a product, and encourages them to complain about any problem. That way, Bean can solve the problem before it disrupts the relationship. Bean's prices are competitive with those of other outdoor sporting specialty stores, but customers are loyal because they like the benefits of the relationship.[10]

The marketing concept applies in nonprofit organizations

The marketing concept is as important for nonprofit organizations as it is for business firms. However, prior to 1970 few people in nonprofits paid attention to the role of marketing. Now marketing is widely recognized as applicable to all sorts of public and private nonprofit organizations, ranging from government agencies, health care organizations, educational institutions, and religious groups to charities, political parties, and fine arts organizations.

Some nonprofit organizations operate just like a business. For example, there may be no practical difference between the gift shop at a museum and a for-profit

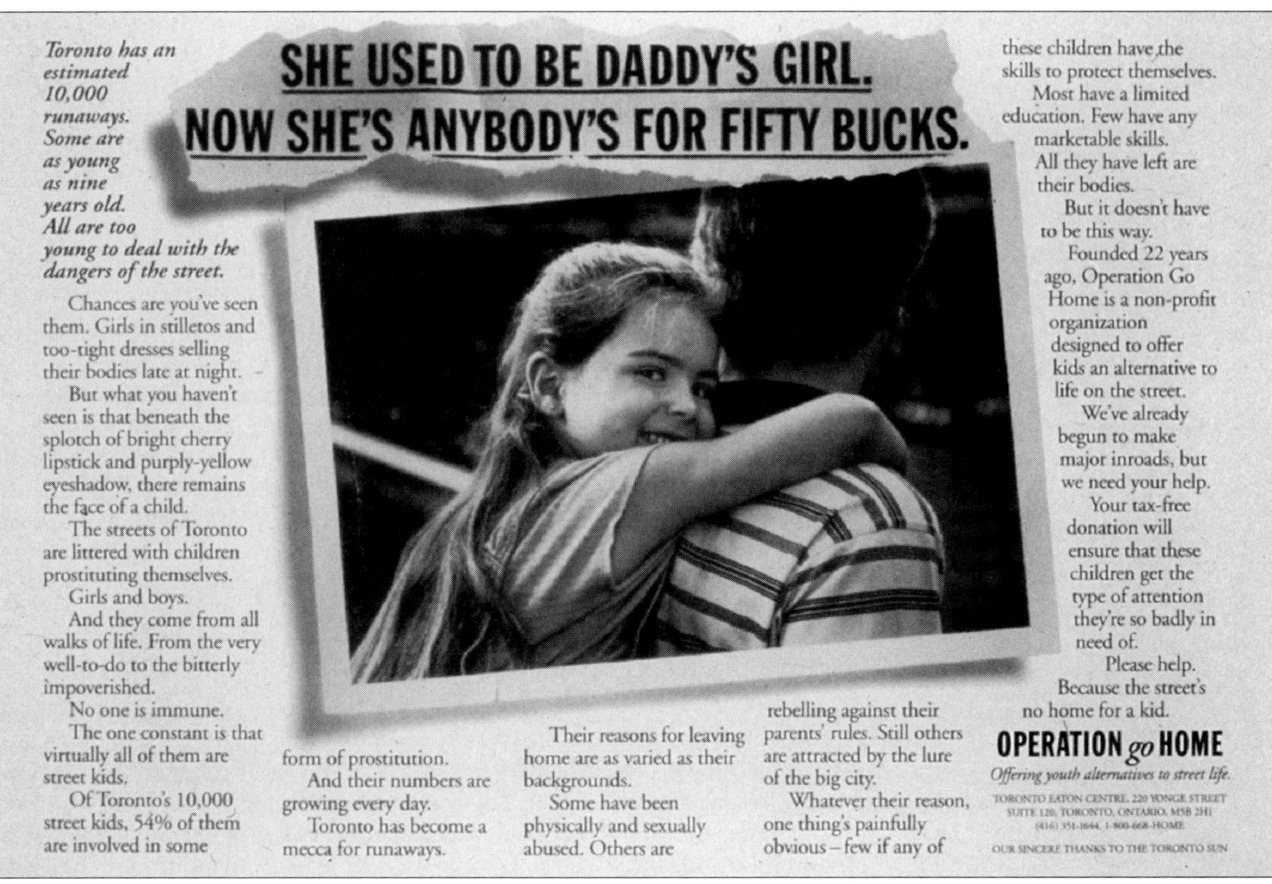

SHE USED TO BE DADDY'S GIRL.
NOW SHE'S ANYBODY'S FOR FIFTY BUCKS.
Toronto has an estimated 10,000 runaways. Some are as young as nine years old. All are too young to deal with the dangers of the street.
Chances are you've seen them. Girls in stilletos and too-tight dresses selling their bodies late at night.
But what you haven't seen is that beneath the splotch of bright cherry lipstick and purply-yellow eyeshadow, there remains the face of a child.
The streets of Toronto are littered with children prostituting themselves.
Girls and boys.
And they come from all walks of life. From the very well-to-do to the bitterly impoverished.
No one is immune.
The one constant is that virtually all of them are street kids.
Of Toronto's 10,000 street kids, 54% of them are involved in some form of prostitution.
And their numbers are growing every day.
Toronto has become a mecca for runaways.
Their reasons for leaving home are as varied as their backgrounds.
Some have been physically and sexually abused. Others are rebelling against their parents' rules. Still others are attracted by the lure of the big city.
Whatever their reason, one thing's painfully obvious – few if any of these children have the skills to protect themselves.
Most have a limited education. Few have any marketable skills.
All they have left are their bodies.
But it doesn't have to be this way.
Founded 22 years ago, Operation Go Home is a non-profit organization designed to offer kids an alternative to life on the street.
We've already begun to make major inroads, but we need your help.
Your tax-free donation will ensure that these children get the type of attention they're so badly in need of.
Please help.
Because the street's no home for a kid.
OPERATION go HOME
Offering youth alternatives to street life.
TORONTO EATON CENTRE, 220 YONGE STREET
SUITE 120, TORONTO, ONTARIO, M5B 2H1
(416) 351-1644, 1-800-668-HOME
OUR SINCERE THANKS TO THE TORONTO SUN

Social service agencies must also be effective marketers.

shop located across the street. On the other hand, some nonprofits differ from business firms in a variety of ways.

Support may not come from satisfied "customers"

As with any business firm, a nonprofit organization needs resources and support to survive and achieve its objectives. Yet support often does not come directly from those who receive the benefits the organization produces. For example, the World Wildlife Fund protects animals. If supporters of the World Wildlife Fund are not satisfied with its efforts—don't think the benefits are worth what it costs to provide them—they will, and should, put their time and money elsewhere.

Just as most firms face competition for customers, most nonprofits face competition for the resources and support they need. A sorority will falter if potential members join other organizations. A shelter for the homeless may fail if supporters decide to focus on some other cause, such as AIDS education. A community theatre group that decides to do a play that the actors and the director like—never stopping to consider what the audience might want to see—may find the theatre is empty and the audience has gone somewhere else. The "Daddy's Girl" advertisement seeking financial support for a social service agency has been recognized as one of the most effective of its kind.

What is the "bottom line"?

As with a business, a nonprofit must take in as much money as it spends or it won't survive. However, a nonprofit organization does not measure "profit" in the same way as a firm. And its key measures of long-term success are also different. For example, the YMCA, universities, and symphony orchestras all seek to achieve different objectives—and need different measures of success.

Profit guides business decisions because it reflects both the costs and benefits of different activities. In a nonprofit organization, it is sometimes more difficult to be objective in evaluating the benefits of different activities relative to what they cost. However, if everyone in an organization agrees to *some* measure of long-run success, this helps serve as a guide to where the organization should focus its efforts.

May not be organized for marketing

Some nonprofits face other challenges in organizing to adopt the marketing concept. Often no one has overall responsibility for marketing activities. A treasurer or accountant may keep the books, and someone may be in charge of operations, but marketing may somehow seem less crucial, especially if no one understands what marketing is all about. Even when some leaders do the marketing thinking, they may have trouble getting unpaid volunteers with many different interests to all agree with the marketing strategy. Volunteers tend to do what they feel like doing!

The marketing concept provides focus

We have been discussing some of the differences between nonprofit and business organizations. However, the marketing concept is helpful in *any* type of organization. Success is unlikely if everyone doesn't pull together to strive for common objectives that can be achieved with the available resources. Adopting the marketing concept helps to bring this kind of focus. After all, each organization is trying to satisfy some group of consumers in some way.[11] For example, Internet Insite 1–2 shows that some nonprofit organizations have Web sites to provide information about their activities and to solicit support.

The marketing concept, social responsibility, and marketing ethics

The marketing concept is so logical that it's hard to argue with it. Yet when a firm focuses its efforts on satisfying *some* consumers—to achieve its objectives—there may be negative effects on society as a whole. This means that marketing managers should be concerned with **social responsibility,** which is a firm's obligation to improve its positive effects on society and to reduce its negative effects. Being socially responsible sometimes requires difficult trade-offs.

Should all consumer needs be satisfied?

Some consumers want products that may not be safe or good for them in the long run. Some critics argue that businesses should not offer cigarettes, high-heeled shoes, alcoholic beverages, sugar-coated cereals, soft drinks, and many processed foods because they aren't "good" for consumers in the long run.

Similarly, motorcycles are one of the most dangerous products identified by the U.S. Consumer Product Safety Commission. Should Harley-Davidson stop production? What about skis, mopeds, and scuba equipment? Who should decide whether these products will be offered to consumers? Is this a micro-marketing issue or a macro-marketing issue?

Charity Begins on the Web

Nonprofit and charitable organizations are facing increasing costs and competition for funds. These organizations have to communicate with a large number of beneficiaries and donors, and the general public, in a cost-effective manner. They have to maintain a high level of service while lowering the costs of fundraising and administrative activities. The Web offers a cost-effective solution. The Web not only enables these organizations to provide detailed and up-to-date information, but also allows them to build ongoing relationships with the various stakeholder groups.

Besides having their own individual presence on the Web, many nonprofit organizations seem to be taking advantage of the "online mall" concept. "Umbrella" sites such as CharityVillage (www.CharityVillage.com) and Catalogue of Nonprofit Agencies and Research (CNAR) (www.cnar.org) provide comprehensive databases of charitable and nonprofit organizations. CNAR's goal is to provide "nonprofit organizations with a centralized medium for communication with the public." CharityVillage claims that it is the "supersite for the nonprofit sector" in Canada. It includes a volunteer bulletin board, information on conferences, fundraising events, and careers in the nonprofit sector, and a comprehensive listing of Canadian nonprofit and charitable organizations.

The level of sophistication in the use of the Internet varies widely among nonprofit and charitable organizations. Most provide details about their activities and services and about fundraising events. Some even provide a "secure server" for those who wish to make a donation online (e.g., Boys and Girls Club of Ottawa-Carleton at www.boys-girls.com).

The David Suzuki Foundation (www.davidsuzuki.org), which focuses on environmental issues and sustainable development, offers an excellent example of how a print media campaign can be linked to a Web campaign. On the Web you can view many of the Foundation's print ads and print materials. The "Major Issue" section is designed to educate the user and makes effective use of graphs and pictures. Those who believe in the cause can act immediately by sending e-mail to provincial or national politicians right from the Web site. There's even an online bookstore. This site demonstrates how a nonprofit organization can use the Web effectively.

Many of Canada's leading businesses are proud sponsors of these nonprofit Web sites. It is not uncommon to see corporate sponsors' logos and names prominently displayed in some of the nonprofit Web sites. For businesses that sponsor these sites, there is opportunity for at least some exposure.

Visit the following Web sites:

1. The Edmonton Symphony Orchestra—www.tgx.com/eso/
2. The Canadian Red Cross—www.redcross.ca

After you browse these sites, evaluate the two Web sites in terms of (a) attractiveness and ease of navigation, and (b) usefulness of content.

Questions to ponder:

a. Who are the "consumers" of these organizations?
b. How effectively are these organizations applying the marketing concept?

Source: This is one of a series of Internet Insites prepared in April 1998 by Dr. Ramesh Venkat of Saint Mary's University for *Basic Marketing;* Ninth Canadian Edition.

Internet Insite 1-2

Ethical Dimensions

Is It an Ethical Issue?

Certainly some complaints about marketing arise because some individual firm or manager was intentionally unethical and cheated the market. At other times, problems and criticism may arise because a manager did not fully consider the ethical implications of a decision. In either case, there is no excuse for sloppiness when it comes to **marketing ethics**—the moral standards that guide marketing decisions and actions. Every individual develops moral standards based on his or her own values. That helps explain why opinions about what is right or wrong often vary from one person to another, from one society to another, and among different groups within a society. It is sometimes difficult to say whose opinions are "correct." Even so, such opinions may have a very real influence on whether an individual's (or a firm's) marketing decisions and actions are accepted or rejected. So marketing ethics are not only a philosophical issue but are also a pragmatic concern. Throughout the text we will be discussing the types of ethical issues individual marketing managers face. In fact, these issues are so important that we will highlight them with the special symbol used in the heading for this section. But we won't be moralizing and trying to tell you how you should think on any given issue. Rather, by the end of the course we hope that *you* will have some firm personal opinions about what is and is not ethical marketing behaviour.

Organizations that have adopted the marketing concept are concerned about marketing ethics as well as broader issues of social responsibility. Individual managers in an organization may have different values. As a result, problems may arise when someone does not share the same marketing ethics as others in the organization. One person operating alone can damage a firm's reputation and even survival. Because the marketing concept involves a companywide focus, it is a foundation for marketing ethics common to everyone in a firm—and helps to avoid such problems.

To be certain that standards for marketing ethics are as clear as possible, many organizations have developed their own written codes of ethics. Consistent with the marketing concept, these codes usually state, at least at a general level, the ethical standards that everyone in the firm should follow in dealing with customers and other people. Many professional societies have also adopted such codes. For example, the American Marketing Association's Code of Ethics—see Exhibit 1–5—sets specific ethical standards for many aspects of the management job in marketing.[12]

What if it cuts into profits?

It seems that being more socially conscious often leads to positive customer response. For example, Gerber had great success when it improved the nutritional quality of its baby food. And many consumers have been eager to buy products that are friendly to the environment (even at a higher price).

Yet as the examples above show, there are times when being socially responsible conflicts with a firm's profit objective. Concerns about such conflicts have prompted critics to raise the basic question: Is the marketing concept really desirable?

Many marketing managers and socially conscious marketing companies are trying to resolve this problem. Their definition of customer satisfaction includes long-range effects—as well as immediate customer satisfaction. They try to balance consumer, company, *and* social interests.

You too will have to make choices that balance these social concerns—either in your role as a consumer or as a manager in a business firm. So throughout the text we will be discussing many of the social issues faced by marketing management.

Exhibit 1-5 Code of Ethics, American Marketing Association

CODE OF ETHICS

Members of the American Marketing Association (AMA) are committed to ethical professional conduct. They have joined together in subscribing to this Code of Ethics embracing the following topics:

Responsibilities of the Marketer

Marketers must accept responsibility for the consequences of their activities and make every effort to ensure that their decisions, recommendations, and actions function to identify, serve, and satisfy all relevant publics: customers, organizations and society.

Marketers' professional conduct must be guided by:

1. The basic rule of professional ethics: not knowingly to do harm;
2. The adherence to all applicable laws and regulations;
3. The accurate representation of their education, training and experience; and
4. The active support, practice and promotion of this Code of Ethics.

Honesty and Fairness

Marketers shall uphold and advance the integrity, honor, and dignity of the marketing profession by:

1. Being honest in serving consumers, clients, employees, suppliers, distributors and the public;
2. Not knowingly participating in conflict of interest without prior notice to all parties involved; and
3. Establishing equitable fee schedules including the payment or receipt of usual, customary and/or legal compensation for marketing exchanges.

Rights and Duties of Parties in the Marketing Exchange Process

Participants in the marketing exchange process should be able to expect that:

1. Products and services offered are safe and fit for their intended uses;
2. Communications about offered products and services are not deceptive;
3. All parties intend to discharge their obligations, financial and otherwise, in good faith; and
4. Appropriate internal methods exist for equitable adjustment and/or redress of grievances concerning purchases.

It is understood that the above would include, *but is not limited to,* the following responsibilities of the marketer:

In the area of product development and management,

- disclosure of all substantial risks associated with product or service usage;
- identification of any product component substitution that might materially change the product or impact on the buyer's purchase decision;
- identification of extra-cost added features.

In the area of promotions,

- avoidance of false and misleading advertising;
- rejection of high pressure manipulations, or misleading sales tactics;
- avoidance of sales promotions that use deception or manipulation.

In the area of distribution,

- not manipulating the availability of a product for purpose of exploitation;
- not using coercion in the marketing channel;
- not exerting undue influence over the reseller's choice to handle a product.

In the area of pricing,

- not engaging in price fixing;
- not practicing predatory pricing;
- disclosing the full price associated with any purchase.

In the area of marketing research,

- prohibiting selling or fund raising under the guise of conducting research;
- maintaining research integrity by avoiding misrepresentation and omission of pertinent research data;
- treating outside clients and suppliers fairly.

Organizational Relationships

Marketers should be aware of how their behavior may influence or impact on the behavior of others in organizational relationships. They should not demand, encourage or apply coercion to obtain unethical behavior in their relationships with others, such as employees, suppliers or customers.

1. Apply confidentiality and anonymity in professional relationships with regard to privileged information;
2. Meet their obligations and responsibilities in contracts and mutual agreements in a timely manner;
3. Avoid taking the work of others, in whole, or in part, and represent this work as their own or directly benefit from it without compensation or consent of the originator or owner;
4. Avoid manipulation to take advantage of situations to maximize personal welfare in a way that unfairly deprives or damages the organization or others.

Any AMA members found to be in violation of any provision of this Code of Ethics may have his or her Association membership suspended or revoked.

Source: Reprinted with permission of the American Marketing Association.

Questions and Problems

1. How do you think consumers would react if a food processor developed a revolutionary new food product that would provide all necessary nutrients in small pills for about $100 per year per person?
2. The American Marketing Association defined marketing as "the process of planning and executing the conception, pricing, promotion and distribution of ideas, goods and services to create exchanges that satisfy individual and organizational objectives." Does this definition consider macro-marketing? Explain your answer.
3. Distinguish between micro- and macro-marketing. Then explain how they are interrelated (if they are).
4. Define the marketing concept in your own words and then explain why the notion of profit is usually included in this definition.
5. Briefly describe how acceptance of the marketing concept might affect the organization and operation of your college or university.
6. Distinguish between production orientation and marketing orientation, illustrating with examples in your local area.
7. Explain why a firm should view its internal activities as part of a total system. Illustrate your answer for (a) a large grocery products producer, (b) a plumbing wholesaler, and (c) a department store chain.
8. Does the acceptance of the marketing concept almost require that a firm view itself as a total system?

Suggested cases

15 Lucas Foods

19 KASTORS, Inc.

31 The Parks Canada Dilemma

Computer-aided problem

Revenue, Cost and Profit Relationships

This problem introduces you to the computer-aided problem software—the PLUS computer program—and gets you started with the use of spreadsheet analysis for marketing decision making. This problem is simple. In fact, you could work it without the PLUS software. But by starting with a simple problem, you will learn how to use the program more quickly and see how it will help you with more complicated problems. Complete instructions for the PLUS software are available from your instructor. However, while you are working with the software, you can press the H key to get help on-screen whenever you need it.

Sue Cline, the business manager at Magna University Student Bookstore, is developing plans for the next academic year. The bookstore is one of the university's nonprofit activities, but any "surplus" (profit) it earns is used to support the student activities centre.

Two popular products at the bookstore are the student academic calendar and notebooks with the school name. Sue Cline thinks that she can sell calendars to 90 percent of Magna's 3,000 students, so she has had 2,700 printed. The total cost, including artwork and printing, is $11,500. Last year the calendar sold for $5.00, but Sue is considering changing the price this year.

Sue thinks that the bookstore will be able to sell 6,000 notebooks if they are priced right. But she knows that many students will buy similar notebooks (without the school name) from stores in town if the bookstore price is too high.

Sue has entered the information about selling price, quantity, and costs for calendars and notebooks in the spreadsheet program so that it is easy to evaluate the effect of different decisions. The spreadsheet is also set up to calculate revenue and profit, based on

Revenue =
(Selling price) × (Quantity sold)

Profit = (Revenue) − (Total cost)

Use the program to answer the questions below. Remember, you can press the H key to get help whenever you need it. Record your answers on a separate sheet of paper.

a. From the Spreadsheet Screen, how much revenue does Sue expect from calendars? How much revenue from notebooks? How much profit will the store earn from calendars? From notebooks?

b. If Sue increases the price of her calendars to $6.00 and still sells the same quantity, what is the expected revenue? The expected profit? (Note: Change the price from $5.00 to $6.00 on the spreadsheet and the program will recompute revenue and profit.) On your sheet of paper, show the calculations that confirm that the program has given you the correct values.

c. Sue is interested in getting an overview of how a change in the price of notebooks would affect revenue and profit, assuming that she sells all 6,000 notebooks she is thinking of ordering. Prepare a table—on your sheet of paper—with column headings for three variables: selling price, revenue, and profit. Show the value for revenue and profit for different possible selling prices for a notebook—starting at a minimum price of $1.60 and adding 8 cents to the price until you reach a maximum of $2.40. At what price will selling 6,000 notebooks contribute $5,400.00 to profit? At what price would notebook sales contribute only $1,080.00? (Hint: Use the What If analysis to compute the new values. Start by selecting "selling price" for notebooks as the value to change, with a minimum value of $1.60 and a maximum value of $2.40. Select the revenue and profit for notebooks as the values to display.)

For additional questions related to this problem, see Exercise 1–4 in the *Learning Aid for Use with Basic Marketing*, Ninth Canadian Edition.

When you finish this chapter, you should:

- Understand what a marketing manager does.
- Know what strategic market planning is—and why it will be the focus of this book.
- Understand target marketing.
- Be familiar with the four Ps in a marketing mix.
- Know the difference between a marketing strategy, a marketing plan, and a marketing program.
- Know about the different kinds of marketing opportunities.
- Understand why opportunities in international markets should be considered.
- Know how to screen and evaluate marketing opportunities, including international opportunities.
- Understand the important new terms (shown in orange).

Chap two

Strategic Market Planning and the Evaluation of Marketing Opportunities

Valcourt, Que.—Transportation giant Bombardier spared no hoopla as it pulled the cover off its latest product, an all-terrain vehicle called the Traxter.

The ATV, essentially a four-wheeled motorcycle, was driven on to the stage by a Bombardier executive amid fireworks, falling artificial snow and the cheers of 2,000 dealers gathered for the annual rollout of the company's 1999 snowmobile models.

However, the Traxter won't go on sale until fall, well past the peak selling period for such vehicles and later than expected. When it does hit the trail, the rugged buggy faces a tough climb for market share in a landscape crowded with competitors.

It's Bombardier's first new recreational product since 1987, when the multinational transportation giant—which also builds aircraft and rail cars—introduced the successful Sea-Doo watercraft.

The ATV market is growing rapidly but Bombardier goes against six well-established contenders including market leaders Honda, Polaris and Yamaha.

Ron Schwarz, an industry analyst with CIBC Wood Gundy, believes Bombardier is much too savvy to spend three years developing the Traxter without expecting to be a major player. "Whenever historically Bombardier has introduced a product, it's an extremely innovative product," said Schwarz, cautioning that "we don't know yet how it will perform."

Another advantage is that Bombardier can use its existing well-developed network of Ski-Doo and Sea-Doo dealers.

Alain Brunelle, president of Bombardier's recreational vehicle division, said the Traxter could help stabilize a cyclical market for its other products. For example, Sea-Doo sales sank last year, prompting the layoff of 850 workers at the Valcourt plant. The Traxter will be manufactured in this small town 100 km east of Montreal, where the world's first snowmobiles were produced 40 years ago and where the Ski-Doo is still built. The factory employs 3,000 at peak production.

The Traxter features a four-stroke, 500-cc engine, developed by Bombardier's Rotax division in Austria.

Last year, 445,158 ATVs were sold in the world, the vast majority in North America. Prices range between $4,200 and $10,500, depending on motor size and other features.

Source: The Canadian Press, "Bombardier Rolls Out New ATV," *The Vancouver Sun*, February 16, 1998, C1.

The management job in marketing

Now that you know about the marketing concept—a philosophy to guide the whole firm—let's look more closely at how a marketing manager helps a firm to achieve its objectives. The marketing manager is a manager, so let's look at the marketing management process.

The **marketing management process** is the process of (1) *planning* marketing activities, (2) directing the *implementation* of the plans, and (3) *controlling* these plans. Planning, implementation, and control are basic jobs of all managers, but here we will emphasize what they mean to marketing managers.

Exhibit 2–1 shows the relationships among the three jobs in the marketing management process. The jobs are all connected, to show that the marketing management process is continuous. In the planning job, managers set guidelines for the implementing job and specify expected results. They use these expected results in the control job to determine whether everything has worked out as planned. The link from the control job to the planning job is especially important. This feedback often leads to changes in the plans—or to new plans.

Marketing managers should seek new opportunities

Exhibit 2–1 shows that marketing managers must seek attractive new opportunities, as customers' needs change or as the organization's ability to meet customers' needs changes. Later in this chapter, we will discuss how marketing managers seek and evaluate opportunities. For now, however, note that marketing managers cannot just plan to maintain the status quo. Markets are dynamic. Consumers' needs, competitors, and the environment keep changing.

Consider Parker Brothers, a company that seemed to have a "Monopoly" in family games. While it continued selling board games, firms like Atari and Nintendo zoomed in with video game competition. Of course, not every opportunity is good for every company. As the Bombardier ATV example shows, really attractive opportunities are those that fit with what the entire company wants—and is able to do.

Exhibit 2–1 The Marketing Management Process

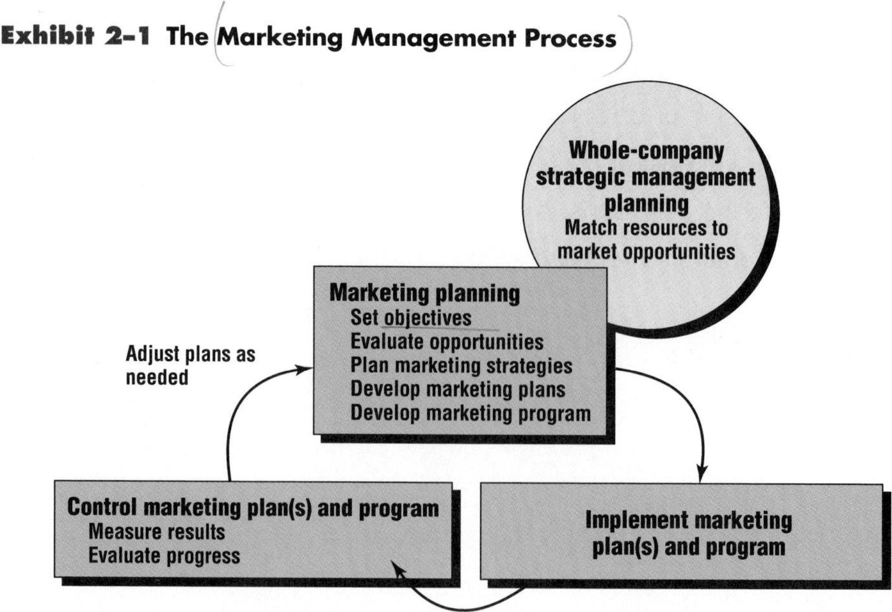

Strategic management planning concerns the whole firm

The job of planning strategies to guide a whole company is called **strategic (management) planning,** which is the managerial process of developing and maintaining a match between an organization's resources and its market opportunities. This is a top-management job that includes planning not only for marketing activities but also for production, research and development, and other functional areas. We'll touch on some of these issues in Chapter 21 when we consider the relationship between marketing and other functional areas. The focus of this text is not on whole-company planning, and you need to understand that marketing department plans are not whole-company plans.

On the other hand, company plans should be market-oriented. And the marketing manager's plans can set the tone and direction for the whole company. So we will use *strategic planning* and *strategic market planning* to mean the same thing.[1]

What is strategic market planning?

Strategic market planning means finding attractive opportunities and developing profitable marketing strategies. But what is a "marketing strategy"? We have used these words rather casually so far. Now let's see what they really mean.

What is a marketing strategy?

A **marketing strategy** specifies a target market and a related marketing mix. It is a "big picture" of what a firm will do in some market. Two interrelated parts are needed:

1. A **target market**—a fairly homogeneous (similar) group of customers to whom a company wishes to appeal.
2. A **marketing mix**—the controllable variables the company puts together to satisfy this target group.

The importance of target customers in this process can be seen in Exhibit 2–2, where the customer—the "C"—is at the centre of the diagram. The customer is surrounded by the controllable variables that we call the *marketing mix*. A typical marketing mix includes some product, offered at a price, with some promotion to tell potential customers about the product, and a way to reach the customer's place.

Exhibit 2-2
A Marketing Strategy

Brøderbund Software's marketing strategy aims at a specific group of target customers—young parents who have a computer at home and want their kids to learn while playing. Brøderbund's strategy calls for a variety of educational software products, ranging from its popular *Print Shop* to *Where in the World Is Carmen Sandiego?* Brøderbund designs all of its software with entertaining graphics and sound, and it tests the software on kids before it's released to be certain that it is easy to use. To make it convenient for target customers to buy the software, Brøderbund works with retailers like EggHead. Retailers are happy to give new Brøderbund products shelf space because they know that Brøderbund's promotion will help bring customers into the store. For example, when Brøderbund released *Where in Time Is Carmen Sandiego?* it not only placed ads in kids' magazines and family-oriented computer magazines but also sent direct-mail flyers to its database of registered customers. Other software publishers sell less expensive games for kids, but parents are loyal to Brøderbund because it consistently does a better job of catering to their needs.[2]

Selecting a market-oriented strategy is target marketing

Note that a marketing strategy specifies some *particular* target customers. This approach is called *target marketing,* to distinguish it from *mass marketing.* **Target marketing** says that a marketing mix is tailored to fit some specific target customers. In contrast, **mass marketing**—the typical production-oriented approach—vaguely aims at "everyone" with the same marketing mix. Mass marketing assumes that everyone is the same, and considers everyone a potential customer. It may help to think of target marketing as the "rifle approach" and mass marketing as the "shotgun approach."

Mass marketers may do target marketing

Commonly used terms can be confusing here. The terms *mass marketing* and *mass marketers* do not mean the same thing. Far from it! Mass market***ing*** means trying to sell to "everyone," as we explained above. Mass market***ers*** like General Foods and Zeller's are aiming at clearly defined target markets. The confusion with mass marketing occurs because their target markets usually are large and spread out.

Target marketing can mean big markets and profits

Target marketing is not limited to small market segments—only to fairly homogeneous ones. A very large market—even what is sometimes called the mass market—may be fairly homogeneous, and a target marketer will deliberately aim at it. For example, a very large group of parents of young children are homogeneous on many dimensions—including their attitudes about changing baby diapers. In the United States alone, this group spends about $3.5 billion a year on disposable diapers—so it should be no surprise that it is a major target market for companies like Kimberly-Clark (Huggies) and Procter & Gamble (Pampers). These days, so many customers in this target market buy disposable diapers that the challenge isn't just offering them a product they want but finding an ecologically sound way to dispose of it!

The basic reason for a marketing manager to focus on some specific target customers is to gain a competitive advantage, by developing a more satisfying marketing mix that should also be more profitable for the firm. Toshiba, for example, established a competitive advantage with travelling business computer users by being the first to offer a powerful laptop computer. Charles Schwab, the discount stock brokerage firm, targets knowledgeable investors who want a convenient, low-cost way to buy and sell shares by phone without a lot of advice (or pressure) from a salesperson.

Developing marketing mixes for target markets

There are many possible ways to satisfy the needs of target customers. A product can have many different features and quality levels. Service levels can be adjusted. The package can be of various sizes, colours, or materials. The brand name and warranty can be changed. Various advertising media—newspapers, magazines, radio, television, the Internet, billboards—may be used. A company's own sales force or other sales specialists can be used. Different prices can be charged. Price discounts may be given, and so on. With so many possible variables, is there any way to help organize all these decisions and simplify the selection of marketing mixes? The answer is yes.

Exhibit 2-3 Marketing Strategy—Showing the Four Ps of a Marketing Mix

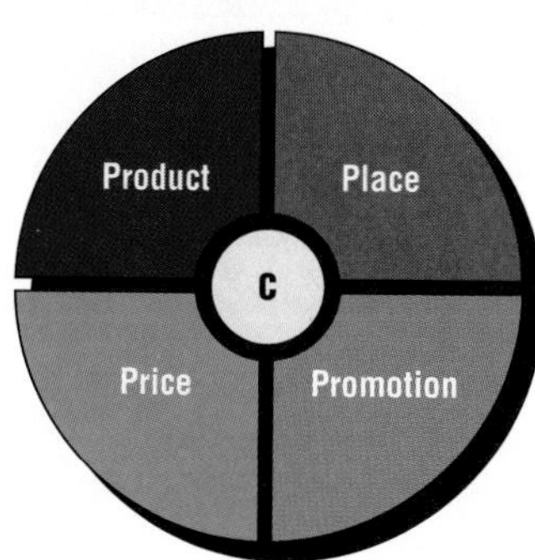

The four Ps make up a marketing mix

It is useful to reduce all the variables in the marketing mix to four basic ones:

Product.
Place.
Promotion.
Price.

It helps to think of the four major parts of a marketing mix as the "four Ps." Exhibit 2–3 emphasizes their relationship and their common focus on the customer, "C."

CUSTOMER IS NOT PART OF THE MARKETING MIX The customer is shown surrounded by the four Ps in Exhibit 2–3. Some students assume that the customer is part of the marketing mix, but this is not so. The customer should be the *target* of all marketing efforts. The customer is placed in the centre of the diagram to show this. The C stands for some specific customers—the target market.

Exhibit 2–4 shows some of the strategy decision variables organized by the four Ps. These will be discussed in later chapters. For now, let's just describe each P briefly.

Product—the good or service for the target's needs

The Product area (Chapters 9 and 10) is concerned with developing the right product for the target market. This offering may involve a physical good, a service, or a blend of both. Keep in mind that Product is not limited to physical goods. For example, the product of H & R Block is a completed tax form. The product of a political party is the set of policies it will work to achieve. The important thing to remember is that your good and/or service should satisfy some customers' needs.

Along with other Product-area decisions shown in Exhibit 2–4, we will talk about developing and managing new products and whole product lines. We will also discuss the characteristics of various kinds of products so that you will be able to make generalizations about product classes. This will help you to develop whole marketing mixes more quickly.

Place—reaching the target

Place (Chapters 11 through 13) is concerned with all the decisions involved in getting the *right* product to the target market's Place. A product isn't much good to a customer if it isn't available when and where it's wanted.

A product reaches customers through a channel of distribution. A **channel of distribution** is any series of firms (or individuals) from producer to final user or consumer.

Exhibit 2-4 Strategy Decision Areas Organized by the Four Ps

Product	Place	Promotion	Price
Physical good Service Features Quality level Accessories Installation Instructions Warranty Product lines Packaging Branding	Objectives Channel type Market exposure Kinds of intermediaries Kinds and locations of stores How to handle transporting and storing Service levels Recruiting intermediaries Managing channels	Objectives Promotion blend Salespeople Kind Number Selection Training Motivation Advertising Targets Kinds of ads Media type Copy thrust Prepared by whom Sales promotion Publicity	Objectives Flexibility Level over product life cycle Geographic terms Discounts Allowances

Exhibit 2-5 Four Examples of Basic Channels of Distribution for Consumer Products

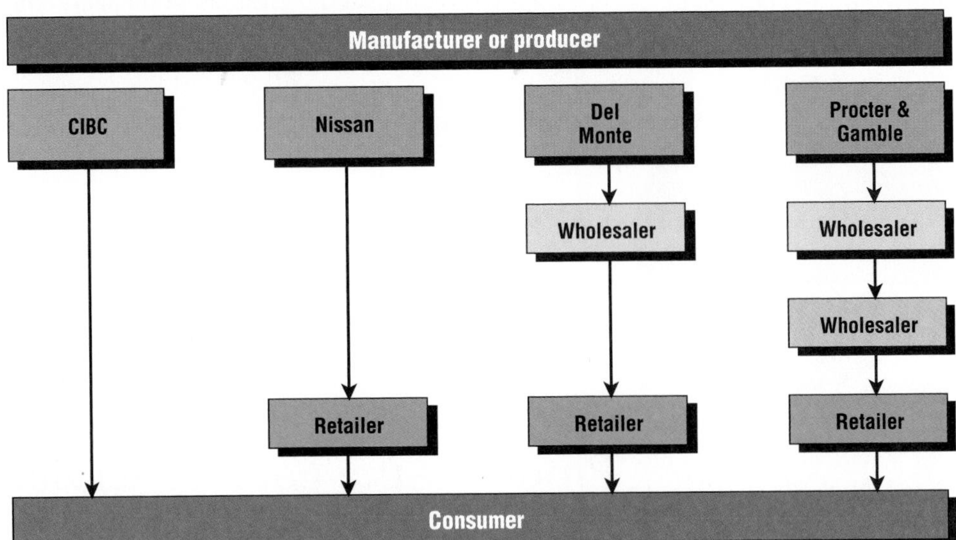

Sometimes, a channel system is quite short. It may run directly from a producer to a final user or consumer. This is especially common in business markets and in the marketing of services. Often, the system is more complex, involving many different kinds of intermediaries and specialists. See Exhibit 2–5 for some examples. And if a marketing manager has several different target markets, several different channels of distribution may be needed.

We will also see how physical distribution service levels and decisions concerning logistics (transporting and storing) relate to the other Place decisions and the rest of the marketing mix.

Promotion—telling and selling the customer

The third P—Promotion (Chapters 14 through 16)—is concerned with *telling* the target market about the right product. Promotion includes personal selling, mass selling, and sales promotion. It is the marketing manager's job to blend these methods.

Personal selling involves direct communication between sellers and potential customers. Personal selling usually happens face to face, but sometimes the communication occurs over the telephone. Personal selling lets the salesperson adapt the firm's marketing mix to each potential customer. But this individual attention comes at a price: personal selling can be very expensive. Often, this personal effort has to be blended with mass selling and sales promotion.

Mass selling is communicating with large numbers of customers at the same time. The main form of mass selling is **advertising**—any *paid* form of nonpersonal presentation of ideas, goods, or services by an identified sponsor. **Publicity**—any *unpaid* form of nonpersonal presentation of ideas, goods, or services—is another important form of mass selling.

Sales promotion refers to those promotion activities—other than advertising, publicity, and personal selling—that stimulate interest, trial, or purchase by final customers or others in the channel. This can involve use of coupons, point-of-purchase materials, samples, signs, catalogues, novelties, and circulars. Sales promotion specialists work with the personal selling and mass selling people.

Price—making it right

In addition to developing the right Product, Place, and Promotion, marketing managers must also decide the right Price (Chapters 17 and 18). In setting a price, they must consider the kind of competition in the target market, and the cost of the whole marketing mix. They must also try to estimate customer reaction to possible prices. Besides this, they also must know current practices as to markups, discounts, and other terms of sale. Further, they must be aware of legal restrictions on pricing.

If customers won't accept the Price, all of the planning effort will be wasted. So you can see that Price is an important area for a marketing manager.

Each of the four Ps contributes to the whole

All four Ps are needed in a marketing mix. In fact, they should all be tied together. But is any one more important than the others? Generally speaking, the answer is no—all contribute to one whole. When a marketing mix is being developed, all (final) decisions about the Ps should be made at the same time. That's why the four Ps are arranged around the customer (C) in a circle—to show that they all are equally important.

Let's sum up our discussion of marketing mix planning thus far. We develop a *Product* to satisfy the target customers. We find a way to reach our target customers' *Place*. We use *Promotion* to tell the target customers (and intermediaries) about the product that has been designed for them. And we set a *Price* after estimating expected customer reaction to the total offering and the costs of getting it to them.

Strategy jobs must be done together

It is important to stress—it cannot be overemphasized—that selecting a target market *and* developing a marketing mix are interrelated. Both parts of a marketing strategy must be decided together. It is *strategies* that must be evaluated against the company's objectives, not alternative target markets or alternative marketing mixes.

Understanding target markets leads to good strategies

A target market's needs virtually determine the nature of an appropriate marketing mix. So marketers must analyze their potential target markets with great care. This book will explore ways to identify attractive market opportunities and develop appropriate strategies. These ideas can be seen more clearly with an example in the home financing market.

The Royal Bank was interested in capturing more of the market looking for financing to purchase a new home. Its strategic planning process involved recognizing the target market's wide ranges of housing needs and of incomes available to meet those needs. The typical home owner owns three different homes during a lifetime. First-time buyers tend to buy a home that has no frills and is functional. A few years later, these people become move-up buyers. Financially better off and with hefty equities from their first homes, they buy larger, more expensive dwellings—usually single-family houses. As years go by, they become empty nesters and move again—often to smaller, more easily maintained dwellings such as bungalows, townhouses, or condominiums.

Each group of home buyers is seeking out different qualities in homes. More important to the Royal Bank, each group also requires different banking services. Understanding this allows the bank to design services for these groups. For first-time home buyers, the Royal provides a series of publications that introduce them to the issues they must be aware of before they invest, including types of mortgages and interest rates. For those planning their move up, the Royal provides a variety of ways they can pay off their mortgages and buy up. And for those selling their empty nest to purchase something more manageable, the bank provides savings accounts that offer high interest for the money they'll have to invest.

Many firms identify several potential target markets for their products but plan their marketing mix around one target market. The Royal Bank chose to concentrate its efforts on selling three markets a particular product that was modified to meet all of their needs. Knowing what it did about each group, the bank offered financing for home purchases (Product), made that financing widely available through all of its branches (Place), and aimed it at low-, middle-, and high-income purchasers through personal consultation and informative brochures (Promotion)—of course, on terms they could live with (Price).[3]

The marketing plan is a guide to implementation and control

Now that the key ideas of strategic market planning have been introduced, we can return to our overview of the marketing management process. You will see how a marketing strategy leads to a marketing plan and ultimately to implementation and control (see Exhibit 2–1 and Internet Insite 2–1, which identifies marketing strategy issues that Web-based marketers must resolve).

Marketing plan fills out marketing strategy

A marketing strategy sets a target market and a marketing mix. It is a "big picture" of what a firm will do in some market. A marketing plan goes further. A **marketing plan** is a written statement of a marketing strategy *and* the time-related details for carrying out the strategy. It should spell out the following in detail:

1. What marketing mix will be offered, to whom (that is, the target market), and for how long.
2. What company resources (shown as costs) will be needed at what rate (month by month, perhaps).
3. What results are expected (sales and profits, perhaps monthly or quarterly).

The plan should also include some control procedures, so that whoever is to carry out the plan will know if things are going wrong. This might be something as simple as comparing actual sales against expected sales—with a warning flag to be raised whenever total sales fall below a certain level.

Implementation puts plans into operation

After a marketing plan is developed, a marketing manager knows *what* needs to be done. Then the manager is concerned with **implementation**—putting marketing plans into operation.

Strategies work out as planned only when they are effectively implemented. Many **operational decisions**—short-run decisions to help implement strategies—may be needed.

Managers should make operational decisions that are consistent with the chosen strategy. Product policies, Place policies, and so on are developed as part of strategic planning. Then operational decisions within these policies probably will be necessary while the basic strategy is carried out. Note, however, that as long as these operational decisions stay within the policy guidelines, managers are making no change in the basic strategy. But what if the controls show that operational decisions are not producing the desired results? Then, the managers may have to reevaluate the whole strategy, rather than just working harder at implementing it.

It's easier to see the difference between strategy decisions and operational decisions if we illustrate these ideas using a shoe company example. In Exhibit 2–6, possible four-P or basic strategy policies are shown in the left-hand column, and likely operational decisions are shown in the right-hand column.

It should be clear that some operational decisions are made regularly—even daily—and that such decisions should not be confused with planning strategy. Certainly, a

Marketing Strategy Issues for the Web

The challenges and opportunities presented by the Web will be discussed in the Insites that follow. As a new advertising medium and distribution channel, the Web holds enormous promise. The Web is slowly replacing traditional media as the primary provider of news and information. The Web is also opening new markets and allowing organizations to communicate more effectively with consumers and their own employees. However, before venturing into online marketspace, a marketer must address the following key questions:

- Should you take your brand online? This would depend on what percentage of your brand's consumers are online. If 50% of your consumers are online, that does not mean you should spend 50 percent, or even 25 percent, of all advertising dollars online. It depends on how much time these consumers are spending online. There may be other, more cost-effective ways of reaching this group.[1]
- What is the nature of your product or service? Products that require personal inspection or testing (experience goods) are harder to sell online.
- What business approach is most appropriate? Should you open an online storefront, or be part of an online mall, or limit yourself to online advertising, or just use the Web as an online catalogue? The answers to these questions will depend on the objectives of your business and your type of product. High-involvement and expensive products that require a lot of information search will benefit from an information-rich Web site presence. Those who are marketing packaged goods, which are inexpensive and low in involvement, may just need to invest in Web advertising.[2]
- Should your online presence complement a presence in traditional channels, or is yours purely an online business? For example, Barnes & Noble has regular bookstores as well as an online bookstore (www.barnesandnoble.com), while Amazon.Com is purely an online bookstore (www.amazon.com).
- Is the market for your product global? If it is, do you want to use the Web to reach overseas customers? Issues such as translation, foreign regulations, foreign exchange, and copyright and tax laws would then have to be considered.
- What is the level of competition online?
- Can you ensure that your Web marketing is in sync with the rest of your marketing plan?
- How much are you going to commit to online marketing? Volvo, the Swedish car manufacturer, was among the first in the automobile industry to establish an online presence. Volvo thought this would lead to increased sales. But visitors to the site used the e-mail feature mainly to complain about problems with their own Volvos. Unfortunately, Volvo did not staff the site with qualified people who could respond properly to these consumer complaints.[3] Even large businesses can make the mistake of committing too little to an Internet presence.

The answers to questions such as these will provide the marketer with a good understanding of whether online marketing is viable or not. It will also help identify the risk factors. Remember, a marketer's job doesn't end with planning. A good plan by itself does not guarantee success. That plan must be carried out effectively.

1. Rex Briggs, "A Roadmap to Online Marketing Strategy, MBInteractive (www.mbinteractive.com).
2. Ibid.
3. Evan L. Schwartz, "Advertising Webonomics 101," in *Wired* (www.wired.com/wired/4.02/webonomics.html).

This is one of a series of Internet Insites prepared in April 1998 by Dr. Ramesh Venkat of Saint Mary's University for *Basic Marketing*, Ninth Canadian Edition.

Exhibit 2-6 Relationship of Strategy Policies to Operational Decisions for Baby Shoe Company

MARKETING MIX DECISION AREA	STRATEGY POLICIES	LIKELY OPERATIONAL DECISIONS
Product	Carry as limited a line of colours, styles, and sizes as will satisfy the target market.	Add, change, or drop colours, styles, and/or sizes as customer tastes dictate.
Place	Distribute through selected "baby products" retailers who will carry the full line and provide good in-store sales support and promotion.	In market areas where sales potential is not achieved, add new retail outlets and/or drop retailers whose performance is poor.
Promotion	Promote the benefits and value of the special design and how it meets customer needs.	When a retailer hires a new salesperson, send current training package with details on product line; increase use of local newspaper print ads during peak demand periods (before holidays, etc.).
Price	Maintain a "premium" price, but encourage retailers to make large-volume orders by offering discounts on quantity purchases.	Offer short-term introductory price "deals" to retailers when a new style is first introduced.

great deal of effort can be involved in these operational decisions. They may take a good part of the sales or advertising manager's time. But they are not the strategy decisions that will be our primary concern.

Our focus has been—and will continue to be—on developing marketing strategies. But it is also important to see that eventually, marketing managers must develop and implement marketing plans. We discuss this more fully in Chapters 19 and 20.[4]

Several plans make a whole marketing program

Most companies implement more than one marketing strategy—and related marketing plan—at the same time. They may have several products—some of them quite different—that are aimed at different target markets. The other elements of the marketing mix may also vary. Gillette's Right Guard deodorant, its Atra Plus razor blades, and its Liquid Paper correction fluid all have different marketing mixes. Yet the strategies for each must be implemented at the same time.[5]

A **marketing program** blends all of the firm's marketing plans into one big plan. See Exhibit 2–7. This program, then, is the responsibility of the whole company. Typically, the whole *marketing program* is an integrated part of the whole company strategic plan we discussed earlier.

Ultimately, marketing managers plan and implement a whole marketing program. In this text, however, we will emphasize planning one marketing strategy at a time, rather than planning—or implementing—a whole marketing program. This is practical because it is important to plan each strategy carefully. Too many marketing managers fall into sloppy thinking. They try to develop too many strategies all at once—and don't develop any very carefully. Good plans are the building blocks of marketing management. We'll talk about merging plans into a marketing program in Chapter 19.

Control is analyzing and correcting what you've done

The control job provides the feedback that leads managers to modify their marketing strategies. To maintain control, a marketing manager uses a number of tools—for example, computer sales analysis, marketing research surveys, and accounting analysis of expenses and profits. A section of Chapter 20 is devoted to the important topic of controlling marketing plans and programs.

Exhibit 2-7 Elements of a Firm's Marketing Program

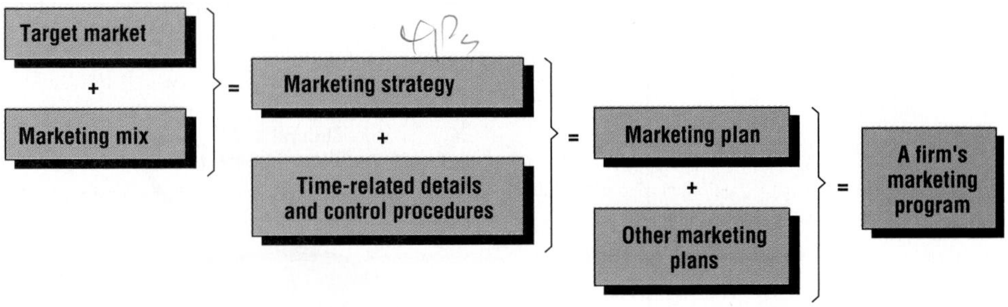

In addition, as we talk about each of the marketing decision areas, we will discuss some of the control problems. This will help you understand how control keeps the firm on course—or shows the need to plan a new course.

All marketing jobs require planning and control

At first, it might appear that only high-level management or really large companies need to be concerned with management and control. This is not true. Every organization needs planning—and without control it's impossible to know if the plans are working.

This means that strategic market planning may be very important to you soon—maybe in your present job, or in your college or university activities, or in deciding on your own career goals. In Appendix C we present some strategic planning ideas to help you set your own career goals and prepare an action plan to get a job. Take a break and look at Appendix C. You'll find it worthwhile!

Strategic planning takes place within a framework

A marketing manager's strategic planning cannot take place in a vacuum. Instead, the manager works with controllable variables within a framework involving many variables that must be considered even though the manager can't control them. Exhibit 2–8 illustrates this framework and shows that the typical marketing manager must be concerned about the competitive environment, economic and technological environment, political and legal environment, and cultural and social environment, as well as the firm's resources and objectives. We will discuss these marketing environment variables in more detail in the next chapter. But clearly, the environment in which the marketing manager operates affects strategic planning.

While market-oriented strategic planning is helpful to marketers, it is also needed by accountants, production and personnel people, and all other specialists. A market-oriented plan lets everybody in the firm know in what "ballpark" they are playing—and what they are trying to accomplish. In other words, it gives direction to the whole business effort. An accountant can't set budgets without a plan, except perhaps by mechanically projecting last year's budget. Similarly, a financial manager can't project cash needs without some idea of expected sales to target customers—and of the costs of satisfying them.

We will use the term *marketing manager* for editorial convenience, but really, when we talk about strategic market planning, we are talking about the planning that a market-oriented manager should do when developing a firm's strategic plans. This kind of thinking should be done—or at least understood—by everyone in the organization who is responsible for planning. And this means even the entry-level salesperson, production supervisor, retail buyer, or personnel counsellor.

Exhibit 2-8 Marketing Manager's Framework

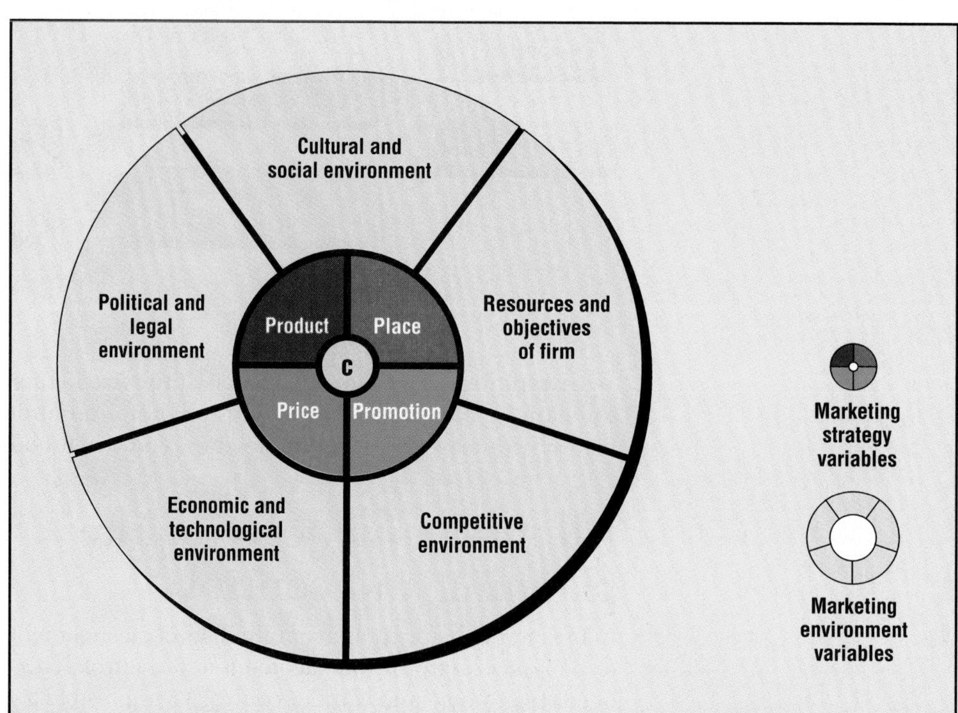

Strategic market planning—the watch industry

We emphasize the planning part of the marketing manager's job for a good reason. The one-time strategy decisions—the decisions that decide what business the company is in and the strategies it will follow—usually determine success, or failure. An extremely good plan might be carried out badly and still be profitable, while a poor but well-implemented plan can lose money. The case history that follows shows the importance of planning. It also shows why we emphasize strategic market planning throughout this text.

The market for watches is dynamic and highly competitive, but Timex has used new technology to develop a line of Indiglo watches that do a better job of meeting the needs of some target customers.

Time for new strategies

Conventional watch makers, both domestic and foreign, had always aimed at customers who thought of watches as high-priced, high-quality symbols to mark special events. Advertising was concentrated around Christmas and graduation time and stressed a watch's symbolic appeal. Expensive jewellery stores were the main retail outlets.

This commonly accepted strategy of the major watch companies ignored people who just wanted to tell the time, and who were interested in a reliable, low-priced watch. So the Timex Company developed a successful strategy around its Timex watches, and became the world's largest watch company. Timex completely upset the watch industry, both foreign and domestic, not only by offering a good product (with a one-year repair or replace guarantee) at a lower price, but also by using new, lower-cost channels of distribution. Its watches were widely available in drugstores, discount houses, and just about any other retail store that would carry them.

But marketing managers at Timex soon faced a new challenge. Texas Instruments, a new competitor in the watch market, took the industry by storm with its low-cost but very accurate electronic watches, using the same channels Timex had developed. Other firms quickly developed a watch that used a more stylish liquid crystal display for the digital readout. Texas Instruments could not change quickly enough to keep up, and the other companies took away its customers. The competition became so intense that Texas Instruments stopped marketing watches altogether.

While Timex and others were focusing on lower-priced watches, Japan's Seiko captured a commanding share of the high-priced gift market for its stylish and accurate quartz watches by obtaining strong distribution. All of this forced many traditional watch makers—like some of the once-famous Swiss brands—to close their factories.

Next, Switzerland's Swatch launched its colourful, affordable plastic watches. It promoted its watches as fashion accessories and set them apart from those of other firms, whose ads squabbled about whose watches were most accurate and dependable. Swatch was also able to attract new intermediaries by focusing its distribution on upscale fashion and department stores. The marketing mix that Swatch developed around its fashion watch idea was so successful that it didn't just increase Swatch's share of the market: the total size of the watch market increased because many consumers bought several watches to match different fashions.

Swatch's success prompted Timex, Seiko, and others to pay more attention to consumer fashion preferences. Timex emphasized better styling to compete in the higher-priced market, and broadened its offering to defend its position in the low- to mid-priced segment.

The economic downturn in the early 1990s brought more changes. Sales of fashion watches levelled off, so Swatch targeted segments with other needs. For example, it introduced a $45 scuba watch guaranteed to keep ticking at depths of 200 metres. The reemergence of value-seeking customers prompted Timex to return to its famous advertising tagline of the 1960s: "It takes a licking and keeps on ticking." Its position as the inexpensive but durable choice has helped it strengthen its distribution in department stores, sporting goods stores, and other channels, and has given it a leg up in getting shelf space for new products such as its Indiglo line of watches. However, just as the new Indiglo technology has allowed Timex to develop new watches, other firms are looking for ways to use technology to open new markets and attract customers with unmet needs. For example, Casio has introduced a watch that includes a remote control for TVs and VCRs. With frequent changes such as these, marketing strategies must constantly be updated and revised.[6]

Creative strategic planning needed for survival

Dramatic shifts in strategy, like those described in the watch industry, may surprise conventional, production-oriented managers. But such changes are becoming much more common and should be expected. Industries or firms that have accepted the marketing concept realize that they cannot define their line of business in terms of the products they currently produce or sell. Rather, they have to think about the basic consumer needs they serve, and how those needs may change in the future. If they are too nearsighted, they may fail to see what's coming until too late.

But planning ahead also involves risk taking. Marketing Demo 2–1 examines how the "bad taste" marketing strategy of WK Buckley, Canada's leading cough syrup manufacturer, has helped it succeed in the Canadian market.

Creative strategic planning is becoming even more important. Domestic and foreign competition threatens those who can't provide superior customer value and find ways to build stronger relationships with customers. New markets, new customers, and new ways of doing things must be found if companies are to operate profitably in the future—and be socially responsible as well.

Marketing Demo 2-1

How Buckley Took On the Big Boys

WK Buckley Ltd. is a Mississauga, Ontario–based company which was established in 1920, when pharmacist William Buckley decided to get into the cough syrup business. Over the past decade, 75-year-old Frank Buckley, who took over the company from his father, has become the marketing spokesman for the company. He appears in a series of quirky ads that make a virtue of the bad taste of Buckley's Mixture to relieve coughs and colds. With his craggy face and quips like "I came by my bad taste honestly. I inherited it from my father" and "It contains oil of pine needles. What did you expect it to taste like?" he has become something of a celebrity. Further, these ads have generated enough consumer interest in new markets to get the product on retailer's shelves.

Buckley's matter-of-fact, down-home honesty has created an image for the company that sets it apart from its mainly well-healed multinational competitors. Since adoption of this "bad taste" campaign eight years ago, Buckley's share of the $97 million Canadian cough-remedy market has grown from 2.2 to 8.1 percent. Although the company plans to increase market share within Canada to 15 percent over the next few years, real growth is expected to come from international markets. Areas such as the United States, Europe, Asia, and other global locations have recently been targeted. In China, for example, Buckley's is negotiating a deal that would see an initial demand for the product that represents 60 percent of Buckley's total current production run.

But the international route is tough for an operation of 23 employees that's battling for shelf space with those multinational competitors. "When Procter & Gamble goes into Wal-Mart, they listen," quips Vice President and General Manager John Meehan. "When Buckley's goes in, they laugh." But Meehan is optimistic. "We built this business on advertising," explains Meehan, "and I think that we can do it elsewhere even if we don't have a $50 million budget like Procter & Gamble."

Through a variety of "off the wall" international campaigns, the company hopes to develop groundswells of interest in niche markets and therefore replicate the successes of the Canadian market. By using the same "bad taste is good medicine" theme translated into the language of its foreign markets, the company plans to capitalize on the success experienced in Canada.

Source: James Pollack, "The Taste of Success," *Marketing Magazine,* January 23, 1995, pp. 11, 13.

Our largest bottle is 200 ml. Anything more would be cruel.

It tastes awful. And it works.

People swear by it. And at it.

It tastes awful. And it works.

On the bright side, you won't have to take it for long.

It tastes awful. And it works.

Exhibit 2-9 Distribution of Different Firms Based on Their Marketing Performance

MARKETING PERFORMANCE:	Total failure	Poor	**Fair**	Good	Exceptional
Marketing share growth	Precipitous decline	Significant decline	**Modest decline**	Increase	Dramatic increase
New Product Success Rate	0%	5%	**10%**	25%	40%+
Advertising ROI	Negative	0%	**1–4%**	5–10%	20%
Promotional programs	Disaster	Unprofitable	**Marginally unprofitable**	Profitable	Very profitable
Customer satisfaction	0–59%	60–69%	**70–79%**	80–89%	90–95%
Customer retention loyalty	0–44%	45–59%	**60–74%**	75–89%	90–94%

Source: Copernicus. The Marketing Investment Strategy Group

Focus on "best practices" for improved results

The case studies and concepts in this chapter highlight effective marketing thinking. Throughout the text, we will continue with this thrust, focusing on marketing frameworks and concepts that produce good results. Some of these are new and innovative, and others are well established. What they have in common is that they all work well.

Sometimes we will warn you about marketing errors, so that you can avoid them. But we won't just give you "laundry lists" of different approaches and then leave it to you to guess what might work. Rather, our focus will be on "best practices" marketing.

There is an important reason for this approach. In too many firms, managers do a poor job planning and implementing marketing strategies and programs. And, as shown in Exhibit 2–9, this type of "death wish" marketing is both costly and ineffective. In fact, you can see that even the average marketing program isn't producing great results—and that accounts for the majority of firms!

Exhibit 2–9 was developed by experts at Copernicus, one of the premier marketing research and consulting firms in the world. As these experts indicate in the chart, some managers are creating marketing programs that produce exceptional results for their companies. This book will help you do exactly that.

What are attractive opportunities?

Strategic market planning tries to match opportunities to the firm's resources (what it can do) and its objectives (what top management wants to do). Successful strategies get their start when a creative manager spots an attractive market opportunity. Yet, an opportunity that is attractive for one firm may not be attractive for another. Attractive opportunities for a particular firm are those which the firm has some chance of doing something about, given its resources and

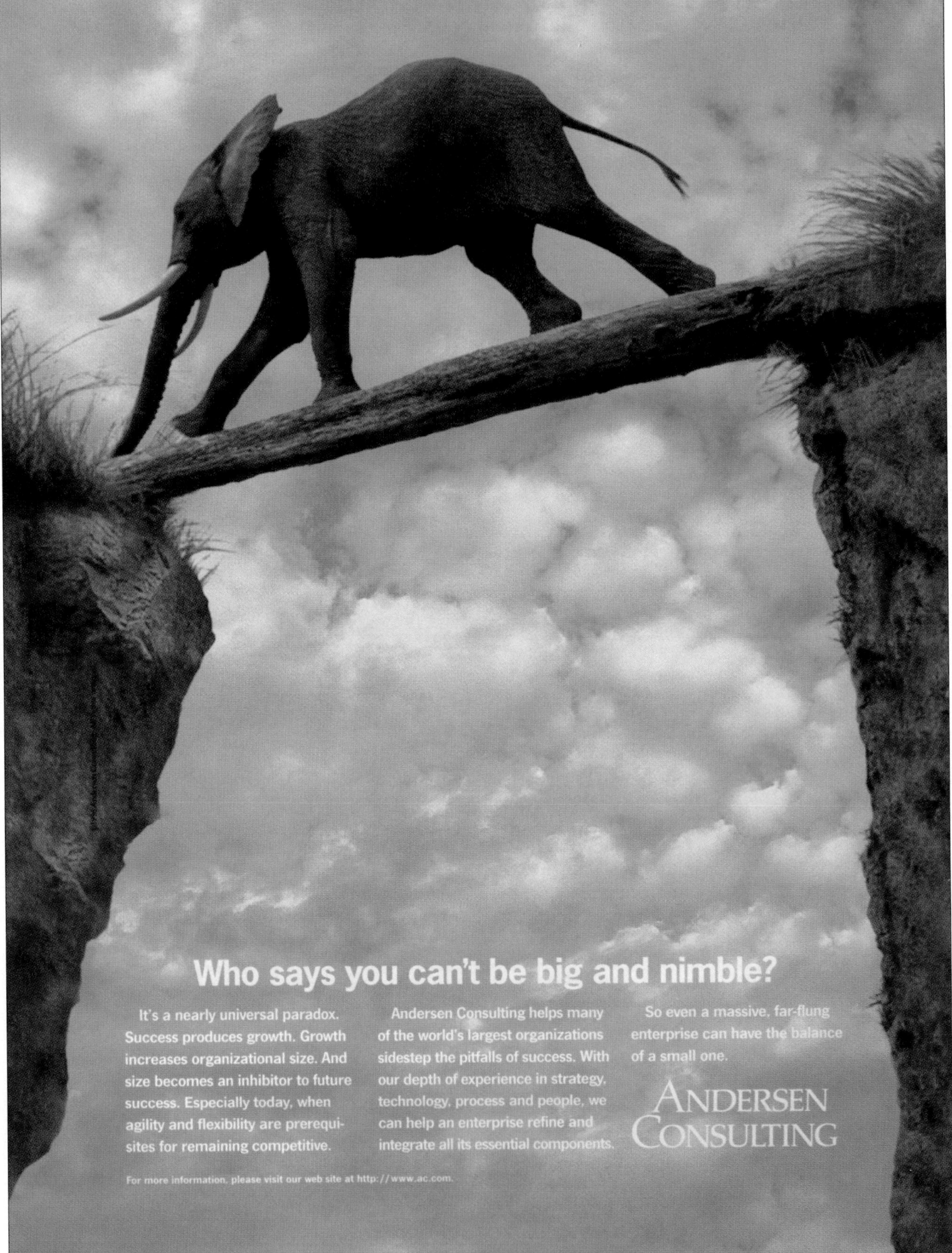
Who says you can't be big and nimble?
It's a nearly universal paradox. Success produces growth. Growth increases organizational size. And size becomes an inhibitor to future success. Especially today, when agility and flexibility are prerequisites for remaining competitive.
Andersen Consulting helps many of the world's largest organizations sidestep the pitfalls of success. With our depth of experience in strategy, technology, process and people, we can help an enterprise refine and integrate all its essential components.
So even a massive, far-flung enterprise can have the balance of a small one.
ANDERSEN CONSULTING
For more information, please visit our web site at http://www.ac.com.

objectives. As the accompanying Andersen Consulting ad suggests, large corporations should not let their size hinder their search for marketing opportunities.

Breakthrough opportunities are best

Throughout this book, we will emphasize finding **breakthrough opportunities**—opportunities that help innovators develop hard-to-copy marketing strategies that will be very profitable for a long time. This is important because there are always imitators who want to "share" the innovator's profits—if they can. It's hard to continue providing superior value to target customers if competitors can easily copy your marketing mix.

Competitive advantage is needed—at least

Even if a manager can't find a breakthrough opportunity, the firm should try to obtain a competitive advantage to increase its chances for profit or survival. **Competitive advantage** means that a firm has a marketing mix that the target market sees as better than a competitor's mix. A competitive advantage may result from efforts in different areas of the firm—cost cutting in production, innovative R&D, more effective purchasing of needed components, or financing for a new distribution facility. Similarly, a strong sales force, a well-known brand name, or good dealers may give it a competitive advantage in pursuing an opportunity. Whatever the source, an advantage only succeeds if it allows the firm to provide superior value and satisfy customers better than some competitor.

Sometimes a firm can achieve breakthrough opportunities and competitive advantage by simply fine-tuning its current marketing mix(es) or developing closer relationships with its customers. Other times it may need new facilities, new people in new parts of the world, and totally new ways of solving problems. But every firm needs some competitive advantage, so that the promotion people will have something unique to sell and so that success won't simply hinge on offering lower and lower prices.[7]

Types of opportunities to pursue

Most people have unsatisfied needs, and alert marketers who see these needs find opportunities all around them. Unfortunately, some opportunities seem obvious only after someone else identifies them. Marketers need a framework for thinking about the kinds of opportunities they may find. Exhibit 2–10 shows the four broad possibilities: market penetration, market development, product development, and diversification. We will look at these separately, but some firms may pursue more than one type of opportunity at the same time.

Market penetration

Market penetration means trying to increase sales of a firm's present products in its present markets, probably through a more aggressive marketing mix. The firm may try to increase customers' rate of use or attract competitors' customers or current nonusers. Marketing Demo 2–2 shows how loyalty marketing can increase corporate profits.

Exhibit 2–10 Four Basic Types of Opportunities

	Present products	New products
Present markets	Market penetration	Product development
New markets	Market development	Diversification

Marketing Demo 2-2

How to Reward Clients Using Loyalty Marketing

Loyalty marketing has become one of the most pervasive marketing techniques of the '90s. The rationale is quite simple—it is commonly accepted that loyal customers are more frequent purchasers and by rewarding loyalty, we will keep these profitable customers as our own.

The techniques used range from sophisticated points programs (frequent flyer clubs, Air Miles participants, membership reward plans) to wallet-sized cards which record your purchase and make you eligible to receive, say, a free coffee or muffin.

The Value of Loyalty

There is much evidence to support the contention that loyalty programs contribute significant amounts to the bottom line. Zellers Inc.'s "Club Z" program has been acknowledged as a key weapon in keeping Wal-Mart at bay. Various frequent flyer programs have shown that customers will actively choose to fly "their" airline to get the points.

In his book *The Loyalty Effect,* Fred Reichheld clearly demonstrates that a five-per-cent improvement in customer loyalty can increase profits by up to 75 per cent. And in *All Consumers are NOT Created Equal,* author Garth Hallberg shows that loyal customers can be motivated to buy even more.

The Key to Loyalty Marketing

There is one critical element in loyalty marketing—recognition. The fundamental success of this approach lies in that it *recognizes and acknowledges* customers who exhibit the behaviour that we value. This simple recognition is a reward to the customer. It becomes more powerful as we add tangible rewards to the recognition—but the rewards are primarily a mechanism to support recognition.

The rewards must reinforce your image and must be rewards that your most loyal customers value. They don't necessarily need to be money or points. For example, Delta Airlines, in a survey of its most loyal frequent flyers, found that this group placed a high value on advance boarding—a "reward" that Delta was easily able to accomodate at very little cost.

A Database Perspective

Loyalty marketing is indeed an important component of the overall marketing mix but it must be viewed in context, as part of a larger effort to maximize return on customer satisfaction.

In a presentation at the National Centre for Database Marketing Conference in December 1996, Dr. Terry Vavra outlined a process to more accurately measure customer value. Vavra's technique includes four key measures. They are: satisfaction, loyalty, profit and potential.

To achieve maximum return, each of these elements must be considered. Highly loyal customers who contribute little profit and low potential need to be treated differently from those who are less loyal but who contribute higher profits and present greater potential profits.

To unlock all of the untapped potential and to effectively manage your customers, you must develop and maintain an accurate database of all customer activity. Without the overall view of profit provided by your database, you may be rewarding unprofitable loyalty.

Source: Brain Broadway, "How To Reward Clients Using Loyalty Marketing," *The Ad Pages, Vancouver's Advertising & Media Directory 1997,* pp. 8, 9, published by BIV Publications Ltd. Reprinted with permission from Brian Broadway.

New promotion appeals alone may not be effective. A firm may need to add more stores in present areas for greater convenience. Short-term price cuts or coupon offers may help. But remember, any firm that cuts prices can expect an immediate response from its competitors.

Obviously, to do effective analysis and planning, marketers need to understand why some people are buying now and what will motivate them to change brands, buy more, or begin or resume buying.

Market development

Market development means trying to increase sales by selling present products in new markets. Firms may try advertising in different media to reach new target customers. Or they may add channels of distribution or new stores in new areas, including overseas. For example, to reach new customers, McDonald's opens outlets in airports, office buildings, zoos, casinos, hospitals, and military bases. And it's rapidly expanding into international markets with outlets in places like Russia, Brazil, Hong Kong, Mexico, and Australia.

Market development may also involve searching for new uses for a product, as when Lipton provides recipes showing how to use its dry soup mixes for chip dip.

Product development

Product development means offering new or improved products for present markets. By identifying the present market's needs, a firm may see ways to add or modify product features, create several quality levels, or add more types or sizes to better satisfy customers. Computer software firms like Microsoft boost sales by introducing new versions of popular programs. Microsoft also develops other types of new products for its customers. Similarly, many ski resorts have developed trails for hiking and mountain bikes, to bring their ski customers back in the summer when the snow is gone and the lodge would otherwise be empty.

Diversification

Diversification means moving into totally different lines of business—perhaps entirely unfamiliar products, markets, or even levels in the production–marketing system. If you stop to think of it, you are familiar with many examples of diversification. Honda is a well established automobile manufacturer. During the 1998 ice storm in Quebec and Ontario, Honda generators were prized possessions. Honda also manufactures and sells power equipment for home gardeners, capitalizing on the current gardening boom.

Diversification presents the most challenging opportunities. Diversification involves both new products *and* new markets. The further the opportunity from what the firm is already doing, the more attractive it may look to the optimists—and the harder it will be to evaluate. Opportunities very different from a firm's current experiences involve higher risks. The landscape is littered with failed efforts at diversification. For example, Holiday Corporation learned fast that making mattresses (like the ones used in its Holiday Inn motels) was *not* one of its strengths.

Which opportunities come first?

Usually, firms find attractive opportunities fairly close to markets they already know. This may allow them to capitalize on changes in their present markets—or more basic changes in the external environment. Moreover, many firms are finding that the easiest way to increase profits is to do a better job of hanging on to the customers they've already won, by meeting their needs so well that they wouldn't consider switching to another firm.

Most firms think first of greater market penetration: they want to increase profits where they already have experience and strengths. Marketers who understand their present markets well may also see opportunities in product development, especially because they already have a way to reach their present customers. But a firm that already has as big a share as it can get in its present markets should consider market development—finding new markets for its present products—including expanding regionally, nationally, or internationally.[8]

How to evaluate opportunities

A progressive firm constantly looks for new opportunities. Once the opportunities are identified, the firm must screen and evaluate them. Usually, a firm can't pursue all available opportunities, so it must try to match its opportunities to its resources and objectives. First, management must quickly screen out the obvious mismatches so that other opportunities can be analyzed more carefully. Let's look at some approaches for screening and evaluating opportunities.

Developing and applying screening criteria

After you analyze the firm's resources (for strengths and weaknesses), the environmental trends the firm faces, and the objectives of top management, you merge them all into a set of product-market screening criteria. These criteria should include both quantitative and qualitative components. The quantitative components summarize the firm's objectives: sales, profit, and return on investment (ROI) targets. (Note: ROI analysis is discussed briefly in Appendix B.) The qualitative components summarize what kinds of businesses the firm wants to be in, what businesses it wants to exclude, what weaknesses it should avoid, and what resources (strengths) and trends it should build on.[9]

Developing screening criteria is difficult, but worth the effort. They summarize in one place what the firm wants to accomplish—in quantitative terms—as well as roughly how and where it wants to accomplish it. The criteria should be realistic—that is, they should be achievable. It should be possible to turn opportunities that pass the screen into strategies that the firm can implement with the resources it has.

Exhibit 2–11 illustrates the product-market screening criteria for a small retail and wholesale distributor. These criteria help the firm's managers eliminate unsuitable opportunities—and find attractive ones to turn into strategies and plans.

Exhibit 2-11 An Example of Product-Market Screening Criteria for a Small Retail and Wholesale Distributor ($5 million annual sales)

1. Quantitative Criteria
- a. Increase sales by $750,000 per year for the next five years.
- b. Earn ROI of at least 25 percent before taxes on new ventures.
- c. Break even within one year on new ventures.
- d. Opportunity must be large enough to justify interest (to help meet objectives) but small enough so company can handle with the resources available.
- e. Several opportunities should be pursued to reach the objectives—to spread the risks.

2. Qualitative Criteria
- a. Nature of business preferred.
  - (1) New goods and services for present customers to strengthen relationships.
  - (2) "Quality" products that do not cannibalize sales of current products.
  - (3) Competition should be weak and opportunity should be hard to copy for several years.
  - (4) Should build on our strong sales skills.
  - (5) There should be strongly felt (even unsatisfied) needs—to reduce promotion costs and permit "high" prices.
- b. Constraints.
  - (1) Nature of businesses to exclude.
    - (a) Manufacturing.
    - (b) Any requiring large fixed capital investments.
    - (c) Any requiring many support people who must be "good" all the time and would require much supervision.
  - (2) Geographic.
    - (a) United States, Mexico, and Canada only.
  - (3) General.
    - (a) Make use of current strengths.
    - (b) Attractiveness of market should be reinforced by more than one of the following basic trends: technological, demographic, social, economic, political.
    - (c) Market should not be bucking any basic trends.

Whole plans should be evaluated

To apply the quantitative part of the screening criteria, you need to forecast the probable results of implementing a marketing strategy, because only implemented plans generate sales, profits, and return on investment (ROI). For a rough screening, you only need to estimate the likely results of implementing each opportunity over a logical planning period. If a product's life is likely to be three years, for example, a good strategy may not produce profitable results for 6 to 12 months. But evaluated over the projected three-year life, the product may look like a winner. When evaluating the potential of possible opportunities (product-market strategies), it is important to evaluate similar things—that is, *whole* plans.

Opportunities that pass the screen—or *all* opportunities, if you don't use screening criteria—should be evaluated in more detail before being accepted as *the* product-market strategic plans for implementation. Usually, a firm has more opportunities than resources and has to choose among them—to match its opportunities to its resources and objectives. The following approaches help firms select among possible plans.

Total profit approach

In the total profit approach, management forecasts potential sales and costs during the life of the plan to estimate likely profitability.

Managers may evaluate the prospects for each plan over a five-year planning period, using monthly and/or annual sales and cost estimates. This is shown graphically in Exhibit 2–12.

Note that managers can evaluate different marketing plans at the same time. Exhibit 2–12 compares a much improved product and product concept (Product A) with a "me-too" product (Product B) for the same target market. In the short run, the me-too product will make a profit sooner and might look like the better choice—if managers consider only one year's results. The improved product, on the other hand, will take a good deal of pioneering, but over its five-year life it will be much more profitable.

Return-on-investment (ROI) approach

Besides evaluating the profit potential of possible plans, firms may also calculate the return on investment (ROI) of resources needed to implement plans. For example, one plan may require a heavy investment in advertising and channel development while another may rely mainly on lower price.

ROI analyses can be useful for selecting among possible plans because equally profitable plans may require vastly different resources and offer different rates of return on investment. Some firms are very concerned about ROI, especially those that borrow money for working capital. There is little point in borrowing to implement strategies that won't return enough to meet the cost of borrowing.

Exhibit 2-12 Expected Sales and Cost Curves of Two Strategies over Five-Year Planning Periods

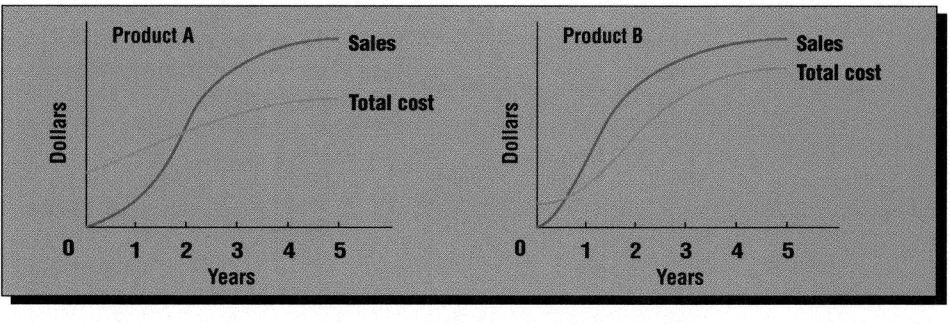

Use planning grids to evaluate a portfolio of opportunities

When a firm has many possibilities to evaluate, it usually has to compare quite different ones. This problem is easier to handle with graphical approaches, such as the nine-box strategic planning grid developed by General Electric and used by many other companies. Such grids can help evaluate a firm's entire portfolio of strategic plans or businesses.

General Electric's strategic planning grid—see Exhibit 2–13—forces company managers to make three-part judgments (high, medium, low) about the business strengths and industry attractiveness of all proposed or existing product-market plans. As you can see from Exhibit 2–13, this approach helps a manager organize information about the company's marketing environments (discussed in the next chapter), along with information about its strategy.

The industry attractiveness dimension helps managers answer this question: "Does this product-market plan look like a good idea?" To answer that question, managers have to judge such factors as the size of the market and its growth rate, the nature of competition, the plan's potential environmental or social impact, and how laws might affect it. Note that an opportunity may be attractive for *some* company, but not well suited to the strengths (and weaknesses) of a particular firm. That is why the GE grid also considers the business strengths dimension.

The business strengths dimension focuses on the ability of the company to pursue a product-market plan effectively. To make judgments along this dimension, a manager evaluates whether the firm has people with the right talents and skills to implement the plan, whether the plan is consistent with the firm's image and profit objectives, and whether the firm could establish a profitable market share given its technical capability, costs, and size.

GE feels that opportunities that fall into the green boxes in the upper left-hand corner of the grid are its best growth opportunities. Managers give these opportunities high marks on both industry attractiveness and business strengths. The red boxes in the lower right-hand corner of the grid, on the other hand, suggest a no-growth policy. Existing red businesses may continue to generate earnings, but they no longer deserve much investment. Yellow businesses are borderline cases—they can go either way. GE may continue to support an existing yellow business but will probably reject a proposal for a new one.

GE's "stoplight" evaluation method is a very subjective, multiple-factor approach. It avoids the traps and possible errors of trying to use oversimplified, single-number criteria, such as ROI or market share. Instead, top managers review detailed written summaries of many factors, and these help them make summary judgments. Then they can make a collective judgment. This approach generally leads to agreement.

Exhibit 2-13 General Electric's Strategic Planning Grid

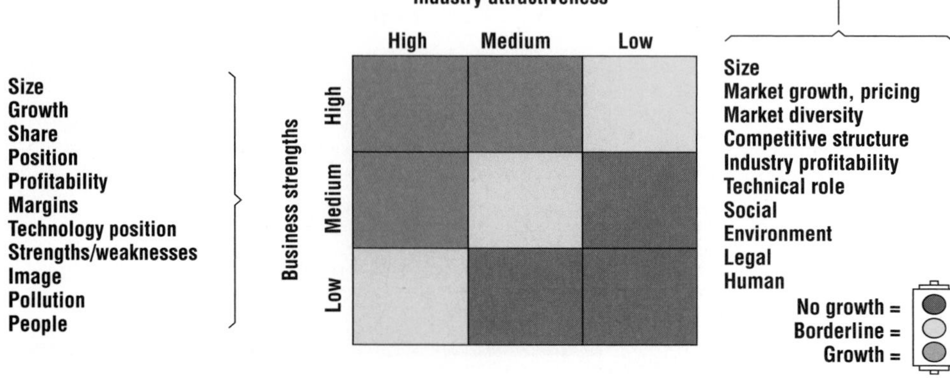

It also helps everyone understand why the company supports some new opportunities and not others.[10]

FACTORS CAN CHANGE TO REFLECT OBJECTIVES General Electric considers various business strength and industry attractiveness factors that reflect its objectives. Another firm might modify the evaluation to emphasize other factors, depending on its objectives and the type of product-market plans it is considering. For example, a small firm with only one product might consider a similar grid—with different criteria—to evaluate new product or market opportunities. While different firms focus on different factors, using many factors helps ensure that managers consider all the company's concerns when evaluating alternative opportunities.

Multiproduct firms have a difficult strategic planning job

Multiproduct firms, like General Electric, obviously have a more difficult strategic planning job than firms with only a few products or product lines aimed at the same or similar target markets. Multiproduct firms have to develop strategic plans for very different businesses. And they have to balance plans and resources so that the whole company reaches its objectives. This means they must analyze alternatives using approaches similar to the General Electric strategic planning grid and only approve plans that make sense for the whole company—even if it means getting needed resources by "milking" some businesses and eliminating others.

Details on how to manage a complicated multiproduct firm are beyond our scope. But you should be aware (1) that there are such firms and (2) that the principles in this text are applicable—they just have to be extended. For example, some firms use strategic business units (SBUs), and some use portfolio management.

Strategic business units may help

SBUs

Some multiproduct firms try to improve their operations by forming strategic business units. A **strategic business unit (SBU)** is an organizational unit (within a larger company) that focuses on some product-markets and is treated as a separate profit centre. By forming SBUs, a company formally acknowledges its very different activities. For example, one SBU of Sara Lee produces baked goods for consumers and restaurants, while another produces and markets Hanes brand T-shirts and underwear.

Some SBUs grow rapidly and require a great deal of attention and resources. Others produce only average profits and should be "milked"—that is, allowed to generate cash for the businesses with more potential. Product lines with poor market position, low profits, and poor growth prospects should be dropped or sold.

Companies that set up strategic business units usually do change their attitudes and methods of operation. They rate managers in terms of achieving strategic plans, as opposed to short-term profits or sales increases. With SBUs, the emphasis is on developing plans; those accepted are implemented aggressively. Under this concept, companies reward some managers for successfully phasing out product lines, while others are rewarded for expanding sales in other markets.

Each manager carries out a market-oriented strategic plan approved by top management. The manager's job is to help develop effective plans and then implement them—to ensure that the company's resources are used effectively and that the firm accomplishes its objectives.

Portfolio management

Some top managements handle strategic planning for a multiproduct firm with an approach called **portfolio management**, which treats alternative products, divisions, or strategic business units as though they were share investments, to be bought and sold using financial criteria. Such managers make trade-offs among very different opportunities. They treat the various alternatives as investments that should be supported, milked, or sold off, depending on profitability and return on investment. In effect, they evaluate each alternative just like a stock market trader evaluates a stock.[11]

This approach makes some sense if alternatives are really quite different. Top managers feel that they can't become very familiar with the prospects for all of their alternatives. So they fall back on the easy-to-compare quantitative criteria. And because the short run is much clearer than the long run, they place heavy emphasis on *current* profitability and return on investment. This puts great pressure on the operating managers to "deliver" *in the short run*—and perhaps even neglect the long run.

Neglecting the long run is risky, and this is the main weakness of the portfolio approach. This weakness can be overcome by enhancing the portfolio management approach with market-oriented strategic plans. These make it possible for managers to more accurately evaluate the alternatives' short-run and long-run prospects.

International opportunities are important

It's easy for a marketing manager to fall into the trap of forgetting about international markets, especially when the firm's domestic market is prosperous. Why go to the trouble of looking elsewhere for opportunities?

The world is getting smaller

International trade is increasing all around the world, and trade barriers are coming down. In addition, advances in communications, especially on the Internet, and in transportation are making it easier and cheaper for even small firms to reach international customers. And national boundaries no longer limit market opportunities. Around the world, potential customers have needs and money to spend. Ignoring these customers doesn't make any more sense than ignoring potential customers in the same town. The real question is whether a firm can effectively use its resources to meet these customers' needs at a profit.

Develop a competitive advantage at home and abroad

If customers in other countries are interested in the products a firm offers—or could offer—serving them may result in even more economies of scale. Lower costs (and prices) may give a firm a competitive advantage both in its home markets *and* abroad. This sort of competitive pressure may actually *force* a marketing manager to expand into international markets. Marketing managers who are only interested in the "convenient" customers in their own backyards may be rudely surprised to find that an aggressive, low-cost foreign producer is willing to pursue those customers—even if doing so is not convenient. Many companies that thought they could avoid the struggles of international competition have learned this lesson the hard way.

A company facing tough competition, thin profit margins, and slow sales growth at home may get a fresh start in another country where demand for its product is just beginning to grow. A marketing manager may be able to "transfer" marketing or technological know-how—or some other competitive advantage—that the firm has already developed. Marketing Demo 2–3 shows that Wulftec International Inc., a Canadian firm with considerable exporting experience, was able to do just that.

Marketing Demo 2-3

Wulftec International Inc. Wins 1997 Canada Export Award and CIBC Job Creation Achievement

Wrapping up the global market has proven easy for Wulftec International Inc. of Ayer's Cliff, Quebec. The company, formed in 1990, designs and manufactures a line of stretch wrapping machinery used in factories across the United States, South and Central America and Europe.

From soft drink cases to farm produce, Wulftec's machines can automatically apply a full web of recyclable polyethylene film or netting around pallets of goods, providing convenient, secure shipment to stores and warehouses worldwide. Some of Wulftec's models can wrap up to 110 pallets an hour, achieving a uniform stretch and consistent appearance that could never be matched by hand.

How do Wulftec's machines work? Take, for example, the company's popular Model WCART-200 (Hurricane). It boasts an arm that rotates a roll of film as it moves up and down the mast of the machine, first stabilizing or unitizing the load, and then continuously wrapping the pallet load from top to bottom.

The wrapping pattern and number of film layers can be programmed by an operator or by the factory's central control computer system. "The plastic, or elastic, acts like a girdle," says Wolfgang Geisinger, Wulftec's President, founder and driving force, with 26 patents under his belt. "Basically, everything is held so tight, it can't move."

Geisinger says Wulftec has been exporting since day one and that the company's adherence to tried-and-true business philosophies has won customers' hearts, and orders, around the globe. "Our philosophy is simple. We hire the best—our employees are second to none and are key to our success. We invest heavily in research and development and we take the time to listen carefully to our customers' needs," he says. "We have also worked hard to develop an effective distribution system that reflects the excellent quality of our product."

This business logic has paid off. In just three years, Wulftec's exports have risen by 483 per cent, up from $1.69 million in 1994 to $9.8 million in 1996. Exports make up 76 per cent of the company's total sales, with customers in the United States, Ireland, France, England, Belgium, Germany, Brazil, Venezuela and Argentina.

At a special ceremony in Quebec City on October 6, 1997, the Honourable Sergio Marchi, Minister for International Trade, and Robert Panet-Raymond, Senior Vice-President, Commercial Banking of CIBC, presented Wulftec International with a prestigious Canada Export Award in recognition of its contribution to creating jobs. In just three years, Wulftec has increased its employee roster by 578 per cent, from 14 to 95 people.

"CIBC is proud to sponsor these awards," adds Mr. Panet-Raymond. "Canada Export Award winners make a key contribution to the Canadian economy by exporting their products and services around the world. At the same time, they are creating jobs here in Canada, and for this they are deserving of our recognition."

The Canada Export Award honours Canadian companies that have excelled in exporting products and services to countries around the world. From more than 200 applicants this year, 10 companies received the fifteenth annual award. Under the theme *Partners in Trade,* Canadian Imperial Bank of Commerce, Export Development Corporation and Stentor, the alliance of Canada's only full-service telecommunications companies, are official sponsors of the 1997 Canada Export Awards, which are presented by the Department of Foreign Affairs and International Trade.

"Canadian companies looking to break into new markets should remember one key thing—respect for different ways of doing business," adds Geisinger. "Learn about the country you want to enter. Learn the language. Learn the culture. Do your best to cater to the unique needs of your customers," he says. "Whatever you do, don't go in with the attitude that you'll only do business your way. Courtesy and respect mean a lot, and if you can demonstrate that you're willing to show both, you'll have an easier time of it, and will also gain your potential customer's trust. Relationships really do count."

Source: Department of Foreign Affairs and International Business, "Wulftec International Inc. Wins 1997 Canada Export Award and CIBC Job Creation Achievement," March 1998. Used with permission of the Department of Foreign Affairs and International Business.

Unfavourable trends in the marketing environment at home, or favourable trends in other countries, may make international marketing particularly attractive. For example, population growth in Canada has slowed and income is leveling off. In other places in the world, population and income are increasing rapidly. Marketing managers for Canadian firms can no longer rely on the constant market growth that drove increased domestic sales for so many years. For many firms, growth—and perhaps even survival—will come only by aiming at more distant customers.

Evaluating opportunities in international markets

The approaches we've discussed so far apply to international markets just as they do to domestic ones. But in international markets it is often harder to fully understand the marketing environment variables. This may make it harder to see the risks involved in particular opportunities. Some countries are politically unstable; their governments and constitutions come and go. An investment that is safe under one government may become a takeover target under another. Further, the possibility of foreign exchange controls—and tax rate changes—can reduce the chance of getting profits and capital back to the home country.

To reduce the risk of missing some basic variable that may help screen out a risky opportunity, marketing managers sometimes need a detailed analysis of the market environment they are considering entering. Such an analysis can reveal facts about an unfamiliar market that a manager in a distant country might otherwise overlook. Further, a local citizen who knows the marketing environment may be able to identify an "obvious" problem ignored even in a careful analysis. Thus, it is very useful for the analysis to include inputs from locals—perhaps cooperative intermediaries.[12]

Risks vary with environmental sensitivity

The farther you go from familiar territory, the greater the risk of making big mistakes. But not all products—or marketing mixes—involve the same risk. Think of the risks as running along a "continuum of environmental sensitivity." See Exhibit 2–14.

Some products are relatively insensitive to the economic and cultural environment they're placed in. These products may be accepted as is, or may require just a little adaptation to make them suitable for local use. Most industrial products are near the insensitive end of this continuum.

At the other end of the continuum, we find highly sensitive products that may be difficult or impossible to adapt to all international situations. Consumer products closely linked to other social or cultural variables are at this end. For example, some of the scanty women's clothing popular in Western countries would be totally inappropriate in Arab countries where women are expected to cover even their faces. Similarly, some cultures view dieting as unhealthy; that explains why products like Diet Pepsi that are popular in North America have done poorly elsewhere. "Faddy" type consumer products are also at this end of the continuum. It's sometimes difficult to understand why such products are well accepted in a home market. This, in turn, makes it even more difficult to predict how they might be received in a different environment.

This continuum helps explain why many of the early successes in international marketing involved basic commodities such as gasoline, soap, transportation vehicles, mining equipment, and agricultural machinery. It also helps explain why some consumer products firms have been successful with basically the same promotion and products in different parts of the globe.

Exhibit 2-14 Continuum of Environmental Sensitivity

Insensitive		Sensitive
Industrial products	Basic commodity-type consumer products	Consumer products that are linked to cultural variables

Yet some managers don't understand the reason for these successes. They think they can develop a global marketing mix for just about *any* product. They fail to see that firms producing and/or selling products near the sensitive end of the continuum should carefully analyze how their products will be seen and used in new environments—and that they must plan their strategies accordingly. American-made blue jeans, for example, have been status symbols in Western Europe and Latin America—and producers have been able to sell them at premium prices through the best intermediaries.[13]

What if risks are still hard to judge?

If the risks of an international opportunity are hard to judge, it may be wise to look first for opportunities that involve exporting. This gives managers a chance to build experience, know-how, and confidence over time. Then the firm will be in a better position to judge the prospects and risks of taking further steps.

Questions and Problems

1. Distinguish clearly between a marketing strategy and a marketing mix. Use an example.
2. Distinguish clearly between mass marketing and target marketing. Use an example.
3. Why is the customer placed in the centre of the four Ps in the diagram of a marketing strategy in Exhibit 2–3? Explain by using a specific example from your own experience.
4. Explain, in your own words, what each of the four Ps involves.
5. Evaluate the text's statement, "A marketing strategy sets the details of implementation."
6. Distinguish between strategy decisions and operational decisions, using a local retailer to illustrate.
7. Distinguish between a strategy, a marketing plan, and a marketing program, using a local retailer to illustrate.
8. Outline a marketing strategy for each of the following new products: (a) a radically new design for a toothbrush, (b) a new fishing reel, (c) a new wonder drug, and (d) a new industrial stapling machine.
9. Provide a specific illustration of why strategic market planning is important for all business people, not just for those in the marketing department.
10. Distinguish between an attractive opportunity and a breakthrough opportunity. Give an example.
11. Explain how new opportunities may be seen by defining a firm's markets more precisely. Illustrate for a situation where you feel there is an opportunity—namely, an unsatisfied market segment—even if it is not very large.
12. Explain the major differences among the four basic types of opportunities discussed in the text, and cite examples for two of these types of opportunities.
13. Explain the components of product-market screening criteria that can be used to evaluate opportunities.
14. Explain the differences between the total profit approach and the return-on-investment approach to evaluating alternative plans.
15. Explain General Electric's strategic planning grid approach to evaluating opportunities.
16. Distinguish between the operation of a strategic business unit and a firm that only pays lip service to adopting the marketing concept.

Suggested cases

1 Marketing a Web Site

2 Disco Jet Canada

32 Sure-Grow Fertilizers

Computer-aided problem

Target Marketing

Marko, Inc.'s managers are comparing the profitability of a target marketing strategy with a mass marketing "strategy." The spreadsheet gives information about both approaches.

The mass marketing strategy is aiming at a much bigger market. But a smaller percentage of the consumers in the market will actually buy this product—because not everyone needs or can afford it. Moreover, because this marketing mix is not tailored to specific needs, Marko will get a smaller share of the business from those who do buy than it would with a more targeted marketing mix.

Just trying to reach the mass market will take more promotion and require more retail outlets in more locations—so promotion costs and distribution costs are higher than with the target marketing strategy. On the other hand, the cost of producing each unit is higher with the target marketing strategy—to build in a more satisfying set of features. But, because the more targeted marketing mix is trying to satisfy the needs of a specific target market, those customers will be willing to pay a higher price.

In the spreadsheet, "quantity sold" (by the firm) is equal to the number of people in the market who will actually buy one each of the product—multiplied by the share of those purchases won by the firm's marketing mix. Thus, a change in the size of the market, the percentage of people who purchase, or the share captured by the firm will affect quantity sold. And a change in quantity sold will affect total revenue, total cost, and profit.

a. On a piece of paper, show the calculations that prove that the spreadsheet "total profit" value for the target marketing strategy is correct. (Hint: Remember to multiply unit production cost and unit distribution cost by the quantity sold.) Which approach seems better—target marketing or mass marketing? Why?

b. If the target marketer could find a way to reduce distribution cost per unit by $.25, how much would profit increase?

c. If Marko, Inc., decided to use the target marketing strategy and better marketing mix decisions increased its share of purchases from 50 to 60 percent—without increasing costs—what would happen to total profit? What does this analysis suggest about the importance of marketing managers knowing enough about their target markets to be effective target marketers?

For additional questions related to this problem, see Exercise 2–3 in the *Learning Aid for Use with Basic Marketing*, Ninth Canadian Edition.

When you finish this chapter, you should:

- Know why company objectives are important in guiding strategic market planning.
- See how the resources of a firm affect the search for opportunities.
- Know the variables that shape the environment of strategic market planning.
- Know how the different kinds of competitive situations affect strategic planning.
- Understand how the economic and technological environment can affect strategic planning.
- Know why the marketing manager must carefully monitor the legal environment.
- Understand the important new terms (shown in orange).

Chapter three

The Changing Marketing Environment

Table 3–1 Environmental Change and the Business Education Response

ENVIRONMENTAL CHANGE	BUSINESS EDUCATION RESPONSE
Canada no longer an isolated economy protected by high tariffs and trade barriers.	First International Business and then Globalization are emphasized.
First mainframes, then PCs, and now the Internet revolutionize business practices.	Information Technology and its applications become central to the entire program.
Large corporations downsize significantly. Small businesses create most of the new jobs.	More emphasis is now placed on small business, "spin-offs," and entrepreneurship.
Women and visible minorities enter the work force in increasing numbers.	Enrolment by women and visible minorities skyrockets. The Management of Diversity becomes an important topic.
"Employment for life" and one career for life are history.	Postsecondary placement offices stress career management.

"The only constant is change." You can expect to hear this statement throughout your business career. Newspaper columns, trade magazines, and books targeted to managers often include discussions of important changes that have already taken place and forecasts of what is to come. Nuala Beck, author of *Shifting Gears: Thriving in the New Economy,* has written some of the best Canadian material of this type.[1] Beck argues that North America's traditional powerhouse industries are no longer the economy's engines of growth. Technology, deregulation, and globalization have combined to create new engines, which are to be found in four strategic sectors: computers and semiconductors; instrumentation; health and medical; and communications/telecommunications. In a follow-up publication, *Excelerate: Growing in the New Economy,* Beck spells out what must be done to prosper in this new economy.[2] Students considering career options, employees concerned about being downsized, and executives worried about the future of their businesses are told how they can adjust to fundamental economic and technological changes.

Beck's books, and others which place more emphasis on population trends and changing lifestyles, are well worth reading. They make it clear that the environmental framework within which marketing decisions must be made is dynamic and cannot be overlooked. But let's consider another way of highlighting the impact of environmental change, using an illustration that's closer to home. Have you ever thought of your degree or diploma program as a product being offered by a postsecondary institution? In fact, these programs very definitely are products, and you are the consumer. How has environmental change affected the business of business education?

Table 3–1 gives examples of environmental changes in the business world over the last fifty years and of how business education has adapted to such changes. The contrast between your degree or diploma program and its predecessor forty or fifty years ago is quite significant. Let's assume that in the late 1950s you enrolled in one of the then very limited number of Canadian business programs. Very few, if any, women would have been in your class. Both students and faculty took it for granted that graduates would become "organization men" with lifetime careers within a major Canadian corporation. University placement offices focused on helping corporate recruiters make "long term" hires. Your curriculum would have reflected these "organization men" and lifetime corporate career assumptions. No real emphasis was placed at that time on computerization, globalization, and entrepreneurship—courses that pervade today's degree and diploma programs.

The business world and academic business programs are very different today than they were fifty years ago. The only constant is change. Degree and diploma programs in business, like all other product offerings, will continue to be affected and shaped by the different types of environmental changes discussed in this chapter.

Marketing's many environments

You saw in the last chapter that finding target market opportunities is the key to effective marketing management. Our discussion of how degree and diploma programs in business have had to respond to many different types of environmental change shows just how important it is that managers continually monitor the world around them and adjust their offerings accordingly. Otherwise, their intended customers will go elsewhere to obtain more up-to-date products.

Five important environmental variables help shape the world within which marketing managers must develop their strategic plans:

- The objectives and resources of the company.
- The competitive environment.
- The economic and technological environment.
- The political and legal environment.
- The cultural and social environment.

The importance of the point we are making here cannot be overemphasized. A marketing manager must formulate a marketing strategy within the context of a constantly changing marketing environment (see Exhibit 2–8). Marketing managers cannot change or shape environmental factors the way they can the elements of a marketing mix. That's why it's useful to recognize such factors for what they are—uncontrollable environmental variables that must be carefully considered when opportunities are being evaluated and when marketing strategies are being selected. In this chapter, we will see how these environmental factors shape opportunities—limiting some possibilities but at the same time making others more attractive.

Objectives should set firm's course

A company must decide where it's going, lest it fall into the trap expressed so well by this quotation: "Having lost sight of our objective, we redoubled our efforts." Company objectives should shape the direction and operation of the whole business.

It is difficult to set objectives that really guide the present and future development of a company. The process forces top management to look at the whole business, relate its present objectives and resources to the external environment, and then decide what the firm wants to accomplish in the future.

It would be convenient if a company could set one objective—such as making a profit—and let that serve as the guide. Actually, however, setting objectives is much more complicated, which helps explain why it's often done poorly, or not done at all.

Three basic objectives provide guidelines

The following three objectives provide a useful starting point for setting a firm's objectives. They should be sought *together* because, in the long run, a failure in even one of the three areas could lead to total failure of the business. A business should:

1. Engage in specific activities that will perform a socially and economically useful function.
2. Develop an organization to carry on the business and implement its strategies.
3. Earn enough profit to survive.[3]

Be socially useful

The first objective says that the company should do something useful for society. This isn't just a "do-gooder" objective. Businesses can't exist without the approval of consumers. If a firm's activities appear to be contrary to the consumer "good," the firm can be wiped out almost overnight by political or legal action—or by consumers' own negative responses.

The first objective also implies that a firm should try to satisfy customer needs. This is why the marketing manager should be heard when the company is setting objectives. That being said, setting whole-company objectives—within resource limits—is ultimately the responsibility of top management. In this sense, whole-company objectives are usually outside the marketing manager's "control."

A firm should define its objectives broadly, setting need-satisfying objectives rather than production-oriented objectives. Because customer needs change, too narrow a view may lead the company into a product-market in which the product itself will soon be obsolete.[4]

Organize to innovate

In a macro or overall sense, consumers in market-directed economies have granted businesses the right to operate, and to make a profit if they can. With this right comes the responsibility for businesses to be dynamic agents of change, adjusting their offerings to meet new needs. Competition is supposed to encourage innovation and efficiency. A business firm should develop an organization which ensures that these consumer-assigned tasks are carried out effectively, and that the firm itself continues to prosper.

Earn some profit

In the long run, a firm must make a profit to survive. But just saying that a firm should try to make a profit isn't enough. Management must specify the time period involved, since many plans that maximize profit in the long run lose money during the first few years. On the other hand, seeking only short-term profits may steer the firm from opportunities that would offer larger long-run profits. Further, trying to maximize profit won't necessarily lead to big profits. Competition in a particular industry may be so fierce as to almost guarantee failure.

A mission statement helps set the course

Our three general objectives provide guidelines, but a firm should develop its own objectives. This is important, but top executives often don't state their objectives clearly. Too often, they say what their objectives were after the fact! If objectives aren't clear from the start, different managers may hold unspoken and conflicting objectives—a common problem in large companies and in nonprofit organizations.

Many firms try to avoid this problem by developing a **mission statement,** which sets out the organization's basic purpose for being. For example, the mission of a public library might be "to serve the minds of the citizens in our community by providing easy access to resources that meet their informational and recreational needs." As illustrated by this example, a good mission statement should focus on a few key goals rather than embracing everything. It should also provide guidelines when managers face difficult decisions. For example, if an employee of the library is trying to decide whether or not to write a proposal for the funding of new computers that will provide Internet access, it should be clear that this is a service that is within the scope of the library's stated mission. On the other hand, if another possible opportunity was to use extra space in the library for exercise equipment, it would appear to be beyond the stated mission. Of course, a mission statement may need to be revised as new market needs arise or as the marketing environment changes. But this would be a fundamental change and not one that is made casually.

The whole firm must work toward the same objectives

A mission statement is important, but it is not a substitute for more specific objectives that provide guidance in screening possible opportunities. For example, top management might set objectives such as "earn 25 percent annual return on investment," "become the market share leader in each of our product-markets," and "introduce at least three innovative and successful products in the next two years."

Of course, when there are a number of specific objectives stated by top management, it is critical that they be compatible. If they're not, frustration and even failure may result. For example, a top management objective of 25 percent annual return on investment may seem reasonable taken by itself. And the objective of introducing new products is reasonable. However, if the costs of developing and introducing the new products cannot be recouped within one year, the return on investment objective is incompatible and impossible to achieve.

Top-management myopia may straitjacket marketing

We are assuming that it is the marketing manager's job to work within the framework of objectives provided by top management. But some of these objectives may limit marketing strategies—and perhaps damage the entire business. This is another reason why it is desirable for the marketing manager to help shape the company's objectives.

Some top managements want a large sales volume or a large market share because they feel this ensures greater profitability. But many large firms with big market shares, like Eastern Airlines, have gone bankrupt. These firms sought large market shares—but earned little profit. Increasingly, companies are shifting their objectives toward *profitable* sales growth rather than just larger market share, as they realize that the two don't necessarily go together.[5]

Company objectives should lead to marketing objectives

You can see why the marketing manager should be involved in setting company objectives. Company objectives guide managers as they search for and evaluate opportunities, and later as they plan marketing strategies. Particular *marketing* objectives should be set within the framework of larger, company objectives. As shown in Exhibit 3–1, firms need to establish a hierarchy of objectives that moves from company objectives to marketing department objectives. For each marketing strategy, firms also need objectives for each of the four Ps—as well as more detailed objectives. For example, in the Promotion area, we need objectives for advertising, for sales promotion, *and* for personal selling.

Xerox provides a good example. One of its company objectives is to achieve high customer satisfaction in every market in which it competes. To this end, the R&D people design equipment to meet specific reliability objectives. Similarly, the production people work to cut manufacturing defects. The marketing department, in turn, sets specific customer satisfaction objectives for every product. This leads to specific promotion objectives to ensure that the sales and advertising people don't promise more than the company can deliver. Service people, in turn, work to respond to almost all service calls within four hours.

Objectives should be realistic and achievable. Objectives are useless if the firm lacks the resources to achieve them.

Exhibit 3-1 A Hierarchy of Objectives

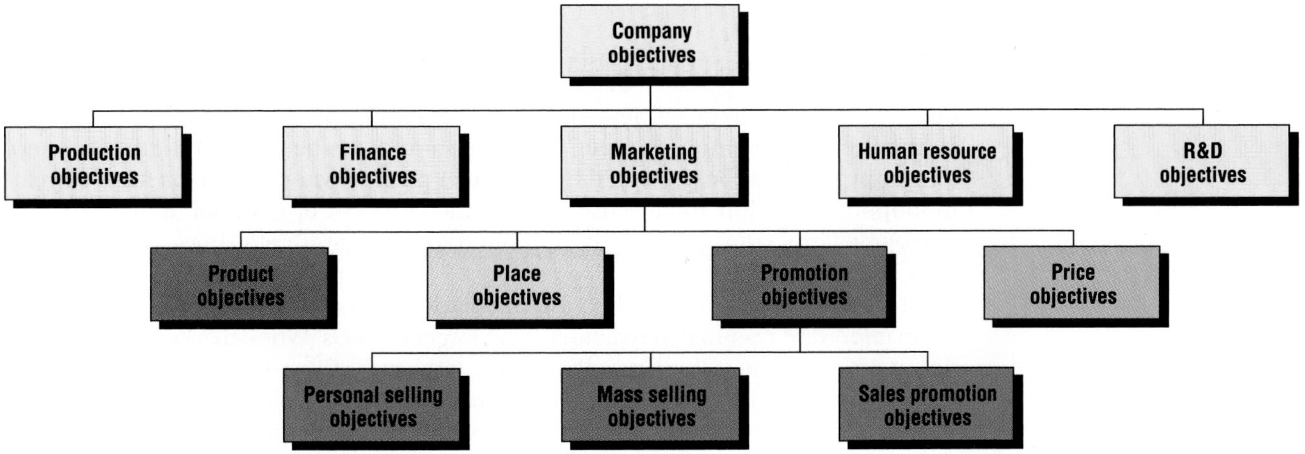

Company resources may limit search for opportunities

Every firm has some resources—hopefully some unique ones—that set it apart from other firms. Breakthrough opportunities—or at least some competitive advantages—come from making use of these strengths while avoiding direct competition with firms having similar strengths.

To find its strengths, a firm must evaluate its functional areas (production, marketing, and finance) as well as its present products and markets. By analyzing successes or failures in relation to the firm's resources, management can discover why the firm was successful in the past—or why it failed.

In the late 1980s, Harley-Davidson's motorcycle business was on the ropes and it was losing customers to Japanese competitors. Studying the Japanese firms helped Harley identify ways to produce higher-quality motorcycles at lower cost. With these resource-use problems resolved, new opportunities opened up—and Harley was again on the road to achieving its objectives.[6]

The pressure of competition focused Harley's attention on manufacturing resources. Other resources that should be considered, as part of an evaluation of strengths and weaknesses, are discussed in the following sections.

Financial strength

Some opportunities require large amounts of capital just to get started. Before a firm makes its first sale, it may require money for R&D, production facilities, marketing research, or advertising. And even a really good opportunity may not be profitable for years. So lack of financial strength is often a barrier to entry into an otherwise attractive market.

Producing capability and flexibility

In many businesses, per unit production costs decrease as the quantity produced increases. This means that smaller producers can be at a great disadvantage when they compete against larger competitors.

On the other hand, new—or smaller—firms sometimes have the advantage of flexibility. They are not handicapped by large, special-purpose facilities that are obsolete or poorly located. U.S. Steel (USX), Bethlehem, and other large steel producers once enjoyed economies of scale. But today they have trouble competing with producers using smaller, more flexible plants. Similarly, poorly located or obsolete retail or wholesale facilities can severely limit strategic market planning.

Marketing strengths

Our marketing strategy framework helps in analyzing current marketing resources. In the Product area, for example, a familiar brand can be a big strength, or a new idea or process may be protected by a *patent.* A patent owner in Canada has a 20-year monopoly to develop and use the new product, process, or material. If one firm has a strong patent, competitors may be limited to second-rate offerings—and their efforts may be doomed to failure.

Good relations with established intermediaries—or control of good locations—can be an important resource in reaching some target markets. When marketing managers decided to introduce the Crest Precision toothbrush, Crest toothpaste had already proved profitable to drugstores, grocery stores, and other retailers who could reach the target market. So these retailers were willing to give Crest shelf space for the toothbrush.

Promotion and Price resources must also be considered. Westinghouse already has a skilled sales force. Marketing managers know these sales reps can handle new products and customers. And low-cost facilities may enable a firm to undercut competitors' prices.

Finally, thorough understanding of a target market can give a company an edge. Many companies fail in new product-markets because they don't really understand the needs of the new customers, or the new competitive environment.

The competitive environment

The **competitive environment** affects the number and types of competitors the marketing manager must face, and how they behave. Although marketing managers usually can't control these factors, they can choose strategies that avoid head-on competition. And, where competition is inevitable, they can plan for it.

Economists describe four basic kinds of market (competitive) situations: pure competition, oligopoly, monopolistic competition, and monopoly. Understanding the differences among these market situations is helpful in analyzing the competitive environment, and our discussion assumes some familiarity with these concepts. (For a review, see Exhibit A–11 and the related discussion in Appendix A.)

The economist's traditional view is that most product-markets head toward either pure competition or oligopoly over the long run. In these situations, a marketing manager competes for customers against competitors who are offering very similar products. Because customers see the different available products (marketing mixes) as close substitutes, competing firms must compete with lower and lower prices, especially in pure competition where there are likely to be large numbers of competitors. Profit margins shrink until they are just high enough to keep the most efficient firms in business. Avoiding pure competition is sensible—and certainly fits with our emphasis on target marketing.

Effective target marketing is fundamentally different from effective decision making in other areas of business. Accounting, production, and financial managers for competing firms can learn about and use the same standardized approaches—and they will work well in each case. In contrast, marketing managers can't just learn about and adopt the same "good" marketing strategy being used by other firms. That just leads to head-on competition—and a downward spiral in prices and profits. So target marketers try to offer customers a marketing mix that is better suited to their needs than competitors' offerings.

Competition-free environments are rare

Most marketing managers would like to have such a strong marketing mix that customers see it as uniquely able to meet their needs. This competition-free ideal is what drives the search for breakthrough opportunities. Yet monopoly situations, in which one firm completely controls a broad product-market, are rare in market-directed economies. Further, governments commonly regulate monopolies. For example, in most parts of the world the prices set by utility companies must be approved by a government agency. Although most marketing managers can't expect to operate with complete control in an unregulated monopoly, they can move away from head-on competition.

Monopolistic competition

In monopolistic competition, a number of different firms offer marketing mixes that at least some customers see as different. Each competitor tries to get control (a monopoly) in its "own" target market. But competition still exists because some customers see the various alternatives as substitutes. A subset of these firms may even compete head-on for the same customers with similar marketing mixes. With monopolistic competition, each firm has its own down-sloping demand curve. But the shape of the demand curve—and elasticity of demand—depends on how similar competitors' products and marketing mixes are. Most marketing managers in developed economies face monopolistic competition.

In monopolistic competition, marketing managers sometimes try to differentiate very similar products by relying on other elements of the marketing mix. For example, Clorox Bleach uses the same basic chemicals as other bleaches. But marketing managers for Clorox may help to set their product apart from other bleaches by offering an improved pouring spout, by producing ads that demonstrate its stain-killing power, or by getting it better shelf positions in supermarkets. Such approaches may not work, especially if competitors can easily imitate the new ideas. Efforts to promote real, but subtle, differences may not do any good either. If potential customers view the different offerings as essentially the same, the market will become more and more competitive, and firms will have to rely on lower costs to obtain a competitive advantage.

Competitor analysis

The best way for a marketing manager to avoid head-on competition is to find new or better ways to satisfy customers' needs. The search for a breakthrough opportunity—or some sort of competitive advantage—requires an understanding not only of customers but also of competitors. That's why marketing managers turn to **competitor analysis,** which is an organized approach for evaluating the strengths and weaknesses of current or potential competitors' marketing strategies. A complete discussion of the possible approaches to competitor analysis is beyond the scope of the first marketing course. Instead, we will briefly cover an approach that works well in many different market situations.

The approach we will discuss is a logical extension of the strategic market planning framework that is the focus of this book. The basic idea is simple: You compare the strengths and weaknesses of your current (or planned) target market and marketing mix with what competitors are currently doing or are likely to do in response to your strategy.

The initial step in competitor analysis is to identify potential competitors. It's useful to start broadly, and from the point of view of target customers. Companies may offer quite different products to meet the same needs, but they are competitors if customers see them as offering close substitutes. For example, disposable diapers, cloth diapers, and diaper rental services all compete in the same generic market concerned with baby care. Identifying a broad set of potential competitors helps marketing managers understand the different ways that customers are currently meeting needs; sometimes it also points to new opportunities. For example, even parents who usually prefer cloth diapers may be interested in the convenience of disposables when they travel.

Usually, however, marketing managers quickly narrow the focus of their analysis to the set of **competitive rivals**—that is, the firms that will be the closest competitors. Rivals offering similar products are usually easy to identify. However, with a really new and different product concept, there may not be a current competitor with a similar product. In that case, the closest competitor may be a firm that is currently serving similar needs with a different product. Although such firms may not appear to be close competitors, they are likely to fight back—perhaps with a directly competitive product—if another firm starts to take away customers.

Anticipate competition

Even if no specific competitors can be identified, marketing managers must consider how long it might take for potential competitors to appear and what they might do. It's easy to make the mistake of assuming that there won't be competition in the future, or of discounting how aggressive competition may become. But a successful strategy attracts others who are eager to jump in for a share of the profit, even if profits only hold up for a short time. That is why it is important for firms to find opportunities where they can sustain a competitive advantage over the longer run.

Finding a sustainable competitive advantage requires special attention to competitors' strengths and weaknesses. For example, it is very difficult to dislodge a competitor who is already a market leader simply by attacking with a strategy that has similar strengths. An established leader can usually defend its position by quickly copying the best parts of what a new competitor is trying to do. On the other hand, an established competitor may not be able to defend quickly if it is attacked where it is weak. For example, Right Guard deodorant built its strong position with an aerosol spray dispenser. But many consumers don't like the messy aerosol cloud—or have become concerned about the effect of aerosols on the environment. That weakness provided Old Spice with a competitive opportunity for a deodorant in a pump dispenser. Right Guard did not quickly fight back with its own pump. The company thought that promoting a pump could hurt sales of its established product—and might even help Old Spice build interest in *its* pump.[7]

Watch for competitive barriers

In a competitor analysis, you also consider **competitive barriers**—the conditions that may make it difficult, or even impossible, for a firm to compete in a market. Such barriers may limit your own plans or, alternatively, block competitors' responses to an innovative strategy.

For example, Exhibit 3–2 summarizes a competitor analysis in the Japanese market for disposable diapers. P&G was about to replace its original Pampers, which were selling poorly, with a new version that offered improved fit and better absorbency. Kao and Uni-Charm, the two leading Japanese producers, both had better distribution networks. Because most Japanese grocery stores and drugstores are very small—about 150 square feet—shelf space is limited and frequent restocking by wholesalers is critical. So, getting cooperation in the channel was a potential competitive barrier for P&G. Uni-Charm further reduced P&G's access to customers when it took advantage of its relationship with retailers to introduce a second, lower-priced brand. To help overcome resistance in the channel, P&G offered wholesalers and retailers better markups and changed to packaging that took less shelf space.[8]

Seek information about competitors

A marketing manager should actively seek information about current or potential competitors. Although most firms try to keep the specifics of their plans secret, much public information may be available. For example, many firms routinely monitor competitors' local newspapers. In one such case, an article discussed a change in the competitor's sales organization. An alert marketing manager realized that the change was made to strengthen the competitor's ability to take business from one of her firm's key target markets. This early warning provided time to make adjustments. Other sources of competitor information include trade publications, alert sales reps, intermediaries, and other industry experts. In business markets, customers may be quick to explain what competing suppliers are offering.

Exhibit 3-2 Competitor Analysis (summary): Disposable Diaper Competition in Japan

	P&G'S CURRENT AND PLANNED STRATEGY	KAO'S STRENGTHS (+) AND WEAKNESSES (–)	UNI-CHARM'S STRENGTHS (+) AND WEAKNESSES (–)
Target market(s)	Upscale, modern parents who can afford disposable diapers	Same as for P&G	Same as for P&G but also budget-conscious segment that includes cloth diaper users (+)
Product	Improved fit and absorbancy (+); brand name imagery weak in Japan (–)	Brand familiarity (+), but no longer the best performance (–)	Two brands—for different market segments—and more convenient package with handles (+)
Place	Distribution through independent wholesalers to both food and drugstores (+), but handled by fewer retailers (–)	Close relations with and control over wholesalers who carry only Kao products (+); computerized inventory reorder system (+)	Distribution through 80% of food stores in best locations (+); shelf space for two brands (+)
Promotion	Heaviest spending on daytime TV, heavy sales promotion, including free samples (+); small sales force (–)	Large, efficient sales force (+); lowest advertising spending (–) and out-of-date ad claims (–)	Advertising spending high (+); effective ads that appeal to Japanese mothers (+)
Price	High retail price (–), but lower unit price for larger quantities (+)	Highest retail price (–), but also best margins for wholesalers and retailers (+)	Lowest available retail price (+); price of premium brand comparable to P&G (–)
Potential competitive barriers	Patent protection (+), limits to access to retail shelf space (–)	Inferior product (–), excellent logistics support system (+)	Economies of scale and lower costs (+); loyal customers (+)
Likely response(s)	Improve wholesaler and retailer margins; faster deliveries in channel; change package to require less shelf space	Press retailers to increase in-store promotion; change advertising and/or improve product	Increase short-term sales promotions; but if P&G takes customers, cut price on premium brand

The Internet is fast becoming a powerful way to get information about competitors. A firm that puts all of its marketing information on a Web site for customers also makes it readily available to competitors. Similarly, computer programs make it easy to search through thousands of online publications and databases for any mention of a competitor. It's also increasingly common to specify what you want and instruct a software "robot" to send you a copy as soon as it's available. This is an incredibly powerful source of information that didn't even exist a few years ago. For more information about this type of Internet news service, go to the PointCast Web site, www.pointcast.com.

The search for information about competitors sometimes raises ethical issues. For example, it's not unusual for people to change jobs and move to a competing firm in the same industry. Such people may have a great deal of information about their old company, but is it ethical for them to use it? Similarly, some firms have been criticized for going too far—for example, waiting at a landfill for competitors' trash to find copies of confidential company reports. In a high-tech version of this practice, computer hackers use the Internet to break into a competitor's computer network. In minutes, hackers can steal information that took years to collect.

Beyond the moral issues, spying on competitors to obtain trade secrets is illegal, and damage awards can be huge. For example, the courts ordered competing firms to pay Procter & Gamble about $125 million in damages for stealing secrets about its Duncan Hines soft cookies. For example, a Frito-Lay employee posed as a potential customer to attend a confidential sales presentation.[9]

Direct competition cannot always be avoided

A firm may find that it cannot avoid highly competitive situations, especially pure competition. Some firms are already in an industry before it becomes intensely competitive. Then as competitors fail, new firms enter the market, possibly because they don't have more attractive alternatives and can at least earn a living. In less-developed economies, this is a common pattern among small retailers and wholesalers. New entrants may not even know how competitive the market is—but they stick it out until they run out of money. Production-oriented firms are more likely to make such a mistake.

Is Canada internationally competitive?

International competitiveness has been defined as the ability to generate more wealth than one's competitors in world markets. Relative competitiveness has a direct impact on jobs, material wealth, and the affordability of our social programs. The most widely used measure, the World Competitiveness Scoreboard, had Canada ranking 10th in international competitiveness in 1998, just marginally below Denmark (8th) and Luxembourg (9th). Our overall ranking between 1994 and 1998 as well as Canada's rankings on various competitiveness factors are highlighted by Internet Illustration 3–1.

The economic environment

The **economic and technological environments** affect how firms—and entire economies—use resources. We will treat the economic and technological environments separately to emphasize that the technological environment provides a *base* for the economic environment. Technical skills and equipment affect how companies convert an economy's resources into output. The economic environment, on the other hand, is affected by how all of the parts of a macroeconomic system interact. This in turn affects such things as national income, economic growth, and inflation. The economic environment may vary from one country to another, but economies around the world are linked.

Economic conditions change rapidly

The economic environment can and does change quite rapidly. The effects can be far-reaching and require changes in marketing strategy.

Even a well-planned marketing strategy may fail if the country goes through a rapid business decline. As consumers' incomes drop, they must shift their spending patterns. They may simply have to do without some products. A weak economy, like the one in Canada and many other parts of the world in the early 1990s, also undermines consumer confidence, even among families whose income is not affected. When consumer confidence is low, people delay making purchases—especially of big-ticket items. Similarly, firms cut back on their own purchases. Many companies aren't strong enough to survive such bad times.

Interest rates and inflation affect buying

Changes in the economy are often accompanied by changes in interest rates—the charge for borrowing money. Interest rates directly affect the total price borrowers must pay for products. In other words, interest rates affect when—and if—they will buy. This is an especially important factor in some business markets. But it also affects consumer purchases of homes, cars, furniture, and other items usually bought on credit.

Changes in interest rates may also have an indirect effect on noncredit purchases. For example, when interest rates dropped significantly in 1991, many families refinanced their homes at the lower rate. They then used the extra money in their pockets for purchases, like clothing, that they had postponed.

Interest rates usually increase during periods of inflation, and inflation is a fact of life in many economies. Canadian inflation levels have recently been quite low. Still, inflation must be considered in strategic planning. When costs are rising rapidly and there are no more cost-cutting measures to take, a marketing manager may have to increase prices. But the decisions of individual marketing managers to raise prices

Internet illustration 3–1

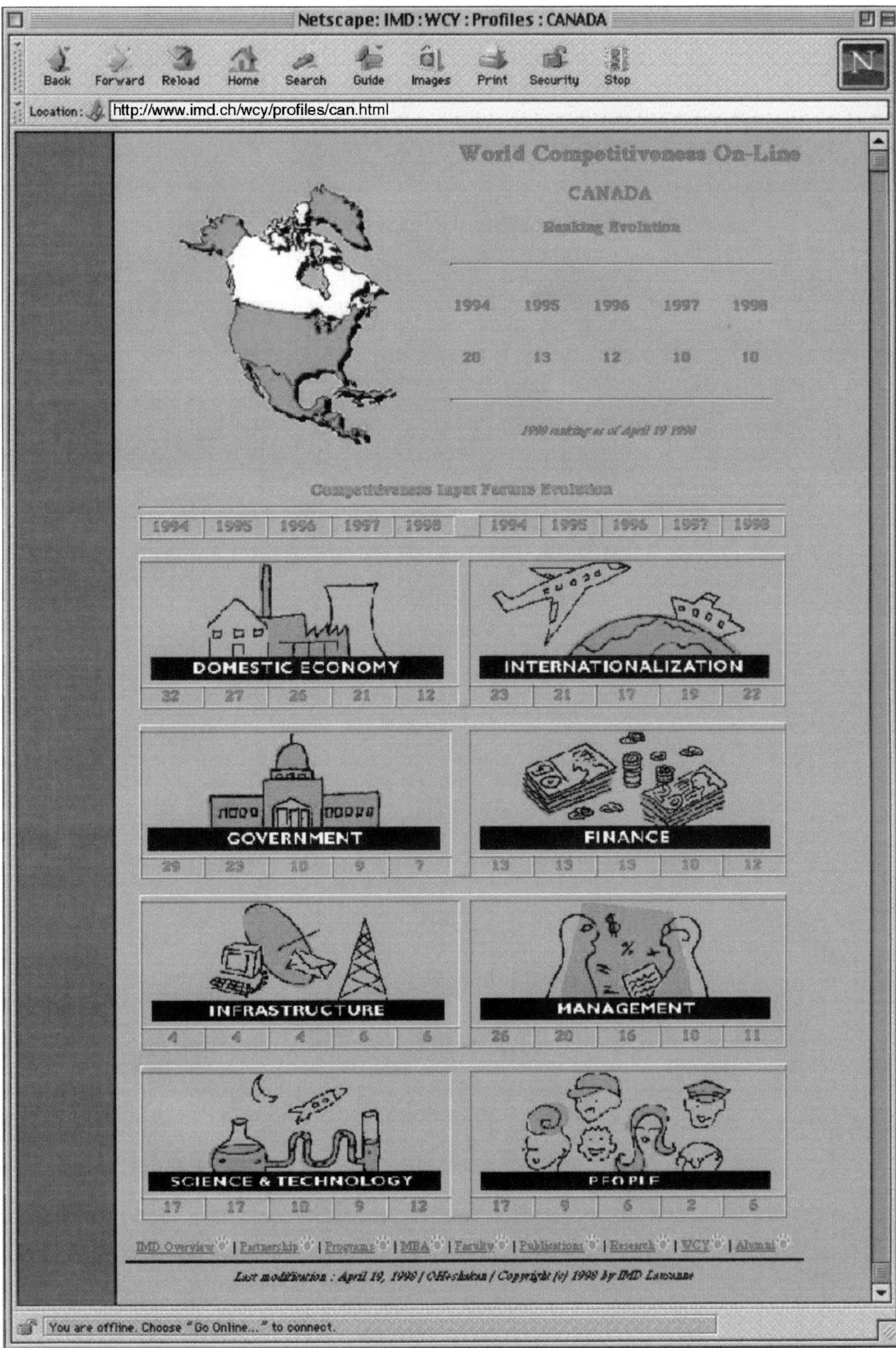

add to macro-level inflation. That can lead to government policies that reduce income, employment, *and* consumer spending.

The global economy is connected

In the past, marketing managers often focused on the economy of their home country. It's no longer that simple. The economies of the world are connected—and at an increasing pace changes in one economy affect others. One reason for this is that the amount of international trade is increasing.

A nation and its trade grow together

All countries trade to some extent—we live in an interdependent world. Trade expands as a country develops and industrializes. In fact, the largest changes in world trade are usually seen in developing economies. Over the last 15 years, for example, exports from Hong Kong, Taiwan, and Singapore have risen dramatically.

Even so, the largest traders are highly developed nations. The United States, Japan, Canada, and the countries of the European Union together account for over half of all world trade. However, each country has its own pattern of trade. Exhibit 3–3 makes it clear that despite Team Canada export initiatives to increase trade with other countries, the U.S. market is three times as important to Canada as the rest of the world combined. The continued importance to the Canadian economy of resource and automotive exports is also highlighted. On the other hand, Internet Insite 3–1 shows how the Internet allows firms of every size to market internationally.

Most countries are eager to sell their goods and services in foreign markets. Yet at the same time, they often don't want their local customers to purchase foreign-made products. They want the money—and the opportunities for jobs and economic growth—to stay in the local economy.

Tariffs and quotas

Taxes and restrictions at national or regional borders greatly reduce the free flow of goods and services between the marketing systems of different countries. **Tariffs**—taxes on imported products—vary depending on whether a country is trying to raise revenue or limit trade. Restrictive tariffs often block all movement. But even revenue-producing tariffs cause red tape, discourage the free movement of products, and increase the prices consumers pay.

Quotas set the specific quantities of products that can move into or out of a country. Tremendous marketing opportunities may exist in a unified Europe, for example, but import quotas (or export controls directed against a specific country) could discourage outsiders from entering.

Trade restrictions can be a major source of conflict. For example, Canada charged the United States with unfair trading practices when a tariff was placed on Canadian softwood lumber shipments. American timber interests had charged that Canadian provinces were unfairly subsidizing their lumber companies, in part by charging low stumpage prices for government-owned trees. Needless to say, Canadian forest product firms disagreed. After years of controversy, a compromise Softwood Lumber Agreement was eventually signed. Nevertheless, the two sides continue to wrangle, with the focus of attention now being whether Canada is living up to the terms of that agreement. The West Coast salmon dispute is another major trade irritant between Canada and the United States.

Global trade is increasing

There are still many obstacles to free trade among nations. And trade wars among nations are likely to continue. Even so, the trend is toward fewer restrictions on international trade. Perhaps the most visible evidence of this was the creation in 1995

Exhibit 3-3 Canada's Largest Trading Partners—1997 (millions of dollars)

CANADIAN EXPORTS BY COUNTRY		CANADIAN IMPORTS BY COUNTRY	
United States	229,091.2	United States	183,421.2
Japan	10,760.7	Japan	12,508.1
United Kingdom	3,592.1	Mexico	6,970.0
South Korea	2,881.3	United Kingdom	6,425.4
Germany	2,624.6	China	6,299.4
China	2,169.4	Germany	5,388.1
Netherlands	1,631.1	France	5,135.8
Hong Kong	1,611.1	Taiwan	3,466.3
Taiwan	1,537.2	Italy	3,056.0
Italy	1,442.0	South Korea	2,821.6
Total (including other countries)	**278,869.1**	**Total** (including other countries)	**271,496.7**

Source: Statistics Canada, adapted from "Exports by Country," Catalogue No. 65-003, January to December 1997, and "Imports by Country," Catalogue No. 65-006, January to December 1997.

Canada's Exports and Imports—1997 (millions of dollars)

	EXPORTS	IMPORTS
Agricultural and fishing products	22,823.6	15,548.9
Energy products	29,441.5	12,038.5
Forestry products	36,406.0	2,372.3
Industrial goods	52,331.4	53,672.4
Machinery and equipment	57,263.3	91,117.5
Automotive products	67,925.9	60,439.1
Consumer goods	8,730.8	29,586.3
Other transactions	3,946.7	6,721.6
Total	**278,869.1**	**271,496.7**

Source: Statistics Canada, adapted from "Canadian International Merchandise Trade," Catalogue No. 65-001, December 1997, Volume 51, Number 12, pp. 23, 35.

of the **World Trade Organization (WTO)**—the only international body dealing with the rules of trade between nations. At its heart are the WTO agreements, which are the legal ground rules for international commerce and for trade policy. The agreements have three main objectives: (1) to help trade flow as freely as possible, (2) to provide an impartial means of settling disputes, and (3) to facilitate further negotiation. In general, the WTO agreements try to encourage competition and discourage protectionism; they also seek to provide more predictable policies.

The WTO evolved from and replaced the **General Agreement on Tariffs and Trade (GATT)**—which was a set of rules governing restrictions on world trade and agreed to by most of the nations of the world. Fifty-three nations signed the first GATT agreement in 1947. After that, there were seven rounds of GATT agreements. Each successive round of talks involved more countries and further reduced tariffs and nontariff trade barriers (such as quotas and unfair product standards). Because each rule affected different countries in different ways, reaching agreement was a slow and complicated process. Some people felt that there was more talk than change, in part because GATT was not even recognized in law as an international organization. Even so, progress was slowly being made. The WTO agreements now cover services and intellectual property as well as goods; GATT was limited to goods. With the formation of the WTO, global trade is becoming an even more important factor in economic development—as well as a more important source of opportunity for individual firms.[10]

Internet Insite 3-1

Globalization of Markets—The Role of the Internet

The phenomenon of globalization has been evident for some years now. Free trade agreements between nations have contributed to growing global trade. NAFTA (www.nafta.net), a trade agreement between the United States, Canada, and Mexico, and GATT, a multilateral agreement to reduce tariffs and trade barriers (see trading.wmw.com/gatt/), have contributed to the growth of international trade. In Asia there is a regional trade cooperation agreement called ASEAN (see www.asean.or.id). Countries with small populations, such as Canada, have much to gain from such free access to foreign markets. Against this backdrop, the Internet, which is a global medium, can be an important vehicle for international trade. The Internet not only is helping smaller firms gain access to foreign markets, but also has the potential to change the fundamental character of national economies.

What is the role of the Internet in this era of globalization? Consider the case of Roswell's Cyberspace Computer Bookstore, a Halifax-based bookstore specializing in computer books (www.roswell.com). Thanks to the Internet and his own entrepreneurship, Roswell James, the owner, converted his traditional bookstore into one with a worldwide storefront. The bookstore carries over 10,000 computer books and can deliver any computer book currently in print. You can browse the "shelves" and search by author, title, subject, or ISBN, or look at recent news releases and book reviews. Roswell will e-mail clients when there are specials and sales or new releases. Customers set up an account first, so that they do not have to submit their credit card information with each order; this eliminates concerns about exchanging such information over the Internet. James, an independent entrepreneur with limited financial resources, now gets orders from countries in Europe and Asia! Most bookstores draw their customers from the local communities. The Internet, on the other hand, has opened an entire global market for a small Halifax business.

Roswell's is just one example. Barnes & Noble, a giant retail bookstore chain in the United States, was a late entrant to Internet marketing when it went online in 1997 (www.barnesandnoble.com). But they project significant growth in their sales due to the large, untapped global market for books in English. Other firms with significant direct-marketing expertise (e.g., 1-800-Flowers) or catalogue sales expertise (e.g., L.L. Bean) have made the transition to the Internet very easily and are cashing in on the global opportunities it offers.

A study by Ernst & Young (www.e&y.com) revealed that 44 percent of retailers who are on the Internet offer their products to customers in foreign countries, with a further 24 percent planning to do so shortly. Similarly, 39 percent of manufacturers offer their products to customers in foreign countries through the Internet, with another 46 percent planning to do so shortly. Not every product or firm will find an attractive foreign market using the Internet. But these figures do suggest that a lot of firms are likely to venture into international markets because of the easier communication and access offered by the Internet.

Currently there are about 50 million Internet users worldwide, most of them in North America. According to some estimates, this figure is likely to increase to 140 million by the year 2000. Other observers are much more optimistic and suggest that over 1 billion people worldwide will be online by the year 2001. Even if the actual figures are somewhere in between, that is still a very sizable number. So the potential offered by the Internet for global expansion is very significant.

The Internet also levels the playing field for smaller firms to some extent. Can you imagine a small business such as Roswell's bookstore becoming a global firm in such a short time without the Internet? Most of the successful online businesses are small startup firms. These firms are successful because they offer consumers value for their money. The size of the firm is almost unimportant. The Internet is ushering in a new era of healthy competition, where small firms with good ideas can survive and even prosper.

Source: This is one of a series of Internet Insites prepared in April 1998 by Dr. Ramesh Venkat of Saint Mary's University for *Basic Marketing*, Ninth Canadian Edition.

NAFTA

The North American Free Trade Agreement (NAFTA) has been successful in developing new investment opportunities for Canadians by decreasing the trade barriers that exist between Canada, the United States, and Mexico. The easing of trade restrictions has allowed exporters in all three countries to open up new markets.

The successes of NAFTA, however, have been countered with concerns such as the "level playing field" issue. Wages in Mexico are much lower than in Canada or the United States. That being so, Mexico, it is argued, will be able to draw labour-intensive jobs away from its two NAFTA partners. Also, Mexico's less restrictive environmental laws may encourage many firms to relocate there from the north. Mexico's fragile economic and political system also worries investors. The very sharp decline in the value of the peso a few years ago made both existing and proposed Mexican investments far less attractive.

Mexico's problems notwithstanding, efforts are being made to expand NAFTA to include countries in Central and South America. A Western Hemisphere Free Trade Agreement may be a long way off, but what's driving such an initiative is clear enough: the U.S. Department of Commerce predicts that by the year 2010 the Western Hemisphere will be buying more American products than Europe or Japan.[11]

Of course, removal of some economic and political barriers—whether across North America or Europe—will not eliminate the need to adjust strategies to reach submarkets of consumers. Centuries of cultural differences will not disappear overnight, and may never disappear. Yet these cooperative arrangements will give firms operating in regions easier access to larger markets, and the countries involved will have a more powerful voice in protecting their own interests.[12]

International countertrade

To overcome the problems of trade restrictions, many firms have turned to **countertrade**—a special type of bartering in which products from one country are traded for products from another country. For example, McDonnell Douglas Helicopter turned to countertrade when the Ugandan government wanted to buy 18 helicopters to help stamp out illegal elephant hunting. Uganda didn't have $25 million to pay for the helicopters, so a countertrade specialist for the helicopter company set up local projects to generate the money. One Ugandan factory turned local pineapples and passion fruit into concentrated juice. The concentrate was sold to European buyers identified by the countertrade specialist. Similarly, soft drink bottlers in Mexico traded locally grown broccoli for Pepsi concentrate; then Pepsi found a market for the broccoli in the United States.

Distribution systems and intermediaries have not yet developed in these countries to handle this sort of exchange. So in pursuing their own opportunities, companies like Pepsi and McDonnell Douglas are stimulating economic development. Deals such as this may seem unusual, but they aren't. Countertrade is becoming an extremely important part of foreign trade for both large and small companies.

What's your money worth?

Changes in the *exchange rate*—how much one country's money is worth in another nation's currency—have an important effect on international trade. When the Canadian dollar is strong, it's worth more in foreign countries. This makes Canadian products more expensive overseas and foreign products cheaper in Canada. But when the Canadian dollar is worth 64 to 68 cents (U.S.), imported goods will cost more, as will the trips Canadian "snowbirds" make to Florida or Arizona.

Marketing managers aren't safe from the forces of changing exchange rates just because their firms are not involved in foreign trade. New competition arises in domestic markets as foreign products gain a competitive edge with lower prices. Many companies find themselves helpless during such economic change. In fact, a country's entire economic system can change as the balance of imports and exports shifts—jobs, consumer incomes, and national productivity are all affected.

Clearly, the marketing manager must watch the economic environment carefully. In contrast to cultural and social conditions, economic conditions change continuously. And the speed of such changes can demand immediate strategy changes.[13]

The technological environment

Technology is the application of science to convert an economy's resources to output. Technology affects marketing in two basic ways: with new products, and with new processes (ways of doing things). For example, we are moving from an industrial society to an information society. Advances in electronic communications have made it possible for people in different parts of the world to communicate face to face through satellite video-conferencing, and to transmit complex design drawings by fax or over the Internet. Computers allow more sophisticated planning and control. These process changes have been accompanied by an exciting explosion of high-tech products, from robots in factories to skin patches that dispense medicines to genetically engineered tomatoes that taste great the year round.

Technology transfer is rapid

New technologies have created important industries that didn't even exist a few years ago. Thirty years ago Microsoft didn't exist. Now it's one of the most profitable companies in the world. With such big opportunities at stake, you can also see why there is such rapid transfer of technology from one part of the world to another. But technology transfer is not automatic. Someone—perhaps you—has to see the opportunity.

Internet technologies are reshaping marketing

Many of the big advances in business have come from early recognition of new ways to do things. There is perhaps no better example of this than the World Wide Web and the Internet. The **Internet** is a system for linking computers around the world. The idea of linking computers in a network is not new. It's been around for years. Furthermore, while we refer to the Internet as a system, it may be more accurate to just think of it as a collection of consistent hardware and software standards. Even so, the Internet expands the network concept to include any computer anywhere. Further, the World Wide Web makes the exchange of information on the Internet easy. As a result, this new technology is radically changing just about every aspect of marketing. We'll be discussing these changes in more detail throughout the text, so for now we'll just illustrate the impact.

Consider the arena of promotion. The invention of TV changed marketing by suddenly making it possible for a sponsor to broadcast a vivid message to millions of people at the same time. Now, the Internet has made it possible for that sponsor to select any of millions of messages and to simultaneously narrowcast any of them to millions of different individuals. It is just as easy for customers to request the information in the first place, or to respond electronically once they have it. In this way the Internet's capability has radically changed our ideas about how firms communicate with customers, and vice versa. Similarly, the Internet is creating totally different approaches to pricing. Airlines are now running online auctions of seats that might otherwise go unsold. When you sell every seat to "the highest bidder," you are really pricing precisely to match supply and demand. To check out an online auction, go to www.onsale.com on the Internet.

In hindsight, new approaches such as these seem obvious, given that the technology is available. But they are not obvious up front, unless you're really looking for them. Marketers should help their firms see such opportunities by trying to understand the "why" of present markets—and what is keeping their firms from being more successful. Then, as new technological developments come along, the mar-

Ethical Dimensions

Technology and Ethical Issues

Marketers must also help their firms decide which technical developments are ethically acceptable. For example, many firms have now installed a system to identify the telephone number of an incoming telephone call. When linked with a computer, this makes it possible for a firm to know which customer is calling even before the customer says the first word. It also makes instantly available detailed information about what a customer has purchased in the past. This is a very powerful technology, but many people feel that this sort of automatic number identification system is an invasion of privacy.

Similarly, with the growing concern about environmental pollution and the quality of life, some attractive technological developments may be rejected because of their long-run effects on the environment. Aseptic drink boxes, for example, are very convenient but difficult to recycle. In a case like this, what's good for the firm and some customers may not be good for the cultural and social environment—or acceptable in the political and legal environment. Being close to the market should give marketers a better feel for current trends, and help firms avoid serious mistakes.

keters will be alert to possible uses of those technologies—and see how opportunities can be turned into profits.[14]

Technology also poses challenges

The rapid pace of technological change opens up new opportunities, but it also poses challenges for marketers. For many firms, success hinges on how quickly new ideas can be brought to market. It's easy for a firm to slip into a production orientation in the flush of excitement that follows a new discovery in an R&D lab. That makes it more important than ever for marketing thinking to guide the production process—starting at the beginning with decisions about where basic R&D effort will be focused.

The political environment

The attitudes and reactions of people, social critics, and governments all affect the political environment. The political environment can also have a dramatic effect on opportunities at a local or international level. Some business managers have become very successful by studying the political environment and developing strategies that take advantage of opportunities related to changing political dimensions.

Nationalism can be limiting

Strong feelings of **nationalism**—the placing of a country's interests before everything else—can affect how marketing systems work. They can affect how marketing managers work as well. In some international markets, nationalistic feelings can reduce sales, or even block all marketing activity. For many years, Japan has made it difficult for outside firms to do business in that country. At the same time, Japan's producers of cars, colour TVs, VCRs, and other products have established profitable markets in the United States, Europe, and other parts of the world. Japan is under pressure to change, but these changes are coming slowly.

In the United States, the "Buy American" policy in many government contracts and business purchases reflects this same attitude. So does support for protecting American producers from foreign competition. This is especially true when it comes to producers of footwear, textiles, production machinery, and cars.[15]

Nationalistic feelings can determine whether a firm can enter a market, because businesses often must get permission to operate. In some political environments this is only a routine formality. In others, a lot of red tape and personal influence are involved, and bribes are sometimes expected. This raises ethical issues for marketing managers—and legal issues, too, since it is illegal for Canadian and American firms to offer such bribes. Clearly, that can make it difficult for an American or Canadian firm to compete with a company from a country that doesn't have similar laws.

Regional groupings increasingly important

Important dimensions of the political environment are likely to be similar among nations that have banded together to have common regional economic boundaries. The moves toward the economic unification of Europe and free trade among the nations of the Western Hemisphere are outstanding examples of this sort of regional grouping.

Unification of European markets

At one time, each of the countries of the European Union (EU) had its own trade rules and regulations. These differences made it difficult and expensive to move products from one country to the others. These countries are now abandoning old political squabbles and nationalistic prejudices in favour of cooperative efforts to reduce taxes and other barriers commonly applied at national boundaries. This unification has eliminated over 300 separate barriers to inter-European trade. Trucks loaded with products spill across the European continent and Britain. The increased efficiency is reducing costs—and the prices European consumers must pay—and creating millions of new jobs. These changes make Europe the largest unified market in the world, and more changes are coming. For example, 11 European countries have agreed to discontinue their own currencies and to adopt a single currency, called the "Euro." These changes have also dramatically altered the opportunities available to marketing managers both in Europe and in other parts of the world.

Consumerism and environmentalism

Some dramatic changes in the political environment, such as the fall of communism in Eastern Europe, happened quickly and were hard to predict. Many important political changes, both within and across nations, have evolved more gradually. Also, what's at the top of the public agenda changes over time. Consumerism and environmentalism are cases in point.

Consumerism is a social movement that seeks to increase the rights and powers of consumers and buyers in relation to sellers and the government. It was much more visible in Canada and the United States 30 years ago, in part due to the tireless efforts of consumer activist Ralph Nader. Consumer boycotts, protest marches, and efforts to attract media attention were quite common. However, such activities are more commonly undertaken today by those concerned with the environment.

Canadian consumerism

Canadian consumerism became an important movement in the late 1960s. One reason for this increased consumer consciousness was the establishment in 1968 of Consumer and Corporate Affairs Canada (CCAC). One department became responsible for administering a number of existing consumer protection laws and a wide variety of new programs designed to further the Canadian consumer's interests.

CCAC moved aggressively in the area of consumer protection. Additional laws were passed and existing legislation was more vigourously enforced. Great emphasis was placed on educating and informing consumers. Complaints received by CCAC were studied to determine the serious problem areas that required corrective action. At the provincial level, consumer protection bureaus and agencies were also greatly strengthened.

Lower profile consumerism

Canadian consumerism has not been nearly as high-profile in recent years. Both CCAC and most of its provincial counterparts have been merged into larger ministries. Consumer protection budgets have been reduced in response to deficit crises at both the provincial and the federal level. The Consumers' Association of Canada encountered organizational problems that led to staff cutbacks and a reduced ability to represent the public interest. Also, *Canadian Consumer* stopped publishing because of financial difficulties.

While consumerism now has a much lower profile, it remains an important feature of the Canadian marketing scene. Government efforts focus on consumer education and consumer awareness. The Web is now being used by the Office of Consumer Affairs to help create that awareness. Specialized groups with a limited focus, such as the Automobile Protection Association with its annual publication, *Lemon-Aid,* are also busy educating and informing consumers. Many Canadian newspapers regularly publish articles on "smart shopping." They also help dissatisfied customers obtain a fair deal from local merchants. Also, consumer-oriented TV programs and radio talk shows frequently deal with marketplace problems.

Environmentalism

Although consumerism has received less attention in recent years, the 1990s brought with them a renewed interest in the environment. Environmentalism was first recognized by some as an important cause in the 1960s. However, widespread uneasiness over what we buy, how we use products, and how we then dispose of consumer waste only surfaced in the late 1980s. Campaigns sponsored by environmental groups, various levels of government, and even businesses now urge Canadians to reduce, to reuse, and to recycle.

Environmental issues are currently receiving far more attention than more traditional consumer protection issues. But like consumerism, the environment may not stay at the top of the public agenda forever. Even so, it's clear that both consumers and manufacturers are looking for environmentally friendly ways of doing things. You can expect to hear a great deal about "sustainable marketing" and "green consumers" over the next few years.

The legal environment

Changes in the economic and political environments often lead to changes in the legal environment and in the ways existing laws are enforced. It's hard for marketing managers to know all the relevant laws, but it's important that they do. The legal environment sets the basic rules for how a business can operate in society. That environment may severely limit some choices, but changes in laws and how they are interpreted also create new opportunities. We, of course, will focus on how the law has evolved in Canada. However, don't forget that laws and their enforcement vary from one country to the next. For example, Canada has not been nearly as aggressive as the United States either in regulating trade practices or in prohibiting proposed mergers.

Anticombines legislation

Canada's Combines Investigation Act was passed to prevent anticompetitive behaviour. Until amended in 1975, difficulties in prosecuting those charged kept it from being effective legislation. Offences had to be treated as violations of criminal law. This meant that the government, to win a case, had to prove guilt "beyond any reasonable doubt." Difficulties in establishing that degree of proof discouraged prosecution. So did a requirement that competition had to be completely or virtually eliminated before the courts could act. These requirements greatly reduced the likelihood that any firm brought to court would be found guilty.

What did the Combines Investigation Act, until it was amended in 1975, actually accomplish? The legislation helped to prevent two kinds of marketing activity: price fixing by competitors, and misleading price advertising. Resale price maintenance was also specifically prohibited in 1951. Aside from these areas, the act had little effect on either prevailing marketing practices or the structure of the Canadian economy. No

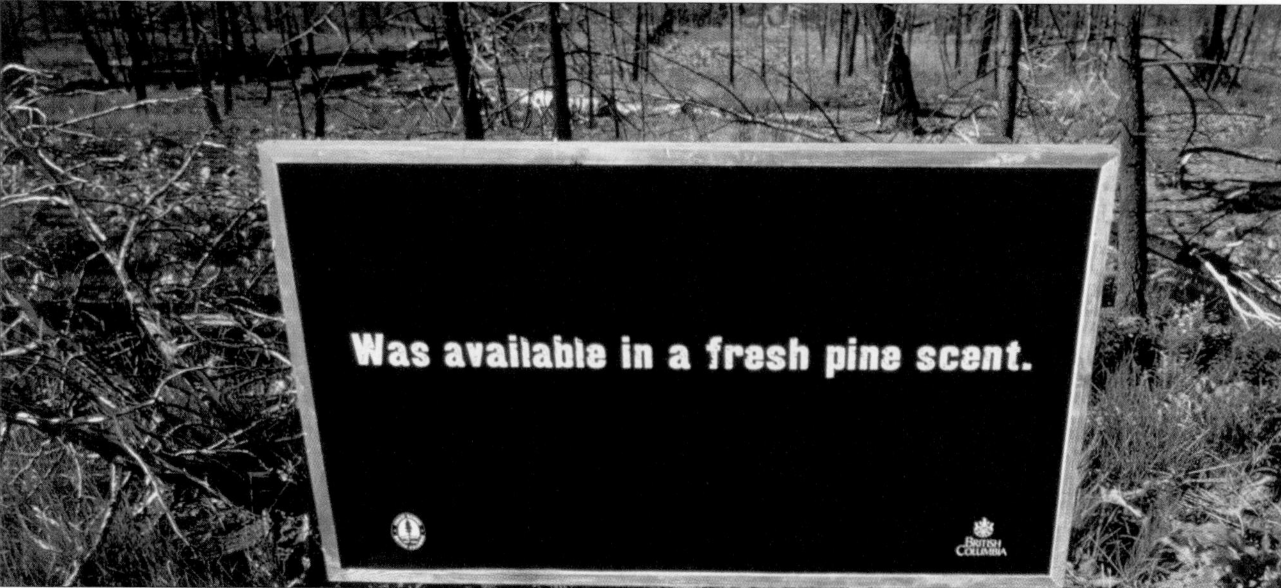

These award-winning B.C. Ministry of Forests' signs reflect environmental concerns.

Marketing Demo 3-1

Record Fine of $550,000 Imposed on Individual for Conspiracy Offence Under the Competition Act

The following is a News Release issued by the Competition Bureau on January 29, 1997:

The Acting Director of Investigation and Research under the Competition Act, Francine Matte, Q.C., announced today that Mr. Pierre Paré, a former senior official with Gestion des Rebuts DMP Inc., has pleaded guilty to one count of conspiracy to unduly lessen competition, and must pay a record fine of $550,000 under the Competition Act.

The Court also imposed a one year jail sentence to be served in the community on Mr. Serge Brière and Mr. Robert Caron, both formerly with Gestion des Rebuts DMP Inc.

This matter follows the guilty plea by Gestion des Rebuts DMP Inc., in April 1996 for a related conspiracy offence; the company was fined $1,950,000.

The offence involved an agreement between competitors to share the market for the hauling and disposal of commercial waste in the Mauricie region of Quebec between 1989 and 1992. The victims of this conspiracy were businesses such as restaurants, corner stores, garages and shopping centres, which lease commercial waste containers.

Mr. Justice Lévesque of the Quebec Superior Court also sentenced Mr. Paré to perform 100 hours of community service. In addition, a Prohibition Order was imposed on the three individuals which requires them to comply with the Act for a period of 10 years.

"Small businesses were denied competition in the commercial waste market because of an agreement that existed among competitors," said Ms. Matte. "This guilty plea sends a strong warning to individuals who seek to avoid liability for Competition Act offences. Individuals cannot promote price fixing and then seek refuge behind a corporation."

The inquiry began in 1992 with the cooperation of certain individuals involved in the conspiracy.

---

firm was ever found guilty of price discrimination. In two key cases brought to court under the merger provisions, the government lost and did not appeal.[16]

The Competition Act

In December 1975, dissatisfaction with the Combines Investigation Act led Parliament to pass Bill C-2, the first part of what became a two-stage revision of the existing legislation. The second series of major changes, dealing primarily with mergers and acquisitions, was not passed until ten years later. The resulting legislation, incorporating both sets of changes, became the Competition Act of 1986.

What was Bill C-2 designed to accomplish? The legislation was tightened up so that it would more effectively regulate then-current marketing practices and make it easier for the government to win cases brought to court. To achieve the latter objective, both the "burden of proof" and the "effective destruction of competition" requirements were somewhat relaxed. To some extent, enforcement has become both easier and more effective. Individuals and organizations—both large and small—have been convicted of deceptive price advertising, bid rigging (so as to share the business), and price fixing. As Marketing Demo 3–1 reveals, significant fines and even jail terms are now a real possibility.

More detail on relevant Competition Act provisions will be presented as each of the four Ps is discussed. However, another round of important changes to the Competition Act may be on the way. As this text was going to press, Parliament was considering amendments that, among other things, would aggressively regulate telemarketing and make it easier to investigate firms suspected of price fixing or bid rigging.

Other federal legislation exists

Other laws and regulations are also designed to protect the consumer interest. See Exhibit 3–4 for a complete listing of the legislation now administered by Industry

Exhibit 3-4 Consumer Legislation Administered by Industry Canada

1. **Fully Administered**
   - Bankruptcy Act and Bankruptcy Rules
   - Boards of Trade Act
   - Canada Business Corporations Act
   - Canada Cooperative Associations Act
   - Canada Corporations Act
   - Competition Act
   - Companies' Creditors Arrangement Act
   - Consumer Packaging and Labelling Act
   - Copyright Act
   - Department of Consumer and Corporate Affairs Act
   - Electricity and Gas Inspection Act
   - Government Corporations Operation Act
   - Hazardous Products Act
   - Industrial Design Act
   - National Trade Mark and True Labelling Act
   - Patent Act
   - Pension Fund Societies Act
   - Precious Metals Marking Act
   - Public Servants Invention Act
   - Tax Rebate Discounting Act
   - Textile Labelling Act
   - Timber Marking Act
   - Trade Marks Act
   - Weights and Measures Act
2. **Administered Jointly with Other Departments**
   - Bills of Exchange Act (with Finance)
   - Canada Agricultural Products Standards Act (with Agriculture)
   - Canada Dairy Products Act (with Agriculture)
   - Fish Inspection Act (with Fisheries and Oceans)
   - Food and Drugs Act (with Health and Welfare)
   - Maple Products Industry Act (with Agriculture)
   - Shipping Conferences Exemption Act (with Transport)
   - Winding-Up Act (with Finance)

Canada, the organization with which Consumer and Corporate Affairs Canada has been merged. Here, we will mention only a few of the many relevant federal laws and regulations. Other laws affecting the four Ps will be discussed in the chapters describing the practices to which they apply.

The Food and Drug Act regulates the sale of foods, drugs, cosmetics, and medical devices. This legislation deals with quality standards, packaging, labelling, and advertising, as well as with the manufacturing practices and selling policies of food and drug manufacturers. Certain forms of misrepresentation in food labelling, packing, selling, and advertising are specifically outlawed by the Food and Drug Act. Many federal units establish product standards and grades. There are also laws concerning the labelling of wool, furs, precious metals, and flammable fabrics.

Provincial and local regulations

Provincial and local laws also affect marketing. There are regulations for starting up a business (licences, examinations, and even tax payments); and in some communities, there are ordinances prohibiting certain activities such as door-to-door selling. Provinces also have attempted to set the store hours for various types of retailers. For example, it wasn't until the early 1990s that Ontario finally legalized Sunday shopping. The sale and advertising of alcoholic beverages are also provincially controlled.

Individual provinces have passed laws that regulate the granting of credit and otherwise call for truth in lending. Purchasers from door-to-door salespeople are often provided with a cooling-off period during which they may cancel a contract. The provinces also exercise their regulatory authority over car dealers, travel agents, and many other types of businesses that deal with large numbers of consumers spending considerable amounts of money.

Perhaps the most significant development on the provincial scene has been the passing of trade practices legislation. Such legislation protects the consumer from unconscionable and deceptive practices. Though the laws passed by different provinces aren't identical, they all attempt to deal with the same set of problems.

The legislative environment in Quebec

Like every other jurisdiction in Canada, Quebec has passed a number of laws to protect its consumers. Quebec's Consumer Protection Act is modelled after, but goes far beyond, trade practices legislation previously passed in British Columbia, Ontario, and Alberta. One unique feature of the Quebec statute is its virtual ban on all advertising directed toward children.

Some laws are intended to ensure the preeminence of the French language in every aspect of Quebec life. Although new Quebec regulations introduced in late 1993 allow for a somewhat greater use of other languages, the primacy of French remains unchanged.

"Let the seller beware"

Traditional thinking about buyer–seller relations has been *let the buyer beware*—but now it seems to be shifting to *let the seller beware.* The emphasis now is on protecting consumers *directly,* rather than *indirectly* by laws designed to preserve competition. Much of the impact of consumer protection legislation tends to fall on manufacturers. They're the producers of the product, and they are expected to stand behind what they make. The courts are placing an ever greater degree of responsibility on manufacturers. Some firms have even been held liable for injuries caused by the user's own carelessness. When this happens, it very definitely becomes a *let the seller beware* world.

Know the laws—follow the courts

Marketers must also stay alert to how legislation is being interpreted and enforced. Often, good legal assistance is required to keep up to date. Managers must accept the political and legal environments as the context within which business must function.

The cultural and social environment

The **cultural and social environment** affects how people live and behave. This in turn affects customer buying behaviour and eventually the economic, political, and legal environments. Many variables make up the cultural and social environment. Some examples are the languages people speak, the type of education they have, their religious beliefs, what type of food they eat, the style of clothing and housing they have, and how they view marriage and family. Because the cultural and social environment has such broad effects, most people don't stop to think about it, how it may be changing, or how it may differ for other people.

A marketing manager can't afford to take the cultural and social environment for granted. Although changes tend to come slowly, they can have far-reaching effects. A marketing manager who sees the changes early may be able to identify big opportunities. Further, within any broad society, different subgroups of people may be affected by the cultural and social environment in different ways. In most countries, the impact of multiculturalism is making such differences even more important to marketers. Because of multiculturalism, special attention must be paid when markets are being segmented. In fact, dealing with cultural differences is often one of the greatest challenges managers face when they are planning strategies, especially for international markets.

We will discuss details of how the cultural and social environment relates to buying behaviour in Chapters 5 through 7. Here we will just use examples to illustrate its impact on strategic market planning.

Cultural similarities and differences

Is there a distinct Canadian culture? If so, how do cultural differences and so-called national characteristics help determine the way Canadians live, work, and consume? It's easy to ask such questions but difficult to answer them in a manner helpful to marketers. All we can do now is indicate some of the cultural similarities and differences that must be taken into consideration.

Seymour Lipset has provided important insights into how we differ from our southern neighbour, the United States. He sees distinct differences that find their roots in the American Revolution. From this event the two countries emerged: one victorious and independent of its British ties, the other content to maintain its links to England.

We appear to have more tolerance for "elites," Lipset believes. We also place less importance on equality. Americans are more religious, more patriotic, and more committed to higher education. Americans don't favour large welfare programs or an active role for government in the economy.

National identity is a very important issue for Canadians, and we look endlessly for qualities that make us distinct. Unfortunately, as Lipset says, we often define ourselves by how we differ from Americans. If they're brash risk-takers, then we're solid, reliable, and decent. Canadians are more class-aware, law-abiding, and group-oriented.[17]

Whether or not we're really the "kinder, gentler" nation may not be easily established. Lipset argues that the two countries differ on the principles that organize them. Nevertheless, similarities in values, living patterns, work roles, family relationships, and consumer behaviour are much more obvious than the differences that might exist between American and Anglo-Canadian families.

Canada is a mosaic

One of the Canadian market's most important characteristics is its distinctive regional differences. The United States is often considered a melting pot. Canada is considered to be a mosaic. Incomes, consumption patterns, lifestyles, dialects, and attitudes vary from province to province. Cultural differences similar to those found between the regions are also common within major urban areas. Large ethnic communities are to be found in Toronto, Montreal, and Vancouver. Food stores, specialty food manufacturers, newsstands, travel agencies, credit unions, and restaurants cater specifically to culturally defined markets. The size and importance of Canada's ethnic market is discussed at length in Chapter 5.

Changing women's roles

Perhaps the shifting role of women in our society best illustrates how the social and cultural environment can affect strategic market planning. Fifty years ago, most people in North America believed that a woman's place was in the home, first and foremost as a wife and mother. Women had less of an opportunity to obtain a higher education, and were completely shut out of many of the most interesting jobs. Obviously, today's world is very different, and so is today's way of thinking about a woman's role in that world.

With better job opportunities, more women are delaying marriage. Once married, they are likely to stay in the work force and have fewer children. The flood of women into the job market boosted economic growth and changed Canadian society in very significant ways. Many stay-at-home jobs that used to be done primarily by women—ranging from family shopping to preparing meals to doing volunteer work—still need to be done by somebody. Husbands and children now do some of these jobs—a situation that has changed the target market for many products. Or a

Marketing Demo 3-2

Women and Offensive Advertising

Most women boycott companies whose advertising they find offensive because of sexist overtones, a new study has found.

And a hefty chunk of these women who snub the offending companies also discuss their objections with friends, although few complain directly to advertisers, said the study, conducted by MediaWatch, a feminist group that monitors how the media portray women.

The study on television and advertising is a wake-up call to marketers who turn a blind eye to women's distaste of sexual stereotypes, said Shari Graydon, president of MediaWatch in Vancouver.

The survey, conducted in consultation with Simon Fraser University's media lab, involved telephone interviews with 625 women in three major cities. MediaWatch said it was identified as the survey's sponsor during the final two questions regarding the respondent's awareness of the organization.

The study is all the more important to marketers because of women's rising purchasing power as they earn more money in the work force and buy a larger array of products—everything from men's clothing to automobiles and computers, the authors said.

The authors found it "somewhat surprising" that women are so dissatisfied with the way they are addressed in the media. Some of the most contentious categories, when it comes to offending women, are fragrance and jeans ads, Ms. Graydon said in an interview.

Still, despite all the huffing and puffing, the troubling truth is that sales of some of the most offensive advertisers, such as Calvin Klein and Chanel, are pretty healthy, she acknowledged.

One ad that drew the ire of many women was for Calvin Klein's Obsession for Men, which appeared in print and television versions. It showed waif-like supermodel Kate Moss, looking barely a teen-ager, lying naked on a couch.

But there are signs that pressure on advertisers in the past few years has paid off, Ms. Graydon and other women's advocates agree.

Canadian car and beer companies have cleaned up their acts considerably, Ms. Graydon said. The beer marketers responded to a growing chorus of complaints about scantily clad women populating their ads. Car companies are realizing that some of their most discriminating consumers are women.

Ms. Graydon praised a Saturn commercial that shows a woman who is so insulted by how she is treated at a rival's dealer (the salesman thinks she's only interested in the vanity mirror or the car's colour) that she becomes a saleswoman for Saturn, where her experience was better.

As the MediaWatch study suggests, marketers who shape the image of women in the media may have to change their practices for purely pragmatic purposes, even if they do not back the feminist cause. "Where arguments about social equity have failed, a desire for profit may prevail," the report concluded.

Still, complaints lodged by MediaWatch, including one about the Obsession ad, have not been upheld by the Canadian Advertising Foundation, said Susan Burke of the foundation.

The foundation found that because the ad pitched a fragrance, it was acceptable to portray a woman in such a vulnerable way, according to Ms. Graydon.

But many other advertisers are catching on to a different message, Susan Skene, marketing director of Hershey Canada Inc, said. "It's an economically sound proposition to target in on women in a way that's not offensive to them."

Source: Marina Strauss, "Advertisers Find That It Pays to Clean Up Their Act," *The Globe and Mail*, Classroom Edition, January 1995, p. 8.

working woman may face a crushing "poverty of time" and look for help elsewhere, thus creating opportunities for frozen food producers, child care centres, dry cleaners, financial services, and the like.

The changing role of women has created real marketing opportunities, as well as a real challenge. For example, a marketing mix targeted at women may require a careful balancing act. Advertisements showing a woman at the office may attract some customers but alienate stay-at-home mothers. Conversely, advertising that shows a woman cheerily doing housework may be criticized by some for reinforcing old stereotypes. Indeed, Marketing Demo 3–2 reveals that some women take offence at much of the consumer advertising they see.

Changes come slowly

A society's basic cultural values and social attitudes are slow to change. A marketing manager's firm can do very little to influence the rate at which such changes occur. Rather than trying, it should keep informed of current attitudes, and work within these constraints as it seeks new and better opportunities.[18]

Questions and Problems

1. Explain how a firm's objectives may affect its search for opportunities.
2. Specifically, how would various company objectives affect the development of a marketing mix for a new type of hiking boot? Assuming this company is just being formed by an outdoorsman with limited financial resources, list the objectives that he may have. Then discuss how they would affect his marketing strategy.
3. Explain how a firm's resources may limit its search for opportunities. Cite a specific example for a specific resource.
4. Discuss how a company's financial strength may have a bearing on the kinds of products it produces. Will it have an impact on the other three Ps as well? If so, how? Use an example in your answer.
5. In your own words, explain how a marketing manager might use a competitor analysis to avoid situations that involve head-on competition.
6. The owner of a small grocery store—the only one in a growing community in the mountains—has just learned that a large supermarket chain plans to open a new store nearby. How difficult will it be for the owner to plan for this new competitive threat? Explain your answer.
7. Discuss the probable impact on your hometown if a major breakthrough in air transportation allowed foreign producers to ship into any Canadian market for about the same transportation cost that domestic producers incur.
8. Will the elimination of trade barriers between countries in Europe eliminate the need to consider submarkets of European consumers? Why or why not?
9. Which way does the Canadian political and legal environment seem to be moving with respect to business-related affairs?
10. Why is it necessary to have so many laws regulating business? Why hasn't Parliament just passed one set of laws to take care of business problems?
11. What and who is the Canadian government attempting to protect in its efforts to preserve and regulate competition?

Suggested Cases

6 The Hand Guard

13 New North Media

17 Huntoon & Balbiera

Computer-aided problem

Competitor Analysis

Mediquip, Inc., produces medical equipment and uses its own sales force to sell the equipment to hospitals. Recently, several hospitals have asked Mediquip to develop a laser-beam "scalpel" for eye surgery. Mediquip has the needed resources, and 200 hospitals will probably buy the equipment. But Mediquip managers have heard that Laser Technologies—another quality producer—is thinking of competing for the same business. Mediquip has other good opportunities it could pursue, so it wants to see if it would have a competitive advantage over Laser Tech.

Mediquip and Laser Tech are similar in many ways, but there are important differences. Laser Technologies already produces key parts that are needed for the new laser product, so its production costs would be lower. It would cost Mediquip more to design the product—and getting parts from outside suppliers would result in higher production costs.

On the other hand, Mediquip has marketing strengths. It already has a good reputation with hospitals, and its sales force calls only on hospitals. Mediquip thinks that each of its current sales reps could spend some time selling the new product and that it could adjust sales territories so only four more sales reps would be needed for good coverage in the market. In contrast, Laser Tech's sales reps call only on industrial customers, so it would have to add 14 reps to cover the hospitals.

Hospitals have budget pressures, so the supplier with the lowest price is likely to get a larger share of the business. But Mediquip knows that either supplier's price will be set high enough to cover the added costs of designing, producing, and selling the new product—and leave something for profit.

Mediquip gathers information about its own likely costs and can estimate Laser Tech's costs from industry studies and Laser Tech's annual report. Mediquip has set up a spreadsheet to evaluate the proposed new product.

a. The initial spreadsheet results are based on the assumption that Mediquip and Laser Tech will split the business 50/50. If Mediquip can win at least 50 percent of the market, does Mediquip have a competitive advantage over Laser Tech? Explain.

b. Because of economies of scale, both suppliers' average cost per machine will vary depending on the quantity sold. If Mediquip had only 45 percent of the market and Laser Tech 55 percent, how would their costs (average total cost per machine) compare? What if Mediquip had 55 percent of the market and Laser Tech only 45 percent? What conclusion do you draw from these analyses?

c. It is possible that Laser Tech may not enter the market. If Mediquip has 100 percent of the market, and quantity purchases from its suppliers will reduce the cost of producing one unit to $6,500, what price would cover all its costs and contribute $1,125 to profit for every machine sold? What does this suggest about the desirability of finding your own unsatisfied target markets? Explain.

For additional questions related to this problem, see Exercise 3–4 in the *Learning Aid for Use with Basic Marketing*, Ninth Canadian Edition.

When you finish this chapter, you should:

- Know about marketing information systems.
- Understand a scientific approach to marketing research.
- Know how to define and solve marketing problems.
- Know about getting secondary and primary data.
- Understand the role of observing, questioning, and using experimental methods in marketing research.
- Understand the important new terms (shown in orange).

Chapter four

Using Marketing Information to Make Better Decisions

Since 1985, social marketing has been a major component of the Canadian government's efforts to reduce tobacco use. Together with legislative measures and anti-tobacco programming that targets vulnerable segments of the population, social marketing is part of a centrally coordinated and multipronged strategy to reduce tobacco demand in Canada.

Health Canada's social marketing campaigns are based on three phases. First, careful analysis of the existing situation and trends; second, the establishment of clear goals and measurable objectives for the initiatives; and finally, the conception, testing, and development of marketing tools.

STRATEGY/SITUATIONAL ANALYSIS Research from the 1994 Health Canada Youth Smoking Survey (the most recent national statistics available) showed that smoking among youth was on the rise in Canada, for the first time in many years. Twenty-four percent of 15- to-19-year-olds in 1994 were current smokers, a rate significantly lower than the 29% in 1985, but higher than the rate of 21% in 1990. [Edward M. Adlaf, Susan J. Bondy. 1994. "Smoking Behaviour." *Youth Smoking Survey, 1994, Technical Report.* p. 38.]

It was apparent to the Health Canada social marketing team that additional market research was needed. With this in mind, they approached the target group directly. In June 1996, a Youth Forum on Tobacco was held to look at new ways of stemming youth smoking. Thirty-six youths from across Canada, of which a full third were smokers, were chosen from various in-school and community-based anti-tobacco programs. Youths attending this forum were asked to evaluate the effectiveness of anti-tobacco programming aimed at the young people of this country. Their response was clear: social marketing activities, particularly broadcast messages, must show and be about real kids, not kids who were hired as actors by advertising agencies. The Youth Forum participants went on to become the Health Minister's Youth Advisory Committee on Tobacco.

The next step was to identify ways to get youths to tell us what is real for them. How do we get their ideas? A unique and new methodology for Health Canada was proposed:

ENLIST "OFF-THE-STREET" YOUTH TO PARTICIPATE DIRECTLY IN THE SOCIAL MARKETING CAMPAIGN This unique idea for Health Canada formed the basis of an interactive social marketing strategy to support tobacco reduction among youth: Health Canada's Challenge to Youth.

On March 10, 1997, the Health Minister launched the Health Canada Challenge to Youth, a tobacco-related contest for young people. "I am asking young people to help us in the fight against youth smoking," said the Minister. "Eighty-five per cent of the 250,000 Canadians who start smoking each year are under the age of 16."

The contest invited 13- to 19-year-olds from across Canada to *Give us your best take on smoking / Donne ta meilleure réplique au tabac.* They were asked to submit a personal 20 second message on how smoking affected them, by calling a toll-free number. The promotional pamphlet read:

> *We're looking for a message that one of your friends, or anyone who's thinking about smoking will listen to. Like why you never tried, or why it's hard to resist the pressure to smoke, or a better way to stop. Whatever you feel is most important.*

Participation in the contest was immediate, with a toll-free line being easy and accessible to virtually all. From March 7 to April 7, 1997, the toll-free lines were opened to young Canadians from across the country.

Collaborations with the Partnerships and Marketing Division of Health Canada were developed to actively promote the Challenge to Youth. Partners included the English and French television stations MuchMusic and Musique Plus, retail outlets of Future Shop, Cineplex Odeon Theatres, and Empire Theatres across Canada.

The contest was promoted across Canada throughout the month-long campaign.

- Four times a day, a 45-second promotional spot was aired on MuchMusic and Musique Plus.
- ClickThrough banners (bought 250,000, delivered 332,937 impressions) were placed on a number of popular youth Web sites.
- Approximately 486 standing displays were positioned in every Cineplex Odeon and Empire Theatre across Canada.
- Standing displays were also set up in 159 English and 80 French Future Shop retail outlets, well established CD sources with youth.

THE RESULTS The contest was a resounding success, with over 19,000 calls received, of which 10,278 valid entries were considered.

Entries were judged on the following criteria: emotional (an honest, sincere message that will create a strong response from teens about smoking); content (a relevant message for teens that is believable and accurate); and originality (to be seen as in one's own words, or a unique message).

After a weekly screening of the calls was performed, the Minister's Youth Advisory Committee on Tobacco selected two winners from each region: Atlantic, Ontario, Quebec, Western and Pacific. The ten winners were flown to Vancouver in April, where they appeared in a Health Canada ad, professionally produced by Palmer Jarvis Communications, giving their winning message about smoking.

In June/July 1997, and again in December/January, two 60-second ads, one in English and one in French, aired in Cineplex Odeon and Empire Theatres across the country. Two English and one French—30 second spots—ran on MuchMusic and Musique Plus during the same time period. Based on the success of the initial run, the ads aired again through a national television buy, skewed to a youth audience, which ran from February 23 to March 31, 1998.

EVALUATION/IMPACT In July 1997, in Toronto, Montreal, and Vancouver, Health Canada conducted a series of 200 interviews with young Canadians from 13 to 19 leaving Cineplex Odeon movie theatres at which Health Canada's commercials had been screened. These "intercept" interviews questioned respondents with regard to their recall of the Health Canada commercial, as well as the interviewees' qualitative response to the advertisements.

The results were phenomenal. Total recall level was 81%, higher than prior in-theatre commercials by Coca-Cola (75% total recall) or Nike (74% total recall). Recall scores were in an equal range by gender (81% male: 80% female), age, and educational level. As well, the sample indicated that recall scores for smokers in the target population (13–19) were the same as for nonsmokers (total recall 79% for smokers and 81% for nonsmokers).

Attendance at the theatres for July 1997 was estimated at 580,000 12- to 17-year-olds and 622,000 18- to 24-year-olds. Both groups combined add up to 29% of the total movie-going audience for the month of July. The ratings for MuchMusic and Musique Plus were equally impressive. The English MuchMusic station showed a weekly reach of 6.5 million viewers, of which 864,000 were in the 12–17 age group. The French Musique Plus reached a weekly audience of over 2 million viewers, with 253,000 falling in the 12–17 age group.

Results from a national telephone survey conducted with over 600 youth ages 12–19 in April 1998 after the television buy were also impressive. Over 80% of the youth felt that these ads were more convincing than any previous anti-tobacco advertising they had ever seen. Further, 77% said that the ads succeeded in convincing them personally of the dangers of smoking. The research also showed a very positive profile of emotional response to the ads, confirming that the advertising approach, peer-to-peer, is very appropriate for the target group.

Although it is still too early to establish what the long-term impact of this campaign on actual behaviour change will be, the results will be monitored over the next five years.

One of the unanticipated benefits of the campaign was the surprisingly positive reaction it drew from parents/adults. Although the feedback has been purely anecdotal at this point, Health Canada has received a significant amount of praise from parents, community groups, and nongovernment organizations in response to the ads. One comment read:

> I am 49 years old with a fourteen year old daughter and 11 yr. old son, and your latest quit smoking ads on TV about what young people have lost, has made a real impression on me. As of today, I am now using the patch, and am attempting to finally quit. Please give my thanks to the real people in these ads, and I hope their lives become better than they are now.

The final tag line in the ads promoted Health Canada's new interactive smoking cessation Web site, quit4life.com. In the first 10 days of the campaign, over 5,400 visits were made to the Web site. Designed to provide further support for teens looking for tips on quitting, the site also provides the opportunity for teens to interact with each other, share their experiences, and learn from each other.

The phenomenal response and success of the campaign clearly indicated the value of listening to one's audience. This peer-to-peer campaign will be used as a model for public education activities over the next five years of the Tobacco Control Initiative.

Health Canada's Challenge to Youth was conceptualized and implemented by the social marketing team at Health Canada: James Mintz, Director of the Partnerships and Marketing Division, and Jane Hazel and Tracy Schoales, the Senior Marketing Consultants who managed the campaign.

Source: James Mintz, Jane Hazel, and Tracy Schoales, "Challenge to Youth: a Health Canada anti-tobacco campaign" (1998). With permission from Health Canada. This article was written for inclusion in *Basic Marketing, Ninth Canadian Edition*.

Marketing managers need information

The successful planning of marketing strategies requires information—information about potential target markets and their likely responses to marketing mixes as well as about competition and other marketing environment variables. Information is also needed for implementation and control. Without good marketing information, managers have to use intuition or guesses—and in today's fast-changing and competitive markets, this invites failure. As described in the Health Canada Challenge to Youth example, the need for good information is just as important to an organization like Health Canada when it develops a social marketing campaign.

Yet managers seldom have all the information they need to make the best decisions. Both customers and competitors can be unpredictable. Getting more information may cost too much or take too long. For example, information on international markets is often incomplete, outdated, or difficult to obtain. So managers often must decide whether they need more information and—if so—how to get it. In this chapter we'll talk about how marketing managers can get the information they need to plan successful strategies.

Radical changes are underway in marketing information

Marketing managers for some companies make decisions based almost totally on their own judgment—with very little hard data. The manager may not even know that he or she is about to make the same mistake that the previous person in that job already made! When it's time to make a decision, they may wish they had more information. But by then it's too late, so they do without.

MIS makes information available and accessible

There is a difference between information that is *available* and information that is readily *accessible.* Some information—such as the details of competitors' plans—is just not available. Other information may be available, but not really accessible without a time-consuming effort. For example, a company may have file cabinets full of records of customer purchases, what was sold by sales reps last month, past marketing plans, or what is in the warehouse. In a sense, all of this information is available. But if a manager can't quickly get this information when it's needed, it isn't useful. By contrast, making the same information instantly accessible over a computer network could be very useful.

Firms realize that it doesn't pay to wait until you have important questions you can't answer. They anticipate the information they will need. They work to develop a *continual flow of information* that is available and quickly accessible when it's needed.

A **marketing information system (MIS)** is an organized way of continually gathering, accessing, and analyzing information that marketing managers need to make decisions.

We won't cover all of the technical details of planning for an MIS. That's beyond the scope of this course. But you should understand what an MIS is so that you know some of the possibilities. We'll be discussing the elements of a complete MIS as shown in Exhibit 4–1. As part of that review, we'll highlight how technology is changing MIS use.

Get more information—faster and easier

Basic MIS concepts are not very different today than they were 20 years ago. However, recent developments in information technology are having a *radical* impact on what information is available to marketing managers and how quickly. A big difference today is how easy it is to set up and use an MIS. A short time ago, connecting

Exhibit 4-1 Elements of a Complete Marketing Information System

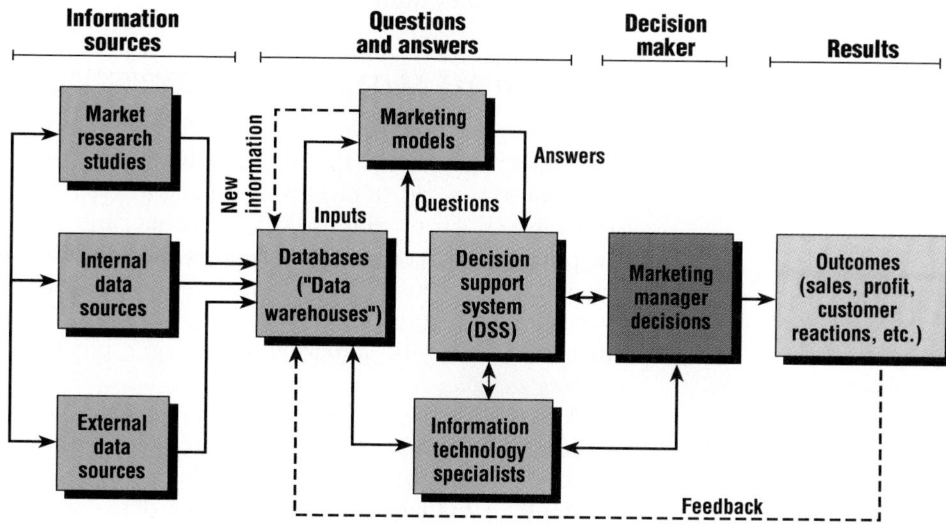

remote computers or exchanging data over networks was very difficult. Now, it's standard and almost automatic. And even a manager with little computer experience can quickly learn to use an MIS. As a result, managers everywhere have access to much more information. It's instantly available, and often just a mouse click away.

Equally important, the *type* of information available is changing dramatically. As recently as 1995, most marketing managers with information needs relied on computers mainly for "number crunching." The multimedia revolution in computing has quickly lifted that limitation. Now it doesn't matter whether marketing information takes the form of a marketing plan, report, memo, spreadsheet, database, presentation, photo, graphic, or table of statistics. It is all being created on computer, so it can be easily stored and accessed by computer. Moreover, new computer programs help find whatever information is available—even if it is "lost" on the computer hard disk of a manager in an office across the ocean. When we talk about a database of marketing information, keep in mind that it may include all types of information, not just numbers.

An Intranet is easy to update

Earlier in the book we covered some of the important ways that the Internet is making more information available—and changing marketing. In addition, many firms, even very small ones, have their own **Intranet**—a system for linking computers within a company. An Intranet works like the Internet. However, to maintain security, access to Web sites on an Intranet is usually limited to employees. Even so, information is available on demand. Further, it's a simple matter to "publish" new information to a Web site as it becomes available. So information can be constantly updated. Prior to this decade, managers could only dream about this sort of capability.

Marketing managers must help develop an MIS

Computers are getting easier to use, but setting up and supporting an MIS still requires technical skill. So in some companies, an MIS is set up by a person or group that provides *all* departments in the firm with information technology support. Or it may be set up by marketing specialists.

These specialists are important, but the marketing manager should play an important role, too. Marketing managers may not know in advance exactly what questions they will have, or when. But they do know what data they've routinely used or needed in the past. They can also foresee what types of data might be useful. They should communicate these needs to the specialists so that the information will be there when they want it.

Decision support systems put managers online

An MIS system organizes incoming information into a *data warehouse*—a place where databases are stored so that they are available when needed. You can think of a data warehouse as a sort of electronic library, where all of the information is indexed extremely well. Firms with an MIS often have information technology specialists who help managers get specialized reports and output from the warehouse. However, to get better decisions, most MIS systems now provide marketing managers with a decision support system. A **decision support system (DSS)** is a computer program that makes it easy for a marketing manager to get and use information *as he or she is making decisions.*

A decision support system usually involves some sort of **search engine**—a computer program that helps a marketing manager find information that is needed. Often, the manager provides a word or phrase to guide the search. For example, a manager who wants sales data for the previous week or day might search for any database or computer file that references the term *unit sales* as well as the relevant data. The search engine would identify any files where that term appeared. If there were many, the manager could narrow the search further (say by specifying the product of interest), or could briefly review the files to find the most appropriate one.

When the search is focused on numerical data, simply finding the information may not go far enough. Thus, a DSS typically helps change raw data—like product sales for the previous day—into more *useful information.* For example, it may draw graphs to show relationships in data—perhaps comparing yesterday's sales to the sales on the same day in the last four weeks.

Some decision support systems go even farther. They allow the manager to see how answers to questions might change in various situations. For example, a manager at Kraft Foods may want to estimate how much sales will increase if the firm uses a certain type of promotion in a specific market area. The DSS will ask the manager for a *personal* judgment about how much business could be won from each competitor in that market. Then, using this input and drawing on data in the database about how the promotion had worked in other markets, the system will make a sales estimate using a marketing model. A **marketing model** is a statement of relationships among marketing variables.

In short, the decision support system puts managers online so that they can study available data and make better marketing decisions faster.[1]

Information makes managers greedy for more

Once marketing managers see how a functioning MIS—and perhaps a DSS—can help their decision making, they are eager for more information. They realize that they can improve all aspects of their planning—blending individual Ps, combining the four Ps into mixes, and developing and selecting plans. Furthermore, they can monitor the implementation of current plans, comparing results against plans and making necessary changes more quickly. (Note: The sales and cost analysis techniques discussed in Chapter 20 are often used in an MIS.) Marketing information systems will become more widespread as networks become easier to use, managers become more sensitive to the possibilities, and more information is available in computer form.

Many firms are not there yet

Of course, not every firm has a complete MIS system. And in some firms that do, managers don't know how to use what's there. A major problem is that many managers are used to doing it the old way—and they don't think through what information they need.

One sales manager thought he was being progressive when he asked his assistant for a report listing each sales rep's sales for the previous month and the current month. The assistant quickly found the relevant information on the firm's Intranet, put it into an Excel spreadsheet, and printed out the report. Later, however, she was surprised to see the sales manager working on the list with a calculator. He was figuring the percentage change in sales for the month and ranking the reps from largest increase in sales to smallest. The spreadsheet software could have done all of that instantly, but the sales manager got what he *asked for*—not what he really needed. An MIS can provide information, but only the marketing manager knows what problem needs solving. It's the job of the manager, not the computer or the MIS specialist, to ask for the right information in the right form.

MIS use is growing rapidly

Some people think that only large firms can develop an effective MIS. Not so! In fact, just the opposite may be true. Low-cost microcomputers make a powerful MIS affordable even for small firms. Further, large firms with complicated marketing programs often face a challenge trying to develop an MIS from scratch. And once a large firm has a system in place it may be very costly to switch to something better. It can be easier for small firms because they are often more focused. They can get started with a simple system and then expand it as needs expand. There is a lot of opportunity in this area for students who are able and willing to apply computer skills to solve real marketing problems.[2]

New questions require new answers

MIS systems tend to focus on recurring information needs. Routinely analyzing such information can be valuable to marketing managers. But it shouldn't be their only source of information for decision making. They must try to satisfy ever-changing needs in dynamic markets. So marketing research must be used to supplement data already available and accessible through the MIS.

What is marketing research?

The marketing concept says that marketing managers should meet the needs of customers. Yet today, many marketing managers are isolated in company offices, far from potential customers. It is just not possible for managers to keep up with all of the changes taking place in their markets.

This means that marketing managers have to rely on help from **marketing research**—procedures to develop and analyze new information to help marketing managers make decisions. One of the important jobs of a marketing researcher is to get the "facts" that are not currently available in the MIS.

Continued improvements in research methods are making marketing research information more dependable. This has encouraged firms to put more money and trust in research. Managers in some consumer product companies don't make any major decisions without the support—and sometimes even the official approval—of the marketing research department. As a result, some marketing research directors rise to high levels in the organization.

Marketing research can provide data to meet the many different informational needs in marketing. It can be useful in copy testing, new product development, and estimating market demand, to name a few areas. Marketing Demo 4–1 provides a detailed listing of all the different types of customized studies that Canadian Facts, one of Canada's largest marketing research firms, can conduct for clients.

Marketing Demo 4-1

How Canadian Facts Meets the Needs of Its Clients with a Diversity of Research Methods

Advertising & communications research

Advertising Pre-Testing / Creative Strategy Testing
Is our creative strategy correct? Will the new creative be effective?

Advertising Tracking
What is the impact of our advertising campaign? What messages are being communicated?

Communications Research
Has the corporate communication program been effective? What level of knowledge exists of the government's energy conservation program?

Direct Mail
Has our mailing reached its designated target? What impact has it had?

Concept & product or service evaluation

Concept Evaluation
Does our new service idea have merit? What level of appeal exists for it?

Name & Packaging Evaluation
Does our package have good shelf recognition and visibility? What image does it convey?

New Product & Service Market Forecasting
What sales levels will be achieved for our new product or service? Should investment be made in a test market for a new product or service?

Product Testing
What effect will a change have on acceptability of our product or service? What is the level of appeal relative to competition?

Public policy & political research

Human Resources
What skill sets are required for critical jobs in our industry sector? What are the attitudes of workers to technological changes in the workplace?

Political Research
What is the level of party support today? How is a particular political candidate viewed?

Program Evaluation
What has been the impact of the government's initiative in a particular area? What policy changes are indicated?

Public Affairs
What are opinion leaders' views of foreign investment restrictions in Canada? How does the public view the government's regulation of my industry?

Public Opinion Studies
What do Canadians believe are the most important issues facing government today? How does the public view the privatization of certain government services?

Market definition & structure

Attitude & Image Studies
What is the image of our brand relative to its competitors? How should it be positioned in the market?

Market Definition & Assessment
How is the market structured? What is the potential for a new service in this region?

Strategic Development & Evaluation
Does our brand have a unique selling proposition? How are the strategic advantages best communicated?

Test Market Assessment
How has the market performed? What is the potential for success on a larger scale?

Other types of research

Business-to-Business Research
What is senior corporate management's attitude toward a new cost control service? Are senior business managers prepared to out-source non-core activities?

Cluster Analysis
How does the market for financial investment products segment? What is the size of each life-style segment in the market?

Customer Satisfaction
What is the meaning of service quality? What elements in customer service are most important to ensure repeat business?

Employee Attitude Surveys
How can company/staff relations be improved? How can we improve productivity?

Legal & Quasi-Legal Surveys
Can a specific advertising claim be made? Is our competitor trading on design elements strongly associated with our product or service?

Perceptual Mapping
What is the direct competitive frame of reference for our product or service? How is our product or service positioned on primary perceptual criteria?

Price Sensitivity
What is the optimum price point? What are consumers willing to pay for a new product or service?

Trade-Off Analysis
What service features or benefits will justify an increase in fee structure? What sacrifices are acceptable when fees are decreased?

Source: Courtesy of Canadian Facts.

Who does the work?

Most large companies have a separate marketing research department to plan and carry out research projects. These departments often use outside specialists, including interviewing and tabulating services, to handle technical assignments. Further, they may call in specialized marketing consultants and marketing research organizations to take charge of a research project.

Small companies (those with less than $4 million to $5 million in sales) usually don't have separate marketing research departments. They often depend on their salespeople or managers to conduct what research they do.

Some nonprofit organizations have begun to use marketing research—usually with the help of outside specialists. For example, many politicians rely on research firms to conduct surveys of voter attitudes.[3]

Effective research requires cooperation

Good marketing research requires much more than just technical tools. It requires cooperation between researchers and marketing managers. Good marketing researchers must keep both marketing research *and* marketing management in mind to be sure their research focuses on real problems.

Marketing managers must be involved in marketing research, too. Many marketing research details can be handled by company or outside experts. But marketing managers must be able to explain what their problems are, and what kinds of information they need. They should be able to communicate with specialists in the specialists' language. Marketing managers may only be "consumers" of research, but they should be informed consumers—able to explain exactly what they want from the research. They should also know about some of the basic decisions made during the research process so that they know the limitations of the findings.

For this reason, our discussion of marketing research won't emphasize mechanics, but rather how to plan and evaluate the work of marketing researchers.

Ethical Dimensions

Issues in Marketing Research

The basic reason for doing marketing research is to get information that people can trust in making decisions. But as you will see in this chapter, research often involves many hidden details. A person who wants to misuse marketing research to pursue a personal agenda can often do so.

Perhaps the most common ethical issues concern decisions to withhold certain information from the research. For example, a manager might selectively share only those results which support his or her point of view. Others involved in a decision might never know they are getting only partial truths. Or during a set of interviews, a researcher may discover that consumers are interpreting a poorly worded question many different ways. If the researcher doesn't admit the problem, an unknowing manager may rely on meaningless results.

Another problem involves more blatant abuses. It is unethical for a firm to contact consumers under the pretense of doing research when the real purpose is to sell something. For example, some political organizations have been criticized for surveying consumers to find out their attitudes about various political candidates and issues. Then, armed with that information, someone else calls back to solicit donations. Legitimate marketing researchers are very concerned about such abuses. If the problem were to become widespread, consumers might not be willing to participate in any research. See Marketing Demo 4–2 for other examples of ethical dilemmas in marketing research.

The relationship between the researcher and the manager sometimes creates an ethical conflict, especially when the research is done by an outside firm. Managers must be careful not to send a signal that the only acceptable results from a research project are ones that confirm their existing point of view. Researchers are supposed to be objective, but that objectivity may be swayed if future contracts depend on getting the "right" results.[4]

Marketing Demo 4-2

Ethical Issues in Data Collection

Misrepresentation of the data collection process stems from two principal sources. The first is representing as research a marketing activity other than research. The second is the abuse of respondents' rights during the data collection process under the rationale of providing better quality research.

Consumers expect to be sold and to be surveyed and they expect to be able to tell the difference without great difficulty. When a selling or marketing activity uses the forms and language of survey research in order to mask the real nature of the activity being performed, it violates the public trust. Some classic examples of this type of practice are:

- The use of survey techniques for selling purposes. In this case, a person answers a few questions only to find him- or herself suddenly eligible to buy a specific product or service. The misuse of the survey approach as a disguise for sales canvassing is a widespread practice that shows no signs of abating.
- The use of survey techniques to obtain names and addresses of prospects for direct marketing. These efforts are usually conducted by mail. Questionnaires about products or brands are sent to households, and response is encouraged by the offer of free product samples to respondents. The listing firms compile the information by implying to the prospective customer that he or she has been interviewed in a market study.

These practices give legitimate research a bad name in the eyes of consumers. Other practices that abuse the rights of respondents and present ethical dilemmas to the researcher are:

- Disguising the purpose of a particular measurement such as a draw or free product choice question.
- Deceiving the prospective respondent as to the true duration of the interview.
- Misrepresenting the compensation in order to gain cooperation.
- Not mentioning to the respondent that a follow-up interview will be made.
- Using projective tests and unobtrusive measures to circumvent the need for a respondent's consent.
- Using hidden tape recorders to record personal interviews (or recording phone conversations without the permission of the respondent).
- Conducting simulated product tests in which the identical product is tried by the respondent except for variations in characteristics such as colour that have no influence on the quality of a product.

Source: ARF position paper, "Phony or Misleading Polls. *Journal of Advertising Research.* Special Issue 26 (January 1987), pp. RC3–RC8; and George S. Day, "The Threats to Marketing Research, *Journal of Marketing Research* 12 (November 1975), pp. 462–67. Taken from David A. Aaker and George S. Day, eds., *Marketing Research,* 4th ed. (New York: John Wiley & Sons), pp. 217, 218.

The scientific method and marketing research

The scientific method, combined with the strategic market planning framework we discussed in Chapter 2, can help marketing managers make better decisions.

The **scientific method** is a decision-making approach that focuses on being objective and orderly in *testing* ideas before accepting them. With the scientific method, managers don't just *assume* that their intuition is correct; instead, they use their intuition and observations to develop **hypotheses**—educated guesses about the relationships between things or about what will happen in the future. Then they test their hypotheses before making final decisions.

A manager who relies only on intuition might introduce a new product without testing consumer response. But a manager who uses the scientific method might say, "I think [hypothesize] that consumers currently using the most popular brand will prefer our new product. Let's run some consumer tests. If at least 60 percent of the consumers prefer our product, we can introduce it in a regional test market. If it doesn't pass the consumer test there, we can make some changes and try again."

The scientific method forces an orderly research process. Some managers don't specify carefully what information they need. They blindly move ahead, hoping that research will provide "the answer." Other managers may have a clearly defined problem or question but lose their way after that. These hit-or-miss approaches waste both time and money.

Five-step approach to marketing research

The **marketing research process** is a five-step application of the scientific method that includes:

1. Defining the problem.
2. Analyzing the situation.
3. Getting problem-specific data.
4. Interpreting the data.
5. Solving the problem.

Exhibit 4–2 shows the five steps in the process. Note that the process may lead to a solution before all of the steps are completed. Or, as the feedback arrows show, researchers may return to an earlier step if needed. For example, the interpreting step may point to a new question, or reveal the need for additional information, before a final decision can be made.

Defining the problem—Step 1

Defining the problem is the most important—and often the most difficult—step in the marketing research process. Sometimes it takes over half the total time spent on a research project. But it's time well spent if the objectives of the research are clearly defined. The best research job on the wrong problem is wasted effort.

The strategic planning framework introduced in Chapter 2 can be useful here. It can help the researcher identify the real problem area, and what information is needed. Do we really know enough about our target markets to work out all of the four Ps? Do we know enough to decide which celebrity to use in an ad, or how to handle a price war in Toronto or Tokyo? If not, we may want to do research rather than rely on intuition.

The importance of understanding the problem, and then trying to solve it, can be seen in the introduction of Fab One Shot, a laundry product developed to clean, soften, and reduce static cling all in one step. Marketing managers were sure that Fab One Shot was going to appeal to heavy users—especially working women with large families. One manager summarized the situation: "Our research showed that while over 50 percent of women were going back to work, 70 percent were still responsible for the family wash . . . and 80 percent use three different laundry products. These women are looking for convenience."

When marketing managers found that other firms were testing similar products, they rushed Fab One Shot into distribution. To encourage first-time purchases, they

Exhibit 4–2 Five-Step Scientific Approach to Marketing Research Process

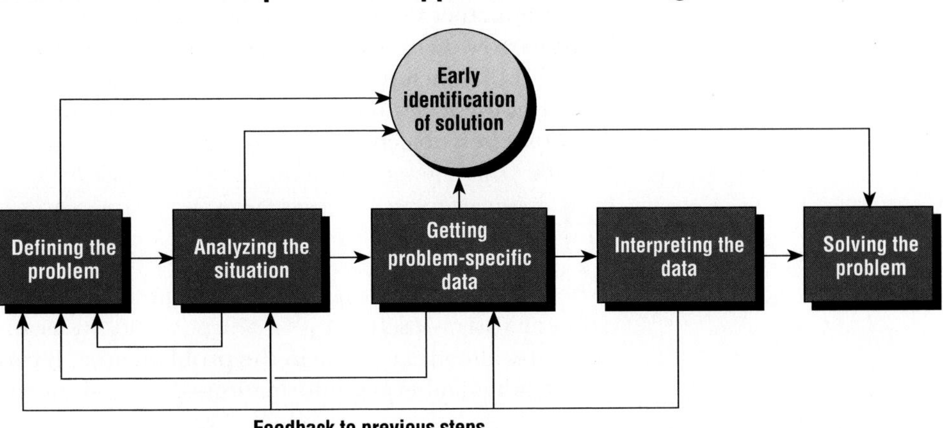

offered introductory price discounts, coupons, and rebates. And they supported the sales promotion with heavy advertising on TV programs that research showed the heavy users watched.

However, research never addressed the problem of how the heavy user target market would react. After the introductory price-off deals were dropped, sales dropped off, too. While the product was convenient, heavy users weren't willing to pay the price—about 25 cents for each washload. For the heavy users, price was a qualifying dimension. And these consumers didn't like Fab's premeasured packets because they had no control over how much detergent they could put in. The competing firms recognized these problems at the research stage—and decided not to introduce their products.

After the fact, it was clear that Fab One Shot was most popular with college and university students, singles, and people living in small apartments. They didn't use much, so the convenience benefit offset the high price. But the company never targeted those segments; rather, it just assumed that it would be profitable to target the big market of heavy users.[5]

The moral of this story is that our strategic planning framework is useful for guiding the problem definition step—as well as the whole marketing research process. First, a marketing manager should understand the target market and what needs the firm can satisfy. Then the manager can focus on lower-level problems—namely, how sensitive the target market is to a change in one or more of the marketing mix ingredients. Without such a framework, marketing researchers may waste time—and money—working on the wrong problem.

Don't confuse problems with symptoms

The problem definition step sounds simple—and that's the danger. It's easy to confuse symptoms with the problem. Suppose a firm's MIS shows that the company's sales are decreasing in certain territories while expenses are remaining the same, resulting in a decline in profits. Will it help to define the problem by asking: How can we stop the sales decline? Probably not. This would be like fitting a hearing-impaired patient with a hearing aid without first trying to find out *why* the patient is having trouble hearing.

It's easy to fall into the trap of mistaking symptoms for the problem, thus confusing the research objectives. Researchers may ignore relevant questions, while analyzing unimportant questions in expensive detail.

Setting research objectives

Sometimes the research objectives are very clear. A manager wants to know if the targeted households have tried a new product and what percentage of them bought it a second time. But research objectives aren't always so simple. The manager might also want to know *why* some didn't buy, or whether they had even heard of the product. Companies rarely have enough time and money to study everything. Managers must narrow their research objectives. One good way is to develop a "research question" list that includes all the possible problem areas. Then managers can consider the items on the list more completely—in the situation analysis step—before they set final research objectives.

Analyzing the situation—Step 2

When the marketing manager thinks the real problem has begun to surface, a situation analysis is useful. A **situation analysis** is an informal study of what information is already available in the problem area. It can help define the problem and specify what additional information—if any—is needed.

Pick the brains around you

The situation analysis usually involves informal talks with informed people. Informed people can be others in the firm, a few good intermediaries who have close contact with customers, or others knowledgeable about the industry. In industrial markets, where relationships with customers are close, researchers may even call the customers themselves. Informed customers may have already worked on the same problem or know about a source of helpful information. As well, their inputs can help to sharpen the problem definition.

Situation analysis helps educate a researcher

The situation analysis is especially important if the researcher is a research specialist who doesn't know much about the management decisions to be made—or if the marketing manager is dealing with unfamiliar areas. Both manager and researcher must be sure they understand the problem area, including the nature of the target market, the marketing mix, competition, and other external factors. Otherwise, the researcher may rush ahead and make costly mistakes, or simply discover facts that management already knows. The following case illustrates this danger.

A marketing manager at the home office of a large retail chain hired a research firm to do in-store interviews to learn what customers liked most—and least—about some of its stores in other cities. Interviewers diligently filled out their questionnaires. When the results came in, it was apparent that neither the marketing manager nor the researcher had done his or her homework. No one had even talked with the local store managers! Several of the stores were in the middle of some messy remodelling, so all the customers' responses concerned the noise and dust from the construction. The research was a waste of money. You can imagine why this retailer—one of the largest in the country—doesn't want to be named! The point is this: Even big companies make marketing research mistakes if they don't take the situation analysis seriously.

Secondary data online or at the library

The situation analysis should also find relevant **secondary data**—information that has already been collected or published. Later, in step 3, we will cover **primary data**—information specifically collected to solve a current problem. Too often, researchers rush to gather primary data at considerable expense before examining relevant secondary data that is already available at little or no cost.

Secondary data can come either from inside the company or from such sources as government agencies, libraries, business periodicals, and trade associations. Much of the inside information is available from the company's own MIS. Often, however, relevant data hasn't been included in that system but is still available from the company's files or from special reports. Obviously, this is the place to start the search for secondary data. After that, the marketing researcher must examine both print-based and online external sources of secondary data.

The Internet has revolutionized the gathering of potentially relevant marketing data. However, a number of important source documents are still only available in a print format or through the purchase of a CD-ROM. This is especially true of materials published before 1995 and for some very comprehensive industrial directories. In other situations, material available for purchase online is still obtainable free of charge at a university or regional Statistics Canada library.

Another important reason to visit libraries is to make use of the expertise of the reference librarians who work in them. These information specialists will know what is available only in print format and what is available online. A librarian's assistance in showing marketing researchers how they can most effectively search data banks and other online sources will also prove invaluable. Of course, prospective market researchers would be well advised to familiarize themselves with online resources and to develop search expertise while still at university or college.

Government data is very useful

Secondary data are compiled in a variety of ways. Governments and international organizations are among the best sources of social, economic, and demographic data. Statistics Canada publishes a great deal of relevant information. Government data are especially useful in estimating the size of markets. In the next chapter—and throughout the book—you will get a feel for the types of data Statistics Canada provides. Provincial and regional governments have units that provide useful information on traffic flows, building permits, school enrolments, and the like. Almost all government data are available at low cost. Much of this information is also available through the Internet and on computer disk.

For leads to more detailed documents, sometimes it makes sense to use summary publications. In Canada, a useful place to start is the Market Research Handbook, which is published every other year by Statistics Canada. For the American market, one of the most useful summaries is the *Statistical Abstract of the United States.* Like an almanac, it is issued every year; it contains 1,500 summary tables from more than 200 published sources. Detailed footnotes guide readers to more specific information on various topics.

How much information is available on countries and markets outside North America? The *United Nations Statistical Yearbook* is one of the finest summaries of worldwide data. Also, most countries with advanced economies have government agencies that help researchers get the data they need. Eurostat, the statistical office for the European Union countries, offers many useful publications packed with both national and regional data. Other useful sources of international information include the World Bank and the Organization for Economic Cooperation and Development (OECD).

Until fairly recently, finding comparable data on less developed economies was not nearly as easy. There were problems with gaining access to such information, as it might only be found in the very largest or most specialized of Canadian libraries. There were also problems associated with timeliness, and with the accuracy of such data. The accessibility problem (but not the problems of timeliness and accuracy) has in large part been overcome by the development of Internet sites providing whatever economic and demographic data are available on most of the world's nations. These sites link to others containing handbooks on "how to do business in" different countries, which have been prepared by large banks or international accounting firms.

Private sources are useful too

Many private research organizations—as well as advertising agencies, newspapers, and magazines—regularly compile and publish data. A good business library is valuable, for sources such as the *Financial Post, Marketing Magazine, The Globe and Mail Report on Business, Journal of Global Marketing,* and the publications of the Conference Board of Canada. Some advertising agencies make their information available at little or no cost to their clients and to buyers of ad space or time. Often a company's suppliers can also provide useful information.

The *Encyclopedia of Associations* lists 75,000 American and international trade and professional associations that can be good sources of information. *Fraser's Canadian Trade Directory* is a source of information on entire industries. A number of firms sell computer CD-ROMs that list all of the businesses in the country. Also, online searching makes it much easier than before to examine a company's financial reports, review all of its press releases, and read stories about the firm that appeared in newspapers or the trade press. In certain lines of business, resources like these may be a big help in estimating both the amount and the nature of competition.[6]

Search engines find information on the Internet

Although much information relevant to your situation analysis may be on the Internet, it won't do you any good if you can't find it. Fortunately, there are a number of good tools for searching on the Internet, and reference books that explain the details of the different tools. However, the basic idea is simple. And, usually, the best way to start is to use a search engine.

Most popular Internet browsers, like Netscape Navigator and Microsoft Internet Explorer, have a menu selection or button to activate an Internet search. In addition, there are hundreds of more specialized search engines. Typically, a user specifies words or a phrase to find and the search engine produces a list of hyperlinks to Web sites where that search string is found. Usually all you do is type in the search string, click on SEARCH, wait while the reference list of links is assembled, and then click on the hyperlink of interest. Then the browser shows the relevant page for that hyperlink on screen. If you want, you can go back to the list and check out another hyperlink.

One of the most popular and useful search engines is at the Web site for Yahoo (www.yahoo.com). It is especially good at searching for Web pages. Another very useful search engine is at the Altavista Web site (www.altavista.digital.com); it does a good job of classifying online documents that include the search string. A search engine that is particularly useful for locating specific people or businesses is at www.hotbot.com. The Northern Light search engine (at www.nlsearch.com) is very good at identifying published articles on the search topic. Keep in mind, however, that these are just a few of the popular search engines. If you want to get an idea of how many are available—and how they are different—go to www.yahoo.com and do a search on the term "search engine."

Most computerized database and index services are now available over the Internet. Some of these are provided by libraries and private firms. For instance, for a fee a user can use Dow Jones' interactive news retrieval system (www.djnr.com) to search the full text of hundreds of publications, including newspapers from around the world. ProQuest Direct, at www.umi.com, is another valuable research tool. It provides access to one of the world's largest collections of information, including summaries of articles from over 5,000 publications. Many articles are available in full-text, full-image format.

Searching the 'Net for secondary data

Internet Insite 4–1 refers you to only a few of the many other thousands of home pages that may contain relevant secondary data. However, the identified sites are "hot-linked" to many—in some cases up to a hundred or more—additional potentially useful data sources.

Syndicated data sources

Another source of information available to researchers is **syndicated data.** This source is a blend of primary and secondary data. Such information is available from private research firms that specialize in supplying data, which they regularly collect to aid marketing managers with specific problems. This data may be collected through surveying, observation, or some combination of the two. The marketing manager subscribes to such a research service and gets regular updates.

Many marketing managers face similar decisions and have similar data needs. So the most economical approach is to have one specialist firm collect and distribute the data to the different users, who share the cost.

When they use syndicated data, companies receive valuable information more quickly and at a lower cost than if the study were conducted for just one subscriber. One problem with using this data source is that no single company can obtain an

Internet Insite 4-1

Key Internet Sources for Secondary Research

A. Online Databases

1. ABI/Inform (Proquest)

Provides you with access to the full text of over 600 core business journals in advertising, marketing, sales, and many other areas. Mainly American but good Canadian and international content.

2. Lexis-Nexis

Full text database of business, legal, and news publications. American, with strong Canadian and international coverage. Start by searching the CANADA Library.

3. CBCA—Canadian Business & Current Affairs

The essential Canadian Index. Covers Canadian newspapers, scholarly journals, popular magazines, and trade journals from 1982 to the present.

These first three sites are fee-for-service databases best accessed (most economically for you) either electronically or by visiting your college or university library.

4. Canadian Corporate Newsnet
http://www.cdn-news.com/

Up-to-the-minute news on thousands of Canadian companies. By setting up a "search profile," you can have information of particular interest sent to your e-mail address.

5. Canada Newswire
http://www.newswire.ca/

The largest news release database in Canada. Searchable by key word, date, organization name, stock symbol, industry, and so on.

B. Canadian Government Sources

1. Government of Canada
http://www.canada.gc.ca/

Provides "hot-link" access to all departments, agencies, and branches of the federal government and to the provinces as well.

2. Industry Canada Strategis
http://www.strategis.ic.gc.ca/

Over 600,000 pages, some of which will almost certainly be relevant to the topic you are researching.

3. Statistics Canada
http://www.statcan.ca/

Canada's official statistical agency. Collects and publishes demographic, economic, and all sorts of other data on Canada and Canadians.

4. Department of Foreign Affairs and International Trade
http://www.dfait-maeci.gc.ca/

Very useful when deciding whether, where, or how to export.

5. Business Development Bank of Canada
http://www.bdc.ca/

Has a major focus on launching and growing a new business, and exporting.

C. Important American Sites

1. FedWorld
http://www.fedworld.gov/

Your point of entry into the U.S. federal government and all of its agencies.

2. STAT-USA/Internet
http://www.stat-usa.gov/

For American economic, trade, and business information. The American equivalent of Strategis but much more "fee for service."

3. U.S. Census Bureau
http://www.census.gov/

The place to obtain U.S. Census data and much more.

4. U.S. Office of Trade and Economic Analysis
http://www.ita.doc.gov/tradestats/

Detailed U.S. foreign trade data by product and by country.

5. U.S. Statistical Resources on the Web
http://www.lib.umich.edu/libhome/documents/center/stats/html/

A final stop to make certain you haven't missed anything at the other U.S. sites.

D. Key Business Publications

1. Marketing Magazine On-Line
http://www.marketingmag.ca/

An incredibly important source of information on Canadian marketing practice.

2. Maclean Hunter On-Line
http://www.mhbizlink.com/

Another important site providing access to a number of trade journals.

3. The Financial Post
http://www.canoe.ca/FP/

A very important source, although finance, not marketing, is its main concern. This site provides links to other Canadian newspapers and to both the Reuters and The Canadian Press business news services.

4. The Globe and Mail Report on Business Magazine
http://www.robmagazine.com

Another essential stop when monitoring the Canadian business scene. This site provides links to *The Globe and Mail* newspaper.

5. Editor and Publisher's Interactive On-line Newspaper Database
http://www.mediainfo.com/

Close to 2,500 (and climbing) online newspaper entries from all over the world.

E. Sites Providing International Information

1. International Business on the WWW
http://www.ciber.bus.msu.edu/busres.htm/

The place to start when searching for information on any country outside North America in which Canadians might wish to do business.

2. Virtual International Business and Economic Sources (VIBES)

http://www.uncc.edu/lis/library/reference/intbus/vibehome/htm/
Another great source of international information.

3. Nijenrode Business Webserver
http://www.nijenrode.sch/nbr/

You will find this site especially useful when European countries are being studied.

4. World Trade Organization
http://www.wto.org/

The best place to start a search for information on regional and world trade.

5. The World Bank
http://www.worldbank.org/
Important economic data, with links to all the other international agencies.

F. Some Specialized Home Sites of Possible Interest

1. Business Ethics

Institute for Business and Professional Ethics, Depaul University
http://condor.depaul.edu/ethics/

2. Information and Technology

Business Research in Information and Technology (BRINT)
http://www.brint.com/

3. Electronic Commerce

The Electronic Commerce Knowledge Center
http://www.knowledgecenters.org/ecenter.asp/

4. Entrepreneurship

Entrepreneurial Edge onLine
http://edgeonline.com/

5. Sustainable Development

IISD Business and Development Program
http://iisdT.iisd.ca/business/

The above are but a few of the many sites on the Web that may provide you with useful secondary data on products, marketing practices, and potential markets. Many other useful sites are identified in the other Internet Insites prepared by Dr. Ramesh Venkat for this text. In addition, the home page for this text (www.mcgrawhill.ca/college/shapiro) will "hotlink" you to hundreds of sites relevant to the topics you are studying. Also, don't forget that most college and university libraries have available through their home pages links to specialized megasites on all sorts of topics. This material, often listed under "Internet Resources," can usually be accessed by everyone, not just by students at the university.

Source: This material was prepared by Dr. Stanley J. Shapiro in May 1998, with guidance from Ms. Elaine Fairey, Business and Economics Librarian at Simon Fraser University. Materials downloaded from the libraries of Queen's University and Simon Fraser University have been used in its preparation.

informational advantage over competitors. Also, the data may not be specifically tailored to address a company's particular problems. Finally, the study may not cover the exact markets or products and services of interest to the user.

Compusearch Market and Social Research Limited is one source of syndicated data in Canada. Compusearch compiles data from Statistics Canada and other secondary sources and repackages the information in a form that is useful to the client. The company gathers detailed demographic and other relevant data by neighbourhoods, sales territories, trading areas, and any other geographic areas of interest to the companies that purchase the data. Compusearch can provide data by neighbourhoods as small as 200 households. This information can be used by clients to identify the characteristics of target markets, to determine where new branches or stores should be located, and to target the most promising consumer groups.

ACNielsen Company of Canada Limited is another source of syndicated data. ACNielsen offers a number of retail indexes such as the Food Index, the Drug Index, the Confectionery/Tobacco Index, and the Mass Merchandiser Index, collectively known as Nielsen's Retail Index Services. For example, the grocery industry is served by the Food Index. This index is based on a sample of 475 grocery stores across Canada, measuring more than 200 product categories. The reports are tailored to clients' needs and contain quantitative results of market size and direction, and brand/size sales volume and share, as well as a host of "reasons why" data.

The Bureau of Broadcast Measurement (BBM) is a nonprofit organization that provides syndicated data on audience estimates for radio stations and programs in Canada. The BBM has approximately 1,000 members and associates from the broadcasting industry. It conducts surveys of radio audiences up to four times a year, depending on the size and competitive nature of the areas surveyed. Radio audiences for more than 150 markets are developed from this sample. Syndicated reports on listenership are made available to members as part of their membership entitlement.

The Print Measurement Bureau (PMB) is another nonprofit Canadian organization that provides syndicated data. It is an industry association that offers standardized readership information on the publications of its member companies. Samples of Canadian residents 12 years of age and older are regularly interviewed. The results of the last two years' worth of data are compiled into an annual report. This report is only available to PMB members. The PMB has recently expanded its services to include the collection of data on the exposure of consumers to other media, their lifestyles, and their product use. Much of this information is subsequently made public.

Situation analysis yields a lot—for very little

The virtue of a good situation analysis is that it can be very informative but takes little time. And it's inexpensive relative to more formal research efforts such as large-scale surveys. Situation analysis can help focus further research or even eliminate the need for it entirely. The situation analyst is really trying to determine the exact nature of the situation—and the problem. In their rush to get out questionnaires, too-hasty researchers may try to skip this step. Often, these researchers find the real problem only when the questionnaires come back—at which point they must start over. One marketing expert put it this way: "Some people never have time to do research right the first time, but they seem to have time to do it over again."

Determine what else is needed

At the end of the situation analysis, you can see which research questions—from the list developed during the problem definition step—remain unanswered. At that point you have to decide exactly what information you need to answer those questions—and how to get it.

This often requires discussion between technical experts and the marketing manager. Often, companies use a written **research proposal**—a plan that specifies what information will be obtained and how—to ensure that no misunderstandings occur later. The research plan may include information about costs, what data will be collected, how it will be collected, who will analyze it and how, and how long the process will take. Then the marketing manager must decide whether it makes sense to go ahead—whether the time and costs involved seem worthwhile. It's foolish to pay $100,000 for information to solve a $50,000 problem! When the decision is not cut and dried, marketing managers should know more about the next steps in the marketing research process.

Getting problem-specific data—Step 3

Gathering primary data

The next step is to plan a formal research project to gather primary data. There are different methods for collecting primary data. Which approach to use depends on the nature of the problem and how much time and money are available.

In most primary data collection, the researcher tries to learn what customers think about some topic, or how they behave under some conditions. There are two basic methods for obtaining information about customers: *questioning* and *observing.* Questioning can range from qualitative to quantitative research. And many kinds of observing are possible.

Qualitative questioning

Qualitative research seeks in-depth, open-ended responses, not yes-or-no answers. The researcher tries to get people to share their thoughts on a topic without giving them many directions or guidelines about what to say.

A researcher might ask different consumers, "What do you think about when you decide where to shop for food?" One person may talk about convenient location, another about service, and others about the quality of the fresh produce. The real advantage of this approach is *depth.* Each person can be asked follow-up questions so that the researcher really understands what *that* respondent is thinking. The depth of the qualitative approach gets at the details; however, the researcher needs a lot of judgment to summarize it all.

Some types of qualitative research don't use specific questions. For example, a cartoon may show a situation such as a woman and a man buying coffee in a supermarket. The respondent may be asked to explain what the woman is saying to the man. Or the consumer might simply be shown a product or an ad and asked to comment.

FOCUS GROUPS STIMULATE DISCUSSION The most widely used form of qualitative questioning in marketing research is the **focus group interview,** which involves interviewing 6 to 10 people in an informal group setting. The focus group also uses open-ended questions, but here the interviewer wants to get group interaction—to stimulate thinking and get immediate reactions. See Marketing Demo 4–3 for an example of focus group interviews with seniors.

A skilled focus group leader can learn a great deal from this approach. A typical session may last an hour, so participants can cover a lot of ground. Sessions are often videotaped, allowing different managers to form their own impressions of what happened.[7] However, a typical problem—and serious limitation—with qualitative research is that it's hard to measure objectively what takes place. The results seem to depend so much on the point of view of the researcher. In addition, people willing to participate in a focus group, especially those who talk the most, may not be representative of the broader target market.

Focus groups can be conducted quickly and at relatively low cost—an average of about $3,500 each. This is part of their appeal. But focus groups are probably being overused. It's easy to fall into the trap of treating an idea arising from a focus group as a "fact" that applies to a broad target market.

To avoid this trap, some researchers use qualitative research to prepare for quantitative research. For example, a regional symphony orchestra wanted to broaden its base of support and increase ticket sales. It hired a marketing research firm to conduct focus group interviews with small groups of current subscribers, former subscribers, and qualified prospects. These interviews helped the marketing managers refine their ideas about what these target "customers" liked and did not like about the orchestra—and what kinds of music future audiences might want. The ideas were then tested with a larger, more representative sample. Interviewers telephoned

Marketing Demo 4-3

A Considered Opinion

The man sitting at the far corner of the large boardroom table stands up before Gail Haarsma has the chance to say her usual goodbye. He makes his own brief speech, complimenting Haarsma's ability to extract comments and opinions from a bunch of grey-haired folk. "It's not an easy thing to do," Haarsma recalls him saying. "You deserve our thanks." With that, the other 12 people in the room stood up as well—clapping!

This is possibly the first standing ovation a focus group moderator has ever received. And Haarsma, consultant for D.R. Harley Consultants in Ottawa, says it's no coincidence her cheerleaders were a group of seniors. "They appreciate being invited, involved and having the opportunity to speak. And they take it seriously. They come prepared to do their best."

This should pique any marketers' interest for two reasons: research done with a group that instinctively takes your queries seriously is going to provide accurate, detailed information on which to build a solid marketing plan; and what can be learned from this research goes beyond quantitative responses—it uncovers some fundamental truths that marketers who target seniors need to know.

Haarsma's firm is becoming known as a specialist in seniors' focus groups, a research method she and colleague Cathy Ladds say is especially suited to learning about seniors. "When testing a product or advertising," says Ladds, "it's the only way to get detailed information from seniors. They won't answer phone surveys."

And the information collected is solid stuff. Haarsma recalls many instances where older focus group participants arrived with prepared notes, and even one instance where a man brought typed, photocopied pages of his comments on a test application form, in case he didn't have a chance to speak.

Christian Fisker, principal of Mature Lifestyles Research Group, has had similar experiences; he recently had one person show up at a group he was conducting for a major bank with another bank's brochures about a service he liked. "He had researched the subject and was expressing what he thought," says Fisker.

Fisker says this thoroughness is also evident in seniors' purchasing habits. "They may visit a sales centre eight times before making the decision to buy. They want to know a lot of details before they buy." In any retail, sales or marketing situation, Fisker advises not to rush them. "They'll walk politely out the door and go elsewhere." Fisker says a sales rep should have a complete information sheet to offer potential clients who are seniors. "They'll take what you give them and read it six or seven times," he says.

Fisker says a focus group with what he calls "mature adults" is also extra-useful because they're far more open than younger participants. "They're at a stage in their life when they're more willing to share information with you. They don't worry what you're going to think. As a result, what you get from them is pretty straightforward."

Haarsma says marketers need to show seniors the same respect seniors give to the research process. An anti-tobacco radio ad she tested for the Ottawa Board of Health provides an example where seniors felt respect was lacking. Specifically tailored to get seniors thinking of the effects of secondhand smoke, the ad depicted a phone conversation between a pregnant woman and her mother, in which the daughter says she will avoid the mother because her smoking is bad for the baby. At first, the group appeared to like the ad. They said it was dramatic, and made an important point. But when one woman, a former smoker, said, "It would offend me," others agreed. It quickly became apparent they were put off by the daughter's manner toward her mother; it didn't convey respect.

In her groups on retail services, Ladds found similar themes; seniors wanted respect for their needs—down to the last detail. Her group members said they preferred stores with wider aisles, larger signs, places to sit down and, above all, knowledgeable, clean-cut sales staff on hand. Haarsma says seniors don't just need or want these things, they expect them.

When the federal government was planning to install an interactive voice response system to handle a deluge of calls about Canada Pension Plans, it took care to design a system that would be accepted and used by seniors. The phone system was tested in three stages by D.R. Harley: first on paper, with Haarsma and Ladds reading the messages to groups of seniors. Then phones were brought in and seniors made calls on the spot. Later, seniors who'd used the system for two months were asked to share their impressions. Many micro lessons came out of the research: seniors wanted slower messages, no more than three or four options, and a clear indication of how to repeat a message. In Northern Quebec, a man of 80 leaned toward Haarsma and said, "Dear, I've got one of those phones with the buttons on the ear piece. If I want to press 'one' for the first option, by the time I get the phone away from my ear, in front of my eyes, adjust my bifocals and focus to find the right button, they're all the way to number seven and I don't know *what's* going on!"

That was a perfect indication, says Haarsma, of what business people and marketers are getting themselves into when they target seniors: details are paramount.

Not only that, older customers reward such thoughtful service with loyalty. Haarsma says one woman in a follow-up group had nothing but praise for the CPP's automated program. "She could tell it was tailored for seniors and she appreciated that."

Source: Anita Lahey, "A Considered Opinion," *Marketing Magazine*, September 23, 1996, p. 22.

500 people and asked them how interested they would be in various orchestra programs, event locations, and guest artists. Then they planned their promotion and the orchestra's program for the year based on the research. The result? Subscription ticket sales nearly doubled from the previous year.[8]

As this example suggests, qualitative research can provide good hypotheses. But we need other approaches, perhaps based on more representative samples and objective measures, to *test* the hypotheses.

Getting objective results

When researchers use identical questions and response alternatives, they can summarize the information quantitatively. Samples can be larger and more representative, and they can use various statistics to draw conclusions. For these reasons, most survey research is **quantitative research,** which seeks structured responses that can be summarized in numbers like percentages, averages, or other statistics. For example, a marketing researcher might calculate what percentage of respondents have tried a new product and then figure an average "score" for how satisfied they were.

Fixed responses

For the sake of simplifying analysis of the replies, survey questionnaires usually provide fixed responses to questions. This multiple-choice approach also makes it easier and faster for respondents to reply. Simple fill-in-a-number questions are also widely used in quantitative research. A questionnaire might ask an industrial buyer, "From approximately how many suppliers do you currently purchase electronic parts?" Fixed responses are also more convenient for computer analysis, which is how most surveys are analyzed.

Measuring attitudes

One common approach to measuring consumers' attitudes and opinions is to have respondents indicate how much they agree or disagree with a questionnaire statement. For example, a researcher interested in what target consumers think about frozen pizzas might include statements like those at the top of Exhibit 4–3.

Another approach is to have respondents *rate* a product, feature, or store. Exhibit 4–3 shows commonly used rating "scales." Sometimes, rating scales are labelled with adjectives like *excellent, good, fair,* and *poor.*

Surveys by mail or phone, or in person

Decisions about which specific questions to ask, and how to ask them, are usually related to how respondents will be contacted—by mail, on the phone, or in person.

MAIL SURVEYS ARE COMMON AND CONVENIENT Mail questionnaires are useful when extensive questioning is necessary. With a mail questionnaire, respondents can complete the questions at their convenience. They may be more willing to fill in personal or family characteristics since a mail questionnaire can be returned anonymously. But the questions must be simple and easy to follow, since no interviewer is there to help.

A big problem with mail questionnaires is that many people don't complete or return them. The **response rate**—the percentage of people contacted who complete the questionnaire—is often around 25 percent in consumer surveys. And it can be even lower. Also, respondents may not be representative. People who are most interested in the questionnaire topic may respond, but answers from this group may be very different from the answers of a typical "don't care" group.[9]

Mail surveys are economical if a large number of people respond. But they may be quite expensive if the response rate is low. Furthermore, it can take a month or more

Exhibit 4-3 Sample Questioning Methods to Measure Attitudes and Opinions

A. Please check your level of agreement with each of the following statements.

	Strongly Agree	*Agree*	*Uncertain*	*Disagree*	*Strongly Disagree*
1. I add extra toppings when I prepare a frozen pizza.	____	____	____	____	____
2. A frozen pizza dinner is more expensive than eating at a fast-food restaurant.	____	____	____	____	____

B. Please rate how important each of the following is to you in selecting a brand of frozen pizza:

	Not at all Important					*Very Important*
1. Price per serving	____	____	____	____	____	____
2. Toppings available	____	____	____	____	____	____
3. Amount of cheese	____	____	____	____	____	____
4. Cooking time	____	____	____	____	____	____

C. Please check the rating that best describes your feelings about the last frozen pizza you prepared.

	Poor	*Fair*	*Good*	*Excellent*
1. Price per serving	____	____	____	____
2. Toppings available	____	____	____	____
3. Amount of cheese	____	____	____	____
4. Cooking time	____	____	____	____

to get the data, which is too slow for some decisions. Moreover, it is difficult to get respondents to expand on particular points. In markets where illiteracy is a problem, it may not be possible to get any response. In spite of these limitations, the convenience and economy of mail surveys makes them popular for collecting primary data.

TELEPHONE SURVEYS—FAST AND EFFECTIVE Telephone interviews are growing in popularity. They are effective for getting quick answers to simple questions. Telephone interviews allow the interviewer to probe and really learn what the respondent is thinking. On the other hand, some consumers find such calls intrusive—about one third refuse to answer any questions. Moreover, the telephone is usually not a very good contact method if the interviewer is trying to get confidential personal information, such as details of family income. Respondents are not certain who is calling or how such personal information might be used.

Research firms, with up to 50 interviewers calling at the same time on long-distance lines, can complete 1,000 or more interviews in one evening. In addition, with computer-aided telephone interviewing, answers are immediately recorded on a computer, which results in fast data analysis. The popularity of telephone surveys is partly due to their speed and high response rates.[10]

PERSONAL INTERVIEW SURVEYS—CAN BE IN-DEPTH A personal interview survey is usually much more expensive per interview than a mail or telephone survey. But it's easier to get and keep the respondent's attention when the interviewer is right there. The interviewer can also help explain complicated directions—and perhaps get better responses. For these reasons, personal interviews are commonly used for research on business customers. To reduce the cost of locating consumer respondents, interviews are sometimes done at a store or shopping mall. This is called a mall intercept interview because the interviewer stops a shopper and asks for responses to the survey.

Researchers have to be careful that having an interviewer involved doesn't affect the respondent's answers. Sometimes, people won't give an answer they consider embarrassing. Or they may try to impress or please the interviewer. Furthermore, in some cultures people don't want to give any information. For example, many people in Africa, Latin America, and Eastern Europe are reluctant to be interviewed. This is also a problem in many low-income, inner-city areas in Canada, where even Statistics Canada interviewers have trouble getting cooperation. When questioning has its limitations, observing may be more accurate or economical.

Observing

As a method, observation does not concern itself with the casual observations that may stimulate ideas in the early steps of a research project. Rather, researchers who are using the observation method are trying to see or record what the subject does naturally. They don't want the observing to *influence* the subject's behaviour.

A museum director wanted to know which of the many exhibits was most popular. A survey didn't help: visitors seemed to want to please the interviewer and usually said that all of the exhibits were interesting. Putting observers near exhibits, to record how long visitors spent at each one, didn't help either. The curious visitors stood around to see what the observer was recording, and that skewed the measures. Finally, the museum floors were waxed to a glossy shine. Several weeks later, the floors around the exhibits were inspected. It was easy to tell which exhibits were most popular, based on how much wax had worn off the floor!

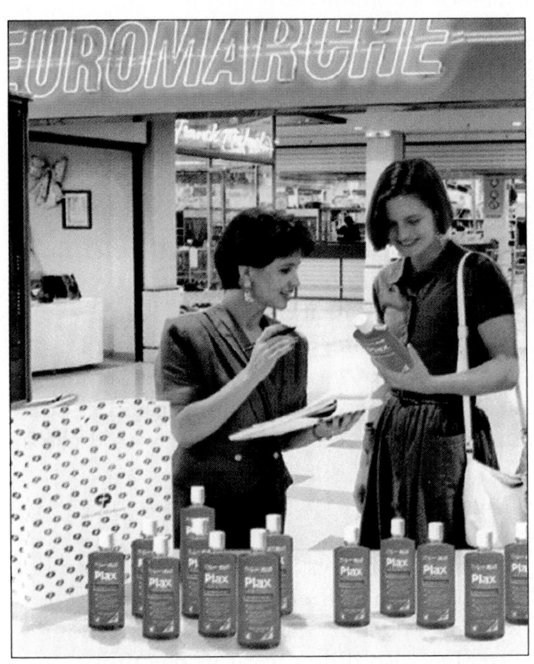

After extensive research with French consumers, including mall intercept interviews like the one shown here, Colgate-France improved the marketing mix for its Plax mouthwash.

In some situations, consumers are recorded on videotape. Later, researchers can study the tape by running the film at very slow speed or actually analyzing each frame. Researchers use this technique to study the routes consumers follow through a grocery store—or how they select products in a department store.

Similarly, many franchise companies use the observation method, to check how well a franchisee is performing. KFC hires people to go to different KFC stores and act like normal customers. Then they report back to KFC on how they were treated, the quality of the service and food, and the cleanliness of the store.

Observation data can be plotted on graphs or maps. A shopping centre developer wondered if one of its centres was attracting customers from all the surrounding areas. The developer hired a firm to record the licence plate numbers of cars in the parking lot. Using registration information, the firm obtained the addresses of all licence holders and plotted them on a map. Very few customers were coming from one large area. The developer aimed direct-mail advertising at that area and generated a lot of new business.

Observation methods are common in advertising research. For example, the ACNielsen Company has developed a device called the *people meter* that adapts the observation method to television audience research. This machine is attached to the TV set in the homes of selected families. It records when the set is on and what station is tuned in. Nielsen uses the results to rate the popularity of TV shows. Some claim that once families get used to the meter, it no longer influences their behaviour. Note, however, that the meter only records what channel is on—not whether anyone is watching.

Checkout scanners see a lot

Computerized scanners at retail checkout counters, a major breakthrough in observing, help researchers collect very specific—and useful—information. Often, this type of data is fed directly into a firm's MIS. Managers of a big department store can see exactly what products have sold each day, and how much money each department earned. But the scanner also has wider applications for marketing research.

Some research firms have set up **consumer panels**—groups of consumers who provide information on a continuing basis. Whenever a panel member shops for groceries, he or she gives an ID number to the clerk, who keys in the number. Then the scanner records every purchase, including brands, sizes, prices, and any coupons used. For a fee, clients can evaluate actual customer purchase patterns, and get answers to their questions about the effectiveness of their discount coupons. Did the coupons draw new customers, or did current customers simply use them to stock up? If consumers switched from another brand, did they go back to their old brand the next time? The answers to such questions are important in planning marketing strategies, and scanners can help marketing managers get the answers.

Some members of the consumer panel are also tied in to a special TV cable system. With this system, a company can direct advertisements to some houses and not others. Researchers can then evaluate the effect of the ads by comparing the purchases of consumers who saw the ads with the purchases of those who didn't.

The use of scanners to "observe" what customers actually do is changing consumer research methods. Companies can turn to firms like Information Resources as a *single source* of complete information about customers' attitudes, shopping behaviour, and media habits.

Data captured by electronic scanners is equally important in business-to-business markets. Increasingly, firms mark their shipping cartons and packages with computer-readable bar codes that make it fast and easy to track inventory, shipments, orders, and the like. As information about product sales or shipments becomes available, it is instantly included in the MIS. That way, a manager can access any detailed piece of information or do an analysis to summarize trends and patterns. Here, as with scanner data on consumers, the information available is so detailed that the possibilities are limited more by imagination—and money—than by technology.[11]

Experimental method controls conditions

A marketing manager can get a different kind of information—with either questioning or observing—using the experimental method. With the **experimental method,** researchers compare the responses of two or more groups that are similar except on the characteristic being tested. Researchers want to learn whether the specific characteristic, which varies among groups, *causes* differences in some response among the groups. For example, a researcher might be interested in comparing responses of consumers who had seen an ad for a new product with those of consumers who had not seen the ad. The "response" might be an observed behaviour, like the purchase of a product, or the answer to a specific question, like "How interested are you in this new product?"

Marketing managers for Mars, the company that makes Snickers candy bars, used the experimental method to help solve a problem. Other candy and snack foods were taking customers. But why? Surveys showed that many consumers thought candy bars were becoming too small. But they also didn't want to pay more for a larger bar. Mars' managers wanted to know whether making their candy bar bigger would increase sales enough to offset the higher cost. To decide, they conducted a marketing experiment.

THIS MAN ACTUALLY GIVES US CREDIBILITY!

HE'S ONE OF THE 2,000 RESPONDENTS IN THE *TARGET SYSTEM*.

The *Target System* has expanded its sampling base. There are now **2,000 respondents** of every stripe and every type within this evolutionary system, making it indispensable to your media planning strategy by ensuring you greater result reliability.

What the *Target System* does is cross-reference habits and consumption figures with the viewing routines of the television audience. Product by product. Program by program. What it gives you is pinpoint accuracy and maximum efficiency in defining your target market. The *Target System*: your most unique, complete and remarkable strategic planning tool.

TARGET
S·Y·S·T·E·M

TVA

The company carefully varied the size of candy bars sold in *different* markets. Otherwise, the marketing mix stayed the same. Then researchers tracked sales in each market area to see the effect of the different sizes. They saw a difference—a big difference—immediately. It was clear that added sales would more than offset the cost of making a bigger candy bar. So marketing managers at Mars made a decision that took them in the opposite direction from other candy companies. And, yes, it proved to be a sweet success.

Test-marketing of new products is another type of marketing experiment. In a typical approach, a company tries variations on its planned marketing mix in a few geographic market areas. The results of the tests help to identify problems or refine the marketing mix before the company decides to go to broader distribution. However, alert competitors may disrupt such tests, perhaps by increasing promotion or offering retailers extra discounts. To avoid these problems, some small firms conduct some of their tests in foreign markets. For example, Carewell, producer of Dentax toothbrushes, tested its new line and various in-store promotions in Singapore and Malta before trying to enter the very competitive North American market. Similarly, a firm that makes baby wipes did its test market experiments in the United Kingdom.

Researchers don't use the experimental method as often as surveys and focus groups because it's hard to set up controlled situations where only one marketing variable is different. But there are probably other reasons, too. Many managers don't understand how much valuable information they can get from this method. Further, they don't like the idea of some researcher "experimenting" with their business.[12]

Interpreting the data—Step 4

After someone collects the data, it has to be analyzed to decide what it all means. In quantitative research, this step usually involves statistics. **Statistical packages**—easy-to-use computer programs that analyze data—have made this step easier. As we noted earlier, some firms provide *decision support systems* so that managers can use a statistical package to interpret data themselves. More often, however, technical specialists are involved at the interpretation step.

Cross-tabulation is one of the most frequently used approaches for analyzing and interpreting marketing research data. It shows the relationship of answers to two different questions. Exhibit 4–4 provides an example. In this case, an Internet provider was interested in learning more about customers who had Internet access at home. With a survey, the firm asked customers if they had moved in the last year. The survey also asked if they had Internet access at home. The answers to the two questions were then cross-tabulated. The results of the analysis showed that customers who had moved in the last year were much more likely than nonmovers to have Internet access at home. So the researchers for the Internet provider concluded that people who had just moved were a prime target market for the service.

Cross-tabulation is popular because the results are usually easy to interpret. But there are many other approaches for statistical analysis, with the best one depend-

Exhibit 4–4 Cross-Tabulation Breakdown of Responses to Internet Provider Consumer Survey

Do You Have Internet Access at Your Home?	Have You Moved in the Last Year?			
	Answers:	No	Yes	Total
	Yes	10.2%	23.4%	15.5%
	No	89.8	76.6	84.5
	Total	100%	100%	100%

Interpretation: 15.5 percent of people in the survey said that they had Internet access in their homes. However, the percentage was much higher (23.4%) among people who had moved in the last year, and lower (10.2%) among people who had not moved.

ing on the situation. The details of statistical analysis are beyond the scope of this book. But a good manager should know enough to understand what a research project can and can't do.[13]

Is your sample really representative?

It's usually impossible for marketing managers to collect all the information they want about everyone in a **population**—the total group they are interested in. Marketing researchers typically study only a **sample**, a part of the relevant population. How well a sample *represents* the total population affects the results. Results from a sample that is not representative may not give a true picture.

The manager of a retail store might want a phone survey to learn what consumers think about the store's hours. If interviewers make all of the calls during the day, the sample will not be representative. Consumers who work outside the home during the day won't have an equal chance of being included. Those interviewed might say that the limited store hours are "satisfactory." Yet it would be a mistake to assume that *all* consumers are satisfied. Marketing managers must be aware of how representative a sample really is.

Random samples

Clearly, getting a representative sample is very important. One method of doing so is **random sampling**, where each member of the population has the same chance of being included in the sample. Great care must be used to ensure that sampling is really random, not just haphazard.

A random sample chosen from a population will tend to have the same characteristics as the population. "Tend to" is important here—the sample will not be exactly the same as the population.

Because of the high cost and difficulty of obtaining a truly random sample, much marketing research is based on nonrandom sampling. Sometimes, nonrandom samples give very good results, especially in industrial markets where the number of customers may be relatively small and fairly similar. But results from nonrandom samples must be interpreted—and used—with care.

Research results

An estimate from a sample, even a representative one, usually varies somewhat from the true value for a total population. Managers sometimes forget this. They assume that survey results are exact. Instead, when interpreting sample estimates, managers should think of them as *suggesting* the approximate value.

When random selection is used to develop the sample, researchers can use various methods to determine the likely accuracy of the sample value. This is done in terms of **confidence intervals**—the range on either side of an estimate that is likely to contain the true value for the whole population. Some managers are surprised to learn how wide that range can be.

Consider a wholesaler who has 1,000 retail customers and who wants to learn how many of these retailers carry a product from a competing supplier. If the wholesaler randomly samples 100 retailers and 20 say yes, then the sample estimate is 20 percent. But with that information the wholesaler can be only 95 percent confident that the percentage of all retailers is in the confidence interval between 12 and 28 percent.[14]

The larger the sample size, the greater the accuracy of estimates from a random sample. With a larger sample, a few unusual responses are less likely to make a big difference.

You can see that the nature of the sample, and how it is selected, makes a big difference in how the results of a study can be interpreted. Managers must consider this when planning data collection, in order to ensure that the final results can be interpreted with enough confidence that they will be useful in strategic market planning. Internet Insite 4–2 shows how those doing marketing research online have been able to overcome sampling problems.

Internet Insite 4-2

Innovation in Online Market Research

Surveysite, a Toronto-based online market research firm, is pioneering market research on the Web (www.surveysite.com), and is an excellent example of how Web technology can be used effectively by market researchers.

When conducting surveys, market researchers would ideally like to draw a random sample of respondents from a given population to ensure validity of the research findings. So far, data collection on the Web has been constrained by the "convenience" sampling that occurs on the Internet. Most commercial Web sites do try to collect consumer feedback information by providing a "feedback" menu option on their home page. According to SurveySite, less than 1 percent of the people who visit a Web site bother to fill out feedback surveys. Usually only *highly satisfied* or *highly dissatisfied* consumers are likely to click on the static feedback buttons. The result is biased samples.

SurveySite's innovative "Pop-up" software may provide the answer to this vexing problem. The Pop-up software first selects visitors at a predetermined interval (for example, every tenth visitor to a Web site). When this visitor browses the site, a small Java™ window pops into view asking the visitor if he or she will complete a short online survey after finishing browsing the site. If the visitor clicks NO, the window disappears; if YES, a small "survey icon" appears in the browser's toolbar. The visitor can continue to browse, or click on the survey icon at any time. When the visitor clicks on the survey icon, an online survey is presented. You can see an online demonstration of this software on SurveySite's Web site.

The interactive nature of the pop-up window, which suddenly appears while the visitor is browsing, seems to enhance the overall response rate for surveys. SurveySite claims that its response rate is comparable to that of telephone surveys. Furthermore, its ability to randomly sample visitors to a Web site increases the validity of the survey results.

SurveySite also maintains a Web Panel, which is a voluntary panel of Web users who periodically respond to surveys regarding various products and services. Using an online chat room, SurveySite is able to conduct focus group studies with these panel members. Panel members may participate from across the country. Here again, SurveySite demonstrates innovative use of Web technology. The online focus group studies cost a fraction of what face-to-face focus groups cost. As well, the anonymity of an online chat room may help elicit insightful and truthful opinions.

From its impressive client list, which includes Timex, TD-Bank, Canadian Tire, Kellogg's, and the Toronto Raptors, it is evident that SurveySite has already made a name for itself in online market research. It is also evident that interactivity on the Web is enabling marketers to get closer to their consumers than ever before. Savvy marketers like SurveySite have just begun to demonstrate some of the possibilities. New frontiers await market researchers in the online world.

To learn more about how Canada's leading market research firms are using the Internet, browse through the Web sites of the following market research firms. Find out what services each firm offers and how it is using the Internet.

1. ACNielsen (www.acnielsen.ca).
2. SurveySite (www.surveysite.com).
3. CF Group Inc. (Burke International Research and *Canadian Facts*) (www.cfgroup.ca).

Source: This is one of a series of Internet Insites prepared in April 1998 by Dr. Ramesh Venkat of Saint Mary's University for *Basic Marketing,* Ninth Canadian Edition.

Validity problems can destroy research

Even when the sampling is carefully planned, it's also important to evaluate the quality of the research data itself.

Managers and researchers should be sure that research data really measure what they are supposed to measure. Many of the variables that marketing managers are interested in are difficult to measure accurately. Questionnaires may let us assign numbers to consumer responses, but that still doesn't mean that the result is precise. An interviewer might ask, "How much did you spend on soft drinks last week?" A respondent may be perfectly willing to cooperate—and be part of the representative sample—but just not be able to remember.

Validity concerns the extent to which data measures what it is intended to measure. Validity problems are important in marketing research because most people want to help and will try to answer, even when they don't know what they're talking about. Further, a poorly worded question can mean different things to different people and invalidate the results. Managers must be sure that they only pay for research results that are representative—and valid.

Poor interpretation can destroy research

Besides sampling and validity problems, a marketing manager must consider whether the analysis of the data supports the *conclusions* drawn in the interpretation step. Sometimes, technical specialists pick the right statistical procedure—their calculations are exact—but they misinterpret the data because they don't understand the management problem. In one survey, car buyers were asked to rank five cars in order from "most preferred" to "least preferred." One car was ranked first by slightly more respondents than any other car, so the researcher reported it as the "most liked car." That interpretation, however, ignored the fact that 70 percent of the respondents ranked the car *last!*

Interpretation problems like this can be subtle but crucial. Some people draw misleading conclusions on purpose in order to get the results they want. Marketing managers must decide whether *all* of the results support the interpretation and are relevant to their problem.

The team approach

Marketing research involves some technical details. But you can see that the marketing researcher and the marketing manager must work together to make sure they really do solve the problem facing the firm. If the whole research process has been a joint effort, the interpretation step can move quickly to making a decision—and solving the problem.

Solving the problem—Step 5

In the problem solution step, managers use the research results to make marketing decisions.

Some researchers, and some managers, are fascinated by the interesting tidbits of information that come from the research process. They are excited if the research reveals something they didn't know before. But if research doesn't have action implications, it has little value and suggests poor planning by the researcher and the manager.

When the research process is finished, the marketing manager should be able to apply the findings in strategic market planning—the choice of a target market or the mix of the four Ps. If the research doesn't provide information to help guide these decisions, the company has wasted research time and money.

We emphasize step 5 because it is the reason for and logical conclusion to the whole research process. This final step must be anticipated during each of the earlier steps.

International marketing research

Marketing research on overseas markets often contributes a great deal to international marketing success. Conversely, export failures are often due to a lack of home-office management expertise concerning customer interests, needs, and other segmenting dimensions as well as environmental factors such as competitors' prices and products. Effective marketing research can help to overcome these problems.

Avoid mistakes with local researchers

Whether a firm is small and entering overseas markets for the first time or already large and well established internationally, there are often advantages to working with local market research firms. These research suppliers know the local situation and are less likely to make mistakes based on misunderstandings of the customs, language, or circumstances of the customers they study.

As we've emphasized, however, it's still important for a marketing manager to work closely with the researchers to be certain that they're not just "doing their own thing" with research that doesn't solve the manager's problems. Just because researchers are experts on doing research in their local settings doesn't mean that they are experts on the specific marketing problems the manager needs to solve. Finding a research supplier with relevant experience helps reduce the likelihood of problems. Many large research firms have a network of local offices around the world to help with such efforts. Similarly, multinational or local advertising agencies and intermediaries can often provide leads as regards the best research suppliers.

Coordination and standardization

When a firm is doing similar research projects in different markets around the world, it makes sense for the marketing manager to coordinate the efforts. After all, if the manager doesn't establish some basic guidelines at the outset, the different research projects may all vary so much that the results can't be compared from one market area to another. When key questions and issues are studied in similar ways, comparisons across markets are possible. Such comparisons give a home-office manager a much better chance of understanding how the markets are similar and how they differ. This can be a key to knowing whether it is appropriate for marketing strategies to be standardized across markets—or alternatively, what customized approaches are necessary.

Multinational companies with operations in various countries often attempt to centralize some market research functions. One reason is to reduce costs or achieve research economies of scale. The centralized approach also improves the firm's ability to transfer experience and know-how from one market area or project to another.

The African, Asian, and Australian unit of Eastman Kodak's International Photographic Division recognized the value of coordinating its marketing research activities. It appointed one or more market research specialists in each subsidiary company throughout the region. The specialists report to local marketing managers but also receive research direction from expert research managers at the head office in the United States. Head office control ensures a high standard of research quality worldwide. For example, the head office coordinates the marketing research training that is handled on a regional basis. Centralized coordination also ensures that research findings in any particular country can be meaningfully compared with those from other countries.

In an international marketing operation, there is even greater opportunity and need to standardize and coordinate elements of a marketing information system. A custom market research survey designed to obtain primary data may only be used one time, and may need to focus on the specifics of the local situation. Yet by their very nature, computer databases and information systems are most useful when they are designed to include the same variables organized consistently over time. Without this, it is impossible for the manager to go into much depth in comparing and contrasting data from different markets.[15]

How much information do you need?

We have been talking about the benefits of good marketing information, but dependable information can be expensive. A big company may spend millions developing an information system. A large-scale survey can cost from $20,000 to $100,000, or even more. The continuing research available from companies such as Information Resources can cost a company well over $100,000 a year. And a market test for 6 to 12 months may cost $200,000 to $500,000 per test market!

Companies that are willing and able to pay the cost often find that marketing information pays for itself. They are more likely to select the right target market and marketing mix, or see a potential problem before it becomes a costly crisis.

What is the value of information?

The high cost of good information must be balanced against its probable value to management. Managers never get all the information they would like to have. Very detailed surveys or experiments may be "too good" or "too expensive" or "too late" if all the company needs is a rough sampling of retailer attitudes toward a new pricing plan—by tomorrow. Money is wasted if research shows that a manager's guesses are wrong—and the manager ignores the facts. For example, GM faced an expensive disaster with its 1986 Riviera, which was released even after extensive research predicted a flop.[16]

Marketing managers must take risks because of incomplete information. That's part of their job and always will be. But they must weigh the cost of getting more data against the likely value. If the risk is not too great, the cost of getting more information may be greater than the potential loss from a poor decision. A decision to expand into a new territory with the present marketing mix, for example, might be made with more confidence after a $25,000 survey. But just sending a sales rep into the territory for a few weeks to try to sell potential customers would be a lot cheaper. And if successful, the answer is in and so are some sales.

Faced with many risky decisions, the marketing manager should only seek help from research for problems where the risk can be reduced at a reasonable cost.[17]

Questions and Problems

1. Discuss the concept of a marketing information system and why it is important for marketing managers to be involved in planning the system.
2. In your own words, explain why a decision support system (DSS) can add to the value of a marketing information system. Give an example of how a decision support system might help.
3. Discuss how output from an MIS might differ from the output of a typical marketing research department.
4. Discuss some of the likely problems facing the marketer in a small firm who is trying to develop a marketing information system.
5. Explain the key characteristics of the scientific method, and show why these are important to managers concerned with research.
6. How is the situation analysis different from the data collection step? Can both these steps be done at the same time to obtain answers sooner? Is this wise?
7. Distinguish between primary data and secondary data and illustrate your answer.
8. If a firm were interested in estimating the distribution of income in the province of Ontario, how could it proceed? Be specific.
9. Go to the library and find (in some government publication) three marketing-oriented "facts" on international markets that you did not know existed or were available. Record on one page and show sources.
10. Explain why a company might want to do focus group interviews rather than individual interviews with the same people.
11. Distinguish between qualitative and quantitative approaches to research, and give some of the key advantages and limitations of each approach.
12. Define response rate and discuss why a marketing manager might be concerned about the response rate achieved in a particular survey. Give an example.
13. Prepare a table that summarizes some of the key advantages and limitations of mail, telephone, and personal interview approaches for administering questionnaires.
14. Would a firm want to subscribe to a shared cost data service if the same data were going to be available to competitors? Discuss your reasoning.
15. Explain how you might use different types of research (focus groups, observation, survey, and experiment) to forecast market reaction to a new kind of disposable baby diaper, which is to receive no promotion other than what the retailer will give it. Further, assume that the new diaper's name will not be associated with other known products. The product will be offered at competitive prices.
16. Marketing research involves expense—sometimes considerable expense. Why does the text recommend the use of marketing research even though a highly experienced marketing executive is available?
17. Discuss the concept that some information may be too expensive to obtain in relation to its value. Illustrate.

Suggested cases

- 8 Diego's
- 31 The Parks Canada Dilemma
- 33 New Brunswick Telephone

Computer-aided problem

Marketing Research

Texmac, Inc., has an idea for a new type of weaving machine that could replace the machines now used by many textile manufacturers. Texmac has done a telephone survey to estimate how many of the old-style machines are now in use. Respondents using the present machines were also asked if they would buy the improved machine at a price of $10,000.

Texmac researchers identified a population of about 5,000 textile factories as potential customers. A sample of these were surveyed, and Texmac received 500 responses. Researchers think the total potential market is about 10 times larger than the sample of respondents. Two hundred twenty of the respondents indicated that their firms used old machines like the one the new machine was intended to replace. Forty percent of those firms said that they would be interested in buying the new Texmac machine.

Texmac thinks the sample respondents are representative of the total population, but the marketing manager realizes that estimates based on a sample may not be exact when applied to the whole population. He wants to see how sampling "error" would affect profit estimates. Data for this problem appear in the spreadsheet. Quantity estimates for the whole market are computed from the sample estimates. These quantity estimates are used in computing likely sales, costs, and profit contribution.

a. An article in a trade magazine reports that there are about 5,200 textile factories that use the old-style machine. If the total market is really 5,200 customers—not 5,000 as Texmac originally thought—how does that affect the total quantity estimate, expected revenue, and profit contribution?

b. Some of the people who responded to the survey didn't know much about different types of machines. If the actual number of old machines in the market is really 200 per 500 firms—not 220 as estimated from survey responses—how much would this affect the expected profit contribution (for 5,200 factories)?

c. The marketing manager knows that the percentage of textile factories that would actually buy the new machine might be different from the 40 percent who said they would in the survey. He estimates that the proportion that will replace the old machine might be as low as 36 and as high as 44 percent—depending on business conditions. Use the What If analysis to prepare a table that shows how expected quantity and profit contribution change when the sample percent varies between a minimum of 36 and a maximum of 44 percent. What does this analysis suggest about the use of estimates from marketing research samples? (Note: Use 5,200 for the number of potential customers and use 220 as the estimate of the number of old machines in the sample.)

For additional questions related to this problem, see Exercise 4–3 in the *Learning Aid for Use with Basic Marketing*, Ninth Canadian Edition.

When you finish this chapter, you should:

- Understand how population growth is shifting in different areas and for different age groups.
- Obtain a feel for the size and importance of Canada's ethnic and French Canadian markets.
- Know about the distribution of income in Canada.
- Know how consumer spending is related to family life cycle and other demographic dimensions.
- Know how to estimate likely consumer purchases for broad classes of products.
- Understand the important new terms (shown in orange).

Chap five

The Canadian Consumer Market: Demographic and Economic Dimensions

Would you ever have expected a book on demography, the statistical study of human populations, to become a Canadian bestseller? That's exactly what happened when David K. Foot, with Daniel Stoffman, wrote *Boom, Bust & Echo.* That book stayed on the Canadian bestseller lists for well over a year. Dr. Foot, one of Canada's most respected demographers, has also won a number of distinguished teacher awards. Both in his book and in his classes at the University of Toronto, he has a unique ability to "make the figures live" by showing how demographics affected the past, influence the present, and will shape the future.

"Demographics explain about two-thirds of everything. They tell us a great deal about which products will be in demand in five years, and they accurately predict school enrollments many years in advance. They allow us to forecast what drugs will be in fashion ten years down the road, as well as what sort of crimes will be on the increase. They help us to know when houses will go up in value, and when they will go down."[1]

Why were over 250,000 copies of *Boom, Bust & Echo* sold? It obviously has something to do with the focus Dr. Foot gave his analysis. That focus is reflected in the book's subtitle: *How to Profit from the Coming Demographic Shift.* Each in his or her own way, that's what the majority of readers were attempting to do. Not only marketers and other corporate types but also city planners, educators, health care administrators, realtors, bureaucrats, and professional investors were among the many Canadians who realized that *Boom, Bust & Echo* was a book well worth reading.

The launch of the book—obviously a new product from the perspective of its publisher—benefited from a very effective promotional plan. However, the book caught on because Dr. Foot and Mr. Stoffman, in less than 250 easily understood pages filled with examples that capture the reader, are able to show that demography has a major influence on every aspect of Canadian life. The list of *Boom, Bust & Echo* chapter titles that we provide here will give you a sense of the arguments being advanced.

CHAPTER 1	**Boomers and Other Cohorts** Why your year of birth is one of the most important things about you.
CHAPTER 2	**The Real Estate Meltdown** Why the real estate boom happened, why it ended, and what the future holds for homeowners and investors.
CHAPTER 3	**Demographic Investing** How to identify the growth markets of the future.
CHAPTER 4	**Jobs and the Corporation** How the demographic shift is transforming the corporation and the nature of work.
CHAPTER 5	**The Rules of Retail** Why stores that offer quality and service will do better than stores that compete solely on the basis of price.
CHAPTER 6	**Tennis, Anyone?** Which leisure activities will grow in popularity and which ones won't.
CHAPTER 7	**The Future of Cities** How demographic change led to the growth of the suburbs, caused the decline of public transit, and altered Canada's crime rate.
CHAPTER 8	**Rethinking Education** Why failure to adapt to demographic change inflated Canada's education costs, and how we can avoid repeating the same mistake.
CHAPTER 9	**The Health Care Crunch** As population aging brings increased pressure on the health care system, reform becomes urgent.
CHAPTER 10	**What's a Family?** How demographic change is transforming family and other social relationships.
CHAPTER 11	**An Older, Wiser Canada** How Canada can survive and prosper in the coming "grey interlude."

Since the material covered is so important to prospective managers, we urge you to read *Boom, Bust & Echo* in the near future. It will be time well spent. But first things first. This chapter should also help prove to you that demography matters. It draws mainly on Census-type materials, with particular emphasis on such topics as population growth by region, ethnic origin, and mother tongue. The age profile of the population and the changing composition of Canadian households are also examined. And because the spending power that people have is another crucial factor in determining the importance of any possible target market, income and how it is distributed are also carefully considered.

Source for inset: Table of Contents, *Boom, Bust & Echo: How to Profit from the Coming Demographic Shift,* by David K. Foot with Daniel Stoffman (Toronto: MacFarlane Walter & Ross, 1996) pp. vii–viii. Reproduced with permission from MacFarlane Walter & Ross.

Getting the facts straight

Demographic and economic data provide marketing managers with critical information about the size, location, and characteristics of possible target markets. You will see how a marketing manager can work with such data to strengthen the company's position in the marketplace. Staying alert to demographic trends and economic conditions will both help you discover new marketing opportunities and give advance warning regarding necessary changes in your existing marketing strategies.

To help build your judgment regarding buyer behaviour, this and the following two chapters will discuss what we know about various kinds of consumers and their buying behaviour. Keep in mind that we are not trying to make generalizations about "average customers" or how the "mass market" behaves. Rather, we are addressing how *some* people in *some* markets will behave. You should expect to find differences.

Fortunately, useful information is available on the economic and demographic dimensions of the Canadian consumer market. Most of it costs very little because it has been collected by government agencies, usually Statistics Canada. When valid data are available, there is no excuse for making decisions based on guesses or rumours. The data in the next few chapters can be used to estimate the potential in different market segments. Check your own assumptions against this data. Now is a good time to get your facts straight.

Population—people buy goods and services

Where do people live?

Exhibit 5–1 shows the population of Canada by province for the years 1982 and 1997. The percentage increase in each province is also indicated. The consumer market in 1997 consisted of over 30 million people, with the bulk of that group (62.2%) living in Quebec and Ontario. Note also that British Columbia and Alberta, with 13.0 and 9.4 percent of the total population respectively, are each larger in population than the four Atlantic provinces combined (7.8 percent).

Quebec and Ontario together contain more than three-fifths of the country's population. They also account for the majority of consumer income and expenditure and for the lion's share of the industrial market. A strong position in these markets is a must for any national marketing strategy. At the same time, their very size can make Quebec and Ontario brutally competitive markets. Also, two very different linguistic and cultural traditions may necessitate distinct marketing approaches. Because Central Canada is so large, some firms pay limited attention to the smaller

Exhibit 5-1 Population of Canada by Province, 1982–97 (estimated, in thousands)

	1982		1997		PERCENT CHANGE
	TOTAL	PERCENT	TOTAL	PERCENT	1982–1997
CANADA	24,658	100%	30,287	100%	22.9%
Newfoundland	569	2.3	564	1.9	−0.9
Prince Edward Island	123	0.5	137	0.5	11.4
Nova Scotia	853	3.5	948	3.1	11.1
New Brunswick	700	2.8	762	2.3	8.9
Quebec	6,463	26.2	7,420	24.5	14.8
Ontario	8,736	35.4	11,408	37.7	30.6
Manitoba	1,038	4.2	1,145	3.8	10.3
Saskatchewan	982	4.0	1,023	3.4	4.1
Alberta	2,326	9.4	2,847	9.4	22.4
British Columbia	2,798	11.3	3,933	13.0	40.1
Yukon	24	0.1	32	0.1	33.3
Northwest Territories	48	0.2	68	0.2	41.7

Source: Statistics Canada, adapted from "Quarterly Demographic Statistics," Catalogue No. 91-002, Volume 11, Number 2, p. 15; and "Quarterly Estimates of Population for Canada, Provinces and Territories," Catalogue No. 91-001, Volume 7, Number 3.

markets in British Columbia, the Prairies, and Atlantic Canada. Yet these regions offer real opportunities to an alert marketer who is looking for areas with fewer competitors, or selling a product of particular interest to people in one of those regions.

Where has population grown the most?

Population figures for a single year don't show the dynamic aspects of markets. The population of Canada more than doubled between 1946 and 1990. But—and this is important to marketers—the population did *not* double everywhere. Firms always try to identify the fastest-growing markets. They want to know both where the more recent growth has been and, even more importantly, where it is likely to be in the future.

Exhibit 5–1 shows that the national growth rate of 22.9 percent for the years 1982 to 1997 was exceeded in only two provinces: British Columbia (40.1 percent) and Ontario (30.6 percent). All the other provinces grew at rates much lower than the national average, except Alberta (22.4 percent), which came close to equalling Canada's overall growth rate.

These different growth rates are especially important to marketers. For example, sudden growth in one area may create demand for many new shopping centres, while new shopping centres in slow-growing areas can create tough competition for existing retailers. But in rapidly growing areas, demand may increase, so profits in even poorly planned facilities may be good.

Exhibit 5–1 represents big-picture data at the national and provincial levels. However, much more detailed data on population are available from Statistics Canada for very small geographical areas. Just as we've considered population changes at the provincial level, a local marketer must divide a city or a big metropolitan area into smaller areas to figure out "where the population's action is."

Local political boundaries don't define market areas

Classifying population by arbitrary city and county boundaries has its limitations. Marketers are more interested in the size of homogeneous marketing areas than in the number of people within political boundaries. This is why Statistics Canada developed

Exhibit 5-2 Total Population of Census Metropolitan Areas, 1981–96 (in thousands)

	1981	1996	*Percentage Change* 1981–1996
Atlantic provinces			
Halifax	277.7	344.1	23.9
St. John's, Newfoundland	154.8	175.2	13.2
Saint John, New Brunswick	121.0	129.4	6.9
Quebec			
Chicoutimi-Jonquière	158.2	167.9	6.1
Montreal	2,862.3	3,365.1	17.6
Ottawa–Hull	743.8	1,039.3	39.7
Quebec	583.8	699.0	19.7
Sherbrooke	125.2	148.9	18.9
Trois-Rivières	125.3	142.0	13.3
Ontario			
Hamilton	542.1	643.0	18.6
Kitchener	287.8	404.2	40.4
London	326.8	413.0	26.4
Oshawa	186.5	275.8	47.9
St. Catharines–Niagara	342.7	391.1	14.1
Sudbury	156.1	166.7	6.8
Thunder Bay	122.0	130.0	6.6
Toronto	3,130.4	4,410.3	40.9
Windsor	250.9	294.1	17.2
Manitoba/Saskatchewan			
Regina	173.2	199.2	15.0
Saskatoon	175.1	223.5	27.7
Winnipeg	592.1	680.3	14.9
Alberta			
Calgary	626.0	853.0	36.4
Edmonton	740.9	890.8	20.2
British Columbia			
Vancouver	1,268.2	1,883.7	48.5
Victoria	241.5	315.2	30.5
Total CMAs	14,314.4	18,385.5	28.4
Total Canada	24,343.2	29,963.6	23.1
Percent CMAs	58.8%	61.4%	

Source: Statistics Canada, adapted from "Annual Demographic Statistics, 1996," Catalogue No. 91-213, pp. 194–6; and "The Daily," Catalogue No. 11-001, April 13, 1987.

a separate population classification, the **Census Metropolitan Area (CMA).** The CMA is the "main labour market area" of a continuous built-up area having 100,000 or more population. It's a zone in which a significant number of people are able to commute on a daily basis to their workplaces in the main built-up area.[2]

In other words, a CMA is an integrated social and economic unit with a large population. CMAs are usually known by the name of their largest city. In 1996 there were 25 CMAs in Canada with a total population of just over 18.3 million. This represents almost 61.4 percent of the 1996 Canadian total. Exhibit 5–2 lists Canada's largest urban areas. These CMAs are major target markets. Toronto, Montreal, and Vancouver, of course, are Canada's largest metropolitan markets. Their combined population has reached 9.7 million, or 32.2 percent of the Canadian total.

In the past fifteen years, some CMAs have grown much faster than others. The big winner has been Vancouver, with a population growth of 48.5 percent, followed closely by Oshawa (47.9 percent), and then by Toronto, Kitchener, Ottawa–Hull, and Calgary. Note, however, the low growth rates of Chicoutimi-Jonquière in Quebec, of Thunder Bay and Sudbury in Ontario, and of Saint John in New Brunswick.

Megalopolis: The continuous city

Twelve of Canada's 25 CMAs fall within Canada's **megalopolis.** This strip of land runs approximately 750 miles, from Quebec City in the east to Windsor in the west, passing through such cities as Trois-Rivières, Sherbrooke, Montreal, Ottawa, Oshawa, Kitchener, Toronto, Hamilton, London, and St. Catharines. This strip, with less than 2 percent of the country's total land mass, contains 40 percent of Canada's population. Another concentration is developing around Vancouver and Victoria. Also, population corridors are building between Calgary and Edmonton, and between Regina and Saskatoon.

Some marketers sell only in metropolitan areas because of the large, concentrated population. Having so many customers packed into a small area can simplify the marketing effort. Fewer intermediaries can be used while still offering products conveniently. One or two local advertising media (city newspaper or TV station) can reach most residents. If a sales force is needed, it will have less wasted travel time and expense because people are closer together.

Metro areas are also attractive markets because they offer greater sales potential than their population alone would indicate. Consumers have more money to spend because wages tend to be higher in these areas. In addition, professional occupations with higher salaries are concentrated in these areas. Densely populated areas offer great opportunities if the competition isn't too strong.

From city to suburbs and then a trickle back

Not only people but also industries have left the cities. This continuing decentralization of industry has moved many jobs closer to the suburbs. We may be developing an urban economic system that's not as dependent on central cities. A growing population must go somewhere, and the suburbs can combine pleasant neighbourhoods with easy transportation to higher-paying jobs nearby or in the city.

Purchase patterns are different in the suburbs. For example, a big-city resident may not need or own a car. But with no mass transportation, living carless in the suburbs is difficult, and in some areas a passenger van to carpool kids and haul lawn supplies or pets is almost a necessity.

Some families, however, have given up on the suburban dream. They found it a nightmare of commuting, yard maintenance, housework, rising local taxes, and gossiping neighbours. These people are leaving suburbia. The movement back to the city is most evident among older— and sometimes wealthier—families. They feel crowded by suburbia's expansion. Their children have left home or are ready to leave. These older families are creating a market for luxury condominiums and high-rise apartments close to downtown and its shopping, recreation, and office facilities. Some young people are also moving into downtown areas, fixing up old homes that still offer convenience and charm at a reasonable price. They are big buyers in the market for "do it yourself" home repair products like paint, insulation, and flooring. They also spend much of their extra money on the city's cultural events and interesting restaurants.

The mobile market

People move, stay a while, and then move again. In fact, the 1996 Census classified nearly half the Canadian population as movers over the previous five years, and about half that group moved to a new community. Both long-distance and local "mobiles" are important market segments. Of course, the approximately 200,000 immigrants to Canada each year also create a tremendous marketing opportunity, especially in Toronto, Vancouver, and Montreal, where most recent immigrants have chosen to live.

Often when people move in the same city, it's to trade up to a bigger or better house or neighbourhood. Those who move tend to be younger, better educated people on the way up in their careers. Their incomes are rising and they have money to spend. Buying a new house may spark many other purchases as well. The old draperies may look shabby in the new house; the bigger yard may require a new lawn mower or even a yard service.

Lately we've been seeing a new development: older or retired people are moving. Some are moving from suburbia to downtown areas in their own city. Others are leaving big cities for smaller towns and cities such as Victoria, British Columbia, and Kingston, Ontario.

Many market-oriented decisions have to be made fairly quickly after moves. People must locate new sources of food, clothing, medical and dental care, and household goods. Once these basic buying decisions are made, they may not change for a long time.

Alert marketers should try to locate these mobile people and inform them of their marketing mixes.[3] The mobile market gives special opportunities to retail chains, national brands, and franchised services that are available in different areas. The customer who moves to a new town may find a familiar supermarket sign down the street and never even try the local competitor.

Not only are Canadians frequent movers, but they also like to travel, try new things, and own second homes, vacation cabins, travel trailers, and boats. This has led to more retail stores, marinas, and recreation areas. More recently, a growing number of Canadians have begun to surf the Net (see Internet Insite 5–1).

Ethnic markets in Canada

Ethnic groups deserve special attention when markets are being analyzed. One basic reason is that people from different ethnic groups may be influenced by very different cultural variables. They may have quite different needs, as well as their own ways of thinking. Canada has long been a multicultural market; rather than disappearing in a melting pot, some important cultural and ethnic dimensions are being preserved and highlighted. This creates both opportunities and challenges for marketers.

Canada's ethnic mix[4]

When completing their 1996 Census forms, about 8.1 million Canadians (about 28 percent of the total population) indicated that they were members of a single or mixed ethnic heritage other than Canadian, English, or French. Many members of this group identified themselves as of European extraction, with Italian (729,000), German (726,000), Ukrainian (332,000), Dutch (314,000), and Polish (266,000) being the backgrounds most frequently cited. The number identifying themselves as Aboriginal was 478,000. A large number of the remaining ethnics would fall into what has come to be known as the "visible minority" category.

Important ethnic communities have existed in Canada almost since Confederation. The same cannot be said about visible minorities. Until Canada introduced a colour-blind immigration policy in 1966, most immigrants were European Caucasians. This is no longer the case. When they completed their 1996 Census forms, some 3.2 million Canadians identified themselves as members of a visible minority. They represented 11.2 percent of the population, up from 6.3 percent in 1986. Exhibit 5–3 provides more detailed information on each visible minority's share of the population, nationally, provincially, and by CMA. Since seven out of every ten visible minority members live in Toronto, Vancouver, or Montreal, similar information is provided for these three CMAs.

Both individually and collectively, ethnic markets are important. This is especially true in Canada's three largest metropolitan markets, where about 80 percent of Canada's entire ethnic population lives. Recent projections indicate that the Chinese,

Who's on the Net?

Who are the consumers on the Web? What are they doing online? And how well are the different segments of the Canadian population represented on the Internet?

Answers to these questions can reveal the demographic and usage patterns on the Web, thus providing valuable information necessary for market segmentation. Several research organizations have been tracking Web demographics and usage patterns. ACNielsen/CommerceNet Survey of the Internet (www.commerce.net/research/) and the GVU's WWW User Survey at Georgia Tech University (www.gatech.edu) are among the most widely cited. ACNielsen/CommerceNet collect data through telephone surveys, and the GVU survey is done online at their Web site. The different methodologies seem to lead to the same conclusion, as evident from the table at the bottom of this page.

It is obvious that Internet demographics are highly skewed toward the upper socioeconomic strata. Interestingly, each GVU Survey has shown a broadening of the Internet demographics. The 7th GVU Survey, for instance, found that only 31 percent of users were women and that average household income was US$57,000. Thus, the trend points toward a growing acceptance and adoption of this new technology.

ACNielsen's Canadian Internet Survey Fall 1997 (www.acnielsen.ca) found that 31 percent of Canadians aged 12 and over have access to the Internet, and out of that group 13 percent have engaged in online shopping or e-commerce (i.e., roughly 4 percent of all Canadians have shopped online). Also, 58 percent of Canadians have had no direct experience with the Internet. Among Internet users, about 50 percent have never clicked on a banner advertisement.

A large number of Canadians are not yet accessing the Web. New technologies such as WebTV and other easy-to-use appliances, as well as decreasing prices of computer hardware, may encourage more consumers to try the Internet. As more and more schools, local libraries, and community centres offer Internet connectivity, more younger as well as low-income citizens will be represented on the Web.

This demographic analysis, however, reveals only a part of the story. What are consumers doing online? According to the 8th GVU Survey, gathering information for personal needs is the most common activity (72 percent), followed by entertainment (65 percent) and education (60 percent). Given a broader definition of "shopping" (shopping/gathering product information), 40 percent said they engaged in this activity. Interestingly, 40 percent of respondents admitted to using the Web simply to waste time!

A study by Price-Waterhouse supported the GVU Survey findings (see the following table). Only 1 percent of online time is devoted to shopping (i.e., actually purchasing over the Internet). So attracting educated, upper-income consumers to your Web site may not be a challenge. Getting these consumers to buy online could be quite a different story.

Frequent Internet Activities

Internet activity	Time spent
Research	43%
E-mail	34
Game playing	9
Reading online news/ magazines (e-zines)	5
Online shopping	1

Source: Price-Waterhouse (www.pricewaterhouse.com)

Here are some questions to ponder: (1) How can marketers use this information about Web demographics? (2) Why is online shopping so low in spite of the attractive demographics? (3) How are men and women likely to differ in their usage of the Web?

Source: This is one of a series of Internet Insites prepared in April 1998 by Dr. Ramesh Venkat of Saint Mary's University for *Basic Marketing*, Ninth Canadian Edition.

Demographics of Internet Users (North America)

Demographic variable	Nielsen/CommerceNet	8th GVU WWW User Survey
Gender	Female–43%, male–57%	Females–38.5%, males–61.5%
Age	18 to 34–43% 55 and over–10%	Average age: 35.7 years
Income	US$50,000 and over–46%	Mean household income: US$53,000
Education	At least college–49%	At least college–47%

Exhibit 5-3 Canada's Visible Minorities

VISIBLE MINORITY POPULATION BY GROUP 1996

	#	%
Total visible minority population	3,197,480	100.0
Chinese	860,150	26.9
South Asian	670,585	21.0
Black	573,860	17.9
Arab/West Asian	244,665	7.7
Filipino	234,200	7.3
Latin American	176,975	5.5
Southeast Asian	172,765	5.4
Japanese	68,135	2.1
Korean	64,835	2.0
Visible minority, n.i.e.[1]	69,745	2.2
Multiple visible minority[2]	61,570	1.9

[1] Includes Pacific Islanders and other visible minority groups
[2] Includes respondents who reported more than one visible minority group
n.i.e.= not included elsewhere

VISIBLE MINORITY POPULATION BY PROVINCE 1996

	Total population	Total visible minority population	Visible minorities as % of total population	Geographic distribution of visible minorities
			%	
Canada	28,528,125	3,197,480	11.2	100.0
Newfoundland	547,155	3,815	0.7	0.1
P.E.I.	132,855	1,520	1.1	0.0
Nova Scotia	899,970	31,320	3.5	1.0
New Brunswick	729,625	7,995	1.1	0.3
Quebec	7,045,085	433,985	6.2	13.6
Ontario	10,642,790	1,682,045	15.8	52.6
Manitoba	1,100,295	77,355	7.0	2.4
Saskatchewan	976,615	26,945	2.8	0.8
Alberta	2,669,195	269,280	10.1	8.4
British Columbia	3,689,760	660,545	17.9	20.7
Yukon Territory	30,650	1,000	3.3	0.0
Northwest Territories	64,125	1,670	2.6	0.1

Visible minority population as a percentage of census metropolitan areas, 1996

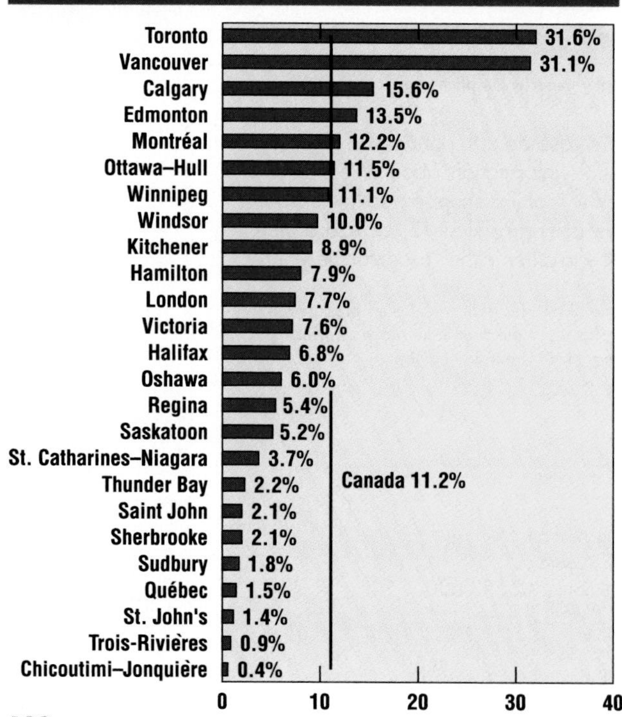

VISIBLE MINORITY POPULATION IN THE TORONTO CENSUS METROPOLITAN AREA 1996

	#	%
Total visible minority population	1,338,090	100.00
Chinese	335,185	25.0
South Asian	329,840	24.7
Black	274,935	20.5
Filipino	99,110	7.4
Arab/West Asian	72,160	5.4
Latin American	61,655	4.6
Southeast Asian	46,510	3.5
Korean	28,555	2.1
Japanese	17,050	1.3
Visible minority, n.i.e.[1]	45,655	3.4
Multiple visible minority[2]	27,435	2.1

[1] Includes Pacific Islanders and other visible minority groups
[2] Includes respondents who reported more than one visible minority group
n.i.e. = not included elsewhere

VISIBLE MINORITY POPULATION IN THE MONTREAL CENSUS METROPOLITAN AREA 1996

	#	%
Total visible minority population	401,425	100.0
Black	122,320	30.5
Arab/West Asian	73,950	18.4
Latin American	46,700	11.6
South Asian	46,165	11.5
Chinese	46,115	11.5
Southeast Asian	37,600	9.4
Filipino	14,385	3.6
Korean	3,500	.9
Japanese	2,315	.6
Visible minority, n.i.e.[1]	3,485	.9
Multiple visible minority[2]	4,875	1.2

[1] Includes Pacific Islanders and other visible minority groups
[2] Includes respondents who reported more than one visible minority group
n.i.e. = not included elsewhere

VISIBLE MINORITY POPULATION IN THE VANCOUVER CENSUS METROPOLITAN AREA 1996

	#	%
Total visible minority population	564,590	100.0
Chinese	279,040	49.4
South Asian	120,140	21.3
Filipino	40,710	7.2
Japanese	21,880	3.9
Southeast Asian	20.370	3.6
Arab/West Asian	18,155	3.2
Korean	17,080	3.0
Black	16,400	2.9
Latin American	13,830	2.4
Visible minority, n.i.e.[1]	6,775	1.2
Multiple visible minority[2]	10,210	1.8

[1] Includes Pacific Islanders and other visible minority groups
[2] Includes respondents who reported more than one visible minority group
n.i.e. = not included elsewhere

Source: Statistics Canada, adapted from "The Daily," Catalogue No. 11-001, February 17, 1998, .

East Indian, and Polish communities will enjoy especially strong growth, both in numbers and in their share of total purchasing power.[5]

"Mainstream" campaigns

To target visible minorities, businesses have two options: include visible minorities in "mainstream" campaigns, or target specific ethnic groups in their mother tongue.

Many ethnic Canadians want to be included in mainstream advertising. According to the Canadian Advertising Foundation, one in five Canadians says that he or she is more likely to buy a product from a firm that makes a point of including visible minorities in its ads. Among visible minorities, that number jumps to nearly one in two (46 percent). Many ethnic consumers are saying: "We drive BMWs; we read *The Globe and Mail* and the *Toronto Star*. Don't look on us as some segregated, marginalized community. Look for us on the main streets of Canada."

Marketers forget that some ethnic groups are well established, with second-, third-, and even eighth-generation families. They consider themselves part of the mainstream and don't want to be reached other than through the mass media. And while new immigrants have strong ties to their cultural heritage, they also seek to assimilate with Canadian society.[6]

Mother-tongue marketing[7]

Although ethnic origin is important to marketers, so is mother tongue (language first spoken at home and still understood). Though not all members of an ethnic community regularly use or even understand their heritage language, obviously those born elsewhere would, and often so do the children of these first-generation immigrants. The 1996 Census showed a marked increase in the percentage of the population who reported their mother tongue as a nonofficial language— from 13.8 percent in 1986 to nearly 17 percent in 1996.

In 1996 the three main mother tongues, other than English and French, were Chinese (reported by 736,000 people), Italian (514,000), and German (471,000). As well, there were 223,000 people reporting Portuguese, 222,000 Polish, and 215,000 Punjabi. The numbers for Tagalog (Filipino), Arabic, and Ukrainian were also each in excess of 150,000. But even though 4.7 million people reported a mother tongue other than English or French in 1996, only 2.8 million of these people spoke a nonofficial language most often at home. Chinese was by far the most frequent of these home languages, followed by Italian, Punjabi, and Portuguese.

Every individual whose "language of comfort" is other than English or French does not present a mother-tongue marketing opportunity. Such individuals have to constitute enough of a marketing segment to be profitably cultivated. There has to be an economical way of reaching them, either in the communities in which they live or through mother-tongue media. In many cases, this can and has been done. Many of those using a given mother tongue tend to live in the same communities, read the same newspapers, and enjoy the same mother-tongue radio and television shows.

Ethnic marketing can pay off

For those who approach target marketing correctly, the benefits are there. One of Canada's major banks showed a 400 percent increase over five years in its Chinese business when it took an aggressive marketing approach. Besides showing Chinese in its mass marketing materials, it also developed Chinese-language ads, direct mail, and in-branch materials, and took a highly visible role supporting community events. Another advertiser, an auto maker, saw a 25 percent boost in sales to the Chinese market after taking an integrated ethnic-marketing approach. As Marketing Demo 5–1 reveals, a rapidly growing ethnic market also creates a demand for specialty retailing.

Marketing Demo 5-1

Huge Asian Supermarket in Burnaby Signals the Birth of a New B.C.

The T&T supermarket occupies one end of the ground floor of Burnaby's Metrotown shopping plaza, and it is what they call in malls an "anchor"—a big store that generates traffic.

A Woodward's store used to be there, but when the chain passed away in 1993—and a part of the old B.C. with it—the T&T moved into the 50,000-square-foot space a few months later, set up shop and, just as symbolically, signalled the birth of a new B.C.

The T&T is the largest Asian supermarket in Canada. It has the familiar look of a North American supermarket, without any brand name recognition. A dozen different tofus command the dairy section where cheese might in Safeway, and the freezers are stocked with potstickers, not perogies. You can find coconut bread, and taro bread, and green apple sponge cake the exact shade of a foam mattress, but damn if you can find a bagel.

The names and variety of the vegetable produce can induce epiglottis seizure: yu choy, gai choy, bok choy, chi choy, don-qua, mo qua, daikon, chun ho, lo bak, yuka, tak koo chai, dai kon lo bok, kapocha, opo. There are Thai pomelos as big as volleyballs.

There are white-fleshed fresh young coconuts skinned into a shape that recalls, oddly, grain silos.

There are fragrant persimmons, as tiny and perfect and red as garnets, and foul-smelling durian, porcupines reincarnated as fruit. There are exquisite-smelling mainland Chinese guava, as small and smooth-skinned as plums, and—unable to find common ground, even in food—Taiwanese guava, big and green and rough-skinned.

Some of the product doesn't quite make the leap in translation. The Hot Kid Big Fried Senbei—a rice cookie—has as its slogan in English, "Digging into boring pie, Getting out of boring time." I have no idea.

In the Filipino section, canned sweet macapuno strings are labelled as "gelatinous mutant coconut." Instructions on a Japanese Lemon Pop drink on "How To Open" demand that we "1. Take out the lid. 2. Take off the ring. 3. Pressure."

Taro root and mung bean ice bars are "quiescently frozen"—demonstrating not only a touching attempt at faithful translation but also that East is East and West is West and never the twain shall meet, popsicle-wise.

The drinks boggle. There are the usual Asian flavors that long ago made their way on to the more sweet-inclined North American palate—guava drink, kiwi drink, passion fruit drink—but there are flavors that the non-Asian can only wonder at: Grass jelly drink. Fresh olive juice drink. Basil seed drink. Pennywort leaves drink. Sour sop drink. Water chestnut drink. Natural barley drink. Chrysanthemum drink. Asparagus drink.

T&T also stocks something called PH Vinegar—a "Personal Health Sour drink," according to the can—and, for action-film fans, Bobo Tea, "A Jackie Chan Product."

The meat section—where the butchers actually serve customers (a nice contrast to Safeway, where butchers barricade themselves behind glass)—reminds us that the Asian appetite encompasses just about anything an animal has to offer. You can not only buy pork stomach, you can buy pork stomach tip. Or pork ears. Or pork heart. Or pork neck bone, pork tails, pork spinal columns.

The oxtails are not the small medallions Caucasians use to make soup with; they are oxtails, the real thing, as long as riding crops. Pale, skeletal duck feet are laid out in neat rows, alongside the smaller, more delicate (and queasiness-inducing) duck tongues.

The hot lunch counter, which attempts to cover as much of the kaleidoscopic Chinese cuisine as it can, offers marinated jelly fish, drunken chicken feet cooked in Chinese wine, preserved pork rind, barbecued quails (sad, naked sparrow-sized roasts) and fried smelt in spicy salt.

"And this," said kitchen manager Alan Wan, pointing to the farthest end of counter "is a kind of North American dish, for the kids." It was a tray of fried chicken. Some things transcend race.

T&T, said store manager David Chen, tries to differentiate itself from the North American-style supermarkets by offering a shopping experience an Asian customer is familiar with—that is, much like a traditional open-air market. This is where the odd amalgam of T&T expresses itself: It borrows the efficiency and cleanliness of a North American supermarket and marries that to the color of an Asian bazaar.

You can see this especially in the seafood section, where crab and lobster and manila clams and rock cod and pink scallops and geoduck—all of them live—languish in big aquarium tanks. It smells of low tide.

On weekends, T&T is packed with shoppers: Chen said they easily do 5,000 customers on a Saturday (about 10 per cent of whom, Chen estimated, are Caucasian.) And its success is telling: While Safeway is closing five stores in the Lower Mainland, T&T is expanding. It now has two stores, with one in Richmond. A third opens this November in Chinatown.

If you haven't seen it, you should give it a try, if only to appreciate this bounty, this rich stew of what the new B.C. has become.

Source: Pete McMartin, The *Vancouver Sun*, September 25, 1996, B1.

Avoid stereotyping

These are the success stories of advertisers who have not forgotten a fundamental principle of marketing: Know your customer. Too many advertisers, however, are not taking the time and care to truly understand who their ethnic consumers are and how to reach them effectively.

The greatest challenge is to get beyond the "them versus us" mentality and the urge to categorize ethnic Canadians, or a given ethnic community, as one homogeneous group. Every black person is not from the Caribbean, for example. A person of Chinese origin could be from Taiwan or Singapore, not just Hong Kong or mainland China. Not all ethnic Canadians are new to this country and speak with an accent, or only speak a language other than English.

The French Canadian market

Who is a French Canadian consumer?

French Canadians can be defined in many ways. The position most often taken is that a French Canadian consumer is anyone whose mother tongue is French or who tends to speak French rather than English at home.[8] However, marketers must realize that a large number of French Canadians are truly bilingual. They watch English-language television and read English-language publications. A significant number of French Canadians who aren't fully bilingual on occasion still prefer to listen to English radio, watch English TV, or read English-language publications. Marketers must carefully study French Canadians' media preferences. They cannot rely exclusively on census discussions of mother tongue or language most often spoken at home.

Where is the French Canadian market?[9]

Is the French Canadian market essentially Quebec, or should it be defined more broadly? For marketing purposes, Quebec and the French Canadian market are not identical. However, a French Canadian market does not exist in every location where a few French-speaking consumers live. Marketers can't afford to develop special programs for very small market segments.

One approach defines the French Canadian market as including Quebec, eight adjacent counties in Ontario, and seven counties in the northern part of New Brunswick. For the fifteen counties taken together, the mother tongue of over half the population is French. In addition, flourishing French Canadian institutions are found in these counties, and French Canadian assimilation into the English culture is somewhat limited. Also, the same areas receive a considerable amount of overflow advertising from Quebec, and they are frequently served by Quebec distributors.[10]

Of the 6.7 million Canadians in 1996 reporting French as their mother tongue, over 90 percent lived in Quebec or the 15 adjacent counties. This figure includes immigrants from France, Haiti, North Africa, Vietnam, and other French-speaking nations. It also includes a substantial Acadian population in New Brunswick. Although unique in many ways, Acadians for marketing planning purposes are usually considered part of the larger "French-speaking" market.

The "other Quebec market"

Some 622,000 individuals who in 1996 reported English as their mother tongue (often classified as anglophones) live in Quebec. In addition, Quebec has an even larger number of "allophone" residents (682,000), who reported some third language as their mother tongue. Although some English-speaking consumers have left Quebec in recent years, the number of Quebec residents with a mother tongue other than French is still larger than the total population of Manitoba or

Saskatchewan. This "other Quebec market" is also less expensive to reach since over 80 percent of these consumers live in and around Montreal. In fact, "other than French-speaking Montreal" would be Canada's fourth-largest city after Toronto, French-speaking Montreal, and Vancouver.

How does consumption differ?

Differences in product use and preference

What differences in product use exist between French Canadians and their English-speaking counterparts? French Quebecers are less likely to drink tea or diet cola, or to eat jam, tuna, cookies, or eggs on a daily basis than are English Canadians. However, they are more likely to use presweetened cereals and regular cola, and to use butter for cooking. They show a strong preference for instant coffee products, giving decaffeinated products a slight edge.

Quebecers feel they give more importance to personal grooming and fashion than do other Canadians. This may explain why 64 percent go to specialized clothing boutiques, compared to 52 percent among other Canadians. Generally, French women in Quebec do not use as much lip gloss, pressed powder, foundation makeup, or perfume, but they are heavier users of perfumed body spray, cologne, and toilet water, as well as lipstick. They also buy more panty hose, swimwear, and hair colouring products (the latter at beauty salons).

French Quebec has a higher proportion of wine drinkers (51 percent versus 44 percent), beer drinkers (50 percent versus 46 percent), and smokers (38 percent versus 29 percent) than the rest of Canada. On the other hand, Quebecers consume less hard liquor. Although French Quebecers represent 60 percent of Canadian drinkers of Geneva gin and 36 percent of cognac drinkers, they show lower rates of regular consumption of hard liquor (10 ounces and more a week).

In terms of leisure and sport activities, there are fewer golfers, joggers, and gardeners in Quebec. The proportion of people who go to movies or entertain at home is also lower. However, there are more cyclists, frequent skiers, woodworkers, dressmakers, and live-theatre fans.

Quebecers are bigger buyers of lottery tickets than most Canadians and are more likely to subscribe to book clubs—but they make fewer personal long-distance phone calls. French Quebecers also generally travel less, be it for business or pleasure.

The financial and banking habits of Quebecers are subject to great differences, partly because of the widespread popularity of the caisses populaires movement. An underdeveloped but growing use of specialty savings tools and trust companies has been recorded.

Purchasing life insurance (65 percent of Quebec adults hold policies, compared to 40 percent for the rest of Canada) is still a strong habit. However, the number of credit card holders is falling: 32 percent of French Quebecers hold two or more cards versus 39 percent for the rest of Canada.[11]

The Print Measurement Bureau's psychographic data show that French Quebecers are more willing to pay premium prices for convenience and premium brands. In terms of other attitudes toward purchasing, French Quebecers give greater credence to advertising than the average Canadian, but they are cautious as to the use of new products, often postponing trials until a product has proven itself. They generally show more brand loyalty, but they will buy another item if it is on special. Furthermore, Quebec consumers buy few "no name" products but make extensive use of cents-off coupons.[12]

These are but a few of the many reported differences in product use and preference. See Marketing Demo 5–2 for a detailed discussion of how North American restaurant chains are attempting to adapt to the Quebec market. It's not always clear what marketers should do when they discover differences in consumption. Should manufacturers of the underconsumed products pay more attention to the Quebec

Marketing Demo 5-2

Fast Food à la Carte

Studies show that Ronald McDonald is second only to Santa Claus in being recognized around the world. The ubiquitous burger clown and his restaurant chain's trademark Golden Arches are a part of the landscape in places as disparate as Russia and South Africa.

But there's at least one place where McDonald's takes its cue from the culture that already exists: none other than Quebec, where the most recognized McDonald's promo plays skillfully on the French language.

The slogan "J'M"—in which the M is the McDonald's logo—is a neat twist on the phrase "J'aime," which means "I like" or "I love." André Lachance, Quebec marketing director at McDonald's Restaurants of Canada Ltd.'s regional office in Dorval, Que., says the long-running slogan is representative of McDonald's philosophy: "All the advertising we do is targeted specifically at the Quebec market. It's a slogan, but it's also a signature: it's powerful because it's what we stand for."

"The beauty of the McDonald's system is in respecting the brand and what it stands for, but the key thing is we want to talk the language of our customers," he says. In Quebec, that means far more than translating made-for-English Canada ads into French.

It means emphasizing humor, like a TV spot promoting November's 25¢ Big Mac deal in which a teenage boy is turned away three times from the house of a prospective date, only to be invited in when the father sees he has a bag of McDonald's takeout. It means sponsoring local initiatives like Quebec City's 2002 Winter Olympics bid. It means creating promotions based on what's going on in the community, like last year's historical place mats commemorating the Montreal Forum. It means offering McLobsters during the popular lobster festival season. It means offering a special combo called the P'tit McDo trio, a play on a common local nickname for McDonald's. And it means adding poutine to the menu.

Poutine, a disgustingly good Quebec-originated concoction of fries with gravy and cheese curds, is not unique to McDonald's. It's also on the menu at Harvey's, Burger King and KFC, three other chains known for catering their fare to Quebecers. Though a 30-year veteran of the Quebec market and a burger-market leader with almost 190 stores, McDonald's is not the only fast-food chain hustling to win the attention of Quebecers. And its tactics appear to be universal.

Dunkin' Donuts (Canada) Ltée of Montreal, which also has about 190 stores in Quebec, representing 85% of its business, has a 35-year history in the province. "Analysis shows the consumer here is different," says marketing director Léo Héroux. "He's in the same age group and has the same profile, but his habits and tastes are different—what he buys, when he buys." Dunkin' Donuts outlets in Quebec sell more yeast-based donuts, like jam-filled brands, and do a steadier, all-day business compared to their counterparts in English Canada, which are busiest at breakfast and sell more "cake donuts," like apple fritters.

The chain airs its TV spots only in Quebec, and emphasizes coupon marketing here more than in other parts of Canada, because redemption rates are higher in the province. It also uses PubliSac, a coupon bag with a wide weekly distribution. "But newspaper inserts do not do well here," says Héroux. "This bag is popular. People seem to like the formula."

Source: Abridged from Anita Lahey, *Marketing Magazine,* November 25, 1996, p. 13.

market? Perhaps there are insurmountable barriers to increasing sales to French Canadians. If so, marketing time and effort could be more profitably spent elsewhere.

Household composition is changing[13]

The "typical" Canadian family is not a young, happily married husband and wife with two children spending all their time in the suburbs. This was never true, and it's even less true now. Although most Canadians eventually marry, they are marrying later, living for years in common law relationships, delaying childbearing, having fewer children, and often getting divorced. Over 20 percent of all marriages are remarriages, and this is resulting in a growing number of "his," "her," and "our" children.

The number of families in Canada climbed 6.6 percent to 7.8 million between 1991 and 1996. Of these, 73.7 percent consisted of married couples, 11.7 percent were living common law, and 14.6 percent were lone-parent families. In total, about 65 percent of all Canadian families had at least one child living at home.

Nontraditional households

Somewhat over 1.8 million unmarried individuals are living together in Canada. About 45 percent of those living common law have children at home. To reach this "common law" market, banks have changed their policies about loans to unmarried couples for homes and cars. Also, insurance companies are designing coverage oriented toward unmarried couples.

Another sizable nontraditional group, single-parent families, more than doubled in importance between 1971 to 1996, rising to over 14.6 percent of all families. By 1996, almost one in every five Canadian children lived in a single-parent family. Over 80 percent of lone-parent families are headed by women. Over two-thirds of these female single parents are in the labour force, the vast majority working full-time. This increase in single-parent families follows from a doubling of the divorce rate between 1971 and 1996.

Single-person households

Once we get rid of the "married couple with two children" image of family life, we must also recognize that the number of households in Canada greatly exceeds the number of families. In addition to the 7.8 million families, there were about 2.6 million individuals, some 11.7 percent of the population 15 and over, living alone in 1996—up from 10 percent in 1986. These households include both young adults, who leave home when they finish school, and divorced "singles." However, the aging of the population—more specifically, an increase in the number of widows—was largely responsible for the growth in this category.

In Canada's urban areas, the percentage of single-person households is even higher. These people need smaller apartments, smaller cars, smaller food packages, and in some cases less expensive household furnishings because they don't have very much money. Other singles have ample discretionary income, and join an attractive target market for luxury goods and services.

Nontraditional households may still be in the minority, but marketers should pay close attention to them. Within a few years, typical "married couple with children" families may well account for only half of all Canadian households.

A look at the future

The world's population is growing rapidly—it may well double over the next 25 years—but this isn't true of Canada. Our own population growth has slowed dramatically. Canada ranks among the slow-growth countries in a world where most developing countries are growing quite rapidly. Many Canadian marketers that previously enjoyed rapid and profitable growth at home are turning to international markets—the United States, Europe, and Asia—where future population growth will be much larger than in our own country.

The falling birthrate

The number of births in Canada fell below the 400,000 mark in 1992. By 1995 the birthrate had fallen to 12.8 live births per thousand of population—the lowest ever seen in Canada. Between 1990 and 1995, international immigration contributed more to Canada's population growth than did natural increase (births minus deaths) over the same period.[14]

Fewer births means less need for "big" family homes and large "family size" food packages. Instead, the demand for small apartments, out-of-home entertainment, travel, and small food packages is increasing. With fewer children, parents can spend more money on each child. For example, expensive bikes, home video games, and designer clothes for children have all done well in recent years. Parents can indulge one or two children more easily than a houseful.

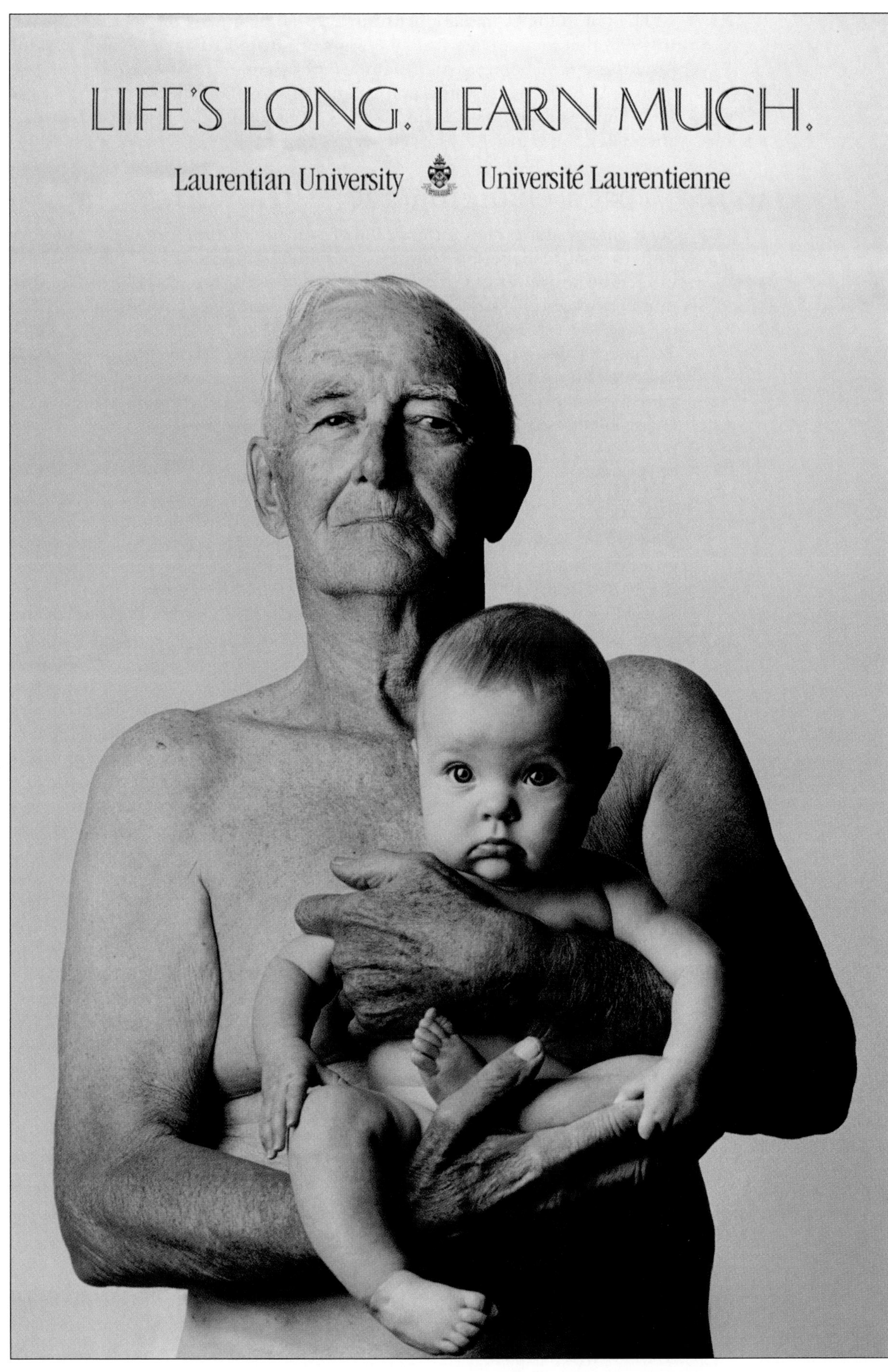
LIFE'S LONG. LEARN MUCH.
Laurentian University Université Laurentienne

The fall in the Canadian birthrate helps explain why the median age is rising. In 1996, that median age was 35.2 years, up from 31.6 in 1986 and 26.3 in 1961. Also, there have been marked changes over time in the size of different age categories. As both the absolute and relative size of older age groupings increased, the number of Canadian teens (10–19) declined by half a million between 1981 and 1991.[15]

What a changing age distribution means

Such changes have had quite an impact on the clothing industry. The focus has shifted from teenage fad followers and their throwaway fashions toward career women buying fewer but better-quality garments for the workplace. The shrinking number of teens has also had an impact on other areas. Grocery prices have gone up over the last few years, but total spending on groceries has not kept pace. Teenagers consume more, per capita, than do either adults or children, and as was indicated above, there were fewer of them to do the consuming. However, that decline has come to an end: the number of teens in Canada remained more or less unchanged between 1991 and 1996.

The baby boom

The main reason for the changing age distribution is that the post–World War II baby boom produced about one-fourth of our present population. This large group crowded into the schools in the 1950s and 1960s and then into the job market in the 1970s. In the 1990s, they're swelling the middle-aged group. And early in the twenty-first century, they'll reach retirement, still a dominant group in the total population. According to one population expert, "It's like a goat passing through a boa constrictor."

Some of the effects of this big market are very apparent. For example, record sales exploded to the beat of rock'n'roll and the Beatles as the baby boom group moved into their record-buying teens. Soon after, universities added facilities and faculty to handle the surge, but then had to cope with excess capacity and loss of revenue when the student-age population dwindled. To relieve financial strain, many universities are now adding special courses and programs for adults to attract the now-aging baby boom students. On the other hand, the "fitness" industry and food producers who offer low-calorie foods are reaping the benefit of a middle-aged "bulge" in the population.

Medical advances are helping people live longer and are also adding to the proportion of senior citizens in the population. The over-65 age group will continue to grow, both absolutely and in percentage terms, for decades to come. These dramatic changes are creating new opportunities for such industries as tourism, health care, and financial services.[16] Marketing Demo 5–3 describes some of the myths and realities involved when targeting the mature market.

Income—markets need people with money

So far, we've been concerned mainly with the *number* of different types of people and *where* they live. But people without money aren't potential customers. And the amount of money people can spend affects the products they're likely to buy. So most marketers study income levels, too.

Changing growth rates

Income comes from producing and selling goods or services in the marketplace. A widely available measure of economic output is the gross domestic product (GDP)—the

Marketing Demo 5-3

Perception vs. Reality in the 50-Plus Market

Debunking Six of the Most Widespread Myths

Today's marketers no longer need to be convinced that the 50-plus age category represents an already huge and ever-growing opportunity to sell a wide range of products and services. But most have no idea how to do it.

How do the 50-plus think? What are their attitudes and behavior as consumers? What are their real concerns, their hot buttons? What are the myths and misconceptions about them?

Ironically, it's what *you* think that will measure your success in this market. Your attitude and the way you treat the mature consumer are almost as important, if not more so, as the services and products targeted at them.

How many of these generally held myths, as originally identified by Age Wave Inc. of California, do you hold?

Myth #1: People over 65 are old. They are not old in today's world, and more importantly, they do not feel old. The definitions of young, middle-aged and old are being expanded upwards daily—it won't be long before we measure old age at 90 or 100.

In any event, age is a poor predictor of who people are and what they need. Health, attitude and lifestage are much more important in determining what you hear, see, buy and do. Grandparents, for example, respond very much the same whether they are 57 or 75.

Myth # 2: Most older people are in ill health. This is no longer the case. While they may have chronic, controlled health problems as they age, they are not necessarily bothered or limited by them. A consumer's potential is better measured by functional abilities, levels of vigor and vitality, and their own feeling of well-being.

Myth # 3: Older minds are not as active as young minds. Of the 40 million or so North Americans over the age of 65, only 10% show any significant loss of memory, and fewer than half of those show serious impairment.

Myth # 4: Older people are not productive. No consistent pattern exists to show the superior productivity of any age group. In the not-too-distant future, older workers will be considered not worn out, but seasoned; not ready to retire, but open to a more flexible and productive work life.

Myth # 5: Older people are unattractive and sexless. Current research shows that men and women continue to feel sensual—dare I say sexy—in later life. In fact, sex and romance continue into later years and may well become deeper and more meaningful.

Myth # 6: Older people are all pretty much the same. No age group is more varied in physical abilities, personal styles, tastes, desires or finances.

When you look at segmenting the 50-plus market, forget the outmoded notion of "seniors" as one unified group sharing many characteristics. They're different people from different generations, with different interests, financial circumstances, preoccupations and needs.

Sweep away these myths and deal instead with the realities of this market. Here are six basic behavior patterns you can take to the bank in developing a 50-plus marketing strategy:

Reality # 1: Mature consumers don't like to be thought of as old. Communicate with them as you would with anyone else. Don't be condescending.

Reality # 2: Mature consumers prefer to be portrayed as attractive and positive. Whether it's a simple brochure or a million-dollar TV campaign, show older people involved in positive activities.

A new mentality is needed in advertising. Ageism still dominates today's marketing, because most ads are produced by young people who haven't been trained about or exposed to the realities of older people. Why not hire someone over the age of 50, at least as a consultant, to deal with this market?

And make sure you are attuned to the special needs and concerns of older women. A quick look at the actuarial tables will show you that more and more of them will make up the bulk of mature consumers.

Reality # 3: Mature consumers are more interested in purchasing experiences than products. Find ways to get them involved. Have them fill out forms or enter contests. Give them choices. Have patience, listen to them, explain in detail.

Reality # 4: Being comfortable is a key psychological need of the older consumer. The less pressure the better. Look for ways to encourage them to trust you or your company. Find out about their hobbies, goals and aspirations.

Reality # 5: Security and safety are crucial factors in the older consumers' decision to buy.

Reality # 6: Convenience and access are just as important as the product itself. A reasonable level of good service will go a long way towards getting their business.

The enormous potential for doing business with the 50-plus market will remain untapped for those who cling to old myths about aging. Those who gain their respect and trust will be happily swamped as they exercise their considerable purchasing power.

Source: David Tafler, *Marketing Magazine,* September 1, 1997, p. 13.

Exhibit 5-4 Gross Domestic Product 1975–1996 (in millions)

YEAR	GROSS DOMESTIC PRODUCT	GROSS DOMESTIC PRODUCT (1992 PRICES)
1975	173,893	445,813
1976	200,296	470,291
1977	221,358	486,562
1978	245,526	506,288
1979	280,309	527,703
1980	315,245	535,007
1981	360,494	557,305
1982	379,734	535,113
1983	411,160	549,843
1984	449,249	581,638
1985	485,139	612,416
1986	511,796	628,575
1987	558,106	654,360
1988	611,785	686,176
1989	656,190	703,577
1990	678,135	705,464
1991	683,239	642,247
1992	698,544	698,544
1993	724,920	716,123
1994	762,251	744,220
1995	799,129	760,309
1996	820,233	769,730

Source: Statistics Canada, adapted from "Canadian Economic Observer," Catalogue No. 11-010; and "Canadian Economic Observer, Historical Statistical Supplement," Catalogue No. 11-210, February 1998.

total value of all goods and services produced in a year. As Exhibit 5–4 shows, Canada's gross domestic product in 1975 was $173.9 billion. By 1985, it had risen to $485 billion—a change of almost 180 percent. Much of that change, however, didn't represent "real" growth but rather the effects of inflation. In 1992 dollars, the relevant figures were $445.8 billion for 1975 and $612.4 billion for 1985. This represents an increase of almost 38 percent over ten years, or an annual growth rate in excess of 3 percent. In retrospect, 3 percent a year growth in real GDP looks quite good. Exhibit 5–4 reveals that there was no meaningful growth at all between 1988 and 1992. Between 1992 and 1996, however, real annual growth in the order of 2 percent resumed.

Family income—no real increase since 1980[17]

Average family income in 1996 was estimated at $56,629. After adjusting for inflation, as measured by changes in the consumer price index, this figure is $2,300 dollars less than it was when family incomes peaked in 1989. Average family income in 1996, after adjusting for inflation, was in fact just $725 above the level recorded in 1980.

The rising income levels of the 1970s broadened markets and drastically changed our marketing system. More families became important customers with money to spend. Many products previously thought of as luxuries could now be sold to mass markets. In this way, the standard of living improved even more because large markets can lead to economies of scale. But as we have just seen, real family incomes haven't really grown since 1980. The recession of the early 1990s and the associated restructuring of Canadian industry caused consumers to lose ground.

Opinions differ as to what will happen to consumer incomes in the future. Some business analysts believe that the lack of growth in real incomes is a sign of worse things to come. They think that Canada's middle-class standard of living is threatened by a decline in the manufacturing sector of the economy. These analysts argue

Exhibit 5-5 Percentage of Total Family Income Going to Different Income Groups

Lowest 20% $0–$25,820	2nd Quintile $25,821–$41,151	Middle Quintile $41,152–$57,793	4th Quintile $57,794–$80,000	Upper Quintile Above $80,000
6.1%	11.9%	17.4%	24.0%	40.6%

Source: Statistics Canada, adapted from "Income Distributions by Size in Canada, 1996," Catalogue No. 13-207, pp. 160–1.

that industries that traditionally paid high wages are now replacing workers with machines to compete with low-cost foreign producers. At the same time, the lower-paying service industries are growing rapidly.

Other analysts aren't so pessimistic. They agree that the percentage of workers earning middle-income wages has decreased. However, they consider this a temporary shift, not a long-term trend. They also argue that given Canada's low interest and inflation rates and its recent success in balancing the budget, this country's economic prospects are strengthening.

Pay close attention to how income is distributed[18]

Exhibit 5–5 makes it clear that higher-income groups still receive a very large share of total income. That chart shows how income is distributed after Canada's families have been divided into five quintiles of equal size, ranging from lowest income to highest. (Comparable information for "unattached individuals" is also available.) The 20 percent of families in the highest-income quintile received over 40 percent of total family income. This gave them extra buying power, especially for luxury items.

At the lower end of the scale are another 1.75 million families. This 20 percent received only about 6.1 percent of total income. Even those in this income group can be an attractive market for some basic commodities, especially food and clothing. Some marketers have chosen to target low-income consumers, usually with a lower-priced marketing mix.

The distribution of income in Canada has varied very little since 1965. The lowest 20 percent have never received more than 6.5 percent of total family income, and the top 20 percent have always received more than 38 percent. But when compared to previous years, the income distribution pattern for 1996 suggests that existing differences are getting even greater. Between 1995 and 1996, the poorest fifth of Canadian families lost 3.1 percent of their income, leaving them with an average income for that year of $17,334. At the same time, the richest fifth saw their incomes grow by 1.8 percent to an average of $114,874.[19]

It's important that you never forget how income is distributed. Serious errors have been made by firms that overestimated the amount of income their target markets had. It's all too easy to make such a mistake. It's often done because of our natural tendency to associate with people like ourselves and to assume that almost everyone lives the same way we do.

The 1996 average family income of just over $56,600 is a useful reference point. A young working couple together can easily go way over this figure. What's being earned may seem like more than enough in the initial flush of making money. However, it's surprising how soon needs and expenses rise to the level of available income. Before long, it's difficult for anyone, even with a relatively high family income, to see how other families could possibly live on much less.

The poverty line

We have already seen that many Canadian families must make do on much less. Even families at the top of the second-lowest income quintile are earning just over $41,000 a year. And according to the most widely used approach to determining who is poor, a very significant proportion of families in the bottom two income quintiles are living in poverty. Statistics Canada has for many years used "low-income cutoffs" as a measure of well being. Families required to spend more than 62 percent of their income on basic necessities like food, shelter, and clothing are said to be "living below the poverty line."[20]

The size of the family unit and the size of the community in which it lives are also considered when calculating "low-income cutoffs." For example, a family of four living in a rural area had a low-income or poverty line cutoff figure of $22,639 in 1997. But it costs considerably more to live in the city than in the country. For a four-person family living in a large metropolitan area, the low-income cutoff figure was $32,759. This Statistics Canada approach has been criticized by some for artificially inflating the number of Canadians reportedly living in poverty.[21] Be that as it may, never forget that millions must make do on considerably less than the family income that most young couples with business degrees can expect to earn.

Exhibit 5–6 shows how total personal income is distributed throughout Canada. It also highlights provincial differences in per capita personal income. Companies often pay a great deal of attention to relative income when examining potential markets. High-income market areas (be they cities, counties, CMAs, or provinces) are usually considered to be most desirable. For example, "upscale" retail dress shops might decide to locate in the suburbs around Toronto because a great many high-income people live in those areas.

Women in the workforce

Between 1976 and 1996, increased female participation in the workforce accounted for two-thirds of all employment growth in Canada. By 1996, 58 percent of all

Exhibit 5–6 Personal Income Geographic Distribution—1996

	PERSONAL INCOME (MILLIONS OF DOLLARS)	PERCENTAGE OF NATIONAL TOTAL	PERSONAL INCOME PER CAPITA (DOLLARS)
Newfoundland	10,254	1.51	17,958
Prince Edward Island	2,563	0.38	18,708
Nova Scotia	18,008	2.65	19,097
New Brunswick	14,346	2.11	18,802
Quebec	158,787	23.36	21,493
Ontario	269,031	39.59	23,910
Manitoba	24,492	3.60	21,409
Saskatchewan	21,369	3.14	20,889
Alberta	65,595	9.65	23,511
British Columbia	91,970	13.53	23,857
Yukon	823	0.12	26,548
Northwest Territories	1,660	0.24	24,776
CANADA	679,605	100.00%	22,681

Source: Statistics Canada, adapted from "Provincial Economic Accounts, 1996," Catalogue No. 13-213, pp. 175–87.

women 15 and over worked outside the home. That year, 45 percent of all paid workers in Canada were women. But women still earn significantly less than men. In 1996, women working full time in the paid workforce made 73.4 percent of the average earnings of their male counterparts. This ratio was up from 68 percent in 1990 and from about 64 percent in the early 1980s. Gender differences for managers and professionals doing roughly comparable work are somewhat smaller, but they still exist.[22]

More money and it's spent differently

In families where the wife works, family spending power is significantly increased. That is why average family income is as high as it is. But many families feel they need this additional income just to make ends meet. Working wives spend more for food and probably choose more expensive, and often already prepared, types of food. Families with working wives also spend more on clothing, alcohol and tobacco, home furnishings and equipment, and cars. In short, when the wife works, it affects the family's spending habits. This fact must be considered when analyzing markets and planning marketing strategies.

Consumer spending patterns are related to population and income

We've been stressing family income and its distribution because consumer budget studies show that most consumers spend their incomes as part of family or household units. These units usually pool their incomes when planning expenditures. However, families don't get to spend all their income. **Disposable income** is what's left after taxes. Out of this disposable income—together with gifts, cash savings, and other assets—the family makes its expenditures. Some families don't spend all of their disposable income—they save part of it. Therefore, we should distinguish between disposable income and actual expenditures when trying to estimate the size of potential target markets.

Discretionary income

Most households spend a good portion of their income on necessities: food, rent or house payments, car and home furnishings payments, insurance, and so on. A family's purchase of luxuries comes from **discretionary income** (what's left of disposable income after paying for necessities).

Discretionary income is a difficult concept because the definition of *necessities* varies from family to family and over time. Most Canadian families don't have enough discretionary income to afford the leisure-class lifestyles seen on TV and in other mass media. On the other hand, some young adults and older people without family responsibilities may have a large share of the total discretionary income in a given area. They may be especially attractive markets for sellers of CD players, cameras, new cars, foreign travel, and various kinds of recreation (tennis, skiing, plays, concerts, and fine restaurants).

Expenditure data

It's obvious that a wealthy family will spend more money than a poor one—and that the money will be spent on different things. But how it's spent and how such spending varies for different target markets are important questions for marketers.

The amount spent on major categories such as food, housing, clothing, transportation, and so on does vary by income level. And the relationships are logical when you realize that many of the purchases in these categories are "necessities."

Exhibit 5-7 Distribution of Average Expenditures by Family Income Group and Unattached Individuals, Canada, 10 Provinces, 1996

	ALL CLASSES	LOWEST QUINTILE	SECOND QUINTILE	THIRD QUINTILE	FOURTH QUINTILE	HIGHEST QUINTILE
Food	12.1%	18.5%	15.6%	13.7%	11.7%	9.6%
Shelter	17.3	31.8	22.4	18.8	16.4	13.2
Principal accommodation	16.3	31.3	21.6	17.9	15.4	11.9
Rented living quarters	4.8	20.5	9.9	6.0	2.9	1.2
Owned living quarters	8.3	5.5	7.2	8.4	9.5	8.3
Water, fuel, and electricity	3.2	5.3	4.4	3.6	3.0	2.3
Other accommodation	1.0	0.5	0.8	0.9	1.0	1.3
Household operation	4.6	6.6	5.6	4.8	4.4	4.0
Communications	1.8	3.3	2.4	2.0	1.6	1.3
Child care expenses	0.6	0.2	0.3	0.5	0.7	0.7
Pet expenses	0.5	0.5	0.6	0.5	0.5	0.4
Other household expenses	1.8	2.5	2.3	1.8	1.7	1.6
Household furnishings and equipment	2.6	2.5	2.8	2.6	2.7	2.6
Clothing	4.3	4.0	4.2	4.3	4.3	4.4
Transportation	12.3	10.6	13.6	13.0	12.8	11.6
Private transportation	11.3	8.8	12.2	12.0	11.9	10.6
Public transportation	1.1	1.8	1.4	1.0	0.8	1.0
Health care	2.1	2.9	2.8	2.3	2.0	1.6
Personal care	1.7	2.3	2.1	1.9	1.7	1.4
Recreation	5.4	4.5	4.6	5.5	5.7	5.5
Reading materials and other printed matter	0.5	0.7	0.6	0.5	0.5	0.5
Education	1.1	1.2	1.1	0.9	1.0	1.3
Tobacco products and alcoholic beverages	2.3	3.6	3.2	2.8	2.2	1.7
Tobacco products	1.1	2.3	1.7	1.4	1.0	0.6
Alcoholic beverages	1.3	1.3	1.5	1.4	1.2	1.1
Miscellaneous expenditures	2.9	2.8	2.8	3.1	3.0	2.8
Total current consumption	69.3	91.9	81.5	74.2	68.5	60.3
Personal taxes	21.9	2.8	11.0	17.2	21.9	30.4
Personal insurance payments and pension contributions	5.3	1.6	3.3	5.3	6.3	5.9
Gifts and contributions	3.5	3.7	4.2	3.3	3.3	3.4
Total expenditure	100.0%	100.0%	100.0%	100.0%	100.0%	100.0%

Source: Statistics Canada, adapted from "Family Expenditures in Canada, 1996," Catalogue No. 62-555.

Exhibit 5–7 can help you understand how potential target customers spend their money. Let's make this more concrete with a simple example. You're a marketing manager for a swimming pool manufacturer. You're considering a mail advertisement to consumers in a neighbourhood where most families fall in the two upper-income quintiles. Let's assume that families in these two quintiles spend an average of $4,600 a year on recreation of all kinds. If you know that it would cost a family at least $3,200 a year for depreciation and maintenance of a pool, it follows that the average family in these two categories would have to make a big shift in its lifestyle in order to purchase a pool.

This type of data won't tell you whether a specific family will buy the pool. But it does supply useful input to help make a sound decision. If more information is needed (perhaps about the strength of the target market's attitudes toward recreation products), then some additional research may be necessary. Perhaps you may want to see a budget study on consumers who already have swimming pools to see how they adjusted their spending patterns and how they felt before and after the purchase.

Other factors also influence spending

Income has a direct bearing on spending patterns, but there are other factors that should not be ignored in any careful analysis of potential markets.

Expenditure patterns in Canada vary by region and with the size and type of family. Differences also exist between renters and home owners. And even among home owners, spending patterns are not the same between those with a mortgage and those without a mortgage.

Location affects spending

Consumer spending data show that the location of a consumer's household affects that household's spending habits. We will not present any more tables here but instead summarize a few important differences. Detailed Statistics Canada data should be analyzed to answer specific questions.

Expenditures on transportation, housing, and food will vary by geographic location. Consumers in urban areas spend a lower percentage of their income on transportation and more on housing than those in rural areas—probably because of higher land and construction costs and greater population density. A rural family spends a larger percentage on food—but lower rural incomes mean that the absolute amount isn't very different.

Lifestage is especially important

Two other demographic dimensions affect spending patterns: age of the adults and age of any children. For example, families of adults spent more money on both food and clothing than families of the same size that also include children. However, age alone does not provide much insight into purchasing patterns. We need to know what stage of life a person is in—setting up house? raising a family? divorcing?[23]

Lifestages, a concept used by the J. Walter Thompson advertising agency in developing promotional campaigns, focuses on the very different stages that each person passes through from birth to death. Marketing Demo 5–4 elaborates on the lifestages concept and, more specifically, on the impact of a first child. The size and distinguishing characteristics of the nine segments into which Canada's adult population can be divided are also discussed. Each of the nine groups has its own spending pattern, which must be taken into consideration when developing a targeted marketing mix. Consider, for example, the very significant variations in the marketplace behaviour of three key lifestages segments—young couples, young parents, and empty nesters. Each group has different spending patterns. Marketers must take this into consideration when developing a marketing mix for particular segments.

YOUNG COUPLES In the past, this group had a transitory phase of three to five years, but due to delayed marriages and childbirth a person may remain in this stage for 10 to 15 years. Young couples live for today, and they like to spend money. They do not automatically buy the brand their parents bought. They look for products that work and they'll quickly try something else that promises to be better than what they are currently using. This group more than any other is on their guard against being ripped off, so firms must be careful to deliver what is promised. However, when a firm can deliver, they are willing to pay extra for what they recognize as a good product.

YOUNG PARENTS The birth of a child brings this group face to face with the inevitability of increasingly scarce resources—both economic and environmental. To this group, the company behind the product is as important as the product itself. These new parents are older, better educated, and more experienced than their predecessors a generation ago. They understand that large corporations have an influence and a role in society beyond the products they make.

Marketing Demo 5-4

J. Walter Thompson's Lifestages

SINGLES: 28% OF CANADIAN ADULTS

At home singles—59% male

- 44% are in school.
- 42% have full-time employment.
- Are a group in transition who tend to live for today.
- Are a difficult audience to reach.

Spend on entertainment and leisure products.

Starting out singles—65% male

- Are financially independent, establishing credit cards and consolidating loans.
- A time of intense experimentation and indulgence.
- Reality and responsibility force rapid maturation.

Spend on entertainment and furnishings for new residences.

Mature singles—59% males

- Are a growing group, as Canadians wait longer to marry, more never marry, and divorces are more common.
- Live leisure-oriented lifestyles.

Spend on their homes/apartments.

Left alone singles—76% female, older than mature singles

- Are surprisingly healthy and relatively happy, with a positive self-image.
- Concerned about health.
- Not very status-conscious, non aspiring.

Spend on necessities, small self-indulgences.

COUPLES: 26% OF CANADIAN ADULTS

Young couples

- Are the happiest of all groups.
- High in self-esteem, with their lives revolving around spouse and work.

Spend on gift buying and purchase of home furnishings (fed by two cheques).

Empty Nesters

- Are relatively carefree.
- Materially well off.
- Enjoy their kids in a different way, no longer making sacrifices.

Spend on trips, classes, eating out, gifts for grandchildren and convenience-oriented appliances.

PARENTS: 47% OF CANADIAN ADULTS

Young Parents

- With children under 12, are driven by the needs of young children, which is a shift from being focussed on themselves.
- Most are juggling parenthood and careers.
- Concerned about the environment and value for money.

Spend on children and home entertainment.

Mature parents—the Boomers

- With more people waiting to have kids, this group is getting older.
- Are blessed with children moving into adolescence, so kids are their biggest worry.
- Fears include drugs/environment.
- More time for new hobbies, entertainment.

Spend on their children, new leisure activities.

Single parents—80% are women

- Are worriers and price shoppers.
- The most dominated by their children.
- Tend to have low self-images.

Spend on the essentials, since they have difficulty making ends meet.[24]

The consumption patterns of this group are driven by the needs of their children. These children make a great many financial, emotional, housing, and logistical demands on their parents. These constraints are compounded by the time limitations imposed by an increasingly necessary two-paycheque household.

EMPTY NESTERS This group represents a second life, not a fleeting hazy few golden years. The empty nesters are composed of aging baby boomers who fully intend to carry on spending. They spend more time than the average person taking vacations, shopping for pleasure, attending arts and cultural events, and going out to dinner, movies, and bars. They are financially well off, as half of them are still working. Their home is paid for, they are no longer sacrificing for others, and they like to spend much of their money on big-ticket items both for themselves and as gifts for their family. Price ceases to have the importance it used to have because this is the time for which they have saved all their lives.

Questions and Problems

1. Discuss how slower population growth (especially the smaller number of young people) will affect businesses in your local community.
2. Discuss the impact of our aging culture on marketing strategy planning.
3. Some demographic characteristics are likely to be more important than others in determining market potential. For each of the following characteristics, identify two products for which this characteristic is *most* important: (a) size of geographic area, (b) population, (c) income, and (d) stage of life cycle.
4. Name three specific examples (specific products or brands, not just product categories) illustrating how demand will differ by geographic location and urban–rural location.
5. Explain how the continuing mobility of consumers as well as the development of big metropolitan areas should affect strategic market planning in the future. Be sure to consider the impact on the four Ps.
6. Explain how redistribution of income has affected marketing planning thus far. Then discuss its likely impact in the future.
7. Explain why the concept of the Census Metropolitan Area (CMA) was developed. Is it the most useful breakdown for retailers?

Suggested cases

3 Blue Metropolis

8 Diego's

When you finish this chapter, you should:

- Understand the economic-buyer model of buyer behaviour.
- Understand how psychological variables affect an individual's buying behaviour.
- Understand how social influences affect an individual's and household's buying behaviour.
- See why the purchase situation has an effect on consumer behaviour.
- Know how time relates to consumer product use.
- Know how consumers use problem-solving processes.
- Have some feel for how a consumer handles all the behavioural variables and incoming stimuli.
- Understand the important new terms (shown in orange).

Chap. six

Behavioural Dimensions of the Consumer Market

They are Tweenies, hear them roar.

From their glitter-polished nails and platform running shoes topped by flair jeans that hang just so on gals, to the de rigeur Hilfiger duds for cool dudes, this group of not-quite-teen boys and girls is the latest darling of the advertising age.

There are 2.4 million of them in Canada, aged nine to 14. And they have an estimated buying power worth an astonishing $1.4 billion annually. According to children's cable channel YTV, the only company which has done extensive market research into tweens, that $1.4 billion represents just the kids' money, cash from birthdays, holidays, babysitting income or allowance. The average allowance, YTV found, is $6 a week.

"This doesn't represent the (buying) influence they exert on their parents," says YTV director of research Julie Look, adding what parents shell out for "gotta-have-it" fashions, or what they spend on snacks, meals out or entertainment, all of which can be influenced by tweens, is on top of that.

Small wonder advertisers, retailers, manufacturers and marketers have recently discovered tweens and begun campaigns targeted just at them.

Nancy Dennis may be the smartest of them all. The 41-year-old retailer opened Ch!ckaboom last November, a store dedicated to the celebration of girl power and the explosion in the tween market. Dubbed "an adventure playground where girls . . . can hang out, have fun and go nuts shopping," the colorful store has doubled its sales each month since opening by catering to the fashion dreams of tweens as young as five.

Dennis decided that unlike other children's retailers, Ch!ckaboom would target the tween, not the one who's most likely paying, the parents.

"That's dramatically different from most children's wear stores and that's the way of the future, says Dennis.

The shopping adventure includes cool clothes, Jewel on the stereo, a book section, wild colors and designs and a fake pony-hide nail polish bar, where tweens experiment with a rainbow of glittery shades.

"It's a cool store," says Emma, 9, as she poses in a trendy camouflage skirt and mesh top.

Shopping at kids' stores often yields dresses that are "too poofy, or too long," adds her sister, Molly, 11. Kids' clothes often aren't cool, she explains, and the fashionable garments in teen stores are too big.

Tweens are loyal to the brands they like. They want quality, a name and a specific image, agree Look and Dennis. And, adds Look, they don't care if they're in lockstep with everybody else—what's important is that they have the same outfits the cool kids have.

"There is no sign that this is a short-term trend," says Kathie Shearer, senior vice-president and media director of TA Media, a media management company.

Shearer points to the cosmetic and personal-care markets, which are both targeting tweens with products like deodorants and shampoo just for them.

While marketers have always aimed products and advertising at kids under 17, the tweens began emerging as a powerful force in recent years. Not little kids, not teens, they were individuals, and companies couldn't ignore them. They stand alone in their tastes, they know exactly what they want to wear, eat and listen to. And they have money. Lots of money.

Kathleen McDonnell, kids and pop culture expert and author of *Kid Culture* (Second Story Press), says she suspects tween power has been around for quite some time. We're just getting around to recognizing and cultivating it.

"We haven't paid much attention to them before. We're concerned about young children and teenagers, and then there is this whole middle group and they have all of a sudden become visible," says McDonnell. "How did they become visible? By being marketed to."

Source: Linda Barnard, "Have Allowance, Will Buy," *Toronto Sun,* March 26, 1998, p. 74.

Consumer behaviour—Why do you buy what you buy?

Specific consumer behaviours vary a great deal for different products and from one target market to the next. That point has been highlighted in the opening discussion of the tween market. In today's global markets, the variations are countless. That makes it impractical to try to catalogue all the detailed possibilities for every different market situation. But there are *general* behavioural principles—frameworks—that marketing managers can apply to learn more about their specific target markets. In this chapter, we'll explore some of the thinking from economics, psychology, sociology, and the other behavioural disciplines. Our approach focuses on developing your skills in working with these frameworks.

The behavioural sciences help you understand the buying process

Most economists assume that consumers are **economic buyers**—people who know all the facts and logically compare choices in terms of cost and value received to get the greatest satisfaction from spending their time and money.

This view assumes that economic needs guide most consumer behaviour. **Economic needs** are concerned with making the best use of a consumer's time and money—as the consumer judges it. Some consumers look for the lowest price. Others will pay extra for convenience. And others may weigh price and quality for the best value. Some economic needs are economy of purchase or use, convenience, efficiency in operation or use, dependability in use, and improvement of earnings.

Clearly, marketing managers must be alert to new ways to appeal to economic needs. Most consumers appreciate firms that offer them improved value for the money they spend. But improved value does not just mean offering lower and lower prices. For example, many consumers face a "poverty of time." So carefully planned Place decisions can make it easier and faster for customers to make a purchase. And products that are designed to work better, or require less service, or last longer, are worth more to the consumer.

In many purchase decisions, the economic value that a purchase offers a customer is important. But most buyer behaviour is not as simple as the economic-buyer model suggests. A product that one person sees as a good value—and is eager to

Exhibit 6-1 A Model of Buyer Behaviour

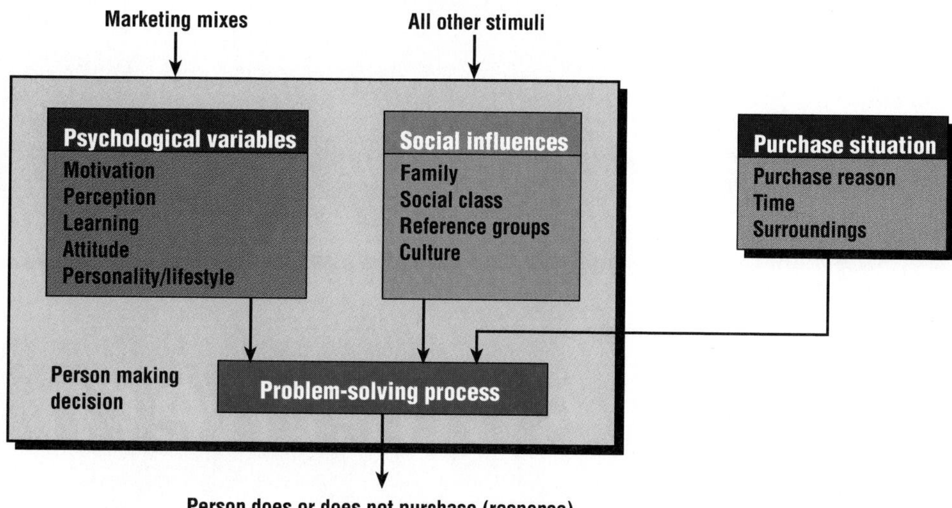

buy—will be of no interest to someone else. So we can't expect to understand buying behaviour without taking a broader view.

How we will view consumer behaviour

Many behavioural dimensions influence consumers. Let's try to combine these dimensions into a model of how consumers make decisions. Exhibit 6–1 shows that psychological variables, social influences, and the purchase situation all affect a person's buying behaviour. We'll discuss these topics in the next few pages. Then we'll expand the model to include the consumer problem-solving process.

Psychological influences within an individual

Everybody is motivated by needs and wants. **Needs** are the basic forces that motivate a person to do something. Some needs involve a person's physical well-being, others, the individual's self-view and relationship with others. Needs are more basic than wants. **Wants** are "needs" that are learned during a person's life. For example, everyone needs water or some kind of liquid, but some people also have learned to want Evian.

When a need is not satisfied, it may lead to a drive. The need for liquid, for example, leads to a thirst drive. A **drive** is a strong stimulus that encourages action to reduce a need. Drives are internal—they are the reasons behind certain behaviour patterns. In marketing, a product purchase results from a drive to satisfy some need.

Some critics imply that marketers can somehow manipulate consumers to buy products against their will. But marketing managers can't create internal drives. Most marketing managers realize that trying to get consumers to act against their will is a waste of time. Instead, a good marketing manager studies what consumer drives, needs, and wants already exist and how they can be satisfied better.

Consumers seek benefits

Each one of us is a bundle of needs and wants. Exhibit 6–2 lists some important needs that might motivate a person to some action. This list, of course, is not complete. But thinking about such needs can help you see what *benefits* consumers might seek from a marketing mix.

When a marketing manager defines a product-market, the needs may be quite specific. For example, the food need might be as specific as wanting a thick-crust pepperoni pizza—delivered to your door hot and ready to eat.

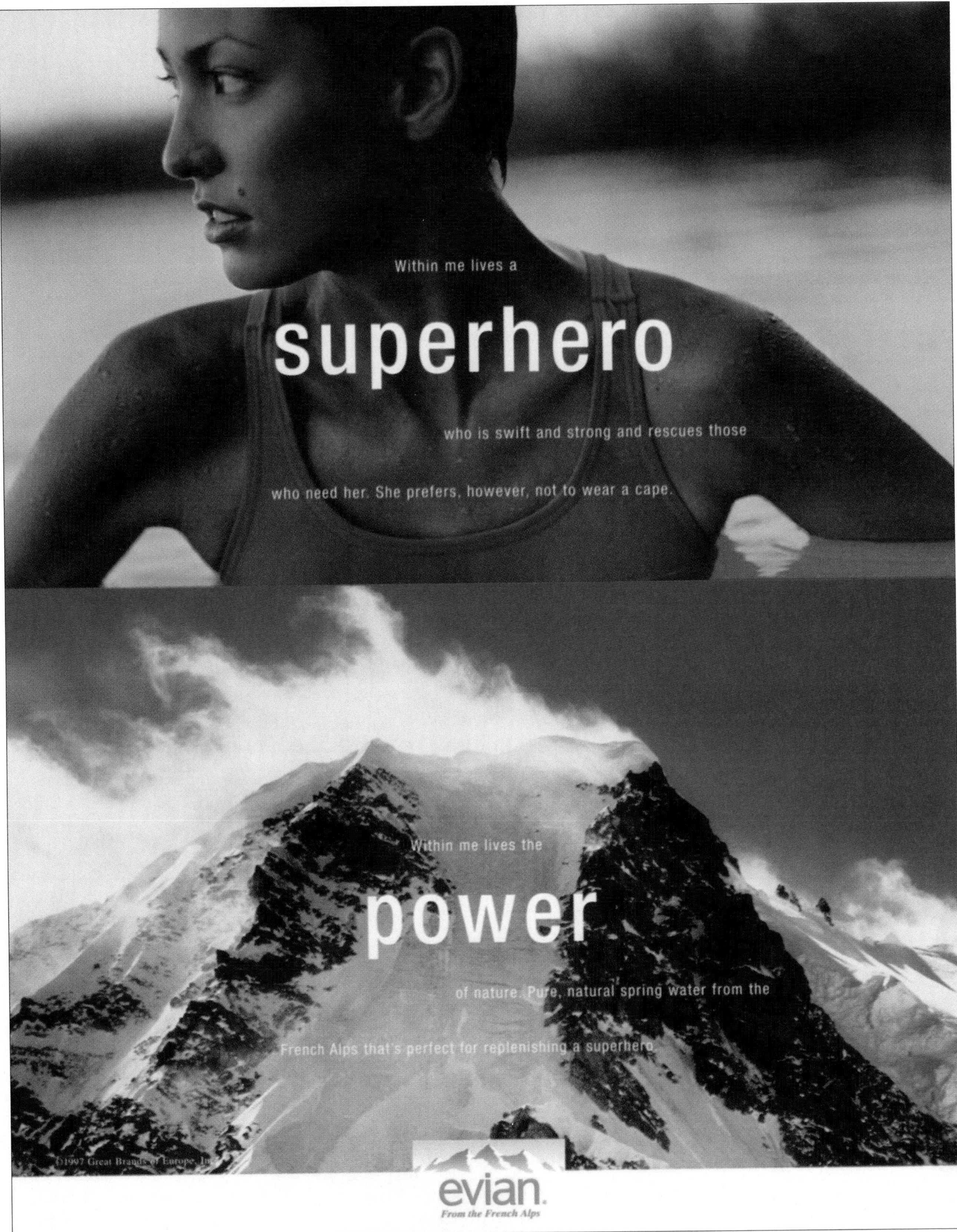

Evian appeals to consumers' "wants."

Exhibit 6-2 Possible Needs Motivating a Person to Some Action

TYPES OF NEEDS	SPECIFIC EXAMPLES			
Physiological needs	Hunger	Thirst	Activity	Sleep
	Sex	Body elimination	Self-preservation	Warmth/coolness
	Rest			
Psychological needs	Aggression	Curiosity	Being responsible	Dominance
	Family preservation	Imitation	Independence	Love
	Nurturing	Order	Personal fulfillment	Playing/competition
	Playing/relaxing	Power	Pride	Self-expression
	Self-identification	Tenderness		
Desire for . . .	Acceptance	Achievement	Acquisition	Affection
	Affiliation	Appreciation	Beauty	Companionship
	Comfort	Fun	Distance/"space"	Distinctiveness
	Esteem	Fame	Happiness	Identification
	Knowledge	Prestige	Pleasure	Recognition
	Respect	Retaliation	Self-satisfaction	Sociability
	Status	Sympathy	Variety	
Freedom from . . .	Fear	Depression	Discomfort	Anxiety
	Pain	Imitation	Loss	Illness
	Harm	Ridicule	Sadness	Pressure

Several needs at the same time

Some psychologists argue that a person may have several reasons for buying—at the same time. Maslow is well known for his five-level hierarchy of needs. We will discuss a similar four-level hierarchy that is easier to apply to consumer behaviour. Exhibit 6–3 illustrates the four levels, along with an advertising slogan showing how a company has tried to appeal to each need. The lowest-level needs are physiological. Then come safety, social, and personal needs. As a study aid, think of the PSSP needs.[1]

Physiological needs are concerned with biological needs—food, drink, rest, and sex. **Safety needs** are concerned with protection and physical well-being (perhaps involving health, food, medicine, and exercise). **Social needs** are concerned with love, friendship, status, and esteem—things that involve a person's interaction with others. **Personal needs,** on the other hand, are concerned with an individual's need for personal satisfaction—unrelated to what others think or do. Examples include self-esteem, accomplishment, fun, freedom, and relaxation.

Motivation theory suggests that we never reach a state of complete satisfaction. As soon as we get our lower-level needs reasonably satisfied, those at higher levels become more dominant. This explains why marketing efforts targeted at affluent consumers in advanced economies often focus on higher-level needs. It also explains why these approaches may be useless in parts of the world where consumers' basic needs are not being met.

It is important to remember, however, that a particular product may satisfy more than one need at the same time. In fact, most consumers try to fill a *set* of needs rather than just one need or another in sequence.

Discovering which specific consumer needs to satisfy may require careful analysis. Consider, for example, the lowly vegetable peeler. Marketing managers for OXO International realized that many people, especially young children and senior citizens, have trouble gripping the handle of a typical peeler. OXO redesigned the peeler with a bigger handle and also coated the handle with dishwasher-safe rubber. This makes cleanup more convenient—and the sharp peeler safer to use when the grip is wet. The attractive grip also appeals to consumers who get personal satisfaction from cooking—and who want to impress their guests.[2]

Exhibit 6-3 The PSSP Hierarchy of Needs

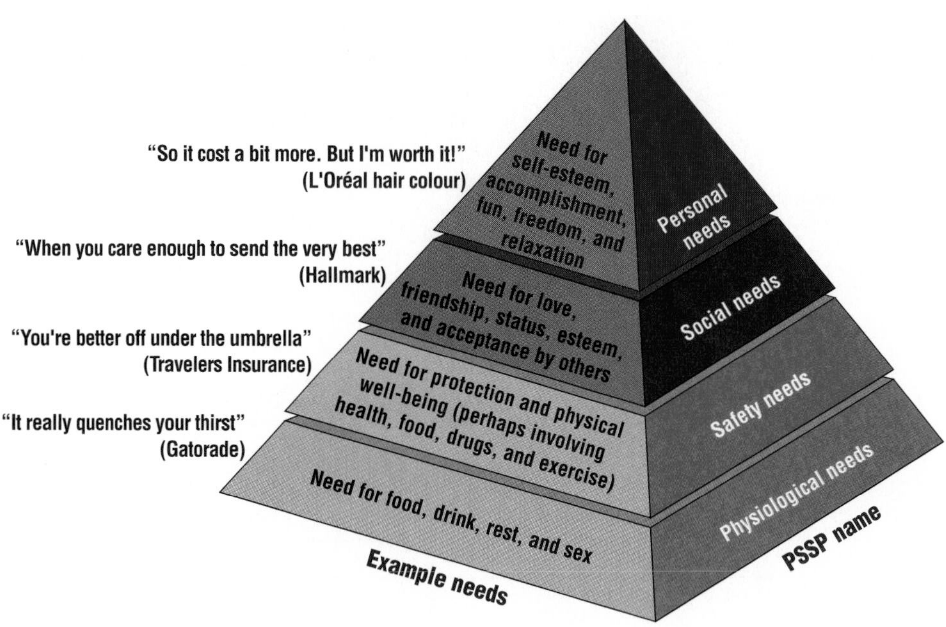

Perception determines what consumers see and feel

Consumers select varying ways to meet their needs, sometimes because of differences in **perception**—how we gather and interpret information from the world around us.

We are constantly bombarded by stimuli—ads, products, stores—yet we may not hear or see anything. This is because we apply the following selective processes:

1. **Selective exposure.** Our eyes and minds seek out and notice only information that interests us.
2. **Selective perception.** We screen out or modify ideas, messages, and information that conflict with previously learned attitudes and beliefs.
3. **Selective retention.** We remember only what we want to remember.

These selective processes help explain why some people are not affected by some advertising—even offensive advertising. They just don't see or remember it!

Our needs affect these selective processes. And current needs receive more attention. For example, Michelin tire retailers advertise some sale in the newspaper almost weekly. Most of the time we don't even notice these ads—until we need new tires. Only then do we tune in to Michelin's ads.

Marketers are interested in these selective processes because they affect how target consumers get and retain information. In other words, marketers are interested in how consumers *learn.*

Learning determines responses

Learning is a change in a person's thought processes caused by prior experience. Learning is often based on direct experience: a little girl tastes her first Dairy Queen cone, and learning occurs! Learning may also be based on associations. When you watch an ad that shows other people enjoying Dairy Queen sundaes, you may conclude that you'd like one too. Consumer learning may result from things that marketers do, or it may result from stimuli that have nothing to do with marketing. Either way, almost all consumer behaviour is learned.[3] For example, Marketing Demo 6–1 shows that marketers of hand sanitizers are trying to make certain that Canadian consumers "learn" to use their product.

Marketing Demo 6-1

Hand Sanitizers Tap into Growing Germ Concern

Germs everywhere, beware. Canadian consumers have your elimination on their minds and marketers are lining up to supply the ammunition.

In the last two months alone, two companies—Belvedere International of Mississauga, Ont. and GOJO Industries of Kuyahoga Falls, Ohio—have launched clear gel "hand sanitizers" in the Canadian market. And with the likes of Reckitt & Colman and Colgate-Palmolive already rolling out similar products to challenge GOJO's Purrell in the U.S., more are expected to follow here faster than you can spell Escherichia coli.

While Canadians have been snapping up germ-killing soaps in droves recently—the antibacterial liquid hand soap category, for instance, grew a whopping 50% to $6.2 million for the 52 weeks ending Jan. 31—these hand sanitizers are a completely new category. Primarily alcohol-based, the gels don't require water like soaps do, and they let consumers "combat germs and help with their hand hygiene on the go," says Rachel Halle, market specialist at GOJO. Purell, for one, claims to kill "99.9% of most common germs in just 15 seconds."

GOJO, which launched Purell in the U.S. in 1996, projects that the market for hand sanitizers will eventually grow to US$100 million south of the border. It brought Purell north in February primarily because drug store chains like PharmaPlus and Shoppers Drug Mart were clamoring for it.

Cathy Wysocki, product manager at Belvedere, which began shipping its OneStep hand sanitizer this month, says germs are "a growing area of concern. There's more and more being written about the flu and colds and how they can be transferred . . . by the hand," she says. Indeed, Purell's PR materials cite a hand hygiene poll conducted by The Strategic Council that reveals 48% of Canadians wash their hands primarily to "kill germs and bacteria."

Alan Middleton, a visiting professor at Rutgers University in Newark and New Brunswick, N.J., agrees that there is an increased concern about germs and bacteria, but with one caveat: "What I deeply suspect it is all about is this search for trying to create some kind of difference for our brands."

At the moment, the main task for GOJO and Belvedere is to educate consumers about the use of the sanitizers, which represents an entirely new behavior. While GOJO is primarily using PR for this purpose—as it did in the U.S.—Belvedere is planning magazine ads and a free-standing insert for the summer/fall period. "The education process is ongoing," Wysocki says.

Source: Lara Mills, *Marketing Magazine,* March 23, 1998, p. 4.

Experts describe a number of steps in the learning process. We've already discussed the idea of a drive as a strong stimulus that encourages action. Depending on the **cues**—products, signs, ads, and other stimuli in the environment—an individual chooses some specific response. A **response** is an effort to satisfy a drive. The specific response chosen depends on the cues and the person's past experience.

Reinforcement of the learning process occurs when the response is followed by satisfaction—that is, reduction in the drive. Reinforcement strengthens the relationship between the cue and the response. And it may lead to a similar response the next time the drive occurs. Repeated reinforcement leads to development of a habit, making the individual's decision process routine. Exhibit 6–4 shows the relationships between the important variables in the learning process.

Exhibit 6-4
The Learning Process

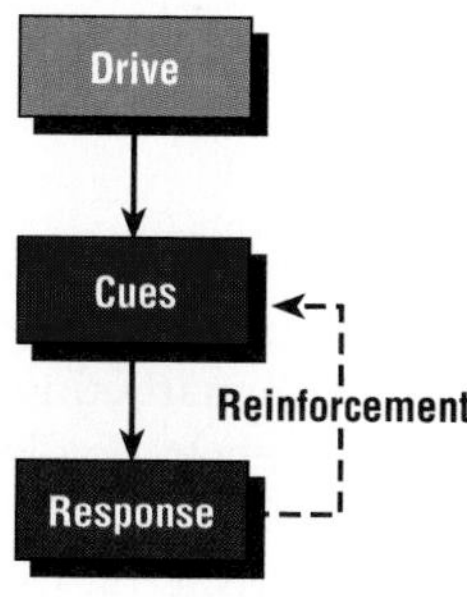

The learning process can be illustrated by a thirsty person. The thirst *drive* could be satisfied in a variety of ways. But if the person happened to walk past a vending machine and saw a 7Up sign—a *cue*—then he might satisfy the drive with a *response*—buying a 7Up. If the experience is satisfactory, positive *reinforcement* will occur, and our friend may be quicker to satisfy this drive in the same way in the future. This emphasizes the importance of developing good products that live up to the promises of the firm's advertising. People can learn to like or dislike 7Up—reinforcement and learning work both ways. Unless marketers satisfy their customers, they must constantly try to attract new ones to replace the dissatisfied ones who don't come back.

Positive cues help a marketing mix

Sometimes marketers try to identify cues or images that have positive associations from some other situation and relate them to their marketing mix. Many people associate the smell of lemons with a fresh, natural cleanliness. So companies often add lemon scent to household cleaning products—like Pledge furniture polish—because it has these associations. Similarly, some shampoos and deodorants are formulated to be clear and packaged in clear bottles because some consumers associate that look with being natural and pure.

Many needs are culturally learned

Many needs are culturally (or socially) learned. The need for food, for instance, may lead to many specific food wants. Many Japanese enjoy sushi (raw fish), and their children learn to like it. Sushi has some popularity in Canada, but it is not the favourite meal of most Canadians.

Some critics argue that marketing efforts encourage people to spend money on learned wants totally unrelated to any basic need. For example, Europeans are less concerned about body odor and buy fewer deodorants than North Americans, who spend millions of dollars on such products. Advertising says that using Ban deodorant "takes the worry out of being close." But is marketing activity the cause of the difference in the two cultures? Most research says that advertising can't convince buyers of something contrary to their basic attitudes.

Attitudes relate to buying

An **attitude** is a person's point of view toward something. The "something" may be a product, an advertisement, a salesperson, a firm, or an idea. Attitudes are an important topic for marketers because attitudes affect the selective processes, learning, and buying decisions.

Because attitudes involve liking or disliking, they have some action implications. Beliefs are not so action-oriented. A **belief** is a person's opinion about something. Beliefs may help shape a consumer's attitudes but they don't necessarily involve any liking or disliking. It is possible to have a belief—say, that Listerine tastes like medicine—without really caring what it tastes like.

In an attempt to relate attitude more closely to purchasing behaviour, some marketers stretch the attitude concept to include consumer "preferences" or "intention to buy." Managers who must forecast how much of their brand customers will buy are particularly interested in the intention to buy. Forecasts would be easier if attitudes were good predictors of intentions to buy. Unfortunately, the relationships usually are not that simple. A person may have positive attitudes toward Jacuzzi whirlpool bathtubs but have no intention of buying one.

Working with existing attitudes

Marketers generally try to understand the attitudes of their potential customers and work with them. It's more economical to work with consumer attitudes than to try to change them. Attitudes tend to be enduring. Changing present attitudes—especially negative ones—is sometimes necessary. But that's probably the most difficult job marketers face.[4]

Meeting expectations

Attitudes and beliefs sometimes combine to form an **expectation**—an outcome or event that a person anticipates or looks forward to. Consumer expectations often focus on the benefits or value that the consumer expects from a firm's marketing mix. This is an important issue for marketers because a consumer is likely to be dissatisfied if his or her expectations are not met. For example, if you are hungry and stop at a fast-food restaurant for a hamburger, you are likely to be dissatisfied if the service is slow, even if the burger tastes great.

A key point here is that consumers may evaluate a product not just on how well it performs but on how it performs *relative to their expectations.* A product that otherwise might get high marks from a satisfied consumer may be a disappointment if there's a gap be-

Ethical Dimensions

Issues May Arise

Part of the marketing job is to inform and persuade consumers about a firm's offering. An ethical issue sometimes arises, however, when consumers have *inaccurate* beliefs. For example, many consumers are confused about which foods are really healthy. Marketers for a number of food companies have been criticized because their packaging and promotion take advantage of inaccurate consumer perceptions about the meaning of the words *lite* or *low-fat*. A firm's lite donuts may have less fat or fewer calories than its other donuts—but that doesn't mean that the donut is *low* in fat or calories. Similarly, promotion of a "children's cold formula" may play off of parents' fears that adult medicines are too strong—even though the basic ingredients in the children's formula are the same and only the dosage is different.

Marketers must also be careful about promotion that might encourage false beliefs, even if the advertising is not explicitly misleading. For example, ads for Ultra Slim-Fast low-fat beverage don't claim that all those who buy the product will lose all the weight they want, but some critics argue that the advertising gives that impression.[5]

tween what the consumer expects and what the consumer gets. Promotion that overpromises can create this problem. Finding the right balance, however, can be difficult. Consider the challenge faced by marketing managers for Van Heusen shirts. In 1994, Van Heusen came up with a new way to treat its shirts so that they looked better when they came out of the wash than previous wash-and-wear shirts. Van Heusen promoted these shirts as "wrinkle-free," and the label showed an iron stuffed in a garbage can. Most people agreed that the new shirt was an improvement. Even so, consumers who bought a shirt expecting it to look as crisp as if it had just been ironed were disappointed.[6]

Personality affects how people see things

Many researchers study how personality affects people's behaviour, but the results have generally been disappointing to marketers. A trait like neatness can be associated with users of certain types of products, like cleaning materials. But marketing managers have not found a way to use personality in strategic market planning.[7] As a result, they've stopped focusing on personality measures borrowed from psychologists and instead have developed lifestyle analyses. More detail on lifestyle analysis is presented in Chapter 8.

Social influences affect consumer behaviour

We've been discussing some of the ways that needs, attitudes, and other psychological variables influence the buying process. Now we'll see that these variables, and the buying process, are also usually affected by relationships with other people. We'll look at how the individual interacts with family, social class, and other groups who may have influence.

Who is the real decision maker?

Relationships with other family members influence many aspects of consumer behaviour. We saw specific examples of this in Chapter 5 when we considered the effects of the family life cycle on family spending patterns. Family members may also share many attitudes and values, consider each other's opinions, and divide various buying tasks. Historically, most marketers in North America targeted the wife as the family purchasing agent. Now, with more women in the workforce and with night and weekend shopping becoming more popular, men and older children do more shopping and decision making. In other countries, family roles vary. For example, in Norway women still do most of the family shopping.

Although only one family member may go to the store and make a specific purchase, when planning marketing strategy it's important to know who else may be involved. Other family members may have influenced the decision or really decided what to buy. Still others may use the product.

You don't have to watch much Saturday morning TV to see that Kellogg's and General Mills know this. Cartoon characters like Cap'n Crunch and Tony the Tiger tell kids about the goodies found in certain cereal packages, and urge them to remind Dad or Mom to pick up that brand on their next trip to the store. But, as illustrated in the Tween case at the beginning of this chapter, kids also influence grown-up purchases. Surveys show that kids often have a big say in a family's choice of products such as apparel, cars, electronics, and health and beauty aids.

Family considerations

A husband and wife may jointly agree on many important purchases, but sometimes they may have strong personal preferences. However, such individual preferences may change if the other spouse has different priorities. One may want to take a family vacation to Disneyland while the other may want a new RCA video recorder and Sony large-screen TV. The actual outcome in such a situation is unpredictable. The preferences of one spouse may change because of affection for the other, or because of the other's power and influence.

Buying responsibility and influence vary greatly depending on the product and the family. A marketer trying to plan a strategy will find it helpful to research the specific target market. Remember, many buying decisions are made jointly, and thinking only about who actually buys the product can misdirect the marketing strategy.[8]

Social class affects attitudes, values, and buying

Up to now, we have been concerned with the individual and the way individuals relate to their families. Now let's consider how society looks at an individual and perhaps the family, in terms of social class. A **social class** is a group of people who have approximately equal social position as viewed by others in the society.

Almost every society has some social class structure. The Canadian class system is far less rigid than in most countries. Children start out in the same social class as their parents, but they can move to a different social class depending on their education and the work they do.

Marketers want to know what buyers in various social classes are like. Simple approaches for measuring social class groupings are based on a person's *occupation, education,* and *type and location of housing.* By using marketing research surveys or studying available census data, marketers can get a feel for the social class of a target market.

Note that income level is not included in this list. There is *some* general relationship between income level and social class. But the income levels of people within the same social class can vary greatly, and people with the same amount of income may be in different social classes.

To develop better marketing strategies, marketing managers need to understand the differences among social classes. Although we use traditional technical terms like *upper, middle,* and *lower,* a word of warning is in order: the terms may seem to imply "superior" and "inferior." But in sociological and marketing usage, no value judgment is intended. We can't say that any one class is "better" or "happier" than another.

The size of Canadian social classes

Dividing a nation's population into distinctly labelled social classes is no easy task. Would-be marketers needn't concern themselves with the specifics of the various ways this has been done in Canada or the United States. The most recent Canadian effort places primary reliance on occupation and education. These data,

Exhibit 6–5 Characteristics and Attitudes of Middle and Lower Classes

MIDDLE CLASSES	LOWER CLASSES
Plan and save for the future	Live for the present
Analyze alternatives	"Feel" what is "best"
Understand how the world works	Have simplistic ideas about how things work
Feel they have opportunities	Feel controlled by the world
Willing to take risks	Play it safe
Confident about decision making	Want help with decision making
Want long-run quality or value	Want short-run satisfaction

from the early 1980s, divide the Canadian consumer public into four major but further divisible social strata: the upper classes (11 percent of the total and divisible in turn into very small upper-upper and lower-upper classes and a considerably larger upper-middle class); the middle class (28 percent of the total); the working class (41 percent); and a lower class (20 percent of the total and divided in turn into upper-lower and lower-lower classes of approximately equal size).[9]

Differences in attitudes and behaviour

The seven Canadian social classes differ in terms of typical occupational and educational profiles, social and geographic horizons, consumption patterns, and personal values. Detailed comparisons reveal that the old saying, "A rich man is simply a poor man with money," isn't true. Given the same income as middle-class people, persons belonging to the lower classes handle themselves and their money very differently. The various classes shop at different stores. They prefer different treatment from salespeople. They buy different brands of products, even when prices are about the same. And they have different spending and saving attitudes. Some of these differences are shown in Exhibit 6–5.

The upper middle class as a case study

The upper-middle class (about 9 percent of the Canadian population) consists of successful professionals, owners of small businesses, and managers of large corporations. These people are concerned about their quality of life. They view their purchases as symbols of success, so they want quality products. They also want to be seen as socially responsible. They support the arts and are community-minded. They are ambitious for their children and, in general, are more future-oriented than lower-class groups. Exhibit 6–6 provides additional information on the upper middle class's consumption behaviour. The information from this and similar descriptions of the other Canadian social classes can be of great value to marketers.

Reference groups are relevant, too

A **reference group** is the people to whom an individual looks when forming attitudes about a particular topic. People normally have several reference groups for different topics. Some they meet face to face. Others they may just wish to imitate. In either case, they may take values from these reference groups and make buying decisions based on what the group might accept.

We're always making comparisons between ourselves and others. So reference groups are more important when others will be able to "see" which product or brand we're using. Influence is stronger for products that relate to status in the group. For one group, owning a swimming pool may be a sign of "having arrived." A consumer's decision to buy or not buy a swimming pool may depend on the opinions of others in that consumer's reference group.[10]

Exhibit 6-6 Consumption Behaviour of Canada's Upper Middle Class

1. Seek out genuine educational experiences for self and children (drama, piano, ballet, Suzuki violin lessons, museums, international student exchanges).
2. Admire those who can speak many languages and often try to learn languages themselves.
3. Believe in high culture (ballet, theatre, opera, art galleries, museums).
4. Participate in sports often associated with prestige and serenity, and those that deliver vigorous exercise (sailing, gliding, horseback riding, golf, tennis, squash, cycling).
5. In clothing, prefer organic materials (cotton, wool, silk, leather) and resist wearing synthetics, such as polyester.
6. Preferred colours tend to be navy blue and pastels. Like preppy Ralph Lauren fashions.
7. More willing to experiment with new dishes (foreign and exotic foods, haute cuisine, ethnic restaurants, and the foreign food and ingredients counters at specialty stores).
8. Generally, are more confident shoppers and decision makers than other classes and more skilful at evaluating products.

Reaching the opinion leaders who are buyers

An **opinion leader** is a person who influences others. Opinion leaders aren't necessarily wealthier or better educated. And opinion leaders on one subject aren't necessarily opinion leaders on another. Capable homemakers with large families may be consulted for advice on family budgeting. Young women may be opinion leaders for new clothing styles and cosmetics. Each social class tends to have its own opinion leaders. Some marketing mixes aim especially at these people, since their opinions affect others and research shows that they are involved in many product-related discussions with "followers." Favourable word-of-mouth publicity from opinion leaders can really help a marketing mix. But the opposite is also true. If opinion leaders aren't satisfied, they're likely to talk about it and influence others.[11]

Culture surrounds the other influences

Culture is the whole set of beliefs, attitudes, and ways of doing things of a reasonably homogeneous set of people. In Chapters 3 and 5, we looked at the broad impact of culture.

People within major cultural groupings tend to be more similar in outlook and behaviour. But sometimes it is useful to think of subcultures within such groupings. For example, within the North American culture, there are various religious and ethnic subcultures. Also, different cultural forces tend to prevail in different regions of the continent.

From a target marketing point of view, a marketing manager will probably want to aim at people within one culture or subculture. When a firm is developing strategies for two cultures, it often needs two different marketing plans.[12]

The attitudes and beliefs we usually associate with culture tend to change slowly. So once marketers develop a good understanding of the culture they are planning for, they should concentrate on the more dynamic variables discussed earlier.

Culture varies in international markets

Planning strategies that consider cultural differences in international markets can be even harder. Each foreign market may need to be treated as a separate market with its own submarkets. In international markets, ignoring cultural differences or assuming that they are not important almost guarantees failure.

For example, when marketing managers for Procter & Gamble first tried to sell the North American version of Cheer to Japanese consumers, they promoted it as

JIMMY. 365 DAYS A YEAR.

The name's Jimmy. And Jimbo or Big Jim are more fitting given its truck heritage. But now with its redesign, this GMC is as comfortable on the way to the ballet as it is to the chalet.

Inside the SLT 4x4 model shown here, you're treated to luxuries like leather seats, electronic climate controls and a smooth quiet ride.

Despite being worthy of the name James, this Jimmy is no prissy luxury car. And its 190 horsepower Vortec engine, shift-on-the-fly 4-wheel drive, and up to 5000-pound towing capacity make sure of that.

Visit your local Pontiac/Buick/GMC dealer for a test drive. And experience this GMC's style and strength for yourself. We know you'll be so at ease with it, you'll prefer to call your sport utility Jimmy.

For more information, visit our web site at www.gmcanada.com™ or call 1-800-GM-DRIVE.

SO REFINED, YOU'LL BE TEMPTED TO CALL IT JAMES.

www.gmcanada.com is a trademark of General Motors Corporation.

What social class would you associate with this GMC Jimmy ad?

an effective all-temperature laundry detergent. But many Japanese wash clothes in cold tap water or leftover bath water, so they don't care about all-temperature washing. In addition, Cheer didn't make suds when it was used with the fabric softeners popular with Japanese consumers. When P&G's marketing managers discovered these problems, they changed Cheer so it wouldn't be affected by the fabric softeners. They also changed Cheer ads to promise superior cleaning *in cold water.* Cheer became one of P&G's best-selling products in Japan.[13]

Time and product use[14]

Decisions made regarding product purchases and product use are based in substantial part on one's perception and use of time and on how time is processed within the mind. The ideas that have been considered in this chapter are all affected by time.

Orientation—Past or future?

Consider products sold with a past orientation and horizon. These are products that will create the feeling of the good old days—for example, cookies like grandma used to make, or music of the 1950s or 1960s. Some high-tech items like the Sony Minicam are sold with a promise of letting you stay in touch with your past. In contrast to this past orientation is the future orientation of some stores and products. The suggestion is that you are buying things ahead of their time.

Activity—Alone or together?

Many products permit or encourage polychronic (doing two things at the same time) time use. The cell phone, for example, enables you to communicate while driving. A Walkman enables you to listen to music while working in the library, riding public transportation, running, or jogging.

In contrast, there are products such as Nintendo that absorb all of your attention and encourage you to do only one thing at a time. People who prefer to do one thing at a time may purchase items that create an environment in which monochronic activity is enhanced. Noise filters, for example, let individuals screen out unwanted noises that could distract from the activity at hand. Voice mail allows individuals to work uninterrupted while calls are recorded for future attention.

Processing—The importance of seasons

Many products are sold or used in cycles, depending on the seasons of the year or the weather. Back-to-school sales are anticipated by retailers and consumers alike. Gardening products and sporting goods are sold on a seasonal basis. Media ads and appropriate retail store decorations remind us (sometimes we think too early) of Valentine's Day, Mother's Day, Father's Day, Halloween, Thanksgiving, and Christmas.

Perceptions of time—How busy are you?

Perceptual time use may greatly affect the kinds of products you will consider. Those who perceive that they are perpetually time poor or overcommitted may look for products that will allow them in some way to repackage or consolidate time use. (See Marketing Demo 6–2). Those who are time rich may actually look for products that help them to use up time. For example, Internet lessons and searching the Net are increasingly popular pastimes for seniors.

Marketing Demo 6-2

Stouffer's Targets "Time Poor" Shoppers

As consumers' lives become more hectic, supermarkets are finding one of their hottest-selling categories is frozen, prepared entrees.

Last year, sales in this category soared 16%, according to ACNielsen of Markham, Ont. Stouffer's is considered the market leader with a 21% share by volume, says Leslie Chester, vice-president, meals division of Stouffer's, whose parent company is Nestlé Canada. According to Chester the Michalena brand has about 15% of the frozen entree market; Swanson, made by Campbell Soup Co., has 13%; Savarin 10%; and Heinz Co. of Canada's Weight Watcher's 5%.

Chester says dinners and entrees is the fastest growing segment of the frozen foods category because people are "time poor" and need "quick, convenient meal solutions." Stouffer's recently launched a frozen line called Pastaria, consisting of six pasta-based entrees. The line will be expanded this year, Chester says, and plans are also in the works to redesign the packaging for Stouffer's Red Box and Lean Cuisine brands.

Most of the growth in the frozen-entree market is in the single-serve products. For the year ending in March 1996, total sales of single-serve frozen entrees were $181 million, according to ACNielsen. And pasta products made up about 30% of that total.

The Pastaria line is being marketed primarily as a lunch meal, a niche that research shows is in great consumer demand, provided the retail price is in the $2 range. Chester says. Frozen entrees usually range from $2 to $4. Pastaria replaces a line called Lunch Express which was not successful because, Chester says, it was perceived as too much of a fast food.

The single-serve, frozen entree category has expanded beyond the low-calorie offerings that dominated it a few years ago to include more flavorful meals. This trend towards good-tasting frozen entrees (which includes everything from stir-frys to Italian pastas), at a low price, is what Stouffer's is playing to with the Pastaria line.

The only consumer advertising being done to support Pastaria is a direct-mail piece and in-package coupons. Chester says most of the marketing budget for the line was spent on packaging and graphics—by Russell Design of Toronto—in the hopes of persuading consumers who see it on the shelf. Russell is also redesigning the boxes for Stouffer's other two lines of frozen entrees.

A Loblaws Cos. spokesperson says the company is looking at possibly expanding its offerings in the category.

Source: Lesley Daw, *Marketing Magazine*, May 12, 1997, p. 4.

Consumers are affected by the purchase situation

Purchase reason can vary

Why a consumer makes a purchase can affect buying behaviour. For example, when you buy a pen to take notes, you might pick up an inexpensive Bic. But you might choose a Cross pen as a gift for a friend.

Time affects what happens

Time influences purchase situations. *When* consumers make a purchase—and the time they have available for shopping—will influence their behaviour. A leisurely dinner induces one sort of behaviour; grabbing a quick latte on the way to work induces another.

Surroundings affect buying, too

Surroundings can affect buying behaviour. The excitement of an auction may stimulate impulse buying. Surroundings may also discourage buying. For example, some people don't like to stand in a checkout line where others can see what they're buying—even if the other shoppers are complete strangers.

Needs, benefits sought, attitudes, motivation, and even how a consumer selects certain products all vary with the purchase situation. So different purchase situations may require different marketing mixes, even when the same target market is involved.[15]

Consumers use problem-solving processes

The variables we've discussed so far affect *what* products a consumer finally decides to purchase. Marketing managers also need to understand *how* buyers use a problem-solving process to select particular products.

Most consumers seem to use the following five-step problem-solving process:

1. Becoming aware of—or interested in—the problem.
2. Recalling and gathering information about possible solutions.
3. Evaluating alternative solutions—perhaps trying some out.
4. Deciding on the appropriate solution.
5. Evaluating the decision.[16]

Exhibit 6–7 presents an expanded version of the buyer behaviour model shown in Exhibit 6–1. Note that this exhibit integrates the problem-solving process with the whole set of variables we've been reviewing.

Exhibit 6–7 An Expanded Model of the Consumer Problem-Solving Process

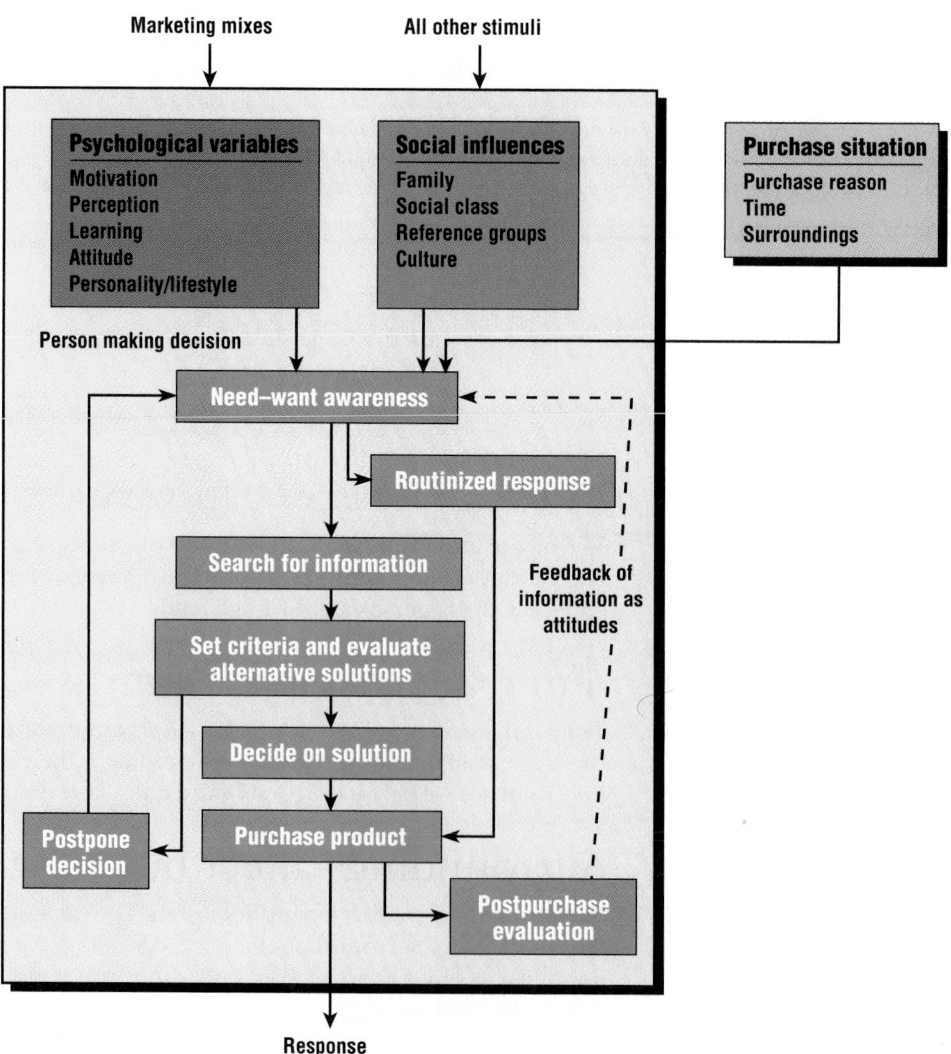

When consumers evaluate information about purchase alternatives, they may weigh differences in brands *and* in the stores where the products may be available. This can be a very complicated evaluation procedure, and depending on their choice of criteria, consumers may make seemingly irrational decisions. When convenient service is crucial, for example, a buyer may pay list price for an unexciting car from a very convenient dealer. Marketers need a way to analyze these decisions.

Grid of evaluative criteria helps

Based on studies of how consumers seek out and evaluate product information, researchers suggest that marketing managers use an evaluative grid showing features common to different products (or marketing mixes). For example, Exhibit 6–8 shows some of the features common to three different cars a consumer might consider.

The grid encourages marketing managers to view each product as a bundle of features or attributes. The pluses and minuses in Exhibit 6–8 indicate one consumer's attitude toward each feature of each car. If members of the target market don't rate a feature of the marketing manager's brand with pluses, it may indicate a problem. The manager might want to change the product to improve that feature, or perhaps use more promotion to emphasize an already acceptable feature. The consumer in Exhibit 6–8 has a minus under gas mileage for the Nissan. If the Nissan really gets better gas mileage than the other cars, promotion might focus on mileage to improve consumer attitudes toward this feature and toward the whole product.

Some consumers will reject a product if they see *one* feature as substandard, regardless of how favourably they regard the product's other features. The consumer in Exhibit 6–8 might avoid the Saab, which he saw as less than satisfactory on ease of service, even if it were superior in all other aspects. In other instances, a consumer's overall attitude toward the product might be such that a few good features could make up for some shortcomings. The comfortable interior of the Toyota (Exhibit 6–8) might make up for less exciting styling, especially if the consumer viewed comfort as really important.

Of course, consumers don't use a grid like this. However, constructing such a grid helps managers think about what evaluative criteria target consumers consider really important, what consumers' attitudes are toward their product (or marketing mix) on each criteria, and how consumers combine the criteria to reach a final decision.[17]

Three levels of problem solving

The basic problem-solving process shows the steps consumers may go through trying to find a way to satisfy their needs, but it doesn't show how long this process will take or how much thought a consumer will give to each step. Individuals who have had a lot of experience solving certain problems can move quickly through some of the steps or almost directly to a decision.

It is helpful, therefore, to recognize three levels of problem solving: extensive problem solving, limited problem solving, and routinized response behaviour.

Exhibit 6–8 Grid of Evaluative Criteria for Three Car Brands

Brands	Common features			
	Gas mileage	Ease of service	Comfortable interior	Styling
Nissan	[–]	+	+	–
Saab	+	[–]	+	+
Toyota	+	+	[+]	[–]

Note: Pluses and minuses indicate a consumer's evaluation of a feature for a brand.

Exhibit 6–9 Problem-solving Continuum

(See Exhibit 6–9.) These problem-solving approaches are used for any kind of product. Consumers use **extensive problem solving** when they are trying to decide how to satisfy a completely new or important need. For example, a music lover who wants higher-quality sound may decide to buy a CD player, but may not have any idea what to buy. After talking with friends to find out about good places to buy a player, she may visit several stores to find out about different brands and their features. After thinking about her needs some more, she may buy a portable Sony unit, which she can use in her apartment or in her car.

Consumers use **limited problem solving** when they're willing to put *some* effort into deciding the best way to satisfy a need. Limited problem solving is typical when a consumer has some previous experience in solving a problem but isn't certain which choice is best at the current time. If our music lover wanted some new CDs for her player, she would already know what type of music she enjoys. She might go to a familiar store and evaluate what CDs they had in stock for her favourite types of music.

Consumers use **routinized response behaviour** when they regularly select a particular way of satisfying a need when it occurs. Routinized response behaviour is typical when a consumer has considerable experience in how to meet a need and has no need for additional information. For example, our music lover might routinely buy the latest recording by her favourite band as soon as it's available.

Most marketing managers would like their target consumers to buy their products in this routinized way. Some firms provide special services for frequent buyers, encourage repeat business with discounts, or do other things to build a good relationship so that the customer purchases from them in a routinized way.

Routinized response behaviour is also typical for **low-involvement purchases**—purchases that have little importance or relevance for the customer. Let's face it—buying a box of salt is probably not one of the burning issues in your life.[18]

Problem solving is a learning process

The reason problem solving becomes simpler with time is that people learn from experience—both positive and negative things. As consumers approach the problem-solving process, they bring attitudes formed by previous experiences and social training. Each new problem-solving process may then contribute to or modify this attitude set. For example, Internet Insite 6–1 discusses the attitude changes that will be required before large numbers of consumers routinely make online purchases.

New concepts require an adoption process

When consumers face a really new concept, their previous experience may not be relevant. These situations involve the **adoption process**—the steps individuals go through on the way to accepting or rejecting a new idea. Although the adoption process is similar to the problem-solving process, learning plays a clearer role and promotion's contribution to a marketing mix is more visible.

In the adoption process, an individual moves through some fairly definite steps:

1. *Awareness.* The potential customer comes to know about the product but lacks details. The consumer may not even know how it works or what it will do.

2. *Interest.* If the consumer becomes interested, he or she will gather general information and facts about the product.

Are Consumers Buying Online?

A storefront on the Internet is a virtual "marketspace," not a physical "marketplace," but it offers consumers the convenience of shopping from home. Every major manufacturer and retailer now has a presence in this marketspace. Mainstream retailers such as The Bay, Sears, and The Gap have a Web presence now. QVC, the home shopping channel, has a Web site called iQVC. But are consumers flocking to these online stores? *Not yet.*

A study by Ernst & Young (www.e&y.com) found that downloading free software and e-mail top the list of activities on the Web, followed by reading news, online banking, and online ticket reservations. The GVU WWW User Survey, conducted by the World Wide Web Consortium (www.gvu.gatech.edu), found that convenience, availability of information, lack of pressure from salespeople, and saving time are the most cited reasons for shopping online. However, most tracking studies of online consumers estimate online shopping at a figure between merely 1 percent (source: Price Waterhouse: www.pw.com) and 4 percent (source: Ernst & Young www.e&y.com) of all online activities. Total Internet shopping in 1997 was estimated at under US$3billion. While Internet use is increasing rapidly, online shopping is not.

Why is the rate of adoption of online shopping so low if indeed there are significant benefits to shopping online? A major concern seems to be the perceived lack of security in online transactions. Most Internet users feel that revealing credit card information over the Internet is not safe. Visa and MasterCard are developing a protocol called Secure Electronic Transaction (SET), which should go a long way toward alleviating consumer fears regarding security. Meanwhile, retailers such as Roswell Cyberspace Computer Book Store in Halifax are insisting that consumers fax all payment information, rather than submitting it through the Internet. Others, such as iQVC, offer a guarantee of full liability coverage for any fraudulent use of the consumer's credit card information. These measures are likely to increase consumer confidence in online shopping.

Many consumers enjoy the social interactions involved in shopping in malls and stores. For these consumers, online storefronts are very good information sources but not nearly as enjoyable as shopping at a real retail store. The GVU WWW User Survey results confirm that most consumers prefer to use the Internet as an information source; in this sense, the Web is fast replacing traditional media as the primary information source for Internet users. However, even these consumers do not yet see the Internet as a substitute for their neighbourhood mall.

The Ernst & Young study and other such surveys (see CyberAtlas: www.cyberatlas.com) reveal that the products most often purchased on the Web are *information-intensive products* such as CD-ROMs, software, books, and financial services. Some types of apparel are being bought online (e.g., replenishment items like women's pantyhose, and clothing from professional sports franchises), but in general, products that require trial and physical examination are not doing well. Products such as software can be tried online (e.g., see Frontpage98 demo at www.microsoft.com/FrontPage) before a purchase decision is made.

There is ample evidence that the Internet has already begun to shape and change consumer behaviour to a significant degree, and will continue to do so as cheaper, faster, and more user-friendly technologies become available. At the same time, the demise of the "brick and mortar" retail malls predicted by experts like Don Tapscott seems a long way off.†

†Don Tapscott, *Digital Economy,* McGraw-Hill, 1996.

Source: This is one of a series of Internet Insites prepared in April 1998 by Dr. Ramesh Venkat of Saint Mary's University for *Basic Marketing,* Ninth Canadian Edition.

Internet Insite 6-1

3. *Evaluation.* A consumer begins to give the product a mental trial, applying it to his or her personal situation.
4. *Trial.* The consumer may buy the product to experiment with it in use. A product that is either too expensive to try or isn't available for trial may never be adopted.
5. *Decision.* The consumer decides on either adoption or rejection. A satisfactory evaluation and trial may lead to adoption of the product and regular use. According to psychological learning theory, reinforcement leads to adoption.
6. *Confirmation.* The adopter continues to rethink the decision and searches for support for the decision—that is, further reinforcement.[19]

Marketing managers for 3M, the company that makes Scotch tape, worked with the adoption process when they introduced Post-it note pads. Test market ads increased awareness—they explained how Post-it notes could be applied to a surface and then easily removed. But test market sales were slow because most consumers were not interested. They didn't see the benefit. To encourage trial, 3M distributed free samples. By using the samples, consumers confirmed the benefit—and once they had used the samples up they started buying Post-its. As Post-it distribution expanded to other market areas, 3M used samples to speed consumers through the trial stage and the rest of the adoption process.[20]

Dissonance may set in

A buyer may have second thoughts after making a purchase decision. The buyer may have chosen from among several attractive alternatives, weighing the pros and cons and finally making a decision. Later doubts, however, may lead to **dissonance**—tension caused by uncertainty about the rightness of a decision. Dissonance may lead a buyer to search for additional information to confirm the wisdom of the decision and so reduce tension. Without this confirmation, the adopter may buy something else next time—or not comment positively about the product to others.[21]

Consumer behaviour in international markets

You're a consumer, so you probably have very good intuition about the many influences on consumer behaviour that we've been discussing. For many different purchase situations you also intuitively know—from experience—which variables are most important. That's good, but it's also a potential trap—especially when developing marketing mixes for consumers in international markets. The less a marketing manager knows about the *specific* social and intrapersonal variables that shape the behaviour of target customers, the more likely it is that relying on intuition will be misleading. We all try to explain things we don't understand by generalizing from what we do know. Yet when it comes to consumer behaviour, many of the specifics do not generalize from one culture to another.

Cadbury's effort to develop a Japanese market for its Dairy Milk Chocolate candy bar illustrates the point. Cadbury's marketing research revealed that Japanese consumers didn't like the high milk-fat content of Cadbury's bar. Cadbury's managers felt that this reaction must be from lack of opportunity to become accustomed to the candy. After all, in most other countries it's the rich taste of the candy that turns consumers into "chocoholics." Yet when Cadbury introduced the bar in Japan, it was a real flop. Taste preferences in other countries simply didn't generalize to Japan.

Sometimes important influences on consumer behaviour are more subtle. When P&G first introduced disposable diapers in Japan, interest was limited. Research suggested that price and health concerns were a sticking point, as was product fit. The diapers leaked because the design was too large for most Japanese babies. However, another powerful cultural force was also at work. At that time, most Japanese mothers were expected to dedicate themselves to caring for their babies. And by tradition, caring mothers always sacrificed their own convenience for the baby's. As a result, many women who could afford the convenience of disposable diapers didn't buy them because they felt guilty using them.

Watch out for stereotypes, and change

Marketers must watch out for oversimplifying stereotypes. Consumers in a foreign culture may be bound by some similar cultural forces, but that doesn't mean they are all the same. Further, changes in the underlying social forces may make certain old views irrelevant.

The stereotype that the typical Japanese executive works very long hours and devotes very little time to family life has been highlighted in the Western media. Yet this view is dated. In today's Japan, many young executives want a more balanced family life. A marketer who didn't recognize this change probably wouldn't fully understand these people, their needs, or buying behaviour in their families.

Developing a marketing mix that really satisfies the needs of a target market takes a real understanding of consumer behaviour—and the varied forces that shape it. So when planning strategies for international markets, it's best to involve locals who better understand the experience, attitudes, and interests of your customers.[22]

Questions and Problems

1. In your own words, explain economic needs and how they relate to the economics orientation model of consumer behaviour. Give an example of a purchase you recently made that is consistent with this model. Give another that is not explained by this model. Explain your thinking.

2. Explain what is meant by a hierarchy of needs, and provide examples of one or more products that enable you to satisfy each of the four levels of need.

3. Cut out (or copy) two recent advertisements: one full-page colour ad from a magazine and one large display from a newspaper. In each case, indicate which needs the ads are appealing to.

4. Explain how an understanding of consumers' learning processes might affect marketing strategy planning. Give an example.

5. How should the social class structure affect the planning of a new restaurant in a large city? How might the four Ps be adjusted?

6. What social class would you associate with each of the following phrases or items?

   a. A gun rack in a pickup truck.
   b. The *National Enquirer.*
   c. *New Yorker* magazine.
   d. People watching soap operas.
   e. TV golf tournaments.
   f. Men who drink beer after dinner.
   g. Families who vacation at a Disney theme park.
   h. Families who distrust banks (keep money in socks or mattresses).
   i. Owners of pit bulls.

   In each case, choose one class, if you can, and then provide some justification for your choice. If you can't choose one class, but rather feel that several classes are equally likely, then so indicate. In those cases where you feel that all classes are equally interested or characterized by a particular item, choose all seven classes.

7. Illustrate how the reference group concept may apply in practice by explaining how you personally are influenced by some reference group for some product. What are the implications of such behaviour for marketing managers?

8. Give two examples of recent purchases where the specific purchase situation influenced your purchase decision. Briefly explain how your decision was affected.

9. Give an example of a recent purchase in which you used extensive problem solving. What sources of information did you use in making the decision?

10. On the basis of the data and analysis presented in Chapters 5 and 6, what kind of buying behaviour would you expect to find for the following products: (a) a haircut, (b) a dishwasher detergent, (c) a printer for a personal computer, (d) a tennis racket, (e) a dress belt, (f) a telephone answering machine, (g) life insurance, (h) an ice cream cone, and (i) a new chequing account? Set up a chart for your answer with products along the left-hand margin as the row headings and the following factors as headings for the columns: (a) how consumers would shop for these products, (b) how far they would go, (c) whether they would buy by brand, (d) whether they would compare with other products, and (e) any other factors they should consider. Insert short answers—words or phrases are satisfactory—in the various boxes. Be prepared to discuss how the answers you put in the chart would affect each product's marketing mix.

Suggested cases

9	Doug Hanson Buys a Car	11	Ralph the Optician
10	Crankcase Transmission		

Computer-aided problem

Selective Processes

Submag, Inc., uses direct-mail promotion to sell magazine subscriptions. Magazine publishers pay Submag $3.12 for each new subscription. Submag's costs include the expenses of printing, addressing, and mailing each direct-mail advertisement plus the cost of using a mailing list. There are many suppliers of mailing lists, and the cost and quality of different lists vary.

Submag's marketing manager, Shandra Debose, is trying to choose between two possible mailing lists. One list has been generated from phone directories. It is less expensive than the other list, but the supplier acknowledges that about 10 percent of the names are out-of-date (addresses where people have moved away). A competing supplier offers a list of active members of professional associations. This list costs 4 cents per name more than the phone list, but only 8 percent of the addresses are out-of-date.

In addition to concerns about out-of-date names, not every consumer who receives a mailing buys a subscription. For example, *selective exposure* is a problem. Some target customers never see the offer—they just toss out junk mail without even opening the envelope. Industry studies show that this wastes about 10 percent of each mailing—although the precise percentage varies from one mailing list to another.

Selective perception influences some consumers who do open the mailing. Some are simply not interested. Others don't want to deal with a subscription service. Although the price is good, these consumers worry that they'll never get the magazines. Submag's previous experience is that selective perception causes more than half of those who read the offer to reject it.

Of those who perceive the message as intended, many are interested. But *selective retention* can be a problem. Some people set the information aside and then forget to send in the subscription order.

Submag can mail about 25,000 pieces per week. Shandra Debose has set up a spreadsheet to help her study effects of the various relationships discussed above—and to choose between the two mailing lists.

a. If you were Debose, which of the two lists would you buy based on the initial spreadsheet? Why?

b. For the most profitable list, what is the minimum number of items that Submag will have to mail to earn a profit of at least $3,500?

c. For an additional cost of $.01 per mailing, Submag can include a reply card that will reduce the percentage of consumers who forget to send in an order to 45 percent. If Submag mails 25,000 items, is it worth the additional cost to include the reply card? Explain your logic.

For additional questions related to this problem, see Exercise 6–3 in the *Learning Aid for Use with Basic Marketing*, Ninth Canadian Edition.

When you finish this chapter, you should:

- Know who the business and organizational customers are.
- See why multiple influence is common in business and organizational purchase decisions.
- Understand the problem-solving behaviour of organizational buyers.
- Know the basic methods used in organizational buying.
- Understand the different types of buyer-seller relationships and their benefits and limitations.
- Know about the number and distribution of manufacturers and why they are an important customer group.
- Know how buying by service firms, retailers, wholesalers, and governments is similar to—and different from—buying by manufacturers.
- Understand the important new terms (shown in orange).

Chap seven

The Buying Behaviour of Business and Organizational Customers

Note: Crila Plastic Industries Ltd. was selected as one of Canada's 50 Best Managed Private Companies for 1997.

Location: Mississauga, Ont.
Business: Plastics
Employees: 350
Annual sales: $50 million

In September 1996, a Floridian named Herb Evans called on Crila Plastic Industries with an idea. On the face of it, the concept seemed mighty unlikely. Evans claimed he represented Geoff House, the owner of a kitchen cabinet company based on the Isle of Wight, better known as a holiday destination in the English Channel than an innovative business centre.

According to Evans, House had invented a plastic that looked and acted exactly like wood. Evans had himself been in a few businesses, including real estate, and it would have been easy to give him the brush-off, particularly since Crila was hardly the only call Evans was making as he tried to drum up interest.

However, marketing and engineering staff studied the proposal and reported to Crila president Peter Clark that the concept, called Extrudawood, looked intriguing.

Clark, in turn, paid attention to their recommendation. "We're a very aggressive marketing organization. Most extrusion companies of our size use commission sales agents. We don't. We have our own 16-member field force so our market information is very acute and gives an edge on opportunities." Evans had drawn up a business plan. "Let me take that home," said Clark. "I love reading business plans."

He read the document over a weekend and flew to the Isle of Wight, where he signed a joint venture deal with House last March for the North American rights to produce Extrudawood.

"It looks, acts, and feels exactly like wood. It can be screwed, nailed, and painted—but it's made of plastic." Crila is not going to patent the chemical makeup of the product or its process. "If you patent it you're essentially telling your competitors how it's done and they'll find a way around the patent," he says.

Production starts early next year, and already the company has sizable orders to produce components for two companies. "One million feet is a nice size order in a year; the two companies are both looking at doing that much each month."

The company still does some decorative extrusions such as automotive trim, vinyl window systems, vending machines, and stick-on furniture mouldings. But custom-engineered extruded components, such as the company will supply using Extrudawood, have become the backbone of the business since Crila acquired Extrusion Plastics Inc. in 1994.

Since that acquisition, the number of engineers employed has risen to 15 from two. Crila has three plants and five divisions, each operating as a separate profit centre. Customers include companies in a wide range of sectors including appliances, automotive, furniture, building components, and leisure products.

Materials employed include rigid and flexible PVC, thermoplastic rubbers, elastomers and olefins, polypropylene, hytrel, polycarbonate alloys, and high impact polystyrene.

At a 25th anniversary celebration in September, Clark unveiled a painting by wildlife artist Richard Stanley. The work shows a pair of mute swans, which mate for life. It is meant to represent the company's commitment to customers, he says.

Source: Rod McQueen, "Canada's 50 Best Managed Private Companies: Crila Plastic Industries Ltd.," *The Financial Post,* December 13, 1997, p. 19.

Business and organizational customers—a big opportunity

When we hear the term *customer,* most of us think about individual final consumers. But many marketing managers aim at customers who are not final consumers. In fact, more purchases are made by businesses and other organizations than by final consumers. As the Crila Plastic Industries case illustrates, the buying behaviour of these customers can be very different from the buying behaviour of final consumers. Developing marketing strategies for these markets requires a solid understanding of who these customers are and how they buy. That is the focus of this chapter.

Business and organizational customers are any buyers who buy for resale or to produce other goods and services. Exhibit 7–1 shows the different types of customers in these markets.

Many characteristics of buying behaviour are common across different types of organizations. That's why the different kinds of organizational buyers are often loosely referred to as "industrial buyers" or "intermediate buyers." As we discuss organizational buying, we will provide examples of buying by many different types of organizations. Later in the chapter, we will highlight some specific characteristics of different customer groups.

Basic purchasing needs are economic

When they make purchase decisions, organizational buyers typically focus on economic factors. They are usually less emotional in their buying than final consumers.

Buyers try to consider the total cost of selecting a supplier and a particular product, not just the initial price of the product. For example, a hospital that needs a new type of X-ray equipment might look at both the original cost and the ongoing costs, at how it would affect doctor productivity, and of course at the quality of the images it produces. The hospital might also consider the seller's reliability and general cooperativeness; its ability to provide speedy maintenance and repair, steady supply under all conditions, and reliable and fast delivery; and any past and present relationships (including previous favours and cooperation in meeting special requests).

The matter of dependability deserves special emphasis. An organization may not be able to function if purchases don't arrive when they're expected. Dependable product quality is important, too. For example, a faulty wire might cause a large piece of equipment to break down, and the costs of finding and correcting the problem could be completely out of proportion to the cost of the wire.

Even small differences are important

Understanding how the buying behaviour of a particular organization differs from that of others can be very important. Even "trivial" differences in buying behaviour may be important because success often hinges on fine-tuning the marketing mix.

Sellers often approach each organizational customer directly, usually through a sales representative. This gives the seller more chance to adjust the marketing mix

Exhibit 7-1 Examples of Different Types of Business and Organizational Customers

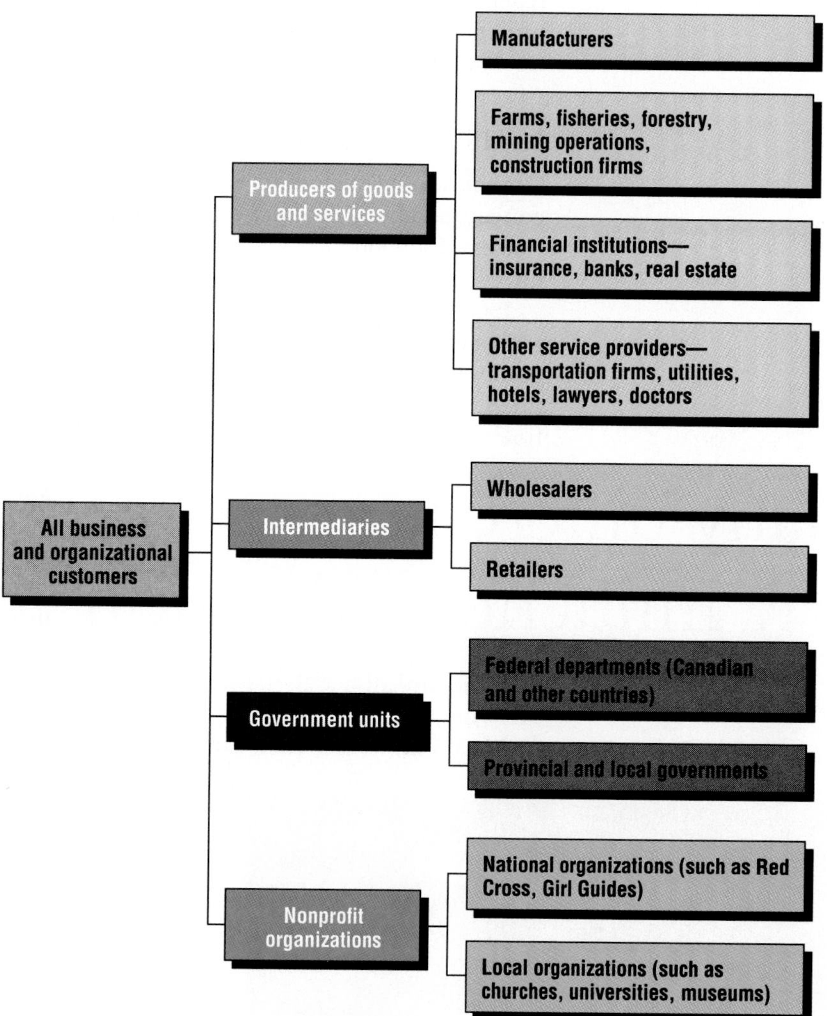

for each individual customer. A seller may even develop a unique strategy for each individual customer. This approach carries target marketing to its extreme. But sellers often need unique strategies to compete for large-volume purchases.

In such situations, the individual sales rep takes much responsibility for strategic planning. The sales rep often coordinates the entire relationship between the supplier and the customer. This may involve working with many people—including top management—in both firms. This is relevant to your career planning, since these interesting jobs are very challenging—and they pay well, too.

Serving customers in international markets

Many marketers discover that there are good opportunities to serve business customers in different countries around the world. Specific business customs do vary from one country to another, and the differences can be important. For example, a salesperson working in Japan must know how to handle a customer's business card with respect. Japanese think of a business card as a symbolic extension of the person who presents it. They consider it rude to write notes on the back of a card or to put it in a wallet while the person who presented it is still in the room. While such cultural differences can be very important, the basic approaches marketers use to deal with business customers in different parts of the world are much less varied than those required to reach individual consumers.

This is probably why the shift to a global economy has been so rapid for many firms. Their business customers in different countries buy in similar ways and can be reached with similar marketing mixes. Business customers, more so than final consumers, are often willing to work with a distant supplier who has developed a superior marketing mix.

Customers may expect quality certification

Organizational customers considering a new supplier or one from overseas may be concerned about product quality. However, this is becoming less of an obstacle because of ISO 9000. **ISO 9000** is a way for a supplier to document its quality procedures according to internationally recognized standards.

ISO 9000 assures a customer that the supplier has effective quality checks in place, without the customer having to conduct its own costly and time-consuming audit. Some customers won't buy from any supplier who doesn't have it. To get ISO 9000 certified, a company basically must prove to outside auditors that it documents in detail how the company operates and who is responsible for quality every step of the way.[1]

Many different people may influence a decision

Many organizations, especially large ones, rely on specialists to ensure that purchases are handled sensibly. These specialists have different titles in different firms (such as purchasing agent, procurement officer, and buyer), but basically they are all **purchasing managers**—buying specialists for their employers. In large organizations, they usually specialize by product area and are real experts.

Most firms look to their purchasing departments to help cut costs and provide competitive advantage. In this environment, purchasing people have a lot of clout. There are good job opportunities in purchasing for capable business graduates.

With
Without
When it comes to the purchasing profession, a C.P.P. designation makes a difference.
The C.P.P. is the only accredited designation for purchasing and supply management professionals in the country. Certified Professional Purchasers have done their homework. They've learned the newest supply management techniques, and they'll continue to do so, since ongoing C.P.P. training demands that they stay current.
In fact, the sole aim of the C.P.P. accreditation program is to provide professionals with the ability to transform purchasing and supply management from an overhead expense into a key competitive advantage in a company's financial strategy.
So when you're weighing the merits of some prospective purchasing professionals, don't forget the extra weight a C.P.P. designation carries. Call us at (416) 977-7111.
C.P.P.
CERTIFIED PROFESSIONAL PURCHASER
Purchasing Management Association of Canada
Association canadienne de gestion des achats

A Certified Professional Purchaser designation is another career option for you to consider.

Salespeople usually have to see a purchasing manager first, before they contact any other employee. These buyers hold important positions and take a dim view of sales reps who try to go around them. Rather than being "sold," these buyers want salespeople to provide accurate information that will help them buy wisely. They like information on new goods and services, and tips on potential price changes, supply shortages, and other changes in market conditions.

Although purchasing managers usually coordinate relationships with suppliers, other people may also play important roles in influencing the purchase decision.

Multiple buying influence in a buying centre

Multiple buying influence means that several people—perhaps even top management—share in making a purchase decision. An example shows how the different buying influences work. Suppose Electrolux, the Swedish firm that produces vacuum cleaners, wants to buy a machine to stamp out the various metal parts it needs. Different vendors are eager for the business. Several people (influencers) help to evaluate the choices. A finance manager worries about the high cost and suggests leasing the machine. The quality control people want a machine that will do a more accurate job—although it's more

Exhibit 7-2 Multiple Influence and Roles in the Buying Centre

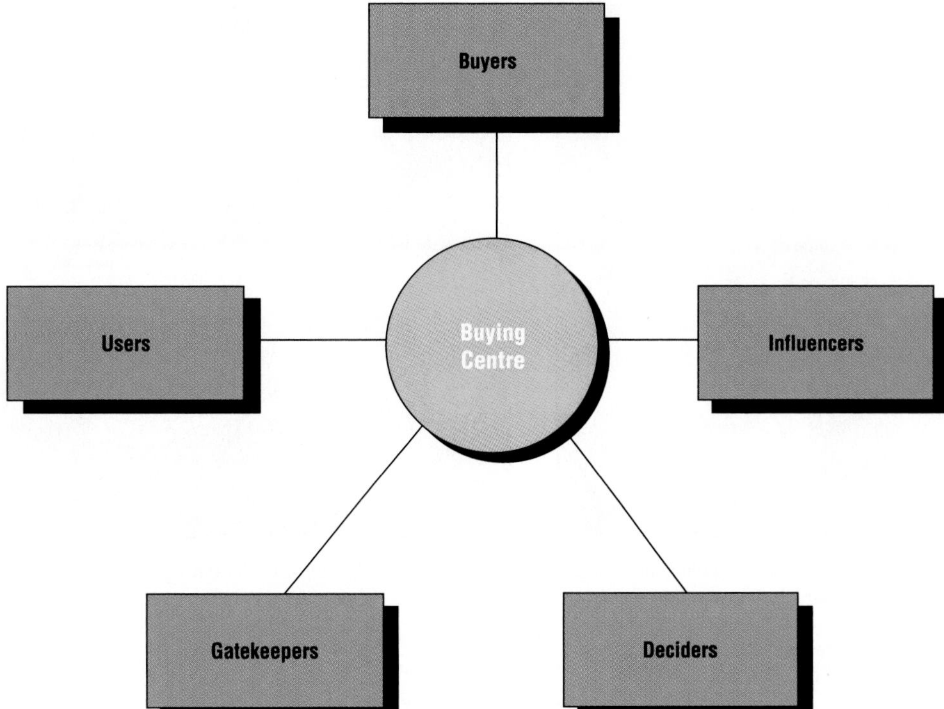

expensive. The production manager is interested in speed of operation. The production line workers and their supervisors want the machine that is easiest to use so that workers can continue to rotate jobs.

The company president (the decider) asks the purchasing department to assemble all the information but retains the power to select and approve the supplier. The purchasing manager's assistant (a gatekeeper) has been deciding what information to pass on to higher-ups as well as scheduling visits for salespeople. After all these buying influences are considered, one of the purchasing agents for the firm (the buyer) will be responsible for making recommendations and arranging the terms of the sale.

It is helpful to think of a **buying centre** as all the people who participate in or influence a purchase. Different people may make up a buying centre from one decision to the next. This makes the marketing job difficult.

The salesperson must study each case carefully. Just learning who to talk with may be hard, but thinking about the various roles in the buying centre can help. See Exhibit 7–2.

The salesperson may have to talk to every member of the buying centre, stressing different topics for each. This complicates the promotion job and may drag it out. On very important purchases—a new computer system, a new building, or major equipment—the selling period may be a year or more.[2]

Vendor analysis

Considering all of the factors relevant to a purchase decision is sometimes a complex task. A supplier or product that is best in one way may not be best in others. To deal with these situations, many firms use **vendor analysis**—a formal rating of suppliers on all relevant areas of performance. The purpose isn't just to get a low price from the supplier on a given part or service. Rather, the goal is to lower the *total costs* associated with purchases. Analysis might show that the best vendor is the one that helps the customer reduce excess inventory, retooling of equipment, or defective parts. By evaluating suppliers on all aspects of how they are working out, buyers can make better decisions.[3]

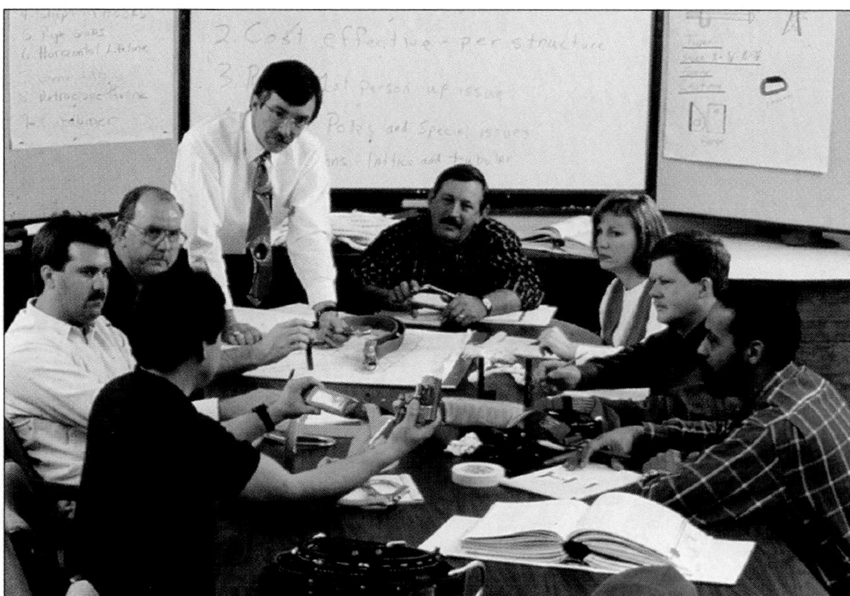

A person who works on a utility firm's high-power wires needs safe, durable climbing gear. A number of different people may influence the decision about which gear the firm should buy.

Behavioural needs are relevant too

Vendor analysis tries to focus on economic factors, but purchasing in organizations may also involve many behavioural dimensions. Purchasing managers and others involved in buying decisions are human—and they want friendly relationships with suppliers.

The different people involved in purchase decisions are also human with respect to protecting their own interests—and their own position in the company. Purchasing managers may want to avoid taking risks that might reflect badly on their decisions. They have to buy a wide variety of products and make decisions involving many factors beyond their control. If a new source delivers late or quality is poor, you can guess who will be blamed. Marketers who can help the buyer avoid risk have a definite appeal. In fact, this may make the difference between a successful and an unsuccessful marketing mix.

Ethical Dimensions

Conflicts May Arise

Although organizational buyers are influenced by their own needs, most are serious professionals who are careful to avoid a conflict between their own self-interest and company outcomes. Marketers must be careful here. A salesperson who offers one of his company pens to a prospect may view the giveaway as part of the promotion effort—but the customer firm may have a policy against any employee accepting *any* gift from a supplier.

Most organizational buyers do their work ethically—and expect marketers to work the same way. Yet there have been highly publicized abuses. For example, some buyers may give contracts to suppliers who offer them vacation trips and other personal favours. Abuses of this sort have prompted many organizations to set up policies that prohibit a buyer from accepting anything from a potential supplier.[4]

Marketers need to take concerns about conflict of interest very seriously. Part of the promotion job is to persuade various individuals who may influence an organization's purchase. Yet the whole marketing effort may be tainted if it even *appears* that a marketer has encouraged a person who influences a decision to put personal gain ahead of company interest.

Purchasing may be centralized

If a large organization has facilities at many locations, much of the purchasing work may be done at a central location. For example, Canadian Tire handles most of the purchase decisions for stores in its retail chain from its head office in Ontario. Many of the purchasing decisions for the federal government are handled by Public Works and Government Services Canada.

With centralized buying, a sales rep may be able to sell to facilities all over a country—or even across several countries—without leaving a base city. This makes selling easier for competitors, too, so the market may be extremely competitive. The importance of such big buyers has led some companies to set up "national account" sales forces that are specially trained to cater to these buyers. A geographically bound salesperson can be at a real disadvantage against such competitors.

Organizational buyers are problem solvers

In Chapter 6, we discussed problem solving by consumers and how it might vary from extensive problem solving to routine buying. In organizational markets, we can adapt these concepts slightly and work with three similar buying processes: a new-task buying process, a modified rebuy process, and a straight rebuy.[5] See Exhibit 7–3.

New-task buying occurs when an organization has a new need and the customer wants a great deal of information. New-task buying can involve setting product specifications, evaluating sources of supply, and establishing an order routine that can be followed in the future if results are satisfactory.

A **straight rebuy** is a routine repurchase that may have been made many times before. Buyers probably don't bother looking for new information or new sources of supply. Most of a company's small or recurring purchases are of this type—but they take only a small part of an organized buyer's time.

The **modified rebuy** is the in-between process where some review of the buying situation is done—though not as much as in new-task buying. Sometimes a competitor will get lazy enjoying a straight rebuy situation. An alert marketer can turn these situations into opportunities by providing more information or a better marketing mix.

Most firms routinize straight rebuys

To save effort and expense, most firms routinize the purchase process whenever they can. When some person wants to make a purchase, a **requisition**—a request to buy something—is filled out. After approval by some supervisor, the requisition is forwarded to the purchasing department for placement with the "best" seller.

Approved requisitions are converted to purchase orders as quickly as possible. Buyers usually make straight rebuys the day they receive the requisition without consulting

Exhibit 7–3 Organizational Buying Processes

Characteristics	Type of process		
	New-task buying	Modified rebuy	Straight rebuy
Time required	Much	Medium	Little
Multiple influence	Much	Some	Little
Review of suppliers	Much	Some	None
Information needed	Much	Some	Little

anyone else. New-task and modified rebuys take longer. If time is important, the buyer may place the order by telephone, fax, or computer.

Computer searching and ordering

Many buyers now delegate a large portion of their routine order placing to computers. They program decision rules that tell the computer how to order and leave the details of following through to the machine. When economic conditions change, buyers modify the computer instructions. When nothing unusual happens, however, the computer system continues to routinely rebuy as needs develop—printing out new purchase orders or electronically sending them to the regular suppliers.

Obviously, it's a big sale to be selected as a major supplier and routinely called up in the buyer's computer program. Such a buyer will be more impressed by an attractive marketing mix for a whole *line* of products than just a lower price for a particular order.[6]

"Shopping" on the Internet adds a wrinkle

The logic of treating routine purchases as rebuys is to reduce the time, hassle, and risk of shopping around. At the same time, however, the creation of Internet Web sites and online order systems is making it easier for some suppliers to steal customers who otherwise would just stick with the convenience of a preferred source. As Internet Insite 7–1 suggests, a rapidly increasing amount of business-to-business marketing is being done online.

When a buyer can do a quick Internet search and check availability and prices of products—especially of standardized items that are available from a number of vendors—differences in price become very visible. A vendor that doesn't offer superior value—perhaps through differentiated service or more convenience—may find itself losing customers.

Of course, the flip side of that is the marketer who wants his or her firm to be found. In today's environment, a good Web site is an important piece of insurance. Even if the Web site doesn't do anything more than list the types of products the firm sells and give an e-mail address—or even a standard telephone number and snail mail address—it is likely to turn up in a search of Web sites.[7]

Ongoing relationships

For straight rebuys, the buyer (or computer) may place an order without even considering other potential sources. Sales reps regularly call on these buyers—but *not* to sell a particular item. Rather, they want to maintain relations, become a preferred source, and/or point out new developments.

New-task buying

Customers in a new-task buying situation are likely to seek information from a variety of sources. See Exhibit 7–4. How much information a customer collects also depends on the importance of the purchase and the level of uncertainty about what choice

Exhibit 7–4 Major Sources of Information Used by Organizational Buyers

	Marketing sources	Nonmarketing sources
Personal sources	• Salespeople • Others from supplier firms • Trade shows	• Buying centre members • Outside business associates • Consultants and outside experts
Impersonal sources	• Advertising in trade publications • Sales literature • Sales catalogues	• Rating services • Trade associations • News publications • Product directories

Business-to-Business Marketing on the Internet

Electronic commerce for consumer products is still in its infancy, with total online sales of consumer products and services for 1997 estimated at about US$1 billion. However, the total value of goods and services traded between companies online (i.e., business-to-business electronic commerce) was estimated at about US$8 billion for 1997. According to Forrester Research Inc., by the year 2002 businesses will buy products and services online worth US$327 billion.

Consumers who shop online mention convenience, choice or variety, and lower prices as the main attractions of online shopping. Businesses and large organizations, on the other hand, want to cut costs, reduce order-processing time, and improve information flow between themselves and their supplier/client organizations. According to Blane Erwin, Director of Forrester's Business Trade and Technologies Strategy unit, these are the main reasons for businesses going online to buy or sell. Currently, business-to-business marketing on the Internet is dominated by hard-goods manufacturers dealing in electronics, computers, airline parts, office supplies, and so on.

Let us examine how different firms in the business-to-business arena are utilizing the Internet in their marketing efforts. International Airline Support Group Inc. (www.iasgroup.com), a leader in the acquisition and sale of aftermarket parts and equipment for different aircraft, has created an online database with search capability where one can find out if a particular airline part is available (www.ipls.com). Another example is Dell Computers (www.dell.com). Dell has created a special section in their Web site for businesses called the Business Center (www.dell.com/business/index.htm); there, it offers businesses the means to "custom design" the computer they want. Dell also has online "specialty stores" that target other large organizational buyers such as universities, governments, and hospitals (http://commerce.us.dell.com/).

Other areas of business-to-business marketing are also utilizing the Internet. Customer service in the business-to-business markets has taken on a whole new dimension. Sun Microsystems (www.sun.com), for example, has created an online service site called Sunsolve Online™, which provides an in-depth, customer-accessible information resource for Sun customers. If you are a Sun customer, you no longer have to hold the telephone line for a customer service representative. You find answers to problems or questions instantly online. By automating a large part of its service and support functions, Sun has been able to provide a higher level of service than before while saving millions of dollars.

Small businesses are using the Internet to gain access to international markets. The Internet provides a low-cost medium for small exporters and importers to communicate with each other. To see some examples of how organizational buyers and sellers meet and transact business online, visit the links at http://ciber.bus.msu.edu/busres/tradlead.htm.

To facilitate the growth of business-to-business electronic commerce, companies such as General Electric are marketing software products that will make electronic commerce more secure. GE Information Services has developed the Trading Process Network (TPN), an Internet-based trading network that "enables buyers and sellers to do business-to-business electronic commerce" (see www.tpn.geis.com).

To understand how business-to-business marketers are using the Internet, George Avlontis and Despina Karayanni, two researchers at the Athens University of Economics and Business, conducted an online study. An e-mail survey was sent to 800 marketing executives in business-to-business firms, with a 10% response rate. The respondents came from such diverse industries as software, equipment manufacturing, computer hardware, and chemicals and plastics. These firms seemed to be using the Internet to gain a marketing advantage over the competition, to build brand identity, to find new customers/markets, and to preserve existing customers. The respondents also felt that the Internet was being used to discover customer needs more quickly, as well as for communicating product benefits and corporate image.

The findings of this study as well as the examples we have seen suggest that the Internet is beginning to emerge as a powerful competitive weapon. Businesses are realizing that the Internet is a more effective communication medium than the good old telephone or fax machine. Not only that, but the Internet also allows for integrating the information systems of suppliers and buyers, the result being efficiencies and cost savings unimaginable just a few years ago. No wonder some experts are very optimistic about the future of electronic commerce in this area.

Some questions to ponder:

1. How will an organizational buyer and an individual consumer (such as you) differ in the use of the Internet?
2. How will a Web site that targets other businesses differ from a Web site that targets individual consumers?

Source: This is one of a series of Internet Insites prepared in April 1998 by Dr. Ramesh Venkat of Saint Mary's University for *Basic Marketing*, Ninth Canadian Edition.

might be best. The time and expense of searching for information may not be justified for a minor purchase. But a major purchase often involves real detective work—and promotion has much more chance to have an impact.

Basic methods in organizational buying

Organizational buyers use four basic approaches to evaluating and buying products: (1) inspection, (2) sampling, (3) description, and (4) negotiated contracts. Understanding the differences in these buying methods is important in strategy planning, so let's look at each approach.

Inspection looks at everything

Inspection buying means looking at every item. It's used for products that are not standardized and that require examination. Here each product is different—as in the case of livestock or used equipment. Such products are often sold in open markets—or at auction if there are several potential buyers. Buyers inspect the goods and either haggle with the seller or bid against competing buyers.

Sampling looks at some

Sampling buying means looking at only part of a potential purchase. As products become more standardized—perhaps because of careful grading or quality control—buying by sample becomes possible. For example, a power company might buy miles of heavy electric cable. A sample section might be heated to the melting point in order to determine that the cable is safe.

People in less-developed economies do a lot of buying by inspection or sampling, regardless of the product. The reason is skepticism about quality, or lack of faith in the seller.

Specifications describe the need

Description (specification) buying means buying from a written (or verbal) description of the product. Most manufactured items and many agricultural commodities are bought this way—often without inspection. When quality can almost be guaranteed, buying by description—grade, brand, or specification—may be satisfactory, especially when there is mutual trust between buyers and sellers. Because this method reduces the cost of buying, buyers use it whenever practical.

Services are usually purchased by description. Since a service is usually not performed until after it's purchased, buyers have nothing to inspect ahead of time.

Once the purchase needs are specified, it's the buyer's job to get the best deal possible. If several suppliers want the business, the buyer will often request competitive bids. **Competitive bids** are the terms of sale offered by different suppliers in re-

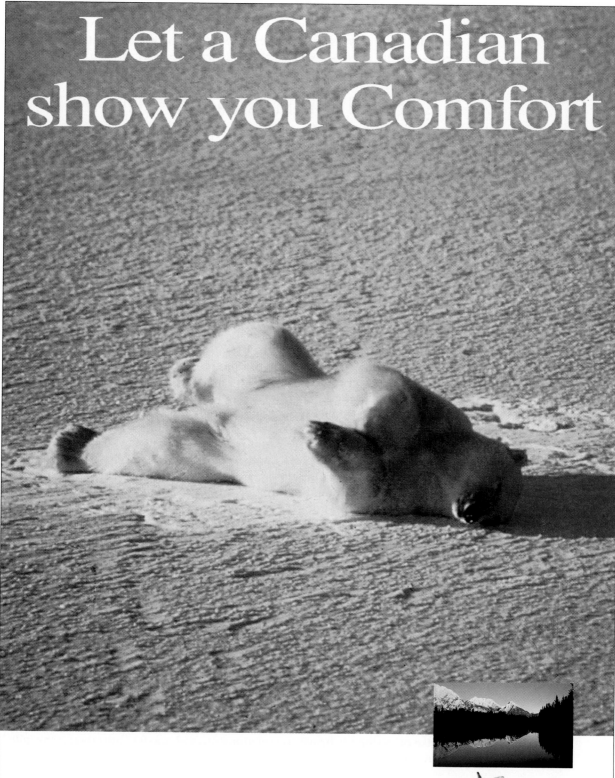

Let a Canadian show you Comfort

Our 747-400 Business Class offers you more room to stretch than any other major airline.

sponse to the buyer's purchase specifications. If different suppliers' quality, dependability, and delivery schedules all meet the specs, the buyer will select the low-price bid. But a creative marketer needs to look carefully at the purchaser's specs—and the need—to see whether other elements of the marketing mix could provide a competitive advantage.

Negotiated contracts handle relationships

Negotiated contract buying means agreeing to a contract that allows for changes in the purchase arrangements.

Sometimes the buyer knows roughly what the company needs but can't fix all the details in advance. Specifications or total requirements may change over time. In such cases, the general project is described, and a basic price may be agreed on—perhaps even based on competitive bids—but with provision for changes and price adjustments up or down.

Buyer–seller relationships in business markets

There are often significant benefits of a close working relationship between a supplier and a customer firm. And such relationships are becoming common. Many firms are reducing the number of suppliers with whom they work, and expecting more in return from the suppliers that remain. The best relationships involve real partnerships where there's mutual trust.

Closely tied firms can often share tasks at lower total cost than would be possible working at arm's length. Costs are sometimes reduced simply by reducing uncertainty and risk. A supplier is often able to reduce its selling price when a customer commits to large orders, or orders over a longer period of time. A large sales volume may produce economies of scale and reduce selling costs.

The customer benefits from lower cost and also is assured a dependable source of supply. A firm that works closely with a supplier can resolve joint problems. For example, it may cost both the supplier and the customer more to resolve the problems of a defective product after it is delivered than it would have cost to prevent the problem. But without the customer's help, it may be impossible for the supplier to identify a solution to the problem. As the head of purchasing at Motorola puts it, "Every time we make an error it takes people at both ends to correct it."

Relationships may reduce flexibility

Although close relationships can produce benefits, they are not always best. A long-term commitment to a partner may reduce flexibility. When competition drives down costs and spurs innovation, the customer may be better off letting suppliers compete for the business. It may not be worth the customer's investment to build a relationship for purchases that are not particularly important, or not made that frequently.

It may at first appear that a seller would *always* prefer to have a closer relationship with a customer, but that is not so. When a customer doesn't want a relationship, trying to build one may cost more than it's worth. Many small suppliers have made the mistake of relying too heavily on relationships with too few customers. One failed relationship may bankrupt the business![8]

Relationships have many dimensions

Relationships are not "all or nothing" arrangements. Firms may have a close relationship in some ways and not in others. It's useful to know about the five key dimensions that characterize most buyer–seller relationships. These are cooperation, information sharing, operational linkages, legal bonds, and relationship-specific adaptations. Purchasing managers for the buying firm and salespeople for the supplier usually coordinate the different dimensions of a relationship. However, as

Exhibit 7-5 Key Dimensions of Relationships in Business Markets

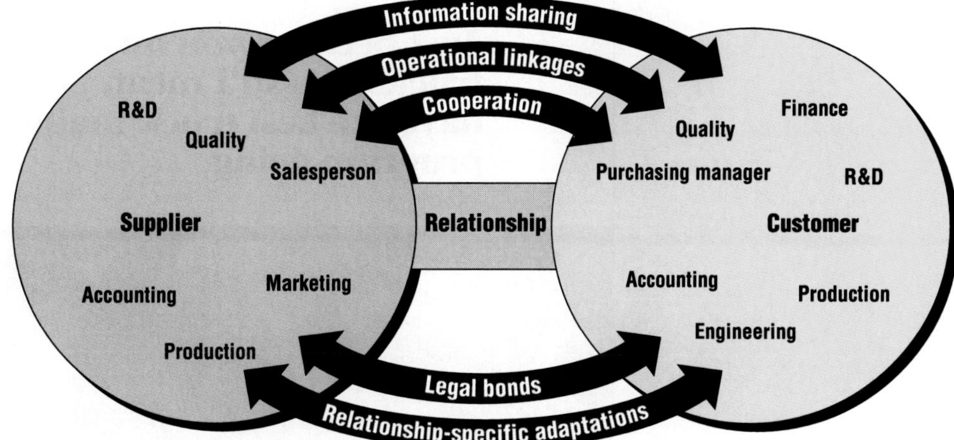

shown in Exhibit 7–5, close relationships often involve direct contacts between a number of people from other areas in both firms.[9]

Cooperation treats problems as joint responsibilities

In cooperative relationships, the buyer and seller work together to achieve both mutual and individual objectives. This doesn't mean that the buyer (or seller) will always do what the other wants. Rather, the two firms treat problems that arise as a joint responsibility.

National Semiconductor (NS) and Siltec, a supplier of silicon wafers, have found clever ways to cooperate and cut costs. For example, workers at the NS plant used to throw away the expensive plastic cassettes that Siltec uses to ship its silicon wafers. Now Siltec and NS cooperate to recycle the cassettes. This helps the environment and also saves more than $300,000 a year, most of which Siltec passes along to NS as lower prices.[10]

Shared information is useful but may be risky

Some relationships involve an open sharing of information that is useful to both the buyer and the seller. This might include the exchange of proprietary cost data, discussion of demand forecasts, and joint work on new product designs. Information might be shared through information systems.

Information sharing can lead to better decisions, reduced uncertainty about the future, and better planning. However, firms don't want to share information if there's a risk that a partner might misuse it. Violations of trust in a relationship are an ethical matter and should be taken seriously. However, as a practical matter, it makes sense to know a partner well before revealing all.

Operational linkages share functions between firms

Operational linkages are direct ties between the internal operations of the buyer and seller firms. These linkages usually involve formal arrangements and ongoing coordination of activities between the firms. Shared activities are especially important when neither firm, working on its own, can perform a function as well as the two firms working together. For example, operational linkages are often required to reduce total inventory costs. Business customers want to maintain an adequate inventory—certainly enough to prevent stock-outs and/or keep production lines moving. On the

Just because you own your trucks, doesn't mean you can't have the best truck maintenance program going.

Rentway Trukcare Guaranteed.

Executive Summary

- *outsourcing of fleet maintenance management*
- *vehicle specification recommendation*
- *complete maintenance management system*
- *guaranteed maintenance costs*
- *full regulatory compliance*
- *North America-wide service network*
- *Rentway – a Trimac Limited subsidiary, 30 years of commitment to quality*

Minimize operating cost and maximize efficiency by specifying the right truck for the job and implementing a quality Preventive Maintenance and repair program. That's what we do with our trucks at Rentway and now, with Trukcare GTD, we can provide the same program to the truck owner too!

Our analysis of your truck needs will ensure that you buy the best truck for the job, and our Trukcare GTD maintenance management program will provide you with fixed operating costs for the economic life of the vehicle. Full maintenance management, scheduled Preventive Maintenance, mechanical repairs, North America-wide road service, replacement equipment...everything you need to operate a quality fleet.

Trukcare GTD – one of the many Truck Fleet Management services available from Rentway.

Call 1-888-RENTWAY.

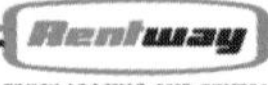

TRUCK LEASING AND RENTAL

Rentway Trukcare GTD offers operational linkages to business customers.

other hand, keeping too much inventory is expensive. Providing a customer with inventory when it's needed may require that a supplier be able to provide **just-in-time delivery**—reliably getting products there *just* before the customer needs them. We'll discuss just-in-time systems in more detail in Chapter 12. For now, we simply point out that just-in-time relationships between buyers and sellers usually require operational linkages (as well as information sharing). For example, an automobile producer may want a supplier of automobile seats to load the delivery truck so that seats are arranged in the colour and style of the cars on the assembly line. This reduces the buyer's costs because the seats only need to be handled one time when they arrive. However, it also means that the supplier's production of seats and systems for loading them on the truck must be closely linked to the customer's production line.

Operational linkages may also involve the routine activities of individuals who almost become part of the customer's operations. Design engineers, salespeople, and service representatives may participate in developing solutions to ongoing problems, conduct regular maintenance checks on equipment, and/or monitor inventory and coordinate orders. At the Chrysler design centre, for example, 30 offices are set aside for full-time use by people employed by suppliers.

Linkages may be customized to a particular relationship, or they may be standardized and operate the same way across many exchange partners. For example, in the channel of distribution for grocery products, many different producers are standardizing their distribution procedures and coordinating with retail chains to make it faster and cheaper to replenish grocery store shelves.

When a customer's operations are dependent on those of a supplier, it may be difficult or expensive to switch to another supplier. For this reason, many buyers try to avoid a relationship that results in these "switching costs."

Contracts spell out obligations

Many purchases are straightforward. The seller's basic responsibility is to transfer title to goods or perform services, and the buyer's basic responsibility is to pay the agreed price. However, in some buyer–seller relationships the responsibilities of the parties are more complex. Then they may be spelled out in a detailed legal agreement. An agreement may apply only for a short period, but long-term contracts are also common.

For example, a customer might ask a supplier to guarantee a 6 percent price reduction for a particular part for each of the next three years and to pledge to virtually eliminate defects. In return, the customer might offer to double its orders and help the supplier boost productivity. This may sound attractive to the supplier, but it may also require new people or facilities. The supplier may not be willing to make these long-term commitments unless the buyer is willing to sign a contract for promised purchases. The contract might spell out what would happen if deliveries are late or if quality is below specification.

When a contract provides a formal plan for the future of a relationship, some types of risk are reduced. But a firm may not want to be legally "locked in" when the future is unclear. Alternatively, some managers figure that even a detailed contract isn't a good substitute for regular, good faith reviews to make sure that neither party is being hurt by changing business conditions.

Harley-Davidson used this approach when it moved toward closer relationships with a smaller number of suppliers. Purchasing executives tossed detailed contracts out the window and replaced them with a short statement of principles to guide relationships between Harley and its suppliers. This "operate on a handshake" approach is typical of relationships with Japanese firms. Many other firms have adopted it. It's great when it works, and a disaster when it doesn't.

Specific adaptations invest in the relationship

Relationship-specific adaptations involve changes in a firm's product or procedures that are unique to the needs or capabilities of a relationship partner. Industrial suppliers often custom design a new product for just one customer. This may require investments in R&D or new manufacturing technologies. Donnelly Corp. is an extreme example. It had been supplying Honda with mirrors for the interiors of its cars. Honda's purchasing people liked Donnelly's collaborative style, so they urged Donnelly to supply its exterior mirrors as well. Donnelly had never been in that business, so it had to build a factory to get started.

Buying firms may also adapt to a particular supplier; a computer maker may design around Intel's memory chip, and independent photo processors say, "We use Kodak paper for the good look" in their advertising. However, buyers often hesitate to make big investments that increase dependence on a specific supplier.

The relationship between Boeing, the giant airplane manufacturer, and one of its suppliers involves relationship-specific adaptation. Boeing is a big customer for machine tools—the equipment it uses to make airplane parts. Like many other manufacturers, Boeing usually designed parts for its planes first and then the supplier whose machines met Boeing's specs at the lowest price got the order. With that approach, neither firm did much adapting to the other. However, it didn't always produce a good result. Boeing had better success when it invited a small set of qualified suppliers to study its operations and recommend how a new landing-gear part could be designed so that the machines to produce them would be more efficient. One supplier, Ingersol, worked with Boeing to design the landing gear so that the total cost of both the parts and the machine to produce them would be lower. The design also helped Boeing speed up its production process. Ingersol put in all this work not knowing if it would win Boeing's business. The investment paid off with an $8 million contract.[11]

Powerful customer may control the relationship

Although a marketing manager may want to work in a cooperative partnership, that may be impossible with large customers who have the power to dictate how the relationship will work. For example, Duall/Wind, a plastics producer, was a supplier of small parts for Polaroid instant cameras. But when Duall/Wind wanted to raise its prices to cover increasing costs, Polaroid balked. Polaroid's purchasing manager demanded that Duall/Wind show a breakdown of all its costs, from materials to labour to profit. As Duall/Wind's president said, "I had a tough time getting through my head that Polaroid wanted to come right in here and have us divulge all that." But Polaroid is a big account—and it got the information it wanted. Polaroid buyers agreed to a price increase only after they were confident that Duall/Wind was doing everything possible to control costs.[12]

Buyers can spread their risk

Even if a marketing manager develops the best marketing mix possible and cultivates a close relationship with the customer, the customer may not give *all* of its business to one supplier. Buyers often look for several dependable sources of supply to protect themselves from unpredictable events such as strikes, fires, or floods in one of their suppliers' plants. That being said, a good marketing mix is still likely to win a larger share of the total business—which can prove to be very important. Moving from a 20 percent to a 30 percent share may not seem like much from a buyer's point of view, but for the seller it's a 50 percent increase in sales![13]

Reciprocity may influence relationship

We've emphasized that most buyer–seller relationships are based on reducing the customer's total procurement costs. However, for completeness we should mention that some relationships are based on reciprocity. **Reciprocity** means trading sales for sales—that is, "if you buy from me, I'll buy from you." If a company's customers also can supply products that the firm buys, then the sales departments of both buyer and seller may try to trade sales for sales. Purchasing managers generally resist reciprocity but often face pressure from their sales departments.

When prices and quality are otherwise competitive, an outside supplier seldom can break a reciprocity relationship. The supplier can only hope to become an alternative source of supply, and wait for the competitor to let its quality slip or prices rise.

Variations in buying by customer type

We've been discussing dimensions of relationships, as well as frameworks that marketing managers often use to analyze buying behaviour in many different types of customer organizations, both in Canada and internationally. However, it's also useful to have more detail about specific types of customers.

Manufacturers are important customers

One of the most striking facts about manufacturers is how few there are compared to final consumers. In the Canadian industrial market, there are fewer than 33,000 manufacturers. Exhibit 7–6 reveals that the vast majority of these are quite small. In

Exhibit 7-6 Canadian Manufacturing Establishments by Number of Employees

	UNDER 5	5 TO 9	10 TO 19	20 TO 49	50 TO 99	100 TO 199	200 TO 499	500 TO 999	1,000 +	HEAD/SALES OFFICES ETC.	TOTAL
Number of establishments	7,406	5,225	5,913	6,898	3,535	2,212	1,154	267	108	n/a	32,718
Percentage of total establishments	22.64%	15.97%	18.07%	21.08%	10.80%	6.76%	3.53%	0.82%	0.33%	n/a	100%
Number of employees	17,113	35,384	82,647	215,656	243,218	307,022	343,760	179,598	219,327	71,435	1,715,160
Percentage of employees	1.00%	2.06%	4.82%	12.57%	14.18%	17.90%	20.04%	10.47%	12.79%	4.16%	100.00%
Percentage of manufacturing shipments	0.50%	0.90%	2.50%	7.10%	9.60%	14.90%	20.90%	11.70%	25.50%	6.40%	100.00%

Source: Statistics Canada, adapted from "Manufacturing Industries of Canada: National and Provincial Areas, 1995," Catalogue No. 31-203.

small plants, the owners may also be the buyers. And they tend to buy less formally than in the relatively few large manufacturing plants that employ the majority of workers and do most of the manufacturing. Less than 5 percent of all manufacturing establishments have 200 or more employees. However, these firms account for just over 58 percent of all manufacturing shipments. It may be desirable, then, to segment industrial markets on the basis of size.

The size distribution of manufacturers varies in other countries. But across the board, the same general conclusion holds: It is often desirable to segment industrial markets on the basis of customer size because large plants do so much of the buying.

Customers cluster in geographic areas

Industrial markets are concentrated in certain geographic areas. Internationally, industrial customers are concentrated in countries that are at the more advanced stages of economic development. Within a country, there is often further concentration in specific areas. In Canada, for example, many factories are concentrated in big metropolitan areas, especially near Montreal and in southern Ontario. Exhibits 7–7 and 7–8 show how Canadian manufacturing is distributed by province and by industry group.

Concentration by industry

We see concentrations not only by size of firm and by geographic location but also by industry. Iron and steel mills cluster in Ontario, while flour mills cluster in Saskatchewan. Paper and allied industries tend to group in Quebec and British Columbia. Other industries have concentration patterns based on the availability of natural or human resources.

Much data is available on industrial markets by SIC codes

What products an industrial customer needs to buy depends on the business it is in. It follows that sales of a product are often concentrated among customers in similar businesses. For example, apparel manufacturers are the main customers for buttons. Marketing managers who can relate their own sales to their customers' type of business can focus their efforts.

Detailed information is often available to help a marketing manager learn more about customers in different lines of business. The federal government regularly collects and publishes data by Standard Industrial Classification (SIC) codes—groups

Exhibit 7-7 Number of Manufacturing Establishments and Value of Shipments by Province

PROVINCE	NUMBER OF ESTABLISHMENTS	PERCENTAGE OF ESTABLISHMENTS	VALUE OF SHIPMENTS ($000,000)	PERCENTAGE VALUE OF SHIPMENTS
Newfoundland	296	0.90%	1,961.50	0.42%
Prince Edward Island	143	0.44%	742.17	0.16%
Nova Scotia	690	2.11%	6,374.31	1.38%
New Brunswick	661	2.02%	8,766.64	1.90%
Quebec	9,983	30.51%	103,739.34	22.43%
Ontario	12,738	38.93%	257,033.30	55.59%
Manitoba	1,053	3.22%	9,060.41	1.96%
Saskatchewan	725	2.22%	5,245.80	1.13%
Alberta	2,509	7.67%	31,257.92	6.76%
British Columbia	3,881	11.86%	38,147.84	8.25%
Yukon and N.W.T.	39	0.12%	72.01	0.02%
CANADA	32,718	100.00%	462,401.25	100.00%

Source: Statistics Canada, adapted from "Manufacturing Industries of Canada: National and Provincial Areas, 1995," Catalogue No. 31-203.

Exhibit 7-8 Value of Manufacturing Shipments by Industry Group

INDUSTRY GROUP	VALUE (000,000)	PERCENTAGE OF TOTAL VALUE
Food	$ 50,276	11.56%
Beverage	7,178	1.65%
Tobacco products	2,831	0.65%
Rubber products	4,157	0.96%
Plastic products	9,347	2.15%
Leather and allied products	975	0.22%
Primary textile	4,021	0.92%
Textile products	3,605	0.83%
Clothing	6,755	1.55%
Wood	26,926	6.19%
Furniture and fixtures	6,298	1.45%
Paper and allied products	30,563	7.03%
Printing and publishing	15,566	3.58%
Primary metal	28,367	6.52%
Fabricated metal products	22,825	5.25%
Machinery	17,835	4.10%
Transportation equipment	99,567	22.90%
Electrical and electrical products	29,395	6.76%
Non-metallic mineral products	7,970	1.83%
Refined petroleum and coal	21,925	5.04%
Chemical products	30,436	7.00%
Other manufacturing	7,958	1.83%
Total	**$434,776**	**100.00%**

Source: Statistics Canada, adapted from "Monthly Survey of Manufacturing," Catalogue No. 31-001, January 1998.

of firms in similar lines of business. The number of establishments, as well as sales volumes and number of employees, broken down by geographic area, are given for each SIC code. A number of other countries collect similar data but use somewhat different classification systems. That's why Canada, the United States, and some other countries are trying to coordinate their data collection efforts by also using the

A firm like Lukens Steel is likely to find that the majority of its customers are concentrated within a few industries, which it can identify by SIC number.

North American Industry Classification System (NAICS, pronounced "Nakes"), an internationally accepted variation of the SIC system. In many other countries, however, data on business customers remains incomplete or inaccurate.

The NAICS is a new development. It was adopted as a standard in 1997, and it will be phased in over time. The phase-in will make it easier to use the new system because in the past data were reported using Standard Industrial Classification (SIC) codes. Many of the codes are similar; check the Web site at www.naics.com for details. However, the move to the new system should help business marketers. The NAICS system is suited for identifying new or fast-changing industries—and for marketers that spells opportunity. NAICS is also more detailed than SIC and works better for services such as financial institutions, health care providers, and firms in the entertainment business. The general logic of NAICS is similar to that of SIC. So, let's take a closer look at how SIC codes work.

In Canada, SIC code breakdowns start with broad industry categories such as food and related products (code 20), tobacco products (code 21), textile mill products (code 22), and apparel (code 23). Within each two-digit industry breakdown, much more detailed information may be available for three-digit and four-digit industries (that is, subindustries of the two- or three-digit industries). Exhibit 7–9 gives an example of more detailed breakdowns within the sawmill and planing mill products industry. But four-digit detail isn't available for all industries in every geographic area. To keep from disclosing competitively useful information, the government does not publish data when only one or two plants are located in any given area.

Many firms find their *current* customers' SIC codes and then look at SIC-coded lists for similar companies that may need the same goods and services. Other companies look at which SIC categories are growing or declining to discover new opportunities. Most trade associations and private organizations that gather data on business markets also use SIC codes.

The SIC system is not perfect. Some companies have sales in several categories but are listed by the government in only one—the code with the largest sales. In addition, some newer manufacturing businesses and some service firms don't fit any of the categories all that well. So although a great deal of good information is available, the codes must be used carefully.[14]

Exhibit 7-9 SIC Analysis of the Sawmill and Planing Mill Products Industry

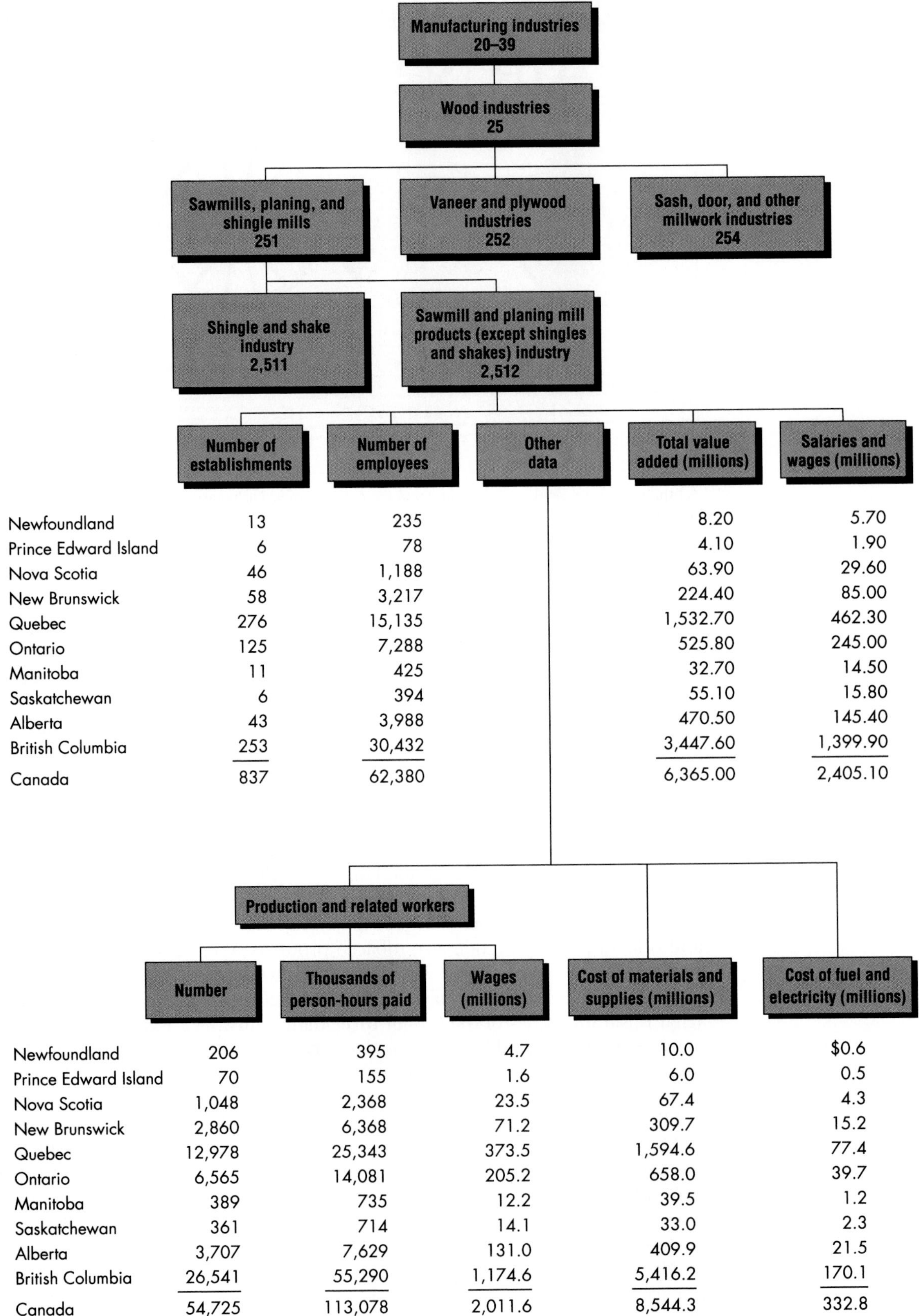

	Number of establishments	Number of employees	Total value added (millions)	Salaries and wages (millions)
Newfoundland	13	235	8.20	5.70
Prince Edward Island	6	78	4.10	1.90
Nova Scotia	46	1,188	63.90	29.60
New Brunswick	58	3,217	224.40	85.00
Quebec	276	15,135	1,532.70	462.30
Ontario	125	7,288	525.80	245.00
Manitoba	11	425	32.70	14.50
Saskatchewan	6	394	55.10	15.80
Alberta	43	3,988	470.50	145.40
British Columbia	253	30,432	3,447.60	1,399.90
Canada	837	62,380	6,365.00	2,405.10

	Number	Thousands of person-hours paid	Wages (millions)	Cost of materials and supplies (millions)	Cost of fuel and electricity (millions)
Newfoundland	206	395	4.7	10.0	$0.6
Prince Edward Island	70	155	1.6	6.0	0.5
Nova Scotia	1,048	2,368	23.5	67.4	4.3
New Brunswick	2,860	6,368	71.2	309.7	15.2
Quebec	12,978	25,343	373.5	1,594.6	77.4
Ontario	6,565	14,081	205.2	658.0	39.7
Manitoba	389	735	12.2	39.5	1.2
Saskatchewan	361	714	14.1	33.0	2.3
Alberta	3,707	7,629	131.0	409.9	21.5
British Columbia	26,541	55,290	1,174.6	5,416.2	170.1
Canada	54,725	113,078	2,011.6	8,544.3	332.8

Source: Statistics Canada, adapted from "Wood Industries, 1994," Catalogue No. 35-250.

Producers of services—smaller and more spread out

Marketing managers need to keep in mind that the service side of the Canadian economy is large and has been growing fast. Service operations are also growing in some other countries. There may be good opportunities in providing these companies with the products they need to support their operations. But there are also challenges.

There are more than 2 million service firms in North America—about six times as many as there are manufacturers. Some of these are big companies with international operations. Examples include The Royal Bank, Four Seasons Hotels, and Canada Post. These firms have purchasing departments that are like those in large manufacturing organizations. But, as you might guess given the large number of service firms, most of them are small. They're also more spread out around the country than manufacturing concerns. Factories often locate where transportation facilities are good, raw materials are available, and it is less costly to produce goods in quantity. Service operations, in contrast, usually have to be close to their customers.

Buying may not be as formal

Purchases by small service firms are often handled by whoever is in charge. This may be a doctor, a lawyer, the owner of a local insurance agency, or the manager of a hotel. Suppliers who usually deal with purchasing specialists in large organizations may have trouble adjusting to this market. Personal selling is still an important part of promotion, but reaching these customers in the first place often requires more advertising. And small service firms may need much more help in buying than a large corporation.

Canon, the familiar name in office copiers, was very successful serving the needs of smaller service firms like law offices. Canon developed promotion materials to help first-time buyers understand differences in copiers. It emphasized that its machines were easy to use and maintain. And it used retail channels to make its copiers available in smaller areas where there wasn't enough business to justify using a sales rep.[15]

Retailers and wholesalers buy for their customers

Most retail and wholesale buyers see themselves as purchasing agents for their target customers—remembering the old saying that "Goods well bought are half sold." Typically, retailers do *not* see themselves as sales agents for particular manufacturers. They buy what they think they can profitably sell. And wholesalers buy what they think their retailers can sell.[16]

Committee buying is impersonal

Some buyers—especially those who work for big retail chains—are annoyed by the number of wholesalers' and manufacturers' representatives who call on them. Space in their stores is limited, and they simply are not interested in carrying every product that some salesperson wants them to sell. Consider the problem facing grocery chains. In an average week, 150 to 250 new items are offered to the buying offices of a large chain like Safeway. If the chain accepted all of them, it would add 10,000 new items during a single year! Obviously, these firms need a way to deal with this overload.[17]

Decisions to add or drop lines or change buying policies may be handled by a *buying committee.* The seller still calls on and gives a pitch to a buyer—but the buyer does not have final responsibility. Instead, the buyer prepares forms summarizing proposals for new products and passes them on to the committee for evaluation. The seller may not get to present her story to the buying committee in person. This rational, almost cold-blooded approach reduces the impact of a persuasive salesperson.

Buyers watch computer output closely

Most larger firms now use sophisticated computerized inventory control systems. Scanners at retail checkout counters keep track of what goes out the door, and computers use this data to update the records. Even small retailers and wholesalers use automated control systems that can print daily unit control reports showing sales of every product. Buyers with this kind of information know, in detail, the profitability of the different competing products. If a product isn't moving, the retailer isn't likely to be impressed by a salesperson's request for more in-store attention or added shelf space.

Reorders are straight rebuys

Retailers and wholesalers usually carry a large number of products. A drug wholesaler, for example, may carry up to 125,000 products. Because they deal with so many products, most intermediaries buy their products on a routine, automatic reorder basis—straight rebuys—once they make the initial decision to stock specific items. Sellers to these markets must understand the size of the buyer's job and have something useful to say and do when they call. For example, they might try to save the intermediary time by taking inventory, setting up displays, or arranging shelves—while trying to get a chance to talk about specific products and maintain the relationship.

Some are not "open to buy"

Retail buyers are sometimes controlled by a miniature profit-and-loss statement for each department or merchandise line. In an effort to make a profit, the buyer tries to forecast sales, merchandise costs, and expenses. The figure for "cost of merchandise" is the amount buyers have budgeted to spend over the budget period. If the money has not yet been spent, buyers are **open to buy**—that is, they have budgeted funds that can be spent during the current period. However, if the budget has been spent, they are no longer in the market and no amount of special promotion or price-cutting is likely to induce them to buy.[18]

Buying and selling are closely related

In wholesale and retail firms, there is usually a very close relationship between buying and selling. Buyers are often in close contact with their firm's customers. The housewares buyer for a local department store, for example, may supervise the salespeople who sell housewares. Salespeople are quick to tell the buyer if a customer wants a product that is not available. Therefore, salespeople should be included in the promotion effort.

Resident buyers may help a firm's buyers

Resident buyers are independent buying agents who work in central markets (Toronto, Paris, Rome, Hong Kong, Montreal, etc.) for several retailer or wholesaler customers based in outlying areas or other countries. They buy new styles and fashions, as well as fill-in items as their customers run out of stock during the year.

Resident buying organizations fill a need. They help small channel members (products and intermediaries) reach each other inexpensively. Resident buyers usually are paid an annual fee based on their purchases.

The farm market

As Marketing Demo 7–1 illustrates, agriculture still plays an important role in the Canadian economy. However, farm incomes are greatly influenced by prices received for crops, cost of supplies purchased, and interest rates.

The number of farms has been declining steadily for many years. At the same time, however, average farm size is continuing to increase. Although there are still many small units, large farms produce most of the output. The modern commercial farm is highly mechanized, highly specialized, and capital-intensive.[19] Owners of large farms tend to run their operations as a business rather than a way of life. They respond to sales presentations stressing savings and increases in productivity. Further, they're more knowledgeable and receptive to change than those running smaller operations—and they may have the money to buy what they need.

For some products, however, farmers share the same motivations as other consumers. This is understandable, since a farmer's home and place of business are the same. Some manufacturers take pride in their office facilities and factories, and a similar pride may affect farmers' purchasing behaviour. Among owners of smaller farms, a new tractor may offer just as much status as a new car would to an urban resident. Also, a farmer's roles in business and as a final consumer sometimes overlap. For example, a station wagon might be used for carrying both feed and the family's groceries.

Farmers tend to specialize in one or a few products such as wheat (or other grains), dairy, and poultry. These specializations have developed in response to geographic and climatic regions. A farmer on the Prairies growing wheat has different needs from a farmer in Ontario or Quebec engaged in the dairy business. And a fruit farmer on the Niagara Peninsula will have different needs from a fruit farmer in British Columbia, where fruit is grown on irrigated terraces.

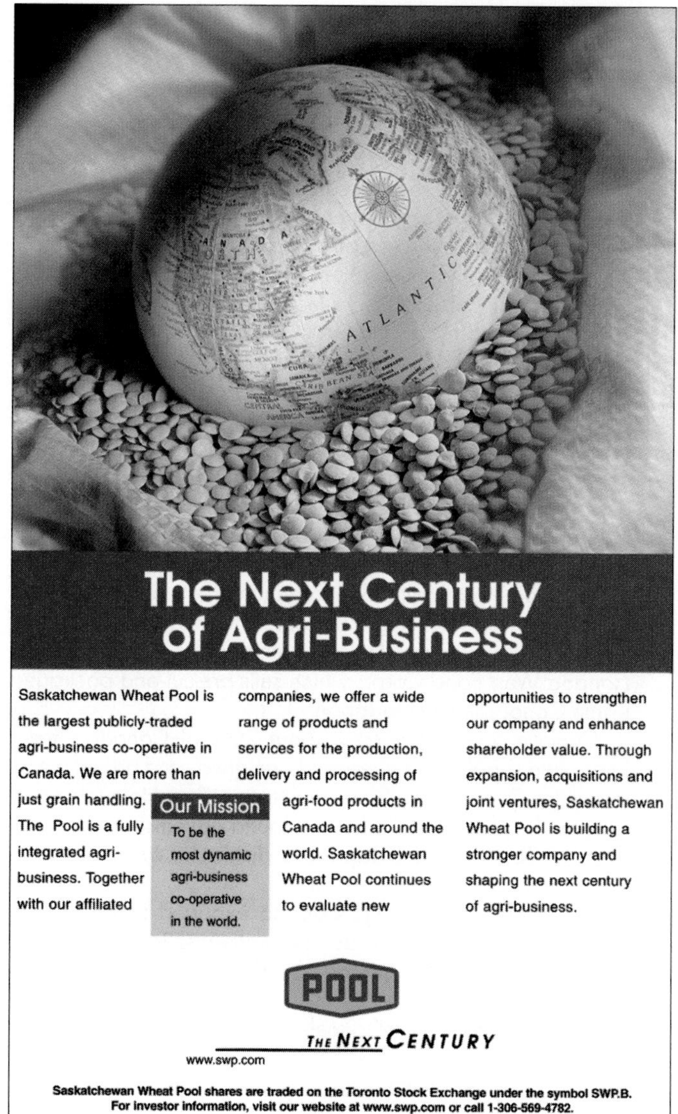

ATLANTIC
The Next Century of Agri-Business
Saskatchewan Wheat Pool is the largest publicly-traded agri-business co-operative in Canada. We are more than just grain handling. The Pool is a fully integrated agri-business. Together with our affiliated companies, we offer a wide range of products and services for the production, delivery and processing of agri-food products in Canada and around the world. Saskatchewan Wheat Pool continues to evaluate new opportunities to strengthen our company and enhance shareholder value. Through expansion, acquisitions and joint ventures, Saskatchewan Wheat Pool is building a stronger company and shaping the next century of agri-business.
Our Mission
To be the most dynamic agri-business co-operative in the world.
POOL
THE NEXT CENTURY
www.swp.com
Saskatchewan Wheat Pool shares are traded on the Toronto Stock Exchange under the symbol SWP.B.
For investor information, visit our website at www.swp.com or call 1-306-569-4782.

The Saskatchewan Wheat Pool plays a key role in agricultural marketing.

Marketing mixes may have to be developed for each type of farm, and occasionally even for individual farmers. Fertilizer producers, for example, have moved far beyond selling an all-purpose bag of fertilizer: Now they're able to blend the exact type needed for each farm. Then they load directly onto fertilizer spreaders that do the job more economically than manual methods. Some producers, in fact, are working directly with farmers, providing a complete service, including fertilizing, weeding, and debugging—all tailored to each individual farmer's needs.

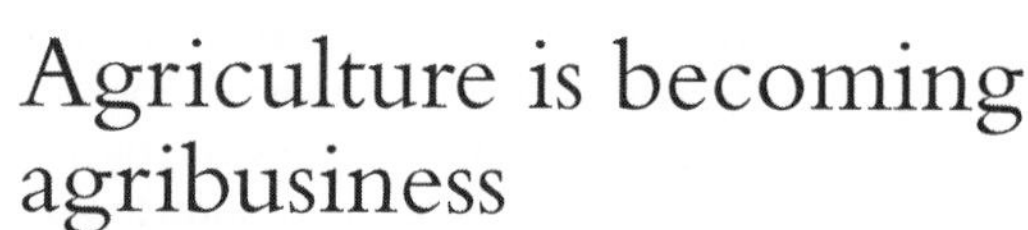

Agriculture is becoming agribusiness

Another important factor is the increasing tendency for farmers to engage in **contract farming.** Here, the farmer obtains supplies and perhaps working capital from local dealers or manufacturers, who agree to purchase the farm's output, sometimes at guaranteed prices. This limits farmers' buying freedom, since they become, in effect, employees. Such arrangements are becoming more common, especially in raising chickens and turkeys and in growing fresh vegetables for commercial canning. For example, a farmer may contract with Maple Leaf Foods, which will supply chicks and feed. The company, in turn, will receive all the chickens that farmer produces. Such arrangements

Marketing Demo 7-1

Rural Sophisticates

Marketing Is Now Second Nature to the Farm Sector

The quaint family farm of yesteryear is undergoing massive changes. Increasingly, the enterprises are likely to be run by college or university educated farmers, a change that's reflected in the way food is being produced, processed, and marketed both at home and abroad.

"There's a saying about farming," says John Murphy, the Royal Bank's Winnipeg-based vice-president of agriculture and agri-business banking, about this evolution. "If you treat farming as a business, it can be a very rewarding way of life. But if you treat farming as a way of life, it can be a very unpleasant business experience."

Canada's agriculture and agri-food industry is big business. The most recent figures show that primary agriculture producers, farmers of crops and livestock, reported $25.6 billion in sales in 1994, while the food and beverage processing industry had wholesale sales of $48.7 billion. This year, some 200,000 farmers (of whom 68,000 are full-time commercial farmers) are expected to buy $11 billion of products from other sectors, like manufacturing, chemical, energy, and finance. That's a projected spending increase of over 1% from 1995.

That level of buying clout commands a lot of respect from marketers, who are boosting the sophistication levels of both their business-to-business and consumer-targeted marketing. Those strategies include defining specific markets and the most effective ways to reach them.

The size of the farming population has shrunk dramatically this century. Today, a mere 3% of Canada's total population lives on farms, compared to close to 32% in 1931. Consequently, avenues like direct mail are doing a better job than traditional mass media in reaching small but diverse and far-flung rural audiences.

The Parker Group, a Calgary-based agri-agency, successfully used direct mail in a relationship-marketing campaign by Vitavax (a seed coating to protect against crop pests and diseases) and the Alberta Wheat Pool. A stuffer in Pool statements encouraged children to become "field investigators" by sending away for a "Sam Spade" science kit that could detect wireworm, fungi, or soil-borne diseases. The kit served several purposes: parents were alerted to potential crop hazards; kids became eligible for prizes; and Vitavax and the Pool gathered data to help quantify their markets.

Trade shows are another effective method of reaching agri-producers. When Sherwin and Sharon Petersen of Rose Valley, Sask., started Buffalo Seeding Systems Ltd. three years ago, they ruled out advertising and opted for face-to-face contact at agri-trade shows.

"Trade shows are the most direct way of marketing. For our products, at this time, it's the best approach," says Sherwin, who attended 32 agri-trade shows during his first year of business.

Paulette Kidd, of Regina's Agribition, Canada's largest annual agricultural trade and livestock show, says exhibitors use such shows to do promotions, brand positioning, and public relations. "Trade shows keep up customer relations," she says.

Business-to-business agri-marketing hasn't lost its human touch, says the Royal Bank's Murphy, who stresses that strong personal relationships still play a major role. The most significant way the Royal Bank reaches its 80,000 farm customers is by having a strong presence in the community with knowledgeable employees who understand farming. "It's really people skills that are the product," says Murphy. "The money's pretty generic."

Still, the bank distributes various collateral materials (produced by Calgary's Fieldstone Marketing & Public Relations) through its branches, and advertises in trade publications. It also produces its own bimonthly newsletter in French and English for farmers.

The other side of the agri-marketing coin is the attempt to reach consumers. Part of the growing marketing awareness of agri-producers is the desire to sell images. Late in February, the Growing Alberta campaign (created by Fieldstone) will be launched by the Canada-Alberta Environmentally Sustainable Agriculture Agreement. The print and electronic campaign will address the industry's economic impact, quality of life, environment, conservation, and food quality and safety.

"Failing to address these issues could affect the future of agriculture in Canada," says Kim McConnell of Fieldstone Marketing, who owns a family farm in Saskatchewan. "Agriculture is a good-news secret and a growth industry. People need to get a handle around it and see the opportunities it has."

One of those opportunities is the chance to crack international markets with niche products. Agri-Food Market Strategies are trade missions jointly funded by industry and the federal government, that have become fundamental to marketing Canadian agri-products abroad.

Still, gaining a foothold in foreign markets can be difficult. "You don't go knocking on doors the way you would in Canada," says Gary Haley, president of Calgary-based Canada West Food Corp., which sells pre-cut and packaged prime Canadian beef to Japan.

Canada West processes about 20% of Canada's fresh lamb, and supplies cut, wrapped, weighed, and priced meats to retailer Overwaitea/Save-on Foods. When Haley decided to enter the Japanese market, he found advertising costs prohibitive. So he hired a Japanese distributor to do Canada West's marketing.

For much of its history, Canada exported its agriculture products as commodities, as raw materials. Today's producers are rethinking that strategy by developing products with the consumer in mind.

Says Fieldstone's McConnell: "Farmers are thinking more about the end user."

Source: Terry Bullick, *Marketing Magazine*, February 19, 1996, pp. 10, 11.

offer security, but they also limit the markets for sellers. It's all part of the move toward bigger and more businesslike agricultural enterprises—what's called **agribusiness.**

Where such contractual arrangements (or actual ownership) are common, marketing managers will have to adjust their marketing mixes. They may have to sell directly to the large manufacturers or dealers handling the arrangements rather than to each farmer.

Farmers are a market, of course, because farm products are themselves marketed. Agricultural marketing is done through a mix of private trading, public sales and auctions, sales under contract, sales through cooperatives, and sales by marketing boards. Methods vary with the type of product, the region, and the preference of producers. Most products, except western grains and a few special crops, are marketed in more than one way.

For many years, large central markets served as price-making centres for agricultural products. These were places where supply and demand forces came together. It's no longer economically feasible, however, for all commodities of a given type to be brought together when buying and selling occurs. With the introduction of standardized grading procedures, this is no longer necessary in any case.

Canada's principal livestock markets are in Montreal, Toronto, Winnipeg, Calgary, and Edmonton, but there are many other outlets ranging from large stockyards to country collection points. Egg sales are regulated by the Canadian Egg Marketing Agency, and the Canadian Turkey Marketing Agency performs similar services for turkey producers. The marketing of fluid milk is a provincial responsibility, with quality, prices, and deliveries regulated by provincial marketing agencies. Fruits and vegetables are distributed through fresh and frozen food markets, canneries, and other processors.

Marketing boards

Marketing boards are an important type of marketing institution for agricultural products. For example, the Canadian Wheat Board is responsible for marketing wheat and barley grown in western Canada. In Ontario, all wheat is sold through the Ontario Wheat Producers' Marketing Board.

Other products sold under marketing boards include hogs, milk, fruit, potatoes and other vegetables, tobacco, poultry, eggs, wood, soybeans, honey, maple products, and pulpwood. There are two federally authorized marketing boards operating in Canada and over 100 provincial ones. Although these boards differ in the powers they can exercise, their mandate generally includes pricing, quotas for production and/or marketing, licensing, promotion, and the control of interprovincial and export trade.[20]

However, the future of marketing boards is uncertain. The new World Trade Organization (WTO) is opposed to making exceptions for supply management schemes in the agricultural sector. Now that a trade deal has been struck, marketing board quotas will be permitted to exist temporarily, but later will be replaced with tariffs, which also will eventually be eliminated.

It is unclear what this will mean for the Canadian agricultural sector. Some say that increased competition from other countries will destroy Canadian farming. Others believe that farmers' incomes will actually increase. Most farmers, however, are against the abolition of marketing boards and the protection they offer in the domestic market.[21]

The government market

Governments in Canada are a very large and concentrated market. On the federal level, for example, much of the buying is done through Public Works and Government Services Canada, a department that purchases billions of dollars' worth of goods and services a year for itself and for other federal departments and agencies. The Department of National Defence is generally Canada's largest single customer. Other major purchasers include the

Ethical Dimensions

Rigged Specs Are an Ethical Concern

At the extreme, a government customer who wants a specific brand or supplier may try to write the description so that no other supplier can meet all the specs. The buyer may have good reasons for such preferences—a more reliable product, prompt delivery, or better service after the sale. This kind of loyalty sounds great, but marketers must be sensitive to the ethical issues involved. Laws that require government customers to get bids are intended to increase competition among suppliers, not reduce it. Specs that are written primarily to defeat the purpose of these laws may be viewed as illegal bid rigging.

Canadian Commercial Corporation (a Crown corporation that helps foreign governments purchase goods made in Canada) and Transport Canada. Collectively, provincial and local governments are even more important markets than the federal government.

The range of goods and services purchased by government is vast, and includes everything from advertising services to appliances. Governments not only run schools, police departments, and military organizations, but also supermarkets, public utilities, research laboratories, offices, hospitals, and liquor stores. And it's expected that government expenditures for these operations will continue to grow. Such opportunities must not be ignored by an aggressive marketing manager.

Government buying methods

Most goods and services are purchased through contracts awarded after a requisition is received from the department that needs these items. Any Canadian business supplying such goods and services is eligible to bid. The only requirements are a desire to sell and evidence of the ability to supply under the terms and conditions of the contract. Any size firm can bid—the overall size of government expenditures is no indication of the size of individual contracts. Despite the overall amount spent by government, firms of all sizes can and do bid for such business, since many thousands of contracts are for relatively small amounts.

Bidding is common

Although bidding procedures vary slightly between departments and levels of government, similar practices are followed. Potential suppliers are invited to tender on a particular contract. The government department in question has drawn up its list of specifications carefully, to clarify what any supplier must bid on and to simplify the selection procedure. The contract is then awarded to the firm submitting the lowest bid that also meets the specifications of the tender call.

Writing specifications isn't easy, and buyers usually appreciate knowledgeable salespeople's help. Salespeople *want* to have input on the specifications so that their product can be considered or even have an advantage. One company may get the business—even with a bid that is not the lowest—because the lower bids don't meet minimum specifications.

Not all government purchases are made this way. Many branded or standardized items are routinely purchased through standing offer arrangements. These offers are issued to suppliers for specific time periods. The suppliers, in turn, agree to supply the goods or services at prearranged prices and delivery conditions. Pharmaceutical supplies, tires and tubes, and petroleum and oil are often bought this way. Invitations to tender on major construction contracts are both advertised and mailed to likely bidders.

Internet Illustration 7-1

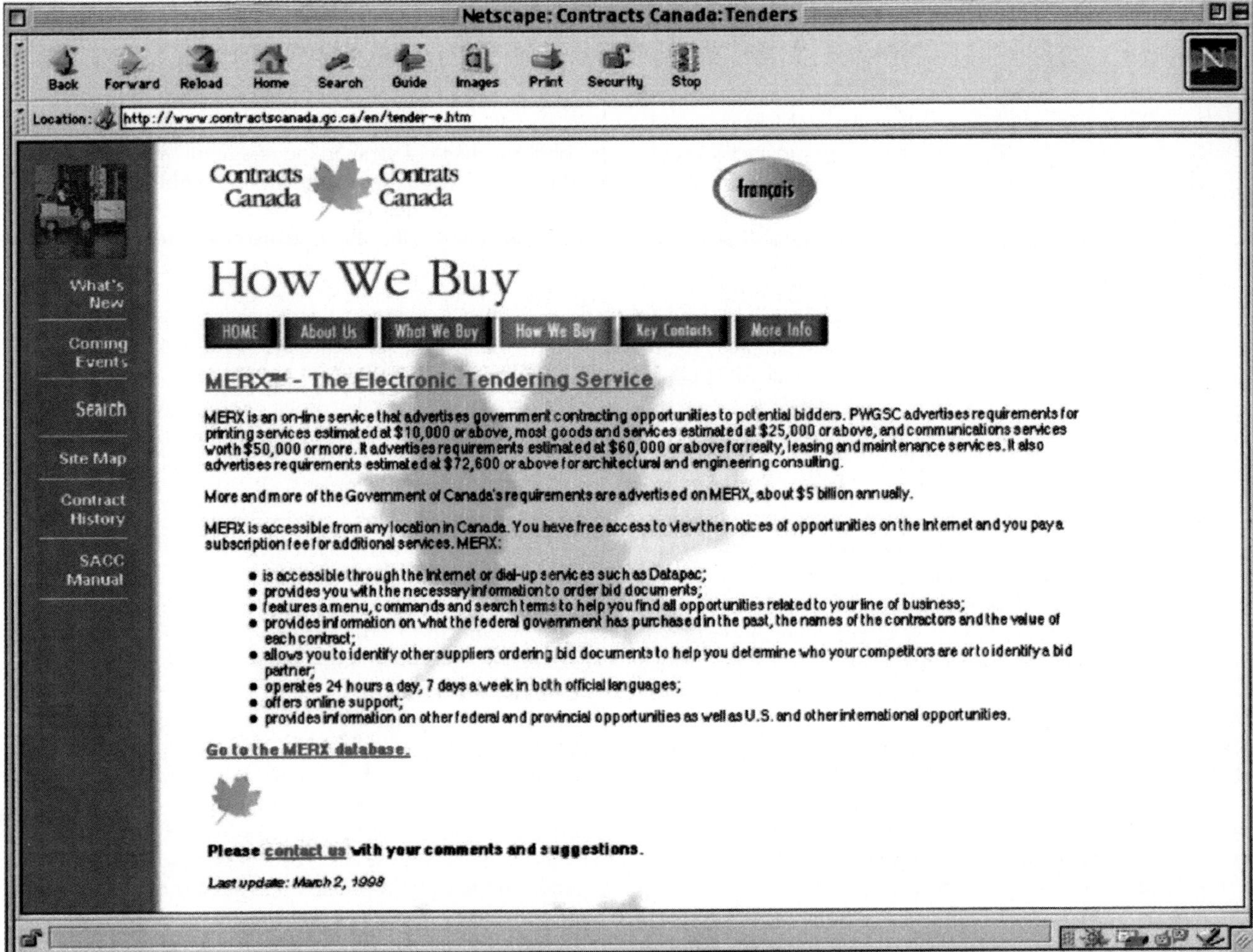

Negotiated contracts are common, too

Contracts may be negotiated for items that are not branded or easily described, or for products that require research and development, or in cases where there is no effective competition. Depending on the government unit involved, the contract may be subject to audit and renegotiation, especially if the contractor makes a larger profit than expected.

Negotiation is often necessary when there are many intangible factors. Unfortunately, this is exactly where favouritism and influence can slip in. Nevertheless, negotiation is an important buying method in government sales—so a marketing mix should emphasize more than just low price.

Learning what government wants

Since almost all government contracts are advertised, a prospective supplier can focus on particular government agencies or departments. Firms can now easily learn about potential government target markets using the assistance available from online government sources. Contracts Canada is an interdepartmental initiative to improve buyer awareness and simplify access to federal government purchasing. Its primary responsibility is to make it easier for Canadian suppliers to do business with the federal government. Contracts Canada also serves as a focal point for supplier and buyer inquiries. Information on past government purchases and forthcoming "opportunities to bid" is available through **Merx—The Electronic Tendering Service** (www.merx.cebra.com). Internet Illustration 7–1

Marketing Demo 7-2

B.C. Only Holdout in Trade Deal

The federal government and every province except B.C. agreed Friday to a watered-down deal to open up the $30-billion-a-year market for goods and services in Canada.

The agreement, reached just as the Canadian Chamber of Commerce issued a scathing assessment of federal-provincial progress on promoting trade, is intended to expand competition in the procurement of goods and services in the so-called MASH sector—municipalities, academic institutions, social services and hospitals.

The deal, aimed at preventing discrimination in the trade of goods and services, includes creation of an electronic tendering system to ensure companies are able to bid on procurement contracts in other provinces.

Federal Industry Minister John Manley said he hopes B.C. will eventually join the agreement when the private sector and local taxpayers see the benefits of freer trade. But Michael Farnworth, B.C.'s new minister of employment and investment, cut short his participation in the meeting and left during lunch.

In 1994, Ottawa and all 10 provinces agreed to sign a treaty to end nontariff barriers to trade between the provinces in everything from government procurement to sales of local brands of beer in other provinces.

The major item on Friday's agenda was to extend government procurement rules to all public and civic institutions within provincial borders.

Businesses across the country that supply those institutions "will have access to much larger potential sales by having access directly to those markets," Manley told reporters. "And secondly, it should enable taxpayers in all those areas to expect that their institutions are going to be able to get the best possible value for their money."

But the agreement, which takes effect a year from now, was altered to exclude the provision of services, such as nursing care. On that basis, B.C. agreed to put the MASH deal into the broader 1994 Agreement on Internal Trade (AIT).

The B.C. government pushed successfully for the exclusions even though it won't be subject to Friday's agreement.

A B.C. official said the province wanted to exclude services in the health and social field because the provinces believed this would invite U.S. competition in this area under the North American Free Trade Agreement.

A federal official said neither Ottawa nor the nine other provinces accepted that argument, but bowed to Victoria's wishes in order to reach Friday's settlement.

Federal governments have been trying for years to lower interprovincial trade barriers, but even the 1994 AIT has been seen as, at best, a modest step because it has feeble enforcement provisions.

The Canadian Chamber of Commerce issued the federal and provincial governments a "failing grade" Friday for their efforts.

"In the almost four years since the Agreement on Internal Trade was signed, regional and sectoral interests have been allowed to dominate the talks, countless deadlines have been missed, and the whole process has been ground to a virtual halt," the Chamber said.

The Chamber said knocking down trade barriers would create at least 200,000 jobs across Canada.

Source: Peter O'Neil, *The Vancouver Sun,* February 21, 1998, A5.

shows how comprehensive that system is. Additional information on the specifics of bidding and tendering is available from Contracts Canada's own Web site (www.contractscanada.gc.ca).

Various provincial and local governments also offer assistance. Industry-oriented magazines and trade associations provide information on how to reach schools, hospitals, highway departments, parks boards, and so on. Of course, marketers interested in selling to provincial and local governments must be aware of any "province first" procurement policies. Most of the provinces tend to favour local suppliers at the expense of firms manufacturing elsewhere. Although a provincial preference in purchasing may make political sense, it poses real problems for firms trying to sell nationally in what is already a very small "Internal Common Market." Marketing Demo 7–2 reports on the successes and failures of one of the periodic efforts to reduce interprovincial trade barriers.

Dealing with foreign governments

Government agencies around the world spend a great deal of money, and they are important target customers for some firms. But selling to government units in foreign countries can be a real challenge. In many cases, a firm must get permission from the government in its own country to sell to a foreign government. Moreover, most government contracts favour domestic suppliers if they are available. Even if such favouritism is not explicit, public sentiment may make it very difficult for a foreign competitor to get a contract. Or the government bureaucracy may simply bury a foreign supplier in so much red tape that there's no way to win.

Questions and Problems

1. Compare and contrast the problem-solving approaches used by final consumers and organizational buyers.
2. Describe the situations that would lead to the use of the three different buying processes for a particular product—lightweight bumpers for a pickup truck.
3. Compare and contrast the buying processes of final consumers and organizational buyers.
4. Briefly discuss why a marketing manager should think about who is likely to be involved in the buying centre for a particular purchase. Is the buying centre idea useful in consumer buying? Explain your answer.
5. If a Canadian hospital were planning to buy expensive MRI scanning equipment (to detect tumors), who might be involved in the buying centre? Explain your answer and describe the types of influence that different people might have.
6. Why would an organizational buyer want to get competitive bids? What are some of the situations when competitive bidding can't be used?
7. How likely would each of the following be to use competitive bids? (a) a small town that needed a road resurfaced, (b) a scouting organization that needed a printer to print its scouting handbook, (c) a hardware retailer that wants to add a new lawn mower line, (d) a grocery store that wants to install a new checkout scanner, (e) a sorority that wants to buy a computer to keep track of member dues. Explain your answers.
8. Discuss the advantages and disadvantages of just-in-time supply relationships from an organizational buyer's point of view. Are the advantages and disadvantages merely reversed from the seller's point of view?
9. IBM has a long-term negotiated contract with Microsoft, a supplier that provides the software operating system for IBM computers. Discuss several of the issues that IBM might want the contract to cover.
10. Would a toy manufacturer need a different marketing strategy for a big retail chain like Toys "Я" Us than for a single toy store run by its owner? Discuss your answer.
11. How do you think a furniture manufacturer's buying habits and practices would be affected by the specific type of product to be purchased? Consider fabric for upholstered furniture, a lathe for the production line, cardboard for shipping cartons, and lubricants for production machinery.
12. Discuss the importance of target marketing when analyzing organizational markets. How easy is it to isolate homogeneous market segments in these markets?
13. Explain how SIC codes might be helpful in evaluating and understanding business markets. Give an example.
14. Considering the nature of retail buying, outline the basic ingredients of promotion to retail buyers. Does it make any difference what kinds of products are involved? Are any other factors relevant?
15. The government market is obviously an extremely large one, yet it is often slighted or even ignored by many firms. Red tape is certainly one reason, but there are others. Discuss the situation. Be sure to include the possibility of segmenting in your analysis.

Suggested Cases

6	The Hand Guard
22	Kelman Mfg. Inc.
30	Le Clair Chemical Company

Computer-aided problem

Vendor Analysis

CompuTech, Inc., makes circuit boards for microcomputers. It is evaluating two possible suppliers of electronic memory chips.

The chips do the same job. Although manufacturing quality has been improving, some chips are always defective. Both suppliers will replace defective chips. But the only practical way to test for a defective chip is to assemble a circuit board and "burn it in"—run it and see if it works. When one chip on a board is defective at that point, it costs $2.00 for the extra labour time to replace it. Supplier 1 guarantees a chip failure rate of not more than 1 per 100 (that is, a defect rate of 1 percent). The second supplier's 2 percent defective rate is higher, but its price is lower.

Supplier 1 has been able to improve its quality because it uses a heavier plastic case to hold the chip. The only disadvantage of the heavier case is that it requires CompuTech to use a connector that is somewhat more expensive.

Transportation costs are added to the price quoted by either supplier, but supplier 2 is farther away, so its transportation costs are higher. And because of the distance, delays in supplies reaching CompuTech are sometimes a problem. To ensure that a sufficient supply is on hand to keep production going, CompuTech must maintain a backup inventory—and this increases inventory costs. CompuTech figures inventory costs—the expenses of finance and storage—as a percentage of the total order cost.

To make its vendor analysis easier, CompuTech's purchasing agent has entered data about the two suppliers on a spreadsheet. He based his estimates on the quantity he thinks he will need over a full year.

a. Based on the results shown in the initial spreadsheet, which supplier do you think CompuTech should select? Why?

b. CompuTech estimates it will need 100,000 chips a year if sales go as expected. But if sales are slow, fewer chips will be needed. This isn't an issue with supplier 2; its price is the same at any quantity. However, supplier 1's price per chip will be $1.95 if CompuTech buys less than 90,000 during the year. If CompuTech only needs 84,500 chips, which supplier would be more economical? Why?

c. If the actual purchase quantity will be 84,500 and supplier 1's price is $1.95, what is the highest price at which supplier 2 will still be the lower-cost vendor for CompuTech? (Hint: You can enter various prices for supplier 2 in the spreadsheet—or use the What If analysis to vary supplier 2's price and display the total costs for both vendors.)

For additional questions related to this problem, see Exercise 7–3 in the *Learning Aid for Use with Basic Marketing,* Ninth Canadian Edition.

When you finish this chapter, you should:

- Know about defining generic markets and product markets.
- Know what market segmentation is and how to segment product-markets into submarkets.
- Know three approaches to choosing the target segment.
- Know dimensions that may be useful for segmenting markets.
- Know what positioning is, and why it is useful.
- Understand the important new terms (shown in orange).

Chapter eight

Finding Target Markets Through Segmentation

One of the most basic forms of segmenting is male and female. Many heavily marketed products are targeted to one or the other of these two segments. In recent years, however, unisex products have entered the marketplace with great success.

Patrick Carroll, the vice-president international of Calvin Klein Cosmetics (Canada) is calculating just how well Klein's "shared fragrances" cKone and cKbe have done in this country, and he's making no bones about why he's in the business.

If 1996 sales are any indication, Carroll will never have to worry about being a pauper. Last year, he says, the Oakville, Ont.-based CK Canada had revenues of about $52 million in its limited area of distribution (mainly department stores plus a smattering of drug stores and perfumeries).

Of the estimated $240-million Canadian market, Calvin Klein fragrances command about a 22% share. That's due in great part to the success of the cKone and cKbe brands, which account for approximately 43% of CK's total sales—or about 10% of the overall fragrances market. That's not small change.

In fact, since the launch of cKone in September 1994 and of cKbe in August 1996, Calvin Klein Cosmetics has made cKone North America's top-selling fragrance, and paved the way for a whole host of entrants to the shared fragrance market. And while consultants say the his 'n' hers perfume trend has reached its peak, CK's followers, such as Paco Rabanne, Roots, The Gap and Banana Republic, are also reporting much success with their slightly different versions of the citrusy scent.

"We've gone from the 'me' fragrances of the '80s to the 'we' fragrances of the 90s," says Marian Bendeth, a fragrance specialist at her own consultancy, Six Scents of Toronto. "Shared scents are not new, but we can thank Calvin Klein for its resurgence."

Jim Hicks, publisher of *Cosmetics* magazine in Toronto, agrees. "Calvin Klein developed a category that didn't exist. [cKone] did so much better than anybody had ever expected. It just blew off the shelves." And while both Hicks and Bendeth maintain that you've got to have good juice to begin with, the success of cKone and cKbe is largely attributable to the offbeat and aggressive advertising by Calvin Klein New York's in-house marketing team.

"Oh, bless him. He's so slick," says Bendeth of Klein's marketing efforts. "He reached out to a new generation of kids that never really thought about him before. With Generation X, the kids want to stand apart. They want something they can call their own. The concept was so eclectic and new to them. Calvin Klein expressed their feelings through his advertising about individuality, but in a shared environment."

And, boy, did they express. In 1996, CK bought space in almost 40 Canadian magazines—including many "alternative" titles such as *Shift* and *Venue,* plus tons of daily newspapers and billboards. Not to mention the spillover from American magazines and TV. According to ACNielsen of Markham, Ont., department stores Sears, Eaton's and The Bay also spent almost $1 million combined to advertise the two unisex scents in 1996.

"Our advertising tends to cut through the clutter," says CK's Carroll. "No matter whether you like it or hate it, people notice it. If you want to be on the cutting edge, you've got to take some risks. Look at these characters," he barks excitedly. "Look at the way they're dressed! We don't just have beautiful people in the ads, we've got all sorts."

Source: Abridged from Mikala Folb, "His + Hers = $$$," *Marketing Magazine*, July 21/28, 1997, p. 20.

cK one
Calvin Klein
a fragrance for a man or a woman

What is a company's market?

Identifying a company's market is an important but sticky issue. In general, a **market** is a group of potential customers with similar needs who are willing to exchange something of value with sellers offering various goods and/or services—that is, ways of satisfying those needs.

Market-oriented managers develop marketing mixes for *specific* target markets. Getting the firm to focus on specific target markets is vital. As shown in Exhibit 8–1, target marketing requires a narrowing-down process to get beyond production-oriented mass market thinking. But firms often misunderstand this narrowing-down process.

Don't just focus on the product

Some production-oriented managers ignore the tough part of defining markets. To make the narrowing-down process easier, they just describe their markets in terms of *products* they sell. For example, producers and retailers of greeting cards might define their market as the "greeting card" market. But this production-oriented approach ignores customers—and customers make a market! This also leads to missed opportunities. Hallmark isn't missing these opportunities. Instead, Hallmark aims at the "personal expression" market. It offers all kinds of products that can be sent as "memory makers"—to express one person's feelings toward another.[1]

From generic markets to product-markets

It's useful to think of two basic types of markets. A **generic market** is a market with *broadly* similar needs and sellers offering various, and often diverse, ways of satisfying those needs. In contrast, a **product-market** is a market with *very* similar needs and sellers offering various *close substitute* ways of satisfying those needs.[2]

A generic market description looks at markets broadly and from a customer's point of view. Status seekers, for example, have several very different ways to satisfy their status needs. A status seeker might buy a new Mercedes, a deluxe tour, or fashions from a French designer. Any one of these *very different* products may satisfy this status need. Sellers in this generic status-seeker market have to focus on the need(s) the customers want satisfied—not on how one seller's product (car, vacation, or designer label) is better than that of another producer.

Exhibit 8-1 Narrowing Down to Target Markets

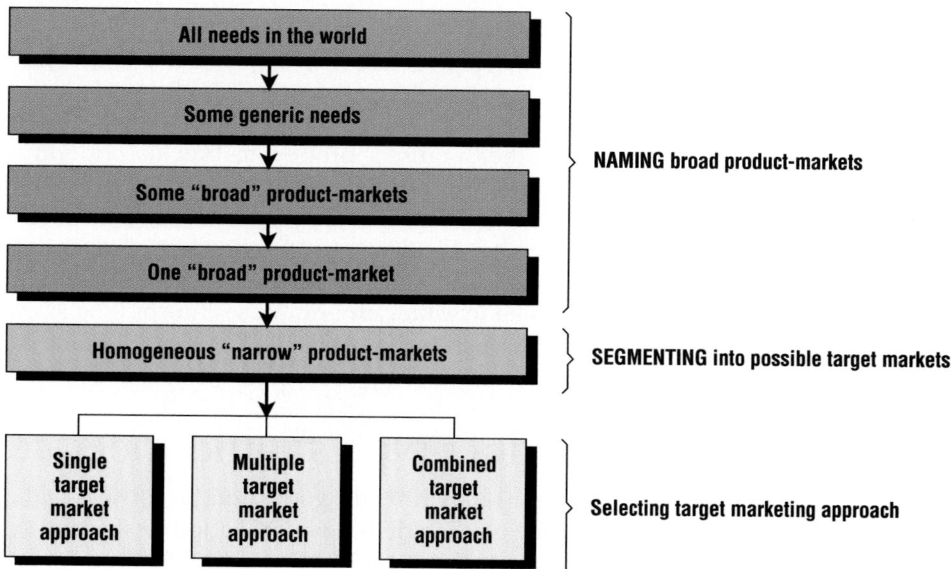

It is sometimes hard to understand and define generic markets because *quite different product types may compete with each other.* But if customers see all these products as substitutes—as competitors in the same generic market—then marketers must deal with this complication.

Suppose, however, that one of our status seekers decides to satisfy this status need with a new, expensive car. Then, in this product-market, Mercedes, Cadillac, and Lexus may compete with each other for the status seeker's dollars. In this *product-market* concerned with cars *and* status (not just transportation!), consumers compare similar products to satisfy their status need.

Most companies quickly narrow their focus to product-markets because of the firm's past experience, resources, or management preferences. And we will usually be thinking of product-markets when we refer to markets. But when looking for opportunities, a marketing manager should consider a broader, generic market view.

Broaden market definitions

Broader market definitions, including both generic market definitions and product-market definitions, can help firms find opportunities. But deciding *how* broad to go isn't easy. Too narrow a definition will limit a firm's opportunities, but too broad a definition makes the company's efforts and resources seem insignificant.

Our strategy planning process helps define relevant markets. Here, we try to match opportunities to a firm's resources and objectives. So the *relevant market for finding opportunities* should be bigger than the firm's present product-market—but not so big that the firm couldn't expand and be an important competitor. A small manufacturer of screwdrivers in Canada, for example, shouldn't define its market as broadly as "the worldwide tool users market" or as narrowly as "our present screwdriver customers." But it may have the production and/or marketing potential to consider "the handyman's hand-tool market in North America." Carefully naming your product-market can help you see possible opportunities.

Naming product-markets and generic markets

Product-related terms do not, by themselves, adequately describe a market. A complete product-market definition includes a four-part description.

What:	1. Product type (type of product and type of service).
To meet what:	2. Customer (user) needs.
For whom:	3. Customer types.
Where:	4. Geographic area.

In other words, a product-market description must include customer-related terms, not just product-related terms. We refer to these four-part descriptions as product-market "names" because most managers label their markets when they think, write, or talk about them. Such a four-part definition can be clumsy, however, so we often use a nickname, such as "golden oldies" for well-to-do Canadian retirees interested in winter cruises. This is fine as long as everyone understands the underlying four-part terms. And the nickname should refer to people, not products, because as we have emphasized, people make markets!

Product type should meet customer needs

Product type describes the goods and/or services that customers want. Sometimes, the product type is strictly a physical good or strictly a service. But marketing managers who ignore the possibility that *both* are important can miss opportunities.

Customer (user) needs refer to the needs the product type satisfies for the customer. At a very basic level, product types usually provide functional benefits such as nourishing, protecting, warming, cooling, transporting, cleaning, holding, saving time, and so forth. Although we need to identify such basic needs first, in advanced economies we must go beyond basic needs to emotional needs—such as needs for fun, excitement, pleasing appearance, and/or status. Correctly defining the need(s) that are relevant to a market is crucial and requires a good understanding of customers. We discussed these topics more fully in Chapters 6 and 7.

Customer type refers to the final consumer or user of a product type. Here, we want to choose a name that describes all present (possible) types of customers.

To define customer type, marketers should identify the final consumer or user of the product type, rather than the buyer—if they are different. For instance, marketers should avoid treating intermediaries as a customer type—unless such people actually use the product in their own business.

The *geographic area* is where a firm competes, or plans to compete, for customers. Naming the geographic area may seem trivial, but understanding the geographic boundaries of a market can suggest new opportunities. Supermarkets in London, or Los Angeles, or Toronto, don't cater to all consumers in these areas, and there may be opportunities to serve unsatisfied customers in the same areas. Similarly, a firm aiming only at the Canadian market may want to expand into world markets.

No product type in generic market names

A generic market description *doesn't include any product-type terms.* It consists of only three parts of a product-market definition, without the product type. This emphasizes that any product type that satisfies the customer's needs can compete in this generic market. Recall that in our status seeker market example, very different product types were competitors. Exhibit 8–2 shows the relationship between generic market and product-market definitions.

By creatively analyzing the needs and attitudes of present and potential target markets, in relation to the benefits offered by a firm and its competitors, you can see new opportunities. Later on, we'll study the many possible dimensions of markets. But for now you should see that defining markets only in terms of current products is not the best way to find new opportunities—or to plan marketing strategies. Internet Insite 8–1 discusses some of the opportunities that the Web provides to alert marketers who wish to target female consumers.

Exhibit 8–2 Relationship between Generic and Product-Market Definitions

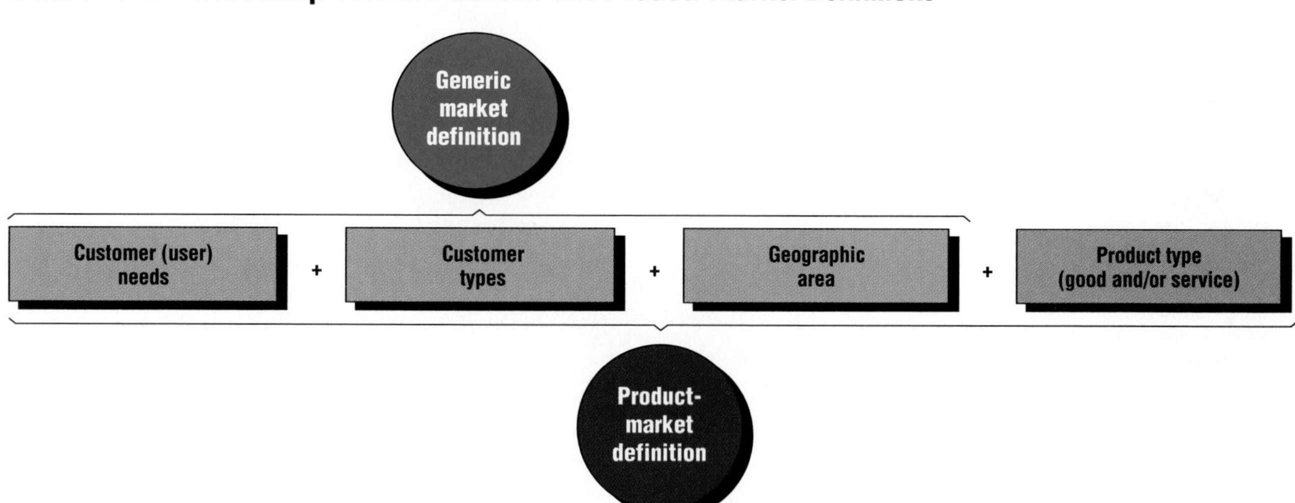

Internet Insite 8-1

Targeting Women on the Web

The demographics of the Internet are somewhat skewed toward the upper-income segment of the population. Internet users are still predominately male and younger, but more women and older people are getting online (see the 8th WWW Survey at www.gvu.gatech.edu/user_surveys/). Marketers have already begun to differentiate between the needs of these different consumer segments.

It is projected that by the year 2000, nearly 48 percent of online users will be women. Currently the figure is about 38.5 percent (www.gvu.gatech.edu/user_surveys/). Women today are managing careers as well as family. Over half of the women online are also moms. As they juggle different tasks and roles, they often don't have the time for shopping or searching for information. Here's where the Internet can play a useful role.

According to a survey by Women's Wire (http://womenswire.com), women feel that they can help their children by going online. They also feel that they can become smarter shoppers (presumably by doing information search and comparison-shopping online). This survey found that 37 percent of the women online were active in financial planning, and visited financial Web sites regularly.

Several Web sites devoted to women and family-oriented women's issues are now online. These include Cybergrrl (www.cybergrrl.com/), Women's Wire (http://womenswire.com), and iVillage (www.ivillage.com). Sites targeting women generally include sections on career, family, child care, fitness and beauty, relationships, and finance. They also invariably include a "chat" feature, with different chat groups devoted to topics of interest to women. Of course, women and men also access many of the same sites.

Most women who are online work full-time (64 percent); also, they are likely to be university or college educated (82 percent) and affluent (average household income: $53,000). These demographics make this segment an attractive target for marketers. Advertising on Web sites devoted to women can be an effective way of reaching this segment. A visit to iVillage or Women.Com will reveal that some of the leading brands are being advertised on these sites. Advertising rates at some of the women's sites such as Women.Com (see www.women.com/fyi/rate.html) suggest that such targeted advertising comes at a high price.

Some questions to ponder:

1. Can you effectively target market on the Web?
2. Can marketers go beyond demographic segmentation and use lifestyle segmentation online? Can you find any examples of that being done on the Web?

Source: This is one of a series of Internet Insites prepared in April 1998 by Dr. Ramesh Venkat of Saint Mary's University for *Basic Marketing*, Ninth Canadian Edition.

Market segmentation defines possible target markets

Market segmentation is a two-step process of (1) *naming* broad product-markets and (2) *segmenting* these broad product-markets in order to select target markets and develop suitable marketing mixes.

This two-step process isn't well understood. Beginners often fail in their early attempts to segment markets because they start with the whole mass market and try to find one or two demographic characteristics with which to segment this market. Customer behaviour is usually too complex to be explained in terms of just one or two demographic characteristics. For example, not all older men—or all young women—buy the same products or brands. Other dimensions usually must be considered, starting with customer needs. Sometimes, many different dimensions are needed to describe the submarkets within a broad product-market.

The first step: Naming broad product-markets

The first step in effective market segmentation involves naming a broad product-market of interest to the firm. Marketers must break apart all possible needs into some generic markets and broad product-markets in which the firm may be able to operate profitably. (See Exhibit 8–1.) No one firm can satisfy everyone's needs. So it must identify various generic needs and select some broad areas—broad product-markets—where it has some resources and experience. This means that a car manufacturer would probably ignore all the possible opportunities in food and clothing markets and focus on the generic market it might call "transporting people in the world" and probably on the broad product-market "cars and trucks for transporting people in the world."

This practical, rough-and-ready approach tries to narrow down the marketing focus to product-market areas where the firm is more likely to have a competitive advantage—or even to find breakthrough opportunities. This process requires considerable thought and judgment about how the firm may obtain a competitive advantage by meeting the needs of some consumers better than any of its competitors.

Market grid is a visual aid to market segmentation

Assuming that any broad product-market (or generic market) may consist of submarkets, picture a market as a rectangle with boxes representing the smaller, more homogeneous product-markets.

Exhibit 8–3, for example, represents the broad product-market of bicycle riders. The boxes show different submarkets. One submarket might focus on people who want basic transportation, another on people who want exercise, and so on. Alternatively, in the generic "transporting market" discussed above, we might see different product-markets of customers for bicycles, motorcycles, cars, airplanes, ships, buses, and others.

Exhibit 8–3 A Market Grid Diagram with Submarkets

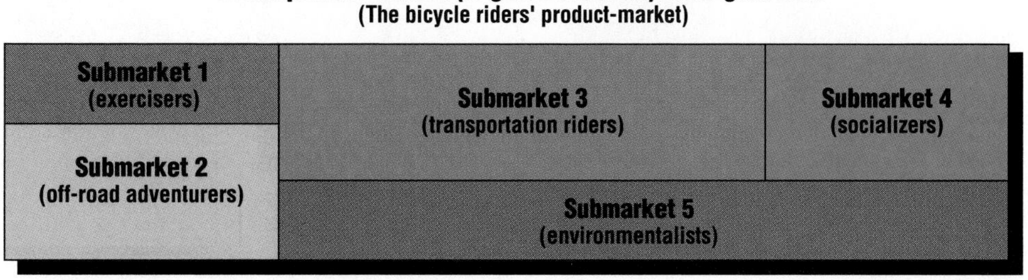

Broad product-market (or generic market) name goes here
(The bicycle riders' product-market)

Submarket 1 (exercisers)

Submarket 2 (off-road adventurers)

Submarket 3 (transportation riders)

Submarket 4 (socializers)

Submarket 5 (environmentalists)

Segmenting—bringing together people with similar needs

Marketing-oriented managers know that **segmenting** involves clustering people with similar needs into a market segment. A **market segment** is a (relatively) homogeneous group of customers who will respond to a marketing mix in a similar way.

This part of the market segmentation process (see Exhibit 8–1) takes a different approach than the naming part. Here, we look for similarities rather than basic differences in needs. Segmenters start with the idea that each person is one of a kind but that it may be possible to combine some similar people into a product-market.

Segmenters see each of these one-of-a-kind people as having a unique set of dimensions. Consider a product-market in which customers' needs differ on two important segmenting dimensions: need for status and need for dependability. In Exhibit 8–4A, each dot shows a person's position on the two dimensions. While each person's position is unique, many people are similar in terms of how much status and dependability they want. So a segmenter may group these people into three (an arbitrary number) relatively homogeneous submarkets—A, B, and C. Group A might be called "status oriented" and Group C "dependability oriented." Members of Group B would want both, and might be called the "demanders."

How far should this bringing together go?

The segmenter wants to combine individual customers into some workable number of relatively homogeneous target markets, and then treat each target market differently.

Look again at Exhibit 8–4A. Remember, we talked about three segments. But this was an arbitrary number. As Exhibit 8–4B shows, there may really be six segments. What do you think—does this broad product-market consist of three segments or six?

Another difficulty with segmenting is that some potential customers just don't fit neatly into market segments. For example, not everyone in Exhibit 8–4B was put into one of the groups. Forcing these individuals into one of the groups would have made these segments more heterogeneous—and harder to please. Further, forming additional segments for them probably wouldn't be profitable: they are too few, and not very similar in terms of the two dimensions. These people are simply too unique to be catered to and may have to be ignored, unless they are willing to pay a high price for special treatment.

The number of segments that should be formed depends more on judgment than on some scientific rule. But the following guidelines can help.

Exhibit 8–4 Every Individual Has His or Her Own Unique Position in a Market—Those with Similar Positions Can Be Aggregated into Potential Target Markets

A. Product-market showing three segments

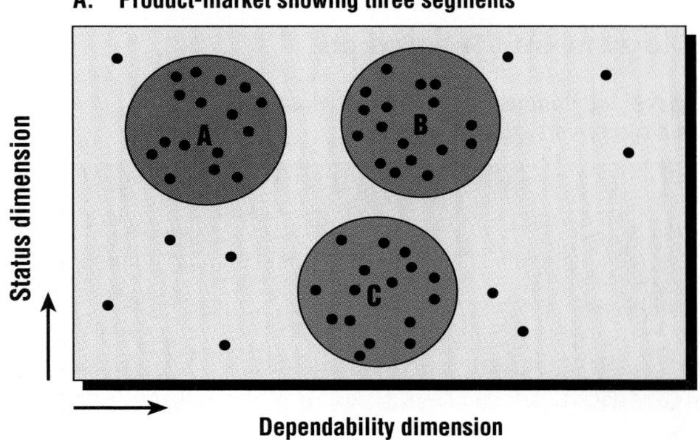

B. Product-market showing six segments

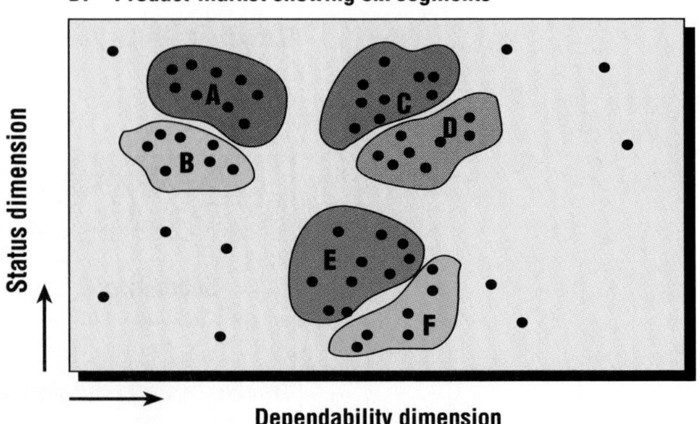

Criteria for segmenting a broad product-market

Ideally, "good" market segments meet the following criteria (see Exhibit 8–5):

1. *Homogeneous (similar) within.* The customers in a market segment should be as similar as possible with respect to their likely responses to marketing mix variables *and* their segmenting dimensions.
2. *Heterogeneous (different) between.* The customers in different segments should be as different as possible with respect to their likely responses to marketing mix variables *and* their segmenting dimensions.
3. *Substantial.* The segment should be big enough to be profitable.
4. *Operational.* The segmenting dimensions should be useful for identifying customers and deciding on marketing mix variables.

It is especially important that segments be *operational.* This leads marketers to include demographic dimensions such as age, income, location, and family size. Information on these dimensions, usually readily available, can be very useful in determining the size of markets and planning marketing mixes. In fact, it is difficult to make some Place and Promotion decisions without such information.

Avoid segmenting dimensions that have no practical operational use. For example, you may find a personality trait such as moodiness among the traits of heavy buyers of a product, but how could you use this fact? Salespeople can't give a personality test to each buyer. Similarly, advertising media buyers or copywriters couldn't make much use of this information. So although moodiness might be related in some way to previous purchases, it would not be a useful dimension for segmenting.

Exhibit 8–5 Criteria for Segmenting

Segmenting dimensions, reponses to four Ps

Homogeneous within

Heterogeneous between

Criteria for segmenting product-markets

Substantial

Operational

Profitable

Useful for identifying customers

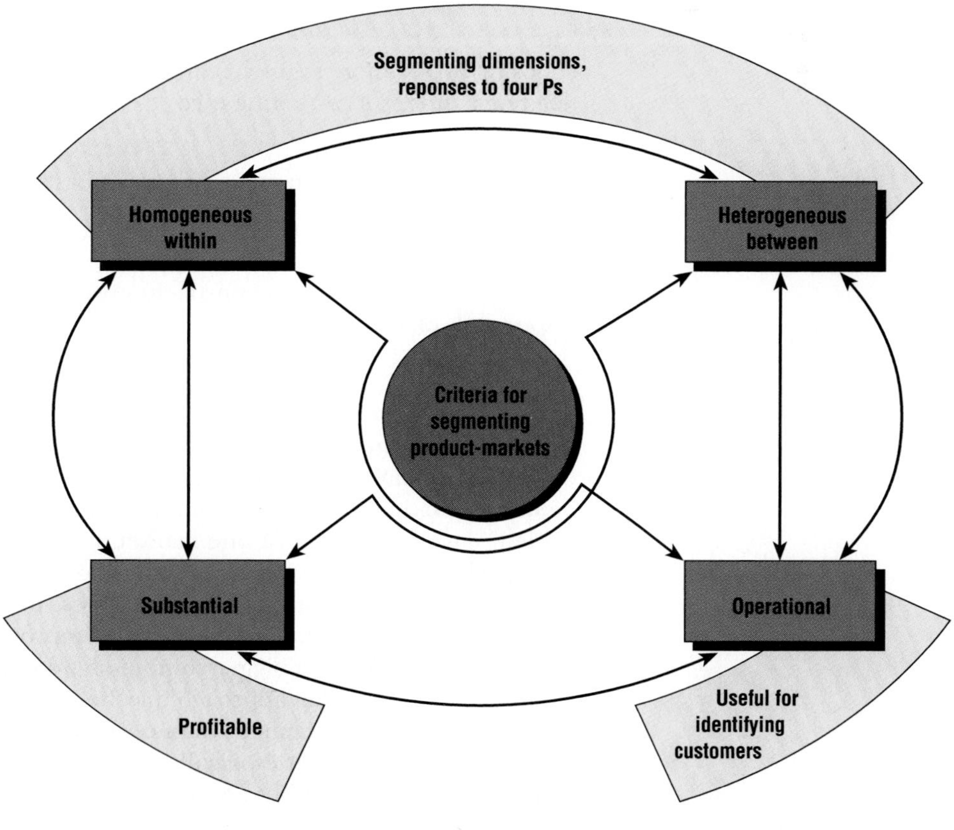

Exhibit 8-6 Target Marketers Have Specific Aims

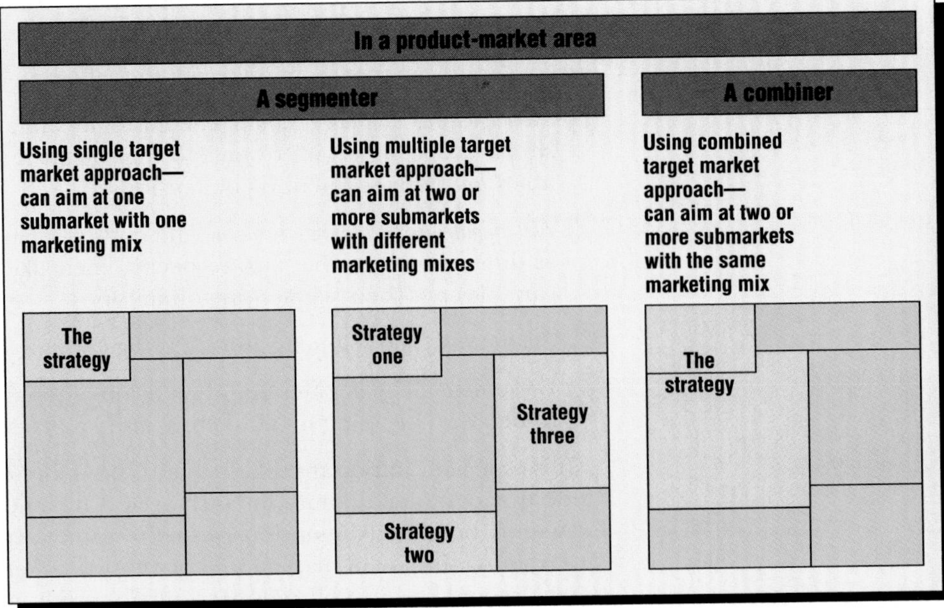

Target marketers aim at specific targets

Once you accept the idea that broad product-markets may have submarkets, you can see that target marketers usually have a choice among many possible target markets.

There are three basic ways of developing market-oriented strategies in a broad product-market.

1. The **single target market approach.** Segmenting the market and picking one of the homogeneous segments as the firm's target market.
2. The **multiple target market approach.** Segmenting the market and choosing two or more segments, then treating each as a separate target market needing a different marketing mix.
3. The **combined target market approach.** Combining two or more submarkets into one larger target market as a basis for one strategy.

Note that all three approaches involve target marketing. They all aim at specific, clearly defined target markets. (See Exhibit 8–6.) For convenience, we call people who follow the first two approaches the *segmenters* and people who use the third approach *combiners.*

Combiners try to satisfy "pretty well"

Combiners try to increase the size of their target markets by combining two or more segments. Combiners look at various submarkets for similarities rather than differences. Then they try to extend or modify their basic offering to appeal to these "combined" customers with just one marketing mix. For example, combiners may try a new package, more service, a new brand, or new flavours. But even when they make product or other marketing mix changes, they don't try to satisfy unique smaller submarkets. Instead, combiners try to improve the general appeal of their marketing mix to appeal to a bigger combined target market.

A combined target market approach may help achieve some economies of scale. It may also require less investment than developing different marketing mixes for different segments, making it especially attractive for firms with limited resources. These potential benefits may be very appealing and make combining seem less risky.

Exhibit 8-7 There May Be Different Demand Curves in Different Market Segments

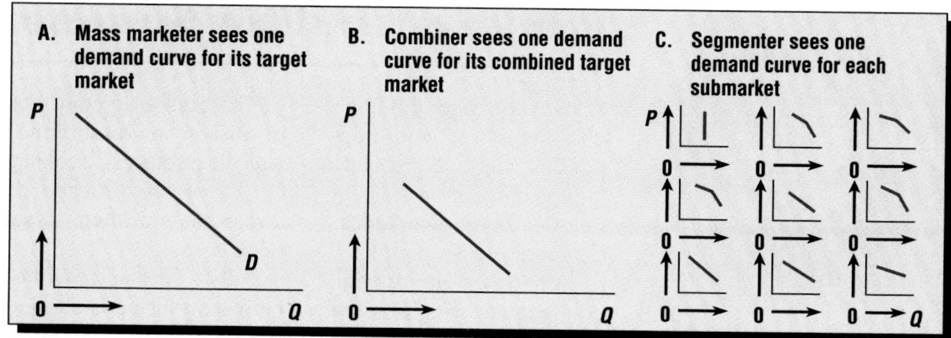

Too much combining is risky

It is tempting to aim at larger combined markets instead of using different marketing mixes for smaller segmented markets. But combiners must be careful not to combine too much. As they enlarge the target market, it becomes less homogeneous, and individual differences within each submarket may begin to outweigh the similarities. This makes it harder to develop marketing mixes that can effectively reach and satisfy potential customers within each of the submarkets.

A combiner faces the continual risk that innovative segmenters will chip away at the various segments of the combined target market by offering more attractive marketing mixes to more homogeneous submarkets. IBM saw this happen very quickly when it first came out with personal computers. Apple took the segment that wanted an easy-to-use computer. Toshiba took travellers who wanted laptop convenience. Compaq got those who wanted the fastest machines. Dell attracted customers who wanted reliability at a low price.

Segmenters try to satisfy "very well"

Segmenters aim at one or more homogeneous segments and try to develop a different marketing mix for each segment. Segmenters usually adjust their marketing mixes for each target market, perhaps making basic changes in the product itself, because they want to satisfy each segment very well.

Instead of assuming that the whole market consists of a fairly similar set of customers (like the mass marketer does), or merging various submarkets together (like the combiner), a segmenter sees submarkets with their own demand curves, as shown in Exhibit 8–7. Segmenters believe that aiming at one, or some, of these smaller markets will satisfy the target customers better and provide greater profit potential for the firm.

Segmenting may produce bigger sales

Note that segmenters are not settling for a smaller sales potential. Rather, they hope to *increase* sales by getting a much larger share of the business in the market(s) they target. A segmenter who satisfies the target market well enough may have no real competition.

AFG Industries, a company that manufactures glass, had a small market share when it was trying to sell glass in the construction market. Then AFG's marketing managers began focusing on the special needs of firms that used tempered and coloured glass in their own production. AFG, using a multiple-target approach, planned marketing mixes for "niche" segments that didn't get attention from the bigger producers. Because of careful segmenting, AFG was soon selling 70 percent of the glass for microwave oven doors and 75 percent of the glass for shower enclosures and patio tabletops. AFG was also earning the best profit margins in its industry.[3] Marketing Demo 8–1 provides another illustration of effective segmentation, this time as applied to Canada's native people.

Marketing Demo 8-1

Bankers' Indian Sunrise

A few years ago, the Bank of Montreal spotted an opportunity in a community that is almost universally ignored by marketers: Canada's native people.

Although many aboriginal people live in dire poverty, significant numbers are moving up economically thanks to rising education levels and the first trickle of land-claims settlements. And the native population, with its high birthrate, is the youngest of any group in Canada, and growing fast.

Determining how best to communicate with people who often had never had a savings account—or even personal I.D. in the form of a driver's license or birth certificate—was a challenge. But Bonnie Shettler, the bank's vice-president of aboriginal affairs, says it was one well worth meeting.

In October 1992, the bank established nine new aboriginal branches in B.C., Alberta, Saskatchewan and the Northwest Territories. Moving into northern outposts like Iqaluit on Baffin Island and agricultural communities like the Cowessess First Nation in southern Saskatchewan, there was a need to treat each community as unique. "This isn't just a traditional market segment like young women who are career oriented," says Shettler. "There isn't just one aboriginal market."

Beyond erecting bricks-and-mortar branches, the bank built relationships with the community. This included such activities as going fishing with native elders, and sponsoring a fundraising dinner for a local filmmaker shooting a movie in Batoche, Sask.

The bank also contributes $50,000 to the MBA program at Saskatchewan Indian Federated College in Regina. As well, it publishes banking information in various dialects. For clients who lacked documentation, the bank took Polaroid shots of them to serve as identification for opening accounts.

What Shettler calls the bank's "grassroots approach" to marketing includes offering customers the option of ordering cheques that include reproductions of works by young native artists. And the bank also runs ads in native publications such as *Windspeaker* in Edmonton.

Shettler won't give numbers, but says the aboriginal banking unit has seen steady growth over four years in loans, mortgages, deposits and commercial accounts, and is profitable.

Other banks are paying attention to the growing economic clout of Indian and Métis people, and the fact that at least 60% of the aboriginal population is under 30. Last fall, the Toronto Dominion Bank signed a deal with the Federation of Saskatchewan Indian Nations to help establish an aboriginal banking system. And CIBC is also using techniques similar to those of the Bank of Montreal in attracting native customers.

"[Mainstream marketing] is not CIBC's approach," says Kevin Lightfoot, manager of community relations at CIBC in Winnipeg. "We do it on a relationship basis, by putting a bank representative in front of them and at their service."

Source: Chris Varcoe, *Marketing Magazine,* July 15, 1996, p. 13.

Should you segment or combine?

Which approach should a firm use? This depends on the firm's resources, on the nature of competition, and—most important—on the similarity of customer needs, attitudes, and buying behaviour.

In general, it's usually safer to be a segmenter—that is, to try to satisfy some customers *very* well instead of many just *fairly* well. That's why many firms use the single or multiple target market approach instead of the combined target market approach. Procter & Gamble, for example, offers many products that seem to compete directly with each other (e.g., Tide versus Cheer, Crest versus Gleem). However, P&G offers "tailormade" marketing mixes to each submarket that is large and profitable enough to deserve a separate marketing mix. Though extremely effective, this approach may not be possible for a smaller firm with more limited resources. A smaller firm may have to use the single target market approach, aiming all its efforts at the one submarket niche where it sees the best opportunity.[4]

Profit is the balancing point

Target marketers develop and implement whole strategies—they don't just segment markets. In practice, cost considerations probably encourage more aggregating, to

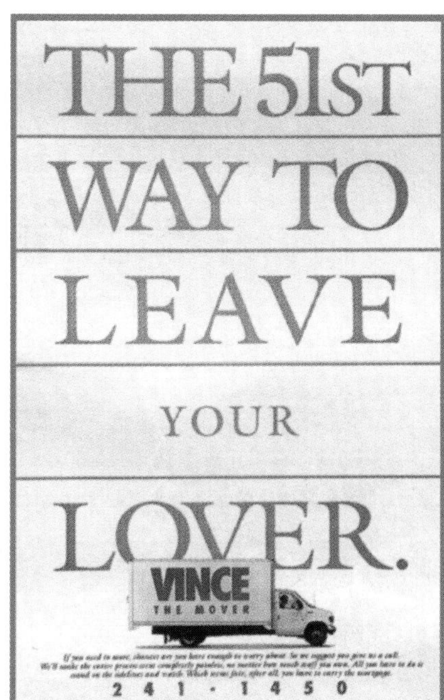

How many segmenting dimensions appear in these ads?

obtain economies of scale, while demand considerations suggest less aggregating, to satisfy needs more exactly.

Profit is the balancing point. It determines how unique a marketing mix the firm can afford to offer to a particular group.

What dimensions are used to segment markets?

Market segmentation forces a marketing manager to decide which product-market dimensions might be useful for planning marketing strategies. The dimensions should help guide marketing mix planning. Exhibit 8–8

Exhibit 8–8 Relation of Potential Target Market Dimensions to Marketing Strategy Decision Areas

POTENTIAL TARGET MARKET DIMENSIONS	EFFECTS ON STRATEGY DECISION AREAS
1. Behavioural needs, attitudes, and how present and potential goods and services fit into customers' consumption patterns.	Affects *Product* (features, packaging, product line assortment, branding) and *Promotion* (what potential customers need and want to know about the firm's offering, and what appeals should be used).
2. Urgency to get need satisfied and desire and willingness to seek information, compare, and shop.	Affects *Place* (how directly products are distributed from producer to customer, how extensively they are made available, and the level of service needed) and *Price* (how much potential customers are willing to pay).
3. Geographic location and other demographic characteristics of potential customers.	Affects size of *Target Markets* (economic potential) and *Place* (where products should be made available) and *Promotion* (where and to whom to target advertising and personal selling).

shows the basic kinds of dimensions we talked about in Chapters 5 through 7—and their probable effect on the four Ps. Ideally, we want to describe any potential product-market in terms of all three types of customer-related dimensions plus a product-type description, because these dimensions will help us develop better marketing mixes.

Many segmenting dimensions considered

Customers can be described by many specific dimensions. Exhibit 8–9 shows some dimensions that are useful for segmenting consumer markets. A few are behavioural dimensions; others are geographic and demographic. Exhibit 8–10 shows some additional dimensions for segmenting markets when the customers are businesses, government agencies, or other types of organizations. Regardless of whether cus-

Exhibit 8-9 Possible Segmenting Dimensions and Typical Breakdowns for Consumer Markets

DIMENSIONS	TYPICAL BREAKDOWNS
Customer-related	
Geographic	
Region	Atlantic provinces; Quebec; Ontario; Prairie provinces; and British Columbia
City, province, CMA size	Under 5,000; 5,000–19,999; 20,000–49,999; 50,000–99,999; 100,000–249,999; 250,000–499,999; 500,000–999,999; 1,000,000–3,999,999; 4,000,000 or over
Demographic	
Age	Infant; under 6; 6–11; 12–17; 18–24; 25–34; 35–49; 50–64; 65 and over
Sex	Male; female
Family size	1–2; 3–4; 5 +
Family life cycle	Young, single; young, married, no children; young, married, youngest child under 6; young, married, youngest child 6 or over; older, married, with children; older, married, no children under 18; older, single; other
Income	Under \$20,000; \$20,000 to \$39,999; \$40,000 to \$59,999; \$60,000 to \$74,999; \$75,000 to \$99,999; \$100,000 and over
Occupation	Professional and technical; managers, officials, and proprietors; clerical, sales; craftspeople, foremen; operatives; farmers; retired; students; housewives and househusbands; unemployed
Education	Grade school or less; some high school; high school graduate; one to two years postsecondary; three to four years postsecondary; five or more years postsecondary
Religion	Catholic; Protestant; Jewish; Muslim; other
Nationality	Canadian; British; French; German; etc.
Social class	Lower-lower; upper-lower; lower-middle; upper-middle; lower-upper; upper-upper
Situation-related	
Benefits offered	
Need satisfiers	PSSP; economic; and more detailed needs
Product features	Situation-specific; but to satisfy specific or general needs
Consumption or use patterns	
Rate of use	Heavy; medium; light; nonusers
Use with other products	Situation-specific (e.g., gas with a travelling vacation)
Brand familiarity	Insistence; preference; recognition; nonrecognition; rejection
Buying situation	
Kind of store	Convenience; shopping; specialty
Kind of shopping	Serious versus browsing; rushed versus leisurely
Depth of assortment	Out of stock; shallow; deep
Type of good	Convenience; shopping; specialty; unsought

Exhibit 8-10 Possible Segmenting Dimensions for Business/Organizational Markets

Type of customer	Manufacturer, service producer, government agency, military, nonprofit, wholesaler or retailer (when end user), etc.
Demographics	Geographic location (region of world, country, region within country, urban → rural) Size (number of employees, sales volume) Primary business or industry (Standard Industrial Classification) Number of facilities
How customer will use product	Installations, components, accessories, raw materials, supplies, professional services
Type of buying situation	Decentralized → centralized Buyer → multiple buying influence Straight rebuy → modified rebuy → new-task buying
Kind of relationship	Weak loyalty → strong loyalty to vendor Single source → multiple vendors "Arm's length" dealings → close partnership No reciprocity → complete reciprocity
Purchasing methods	Vendor analysis, inspection buying, sampling buying, specification buying, competitive bids, negotiated contracts, long-term contracts

tomers are final consumers or organizations, segmenting a broad product-market may involve using several different dimensions at the same time. Which ones are most important depends on the specific product-market.[5]

With so many possible segmenting dimensions, and knowing that several dimensions may be needed to show what is really important in specific product-markets, how should we proceed?

Qualifying and determining dimensions

To select the important segmenting dimensions, think about two different types of dimensions. **Qualifying dimensions** are those relevant to including a customer type in a product-market. **Determining dimensions** are those that actually affect the customer's purchase of a specific product or brand in a product-market.

A prospective car buyer, for example, has to have enough money—or credit—to buy a car and insure it. Our buyer also needs a driver's licence. This still doesn't guarantee a purchase. He or she must also have a real need—such as a job that requires "wheels," or kids who have to be carpooled. This need may motivate the purchase of *some* car. But these *qualifying* dimensions don't determine what specific brand or model car the person may buy. That depends on more specific interests, such as the kind of safety, performance, or appearance the customer wants. *Determining* dimensions related to these needs will affect the specific car the customer purchases.

Determining dimensions may be very specific

How specific the determining dimensions are depends on whether you are concerned with a general product type or a specific brand. (See Exhibit 8–11.) The more specific you want to be, the more particular the determining dimensions may be. In a particular case, the determining dimensions may seem minor. But they are important because they *are* the determining dimensions. In the car status-seekers' market, for example, paint colours or brand name may determine which cars people buy.

Ethical Dimensions

Selecting Segmenting Dimensions

Marketing managers sometimes face ethical decisions when selecting segmenting dimensions. Problems may arise when a firm targets customers who are somehow at a disadvantage in dealing with the firm or who are unlikely to see the negative effects of their own choices. For example, some people criticize shoe companies for targeting poor, inner-city kids who see expensive athletic shoes as an important status symbol. Many firms, including producers of infant formula, have been criticized for targeting consumers in less-developed nations. Encyclopedia publishers have been criticized for aggressive selling to less-educated parents who want their children to have better opportunities but who don't seem to understand that the "pennies a day" credit terms add up to more than they can really afford. Some nutritionists criticize firms that market soft drinks, candy, and snack foods to children.

Sometimes a marketing manager must decide whether a firm should serve customers it really doesn't want to serve. For example, banks sometimes offer marketing mixes that are attractive to wealthy customers but that basically drive off low-income consumers.

People often differ about what segmenting dimensions are ethical in a given situation. Marketing managers need to consider not only their own views but also the views of other groups in society. Even when there is no clear "right" answer, negative publicity may be very damaging.[6]

Exhibit 8-11 Finding the Relevant Segmenting Dimensions

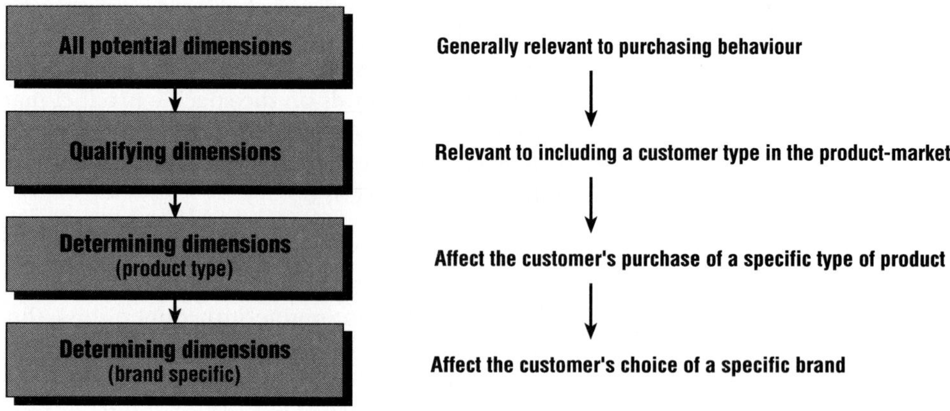

Qualifying dimensions are important, too

The qualifying dimensions help identify the core features that must be offered to everyone in a product-market. Qualifying and determining dimensions work together in marketing strategy planning.

Different dimensions needed for different submarkets

Note that each different submarket within a broad product-market may be motivated by a different set of dimensions. In the snack food market, for example, health food enthusiasts are interested in nutrition, dieters worry about calories, and economical shoppers with lots of kids may want volume to "fill them up." The related submarkets might be called *health-conscious snack food market, dieters' snack food market,* and *kids' snack food market.* They would be in different boxes in a market grid diagram for snack food customers.

The above approach applies in business markets too

We can apply the above approach to segmenting markets when the customers (or final users) are business organizations rather than individual consumers. There are two main differences. The first difference is in selecting the broad product-market. Business markets, especially in industrial settings, often have different needs.

Business organizations usually make purchases to meet basic functional needs. Their demands derive from final consumer demands—so the business (or nonprofit organization) market makes purchases that help it produce finished goods or services. Such firms may buy physical goods and do the work themselves, or they may pay someone else to provide the service as well.

In defining the relevant broad product-market using both geographic dimensions and basic functional needs, we are usually ensuring that our focus is broad enough—that is, not exclusively on the product now being supplied to present customers. But we are also avoiding expanding our focus to "all the business needs in the world."

Businesses also should focus on needs

As with consumer markets, it is better to focus on needs satisfied by products, rather than on product characteristics themselves. We may find new ways of satisfying a need—and completely surprise and upset current producers—when we avoid defining the product-market too narrowly.

The other main difference in segmenting industrial markets is that we use segmenting dimensions like those discussed in Chapter 7.

International marketing requires even more segmenting

Success in international marketing requires even more attention to segmenting. There are over 228 nations, each with a unique culture! These nations vary greatly in language, customs (including business ethics), beliefs, religion, race, and income distribution patterns. All of this can complicate the segmenting process. Even worse, firms entering international markets often find that critical data are less available—and less dependable. This is one reason why some firms insist that local operations and decisions be handled by local representatives. They, at least, have a "feel" for their markets.

The process of segmenting international markets may require more dimensions, but is basically the same as for domestic markets. The only addition is that marketers should segment by country or region, and look at demographic, cultural, and other characteristics, including stage of economic development, to help them find reasonably similar submarkets. Then depending on whether the firm is aiming at final consumers or business markets, marketers should continue to segment the markets as discussed earlier.

More sophisticated techniques may help in segmenting

VALS 2 is widely used

Segmenting is not an easy process, and many sophisticated techniques have been developed to help managers with this task. One method that assists marketing managers for consumer products firms is known as VALS 2 (values, attitudes, and lifestyles). SRI International, a research firm, developed this approach to describe a firm's target market in terms of a set of typical VALS 2 lifestyle groups (segments). An advantage of this approach is that SRI has developed very detailed information about the various VALS 2 groups. The VALS 2 approach has been used to profile consumers in the United Kingdom, Germany, Japan, Canada, and the United States. The disadvantage of VALS 2 and other similar approaches is that they may not be very specific to the marketing manager's target market.

To obtain a better understanding of the VALS system, check out the SRI Web site at http://future.sri.com/vals/valshome.html/. SRI has developed a segmentation scheme for the Internet called "iVALS," which considers consumer demographics as well as why and how consumers use the Internet. You can fill out the iVALS survey online and find out the iVALS category to which you belong.

The Goldfarb segments[7]

The Goldfarb organization has developed the best known made-in-Canada approach to lifestyle segmentation. The Goldfarb Segments are based on a sample of 1,400 adult Canadians, who responded to approximately 200 questions. These questions dealt with attitudes toward life, goals, values, stands on moral issues, and life satisfaction. An individual was assigned to a segment on the basis of his or her "dominant" attitudinal and behavioural characteristics. This does not mean that some of these characteristics will be completely dissimilar to those found in one or more other Goldfarb segments. However, the dominant characteristics are the primary factors that influence the behaviour of individuals in a given segment.

Six lifestyle segments emerged from this process. The six segments were classified according to two broad categories: *more traditional* and *less traditional.* As you can see in Exhibit 8–12, the more traditional segments, representing 52 percent of the adult population, include the day-to-day watchers, the old-fashioned puritans, and the responsible survivors. The less traditional segments, representing 48 percent of the adult population, include the joiner-activists, the disinterested self-indulgents, and the aggressive achievers. Exhibit 8–12 also highlights selected lifestyle and behavioural characteristics of each segment.

Exhibit 8–12 The Goldfarb Segments

SEGMENT	PERCENT OF POPULATION	CHARACTERISTICS
More traditional		
Day-to-day watchers (Conformistes)	24%	Traditional value structure; prefer the tried and true; research their purchases; satisfied with life as it is.
Old-fashioned puritans (Prudes démodés)	16%	Conservative; afraid of change; home and family oriented; least likely to try new brands; least likely to own credit cards; heavily insured.
Responsible survivors (Casaniers diligents)	12%	Respect the status quo; usually want and seek advice; enjoy self-rewards; very brand loyal; heavy TV viewers.
	52%	
Less traditional		
Joiner-activists (Réformistes)	21%	Nonconformists; dynamic, leading edge thinkers; quality and convenience oriented; like new technology; willing to spend; eat out frequently; heavy pleasure trip takers.
Disinterested self-indulgents (Hédonistes non-engagés)	17%	Insular and self-oriented; interested in self-gratification, risk-oriented; impulse purchasers; borrow heavily; heavy lottery ticket buyers; like product innovation.
Aggressive achievers (Conquérants aggressifs)	10%	Success-oriented; want to be leaders; need to have psyches stroked; love status-signalling products; flaunt material possessions.
	48%	

Source: Berkowitz et al., *Marketing, Third Canadian Edition*, McGraw-Hill Ryerson, 1998, p. 156.

Exhibit 8-13 Lifestyle Dimensions (and some related demographic dimensions)

DIMENSION	EXAMPLES		
Activities	Work	Vacation	Community
	Hobbies	Entertainment	Shopping
	Social events	Club membership	Sports
Interests	Family	Community	Food
	Home	Recreation	Media
	Job	Fashion	Achievements
Opinions	Themselves	Business	Products
	Social issues	Economics	Future
	Politics	Education	Culture
Demographics	Income	Geographic area	Occupation
	Age	City size	Family size
	Family life cycle	Dwelling	Education

Both VALS 2 and the Goldfarb Segments are based on a segmentation approach known as psychographics or lifestyle analysis. This involves analyzing a person's activities, interests, and opinions—sometimes referred to as AIOs. Exhibit 8–13 identifies a number of variables for each of the AIO dimensions, along with some demographics used to add detail to the lifestyle profile of a target market.

Lifestyle analysis assumes that marketers can plan more effective strategies if they know more about their target markets. Understanding the lifestyles of target customers has been especially helpful in providing ideas for advertising themes. For example, will it help Mercury marketing managers to know that an average member of the target market for a Sable station wagon is 34.8 years old and married, lives in a three-bedroom home, and has 2.3 children?

Lifestyles help marketers paint a more human portrait of the target market. For example, lifestyle analysis may show that the 34.8-year-old is also a community-oriented consumer with traditional values who especially enjoys spectator sports and spends much time in other family activities. An ad might show the Sable being used by a happy family at a ball game, so that the target market could really identify with the ad. And the ad might be placed in a magazine like *Sports Illustrated,* whose readers match the target lifestyle profile.

BC Transit also used psychographics

Markets can be segmented in many different ways. Marketing Demo 8–2 illustrates how BC Transit segmented its market in terms of demographics, the purpose of the trip, and psychographics.

Clustering can help

Clustering techniques are often used to identify market segments. Cluster analysis tries to find similar patterns within sets of data. Clustering groups customers who are similar on their segmenting dimensions into homogeneous segments. Clustering approaches use computers to do what previously was done with much intuition and judgment.

The data to be clustered might include such dimensions as demographic characteristics, the importance of different needs, attitudes toward the product, and past buying behaviour. Computerized statistical programs are used to search all the data for homogeneous groups of people. When such groups are found, marketers study the dimensions of the people in the groups to see why the computer clustered them together. The results sometimes suggest new, or at least better, marketing strategies.[8]

Marketing Demo 8-2

Market Segmentation at BC Transit

BC Transit has identified two ways to increase ridership in its target market—maintain a highly satisfied customer base with few customer dropouts, or develop new ridership among the nonuser segment. BC Transit set out to identify its target market by using the nature and purpose of the trip and demographic data to segment the market into identifiable groups. It was able to identify nine segments.

1. *Educational/school-based trips.* This applies to three groups: ages 5–17, who require transit to public schools; ages 14–18, who require service to school and who will use transit for other purposes; and those requiring transit to postsecondary institutions.
2. *Commuter/work-based trips.* This is the largest segment, generating the greatest number of trips. This segment consists of the urban- and suburban-based commuters who require service from 6:30 AM to 9:00 AM and from 4:00 PM to 6:00 PM.
3. *Seniors, ages 65+.* This segment is the fastest-growing segment, with an increasing demand for convenient service.
4. *Accessible.* This encompasses the disabled community, who need specialized service.
5. *Tourist.* The Lower Mainland is a growing tourist destination. As a result, there is considerable demand for transit service to tourist attractions and destinations. This demand is fairly constant from year to year but fluctuates on a seasonal basis.
6. *Sport/special event.* Transit needs for the large crowds that occur throughout the year.
7. *Shoppers.* This segment requires service generally during midday to and from the major shopping/urban centres.
8. *Leisure/recreation.* Routing and frequency demands vary considerably, but service is generally required during the midday, afternoon, and evening periods.
9. *Medical/dental/banking.* Demand for service is generally heaviest during midday for this segment, and service is generally to the urban centres.

BC Transit has also used psychographics to understand more precisely the motivations people have for using public transit and to discover strategies for building ridership. This analysis revealed six clusters of transit user (or non-user) types.

1. *Captives.* This group contained 23 percent of the total sample and represented 67 percent of total transit volume. These are individuals who have no private vehicle and, therefore, have no alternative to public transit (other than carpooling). This group tends to be female, nonethnic, and of low socioeconomic status.
2. *Transit advocates.* This group, making up 14 percent of the total sample, represented 16 percent of total transit volume. Transit advocates are sensitive to the stress and cost of driving. They consistently rate transit positively in all areas and use transit frequently.
3. *Critical transit users.* This group accounted for 11 percent of the sample and 8 percent of total transit volume. These individuals tend to be high-income women who use transit a moderate amount but who negatively evaluate the service.
4. *Grudging transit users.* This group contained 15 percent of the total sample but accounted for only 7 percent of total transit volume. Its members tend to be young, mobile, high socioeconomic status, non-ethnic men. People in this group tend to use their cars to run errands and feel that the convenience of a car is important.
5. *Car lovers.* This group included 22 percent of the total sample but accounted for only 2 percent of total transit volume. Its members tend to be ethnic, unfamiliar with transit, and concerned about the safety of the transit system. They are possible converts to transit.
6. *Committed non-users.* This group contained 15 percent of the sample but made only 1 percent of all transit trips. Its members are disproportionately retired men. All aspects of transit service are unimportant to this group. Transit is entirely irrelevant to them.

Source: Bruce Campbell, Ph.D., Campbell, Goodell, Traynor Consultants. Courtesy of BC Transit.

A cluster analysis of the toothpaste market, for example, might show that some people buy toothpaste because it tastes good (the sensory segment), while others are concerned with the effect of clean teeth and fresh breath on their social image (the sociables). Still others worry about decay or tartar (the worriers), and some are just interested in the best value for their money (the value seekers). Each of these market segments calls for a different marketing mix, although some of the four Ps may be similar.

Finally, a marketing manager has to decide which one (or more) of these segments will be the firm's target market(s).

You can see that clustering techniques only *aid* managers. Managers still need judgment to develop an original list of possible dimensions and to name the resulting clusters.

Customer database can focus the effort

A variation of the clustering approach involves the use of a customer database. The seller fine-tunes the marketing effort with information from the database. This usually includes data on a customer's past purchases as well as other segmenting information. For example, an auto-repair garage that keeps a database of customer oil changes can send a reminder postcard when it's time for the next oil change. Similarly, a florist that keeps a database of customers who have ordered flowers for Mother's Day or Valentine's Day can call them in advance with a special offer. A firm that operates over the Internet may have a special advantage with these database-focused approaches. It may be able to communicate with customers via e-mail; such an effort would be not only targeted, but also very inexpensive. For an illustration of how this works, see the opening discussion in Chapter 14 about how Canadian Tire uses a weekly electronic flyer to push product information into customers' e-mail.

Positioning helps identify product-market opportunities

As we've emphasized throughout, the reason for focusing on a specific target market, by using marketing segmentation approaches or tools such as cluster analysis and data bases, is so that you can fine-tune the entire marketing mix to appeal to some group of potential customers better than your competitors. By *differentiating* its marketing mix to do a better job of meeting customers' needs, a firm builds a competitive advantage. In other words, target customers will view the firm's position in the market as uniquely suited to their preferences and needs. Further, because everyone in the firm is clear about what position it wants to achieve with customers, Product, Promotion, and other marketing mix decisions can be blended better to achieve the desired objectives.

The marketing manager may want customers to see the firm's offering as unique, but that is not always possible. Me-too imitators may come along and copy the firm's strategy. Further, even when a firm's marketing mix is different, busy consumers will not always recognize it. Thus, when looking for opportunities, it's important for the marketing manager to know how customers *do* view the firm's offering. That's where another important approach—*positioning*—comes in.

Positioning—Where you fit

Positioning shows how customers locate proposed and/or present brands in a market. Like cluster analysis and trade-off analysis, positioning requires some formal marketing research but may be helpful when competitive offerings are quite similar. The results are usually plotted on graphs to help show how consumers view the competing products. Usually, the products' positions are related to two or three product features that are important to the target customers.

Assuming that the picture is reasonably accurate, managers then decide whether they want to leave their product (and marketing mix) alone or reposition it. This may mean *physical changes* in the product or simply *image changes based on promotion.* For example, most beer drinkers can't pick out their favourite brand in a blind test, so physical changes may not be necessary (and may not even work) to reposition a beer brand.

Managers make the graphs for positioning decisions by asking product users to make judgments about different brands—including their "ideal" brand. They then use computer programs to summarize the ratings and plot the results. The details of positioning techniques—sometimes called "perceptual mapping"—are beyond the scope of this text. But Exhibit 8–14 shows the possibilities.[9]

Exhibit 8-14 "Product Space" Representing Consumers' Perceptions of Different Brands of Bar Soap

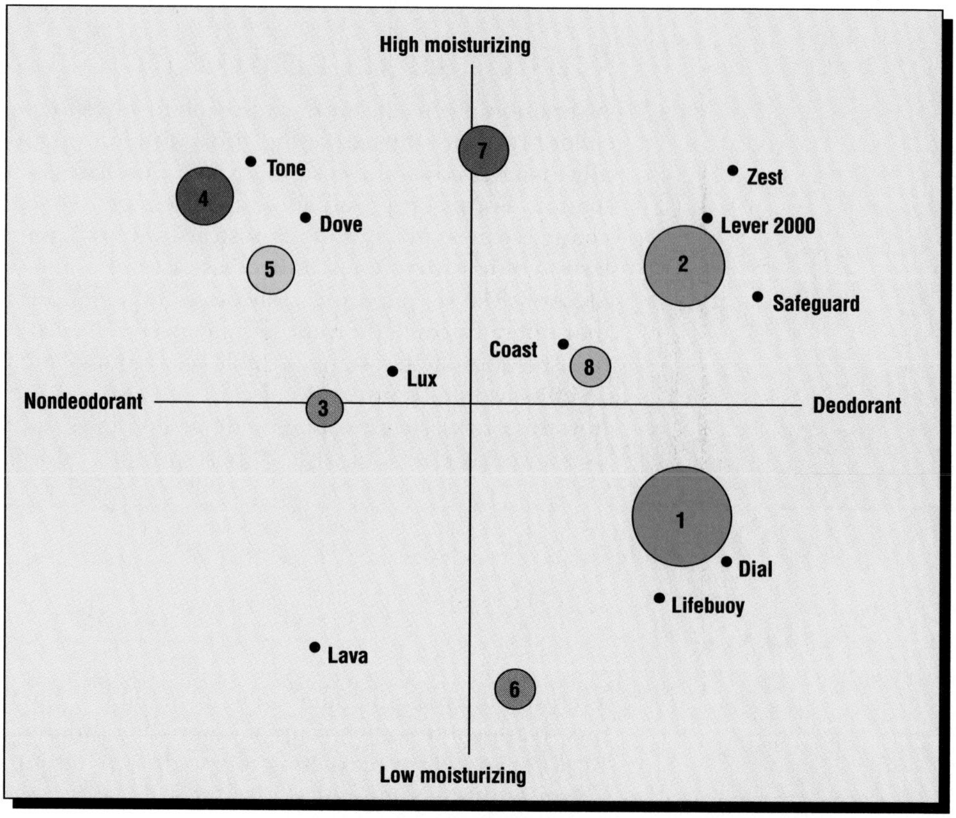

Exhibit 8–14 shows the "product space" for different brands of bar soap using two dimensions—the extent to which consumers think the soaps moisturize and deodorize their skin. For example, consumers see Dial as quite low on moisturizing but high on deodorizing. Lifebuoy and Dial are close together, implying that consumers think of them as similar on these characteristics. Dove is viewed as different and is farther away on the graph. Remember that positioning maps are based on *customers' perceptions,* and that the actual characteristics of the products (as determined by a chemical test) may well be different!

The circles in Exhibit 8–14 show different sets (submarkets) of consumers clustered near their ideal soap preferences. Groups of respondents with a similar ideal product are circled to show apparent customer concentrations. In this graph, the size of the circles suggests the size of the segments for the different ideals.

Ideal clusters 1 and 2 are the largest and are close to two popular brands—Dial and Lever 2000. It appears that customers in cluster 1 want more moisturizing than they see in Dial and Lifebuoy. However, exactly what these brands should do about this isn't clear. Perhaps both of these brands should leave their physical products alone, but emphasize moisturizing more in their promotion to make a stronger appeal to those who want moisturizers. A marketing manager talking about this approach might simply refer to it as "positioning the brand as a good moisturizer." Of course, whether the effort is successful depends on whether the whole marketing mix delivers on the promise of the positioning communication.

COMBINING VERSUS SEGMENTING Positioning analysis may lead a firm to combining rather than segmenting, if managers think they can make several general appeals to different parts of a "combined" market. For example, by varying its promotion, Coast might try to appeal to segments 8, 1, and 2 with the same product. These segments are all quite similar (close together) in what they want in an ideal brand. On the other hand, there may be clearly defined submarkets, and some parts of the market may be "owned" by one product or brand. In this case, repositioning efforts—moving the firm's own product into another segment of the general market area where competition is weaker—may be more practical.

Positioning as part of broader analysis

Positioning helps managers understand how customers see their market. It is a visual aid to understanding a product-market. The first time such an analysis is done, managers may be shocked to see how much customers' perceptions of a market differ from their own. For this reason alone, positioning is useful. But positioning usually focuses on specific product features and brands that are close competitors in the product-market. Thus, it is a product-oriented approach. Important *customer*-related dimensions, including needs and attitudes, may be overlooked.

Premature emphasis on product features is dangerous in other ways as well. As our bar soap example shows, starting with a product-oriented definition of a market and how bar soaps compete against other bar soaps can make a firm miss more basic shifts in markets. For example, bars might be losing popularity to liquid soaps. Or other products, like bath oils or facial cleansers, may be part of the relevant competition. Managers wouldn't see these shifts if they looked only at alternative bar soap brands—the focus is just too narrow.

It's also important to realize that the way consumers look at a product isn't a matter of chance. Let's continue with our bar soap example. While many consumers do think about soap in terms of moisturizing and deodorizing, other needs shouldn't be overlooked. For example, some consumers are especially concerned about wiping out germs. Marketers for Dial soap recognized this need and developed ads that positioned Dial as "the choice" for these target customers.

As we emphasize throughout the text, you must understand potential needs and attitudes when planning marketing strategies. If customers treat different products as substitutes, then a firm must position itself against those products, too. It can't just focus on a few product characteristics or benefits if they aren't the determining dimensions of the target market. Thus, it's usually best to rely on positioning approaches when they are part of a broader analysis. This helps ensure that the entire marketing mix is positioned for competitive advantage.

Questions and Problems

1. Explain what market segmentation is.
2. List the types of potential segmenting dimensions, and explain which you would try to apply first, second, and third in a particular situation. If the nature of the situation would affect your answer, explain how.
3. Explain why segmentation efforts based on attempts to divide the mass market using a few demographic dimensions may be very disappointing.
4. Illustrate the concept that segmenting also involves combining by referring to the admissions policies of your own college or university and a nearby one.
5. Review the types of segmenting dimensions listed in Exhibit 8–9, and select the ones you think should be combined to fully explain the market segment you personally would be in if you were planning to buy a new watch today. List several dimensions, and try to develop a shorthand name, such as "fashion oriented," to describe your own personal market segment. Then try to estimate what proportion of the total watch market would be accounted for by your market segment. Next, explain whether there are any offerings that come close to meeting the needs of your market. If not, what sort of a marketing mix is needed? Would it be economically attractive for anyone to try to satisfy your market segment? Explain.
6. Identify the determining dimension or dimensions that explain why you bought the specific brand you did in your most recent purchase of a (a) soft drink, (b) shampoo, (c) shirt or blouse, and (d) larger, more expensive item, such as a bicycle, camera, or boat. Try to express the determining dimension(s) in terms of your own personal characteristics rather than the product's characteristics. Estimate what share of the market would probably be motivated by the same determining dimension(s).
7. Explain how "positioning" can help a marketing manager identify target market opportunities.

Suggested Cases

- 4 Starbucks Pouring Hot in Canada
- 5 Parker's Classics
- 23 Ontario Rutabaga Council
- 31 The Parks Canada Dilemma

Computer-aided problem

Segmenting Customers

The marketing manager for Micro Software Company is seeking new market opportunities. He is focusing on the word processing market and has narrowed it down to three segments: the Fearful Typists, the Power Users, and the Specialists. The Fearful Typists don't know much about computers—they just want a fast way to type letters and simple reports without errors. They don't need a lot of special features. They want simple instructions and a program that's easy to learn. The Power Users know a lot about computers, use them often, and want a word processing program with many special features. All computer programs seem easy to them, so they aren't worried about learning to use the various features. The Specialists have jobs that require a lot of writing. They don't know much about computers but are willing to learn. They want special features needed for their work—but only if they aren't too hard to learn and use.

The marketing manager prepared a table summarizing the importance of each of three key needs in the three segments:

Market Segment	Importance of Need (1=not important; 10=very important)		
	Features	**Easy to use**	**Easy to learn**
Fearful typists	3	8	9
Power users	9	2	2
Professional specialists	7	5	6

Micro's sales staff conducted interviews with seven potential customers, who were asked to rate how important each of these three needs were in their work. The manager prepared a spreadsheet to help him cluster (aggregate) each person into one of the segments, along with other similar people. Each person's ratings are entered in the spreadsheet, and the clustering procedure computes a similarity score that indicates how similar (a low score) or dissimilar (a high score) the person is to the typical person in each of the segments. The manager can then assign potential customers to the segment that is most similar (that is, the one with the *lowest* similarity score).

a. The ratings for a potential customer appear on the first spreadsheet. Into which segment would you assign this person?

b. The responses for seven potential customers who were interviewed are listed in the table below. Enter the ratings for a customer in the spreadsheet and then write down the similarity score for each segment. Repeat the process for each customer. Based on your analysis, indicate the segment to which you would assign each customer. Indicate the size (number of customers) of each segment.

c. In the interview, each potential customer was also asked what type of computer he or she would be using. The responses are shown in the table along with the ratings. Group the responses based on the customer's segment. If you were targeting the Fearful Typists segment, what type of computer would you focus on when developing your software?

d. Based on your analysis, which customer would you say is *least* like any of the segments? Briefly explain the reason for your choice.

For additional questions related to this problem, see Exercise 8–4 in the *Learning Aid for Use with Basic Marketing,* Ninth Canadian Edition.

Potential customer	Importance of Need (1=not important; 10=very important)			Type of computer
	Features	**Easy to use**	**Easy to learn**	
A.	8	1	2	Dell
B.	6	6	5	IBM
C.	4	9	8	Macintosh
D.	2	6	7	Macintosh
E	5	6	5	IBM
F.	8	3	1	Dell
G.	4	6	8	Macintosh

When you finish this chapter, you should:

- Understand what "Product" really means.
- Know the key differences between goods and services.
- Know the differences among the various consumer and business product classes.
- Understand how the product classes can help a marketing manager plan marketing strategies.
- Understand what branding is and how to use it in strategic planning.
- Understand the importance of packaging in strategic planning.
- Understand the role of warranties in strategic planning.
- Understand the important new terms (shown in orange).

Chapter nine

Product Planning for Goods and Services

LOOKING FOR COOL CLOTHES, LIVELY MUSIC AND LOTS OF FUN UNDER ONE ROOF?

Join us as we celebrate the Fall '98 arrivals with exclusive events, informal modelling, refreshments and exciting prizes. Don't miss any of it!

Wednesday, September 16
• The launch of Burberrys, K.S. Selection and Teenflo
12 to 2

Thursday, September 17
• Career wear day featuring Holt Renfrew brand
12 to 2

Friday, September 18
• Career wear day featuring Dana Buchman, Anne Klein and Episode
11 to 3

Saturday, September 19
• Weekend wear day featuring Holt Renfrew Sport, Emanuel Liberté and Ellen Tracy & Co.
1 to 4

HOLT RENFREW
240 Sparks Street • (613) 238-2200

Holt Renfrew & Co. Ltd. is poised to put a heavy marketing push behind its private labels as the high-end retailer borrows a page from sister company Loblaw Cos. Ltd. and its successful President's Choice line.

The company plans to expand its retail space by 25 per cent over the next 18 months, with more displays of its own Holt Renfrew brand in separate shops within the stores.

More of the private label merchandise will consist of hip, so-called "fashion-forward" clothing that is generally only available under big-name designer labels at top prices, insiders say.

For example, a stylish Prada suit sells for $2,000 to $4,000. But the Holt Renfrew equivalent will go for $300 to $700, still cut from high-quality fabrics, company officials say.

As well, the retailer is looking to export its in-house labels—test marketing started recently in Japan.

"We think the President's Choice label is absolutely a role model," Joel Rath, president of the Toronto-based company, said in a recent interview. "We have to work to be a destination."

The chain of 12 stores does carry exclusive designer fashions, but in recent years has broadened its appeal with more affordable private label goods—everything from soaps to sweaters. The off-brand merchandise now rings up 28 per cent of its business, up from 16 per cent five years ago.

Soon the chain's advertising will place even greater emphasis on private brands. Holt's will tell the story behind the products—how they were developed, their history and characteristics—thus taking a leaf from Toronto-based Loblaw and its chatty Insider Reports.

Holt Renfrew's private label strategy has helped it survive in an era when other carriage-trade retailers, such as Toronto's Creeds and Ira Berg, have gone broke, victims of tight-fisted customers and tough economic times.

"You can count on one hand the number of high-end fashion retailers left in the country," says retail consultant Len Kubas in Toronto. "I'm impressed with the kind of communications Holt Renfrew maintains with their regular customers, and how they treat their customers . . . I think they're consummate marketers."

The company's Club Select loyalty program rewards buyers who use the Holt Renfrew charge card. Shoppers collect air mile points or gift certificates for purchasing certain amounts. The retailer also sends customers its glossy *Point of View* magazines, which act as a vehicle to tout new merchandise.

Holt's has stepped up in-store events to draw crowds, including fashion shows and appearances by well-known designers. The company subscribes to the view that retail is entertainment. It tries to constantly upgrade the stores with fresh looks. The expanded Yorkdale site in Toronto, for example, will boast underground valet parking and what Holt's calls "comfort zones" for shoppers to relax and make phone calls.

Of course, it helps to have a rich parent. Holt's was bought about a decade ago by a Weston family holding company, which also has a controlling interest in George Weston Ltd., Loblaw's owner. Weston boss Galen Weston reportedly wanted an outlet for wife Hilary's merchandising talents. She recently moved on to become Ontario's Lieutenant-Governor.

But deep pockets don't guarantee good fortunes in retail. The Eaton family floundered for almost a decade with its department store chain, which last month was pushed into bankruptcy protection.

Holt's stands on stronger ground. The company turned a profit last year, although Mr. Rath won't provide details. It rang up roughly $300-million in annual sales in 1996, about double the amount of five years ago when Mr. Rath stepped into the top job.

The Westons were wise enough to delegate management authority to retail experts such as Mr. Rath. That's in sharp contrast to the Eatons, who took on a lot of the senior duties themselves or hired financial managers to run the show rather than merchants, observers say.

Mr. Rath, on the other hand, is a U.S. veteran who has held executive positions at such major chains as Sears Roebuck and Nieman Marcus, which is one of the leaders in upscale retailing.

Last month, Mr. Weston announced the parent was pouring another $25-million into Holt's for expansion. The chain will replace Toronto's Yorkdale store and the one in Quebec City's Place Ste. Foy with larger spaces in the same malls.

And the flagship downtown Toronto store will get bigger, taking on an Estee Lauder spa, new boutiques and even a barber shop next to the enlarged men's section.

Understandably, Harry Rosen is one of the upscale retailers in Canada carefully watching Holt's every move. Holt's tried to buy the men's clothing chain last year, but Mr. Rosen steadfastly resisted. Instead, he snatched the chain back from Dylex Ltd., which was looking to unload its 51-per-cent interest.

Mr. Rath acknowledges he is sniffing out the Eaton's stores that are on the block but "there's nothing concrete at this time." Holt's is searching for a new downtown Calgary location and is negotiating a second outlet in Vancouver with an undisclosed party.

What is certain is that Holt's is pulling out all stops for its private labels. The retailer recently hired Ian Hylton, a former Holt's buyer, as international marketing director. Mr. Hylton has the mandate to bolster Holt's private label sales outside of Canada.

Last week, Mr. Hylton paid a visit to Dublin's Brown Thomas department store, which plans to carry Holt's goods. No doubt, a U.S. chain will be next on his shopping list. ●

Source: Marina Strauss, "Holt Renfrew Brands A Strategy," *The Globe and Mail,* March 20, 1997, B13. Reprinted with permission from *The Globe and Mail.*

The product area involves many strategy decisions

The Holt Renfrew case highlights some important topics we'll discuss in this chapter and the next. Here we'll start by looking at how customers see a firm's product. Later we'll talk about product classes to help you better understand strategic market planning. We'll also talk about branding, packaging, and warranties. As shown in Exhibit 9–1, there are many strategy decisions relating to the Product area.

What is a product?

When Toyota sells a new RAV4, is it just selling a certain number of nuts and bolts, some sheet metal, an engine, and four wheels?

When Air Jamaica sells a ticket for a flight to the Caribbean, is it just selling so much wear and tear on an airplane and so much pilot fatigue?

The answer to these questions is *no.* Instead, what these companies are really selling is the satisfaction, use, or benefit the customer wants.

Exhibit 9-1 Strategic Planning for Product

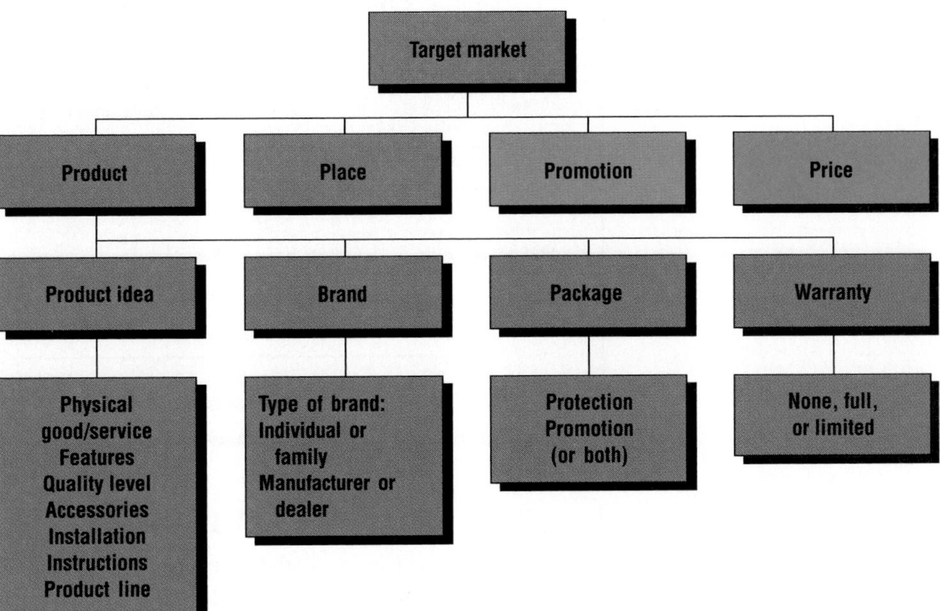

All that most consumers care about is that their cars look good and keep running. And when they take a trip on Air Jamaica, they really don't care how hard it is on the plane or the crew: they just want a safe, comfortable trip. In the same way, when producers or intermediaries buy a product, they're interested in the profit they can make from its purchase, through use or resale.

Product means the need-satisfying offering of a firm. The idea of "Product" as potential customer satisfaction or benefits is very important. Many business managers get wrapped up in the technical details involved in producing a product. But that's not how most customers view the product. Most customers think about a product in terms of the total satisfaction it provides. That satisfaction may require a "total" product offering that is really a combination of the right kind of service, a physical good with the right features, useful instructions, a convenient package, a trustworthy warranty, and perhaps even a familiar name that has satisfied the consumer in the past.

Product quality and customer needs

Product quality should also be determined by how customers view the product. From a marketing perspective, **quality** means a product's ability to satisfy a customer's needs or requirements. This definition focuses on the customer and on how the customer thinks a product will fit some purpose. For example, the "best" credit card may not be the one with the highest credit limit but the one that's accepted where a consumer wants to use it. Similarly, the best-quality clothing for casual wear on campus may be a pair of jeans—not a pair of dress slacks made of a higher-grade fabric.

Among different types of jeans, the one with the strongest stitching and the most comfortable or durable fabric may well be perceived as having the highest grade or *relative quality* for its product type. Marketing managers often focus on relative quality when comparing their products to competitors' offerings. However, a product with better features is not a high-quality product if the features aren't what the target market wants.

Quality and satisfaction depend on the total product offering. If potato chips get stale on the shelf because of poor packaging, the consumer will be dissatisfied. A broken button on a shirt will disappoint the customer, even if the laundry did a nice job cleaning and pressing the collar. A VCR is a poor-quality product if it's hard for a consumer to program it.[1]

Exhibit 9-2 Examples of Possible Blends of Physical Goods and Services in a Product

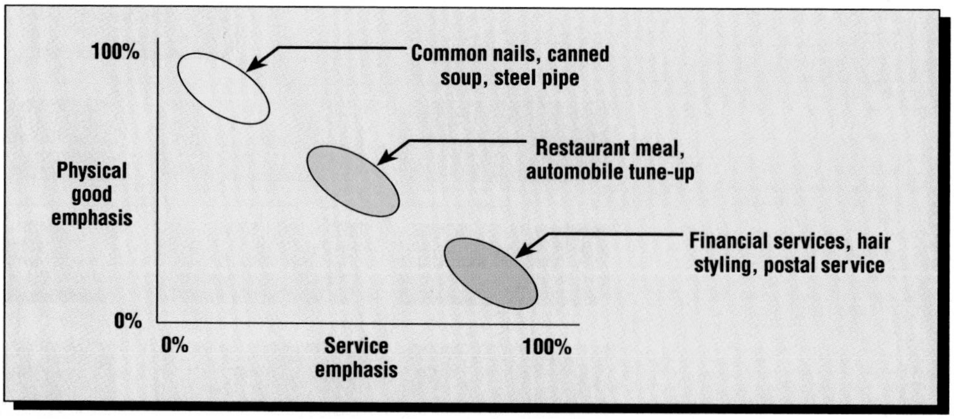

Goods and/or services are the product

You already know that a product may be a physical *good* or a *service* or a *blend* of both. Yet it's too easy to slip into a limited, physical-product point of view. We want to think of a product in terms of the needs it satisfies. If a firm's objective is to satisfy customer needs, service can be part of its product (or service alone may *be* the product), and must be provided as part of a total marketing mix.

Exhibit 9–2 shows this bigger view of Product. It shows that a product can range from a 100 percent emphasis on physical goods (example: commodities like common nails) to a 100 percent emphasis on service (example: advice from a lawyer). Regardless of the emphasis, the marketing manager must consider most of the same elements in planning products and marketing mixes. We usually won't make a distinction between goods and services but will call all of them *Products*. Sometimes, however, understanding the differences between goods and services can help fine-tune strategic market planning. So let's look at some of these differences next.

Differences in goods and services

A good is a physical thing that can be seen and touched. You can try on a Benetton shirt, thumb through the latest issue of *People* magazine, or smell Colombian coffee as it brews. A good is a *tangible* item. When you buy it, you own it. And it's usually pretty easy to see exactly what you'll get.

On the other hand, a **service** is a deed performed by one party for another. When you provide a customer with a service, the customer can't keep it. Rather, a service is experienced, used, or consumed. You go see a Touchstone Studios movie, but afterwards all you have is a memory. You ride on a ski lift at Whistler, but you don't own the equipment. Services are not physical, rather they are *intangible.* You can't "hold" a service. And it may be hard to know exactly what you'll get when you buy it.

Most products are a combination of tangible and intangible elements. Petro-Canada gas and the credit card to buy it are tangible—the credit the card grants is not. A McDonald's hamburger is tangible—but the fast service is not.

Is the product produced before it's sold?

Goods are usually produced in a factory and then sold. A Sony TV may be stored in a warehouse or store waiting for a buyer. In contrast, services are often sold first, then produced. And they're produced and consumed in the same time frame. Goods producers may be far away from the customer, but service providers often work in the customer's presence.

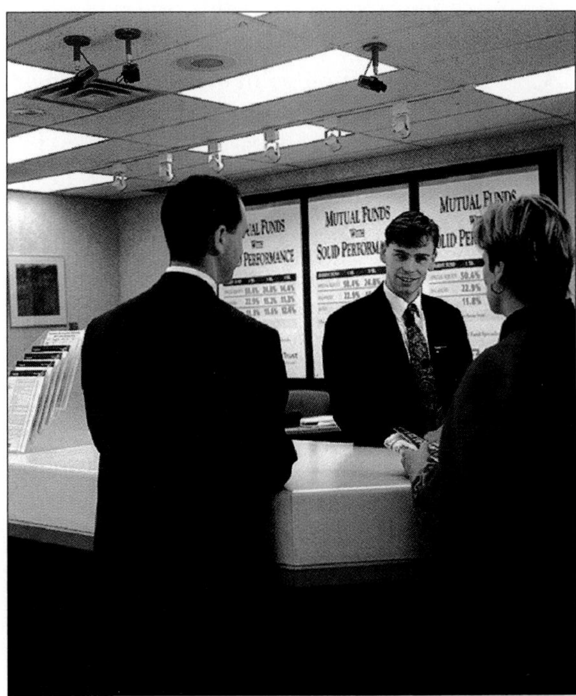

Because a service is a deed performed by one party for another, providing consistent service quality can be a challenge.

A worker in a Sony TV factory can be in a bad mood, and customers will never know. But a rude bank teller can drive customers away.

Services can't be stored or transported

Services are perishable: they can't be stored. This makes it harder to balance supply and demand. An example explains the problem.

Bell Canada sells long-distance telephone services. Even when demand is high—during peak business hours or on Mother's Day—customers expect the service to be available. They don't want to hear "Sorry, all lines are busy." So Bell Canada must have enough equipment and employees to deal with peak demand times. But when customers aren't making many calls, Bell Canada's facilities are idle. Bell Canada might be able to save money with less capacity (equipment and people), but then it would sometimes have to face dissatisfied customers.

It's often difficult to achieve economies of scale when the product emphasis is on service. Services can't be produced in large, economical quantities and then transported to customers. In addition, *services often have to be produced in the presence of the customer.* So service suppliers often need duplicate equipment and staff at places where the service is actually provided. Merrill Lynch sells investment advice along with financial products worldwide. That advice could, perhaps, be produced more economically in a single building in Toronto. But Merrill Lynch has offices all over the world. Customers want a personal touch from the stockbroker telling them how to invest their money.[2]

Whole product lines must be developed too

A **product assortment** is the set of all product lines and individual products that a firm sells. A **product line** is a set of individual products that are closely related. The seller may see them as related because they're produced and/or operate in a similar way, sold to the same target market, sold through the same types of outlets, or priced at about the same level. For example, Loblaw's, under its President's Choice brand and other labels, has many product lines in its product assortment—including tea, snacks, diapers, and shampoo. But Tilden has one product line—different types of cars to rent. An **individual product** is a particular product within a product line. It usually is differentiated by brand, level of service offered, price, or some other characteristic. For example, each size of a brand of soap is an individual product. Intermediaries usually think of each separate product as a stockkeeping unit (sku) and assign it a unique sku number.

Exhibit 9–3 Product Classes

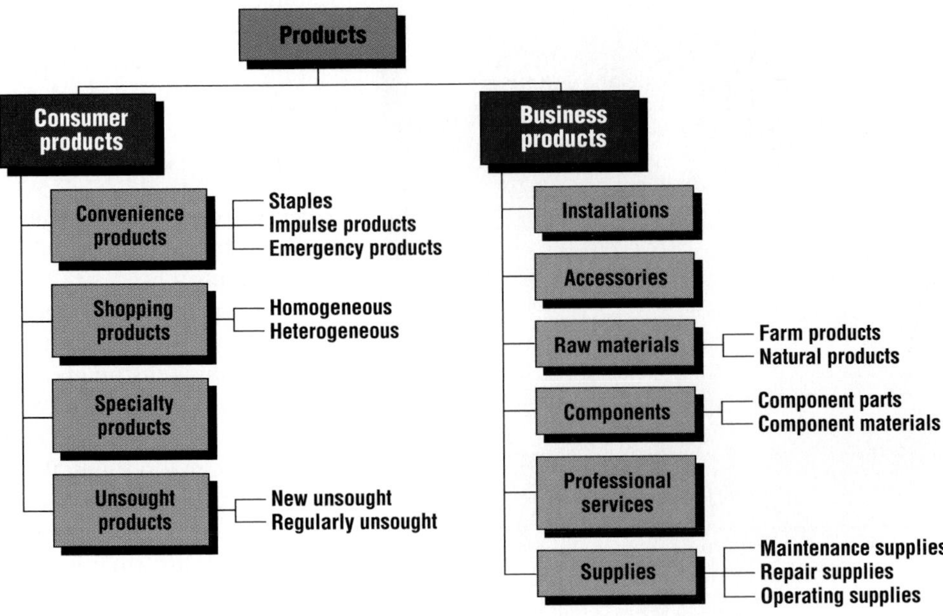

Product classes help plan marketing strategies

You don't have to treat *every* product as unique when planning strategies. Some product classes require similar marketing mixes. These product classes are a useful starting point for developing marketing mixes for new products—and for evaluating present mixes. Exhibit 9–3 summarizes the product classes.

Product classes start with type of customer

All products fit into one of two broad groups, based on the type of customer that will use them. **Consumer products** are products meant for the final consumer. **Business products** are products meant for use in producing other products. The same product *might* be in both groups: consumers buy Mazola Corn Oil to use in their own kitchens, but food processing companies and restaurants buy it in large quantities as an ingredient in the products they sell. But selling the same product to both final consumers and business customers requires (at least) two different strategies.

There are product classes within each group. Consumer product classes are based on *how consumers think about and shop for products.* Business product classes are based on *how buyers think about products and how they'll be used.*

Consumer product classes

Consumer product classes can be divided into four groups: (1) convenience, (2) shopping, (3) specialty, and (4) unsought. Each class is based on the way people buy products. See Exhibit 9–4 for a summary of how these product classes relate to marketing mixes.[3]

Convenience products—purchased quickly with little effort

Convenience products are products that consumers need but aren't willing to spend much time or effort shopping for. These products are bought often, require little service or selling, don't cost much, and may even be bought out of

Exhibit 9-4 Consumer Product Classes and Marketing Mix Planning

CONSUMER PRODUCT CLASS	MARKETING MIX CONSIDERATIONS	CONSUMER BEHAVIOUR
Convenience products		
Staples	Maximum exposure with widespread, low-cost distribution; mass selling by producer; usually low price; branding is important.	Routinized (habitual), low-effort, frequent purchases; low involvement
Impulse	Widespread distribution with display at point of purchase.	Unplanned purchases bought quickly.
Emergency	Need widespread distribution near probable point of need; price sensitivity low.	Purchase made with time pressure when a need is great.
Shopping products		
Homogeneous	Need enough exposure to facilitate price comparison; price sensitivity high.	Customers see little difference among alternatives, seek lowest price.
Heterogeneous	Need distribution near similar products; promotion (including personal selling) to highlight product advantages; less price sensitivity.	Extensive problem solving; consumer may need help in making a decision.
Specialty products	Price sensitivity is likely to be low; limited distribution may be acceptable, but should be treated as a convenience or shopping product (in whichever category product would typically be included) to reach persons not yet sold on its specialty product status.	Willing to expend effort to get specific product, even if not necessary; strong preferences make it an important purchase.
Unsought products		
New unsought	Must be available in places where similar (or related) products are sought; needs attention-getting promotion.	Need for product not strongly felt; unaware of benefits or not yet gone through adoption process.
Regulary unsought	Requires very aggressive promotion, usually personal selling.	Aware of product but not interested; attitude toward product may even be negative.

habit. A convenience product may be a staple, an impulse product, or an emergency product.

Staples are products that are bought often, routinely, and without much thought. Examples include breakfast cereal, canned soup, and most other packaged foods used almost every day in almost every household.

Impulse products are products that are bought quickly, as *unplanned* purchases, because of a strongly felt need. True impulse products are items that the customer hadn't planned to buy, decides to buy on sight, may have bought the same way many times before, and wants right now. If the buyer doesn't see an impulse product at the right time, the sale may be lost.[4]

Emergency products are products that are purchased immediately when the need is great. The customer doesn't have time to shop around when a traffic accident occurs, a thunderstorm begins, or an impromptu party starts. The price of the ambulance service, raincoat, or ice cubes won't be important.

Shopping products are compared

Shopping products are products that a customer feels are worth the time and effort to compare with competing products. Shopping products can be divided into two types—homogeneous and heterogeneous—depending on what customers are comparing.

Homogeneous shopping products are shopping products the customer sees as basically the same—and wants at the lowest price. Some consumers feel that certain sizes and types of refrigerators, television sets, washing machines, and even cars are very similar. So they shop for the best price.

Firms may try to emphasize and promote their product differences to avoid head-to-head price competition. For example, kitchen appliance manufacturers and dealers regularly promote their product differences. But if consumers don't think the differences are real or important, they'll just look at price.

Heterogeneous shopping products are shopping products the customer sees as different—and wants to inspect for quality and suitability. Furniture, clothing, dishes, and some cameras are good examples. Often, the consumer expects help from a knowledgeable salesperson. Quality and style matter more than price. In fact, once the customer finds the right product, price may not matter at all—as long as it's reasonable. For example, you may have asked a friend to recommend a good dentist without even asking what the dentist charges.

Branding may be less important for heterogeneous shopping products. The more consumers compare price and quality, the less they rely on brand names or labels. Some retailers carry competing brands so that consumers won't go to a competitor to compare items.

Specialty products—no substitutes, please!

Specialty products are consumer products that the customer really wants—and makes a special effort to find. Shopping for a specialty product doesn't mean comparing—the buyer wants that special product and is willing to search for it. It's the customer's *willingness to search*—not the extent of searching—that makes it a specialty product.

Any branded product that consumers insist on by name is a specialty product. Marketing managers want customers to see their products as specialty products and ask for them over and over again. Building that kind of relationship isn't easy: it means satisfying the customer every time. However, that's easier and a lot less costly than trying to win back dissatisfied customers or attract new customers who may not be seeking the product at all.

Unsought products need promotion

Unsought products are products that potential customers don't yet want or know they can buy. So they don't search for them at all. In fact, consumers probably won't buy these products if they see them—unless Promotion can show their value.

There are two types of unsought products. **New unsought products** are products offering really new ideas that potential customers don't know about yet. Informative promotion can help convince customers to accept the product, thus ending its unsought status. Yoplait Yogurt, Litton's microwave ovens, and Sony's videotape recorders are all popular items now, but initially they were new unsought products.

Regularly unsought products are products—like gravestones, life insurance, and encyclopedias—that stay unsought but not unbought forever. There may be a need, but potential customers aren't motivated to satisfy it. For this kind of product, personal selling is *very* important.

Many nonprofit organizations try to "sell" their unsought products.

One product may be seen several ways

We've been looking at product classes one at a time. But the same product might be seen in different ways by different target markets at the same time. For example, a product viewed as a staple by most consumers in the United States, Canada, or some

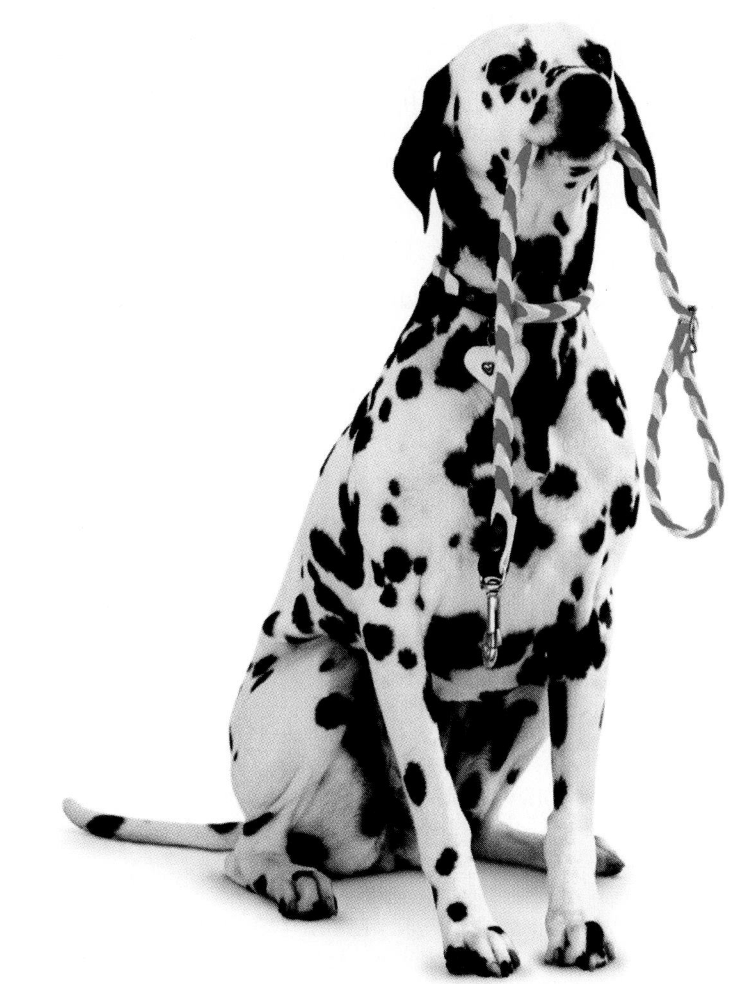

How Come Nobody Ever Says They're 'Healthy As A Dog?'
One of the many misconceptions about exercise is that everyday activities like walking your best friend does little to improve your health. In fact, nothing could be further from the truth. The daily bound with 'Spot' is great for both of you. And, considering how eager he is to go whenever you are, says a lot about how little it takes to be active and feel good. Just 30 minutes a day, most days of the week, for a whole new leash...er, lease, on life. Of course, if you don't have a dog, there's nothing stopping you from taking yourself for a daily walk. (Leash optional)
Sharing a Healthier Future™ with
PARTICIPACTION ®

To some consumers, health is an "unsought product."

similar affluent country may be seen as a heterogeneous shopping product by consumers in another country. The price may be much higher when considered as a proportion of the consumer's budget, and the available choices may be very different. Similarly, a convenient place to shop often means very different things in different countries. In Japan, for example, retail stores tend to be much smaller and carry smaller selections of products.

Business products are different

Business product classes are also useful for developing marketing mixes, since business firms use a system of buying related to these product classes. Before looking at how business products are different, however, we'll note some important similarities that affect strategic market planning.

One demand derived from another

The big difference in the business products market is **derived demand**—the demand for business products derives from the demand for final consumer products. For example, car manufacturers buy about one-fifth of all steel products. Even a steel company with a good marketing mix will lose sales to car manufacturers if demand for cars drops.[5]

Price increases might not reduce quantity purchased

Total *industry* demand for business products is fairly inelastic. Business firms must buy what they need to produce their own products. Even if the cost of basic silicon doubles, for example, Intel needs it to make computer chips. The increased cost of the silicon won't have much effect on the price of the final computer—or on the number of computers consumers demand. Sharp business buyers try to buy as economically as possible. So the demand facing *individual sellers* may be extremely elastic—if similar products are available at a lower price.

Tax treatment affects buying too

How a firm's accountants—and the tax laws—treat a purchase is also important to business customers. An **expense item** is a product whose total cost is treated as a business expense in the year it's purchased. A **capital item** is a long-lasting product that can be used and depreciated for many years. Often it's very expensive. Customers pay for the capital item when they buy it, but for tax purposes the cost is spread over a number of years.

Business product classes—how they are defined

Business product classes are based on how buyers see products—and how the products will be used. The classes of business products are (1) installations, (2) accessories, (3) raw materials, (4) components, (5) supplies, and (6) professional services. Exhibit 9–5 relates these product classes to marketing mix planning.

Installations

Installations, such as buildings, land rights, and major equipment, are important capital items. One-of-a-kind installations, such as office buildings and custom-made machines, generally require special negotiations for each sale. Standardized major equipment is treated more routinely. Even so, negotiations for installations involve top management, and can stretch over months or even years.

Installations are a boom-or-bust business. When sales are high, businesses want to expand capacity rapidly. And when the potential return on a new investment is very attractive, firms may accept any reasonable price. But during a downswing, buyers have little or no need for new installations and sales fall off sharply.[6]

Exhibit 9-5 Business Product Classes and Marketing Mix Planning

BUSINESS PRODUCT CLASSES	MARKETING MIX CONSIDERATIONS	BUYING BEHAVIOUR
Installations	Usually requires skillful personal selling by producer, including technical contacts, and/or understanding of applications; leasing and specialized support services may be required.	Multiple buying influence (including top management) and new-task buying are common; infrequent purchase, long decision period, and boom-or-bust demand are typical.
Accessory equipment	Need fairly widespread distribution and numerous contacts by experienced and sometimes technically trained personnel; price competition is often intense, but quality is important.	Purchasing and operating personnel typically make decisions; shorter decision period than for installations.
Raw materials	Grading is important, and transportation and storing can be crucial because of seasonal production and/or perishable products; markets tend to be very competitive.	Long-term contracts may be required to ensure supply.
Component parts and materials	Product quality and delivery reliability are usually extremely important; negotiation and technical selling typical on less-standardized items; replacement after market may require different strategies.	Multiple buying influence is common; competitive bids used to encourage competitive pricing.
Maintenance, repair, and operating (MRO) supplies	Typically require widespread distribution or fast delivery (repair items); arrangements with appropriate intermediaries may be crucial.	Often handled as straight rebuys, except important operating supplies may be treated much more seriously and involve multiple buying influence.
Professional services	Services customized to buyer's need; personal selling very important; inelastic demand often supports high prices.	Customer may compare outside service with what internal people could provide; needs may be very specialized.

Specialized services

Suppliers sometimes include special services with an installation at no extra cost. A firm that sells (or leases) equipment to dentists, for example, may install it and help the dentist learn to use it.

Accessories

Accessories are short-lived capital items—tools and equipment used in production or office activities. Examples include Canon's small copy machines, Rockwell's portable drills, and Steelcase's filing cabinets.

Since these products cost less and last a shorter time than installations, multiple buying influence is less important. Operating people and purchasing agents, rather than top managers, may make the purchase decision. As with installations, some customers may wish to expense the cost by leasing or renting.

Accessories are more standardized than installations. And they're usually needed by more customers. For example, IBM sells its robotics systems, which can cost over $1 million, as custom installations to large manufacturers. But IBM's Thinkpad computers are accessory equipment for just about every type of modern business all around the world.

Raw materials

Raw materials are unprocessed expense items, such as logs, iron ore, wheat, and cotton, that are moved to the next production process with little handling. Unlike installations and accessories, *raw materials become part of a physical good, and are expense items.*

We can break raw materials into two types: (1) farm products and (2) natural products. **Farm products** are grown by farmers, for example, oranges, wheat, sugar cane, cattle, poultry, eggs, and milk. **Natural products** are products that occur in nature, such as fish and game, timber and maple syrup, and copper, zinc, iron ore, oil, and coal.

The need for grading is one of the important differences between raw materials and other business products. Nature produces what it will, and someone must sort and grade raw materials to satisfy various market segments. Top-grade fruits and vegetables may find their way into the consumer products market. Lower grades, which are treated as business products, are used in juices, sauces, and soups.

Most buyers of raw materials want ample supplies in the right grades for specific uses: fresh vegetables for Green Giant's production lines, or logs for International Paper's paper mills. To ensure steady quantities, raw materials customers often sign long-term contracts—sometimes at guaranteed prices.

Component parts and materials

Components are processed expense items that become part of a finished product. Component *parts* are finished (or nearly finished) items that are ready for assembly into the final product. Disk drives installed in personal computers, air bags in cars, and motors for appliances are examples. Component *materials* are items such as wire, paper, textiles, and cement. They have already been processed, but must be processed further before becoming part of the final product. Since components become part of the firm's own product, quality is extremely important.

Components are often produced in large quantity to meet standard specifications. However, some components are custom made. When they are, teamwork between the buyer and seller may be needed to arrive at the right specifications. So a buyer may find it attractive to develop a close partnership with a dependable supplier. And top management may be involved if the price is high or the component is extremely important to the final product.

Since component parts go into finished products, a replacement market often develops. This *after market* can be both large and very profitable. Car tires and batteries are two examples of components originally sold in the *OEM (original equipment market)* that become consumer products in the after market. The target markets are different, and different marketing mixes are usually necessary.[7]

Supplies for maintenance, repair, and operations

Supplies are expense items that do not become part of a finished product. Buyers may treat these items less seriously. When a firm cuts its budget, orders for supplies may be the first to go. Supplies can be divided into three types: (1) maintenance, (2) repair, and (3) operating supplies. Thus, their common name: MRO supplies.

Maintenance and small operating supplies are like convenience products: the item will be ordered because it is needed, but buyers won't spend much time on it. Branding may become important because it makes buying easier for such "nuisance" purchases. Breadth of assortment and the seller's dependability are also important. Intermediaries usually handle the many supply items.[8]

If operating supplies are needed regularly and in large amounts, they receive special treatment. Many companies buy coal and fuel oil in railway-car quantities. Usually there are several sources for such commodity products, and large volumes may be purchased in highly competitive international markets.

Professional services

Professional services are specialized services that support a firm's operations. They are usually expense items. Engineering and management consulting services can improve the plant layout and/or the company's efficiency. Computer services can process data. Design services can supply designs for physical plant, products, and promotion materials. Advertising agencies can help promote the firm's products, and food services can improve morale.

Here the *service* part of the product is emphasized. Goods may be supplied, as coffee and doughnuts are with food service, but the customer is interested mainly in the service.

Managers compare the cost of buying professional services outside the firm with the cost of having company people do them. For special skills needed only occasionally, an outsider may be the best source. Further, during the last decade many firms have tried to cut costs by downsizing the number of people they employ. In many cases, work that was previously done by an employee is now provided as a service by an independent supplier. Clearly, the number of service specialists is growing in our complex economy. See Marketing Demo 9–1 for an example of Canada's success in exporting professional services.

Branding needs a strategy decision too

There are so many brands, and we're so used to seeing them, that we take them for granted. But branding is an important decision area, so we will treat it in some detail.

What is branding?

Branding means the use of a name, term, symbol, or design, or a combination of these, to identify a product. It includes the use of brand names, trademarks, and practically all other means of product identification.

Brand name has a narrower meaning. A **brand name** is a word, a letter, or a group of words or letters. Examples include Blockbuster Video, WD-40, 3M Post-its, and IBM Aptiva computers.

Trademark is a legal term. A **trademark** includes only those words, symbols, or marks that are legally registered for use by a single company. A **service mark** is the same as a trademark except that it refers to a service offering.

The word *Buick* can be used to explain these differences. The Buick car is branded under the brand name Buick (whether it's spoken or printed in any manner). When "Buick" is printed in a certain kind of script, however, it becomes a trademark. A trademark need not be attached to the product. It need not even be a word—it can be a symbol.

These differences may seem technical. But they are very important to business firms that spend a lot of money to protect and promote their brands.

Brands meet needs

Well-recognized brands make shopping easier. Think of trying to buy groceries, for example, if you had to evaluate the advantages and disadvantages of each of 25,000 items every time you went to a supermarket. Many customers are willing to buy new things, but having gambled and won, they like to buy a sure thing the next time.

Brand promotion has advantages for branders as well as customers. A good brand reduces the marketer's selling time and effort. And sometimes a firm's brand name is the only element in its marketing mix that a competitor can't copy. Also, good brands can improve the company's image, and speed up acceptance of new products marketed under the same name. For example, many consumers quickly tried Snickers ice cream bars when they were introduced because they already knew they liked Snickers candy bars.[9]

Conditions favourable to branding

Can you recall a brand name for file folders, bed frames, electric extension cords, or nails? As these examples suggest, it's not always easy to establish a respected brand.

Marketing Demo 9-1

The Noticeable Export Gains of "Invisibles"

It's easy to keep track of the goods we export because goods are so wonderfully tangible. All of us, at one time or another, have seen trucks and trains and ships loaded with the cars, grain, lumber and machinery that Canadians are exporting to customers abroad.

But there are also exports we don't see. With good reason, statisticians sometimes call them "invisibles," because they consist of a wide range of things that cannot be seen but are very real commercially.

They are mainly business services and rights for which fees and royalties are paid.

Canada's exports of these items have been soaring in recent years. You might be surprised to discover just what kind of things we are getting good at selling to foreigners.

Did you know, for example, that since 1990, Canadian exports of architectural and engineering services have increased almost fivefold? Or that royalties and licence fees paid to Canadians by foreigners have almost tripled? Or that exports of computer services have more than doubled?

Growth like that sounds wildly impressive, so it's important to keep some perspective. Compared with the $281-billion in goods we exported last year, our $18-billion in exports of all commercial services looks rather puny, even if it is twice what we earned in 1990. And while we ran a $41-billion surplus in goods last year, we had a $3.9-billion deficit in business services.

From 1988 to 1996, while exports of goods grew 96 per cent, sales of business services to foreigners expanded 126 per cent, so it's evident that service companies are not shy about getting into the export game.

So what are we selling?

Our top export is insurance, almost $4-billion worth of it last year. It has grown rapidly from $2-billion in 1990, but not fast enough to keep up with imports of insurance, which hit $4.6-billion in 1996. Clearly, insurance is increasingly becoming a hot trade item as Canadian companies exploit their specialties abroad and foreign insurers try to win Canadian customers.

The next-biggest category of exports takes in communications services—everything from couriers to the most sophisticated forms of telecommunications, like teleconferencing and electronic data exchange. It was worth about $1.9-billion in exports last year and it's one category where we usually run a surplus.

Third on the list is research and development, which counts everything done by Canadian scientists and other researchers who worked for foreign clients. It was worth $1.7-billion in 1996, up from $700-million in 1990. Canadian companies are much less inclined to buy their R&D from abroad. We've run surpluses in this category since 1985.

The fourth-ranked export item is something Statistics Canada calls architectural and engineering services, which brought in revenues of almost $1.6-billion in 1996, a huge leap from $330-million in 1990.

Canada's big engineering firms have a long history of winning contracts to work on large construction projects abroad—like hydroelectric dams or transit systems. But it seems that when work dried up in Canada during the recession and slow-growth recovery of the 1990s, the companies intensified their search for foreign customers who would buy their design and consulting services.

This is an area where Canadians are clear world-beaters. We consistently run surpluses in this category, sums that amounted to more than $1.1-billion in each of the past two years.

These four areas are the biggest in sheer volume. But to find the fastest-growing export items, you have to go to a couple of smaller categories.

Royalties and licence fees brought in about $500-million last year, triple the 1990 level. This includes the money Canadians earn from the intellectual property they create—patents, trademarks, copyrights, software and franchises. However, our payments to foreigners are even bigger and also rising at a rapid clip. Last year, we paid some $2.7-billion to be able to use products they had created.

Computer services are another hot growth area. This covers the design, engineering and management of computer systems and includes the production of original software. It brought in more than $1.2-billion last year, compared with $500-million in 1990. It's another area where we sell more than we buy from other countries. Last year, the surplus in computer services amounted to $300-million.

You won't hear about these export items in the regular monthly reports on Canada's trade, because they count only goods. Exports of services are measured less frequently and reported less prominently.

Business services may be invisible, but it's evident that a growing number of Canadians are finding new customers abroad who are willing to pay some very tangible dollars for these intangible products.

Source: Bruce Little, *The Globe and Mail,* August 11, 1997, A6. Reprinted with permission from *The Globe and Mail.*

The following conditions are favourable to successful branding:

1. The product is easy to identify by brand or trademark.
2. The product quality is the best value for the price and the quality is easy to maintain.
3. Dependable and widespread availability is possible. When customers start using a brand, they want to be able to continue using it.
4. Demand is strong enough that the market price can be high enough to make the branding effort profitable.
5. There are economies of scale. If the branding is really successful, costs should drop and profits should increase.
6. Favourable shelf locations or display space in stores will help. This is something retailers can control when they brand their own products. Producers must use aggressive salespeople to get favourable positions.

In general, these conditions are less common in less-developed economies—which may explain why efforts to build brands in less-developed nations often fail.

Achieving brand familiarity is not easy

The earliest and most aggressive brand promoters were the patent medicine companies. They were joined by the food manufacturers, who grew in size in the latter half of the nineteenth century. Some of the brands started in the 1860s and 1870s (and still going strong) are Borden's Condensed Milk, Quaker Oats, Pillsbury's Best Flour, and Ivory Soap. Today, familiar brands exist for most product categories, ranging from crayons (Crayola) to rental car services (Hertz). However, which brand is familiar often varies from one country to another.

Brand acceptance must be earned with a good product and regular promotion. **Brand familiarity** relates to how well customers recognize and accept a company's brand. The degree of brand familiarity affects the planning for the rest of the marketing mix—especially where the product should be offered and what promotion is needed.

Five levels of brand familiarity

Five levels of brand familiarity are useful for strategy planning: (1) rejection, (2) nonrecognition, (3) recognition, (4) preference, and (5) insistence.

Some brands have been tried and found wanting. **Brand rejection** means that potential customers won't buy a brand unless its image is changed. Rejection may suggest a change in the product, or perhaps only a shift to target customers who have a better image of the brand. Overcoming a negative image is difficult and can be very expensive.

Brand rejection is a big concern for service-oriented businesses because it's hard to control the quality of service. A business traveller who gets a dirty room in a Hilton Hotel in Caracas, Venezuela, may not return to any Hilton anywhere. Yet it's difficult for Hilton to ensure that every maid does a good job every time.

Some products are seen as basically the same. **Brand nonrecognition** means final consumers don't recognize a brand at all—even though intermediaries may use the brand name for identification and inventory control.

Brand recognition means that customers remember the brand. This can be a big advantage if there are many "nothing" brands on the market. Even if consumers can't recall the brand without help, they may be reminded when they see it in a store among other less familiar brands.

Most branders would like to win **brand preference,** which means that target customers usually choose the brand over other brands, perhaps out of habit or because of favourable past experience.

Exhibit 9-6 Characteristics of a Good Brand Name

• Short and simple • Easy to spell and read • Easy to recognize and remember • Easy to pronounce • Can be pronounced in only one way • Can be pronounced in all languages (for international markets)	• Suggestive of product benefits • Adaptable to packaging/labelling needs • Not offensive, obscene, or negative • Always timely (does not get out-of-date) • Adaptable to any advertising medium • Legally available for use (not in use by another firm)

Brand insistence means customers insist on a firm's branded product and are willing to search for it. This is an objective of many target marketers.

The right brand name can help

A good brand name can help build brand familiarity. It can help tell something important about the company or its product. Exhibit 9–6 lists some characteristics of a good brand name. Some successful brand names seem to break all these rules, but many of these got started when there was less competition.

Companies that compete in international markets face a special problem in selecting brand names. A name that conveys a positive image in one language may be meaningless in another. Or worse, it may have unintended meanings. GM's Nova car is a classic example. GM stuck with the name Nova when it introduced the car in South America. It seemed sensible, because Nova is the Spanish word for star. However, Nova also sounds the same as the Spanish words for "no go." Consumers weren't interested in a no-go car, and sales didn't pick up until GM changed the name.[10]

A respected name builds brand equity

Because it's difficult and expensive to build brand recognition, some firms prefer to buy established brands rather than try to build their own. The value of a brand to its current owner or to a firm that wants to buy it is sometimes called **brand equity**—the value of a brand's overall strength in the market. For example, brand equity is likely to be higher if many satisfied customers insist on buying the brand and if retailers are eager to stock it. That almost guarantees ongoing profits from the brand and increases the brand's value. Internet Insite 9–1 discusses some of the most successful initial efforts at building brands on the Web.

Protecting Canadian trademarks and brand names

The law protects the owners of trademarks and brand names. Ownership of brand names and trademarks is generally established by distinctiveness and continued use.

Since the basic right is found in "use," a Canadian firm need not register its trademark under the **Trademarks Act.** But when a trademark is so registered, the registering firm is legally protected against any other company using a trademark that might be confused with its own. In contrast, the holder of an unregistered trademark couldn't sue a firm merely for using a similar trademark. The owner of an unregistered trademark would have to prove that some other firm was deliberately using that name to confuse consumers by "passing off" its products as those of the trademark holder.

Canadian and U.S. laws differ in the types of trademark protection they provide. There's less chance of a Canadian trade name being ruled "generic" or a common descriptive term—and therefore no longer protectable by its original owner. For

Building Brands on the Web

The virtual marketspace on the Web is seen as the great equalizer, as the level playing field where small firms can compete with large ones. The relatively low cost of setting up an electronic storefront makes it easier for entrepreneurs with limited resources to gain access to the growing virtual marketspace. Does this spell the end of dominant brands? Not really. Concerns about online security and the information overload that occurs during Internet searches are two reasons why online consumers seem to be gravitating toward well-known, trusted brands.

Established brands such as IBM are using the Web to reach out to new segments. IBM, in an effort to develop brand awareness among younger people, is providing online interactive games such as "hoop," football, and tennis (www.ibm.com/sports/). IBM knows that kids, the consumers of tomorrow, can be reached effectively through sports. The Web allows IBM to build not only awareness, but also a relationship with youth.

Kraft, another household name, has an Interactive Kitchen (www.kraftfoods.com) where consumers can personalize their meal plans, read recipes and culinary tips, and fill their online shopping carts with Kraft products. Sony has leveraged its strong brand equity and established a Web site called The Station (www.sony.com). Here, you can play the Wheel of Fortune and many other games, chat with famous musicians, listen to music, and while you are at it also buy Sony products.

These are some examples of successful Web sites, where marketers have been able to engage consumers through the use of interactive features. These sites allow consumers to participate actively and have fun. In the process, consumer involvement in the product is bound to increase, leading to strengthened brand identification and loyalty. Manufacturers who were far removed from consumers are now learning to build relationships with consumers. For these established brands, this Web-based marketing approach is a significant departure from "in your face" marketing. This is soft-sell at its best.

Some new brands were actually born in the virtual marketspace and are quickly establishing strong identities. *Wired,* the first real e-zine (or electronic magazine), understood the Internet culture (www.wired.com). It describes itself as a magazine that "charts the impact of technology on business, culture, life." It is targeted to the techno-savvy, and speaks to the needs and interests of the Web community. There are threaded discussions and articles that keep you on top of developments in the digital world. It is a free, advertising supported Web site—a less conventional but still effective business model.

Among the many online stores selling wine, Virtual Vineyard, a California-based company (www.virtualvineyard.com), stands out. You can visit the food shop, wine shop, or gift shop, educate yourself on various wines, and have your questions answered by experts.

And then there is Amazon.Com—"Earth's Biggest Bookstore" (www.amazon.com). Not only does this online store handle over 2.5 million titles, but its Web site offers book reviews, various contests, and keyword and author search capability. You can browse or buy from the convenience of your home, and even be the book critic of the week. Clearly, firms like Virtual Vineyard and Amazon.Com understand how to use the Web, and offer value that is not matched by traditional retailers.

The Web offers everyone a chance—established players as well as newcomers. Marketers who see the Web as more than just an online catalogue, who try to educate the consumer, and who use interactive tools to engage the consumer, are the ones who are succeeding. Success in the virtual marketspace still depends on some old-fashioned ideas, such as creating value and offering service, reliability, convenience, and savings. Brand managers are just discovering that this medium offers a whole new way of building customer relationships and brand loyalty.

References

1. Gerry McGovern, "Building Brands: Brick-by-Brick," in *ClickZ Today,* April 28, 1998, (www.clickz.com).

2. Alice Z. Cuneo, "Cyberbrand Study: Web Branding Opens Links to Customers," in *NetMarketing* (www.netb2b.com).

3. Rex Briggs, "A Roadmap to Online Marketing Strategy," *MBInteractive* (www.mbinteractive.com).

Source: This is one of a series of Internet Insites prepared in April 1998 by Dr. Ramesh Venkat of Saint Mary's University for *Basic Marketing,* Ninth Canadian Edition.

Private label
eating you alive?
Bite back!
At The Thomas Pigeon Design Group, we create brand identities that give teeth to national brands. Teeth to cut through cluttered store shelves. Teeth to take a bite out of private label. Our proprietary seven-step process has helped leading national brands in Canada and the U.S. realize sensational sales results. Brands like Hostess, Claritin, Jell-O, and Carefree. Brands like Cracker Barrel, Ramses, Dream Whip, Primo and Miss Vickies. To find out how we can put more bite into your brand's image, call Thomas Pigeon or Allan MacTaggart today.
Dedicated to building national brands through effective package design
(905) 338-8300

THOMAS
PIGEON
DESIGN

example, Bayer Aspirin is still a protected trademark in Canada, even though *aspirin* has become a generic term in the United States.[11]

You must protect your own

A brand can be a real asset to a company. Every firm should try to ensure that its brand doesn't become the generic term for its kind of product. When this happens, the brand name or trademark falls into the public domain, and the owner loses all rights to it. This happened in the United States with the names cellophane, aspirin, shredded wheat, and kerosene. Teflon, Scotch Tape, and Xerox also came close to becoming common descriptive terms there. And Miller Brewing Company tried, unsuccessfully, in the U.S. courts to protect its Lite beer by suing other brewers who wanted to use the word *light*.[12]

Ethical Dimensions

Counterfeiting Is Accepted in Some Cultures

Even when products are properly registered, counterfeiters may make unauthorized copies. Many well-known brands, ranging from Levi's jeans to Rolex watches to Zantax ulcer medicine, face this problem. Counterfeiting is especially common in developing nations. In China, most videotapes and CDs are bootleg copies. Counterfeiting is big business in some countries, so efforts to stop it may meet with limited success. There are also differences in cultural values. In South Korea, for example, many people don't see counterfeiting as unethical.[13]

What kind of brand to use?

Branders of more than one product must decide whether they are going to use a **family brand**—the same brand name for several products—or individual brands for each product. Examples of family brands are Keebler snack food products and Sears' Kenmore appliances.

The use of the same brand for many products makes sense if all are similar in type and quality. The main benefit is that the goodwill attached to one or two products may help the others. Money spent to promote the brand name benefits more than one product, and this cuts promotion costs for each product.

A special kind of family brand is a **licensed brand**—a well-known brand that sellers pay a fee to use. For example, the familiar Sunkist brand name has been licensed to many companies for use on more than 400 products in 30 countries.[14]

Individual brands for outside and inside competition

A company uses **individual brands**—a separate brand name for each product—when it's important for the products to each have a separate identity, as when products vary in quality or type.

If the products are really different, such as Elmer's glue and Borden's ice cream, individual brands can avoid confusion. Some firms use individual brands with similar products to make segmentation and positioning efforts easier. Unilever, for example, markets Aim, Close-Up, and Pepsodent toothpastes, but each involves different positioning efforts.

Sometimes firms use individual brands to encourage competition within the company. Each brand is managed by a different group within the firm. They argue that if anyone is going to take business away from their firm, it ought to be their own brand. However, many firms that once used this approach have reorganized. Faced with slower market growth, they found they had plenty of competitive pressure from other firms. The internal competition just made it more difficult to coordinate different marketing strategies.[15]

Generic "brands"

Products that some consumers see as commodities may be difficult or expensive to brand. Some manufacturers and intermediaries have responded to this problem with **generic products**—products that have no brand at all other than identification of their contents and the manufacturer or intermediary. Generic products are usually offered in plain packages at lower prices.[16]

Who should do the branding?

Manufacturer brands versus dealer brands

Manufacturer brands are brands created by producers. These are sometimes called "national brands" because the brand is promoted all across the country or in large regions. Note, however, that many manufacturer brands are now distributed globally. Such brands include Kellogg's, Whirlpool, Ford, and IBM. Many creators of service-oriented firms—like McDonald's, Orkin Pest Control, and Midas Muffler—promote their brands this way too.

Dealer brands, also called **private brands,** are brands created by intermediaries. Examples of dealer brands include Safeway, Home Hardware, and The Bay. Some of these are advertised and distributed more widely than many national brands.

Who's winning the battle of the brands?

The **battle of the brands**—that is, the competition between dealer brands and manufacturer brands—is just a question of whose brands will be more popular, and who will be in control.

At one time, manufacturer brands were much more popular than dealer brands. Now sales of both kinds of brands are about equal. That being said, sales of dealer brands are expected to continue growing. Intermediaries have some advantages in this battle. With the number of large wholesalers and retail chains growing, they are better able to arrange reliable sources of supply at low cost. They can also control the point of sale and give the dealer brand special shelf position or promotion.

Consumers benefit from the battle. Competition has already narrowed price differences between manufacturer brands and well-known dealer brands.[17]

The strategic importance of packaging

Packaging involves promoting and protecting the product. Packaging can be important to both sellers and customers. It can make a product more convenient to use or store. It can prevent spoiling or damage. Good packaging makes products easier to identify and promotes the brand at the point of purchase and even in use.

PACKAGING CAN MAKE THE DIFFERENCE A new package can make *the* important difference in a new marketing strategy, by meeting customers' needs better. Sometimes a new package makes the product easier or safer to use. For example, Quaker State oil comes with a twist-off top and pouring spout to make it more

Marketing Demo 9-2

The Drive for Shelf Impact

Why Package Design Is Taking on a Bigger Role in the Marketing Mix

Package design's increasing importance is a fact of marketing life. With time-starved, usually impatient consumers to satisfy, a well-designed package can mean the difference between galloping sales success and flatlining off to nowhere. But what's driving companies in so many product categories to overhaul their designs regularly, or at least to tweak them with a compulsion verging on the neurotic?

The first explanation is nothing more complicated than cluttered store shelves. There is a bewildering variety of products available to the consumer today, thanks in no small part to most Canadians' comparative affluence. And, say observers, it's this clutter that has raised the stakes for marketers.

Shelf impact is one of a brand's most important aspects, says designer Martin Kuster, president of Hunter Straker in Toronto. The product's packaging has to fairly leap out at the consumer, because, he says, "If you're not seen, tough luck."

Richard Loh, president of Marketing by Design, also in Toronto, agrees that package design must stand out in the store. "It's got to say, 'Pick me up and take me home,' " he says.

Réjean Leblanc, vice-president of marketing at Goodhue & Associés in Montreal, agrees. Since 70% or so of all purchase decisions are made on the spot, he says, package design has to "seduce" the consumer from the shelf.

Meredith Gray, marketing director, North America, for Houbigant (Canada) in Laval Que., says for the fragrance business, as for other industries, shelf clutter is an issue that affects package design. There are lots of fragrances on the market already, says Gray, and in a promotions-driven business such as hers, promotional items just add to the problem. "It really has to have standout packaging just to get (consumers') interest," says Gray.

Ken Jure, director of marketing, consumer products, at Fuji Photo Film Canada in Mississauga, Ont., says film is an impulse buy, and package design plays an important part in the purchase decision for many people. The graphics of the package have to convey the product's quality, Jure continues, noting that Fuji is now introducing its Superior brand of film, which uses gold coloring to replace its current offering, Super G Plus . . .

Predicting the future of package design is not without its pitfalls, although there are some ideas that occur over and over. Designer Micahel Dangelmaier, a partner at Karo in Calgary, says the environmental movement has had a strong impact on design and will continue to exert an influence. Packaging will likely become more adaptable, says Dangelmaier, so it can be reused.

There will also be continued emphasis on simplicity, thinks Kuster. He says in five years or so package design will be simpler thanks to consumers' decreasing attention spans and product usage getting simpler. No more pouches in boxes, he predicts. And perhaps there will even be less box.

One definite trend in package design is transparency, so consumers can actually see some of what they're buying. Kellogg has already sold Rice Krispie Treats in boxes with transparent panels, for example, and Loh recalls transparent cans being introduced in Britain about a decade ago. The ultimate in package design for some categories, marketers seem to be saying, is giving consumers a look at the actual product itself.

Source: Abridged from David Chilton, *Marketing Magazine,* March 23, 1998, p. 16.

convenient for customers at self-service gas stations. And most drug and food products now have special seals to prevent product tampering.

PACKAGING SENDS A MESSAGE Packaging can tie the product to the rest of the marketing strategy. Packaging for Eveready batteries features the pink bunny, who reminds consumers that the batteries are durable. A good package sometimes gives a firm more promotion effect than it could get with advertising. Customers see the package in stores, when they're actually buying. Shelf impact is important. As Marketing Demo 9–2 indicates, cluttered store shelves require marketers to pay close attention to package design.

PACKAGING MAY LOWER DISTRIBUTION COSTS Better protective packaging is very important to manufacturers and wholesalers, who sometimes have to pay the cost of goods damaged in shipment. Retailers need protective packaging too. It can reduce storing costs by cutting breakage, spoilage, and theft. Good packages save space and are easier to handle and display.[18]

Exhibit 9-7
Illustration of a Universal Product Code

UNIVERSAL PRODUCT CODES ALLOW MORE INFORMATION To speed handling of fast-selling products, government and industry representatives have developed a **universal product code (UPC)** that identifies each product with marks readable by electronic scanners. A computer then matches each code to the product and its price. Supermarkets and other high-volume retailers use these codes. They reduce the need to mark the price on every item. They also reduce errors by cashiers and make it easy to control inventory and track sales of specific products. Exhibit 9–7 shows a universal product code mark.

The codes help consumers too, by speeding up the checkout process. Also, most systems now include a printed receipt showing the name, size, and price of each product bought.

What is socially responsible packaging?

Some consumers say that some package designs are misleading—perhaps on purpose. Who hasn't been surprised by a candy bar half the size of the package? Others feel that the great variety of packages makes it hard to compare values. And some are concerned about whether the packages are degradable or can be recycled.

The task of adopting "greener" packaging isn't simple. In addition to establishing costs and benefits, simply coordinating solutions between producers, governments, and citizen organizations is an enormous task. In order to help Canadians identify better packaging and products, the "Ecologo" appearing on this page has been adopted.

Federal law tries to help

The **Hazardous Products Act** gives Industry Canada the authority either to ban or to regulate the sale, distribution, and labelling of hazardous products.

Ethical Dimensions

Ethical Decisions Remain

Although various laws provide guidance on many packaging issues, many areas still require marketing managers to make ethical choices. For example, some firms have been criticized for designing packages that conceal a downsized product, giving consumers less for the money. Similarly, some retailers design packages and labels for their private-label products that look just like—and are easily confused with—manufacturer brands. Are efforts such as these unethical, or are they simply an attempt to make packaging a more effective part of a marketing mix? Different people will answer differently.

Some marketing managers promote environmentally friendly packaging on some products while simultaneously increasing the use of problematic packages on others. Empty packages now litter our streets, and some plastic packages will lie in a city dump for decades. But some consumers like the convenience that accompanies these problems. Is it unethical for a marketing manager to give consumers with different preferences a choice? Some critics argue that it is; others praise firms that give consumers a choice.

Many critics feel that labelling information is too often incomplete or misleading. Do consumers really understand the nutritional information required by law? Further, some consumers want information that is difficult—perhaps even impossible—to provide. For example, how can a label accurately describe a product's taste or texture? But the ethical issues focus on how far a marketing manager should go in putting potentially negative information on a package. For example, should Häagen-Dazs affix a label that says, "This product will clog your arteries"? That sounds extreme, but what type of information *is* appropriate?[19]

Since 1971, all products considered potentially hazardous (such as cleaning substances, chemicals, and aerosol products) have had to carry on their labels an appropriate symbol that reveals both the possible danger and the necessary precautions. The symbols chosen indicate whether the product is poisonous, flammable, explosive, or corrosive.

The **Consumer Packaging and Labelling Act** calls for bilingual labels and for the standardization of package sizes and shapes. It also requires that all food products be labelled in metric terms as well as in traditional Canadian measures. When reference is made on a label or package to the number of servings being provided, the average size of these servings must also be indicated. The term *best before* must appear in both official languages along with a date reflecting the product's durability.

Labelling requirements for certain specified products are also set forth in the National Trademark and True Labelling Act, the Textile Labelling Act, and the Precious Metals Marking Act. The Textile Care Labelling Program provides for all garments and other textiles to be labelled with washing or dry cleaning instructions. Similarly, the CANTAG program now being widely used provides customers with performance, capacity, and energy consumption data on major appliances.

Unit-pricing is a possible help

Some retailers—especially the large supermarket chains—make it easier for consumers to compare packages with different weights or volumes. They use **unit-pricing,** which involves placing the price per ounce (or some other standard measure) on or near the product. This makes price comparison easier.[20]

Warranty policies are a part of strategy planning

A **warranty** explains what the seller promises about its product. Deciding on warranty policies is part of strategy planning. A marketing manager should decide whether to offer a specific warranty, and if so what the warranty will cover and how it will be communicated to target customers. In this area, the legal environment—as well as customer needs and competitive offerings—must be considered.

Both the common law and sale-of-goods legislation say that producers must stand behind their products, even if they don't offer a specific warranty. A written warranty provided by the seller may promise more than the common law provides; however, it may actually *reduce* the responsibility a producer would have under common law.

Provincial and federal laws attempt to see that any warranty offered is fair to the consumer, easy to understand, and precise as to what is and what isn't covered. Before this increased government concern, some firms simply said their products were "fully warranted" or "absolutely guaranteed" without either specifying a time period or spelling out the meaning of the guarantee.

On the federal level, protection against misleading warranties is provided by the Competition Act. Specifically prohibited are warranties that seem unlikely to be carried out, warranties where excessive labour or handling charges are used to cover the manufacturer's cost of allegedly replacing defective parts "free of charge," and warranties that reduce a purchaser's usual rights under common law.[21]

Warranty may improve the marketing mix

Some firms use warranties to improve the appeal of their marketing mix. They design more quality into their goods or services and offer refunds or replacement—not just repair—if there is a problem. Xerox uses this approach with its copy machines. Its three-year warranty says that a customer who is not satisfied with a copier—for *any* reason—can trade it for another model. This type of warranty sends a strong signal. A buyer doesn't have to worry about whether the copier will work as expected, or whether service calls will be prompt, or even whether the Xerox salesperson or dealer has recommended the appropriate model.

Service guarantees

Customer service guarantees are becoming more common as a way to attract and keep customers. Pizza Hut guarantees a luncheon pizza in five minutes or it's free. General Motors set up a fast-oil-change guarantee to compete with fast-lube specialists who were taking customers away from dealers. If the dealer doesn't get the job done in 29 minutes or less, the next oil change is free. The Hampton Inn motel chain guarantees "100% satisfaction." All employees—even the cleaning crews—are empowered to offer an unhappy customer a discount or refund on the spot.

There's more risk in offering a service guarantee than a warranty on a physical product. An apathetic employee or a service breakdown can create a big expense. However, without the guarantee, dissatisfied customers may just go away mad without ever complaining. When customers collect on a guarantee, the company can clearly identify the problem. Then the problem can be addressed.

Warranty support can be costly

The cost of warranty support ultimately must be covered by the price that consumers pay. This has led some firms to offer warranty choices. The basic price for a product may include a warranty that covers a short time period or that covers parts but not labour. Consumers who want more or better protection pay extra for an extended warranty or a service contract.[22]

Questions and Problems

1. Define, in your own words, what a Product is.

2. Discuss several ways in which physical goods are different from pure services. Give an example of a good and then an example of a service that illustrates each of the differences.

3. What products are being offered by a shop that specializes in bicycles? By a travel agent? By a supermarket? By a new car dealer?

4. What kinds of consumer products are the following? (a) watches, (b) automobiles, (c) toothpastes. Explain your reasoning.

5. Consumer services tend to be intangible, and goods tend to be tangible. Use an example to explain how the lack of a physical good in a pure service might affect efforts to promote the service.

6. How would the marketing mix for a staple convenience product differ from one for a homogeneous shopping product? How would the mix for a specialty product differ from the mix for a heterogeneous shopping product? Use examples.

7. Give an example of a product that is a *new* unsought product for most people. Briefly explain why it is an unsought product.

8. In what types of stores would you expect to find (a) convenience products, (b) shopping products, (c) specialty products, and (d) unsought products?

9. Cite two examples of business products that require a substantial amount of service in order to be useful.

10. Explain why a new law office might want to lease furniture rather than buy it.

11. Would you expect to find any wholesalers selling the various types of business products? Are retail stores required (or something like retail stores)?

12. What kinds of business products are the following? (a) lubricating oil, (b) electric motors, (c) a firm that provides landscaping and grass mowing for an apartment complex. Explain your reasoning.

13. How do raw materials differ from other business products? Do the differences have any impact on their marketing mixes? If so, what specifically?

14. For the kinds of business products described in this chapter, complete the following table (use one or a few well-chosen words).

15. Is there any difference between a brand name and a trademark? If so, why is this difference important?

16. Is a well-known brand valuable only to the owner of the brand?

17. Suggest an example of a product and a competitive situation where it would *not* be profitable for a firm to spend large sums of money to establish a brand.

18. List five brand names and indicate what product is associated with the brand name. Evaluate the strengths and weaknesses of the brand name.

19. Explain family brands. Should Toys "Я" Us develop its own dealer brands to compete with some of the popular manufacturer brands it carries? Explain your reasons.

20. In the past, Sears emphasized its own dealer brands. Now it is carrying more well-known

PRODUCTS	1	2	3
Installations			
Buildings and land rights			
Major equipment			
Standard			
Custom-made			
Accessories			
Raw materials			
Farm products			
Natural products			
Components			
Supplies			
Maintenance and small operating supplies			
Operating supplies			
Professional services			

1. *Kind of distribution facility(ies) needed and functions they will provide.*
2. *Calibre of salespeople required.*
3. *Kind of advertising required.*

manufacturer brands. What are the benefits to Sears of carrying more manufacturer brands?

21. What does the degree of brand familiarity imply about previous and future promotion efforts? How does the degree of brand familiarity affect the Place and Price variables?

22. You operate a small hardware store with emphasis on manufacturer brands and have barely been breaking even. Evaluate the proposal of a large wholesaler who offers a full line of dealer-branded hardware items at substantially lower prices. Specify any assumptions necessary to obtain a definite answer.

23. Give examples where packaging costs probably (a) lower total distribution costs and (b) raise total distribution costs.

24. Is it more difficult to support a warranty for a service than for a physical good? Explain.

Suggested cases

11 Ralph the Optician

15 Lucas Foods

19 Kastors, Inc.

Computer-aided problem

Branding Decision

Wholesteen Dairy, Inc., produces and sells Wholesteen brand condensed milk to grocery retailers. The overall market for condensed milk is fairly flat, and there's sharp competition among dairies for retailers' business. Wholesteen's regular price to retailers is $8.88 a case (24 cans). FoodWorld—a fast-growing supermarket chain and Wholesteen's largest customer—buys 20,000 cases of Wholesteen's condensed milk a year. That's 20 percent of Wholesteen's total sales volume of 100,000 cases per year.

FoodWorld is proposing that Wholesteen produce private-label condensed milk to be sold with the FoodWorld brand name. FoodWorld proposes to buy the same total quantity as it does now, but it wants half (10,000 cases) with the Wholesteen brand and half with the FoodWorld brand. FoodWorld wants its brand in cans that cost $.01 less than Wholesteen pays for a can now. But FoodWorld will provide preprinted labels with its brand name, which will save Wholesteen an additional $.02 a can.

Wholesteen spends $70,000 a year on promotion to increase familiarity with the Wholesteen brand. In addition, Wholesteen gives retailers an allowance of $.25 per case for their local advertising, which features the Wholesteen brand. FoodWorld has agreed to give up the advertising allowance for its own brand, but it is only willing to pay $7.40 a case for the milk that will be sold with the FoodWorld brand name. It will continue under the old terms for the rest of its purchases.

Sue Glick, Wholesteen's marketing manager, is considering the FoodWorld proposal. She has entered cost and revenue data on a spreadsheet, so that she can see more clearly how the proposal might affect revenue and profits.

a. Based on the data in the initial spreadsheet, how will Wholesteen profits be affected if Glick accepts the FoodWorld proposal?

b. Glick is worried that FoodWorld will find another producer for the FoodWorld private-label milk if Wholesteen rejects the proposal. This would immediately reduce Wholesteen's annual sales by 10,000 cases. FoodWorld might even stop buying from Wholesteen altogether. What would happen to profits in these two situations?

c. FoodWorld is rapidly opening new stores, and sells milk in every store. The FoodWorld buyer says that next year's purchases could be up to 25,000 cases of Wholesteen's condensed milk. But Sue Glick knows that FoodWorld may stop buying the Wholesteen brand and want all 25,000 cases to carry the FoodWorld private-label brand. How will this affect profit? (Hint: Enter the new quantities in the "proposal" column of the spreadsheet.)

d. What should Wholesteen do? Why?

For additional questions related to this problem, see Exercise 9–5 in the *Learning Aid for Use with Basic Marketing,* Ninth Canadian Edition.

When you finish this chapter, you should:

- Understand how product life cycles affect strategic planning.
- Know what is involved in designing new products and what "new products" really are.
- Understand the new-product development process.
- See why product liability must be considered in screening new products.
- Understand the need for product, brand, or category managers.
- Understand the important new terms (shown in orange).

Chapter ten

Product Management and New Product Development

Nestlé Canada has announced a shopping cart full of brand extensions and repositionings.

Soon consumers will see new chocolate bars with familiar names, new desserts, new frozen entrees and a new name on all O-Pee-Chee candies. And British Columbians are already drinking cans of iced coffee.

Bob Leonidas, senior vice-president of consumer communications, says the new products are in response to consumer demand. And many of those are in chocolate and confections, Leonidas explains, because those are impulse buying areas with no ceiling on the market.

Kit Kat Sticks, a 14-gram version of the chocolate wafer bar, are already available at check-out counters for 39 cents. These will compete in the light chocolate snack market with Cadbury's new Time Out bar.

Triple Chocolate Coffee Crisp, with more chocolate and less coffee flavour, will hit store shelves later this fall and will be supported by a TV campaign. According to Nestlé, Coffee Crisp is the number-one-selling chocolate bar in Canada, with a market share of 5.8%, followed by Kit Kat with 5.5%.

A trend towards white chocolate has led to White Crunch, as well as two products targeted at children, Milkybar Biscuit and Milkybar Dots.

Nestlé has also launched four Nestlé Classique bars to compete in the higher-end, imported chocolate market against such products as Kraft Canada's Toblerone. New products launching in time for Christmas will be After Eight Collection boxed chocolates and a Yule-log-style product called the After Eight Ice Cream Dessert, which will be supported by magazine ads.

O-Pee-Chee candies, which Nestlé acquired in November 1996, are being rebranded as Willy Wonka, the brand name the candies carry in the U.S. The rebranding will be completed by the end of the year and advertising for Willy Wonka will begin next year. New products are also being added to the lineup, including Gummy Sweetarts and Fizzy Jerkz. Blair Nuess, Willy Wonka brands marketing manager, says the newest trends in kids' candy are different textures and sour tastes.

Getting to the main course, Nestlé has added more SKUs to its recently rebranded Stouffer's Home Style frozen entree line. Prior to May, the line was simply known as Stouffer's. There are also four new products in the Stouffer's Pastaria line, first introduced in March.

To wash this all down, Nestlé is test marketing a new cold, canned coffee beverage, Nescafé Ice in British Columbia.

Not to ignore four-legged consumers, last month Nestlé repositioned its Dr. Ballard dog food as a super-premium brand available only in pet stores and through veterinarians, says Diane Robertson, pet food project manager. The Alpo brand remains in grocery stores.

Source: Lesley Daw, "Nestlé Marketing Assault Aims Wide," Marketing Magazine, October 6, 1997, p. 3.

Managing products over their life cycles

The new product introductions, brand extensions, repositionings, and rebrandings described in the opening Nestlé Canada story are repeated over and over again in product-markets worldwide. In the same way, cellular phones are replacing short-wave radios and CBs and making it possible for people to communicate from places where it was previously impossible. Cassette tapes replaced vinyl records, and now CDs and digital audiotape are being challenged by new formats. Switchboard operators in many firms have been replaced by answering machines, and answering machines are being replaced by voice mail.

Obviously, products, markets, and competition change over time. This makes marketing management an exciting challenge. As Internet Insite 10–1 shows, developing new products and managing existing products to meet changing conditions is essential to the success of every firm. In this chapter we will look at some important ideas in these areas.

Products, like consumers, go through life cycles. So product planning and marketing mix planning are important. Competitors are always developing and copying new ideas and products, making existing products out-of-date more quickly than ever.

Product life cycle has four major stages

The **product life cycle** describes the stages a new product idea goes through from beginning to end. The product life cycle is divided into four main stages: (1) market introduction, (2) market growth, (3) market maturity, and (4) sales decline.

A particular firm's marketing mix usually must change during the product life cycle. There are several reasons why. Customers' attitudes and needs may change over the product life cycle. The product may be aimed at entirely different target markets at different stages. And the nature of competition is that it moves toward pure competition or oligopoly.

Further, total sales of the product, by all competitors in the industry, vary in each of its four stages. They move from very low in the market introduction stage, to high at market maturity, and then back to low in the sales decline stage. More important, the profit picture changes, too. These general relationships can be seen in Exhibit 10–1. Note that sales and profits do not move together over time. *Industry profits decline while industry sales are still rising.*[1]

Market introduction—investing in the future

In the **market introduction** stage, sales are low as a new idea is first introduced to a market. Customers aren't looking for the product. They don't even know about it. Informative promotion is necessary to tell potential customers about the benefits and uses of the new product concept.

Exhibit 10–1 Life Cycle of a Typical Product

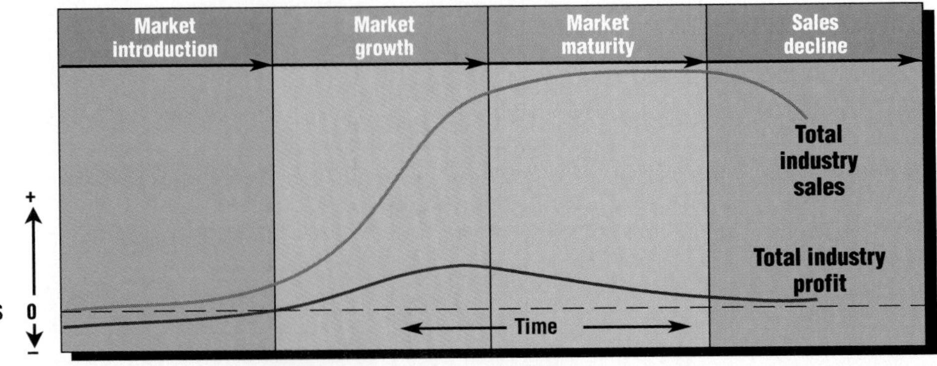

New Products on the Web

In an era of increasing competition and growing consumer expectations, only products and services that offer superior value to consumers can succeed. On the Internet, innovative marketers are offering precisely such products. Here are some examples.

Financial Services

Online trading in stocks allows serious investors to make "real-time" decisions. Besides allowing customers to buy and sell stocks from around the world through the Internet, right from the comfort of their home, online financial service companies offer consumers a great deal of useful information. Charles Schwab (www.eschwab.com) offers extensive information on mutual funds as well as complete brokerage services online. Quote.Com (www.quote.com) allows you not only to trade online and to have access to detailed industry reports, but also to dynamically monitor your stock portfolio online! Timely and accurate information is important to investors, and so is security of transactions. These online financial services satisfy both needs.

Travel and Leisure

Most consumers do some research and planning before they embark on a vacation. Travel agents have usually been the main source of information about travel destinations. With the advent of Internet Marketing, that has changed forever. Now you can plan your vacation online. At Epicurious (www.epicurious.com), you can select a vacation to suit your every need. Their search engine will point out the ideal holiday destination for you based on your choice of climate, region, activities, and cost! In addition, the Web site is filled with useful information for travellers. After you plan your vacation, if you want to look for cheap airline tickets and last-minute deals, check out Priceline (www.priceline.com) and Travelocity (www.travelocity.com). Planning travel and making airline and hotel bookings has long been a demanding task. The new online services make travel planning a pleasure.

Entertainment and Games

The interactive qualities of the Internet are fully exploited by sites that offer Web-based games. Sony has leveraged its prestigious brand name and created an interesting online game site called The Station™ (www.station.sony.com). Interactive games abound on the Internet. If you are in the mood for some fun and games on the Web, try the Yahoo! directory (www.yahoo.com/Recreation/Games/Internet_Games/Interactive_Web_Games).

If interactive online games aren't your cup of tea, and you prefer movies instead, try Film.Com (www.film.com). In their Screening Room, you can play short films on your computer through RealPlayer™. If you are a real film buff, you may want to visit the Internet Movie Database (us.imdb.com), where you will find everything you wanted to know about films. The Internet's potential for entertainment is enormous. Cable modems and other advances in technology will soon bring that potential to fruition.

Books and E-Zines

Wired is the forerunner to many of today's e-zines and continues to be a source of rich information for anyone interested in the Internet. The *Webmonkey*, a spin-off, caters to the technically inclined (www.wired.com). Another e-zine that originated on the Web is *Slate* (www.slate.com), sponsored by Microsoft. It's a complete magazine in digital form. Traditional magazines such as *Time* have also discovered the Internet and have adapted quite successfully (www.pathfinder.com). Check out *TV Guide* (yes, *TV Guide*) online and see how they are using the capabilities of the Internet to offer consumers much more than what they offer in the print version (www.tvguide.com). The e-zines offer information in a format that is more entertaining than print.

In addition to getting your daily dose of news and entertainment on the Internet, you can also now order the latest book by your favourite author with just a few keystrokes. Try Amazon.Com (www.amazon.com) or BarnesandNoble.Com (www.barnesandnoble.com). If you are interested in just computer books, then the Halifax-based Roswell's Cyberspace Computer Bookstore (www.roswell.com) may be the place for you. They carry over 10,000 computer book titles and can deliver almost anywhere in the world! Convenience, wide selection, and low prices are the key consumer benefits offered by these online bookstores.

Food and Beverages

It was only natural that the fast communication capability of the Internet would find a use in the home delivery of food. Among the first to offer a food delivery service on the Internet was Waiters on Wheels, a California-based company (www.waitersonwheels.com). You can order from an extensive menu listing offerings from several local restaurants, and Waiters on Wheels will deliver the food. If you would like some California wine to go with your food, you can order that too via the Internet from Virtual Vineyards (www.virtualvineyard.com). Along with description and price, you also get expert advice and a detailed taste chart to guide your wine selection.

In each example discussed here, it is clear that these services not only are unique, but also offer real value to consumers. That is the key to successful new product development. Consumers are rapidly adopting such services. A recent study by Price Waterhouse (www.pw.com) showed that the Internet is displacing other activities. According to the Price Waterhouse Consumer Technology Survey, one-third of respondents used the Internet instead of watching TV, and nearly one-third used the Internet instead of reading a "book, newspaper or magazine." From these data it is clear that for many consumers the Internet is already the first choice as an entertainment and information source. As more consumers gain access to the Internet and as technology becomes more user-friendly, this trend is likely to continue.

Source: This is one of a series of Internet Insites prepared in April 1998 by Dr. Ramesh Venkat of Saint Mary's University for *Basic Marketing*, Ninth Canadian Edition.

Even though a firm promotes its new product, it takes time for customers to learn that the product is available. Most companies experience losses during the introduction stage because they spend so much money for Promotion, Product, and Place development. Of course, they invest the money in the hope of future profits.

Market growth

In the **market growth** stage, industry sales grow fast, and industry profits rise—but then start falling. The innovator begins to make big profits as more and more customers buy. But competitors see the opportunity and enter the market. Some just copy the most successful product or try to improve it to compete better. Others try to refine their offerings to do a better job of appealing to some target markets. The new entries result in much greater product variety.

This is the time of biggest profits *for the industry. But it is also when industry profits begin to decline* as competition increases. See Exhibit 10–1.

Some firms make big strategic planning mistakes at this stage by not understanding the product life cycle. They see the big sales and profit opportunities of the early market growth stage but ignore the competition that will soon follow. By the time they realize their mistake, it may be too late. Marketing managers who pay attention to competitor analysis are less likely to encounter this problem.

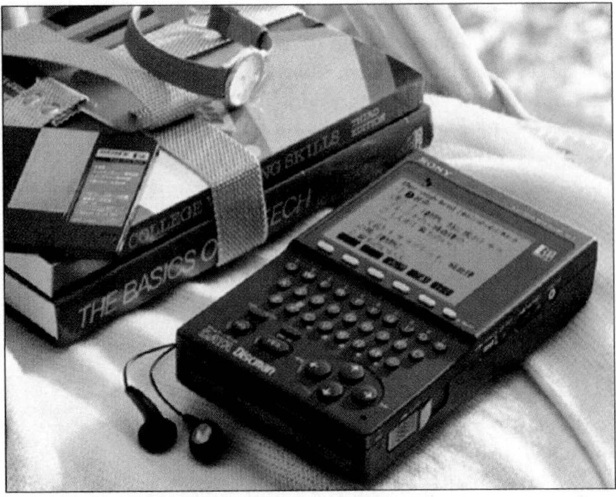

A product like Sony's Data Discman needed informative promotion during the market introduction stage of the product life cycle, so that customers would know about its benefits and uses.

Market maturity

During the **market maturity** stage, industry sales level off and competition gets tougher. Many aggressive competitors have entered the race for profits (except in oligopoly situations). Industry profits go down throughout the market maturity stage because promotion costs rise, and because some competitors cut prices to attract business. Less efficient firms can't compete with this pressure, and drop out of the market.

New firms may still enter the market at this stage, increasing competition even more. Note that late entries skip the early life-cycle stages, including the profitable market growth stage. And they must try to take a share of the saturated market from established firms, which is difficult and expensive. Satisfied customers who are happy with their current relationship typically won't be interested in switching to a new brand.

Persuasive promotion becomes more important during the market maturity stage. Products may differ only slightly if at all. Most competitors have discovered the most effective appeals, or quickly copied the leaders. The various products become almost the same in the minds of potential consumers.

In Canada, the markets for most cars, boats, television sets, and many household appliances are in market maturity.[2] This stage may continue for many years, until a basically new product idea comes along—even though individual brands or models come and go.

Sales decline

During the **sales decline** stage, new products replace the old. Price competition from dying products becomes more vigorous, but firms with strong brands may make profits until the end because they successfully differentiated their products.

They may keep some sales by appealing to the most loyal customers or to those who are slow to try new ideas. These buyers may switch later, smoothing the sales decline.

Product life cycles relate to specific markets

Remember that a product life cycle describes industry sales and profits for a *product idea* within a particular product-market. The sales and profits of an individual product, model, or brand may not, and often do not, follow the life cycle pattern. They may vary up and down throughout the life cycle, sometimes moving in the opposite direction of industry sales and profits. Further, a product idea may be in a different life cycle stage in different markets.

Individual brands may not follow the pattern

A given firm may introduce or withdraw a specific product during any stage of the product life cycle. A "me too" brand introduced during the market growth stage, for example, may not be well received at all and suffer a quick death. Or it may reach its peak and start to decline even before the market maturity stage begins. Market leaders may enjoy high profits during the market maturity stage, even though industry profits are declining. Sometimes the innovator brand loses so much in the introduction stage that it has to drop out just as others are reaping big profits in the growth stage.

Strategy planners who naïvely expect sales of one firm's individual brand to follow the general product life-cycle pattern are likely to be rudely surprised. In fact, it may be more sensible to think in terms of "product-market life cycles" rather than product life cycles. Even so, we will use the term *product life cycle* because it is commonly accepted and widely used.

Each market should be carefully defined

How we see product life cycles depends on how broadly we define a product-market. For example, as of 1997 about 86 percent of all Canadian households owned a microwave oven.[3] Although microwave ovens appear to be at the market maturity stage here, in many other countries they're still early in the growth stage. Even in European countries like Switzerland and Italy, fewer than 15 percent of all households own a microwave oven. As this example suggests, a firm with a mature product can sometimes find new growth in international markets.

How broadly we define the needs of customers in a product market also affects how we view product life cycles, and who the competitors are. Consider the needs related to storing and preparing foods. Wax paper sales in North America started to decline when Dow introduced Saran Wrap. Then, in the early 1970s, sales of Saran Wrap (and other similar products) fell sharply when small plastic storage bags became popular. However, sales picked up again by the end of the decade. The product didn't change, but customers' needs did. Saran Wrap filled a new need because it worked well in microwave cooking.

If a market is defined broadly, there may be many competitors, and the market may appear to be in market maturity. On the other hand, if we focus on a narrow submarket, and a particular way of satisfying specific needs, then we may see much shorter product life cycles as improved product ideas come along to replace the old.

Product life cycles vary in length

How long an entire product life cycle takes varies widely across products. So does the length of each stage. The cycle may vary from 90 days in the case of toys like the Ghostbusters line, to possibly 100 years for gas-powered cars.

Some products move fast

A new product idea will move through the early stages of the life cycle more quickly when it has certain characteristics. The fast adoption of NutraSweet low-calorie sweetener in the North American market is a good example. NutraSweet offered a real comparative advantage—fewer calories compared to sugar, without the bitter aftertaste of other sweeteners. Free samples of NutraSweet chewing gum made it easy for consumers to try the product without any risk. And it was easy to communicate its benefits. NutraSweet worked well in many products, such as diet soft drinks, that were already a part of consumers' lifestyles. However, in less-developed countries where malnutrition, not dieting, is the problem, NutraSweet does not have the same comparative advantage.[4]

Product life cycles are getting shorter

The life of different products varies, but in general, product life cycles are getting shorter. This is partly due to rapidly changing technology. One new invention may make possible many new products that replace old ones. Electronic microchips led to hundreds of new products, from Texas Instruments' calculators and Pulsar digital watches in the early days to microchip-controlled heart valves now.

Patents for a new product may not provide much protection from competitors, who can often find ways to copy the product idea without violating a specific patent. Worse, some firms find out that an unethical competitor simply disregarded the patent protection. Patent violations by foreign competitors are very common. A product's life may be over before a case can get through court bottlenecks. The patent system internationally needs significant improvement if it is to really protect firms that develop innovative ideas.[5]

Although life cycles keep moving in the advanced economies, many advances bypass most consumers in less-developed economies. These consumers struggle at the subsistence level, without an effective macro-marketing system to stimulate innovation. Some of the innovations and economies of scale in the advanced societies do trickle down to benefit such consumers. Inexpensive antibiotics and drought-resistant plants, for example, are making a life-or-death difference.

The early bird usually makes the profits

The increasing speed of product life cycles means that firms must be developing new products all the time. Furthermore, they must try to offer marketing mixes that will make the most of the market growth stage, when profits are highest.

The pioneer in a product-market may have a big advantage. However, during the growth stage, competitors are likely to introduce product improvements. Fast changes in marketing strategy may be required here because profits don't necessarily go to the innovator. Sometimes fast copiers of the basic idea will share in the market growth stage. Sony was a pioneer in developing videocassette recorders, and one of the first on the market. Other firms quickly followed, and the competition drove down prices

Exhibit 10-2 Patterns of Fashion, Fad, and Style Cycles for Fashion Products

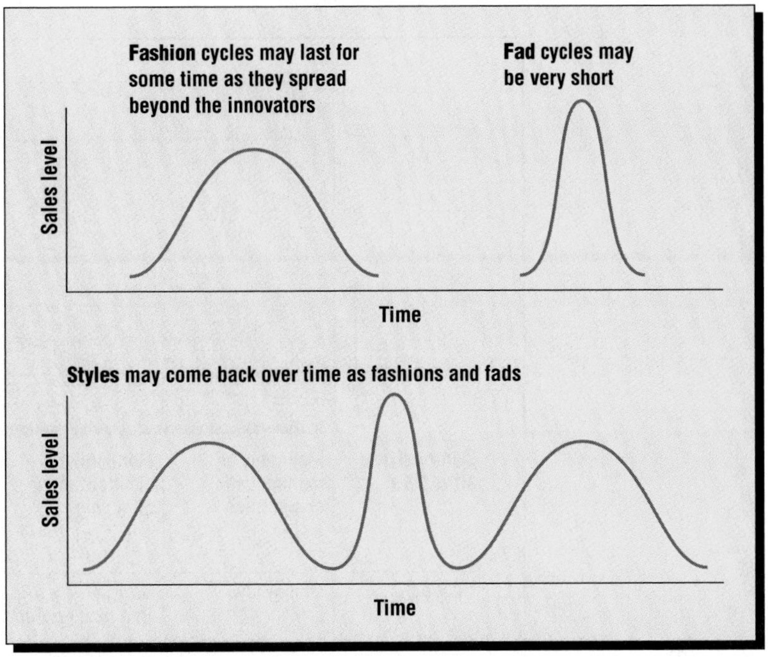

and increased demand. But Sony stuck to its Beta format VCRs while most consumers were buying VHS-format machines. By the time Sony finally offered a VHS-format machine, VCR sales had ebbed, and competitors controlled the market.[6]

The short happy life of fashions and fads

The sales of some products are influenced by **fashion**—the currently accepted or popular style. Fashion-related products tend to have short life cycles. What is currently popular can shift rapidly. Marketing managers who work with fashions often have to make really fast product changes.

How fast is fast enough? The Limited, a retail chain that specializes in women's fashions, tracks consumer preferences every day through point-of-sale computers. Based on what's selling, new product designs are sent by satellite to suppliers around North America and in Hong Kong, South Korea, and Singapore. Within days, clothing from those distant points begins to collect in Hong Kong. About four times a week, a chartered jet brings it to the Limited's distribution centre in Ohio, where items are priced and then shipped to stores within 48 hours. In spite of the speed of this system, a top manager at the Limited has commented that it's "not fast enough" for the 1990s.[7]

A **fad** is an idea that is fashionable only to certain groups who are enthusiastic about it. But these groups are so fickle that a fad is even more short-lived than a regular fashion. Many toys, like the Velcro-covered Super Grip Ball and Hasbro's Transformers, do well during a short-lived cycle. Some teenagers' music tastes are fads. Exhibit 10–2 summarizes the shape of typical life cycles for fashions, fads, and styles. Note that the pattern for a style may go up and down as it comes back into fashion over time.[8]

Planning for different stages of the product life cycle

Where a product is in its life cycle, and how fast it's moving to the next stage, should affect strategic market planning. Marketing managers must make realistic plans for the later stages. Exhibit 10–3 shows the relationship of the product life cycle to the marketing mix variables. The technical terms in this figure are discussed later in the book.

Exhibit 10–3 Typical Changes in Marketing Variables over the Product Life Cycle

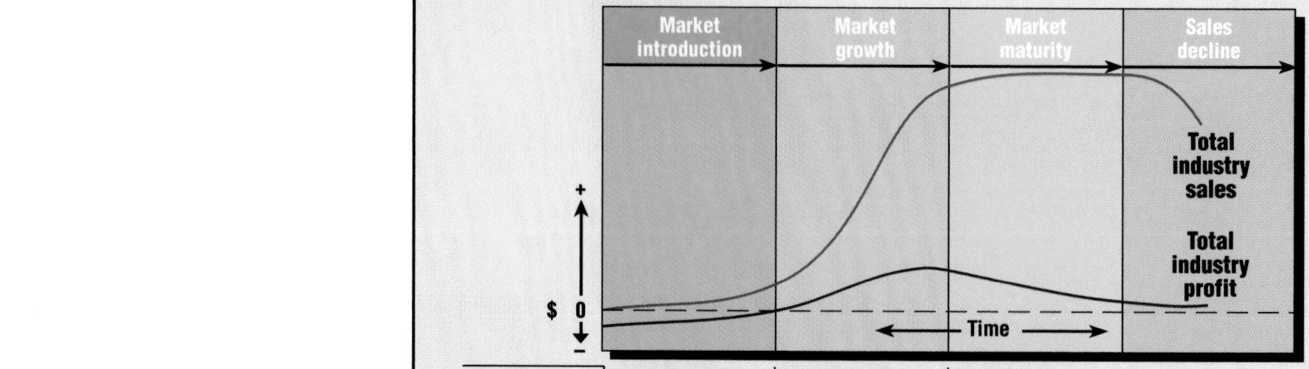

	Market introduction	Market growth	Market maturity	Sales decline
				Total industry sales
$ + 0 −		← Time →		Total industry profit
Competitive situation	Monopoly or monopolistic competition	Monopolistic competition or oligopoly	Monopolistic competition or oligopoly heading toward pure competition →	→
Product	One or few	Variety—try to find best product Build brand familiarity	All "same" Battle of brands	Some drop out
Place	Build channels Maybe selective distribution →	Move toward more intensive distribution →	→	→
Promotion	Build primary demand Pioneering/informing	Build selective demand → Informing/persuading →	Persuading/reminding (frantically competitive)	→
Price	Skimming or penetration	Meet competition (especially in oligopoly) → or Price dealing and price cutting →	→	→

Introducing new products

Exhibit 10–3 shows that a marketing manager has to do a lot of work to introduce a really new product. Money must be spent developing the new product. Even if the product is unique, this doesn't mean that everyone will immediately come running to the producer's door. The firm will have to build channels of distribution, perhaps offering special incentives to win cooperation. Promotion is needed to build demand *for the whole idea,* not just to sell a specific brand. Because all this is expensive, it may lead the marketing manager to try to "skim" the market, charging a relatively high price to help pay for the introductory costs.

The correct strategy, however, depends on how quickly the new idea will be accepted by customers—and how quickly competitors will follow with their own products. When the early stages of the cycle will be fast, a low initial (penetration) price may help develop loyal customers early and keep competitors out.

Also relevant is how quickly the firm can change its strategy as the life cycle moves on. Some firms are very flexible. They can compete effectively with larger, less adaptable competitors by adjusting their strategies more frequently.

Exhibit 10-4 Examples of Three Strategic Marketing Choices for a Firm in a Mature Product-Market

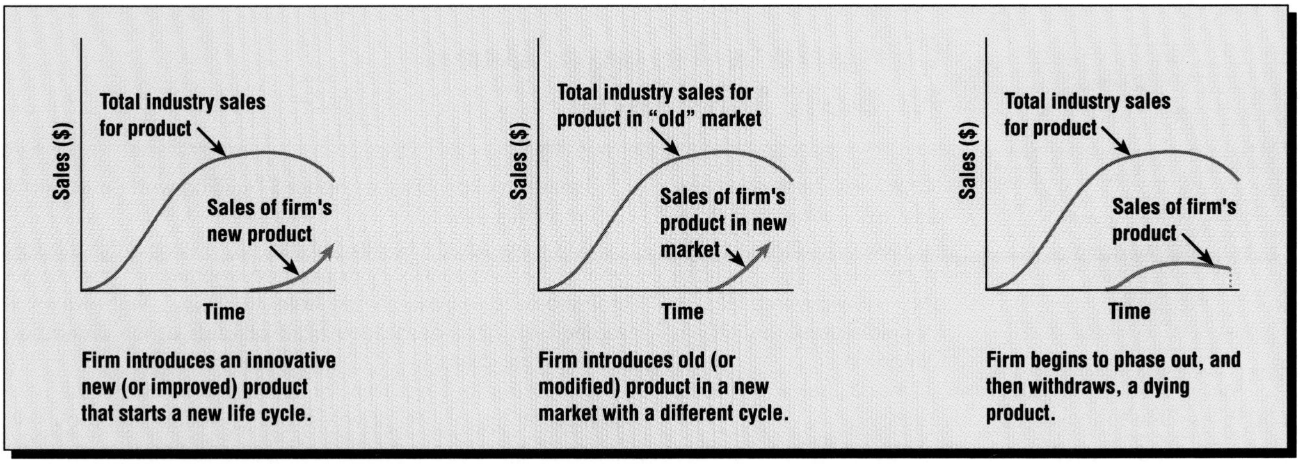

Sales ($)
Total industry sales for product
Sales of firm's new product
Time

Firm introduces an innovative new (or improved) product that starts a new life cycle.

Sales ($)
Total industry sales for product in "old" market
Sales of firm's product in new market
Time

Firm introduces old (or modified) product in a new market with a different cycle.

Sales ($)
Total industry sales for product
Sales of firm's product
Time

Firm begins to phase out, and then withdraws, a dying product.

Managing maturing products

It's very important for a firm to have some competitive advantage as it moves into market maturity. Even a small advantage can make a big difference, and some firms do very well by carefully managing their maturing products. They are able to capitalize on a slightly better product, or perhaps lower production and/or marketing costs. Or perhaps they are simply more successful at promotion and so better at differentiating their product from those of competitors. See, for example, the accompanying ad for Kellogg's™ Special K™ cereal. Another example: Graham crackers, with flat sales, were competing in a mature market. Nabisco used the same ingredients to create bite-sized Teddy Grahams and then promoted them heavily. These changes captured new sales and profits.[9]

In market maturity, industry profits decline. Top managers must see this, or they will continue to expect the attractive profits of the market growth stage—profits that are no longer possible. They may set impossible goals for the marketing department, causing marketing managers to think about deceptive advertising or some other desperate attempt to reach impossible objectives.

Product life cycles keep moving. But that doesn't mean a firm should just sit by as its sales decline. There are other choices. A firm can improve its product or develop an innovative new product for the same market. Or it can develop a strategy for its product (perhaps with modifications) targeted at a new market. For example, it might find a market in a country where the life cycle is not so far along, or it might try to serve a new need. Or the firm can withdraw the product before it completes the cycle, and refocus on better opportunities. See Exhibit 10–4, and Marketing Demo 10–1, which describes how a Canadian company adapted its chewable vitamins for sales in Japan.

Develop new strategies for different markets

In a mature market, a firm may be fighting to keep or increase its market share. But if the firm finds a new use for the product, it may need to try to stimulate overall demand. Du Pont's Teflon is a good example. It was developed more than 50 years ago and has enjoyed sales growth as a nonstick coating for cookware, as an insulation for aircraft wiring, and as a lining for chemically resistant equipment. But marketing managers for Teflon are not waiting to be stuck with declining profits in those mature markets. They constantly develop strategies for new markets where Teflon will meet needs. For example, Teflon is now selling well as a special coating for the wires used in high-speed communications between computers.[10]

Marketing Demo 10-1

Canada's Image Used to Sell Vitamins

TOKYO—A poster on display at hundreds of drugstores across Japan depicts a sparkling glacial lake and snow-covered Rocky Mountain peaks beneath a Canadian flag.

"This product is imported from Canada, home of forests and lakes," the Japanese ad copy reads.

It's an image that can sell just about anything Canadian here—from building products to bottled water and travel packages.

In this case, however, the advertisement is a pitch for chewable vitamin tablets made by C. E. Jamieson & Co. Ltd. in the somewhat less picturesque city of Windsor, Ont., clear across the country from the Rockies.

No matter. The pitch works and it has helped Jamieson, Canada's leading vitamin producer, crack the tough Japanese retail market after four years of false starts and an investment of at least $250,000.

"It's come out loud and clear to us that the image of Canada to the Japanese is one of clean, pure and trusting," Jamieson president Vic Neufeld said. "It was obvious for us to play on that image."

But as many Canadian companies exporting to Japan know, it's not positioning a product that is most difficult, but finding a suitable local partner to make it sell.

For Jamieson, the partner was the Tokyo-based Oriex drugstore chain, with 2,300 co-operative outlets located from Okinawa in the south to Hokkaido in the north. Oriex, which operates a massive automated distribution centre near Tokyo, is one of the largest drugstore operators and leading food importers in Japan.

Jamieson, a private company controlled by chairman Eric Margolis of Toronto, signed a modest contract last year to produce a line of private-label, chewable vitamins for Oriex.

The company's initial foray may be relatively small compared with the overall size of the Japanese market, or even Jamieson's worldwide sales, estimated to be worth more than $60-million a year. The Japanese over-the-counter market for vitamins is worth $3-billion a year, typically consumed in liquid or tablet form.

But Mr. Neufeld said the company expects to parlay an initial shipment of 100,000 vitamin bottles (each of which sells for the equivalent of nearly $7 in Japan and has a Canadian flag on the label) into a $5-million business within three years by expanding the range of products it sells. That would make Japan Jamieson's second-largest export market after the United States.

"The numbers could be astronomical," said Mr. Neufeld, who will visit Oriex again later this month to sign what he hopes will be an even larger order.

Jamieson expects to sell about $1-million worth of vitamins in Japan this year.

It has not been easy to get this far. It took Jamieson two years to find a suitable partner and another full year of negotiations to make its first sale to Oriex, with which it teamed up after assistance from officials at the Canadian Embassy in Tokyo.

For Oriex, buying from Jamieson is part of a strategy to source many of its private-label products from outside Japan. Kouji Murakoshi, Oriex's general manager, said the company plans to make Canada its most important foreign counterpart.

"Consumers are more confident because it's a Canadian product," he said. "The image of Canada to the Japanese people is much greater than America."

. . . But Jamieson could not simply slap new labels on the products it already sells in Canada or other parts of the world. The two companies spent 10 months working out a formulation that was acceptable to the Japanese government, which maintains strict health regulations that are the bane of food and drug exporters around the world.

Jamieson removed all dyes from its vitamins, replaced artificial flavours with acceptable natural flavours and found a substitute for vegetable magnesium sterate as a lubricant.

It also had to meet strict size regulations, which require that any vitamins sold as food products must be exactly 15 millimetres wide.

But an opportunity to grab even a small piece of Japan's ballooning health care market can be worth the hassle. Sales of all sorts of medical-related products, including drugs and equipment, are growing at double-digit rates every year, in part because of the rapidly aging Japanese population.

. . . None of this is a guarantee that the road ahead will be easy for Jamieson. Mr. Neufeld said that since Jamieson entered the market late last year, some of the major drug makers that dominate Japan's over-the-counter vitamin market have begun to sell chewable vitamins as well.

So far, the rival products are tough to chew and cost as much as three times more. But Mr. Neufeld is aware that the Japanese could soon match his formula and start making similar products domestically. "They are very clever and one day the big pharmaceutical giants will copy us," he said.

But Mr. Neufeld said Jamieson spent a long time developing its relationship with Oriex and is confident that it can withstand any competitive pressures.

"Without a relationship you'll fail in Japan," he said. "They constantly test your commitment to the market and to them as a partner. But once it's determined that you are someone they can trust, you've conquered the biggest hurdle."

Source: Barrie McKenna, *The Globe and Mail*, May 6, 1997, B19.

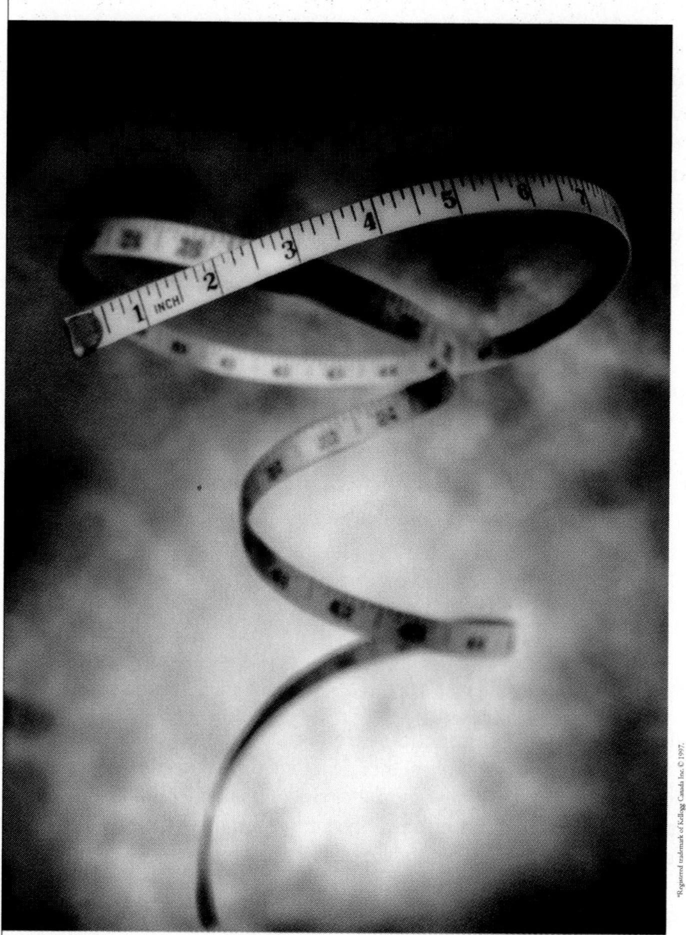

DON'T LET IT MEASURE YOUR SELF-ESTEEM.

It's unfortunate that something as insignificant as a tape measure can have such an impact on how we feel about ourselves. Don't let it. It can't measure who you are. Exercise. Refuse to skip meals. Start with a balanced breakfast every morning and go from there. Kellogg's Special K* cereal is fat free and a source of nine essential nutrients so it's a light, sensible way to start your day. After all, looking your best is about being strong and healthy. And the standards you measure yourself by should be your own.*

Look good on your own terms.

*Registered trademark of Kellogg Canada Inc. © 1997.

Phasing out dying products

Not all strategies have to be exciting growth strategies. If prospects are poor in some product-market, a phase-out strategy may be needed. The need for phasing out becomes more obvious as the sales decline stage arrives. But even in market maturity, it may be clear that a particular product is not going to be profitable enough to reach the company's objectives using the current strategy. Then the wisest move may be to develop a strategy that helps the firm phase out of the product-market—perhaps over several years.

Phasing out a product may involve some difficult implementation problems. But phase-out is also a *strategy*—and it must be market-oriented to cut losses. In fact, it is possible to milk a dying product for some time if competitors move out more quickly. This situation occurs when there is still ongoing (though declining) demand, and when some customers are willing to pay attractive prices to get their old favourite.

New product planning

Competition is strong and dynamic in most markets. So it is essential for a firm to keep developing new products—and improving its current products—to meet changing customer needs and competitors' actions. Not having an active new-product development process means that, consciously or subconsciously, the firm has decided to milk its current products and go out of business. New-product planning is not an optional matter. In today's dynamic markets, it has to be done just to survive.

What is a new product?

A **new product** is one that is new *in any way* for the company concerned. A product can become "new" in many ways. A fresh idea can be turned into a new product and start a new product life cycle. For example, for some medications, Alza Corporation's time-release skin patches are replacing pills and injections.

Variations on an existing product idea can also make a product new. Oral B changed its conventional toothbrush to include a strip of colored bristles that fade as you brush; that way you know when it's time for a new brush. Even small changes in an existing product can make it new.[11]

Product is "new" only 12 months

A firm can call its product new for only a limited time. Twelve months is the limit according to Industry Canada. To be called new, a product must be entirely new or changed in a "functionally significant or substantial respect." While 12 months may seem a very short time for production-oriented managers, it may be reasonable, given the fast pace of change for many products.

Ethical Dimensions

New-Product Planning

New product decisions, and decisions to abandon old products, often involve ethical considerations. For example, some firms (including the firm that develops drugs used in treating AIDS) have been criticized for holding back important new product innovations until patents run out—or sales slow down—on their existing products. Others have been criticized for "planned obsolescence"—that is, for releasing new products that the company plans to soon replace with improved new versions. Similarly, wholesalers and retailers complain that producers too often keep their new-product introduction plans a secret and leave intermediaries with dated inventory that they can sell only at a loss.

Criticisms are also levelled at firms that constantly release minor variations of products that already saturate markets. Consider what's happening with disposable diapers. Marketing managers may feel that they're serving some customers' needs better when they offer diapers in boys' and girls' versions and in a variety of sizes, shapes, and colours. But many retailers feel that the new products are simply a ploy to get more shelf space. Further, some consumers complain that the bewildering array of choices makes it impossible to make an informed choice.

Different marketing managers have very different reactions to such criticisms. It is fair to say, however, that product management decisions often have a significant effect on customers and intermediaries. A too casual decision may lead to a negative backlash that affects the firm's strategy or reputation.[12]

An organized new-product development process is critical

For many firms, the key to success and survival is identifying and developing new product ideas, along with effective strategies to go with them. But this isn't easy. New-product development demands money, effort, time, and talent—and even then, the risks and costs of failure are high. Experts estimate that consumer packaged-goods companies spend at least $20 million to introduce a new brand. Gillette spent six years and more than US$750 million developing its MACH3 three-bladed razor. Another US$300 million is to be spent worldwide on marketing this product in the first year after its launch.[13]

Between 70 and 80 percent of all new brands flop. In the service sector, the front-end cost of a failed effort may not be as high, but it can have a devastating long-term effect if dissatisfied consumers turn elsewhere for help.[14]

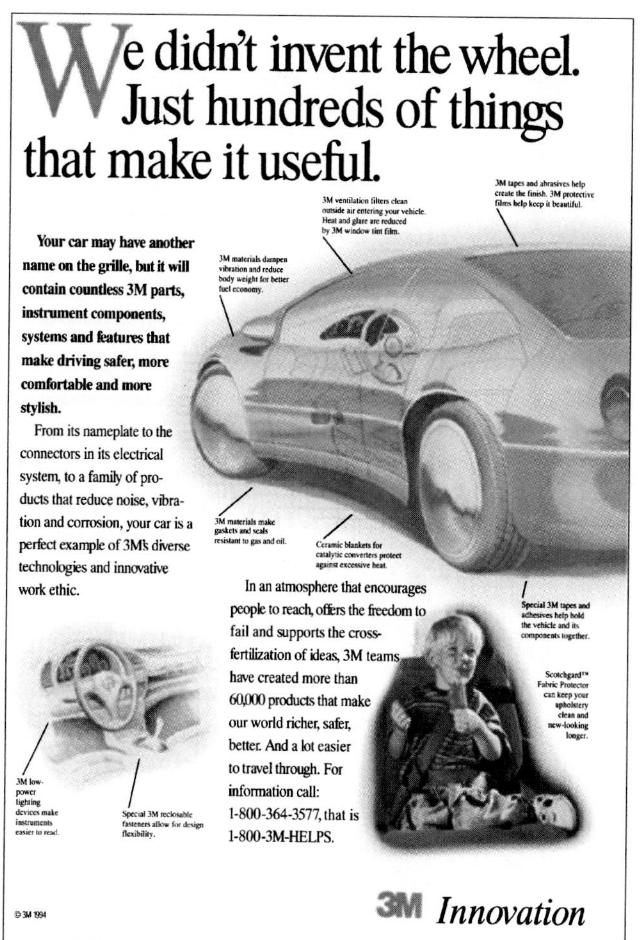

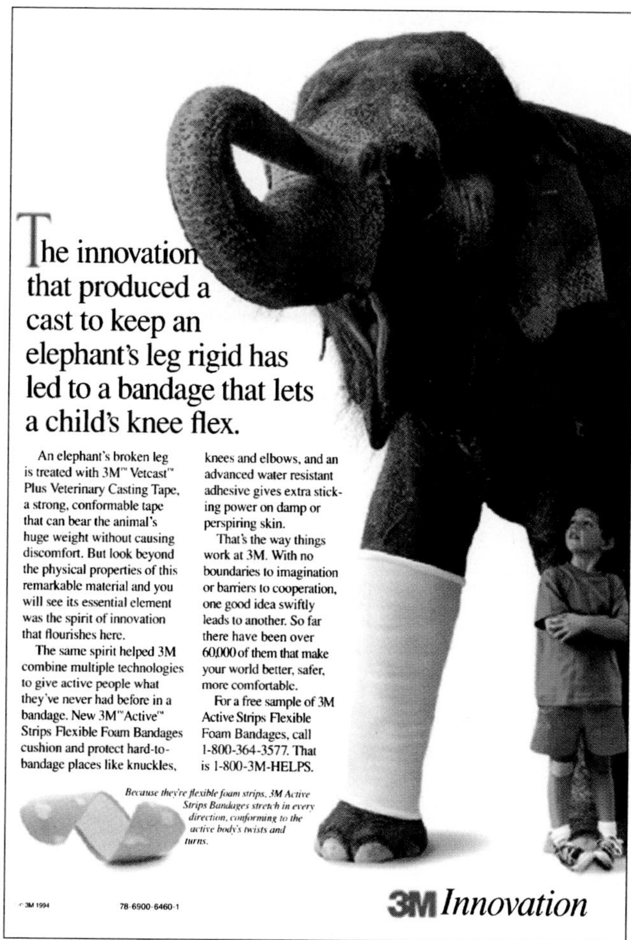

Generating innovative and profitable new products requires creativity—and an organized new-product development process.

Why new products fail

A new product may fail for many reasons. Most often, companies fail to offer a unique benefit, or they underestimate the competition. Sometimes the idea is good but the company has design problems; or the product costs much more to produce than was expected. Some companies rush to get a product on the market without developing a complete marketing plan.[15]

But moving too slowly can be a problem too. With the fast pace of change for many products, speedy entry into the market can be a competitive advantage. A few years ago, marketers at Xerox were alarmed that Japanese competitors were taking market share with innovative new copiers. It turned out that the competitors were developing new models twice as fast as Xerox and at half the cost. For Xerox to compete, it had to slash its five-year product development cycle.[16]

Five steps to new-product success

To move quickly and also avoid expensive new-product failures, many companies follow an organized new-product development process. The following pages describe such a process, which moves logically through five steps: (1) idea generation, (2) screening, (3) idea evaluation, (4) development (of product and marketing mix), and (5) commercialization.[17] (See Exhibit 10–5.)

An important element in this new-product development process is ongoing evaluation of a new idea's likely profitability and return on investment. The hypothesis tested is that the new idea will *not* be profitable. This puts the burden on the new idea to prove itself or be rejected. Such a process may seem harsh, but most new ideas have some basic flaw. Marketers try to discover those flaws early, and either find

Exhibit 10-5 New-Product Development Process

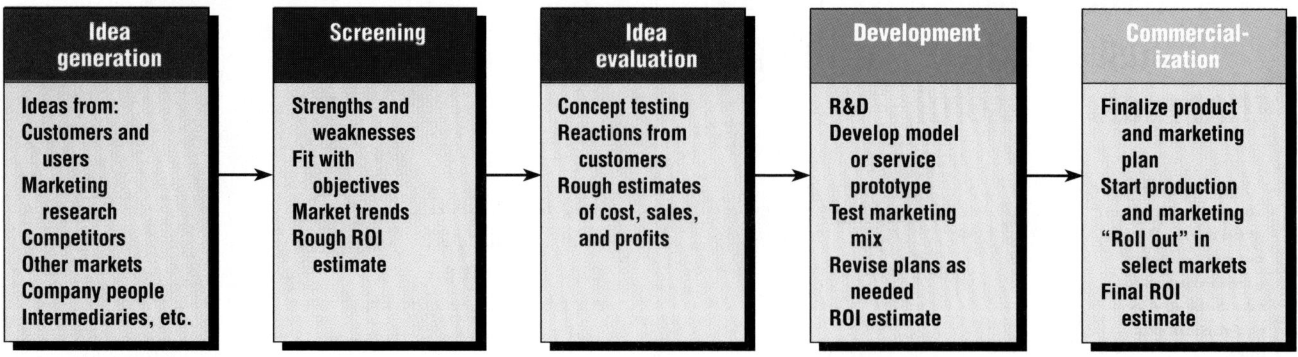

a remedy or reject the idea completely. Applying this process requires careful analysis of the idea *before* the company spends money to develop and market a product. This is a major departure from the usual production-oriented approach, in which a company develops a product first and then asks sales to "get rid of it."

Step 1: Idea generation

Finding new-product ideas can't be left to chance. Companies need a formal procedure for seeking new ideas. Although later steps eliminate many ideas, a company must have some that succeed.

New ideas can come from a company's own sales or production staff, intermediaries, competitors, consumer surveys, or other sources such as trade associations, advertising agencies, and government agencies. By analyzing new and different views of the company's markets and studying present consumer behaviour, a marketing manager can spot opportunities that have not yet occurred to competitors—or even to potential customers. For example, ideas for new service concepts may come directly from analysis of consumer complaints.

No one firm can always be first with the best new ideas. So in their search for ideas, companies should pay attention to what competitors are doing. New-product specialists at Ford Motor Company buy other firms' cars as soon as they're available. Then they take the cars apart to get ideas for improvements.[18]

Many firms now "shop" in international markets for new ideas. Jamaica Broilers, a poultry producer in the Caribbean, moved into fish farming. It learned that many of the techniques it was using to breed chickens were also successful on fish farms in Israel.[19]

Research shows that many new ideas in business markets come from customers who identify a need they have. Then they approach a supplier with the idea—and perhaps even with a particular design or specification. These customers become the lead users of the product, but the supplier can pursue the opportunity in other markets.[20]

Step 2: Screening

Screening involves evaluating the new ideas with the product-market screening criteria described in Chapter 2. Recall that these criteria include the combined output of a resource (strengths and weaknesses) analysis, a long-run trends analysis, and a thorough understanding of the company's objectives. Further, a "good" new idea should eventually lead to a product (and marketing mix) that will give the firm a competitive advantage—hopefully, a lasting one.

Opportunities with better growth potential are likely to be more attractive. We discussed this idea earlier when we introduced the GE planning grid (see Exhibit 2–13). Now, however, you know that the life cycle stage at which a firm's new product enters the market has a direct bearing on its prospects for growth. Clearly, screening should consider how the strategy for a new product will hold up over the whole product life cycle. In other words, screening should consider how attractive the new product will be in both the short term and the long term.

SOME COMPANIES SCREEN BASED ON CONSUMER WELFARE The firm's final choice in product design should fit with the company's overall objectives and make good use of the firm's resources. But it's also desirable to create a need-satisfying product that will appeal to consumers in the long run as well as the short run. Ideally, the product will increase consumer welfare, too, and not just satisfy a whim. Different kinds of new-product opportunities are shown in Exhibit 10–6. Obviously, a socially responsible firm will try to find desirable opportunities rather than deficient ones. This may not be as easy as it sounds, however. Some consumers want "pleasing products" instead of "desirable products." They emphasize immediate satisfaction and give little thought to their own long-term welfare. And some competitors are quite willing to offer what consumers want in the short run. Generating "socially responsible" new-product ideas is a challenge for new-product planners. Consumer groups are helping to force this awareness on more firms.

SAFETY MUST BE CONSIDERED Real acceptance of the marketing concept certainly leads to the design of safe products. But some risky products are purchased because they provide thrills and excitement—for example, bicycles, skis, hang gliders, and bungee jumps. Even so, safety features usually can be added—and they're desired by some potential customers.

The **Hazardous Products Act** gives Industry Canada the authority either to ban outright or to regulate the sale, distribution, labelling, and advertising of potentially dangerous products. This act reemphasizes the need for business people to become more safety-oriented.

Exhibit 10-6 Types of New-Product Opportunities

Long-run consumer welfare	Immediate satisfaction: High	Immediate satisfaction: Low
High	Desirable products	Salutary products
Low	Pleasing products	Deficient products

Adopting the marketing concept should lead to the development of safe products.

Product safety complicates strategic planning because not all customers—even those who want better safety features—are willing to pay more for safer products. Some features cost a lot to add and increase prices considerably. These safety concerns must be considered at the screening step, because a firm can later be held liable for unsafe products.

PRODUCTS CAN TURN TO LIABILITIES **Product liability** means the legal obligation of sellers to pay damages to individuals who are injured by defective or unsafe products. Product liability is a serious matter. Liability settlements may exceed not only a company's insurance coverage but its total assets! Some experts predict that this could happen to Dow-Corning because of its liability for faulty silicone breast implants.

The courts have been enforcing a very strict product liability standard. Producers may be held responsible for injuries related to their products, no matter how the items are used or how well they are designed. Riddell (whose football helmets protect the pros) was hit with a $12 million judgment in a case involving a high school football player who broke his neck. The jury concluded that Riddell should have put a sticker on the helmet to warn players of the danger of butting into opponents! Cases and settlements like this are common.

Product liability is a serious ethical and legal matter. Many countries are attempting to change their laws so that they will be fair to both firms and consumers. But until product liability questions are resolved, marketing managers must be even more sensitive when screening new-product ideas.[21]

ROI IS A CRUCIAL SCREENING CRITERION Getting by the initial screening criteria doesn't guarantee success for the new idea. But it does show that at least the new idea is in the right ballpark *for this firm.* If many ideas pass the screening criteria, a firm must set priorities to determine which ones go on to the next step in the process. This can be done by comparing the ROI (return on investment) for each idea (assuming the firm is ROI-oriented). The most attractive alternatives will then be pursued first.

Step 3: Idea evaluation

When an idea moves past the screening step, it is evaluated more carefully. Companies can often estimate likely costs, revenue, and profitability at this stage. And market research can help identify the size of potential markets.

Note that an actual product has not yet been developed—and this can handicap the firm in getting feedback from customers. For help in idea evaluation, firms use **concept testing**—getting reactions from customers about how well a new product idea fits their needs. Concept testing uses market research, ranging from informal focus groups to formal surveys of potential customers.

Product planners must think about wholesaler and retailer customers as well as final consumers. Intermediaries may have special concerns about handling a proposed product. An ice cream maker was considering a new line of ice cream novelty products, and had visions of a hot market in California. But he had to drop his idea when he learned that grocery store chains wanted payments of $20,000 each just to stock his frozen novelties in their freezers.[22]

Whatever research methods are used, the idea evaluation step should gather enough information to help managers decide whether there is an opportunity, whether it fits with the firm's resources, *and* whether there is a basis for developing a competitive advantage. With such information, the firm can estimate likely profit from the various market segments and decide whether to continue the new-product development process.[23]

Step 4: Development

Product ideas that survive the screening and idea evaluation steps must now be analyzed further. Usually, this involves some research and development (R&D) and engineering to design and develop the physical part of the product. In the case of a new service offering, the firm will work out the details of what training, equipment, staff, and so on will be needed to deliver on the idea. Input from the earlier efforts helps guide this technical work.

New computer-aided design (CAD) systems are sparking a revolution in design work. Designers can develop lifelike 3-D colour drawings of packages and products. Then the computer allows the manager to look at the product from different perspectives, just as if it were real. Changes can be made almost instantly. And once the designs are finalized, they can be fed directly into computer-controlled manufacturing systems. Motorola and Timex have found that these systems cut their design development time in half, and give them a leg up on competitors.

Even so, it is still a good idea to test models and early versions of the product in the market. This process may have several cycles. A manufacturer may build a model of a physical product or produce limited quantities; a service firm may try to train a small group of service providers. Product tests with customers may lead to revisions, *before* the firm commits to full-scale efforts.

With actual goods or services, potential customers can react to how well the product meets their needs. Focus groups, panels, and larger surveys can get reactions to specific features and to the whole product idea. Sometimes that reaction kills the idea. For example, Coca-Cola Foods believed it had a great idea with Minute Maid Squeeze-Fresh—frozen orange juice concentrate in a squeeze bottle. In tests, however, Squeeze-Fresh bombed. Consumers loved the idea but hated the product. It was messy to use, and no one knew how much concentrate to squeeze in the glass.[24]

In other situations, testing can lead to the revision of product specifications for different markets. Sometimes a complex series of revisions may be required. Months or even years of research may be necessary to ascertain precisely what different market segments will find acceptable.

Firms often use full-scale market testing to get reactions in real market conditions, or to test variations in the marketing mix. For example, a firm may test alternative brands, prices, or advertising copy in different test cities. Note that the firm is testing the whole marketing mix, not just the product.

Market tests can be very expensive. But *not* testing is also dangerous. Frito-Lay was so sure it understood consumers' snack preferences that it introduced a three-item cracker line without market testing. Even with network TV ad support, MaxSnax met with overwhelming consumer indifference. By the time Frito-Lay pulled the product from store shelves, it had lost $52 million.[25]

After the market test, the firm can estimate likely ROI for various strategies to determine whether the idea will be moved on to commercialization.[26]

Step 5: Commercialization

A product idea that survives this far can finally be placed on the market. Putting a product on the market is expensive. Manufacturing or service facilities have to be set up. Goods have to be produced to fill the channels of distribution, or people must be hired and trained to provide services. Further, introductory promotion is costly, especially if the company is entering a very competitive market.

Because of the size of the job, some firms introduce their products city by city or region by region—in a gradual "roll out"—until they have complete market coverage. Roll-outs also permit more market testing, although that is not their purpose. But marketing managers also need to pay close attention to control, to ensure that the implementation effort is working and that the strategy is on target.

New product development: a total company effort

Companies that are particularly successful at developing new goods and services seem to have one trait in common: enthusiastic top-management support for new-product development.[27]

In addition, rather than leaving new-product development to anyone who happens to be interested (perhaps in engineering, R&D, or sales), successful companies put someone in charge—a person, department, or team.

A new-product development team with people from different departments helps ensure that new ideas are carefully evaluated, and that profitable ones are quickly brought to market. It's important to choose the right people for the job. Overly conservative managers may kill too many—or even all—new ideas. Or committees may create bureaucratic delays that make the difference between a product's success or failure.

Market needs guide R&D effort

From the idea generation stage to the commercialization stage, the R&D specialists, the operations people, and the marketing people must work together to evaluate the feasibility of new ideas. It isn't sensible for a marketing manager to develop elaborate marketing plans for goods or services that the firm simply can't produce—or produce profitably. It also doesn't make sense for R&D people to develop a technology or product that does not have potential for the firm and its markets. Clearly, a balancing act is involved here.

Need for product managers

When a firm has only one or a few related products, everyone is interested in them. But when a firm has products in several different product categories, management may decide to put someone in charge of each category—or each brand—to ensure that attention to each product is not lost in the rush of everyday business. **Product managers** or **brand managers** manage specific products, often taking over the jobs formerly handled by an advertising manager. That gives a clue to what is often their major responsibility— Promotion—since the products have usually already been developed by the new-product people.

Product managers are especially common in large companies that produce many kinds of products. Several product managers may serve under a marketing manager. Sometimes these product managers are responsible for the profitable operation of a particular product's entire marketing effort. Then they have to coordinate their efforts with others, including the sales manager, advertising agencies, production and research people, and even channel members. This is likely to lead to difficulties if product managers have no control over the marketing strategy for other related brands, or authority over other functional areas whose efforts they are expected to direct and coordinate!

To avoid these problems, in some companies the product manager serves mainly as a "product champion" concerned with planning the promotion effort and getting it implemented. A higher-level marketing manager with more authority coordinates the efforts and integrates the marketing strategies for different products into an overall plan.

The activities of product managers vary greatly with their experience and aggressiveness, and with the company's organizational philosophy. Today, companies are emphasizing marketing *experience*, because this important job takes more than academic training and enthusiasm.[28]

Will category managers replace brand managers?*

Many firms now have category managers rather than brand managers. What's the difference? Briefly, category managers are no longer responsible only for demand stimulation but have expanded their responsibil-

*This material was written by Professor Robert D. Tamilia, of the University of Quebec at Montreal (UQAM), for *Basic Marketing*, Ninth Canadian Edition.

ities to include the supply side as well. That is, category managers are also involved in the buying function. They no longer focus their attention on specific brands but rather on product categories, including entire product lines (such as soaps and detergents, hair-care or pet-care products). Such product categories can be managed as business units within the firm, similar to the management of SBUs (strategic business units). Category management follows the entrepreneurial model in which managers have complete responsibility for various product categories under their supervision.

Consumer packaged-goods companies have had to restructure their brand management marketing approach to correspond more to the way large retailers and wholesalers are now buying and merchandising such product lines in-store. Retailers' own category management systems focus on both buying and selling, not for individual brands but for product categories as a whole. After all, retailers are more concerned with the marketing of product categories than with individual brands supplied by just one firm. As a result, they are now requiring that their suppliers help them sell more quickly within a product category with high stock turnover rates and profitable margins.

Category managers, by definition, need to work more closely with retailers and other resellers in the supply chain. They form closer alliances in order to ensure better coordination between promotional activities and the logistics work (i.e., resellers' work) required to move and store products on store shelves.

Less units rather than more?

Under the traditional brand management system, brand managers would add more brand sizes, more flavours, and more brand variety (i.e., brand line extensions) in order to make the brand more competitive, to keep up with competitors' attempts at product differentiation, or to rejuvenate their brand. For example, hundreds of laundry detergent products are on the market, with each of the leading brands available in a multitude of SKUs (stock keeping units), such as cold wash, low temperature, bleach or bleach-free, odorless, lemon-scented or natural, powder, liquid, and low suds. All of these are available in a bewildering assortment of package sizes and refills.

Marketing practices under brand management did not seem to question the need to have a brand available in such a confusing array of choices. But such promotion-based marketing efforts resulted in a tremendous rise in the number of brand-related SKUs. Either their distribution costs were unknown, or their cost responsibilities lay elsewhere than with brand managers.

Category managers, at either the retail or the manufacturer level, are now more knowledgeable when it comes to the logistical costs of having too many SKUs. They are also better able to assess costs, using a cost accounting procedure called ABC (activity based accounting). This software-based costing procedure examines all of the various costs associated with supplying and selling SKUs in the store. With the use of ABC and its variant, DPP (direct product profit), category managers working for large retailers can develop better and even optimal planograms for specific product categories—or even for individual stores.

For many brands, the analysis of demand and of supply costs has led to a rather dramatic change in the number of SKUs. For example, Procter and Gamble has managed to reduce its number of SKUs by 34 percent, and hopes to make a further reduction of 20 percent by the year 2000. Another example is Lever Pond's Vaseline products. In 1995, a total of 29 SKUs were associated with the Vaseline brand. This number has since been reduced to 15. Similarly, Scott Paper has managed to pare down its number of SKUs by 20 percent since 1995.[29]

Questions and Problems

1. Explain how industry sales and industry profits behave over the product life cycle.
2. Cite two examples of products that you feel are currently in each of the product life-cycle stages. Consider services as well as physical goods.
3. Explain how you might reach different conclusions about the correct product life-cycle stage(s) in the worldwide automobile market.
4. Explain why individual brands may not follow the product life-cycle pattern. Give an example of a new brand that is not entering the life cycle at the market introduction stage.
5. Discuss the life cycle of a product in terms of its probable impact on a manufacturer's marketing mix. Illustrate using personal computers.
6. What characteristics of a new product will help it to move through the early stages of the product life cycle quickly? Briefly discuss each characteristic, illustrating with a product of your choice. Indicate how each characteristic might be viewed in some other country.
7. What is a new product? Illustrate your answer.
8. Explain the importance of an organized new-product development process and illustrate how it might be used for (a) a new hair care product, (b) a new children's toy, and (c) a new subscribers-only cable television channel.
9. Discuss how you might use the new-product development process if you were thinking about offering some kind of summer service to residents in a beach resort town.
10. Explain the role of product or brand managers. When would it make sense for one of a company's current brand managers to be in charge of the new-product development process? Explain your thinking.
11. If a firm offers one of its brands in a number of different countries, would it make sense for one brand manager to be in charge, or would each country require its own brand manager? Explain your thinking.
12. Discuss the social value of new-product development activities that seem to encourage people to discard products that are not all worn out. Is this an economic waste? How worn out is all worn out? Must a shirt have holes in it? How big?

Suggested Cases

13 New North Media	33 New Brunswick Telephone
32 Sure-Grow Fertilizers	34 Rocky Mountain House Co-op

Computer-aided problem

Growth Stage Competition

AgriChem, Inc., has introduced an innovative new product—a combination fertilizer, weed killer, and insecticide that makes it much easier for soybean farmers to produce a profitable crop. The product introduction was quite successful, with 1 million units sold in the year of introduction. And AgriChem's profits are increasing. Total market demand is expected to grow at a rate of 200,000 units a year for the next five years. Even so, AgriChem's marketing managers are concerned about what will happen to sales and profits during this period.

Based on past experience with similar situations, they expect one new competitor to enter the market during each of the next five years. They think this competitive pressure will drive prices down about 6 percent a year. Further, although the total market is growing, they know that new competitors will chip away at AgriChem's market share—even with the 10 percent a year increase planned for the promotion budget. In spite of the competitive pressure, the marketing managers are sure that familiarity with AgriChem's brand will help it hold a large share of the total market—and give AgriChem greater economies of scale than competitors. In fact, they expect that the ratio of profit to dollar sales for AgriChem should be about 10 percent higher than for competitors.

AgriChem's marketing managers have decided the best way to get a handle on the situation is to organize the data in a spreadsheet. They have set up the spreadsheet so that they can change the "years in the future" value and see what is likely to happen to AgriChem and the rest of the industry. The starting spreadsheet shows the current situation with data from the first full year of production.

a. Compare AgriChem's market share and profit for this year with what is expected next year—given the marketing managers' current assumptions. What are they expecting? (Hint: Set number of years in the future to 1.)

b. Prepare a table showing AgriChem's expected profit, and the expected industry revenue and profit, for the current year and the next five years. Briefly explain what happens to industry sales and profits and why. (Hint: Use the What If analysis to vary the number of years in the future value in the spreadsheet from a minimum of 0—the current year—to a maximum of 5. Display the three values requested.)

c. If market demand grows faster than expected—say, at 280,000 units a year—what will happen to AgriChem's profits and the expected industry revenues and profits over the next five years? What are the implications of this analysis?

For additional questions related to this problem, see Exercise 10–3 in the *Learning Aid for Use with Basic Marketing*, Ninth Canadian Edition.

When you finish this chapter, you should:

- Understand how and why marketing specialists develop to make channel systems more effective.
- Understand what product classes suggest about Place objectives.
- Understand why some firms use direct channel systems while others rely on intermediaries and indirect systems.
- Understand how to develop cooperative relationships—and avoid conflict—in channel systems.
- Know how channel members in vertical marketing systems shift and share functions to meet customer needs.
- Understand the differences between intensive, selective, and exclusive distribution.
- Understand the important new terms (shown in orange).

Chap eleven

Place and Development of Channel Systems

Connors Brothers' history as an export company stretches back into the last century, and it is well-placed to continue to expand this tradition as it approaches the next century.

Founded in 1893, the company was shipping its canned fish to New England from the beginning. Now with four plants in Canada and the United States, and 1,800 employees, the company is the largest producer of canned sardines and herring in North America.

The largest of these plants is still where it all started—in Blacks Harbour, New Brunswick. The company ships close to a million cases of Brunswick label canned fish a year from Blacks Harbour to 35 countries. Another half-million cases are shipped from their other plants—two in Canada and one in the U.S. Indeed, 75% of the company's output is sold outside of Canada. As the company deals with a consumer product, the strategy is the same for every market: develop distribution and get the product in the stores.

Finding the right distributor falls to Heinz Scharer, international sales manager. In some cases this can be relatively easy, especially in established markets, where brokers can be pounding down your door.

"It's easier when you have a track record with the product," says Scharer. "Brokers want the line. In Trinidad and Tobago we have brokers coming to our door quite regularly. In the Caribbean, the canned seafood section is really the Brunswick section. It helps that we've been exporting there for 80 years. But you can't take anything for granted. You still have to market."

Recently, Connors Brothers has been marketing more heavily in the Caribbean, to support the introduction of canned tuna and salmon. The higher-value product has given the company a little space to market beyond its standard in-store promotions.

Finding a distributor in a new market presents much more difficult challenges. Even a relationship which seems to be going well can turn sour.

Connors Brothers entered the Mexican market in typical fashion, at a trade show. In this case, it was the ANTAD food trade show in 1992 in Guadalajara. In general, and particularly for ANTAD, the Canadian embassy is a good source of local market information.

"The Canadian government is involved with ANTAD," says Scharer. "They would invite all the major retailers and brokers and have a reception."

The company found a broker, and Mexican sales grew rapidly. Within a year-and-a-half, a decision was made to hire a general manager to oversee Mexico, creating the company's only foreign office outside of the U.S. Given the size of the market, and the growth in sales, the company decided to have one of their own people keeping an eye on the operation. While reporting to Connors Brothers, the general manager sat in the office of the company's broker and worked closely with the broker's sales and accounting staff.

Then, a couple of years ago, the relationship began to come apart. "The broker's staff weren't working to the best of their ability, and we weren't able to get the information we required," says Scharer.

The broker was having financial difficulties, which became insurmountable when the peso crashed. The decision to change brokers was not made lightly. The Mexican government had questions about who was the true employer of the broker's staff—the broker or Connors Brothers—and who would be responsible for severance packages. Sorting out the mess took a year-and-a-half.

"There was a compromise between our broker and ourselves," says Scharer. "The government didn't have to act. The lawyers worked it out."

This episode will make the company more cautious in the future. Prospective brokers from now on can expect a thorough check of their history. Fortunately, the Mexican market is still a lucrative one, and the relationship was not a complete disaster.

"They did have the contacts to get the product established," says Scharer. "It could have been worse."

Problems like this are unusual, and Connors Brothers does its best to avoid them. For example, it uses an exclusivity clause in its contracts to keep its brokers from selling a competitor's products, in order to avoid possible conflict of interest.

Finding the right distributor for a new market is not always difficult. Connors Brothers has made in-roads into the Eastern European market on the strength of their international reputation.

"In Eastern Europe it's ex-pats in Canada that made the contact; they got a hold of us," says Scharer. "That's very odd, really. But it did happen back to back in both the Czech Republic and Poland."

Eastern Europe is something of a ready-made market for the company, because Eastern Europeans are already big eaters of canned fish—particularly herring. Local suppliers' inability to meet the demands of changes in the Eastern European marketplace is creating a big opportunity.

"A lot of retail chains are being bought out by major Western European retailers, who want a constant supply of product," says Scharer. "We're really growing in those western-style supermarkets."

Connors Brothers is hoping to build on the Eastern European success with the introduction of salmon and tuna, but the really big catch is still out of reach.

"Russia will be very difficult," says Scharer. "They can't afford the product, but they're very big consumers of canned fish. We went to a trade show at the end of 1996. The embassy was a big help there with set-ups at the show, and they gave us a list of major wholesalers and importers of canned goods."

Connors Brothers learned the potential is there, but the infrastructure is sadly lacking. Distribution is difficult, and the banking situation is worse. Because no Russian banks are recognized internationally, brokers can't provide letters of credit to importers. Somehow they have to come up with the cash instead.

"You have to be creative," says Scharer. "There will be a way."

Source: Kevin Yarr, "In the Can," *Atlantic Progress,* May 1997, pp. 19–22. Reprinted with permission from Kevin Yarr.

Place decisions—an important part of marketing strategy

Offering customers a good product at a reasonable price is important to a successful marketing strategy. But it's not the whole story. As the Connors Brothers example indicates, managers must also think about **Place**—making goods and services available in the right quantities and locations, when customers want them.

In this chapter and the next, we'll deal with the many important strategy decisions that a marketing manager must make concerning Place. Exhibit 11–1 gives you an overview. We'll start by discussing the types of channels that are needed to meet cus-

Exhibit 11-1 Strategy Decision Areas in Place

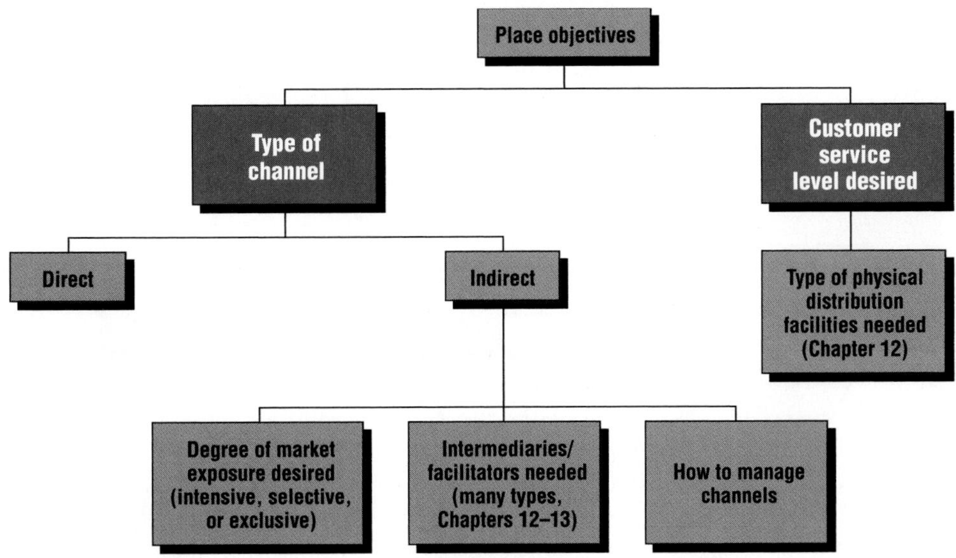

tomers' needs. We'll show why specialists are often involved and how they come together to form a **channel of distribution**—any series of firms or individuals who participate in the flow of products from producer to final user or consumer. We'll also consider how to manage relations among channel members to reduce conflict and improve cooperation.

All economies need marketing systems

In a **pure subsistence economy,** each family unit produces everything it consumes. There is no need to exchange goods and services. Each producer-consumer unit is totally self-sufficient, although usually its standard of living is relatively low. No marketing takes place because *marketing doesn't occur unless two or more parties are willing to exchange something for something else.*

What is a market?

The term *marketing* comes from the word **market,** which is a group of potential customers with similar needs who are willing to exchange something of value with sellers offering various goods and/or services—that is, ways of satisfying those needs. Of course, some negotiation may be needed. This can be done face to face at some physical location (for example, a farmers' market). Or it can be done indirectly, through a complex network of intermediaries who link buyers and sellers living far apart.

In primitive economies, exchanges tend to occur in central markets. **Central markets** are convenient places where buyers and sellers can meet one on one to exchange goods and services. We can understand marketing better by seeing how and why central markets develop.

Central markets help exchange

Imagine a small village of five families, each with a special skill for producing some need-satisfying product. After meeting basic needs, each family decides to specialize. It's easier for one family to make two pots and another to make two baskets than for each one to make one pot and one basket. Specialization makes labour more efficient and more productive. It can increase the total amount of form utility created (see Chapter 1). Specialization also can increase the task utility in producing services. For the moment, however, we'll focus on products that are physical goods.

Exhibit 11-2

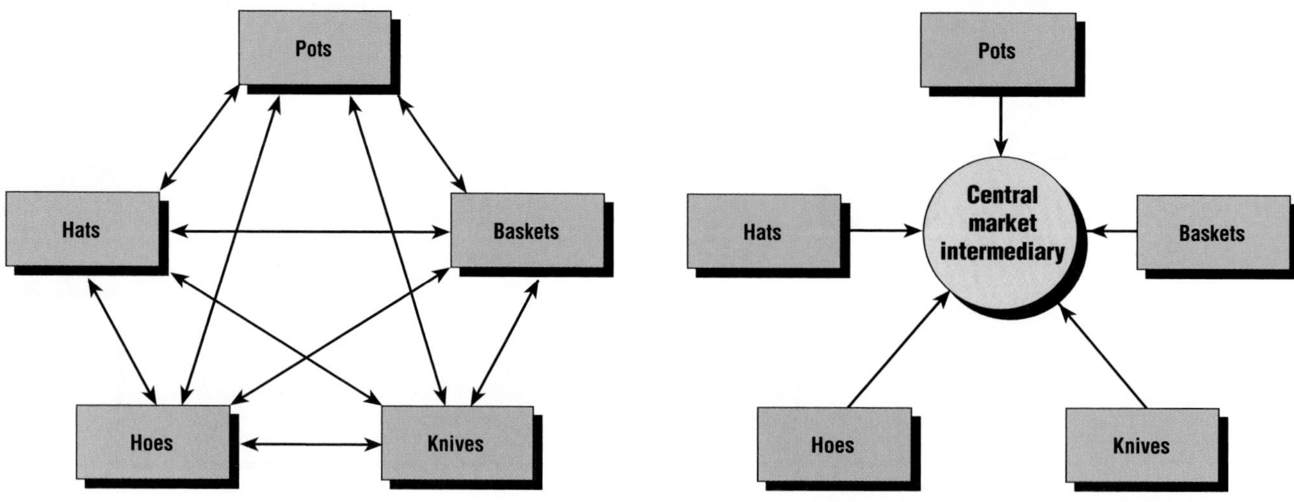

If each of these five families specializes in one product, they will all have to trade with one another. As Exhibit 11–2A shows, it will take the five families ten separate exchanges to obtain some of each of the products. If the families live near one another, the exchange process will be relatively simple. But if they are far apart, travel back and forth will take time. Who will do the travelling, and when?

Faced with this problem, the families may agree to come to a central market and trade on a certain day. Then each family needs to make only one trip to the market to trade with all the others. This reduces the total number of trips to five, which makes exchange easier, leaves more time for producing and consuming, and also provides for social gatherings.

A monetary system simplifies trading

While a central meeting place simplifies exchange, the individual bartering transactions still take a lot of time. Bartering only works when someone else wants what you have, and vice versa. Each trader must find others who have products of about equal value. After trading with one group, a family may find itself with extra baskets, knives, and pots. Then it will have to find others willing to trade for these products.

A common monetary system changes all this. Sellers only have to find buyers who want their products and agree on the price. Then sellers are free to spend this income to buy whatever they want. (If some buyers and sellers use *different* monetary systems—that is, if some use dollars and others use yen—they must also agree on the rate at which the money will be exchanged.)

Intermediaries help exchange even more

The development of a central market and a money system simplifies the exchange process among the five families in our imaginary village. But the families still need to make ten separate transactions. So it still takes a lot of time and effort for the five families to exchange goods.

This clumsy exchange process is made much simpler by an **intermediary**—someone who specializes in trade rather than production. An intermediary is willing to buy each family's goods and then sell each family whatever it needs. The intermediary charges for this service, of course. But this charge may be more than offset by savings in time and effort.

In our simple example, using an intermediary at a central market reduces the necessary number of exchanges for all five families from 10 to 5 (see Exhibit 11–2B). Each family has more time for production, consumption, and leisure. Also, each family can specialize in producing what it produces best, which creates more form and task utility. Meanwhile, by specializing in trade, the intermediary provides additional time, place, and possession utility. In total, all the villagers may enjoy greater economic utility—and greater consumer satisfaction—by using an intermediary in the central market.

Note that the reduction in transactions that results from using an intermediary in a central market becomes more important as the number of families increases. For example, if the population of our imaginary village increases from 5 to 10 families, 45 transactions are needed without an intermediary. When an intermediary is used, only one transaction is required for each family.

Today, such intermediaries are known as *wholesalers* and *retailers*. The advantages of working with intermediaries increase with increases in the number of producers and consumers, their distance from or difficulties in communicating with one another, and the number and variety of competing products. That is why there are so many wholesalers and retailers in modern economies.

Effective marketing links producers and consumers

Effective marketing means delivering the goods and services that consumers want and need. It means getting products to them at the right time, in the right place, and at a price they're willing to pay. It means keeping consumers satisfied after the sale, and bringing them back to purchase again when they are ready. That's not an easy job, especially when you think about the variety of goods and services that a highly developed economy can produce, and the many kinds of goods and services that consumers want.

Effective marketing in an advanced economy is more difficult because producers and consumers are often separated in several ways. As Exhibit 11–3 shows, exchange between producers and consumers is hampered by spatial separation, separation in time, separation of information and values, and separation of ownership. "Discrepancies of quantity" and "discrepancies of assortment" further complicate exchange

Figure 11–3 Marketing Facilitates Production and Consumption

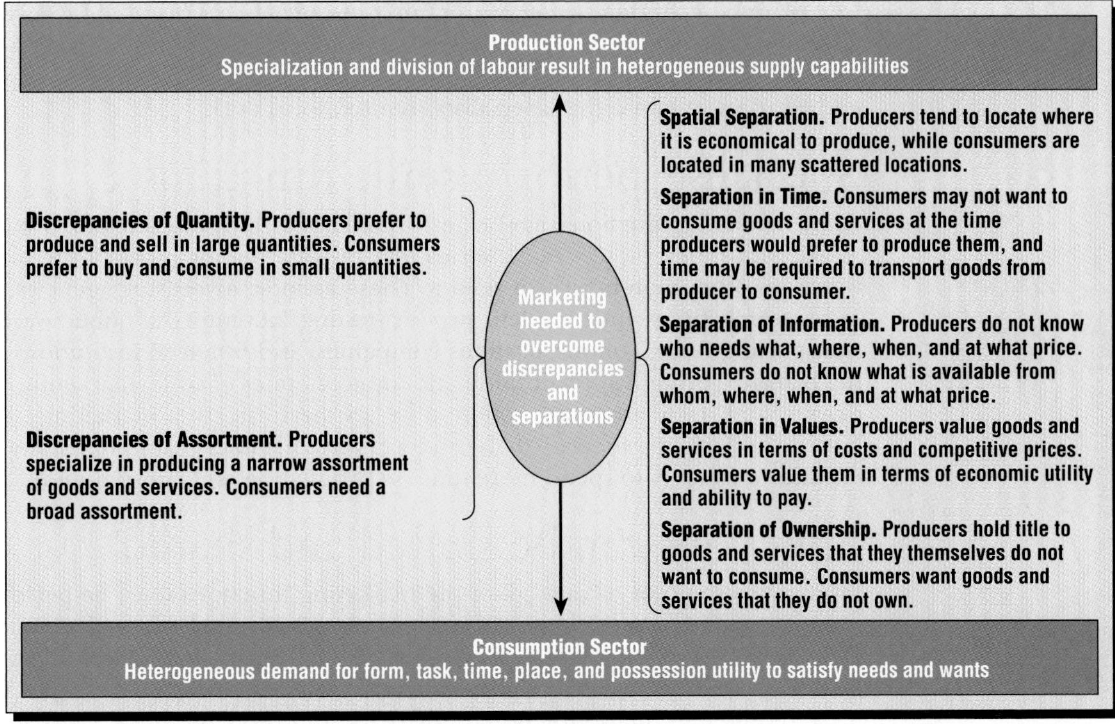

between producers and consumers. That is, each producer specializes in producing and selling large amounts of a narrow assortment of goods and services, but each consumer wants only small quantities of a wide assortment of goods and services.[1]

Marketing functions help narrow the gap

The purpose of a marketing system is to overcome these separations and discrepancies. The "universal functions of marketing" help do this.

The **universal functions of marketing** are these: buying, selling, transporting, storing, standardization and grading, financing, risk taking, and market information. They must be performed in all marketing systems. *How* these functions are performed, and *by whom*, may differ among nations and economic systems. But they are needed in any marketing system. Let's take a closer look at them now.

Exchange usually involves buying and selling. The **buying function** means looking for and evaluating goods and services. The **selling function** involves promoting the product. It includes the use of personal selling, advertising, and other direct and mass selling methods. This is probably the most visible function of marketing.

The **transporting function** involves moving goods from one place to another. The **storing function** involves holding goods until customers need them.

Standardization and grading involve sorting products according to size and quality. This makes buying and selling easier by reducing the need for inspection and sampling. **Financing** provides the necessary cash and credit to produce, transport, store, promote, sell, and buy products. **Risk taking** involves bearing the uncertainties that are part of the marketing process. A firm can never be sure that customers will want to buy its products. Products can also be damaged, stolen, or outdated. The **market information function** involves the collection, analysis, and distribution of all the information needed to plan, carry out, and control marketing activities, whether in the firm's own neighbourhood or in a market overseas.

Who performs marketing functions?

From a macro-level point of view, these marketing functions are all part of the marketing process, and must be done by someone. None of them can be eliminated. In a planned economy, some of the functions may be performed by government agencies. Others may be left to individual producers and consumers. In a market-directed system, marketing functions are performed by producers, consumers, and a variety of marketing specialists (see Exhibit 11–4).

Specialists perform some functions

Some marketing functions may be performed not only by intermediaries but also by a variety of other **facilitators**—firms that provide one or more of the marketing functions other than buying or selling. These include advertising agencies, marketing research firms, independent product-testing laboratories, public warehouses, transporting firms, communications companies, and financial institutions (including banks). Through specialization and/or economies of scale, marketing intermediaries and facilitators are often able to perform the marketing functions better—and at a lower cost—than producers or consumers can. This allows producers and consumers to spend more time on production and consumption.

Functions can be shifted and shared

From a macro point of view, all of the marketing functions must be performed by someone. But *from a micro point of view, not every firm must perform all of the functions. Furthermore, not all goods and services require all the functions at every level of their production.* "Pure services," such as a plane ride, don't need storing, for example. But storing is required in the production of the plane and while the plane is not in service.

Exhibit 11-4 Model of a Market-Directed Macro-Marketing System

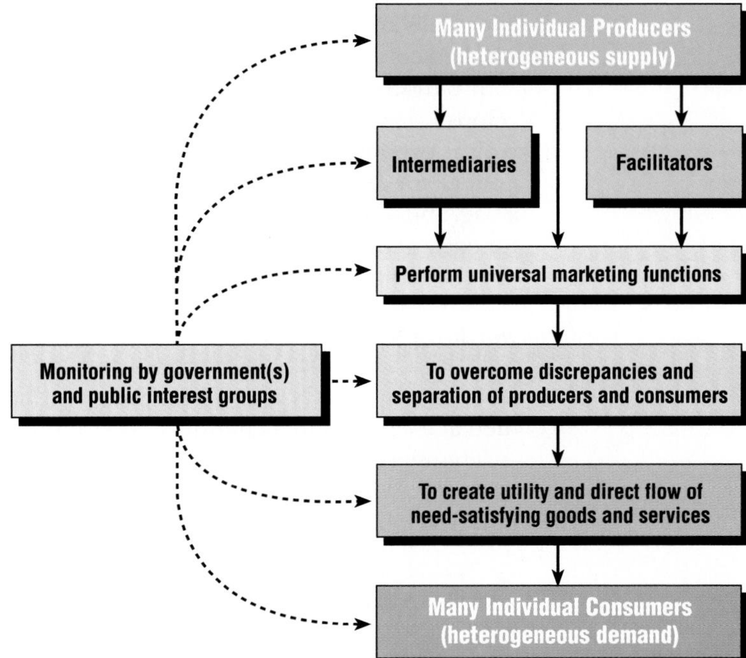

Some marketing specialists perform all the functions. Others specialize in only one or two. Marketing research firms, for example, specialize only in the market information function. The important point to remember is this: *Responsibility for performing the marketing functions can be shifted and shared in a variety of ways, but no function can be completely eliminated.*

Discrepancies and separations require specialists

The assortment and quantity of products customers want may be different from the assortment and quantity of products companies produce. Producers are often located far from their customers and may not know how best to reach them. Customers for their part may not know about their choices. Specialists arise in response to these discrepancies and separations. (See Exhibit 11–3).[2]

Intermediaries supply needed information

Customers don't always have "perfect information" about all producers, nor do all producers know which customers need what product, where, when, and at what price. Specialists help provide information to bring buyers and sellers together. For example, a local independent insurance agent may help consumers decide which policy—and which insurance company—best fits their needs.

Intermediaries who are close to their customers are often in a better position to forecast demand more accurately. This information can help reduce inventory costs in the whole channel, and may help the producer smooth out production.

As illustrated in the Connors Brothers example, most producers seek help from specialists when they first enter international markets. Specialists can provide crucial information about customer needs, as well as insights into the particular marketing environment.

Discrepancies of quantity and assortment

Discrepancy of quantity refers to the difference between the quantity of products it is economical for a producer to make and the quantity final users or consumers normally want. For example, most manufacturers of golf balls produce large quantities—perhaps 500,000 in a given time period. The average golfer, however, wants only a few balls at a time. Adjusting for this discrepancy usually requires intermediaries—wholesalers and retailers.

Producers typically specialize by product, and therefore another discrepancy develops. **Discrepancy of assortment** refers to the difference between the lines a typical producer makes and the assortment final consumers or users want. Most golfers, for example, need more than golf balls. They want golf shoes, gloves, clubs, a bag, and—of course—a golf course to play on. And they usually don't want to shop for each item separately. So again, there is a need for wholesalers and retailers to adjust these discrepancies.

Adjust discrepancies with regrouping activities

Regrouping activities adjust the quantities and/or assortments of products handled at each level in a channel of distribution.

There are four regrouping activities: accumulating, bulk-breaking, sorting, and assorting. When one or more of these activities are needed, a marketing specialist may develop to fill this need.

Adjusting quantity discrepancies

Accumulating involves collecting products from many small producers. Much of the coffee that comes from Colombia is grown on small farms in the mountains. Accumulating the small crops into larger quantities is a way of getting the lowest transporting rate, and of making it more convenient for distant food processing companies to buy and handle it. Accumulating is especially important in less-developed countries and in other situations, like agricultural markets, where there are many small producers.

Accumulating is also important with professional services, which often involve the combined work of a number of individuals, each of whom is a specialized producer. A hospital makes it easier for patients by accumulating the services of a number of health care specialists, many of whom may not actually work for the hospital.

Bulk-breaking involves dividing larger quantities into smaller quantities as products get closer to the final market. Bulk-breaking may involve several levels of intermediaries. Wholesalers may sell smaller quantities to other wholesalers, or directly to retailers. Retailers continue breaking bulk as they sell individual items to their customers.

Adjusting assortment discrepancies

Different types of specialists adjust assortment discrepancies. They perform two types of regrouping activities: sorting and assorting.

Sorting means separating products into grades and qualities desired by different target markets. For example, a wholesaler that specializes in serving convenience stores may focus on smaller packages of frequently used products; a wholesaler working with restaurants and hotels may handle only very large institutional sizes.

Assorting means putting together a variety of products to give a target market what it wants. This usually is done by those closest to the final consumer or user—that is, by retailers or wholesalers, who try to supply a wide assortment of products for the convenience of their customers. Thus, a wholesaler selling tractors and mowers to golf courses might also carry grass seed, fertilizer, and even golf ball washers or irrigation systems.

Watch for changes

Sometimes these discrepancies are adjusted badly, especially when consumer wants and attitudes shift rapidly. When cellular phones suddenly became popular, an opportunity developed for a new specialist. Cellular phone dealers came on the scene to help customers figure out what type of cellular phone and service would meet their needs. After all, the traditional phone companies didn't initially offer these ser-

Marketing Demo 11-1

Fast On-Site Hose Service

Finning Launches New 24-Hour Mobile Hydraulic Hose Repair Service in B.C.'s Lower Mainland

Quick emergency hydraulic hose repairs on the job site throughout the greater Vancouver area—that's the goal of a pilot product support program launched in the Lower Mainland last fall.

"The operative word around here is speed," says Finning hose and fitting specialist Ron Konrad from the new service's truck dispatch centre in Coquitlam. "Our goal with this program is instant response. We want to be at the customer's job site virtually anywhere in the Lower Mainland within 20 to 30 minutes. And then get the machine back working just as quickly."

To do that, the company is using four new specially equipped hose service trucks, each with its own fully qualified hose technician. Although dispatched out of a central location, the trucks are strategically located throughout the Lower Mainland to speed response time.

"We have divided the Lower Mainland into four service areas and station one truck in each at all times," says Konrad.

. . . Each unit is fully equipped to complete virtually any hose assembly or repair at the job site. The trucks carry a wide selection of Cat hose, couplings and adaptors, hose press, and computerized crimper.

Konrad stresses that the new service encompasses both Caterpillar and non-Cat machines.

"These trucks are completely equipped for on-site hose manufacturing for almost any mobile machine. They carry a full range of Cat hose and reusable couplings, adaptors, and standard, metric or DIN fittings. The onboard inventory in each truck is replenished daily."

He adds: "We developed this service with one thing in mind: to be able to complete the repair faster than the customer can do himself by sending his mechanic or operator to the nearest branch to get the hose or assembly he needs, then go back to the job site to do the repair. We can save the company time and money—and have the machine back working faster—by calling the hose van instead."

Konrad says the program is based on a similar service operated successfully by Finning in the UK for some time. The concept and design layout for the trucks was developed in close concert with Caterpillar, which wants to see other Cat dealers mount similar programs, he says.

"For any machine owner, uptime is what it is all about. It has been estimated that up to 30 per cent of machine downtime is related to a hydraulic hose failure."

While the new service targets emergency repairs, the technicians are also available for routine, scheduled on-site hose inspections for fleet operators or at industrial plant operations. "The idea is to change out a suspect hose or coupling prior to failure. The trucks are also equipped to do on-site hydraulic oil particle count analysis, which can be done at the same time. A lot of customers have told us that this is a service they would very much like to see."

Konrad says some Lower Mainland customers may recall that the company tried a similar program on a trial basis several years ago. "It involved a single service truck that couldn't provide the response time we or the customers wanted in an area this large. It also wasn't available 24 hours and it was restricted to Cat machines. We've addressed all of these drawbacks with this service. The response from customers so far has been fantastic. This is a pilot program and we'll be looking at it closely in terms of expanding it to other centres in the future."

Source: *Tracks & Treads,* a Finning (Canada) Publication, 1998, Volume 37, No. 1, p. 3.

vices. However, it cost the sellers of cellular services about $300 per customer to sell through dealers. As the market grew and the competition for customers heated up, electronics stores wanted a piece of the action, and they were willing to take a smaller markup. Now that the market is much more established, many cellular service providers are finding it cheaper to use their own salespeople.

Specialists should develop to adjust discrepancies *if they must be adjusted.* But there is no point in having intermediaries just because that's the way it has been done in the past. Sometimes a breakthrough opportunity can come from finding a better way to reduce discrepancies—perhaps by eliminating some steps in the channel. For example, as described in Marketing Demo 11–1, Finning (Canada), a division of Finning International Inc., launched a 24-hour mobile, on-site hose repair service for its customers.

Many small manufacturers of business products have found that with an Internet Web site they can now reach more customers in distant markets than was previously possible with independent manufacturer's reps, who sold on commission but otherwise left distribution to the firm. If it costs the firm less to establish an order-taking Web site and advertise it in a trade magazine, the cost advantage can translate to lower prices and a marketing mix that is a better value for some target segments.[3]

Place decisions are guided by ideal place objectives

All marketing managers want to be sure that their goods and services are available in the right quantities and locations, when customers want them. But customers may have different needs with respect to time, place, and possession utility as they make different purchases.

To more quickly reach its Place objectives in the Japanese market and achieve widespread, low-cost distribution, GE agreed to form a joint venture with Hitachi. The joint venture distributes 75 different types of light bulbs through a network of 100 wholesalers who serve 10,000 established Hitachi retail outlets.

Product classes suggest place objectives

You've already seen this in Chapter 9 with the product classes, which summarize consumers' urgency to have needs satisfied and willingness to seek information, shop, and compare. Now you should be able to use the product classes to handle Place decisions.

Exhibit 9–4 showed the relationship between consumer product classes and ideal Place objectives. Similarly, Exhibit 9–5 showed the business product classes and how they relate to customer needs. Study these exhibits carefully. They set the framework for making Place decisions. In particular, the product classes help us decide how much market exposure we'll need in each geographic area.

Place system is not automatic

Several different product classes may be involved if different market segments view a product in different ways. Thus, just as there is no automatic classification for a specific product, we can't automatically decide the one best Place arrangement.

Place decisions have long-run effects

The marketing manager must also consider Place objectives in relation to the product life cycle (see Exhibit 10–3). Place decisions have long-run effects. They're usually harder to change than Product, Price, and Promotion decisions. It can take years and a great deal of money to develop effective working relationships with others in the channel. Legal contracts with channel partners may also limit changes. And it's hard to move retail and wholesale facilities once they're set up. Yet as products mature, they typically need broader distribution to reach different target customers.

The distribution of premium pet foods followed this pattern. Most pet food producers reached consumers through supermarkets. Yet supermarkets weren't willing to put much emphasis on specialized pet foods because there wasn't much demand. Marketing managers for Hill's Science Diet products concentrated on getting distribution through pet shops and veterinary offices. By 1991, pet owners were spending over $1 billion a year for premium-priced food from pet stores and vets. What's more, the profit margins on the specialty foods are high. Seeing this growth, Purina, Kal Kan, and other producers developed new products and worked with their supermarket channels to set up special "nutrition centres" on the pet food aisle. But Science Diet plans to stick with its current channels to expand distribution into 28 other countries. In pet stores across Japan, for example, Science Diet is attracting new customers with special displays featuring samples and free literature.[4]

Channel system may be direct or indirect

One of the most basic Place decisions producers must make is whether to handle the entire distribution themselves, or use wholesalers, retailers, and other specialists. Intermediaries, in turn, must select the producers they'll work with.

Why a firm might want to use direct distribution

Many firms prefer to distribute direct to final customers because they want to control the entire marketing job. They may think they can serve target customers at a lower cost or do the work more effectively than intermediaries. Usually, intermediaries carry the products of several competing producers, so they aren't willing to give any one item the special emphasis its producer wants.

The Internet now makes it easier

The Internet is giving many firms direct access to prospects and customers whom it would have been difficult or impossible to reach in the past. Even very small, specialized firms may be able to establish a Web page and draw customers from all over the world. Of course, there are limitations to this approach. If a customer wants a salesperson to demonstrate a product, then a "virtual store" may not be adequate. However, the concept of distribution over the Internet is just in the introductory stage. Very soon, firms will use live camera "feeds" while talking with the customer over an Internet video phone. Whether it's with the help of technology or by other more traditional means, there often *are* great advantages in selling direct to the final user or consumer.

Direct contact with customers

When a firm is in direct contact with its customers, it is more aware of changes in customer attitudes. It is better able to adjust its marketing mix quickly because there is no need to convince other channel members to help. If a product needs an aggressive selling effort or special technical service, the marketing manager can ensure that the sales force receives the necessary training and motivation.

Suitable intermediaries are not available

A firm may have to go direct if suitable intermediaries are not available—or will not cooperate. Intermediaries who have the best contacts with the target market may be hesitant to add unproven products, especially really new products that don't fit well with their current business.

Common with business customers and services

Many business products are sold direct-to-customer. Rolm, for example, sells its computerized voice mail systems direct. This is understandable, since in business markets there are fewer transactions, orders are larger, and customers may be concentrated in a small geographic area.

Many service firms also use direct channels. If the service must be produced in the presence of customers, there may be little need for intermediaries. An accounting firm like Arthur Andersen, for example, must deal directly with its customers. However, many firms that produce physical goods turn to specialist intermediaries to help provide the services customers expect as part of the product. Maytag may hope that its authorized dealers don't get many repair calls, but the service is available when customers need it. Here the intermediary produces the service.[5]

Large supermarket chains accumulate products from many producers at their distribution centres and then break bulk to provide the convenient assortments that consumers expect to find at individual stores.

Don't be confused by the term *direct marketing*

An increasing number of firms now rely on **direct marketing**—direct communication between the seller and the individual customer using a promotion method other than face-to-face personal selling. Sometimes direct marketing promotion is coupled with direct distribution from the producer to consumers. Stokes Seeds Limited, for example, sells the seeds it grows direct to consumers with a mail catalogue. However, many firms that use direct marketing promotion distribute their products through intermediaries. So the term *direct marketing* is concerned mainly with the Promotion area, not Place decisions. We'll talk about direct marketing promotion in more detail in Chapter 14.

When indirect channels are best

Even when a producer wants to handle the entire distribution job, sometimes it's simply not possible. Customers often have established buying patterns. For example, Square D, a producer of electrical supplies, may want to sell directly to big electrical contractors. But if contractors like to make all of their purchases in one convenient stop—at a local electrical wholesaler—the only practical way to reach them is through a wholesaler.

Similarly, consumers are spread throughout many geographic areas and often prefer to shop for certain products at specific places. For example, a consumer may see a Pharmasave drugstore as *the* place to shop for convenience items. This is why most consumer products use indirect channels.[6]

Direct distribution usually requires a significant investment in facilities and people. A new company may want to avoid that investment by working with established intermediaries. Such intermediaries may further reduce a producer's need for working capital by buying the producer's output and carrying it in inventory until it's sold.

Some intermediaries play a critical role by providing credit (working capital) to customers at the end of the channel. An intermediary who knows local customers can help reduce credit risks.

The most important reason for using indirect channels of distribution is that intermediaries can often help producers serve customer needs better and at lower cost.

Effects of the Internet

We have already seen that the Internet will allow many providers of goods and services to deal directly with the consumer. No one knows for sure at this time how electronic commerce will affect distribution channels. However, Internet Insite 11–1 highlights some interesting developments in this area.

Disintermediation and Cybermediaries

The Internet provides manufacturers with the ability to sell directly to consumers, bypassing intermediaries. "The Internet has the ability to remove the middleman, the opportunity to take out layers of mark-up and cost—hence the term disintermediation," says Charlie Hamlin, executive VP of interactive business development at NFO Research Inc (Greenwich, Conn.). "It [disintermediation] consists of any direct transaction or exchange of goods or services that bypasses someone typically involved in such a transaction."[1]

The most popular items purchased online are PC software, books, CDs/tapes, PC hardware, airline tickets, clothes, and consumer electronics. If a publisher can sell books directly to consumers from its Web site (see McGraw-Hill at www.pbg.mcgraw-hill.com), or if an airline can now more effectively sell tickets directly to passengers (see Air Canada at www.aircanada.ca), what will become of intermediaries? In some instances traditional channels may disappear; in other instances traditional channels may have to play a diminished or perhaps different role.

Dealernet is a company that offers a one-stop information site for automobile purchasers (www.dealernet.com). It provides an extensive database of information about all models of cars, comparisons of prices and models, online applications for financing, information on car insurance, information on automotive parts, and a search feature to locate a dealer near your home. While Dealernet does not eliminate car dealers, it has taken over a lot of the services offered by such dealers. In doing so, it is forcing car dealers to redefine their role.

Most airlines now provide travellers with the ability to check fares and frequent-flier points, as well as to make ticket reservations online. Some even entice them to their Web sites with unbelievably low prices. American Airlines (www.americanair.com) offers a special rate, branded as "Net SAAVer Fares," only to its online customers. American Airlines is able to pass on the savings in travel agent commissions to these consumers. This is clearly a threat to traditional travel agents. Will such agents become a dying breed, or will they redefine their role to justify their existence?

It may not be an exaggeration to say that with the advent of Internet and interactive technologies, any business now serving as an intermediary between a product or service supplier and a final consumer could be at risk.[2] But some experts argue that "disintermediation is not a *fait accompli* for the [retail] industry in general. Smart retailers know that they can exist and prosper in the era of online shopping if they approach their operations from a new perspective.[3] They point to successful firms such as L.L. Bean, a company that has leveraged its existing strengths in distribution and has used the Web to reach new markets in Japan, as examples of how smart retailers can prosper in an era of electronic commerce.

Deborah Cross of Computer Sciences Corp. has identified three categories of retailers who are vulnerable to disintermediation:[4]

- Those whose products or services can be offered digitally—for example, providers of software, music, magazines, newspapers.
- Those who deal in lower-priced, frequently purchased items not requiring expert knowledge—in other words, retailers with non-strategic consumer relationships.
- Those who cater to computer-literate, Internet-savvy individuals. These are the consumers who are buying computers and even personalized items such as clothing online.

While the role of intermediaries is likely to change drastically, it is premature to mourn over or rejoice at the "death of the middleman." New, online intermediaries, or "cybermediaries," are now emerging as the link between the supplier and the end consumer. The cybermediary leverages the technological capability of the Internet and forms an important link between consumers and producers.[5]

Given the vast amount of information available on the Web, it is inevitable that consumers are going to need assistance in sifting through the information avalanche. Search engines and directories such as Yahoo! Lycos, and Altavista are cybermediaries. Andersen Consulting has even created an automated intermediary named BargainFinder, which is a prototype for an intelligent agent that can search the Web to find the lowest-priced music CDs (http://bf.cstar.ac.com/bf/). The concept can easily be expanded to other product categories. Online publishers and content providers such as *Wired* magazine (www.wired.com) become cybermediaries as they connect consumers to producers with banner ads and product listings.

When consumers engage in online shopping, they have to make payments to sellers. Credit card companies such as VISA (www.visa.com) and firms such as Digicash (www.digicash.com), which offers an electronic equivalent of cash, have stepped in to offer an important service here. Clearly, in the electronic marketspace a new breed of intermediary is beginning to play a useful bridging role.[6]

As some traditional retailers give way to the new breed of online retailers, the traditional store-based retailers face challenging times. However, disintermediation does not mean the end of traditional intermediaries. Shopping malls will continue to exist and even grow for the simple reason that for most consumers the term "shopping" means a lot more than buying things. For some it is a pleasurable experience. For others it is a necessary social ritual, a place to spend time with friends and family. While online shopping offers convenience and even savings, many consumers will continue to prefer the brick-and-mortar shopping mall to the chic cybermall.

1. Paul Hawken, "Disintermediation: Cutting Out the Middlemen," *Modern Office Technology,* August 1995, p. 16.
2. John Hagel III and Thomas R. Eisenmann, "Navigating the Multimedia Landscape," *The McKinsey Quarterly,* No. 3, 1994.
3. Deborah Cross, "Are You a Candidate for Disintermediation?" *RT Online,* September 1997 (www.retailtech.com/archive/candidat.htm).
4. Ibid.
5. Mitra Barun Sarkar, Brian Butler, and Charles Steinfeld, "Intermediaries and Cybermediaries: A Continuing Role for Mediating Players in the Electronic Marketplace," *Journal of Computer-Mediated Communication,* December 1995.
6. Ibid.

Source: This is one of a series of Internet Insites prepared in April 1998 by Dr. Ramesh Venkat of Saint Mary's University for *Basic Marketing,* Ninth Canadian Edition.

Channel relationship must be managed

Specialist intermediaries can help make a channel more efficient. But there may be problems getting the different firms in a channel to work together well. How well they work together depends on the type of relationship they have. This should be carefully considered, since marketing managers usually have choices about what type of channel system to join, or develop.

The entire channel should have a product market commitment

Ideally, all of the members of a channel system should have a shared *product-market commitment,* with all members focusing on the same target market at the end of the channel and sharing the various marketing functions in appropriate ways. Unfortunately, many marketing managers overlook this idea because it's not the way their firms traditionally handle channel relationships.

Traditional channel systems involve weak relationships

In **traditional channel systems,** the various channel members make little or no effort to cooperate with one another. They buy and sell from each other, and that's the extent of their relationship. Each channel member does only what it considers to be in its own best interests. It doesn't worry about other members of the channel. This is shortsighted, but it's easy to see how it can happen. The objectives of the various channel members may be different. General Electric wants a wholesaler of electrical building supplies to sell GE products. But a wholesaler who works with different producers may not care whose products get sold. The wholesaler just wants happy customers and a good profit margin.

Traditional channel systems are still typical—and very important—in some industries. The members of these channels have their independence, but they may pay for it too. As we will see, such channels are declining in importance, and for good reason.

Conflict gets in the way

Because members of traditional channel systems often have different objectives, and different ideas about how things should be done, conflict is common.

There are two basic types of conflict in channels of distribution. *Vertical conflicts* occur between firms at different levels of the channel of distribution. For example, a producer and a retailer may disagree about how much shelf space or promotion effort the retailer should give the producer's product.

Recently, there has been vertical conflict between the big recording companies—including Sony, Warner Music, and Capitol-EMI—and their retail outlets, which want to sell used CDs as well as new releases. The recording companies argue that the used CDs eat into their sales and deprive artists of royalties. When Wherehouse Entertainment (one of the largest American retail music chains) started to sell used CDs, at about half the price of new ones, several recording companies announced that they would halt cooperative advertising payments to any retailer that sold used CDs.[7]

Horizontal conflicts occur between firms at the same level in the channel of distribution. For example, a furniture store that keeps a complete line of furniture on display isn't happy to find out that a store down the street is offering customers lower prices on special orders of the same items. The discounter is getting a free ride from the competing store's investment in inventory. And nothing gets an independent retailer more charged up than finding out that a chain store is selling some product for less than the wholesale price the independent pays.

Cooperative relationships share common objectives

Usually the best way to avoid conflict is to get everyone focused on the same basic objective—satisfying the customer at the end of the channel. This leads us away from traditional channels to the channel captain concept.

Each channel system should act as a unit, with each member of the channel collaborating to serve customers at the end of the channel. With this approach, cooperation is everyone's responsibility. However, some firms are in a better position to take the lead in the relationship and in coordinating the entire channel effort. This situation calls for a **channel captain**—a manager who helps direct the activities of an entire channel and tries to avoid, or solve, channel conflicts.

The concept of a single channel captain is logical. But some traditional channels don't have a recognized captain. The various firms don't act as a coordinated system.

But like it or not, firms are interrelated—even if poorly—by their policies. So it makes sense to try to avoid channel conflicts by planning for channel relations. The channel captain arranges for the necessary functions to be performed in the most effective way.

Some producers lead their channels

In the United States, producers often take the lead in channel relations. Intermediaries often wait to see what the producer intends to do, and wants *them* to do. After marketing managers for L'eggs set Price, Promotion, and Place policies, wholesalers and retailers decide whether their roles will be profitable, and whether they want to join in the channel effort.

Some intermediaries are channel captains

The channel captains in Canada are more often large wholesalers or retailers. They analyze their customers' needs and then seek out producers who can provide products at reasonable prices. This is becoming more common in the United States, and it is already typical in many foreign markets. In Japan, for example, very large wholesalers (trading companies) are often the channel captains.

Most pet food companies focus on distribution through grocery stores, but Science Diet brand premium pet foods reach consumers in North America and Japan through a different channel—veterinary offices and pet stores. Because Science Diet has developed cooperative relationships with other members of this channel, Science Diet products often get special promotion support at the point of purchase.

Channel captains who are intermediaries often develop their own dealer brands. Large retailers like Sears and Zellers in effect act like producers. They specify the entire marketing mix for a product and then delegate production to a factory.

Intermediaries are closer to the final user or consumer and are in an ideal position to assume the channel captain role. Intermediaries—especially large retailers—may even dominate the marketing systems of the future.[8]

Vertical marketing systems focus on final customers

Many marketing managers accept the view that a coordinated channel system can help everyone in the channel. These managers are moving their firms away from traditional channel systems and are instead developing or joining vertical marketing systems.

Vertical marketing systems are channel systems in which the entire channel focuses on the same target market at the end of the channel. Such systems make sense—and are growing—because if the final customer doesn't buy the product, the entire channel suffers. There are three types of vertical marketing systems: corporate, administered, and contractual. Exhibit 11–5 summarizes some characteristics of these systems and compares them with traditional systems.

Corporate channel systems shorten channels

Some corporations develop their own vertical marketing systems by internal expansion and/or by buying other firms. With **corporate channel systems**—corporate ownership all along the channel—we might say the firm is going "direct." But actually the firm may be handling manufacturing, wholesaling, *and* retailing—so it's more accurate to think of the firm as a vertical marketing system.

Corporate channel systems often develop by **vertical integration**—the acquisition of firms at different levels of channel activity. Bridgestone, for example, has rubber plantations in Liberia, tire plants in Ohio, and wholesale and retail outlets all over the world.

Exhibit 11-5 Characteristics of Traditional and Vertical Marketing Systems

Characteristics	Type of channel			
		Vertical marketing systems		
	Traditional	Administered	Contractual	Corporate
Amount of cooperation	Little or none	Some to good	Fairly good to good	Complete
Control maintained by	None	Economic power and leadership	Contracts	Ownership by one company
Examples	Typical channel of "inde-pendents"	General Electric, Miller Beer, O.M. Scott & Sons (lawn products)	McDonald's, Holiday Inn, IGA, Home Hardware, Super Valu, Coca-Cola, Chevrolet	Florsheim Shoes, Sherwin-Williams

Vertical integration has many possible advantages: stable sources of supply, better control of distribution, better quality control, larger research facilities, greater buying power, and lower executive overhead. Provided that the discrepancies of quantity and assortment are not too great at each level in a channel—that is, that the firms fit together well—vertical integration can be extremely efficient and profitable. It can also benefit consumers through lower prices and better products.

Firms cooperate in administered and contractual systems

Firms can often gain the advantages of vertical integration without building an expensive corporate channel. A firm can develop *administered* or *contractual* channel systems instead. In **administered channel systems,** the channel members informally agree to cooperate with one another. They can agree to routinize ordering, standardize accounting, and coordinate promotion efforts. In **contractual channel systems,** the channel members agree by contract to cooperate with one another. With both of these systems, the members achieve some of the advantages of corporate integration while retaining some of the flexibility of a traditional channel system. In fact, opportunities to reduce costs and to provide customers with superior value are growing in these systems as new information technologies help channel partners share data to make products flow more efficiently through the channel.

For example, an appliance producer has developed an informal arrangement with the independent wholesalers in its administered channel system. It agrees to keep production and inventory levels in the system balanced by using sales data from the wholesalers. Every week, its managers do a thorough analysis of up to 130,000 major appliances located in the many warehouses operated by its 87 wholesalers. Because of this analysis, both the producer and the wholesalers can be confident that they have enough inventory but not the expense of too much. And the producer has better information for planning its manufacturing and marketing efforts.

Intermediaries in the grocery, hardware, and drug industries develop and coordinate similar systems. Computerized checkout systems track sales. The information is sent to the wholesaler's computer, which enters orders automatically when needed. This reduces buying and selling costs, inventory investment, and customer frustration with out-of-stock items throughout the channel.

Vertical marketing systems compete well

Smoothly operating channel systems are more efficient and successful. In the consumer products field, vertical systems have a healthy majority of retail sales and should continue to increase their share in the future. Vertical marketing systems are becoming the major competitive units in the Canadian distribution system, and are growing rapidly in other parts of the world as well.[9]

The best channel system should achieve ideal market exposure

You may think that all marketing managers want their products to have maximum exposure to potential customers. This isn't true. Some product classes require much less market exposure than others. **Ideal market exposure** makes a product available widely enough to satisfy target customers' needs but not exceed them. Too much exposure only increases the total cost of marketing.

Ideal exposure may be intensive, selective, or exclusive

Intensive distribution involves selling a product through all responsible and suitable wholesalers or retailers who will stock and/or sell the product. **Selective distribution** involves selling through only those intermediaries who will give the product special attention. **Exclusive distribution** involves selling through only one intermediary in a particular geographic area. As we move from intensive to exclusive distribution, we give up exposure in return for some other advantage, including, but not limited to, lower cost.

Sell it where they buy it

Intensive distribution is commonly needed for convenience products and business supplies. Customers want such products nearby.

The seller's intent is important here. Intensive distribution refers to the *desire* to sell through *all* responsible and suitable outlets. What this means depends on customer habits and preferences. If target customers normally buy a certain product at a certain type of outlet, ideally, you would specify this type of outlet in your Place policies. If customers prefer to buy Sharp portable TVs only at TV stores, you would try to sell all TV stores to achieve intensive distribution. Today, however, many customers buy small portable TVs at a variety of convenient outlets, including nearby drugstores, a local Kmart, or over the phone from the Sharper Image catalogue. This means that an intensive distribution policy requires use of all these outlets, and more than one channel, to reach one target market.

Sell it where it sells best

Selective distribution covers the broad area of market exposure between intensive and exclusive distribution. It may be suitable for all categories of products. Only the better intermediaries are used here. Companies usually use selective distribution to gain some of the advantages of exclusive distribution, while still achieving fairly widespread market coverage.

A selective policy might be used to avoid selling to wholesalers or retailers who (1) have a poor credit rating, (2) have a reputation for making too many returns, (3) place orders that are too small to justify making calls or providing service, or (4) are not in a position to do a satisfactory job.

Selective distribution is becoming more popular than intensive distribution, with more firms realizing they don't need 100 percent coverage of a market to justify or support national advertising. Often the majority of sales come from relatively few customers, and the others buy too little compared to the cost of working with them. That is, they are unprofitable to serve. This is "the 80/20 rule"—80 percent of a company's sales often come from only 20 percent of its customers *until the firm becomes more selective in choosing customers.*

Esprit, a producer of colourful, trendy clothing, was selling through about 4,000 department stores and specialty shops nationwide. But it found that about half of the stores generated most of its sales. Sales analysis also showed that sales in Esprit's own stores were about 400 percent better than sales in other sales outlets. As a result, Esprit cut back to about 2,000 outlets and opened more of its own stores—and profits increased.[10]

Selective distribution makes sense for shopping and specialty products and for those business products that need a special effort from channel members. Wholesalers and retailers are more willing to promote products aggressively when they know they're going to obtain the majority of sales through their own efforts. They may carry more stock and wider lines, do more promotion, and provide more service—all of which leads to more sales.

Exclusive distribution sometimes makes sense

Exclusive distribution is just an extreme case of selective distribution: the firm selects only one intermediary in each geographic area. Besides the various advantages of selective distribution, producers may want to use exclusive distribution to help control prices and the service offered in a channel. It's also attractive to intermediaries because they know they don't face local competition selling the same products.

But is limiting market exposure legal?

Marketing managers must operate within the law, and any consideration of Place must raise the question of the legality of limiting market exposure.

As long as there is no abuse of a dominant position, exclusive distribution as such isn't illegal in Canada. Indeed "vertical" exclusive distribution contracts between a manufacturer and an intermediary have never been successfully challenged in the courts. "Horizontal" arrangements among competing retailers, wholesalers, and/or manufacturers operating at the same level would almost certainly be judged a violation of the Competition Act. However, it would have to be proven that such agreements had "unduly lessened competition."

The Competition Tribunal has the authority to review vertical agreements and to act against those judged as having an adverse effect on competition. The 1975 amendments to the Combines Act (now called the Competition Act) also specified that "unduly lessening competition" meant lessening it to any extent judged detrimental to the public interest. (Previously, it had to be shown that competition would be completely or virtually eliminated.) However, the same amendments allowed temporary exclusive dealing arrangements in order to permit the introduction of a new product or where there is some technological justification for such a policy.

Consignment selling and refusal to supply

The Competition Tribunal can also bar **consignment selling** when such a policy is being used to (1) fix the price at which a dealer sells the products so supplied or (2) discriminate between those receiving the product for resale. Until this change was made, a supplier could control the selling price by dealing only on consignment and by specifying the commission level built into the ultimate price. Alternatively, a supplier could allow a favoured customer on consignment a larger commission than other customers.

The Tribunal can also help someone injured by a **refusal to supply.** This applies when a firm or individual is unable to obtain, on the usual terms, adequate supplies of an article or service not generally in short supply. This amendment doesn't make refusal to supply an offence in itself. However, a complaint concerning such practices can be brought to the Competition Tribunal. If the complaint is upheld, the Tribunal can order that one or more suppliers accept that customer on usual trade terms.

Channel systems can be complex

Trying to achieve the desired degree of market exposure can lead to complex channels of distribution. Firms may need different channels to reach different segments of a broad product-market, or to ensure they reach each segment.

Exhibit 11–6 shows the many channels used by a company that produces roofing shingles. It also shows (roughly) what percentage of the sales go to different channel members. Shingles are both consumer products (sold to do-it-yourselfers) and business products (sold to building contractors and roofing contractors). This helps explain why some channels develop. But note that the shingles go through different wholesalers and retailers: independent and chain lumberyards, hardware stores, and mass merchandisers. This can cause problems because different wholesalers and retailers want different markups. It also increases competition—including price competition. And the competition among different intermediaries may result in conflicts between the intermediaries and the producer.

Exhibit 11–6 Roofing Shingles Are Sold Through Many Kinds of Wholesalers and Retailers

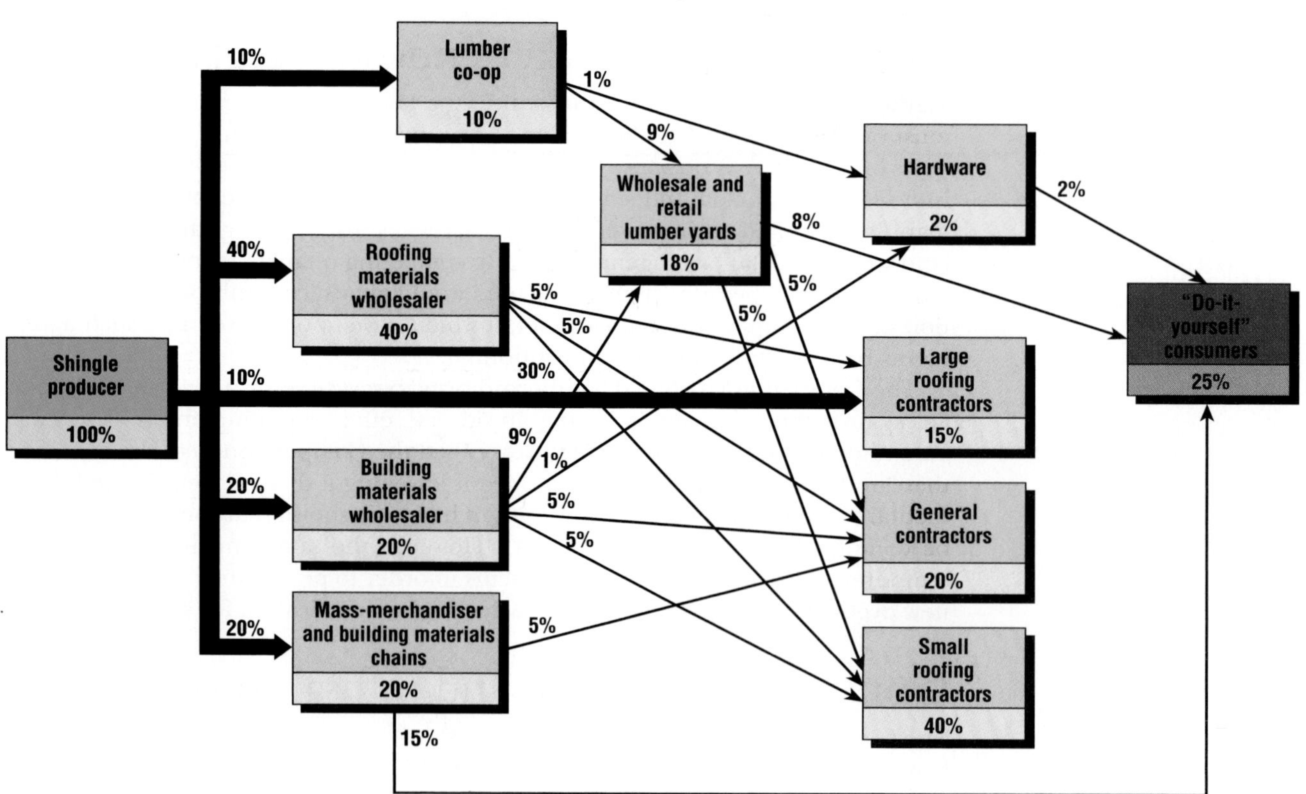

Dual distribution systems may be needed

Dual distribution involves a producer using several competing channels to reach the same target market—perhaps using several intermediaries in addition to selling directly. Dual distribution is becoming more common. Big retail chains want to deal directly with producers. They want large quantities and low prices. The producer sells directly to retail chains and relies on wholesalers to sell to smaller accounts. Some established intermediaries resent this because they don't appreciate *any* competition—especially price competition set up by their own suppliers.

Other times, producers are forced to use dual distribution because their present channels are doing a poor job or aren't reaching some potential customers. For example, Reebok International had been relying on local sporting goods stores to sell its shoes to high school and university athletic teams. But Reebok wasn't getting much of the business. When it set up its own team sales department to sell direct to the schools, it got a 30,000 unit increase in sales.[11]

Ethical Dimensions

Decision Making for Channel Issues

A shared product-market commitment guides cooperative relationships among channel members as long as the channel system is competitive. However, if customers' Place requirements change, the current channel system may lose its effectiveness. The changes required to serve customer needs may hurt one or more members of the channel. The most difficult ethical dilemmas in the channels area arise in situations like this—because not everyone can win.

For example, wholesalers and the independent retailers they serve in a channel of distribution may trust a producer channel captain to develop marketing strategies that will work for the whole channel. However, the producer may conclude that everyone in the channel will ultimately fail if it continues exclusive distribution. It may decide that consumers—and its own business—would be best served by a change (say, dropping current intermediaries and selling direct to big retail chains). A move of this sort, if implemented immediately, may not give current intermediaries a chance to make adjustments of their own. The more dependent they are on the producer, the more severe the impact will likely be. It's not easy to determine the best or most ethical solution in these situations. However, marketing managers must think carefully about the implications of strategy changes in the Place area, because they can have very severe consequences for other channel members. In channels, as in any business dealings, relationships of trust must be treated with care.[12]

Reverse channels should be planned

Most firms focus on getting products to their customers. But some marketing managers must also plan for **reverse channels**—channels used to retrieve products that customers no longer want. The need for reverse channels may arise because of product recalls, errors in completing orders, warranty work, or recycling needs (as with soft-drink bottles). And, of course, at some point or other, most consumers buy something in error and want to return it.

When marketing managers don't plan for reverse channels, the firm's customers may be left to solve "their" problem. That usually doesn't make sense. So a complete plan for Place may need to consider an efficient way to return products, with policies that different channel members agree on.[13]

Questions and Problems

1. Give two examples of service firms that work with other channel specialists to sell their products to final consumers. What marketing functions is the specialist providing in each case?
2. Discuss some reasons why a firm that produces installations might use direct distribution in its domestic market but use intermediaries to reach overseas customers.
3. Explain discrepancies of quantity and assortment, using the clothing business as an example. How does the application of these concepts change when selling steel to the automobile industry? What impact does this have on the number and kinds of marketing specialists required?
4. Explain the four regrouping activities, using an example from the building supply industry (nails, paint, flooring, plumbing fixtures, etc.). Do you think that many specialists develop in this industry, or do producers handle the job themselves? What kinds of marketing channels would you expect to find in this industry, and what functions would various channel members provide?
5. Insurance agents are intermediaries who help other members of the channel by providing information and handling the selling function. Does it make sense for an insurance agent to specialize and work exclusively with one insurance provider? Explain.
6. Discuss the Place objectives and distribution arrangements that are appropriate for the following products (indicate any special assumptions you have to make to obtain an answer):
   a. A postal scale for products weighing up to two pounds.
   b. Children's toys: (1) radio-controlled model airplanes costing $80 or more, (2) small rubber balls.
   c. Heavy-duty, rechargeable, battery-powered nut tighteners for factory production lines.
   d. Fibreglass fabric used in making roofing shingles.
7. Give an example of a producer that uses two or more different channels of distribution. Briefly discuss what problems this might cause.
8. Explain how a channel captain can help traditional independent firms compete with a corporate (integrated) channel system.
9. Find an example of vertical integration within your city. Are there any particular advantages to this vertical integration? If so, what are they? If there are no such advantages, how do you explain the integration?
10. What would happen if retailer-organized channels (either formally integrated or administered) dominated consumer product marketing?
11. How does the nature of the product relate to the degree of market exposure desired?
12. Why would intermediaries want to be exclusive distributors for a product? Why would producers want exclusive distribution? Would intermediaries be equally anxious to get exclusive distribution for any type of product? Explain, with reference to the following products: candy bars, batteries, golf clubs, golf balls, steak knives, televisions, industrial woodworking machinery.
13. Explain the present legal status of exclusive distribution. Describe a situation where exclusive distribution is almost sure to be legal. Describe the nature and size of competitors and the industry, as well as the nature of the exclusive arrangement. Would this exclusive arrangement be of any value to the producer or intermediary?
14. Discuss the promotion a new grocery-products producer would need in order to develop appropriate channels and move products through those channels. Would the nature of this job change for a new producer of dresses? How about for a new, small producer of installations?

Suggested cases

14 Dalton Olds, Inc.

26 Cutter's, Inc.

29 Parker Instruments Ltd.

Computer-aided problem

Intensive versus Selective Distribution

Hydropump, Inc., produces and sells high-quality pumps to business customers. Its marketing research shows a growing market for a similar type of pump aimed at final consumers, for use with Jacuzzi-style tubs in home remodelling jobs. Hydropump will have to develop new channels of distribution to reach this target market because most consumers rely on a retailer for advice about the combination of tub, pump, heater, and related plumbing fixtures they need. Hydropump's marketing manager, Robert Black, is trying to decide between intensive and selective distribution. With intensive distribution, he would try to sell through all the plumbing supply, bathroom fixture, and hot-tub retailers who will carry the pump. He estimates that about 5,600 suitable retailers would be willing to carry a new pump. With selective distribution, he would focus on about 280 of the best hot-tub dealers (two or three in the hundred largest metropolitan areas).

Intensive distribution would require Hydropump to do more mass selling—primarily advertising in home renovation magazines—to help stimulate consumer familiarity with the brand and convince retailers that Hydropump equipment will sell. The price to the retailer might have to be lower too (to permit a bigger markup) so they would be motivated to sell Hydropump rather than some other brand offering a smaller markup.

With intensive distribution, each Hydropump sales rep could probably handle about 300 retailers effectively. With selective distribution, each sales rep could handle only about 70 retailers because more merchandising help would be necessary. Managing the smaller sales force and fewer retailers—with the selective approach—would require less manager overhead cost.

Going to all suitable and available retailers would make the pump available through about 20 times as many retailers and have the potential of reaching more customers. However, many customers shop at more than one retailer before making a final choice—so selective distribution would reach almost as many potential customers. Furthermore, if Hydropump used selective distribution, it would get more in-store sales attention for its pump—and a larger share of pump purchases—at each retailer.

Black has decided to use a spreadsheet to analyze the benefits and costs of intensive versus selective distribution.

a. Based on the initial spreadsheet, which approach seems to be the most sensible for Hydropump? Explain.

b. A consultant points out that even selective distribution needs national promotion. If Black has to increase advertising and spend a total of $100,000 on mass selling to be able to recruit the retailers he wants for selective distribution, would selective or intensive distribution be more profitable?

c. With intensive distribution, how large a share (percent) of the retailers' total unit sales would Hydropump have to capture to sell enough pumps to earn $200,000 profit?

For additional questions related to this problem, see Exercise 11–3 in the *Learning Aid for Use with Basic Marketing*, Ninth Canadian Edition.

When you finish this chapter, you should:

- Understand why physical distribution (logistics) is such an important part of Place and strategic market planning.
- Understand why the physical distribution customer service level is a marketing strategy variable.
- Understand the physical distribution concept and why it requires coordination of storing, transporting, and related activities.
- Know about the advantages and disadvantages of the various transporting methods.
- Know how inventory decisions and storing affect marketing strategy.
- Understand the distribution centre concept.
- See how computers help improve coordination of physical distribution in channel systems.
- Understand the important new terms (shown in orange).

Chapter twelve

Logistics and Distribution

OVER SIBERIA—Captain Bob Sherrit lifts his eyes from the instrument cluster of the Boeing 747–400 and nods toward the cockpit windows. "We just entered Russian airspace," he says.

It is no big deal, the way he says it. But it is. Fifteen years ago a Korean Airlines jet, straying into Siberian air, was blasted out of the sky. Today, Canadian Airlines International pays a handsome fee to cut across both Russian and Chinese airspace. By doing so, it evades winter headwinds across the Pacific, getting Flight 7 from Vancouver to Hong Kong an hour earlier.

An hour is a precious thing, not just for the 400 passengers for whom the trip to Hong Kong is a multiple-meal, three-movie marathon, or for Canadian, which has calculated to the minute the $113,000 cost of operating one of the world's largest commercial airliners on this route.

There is also the cargo to consider. Thousands of kilograms of trade goods are loaded into containers or roped onto pallets, riding two levels down from the flight deck in a hold tall enough for a man to stand in.

Every touchdown of a 747 on the Hong Kong–Vancouver route is said to create almost a person-year's worth of employment, and much of that grows from the goods in its belly.

Freight—fish, flowers, dried geckos on a stick—is an unseen passenger on many, if not most of the 343,000 annual flights to and from Vancouver International, growing lock-step with an airport now employing more than 17,000. It is the difference between profit and loss on many routes.

Air cargo is the hypersensitive barometer of the impatient global economy. The Asian currency crisis, estimated to have trimmed a percentage point off B.C.'s economic activity, has also dimmed freight growth projections, but only in the short-term.

Global revenues for courier and cargo may double to $200 billion within 10 years, one study predicts. It is the air force of an economic ideology no one expects to change anytime soon: buy low there, sell high here, deliver anywhere—but only the instant it is paid for . . .

"The whole grease of international commerce and international trade and of high-speed globalization is air freight," says Dave Frank, managing director of the International Commercial Centre, part of Vancouver International's cargo village.

The village/travel agency for some 261,000 tonnes annually of such things as pest-eating lady bugs, iced human eyeballs, mushrooms, fruit salad and ceramic tile sprawls along the southern side of the airport's Miller Road. It is a windowless world of warehouses, air freighters and belly holds; of space and weight, of time and motion.

Everyone in the business has a favourite story. The jumbo jet loaded with pigs. The monkeys who broke out of their cages and into the passenger luggage. A human heart for transplant.

Walking through the village one day, Frank summed up its governing economic imperative: "Whenever a product is not moving, it is costing money. Period."

Today, in the morning hours before the 1:20 P.M. departure of Flight 7, the dominant product in Canadian's warehouse is seafood, bound for Hong Kong and other destinations. Thousands of kilograms of boxed farmed fresh salmon are headed for Hong Kong and Narita, Japan. Squeaking scratches emanate from two pallets of Styrofoam boxes filled with Cuban lobsters intent on escape. Vancouver, where they have spent a day rejuvenating in salt water tanks, is mid-way in their 60-hour race to the platters of Beijing's emerging upper-class . . .

The [return trip] waybills reflect the difference in the return trade: cartons of ladies' jackets for Downsview, shoes for Burlington, computer components for Markham, plastic toys for Montreal, Quartz watches, wallets, samples of next season's Christmas lights, Chinese magazines for Vancouver, books for Richmond, music discs for Surrey . . .

Source: Abridged from Ken MacQueen, "Trade That Shaped B.C. Soars into New Era: Wings of Commerce," *The Vancouver Sun,* March 14, 1998, A1, A14.

Physical distribution gets it to customers

The right channel of distribution is crucial in getting products to the target market's Place. Whenever the product includes a physical good, like the cargo in the Canadian Airlines International jet, Place requires physical distribution (PD) decisions. **Physical distribution** (PD) is the transporting and storing of goods to match target customers' needs with a firm's marketing mix, both within individual firms and along a channel of distribution. **Logistics** is another common name for physical distribution.

PD costs are very important both to firms and to consumers. PD costs vary from firm to firm and, from a macro-marketing perspective, from country to country. However, for many goods, firms spend half or more of their total marketing dollars on physical distribution activities. The total amount of money involved is so large that even small improvements in this area can have a big effect on an entire macro-marketing system—and consumers' quality of life. And there's room for improvement. For example, many supermarket chains and the producers that supply them are collaborating to develop a system, called efficient consumer response (ECR), that may eventually cut grocer's costs—and prices—by more than 11 percent. The basic idea of ECR involves paperless computerlinks between grocers and their suppliers. These links will lead to better merchandise assortments and to a continuous replenishment of shelves based on what actually sold each day. Obviously, this kind of innovation doesn't happen overnight, but you can see that more effective approaches to distribution have the potential to save firms—and their customers—massive amounts of money.[1] See Marketing Demo 12–1 for a more detailed discussion of efficient consumer response.

Physical distribution and customer service

From the beginning, we've emphasized that strategic market planning is based on meeting customers' needs. Planning for physical distribution and Place is no exception. So let's start by looking at PD through a customer's eyes.

Customers want products—not excuses

Customers don't care how a product was moved or stored, or what some channel member had to do to provide it. Rather, customers think in terms of the physical distribution **customer service level**—how rapidly and dependably a firm can deliver what they want. Marketing managers need to understand the customer's point of view.

What does this really mean? It means that Toyota wants to have enough windshields delivered to make cars *that* day—not late so that production stops *or* early so that there are a lot of extras to move around or store. It means that business executives who

Marketing Demo 12-1

What Is Efficient Consumer Response?

ECR, which stands for efficient consumer response, is an attempt on the part of the food industry as a whole to improve its distribution practices. ECR arose in the United States in 1993 in response to the grocery industry's concern over the new "category killers" entering their markets (e.g., Wal-Mart's Sam's Club, Price Club/Costco). Because of their superior logistics management skills and highly sophisticated information systems, these new competitors had a major advantage over the more traditional supermarket industry.

ECR is a business philosophy involving a partnership of manufacturers, wholesalers, and retailers. The basic premise is that today's information technology can and should be harnessed to the industry's logistical chain, with the goal of revamping the entire food distribution network, from plant to store shelves.

The term ECR is somewhat misleading, in that the concept relates to the members of the distribution supply network more than to the final consumers. This is not to suggest that consumers are not an integral part of ECR.

Data on consumer purchases are recorded at checkout counters. These point of sale scanner data enable category managers to track sales of individual brands. For example, ACNielson's HomeScan consumer panel of over 7,000 families provides much-needed consumer data to retailers and to other members of the channel.

The households on the HomeScan panel amount to a single-source data system. ACNielson already knows much about them, in terms of their demographics, the languages they speak, and the media they read, hear, and watch. ACNielson also knows the consumption patterns of each household on the panel, both by brands and across a large variety of product and service categories. In other words, the data provided by the panel reveal who uses what products how often. When combined with other available information (demographic, lifestyle, psychometric, and so on), a highly detailed profile emerges of over 7,000 consumer households.

Having blended all these various data, category managers can develop more astute store-level merchandising plans, and improve their buying practices. They can manage their shelf space better, and select SKUs more scientifically for each product category. For those who adopt it, ECR, used along with category management and Activity Based Costing, results in stronger sales, more efficient merchandising practices, and a general increase in productivity.

By managing its logistics more soundly, the grocery industry as a whole will become more responsive, flexible, and competitive—provided, of course, that its members adhere to ECR approaches. The use of new technologies such as computer-assisted ordering, electronic data interchange, universal product codes, and uniform vendor codes, will help rejuvenate this industry and revolutionize its business practices.

It is difficult for a single firm to coordinate its logistic activities among its various exchange partners. It is even harder for an entire industry to do so, especially when that industry is as complex as the food business.

The amount of work that is going to be necessary to coordinate logistics among all the many different members of the food distribution channel is simply awesome. Customer service standards and performance evaluations will need to be set according to members' requirements. The data collection processes will be expensive to put in place, but this cost will be more than justified by the benefits to the members of the supply chain, once their operations are standardized.

The various committees that have been established on both sides of the border show how committed the food industry is to doing more with less and to improving its efficiency. The resulting cost savings, which will amount to billions of dollars, are certain to result in lower food prices for consumers.

As many as 30 Canadian companies and seven industry associations are presently involved in implementing the ECR food distribution philosophy. These companies include National Grocers Co., the Oshawa Group, the Great Atlantic and Pacific Company of Canada, Nestlé Canada, Procter and Gamble, and Kraft Canada. Also involved are the Canadian Association of Drug Stores, the Food and Consumer Products Manufacturers of Canada, and the Canadian Council of Grocery Distributors.

ECR is not without its critics. The approach has some social implications. When one link in the logistical network breaks down, product availability may be seriously compromised. For example, a major strike by truckers in France showed just how interdependent logistical activities are under ECR. Because of the strike, consumers in certain markets were left with dangerously low levels of food. Others maintain that ECR is merely an attempt on the part of manufacturers to counterbalance the increasing dominance of retailers, who are demanding so much from them that brand equity and brand loyalty are suffering.

Whatever the rationale behind ECR, this new coordinated management approach to food distribution is bound to change the way the industry operates. Logistics management, as a means for cutting costs and improving performance, will become an increasingly important factor in the food industry.

*References: Kurt Salmon Associates, Inc. (1993), *Efficiency Consumer Response: Enhancing Consumer Value in the Grocery Industry,* Washington, D.C.: The Research Department, Food Marketing Institute.

Chain Store Age (1995), "The Grocery Industry and ECR," (November), pp. 92–4.

Ross, Dale (1996), "ECR Evolution," *Materials Management and Distribution,* (May).

Source: Marketing Demo 12–1 was written by Professor Robert D. Tamilia, University of Québec at Montréal (UQAM), for *Basic Marketing,* Ninth Canadian Edition.

rent cars from Tilden want them to be ready when they get off the plane. It means you want your Pringles potato chips to be whole when you buy them—not crushed into crumbs from rough handling in a warehouse.

Physical distribution is often invisible

PD is, and should be, a part of marketing that is "invisible" to most consumers. It only gets their attention when something goes wrong. At that point, it may be too late to do anything that will keep them happy.

In countries where physical distribution systems are inefficient, consumers face shortages and inconvenient waits for the products they need. In contrast, most consumers in the United States and Canada don't think much about physical distribution. This probably means that these market-directed macro-marketing systems work pretty well—that a lot of individual marketing managers have made good decisions in this area. But it doesn't mean that the decisions are always clear-cut or simple. In fact, many trade-offs may be required.

Trade-offs of costs, service, and sales

Most customers would prefer very good service at a very low price. But that combination is hard to provide because it usually costs more to provide higher levels of service. So most physical distribution decisions involve trade-offs between costs, the customer service level, and sales.

If you want a new Compaq computer and the computer store where you would like to buy it doesn't have it on hand, you're likely to buy it elsewhere. If that model Compaq is hard to get, you may just switch to some other brand. Perhaps the first store could keep your business by guaranteeing next-day delivery of your computer—by using special airfreight delivery from the factory. Here, the manager is trading the cost of storing a large inventory for the extra cost of speedy delivery—assuming that the computer is available in inventory *somewhere* in the channel. Missing one sale may not seem that important, but it all adds up. In fact, Compaq Computer estimates that it lost between $500 million and $1 billion in sales in 1994 because its computers weren't available when and where customers were ready to buy them.

Exhibit 12–1 illustrates trade-off relationships like those highlighted in the Compaq example. For example, faster but more expensive transportation may reduce the need for costly inventory of computers. There is also a trade-off between the service level and sales. If the service level is too low—if products are not available on a timely and dependable basis—customers will buy elsewhere, and sales will be lost. Alterna-

Exhibit 12–1 Trade-Offs Among Physical Distribution Costs, Customer Service Level, and Sales

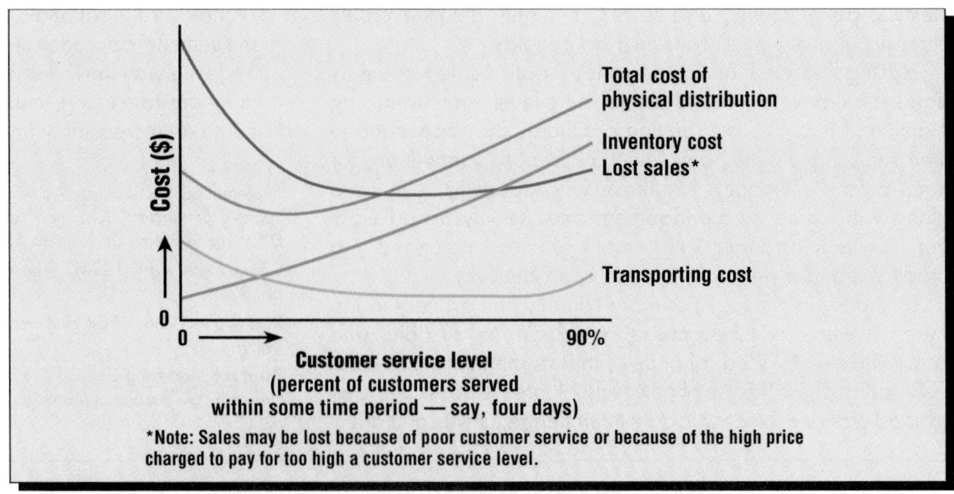

tively, the supplier may hope that a higher service level will attract more customers or motivate them to pay a higher price. But if the service level is higher than customers want or are willing to pay for, sales will be lost.

The important point is that many trade-offs must be made in the PD area. These trade-offs can be complicated. The lowest-cost approach may not be best if customers aren't satisfied. A higher service level may make a better strategy. Further, if different channel members or target markets want different customer service levels, several different strategies may be needed.[2]

Many firms are trying to address these complications by using information technology to improve service levels and cut costs at the same time. As you'll see, better information flows make it easier to coordinate the different activities and cut inefficiencies that don't add value for the customer.

Physical distribution concept focuses on the whole distribution system

The **physical distribution (PD) concept** reflects a belief that all transporting, storing, and product-handling activities of a business and a whole channel system should be coordinated as one system that seeks to minimize the cost of distribution for a given customer service level. Lower costs and better service help to increase customer value. It may be hard to see this as a startling development. But until just a few years ago, even the most progressive companies treated physical distribution functions as separate and unrelated activities.

Within a firm, responsibility for different distribution activities was spread among various departments—production, shipping, sales, warehousing, and others. No one person was responsible for coordinating storing and shipping decisions, or for seeing how they related to customer service levels. Some firms even failed to calculate the costs for these activities, so they never knew the *total* cost of physical distribution. If it was unusual for distribution to be coordinated within a firm, it was even rarer for different firms in the channel to collaborate. Each just did its own thing.[3]

Unfortunately, in too many firms old-fashioned ways persist, with a focus on individual functional activities rather than on the whole physical distribution system. Trying to reduce the cost of individual functional activities may actually increase total distribution costs, not just for the firm but for the whole channel. It may also lead to the wrong level of customer service. Well-run firms now avoid these problems by paying attention to the physical distribution concept.

Decide what service level to offer

With the physical distribution concept, firms work together to decide which aspects of service are most important to customers at the end of the channel, and which specific service level to provide. Then they search for the least expensive way to achieve the target level of service.

Exhibit 12–2 lists a variety of factors that may influence the customer service level (at each level in the channel). The most important aspects of customer service depend on target market needs. Xerox might focus on how long it takes to deliver copy machine repair parts once it receives an order. When a copier breaks down, customers want the repair "yesterday." The service level might be stated as follows: "We will deliver 90 percent of all emergency repair parts within 8 business hours, and the remainder within 24 hours." Such a service level might require that almost all such parts be kept in inventory, that the most commonly needed parts be available on the service truck, that order processing be very fast and accurate, and that parts not available locally be sent by airfreight. If Xerox doesn't make the part, it would need to be sent directly from Xerox's supplier. Obviously, supplying this service level will affect the total cost of the PD system. But it may also beat competitors who don't provide this service level.

Exhibit 12-2 Examples of Factors That Affect PD Service Level

- **Advance information on product availability**
- **Time to enter and process orders**
- **Back order procedures**
- **Where inventory is stored**
- **Accuracy in filling orders**
- **Damage in shipping, storing, and handling**
- **Order status information**
- **Advance information on delays**
- **Time needed to deliver an order**
- **Reliability in meeting delivery date**
- **Complying with customer's instructions**
- **Defect-free deliveries**
- **How needed adjustments are handled**
- **Procedures for handling returns**

In highly competitive situations where the firm has little else to differentiate its marketing mix, increasing service levels may be very profitable. Dow sells homogeneous basic chemicals that are also sold by many other suppliers. Increasing the service level—perhaps through faster delivery or wider stocks—may allow Dow to make headway in a market without changing Product, Price, or Promotion. Competitors may not realize what has happened, or that Dow's improved customer service level makes its marketing mix better.[4]

Find the lowest total cost for the right service level

The **total cost approach** involves evaluating each possible PD system and identifying *all* of the costs of each alternative. This approach uses the tools of cost accounting and economics. Costs that might otherwise be ignored, such as inventory carrying costs, are considered. The possible costs of lost sales due to a lower customer service level may also be considered. The following simple example clarifies why the total cost approach is important.

A cost comparison of alternative systems

The Good Earth Vegetable Company was shipping produce to distant markets by train. The cost of shipping a ton of vegetables by train averaged less than half the cost of airfreight, so the company assumed that rail was the best method. But then Good Earth managers did a more complete analysis. To their surprise, they found that the airfreight system was faster and cheaper.

Exhibit 12–3 compares the costs for the two distribution systems—airplane and railway. Because shipping by train was slow, Good Earth had to keep a large inventory in a warehouse to fill orders on time. And the company was also surprised at the extra cost of carrying the inventory in transit. Good Earth's managers also found that the cost of spoiled vegetables during shipment and storage in the warehouse was much higher when they used rail shipping.

In this case, total cost analysis showed that airfreight, while more costly by itself, provided better service than the conventional means—and at a lower total distribution cost. This case also illustrates why it is important to look beyond individual functional elements of PD and consider the costs and service level of an entire system. This broader focus should consider how the whole channel operates, not just individual firms.

Many firms are now applying this type of thinking to improve value to customers—and profits. For example, after two years of work with the total cost approach, National Semiconductor cut its standard delivery time in half, reduced distribution costs 2.5 percent, and increased sales by 34 percent. In the process, it shut down six warehouses around the globe and started to airfreight microchips to its worldwide customers from a new, 125,000 square foot distribution centre in Singapore. In advance of these changes, no one would have said that this was the obvious thing to do. But it proved to be the smart thing.

Exhibit 12-3 Comparative Costs of Airplane versus Rail and Warehouse

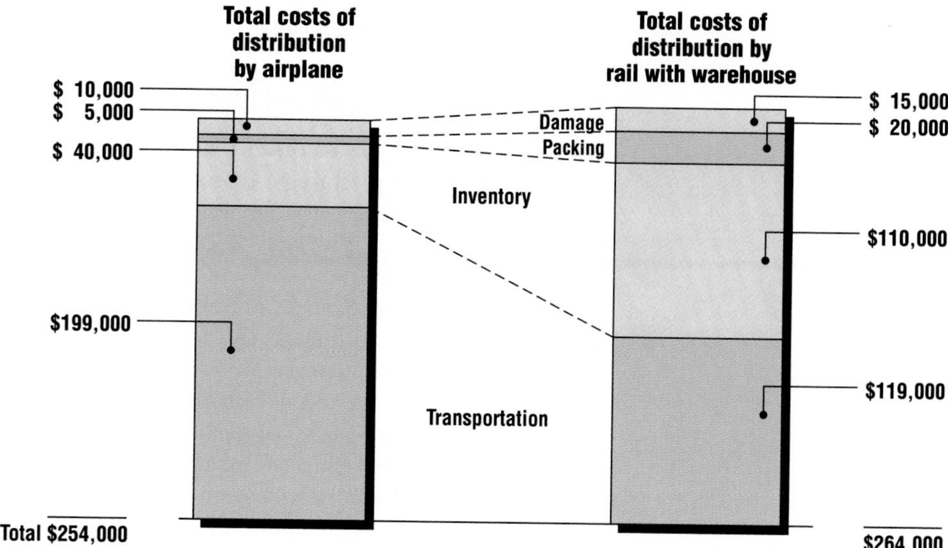

Identifying all the alternatives is sometimes difficult

It's important for firms to compare the costs and benefits of all practical PD alternatives, including how functions can be shared in the channel. Sometimes, however, there are so many possible combinations that it is difficult to consider each one thoroughly. For example, there may be hundreds of possible locations for a warehouse. And each location may require different combinations of transporting, storing, and handling costs. Some companies use computer simulation to compare the many possible alternatives. But typically, the straightforward total cost analysis discussed above is practical, and will show whether there is need for a more sophisticated analytical approach.[5]

Coordinating logistics activities among firms

As marketing managers develop the Place part of a strategy, it is important for them to decide how physical distribution functions can and should be divided within the channel. Who will store, handle, and transport the goods—and who will pay for these services? Who will coordinate all of the PD activities?

There is no "right" sharing arrangement. Physical distribution can be varied endlessly in a marketing mix and in a channel system. And competitors may share these functions in different ways, with different costs and results.

How PD is shared affects the rest of a strategy

How the PD functions are shared affects the other three Ps, especially Price. The sharing arrangement can make or break a strategy. Consider Channel Master, a firm that wanted to take advantage of the growing market for the dishlike antennas used by motels and other businesses to receive TV signals from satellites. The product looked like it could be a big success, but the small company didn't have the money to invest in a large inventory. So Channel Master decided to work only with wholesalers who were willing to buy (and pay for) several units, which would be used for demonstrations and to ensure that buyers got immediate delivery.

In the first few months, Channel Master earned $2 million in revenues simply by providing inventory for the channel. And the wholesalers paid the interest cost of carrying inventory—over $300,000 the first year. Here, the wholesalers agreed to share the risk of the new venture—but this was a good decision for them. They won many sales from a competing channel whose customers had to wait several months for delivery. And by getting off to a strong start, Channel Master became a market leader.

A coordinated effort reduces conflict

PD decisions interact with other Place decisions, the rest of the marketing mix, and the whole marketing strategy. If firms in the channel do not plan and coordinate how they will share PD activities, PD is likely to be a source of conflict rather than a basis for competitive advantage. Holly Farms' problems in introducing a new product illustrate this point.

Marketers at Holly Farms were encouraged when preroasted chicken performed well in a market test. But channel conflict surfaced when they moved to broader distribution. As with other perishable food products, the Holly Farms label indicated a date by which the chicken should be sold. Many grocers refused to buy the roast chicken because they were concerned that they had only a few days after it was delivered to sell it. They didn't want it to spoil—at their expense—on the shelf. They also didn't want to sell their customers something that wasn't fresh.

Shelf life had not been a problem with Holly Farms' raw chicken. It sold in higher volume and moved off shelves more quickly. The source of the problem with the roast chicken was that it took nine days to ship from the plant to distant stores. Coupled with slow turnover, that didn't leave grocers enough selling time. To address the problem, Holly Farms changed its transportation arrangements. It also developed new packaging that allowed grocers to store the chicken longer. Holly Farms also shifted its promotion budget to put more emphasis on in-store promotions to speed up sales once the chicken arrived. Having made these changes, Holly Farms was able to win cooperation in the channel and establish its product in the market.[6]

JIT requires a close, cooperative relationship

We introduced the concept of just-in-time (JIT) delivery in Chapter 7. Now that you know more about PD alternatives, it's useful to consider some of the strategic marketing implications of this approach.

A key advantage of JIT for business customers is that it reduces their PD costs—especially storing and handling costs. However, if the customer doesn't have any backup inventory, there's no "security blanket" if something goes wrong. If a supplier's delivery truck gets stuck in traffic, if there's an error in what's shipped, or if there are any quality problems when the products arrive, the customer's business stops. Thus, a JIT system requires that suppliers have extremely high quality control in production and in every PD activity, including PD service.

For example, to control the risk of transportation problems, JIT suppliers often locate their facilities close to important customers. Trucks may make smaller and more frequent deliveries—perhaps even several times a day. As this suggests, a JIT system usually requires a supplier to be able to respond to very short order lead times. In fact, a supplier's production often needs to be based on the customer's production schedule. If that isn't possible, the supplier must have adequate inventory to meet the customer's needs. Moreover, the supplier may in turn need better service from firms that it relies on for, say, raw materials or supplies.

You can see that the JIT system shifts greater responsibility for PD activities backward in the channel. If the supplier can be more efficient than the customer could be in controlling PD costs, and still provide the customer with the service level required, this approach can work well for everyone in the channel. However, it should be clear that JIT is not always the best or lowest cost approach. It may be better for a supplier to produce and ship in larger, more economical quantities, if the savings offset the distribution system's total inventory and handling costs.

While not every firm can or should use a just-in-time approach, it is an important idea. It focuses attention on the need to coordinate the PD system throughout the channel. It also highlights the value of close working relationships and effective communication between marketers and their customers. Whether or not a firm uses the JIT approach, good information is often the key to coordinating PD activities and improving the customer service level.[7]

Chain of supply may involve even more firms

In our discussion, we have taken the point of view of a marketing manager. This focuses on how logistics should be coordinated to meet the needs of customers at the end of the channel of distribution. Now, however, we should broaden the picture somewhat, because the relationships within the distribution channel are sometimes part of a broader network of relationships in the **chain of supply**—the complete set of firms and facilities and logistics activities involved in procuring materials, transforming them into intermediate or finished products, and distributing them to customers. For example, Toyota not only works with dealers and customers farther down its channel of distribution, but also coordinates its activities with those of the supplier firms from which it buys parts, supplies, and raw materials. In turn, those firms are linked to other suppliers who come even earlier in the chain of supply. What happens at each link along the chain can affect coordination farther down the chain. If the firm that produces seats for Toyota doesn't get the fabric from its supplier on time, the seats will be delayed en route to Toyota and the car will be slow getting to the dealer and consumer.

Ideally, all of the firms in the chain of supply should work together to meet the needs of the customer at the very end of the chain. That way, at each link along the chain the shifting and sharing of logistics functions and costs is handled to result in maximum value for the final customer. Further, all of the firms in the whole chain of supply are able to do a better job of competing against competitors who are involved in other chains of supply.

The practical reality is that coordination across the whole chain of supply doesn't always happen. The customer service level that a marketing manager needs to compete may not be possible if firms earlier in the chain of supply can't or won't do what is needed. In these situations the purchasing and manufacturing departments can't be expected to do the impossible. Resolving this sort of problem requires strategic decisions by the firm's top management. For example, the CEO may have to acquire and vertically integrate its own sources of supply. However, if that can't happen, the firm may need to change marketing strategies, and target markets where it has a better chance of competing.

Because of the challenges of coordinating logistics functions across the complete chain of supply, some firms have put a high- level executive in charge of chain-of-supply decisions. This person works with people in marketing, procurement, manufacturing, and other areas to find the best ways to address problems that arise. Yet it's still difficult for a manager in any one company to know what kind of logistics-sharing arrangement will work best, or even be possible, with a whole series of other companies. Because of that, many firms turn to outside experts for help. For example, there are now specialists who design computer systems that link all of the firms in a chain of supply. Similarly, there are consultants who use computer models to figure out the best locations for inventory, or the best way to shift logistics functions among firms.[8]

Better information helps coordinate PD

Coordinating all of the elements of PD has always been a challenge, even in a single firm. Trying to coordinate PD throughout the whole supply chain is even tougher. Keeping track of inventory levels, when to order, and where goods are when they move is complicated. Computers are becoming more and more important in finding solutions to these challenges.

Many firms now update their marketing information systems continuously so that they can immediately find out what products have sold, the level of the current inventory, and when goods being transported will arrive. And coordination of physical distribution decisions throughout channels of distribution continues to improve, with more and more firms able to have their computers "talk to each other" directly.

Ethical Dimensions

Ethical Issues in Physical Distribution

Most of the ethical issues that arise in the PD area concern communications about product availability. For example, some critics say that marketers too often take orders for products which are not available or which they cannot deliver as quickly as customers expect. Yet a marketing manager can't always know precisely how long it will take before a product will be available. It doesn't make sense for the marketer to lose a customer if it appears that he or she can satisfy the customer's needs. But the customer may be inconvenienced or face added cost if the marketer's best guess isn't accurate. Similarly, some critics suggest that stores too often run out of the products they promote to attract consumers to the store. Yet it may not be possible for the marketer to predict demand, or to know when placing an ad that deliveries won't arrive. Different people have different views about how a firm should handle such situations.

Some suppliers criticize customers for abusing efforts to coordinate PD activities in the channel. For example, some retailers hedge against uncertain demand by telling suppliers they plan to place an order, but then they don't *confirm* the order until the last minute. If sales in the store are slow, they want to be able to say that it wasn't an order in the first place. This shifts the uncertainty to the supplier and reduces the retailer's inventory costs. Is this unethical? Some think it is.

Electronic data interchange sets a standard

Until recently, differences in computer systems from one firm to another hampered the flow of information. Many firms are now attacking this problem by adopting **electronic data interchange (EDI)**—an approach that puts information in a standardized format easily shared between different computer systems. Purchase orders, shipping reports, and other paper documents are being replaced with computerized EDI. With EDI, a customer transmits its order information directly to the supplier's computer. The supplier's computer immediately processes the order, and schedules production, order assembly, and transportation. Inventory information is updated automatically, and status reports are available instantly. The supplier may then use EDI to send the updated information to the transportation provider's computer. This type of system is now very common. In fact, almost all international transportation firms rely on EDI links with their customers.[9]

This improved information flow and coordination affect other PD activities as well. Instantaneous order processing or the use of an EDI system or the Internet can have the same effect on the customer service level as faster, more expensive transportation. And knowing what a customer has in stock can improve a supplier's own inventory planning—and reduce costs in the whole channel.

Better coordination of PD activities is a key reason for the success of Pepperidge Farm's line of premium cookies. It was making the wrong products and delivering them—too slowly—to the wrong market. Poor information was the problem. Now the company has an almost instantaneous EDI link between sales, delivery, inventory, and production. Many of the company's 2,200 drivers use hand-held computers to record the inventory at each stop along their routes. They use the Internet to transmit the information into a computer at the bakeries, so that cookies in short supply will be produced. The right assortment of fresh cookies is quickly shipped to local markets, and delivery trucks are loaded with what retailers need that day. Pepperidge Farm now moves cookies from its bakeries to store shelves in about three days; most cookie producers take about ten days. That means fresher cookies for consumers, and helps support Pepperidge Farm's high-quality positioning and premium price.[10]

In summary, using computers to share information and coordinate activities is helping some firms and channels compete successfully for customers—and increase their own profits. Now that you see why the coordination of physical distribution activities is so important, let's take a closer look at some of the PD decision areas.

The transporting function adds value to a marketing strategy

Transporting is the marketing function of moving goods. Transportation provides time and place utilities—at a cost. Unless the cost is less than the value added to products by moving them, there is little reason to ship in the first place.

Transporting can help achieve economies of scale in production. If production costs can be reduced by producing larger quantities in one location, these savings may more than offset the added cost of transporting the finished products to customers. Without low-cost transportation, both within countries and internationally, there would be no mass distribution as we know it today.

Transporting can be costly

Transporting costs may limit the target markets a marketing manager can consider. Shipping costs increase delivered cost—and that's what really interests customers. Transport costs add little to the cost of products that are already valuable relative to their size and weight. But transporting costs can be a large part of the total cost for heavy products of low value—like many minerals and raw materials. Exhibit 12–4 shows transporting costs as a percentage of total sales dollars for several products.[11]

Governments may influence transportation

Governments often play an important role in the development of a country's transportation system, including its roads, harbours, railways, and airports. And different countries regulate transportation differently, although regulation has in general been decreasing.

Now you have more transporting choices

Today, most of the regulations governing transportation in Canada—and in many other countries—have been relaxed. For example, as part of their economic unification, most European countries are easing their transporting regulations. The construction of the tunnel under the English Channel is a dramatic example of the changes taking place. The "Chunnel" allows trains to speed between England and the rest of Europe.

Exhibit 12-4 Transporting Costs as a Percentage of Selling Price for Different Products

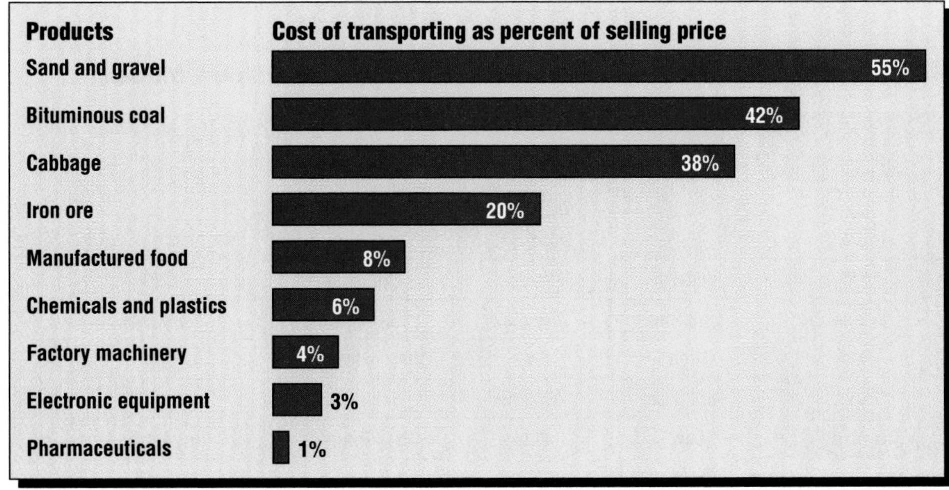

As regulations have decreased, competition in the transportation industry has increased. As a result, a marketing manager generally has many carriers in one or more modes competing for the firm's transporting business. Or a firm can do its own transporting. So knowing about the different modes is important.[12]

Which transporting alternative is best?

The transporting function should fit into the overall marketing strategy. But picking the best transporting alternative can be difficult. The "best" alternative depends on the product, on other physical distribution decisions, and on what service level the company wants to offer. The best alternative should be as low cost as possible, and should also provide the required level of service (e.g., speed and dependability). Exhibit 12–5 shows that different modes of transportation have different strengths and weaknesses. Cost is *not* the only criterion for selecting the best transportation mode. Marketing Demo 12–2 describes the services of a Canadian transportation company that assists shippers to find the best transportation mode.[13]

Railways—large loads at low cost

Railways are the workhorse of the Canadian transportation system. They carry more freight over more miles than any other mode. In Canada, as in other countries, they carry heavy and bulky goods—such as raw materials, steel, chemicals, cars, canned goods, and machines—over long distances. By handling large quantities, the railways are able to transport at relatively low cost.

Because railway freight moves more slowly than truck shipments, it is not as well suited for perishable items or those in urgent demand. Railways are most efficient at handling full carloads of goods. Less-than-carload (LCL) shipments take a lot of handling and rehandling, which means they usually move more slowly and at a higher price per pound than carload shipments.

Competition has forced railways to innovate

Railways earned low profits for many years, in part because trucks took a large share of the most profitable business. Now railways are cutting costs and improving services to improve profits. Reduced government regulation helped. Many railways merged to reduce overlap in equipment and routes. Others increased prices where competition from truck and water transport was weak.

Railways now cater to the needs of new target customers with a variety of specially designed railcars and services, ranging from double-decker railcars to computerized

Exhibit 12-5 Benefits and Limitations of Different Transport Modes

	Transporting Features					
Mode	Cost	Delivery speed	Number of locations served	Ability to handle a variety of goods	Frequency of scheduled shipments	Dependability in meeting schedules
Rail	Medium	Average	Extensive	High	Low	Medium
Water	Very low	Very slow	Limited	Very high	Very low	Medium
Truck	High	Fast	Very extensive	High	High	High
Air	Very high	Very fast	Extensive	Limited	High	High
Pipeline	Low	Slow	Very limited	Very limited	Medium	High

Marketing Demo 12-2

Wheels International Freight Systems Inc.

One of Canada's 50 Best Managed Private Companies for 1997

Location: Etobicoke, Ont.
Business: Trucking
Employees: 75
Annual Sales: $70 million

Just as there are contrarian investors, there are contrarian truckers.

Rather than build up its own fleet, Wheels International has created an organization without assets. "I wasn't in a position to inherit my father's company so we didn't have the assets my competition did," says president Doug Tozer. "We had to find another way."

Wheels International acts like a travel agent, working with customers to find the best transportation routes using any trucking company, airline or railway.

Unencumbered by costs, capital financing and driver selection, Wheels is a full service transportation company with annual growth rates averaging more than 30% since the firm was founded in 1988.

A highway division offers flat beds, refrigerated units, air ride, bulk trainers and containers. There is also intermodal, ocean freight forwarding and direct service to Mexico through the company's own facility in Laredo, Tex.

"We took over the customer's power by getting between them and whatever service they're using. Rather than have the assets, we had the stick of being able to pick which railway we used. I don't replace the carrier, I'm educating the shipper and bringing value to them."

Clients include Goodyear Tire & Rubber Co., Hudson's Bay Co., Canadian Tire Corp. and Quaker Oats Co.

"We have a blank piece of paper in front of us whenever we look at a project. The same fibre runs through every business: organizing and managing the best process. Sometimes we take on assets, but that means less time to focus on opportunity."

The company has 250 trailers, for example, but most are owner operated and under contract to Wheels.

"I tell my customers that I don't have to manage my own assets so I can be more flexible to manage what they want," Tozer says.

New technology has meant cost reductions. "The real savings in any transportation business is in handling the flow of information. Bills of lading can now all be processed with signature capture. Paperwork that used to be done 10 times at a cost of $200 can now be handled for 1/10th of that using signature capture."

Source: Rod McQueen, "Canada's 50 Best Managed Private Companies: Wheels International Freight Systems Inc.," *The Financial Post,* December 13, 1997, p. 47.

---

freight-tracking systems.[14] Intermodal transport is also becoming more common. CN has built a tunnel at Sarnia in order to serve the American market more efficiently.

To offset the shortcomings of low speed and high cost and still get business from small shippers, some railways encourage **pool car service,** which allows groups of shippers to pool their shipments of like goods into a full car. Sometimes, local retailers buying from a single area like Vancouver combine their shipments in single cars. Local truckers then deliver the goods when they arrive.

Another example of a special railway service is **diversion in transit,** which allows redirection of carloads already in transit. A Florida grower can ship a carload of oranges toward Canada as soon as they're ripe. While they head north, the grower can find a buyer or identify the market with the best price. Then—for a small fee—the railway will reroute the car to this destination.

Trucks—more expensive, but flexible

The flexibility of trucks makes them better at moving small quantities of goods for shorter distances. They can travel on almost any road. They go where the rails can't. That's why at least 75 percent of consumer products travel at least part of the way from producer to consumer by truck. And in countries with good highway systems, trucks can give extremely fast service. Truckers also compete with railways for high-value items.

Critics complain that trucks congest traffic and damage highways. But trucks are essential to our present macro-marketing system.[15]

SOME THINGS ARE WORTH THE WAIT.

YOUR DELIVERY ISN'T ONE OF THEM.

Whoever said "good things come to those who wait" never worked in the transportation business.

We're Epic Express, a new freight transportation company that's dedicated to total customer satisfaction, and eliminating the word "wait" from your business vocabulary.

This dedication to shippers in Ontario and Quebec is why we offer time-definite deliveries, where you set the delivery times yourself.

It's why we provide a superior tracking and tracing system, so you'll never have to wait for shipment information at any point in transit. And it's why we've assembled an experienced, customer-focused staff, ready to provide expedient solutions to your transportation needs.

At Epic Express, we're driven by ideas that will help your business become more competitive and more profitable. Don't wait. Call us today at 1-800-387-6759.

EPIC EXPRESS

A NEW ROAD IN TRANSPORTATION

Water transportation is slow—but it's very important for international shipments.

Ship it overseas—but slowly

Water transportation is the slowest shipping mode, but usually the lowest-cost way of shipping heavy freight. Water transportation is very important for international shipments and often the only practical approach. This explains why port cities like Halifax, Vancouver, Rotterdam, Osaka, and Singapore are important centres for international trade.

Inland waterways are important, too

Inland waterways such as the St. Lawrence Seaway in Canada and the Rhine and Danube in Europe are also important, especially for bulky, nonperishable products like iron ore, grain, steel, petroleum products, cement, gravel, sand, and coal. However, when winter ice closes freshwater harbours, alternative transportation must be used. Some shippers, such as those moving iron ore, ship their total annual supply during the summer months and store it near their production facilities for winter use. Here, low-cost transporting combined with storing reduces *total* cost.

Pipelines are used mainly by the petroleum industry

In Canada, pipelines carry all of the natural gas, most of the crude oil, and more than half of all the liquefied natural gas moving between processing plants and markets. Most of this pipeline runs from Alberta and Saskatchewan to eastern Canada and the United States. Oil pipeline companies are common carriers. They carry oil for a fixed charge, while in most cases gas pipeline companies own the gas being transported.[16]

Airfreight is expensive but fast and growing

The most expensive cargo transporting mode is airplane—but it is fast! Airfreight rates usually are at least twice as high as trucking rates, but the greater speed may offset the added cost. Trucks took the cream of the railways' traffic. Now airplanes are taking the cream of the cream.

High-value, low-weight goods—high-fashion clothing, parts for the electronics and metal-working industries, and so on—are often shipped by air. Airfreight is also creating new transporting business. As illustrated in the Canadian Airlines International example, which introduced this chapter, perishable products that previously could not be shipped are now being flown across continents and oceans. Flowers and bulbs from Holland, for example, are now jet-flown to points all over the world. Airfreight is also becoming very important for small emergency deliveries, such as repair parts, special orders, and business documents that must be somewhere the next day.

Airplanes may cut the total distribution cost

An important advantage of using airplanes is that the cost of packing, unpacking, and preparing the goods for sale may be reduced or eliminated. Planes may help a firm reduce inventory costs by eliminating outlying warehouses. Valuable by-products of airfreight's speed are less spoilage and damage and reduced theft. Although the *transporting* cost of air shipments may be higher, the *total* cost of distribution may be lower. More and more firms now realize this, and airfreight firms like DHL Worldwide Express, FedEx, Purolator, and Priority Courier are enjoying rapid growth.

These firms play an especially important role in the growth of international business. While the bulk of international cargo moves on ships, the speed of airfreight opens up global markets for many businesses that previously had only domestic opportunities. For example, DHL Worldwide Express offers 24-hour delivery service from Tokyo to Los Angeles, from New York to Rome, and from London to Chicago. For a firm whose products are valuable relative to their weight and size, the cost of air deliveries may seem trivial when compared to the sales potential of competing in new markets.[17]

Containers move between modes easily

We've described the modes separately, but products often move by several different modes and carriers during their journey. This is especially common for international shipments. Japanese firms such as Sony ship stereos to the United States, Canada, and Europe by boat. When they arrive at the dock, they are loaded on trains and sent across the continent. Then the units are delivered to a wholesaler by truck or rail.

Loading and unloading goods several times used to create real problems. Parts of a shipment would become separated or be damaged or stolen. And handling the goods, perhaps many times, raised costs and slowed delivery. Many of these problems have been reduced through **containerization**—the grouping of individual items into an economical shipping quantity and sealing them in protective containers for transit to the final destination. This protects the products and simplifies handling during shipping. Some containers are as large as truck bodies.

Piggyback—a ride on two or more modes

Piggyback service means loading truck trailers, or flatbed trailers carrying containers, on railcars to provide both speed and flexibility. Railways now pick up truck trailers at the producer's location, load them onto specially designed rail flatcars, and haul them as close to the customer as rail lines run. The trailers are then hooked up to a truck tractor and delivered to the buyer's door. Similar services are offered on oceangoing ships, which allows door-to-door service between cities around the world.

To better coordinate the flow of products between modes, transportation companies like CSX now offer customers a complete choice of different transportation modes. Then CSX, not the customer, figures out the best and lowest-cost way to shift and share transporting functions between the modes.[18]

Transportation choices also affect environmental costs

Marketing managers must be sensitive to the environmental effects of transportation decisions. Some say trucks cause air pollution in already crowded cities. People who live near airports suffer the consequences of noise pollution. A damaged pipeline can spew thousands of gallons of oil before it can be repaired. The *Exxon Valdez* oil spill in Alaska is a dramatic example of the kind of environmental disaster that can happen when a transportation accident occurs.

Many firms are taking steps to reduce these problems. For example, Conoco, a subsidiary of Du Pont, is building ships with double-hulls to reduce the risk of leaks. Some trucking and railway firms establish elaborate safety procedures for dealing with toxic cargo. Today, the public *expects* companies to manufacture, transport, sell, and dispose of products in an environmentally sound manner. If companies are environmentally unsafe, some consumers will show dissatisfaction through their market choices. However, these environmental efforts increase the cost of distribution.[19]

Economies of scale in transporting

Most transporting rates—the prices charged for transporting—are based on the idea that large quantities of a good can be shipped at a lower transport cost per pound than small quantities. Whether a furniture truck delivers one sofa or a full carload, the furniture company still has to pay for the driver, the truck, the gas, and other expenses like insurance.

Transporters often give much lower rates for quantities that make efficient use of their transport facilities. Thus, transport costs per pound for less-than-full carloads or truckloads are often twice as high as for full loads. These quantity rate differences are a big reason why some wholesalers exist at all. They buy in large quantities to get the advantage of economies of scale in transporting. Then they sell in the smaller quantities their customers need.

Freight forwarders accumulate economical shipping quantities

Freight forwarders combine the small shipments of many shippers into more economical shipping quantities. Freight forwarders do not own their own transporting facilities, except perhaps for delivery trucks. Rather, they wholesale air, ship,

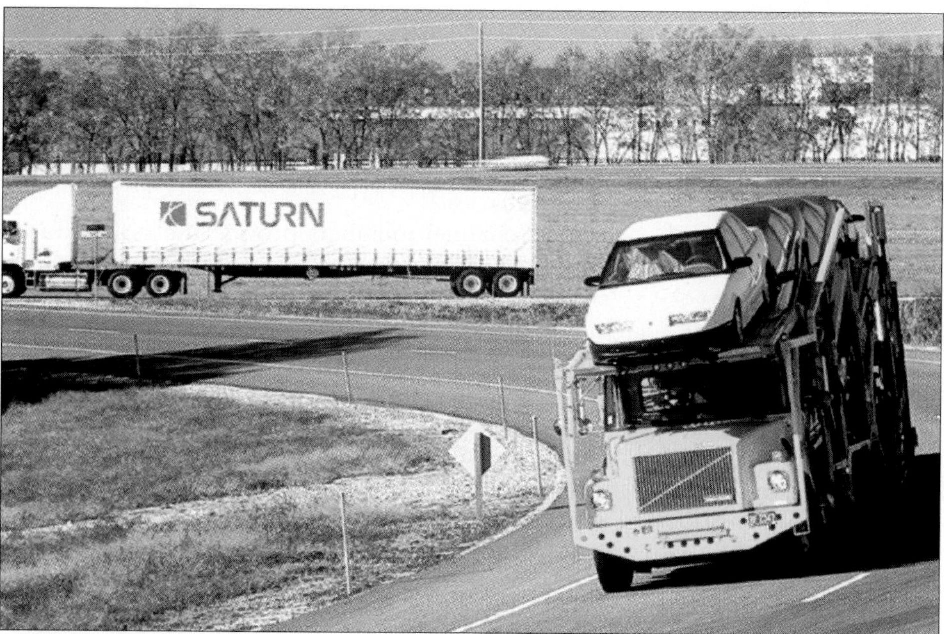

Many firms have their own truck fleets, but Saturn decided it was better to develop a close relationship with Ryder, a supplier of transportation services. Ryder helped design Saturn's state-of-the-art system for just-in-time delivery of components to the assembly line—and it also transports finished cars to dealers.

rail, and truck space. They accumulate small shipments from many shippers and reship in larger quantities to obtain lower transporting rates.

Freight forwarders are especially useful in arranging international shipping. They handle a large percentage of the general cargo shipped from Canadian ports to foreign countries. They are also very helpful for handling international airfreight. For example, Air Express International specializes in helping marketing managers find the most efficient air cargo firm to speed deliveries around the world.[20]

Should you do it yourself?

To cut transporting costs, some marketing managers do their own transporting rather than buy from specialists. Large producers, such as Levi Strauss, often buy or lease their own truck fleets. Shell Oil and other large petroleum, iron ore, and gypsum rock producers have their own ships. Some firms now buy their own planes for airfreight.[21]

The storing function and marketing strategy

Storing is the marketing function of holding goods. It provides time utility. **Inventory** is the amount of goods being stored.

Having products on hand when customers want them may make the difference between a satisfied customer and a lost sale. Yet deciding on the right inventory level is difficult when it's hard to forecast likely demand. A firm that is stocked out when its customers are ready to buy may not only lose the sale but also create a dissatisfied customer and damage the relationship and the possibility of future sales. Kmart ran into this problem. A number of consumers decided it was no longer a convenient place to shop when stores repeatedly ran out of basic staples that consumers expected to find.

Storing is necessary when production of goods doesn't match consumption. This is common with mass production. Nippon Steel, for example, might produce thousands of steel bars of one size before changing the machines to produce another size. Changing the production line can be costly and time-consuming. It's often cheaper to produce large quantities of one size—and store the unsold quantity—than to have shorter production runs. In this way, storing goods allows the producer to achieve economies of scale in production.

Storing varies the channel system

Storing allows producers and intermediaries to keep stocks at convenient locations, ready to meet customers' needs. In fact, storing is one of the major activities of some intermediaries.

Most channel members provide the storing function for some length of time. Even final consumers store some things for their future needs.

Which channel members store the product, and for how long, affects the behaviour of all channel members. For example, the producer of Snapper lawn mowers tries to get wholesalers to inventory a wide selection of its machines. That way, retailers can carry smaller inventories, since they can be sure of dependable local supplies. And they may decide to sell Snapper, rather than Toro or some other brand that they would have to store at their own expense.

If final customers "store" the product, more of it may be used or consumed. Coke wants customers to buy sixpacks and 2-litre bottles. Then consumers have an "inventory" in the refrigerator when thirst hits. Of course, consumers aren't always willing or able to hold the inventory. In China, for example, Coke had little success until it gave up pushing 2-litre bottles and switched to single-serving 75 ml bottles. Only 1 out of 10 Chinese families has a refrigerator, so they didn't have a good way to store a bottle once it was open.

Goods are stored at a cost

Storing can increase the value of goods, but *storing always involves costs* too. Car dealers, for example, must store cars on their lots while they wait for the right customer. The interest expense of money tied up in the inventory is a major cost. In addition, if a new car on the lot is dented or scratched, there is a repair cost. If a car isn't sold before the new models come out, its value drops. There is also a risk of fire or theft, so the retailer must carry insurance. And, of course, dealers incur the cost of the display lot where they store the cars.

In today's competitive markets, most firms watch their inventories closely. The total direct and indirect costs of unnecessary inventory can make the difference between a profitable strategy and a loser. On the other hand, a marketing manager must be very careful in making the distinction between unnecessary inventory and inventory that may be needed to provide the kind of service customers expect.[22]

Rapid response cuts inventory costs

Many firms are finding that they can cut inventory costs and still provide the desired customer service, if they can reduce the time it takes to replace items that are sold. This is one important reason why the JIT and ECR approaches we discussed earlier in the chapter have been widely adopted. These approaches work because the firms involved use EDI, the Internet, and similar computerized approaches to share information and speed up the order cycle and delivery process.

Rapid replenishment of inventories is not the only reason inventory costs have been reduced. Firms that use the information from JIT and ECR systems often can see benefits to dropping some of the items they stock and sell. P&G is a vivid example. Between 1991 and 1996 it introduced many new products, but cut its total number of SKUs (individual stock-keeping units) by 34 percent. P&G hasn't stopped selling bar soap, but it has cut the number of sizes and colours for some of its brands. After the cuts, sales of the remaining products went up and costs came down. With fewer products, P&G can put more marketing effort behind those it has kept, and its customer-retailers are more willing to push products that turn over quickly. Reducing the number of SKUs does reduce consumer choice, but there is a point where additional choice doesn't add enough value for consumers to justify the extra expense—including the higher inventory costs.[23]

Specialized storing facilities can be very helpful

Specialized storing facilities may reduce costs and serve customers better.

Private warehouses are common

Private warehouses are storing facilities owned or leased by companies for their own use. Most manufacturers, wholesalers, and retailers have some storing facilities either in their main buildings or in a warehouse district.

Firms use private warehouses when a large volume of goods must be stored regularly. Private warehouses can be expensive, however. If the need changes, the extra space may be hard, if not impossible, to rent to others.

Public warehouses fill special needs

Public warehouses are independent storing facilities. They can provide all the services that a company's own warehouse can provide. A company may choose a public warehouse if it doesn't have a year-long need for space. For example, Tonka Toys

Exhibit 12-6 A Comparison of Private Warehouses and Public Warehouses

Characteristics	Type of warehouse	
	Private	Public
Fixed Investment	Very high	No fixed investment
Unit cost	High if volume is low Very low if volume is very high	Low: charges are made only for space needed
Control	High	Low managerial control
Adequacy for product line	Highly adequate	May not be convenient
Flexibility	Low: fixed costs have already been committed	High: easy to end arrangement

uses public warehouses because its business is seasonal. Tonka pays for the space only when it is used. Public warehouses are also useful for manufacturers who must maintain stocks in many locations, including foreign countries. See Exhibit 12–6 for a comparison of private and public warehouses.[24]

The right facilities cut handling costs

The cost of physical handling is a major storing cost. To reduce these costs, modern one-storey buildings away from downtown traffic are replacing the old multistory warehouses. They eliminate the need for elevators, and permit the use of power-operated lift trucks, battery-operated motor scooters, roller-skating order pickers, electric hoists for heavy items, and hydraulic ramps to speed loading and unloading. Most of these new warehouses use lift trucks and pallets (wooden trays that carry many cases) for vertical storage and better use of space. Computers monitor inventory, order needed stock, and track storing and shipping costs. Some warehouses even have computer-controlled order picking systems that speed the process of locating and assembling the assortment required to fill an order.[25]

The distribution centre—a different kind of warehouse

Is storing really needed?

Discrepancies of assortment or quantity between one channel level and another are often adjusted at the place where goods are stored. It reduces handling costs to regroup and store at the same place—*if both functions are required.* But sometimes regrouping is required when storing isn't.

Don't store it, distribute it

A **distribution centre** is a special kind of warehouse designed to speed the flow of goods and avoid unnecessary storing costs. Anchor Hocking moves over a million pounds of its housewares products through its distribution centre each day. Faster inventory turnover and easier bulk-breaking reduce the costs of carrying inventory. This is important; as mentioned earlier, these costs may run as high as 40 percent of the value of the average inventory each year. The lower costs and faster turnover lead to bigger profits.

Today, the distribution centre concept is widely used by firms at all channel levels. Many products buzz through a distribution centre without ever sitting on a shelf; workers and equipment immediately sort the products as they come in and then move them to an outgoing loading dock and the vehicle that will take them to their next stop. While these "cross-docking" approaches have become more efficient, the basic benefits of the distribution centre approach are still the same as they were over 25 years ago when the idea was pioneered. A good way to see how the distribution centre works is to consider an early application.

Pillsbury's overwhelmed distribution system

Pillsbury, the manufacturer of baking products, used to ship in carload quantities directly from its factories to large intermediaries. Initially, plants were as close to customers as possible, and each plant produced the whole Pillsbury line. As lines expanded, however, no single plant could produce all the various products. When customers began to ask for mixed carload shipments and faster delivery, Pillsbury added warehouse space and started hauling goods from plant to plant.

Over time, Pillsbury set up 100 branch warehouses controlled by 33 sales offices. Accounting, credit, and other processing operations were duplicated in each sales office. PD costs were high, but the customer service level was still a problem. It took Pillsbury a week just to process an order. And the company had no effective control over its inventories. Pillsbury needed to change to distribution centres.

The distribution centre brings it all together

Pillsbury first specialized production at each plant to a few product lines. Then Pillsbury sent carload shipments directly to the distribution centres, which almost eliminated storing at the factories. The distribution centres were controlled by four regional data processing centres, which quickly determined where and when goods were to be shipped. Centralized accounting got invoices to customers faster, resulting in quicker payment. Because each distribution centre always had adequate inventory, it could ship orders the most economical way. And because the field sales organization no longer handled physical distribution or inventory, it could focus on sales. Pillsbury could guarantee customers delivery within three days.

There are many variations of the distribution centre. The Pillsbury example shows it within an integrated operation. But public warehouses offer similar services.

McKesson is a leading distributor of drugs, and effective use of technology has been a key reason for its success. The space age gizmo on this man's arm combines a scanner, a computer, and a two-way radio, to speed up order assembly and delivery from McKesson's distribution centre.

Managers must be innovative to provide superior value

More competitive markets, improved technology (see Internet Insite 12–1), coordination among firms, and efficient new distribution centres are bringing big improvements to the PD area. Yet, the biggest challenges may be more basic. As we've emphasized here, physical distribution activities transcend departmental, corporate, and even national boundaries. So seeing and taking advantage of the opportunities for improvement often requires cooperation all along the channel system. Too often, such cooperation doesn't exist—and changing ingrained ways of doing things is hard. But marketing managers who push for innovations in these areas are likely to win customers away from firms, and from whole channel systems, that are stuck on doing things in the old way.[26]

Internet Insite 12-1

Electronic Commerce and Supply Chain Management

Individual consumers who shop online may place orders for a few items. Traditional retailers who have recently migrated to the world of electronic commerce have quickly realized that they are not set up to process and ship individual orders. Rather, theirs is a world of palletized delivery. Consumer product companies are also accustomed to bulk distribution, which gives them economies of scale.

Most retailers who have invested heavily in traditional distribution infrastructure have Internet order processing systems that are separate from their current distribution systems. According to AC-Nielsen, only about 4 percent of Canadians have shopped online (www.acnielsen.ca). This low volume of Internet shopping makes it difficult to plan distribution models that provide efficiency and lower costs.

As retailers and manufacturers search for answers to their distribution dilemmas, new online companies that specialize in delivery and order fulfilment are emerging. For example, NetGrocer (www.netgrocer.com) specializes in the delivery of grocery and other products. You can select what you want on screen, from a wide variety of products and brand names. For a small fee, the items are then delivered to you at home. NetGrocer claims that its prices are 20 percent lower than supermarket prices!

Manufacturers and retailers who go online have three choices in terms of reaching the consumer.[1] The most common seems to be "third-party distribution." This involves delivery of online orders through Federal Express, UPS, or even Canada Post. Online retailers such as JC Penney (www.jcpenney.com) use this method. This approach is usually used for high-value merchandise. Some online manufacturers and retailers prefer "accumulation distribution." Accumulation distributors collect low-value merchandise from many manufacturers and retailers and deliver the products to Internet shoppers. NetGrocer is one such distributor. Conventional distributors and wholesalers, who have warehouse space and technology, can also take on this role. Lastly, it is also possible to have "hybrid distribution," whereby low-value items are shipped through accumulation distributors and high-value items are shipped through third-party providers.[2]

Internet order fulfilment is expensive. Most established firms that have recently moved online are not equipped to handle order fulfilment. Many are sensibly outsourcing this activity. Even so, electronic commerce does offer considerable scope for cost reductions in the fulfilment area. It allows for paperless transactions. In many cases these transactions are fully automated. A customer service representative is not required to take the online order. Direct benefits include lower operating costs and improved customer service. NetGrocer, for example, will deliver products from different suppliers through Federal Express, and will then allow the consumer to track the shipment online!

Advances in Internet technologies will increasingly allow linkages between manufacturers/distributors and their customers and suppliers. As electronic commerce increases, the rules of distribution are rapidly being rewritten.[3]

1. "Solving The Fulfillment Issue," Ernst & Young Internet Shopping Survey (www.e&y.com).
2. Ibid.
3. "Internet Offers Potential to Improve Supply Chain Integration" (www.gt.com/gtonline/mandist/)

Source: This is one of a series of Internet Insites prepared in April 1998 by Dr. Ramesh Venkat of Saint Mary's University for *Basic Marketing,* Ninth Canadian Edition.

Questions and Problems

1. Explain how adjusting the customer service level could improve a marketing mix. Illustrate.
2. Briefly explain which aspects of customer service you think would be most important for a producer that sells fabric to a firm that manufactures furniture.
3. Briefly describe a purchase you made where the customer service level had an effect on the product you selected or where you purchased it.
4. Discuss the types of trade-offs involved in PD costs, service levels, and sales.
5. Explain the total cost approach and why it may be controversial in some firms. Give examples of how conflicts might occur between different departments.
6. Discuss the relative advantages and disadvantages of railways, trucks, and airlines as transporting methods.
7. Discuss some of the ways that air transportation can change other aspects of a Place system.
8. Indicate the nearest location where you would expect to find large storage facilities. What kinds of products would be stored there? Why are they stored there instead of some other place?
9. When would a producer or intermediary find it desirable to use a public warehouse rather than a private warehouse? Illustrate, using a specific product or situation.
10. Differentiate between a warehouse and a distribution centre. Explain how a specific product would be handled differently by each.
11. Discuss some of the ways that computers are being used to improve PD decisions.
12. Explain why a just-in-time delivery system would require a supplier to pay attention to quality control. Give an example to illustrate your points.
13. Discuss the problems a supplier might encounter in using a just-in-time delivery system with a customer in a foreign country.

Suggested cases

15 Lucas Foods

22 Kelman Mfg. Inc.

30 Le Clair Chemical Company

Computer-aided problem

Total Distribution Cost

Proto Company has been producing various items made of plastic. It recently added a line of plain plastic cards that other firms (such as banks and retail stores) will imprint to produce credit cards. Proto offers its customers the plastic cards in different colours, but they all sell for $40 per box of 1,000. Tom Phillips, Proto's product manager for this line, is considering two possible physical distribution systems. He estimates that if Proto uses airfreight, transportation costs will be $7.50 a box, and its cost of carrying inventory will be 5 percent of total annual sales dollars. Alternatively, Proto could ship by rail for $2 a box. But rail transport will require renting space at four regional warehouses—at $26,000 a year each. Inventory carrying cost with this system will be 10 percent of total annual sales dollars. Phillips prepared a spreadsheet to compare the cost of the two alternative physical distribution systems.

a. If Proto Company expects to sell 20,000 boxes a year, what are the total physical distribution costs for each of the systems?

b. If Phillips can negotiate cheaper warehouse space for the rail option so that each warehouse costs only $20,000 per year, which physical distribution system has the lowest overall cost?

c. Proto's finance manager predicts that interest rates are likely to be lower during the next marketing plan year and suggests that Tom Phillips use inventory carrying costs of 4 percent for airfreight and 7.5 percent for railways (with warehouse cost at $20,000 each). If interest rates are in fact lower, which alternative would you suggest? Why?

For additional questions related to this problem, see Exercise 12–3 in the *Learning Aid for Use with Basic Marketing*, Ninth Canadian Edition.

When you finish this chapter, you should:

- Understand the importance of retailing as a sector of the Canadian economy.
- Know how producers and wholesalers view retailers as members of the channel of distribution.
- See why belonging to a chain or a buying group can be important to a retailer.
- Understand how retailers should plan their marketing strategies.
- Know how technology and globalization are having an impact on retailing.
- Know the various kinds of merchant wholesalers and agent middlemen and the strategies they use.
- Know what progressive wholesalers are doing to modernize their operations and marketing strategies.
- Understand the important new terms (shown in orange).

Chap thirteen

Retailers, Wholesalers, and Strategic Planning*

*The retailing section of this chapter draws very heavily from material previously written for *Basic Marketing*, Eighth Canadian Edition, by Professors Paulette Padanyi and Margaret Sutcliffe of Ryerson Polytechnic University.

Ever wonder why foreign chains such as IKEA, the Body Shop plc and the Gap Inc. can walk right into Canada and grab a huge bite of the retail market? Indeed, the number of foreign operators in Canada has jumped dramatically in the past decade. Since 1985, there has been a fivefold increase in the number of major U.S. retailers operating in Canada, according to a research report conducted by Ryerson Polytechnic University's Centre for the Study of Commercial Activity. Meanwhile, only a few of Canada's top retailers have attempted to expand outside our national boundaries. Yet according to the Ryerson report, released in late 1996: "Canadian retailers must consider international expansion, or face diminishing profits in their home market in the long-term." What's more, the report suggests that "the best opportunities for international expansion exist now."

Michael Budman doesn't need to be reminded of this urgency. The hyperenergetic co-owner of Roots Canada Ltd. has been pursuing growth outside the country aggressively ever since he and his partner, Don Green, founded their integrated clothing company 23 years ago. Although Budman thinks there's room for more stores inside Canada—Roots already boasts 95 outlets across the country—he's got his sights on some of the world's biggest consumer markets. Roots now has half a dozen stores in the U.S. and 15 franchises in Asia . . .

Budman and Green have taken Roots a long way since the introduction of its first product—the weird-looking "negative heel" shoe—24 years ago. Roots now sells everything from mouse pads to expensive leather furniture and has recently branched out into the highly profitable world of trendy licensed products, including watches, bottled fragrances and eye-wear. Annual revenue now exceeds $100 million, and Budman figures that sales could double within five years, especially if the company pursues its expansionist agenda in the U.S.

Fundamentally, however, Roots is still the same company Budman and Green established back in 1973 with some personal savings and a $20,000 loan from Green's dad. Although they are now "seriously considering" taking Roots public, the two men are committed to maintaining its "core values," which reflect a personal attachment to Canada. Although Budman and Green are both natives of Detroit, they spent many childhood summers camping out in Ontario's Algonquin Provincial Park. The Canadian wilderness still forms the backbone of Roots' marketing image, particularly in Asia, where the company's products are increasingly popular. "Asians are enamored with our rugged, natural environment," Budman says. "They like that shtick." The Canadian angle may be pure gimmick, but 95% of the items sold in Roots stores are manufactured in this country. That translates into hundreds of well-paying jobs that might otherwise be farmed out to Third World sweatshops.

The fact is, Roots is not a typical retail outfit—as Budman never fails to point out. "We have our own culture. We've always been completely accountable for the products we sell. We manage our own factories, monitor working conditions, sign the cheques. We live and die by our brand." Apparently, Budman lives in his brand as well. Today, he's decked out in a black Roots turtleneck and vest. His son is similarly attired. Wife Diane is proudly sporting a blue Roots cap.

If ever there was a company focused on "lifestyle," it's got to be Roots. "That's a very prominent niche, and Roots really caters to it," says retail analyst Strapagiel. "The lifestyle market has not been encroached upon by the big-box stores." Although Strapagiel warns that consumers may be starting to cut back on "extra" items such as clothing, another school of thought insists that casual clothing retailers are in for many years of solid growth. According to the Retail Council of Canada, office workers will be dressing casual 50% of the time by the year 2000. It's a style Budman has been promoting all his working life. ●

Source: Brian Hutchinson, "Merchants of Boom: Roots Canada Ltd." *Canadian Business,* May 1997, pp. 46–48. Reprinted by permission of *Canadian Business.*

Wholesalers and retailers plan their own strategies

In Chapter 11, we discussed the role that wholesalers and retailers play as members in channel systems. In this chapter, we'll focus on the main questions that retailers and wholesalers must consider in developing their own strategies.

We'll start with the strategies used by different types of retailers and how they are evolving. Understanding how and why retailing changes will help you know what to expect in the future. Then, we'll consider the different types of wholesalers and how they meet the needs of their suppliers and customers.

The nature of retailing

Retailing covers all of the activities involved in selling goods and services to final consumers for nonbusiness use. The term *retailer* is applied to businesses whose primary function is to sell products to consumers for their personal use. Producers or wholesalers who deal directly with final consumers can be said to be engaged in retailing. However, they would not generally be called retailers because retailing is not their *primary* function.

Retailers come in all sizes

Retailers vary significantly in size. They range from large chains like Loblaw's to the company that stocks the vending machines in your student centre to the woman who sells knitted wear at a local crafts market. The total number of sales transactions handled at the retail level is much greater than the number handled at other channel levels. As a result, retailing is a very labour-intensive business. In Canada, over 1.3 million people are employed in retailing, mostly at the counter sales and supervisory levels.[1]

Retailing involves many small sales transactions

Retailing is also a very competitive business, with about 225,000 outlets fighting for the close to $250 billion (that's $250,000,000,000) a year that Canadian consumers spend on goods and services.[2] Thousands of these retailers go out of business each year. Nothing does more to highlight the competitiveness of Canadian retailing than the fact that the Eaton's chain, a long-established retailing landmark, very nearly went bankrupt in early 1997. Also, a faltering Woolworth chain in Canada was sold to Wal-Mart, and more recently, The Hudson's Bay Company purchased K-Mart's money-losing Canadian stores. The Bay closed some 40 of these outlets while merging the rest of K-Mart with the Zellers chain it also owns.

Retailing is very competitive

The influx of international megastores will make Canadian retailing even more competitive over the next few years. This will require increased emphasis on sophisticated management techniques. The old adage, "If the retailing effort isn't effective,

Weekly supermarket flyers vie for consumers' attention.

everyone in the channel suffers—and some products aren't sold at all," will become even truer in the next few decades.[3]

Retailers must deal with both producers and consumers

Retail management can be looked at from two perspectives—the way that marketing-oriented producers relate to retailers, and the way that marketing-oriented retailers must view themselves if they are to succeed in a highly competitive environment. You will be presented with both perspectives in the next two sections. Then, we will discuss the impact of technology and globalization on retailing, and what to expect in the future.

The retailer as a distributor of goods

From the standpoint of a goods producer–marketer like Procter & Gamble, retailers are the last link in an *indirect* channel of distribution to the final consumer. Selection of the right number and type of retailers is critical to achieving the producer's strategic place objectives. Choosing the right number affects the *degree of market exposure desired*—intensive, selective, or exclusive distribution. Choosing the right type affects the *channel management and control needed to execute marketing plans;* it has an impact on the breadth and depth of the product line's distribution, on the type of product knowledge/assistance that will be provided to consumers by the retailer's staff, and on how consistent the line's pricing and promotion will be with the producer's marketing plans.

Scrambled merchandising—problems and opportunities

Selection of the retailers to use in a channel of distribution is not easy. There are about 225,000 retail stores in Canada, including food stores, drugstores, florists, hardware stores, and so on.

Even though we commonly call them "food stores" or "drugstores" or "florists," and so on, many retail outlets are moving toward "scrambled merchandising"—carrying any product line they think they can sell profitably. This is making it increasingly difficult for producers to choose the retailers with which they should deal. However, it is also providing more opportunities for producers to reach their potential customers. And scrambled merchandising can result in a competitive advantage for those producers who are able to keep ahead of competition in seeking out retailers who are willing to broaden their existing product assortments. See Marketing Demo 13–1 for an example of how "traditional" grocery retailers have lost sales to other types of retailers also selling groceries.

Marketing Demo 13-1

The Worst of Times for Grocers

It was a horrific year for the grocery industry in Canada. Total sales of grocery products in 1996 actually declined by 3.2%, the first decline in 45 years of tracking by the industry magazine *Canadian Grocer*.

Sales at chain supermarkets, including major banner convenience stores, declined by 0.5%. But independents took a whopping 6.7% hit. Ontario and Quebec were hit the hardest, with overall sales declines of 6.0% and 7.9%, respectively. (Quebec also suffered the loss of 142 franchise independents and 533 unaffiliated independents.)

The lost sales at traditional grocers appear to be going to alternative-format stores that now sell groceries. These include warehouse club stores (especially in Quebec, Ontario, Alberta and B.C.), mass merchandisers, drug stores and all the other non-traditional grocery outlets where consumers can buy food products today.

While it is true that the total dollar sales of grocery product through alternative formats are not known, it is known that sales through warehouse club stores, mass merchandisers, drug stores and so on represent about 19.6% of total grocery volume in Canada. This means those outlets account for a minimum of $10.6 billion of the estimated $64-billion total universe of grocery sales. Traditional grocery store sales account for $48.3 billion, and department stores and "all others" make up the remaining $4.7 billion.

Quebec and Ontario have been the hardest hit by warehouse club stores. As of August 1996, PriceCostco had 14 outlets in Quebec and 17 in Ontario. In addition, grocery sales through warehouse clubs and other non-traditional retailers are growing rapidly.

Since 1990, when these types of stores had 11.4% of the Quebec market in grocery products, they have now grown to represent 20.4%. In Ontario in 1990, they had captured 12%. Today they have 21%. In Alberta, they have 17.5%, and in B.C., the third province where traditional grocery store sales declined last year, nontraditional retailers have captured a very significant 22.5% of the grocery market.

With very few exceptions, those corporate grocery giants that did manage to show reasonable sales gains last year did it by purchasing competitors, building larger stores to replace existing ones and opening new stores in areas where they were not previously strong players.

The sector's future looks like it will bring more of the same—flat sales, more store closings and a very, very tough marketplace. Only the very best, and the toughest, are assured success.

Source: George Condon, *Marketing Magazine*, May 26, 1997, p. 12. Excerpted from *Canadian Grocer*.

Select retailers with the right image

Selection of retail outlets for a channel of distribution must also take into account that retailers access consumers in a variety of different ways. Retailers can be located in highly planned regional shopping centres in the suburbs or they can be part of unplanned clusters of stores at major urban intersections. They can be stand-alone operations on side streets in small towns or they can reach consumers through in-home methods not involving stores at all. Ideally, a producer wants to be aligned with retailers that will reinforce and enhance that producer's product positioning.

Chains—the most efficient retailers for producers

Acquiring their own retailing outlets might strike you as an easy way for producers to achieve their Place objectives. This type of vertical integration has been achieved by Hallmark Cards. However, most small to medium-sized producers, such as Clairol and Irwin Toys, and many large producers, such as Kraft–General Foods and Lever Brothers, lack either the financial means or the retail management expertise to undertake vertical integration. These firms tend to gravitate toward chains as their primary distribution outlets. They do so because selling products to chains is very efficient. Producers can obtain large orders and maximize the number of consumers their products reach while making relatively few sales calls on retail headquarters. The chains benefit because their large orders qualify for maximum volume dis-

Exhibit 13-1 Canada's Billion-Dollar Retailers, 1996–97, Sales and Net Income (in 000,000's)

RANK	ORGANIZATION	SALES	NET INCOME
1.	George Weston Ltd.	12,709.0	239.0
2.	Loblaw Cos.	9,847.5	173.7
3.	Oshawa Group Ltd.	6,383.5	55.2
4.	Hudson's Bay Co.	6,007.2	36.1
5.	Provigo	5,832.5	38.8
6.	Canada Safeway Ltd.	4,733.7	157.4
7.	Sears Canada Inc.	3,955.9	34.3
8.	Canadian Tire Corp Ltd.	3,907.9	131.9
9.	Zellers Inc.	3,578.5	116.4
10.	Westfair Foods Ltd.	3,352.9	90.6
11.	Metro-Richelieu, Inc.	3,266.0	61.0
12.	Empire Co. Ltd.	2,915.2	42.1
13.	Price Costco Canada Inc.	2,702.0	N/A
14.	Great A&P Tea Co. Canada Ltd.	2,372.3	N/A
15.	Westburne Inc.	2,080.6	37.7
16.	Brewer's Retail Inc.	2,060.2	N/A
17.	Liquor Control Board of Ontario	1,909.8	666.7
18.	Hudon & Deaudelan Ltee	1,797.0	N/A
19.	McDonald's Restaurants of Canada Ltd.	1,740.3	N/A
20.	T. Eaton Co. Ltd.	1,672.1	(92.5)
21.	Jean Coutu Group (PJC) Inc.	1,614.2	46.4
22.	Société des Alcools du Québec	1,312.0	350.9
23.	Future Shop Ltd.	1,303.8	17.2
24.	Dylex Ltd.	1,236.0	22.9

Source: Based on *Canadian Business* "Performance 500," June 1997, pp. 135–87.

counts. As a result of this mutually beneficial relationship between producers and large retailers, chains dominate the Canadian retail landscape. See Exhibit 13–1 for more data on Canada's largest retailers.

Different types of chains exist

There are several different types of chains to which producers can sell. Most of Canada's major retail firms are **corporate chains.** Statistics Canada defines a corporate chain as "an organization operating four or more retail outlets in the same kind of business, under the same legal ownership." Corporate retail chains usually deal directly with producer-marketers. They sometimes charge producers fees for initially agreeing to carry their products. These chains are major marketers who make their own Product, Price, Place, and Promotion decisions.[4]

Competitive pressure arising from the buying efficiency of corporate chains has encouraged the development of both cooperative chains and voluntary chains. **Cooperative chains** are retailer-sponsored groups, formed by independent retailers, that run their own buying organizations and conduct joint promotion efforts. Sales of cooperative chains are rising as they are learning how to compete with corporate chains. Examples of co-op chains include Associated Grocers, Certified Grocers, and Home Hardware. **Voluntary chains** are wholesaler-sponsored groups that work with independent retailers. Some are linked by contracts stating common operating procedures and requiring the use of common storefront designs, store names, and joint promotion efforts. Examples include IGA and SuperValu.

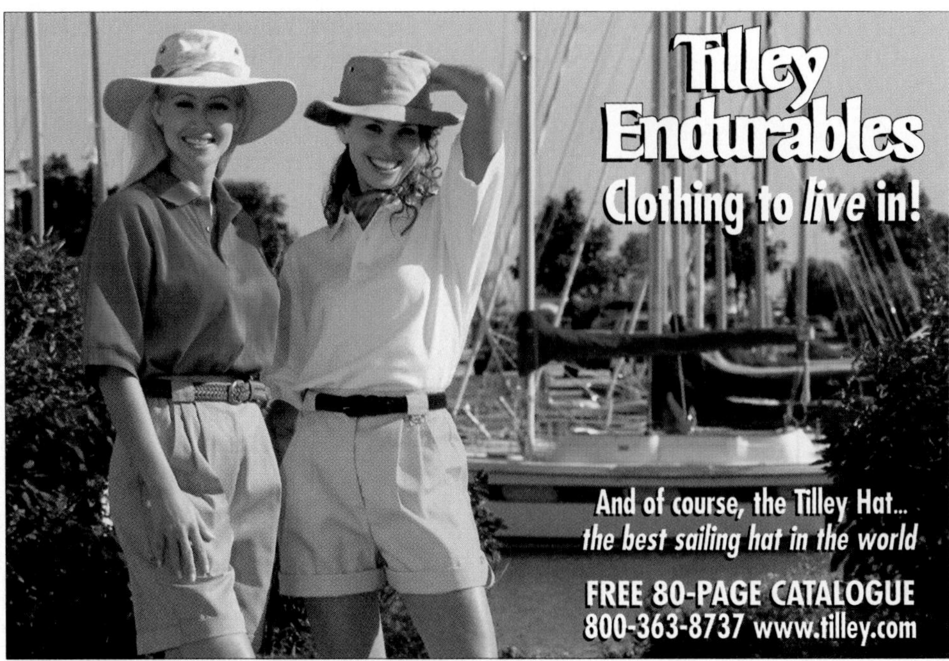

Catalogue sales to time-strapped consumers are increasing.

Franchisers form chains, too

Franchise operations are another means for retailers to group together to compete with chains and offer efficient product distribution to producers. In a franchise operation, the franchiser develops a good marketing strategy, which the retail franchise holders then carry out in their own units. The largest and best established retail franchise operation in Canada is Canadian Tire. Each franchise holder benefits from the relationship with the franchiser and its experience, buying power, and image. In return, the franchise holder usually signs a contract to pay fees and commissions, and to strictly follow franchise rules designed to continue the successful strategy.[5]

Independent retailers are underutilized

Producers seek out many different types of retail chains or buying groups to include in their channels of distribution. But what about using small, independent retailers who have not affiliated themselves in any way with other operations? With the notable exception of the fashion/apparel industry, both large and small producer-marketers usually deal indirectly with independent retail operations through wholesalers. Wholesaling intermediaries (discussed later in this chapter) help them find appropriate small retailers to carry their product lines, and provide local warehousing and sales assistance as needed. However, for most producers independent retailers represent a small portion of sales—on average, less than 25 percent. Therefore, they are generally given the least consideration among the retail alternatives facing producers.

An interesting untapped opportunity could involve smaller producers linking directly with independent retailers. Such linkups could be a viable way to develop innovative, customized products. These products could differentiate smaller producers and retailers from larger ones, allowing the smaller players to survive the many changes that are occurring in the retail industry.

Nonstore retailing is another option

Other potential retail operations with which producers can link up are not even store-based. Some of these options, such as catalogue selling, door-to-door selling, and automatic vending, have existed for many years.

Catalogue selling originated in the nineteenth century as a way to serve rural customers but is now used to reach time-strapped urbanites. Catalogues are mailed to potential or previous customers' homes. Purchase orders are mailed back to the retailer for handling.

Door-to-door selling is on the decline in Canada because more adults are working outside the home and it's getting harder to find someone at home during the day. However, some firms continue to use this method of distribution.

Automatic vending—selling and delivering products through vending machines—is becoming more popular because more and more consumers appreciate their convenience. The major disadvantage with automatic vending is the higher retail prices that must be charged for producers' branded items. Since machines are expensive to buy, stock, and repair relative to the volume they sell, the vending industry must charge higher prices. However, as costs come down—and as consumers' desire for convenience rises—we will see more growth in this method of retailing. Automatic bank teller machines are examples of how technology is changing automatic vending.[6]

Direct-mail and **television retailing** are becoming more popular, especially for dual-career families. Typically, consumers see the offerings through flyers delivered to their homes or in ads on TV. They mail in or phone in their orders to a vendor, charging their purchases to a credit card. Most experts think that the coming explosion in the number of available cable channels—and interactive cable services—will greatly increase television retailing.[7]

Retailing on the Internet

Wal-Mart now sells from a Web site, and one could view that development as just another aspect of how low-margin mass merchandisers are trying to appeal to a large target market with wide (or deep) assortments of products at discount prices. Or one might view the Internet as just another way to provide convenient in-home shopping, with an electronic catalogue on a remote computer. After all, that's the way most people saw earlier dial-up systems such as Prodigy—a joint venture between Sears and IBM that fizzled because it was too complicated.

All types of retailers are now establishing a presence on the Internet. This has the potential, over time, to dramatically reshape many aspects of retail selling. So rather than just treating it as a new way that some types of retailers are varying their old strategies, let's look at the Internet in terms of what it is likely to become—something that is *really* different.

It's still in its infancy

Don't confuse the "big bang" that the Internet may have on retailing (and consumer shopping behaviour) with the reality of its immediate economic impact on the retail system. So far, that impact is pretty limited. In 1997 consumers worldwide spent about US$2.7 billion on the Internet. To put that in perspective, it took about 3 percent of Wal-Mart's stores to rack up the same sales. Looking ahead, retail sales on the Internet are expected to grow to only about US$8 billion by 2002. So in absolute dollars, retailing on the Internet is in its infancy. However, it has the potential to grow very rapidly in both sales and impact. Taking these two vantage points in combination, it's useful to consider what's different about it today and how it will evolve.

Product assortments are not limited by location

As we noted earlier, traditional thinking about retailing looks at product assortments from the perspective of location and shopping convenience. On the Internet, by contrast, a consumer can get to a very wide assortment—perhaps from different sellers—by clicking from one Web site to the next. The assortment moves toward being unlimited.

Convenience takes on new meanings

The Internet makes it very convenient to shop, but is very inconvenient in other ways. You have to plan ahead. When you buy something on the Internet, you don't have it to hold. Someone has to deliver it, and that involves delays and costs.

Surfing around the Internet is convenient for people who are facile with computers, but many consumers are not. It should be no surprise that the majority of retail dollars spent via the Internet so far are for computer-related stuff. That target market visits the Internet store. But many people don't.

It is expected, however, that access to the Internet will evolve quickly. Cable operators and telephone companies are in a race with other firms, and new technologies are being developed all the time. Web TV already makes it easy, but it is just the start. Costs will continue to come down, and within a decade the majority of Canadian homes will have some sort of access to the Internet.

More and less information at the same time

On the Web, a consumer can't touch a product or really inspect it. For many products, consumers want to be able to do that, or at least they're used to doing it. On the other hand, a consumer in a retail store often finds it hard to get any information, to say nothing about good information. At a Web site it's often possible to get much more information with just a mouse click, even though only the product and a brief description are presented on the initial page.

It's also possible to access a much broader array of information. Ziff-Davis Publishing, for example, has a comprehensive Web site (www.zdnet.com) with product reviews, feature comparisons, performance tests, and other data on every computer-related product imaginable. Similar sites are being developed for everything from automobiles to vitamins. Better information will make many consumers better shoppers, even if they buy in a store rather than online.

More powerful computers are also opening up many more possibilities for multimedia information—not just pictures but full-motion product demo videos and audio explanations. Also, the Internet is quickly turning into a medium for video conferencing. It's predicted that by 2002 about 11 percent of all long-distance calls will be handled over the Internet. So it is likely that in the near future, consumers will not only be able to get computer-provided help during a visit to a Web site, but also help from a real person.

Lost in the "aisles" of the Internet

If you know what you want, and it's one thing, you can usually find it fast on the Internet. You can look for "Revo sunglasses" with a search engine and get a list of sellers and see pictures of every style made. It's quick and easy. If you don't know exactly what you're looking for, however, you may get too much information or the wrong information. It's hard to narrow a search when you don't know what you're looking for. Clearly, for the appeal of Internet retailing to spread there will need to be better "virtual malls"—databases with lots of information that can be viewed in lots of ways. This will make it easier for customers to get the information they want and to avoid the clutter that is, at best, irrelevant.

How fast and how soon?

All forms of traditional retailing could be seriously affected by the rapid development of **electronic commerce,** a term used to describe the exchange of valuable information, goods, and services that occurs between connected computers. However, it is impossible at this time to predict just how important that form of retailing will become. A very significant volume of sales will be made online by 2005. But will such sales account for 2, 5, 10, or 20 percent, or even more, of total Canadian retail sales? And will most of this business be done primarily by conventional retailers who add home pages, or will it be done primarily by new organizations selling through electronic malls?

Will sales through the Internet turn out to be additional business for mail order retailers, or will most of these purchases be made by customers who would otherwise have ordered by mail? How fast will consumers get over their current reluctance to send credit card information over the Internet? How many Canadians either will not be able to afford Internet access or will refuse to make any purchases online? How many consumers enjoy "going shopping" and will see no reason to give up a pleasurable experience? These are some of the important retailing questions that will be answered over the next few years. For further discussion of some of these issues, see Internet Insite 13–1.

The retailer as a strategic manager

Retailers are not simply outlets through which producers can access their final consumers. Retail operations are also competitive businesses that must be strategically managed to achieve both short-term customer satisfaction and long-term customer loyalty. In North America, the recognition that stores are products in themselves (and not just a collection of producers' products) has led many retailers to question whether their suppliers (i.e., their wholesalers and producers) should be in charge of the channels of distribution. This, in turn, has encouraged established retailers to use the strategic market planning process to become much more aggressive in managing their own businesses.[8]

Often, among small retailers, the motive for getting into retailing is "to be my own boss!"[9] The approach taken is to set up a store that carries products that the new entrepreneur likes or that provides services he or she personally needs. This production-oriented approach is one of the key reasons why about three-fourths of all new retailing ventures fail during their first year. Small retailers must also use the strategic marketing planning process.[10]

Organizations such as the Retail Council of Canada, Ernst & Young, and Morris Saffer Advertising are trying to help both large and small retailers switch their decision making from being tactical to being strategic in nature.[11]

Retailers must understand their markets

To be successful, retailers must know the size of the "trading area(s)" (the market or markets) in which they wish to operate. They must assess whether the population and income of the area(s) can support another outlet with the type of goods or services they plan to offer. They must analyze the growth trend in their market(s), recognizing that in North America, population and disposable incomes are not increasing very much. This, along with the fact that many consumers have now maxed out their credit, means that new businesses should assume that their revenue will have to come from competitors' business.

Retailers must analyze their marketing environment

Retailers must also understand their marketing environment. Many municipal, provincial, and federal laws and regulations have an impact on retail operations. Furthermore, local "culture" and outside factors such as tourism can affect decisions such as store hours. Most importantly, retailers must be familiar with the business strategies of direct and indirect competitors in their trading area(s).

Having drawn on such information, retailers can develop target market, positioning, and marketing mix strategies that can provide them with a competitive advantage. In terms of marketing planning, note well that successful retailers such as Benetton do not try to be all things to all people. They have developed loyal customer bases because they have provided their stores with distinct target markets and images.

Internet Insite 13-1

Issues in Online Retailing

The Internet is fast emerging as a shopping channel with unquestionable advantages both to online retailers and to consumers. Even though only 4 percent of Canadians have made online purchases so far (see www.acnielsen.ca), the potential is enormous. This conclusion is well supported by a research study done by Ernst & Young (www.ey.com).

Several traditional retailers such as Wal-Mart (www.wal-mart.com) and J.C. Penney's (www.jcpenney.com) currently offer full-fledged online shopping Web sites. Others, such as The Bay (www.hudsonsbay.com) and Eaton's (www.eatons.com) offer limited online services at present. Some of the major traditional retailers have yet to establish a significant online presence.

Low consumer confidence regarding the security of online transactions has so far hampered the growth of online retailing. But that may change soon. Two recent developments may reduce consumer fears about fraud in online transactions. First, Visa and Mastercard, along with American Express, have established a "single technical standard" for safeguarding credit card purchases over the Internet called Secure Electronic Transaction (SET™) (see www.setco.com). Second, the Canadian Institute of Charted Accountants (www.cica.ca) has established a set of principles and guidelines to address business-to-consumer transactions on the Internet. These guidelines, named WebTrust™, are aimed at alleviating consumer concerns about the security of electronic transactions. An online retailer who follows the WebTrust™ guidelines and SET™ standards can display these logos on its Web site, and thus gain consumer confidence.

While some traditional retailers have been uncertain how to integrate the Web into their marketing strategy, Internet-only retailers such as Amazon.Com (www.amazon.com), CDnow (www.Cdnow.com), and eToys (www.eToys.com) have quickly emerged as major players in their respective categories. These retailers specialize in one category (books, CDs, toys, etc.), and offer an extensive choice, great value, and efficient, reliable order fulfilment.

Success is by no means guaranteed online. A retailer should answer some basic questions before going online. Is my product suitable for the Web? Am I likely to find my target market online? If I go online, can I lower my costs, or maintain those costs while increasing service quality? In their survey of retailers, Ernst & Young found that among those not involved in electronic commerce, the most common reason for staying away was inappropriateness of the product for the Web (47 percent), lack of advantages or opportunities (24 percent) and higher costs (17 percent).

Online entry strategies vary widely. Some retailers heavily discount their prices to attract consumers to their Web sites. Most established retailers who are using the online channel as a supplement to their conventional channels try to maintain similar prices. This strategy allows them to preserve product positioning (or "store positioning"). The Web, however, facilitates greater comparison-shopping. With very little effort, one can check the price of products in different online stores. This is likely to increase the pressure on retailers.

The key to retail success is often said to be "location, location, and location." Is this true online? Obviously, your Web site should be easy to find. Most customers seem to find Web sites through search engines, so the more search engines you arrange to be listed under, the better access you are providing to your online store. Should you locate your store in an online shopping mall? (See California Mall at www.californiamall.com and The Internet Mall at www.internetmall.com). While online malls offer some advantages, such as a built-in shopping cart (and order processing system), one should consider the traffic generated by the mall and costs before choosing to locate in an online mall. A disadvantage of online malls is that stores are grouped according to product/service category, making your nearest competitors your neighbour; this increases the likelihood of comparison-shopping. An online mall, however, may be an attractive option for smaller retailers.

The online retailer has to deal with questions regarding location, positioning strategy, pricing, and assortment of goods to be carried. But going online has different implications for different retailers. For catalogue retailers such as L.L. Bean (www.llbean.com), the Web may be a threat because shopping online is very much like catalogue shopping. For that reason, these retailers have made a quick entry online to protect their market share. For other retailers, such as J.C. Penney and Wal-Mart, the Web may be a means of reducing costs or reaching new markets or improving customer relations.

The Ernst & Young survey found that 37 percent of retailers are either currently selling online or plan to do so shortly. That is good news for consumers. As online competition increases, consumers are certain to benefit.

Source: This is one of a series of Internet Insites prepared in April 1998 by Dr. Ramesh Venkat of Saint Mary's University for *Basic Marketing*, Ninth Canadian Edition.

Target marketing is key

In defining the target market(s) for a retail operation, you must pay particular attention to whether the store is targeting buyers, or users, or both. For example, which group should be the target for a ladies' lingerie store—women (purchasing for themselves), or men (purchasing for gifts), or both? A different marketing strategy would be developed and implemented in light of the retailer's answer to that question.

Consumers have emotional and social motives

The target market's shopping needs relative to the type of outlet planned must be determined (preferably through market research).[12] Consumers consider many factors when choosing particular retailers. These factors can be based on emotional and social needs as well as economic needs.

Some people get an ego boost from shopping in a store with a prestige image. Others just want to shop in a store where they don't feel out of place. This kind of social influence can be subtle, but different stores do seem to attract customers from different social classes and cultural backgrounds. Zellers succeeds with a "budget" image that appeals to lower-income customers. Holt Renfrew, on the other hand, works at its upper-income image. Most people like to shop where salespeople and other customers are similar to themselves.

The atmosphere at a retail store may also affect how consumers view a retailer. How merchandise is displayed, and the decorations, colours, and finishes used, and even the temperature, sounds, and smell of a store, all contribute to "atmospherics" and store image. The right combination of these things may attract more target customers and encourage increased spending.[13]

Economic needs—which store has the best value?

Factors related to economic needs are also very important when a consumer selects a retailer.[14] Some of these factors are listed below:

- *Price.* Value offered, credit available, special discounts.
- *Location.* Convenience, parking, safety.
- *Product selection.* Width and depth of assortment, quality.
- *Special services.* Home delivery, special orders, gift wrap.
- *Helpful salespeople.* Courteous, knowledgeable, fast checkout.
- *Fairness in dealings.* Honesty, return privileges.

Retail marketing mixes have seven Ps

The retailer must consciously develop a marketing mix that is capable of satisfying the emotional, social, and economic needs of its target market(s). A retailer's marketing mix can be said to consist of seven key variables:

1. *Product.* Merchandise assortment, quality.
2. *Personnel.* Type and quality of assistance available.
3. *Personalized services.* Return policies, ability to customize, hours, other extras.
4. *Price.* Value relative to quality.
5. *Place.* Store location, parking facilities, exterior elements.
6. *Physical facilities.* Store layout, washrooms, interior elements.
7. *Promotion.* Advertising, sales promotion, including price features, in-store display.

Marketing Demo 13-2

Consumers Make Point: No Service, No Spending

No shoes, no service is giving way to a new retail mantra of the '90s: No service, no shoppers.

A survey by the Angus Reid Group concludes that retailers who keep their customers waiting more than two minutes for service will see more than half walk out of the door, many never to return.

"There is a different kind of consumer than there was 10 years ago," John Wright, senior vice-president of the Angus Reid Group, said from his office in Toronto.

"Now the commodity has moved away from being the product being sold, to being the consumer. The commodity is no longer sitting on the retailer's shelf. The commodity is standing in front of the cash register."

"It has become a privilege to have a customer in your store."

The survey, conducted for Ernst & Young at the start of the Christmas shopping period, showed 54 per cent of consumers refuse to wait more than two minutes for service.

Wealthier Canadians have the least patience, with only 46 per cent of those earning at least $60,000 a year willing to wait longer than five minutes, compared with 63 per cent of Canadians with incomes under $30,000 willing to wait that long.

Men are also more impatient. Only 46 per cent of them will wait more than five minutes, compared with 54 per cent of women who will endure longer waits.

When customers walk, 40 per cent will never darken the retailer's door again.

"Consumers don't have a lot of time; they don't have a lot of money, although they have more now than even 24 months ago," Wright said. "In the old days, they would have lined up at the counter because they had nowhere else to go. Now they have more choice."

Management may be the last to hear from disgruntled consumers. Poor service prompts 84 per cent of consumers to go to the competition; 80 per cent leave without spending a dime and 80 per cent return less often.

Fewer than half, 47 per cent, would complain to management.

The most common shopping complaints include:

- Can't find help.
- Long lines or waits.
- Rude, aggressive or overly friendly staff.
- Inexperienced staff.

Wright said that demographically consumers fall into two main groups when it comes to customer service expectations. The baby-boomer types have been around long enough, so while they may have grown up with shoddy service, they don't want to settle for that any more.

The younger generations have been raised in an era in which choice is a given, so they simply don't accept poor service. They are accustomed to being able to go to the competition for the same price and selection.

The survey was based on 1,519 telephone interviews from Nov. 17–28, [1997]. Results are said to be accurate within 2 1/2 per cent, plus or minus, 19 times out of 20. The margin of error will be larger within specific regions and for other subgroups of the population.

Source: Gillian Shaw, *The Vancouver Sun*, January 31, 1998, H1, H11.

Retail marketing mixes must anticipate change

A retailer's marketing mix must be internally consistent with the long-term positioning and imagery chosen to achieve customer loyalty. At the same time, it must be well balanced because the resources of the business are limited. In setting up a mix, a wise retailer understands not only what the customers' needs are but also how customers prioritize these needs. Understanding what's important to customers allows a retailer to better deal with the rapid competitive changes that typify the retail industry. A recent survey shows just how important customer service has become (see Marketing Demo 13–2).

For example, a retailer who wants to set up a prestige store, such as Ashley's China, may have to deal with the following customer expectations, in order of importance: product selection, helpful and knowledgeable salespeople, store atmosphere, location, and price. A retail mix designed to respond to these needs may entail, in order of priority:

1. *Product.* Classic merchandise, plus some newer-design quality lines appealing to innovators and early adopters.
2. *Personnel.* Well-trained staff capable of catering to customers' social, psychological, and information needs.

3. *Personalized services.* Purchase customization, status wrapping and packaging, shipping anywhere in North America.
4. *Price.* High profit margin/low turnover prices.
5. *Place.* An upscale commercial district location, possibly near an upscale residential area.
6. *Physical facilities.* Luxurious appointments (chandeliers, carpets, etc.), spacious layout, elegant displays.
7. *Promotion.* Frequent advertising in media read or seen by upper-income or status-oriented customers; infrequent sales.

Suppose a new competitor opened nearby offering similar merchandise at lower prices but with fewer services and less attractive facilities. Should Ashley's retaliate immediately by lowering its prices? Some retailers faced with this situation would do so. However, it is not necessarily the best response. Why not? Because the right personalized services and physical surroundings are more important to our retailer's customers than low price. As well, Ashley's might trigger a costly price war with the new entrant that would undermine its long-term prestige positioning.

Retailers must be good managers of people

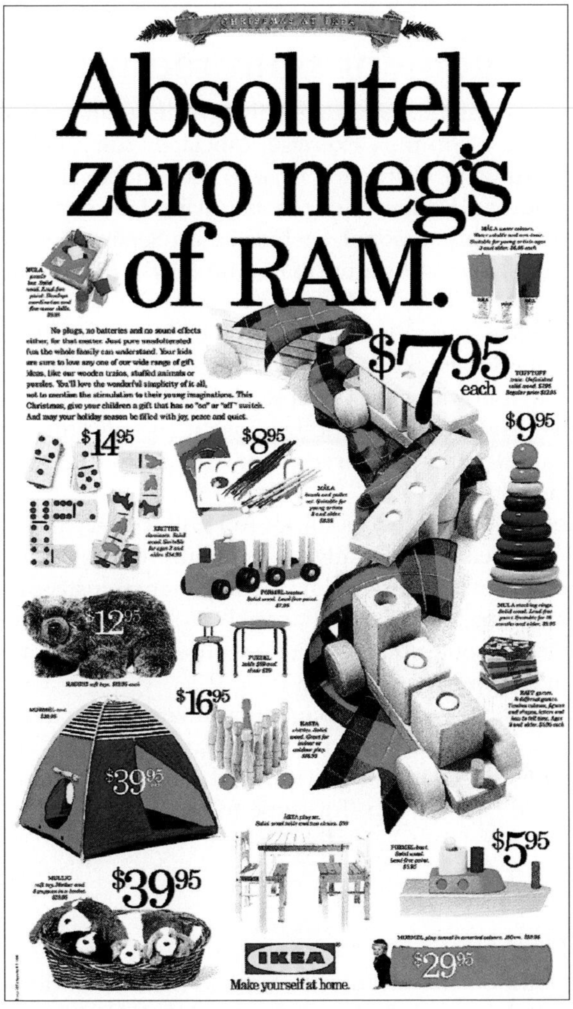

Changes in today's marketing environment are increasing the importance of the personnel and personalized services variables in the retailer's marketing mix. These changes are due to two factors: demographic trends, and technological advances.

As the baby boomers age, they are becoming increasingly risk aversive. They are demanding more assistance from sales staff and are expecting store personnel to have a reasonable knowledge of all the products that the store carries. In addition, they have the disposable income to pay for extras that will customize the goods or services to their needs.

At the same time, technological advances are increasing the expectations of *all* consumers with regard to both the amount of information and the degree of product customization available.

Given these expectations, retailers are beginning to see their employees as key to meeting today's customer demands. They are recognizing that their counter sales and supervisory personnel are valuable human assets who must be properly managed and nurtured. To enhance job satisfaction and create a sense of "ownership" toward the retail operation, employees are increasingly being allowed to solve customer problems without supervisory intervention. For example, many are now allowed to discount damaged merchandise based on their own judgment. Some retailers are also asking their employees for promotional ideas. Many are providing in-house training and other educational programs to improve employee effectiveness and efficiency.[15]

Retailers must place more emphasis on human resource management if they are to become more proactive in dealing with their customers. Such an emphasis will also help retailers find the strength to act as channel captains and thus deal more aggressively with producers and wholesalers.

The retailing approach IKEA developed in Sweden is also popular in North America.

Exhibit 13-2 Illustrative Gross Margins in Selected Retail Trades

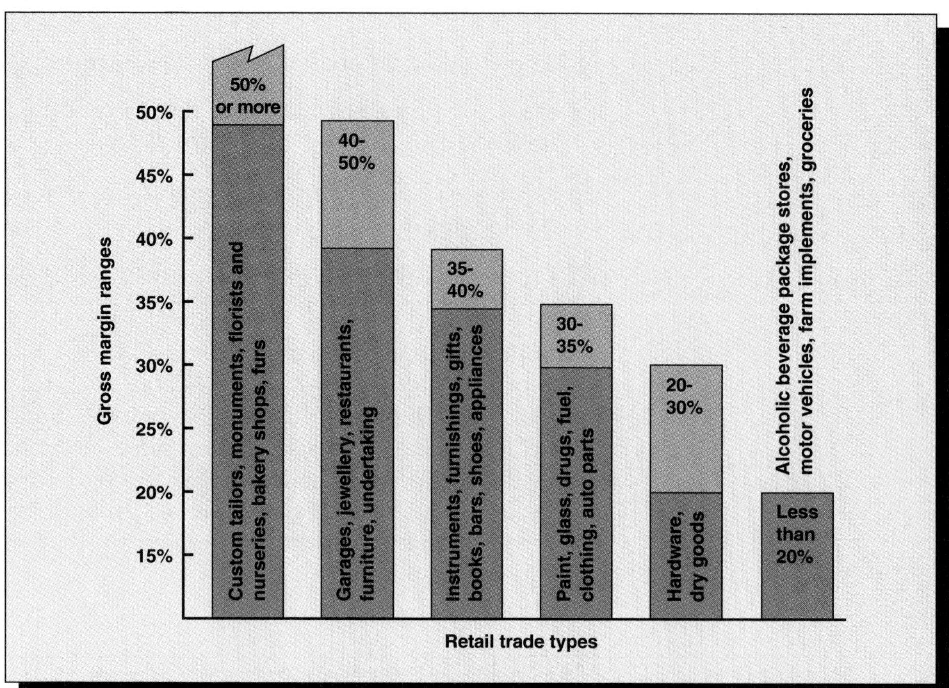

Strong financial management skills required

Retailers must also manage their marketing mixes strategically in order to maximize profitability. Financial management is a complex exercise, especially for retailers who make frequent use of sales to draw in customers or who have perishable or fashion-oriented products, as do food and department stores. It is also very challenging for retail operations that are highly seasonal, such as Laura Secord Chocolates. In all of the above circumstances, managers must maximize profits during the peak periods to carry them through the valleys.

In order to forecast peaks and valleys, a retailer needs a well-laid-out marketing plan with a detailed promotional calendar. For example, to set the initial retail price for an item, a retailer must know the following: (1) the cost of the product, (2) the expenses associated with selling the product, (3) the desired profit (or markup) on the product, and (4) the number and level of price reductions (or markdowns) to be taken on the product before it is sold.

Profit potential varies significantly by store type, as shown in Exhibit 13–2. This is due, in part, to the different markup levels traditionally taken in different retail sectors. However, the extent of financial control exercised by management is just as important. In fact, scrambled merchandising is caused by managers seeking to improve their businesses' financial outlook. Based on Exhibit 13–2, can you see why hardware stores often carry gift items and small appliances?

Other tools that retailers can use to analyze and manage their financial situations are operating statements and ratios, stockturn rates, return on investment (ROI), and return on assets (ROA). Appendix B—Marketing Arithmetic, which is found after Chapter 22, provides formulas and explanations for these tools.

If you're successful, what are your growth options?

Successful retailers must at some point decide whether to expand their operations. Some, like Ed Mirvish of Honest Ed's in Toronto, elect to remain single units. Others elect to branch out. Such retailers have three choices in developing a growth strategy: horizontal expansion, or vertical integration, or both.

Ethical Dimensions

Competitive Pressures and Marketing Practices

Most retailers face intense financial and competitive pressures. The desperation that comes with such pressures has pushed some retailers toward questionable marketing practices.

Critics argue, for example, that retailers too often advertise special sale items to bring price-sensitive shoppers into the store but then don't stock enough to meet demand. Other stores have been criticized for pushing consumers to trade up to more expensive items. What is ethical and unethical in such situations, however, is subject to debate. Retailers can't always anticipate demand perfectly, and deliveries may not arrive on time. Similarly, encouraging trade-ups may be a sensible part of a strategy—if it's done honestly.

Some abuses are more clear-cut. For example, one of the leading retailers of automotive services in North America once took out nationwide ads to apologize for problems it created with a new system designed to increase sales. On the surface, it seemed simple. Store managers were paid a percentage on sales. However, some of them abused the chain's customers by suggesting unnecessary repairs.

In retailing, as in other types of business, the marketing concept should guide firms away from unethical treatment of customers. However, a retailer who is worried about survival may be prepared to compromise on the need to satisfy customers in both the short and long term.[16]

Horizontal expansion can be achieved by adding more stores, or more product lines, or more forms of retailing. Adding additional stores to reach more target market customers can ultimately lead to becoming a local, national, or international chain operation. Adding more product lines can lead to improved profitability (if more profitable lines than those initially sold are involved) and to more complete servicing of a customer's needs. It can also lead to scrambled merchandising and thus a broader set of competitors to watch. Adding more forms of retailing can entail expanding into nonstore operations (e.g., catalogue shopping) or even opening a new chain to target new customer groups.

Vertical integration by retailers can involve them acquiring wholesaling and/or manufacturing operations. Many of Loblaws' PC brands are produced at Sunfresh Limited, its manufacturing arm, and then distributed to the various Loblaws outlets via the company's wholesaling arm, National Grocers. Vertical integration can also involve private-label branding and specification buying. Here, a producer provides the retailer with a unique product or products that the producer cannot sell to others.

Retail management is complex and challenging

Whatever their size, successful retailers have learned to develop strategic retail management programs capable of achieving predetermined short- and long-term business objectives.

As indicated in Exhibit 13–3, there are several key components that must work together to form an effective retail management program. The company's long-term objectives—generally a combination of diverse goals such as customer loyalty and maximum profits—must be set and kept in balance. These objectives, along with the needs and expectations of the firm's target market(s) and the realities of the marketing environment, must be taken into account in selecting the strategic marketing, human resource, and financial elements that become the firm's business plan.

Besides achieving the retailer's long-term objectives, the resulting plan must also meet the short-term objectives of providing day-to-day customer satisfaction and reaching annual profit margin targets, both of which are necessary to ensure year-to-year survival.

Exhibit 13-3 Components of a Strategic Retail Management Program

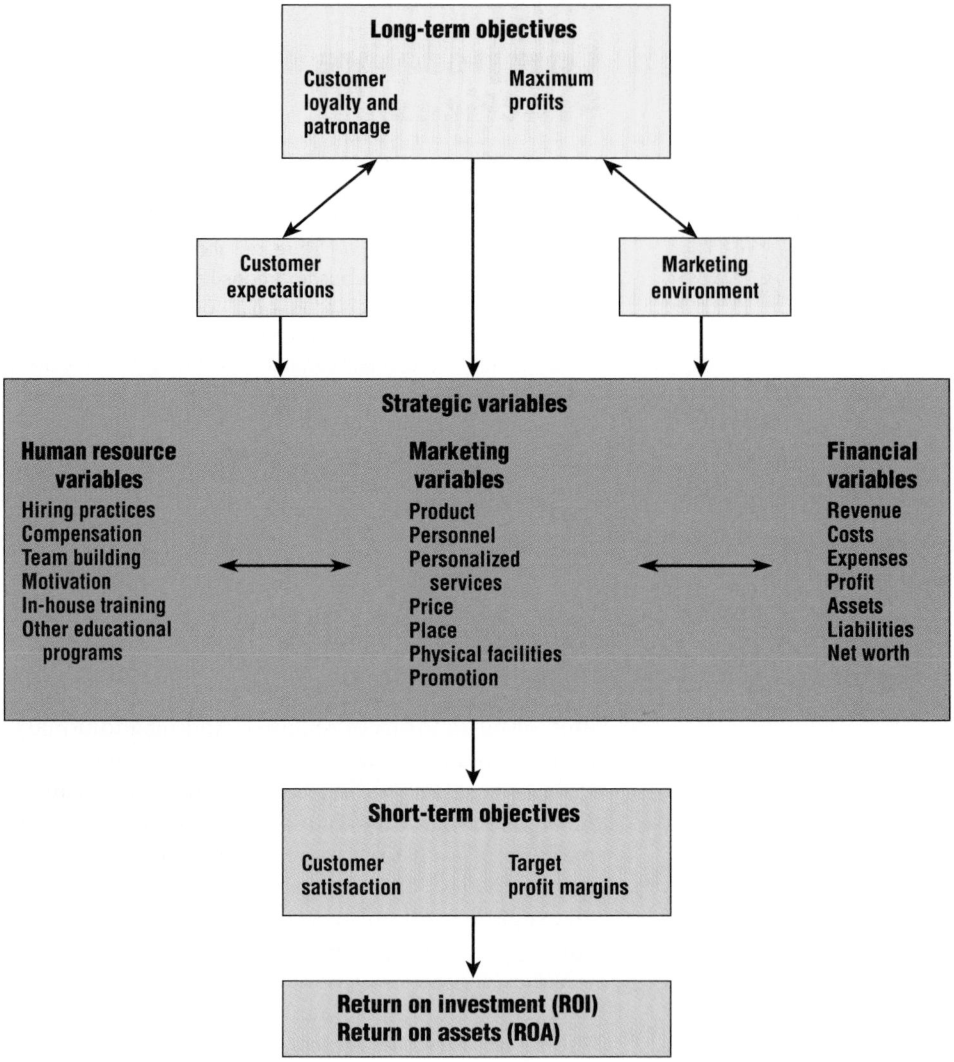

Short-term profit performance is the basis for the ROI and ROA measures used to establish how effectively the operation is using its resources. In turn, these measures help the retailer obtain loans and other financial support for investment in the operation. Continuous upgrading of assets is necessary to keep on top of customer expectations, to adjust to competitive and environmental changes, and thus to continue to achieve the operation's long-term goals.

All of the components in a strategic retail management program are interrelated, more so than a simple model can indicate. In other words, retail management is an ongoing, dynamic process. Changes in consumer expectations and the marketing environment are not unusual. Such changes can require frequent plan modifications during any given year. However, alert retail managers anticipate major changes and include contingency options in their annual business plans. Managers who fail to anticipate changes run the risk of making plan modifications that appear to be the right thing to do in the short run but have a negative impact on the firm's long-term objectives.

The impact of technology

Like many business sectors, retailing is being significantly affected by technology. This, in turn, is influencing how retailers deal with both their customers and their suppliers.

In terms of dealing with customers, recent innovations include the following:

- *Levi's mass customization system.* Consumers can custom order Levi's jeans to their own specifications using a computer terminal available at participating retailers.
- *The Interac® Direct Payment system.* Using their banking cards, consumers can make payments directly from their banking accounts, thereby eliminating the approval process associated with using cheques as well as the interest charges that accompany the use of credit cards.[17]
- *Online comparison shopping and electronic commerce.* We have already seen that these related activities are obviously going to have a major, if still unpredictable, impact both on how customers gather information and on how they actually purchase goods and services.

It has generally been assumed that technological advances depersonalize commercial transactions. However, some observers have argued that the innovations noted above do *not* distance retailers from their customers; rather, they increase the ease with which retailers and customers can interact and thus are in keeping with the underlying social nature of retailing. With which of these points of view do you agree?

Technology and retailer–supplier relations

In terms of dealing with suppliers, the development of scanner data has been a very important innovation. Scanner data, which are generated at the checkout counter when consumers pay for their purchases, were initially used for inventory control. Now such data are also being used to provide retailers with their own source of market share information by product category. A decade ago, retailers were dependent on suppliers for this type of information.[18]

Electronic data interchange (EDI) is a more recent innovation. As outlined in Chapter 12, EDI involves setting up a computer link between suppliers and retailers that allows for the very fast handling of purchase orders and expedites the shipment of goods. Such a system has been a key contributor to Wal-Mart's highly successful consumer pricing and service strategies.[19]

Globalization in retailing

Historically, new retailing approaches that have succeeded in one developed country have quickly spread to others. Self-service approaches that started with supermarkets in North America are now found in many retail operations around the world. Similarly, mass-merchandising and superstore concepts were pioneered in Australia and Europe and then brought to North America.[20]

On the other hand, retailing in less developed nations has typically involved small shops selling very small quantities, often to a small number of consumers. A lack of personal financial resources has been a contributing factor to this situation. Consumers in these countries often haven't had the incomes to support mass distribution. As well, the governments of some countries in Asia, Europe, and South America have severely limited the evolution of retailing through laws designed to protect small shopkeepers by keeping out large stores. Also, religious beliefs or societal norms have prevented retailers from opening on weekends or evenings, and this makes them less convenient for customers.[21]

Megaretailers are "going global"

Changes are taking place, however. Using sophisticated strategic management skills and enhanced technological capacity to run large, highly efficient operations, megaretailers are beginning to expand throughout the world. These megaretailers include U.S.-based operations such as Wal-Mart and Toys "Я" Us and European companies such as Benetton, Makro, and Marks & Spencer. These companies are seeking new markets because their home bases are saturated with competition. At home, they are sharing stagnant consumer markets with an increasing number of firms attempting to copy their success. They need to enter new markets to grow.[22]

They are targeting emerging economies

The new markets that the megaretailers are targeting include emerging economies such as Mexico, Southeast Asia, and China. In these countries, the use of credit to make purchases is beginning to gain acceptance. Furthermore, much of the population is younger than 18 and will move into the prime spending years over the next two decades. Will megaretailers be able to establish long-term operations in these markets? This will depend on how successfully they adapt their marketing mixes to new cultures. It will also depend on their ability to build the physical distribution networks needed to stock and maintain their store shelves. Also, and as proof that the economic environment is always important, foreign retailers have had to adjust in recent years both to a peso crisis in Mexico and to major financial problems throughout Southeast Asia.

Canada is also attractive to megaretailers

Many American chains have been attracted to Canada in recent years by our low exchange rate and the North American Free Trade Agreement. Some, such as Toys "Я" Us, Business Depot, Winners, and The Gap, have done quite well. Wal-Mart, in particular, has rapidly become a very major player in the Canadian department store sector. Other American big-box warehouse stores have also successfully invaded Canada. There are now some 57 American and 20 non-American retailers operating in Canada. Foreign-controlled space now amounts to almost 70 million square feet, or approximately 17 percent of the total Canadian market, excluding food and automotive. There are now about 2 square feet of American retail space for every person in Canada.[23]

But the defensive marketing actions taken by established Canadian retailers have surprised some American firms. For example, Home Depot entered Canada in February 1994 by acquiring 75 percent of Aikenhead's Home Improvement Warehouse. By June of 1995, Home Depot had decided to scale back its operations in Canada because of the unexpectedly strong response of Canadian do-it-yourself chains such as Revelstoke Home Centres Ltd. In the mid and late 1990s, Canadian Tire has also more than held its own against foreign-owned entrants into Canada.

Canadian retailers are expanding globally

Can Canadian retail organizations successfully perform on a larger stage? Can they "compete with the best"? Canadian retailers have been criticized for not being aggressive enough in the global marketplace. There is concern that the resulting lack of managerial experience and sophistication will ultimately increase Canadian firms' vulnerability to take-over by foreign-based retailers. Others have argued that our domestic focus has been the reason that Canadian retailers have recently looked abroad for senior managers with both American and international experience.

Some attempts at expansion into the United States by major Canadian retailers have failed (example: Canadian Tire). However, generalities about a lack of Canadian retail aggressiveness may be unwarranted. There are at least 21 Canadian retailers currently operating in the United States out of a total of 46 that have entered—a 46 percent survival rate. A further eight Canadian retailers are operating internationally in locations other than the United States. The American market is an extremely challenging one. Some of the Canadian retailers operating in the United States are performing well, while others are struggling. Future Shop is but one of many Canadian chains that at one time experienced serious losses. But other firms, such as Club Monaco, are succeeding both in the United States and in other international markets.[24]

What is a wholesaler?

It's hard to define what a wholesaler is because there are so many different wholesalers doing different jobs. Some of their activities may even seem like manufacturing. As a result, some wholesalers call themselves "manufacturer and dealer." Some like to identify themselves with such general terms as merchant, jobber, dealer, or distributor. Others just take the name commonly used in their trade, without really thinking about what it means.

To avoid a long, technical discussion on the nature of wholesaling, we'll use the Statistics Canada definition:

Wholesalers are primarily engaged in buying merchandise for resale to retailers; to industrial, commercial, institutional, and professional users; to other wholesalers; for export; to farmers for use in farm production; or acting as agents in such transactions.

Mixed activity businesses (such as firms engaged in both wholesaling and retailing, contracting, service trades, manufacturing, and so on) are considered to be in wholesale trade whenever they derive the largest portion of their gross margin from their wholesaling activity.[25]

Possible wholesaling functions

Wholesalers may perform certain functions for both their suppliers and their own customers—in short, for those above and below them in the channel. *Wholesaling functions* really are variations of the basic marketing functions—buying, selling, grading, storing, transporting, financing, risk taking, and gathering market information. Wholesaling functions are basic to the following discussion because decisions about what combination of functions to perform are a key part of a wholesaler's strategy planning. Keep in mind that *not all* wholesalers provide all of our functions.

What a wholesaler might do for customers

Wholesalers perform a variety of activities that benefit their customers:

- *Regroup goods.* Provide the quantity and assortment customers want at the lowest possible cost.
- *Anticipate needs.* Forecast customers' demands and buy accordingly.
- *Carry stocks.* Carry inventory so that customers don't have to store a large inventory.
- *Deliver goods.* Provide prompt delivery at low cost.
- *Grant credit.* Give credit to customers, perhaps supplying their working capital. Note: This financing function may be very important to small customers; sometimes it's the main reason they use wholesalers instead of buying directly from producers.
- *Provide information and advisory service.* Supply price and technical information as well as suggestions on how to install and sell products. Note: The wholesaler's sales reps may be experts in the products they sell.
- *Provide part of the buying function.* Offer products to potential customers so that they don't have to hunt for supply sources.
- *Own and transfer title to products.* Help complete a sale without the need for other intermediaries, thereby speeding the whole buying and selling process.

What a wholesaler might do for producer-suppliers

Wholesalers also benefit producer-suppliers:

- *Provide part of a producer's selling function.* Approach producer-suppliers instead of waiting for their sales reps to call.

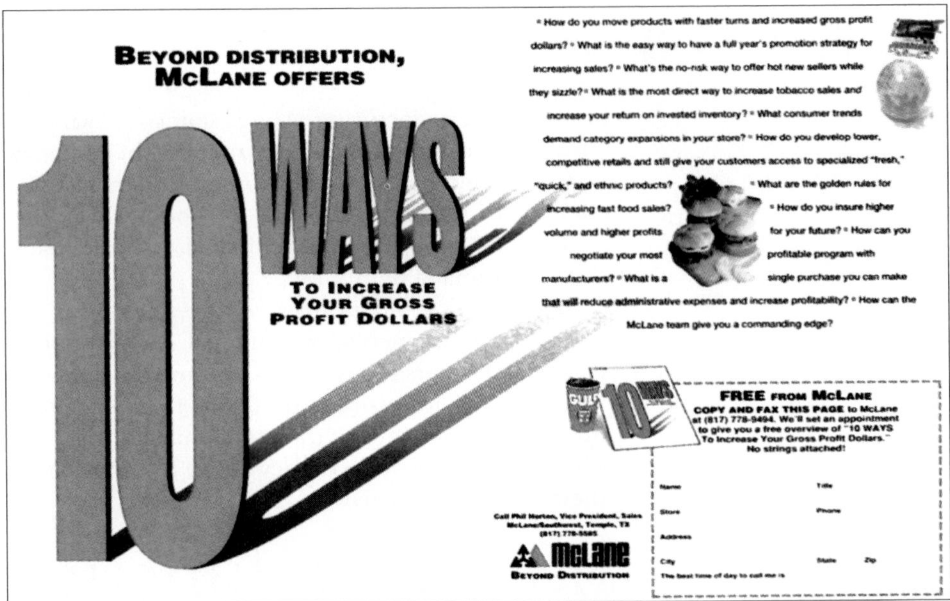

A wholesaler often helps its customers by carrying needed products and providing prompt delivery at low cost.

- *Store inventory.* Reduce a producer's need to carry large stocks, thus cutting the producer's warehousing expenses.
- *Supply capital.* Reduce a producer's need for working capital by buying the producer's output and carrying it in inventory until it's sold.
- *Reduce credit risk.* Sell to customers the wholesaler knows, and take the loss if these customers don't pay.
- *Provide market information.* As an informed buyer and seller closer to the market, reduce the producer's need for market research.

Functions are crucial in many channels

You will see the importance of these wholesaling functions by looking at a specific case. George Mariakakas is a heating contractor. His company sells heating systems, and his crew installs them in new buildings. Mariakakas gets a lot of help from Air Control Company, the wholesaler who supplies this equipment. When Mariakakas isn't certain what type of furnace to install, Air Control's experts give him good technical advice. Air Control also stocks an inventory of products from different producers. This means that Mariakakas can order a piece of equipment when he's ready to install it. He doesn't have to tie up capital in a big inventory, or wait for a part to be shipped cross-country from a producer. Air Control even helps finance his business. Mariakakas doesn't have to pay for his purchases until 30 days after he takes delivery. By then, he has finished his work and been paid by his customers. Mariakakas's whole way of doing business would be different without this wholesaler providing wholesaling functions.

Different kinds of wholesalers perform different functions

You will reach a better understanding of wholesalers and their strategies when you look at them as members of channels. In Chapter 11, we discussed in general terms the functions that a channel intermediary can provide (when we explained why a producer might use an indirect channel of distribution). Moreover, wholesaling functions are simply variations on the basic marketing functions—buying, selling, grading, storing, transporting, financing, risk taking, and informa-

Exhibit 13-4 Types of Wholesalers

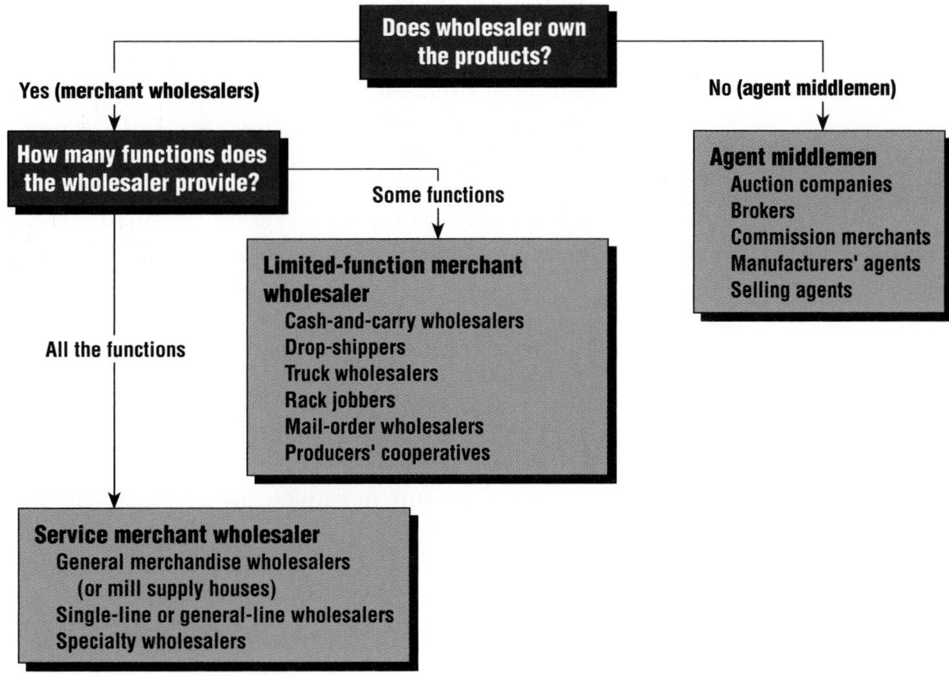

tion gathering—also discussed in Chapter 11. Now we will further develop these ideas by showing how different types of wholesalers perform different functions for their suppliers and customers.

Exhibit 13–4 provides an overall view of the various kinds of wholesalers described in more detail below. It highlights the fact that a major difference between merchant and agent wholesalers has to do with whether they *own* the products they sell.

Merchant wholesalers are the most numerous

Merchant wholesalers own (take title to) the products they sell. They often specialize by certain types of products or customers. For example, Fastenal is a wholesaler that specializes in distributing threaded fasteners used by a variety of manufacturers. It owns (takes title to) the fasteners for some period before selling to its customers. Most wholesaling establishments in North America are merchant wholesalers. Such wholesalers are even more common in other countries. Japan is an extreme example. In its unusual multitiered distribution system, products are often bought and sold by a series of merchant wholesalers on their way to the business user or retailer.

Service wholesalers provide all the functions

Service wholesalers are merchant wholesalers who provide all the wholesaling functions. Within this basic group are three types: (1) general merchandise, (2) single-line, and (3) specialty.

General merchandise wholesalers are service wholesalers who carry a wide variety of nonperishable items such as hardware, electrical supplies, plumbing supplies, furniture, drugs, cosmetics, and automobile equipment. With their broad lines of convenience and shopping products, they serve hardware stores, drugstores, and small department stores. *Mill supply houses* operate in a similar way, but carry a broad variety of accessories and supplies to serve the needs of manufacturers.

Single-line (or general-line) wholesalers are service wholesalers who carry a narrower line of merchandise than general merchandise wholesalers. For example, they may carry only food, or wearing apparel, or certain types of industrial tools or supplies. In consumer products, they serve the single- and limited-line stores. In business products, they cover a wider geographic area and offer more specialized service.

Specialty wholesalers are service wholesalers who carry a very narrow range of products, and offer more information and service than other service wholesalers. A consumer products specialty wholesaler might carry only health foods or oriental foods instead of a full line of groceries.

A specialty wholesaler of business products may limit itself to fields requiring special technical knowledge or service. Richardson Electronics is an interesting example. It specializes in distributing replacement parts, such as electron tubes, for old equipment that many manufacturers still use on the factory floor. Richardson describes itself as "on the trailing edge of technology," but its unique products, expertise, and service are valuable to its target customers, many of whom operate in countries where new technologies are not yet common.[26]

Limited-function wholesalers

Limited-function wholesalers provide only *some* wholesaling functions. Exhibit 13–5 shows the functions typically provided—and not provided. In the following paragraphs, we will discuss the main features of these wholesalers. Although less numerous in some countries, these wholesalers are very important for some products.

Cash-and-carry wholesalers

Cash-and-carry wholesalers operate like service wholesalers, except that the customer must pay cash.

Some retailers, such as small auto repair shops, are too small to be served profitably by a service wholesaler. So service wholesalers set a minimum charge—or just

Exhibit 13-5 Functions Provided by Different Types of Limited-Function Merchant Wholesalers

FUNCTIONS	CASH-AND-CARRY	DROP SHIPPER	TRUCK	MAIL ORDER	COOPERATIVES	RACK JOBBERS
For customers						
Anticipates needs	X		X	X	X	X
"Regroups" products (one or more of four steps)	X		X	X	X	X
Carries stocks	X		X	X	X	X
Delivers products			X		X	X
Grants credit		X	Maybe	Maybe	Maybe	Consignment (in some cases)
Provides information and advisory services		X	Some	Some	X	
Provides buying function		X	X	X	Some	X
Owns and transfers title to products	X	X	X	X	X	X
For producers						
Provides producers' selling function	X	X	X	X	X	X
Stores Inventory	X		X	X	X	X
Helps finance by owning stocks	X		X	X	X	X
Reduces credit risk	X	X	X	X	X	X
Provides market information	X	X	Some	X	X	Some

refuse to grant credit to a small business that may have trouble paying its bills. Or the wholesaler may set up a cash-and-carry department to supply the small retailer for cash on the counter. The wholesaler can operate at lower cost because the retailers take over many wholesaling functions. And using cash-and-carry outlets may enable the small retailer to stay in business. These cash-and-carry operators are especially common in less-developed nations, where very small retailers handle the bulk of retail transactions. In Canada, big warehouse clubs are taking some of this business.

Drop-shippers don't handle products

Drop-shippers own (take title to) the products they sell—but they do *not* actually handle, stock, or deliver them. These wholesalers are mainly involved in selling. They get orders and pass them on to producers. Then the producer ships the order directly to the customer. Drop-shippers commonly sell bulky products (like lumber), for which additional handling would be expensive and possibly damaging.

Truck wholesalers deliver—at a cost

Truck wholesalers specialize in delivering products that they stock in their own trucks. By handling perishable products in general demand—tobacco, candy, potato chips, and salad dressings—truck wholesalers may provide almost the same functions as full-service wholesalers. Their big advantage is that they promptly deliver perishable products that regular wholesalers prefer not to carry. A 7-Eleven store that runs out of potato chips on a busy Friday night doesn't want to be out of stock all weekend!

Mail-order wholesalers reach outlying areas

Mail-order wholesalers sell out of catalogues, which may be distributed widely to smaller industrial customers or to retailers who might not be called on by other intermediaries. These wholesalers operate in the hardware, jewellery, sporting goods, and general merchandise lines. For example, Inmac uses a catalogue to sell a complete line of computer accessories. Inmac's catalogues are printed in six languages and distributed to business customers in the United States, Canada, and Europe. Many of these customers don't have a local wholesaler.[27]

Producers' cooperatives do sorting

Producers' cooperatives operate almost as full-service wholesalers, with the "profits" going to the cooperative's customer-members. Cooperatives develop in agricultural markets where there are many small producers. Examples of such organizations are Sunkist (citrus fruits), Sunmaid Raisin Growers Association, and B.C. Hothouse, which serves cucumber, tomato, and pepper growers in British Columbia's Lower Mainland.

To improve the quality of farm products offered to the market, successful producers' cooperatives emphasize sorting. Some also brand these improved products and then promote the brands. For example, the California Almond Growers Exchange has captured most of the retail market with its Blue Diamond brand. Colombian Coffee producers use ads and a trademark featuring "Juan Valdez" and his donkey, to encourage consumers to buy brands of coffee made from their beans.

Farmers' cooperatives in the United States and marketing boards in Canada sometimes succeed in restricting output and increasing prices by taking advantage of the normally inelastic demand for agricultural commodities. In most businesses, it is not legal for a wholesaler to arrange for producers to band together to "fix" prices and output in this way. However, for more than 50 years, American agricultural cooperatives have been specifically excluded from these regulations.[28] In Canada, marketing boards are sometimes also allowed to exercise similar powers. More often, however, the marketing board is the sole sales agent but cannot assign quotas or otherwise try to control supply.

Rack jobbers sell hard-to-handle assortments

Rack jobbers specialize in hard-to-handle assortments of products that a retailer doesn't want to manage. Usually, they display the products on their own wire racks. For example, a grocery store or mass-merchandiser may rely on a rack jobber to decide which paperback books or magazines it sells. The wholesaler knows which titles sell in the local area, and applies that knowledge in many stores. Rack jobbers are usually paid cash for what is sold or delivered.

Costs and profits vary with the product sold

Is the cost of doing business the same for all classes of wholesale merchants? Gross margins, as a percentage of net sales, average 20.1 percent for the entire category. However, specific margins range from 11.0 percent for those wholesaling farm products to 30.0 percent for machinery and equipment wholesalers. Why do such differences exist? It obviously costs more to assemble some products than it does others. The services demanded by customers for one product category may also cost more to provide than those demanded by purchasers of other items. Finally, one wholesale business may be much more labour-intensive than another. Wholesale merchants with high gross margins aren't necessarily the most profitable. Many of these firms also have high operating costs.

Agent middlemen are strong on selling

Agent middlemen are wholesalers who do not own the products they sell. Their main purpose is to help in buying and selling. They usually provide even fewer functions than the limited-function wholesalers, so they may operate at relatively low cost—sometimes 2 to 6 percent of their selling price.

They are important in international trade

Agent middlemen are common in international trade. Many markets have only a few well-financed merchant wholesalers. The best many producers can do is get local representation through agents, and then arrange financing through banks that specialize in international trade.

Agent middlemen are usually experts on local business customs and rules concerning imported products in their respective countries. Sometimes a marketing manager can't work through a foreign government's red tape without the help of a local agent.

They are usually specialists

Agent middlemen—like merchant wholesalers—typically specialize by customer type and by product or product line. So it's important to determine exactly what each one does. In the following paragraphs, we'll mention only the most important points about each type. Study Exhibit 13–6 for details on the functions provided by each.

Manufacturers' agents—freewheeling sales reps

A **manufacturers' agent** sells similar products for several noncompeting producers, for a commission on what is actually sold. Such agents work almost as members of each company's sales force, but they're really independent middlemen. More than half of all agent middlemen are manufacturers' agents.

Their big plus is that they already call on some customers and can add another product line at relatively low cost—and at no cost to the producer until something sells! If an area's sales potential is low, a company may use a manufacturers' agent because the agent can do the job at low cost. Small producers often use agents everywhere because their sales volume is too small to justify their own sales force.

Exhibit 13-6 Functions Provided by Different Types of Agent Middlemen

FUNCTIONS	MANUFACTURERS' AGENTS	BROKERS	COMMISSION MERCHANTS	SELLING AGENTS	AUCTION COMPANIES
For customers					
Anticipates needs	Sometimes	Some			
"Regroups" products (one or more of four steps)	Some		X		X
Carries stocks	Sometimes		X		Sometimes
Delivers products	Sometimes		X		
Grants credit			Sometimes	X	Some
Provides information and advisory services	X	X	X	X	
Provides buying function	X	Some	X	X	X
Owns and transfers title to products		Transfers only	Transfers only		
For producers					
Provides selling function	X	Some	X	X	X
Stores inventory	Sometimes		X		X
Helps finance by owning stocks					
Reduces credit risk				X	Some
Provides market information	X	X	X	X	

Agents can be especially useful for introducing new products. For this service, they may earn 10 to 15 percent commission. (In contrast, their commission on large-volume established products may be quite low—perhaps only 2 percent.) A 10 to 15 percent commission may seem small for a new product with low sales. Once a product sells well, however, a producer may think the rate is high and begin using its own sales reps. Agents are well aware of this possibility. That's why most try to work for many producers and avoid being dependent on only one line.

Manufacturers' agents are very useful in fields where there are many small manufacturers who need to contact customers. They may cover a very narrow geographic area, such as a city or province. However, they are also important in international marketing, and an agent may take on responsibility for a whole country.

Import and export agents handle international trade

While manufacturers' agents operate in every country, **export or import agents** are basically manufacturers' agents who specialize in international trade. These agent middlemen help international firms adjust to unfamiliar market conditions in foreign markets.[29]

Brokers provide information

Brokers bring buyers and sellers together. Brokers usually have a *temporary* relationship with the buyer and seller while a particular deal is negotiated. They are especially useful when buyers and sellers don't come into the market very often. The broker's product is information about what buyers need—and what supplies are available. They may also aid in buyer–seller negotiations. If the transaction is completed, they earn a commission from whichever party hired them. **Export and import brokers** operate like other brokers, except that they specialize in bringing together buyers and sellers from different countries.

Selling agents—almost marketing managers

Selling agents take over the entire marketing job of producers—not just the selling function. A selling agent may handle the entire output of one or more producers—even competing producers—with almost complete control of pricing, selling, and advertising. In effect, the agent becomes each producer's marketing manager.

Financial trouble is one of the main reasons a producer calls in a selling agent. The selling agent may provide working capital but may also take over the affairs of the business.

A **combination export manager** is a blend of manufacturers' agent and selling agent, and handles the entire export function for several producers of similar but noncompeting lines.

Commission merchants handle distant markets

Commission merchants and **export or import commission houses** handle products shipped to them by sellers, complete the sale, and send the money—less their commission—to each seller.

Commission agents are common in agricultural markets where farmers must ship to big-city central markets. They need someone to handle the products there, as well as sell them, since a farmer can't go with each shipment. Commission agents are sometimes used in other trades, such as textiles. Here, many small producers want to reach buyers in a central market—perhaps one in a distant country—without having to maintain their own sales forces.

Auction companies—speed up the sale

Auction companies provide a place where buyers and sellers can come together and complete a transaction. There aren't many auction companies, but they are important in certain lines such as livestock, furs, tobacco, and used cars. For these products, demand and supply conditions change rapidly, and the product must be seen in order to be evaluated. The auction company brings buyers and sellers together. Buyers inspect the products, then demand and supply interact to determine the price.

Manufacturers' sales branches are also wholesalers

Manufacturers' sales branches are separate businesses that producers set up away from their factories. For example, computer producers such as IBM set up local branches in markets around the world to provide service, display equipment, and handle sales. Although there aren't many of these branches, they account for a significant proportion of total wholesale sales. One reason sales per branch are so high is that the branches are usually placed in the best market areas. This also helps explain why their operating costs are lower. But cost comparisons between various channels can be misleading, since the cost of selling is not always charged to a manufacturer's sales branch. If all the expenses associated with running such branches were properly allocated to them, their apparent cost savings might disappear.

Statistics Canada periodically collects data showing the number, kind, location, and operating expenses of manufacturers' sales branches. Similar data are available for many other countries. This type of information helps marketers analyze competitors' distribution systems and probable costs. If those competitors are using sales branches, it could mean that in a given country or region no good specialists are available—at least none that could provide the functions needed.

Wholesaling is big business

Would you have expected the total volume of sales made by the different types of wholesalers to be greater than what was made by retailers? That is in fact the case both in Canada and the United States. We tend to forget that industrial distributors selling to industry are a type of wholesaler, so their sales fall into this category. Also, some consumer and industrial products are bought and sold by more than a single wholesaler on their way to market.

Some $287.2 billion of sales were made at the wholesale level in Canada in 1992. About 65,000 wholesale merchants accounted for $248.7 billion, or 86.6 percent of that total. Some 2,000 agents and brokers—the other segment of the wholesale trade sector—accounted for $38.5 billion, the remaining 13.4 percent. As was mentioned earlier, a substantial volume of wholesaling is also done by somewhat under 7,000 manufacturers' sales branches. In 1992, sales by such branches reached $33.0 billion, which is not all that much less than the amount of business done by the agent and broker category. By 1997, sales by wholesale merchants had risen to $287.1 billion. Unfortunately, comparable data for the agent and broker category and for manufacturers' sales branches were not available.[30]

Wholesaling has changed over the years

In earlier days, wholesalers dominated distribution channels in Canada and most other countries. The many small producers and small retailers needed their services. This situation still exists in many countries, especially those with less-developed economies. However, in the developed nations, as producers became larger, some bypassed the wholesalers. Similarly, large retail chains often took control of functions that had been handled by wholesalers. In light of these changes, many people predicted a gloomy future for wholesalers.

Producing profits, not chasing orders

Yet partly due to new management and new strategies, wholesalers have held their own, and many are enjoying significant growth. To be sure, many still operate in the old ways, and wholesaling is changing less rapidly than retailing. But progressive wholesalers are showing greater interest in their customers and in channel systems. Some offer more services. Others are developing voluntary chains that bind them more closely to their customers.

Modern wholesalers no longer require all customers to pay for all the services they offer. Now some wholesalers offer basic service at minimum cost, and then charge additional fees for any special services required.

Most modern wholesalers have streamlined their operations to cut unnecessary costs and improve profits. To cut costs, they use computers to keep track of inventory and to order new stock as needed. Computerized sales analysis helps them identify and drop unprofitable products. Wholesalers are also more selective in picking customers. They use a selective distribution policy when cost analysis shows that many of their smaller customers are unprofitable. With these less desirable customers gone, wholesalers are able to give more attention to more profitable customers.

Progress—or fail

Many wholesalers are also modernizing their warehouses and physical handling facilities. They mark products with bar codes that can be read with hand-held scanners, so that inventory, shipping, and sales records can be easily and instantly updated. Computerized order-picking systems speed the job of assembling orders. New storing facilities are carefully located to minimize the costs of both incoming freight and deliveries. Delivery vehicles travel to customers in a computer-selected sequence that reduces the number of miles travelled. And wholesalers who serve manufacturers are rising to the challenge of just-in-time delivery systems, and are making renewed efforts to add value in the distribution channel.

Perhaps good-bye to some

Not all wholesalers are progressive, and some of the smaller, less efficient ones may fail. Efficiency and low cost, however, are not all that's needed for success. Some wholesalers will disappear as the functions they once provided are shifted and shared in different ways in the channel. Cost-conscious buyers for Wal-Mart and other chains are refusing to deal with some of the intermediaries who represent small producers. They want to negotiate directly with the producer—not just accept the price traditionally available from a wholesaler. Similarly, more producers are seeing advantages in having closer direct relationships with fewer suppliers, and they're paring the vendor roles to exclude wholesalers who do a poor job of meeting their needs. Also, efficient delivery services such as UPS and FedEx are making it easy and inexpensive for many producers to ship directly to their customers—even ones in foreign markets.[31]

Survivors will need effective strategies

To survive, each wholesaler must develop a good marketing strategy. Profit margins are not large in wholesaling; typically, they range from less than 1 percent to 2 percent. And they've declined in recent years as the competitive squeeze has tightened.

The wholesalers who do survive will need to be efficient, but that doesn't mean they'll all have low costs. Some wholesalers' higher operating expenses result from the strategies they select—including the special services they offer to *some* customers.

What will happen to retailers and wholesalers in the future

A common theme in this chapter and the two before it is that channels of distribution are in the midst of dynamic changes. There have been dramatic improvements due to more efficient ways of coordinating logistics. The Internet, as the backbone for a whole new form of electronic commerce, is another force for

Ethical Dimensions

Relations with Wholesalers

There's no doubt that some wholesalers are being squeezed out of business. Some critics—including many of the wholesalers affected by these changes—argue that it's unethical for powerful suppliers or customers to simply cut out wholesalers who spend money and time—perhaps decades—developing markets. Laws, as well as contracts between channel members, sometimes define what changes are or are not legal. But in some cases, the ethical issues are more ambiguous.

For example, as part of a broader effort to improve profits, Amana notified Cooper Distributing Co. that it intended to cancel their distribution agreement—in 10 days. Cooper had been handling Amana appliances for 30 years, and Amana products represented 85 percent of Cooper's sales. Amana's explanation to Cooper? "It's not because you're doing a bad job: We just think we can do it better."

Situations like this arise often. They may be cold-hearted, but are they unethical? Many argue that it isn't fair for Amana to cut off the relationship on such short notice. But most wholesalers realize that their business is always at risk, if they don't perform channel functions better or cheaper than what their suppliers or customers can do themselves.[32]

change. But even before all of this, the evolution of retailing and wholesaling was ongoing. Intermediaries that find new and better ways to add value prosper.

It can't be overemphasized that such changes are ongoing. Clearly, we have just seen the tip of the iceberg when it comes to the impact that the Internet—and related technologies that will evolve in the future—will have on Place. There is an explosion in the number and variety of firms that are trying to figure out how to establish a presence on the Web. Many of them are reshaping competition in the product-markets in which they compete.

On the other hand, the adoption process that is underway is typical of other innovations. Much of the initial change has simply been an adjustment to what was done in the past. The catalogue becomes electronic. E-mail supplements toll-free phone orders. A retailer opens a new Web site instead of a new store. The technology is revolutionary and exciting, but much of what firms are doing with it so far is evolutionary. Revolutionary change will come, and will bring greater rewards to the innovators.

Imagine, for example, what it would take for you—and everyone you know—to do a lot of your routine shopping on the Internet. What new marketing functions would be needed, and who would provide them? What would the channel system look like? What new kind of intermediary will develop and what will it do? Let's consider one scenario.

After you surf the Net and put products in your virtual shopping basket at one or more Web sites, what should happen next? Perhaps the seller will start by assembling your items in a carton with a bar code for your personal name, address, and account. Then, that carton, along with cartons for all of the other orders that come into that Web site, will be taken quickly in large, economical batches to an intermediary. The computer-controlled sorting system at the intermediary's 5 acre facility will scan each carton for its bar code and route it to the sorting area for the truck that serves you and each of your neighbours. After a night of accumulating all the cartons that are directed to you from different sellers, the intermediary will place the cartons on a delivery vehicle in the right sequence so that they can be efficiently unloaded as the truck passes each customer on its route. Of course, you're not home. With the money you've saved by not running all over town burning gas, you're off on a vacation; you have time to take off because day after day you're not waiting in traffic and checkout lines. Although you're not home, you have a special cabinet—with a combination lock—mounted to the side of your house, where the delivery person leaves your purchases.

This little drama may seem far-fetched today. But it, or something like it, probably isn't far off. Specialist intermediaries will develop to make distribution *after* an Internet purchase more efficient, just as intermediaries developed to make distribution more efficient *prior* to purchases in retail stores. What is described above isn't very different from what UPS does, one package at a time, when it makes deliveries from manufacturers to retailers. But the cost per package is much higher than it would be if everybody received deliveries every day. It's like the difference between the cost of regular mail and special delivery.

If the after-purchase distribution problem is handled, who will the seller be? Will the Internet merchants of tomorrow be an evolved form of the retailers of today? Or will current-day wholesalers be in a better position to catch that prize? Some wholesalers are already working with very large assortments. Or in a world where you can conveniently surf from one specialized seller to another, will the breadth of assortment from any one seller be irrelevant? That could put producers in a stronger position. Perhaps none of these traditional forms of business will lead the way, but rather it will be a firm that takes birth on the Net to meet customers' needs in a completely new and unique way. The answers to these questions will take time, but they are taking shape even as you read. Already new intermediaries are coming on the scene.[33]

Let's admit it. You can only speculate about where net commerce will lead. But perhaps it's good to speculate a little. The way markets work in the future will depend on people like you, and the creative innovations that you speculate about, study, analyze, and ultimately turn into profitable marketing strategies. The competition will be tough, but hopefully you're now on your way to being up to the challenge.

Questions and Problems

1. Select a specific product. If you were the marketing manager for this product, what type of a retail operation would you want to use in your channel of distribution and why? Remember to consider nonstore as well as store-based retailers.
2. What advantages does a retail chain have over a retailer who operates with a single store? Does a small retailer have any advantages in competing against a chain? Explain your answer.
3. Discuss the advantages and disadvantages of small retailers and small producers linking up to distribute unique products to consumers.
4. Discuss the changes in the marketing environment that you think explain why direct-mail and television retailing have been growing so rapidly.
5. This chapter asserts that stores are products in themselves, not just a collection of producers' products. Do you agree or disagree? Explain your position.
6. Select a specific store in your community and interview the owner or manager. What combination of marketing, human resource, and financial strategies is used in this store? What opportunities are there for improvement?
7. List some recent technological innovations that have been adopted by stores in your community. Discuss the consumer and retailer benefits associated with their use.
8. Are the opportunities for international expansion as good for store-based retailers as they are for goods producers? Explain your answer.
9. Discuss the potential of electronic shopping from the standpoint of international retailing.
10. If you managed a small retail store in your community, how would you go about keeping yourself informed both about your customers' attitudes and expectations toward shopping and, as well, about all the other changes expected to occur in retailing over the next few years?
11. What risks do merchant wholesalers assume by taking title to goods? Is the size of this risk about constant for all merchant wholesalers?
12. Why would a manufacturer set up its own sales branches if established wholesalers were already available?
13. What is an agent intermediary's marketing mix? Why do you think that many merchant wholesalers handle competing products from different producers, while manufacturers' agents usually handle only noncompeting products from different producers?
14. Discuss the future growth and nature of wholesaling if low-margin retail chains and scrambled merchandising continue to become more important. How will wholesalers have to adjust their mixes? Will wholesalers be eliminated? If not, what wholesaling functions will be most important? Are there any particular lines of trade where wholesalers may have increasing difficulty?
15. What alternatives does a producer have if it is trying to expand distribution in a foreign market and finds that the best existing merchant wholesalers won't handle imported products?
16. Discuss how computer systems affect wholesalers' and retailers' operations.
17. Do wholesalers and retailers need to worry about new-product planning just as a producer needs to have an organized new-product development process? Explain your answer.

Suggested cases

10 Crankcase Transmission

11 Ralph the Optician

16 Runners World

Computer-aided problem

Selecting Channel Intermediaries

Art Glass Productions, a producer of decorative glass gift items, wants to expand into a new territory. Managers at Art Glass know that unit sales in the new territory will be affected by consumer response to the products. But sales will also be affected by which combination of wholesalers and retailers Art Glass selects. There is a choice between two wholesalers. One wholesaler, Giftware Distributing, is a merchant wholesaler that specializes in gift items; it sells to gift shops, department stores, and some mass-merchandisers. The other wholesaler, Margaret Degan & Associates, is a manufacturers' agent that calls on many of the gift shops in the territory.

Art Glass makes a variety of glass items, but the cost of making an item is usually about the same—$5.20 a unit. The items would sell to Giftware Distributing at $12.00 each—and in turn the merchant wholesaler's price to retailers would be $14.00—leaving Giftware with a $2.00 markup to cover costs and profit. Giftware Distributing is the only reputable merchant wholesaler in the territory, and it has agreed to carry the line only if Art Glass is willing to advertise in a trade magazine aimed at retail buyers for gift items. These ads will cost $8,000 a year.

As a manufacturers' agent, Margaret Degan would cover all of her own expenses and would earn 8 percent of the $14.00 price per unit charged the gift shops. Individual orders would be shipped directly to the retail gift shops by Art Glass—using United Parcel Service (UPS). Art Glass would pay the UPS charges at an average cost of $2.00 per item. In contrast, Giftware Distributing would anticipate demand and place larger orders in advance. This would reduce the shipping costs, which Art Glass would pay, to about $.60 a unit.

Art Glass's marketing manager thinks that Degan would only be able to sell about 75 percent as many items as Giftware Distributing—since she doesn't have time to call on all of the smaller shops and doesn't call on any department stores. On the other hand, the merchant wholesaler's demand for $8,000 worth of supporting advertising requires a significant outlay.

The marketing manager at Art Glass decided to use a spreadsheet to determine how large sales would have to be to make it more profitable to work with Giftware and to see how the different channel arrangements would contribute to profits at different sales levels.

a. Given the estimated unit sales and other values shown on the initial spreadsheet, which type of wholesaler would contribute the most profit to Art Glass Productions?

b. If sales in the new territory are slower than expected, so that the merchant wholesaler was able to sell only 3,000 units—or the agent 2,250 units—which wholesaler would contribute the most to Art Glass's profits? (Note: Assume that the merchant wholesaler only buys what it can sell—that is, it doesn't carry extra inventory beyond what is needed to meet demand.)

c. Prepare a table showing how the two wholesalers' contributions to profit compare as the quantity sold varies from 3,500 units to 4,500 units for the merchant wholesaler and 75 percent of these numbers for the manufacturers' agent. Discuss these results.

(Note: Use the What If analysis to vary the quantity sold by the merchant wholesaler, and the program will compute 75 percent of that quantity as the estimate of what the agent will sell.)

For additional questions related to this problem, see Exercise 13–4 in the *Learning Aid for Use with Basic Marketing,* Ninth Canadian Edition.

When you finish this chapter, you should:

- Know the advantages and disadvantages of the promotion methods a marketing manager can use in strategic planning.
- Understand the integrated marketing communications concept and why most firms use a blend of different promotion methods.
- Understand the importance of promotion objectives.
- Know how the communication process affects promotion planning.
- Understand how direct-response promotion is helping marketers develop more targeted promotion blends.
- Understand how new customer-initiated interactive communication is different.
- Know how typical promotion plans are blended to get an extra push from intermediaries and help from customers in pulling products through the channel.
- Understand how promotion blends typically vary over the adoption curve and product life cycle.
- Understand how to determine how much to spend on promotion efforts.
- Understand the important new terms (shown in orange).

Chap fourteen

Promotion—Introduction to Integrated Marketing Communications

. . . As director of sales and marketing at Toronto-based Canadian Tire Corp., Karl Bruenjes oversaw the September launch of the eFLYER, a weekly electronic brochure that "pushes" product information into customers' e-mail.

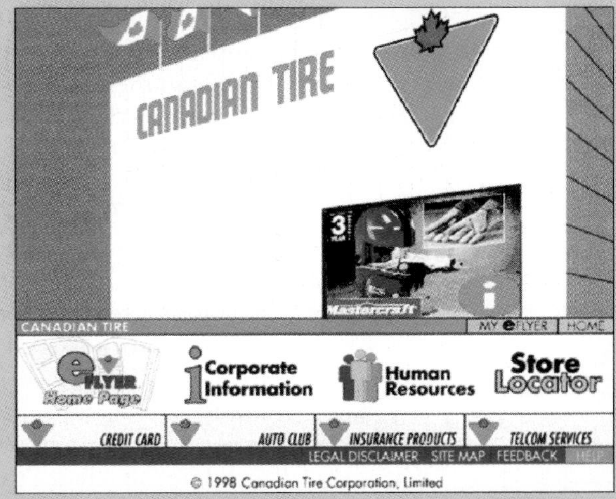

Thirty thousand people signed up for the service during its first four months, he says. And interest is growing, with the latest figure pegged at 55,000 subscribers. Bruenjes says the program has been a success: Canadian Tire's goal was 50,000 eFLYER customers after a year, and it has coasted to that number in half the time.

As more people turn to the Net as a place to shop, marketers ranging from huge retail chains to small-time operators, like Bill and Joe selling software out of their basement, are creating Web sites to meet the demand. CDs and books, once the mainstays of online stores, are now sharing band-width with apparel, furniture, fitness equipment, electronics and outdoor leisure items. Consumers have the option of buying these items in cyberstores or through site catalogues, depending on what retailers offer online.

There's no consensus on the value of Net sales in Canada. But Deloitte & Touche Consulting Group in Toronto estimates that last year they reached about $255 million, out of a worldwide total of $12.8 billion. The firm predicts that online sales in this country will soar 27-fold in just five years—the same rate of growth as globally. By 2002, it forecasts sales will total a massive $6.9 billion in Canada and $348 billion worldwide.

That increase is based on the assumption that online security issues will be resolved by then, says Adel Melek, senior manager of Deloitte & Touche's e-commerce group. He says consumers' concerns about insecure personal information remain the biggest hindrance to e-commerce.

Canadian Tire has sidestepped this problem by providing a service that doesn't require customers to make purchases over the Net. This is how the eFLYER works: A consumer registers for it at the company's Web site (www.canadiantire.ca) and specifies merchandise preferences. For example, a handyman requesting information on power tools may receive a customized eFLYER featuring drills, jigsaws and routers, complete with product descriptions, photos and prices. A customer can print a shopping list of product choices that may make him or her eligible for double-Canadian Tire money or double Options points, depending on the payment method.

While Canadian Tire wants to track whether higher sales are associated with the eFLYER, Bruenjes says that's very difficult, because the same products are advertised in other media. He will reveal that the average transaction value by people who use the eFLYER's shopping list function is "at least twice what it is for our typical customer," though he remains tight-lipped about the actual amount.

Bruenjes attributes the eFLYER's appeal, in part, to the fact that "the Canadian Tire (print) flyer is the most read and most well-liked flyer in Canada," according to company research. (It sends nine million flyers to Canadian households every week, and distributes another nine million catalogues twice a year, reaching about 80% of all households.) The eFLYER has also found success because the Net-savvy population is skyrocketing. "So having that available in an e-mail format to them every week is obviously attractive," says Bruenjes . . .

The eFLYER concept came to the forefront during focus group discussions shortly after Canadian Tire created its corporate Web site last April. Some participants said they wanted to see products online.

The eFLYER was not designed to be transactionally based because "90% of the population need to travel no more than 15 minutes to get to a Canadian Tire store," says Bruenjes. Moreover, the need to transact online and have the product delivered to your house did not come out strongly during discussions, he says.

Security of personal information—namely credit card numbers—was another factor in the decision to embrace just an online flyer. Bruenjes believes that people's attitudes about transmitting credit card information will eventually change, but he expects the "level of discomfort" to continue over the next six months . . .

While Canadian Tire may look at "some product lines" in the future, Bruenjes says he'd need "a pretty strong indication" that customers favor full blown e-commerce. Prior to that kind of investment, he says, the company must consider whether it wants to wind up delivering "everything from a box of Tide to a lawn tractor". . .

Source: Abridged from Fawzia Sheikh, "Custom E-Flyers," *Marketing Magazine,* March 16, 1998, p. 11.

Several promotion methods are available

Promotion is communicating information between seller and potential buyer or others in the channel to influence attitudes and behaviour. The marketing manager's main promotion job is to tell target customers that the right Product is available at the right Place at the right Price.

What the marketing manager communicates is determined by target customers' needs and attitudes. *How* the messages are delivered depends on what blend of the various promotion methods the marketing manager chooses.

A marketing manager can choose from several promotion methods—personal selling, mass selling, and sales promotion (see Exhibit 14–1). Further, because the different promotion methods have different strengths and limitations, a marketing manager usually uses them in combination. And, as with other marketing mix decisions, it is critical that the marketer manage and coordinate the different promotion methods as an integrated "whole," not as separate and unrelated parts. Further, to be effective promotion must work well with the other elements of the marketing mix and be matched with the needs and interests of a specific target market.

Exhibit 14–1 Basic Promotion Methods and Strategic Planning

Personal selling—flexibility is its strength

Personal selling involves direct spoken communication between sellers and potential customers. Face-to-face selling provides immediate feedback, which helps salespeople to adapt. Although salespeople are included in most marketing mixes, personal selling can be very expensive. So it's often desirable to combine personal selling with mass selling and sales promotion.

Mass selling involves advertising and publicity

Mass selling involves communicating with large numbers of potential customers at the same time. It's less flexible than personal selling, but when the target market is large and scattered, mass selling can be less expensive.

Advertising is the main form of mass selling. **Advertising** is any *paid* form of nonpersonal presentation of ideas, goods, or services by an identified sponsor. It includes the use of traditional media like magazines, newspapers, radio and TV, billboards, and direct mail, as well as new media such as the Internet. While advertising must be paid for, another form of mass selling—publicity—is "free."

Publicity avoids media costs

Publicity is any *unpaid* form of nonpersonal presentation of ideas, goods, or services. Of course, publicity people are paid. But they try to attract attention to the firm and its offerings *without having to pay media costs.* For example, book publishers try to get authors on TV talk shows because this generates a lot of interest—and book sales—without the publisher paying for TV time. As seen in the accompanying ad, Canada NewsWire Ltd. uses a mix of modern technologies to help Canadian firms distribute their press releases.

Coleco's publicity to introduce its Cabbage Patch dolls is a classic example. It held press parties for reporters and their children. A number of reporters wrote human interest stories about their kids "adopting" the cute dolls. Those stories prompted more media attention—and a very successful product introduction—without Coleco doing any introductory advertising.[1]

If a firm has a really new message, publicity may be more effective than advertising. Trade magazines, for example, may carry articles featuring the newsworthy products of regular advertisers—in part because they *are* regular advertisers. The firm's publicity people write the basic copy and then try to convince magazine editors to print it. Each year, magazines print photos and stories about new cars, and often the source of the information is the auto producers. A consumer might not pay any attention to an ad but read carefully a long magazine story with the same information.

Some companies prepare videotapes designed to get free publicity for their products on TV news shows. For example, after learning that Seattle Mariner Jay Buhner loves Cheerios, a General Mills marketing manager had 162 boxes of the cereal stuffed into his spring-training locker. Then he made a videotape of Buhner's surprise on opening his locker. When the videotape was offered to TV stations, it was shown on news programs in 12 major markets around the country. It cost virtually nothing to produce the video, but it would have cost hundreds of thousands of dollars to get as much attention with advertising on the evening news.[2]

Sales promotion tries to spark immediate interest

Sales promotion refers to promotion activities (excluding advertising, publicity, and personal selling) that stimulate interest, trial, or purchase by final customers or others in the channel. Sales promotion may be aimed at consumers, at

Linking all the pieces into your communications solution

We're Canada NewsWire

Your Multi-Technology Approach To Corporate Communications.

When you've got something important and urgent to say about your organization, we'll deliver your message to the right people in the media, business and financial communities wherever they are -- across Canada and around the world.

And if your organization is publicly listed, we can ensure simultaneous real-time distribution and receipt of the financial information you must disclose to your stakeholders, brokers, analysts and money managers.

No one else can reach the people who count faster or more accurately. That's because CNW can put ALL the appropriate leading-edge communications technologies to work for you — everything from ENHANCED FAX to ON-LINE DATABASES to the INTERNET to SATELLITE VIDEO-CONFERENCING *PLUS* the MOST EXTENSIVE CANADIAN ON-LINE NETWORK reaching the media and the financial communities. Our representatives will help you choose the best methods and technologies to deliver YOUR message to YOUR audience the way THEY prefer to receive it.

Whether it's the announcement of a major new appointment ... a company takeover ... a stock split ... timely disclosure of financial information ... translation of your news releases into other languages ... or a public relations crisis where you must immediately publicize your company's reaction ... you can trust CNW to put together ALL the pieces of the communication puzzle to ensure the successful dissemination of your company's message.

For all your communications solutions call your nearest CNW office, or E-mail us at cnw@newswire.ca *today!*

Vancouver (604) 669-7764 Calgary (403) 269-7605
Toronto (416) 863-9350 Ottawa (613) 563-4465
Montreal (514) 878-2520 Halifax (902) 422-1411

Canada NewsWire

Give us your message. We'll give you the world.

Marketing Demo 14-1

The Tasting Race

Sampling is nothing new. Yet although shoppers have been nibbling on little cubes of cheese on toothpicks in grocery stores for years, these days they're being offered more samples of more types of food than ever before. Grocery shoppers, at a peak time, may be offered as many as 10 samples of everything from plain crackers to hot entrees.

Sampling is on the rise everywhere, and in-store sampling is no exception. Provigo, for instance, tripled the number of samplings in its stores in 1995 from 5,000 to 15,000. And sampling is continuing to grow at the Quebec grocery giant, which this spring started offering samples of complete, easy-to-prepare meals.

Sampling is becoming a more important part of the marketing mix because of the number of new, high-end products and different products being introduced. And in-store sampling is a win-win proposition: marketers get direct access to consumers to generate trial, and retailers add some excitement to the shopping experience and drive sales of the sampled products. But, with this growth, companies are forced to become more innovative with what they are sampling and to ensure that their booths stand out from the crowd.

Almost every new or relaunched product uses sampling, because it offers consumers a risk-free way to try the product, fulfilling the first step of the progression from trial to repeat use to brand loyalty. Tim Carter, vice-president of public affairs for The Oshawa Group of Toronto, owners of the IGA and Price Chopper grocery banners, says sampling is "the best way to get across to consumers the quality of a product fast."

Sue Martin, product manager for tomato products and condiments at H.J. Heinz Co. of Canada, explains that marketers need to do "anything we can do to get the product into the consumer's mouth before she has to take the risk of buying it."

Recently, Toronto-based Heinz used in-store sampling to launch Heinz/McIlhenny Tobasco Hot Ketchup, which has been available in Canada since last October.

Sampling in the grocery store allows marketers access to consumers right where they are making their purchase decisions—"at the moment of truth," says Bern Gorecki, VP of marketing and sales at InStore Focus, a Toronto-based sampling company.

Sampling also adds a personal element to advertising that is otherwise impersonal. As Gorecki says, it "brings the brand to life." He explains that the sample is the company's opportunity to prove all the promises it makes in its advertising. The human element also allows the consumer to ask questions about the product or how to prepare it and even offer feedback, he adds . . .

But sampling is not the answer for all new products. Carter says in order to sample a product the company should be confident that it has the best-tasting entry in the category. He says companies should sample products if the primary selling feature is taste, not price . . .

Source: Abridged from Lesley Daw, *Marketing Magazine*, August 18–25, 1997, S1.

Exhibit 14-2 Example of Sales Promotion Activities

Aimed at final consumers or users	Aimed at intermediaries	Aimed at company's own sales force
Contests	Price deals	Contests
Coupons	Promotion allowances	Bonuses
Aisle displays	Sales contests	Meetings
Samples	Calendars	Portfolios
Trade shows	Gifts	Displays
Point-of-purchase materials	Trade shows	Sales aids
Banners and streamers	Meetings	Training materials
Trading stamps	Catalogues	
Sponsored events	Merchandising aids	

intermediaries, or even at a firm's own employees (see Exhibit 14–2). Relative to other promotion methods, sales promotion can usually be implemented quickly and get results sooner. In fact, most sales promotion efforts are designed to produce immediate results. For an example, see Marketing Demo 14–1, which describes in-store sampling of food products.

Food sampling is increasing, and you soon may have "lunch" at the supermarket.

Costs of advertising vs. personal selling or sales promotion

Because advertising is all around them, many people think that promotion money gets spent mainly on advertising. The many ads you see in magazines and newspapers and on TV are impressive—and costly. But all the special sales promotions—coupons, sweepstakes, trade shows, event sponsorships, and the like—add up to even more money. Also, salesclerks complete most retail sales, while behind the scenes, much personal selling goes on in the channels and in other business markets. In total, firms spend less money on advertising than on personal selling or sales promotion.

That being said, the amount of emphasis on each promotion method usually varies with each specific marketing strategy, which in turn depends on the target market and other elements of the marketing mix. Different promotion methods have different strengths and limitations. But they also complement each other, and some communication tasks can be handled better or more economically with one method than with another. In sum, to get the entire promotion job done, most firms use a blend of the three promotion methods.

We'll talk about individual promotion methods in more detail in the next two chapters. First, however, you need to understand the role of the entire promotion blend—personal selling, mass selling, and sales promotion combined—so that you can see how promotion fits into the rest of the marketing mix.

Someone must plan, integrate, and manage the promotion blend

Each promotion method has its own strengths and weaknesses, and in combination they provide a comprehensive set of tools for marketing communications. And each method involves its own distinct activities and requires different types of expertise.

This is why it's usually the responsibility of specialists—such as sales managers, advertising managers, and promotion managers—to develop and implement the detailed plans for the various parts of the overall promotion blend.

Sales managers manage salespeople

Sales managers are concerned with managing personal selling. Often the sales manager is responsible for building good distribution channels and implementing Place policies. In smaller companies, the sales manager may also act as the marketing manager, and be responsible for advertising and sales promotion.

Advertising managers work with ads and agencies

Advertising managers manage their company's mass selling efforts on television, and in newspapers, magazines, and other media. Their job is to choose the right media and develop the ads. Advertising departments within a firm may help in these efforts, or outside advertising agencies may be used. The advertising manager may handle publicity as well. Or it may be handled by an outside agency or by whoever handles **public relations**—communication with noncustomers, including labour, public interest groups, shareholders, and the government.

Sales promotion managers need many talents

Sales promotion managers manage their company's sales promotion efforts. In some companies a sales promotion manager has independent status and reports directly to the marketing manager. If a firm's sales promotion spending is substantial, it probably *should* have a specific sales promotion manager. Sometimes, however, the sales or advertising departments handle sales promotion efforts, or sales promotion is left as a responsibility of individual brand managers. Whoever the manager is, sales promotion activities vary so much that many firms use both inside and outside specialists.

The marketing manager talks to all, blends all

Although many specialists may be involved in planning for and implementing specific promotion methods, determining the blend of promotion methods is a strategy decision, and the responsibility of the marketing manager.

The various promotion specialists tend to focus on what they know best and on their own areas of responsibility. A creative Web page designer or advertising copy writer in Toronto—even a very good one—may have no idea what a salesperson does during a call on a wholesale distributor. Also, because of differences in outlook and experience, the advertising, sales, and sales promotion managers often have trouble working together as partners or equals. Too often they view other promotion methods as using up budget money they want.

The marketing manager must weigh the pros and cons of the various promotion methods, and devise an effective promotion blend that brings together the various departments and personalities and coordinates their efforts. Then, the advertising, sales, and sales promotion managers should develop the details consistent with what the marketing manager wants to accomplish.

Consistent and complete messages equal integrated marketing communications

An effective blending of all of the firm's promotion efforts should result in **integrated marketing communications**—the intentional coordination of every communication from a firm to a target customer to convey a consistent and complete message.

Different promotion methods handle different parts of the overall communication job, but the methods are coordinated so that the sum is greater than the parts. The separate messages are complementary; they are also consistent.

It seems obvious that a firm's various communications to a target market should be consistent. However, when a number of different people are working on different promotion elements, they are likely to see the same big picture only if a marketing manager ensures that it happens. The challenge of consistency is usually greater when different aspects of the promotion effort are handled by different firms at different levels in the distribution channel. As we've discussed, different channel members may have conflicting objectives, especially if they don't have a common focus on the consumer or business user at the end of the channel.

As a starting point, to get effective coordination and consistency everyone involved with the promotion effort must understand clearly the plan for the overall marketing strategy. They all need to understand the role of each of the different promotion methods and how they will work together to achieve specific promotion objectives.[3]

Which methods to use depends on promotion objectives

The different promotion methods are all different forms of communication. But good marketing managers aren't interested simply in communicating: they want communication that encourages customers to choose a *specific* product. They know that if they have a better offering, informed customers are more likely to buy. Therefore, they're interested in (1) reinforcing present attitudes or relationships that might lead to favourable behaviour or (2) actually changing the attitudes and behaviour of the firm's target market.

In terms of demand curves, promotion may help the firm make its present demand curve more inelastic, or shift the demand curve to the right, or both. These possibilities are shown in Exhibit 14–3. The buyer behaviour model introduced in Chapter 6 showed the many influences on buying behaviour. You saw there that changing buyer behaviour is a tough job—but that is precisely the objective of Promotion.

Informing, persuading, reminding—the basic promotion objectives

For a firm's promotion to be effective, its promotion objectives must be clearly defined. The right promotion blend depends on what the firm wants to accomplish. It's helpful to think of the three basic promotion objectives: *informing, persuading,* and *reminding* target customers about the company and its marketing mix. All three

Exhibit 14–3 Promotion Seeks to Shift the Demand Curve

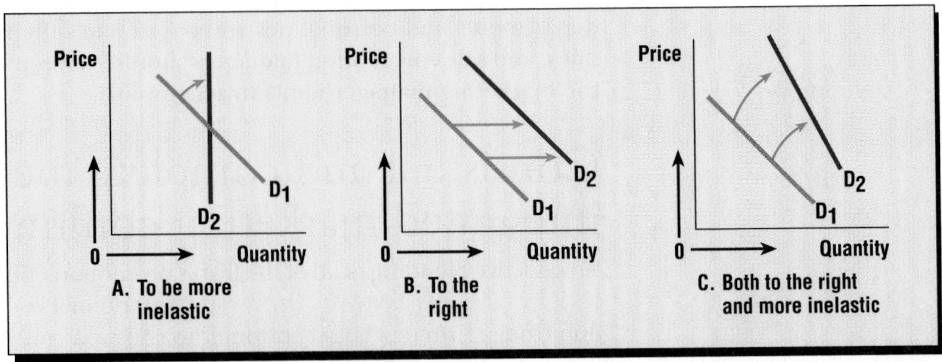

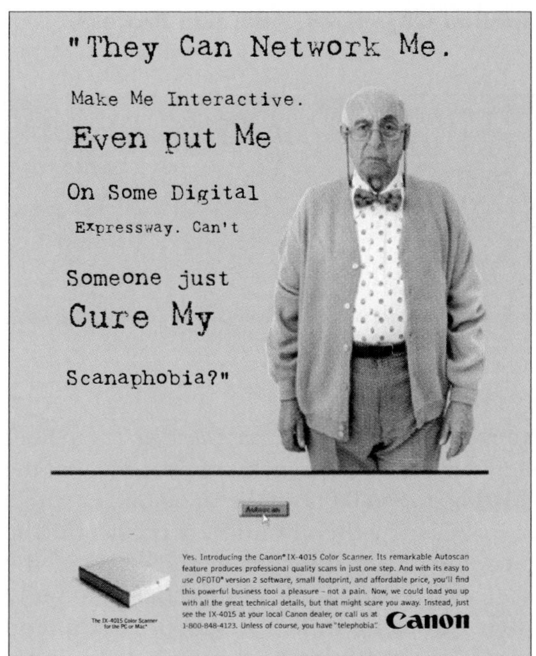

"They Can Network Me.
Make Me Interactive.
Even put Me
On Some Digital
Expressway. Can't
Someone just
Cure My
Scanaphobia?"
Yes. Introducing the Canon® IX-4015 Color Scanner. Its remarkable Autoscan feature produces professional quality scans in just one step. And with its easy to use OFOTO® version 2 software, small footprint, and affordable price, you'll find this powerful business tool a pleasure – not a pain. Now, we could load you up with all the great technical details, but that might scare you away. Instead, just see the IX-4015 at your local Canon dealer, or call us at 1-800-848-4123. Unless of course, you have "telephobia".
The IX-4015 Color Scanner for the PC or Mac®
Canon

Canon's colour scanner is a technical product, but Canon recognizes that its promotion must be effective in communicating with target customers who neither know nor like a lot of technical jargon.

objectives involve changing buyer behaviour by providing more information.

Even more useful is a more specific set of promotion objectives that outline *exactly who* you want to inform, persuade, or remind, and *why*. This set of objectives is unique to each company's strategy—and specific objectives vary by promotion method. We'll talk about more specific promotion objectives in the next two chapters. Here we'll limit ourselves to the three basic promotion objectives, and how you can reach them.

Informing is educating

Potential customers must know something about a product if they are to buy at all. A firm with a really new product may not have to do anything but inform consumers about it—and show that it meets consumer needs better than other products. When Volkswagen reintroduced its Beetle, both the unique styling of the car and its nostalgia appeal simplified the promotion job. Excitement about the Beetle generated a lot of free publicity in car magazines and newspapers. Salespeople refereed arguments between desperate customers at North American VW dealerships.[4]

Persuading usually becomes necessary

When competitors offer similar products, the firm must not only inform customers that its product is available but also persuade them to buy it. A *persuading* objective means that the firm will try to develop a favourable set of attitudes so that customers will buy—and keep buying—its product. Promotion with a persuading objective often focuses on reasons why one brand is better than competing brands. To help convince consumers to buy Tylenol rather than some other firm's brand, Johnson & Johnson's ads position Tylenol as the safe and effective pain relief medicine that is typically used by hospitals.

Reminding may be enough, sometimes

When target customers already have positive attitudes about a firm's marketing mix—or a good relationship with a firm—a *reminding* objective may be suitable. This objective can be extremely important. Even though customers have been attracted and sold once, they are still targets for competitors' appeals. Reminding them of their past satisfaction may keep them from shifting to a competitor. Campbell realizes that most people know about its soup, so much of its advertising is intended to remind.

Promotion objectives relate to adoption process

In Chapter 6, we looked at consumer buying as a problem-solving process in which buyers go through six steps—awareness, interest, evaluation, trial, decision, and confirmation—on the way to adopting (or rejecting) an idea or product. Now we see that the three basic promotion objectives relate to these six steps (see Exhibit 14–4). *Informing* and *persuading* may be needed to affect the potential customer's knowledge and attitudes about a product—and then bring about its adoption. Later promotion can simply *remind* the customer about that favourable experience, and reinforce the adoption decision.

The AIDA model is a practical approach

The basic promotion objectives and adoption process fit very neatly with another action-oriented model, called AIDA, which we will use in this and the next two chapters to guide some of our discussion.

Exhibit 14-4 Relationship of Promotion Objectives, Adoption Process, and AIDA Model

Promotion objectives	Adoption process (Chapter 6)	AIDA model
Informing	Awareness Interest	Attention Interest
Persuading	Evaluation Trial	Desire
Reminding	Decision Confirmation	Action

The **AIDA model** consists of four promotion jobs: (1) to get *Attention,* (2) to hold *Interest,* (3) to arouse *Desire,* and (4) to obtain *Action.* (As a memory aid, note that the first letters of the four key words spell *AIDA*—the well-known Verdi opera.)

Exhibit 14–4 shows the relationship between the adoption process and the AIDA model. Getting attention is necessary to make consumers aware of the company's offering. Holding interest gives the communication a chance to build the consumer's interest in the product. Arousing desire affects the evaluation process and perhaps builds preference. And obtaining action includes gaining trial, which may lead to a purchase decision. Continuing promotion is needed to confirm the decision, and to encourage an ongoing relationship and additional purchases.

Promotion requires effective communication

Promotion is wasted if it doesn't achieve its objectives. And that happens when it doesn't communicate effectively. There are many reasons why a promotion message may be misunderstood or not heard at all. Here it's useful to think about an entire **communication process,** which involves a source trying to reach a receiver with a message. Exhibit 14–5 shows the elements of the communication process. Here a **source**—the sender of a message—is trying to deliver a message to a **receiver**—a potential customer. Research shows that customers evaluate not only the message but also the source of the message in terms of trustworthiness and credibility. For example, American Dental Association (ADA) studies show that Listerine mouthwash helps reduce plaque buildup on teeth. Listerine mentions the ADA endorsement in its promotion to help make the promotion message credible.

A major advantage of personal selling is that the source—the seller—can get immediate feedback from the receiver. It's easier to judge how the message is being received, and to change it if necessary. Mass sellers usually must depend on marketing research or total sales figures for feedback, and that can take too long. As we'll discuss later in this chapter, this has prompted some marketers to include toll-free telephone numbers and other ways of building direct-response feedback from consumers into their mass selling efforts.

The **noise** (see in Exhibit 14–5) is any distraction that reduces the effectiveness of the communication process. Conversations and snack-getting during TV ads are noise. The clutter of competing ads in a newspaper is noise. Advertisers planning messages must recognize that many possible distractions—noise—can interfere with communications.

"Colombian Coffee on ice."

Compare this Juan Valdez Colombian coffee ad to the AIDA model.

Exhibit 14–5 The Traditional Communication Process

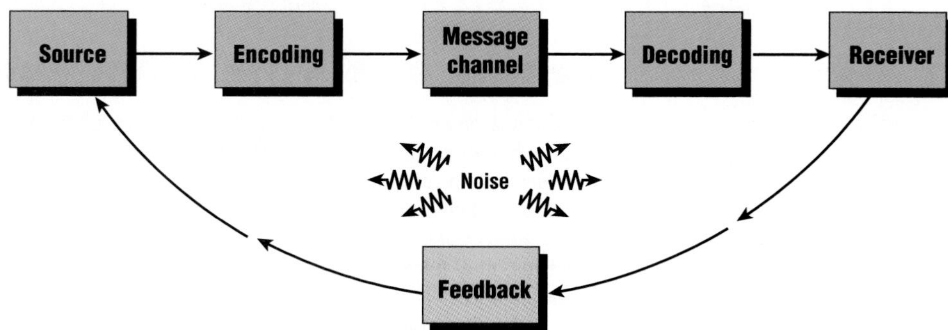

Exhibit 14–6 This Same Message May Be Interpreted Differently

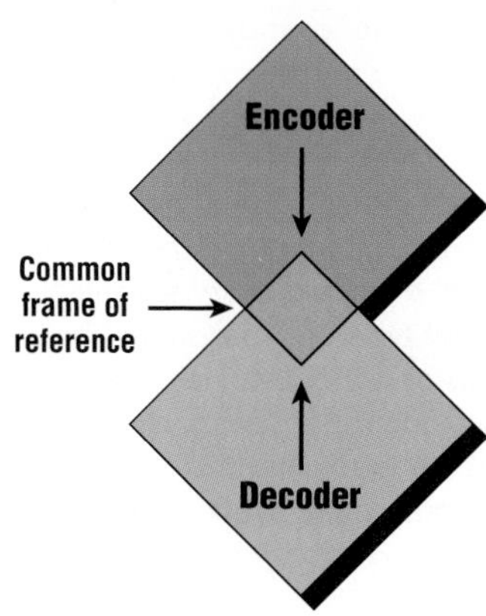

Encoding and decoding need a common frame of reference

The basic difficulty in the communication process occurs during encoding and decoding. **Encoding** relates to the source deciding what it wants to say and translating it into words or symbols that will have the same meaning to the receiver. **Decoding** has to do with the receiver translating the message. This process can be very tricky. The meanings of various words and symbols may differ depending on the attitudes and experiences of the two groups. People need a common frame of reference in order to communicate effectively (see Exhibit 14–6). Maidenform encountered this problem with its promotion aimed at working women. The company ran a series of ads depicting women stockbrokers and doctors wearing Maidenform lingerie. The men in the ads were fully dressed. Maidenform was trying to show women in positions of authority, but some women felt the ad presented them as sex objects. In this situation, the promotion people who encoded the message didn't understand the attitudes of the target market—and how they would decode the message.[5]

Message channel is important too

The communication process is complicated even more because the receiver knows the message is coming not only from a source but also through some **message channel**—the carrier of the message. A source can use many message channels to deliver a message. The salesperson does it in person with voice and action. Advertising must do it with magazines, newspapers, radio, and TV, or with less traditional media such as e-mail or Internet Web sites. A particular message channel may enhance or detract from a message. A TV ad, for example, can *show* that Dawn dishwashing detergent "takes the grease away"; the same claim in a newspaper ad might not be very convincing. On the other hand, a receiver may attach value to a product if the message comes in a well-respected newspaper or magazine. Some consumers buy products advertised in *Good Housekeeping* magazine, for example, because they have faith in its seal of approval.[6]

The same message may be interpreted differently

Different audiences may see the same message in different ways, or interpret the same words differently. Such differences are common in international marketing when cultural differences or translation are problems. In Taiwan, the translation of the Pepsi slogan "Come alive with the Pepsi Generation" came out as "Pepsi will bring your ancestors back from the dead." When Frank Perdue said, "It takes a tough man to make a tender chicken," Spanish speakers heard "It takes a sexually stimulated man to make a chicken affectionate." Worse, a campaign for Schweppes Tonic Water in Italy translated the name into Schweppes Toilet Water. Many firms run into problems like this.[7]

Ethical Dimensions

Honest and Fair Communications

Promotion is one of the most often criticized areas of marketing, and many of the criticisms focus on whether communications are honest and fair. Marketers must sometimes make ethical judgments when planning promotions.

Video publicity releases provide an interesting example. When a TV news program broadcasts a video publicity release, consumers don't know it was prepared to achieve marketing objectives; they think the news staff are the source. That may make the message more credible, but is it fair? Many say yes—as long as the publicity information is truthful. But grey areas remain. Consider, for example, a SmithKline Beecham video about a prescription heart attack drug. An estimated 27 million consumers saw the video on various TV news programs. The video included a laundry list of possible side effects and other warnings, just as is required for normal drug advertising. But there's never any guarantee that the warnings won't be edited out by local TV stations.

Critics raise similar concerns about the use of celebrities in advertisements. A person who plays the role of an honest and trustworthy person on a popular TV series may be a credible message source in an ad, but is using such a person misleading to consumers? Some critics believe it is. Others argue that consumers recognize advertising when they see it and know celebrities are paid for their endorsements.

The most common criticisms of promotion relate to promotional messages that make exaggerated claims. What does it mean for an ad or a salesperson to claim that a product is the "best available"? Is that the personal opinion of people in the firm, or should every statement—even very general ones—be backed up by objective proof? What type of proof should be required? Some promotional messages do misrepresent the benefits of a product. However, most marketing managers want to develop ongoing relationships with—and repeat purchases from—their customers. They realize that customers won't come back if the marketing mix doesn't deliver what the promotion promises. Further, consumers are becoming more sceptical about all the claims they hear and see. As a result, most marketing managers work to make promotion claims specific and believable.[8]

Problems occur even when there is no translation. For example, a new children's cough syrup was advertised as extra-strength. The advertising people thought they were assuring parents that the product worked well. But Moms and Dads avoided the product because they feared that it might be too strong for their children.

Integrated direct-response promotion is very targeted

The challenge of developing promotions that reach *specific* target customers has prompted many firms to turn to direct marketing—that is, direct communication between a seller and an individual customer using a promotion method other than face-to-face personal selling. Most direct marketing communications are designed to prompt immediate feedback—a direct response—by customers. That's why this type of communication is often called *direct-response promotion.*

Early efforts in the direct-response area focused on direct-mail advertising. A carefully selected mailing list (from the many available) allowed advertisers to reach a specific target audience with specific interests. Direct-mail advertising proved to be very effective when the objective was to get a direct response by customers.

Now it's more than direct-mail advertising

Achieving a measurable, direct response from specific target customers is still the heart of direct promotion. But the promotion medium is evolving to include not only mail but also telephone, print, computer networks, broadcast, and even interactive video. The customer's response may be a purchase (or donation), a question, or a request for more information. More often than not, the customer responds by calling a toll-free telephone number, or—in the case of business markets—by sending a fax. A knowledgeable salesperson talks with the customer on the phone and follows up. That may involve filling an order and having it shipped to the customer, or putting an interested prospect in touch with a salesperson, who then makes a personal visit. There are, however, many variations on this approach. For example, some firms route incoming information-request calls to a computerized answering system. The caller indicates what information is required by pushing a few buttons on the telephone keypad, and then the computer instantly sends requested information to the caller's fax machine.

Direct-response promotion often is an important component of integrated marketing communications programs and is closely tied to other elements of the marketing mix. What distinguishes this general approach is that the marketer targets more of its promotion effort at specific individuals, who respond directly.

A promotion campaign that marketing managers developed for Ryder Systems' move-it-yourself rental trucks illustrates these ideas. Ryder's marketing strategy focused on quality trucks and service rather than on bargain-basement prices. Ryder's objective was to increase truck rentals and sales of supplies while maintaining its premium prices. Most other rental firms were competing with lower prices, hoping for gains in market share to offset a market that was shrinking because of a weak economy.

To reach the target market—consumers who were considering a move—Ryder placed 60-second ads on popular TV shows whose audience demographics matched Ryder's target market. The ads touted Ryder quality and also offered consumers a free home-moving guide and planning kit. All the consumer had to do to get the promotional brochure was call a toll-free telephone number. The brochure provided useful information about moving—including details on how Ryder's comfortable trucks and helpful services could make the move easier. It also included a discount coupon for Ryder supplies (including furniture pads and locks) that consumers could redeem at any Ryder dealer. Equally important, the computerized mailing list (database) of people who called for the brochure served as a targeted list of prospects for Ryder's telemarketing salespeople. When one of them identified a good prospect, the final personal selling job was turned over to a local Ryder dealer. The dealer's personal attention helped to resolve consumer questions and get rental contracts. Further, because the entire promotion effort was consistent in differentiating Ryder's quality services, the dealers were able to charge a higher price than competitors.[9]

Target customer directly with a database

As the Ryder case suggests, direct-response promotion usually relies on a customer (or prospect) database to target specific individuals. The computerized database includes customers' names and addresses (or telephone numbers) as well as past purchases and other segmenting characteristics. Individuals (or segments) who respond to direct promotion are the target for additional promotion. For example, a customer who buys lingerie from a catalogue once is a good candidate for a follow-up. The follow-up might extend to other types of clothing. Greenpeace and the Cousteau Society send mail advertisements to people interested in environmental issues. They ask for donations or other types of support.

BMW and other car companies have found that videotapes are a good way to provide consumers with a lot of information about a new model. However, it's too expensive to send tapes to everyone. To target the mailing, BMW first sends likely car buyers (high-income consumers who own a BMW or competing brand) personalized direct-mail ads that offer a free videotape. Interested consumers send back a return card. Then BMW sends the advertising tape and updates its database so that a dealer will know to call the consumer.

Ethical Dimensions

Direct-Response Methods

Direct-response promotion and database targeting have become an important part of many marketing mixes, and more and more customers find direct-response very convenient. But not everyone is enthusiastic. Some critics argue that thousands of acres of trees are consumed each week just to make the paper for direct-response "junk mail" that consumers don't want. Other critics worry about privacy issues related to how a direct-response database might be used, especially if it includes detailed information about a consumer's purchases. Similarly, many consumers don't like getting direct promotion telephone solicitations anytime, but especially in the evening and at meal times when they seem to be particularly frequent. Most firms who use direct-response promotion are very sensitive to these concerns and take steps to address them.[10]

The customer may initiate the communication process

Traditional thinking about promotion—and for that matter about the communication process—has usually been based on the idea that it's the seller (source) who initiates the communication. Of course, for decades consumers have been looking in the Yellow Pages for information or asking retail salespeople for help. Similarly, it's not news that organizational buyers call potential vendors to ask questions or request bids.

Even so, marketers usually think of buyers as more or less passive message receivers in the communication process—at least until the marketer has done something to stimulate attention, interest, and desire. That's one reason why targeting is so important—so that the promotion effort and expense isn't wasted on someone who isn't at all interested. Moreover, the need for a blend of promotion methods is built on the idea that at any given point you can only get a customer's attention and interest for a few seconds—or a few minutes if you're really lucky. As we noted above, even with highly targeted direct-response promotion, the marketer typically takes the first step with promotion to get the interaction started.

New electronic media enable interactive communication

As shown in the Canadian Tire eFLYER case at the start of this chapter, we are seeing the start of some big changes—and these changes are ushering in new types of marketing opportunities. In the information age, it is much easier for customers to search for information on their own. In fact, the buyer may be able to access a great deal of information and place an order without any direct involvement by the seller. The new interactive information technologies enabling this change take many different forms. Some of the most important are the World Wide Web and e-mail listservers on the Internet, caller-controlled fax-on-demand, computerized telephone voice-messaging systems, video kiosks in malls, CD-ROM and DVD disks on personal computers, and Web TV.

New variations on these interactive technologies are being developed all the time. For example, in England, where interactive cable TV systems are already typical, consumers have access to a system called Teletext. With Teletext, they can use their standard TV remote control unit to search through thousands of on-screen pages of information—ranging from the schedules for flights from London's airports, to the current weather, to advertising for automobiles and specials at the local supermarket. The benefits of Teletext are very similar to the benefits of the World Wide Web on the Internet, but this system is even simpler to use. Similar systems will become more available in other countries as government regulations change and as cable companies upgrade their equipment.

Exhibit 14-7 A Model of Customer-Initiated Interactive Communication

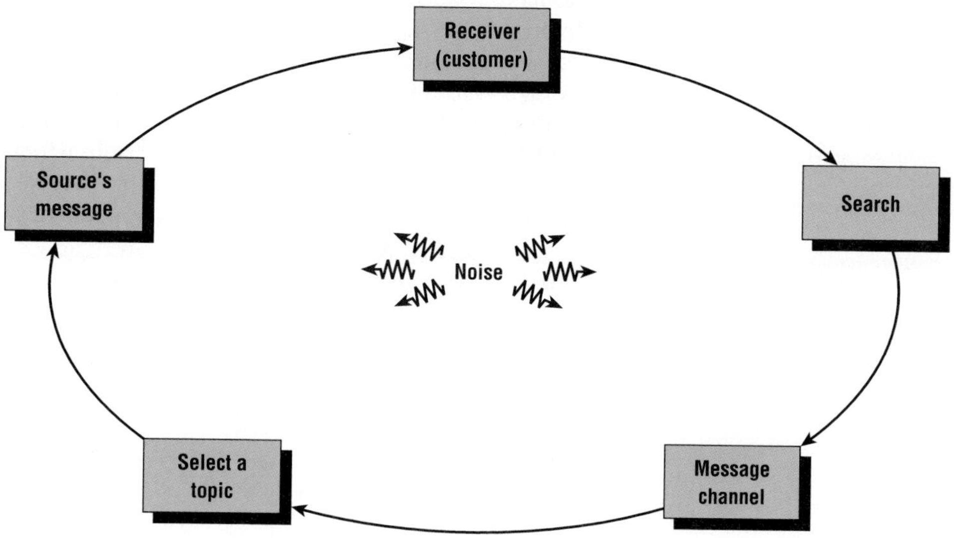

This type of customer-initiated information search and/or communication represents a change that will become prevalent for more types of purchases in the future, so we should think about it in more detail. Let's start by contrasting the simple model of customer (receiver) initiated interactive communication shown in Exhibit 14–7. At first it doesn't seem that different from the traditional communication model we considered earlier (Exhibit 14–5). You will see, however, that the differences are significant.

Consumer initiates communication with a search process

In the model in Exhibit 14–7, a customer initiates the process with a decision to search for information in a particular message channel. In the new information environment, perhaps the most far-reaching message channel to search is the Internet. As was the case before, the message channel is still the carrier of the message, but "searchable" message channels usually feature an archive of preexisting messages on a number of topics. In some situations, many topics—even millions—may be available.

In the next step, the consumer selects one specific topic on which to receive a message. A topic might be selected in a variety of ways, depending on the message channel. The most typical approaches involve using a mouse, a remote control device, or a keypad to highlight a selection from some sort of initial list (such as a table of contents or index). Of course, other approaches are common. For example, many dial-up telephone systems are using voice-recognition systems. Or in the case of the Internet, you might enter a word or phrase and then ask the computer to search for a list of topics that use that word.

Consumer decides how much information to get

Once a specific topic is selected, the message for that topic is displayed. Typically, the message is quite brief, but it may also include information about a simple way to get more detailed information, select another related topic, return to the original selection process, or quit the search. After each message the consumer can decide whether to search further (say, to get more detail on an initial topic or to broaden the search to other topics). This interactive approach makes it easy for the consumer to conveniently get as much or as little information as desired and to spend as little or as much time searching as seems worthwhile. However, noise may still be a problem; for example, a consumer who wants information about a specific product may waste a lot of time and not find what is needed, because it was not available on the message channel or it was too hard to find. This can be very frustrating for the consumer. This is why some firms are creating ways that a consumer can click on a Web site choice and in doing so establish voice communication with a real person at a 24-hour-a-day calling centre. For example, Mercedes-Benz has been testing AT&T's "interactiveAnswers" approach, in which a person at the calling centre telephones the customer and provides the precise product information needed. Other firms are using variations of this approach, including live teleconferencing over the Internet. Many personal computers now come equipped with everything needed for this type of Internet teleconferencing.

Action—including purchase—may be immediate

Even without a voice link to a live salesperson, the "action" required to make a purchase via interactive media is usually very fast and easy, because increasingly, one of the selections available for the customer is "how to buy." At many Internet sites, for example, a consumer can click on a selected item to place it in a virtual shopping cart, charge it to a credit card, and arrange for shipping by a service like UPS.

Custom communications will be more personalized

As you can see, the traditional principles of communication that we discussed earlier in the chapter are still important in customer-initiated interactive communication. At the same time, the new interactive approach allows the marketer to customize communication to the needs of the consumer. As new approaches develop in this arena, we are likely to see more and more promotion targeted at single-person "segments."

The multimedia capabilities of the new electronic media mean that many types of information—pictures, graphs, words, video, and sounds—can be combined and used in one place. As a result, one advantage of the new electronic media is that they serve as an archive for all of the different promotional materials that a firm develops. This allows managers with responsibilities for different specialties to see how their materials work with the rest of the firm's promotion blend—so there is even more incentive to develop integrated communication.[11]

How typical promotion plans are blended and integrated

Most marketing managers try to integrate and blend the three different promotion methods because some promotion jobs can be done more economically one way than another. But what blend is right in a particular situation?

There is no one *right* promotion blend for all situations. Each must be developed as part of a marketing mix, and should be designed to achieve the firm's promotion objectives in each marketing strategy. For example, if the channel of distribution for a firm's product involves intermediaries, the marketing manager must consider the promotion blend that is appropriate in the channel as well as what type of promotion should be targeted at customers at the end of the channel. Similarly, the emphasis among the three types of promotion typically varies depending on whether the customers at the end of the channel are business users or final consumers. Let's take a closer look at typical promotion blends in these different situations.

A push in the channel with promotion to intermediaries

When a channel of distribution involves intermediaries, their cooperation can be crucial to the success of the overall marketing strategy. **Pushing** (a product through a channel) means using normal promotion efforts—personal selling, advertising, and sales promotion—to help sell the whole marketing mix to possible channel members. This approach emphasizes the importance of building a channel and securing the wholehearted cooperation of channel members to push the product down the channel to the final user.

Producers usually take on much of the responsibility for the pushing effort in the channel. However, most wholesalers also handle at least some of the promotion to retailers or other wholesalers further down the channel. Similarly, retailers often handle at least some of the promotion in their local markets. When different firms in the channel handle different aspects of communicating to final consumers or business users, the overall promotion effort is most likely to be effective when all of the individual messages are carefully integrated—that is, coordinated, consistent, and complete.

Promotion to intermediaries stresses personal selling

Salespeople handle most of the important communication with intermediaries. Intermediaries don't want empty promises; they want to know what they can expect in return for their cooperation and help. A salesperson can answer questions about what promotion will be directed toward the final consumer, discuss each channel member's part in marketing the product, and provide important details on pricing, markups, promotion assistance, and allowances.

A salesperson can help the firm determine when it should adjust its marketing mix from one intermediary to another. In highly competitive urban areas, for example, mixes may emphasize price.

When a number of suppliers offer similar products and compete for attention and shelf space, the wholesaler or retailer usually pays attention to the one with the best profit potential. In these situations, the sales rep must convince the intermediary that demand for the product exists and that making a profit will be easy. A firm can make the sales rep's job easier by targeting special sales promotion at intermediaries too.

Sales promotions targeted at intermediaries usually focus on short-term arrangements that will improve the intermediaries' profits. For example, a soft-drink bottler might offer a convenience store a free case of drinks with each two cases it buys. The free case improves the store's profit margin on the entire purchase. Or a supplier might offer a price discount if the retailer uses a special point-of-purchase display. Other types of sales promotions, such as contests that offer vacation trips for high-volume intermediaries, are also common.

Firms run ads in trade magazines to recruit new intermediaries or to inform channel members about a new offering. Trade ads usually encourage intermediaries to contact the supplier for more information, and then a salesperson takes over.

Push within a firm—with promotion to employees

Some firms emphasize promotion to their own employees—especially salespeople or others in contact with customers. This type of *internal marketing* effort is basically a variation on the pushing approach. One objective is to inform employees about important elements of the marketing strategy, so that they'll work together as a team to implement it. Some firms use promotion to motivate employees to work harder at specific jobs, such as providing customer service or achieving higher sales. For example, many firms use sales contests and award free trips to big sellers.

Some companies design the ads they target at customers so that the ads also communicate to employees—and boost the employees' image. This is typical in service-oriented industries where the quality of the employees' efforts is a big part of the product. For example, some Delta Airlines ads use the theme "we like to fly, and it shows." Although the ads communicate mainly to customers, they remind Delta's employees that the service they provide is crucial to the marketing strategy—and to customer satisfaction.

Pulling the product through the channel

Whatever promotion a firm uses to get help from channel members or employees in pushing a product, most producers focus a significant amount of promotion on the customers at the end of the channel. This helps stimulate demand for the firm's offering and can help pull the product through the channel of distribution. **Pulling** means getting customers to ask intermediaries for the product.

Pulling and pushing are usually used in combination (see Exhibit 14–8, and Internet Insite 14–1 for an example of how these concepts apply to the Web). However, if intermediaries won't work with a producer—perhaps because they're already carrying a competing brand—a producer may try to use a pulling approach by itself. This involves a highly aggressive and expensive promotion to final consumers or users (perhaps using coupons or samples) that temporarily bypasses intermediaries. If the promotion works, the intermediaries will be forced to carry the product to satisfy customer requests. However, this approach is risky. Companies can waste an expensive promotion effort if customers lose interest before reluctant intermediaries make the product available. At minimum, intermediaries should be told about the planned pulling effort, so that they can be ready if the promotion succeeds.

Who handles promotion to final customers at the end of the channel varies in different channel systems, depending on the mix of pushing and pulling. Further, the promotion blend typically varies depending on whether customers are final consumers or business users.[12]

Exhibit 14–8 Promotion May Encourage Pushing in the Channel, or Pulling by Customers, or Both

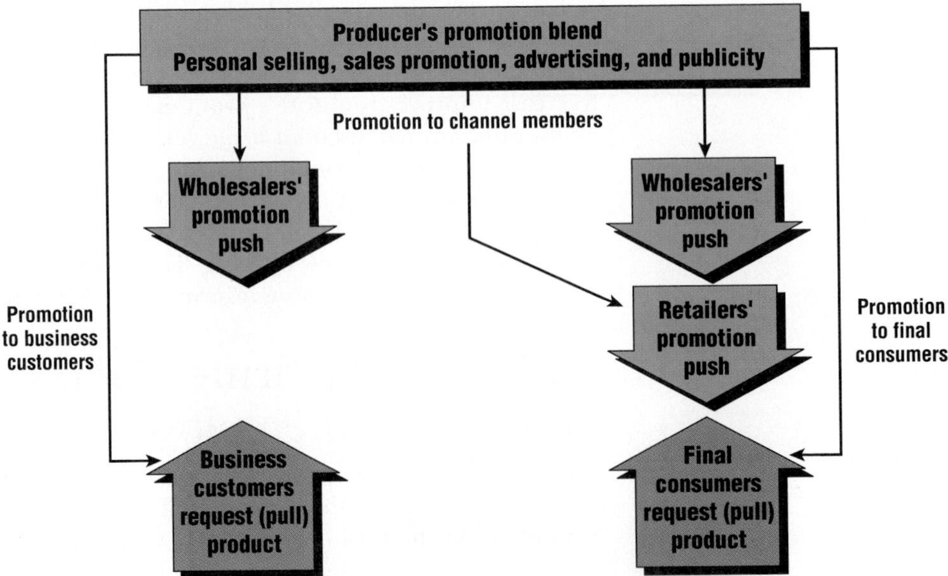

Push versus Pull on the Web

On the Web, information is provided to consumers who actively seek it. The Web is both an active and an interactive medium, not a passive medium.[1] Those who are browsing have control over the information they see.[2] The Web is a *pull* medium. But while there are many ways of attracting browsers (consumers) to a Web site, some content providers would like to actively "push" their content to the browser. This is done using what is known as push technology. The Web can also push content to browsers' desktop machines, using multiple Web channels. Push technology assures content providers that an audience of a certain given profile is indeed being exposed to the content (and all the advertising that goes with it).[3]

In the pull model, the browser asks for information by performing a search, for example. In the push model, information is automatically delivered to your computer based on some criteria such as time of day. As an example, you can have "customized" news from *The Globe and Mail* (www.globeandmail.com) or CNN (www.cnn.com) delivered to your computer. You customize by choosing the news categories in which you are interested.

One of the software companies specializing in push technology is PointCast™ (www.pointcast.com). This software is freely available. Microsoft and Netscape have similar products. To see how PointCast works, go to the CNN site. PointCast collects information from different content sites such as *The Globe and Mail*, CNN, and the *Wall Street Journal*. It allows you to choose news categories such as business and finance, sports, and politics. These categories are like specialty television channels. Updated information is delivered to your computer every few hours.

All this is free. But there's a catch. In exchange for this personalized news service, you have to fill out an online form with detailed personal information. This information is used to target advertising in your direction. When you open your browser to read your free personalized news, you also get advertising that is specific to your interests or needs. Is this a good thing, a small price to pay for the convenience? Or is it an excessive intrusion into your privacy? What do you think?

If Web content providers adopt push technologies, the Web will soon start resembling other traditional push media. Thus, while push technology offers an advantage in terms of targeting the message to the right audience, it also has its drawbacks. In the long term, both push and pull models will continue to exist on the Web. Those who want to do specific research or information search, or just browse for fun, will adopt the pull approach. Others may prefer the convenience of push, even if it results in the loss of a little privacy.

[1] Donna Hoffman and Thomas P. Novak, "Marketing in Hypermedia Computer-Mediated Environments: Conceptual Foundations," Working Paper No. 1 (Revised July 11, 1995), Project 2000: Research Program on Marketing in Computer-Mediated Environments.

[2] Marketing and the Internet (www.cybersolve.com)

[3] Ibid.

Source: This is one of a series of Internet Insites prepared in April 1998 by Dr. Ramesh Venkat of Saint Mary's University for *Basic Marketing,* Ninth Canadian Edition.

Internet Insite 14–1

Promotion to final consumers

The large number of consumers almost forces producers of consumer products and retailers to emphasize mass selling and sales promotion. Sales promotion, such as contests and free samples, may build consumer interest and short-term sales of a product. Effective mass selling may build enough brand familiarity that little personal selling is needed—as in self-service and discount operations.

If a product has already won brand preference or insistence—perhaps after years of satisfactory service—aggressive personal selling may not be needed. Reminder-type advertising may be all that's necessary to maintain a positive relationship. Hershey Chocolate long prided itself on not having to do any advertising in the United States! However, Hershey had to start advertising when competitors entered the market and took away customers.

Personal selling can be effective as well. Some retailers—specialty shops in particular—rely heavily on well-informed salespeople. Technical products (such as camcorders and computers) and personal services (such as health care and estate planning) may also require personal selling. Direct selling firms like Avon and Amway also rely on personal selling. But aggressive personal selling to final consumers usually is found in relatively expensive channel systems, such as those for fashionable clothing, furniture, consumer electronics, and automobiles.

Promotion to business customers

Producers and wholesalers who target business customers usually emphasize personal selling. This is practical, because these customers are much less numerous than final consumers and their purchases are typically larger.

Moreover, business customers may have technical questions or need adjustments in the marketing mix. An extremely technical business product may require a heavy emphasis on personal selling, using technically trained salespeople. This is the only sure way to make the product understood and get feedback on how customers use it. The technical sales rep meets with engineers, production managers, purchasing agents, and top managers, and can adjust the sales message to the needs of these various influences.

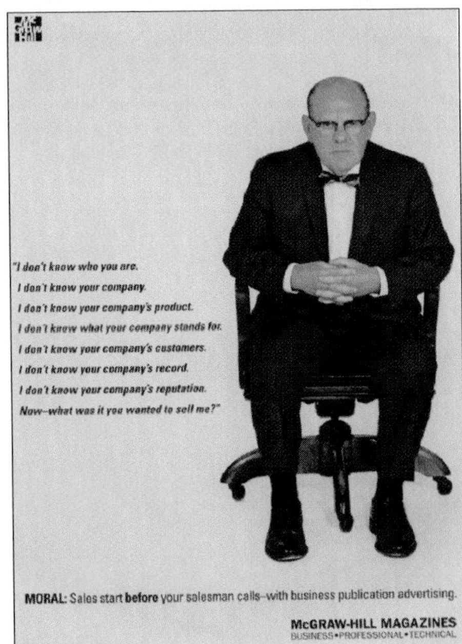

The classic McGraw-Hill ad on the left, which first appeared in 1958, suggests that it is seldom practical for personal selling to carry the whole promotion load—even in business markets. The new version of the ad is more up-to-date, but the message is the same.

Sales reps can be more flexible in adjusting their companies' appeals to suit each customer—and personal contact is usually required to close a sale. A salesperson is also able to call back later to follow up with additional information, resolve any problems, and nurture the relationship with the customer.

While personal selling dominates in business markets, mass selling is also necessary. A typical sales call on a business customer costs $200.[13] That's because salespeople spend less than half their time actually selling. The rest is consumed by such tasks as travelling, paperwork, sales meetings, and strictly service calls. So it's seldom practical for salespeople to carry the entire promotion load. A firm invests too much in its salespeople to use their time and skill for jobs that could be handled in less costly ways.

Ads in trade magazines, for instance, can inform potential customers that a product is available; and most trade ads give a toll-free telephone or fax number to stimulate direct inquiries. Domestic and international trade shows also help identify prospects. Even so, sellers who target business customers usually spend only a small percentage of their promotion budget on mass selling and sales promotion.

Each market segment may need a unique blend

Knowing what type of promotion is typically emphasized with different targets is useful in planning the promotion blend. But each unique market segment may need a separate marketing mix—and a different promotion blend. Some mass-selling specialists miss this point. They think mainly in terms of mass marketing rather than target marketing. Aiming at large markets may be desirable in some situations, but promotion aimed at everyone can end up hitting no one. In developing the promotion blend, be careful not to slip into a shotgun approach when what you really need is a rifle approach—with a more careful aim.

Adoption processes can guide promotion planning

The AIDA and adoption processes look at individuals. This emphasis on individuals helps us understand how promotion affects how people behave. But it's also useful to look at markets as a whole. Different segments of customers within a market may behave differently, with some taking the lead in trying new products and, in turn, influencing others.

Promotion must vary for different adopter groups

Research on how markets accept new ideas has led to the adoption curve model. The **adoption curve** shows when different groups accept ideas. It shows the need to change the promotion effort as time passes. It also emphasizes the relationships among groups, and shows that some groups act as leaders in accepting a new idea.

Exhibit 14–9 shows the adoption curve for a typical successful product. Some of the important characteristics of each of these customer groups are discussed below. Which one are you?

Innovators don't mind taking some risks

The **innovators** are the first to adopt. They are eager to try new ideas, and willing to take risks. Innovators tend to be young and well educated. They are likely to be mobile and to have many contacts outside their local social group and community. Business firms in the innovator group are often aggressive small companies with an entrepreneurial view and a willingness to take the risk of doing something new and different. However, large firms, especially specialized ones, may be in the innovator group.

Exhibit 14-9 The Adoption Curve

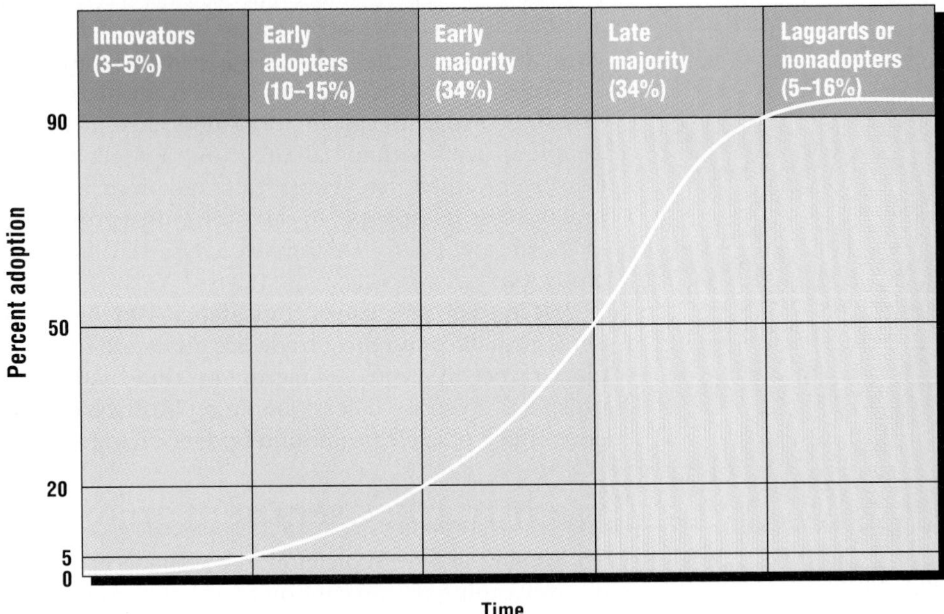

An important characteristic of innovators is that they rely on impersonal and scientific information sources—or other innovators—rather than on salespeople. They often search for information. For example, they might do a search on the Internet, read articles in technical publications, or look for informative ads in special interest magazines.

Early adopters are often opinion leaders

Early adopters are well respected by their peers, and often are opinion leaders. They tend to be younger, more mobile, and more creative than later adopters. But unlike innovators, they have fewer contacts outside their own social group or community. Business firms in this category also tend to be specialized.

Of all the groups, this one tends to have the greatest contact with salespeople. Mass media are important information sources as well. Marketers should be very concerned about attracting and selling the early adopter group. Their acceptance is really important in reaching the next group, because the early majority look to the early adopters for guidance. The early adopters can help the promotion effort by spreading *word of mouth* information and advice among other consumers.

OPINION LEADERS HELP SPREAD THE WORD Marketers know the importance of personal conversations and recommendations by opinion leaders. If early groups reject the product, it may never get off the ground. For example, some moviegoers are the first to see new movies. If they think a movie is dull, they quickly tell their friends not to waste their time and money. Consumers are even more likely to talk about a negative experience than a positive experience.

But if opinion leaders accept a product, what they say about it can be very important. Such word-of-mouth publicity may do the real selling job, long before the customer ever walks into the retail store.

Some companies try to target promotion to encourage opinion leadership and word-of-mouth publicity. When Canon introduced a new, high-quality, automatic 35mm camera, it prepared special ads designed to help opinion leaders explain to others how the camera worked. Other firms take a simpler approach: their ads just say "tell your friends." The Internet is providing even small companies with a low-cost way to encourage word of mouth. An interesting Web page can attract attention—and customers. For example, a retail shop called Hot Hot Hot, which carries a huge variety of hot sauces for food, established a Web site. Very quickly, largely because of word of mouth, 1,500 people were visiting the Web page each day.[14]

Early majority group is deliberate

The **early majority** avoid risks and wait to consider new ideas until after many early adopters have tried and liked them. Average-sized business firms that are less specialized often fit in this category. If successful companies in their industry adopt the new idea, they will too.

The early majority have a great deal of contact with mass media, salespeople, and early adopter opinion leaders. Members usually aren't opinion leaders themselves.

Late majority is cautious

The **late majority** are cautious about new ideas. Often they are older than the early majority group, and more set in their ways. So they are less likely to follow opinion leaders and early adopters. In fact, it may take strong social pressure from their own peer group to get them to adopt a new product. Business firms in this group tend to be conservative, smaller-sized firms with little specialization.

The late majority make little use of marketing sources of information—mass media and salespeople. They tend to be oriented more toward other late adopters rather than outside sources they don't trust.

Laggards or nonadopters hang on to tradition

Laggards or **nonadopters** prefer to do things the way they've been done in the past and are very suspicious of new ideas. They tend to be older and less well educated. They may also be low in social status and income. The smallest businesses with the least specialization often fit this category. They cling to the status quo and think it's the safe way.

The main source of information for laggards is other laggards. This certainly is bad news for marketers who are trying to reach an entire market quickly, or who want to use only one promotion method. In fact, it may not pay to bother with this group.[15]

Promotion blends vary over the life cycle

A new product concept seldom becomes a spectacular success overnight. The adoption curve helps explain why. The adoption curve also helps explain why a new product goes through the product life-cycle stages described in Chapter 10—market introduction, market growth, market maturity, and sales decline. During these stages, promotion blends may have to change in order to achieve different promotion objectives.

Market introduction stage—"this new idea is good"

During market introduction, the basic promotion objective is informing. If the product is a really new idea, the promotion must build **primary demand**—that is, demand for the general product idea, not just for the company's own brand. Multimedia computers, personal information managers, and electric cars are good examples of product concepts for which primary demand is just beginning to grow. There may be few potential innovators during the introduction stage, and personal selling can help find them. Firms also need salespeople to find good channel members and persuade them to carry the new product. Sales promotion may be targeted at salespeople or channel members to get them interested in selling the new product. And sales promotion may also encourage customers to try it.

Market growth stage—"our brand is best"

In the market growth stage, more competitors enter the market, and promotion emphasis shifts from building primary demand to stimulating **selective demand**—that is, demand for a company's own brand. The main job is to persuade customers to buy, and then keep buying, the company's product.

Now that more potential customers are trying and adopting the product, mass selling may become more economical. But salespeople and personal selling must still work in the channels, expanding the number of outlets and cementing relationships with current channel members.

Market maturity stage—"our brand is better, really"

In the market maturity stage, even more competitors have entered the market. Promotion becomes more persuasive. At this stage, mass selling and sales promotion may dominate the promotion blends of consumer products firms. Business products may require more aggressive personal selling, perhaps supplemented by more advertising. The total dollars allocated to promotion may rise as competition increases.

If a firm already has high sales relative to its competitors, it may have a real advantage in promotion at this stage. If, for example, Nabisco has twice the sales for a certain type of cookie as Keebler, its smaller competitor, and they both spend the same *percentage* of total sales on promotion, Nabisco will be spending twice as much and will probably communicate to more people. Nabisco may get even more than twice as much promotion because of economies of scale.

Firms that have strong brands can use reminder-type advertising at this stage to make sure customers remember the product name. Similarly, many firms turn to various types of frequent-buyer promotions, or to newsletters and other communications targeted at current customers, to strengthen the buyer–seller relationship and keep customers loyal. In a stagnant market, this may be much less expensive—and more effective—than persuasive efforts to win customers away from competitors.

Sales decline—"Let's tell those who still want our product"

During the sales decline stage, the total amount spent on promotion usually decreases as firms try to cut costs to remain profitable. Since some people may still want the product, firms need more targeted promotion to reach these customers.

On the other hand, some firms may increase promotion to try to slow the cycle at least temporarily. Crayola had almost all of the market for children's crayons, but sales were slowly declining as new kinds of markers came along. Crayola slowed the cycle with more promotion spending and with a message to parents to buy their kids a "fresh box."

Nature of competition requires different promotion

Firms in monopolistic competition may favour mass selling because they have differentiated their marketing mixes and have something to talk about. As a market tends toward pure competition—or oligopoly—it is difficult to predict what will happen. Competitors in some markets try to outpromote each other. The only way for a competitor to stay in this kind of market is to match rivals' promotion efforts, unless the entire marketing mix can be improved in some other way. We see a lot of such competitive advertising in our daily newspapers, and in cents-off coupons at grocery store checkout counters.

In markets that are drifting toward pure competition, some companies will resort to price-cutting. Lower prices may be offered to intermediaries, or customers, or both. This *may* increase the number of units sold—temporarily—but it may also reduce total revenue and the amount available for promotion *per unit.* And competitive retaliation, perhaps in the form of short-term sales promotions, may reduce the temporary sales gains and drag price levels down faster. The cash flowing into the business may decline, and promotion spending may have to be cut back.[16]

Setting the promotion budget

There are some economies of scale in promotion. An ad on national TV may cost less *per person reached* than an ad on local TV. Similarly, citywide radio, TV, and newspapers may be cheaper than neighbourhood newspapers or direct personal contact. But the *total cost* for some mass media may force small firms, or those with small promotion budgets, to use promotion alternatives that are more expensive per contact. For example, a small retailer might want to use local television but find that there is only enough money for a Web page on the Internet, an ad in the Yellow Pages, and an occasional newspaper ad.

Smaller producers and firms that offer relatively undifferentiated consumer products emphasize personal selling first and rely mainly on sales promotion for the balance. The objective is to build good channel relations and encourage channel members to recommend and push the product. Note that here we are referring to percentages in the promotion blend, and not the level of expenditures. Setting the overall level of promotion spending—and the amount to spend on each type of promotion—is an important but difficult decision.

Budgeting for promotion using a percentage of sales

The most common method of budgeting for promotion expenditures is to compute a percentage of either past sales or sales expected in the future. The virtue of this method is its simplicity. A similar percentage can be used automatically each year, thus eliminating the need to keep evaluating the kind and amount of promotion effort needed and its probable cost. This method allows executives who aren't too tuned in to the marketing concept to write off a certain percentage or number of dollars, while controlling the total amount spent. When a company's top managers have this attitude, they often get what they deserve—something less than the best results.

Find the task, budget for it

Just because budgeting a certain percentage of past or forecast sales is common doesn't mean that it's smart. This mechanical approach leads to expanding marketing expenditures when business is good and cutting back when business is poor. It may in fact be desirable to increase marketing expenditures when business is good. But when business is poor, this approach may just make the problem worse, if weak promotion is the reason for declining sales. The most sensible approach may be to be *more,* not less, aggressive!

Other methods of budgeting for marketing expenditures are as follows:

1. Match expenditures with competitors.
2. Set the budget as a certain number of cents or dollars per sales unit (by case, by thousand, or by ton), using the past year or estimated year ahead as a base.
3. Base the budget on any uncommitted revenue, perhaps including budgeted profits. Companies with limited resources may use this approach. Or a firm may be willing to sacrifice some or all of its current profits for future sales—that is, it may look at promotion spending as an *investment* in future growth.

4 Base the budget on the job to be done. For example, the spending level might be based on the number of new customers desired and the percentage of current customers that the firm must retain to leverage investments in already established relationships. This is called the **task method**—basing the budget on the job to be done.

Task method—budgeting without agony

In the light of our continuing discussion about planning marketing strategies to reach objectives, the most sensible approach to budgeting promotion expenditures is the task method. In fact, this approach makes sense for *any* marketing expenditure, but here we'll focus on promotion.

A practical approach is to determine which promotion objectives are most important to the overall strategy, and which promotion methods are most economical and effective for the communication tasks relevant to each objective. There's never enough money to do all of the promotion that you might want to do. However, this approach helps you set priorities so that the money you spend produces specific results.

The amount budgeted using the task method can be stated as a percentage of sales. But you should see that calculating the right amount is much more involved than picking up a past percentage. It requires careful review of the specific promotion (and marketing) tasks to be accomplished and how each task fits with others to achieve the overall objectives. The costs of these tasks are then totalled to determine how much should be budgeted for promotion (just as money is allocated for other marketing activities required by the strategy). In other words, the firm can assemble its total promotion budget directly from detailed plans rather than by simply relying on historical patterns or ratios.

This method also helps to eliminate budget fights between different promotion areas. Such conflicts may arise if managers and specialists responsible for different promotion methods see themselves as pitted against one another for limited budget dollars. However, the task method of budgeting encourages everyone—the marketing manager *and* the specialists—to focus on the overall strategy and what promotion objectives need to be achieved. The specialists may still make their own proposals and suggestions about how best to perform tasks and achieve the objectives. But the budget allocations are then based on the most effective ways of getting things done—not on what the firm did last year, or what some competitor does, or even on internal "politics." With this approach, different promotion specialists are also more likely to recognize that different tasks and objectives are best served with different methods—and that they must all work together to achieve truly integrated marketing communications.[17]

In this chapter our focus has been on blending the different promotion methods into an integrated whole. We've emphasized that different methods—publicity, personal selling, advertising, and sales promotion—are complementary. In different situations they must be combined in different ways to achieve an effective and integrated overall promotion blend. The concepts we've been discussing apply to all types of marketing communications. Yet to be more skilled in matching specific promotion methods to specific tasks and objectives, it will help to know more about the strategy decisions involved in managing the major promotion areas. So that will be our focus in the next two chapters.

Questions and Problems

1. Briefly explain the nature of the three basic promotion methods available to a marketing manager. What are the main strengths and limitations of each?
2. In your own words, discuss the integrated marketing communications concept. Explain what its emphasis on "consistent" and "complete" messages implies with respect to promotion blends.
3. Relate the three basic promotion objectives to the four jobs (AIDA) of promotion using a specific example.
4. Discuss the communication process in relation to a producer's promotion of an accessory product—say, a new electronic security system businesses use to limit access to areas where they store confidential records.
5. If a company wants its promotion to appeal to a new group of target customers in a foreign country, how can it protect against its communications being misinterpreted?
6. Promotion has been the target of considerable criticism. What specific types of promotion are probably the object of this criticism? Give a specific example that illustrates your thinking.
7. With direct-response promotion, customers provide feedback to marketing communications. How can a marketing manager use this feedback to improve the effectiveness of the overall promotion blend?
8. How can a promotion manager target a message to a certain target market with electronic media (like the Internet) when the customer initiates the communication? Give an example.
9. What promotion blend would be most appropriate for producers of the following established products? Assume average- to large-sized firms in each case, and support your answer.
   a. Chocolate candy bar.
   b. Car batteries.
   c. Pantyhose.
   d. Castings for truck engines.
   e. A special computer used by manufacturers for control of production equipment.
   f. Inexpensive plastic rainhats.
   g. A digital tape recorder that has achieved specialty-product status.
10. A small company has developed an innovative new spray-on glass cleaner that prevents the buildup of electrostatic dust on computer screens and TVs. Give examples of some low-cost ways the firm might effectively promote its product. Be certain to consider both push and pull approaches.
11. Would promotion be successful in expanding the general demand for: (a) raisins, (b) air travel, (c) golf clubs, (d) walking shoes, (e) high-octane unleaded gasoline, (f) single-serving, frozen gourmet dinners, and (g) cement? Explain why or why not in each case.
12. Explain how an understanding of the adoption process would help you develop a promotion blend for digital tape recorders, a new consumer electronics product that produces high-quality recordings. Explain why you might change the promotion blend during the course of the adoption process.
13. Explain how opinion leaders affect a firm's promotion planning.
14. Discuss how the adoption curve should be used to plan the promotion blend(s) for a new automobile accessory—an electronic radar system that alerts a driver if he or she is about to change lanes into the path of a car that is passing through a "blind spot" in the driver's mirrors.
15. If a marketing manager uses the task method to budget for marketing promotions, are competitors' promotion spending levels ignored? Explain your thinking, and give an example that supports your point of view.
16. Discuss the potential conflict among the various promotion managers. How could this be reduced?

Suggested cases

5 Parker's Classics

21 Honda Hit • Run • Throw

27 Lever, Ltd.

Computer-aided problem

Selecting a Communications Channel

Helen Troy, owner of three Sound Haus stereo equipment stores, is deciding what message channel (advertising medium) to use to promote her newest store. Her current promotion blend includes direct-mail ads that are effective for reaching her current customers. She also has knowledgeable salespeople who work well with consumers once they're in the store. However, a key objective in opening a new store is to attract new customers. Her best prospects are professionals in the 25–44 age range with incomes over $38,000 a year. But only some of the people in this group are audiophiles who want the top-of-the-line brands she carries. Troy has decided to use local advertising to reach new customers.

Troy narrowed her choice to two advertising media: an FM radio station and a biweekly magazine that focuses on entertainment in her city. Many of the magazine's readers are out-of-town visitors interested in concerts, plays, and restaurants. They usually buy stereo equipment at home. But the magazine's audience research shows that many local professionals do subscribe to the magazine. Troy doesn't think that the objective can be achieved with a single ad. However, she believes that ads in six issues will generate good local awareness with her target market. In addition, the magazine's colour format will let her present the prestige image she wants to convey in an ad. She thinks that will help convert aware prospects to buyers. Specialists at a local advertising agency will prepare a high-impact ad for $2,000, and then Troy will pay for the magazine space.

The FM radio station targets an audience similar to Troy's own target market. She knows repeated ads will be needed to ensure that most of her target audience is exposed to her ads. Troy thinks it will take daily ads for several months to create adequate awareness among her target market. The FM station will provide an announcer and prepare a tape of Troy's ad for a one-time fee of $200. All she has to do is tell the station what the message content for the ad should say.

Both the radio station and the magazine gave Troy reports summarizing recent audience research. She decides that comparing the two media in a spreadsheet will help her make a better decision.

a. Based on the data displayed on the initial spreadsheet, which message channel (advertising medium) would you recommend to Troy? Why?

b. The agency that offered to prepare Troy's magazine ad will prepare a fully produced radio ad—including a musical jingle—for $2,500. The agency claims that its musical ad will have much more impact than the ad the radio station will create. The agency says its ad should produce the same results as the station ad with 20 percent fewer insertions. If the agency claim is correct, would it be wise for Troy to pay the agency to produce the ad?

c. The agency will not guarantee that its custom-produced radio ad will reach Troy's objective—making 80 percent of the prospects aware of the new store. Troy wants to see how lower levels of awareness—between 50 percent and 70 percent—would affect the advertising cost per buyer and the cost per aware prospect. Use the What If analysis to vary the percentage of prospects who become aware. Prepare a table showing the effect on the two kinds of costs. What are the implications of your analysis?

For additional questions related to this problem, see Exercise 14-3 in the *Learning Aid for use with Basic Marketing,* Ninth Canadian Edition.

Chapter fifteen

Personal Selling

When you finish this chapter, you should:

- Understand the importance and nature of personal selling.
- Know the three basic sales tasks and what the various kinds of salespeople are expected to do.
- Know what the sales manager must do—including selecting, training, and organizing salespeople—to carry out the personal selling job.
- Understand how the right compensation plan can help motivate and control salespeople.
- Understand when and where to use the three types of sales presentations.
- Understand the important new terms (shown in orange).

Vaughn Wyant, president of Jubilee Ford Sales Ltd., learned the car trade in England. Wyant moved back to his hometown of Saskatoon in 1983 and bought the local Ford dealership. Sales were pretty much flat—until Wyant decided to build his own super salesforce. By hiring a new team of motivated sellers and focussing them on customer service, Wyant drove up sales from $34 million in 1993 to more than $60 million last year, when he was named the Prairie region's Retail Entrepreneur of the Year. Jubilee is now the largest car dealership in Saskatchewan.

Keys to that success? Wyant insists his "product specialists" know everything from technical specs to what's in the competitor's showroom, so the dealership hosts regular seminars and encourages staff to take courses offered by Ford. In turn, Wyant delivers a steady stream of tire-kickers with regular print and broadcast advertising: "My job is to create traffic, to make the phones ring so the salespeople can do their job." To keep the team on track, sales manager Blair Pizzey conducts daily sales huddles. "Communication is very important," he says. "You have to let them in on what your plan is and what your goals are."

Most important, Wyant leads by example. Indeed, he is still likely to be found chatting up clients on the showroom floor. "The most important function in any business," he says, "is selling."

Even in these days of infomercials and electronic commerce, few companies can excel without a knowledgeable, professional sales team. "The reason why a salesforce is necessary is that we represent a certain authority or expertise," says Howard Wallace, v-p of sales for the Americas at Hummingbird Communications Ltd. The North York, Ont., software developer's reps not only sell product, but solve customers' distribution and technical problems. In fact, the firm now employs 70 salespeople, up from just one—Wallace—in 1991. That new commitment to sales has helped drive phenomenal growth at Hummingbird, which has ranked near the top of the PROFIT 100 list of Canada's Fastest-Growing Companies for the past two years.

But the move away from quota-driven order-takers to full-service, more consultative selling has its price. "Relationship selling" often means longer sales cycles, complex commission structures and custom-tailored sales strategies—which demands more management participation.

You have to sharply define the responsibilities and goals of your salesforce. You have to better co-ordinate sales-related functions, from advertising to production to distribution, ensuring your company's products and services are available at the right place and time. Most of all, you have to build teams with the skills, tools and desire required to succeed in the new business environment.

Vaughn Wyant considers it one of the best moves he's ever made. Five years ago, he took a hard look at his car dealership, and decided some of his top salespeople had to go. Within two years, they were replaced by a half-dozen "kids"—including a farmboy and newly-minted college grads—all supervised by a manager in his mid-20s.

Since the overhaul, Jubilee's new vehicle sales alone have shot up about 30%—growth Wyant couldn't have expected from his previous crew. "A lot of people in our business would get out of bed, come to work, stand around and wait for customers to come in the door," says Wyant. He knew grabbing market share demanded salespeople who liked cars, liked people, and placed customer service above all. That meant letting go of some of the old guard. But now, he says, "We don't miss those guys at all."

As Wyant discovered, the first pillar of a strong sales team is the people themselves. So you have to know how to recruit. "We make most of our mistakes in the hiring stage," says Ron Clayson of the Clayson Group, a sales training firm in Toronto. "We say, 'Hey, this is not quite who we're looking for, but let's give them a chance'." The result: sales duds who never earn a dime.

Other companies never really know who they're hiring, says Brian Jeffrey, president of SalesForce Training & Consulting Inc. in Ottawa. He recommends putting promising candidates through a series of interviews in which several employees participate. To avoid sales slugs, he suggests posing tough questions about sales fundamentals, such as the definition of a "trial close" or a "unique selling proposition." After an interview, compare notes with your colleagues. And always check references.

What's the mark of a top salesperson? "You want someone who is a bit of a driver, persistent, not afraid of cold calls—if he doesn't close it, he's on to the next one," suggests Jeffrey. But even candidates with all those qualities might not be right for your opening. Your sales team requires a mix of sales styles: for instance, "finders" of new clients and "minders" of established accounts. "People think it contradicts the definition, but a good team is made up of people who each bring special skills," says Kit Grant of Calgary-based Grant Training Systems Inc. "A good team is not a group of clones."

Source: Abridged from Michael G. Crawford, "Building the Perfect Sales Force," *Profit Magazine,* April/May 1997. Reprinted with permission from Michael G. Crawford.

The importance and role of personal selling

Promotion is communicating with potential customers. Personal selling is often the best way to do it. Almost every company can benefit from personal selling. While face to face with prospects, salespeople can get more attention than an advertisement or a display. They can adjust what they say or do to take into consideration culture and other behavioural influences on the customer. They can ask questions to find out about a customer's specific interests. They can also stay in tune with the prospect's feedback and adjust the presentation as they move along. If and when the prospect is ready to buy, the salesperson is there to ask for the order. And afterwards, the salesperson is there to ensure that the customer is satisfied and that the relationship between the customer and the firm continues to be mutually beneficial.

Personal selling requires strategy decisions

As was described in the Jubilee Ford Sales Ltd. case, marketing managers must decide how much—and what kind of—personal selling effort each marketing mix needs. Specifically, as part of their strategic planning, they must decide: (1) how many salespeople they need, (2) what kind of salespeople they need, (3) what kind of sales presentation to use, (4) how to select and train salespeople, and (5) how to supervise and motivate them. The sales manager provides inputs into these strategy decisions, and then implements the personal selling part of the marketing strategy.

In this chapter, we'll discuss the importance and nature of personal selling so that you'll understand the strategic decisions that sales and marketing managers face. These strategic decisions are shown in Exhibit 15–1.

Exhibit 15-1 Strategic Planning for Personal Selling

Personal selling techniques vary country to country

We'll also discuss a number of frameworks and how-to approaches that guide management's strategic decisions. Because these approaches apply equally to domestic and international markets, we won't emphasize that distinction in this chapter. This does not mean, however, that personal selling techniques don't vary from one country to another. On the contrary, in dealing with *any* customer, the salesperson must be very sensitive to cultural influences and to other factors that may affect communication. For example, a Japanese customer and an Arab customer may respond differently to subtle aspects of a salesperson's behaviour. The Arab customer may expect to be very close to a salesperson, perhaps only two feet away, while they talk. The Japanese customer may consider that distance rude. Similarly, what topics of discussion are considered sensitive, how messages are interpreted, and which negotiating styles are used vary from one country to another. A salesperson must know how to communicate effectively with each customer, wherever and whoever that customer is, but those details are beyond the strategic planning focus of this text.[1]

Personal selling is important

We've already seen that personal selling is important in some promotion blends—and absolutely essential in others. You would better appreciate the importance of personal selling if you regularly had to meet payrolls and somehow—almost miraculously—your salespeople kept coming in with orders just in time to keep the business from closing.

Personal selling is often a company's largest single operating expense. This is another reason why it is important to understand the decisions in this area. Bad sales management decisions can be costly not only in lost sales but also in out-of-pocket expenses.

Every economy needs and uses many salespeople. In Canada, about 1.3 million people in the total labour force are involved in sales work.[2] That's about 20 times more people than are employed in Canada in advertising. Any activity that employs so many people—and is so important to the economy—deserves study. Looking at what salespeople do is a good way to start.

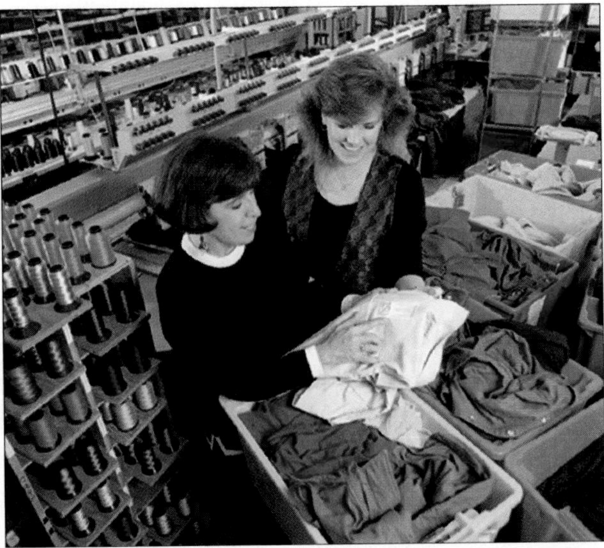

While face to face with prospects, salespeople can adjust what they say or do to take into consideration culture and other behavioural influences.

Helping customers buy is good selling

Good salespeople don't just try to *sell* the customer. Rather, they try to *help the customer buy,* by understanding the customer's needs and presenting the advantages and disadvantages of their products. Such helpfulness results in satisfied customers and long-term relationships. And strong relationships often form the basis for a competitive advantage, especially for firms that target business markets.

Salespeople represent the whole company, *and* customers

The salesperson is a representative of the entire company, and is responsible for explaining its total effort to target customers rather than just pushing products. The salesperson may provide information about products, explain and interpret company policies, and even negotiate prices or diagnose technical problems.

The sales rep is often the only link between the firm and its customers, especially if customers are far away. When a number of people from the firm are involved with the customer organization—which is increasingly common as more and more suppliers and customers form closer relationships—it is usually the sales rep who coordinates the relationship for his or her firm (see Exhibit 7–5).

The salesperson also represents the *customer* back inside the selling firm. Recall that feedback is an essential part of both the communication process *and* the management process of planning, implementing, and control. For example, the sales rep is the likely one to explain to the production manager why a customer is unhappy with product quality—or to the logistics manager why slow shipments are causing problems.

As evidence of these changing responsibilities, some companies now give their salespeople such titles as field manager, sales consultant, market specialist, account representative, or sales engineer.

Sales force aids in market information function

The sales force also aids in the marketing information function. The sales rep may be the first to hear about a new competitor's strategy. And as the following example shows, sales reps who are attuned to customers' needs can be a key source of ideas for new products.

Ballard Medical Products is a small producer that competes with international giants in the hospital supply business. A key factor in Ballard's success is that its salespeople are trained as information specialists who seek and report on customer feedback. At each hospital, they work closely with the doctor and nurse specialists who use Ballard products. And when one of those people says, "We need a product that would solve this problem," the Ballard sales rep probes the customer's needs and then follows up with inputs to Ballard's new-product development group.[3]

Salespeople can be strategic planners too

Some firms expect salespeople to be marketing managers in their own territories. And some become marketing managers by default because top management hasn't provided detailed strategy guidelines. Either way, salespeople may take the initiative to fill the gap. The salesperson may decide (1) which target customers to aim at, (2) which particular products to emphasize, (3) which intermediaries to call on or to work with the hardest, (4) how to use promotion money, and (5) how to adjust prices.

A salesperson who can put together profitable strategies and implement them well can rise very rapidly. The opportunity is there for those who are prepared and willing to work.[4]

What kinds of salespeople are needed?

If a firm has too few salespeople, or the wrong kind, some important personal selling tasks may not be completed. And having too many salespeople, or the wrong kind, wastes money. A sales manager needs to find a good balance—the right number and the right kind of salespeople. This balance may change over time with changes in strategy or the firm's environment. That's why many firms have been restructuring their sales forces.

One of the difficulties in determining the right number and kind of salespeople is that every sales job is different. While an engineer or accountant can look forward to fairly specific duties, the salesperson's job changes constantly. However, there are three basic types of sales tasks. This gives us a starting point for understanding what selling tasks need to be done, and how many people are needed to do them.

Personal selling is divided into three tasks

The three **basic sales tasks** are order getting, order taking, and supporting. For convenience, we'll describe salespeople by these terms—referring to their primary task—*although one person may do all three tasks in some situations.*

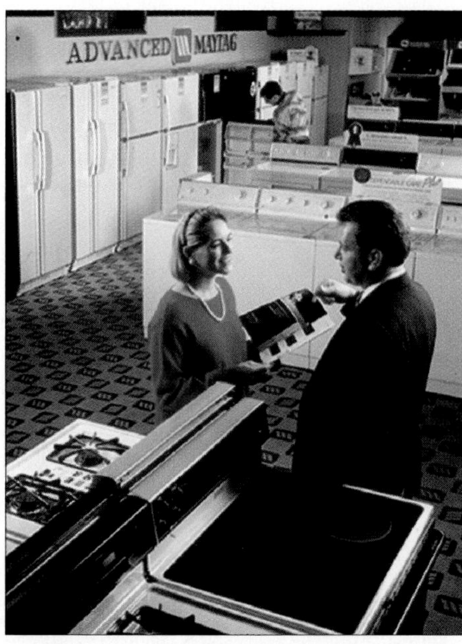

Consumers who are interested in shopping products often want help from a well-informed salesperson.

Order getters—develop new business relationships

Order getters concern themselves with establishing relationships with new customers and developing new business. **Order getting** means seeking possible buyers with a well-organized sales presentation designed to sell a good, service, or idea.

Order getters must know what they're talking about—not just be personal contacts. Order-getting salespeople work for producers, wholesalers, and retailers. Most of them are well paid; many earn more than $80,000 a year.

Producers' order getters—find new opportunities

Producers of all kinds of products—especially business products—have a great need for order getters. Order getters locate new prospects, open new accounts, see new opportunities, and build channel relationships.

When top-level people participate in a purchase decision, they are more interested in ways to improve profits than in technical details. Good order getters cater to this interest. They identify ways to solve problems, and then sell concepts and ideas, not just physical products. The products they supply are merely the means of achieving the customer's end.

Order getters for professional services—and for other products where service is a crucial element of the marketing mix—face a special challenge. The customer usually can't inspect a service before deciding to buy. The order getter's communication and relationship with the customer may be the only basis on which to evaluate the quality of the supplier.

An order getter in business markets needs the know-how to help customers solve their problems. Often the order getter needs to understand a customer's entire business as well as technical details about the product and its applications. For example, a salesperson for automated manufacturing equipment must understand everything about a prospect's production process as well as the technical details of converting to computer-controlled equipment.

Wholesalers' order getters almost hand it to customers

Agent intermediaries often are order getters—particularly the more aggressive manufacturers' agents and brokers. They face the same tasks as producers' order getters. Unfortunately for them, once the order getting is done and the customers become established and loyal, producers may try to eliminate the agents and save money by using their own order takers.

Progressive merchant wholesaler sales reps are developing into consultants and store advisors rather than just order takers. Such order getters may become retailers' partners in the job of moving goods from the wholesale warehouse through the retail store to consumers. These order getters almost become a part of the retailer's staff. They help plan displays, write orders, and conduct demonstrations. They also plan advertising, special promotions, and other retailing activities.

Retail order getters influence consumer behaviour

Convincing consumers of the value of products they haven't seriously considered takes a high level of personal selling ability. Order getters for unsought products (see Exhibit 9–4) must help customers see how a new product can satisfy needs now being filled by something else. Early order getters for microwave ovens, for example, faced a tough job. They had to convince sceptical customers that this new kind of cooking was safe and that it would be more convenient than traditional approaches—once the customer got used to it. Without order getters, many of the products we now rely on, from mutual funds to air conditioners, might well have died in the market introduction stage. The order getter helps bring products out of the introduction stage into the market growth stage. Without sales and profits in the early stages, the product may fail—and never be offered again.

Order getters are helpful for selling *heterogeneous* shopping products. Consumers shop for many of these items on the basis of price and quality. They welcome useful information. Cars, furniture and furnishings, cameras, jewellery, and fashion items can be sold effectively by an aggressive, helpful order getter. Thoughtful advice, based on an understanding of the consumer and a thorough knowledge of the product and its alternatives, may really help consumers and bring profits to the salesperson and retailer.

Order takers—nurture relationships to keep the business coming

Order takers sell to regular or established customers, complete most sales transactions, and maintain relationships with their customers. After a customer becomes interested in a firm's products through an order getter or supporting salesperson, or through advertising or sales promotion, it is an order taker who usually answers any final questions and completes the sale. **Order-taking** is the routine completion of sales made regularly to target customers. The routine completion of sales usually requires ongoing follow-up with the customer, to ensure that the customer is totally satisfied and that the relationship will continue in the future.

Sometimes sales managers or customers use the term *order taker* as a put-down when referring to salespeople who don't take any initiative. While a particular salesperson may perform poorly enough to justify criticism, it's a mistake to downgrade the function of order-taking. Order-taking is extremely important. Many firms lose

"I hate this weather. I hate my dog. I hate this chair. I hate being stuck in Customer Service. Now, what do you want?"

sales just because no one ever asks for the order—and closes the sale. Moreover, the order taker's job is not limited to taking orders. Even in business markets where customers place routine orders with computerized order systems and EDI, order takers do a variety of important jobs.

Producers' order takers—train, explain, and collaborate

Once industrial, wholesale, or retail accounts are established, regular follow-up is necessary. Order takers work on improving the entire relationship with the customer, not just on completing a single transaction. Even if computers handle routine reorders, someone has to explain details, make adjustments, handle complaints, explain or negotiate new prices and terms, place sales promotion materials, and keep customers informed of new developments. Someone may have to train customers' employees. All these activities are part of the order taker's job. And a failure to meet a customer's expectations on any of these activities could jeopardize the relationship and future sales.

Producers' order takers often have a regular route with many calls. To handle these calls well, they must have energy, persistence, enthusiasm, and a friendly personality that wears well over time. They sometimes have to take the heat when something goes wrong with some other element of the marketing mix.

Firms sometimes use order-taking jobs to train potential order getters and managers. Such jobs give newer employees an opportunity to meet key customers and to better understand their needs. And frequently, they run into some order-getting opportunities. Order takers who are alert to order-getting opportunities can make a big difference in generating new sales.

Wholesalers' order takers keep in touch

While producers' order takers usually handle relatively few items—and sometimes even a single item—wholesalers' order takers may sell 125,000 items or more. Most wholesale order takers just sell out of their catalogue. They have so many items that they can't possibly give aggressive sales effort to many—except perhaps newer or more profitable items. There are just too many items to single any out for special attention.

The wholesale order taker's main job is to maintain close contact with customers—perhaps once a week—and fill any needs that develop. After writing up the order, the order taker normally checks to make sure the company fills the order promptly and accurately. The order taker also handles any adjustments or complaints, and generally acts as a liaison between the company and its customers.

Such salespeople are usually the low-pressure type—friendly and easygoing. Usually these jobs aren't as high paying as the order-getting variety; on the other hand they attract many because they aren't as taxing. They require relatively little travelling, and there is little or no pressure to get new accounts. There can be a social aspect too. The salesperson sometimes becomes good friends with customers.

Retail order takers play a vital role

Order-taking may be almost mechanical at the retail level—for example, at the supermarket checkout counter. Even so, retail order takers play a vital role in a retailer's marketing mix. Customers expect prompt and friendly service. They will find a new place to shop rather than deal with a salesclerk who is rude about having to complete a sale (see Marketing Demo 13–2). Some retail clerks are poor order takers because they aren't paid much—often only the minimum wage.

Supporting sales force—informs and promotes in the channel

Supporting salespeople help the order-oriented salespeople, but don't try to get orders themselves. Their activities are aimed at enhancing the relationship with the customer and getting sales in the long run. In the short run, they are ambassadors of good will who may provide specialized services and information. Almost all supporting salespeople work for producers, or for intermediaries who do this supporting work for the producers. There are two types of supporting salespeople: missionary salespeople and technical specialists.

Missionary salespeople can increase sales

Missionary salespeople are supporting salespeople who work for producers, calling on their intermediaries and their customers. They try to develop good will and stimulate demand and help the intermediaries train their salespeople, and often take orders for delivery by the intermediaries. Missionary salespeople are sometimes called *merchandisers* or *detailers.*

Producers who rely on merchant wholesalers to obtain widespread distribution often use missionary salespeople. The sales rep can give a promotion boost to a product that otherwise wouldn't get much attention from the intermediaries because it's just one of many they sell. A missionary salesperson for cold remedy products, for example, might visit druggists during the cold season and encourage them to use a special end-of-aisle display for Vicks' cough syrup—and then help set it up. The wholesaler that supplies the drugstore would benefit from any increased sales but might not take the time to urge use of the special display.

An imaginative missionary salesperson can double or triple sales. Naturally, this doesn't go unnoticed. Missionary sales jobs are often a route to order-oriented jobs. In fact, this position is often used as a training ground for new salespeople. Recent university grads are often recruited for these positions.

Technical specialists know product applications

Technical specialists are supporting salespeople who provide technical assistance to order-oriented salespeople. Technical specialists usually are science or engineering graduates with the know-how to understand the customer's applications and explain the advantages of the company's product. They are usually more skilled at showing the technical details of their product than at trying to persuade customers to buy it. Before the specialist's visit, an order getter probably has stimulated interest. The technical specialist provides the details.

Three tasks may have to be blended

We have described three sales tasks—order-getting, order-taking, and supporting. However, a particular salesperson might be given two—or all three—of these tasks. Ten percent of a particular job may be order-getting, 80 percent order-taking, and the additional 10 percent supporting. Another company might have many different people handling the different sales tasks. This can lead to **team selling,** which involves different sales reps working together on a specific account. Sometimes one or more of the "sales reps" on a team may not be from the sales department at all. If improving the relationship with the customer calls for technical support from the quality control manager, then that person becomes a part of the team, at least temporarily.

Our New Equipment is Worth Millions. Our Expert People Are Priceless.

We've always been dedicated to providing the best service in the industry. To demonstrate our commitment, we've invested $8 million in our customers' future business. With state-of-the-art technology, we can offer faster delivery, higher quality and more competitive prices than ever before. Combine that with the expertise and friendly advice of our talented staff and you've got a printing company with a winning formula for our customers' guaranteed success. Call today and profit from our investment.

QUEBECOR PRINTING
VANCOUVER

1070 S.E. Marine Drive, Vancouver, B.C. V5X 2V4 Tel (604) 321-2231 Fax (604) 322-2308

Producers of high-ticket items often use team selling. Different specialists handle different parts of the job, but the whole team coordinates its efforts to achieve the desired result.[5]

The right structure helps assign responsibility

A sales manager must organize the sales force so that all the necessary tasks are done well. A large organization may have different salespeople specializing by different selling tasks *and* by the target markets they serve.

Different target markets, different selling tasks

Sales managers often divide sales force responsibilities based on the type of customer involved. For example, Bigelow—a company that makes quality carpet for homes and office buildings—has divided its sales force into two groups of specialists. Some Bigelow salespeople call only on architects to help them choose the best type of carpet for new office buildings. Often no selling is involved because the architect only suggests specifications and doesn't actually buy the carpet.

Other Bigelow salespeople call on retail carpet stores. These reps encourage the store manager to keep a variety of Bigelow carpets in stock. They also take orders, help train the store's salespeople, and try to solve any problems that arise.

Big accounts get special treatment

Very large customers often require special selling effort—and relationships with them are treated differently. Moen, a maker of plumbing fixtures, has a regular sales force to call on building material wholesalers and an élite **major accounts sales force** that sells directly to large accounts, such as major retail chain stores that carry plumbing fixtures.

You can see why this sort of special attention is justified when you consider Procter & Gamble's relationship with Wal-Mart. Although P&G is an international powerhouse, its total sales in every country except the U.S. and Germany add up to less than its sales to Wal-Mart. That's why the P&G sales team that calls on Wal-Mart lives in Bentonville, Arkansas, where Wal-Mart is based.[6]

Specialists in telephone selling

Some firms have a group of salespeople who specialize in **telemarketing**—using the telephone to "call" on customers or prospects. A phone call has many of the benefits of a personal visit—for example, salespeople are able to modify the message as feedback is received. The big advantage of telemarketing is that it saves time and money. When customers are small or in hard-to-reach places, telemarketing may be the only economical approach. Many firms find that a telemarketing sales force can build profitable relationships with customers who would otherwise be ignored.

Telemarketing is often used when many prospects must be contacted in order to reach one who is actually interested in buying. When telemarketing is used in these circumstances, many consumers consider it to be an invasion of privacy. The high-pressure tactics of some telemarketers have resulted in the Canadian government proposing changes to the Competition Act to regulate this form of selling.

Sales tasks are done in sales territories

Often companies organize selling tasks on the basis of a **sales territory**—a geographic area that is the responsibility of one salesperson or several working together. Depending on the market potential, a territory might be a region of a country, or a province, or part of a city. Companies such as Lockheed Aircraft Corporation often consider a whole country as *part* of a sales territory for one salesperson.

Carefully set territories can reduce travel time and the cost of sales calls. Assigning territories can also help reduce confusion about who has responsibility for a set of selling tasks. Consider the case of the Hyatt Hotel chain. Formerly, each hotel had its own salespeople to get bookings for big conferences and business meetings. That meant that professional associations and other prospects who had responsibility for selecting meeting locations might be called on by sales reps from 20 or 30 different Hyatt hotels in different parts of the world. Now, the Hyatt central office divides up responsibility for working with specific accounts; one rep calls on an account and then tries to sell space in the Hyatt facility that best meets the customer's needs.

Sometimes simple geographic division isn't possible. A company's various products may require very different knowledge or selling skills—even though those products sell in the same territory or to the same customer. For example, Du Pont makes special films for hospital X-ray departments as well as chemicals used in laboratory blood tests. But a salesperson who can talk to a radiologist about the best film for a complex X-ray probably can't be expected to know everything about blood chemistry! As Internet Insite 15–1 suggests, the Web is significantly affecting not only sales territories but also many other aspects of sales management.

The number of salespeople needed depends on the workload

Once the important selling tasks are specified and the responsibilities divided, the sales manager must decide how many salespeople are needed. The first step is estimating how much work can be done by one person in some time period. Then the sales manager can make an educated guess about how many people are required in total, as the following example shows.

For many years, the Parker Jewelry Company was very successful selling its silver jewellery to department and jewellery stores in Western Canada. But top managers wanted to expand into the big urban markets of Quebec and Ontario. They realized that most of the work for the first few years would require order getters. They felt that a salesperson would need to call on each account at least once a month to get a share of this competitive business. They estimated that a salesperson could make only five calls a day on prospective buyers and still have time for travel, waiting, and follow-up on orders that came in. This meant that a sales rep who made calls 20 days a month could handle about 100 stores (5 a day × 20 days).

The managers used a personal computer and a CD-ROM database that included all of the telephone Yellow Pages listings for the country. This allowed them to quickly list and get a count of the total number of jewellery departments and stores in their target market. Then they simply divided the total number of stores by 100 to estimate the number of salespeople needed. This also helped them set up territories, by defining areas that included about 100 stores for each salesperson. Obviously, managers might want to fine-tune this estimate for differences in territories such as travel time. But the basic approach can be adapted and applied to many different situations.[7]

When a company is starting a new sales force, managers are concerned about its size. But many established firms ignore this issue. The manager forgets that over time, the right number of salespeople may change as selling tasks change. Then, when a problem becomes obvious, the manager tries to change everything in a hurry—a big mistake! Consideration of what type of salespeople and how many should be ongoing. If the sales force needs to be reduced, it doesn't make sense to let a lot of people go all at once—especially when that could be avoided with some planning. Conversely, finding and training effective salespeople is an ongoing job.

Enhancing Personal Selling Effectiveness

Direct online selling to consumers works for some products and services. But Web-based marketing does not necessarily lead to the replacement of salespeople. Some expensive or highly technical products do require careful educating of the consumer and repeated contacts before closing the sale.[1] Also, in many business-to-business marketing situations personal selling will continue to play a key role in the overall promotional mix. But the Internet can help salespeople perform their jobs more effectively.

The Internet is slowly replacing other media as a source of product information. The GVU7 survey reports that 86 percent of surfers use the Web for gathering information.[2] Commercial Web sites usually have an online "contact or feedback" feature, where consumers can request more information or place an inquiry. Furthermore, Web site tracking software can provide information on visitors, including e-mail addresses and organization names. All this information reduces the legwork that a salesperson must do. The Web can thus play a useful role in sales prospecting. If someone takes the trouble to fill out an online inquiry or information request form, that becomes a rather useful sales lead.

Besides providing such sales leads, technology can now help in sales force training and management. This is where the *Intranet* comes into the picture. The Internet is an open external network of millions of computers. Information on the Internet is publicly available. Corporate Intranets, on the other hand, are closed internal networks where information can be accessed through browsers (such as Netscape or Internet Explorer) only by the employees of the organization. Large organizations that have salespeople in different regions find Intranets a very effective means of disseminating up-to-date information. A salesperson can log on to a corporate Intranet through a modem from an airplane or from a hotel room and have immediate access to the corporate database. Price lists, product specifications, product updates, sales presentations, customer testimonials, and current information about industry trends and competition are some of the data available on the Intranet for marketing and sales staff.

Intranets are also a very effective tool in sales training. Self-learning manuals, interactive tutorials, and audio and video presentations can be delivered through Intranets. Salespeople in different locations need no longer congregate in the regional or head office for training. This cost-effective training solution works well for technical products. To learn more about Intranets, visit The Intranet Journal (www.intranetjournal.com).

In some situations a direct online sales strategy can lower costs by reducing or eliminating the sales staff. Many organizations will continue to rely heavily on personal selling, but even here, the Internet can greatly improve sales force effectiveness.

[1] Ralph F. Wilson, "Developing Sales Leads from Your Web Site," *Web Marketing Today,* Issue 36, September 1, 1997 (www.wilsonweb.com)

[2] GVU WWW User Survey 7 (www.gvu.gatech.edu/usersurveys?)

Source: This is one of a series of Internet Insites prepared in April 1998 by Dr. Ramesh Venkat of Saint Mary's University for *Basic Marketing,* Ninth Canadian Edition.

Internet Insite 15-1

Information technology provides tools to do the job

Personal selling involves communication, and just as in every other aspect of communication, rapid developments in information technology are having a profound impact on personal selling. How sales tasks and responsibilities are planned and handled is changing in many companies because of the new tools that are becoming available. It is usually the sales manager's job—perhaps with help from specialists in technology—to decide what type of tools are needed and how they will be used.

To get a clearer sense of what is involved, consider a day in the life of a typical major accounts sales representative for a large consumer packaged goods firm: Over a hasty breakfast, she reviews the day's events on her laptop's organizer, logs onto the company network, and sorts through the dozen e-mail messages she finds there. One is from a buyer for a supermarket chain. He's worried that his store's sales in the disposable diaper category are off 10 percent and wants to know if the rep can help. Working from her home PC, the rep dials into an online database and downloads sales trend data for the chain and its competitors. A spreadsheet analysis of the data suggests that the chain is losing sales in the disposable diaper category to new competition from warehouse clubs. Next, the rep places a conference call with a diaper brand manager and a company sales promotion specialist to seek their advice. She then prepares a written recommendation that the buyer include and frequently promote larger-size diaper packages of both her company's and competitors' brands in the chain's merchandise mix. She also prepares a PowerPoint presentation, complete with full-colour graphics, which she will deliver to the buyer on her laptop PC at a later meeting. Before leaving home, the rep e-mails an advance copy of the report to the buyer and prints a colour copy for her manager.

New software and hardware—a competitive edge

This example uses a consumer packaged goods setting, but the basic idea applies in all types of sales settings, especially in business markets. Many of today's sales reps rely on an array of software and hardware that was hardly imaginable even a decade ago (see Marketing Demo 15–1). The information technology explosion has put new software for spreadsheet analysis, electronic presentations, time management, sales forecasting, customer contact, and shelf space management at the salesperson's fingertips. New but now commonplace hardware includes everything from cellular phones, fax machines, laptop computers, and pagers to personalized videoconferencing systems. In many situations these technologies are dramatically changing the ability of sales reps to meet the needs of their customers while achieving the objectives of their jobs.

However, the availability of these technologies does not change the basic nature of the sales tasks that need to be accomplished. What they do change is how—and how well—the job is done. Yet this is not simply a matter of implementation that is best left to individual sales reps. A key reason is that many of these tools may be necessary just to compete effectively. If competitors have the tools and they can do a better job of meeting customers' needs and providing service, a sales manager may have no choice. For example, if customers expect to be able to send an e-mail and get a quick response from a sales rep, a sales organization that does not have this capability will be at a real disadvantage in getting or keeping that customer's business.

Moreover, many of these technologies must be in place for the whole sales organization if the new system is to work properly. For example, it doesn't help much that a salesperson is able to use a laptop computer to dial in to the company if the data the rep needs are not available, online and up to date, in an easily accessible format.

On the other hand, these tools have associated costs. There is the obvious expense of buying the technology. But there is also the time cost of teaching everyone how to use it. Often, that is not a simple matter. Some salespeople who have done the sales job well for a long time "the old fashioned way" resent being told that they have to change what they are doing—even if it's what customers expect. And the flip side of that is that some customers don't want to deal with anything electronic. They don't want e-mail, spreadsheets, or faxes. They want personal attention. And to them, personal attention means a voice and face that they recognize. In some cases that means that the technology is a tool in the background. It is not seen or felt, but its positive impact can be observed. Of course, if a firm expects salespeople to be able to use these technologies, that requirement needs to be included when it comes to selecting and training people for the job.

Sound selection and training help build a sales force

It is important to hire *well qualified* salespeople. But the selection in many companies is a hit-or-miss affair, done without serious thought about exactly what kind of person the firm needs. Managers may hire friends and relations—or whoever is available—because they feel that the only qualification for a sales job is a friendly personality. This approach leads to problems.

Progressive companies are more careful. They constantly update a list of possible job candidates. They schedule candidates for multiple interviews with various executives, do thorough background checks, and even use psychological tests. Unfortunately, such techniques can't guarantee success. But a systematic approach based on several different inputs results in a better sales force.

One problem in selecting salespeople is that two different sales jobs with identical titles may involve very different selling tasks, and require different skills. A carefully prepared job description helps avoid this problem.

Job descriptions—in writing and specific

A **job description** is a written statement of what a salesperson is expected to do. It might list 10 to 20 specific tasks. Each company must write its own job specifications, which should provide clear guidelines about what selling tasks the job involves. This is critical in order to determine the kind of salespeople who should be selected—and later it provides a basis for seeing how they should be trained, how well they are performing, and how they should be paid.

Good salespeople are trained, not born

The idea that good salespeople are born may have some truth, but it isn't the whole story. A salesperson needs to be taught—about the company and its products, about giving effective sales presentations, and about building strong relationships with customers. But this isn't always done. Many salespeople fail, or do a poor job, because they haven't had good training. Firms often hire new salespeople and immediately send them out on the road, or the retail selling floor, with no grounding in the basic selling steps and no information about the product or the customer. This isn't enough!

The kind of training needed depends on the job

It's up to sales and marketing management to ensure that the salespeople know what they're supposed to do and how to do it. Saturn car dealers faced this problem. They wanted customer-oriented salespeople who would satisfy customer's needs rather than just aggressively "push iron." Many salespeople who had been selling for other car companies found it hard to adjust to Saturn's philosophy. Saturn's training program addressed these problems. Now Saturn salespeople earn some of the highest customer satisfaction ratings in the automobile industry.

Sales training should be modified based on the experience and skills of the group involved. But the company's sales training program should cover at least the following areas: (1) company policies, (2) product information, (3) building relationships with customer firms, and (4) professional selling skills.

Selling skills can be learned

Many firms spend the bulk of their training time on product information and company policy. They neglect training in selling techniques because they think selling is something anyone can do. But training in selling skills can pay off. For example, it can help salespeople learn how to be more effective in cold calls on new prospects, in listening carefully to identify a customer's real problems, and in closing the sale.

Training on selling techniques often starts in the classroom with lectures, case studies, and videotaped trial presentations and demonstrations. Then a complete training program adds on-the-job observation of effective salespeople and coaching from sales supervisors. Many companies also use weekly sales meetings, annual conventions, and regular newsletters—as well as ongoing training sessions—to keep salespeople up to date.[8]

Compensating and motivating salespeople

To recruit and keep good salespeople, a firm has to develop an attractive compensation plan designed to motivate. Ideally, sales reps should be paid in such a way that what they want to do—for personal interest and gain—is in the company's interest too. Most companies focus on financial motivation, but public recognition, sales contests, and simple personal recognition for a job well done can be highly effective in encouraging greater sales effort.[9] Our main emphasis here, however, will be on financial motivation.[10]

Two basic decisions must be made in developing a compensation plan: (1) the level of compensation and (2) the method of payment.

Marketing Demo 15-1

Salespeople Work Smarter—with Their Fingertips

Laptop computers help more salespeople work smarter, not just harder. Salespeople use computers in many different ways.

Without a laptop, it was impossible for a wholesaler's salespeople to master Cincinnati Milacron's product line. Now a computer asks a series of questions and then helps the salesperson figure out which of 65,000 grinding wheels and hundreds of cutting fluids to sell to each metal shop. After adding this system, Milacron doubled its market share—without adding new salespeople.

Laptops help keep salespeople for London Fog clothing up to date when they're on the road calling on accounts. Early each morning before leaving the hotel, the sales reps call into the company's central computer. It downloads to the laptops all the latest information about product availability, prices, customers' accounts, and the like. Later in the day, when a customer has a question about product delivery, the sales rep can answer it instantly—without scheduling another appointment or even calling the home office.

Salespeople for Metropolitan Life Insurance use laptops to help customers analyze the financial implications of different investments. For example, when the manager of a pension fund wanted to see what would happen if she switched money from one investment to another, the salesperson used spreadsheet software on the laptop to do the analysis on the spot. The customer was convinced, and the sales rep closed a $633,000 sale.

When Hewlett-Packard equipped a group of salespeople with laptops, the machines helped improve communications and reduced the amount of time spent in meetings at the home office. As a result, salespeople were able to spend 27 percent more time with customers—and sales rose by 10 percent.

Results like these explain why the number of companies equipping their salespeople with laptops is growing so rapidly. New laptops that include built-in cellular phones that can send and receive faxes are attracting even more companies.[11]

"This was when we had the execution."

Compensation varies with job and skills

To attract good salespeople, a company must pay at least the going market wage for different kinds of salespeople. To be sure it can afford a specific type of salesperson, when writing the job description the company should estimate how valuable such a salesperson will be. A good order getter may be worth $50,000 to $100,000 to one company but only $25,000 to another, simply because the second firm doesn't have enough to sell! In such a case, the second company should rethink its job specifications or completely change its promotion plans, because the going rate for good order getters is much higher than $25,000 a year.

If a job requires extensive travel, aggressive pioneering, or contacts with difficult customers, the pay may have to be higher. But the salesperson's compensation level should compare, at least roughly, with the pay scale of the rest of the firm. Normally, salespeople earn more than the office or production force but less than top management.

Payment methods vary

Given some general level of compensation, there are three basic methods of payment: (1) *straight salary,* (2) *straight commission,* or (3) a *combination plan.* Straight salary normally supplies the most security for the salesperson, and straight commission the most incentive to get sales. These two represent extremes. Most companies want to offer their salespeople some balance between incentive and security, so the most popular method of payment is a combination plan that includes some salary and some commission. Bonuses, profit sharing, pensions, stock plans, insurance, and other fringe benefits may be included too.

Salary gives control—if there is close supervision

A salesperson on straight salary earns the same amount regardless of how he or she spends time. So the salaried salesperson is expected to do what the sales manager asks, whether it is order-taking, supporting sales activities, solving customer problems, or completing sales call reports. However, the sales manager maintains control *only* by close supervision. This means that straight salary or a large salary element in the compensation plan increases the amount of sales supervision needed.

If such personal supervision would be difficult, a manager may get better control with a compensation plan that combines some commission (or even a straight commission) with built-in direction. For example, if a company wants its salespeople to devote more time to developing new accounts, it can pay higher commissions for first orders from a new customer. However, a salesperson on a straight commission tends to be his or her own boss. The sales manager is less likely to get help on sales activities that won't increase the salesperson's earnings.

Incentives can be direct or indirect

The incentive effect of compensation works best when there is a direct relationship between the salesperson's effort and results. The relationship between individual effort and results is less direct if a number of people are involved in the sale—engineers, top management, or supporting salespeople. Here, each one's contribution is less obvious, and greater emphasis on salary may make more sense.

When a company wants to expand sales rapidly, it usually offers strong incentives to order-getting salespeople. Strong incentives may also be sensible when the company's objectives are shifting or varied. In this way, the salesperson's activities and efforts can be directed and shifted as needed. One trucking company, for example, has a sales incentive plan that pays higher commissions on business needed to balance freight movements, depending on how heavily traffic has been moving in one direction or another.

An incentive compensation plan can help motivate salespeople, but you have to be certain that the incentives are really aligned with the firm's objectives. For example, some critics believe that IBM's sales commission plan resulted in IBM salespeople pushing customers to buy computers they didn't need; the sales reps got the sale and income, but then customers who were dissatisfied with what they'd purchased broke off their relationship with IBM and turned to other suppliers. Now, IBM is trying to more carefully align its incentive plan with a customer orientation. For example, most IBM sales reps receive incentive pay based on both customer satisfaction ratings and the profitability of the sales they get. Finding the right balance between these two criteria isn't easy. But many firms use variations of this approach, because incentives that focus only on short-term or first-time sales may not be best for motivating sales reps to develop long-term, need-satisfying relationships with their customers.

Flexibility is desirable—but difficult to achieve

Flexibility is probably the most difficult aspect to achieve. One major reason that combination plans have become more popular is that they offer a way to meet varying situations. We'll consider four major kinds of flexibility.

Flexibility in selling costs is especially important for most small companies. With limited working capital and uncertain markets, small companies like straight commission—or combination plans with a large commission element. When sales drop off, costs do too. Such flexibility is similar to using manufacturers' agents who get paid only if they deliver sales. This advantage often dominates in selecting a sales compensation method. Exhibit 15–2 shows the general relationship between personal selling expense and sales volume for each of the basic compensation alternatives.

Exhibit 15-2 Relation Between Personal Selling Expenses and Sales Volume, for Three Basic Personal Selling Compensation Alternatives

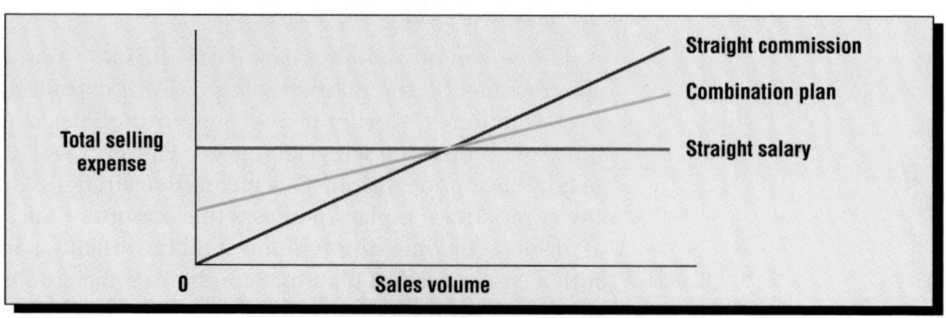

Sales potential usually differs from one sales territory to another, so it is desirable for a compensation plan to offer *flexibility among territories.* Unless the pay plan allows for territory differences, the salesperson in a growing territory may have rapidly increasing earnings, while the sales rep in a poor area will have little to show for the same amount of work. Such a situation isn't fair, and can lead to high turnover and much dissatisfaction. A sales manager can take such differences into consideration when setting a salesperson's **sales quota**—the specific sales or profit objective a salesperson is expected to achieve.

Flexibility among people is important because most companies' salespeople vary in their stage of professional development. Trainees and new salespeople usually require a special pay plan with emphasis on salary. This provides at least some stability of earnings.

Flexibility among products is desirable because most companies sell several different products with different profit potentials. Unless firms recognize this fact, the salespeople may push the products that sell best and ignore overall company profit. A flexible commission system can more easily adjust to changing profit potentials.

Try to keep plan simple

A final consideration is the need for simplicity. Complicated plans are hard for salespeople to understand. Salespeople become dissatisfied when they can't see a direct relationship between their effort and their income. Simplicity is best achieved with straight salary. But in practice, it's usually better to sacrifice some simplicity to gain some incentive, flexibility, and control.[12]

Personal selling techniques—prospecting and presenting

We've stressed the importance of training in selling techniques. Now let's discuss these ideas in more detail so that you understand the basic steps each salesperson should follow. Exhibit 15–3 shows the steps we'll consider. You can see that the salesperson is carrying out a planned communication process—as we discussed in Chapter 14.

Prospecting—narrowing down to the right target

Narrowing the personal selling effort down to the right target requires constant, detailed analysis of markets and much prospecting. Basically, **prospecting** involves following all the leads in the target market to identify potential customers.

Finding live prospects who will help make the buying decision isn't as easy as it sounds. In business markets, for example, the salesperson may need to do some hard detective work to find the real purchase decision makers.

Most salespeople use the telephone for much of their detective work. A phone call often saves the wasted expense of personal visits to prospects who are not interested—or it can provide much useful information for planning a follow-up sales visit. Some hot prospects can even be sold on the phone.

Some companies provide prospect lists to make this part of the selling job easier. For example, one insurance company checks the local newspaper for marriage announcements. Then a salesperson calls to see if the new couple is interested in finding out more about life insurance.[13]

Keep good relationships healthy

While prospecting focuses on identifying new customers, established customers require attention too. It's often time-consuming and expensive to establish a relationship with a customer, so once established it makes sense to keep the relationship

Exhibit 15-3 Key Steps in the Personal Selling Process

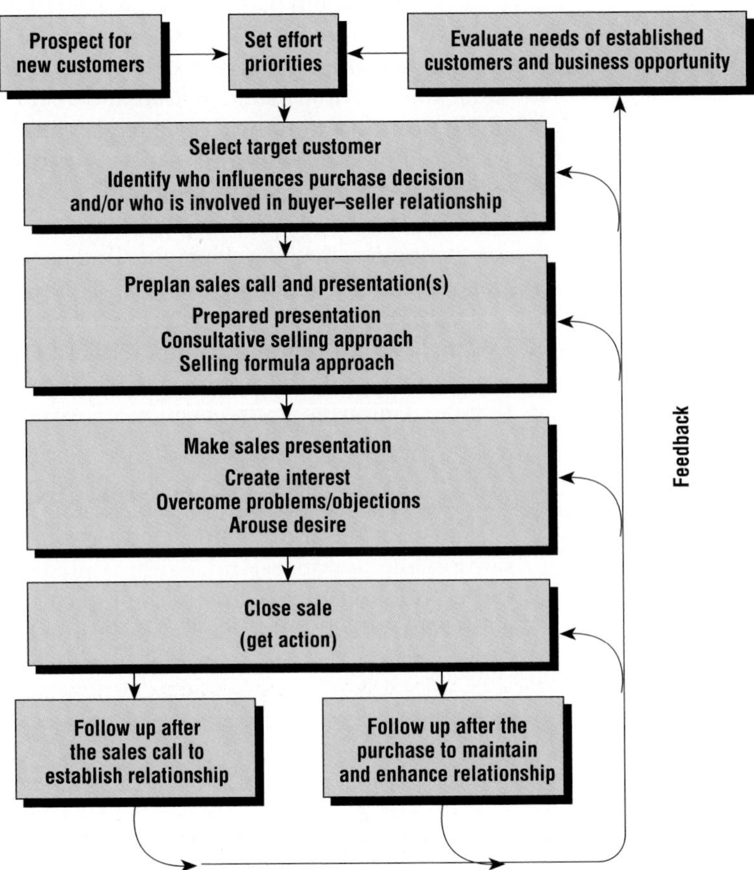

healthy. That requires the rep to routinely review active accounts, rethink customers' needs, and reevaluate each customer's long-term business potential. Some small accounts may have the potential to become big accounts, and some accounts that previously required a lot of costly attention may no longer warrant it. So a sales rep may need to set priorities for new prospects as well as existing customers.

How long to spend with whom?

Once possible prospects—and customers who need attention—have been identified, the salesperson must decide how much time to spend with each one. A sales rep must "qualify" customers to see if they deserve more effort. The salesperson usually makes these decisions by weighing the potential sales volume as well as the likelihood of a sale. This requires judgment. But well-organized salespeople usually develop some system because they have too many demands on their time.

Some firms provide their reps with personal computers and specially developed computer programs to help with this process. Most of them use some grading scheme. A sales rep might estimate how much each account is likely to purchase as well as the probability of getting the business, given the competition. The computer then combines this information and grades each prospect. Attractive accounts may be labelled A—and the salesperson may plan to call on them weekly until the sale is made, the relationship is in good shape, or the customer is moved into a lower category. B customers might offer somewhat lower potential and be called on monthly. C accounts might be called on only once a year, unless they happen to contact the salesperson. And D accounts might be transferred to a telemarketing group.[14]

Three kinds of useful sales presentations

Once the salesperson selects a target customer, it's necessary to make a **sales presentation**—a salesperson's effort to make a sale or address a customer's problem. But someone has to plan what kind of sales presentation to make. This is a strategy decision. The kind of presentation should be set before the sales rep goes calling. And in situations where the customer comes to the salesperson—in a retail store, for instance—planners have to make sure that customers are brought together with salespeople.

For sales presentations, a marketing manager has a choice between two basic approaches: the prepared approach, and the consultative selling approach. Another approach—the selling formula approach—is a combination of the two. Each of these has its place.

The prepared sales presentation

The **prepared sales presentation** approach uses a memorized presentation that is not adapted to each individual customer. This approach says that a customer faced with a particular stimulus will give the desired response—in this case, a yes answer to the salesperson's prepared statement, which includes a **close,** the salesperson's request for an order.

If one trial close doesn't work, the sales rep tries another prepared presentation and attempts another closing. This can go on for some time, until the salesperson runs out of material or the customer either buys or decides to leave. Exhibit 15–4 shows the relative participation of the salesperson and customer in the prepared approach. Note that the salesperson does most of the talking.

Firms may rely on the canned approach when only a short presentation is practical. It's also sensible when salespeople aren't very skilled. The company can control what they say—and in what order. But a canned approach has a weakness. It treats all potential customers alike. It may work for some and not for others, and the salespeople probably won't know why or learn from experience. A prepared approach is sometimes suitable for simple sales, but it is not considered good selling for complicated situations.

Consultative selling

The **consultative selling approach** involves developing a good understanding of the individual customer's needs before trying to close the sale. This name is used because the salesperson is almost acting as a consultant to help identify and solve the customer's problem. With this approach, the sales rep makes some general benefit statements to get the customer's attention and interest. Then the salesperson asks questions and *listens carefully* to understand the customer's needs. Once they agree on needs, the seller tries to show the customer how the product fills those needs—and to close the sale. This is a problem-solving approach in which the customer and

Exhibit 15-4
Prepared Approach to Sales Presentation

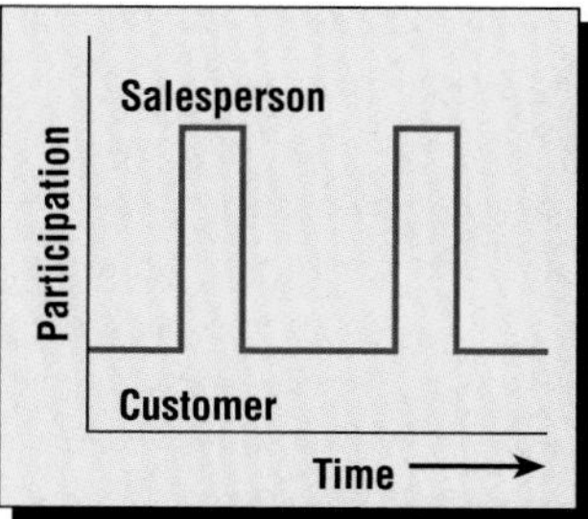

Exhibit 15-5
Consultative Selling Approach to Sales Presentation

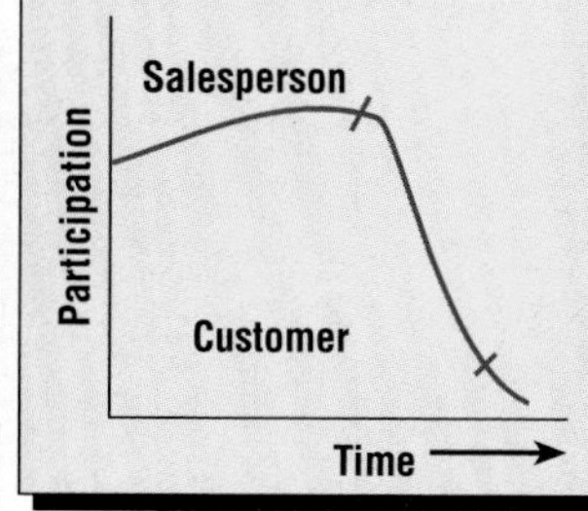

Exhibit 15-6
Selling-Formula Approach to Sales Presentation

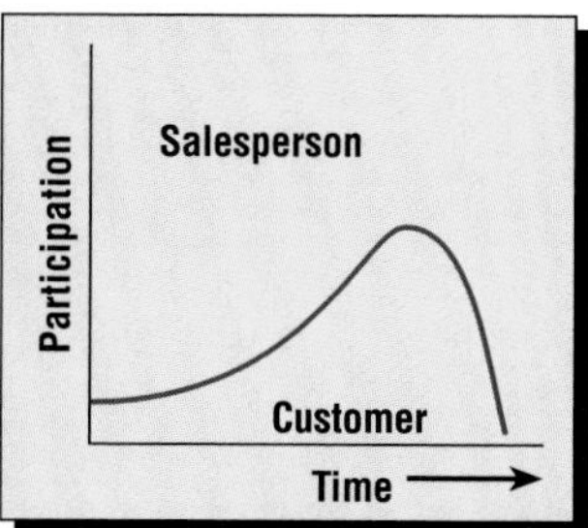

salesperson work together to satisfy the customer's needs. That's why it's sometimes called the need-satisfaction approach. Exhibit 15–5 shows the participation of the customer and the salesperson during such a sales presentation.

The consultative selling approach is most useful when there are many subtle differences among the customers in one target market. In the extreme, each customer may be thought of as a separate target market—with the salesperson trying to adapt to each one's needs and attitudes. With this approach, the sales rep may even conclude that the customer's problem is better solved with someone else's product. That might result in one lost sale, but it also is likely to build real trust and more sales opportunities over the life of the relationship with the customer. That's why this kind of selling is becoming typical in business markets, where the salesperson has already established a close relationship with a customer.

Selling formula approach—some of both

The **selling formula approach** starts with a prepared presentation outline—much like the prepared approach—and then leads the customer through some logical steps to a final close. The prepared steps are logical because we assume that we know something about the target customer's needs and attitudes.

Exhibit 15–6 shows the selling formula approach. At the beginning of the presentation, to communicate key points early, the salesperson does most of the talking. This part of the presentation may even have been prepared as part of the marketing strategy. As the sales presentation moves along, however, the salesperson brings the customer into the discussion to help clarify just what needs this customer has. The salesperson's job is to discover the needs of the particular customer so as to know how to proceed. Once it is clear what kind of customer this is, the salesperson comes back, to show how the product satisfies this specific customer's needs—and to close the sale.

This approach can be useful for both order-getting and order-taking situations, where potential customers are similar and firms must use relatively untrained salespeople. Some office equipment and computer producers use this approach. They know the kinds of situations their salespeople meet, and roughly what they want them to say. Using this approach speeds training and makes the sales force productive sooner.

AIDA helps plan sales presentations

AIDA—Attention, Interest, Desire, Action. Most sales presentations follow this AIDA sequence. The time a sales rep spends on each of the steps may vary depending on the situation and the selling approach being used. But it is still necessary to begin a presentation by getting the prospect's *attention,* and hopefully, to move the customer to *action.*[15]

Each sales manager—and salesperson—needs to think about this sequence in deciding what sales approach to use and in evaluating a possible presentation. Will the presentation get the prospect's attention quickly? Will it be interesting? Will the benefits be clear? Does the presentation consider likely objections so that the sales rep can close the sale when the time is right? These may seem like simple things. But too often they aren't done at all—and a sale is lost.

Ethical Dimensions

Truth and Honesty in Personal Selling

As in every other area of marketing communications, ethical issues arise in the personal selling area. The most basic issue, plain and simple, is whether a salesperson's presentation is honest and truthful. But addressing that issue is a no-brainer. No company is served well by a salesperson who lies or manipulates customers to get their business.

On the other hand, most sales reps sooner or later face sales situations in which they must make more difficult ethical decisions about how to balance company interests, customer interests, and personal interests. Conflicts are less likely to arise if the firm's marketing mix really meets the needs of its target market. Similarly, they are less likely to arise when the firm sees the value of developing a longer-term relationship with the customer. Then, the salesperson is arranging a happy marriage. By contrast, ethical conflicts are more likely when the sales rep's personal outcomes (such as commission income) or the selling firm's profits hinge on making sales to customers whose needs are only partially met by the firm's offering.

Ideally, companies can avoid conflicts by supporting their salespeople with a marketing mix that really offers target customers unique benefits. Moreover, top executives, marketing managers, and sales managers set the tone for the ethical climate in which salespeople operate. If they set impossible goals or project a "do-what-you-need-to-do" attitude, a desperate salesperson may yield to the pressure of the moment. When a firm clearly advocates ethical selling behaviour and makes it clear that unfair selling techniques are not acceptable, the salesperson is not left trying to swim "against the flow."[16]

Questions and Problems

1. What strategy decisions are needed in the personal selling area? Why should the marketing manager make these strategy decisions?
2. What kind of salesperson (or what blend of the basic sales tasks) is required to sell the following products? If there are several selling jobs in the channel for each product, indicate the kinds of salespeople required. Specify any assumptions necessary to give definite answers.
   a. Laundry detergent.
   b. Costume jewellery.
   c. Office furniture.
   d. Men's underwear.
   e. Mattresses.
   f. Corn.
   g. Life insurance.
3. Distinguish among the jobs of producers', wholesalers', and retailers' order-getting salespeople. If one order getter is needed, must all the salespeople in a channel be order getters? Illustrate.
4. Discuss the role of the manufacturer's agent in a marketing manager's promotion plans. What kind of salesperson is a manufacturer's agent? What type of compensation plan is used for a manufacturer's agent?
5. Discuss the future of the specialty shop if producers place greater emphasis on mass selling because of the inadequacy of retail order-taking.
6. Compare and contrast missionary salespeople and technical specialists.
7. Explain how a compensation plan could be developed to provide incentives for experienced salespeople and yet make some provision for trainees who have not yet learned the job.
8. How would a straight commission plan provide flexibility in the sale of a line of women's clothing products that continually vary in profitability?
9. How would our economy operate if personal salespeople were outlawed? Could the economy work? If so, how? If not, what is the minimum personal selling effort necessary? Could this minimum personal selling effort be controlled by law?

Suggested Cases

18 Blackburn Company

20 Bemis Cable Inc.

26 Cutters, Inc.

28 Imperial Lumber Limited

Computer-aided problem

Sales Compensation

Franco Welles, sales manager for Nanek, Inc., is trying to decide whether to pay a sales rep for a new territory with straight commission or a combination plan. He wants to evaluate possible plans—to compare the compensation costs and profitability of each. Welles knows that sales reps in similar jobs at other firms make about $36,000 a year.

The sales rep will sell two products. Welles is planning a higher commission for Product B, because he wants it to get extra effort. From experience with similar products, he has some rough estimates of expected sales volume under the different plans, and various ideas about commission rates. The details are found in the spreadsheet. The program computes compensation, and how much the sales rep will contribute to profit. "Profit contribution" is equal to the total revenue generated by the sales rep minus sales compensation costs and the costs of producing the units.

a. For the initial values shown in the spreadsheet, which plan—commission or combination—would give the rep the highest compensation, and which plan would give the greatest profit contribution to Nanek, Inc.?

b. Welles thinks a sales rep might be motivated to work harder and sell 1,100 units of Product B if the commission rate (under the commission plan) were increased to 10 percent. If Welles is right (and everything else stays the same), would the higher commission rate be a good deal for Nanek? Explain your thinking.

c. A sales rep interested in the job is worried about making payments on her new car. She asks if Welles would consider paying her with a combination plan but with more guaranteed income (an $18,000 base salary) in return for taking a 3 percent commission on Products B and A. If this arrangement results in the same unit sales as Welles originally estimated for the combination plan, would Nanek, Inc., be better off or worse off under this arrangement?

d. Do you think the rep's proposal will meet Welles' goals for Product B? Explain your thinking.

For additional questions related to this problem, see Exercise 15–3 in the *Learning Aid for Use with Basic Marketing,* Ninth Canadian Edition.

When you finish this chapter, you should:

- Understand why a marketing manager sets specific objectives to guide the advertising effort.
- Understand when the various kinds of advertising are needed.
- Understand how to choose the "best" medium.
- Understand how to plan the "best" message—that is, the copy thrust.
- Understand what advertising agencies do, and how they are paid.
- Understand how to advertise legally.
- Understand the importance and nature of sales promotion.
- Know the advantages and limitations of different types of sales promotion.
- Understand the important new terms (shown in orange).

Chap sixteen

Advertising and Sales Promotion

On the TV show *Seinfeld,* face-painting [wasn't] looked upon kindly. After all, Elaine ditched her boyfriend, the monosyllabic mechanic, when he tried to show some spirit— facially—for his favorite hockey team.

But then along came Molson Breweries, which, with its "I AM Canadian" campaign, turned a painted face into one that launched a thousand beer bottles. Or, rather, make that 37 million bottles—the volume equivalent of Molson's gains in 1996 over 1994. And with the campaign's funky, youth-targeted images, Molson Canadian chugged its way from beer brand to pop culture icon.

Two years earlier, though, things weren't looking so good for poor, neglected Molson Canadian. The "innovation wars" of 1993 between Molson and Labatt had brewed up a caseful of new beer brands: Dry, Ice, Red and assorted "light" and "strong" variations. By the time Molson turned its attention back to Canadian, the brand had lost energy—and market share.

Something had to be done. Canadian had to be revitalized, but how? The challenge was to re-ignite the brand at its youth core and reaffirm its relevance to the entry level drinker. But recruiting 19- to 24-year-old drinkers to a mature brand with negative momentum was an unprecedented move. And now, freshman drinkers wanted to be portrayed as more than mere partyers. They didn't want to learn, as the existing Molson Canadian campaign suggested, "What Beer's All About." It was time for something completely new.

Molson's agency of 25 years, MacLaren McCann Canada Inc. of Toronto, knew that drinkers tend to wear their beer brand on their sleeves (sometimes quite literally). For this campaign to be successful, it needed to reach deep into the hearts, souls and minds of young Canadians, provoking a sense of personal pride in being themselves and in being Canadian. But in a market with limited competitive advantage because of government regulations and manufacturer practice, it wasn't enough to simply target Canadian youth. This campaign had to earn the right to *become* the defining voice of Canadian youth.

The ensuing commercials—a multilayering of stream-of-consciousness insights, original music and visuals of real people doing their thing—were placed in suitably hip locales: TV programs for young adults, urban entertainment newspapers, bar and restaurant bathrooms, and college and university campuses. And then Molson turned "I AM" into a cyber concept, becoming the first in its category with a web site, "I AM Online."

As a result of the campaign, Molson Canadian recovered 12% of its share in the Ontario market (1996 vs. 1994) and 8% in English Canada overall. And from a long-term perspective, the brand grew against entry level drinkers, with penetration of the 19-to-24 age group up 13% in 1996 vs. 1994. But even more significant is that Molson Canadian saw a huge increase of 39% with the "college educated" crowd, who tend to be opinion leaders and can influence brand preferences of their peers. But beyond all the numbers and figures, where's the proof this campaign actually got to the heart of what it means to be Canadian? Well, first of all, it's been reproduced. At sporting events, crowd members sometimes hold up maple leaf signs that say "I AM." And the campaign continues to evolve. In recent ads to promote Oktoberfest celebrations in Kitchener/Waterloo, Ont., Molson featured a guy with his face painted like the German flag. The slogan? "I AM Bavarian," of course.

Source: "1997 Cassies Awards: I AM Canadian, Beverages Category—Gold," *Marketing Magazine*, November 3, 1997, p. 8.

Advertising, sales promotion, and marketing strategy decisions

Mass selling makes widespread distribution possible. Although not as flexible as personal selling, advertising can often reach large numbers of potential customers at the same time. It can inform and persuade customers, and help position a firm's marketing mix as the one that meets customers' needs. Sales promotion aimed at final customers, channel members, or a firm's own employees can often sway the target to immediate action. In the past decade, spending on sales promotion has grown at a rapid rate, especially in mature consumer-products markets where marketing managers want more attention from intermediaries and a larger share of consumers' purchases. Today, most promotion blends contain advertising and sales promotion as well as personal selling and publicity.

Advertising contacts vary in cost and results. This means that marketing managers—and the advertising managers who work with them—have important strategy decisions to make. As the Molson Breweries case illustrates, they must decide(1) who their target audience is, (2) what kind of advertising to use, (3) how to reach customers (via which types of media), (4) what to say to them (the copy thrust), and (5) who will do the work—the firm's own advertising department or outside agencies. See Exhibit 16–1.

Exhibit 16-1 Strategic Planning for Advertising

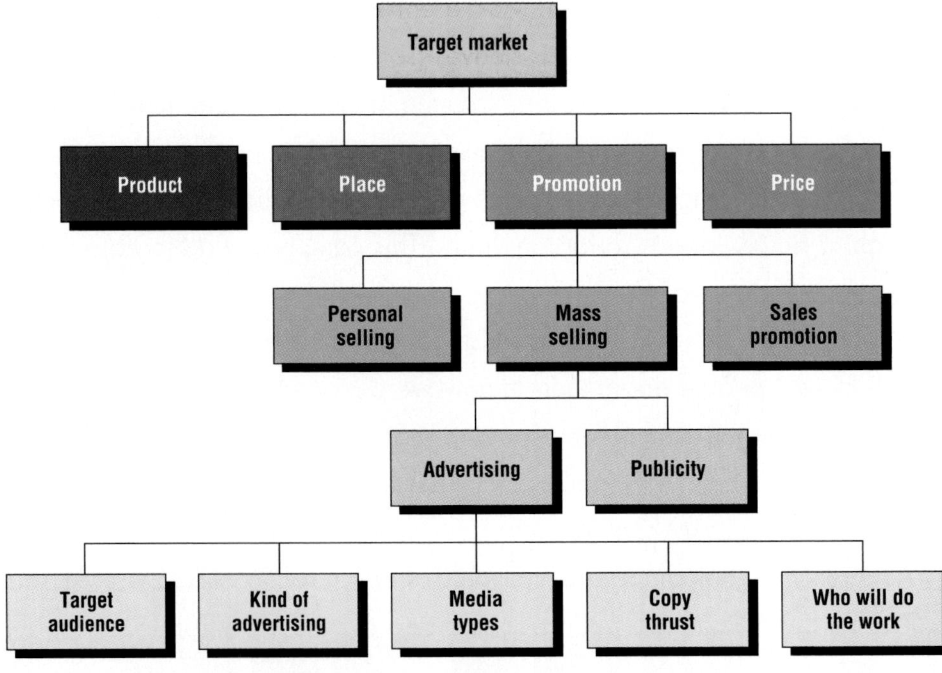

International dimensions are important

The basic strategic planning decisions for advertising and sales promotion are the same regardless of where in the world the target market is located. From the outset, however, remember that the choices available to a marketing manager within each of the decision areas may vary dramatically from one country to another. Print ads are useless if the target audience can't read. Commercial television may not be available. If it is, government may limit the type of advertising permitted or when ads can be shown. Radio broadcasts in a market area may not be in the target market's language. Cultural, social, and behavioural influences may limit what type of advertising messages can be communicated.

International dimensions may also have a significant impact on sales promotion alternatives. For example, in countries with a large number of very small retailers, some types of trade promotion are difficult, or even impossible, to manage. A typical Japanese grocery retailer with only 200 square feet of space, for example, doesn't have room for *any* special end-of-aisle displays. Consumer promotions may be affected too. Polish consumers, for example, are sceptical about product samples. They figure that if it's free, something's amiss. In some developing nations, samples can't be distributed through the mail, because they're routinely stolen before they get to customers. Similarly, coupons won't work unless consumers can redeem them, and in some regions there is no clearinghouse to redeem them. And some countries ban consumer sweepstakes, because they see it as a form of gambling.

Throughout this chapter we'll consider a number of these international promotion issues, but our main focus will be on the array of choices available in Canada and other advanced, market-directed economies.[1]

The importance of advertising

Canadian expenditures

Canadian expenditures on advertising media are substantial. A new method of estimating them (one that excludes production costs, classified advertising revenues, and agency commissions) suggests that such expenditures in 1996 approached $7.4 billion. Exhibit 16–2 reveals how much of that amount was paid to daily newspapers, television,

Exhibit 16–2 Net Canadian Advertising Revenues

	REVENUES (MILLIONS OF $)					
MEDIUM	1994	% OF TOTAL	1995	% OF TOTAL	1996	% OF TOTAL
Television*	1,769	25%	1,844	26%	1,976	27%
Daily newspapers†	1,319	19	1,368	19	1,315	18
Catalogues, direct mail	1,071	15	991	14	1,110	15
Yellow pages, directories‡	847	12	864	12	892	12
Radio	741	11	769	11	797	11
Weeklies/community newspapers	562	8	579	8	597	8
Consumer magazines	260	4	265	4	268	4
Trade publications	170	3	175	2	177	2
Outdoor & transit	132	2	167	2	200	2
Other print (religious, school, farm, weekend)	91	1	37	1	37	1
Total, all media	6,962		7,059		7,368	

*Includes specialty services.
†Excludes classified.
‡Excludes city directories.

Source: Canadian Media Directors' Council's Media Digest 1998–99, p. 11, published by *Marketing Magazine,* as compiled by TVB from Statistics Canada, CRTC, CDNA, Magazines Canada, Mediacom/ACN, Tele-Direct and Industry Estimates.

catalogues and direct mail, and the remaining media options. That television and newspapers account for so much of the total is probably no surprise to you. But would you have guessed that advertising expenditures in the Yellow Pages and other directories exceed those for radio? Wouldn't you have expected consumer magazines to account for considerably more than 4 percent of all media spending? In the next few years the Internet also seems certain to become an important advertising medium (see Internet Insite 16–1).

Canadian firms and industries differ in the percentage of their sales spent on advertising. This difference reflects advertising's relative importance to the firm's or industry's marketing mix. Significant differences also exist in the amount spent advertising different types of products. Marketing Demo 16–1 classifies advertising expenditures by product category. The text accompanying the chart points out that significant changes can occur from year to year. It also shows how much of total spending is accounted for by the categories at the top of the list.

Less costly than personal selling

Clearly, advertising is an important factor in certain markets, especially consumer goods markets. Nevertheless, in total, much less is spent on advertising than on personal selling. And although total advertising expenditures are large, the advertising industry itself employs relatively few people. Probably fewer than 60,000 people work directly in Canadian advertising. This figure includes everyone who helps create or sell advertising for the different advertising media as well as those in advertising agencies. It also includes those working for retailers, wholesalers, and manufacturers who either create their own advertising or at least manage that activity.[2]

Advertising objectives are a strategic decision

Every ad and every advertising campaign should have clearly defined objectives. These should grow out of the firm's overall marketing strategy—and the jobs assigned to advertising. It isn't enough for the marketing manager to say, "Promote the product." The marketing manager must decide exactly what advertising should do.

Advertising objectives should be more specific than personal selling objectives. One of the advantages of personal selling is that a salesperson can shift the presentation for a specific customer. Each ad, however, must be effective not just for one customer but for thousands—or millions—of them.

The marketing manager sets the overall direction

The marketing manager might give the advertising manager one or more of the following specific objectives, along with the budget to accomplish them:

1. Help introduce new products to specific target markets.
2. Help position the firm's brand or marketing mix by informing and persuading target customers or intermediaries about its benefits.
3. Help obtain desirable outlets and tell customers where they can buy a product.
4. Provide ongoing contact with target customers—even when a salesperson isn't available.
5. Prepare the way for salespeople by presenting the company's name and the merits of its products.
6. Get immediate buying action.
7. Help to maintain relationships with satisfied customers and confirm their purchase decisions.

An Introduction to Internet Advertising

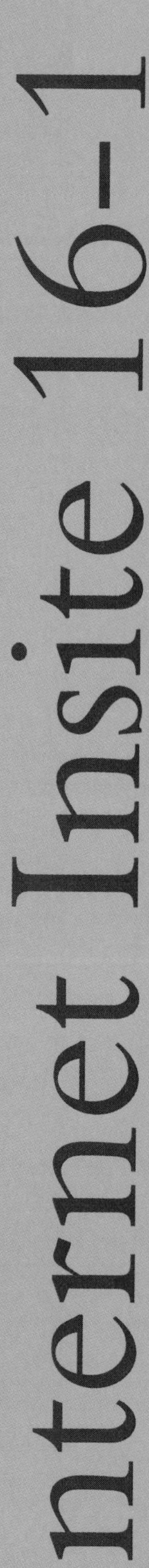

Advertising space on Web sites is typically sold on the basis of "cost per thousand impressions" or CPM. An impression (also called "exposure" or "page view") occurs when a visitor to a Web site views a page where the ad is displayed, irrespective of whether the ad itself is seen or not. To ensure a reasonable chance of the viewer actually seeing the ad, providers of online advertising space use different tactics. Many online content providers such as TIME (www.pathfinder.com) and *The Globe and Mail* (www.globeandmail.ca) tend to place most of their banner ads at the top of the page, thereby increasing the likelihood of the visitor actually seeing the ad before scrolling down the page. Others, such as *Wired* (www.hotwired.com), prefer not to leave anything to chance, and put the banner ad in the page, thus ensuring that the banner is visible even as the visitor scrolls down the page.

Unlike newspaper, TV, or magazine ads, advertisements on the Web can be made interactive. Banner ads tend to entice visitors to "click" on them through various means, including animation, contests, and free promotions. The number of "click-throughs" is treated as a measure of effectiveness. Clicking on the banner ad takes the visitor to another page that usually has more detailed information about the product or service. The problem is that not everyone who sees a banner ad is likely to click. In fact, click-through rates are typically between 3 and 5 percent. Web sites selling ad space prefer to charge based on CPM, rather than "click-throughs."

How much does Web advertising cost? Typically, for up to 100,000 impressions the cost can range from $20 to $100 per thousand. Most popular sites offer volume and frequency discounts for large advertisers. It has to be emphasized that 100,000 impressions does not mean 100,000 unique visitors, since individuals often visit the same page several times. If a site reports 100,000 impressions or page views, that may translate to between 10,000 and 40,000 different individuals.

On the Web, advertising measurement is done through tracking software and Web server logs. The ubiquitous Web counter, which announces that you are the 10,000th visitor to a page, is often connected to more sophisticated tracking software that can capture information such as browser being used, previous Web site visited (in other words, whether the visitor is coming from a site that carries our banner ad), pages seen at the present Web site, country of origin, time of visit, and so on. Further, some Web sites attach a "cookie" file, which is a small text file that resides on the user's computer hard disk. This file can contain information about previous visits to a particular Web site. While this information is of great value to the advertiser, there are serious privacy concerns for most Web users (visit http://consumer.net for more information on Internet privacy). Current Web browsers allow users to "disable" cookies, if they do not wish their Web browsing pattern to be publicly revealed.

Page impressions can be undercounted, for instance, as a result of "caching." With caching, the page displaying the ad is delivered once, and then stored locally on the user's computer hard disk. When the user types that URL (or Web site address) at a later time, the page may now be loaded from the user's hard disk. Even though the user may see the banner ad for a second time through this process, this second impression is not counted because the page did not download from the server that carries the banner ad. Sites selling advertising space use surveys and subscription information to validate or refine the estimates provided by tracking software.

Some advertisers are linking rewards to performance. Amazon.Com (www.amazon.com), an Internet book store that is a real success story, is a prime example. Amazon.Com allows certain Web sites to become Amazon "Associates." Amazon.Com does not pay associates for carrying its banner or for making book recommendations. They are paid only if a book purchase originates from the associate's Web site. Again, tracking technology allows for such innovations in advertising. If you are curious as to how this works, go to Yahoo! (www.yahoo.com) and search for your favourite hobby. When the search results are presented, you will see an Amazon.Com banner with links to related books!

To learn more about Internet advertising, visit the following sites:

1. Internet Advertising Bureau (www.iab.net).
2. Ad Resource (www.adresource.com).
3. Internet Advertising Resource Guide (www.admedia.org).

Source: This is one of a series of Internet Insites prepared in April 1998 by Dr. Ramesh Venkat of Saint Mary's University for *Basic Marketing*, Ninth Canadian Edition.

Ignore this.

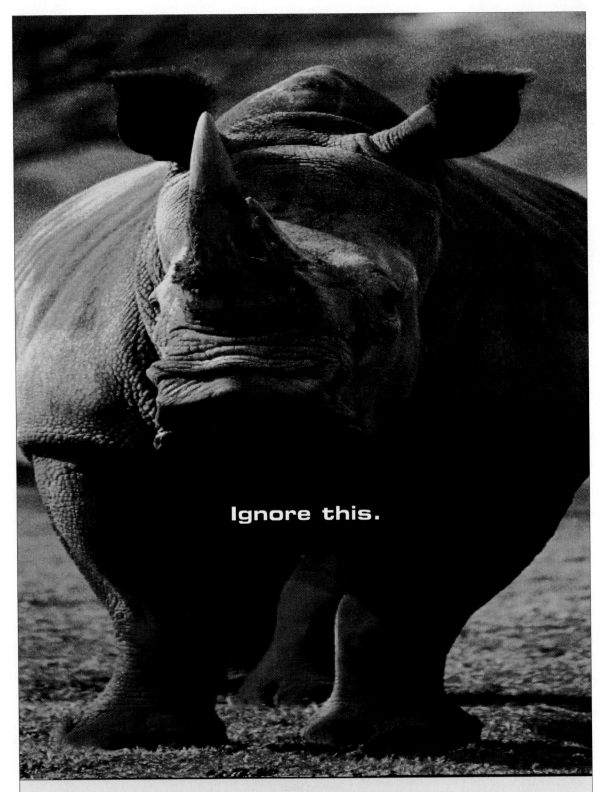

Outdoor advertising and rhinos have a lot in common. They're big, bold and attention-grabbing. So next time you're advertising in B.C. and want to stop your target audience in their tracks, call (604) 291-1229. We're Seaboard Advertising.
We can deliver the same impact as this rhino, and nobody will get hurt.

Marketing Demo 16-1

Canada's Top 25 Advertising Categories

Ad spending patterns were highly erratic in 1996. Total spending grew by 3.4%, but this average disguises sharp contrasts between boom-time conditions in some categories and steep declines in others.

Estimates supplied to *Marketing* by ACNielsen of Markham, Ont. show that the gigantic retail category logged a decline of 2.7% in ad spending during 1996. With inflation at about 2%, this meant a small but significant decline in real terms for this category. Two other huge categories were virtually flat: automotive (down 1.2%) and food (up 1.2%).

But while spending languished in some mega-categories, 11 other sectors were smoking. Financial services and insurance services led the way, with a spectacular 27.8% rise, followed by home entertainment (23.8%), schools (23.1%), publishing (22.9%), sporting goods and recreational products (17.8%), travel and transportation (17.2%), media (13.2%), business equipment and services (12.7%), oil companies (12.7%), restaurants (12.4%) and local auto dealer advertising (11.1%).

While these 11 categories zoomed upward at a double-digit clip, five others headed just as fast the other way. The government category showed the biggest decline, down a thumping 35.3%. The other double-digit shrinkers were mail order (29.5%), lotteries (20.2%), apparel (14.5%) and hair products (11.8%).

Overall, twice as many categories were growing fast as shrinking fast, which explains the overall growth rate of 3.4%. But the fact that five of the top 25 advertiser categories saw such big drops is a reminder that these days the entire economy seldom moves in sync.

The table here features figures from ACNielsen's *Annual Summary of Advertising Expenditures in Canada* reports for 1994–96. These reports track media spending in TV, radio, dailies, magazines and out of home.

In 1996, ACNielsen estimates that the 3,841 companies measured spent $4.8 billion on advertising. It allocated this total into 851 classes, then grouped it into 54 categories. The top [10] categories shown here accounted for [$3.536] billion in spending, [out of the $4,800.4 billion total for 1996].

The figures also confirm how crucial a handful of categories are to total spending. The top three alone accounted for 38% of the $4.8 billion ad pie in 1996. This proportion rose to 53% for the top five and an utterly dominant 74% for the top 10.

1996 Rank	**Category**	**Ad Spending ($ Millions) 1996**	**1995**
1	Retail	892.4	917.6
2	Automotive: Cars; Minivans; Trucks; Vans; Dealer Assocs.	508.4	514.4
3	Business Equipment & Services	445.3	395.0
4	Food	400.3	395.7
5	Entertainment	321.1	300.9
6	Financial & Insurance Services	273.3	213.8
7	Travel & Transport.	213.4	182.1
8	Restaurants; Catering Services; Night Clubs	210.0	186.9
9	Local Automotive Dealer Advtg.	152.7	137.4
10	Cosmetics & Toiletries	119.5	126.9
TOTALS FOR ALL 54 CATEGORIES		4800.4	4641.1

Source: Jim McElgunn, "Canada's Top 25 Advertising Categories," *Marketing Magazine,* October 20, 1997, p. 46, from information provided by ACNielsen, Markham, Ontario.

If you want half the market, say so!

The objectives listed above are not as specific as they could be. If a marketing manager really wants specific results, they should be clearly stated. A general objective is: "To help expand market share." This could be rephrased more specifically: "To increase shelf space in our cooperating retail outlets by 25 percent during the next three months."

Objectives guide implementation too

The specific objectives obviously affect implementation. Advertising that may be right for encouraging new customers to switch from a competing brand may be all wrong for appealing to established customers with whom a firm already has a good relationship. As Exhibit 16–3 shows, the type of advertising that achieves objectives for one stage of

Exhibit 16-3 Examples of Different Types of Advertising over Adoption Process Stages

the adoption process may be off target for another. For example, most advertising for cameras in North America, Germany, and Japan focuses on foolproof pictures or state-of-the-art design because most consumers in these countries already own *some* camera. In Africa, where only about 20 percent of the population owns a camera, ads must sell the whole concept of picture-taking.

Objectives determine the kinds of advertising needed

The advertising objectives largely determine which of two basic types of advertising to use—product or institutional.

Product advertising tries to sell a product. It may be aimed at final users or at channel members.

Institutional advertising tries to promote an organization's image, reputation, or ideas, rather than a specific product. Its basic objective is to develop good will or improve an organization's relations with various groups—not only customers but also current and prospective channel members, suppliers, shareholders, employees, and the general public. The British government, for example, uses institutional advertising to promote England as a place to do business.

Product advertising—know us, like us, remember us

Product advertising falls into three categories: pioneering, competitive, and reminder advertising.

PIONEERING ADVERTISING—BUILDS PRIMARY DEMAND **Pioneering advertising** tries to develop primary demand for a product category rather than demand for a specific brand. Pioneering advertising is usually done in the early stages of the product life cycle. It informs potential customers about the new product and helps turn them into adopters. When Merrell Dow Pharmaceutical introduced a prescription drug to help smokers break the habit, its pioneering ad didn't even mention the name of the drug. Instead it informed smokers who wanted to quit that doctors could now help them overcome their nicotine dependence.

COMPETITIVE ADVERTISING—EMPHASIZES SELECTIVE DEMAND **Competitive advertising** tries to develop selective demand for a specific brand. As the product life cycle moves along, a firm is forced into competitive advertising to hold its own against competitors.

Competitive advertising may be direct or indirect. The **direct type** aims for immediate buying action. The **indirect type** points out product advantages to affect future buying decisions.

Most of Canadian Airlines' advertising is of the competitive variety. Much of it tries for immediate sales, so the ads are the direct type, with prices, timetables, and

Many nonprofit organizations—including Mothers Against Drunk Driving—rely on marketing to help achieve their objectives.

phone numbers to call for reservations. Some are the indirect type. They focus on the quality of service and number of cities served, and suggest you mention Canadian's name the next time you talk to your travel agent.

Comparative advertising is even rougher. **Comparative advertising** involves making specific brand comparisons using actual product names. A comparative ad for Advil shows pictures of competing pain relievers; then the ad copy makes specific superiority claims that it is longer-lasting and easier on the stomach. In the same vein, Sprint Canada and AT&T Canada battle it out in TV ads, each claiming that their long-distance services are the better value.

Many countries forbid comparative advertising, but that situation is changing. For example, Japan banned comparative advertising until about ten years ago, when the restrictions were relaxed. Japan's move followed an earlier change in the United States. The Federal Trade Commission decided to encourage comparative ads, after banning them for years, because it thought that lifting the ban would increase competition and provide consumers with more useful information. But this approach led to legal as well as ethical problems, and some advertisers and their agencies now back away from comparative advertising even in countries like Canada, where it is allowed. A Canadian comparative advertising legal case is discussed in Marketing Demo 16–2.

Superiority claims are supposed to be fair, factual, and supported by research evidence—but the guidelines aren't clear. Some firms just keep running tests until they get the results they want. Others talk about minor differences that don't reflect a product's overall benefits. Some comparative ads leave consumers confused—or even angry if the product they're using is criticized. Comparative ads can also backfire by calling attention to competing products that consumers had not previously considered.[3]

Comparative advertising may be a can of worms that some advertisers wish they hadn't opened. But comparative ads seem to attract attention. So some advertisers will probably continue using this approach—at least in countries that allow it.[4]

Reminder advertising tries to keep the product's name before the public. It may be useful when the product has achieved brand preference or insistence—perhaps in the market maturity or sales decline stages. It is used primarily to reinforce previous promotion. Here, the advertiser may use soft-sell "reminders" that simply mention or show the name. Sunkist, for example, often relies on reminder ads because most consumers already know the brand name and—after years of promotion—associate it with high product quality.

Marketing Demo 16-2

Moisture and Misleading Advertising

Why the Ontario Court Denied Unilever an Injunction against P&G's Comparative Soap Ads

If you are considering attacking a competitor through comparative advertising, ask yourself the following question: Is there sufficient support for the comparative claim I propose to make? This is what the court will ask should your ad be challenged on the basis that it constitutes misleading advertising.

The importance of a factual basis for claims made in comparative advertising was once again highlighted in the Feb. 23 [1996] decision of the Ontario Court of Justice (General Division) in *UL Canada Inc. v. Procter & Gamble Inc.* (*Marketing*, Mar. 11 [1996], p. 4).

UL had asked the court for an interlocutory injunction to restrain P&G from running a television commercial and distributing literature advertising its Oil of Olay bath bar as superior in moisture retention to the "leading beauty bar." UL argued that P&G's superiority claim is a "direct and disparaging comparison" with UL's Dove bar and that this claim constitutes misleading advertising.

When considering an application for an interlocutory injunction, the court asks three questions: (a) Is there a serious issue to be tried? (b) Will the applicant be irreparably harmed if the injunction is refused? and (c) Does the balance of convenience favor granting the injunction?

With respect to the first question, the challenged advertisements essentially claim that more skin moisture is retained when using Oil of Olay than when using the leading beauty bar. The primary issue the court was concerned with was the adequacy and propriety of P&G's tests regarding the comparative effect of product usage on skin for both the Olay bar and Dove bar. After listening to expert evidence as to the propriety of tests conducted by both P&G and UL, Madam Justice Dunnet concluded that there was scientific evidence to establish a reasonable basis for the superiority claim and thus substantiate P&G's claim and defeat UL's application. Consequently, there was no serious issue to be tried.

With respect to the second question, the court held that UL did not provide sufficient evidence to establish what losses it has and will suffer, to prove that any market loss which it has suffered or may suffer would be permanent, or that any losses are not calculable. Nor did it present any substantive evidence that any harm to its goodwill or reputation would be irrevocable.

The answer to the third question requires a consideration of which of the two parties will suffer the greater harm from the granting or refusing of an interlocutory injunction. The court concluded that any losses suffered by UL would be strictly financial, and that the corporation has the ability to absorb the losses without affecting its long-term viability. P&G, on the other hand, would have to pull its advertisements, which might call into question its credibility and reputation. Moreover, considerable expense and inconvenience would be involved, both to P&G and others such as retailers. Therefore, the balance of convenience did not favor granting the injunction.

Also of note is the fact that even though neither UL, nor its Dove brand beauty bar, were referred to by name in any of the ads, the court found that the words "leading beauty bar" in P&G's ads refer to the Dove bar. The court noted that, since 1967, UL's Dove has become the leading beauty bar in this country by both dollar and tonnage market share and the leading product in the personal wash-bar soap category.

Advertising can be an effective tool in persuading the public to utilize a particular product or service. By its nature, it is one-sided and usually does not convey a full and balanced analysis. For this reason the courts are generally reluctant to intervene in the competitive marketplace unless advertisements are clearly unfair. Comparative advertising is undoubtedly one of the most effective advertising methods. Clearly, though, because of the substantial cost of launching an advertising campaign, avoiding scrutiny of the courts is an important goal of every marketing department. The Oil of Olay case demonstrates the importance of having convincing evidence of adequate supporting tests before embarking on a comparative campaign.

Source: Angela Di Padova, Fasken Campbell Godfrey, Toronto, for *Marketing Magazine*, March 18, 1996, p. 20.

Institutional advertising—remember our name

Institutional advertising usually focuses on the name and prestige of an organization or industry. It may seek to inform, persuade, or remind.

Many Japanese firms, such as Hitachi, emphasize institutional advertising, in part because they often use the company name as a brand name.

Companies sometimes rely on institutional advertising to present the company in a favourable light—perhaps to overcome image problems. Ads for an oil company, for example, might highlight its concern for the environment.

Some organizations use institutional advertising to advocate a specific cause or idea. Insurance companies and organizations like Mothers Against Drunk Driving, for example, use these advocacy ads to encourage people not to drink and drive.[5]

Coordinating advertising efforts with cooperative relationships

Sometimes a producer knows that an advertising job can be done more effectively or more economically by someone farther along in the channel. Alternatively, a large retail chain may approach manufacturers with a catalogue or program, and tell them how much it will cost to participate. In either case, the producer may offer **advertising allowances**—price reductions to firms farther along in the channel to encourage them to advertise or otherwise promote the firm's products locally.

Cooperative advertising involves intermediaries and producers sharing in the cost of ads. This helps wholesalers and retailers compete in their local markets. It also helps the producer get more promotion for the advertising dollar, because media usually give local advertisers lower rates than national or international firms. In addition, a retailer or wholesaler who is paying a share of the cost is more likely to follow through.

Integrated communications

Coordination and integration of ad messages in the channel is another reason for cooperative advertising. One big, well-planned, integrated advertising effort is often better than many different—perhaps inconsistent—local efforts. Many franchise operations like the idea of communicating with one voice. KFC, for example, encourages its franchises to use common advertising materials. Before, many developed their own local ads—with themes like "Eight clucks for four bucks"—that didn't fit with the company's overall marketing strategy.

However, allowances and support materials alone don't ensure cooperation. When channel members don't agree about the advertising program, it can be a serious source of conflict. For example, Benetton, the Italian sportswear company, wanted its "United Colors" ad campaign to be controversial. Pictures showed a dying AIDS victim and a torn, bloody uniform from the war in Bosnia. Most Europeans—including many of Benetton's retailer–franchisees—saw the ads as a tasteless attempt to exploit suffering. To protest the ads, a group of German franchisees stopped paying their franchise fees and sued Benetton for damages. This is an extreme example, but even in routine situations a marketing manager should consider the likely reaction of other channel members before implementing any advertising program.[6]

Choosing the "best" medium—how to deliver the message

What is the best advertising medium? There is no simple answer to this question. Effectiveness depends on how well the medium fits with the rest of a marketing strategy. That is, it depends on (1) your promotion objectives, (2) which target markets you want to reach, (3) the funds available for advertising, and (4) the nature of the media—including who they *reach,* with what *frequency,* with what *impact,* and at what *cost.* Exhibit 16–4 provides an overview of the media options available in Canada.

Ethical Dimensions

Advertising Allowance Programs

Ethical issues sometimes arise concerning advertising allowance programs. For example, a retailer may run one producer's ad to draw customers to the store but then sell them another brand. Is this unethical? Some producers think it is. A different view is that retailers are obligated to the producer to run the ad—but obligated to consumers to sell them what they want, no matter whose brand it may be. A producer can often avoid the problem with a strategy decision, by setting the allowance amount as a percentage of the retailer's *actual purchases.* That way, a retailer who doesn't produce sales doesn't get the allowance.

Sometimes a retailer takes allowance money but doesn't run the ads at all. Some producers close their eyes to this problem because they don't know what to do about intense competition from other suppliers for the retailer's attention. But there are legal and ethical problems with that response as well. Basically, the allowance may have become a disguised price concession that results in price discrimination, which is illegal in Canada and the United States. So smart producers insist on proof that the advertising was really done.[7]

Exhibit 16-4 A Capsule View of Major Canadian Media

Television	43 television markets covered by 131 commercial television stations, most of which belong to 1 of 17 networks. There are 21 specialty networks.
Radio	867 radio stations (350 AM and 517 FM).
Daily newspapers	110 daily newspapers with an average daily paid circulation of 4.6 million. Gross circulation as a percentage of households is approximately 63%.
Consumer magazines	Over 500 consumer magazines ranging in content from general editorial to special interest categories (such as photography and music).
Business publications	Listed in *Canadian Advertising Rates and Data* (CARD) with circulations of 20,000 plus.
Direct marketing	Direct mail is the most common form of direct marketing.
Ethnic press	174 publications covering 44 ethnic groups other than English and French.
Farm publications	98 farm publications whose circulation ranges from 1,000 copies to large, mass-appeal publications with over 200,000 circulation.
Community newspapers	Approximately 900, with an average weekly circulation of over 9.0 million
Weekend newspapers	Essentially a Quebec phenomenon: 11 such papers are published in French.
Religious publications	25 publications listed under the religious category in CARD; they range in circulation from 1,300 to over 270,200.
University and school publications	Over 212 university, community college, alumni, and scholarly publications.
Outdoor advertising	Poster space is available in more than 400 Canadian municipalities.
Transit Advertising	Available in 90 markets across Canada, including 24 suburban markets, which can be booked separately.

Source: Based on the Canadian Media Directors' Council's *Media Digest* 1997–98, published by *Marketing Magazine.*

Exhibit 16–5 shows some pros and cons of major kinds of media—and some typical costs. However, some of the advantages noted in this table may not apply in all markets. For example, direct mail may not be a wise choice in a less-developed country with a weak postal system or high rate of illiteracy. Similarly, TV audiences are often less selective, but a special-interest cable TV show may reach a very targeted audience.[8]

Specify promotion objectives

Before you can choose the best medium, you have to decide on your promotion objectives. If the objective is to increase interest and that requires demonstrating product benefits, TV may be the best alternative. If the objective is to inform, using a detailed story and precise pictures, then magazines may be better. For example, Jockey switched its advertising to magazines from television when it decided to show the variety of colours, patterns, and styles of its men's briefs. Jockey felt that it was too hard to show the details in a 30-second TV spot. Further, Jockey felt that there were problems with modelling men's underwear on television. However, Jockey might have stayed with TV had it been targeting consumers in France or Brazil, where nudity in TV ads is common.[9]

Match your market with the media

To guarantee good media selection, the advertiser first must *clearly specify* its target market. Then the advertiser can choose media that reach target customers.

The media available in a country may limit the choices. In less-developed nations, for example, radio is often the only way to reach a broad-based market of poor consumers who can't read or afford television.

Usually, however, the main problem is how to select media that will reach the target audience effectively. Most of the major media use marketing research to develop profiles of the people who buy their publications, or live in their broadcasting area.

Another problem is that the audience for media that *do* reach your target market may also include people who are *not* in the target group. But *you pay for the entire audience the media deliver*—including those who aren't potential customers. For example, Delta Faucet, a faucet manufacturer that wanted its ads to reach plumbers, placed ads on ESPN's Saturday college football telecasts. Research showed that many plumbers watched the ESPN games. Yet plumbers are only a very small portion of the total college football audience—and the size of the total audience determined the cost of the advertising time.

The cost of reaching the real target market goes up fastest when the irrelevant audience is very large. Ads run during the Olympics, for example, reach a very large audience, but that audience is also very diverse. Research suggests that many of the firms that sponsored ads on these big-audience shows would have gotten more bang for the buck by placing ads on shows that reached more-targeted audiences.[10]

Because it is so difficult to evaluate alternative media, some media analysts focus on objective measures, such as cost per thousand of audience size or circulation. But advertisers preoccupied with keeping these costs down may ignore the relevant segmenting dimensions—and slip into mass marketing.

Some media help zero in on specific target markets

Today, the major media direct more attention to reaching smaller, more defined target markets. The most obvious evidence of this is in the growth of spending on direct-mail advertising to consumers listed in a database. However, other major media are becoming more targeted as well.

National print media may offer specialized editions. *Time* magazine, for example, offers not only several regional and metropolitan editions but also special editions

Exhibit 16-5 Media Characteristics—Information on the Strengths and Weaknesses of Media as Advertising Vehicles

	Newspapers	Consumer magazines	Radio	Televison
Features	Broad information, life-style travel and entertainment, plus highly localized news of community activities through community weeklies.	Special interests and selective audiences. Usually high-quality reproduction. Long life.	Highly varied from hard rock to all talk, easy listening to country and western. A flexible medium.	Mass audience. Highly visible. Ubiquitous medium for instant exposure of pictures and ideas. High impact.
Audience	Broad: 60% of adults daily, 82% weekly. Higher among educated, older, affluent consumers. Total coverage with weeklies.	Selective, from hobbyists to investors, athletes to cooks. Also some general-interest magazines.	Varies by station and by time of day. Reaches 94% of Canadians weekly. Per capita listening: 21 hours weekly. Small audiences per program.	Broad; whole family. Varies by time of day but reaches 96% of Canadians weekly. 23 viewing hours weekly per capita. Large audiences per program. 78% of homes are equipped with VCRs, 76% cable penetration.
Location	Usually one daily per town; more in larger cities. Weeklies service target audiences, specific neighbourhoods, and suburban markets, and fill in holes not reached by dailies.	Most national, some regional. National magazines often have regional editors. Some are specific to one city. Many offer advertisers regional splits.	All markets. Major urban centres have up to 20 stations. Smallest cities usually have at least several.	Several TV stations in most cities. Many have more than four. Repeater stations and satellite ensure almost universal coverage.
Cost	Cost to cover 17 markets with 1/2-page ad in each of 18 dailies: $24,400.	Extreme variations, but a reasonable average is $3,500 for full-page four-colour for local publications.	To reach 40% of the Vancouver market an average of five times per week costs $11,000 to $13,000 weekly.	Costly for top-rated programs: $30,000 per week in Vancouver to reach 50% of the market four times per week. In B.C., $40,000 per week. Production costs can be $10,000 and more.
Best way to use	Local medium. Action and sales. Low costs (of media and production) for local advertisers. To convey information and for tie-ins with promotions. Maximum flexibility—size, timing.	Match specific products or product classes with editorial content.	Frequency medium. Selective exposure among pinpointed audiences. On-air personalities, short-term action, promotions.	Broad exposure. Product demonstration. Name identity. Awareness. Image. Lifestyle. High impact. Action.
Disadvantages	High cost for national campaigns. Nonselective audience. Limited appeal to young; reading patterns spotty. Short life. Limited readership data for weeklies.	Varies. Some are strong, some weak. Advertising clutter in some publications. Long lead times. Circulation patterns may not match product distribution.	Fragmented audience. Advertising and editorial clutter. Often used as background.	Cost may be prohibitive. Difficult to break through threshold of awareness and keep attention. Production can be extremely expensive. Clutter. Long lead times.

for university students, educators, doctors, and business managers. Magazines like *Newsweek*, France's *Paris Match International*, and Germany's *Wirtschaftwoche* provide international editions.

Many magazines serve only special interest groups, such as fishermen, soap opera fans, new parents, professional groups, and personal computer users. In fact, the most profitable magazines seem to be the ones aimed at clearly defined markets. Many specialty magazines also have international editions.

Outdoor	Transit	Direct mail	Yellow Pages
Many types, including billboards and backlit posters. Highly visible, good quality on backlits. Obtrusive. Limited applications for many companies.	Interior and exterior panels. Highly visible. Requires concise message.	Increasingly popular. Highly selective and personal. Efficient for narrow target audiences and both small and large advertisers.	Mass medium reaching most users and owners of telephones. Supported by phone company advertising. Readily accessible to consumers 24 hours per day, 365 days a year.
Very broad; anyone outdoors. Age, income, sex vary by location, but it's used to "cover the world."	Exterior reaches similar audience to outdoor billboards. Interior tends to cover students and a clerical/sales/technical audience versus business audience.	Completely controlled. Direct-mail lists available from internal and external sources to cover almost every conceivable market.	Qualified prospects searching for a specific product/service.
Billboards: anywhere there are cars and highways, especially in cities. Backlits: large urban centres. Restricted locations in B.C.	Anywhere there is a transit system. (In Vancouver, includes SkyTrain)	Controlled by the mailer.	There is a Yellow Pages directory in every market, in addition to specialized editions.
$40,000 to achieve a minimally effective billboard campaign for one month in B.C. (approx. 70 posters). Backlits: $8,000 per month in Vancouver for approximately five locations.	Exterior: $10,000–$20,000 to achieve a minimum one-month campaign in B.C.; $12,000 in Greater Vancouver. Interior: $3,000 for B.C.; $3,000 in Victoria.	Average cost to rent 1,000 names is $125. Costs of the entire mailing can run $300–$1,000 per 1,000 names.	Directories are published by different phone companies in different markets with varying standards and rates. Little or no production costs.
Broad awareness. Reinforce main campaign, name, and image.	Broad awareness. Simple, uncomplicated messages.	Personalized advertising effort.	Reaches consumers at information-search or vendor-identification use when looking to make a purchase, or visitors/new residents of area.
Limited ability to convey product information. Inability to narrow audience. Some local regulatory restrictions. Costly production.	Short exposure time. Difficult to target against a narrow audience. Limited copy detail available.	No editorial environment to attract and hold audience. Low response rate. "Junk mail" image.	More of a directional/information medium versus creative. Must give full service details in ad to maximize value.

Source: Adapted from Wright, Winter, Zeigler, and O'Dea, *Advertising* (McGraw-Hill Ryerson Ltd.), with research assistance from *Palmer Jarvis Advertising.* Reproduced in *The Ad Pages,* 1995, pp. 4–5.

There are trade magazines in many fields, such as chemical engineering, furniture retailing, electrical wholesaling, farming, and the defence market. *Canadian Advertising Rates and Data* provides a guide to the hundreds of magazines now available in Canada. Similar guides exist in most other countries.

In addition to trade magazines bought at newsstands or through subscription, there's an important class of magazine in Canada called *controlled circulation.* These magazines are distributed free to special interest groups; the publisher gets all its

LAST YEAR CHATELAINE READERS SPENT MORE MONEY ON TRUCKS AND MINI VANS THAN THEY DID ON BREAD AND BUTTER.

In the next twelve months Chatelaine readers are 34% more likely to buy a car than the average Canadian adult. In fact, they intend to spend almost 4 billion dollars on cars. They also buy sporting equipment, furniture and vacations as well as food and clothing for themselves and their family. This makes them an economic force just waiting to be tapped.*

Chatelaine is the largest paid circulation woman's magazine in Canada. It's where Canadian women in the busiest years of their lives get it all together. And it's where you can get together with them.

CHATELAINE. WHERE CANADIAN WOMEN GET IT ALL, TOGETHER.

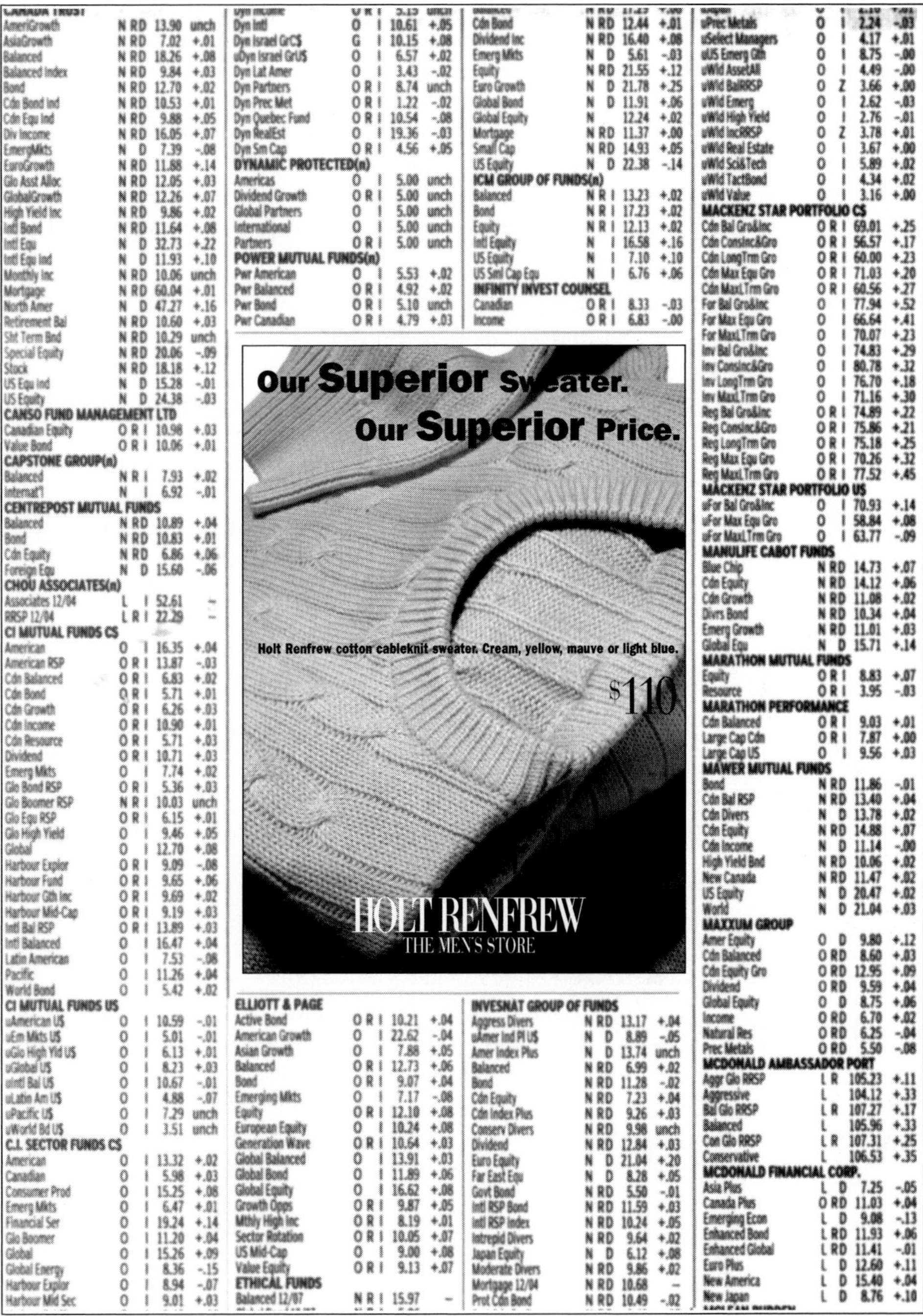

Fund			Price	Chg
AmeriGrowth	N	RD	13.90	unch
AsiaGrowth	N	RD	7.02	+.01
Balanced	N	RD	18.26	+.08
Balanced Index	N	RD	9.84	+.03
Bond	N	RD	12.70	+.02
Cdn Bond Ind	N	RD	10.53	+.01
Cdn Equ Ind	N	RD	9.88	+.05
Div Income	N	RD	16.05	+.07
EmergMkts	N	D	7.39	-.08
EuroGrowth	N	RD	11.88	+.14
Glo Asst Alloc	N	RD	12.05	+.03
GlobalGrowth	N	RD	12.26	+.07
High Yield Inc	N	RD	9.86	+.02
Intl Bond	N	RD	11.64	+.08
Intl Equ	N	D	32.73	+.22
Intl Equ Ind	N	D	11.93	+.10
Monthly Inc	N	RD	10.06	unch
Mortgage	N	RD	60.04	+.01
North Amer	N	D	47.27	+.16
Retirement Bal	N	RD	10.60	+.03
Sht Term Bnd	N	RD	10.29	unch
Special Equity	N	RD	20.06	-.09
Stock	N	RD	18.18	+.12
US Equ Ind	N	D	15.28	-.01
US Equity	N	D	24.38	-.03
CANSO FUND MANAGEMENT LTD				
Canadian Equity	O	R I	10.98	+.03
Value Bond	O	R I	10.06	+.01
CAPSTONE GROUP(n)				
Balanced	N	R I	7.93	+.02
Internat'l	N	I	6.92	-.01
CENTREPOST MUTUAL FUNDS				
Balanced	N	RD	10.89	+.04
Bond	N	RD	10.83	+.01
Cdn Equity	N	RD	6.86	+.06
Foreign Equ	N	D	15.60	-.06
CHOU ASSOCIATES(n)				
Associates 12/04	L	I	52.61	–
RRSP 12/04	L	R I	22.29	–
CI MUTUAL FUNDS C$				
American	O	I	16.35	+.04
American RSP	O	R I	13.87	-.03
Cdn Balanced	O	R I	6.83	+.02
Cdn Bond	O	R I	5.71	+.01
Cdn Growth	O	R I	6.26	+.03
Cdn Income	O	R I	10.90	+.01
Cdn Resource	O	R I	5.71	+.03
Dividend	O	R I	10.71	+.03
Emerg Mkts	O	I	7.74	+.02
Glo Bond RSP	O	R I	5.36	+.03
Glo Boomer RSP	N	R I	10.03	unch
Glo Equ RSP	O	R I	6.15	+.01
Glo High Yield	O	I	9.46	+.05
Global	O	I	12.70	+.08
Harbour Explor	O	R I	9.09	-.08
Harbour Fund	O	R I	9.65	+.06
Harbour Gth Inc	O	R I	9.69	+.02
Harbour Mid-Cap	O	R I	9.19	+.03
Intl Bal RSP	O	R I	13.89	+.03
Intl Balanced	O	I	16.47	+.04
Latin American	O	I	7.53	-.08
Pacific	O	I	11.26	+.04
World Bond	O	I	5.42	+.02
CI MUTUAL FUNDS US				
uAmerican US	O	I	10.59	-.01
uEm Mkts US	O	I	5.01	-.01
uGlo High Yld US	O	I	6.13	+.01
uGlobal US	O	I	8.23	+.03
uIntl Bal US	O	I	10.67	-.01
uLatin Am US	O	I	4.88	-.07
uPacific US	O	I	7.29	unch
uWorld Bd US	O	I	3.51	unch
C.I. SECTOR FUNDS C$				
American	O	I	13.32	+.02
Canadian	O	I	5.98	+.03
Consumer Prod	O	I	15.25	+.08
Emerg Mkts	O	I	6.47	+.01
Financial Ser	O	I	19.24	+.14
Glo Boomer	O	I	11.20	+.04
Global	O	I	15.26	+.09
Global Energy	O	I	8.36	-.15
Harbour Explor	O	I	8.94	-.07
Harbour Mid Sec	O	I	9.01	+.03

Fund			Price	Chg
Dyn Intl	O	I	10.61	+.05
Dyn Israel GrC$	G	I	10.15	+.08
uDyn Israel GrUS	O	I	6.57	+.02
Dyn Lat Amer	O	I	3.43	-.02
Dyn Partners	O	R I	8.74	unch
Dyn Prec Met	O	R I	1.22	-.02
Dyn Quebec Fund	O	R I	10.54	-.08
Dyn RealEst	O	I	19.36	-.03
Dyn Sm Cap	O	R I	4.56	+.05
DYNAMIC PROTECTED(n)				
Americas	O	I	5.00	unch
Dividend Growth	O	R I	5.00	unch
Global Partners	O	I	5.00	unch
International	O	I	5.00	unch
Partners	O	R I	5.00	unch
POWER MUTUAL FUNDS(n)				
Pwr American	O	I	5.53	+.02
Pwr Balanced	O	R I	4.92	+.02
Pwr Bond	O	R I	5.10	unch
Pwr Canadian	O	R I	4.79	+.03
ELLIOTT & PAGE				
Active Bond	O	R I	10.21	+.04
American Growth	O	I	22.62	-.04
Asian Growth	O	I	7.88	+.05
Balanced	O	R I	12.73	+.06
Bond	O	R I	9.07	+.04
Emerging Mkts	O	I	7.17	-.08
Equity	O	R I	12.10	+.08
European Equity	O	I	10.24	+.08
Generation Wave	O	R I	10.64	+.03
Global Balanced	O	I	13.91	+.03
Global Bond	O	I	11.89	+.06
Global Equity	O	I	16.62	+.08
Growth Opps	O	R I	9.87	+.05
Mthly High Inc	O	R I	8.19	+.01
Sector Rotation	O	R I	10.05	+.07
US Mid-Cap	O	I	9.00	+.08
Value Equity	O	R I	9.13	+.07
ETHICAL FUNDS				
Balanced 12/07	N	R I	15.97	–

Fund			Price	Chg
Cdn Bond	N	RD	12.44	+.01
Dividend Inc	N	RD	16.40	+.08
Emerg Mkts	N	D	5.61	-.03
Equity	N	RD	21.55	+.12
Euro Growth	N	D	21.78	+.25
Global Bond	N	D	11.91	+.06
Global Equity	N		12.24	+.02
Mortgage	N	RD	11.37	+.00
Small Cap	N	RD	14.93	+.05
US Equity	N	D	22.38	-.14
ICM GROUP OF FUNDS(n)				
Balanced	N	R I	13.23	+.02
Bond	N	R I	17.23	+.02
Equity	N	R I	12.13	+.02
Intl Equity	N	I	16.58	+.16
US Equity	N	I	7.10	+.10
US Sml Cap Equ	N	I	6.76	+.06
INFINITY INVEST COUNSEL				
Canadian	O	R I	8.33	-.03
Income	O	R I	6.83	-.00
INVESNAT GROUP OF FUNDS				
Aggress Divers	N	RD	13.17	+.04
uAmer Ind Pl US	N	D	8.89	-.05
Amer Index Plus	N	D	13.74	unch
Balanced	N	RD	6.99	+.02
Bond	N	RD	11.28	-.02
Cdn Equity	N	RD	7.23	+.04
Cdn Index Plus	N	RD	9.26	+.03
Conserv Divers	N	RD	9.98	unch
Dividend	N	RD	12.84	+.03
Euro Equity	N	D	21.04	+.20
Far East Equ	N	D	8.28	+.05
Govt Bond	N	RD	5.50	-.01
Intl RSP Bond	N	RD	11.59	+.03
Intl RSP Index	N	RD	10.24	+.05
Intrepid Divers	N	RD	9.64	+.02
Japan Equity	N	D	6.12	+.08
Moderate Divers	N	RD	9.86	+.02
Mortgage 12/04	N	RD	10.68	–
Prot Cdn Bond	N	RD	10.49	-.02

Fund			Price	Chg
uPrec Metals	O	I	2.24	-.03
uSelect Managers	O	I	4.17	+.01
uUS Emerg Gth	O	I	8.75	-.00
uWld AssetAll	O	I	4.49	-.00
uWld BalRRSP	O	Z	3.66	+.00
uWld Emerg	O	I	2.62	-.03
uWld High Yield	O	I	2.76	-.01
uWld IncRRSP	O	Z	3.78	+.01
uWld Real Estate	O	I	3.67	+.00
uWld Sci&Tech	O	I	5.89	+.02
uWld TactBond	O	I	4.34	+.02
uWld Value	O	I	3.16	+.00
MACKENZ STAR PORTFOLIO C$				
Cdn Bal Gro&Inc	O	R I	69.01	+.25
Cdn ConsInc&Gro	O	R I	56.57	+.17
Cdn LongTrm Gro	O	R I	60.00	+.23
Cdn Max Equ Gro	O	R I	71.03	+.20
Cdn MaxLTrm Gro	O	R I	60.56	+.27
For Bal Gro&Inc	O	I	77.94	+.52
For Max Equ Gro	O	I	66.64	+.41
For MaxLTrm Gro	O	I	70.07	+.23
Inv Bal Gro&Inc	O	I	74.83	+.29
Inv ConsInc&Gro	O	I	80.78	+.32
Inv LongTrm Gro	O	I	76.70	+.18
Inv MaxLTrm Gro	O	I	71.16	+.30
Reg Bal Gro&Inc	O	R I	74.89	+.22
Reg ConsInc&Gro	O	R I	75.86	+.21
Reg LongTrm Gro	O	R I	75.18	+.25
Reg Max Equ Gro	O	R I	70.26	+.32
Reg MaxLTrm Gro	O	R I	77.52	+.45
MACKENZ STAR PORTFOLIO US				
uFor Bal Gro&Inc	O	I	70.93	+.14
uFor Max Equ Gro	O	I	58.84	+.08
uFor MaxLTrm Gro	O	I	63.77	-.09
MANULIFE CABOT FUNDS				
Blue Chip	N	RD	14.73	+.07
Cdn Equity	N	RD	14.12	+.06
Cdn Growth	N	RD	11.08	+.02
Divrs Bond	N	RD	10.34	+.04
Emerg Growth	N	RD	11.01	+.03
Global Equ	N	D	15.71	+.14
MARATHON MUTUAL FUNDS				
Equity	O	R I	8.83	+.07
Resource	O	R I	3.95	-.03
MARATHON PERFORMANCE				
Cdn Balanced	O	R I	9.03	+.01
Large Cap Cdn	O	R I	7.87	+.00
Large Cap US	O	I	9.56	+.03
MAWER MUTUAL FUNDS				
Bond	N	RD	11.86	-.01
Cdn Bal RSP	N	RD	13.40	+.04
Cdn Divers	N	D	13.78	+.02
Cdn Equity	N	RD	14.88	+.07
Cdn Income	N	D	11.14	-.00
High Yield Bnd	N	RD	10.06	+.02
New Canada	N	RD	11.47	+.02
US Equity	N	D	20.47	+.02
World	N	D	21.04	+.03
MAXXUM GROUP				
Amer Equity	O	D	9.80	+.12
Cdn Balanced	O	RD	8.60	+.03
Cdn Equity Gro	O	RD	12.95	+.09
Dividend	O	RD	9.59	+.04
Global Equity	O	D	8.75	+.06
Income	O	RD	6.70	+.02
Natural Res	O	RD	6.25	-.04
Prec Metals	O	RD	5.50	-.08
MCDONALD AMBASSADOR PORT				
Aggr Glo RRSP	L	R	105.23	+.11
Aggressive	L		104.12	+.33
Bal Glo RRSP	L	R	107.27	+.17
Balanced	L		105.96	+.33
Con Glo RRSP	L	R	107.31	+.25
Conservative	L		106.53	+.35
MCDONALD FINANCIAL CORP.				
Asia Plus	L	D	7.25	-.05
Canada Plus	O	RD	11.03	+.04
Emerging Econ	L	D	9.08	-.13
Enhanced Bond	L	RD	11.93	+.06
Enhanced Global	L	RD	11.41	-.01
Euro Plus	L	D	12.60	+.11
New America	L	D	15.40	+.04
New Japan	L	D	8.76	+.10

Our Superior Sweater.
Our Superior Price.
Holt Renfrew cotton cableknit sweater. Cream, yellow, mauve or light blue.
$110
HOLT RENFREW
THE MEN'S STORE

A retail ad in the middle of the daily stock market report grabs attention.

revenue from advertising. The largest of these is *Homemaker's*. With its French counterpart, *Madame au Foyer*, it offers a combined circulation of over 1.9 million delivered to preselected homes in middle- and upper-income areas. In addition, some magazines are sent without charge to narrow, well-defined segments.

Radio has become a more specialized medium. Some stations cater to particular ethnic and racial groups, such as the Chinese community, Indo-Canadians, and French Canadians. Others aim at specific target markets with rock, country, or classical music. Stations that play golden oldies have been popping up around North America to appeal to the baby boomer crowd.

Cable TV channels such as MuchMusic, CBC Newsworld, TSN, and YTV also target specific audiences. TSN, for example, has an audience heavily weighted toward affluent male viewers. MuchMusic appeals most strongly to young, affluent viewers.

Infomercials—long commercials that are broadcast with a TV show format—give a glimpse of how targeted cable TV will become when consumers have access to hundreds or perhaps even thousands of TV channels. With so many channels competing for consumer attention, most channels will succeed only if they offer programs and commercials that are very specific to the interests and needs of smaller, more homogeneous target markets.

Specialized media are small—but gaining

The *major* advertising media listed in Exhibit 16–5 attract the vast majority of advertising media budgets. But advertising specialists are always looking for cost-effective new media that will help advertisers reach their target markets. For example, one company successfully sells space for signs on bike racks that it places in front of 7-Eleven stores. In Eastern Europe, where major media are still limited, companies like Campbell's pay to put ads on bus shelters. Hotels and auto rental companies buy space on advertising boards placed in the restrooms on airplanes.

In recent years, these specialized media have gained in popularity. They get the message to the target market close to the point of purchase and away from the usual advertising clutter in the mass media. For example, Actmedia sells advertising space on little message boards that hang on shopping carts and shelves in grocery stores and drugstores.[11]

There are too many specialized media to go into all of them in detail here. But all of them require the same type of strategic decisions as the more typical mass media.

"Must buys" may use up available funds

Selecting which media to use is still pretty much an art. The media buyer may start with a budgeted amount and try to buy the best blend to reach the target audience.

Some media are obvious "must buys"—for example, *the* local newspaper for a retailer in a small or medium-sized town. Most firms serving local markets view a Yellow Pages listing as a must buy. These ads may even use up the available funds.

Because TV advertising costs so much, many firms are moving away from television—especially the networks—and experimenting with combinations of other media. Very targeted media, like direct-mail advertising and point-of-purchase advertising, are growing rapidly as a result of this shift. But an even bigger media revolution is brewing—and it has the potential to radically change the nature and role of advertising.

Advertising on the Internet: new opportunities and new challenges

Advertising on the Internet is growing rapidly as mainstream advertisers join the innovators in the quest for more efficient ways to reach target customers with promotion. The advertising messages take many forms, ranging from displays that basically look like traditional print ads to button and banner ads. An Internet *banner ad* is a headline that appears on a Web page. Its purpose is to attract the interest of people in the advertiser's target market and encourage them to visit the advertiser's Web site for more information. As Internet Insite 16–2 indicates, banner ads on the Web have rapidly increased in number. A button is usually much smaller—perhaps just showing the advertiser's name or symbol.

Internet ads seek a direct response—a click

Whatever specific form an ad takes, it is usually "linked" to the advertiser's Web site. In other words, a viewer responds to an ad by clicking on it with a mouse, and more detailed information appears on the viewer's display. The information may include

Making Your Banner Ads Effective

Internet Insite 16-2

Advertising on the Internet is now almost a $1 billion industry. That is still minuscule compared to what advertisers spend on print and television. But this "new medium" has made even sceptical advertisers stand up and take notice. Every major brand name is now featured in an Internet advertisement. As you surf the Net, you see banner ads popping up carrying household names such as Microsoft, IBM, DEC, Oldsmobile, Honda, Toyota, P&G, and Office Depot.

Some big advertisers are simply testing the Internet, not worrying about the returns for now. For most advertisers, however, that is not the case. The cost–benefit ratio has to justify choosing the Internet over other media for advertising. Are banner ads effective? Some research evidence is beginning to shed light on this important question.

Doubleclick (www.doubleclick.net), an Internet advertising agency, based on its research, has concluded that the following creative elements can increase the effectiveness of banner advertising:

- Animation—can increase consumer response rates by up to 25 percent.
- Cryptic messages—can increase click-through rates (number of users clicking on the banner) by 18 percent, but can also miss the target audience.
- Posing a question—can increase response by 15 percent.
- Call to action such as "click here"—can increase response by 15 percent.
- Use of free offers—can improve click-throughs dramatically.

Creative copy is important, but good copy alone cannot sell a product. Proper targeting and positioning will lead to a better response. The banner ad must be placed in the appropriate Web site based on the demographics and interests of targeted consumers. Advertisements targeted to women may be more effective in sites like iVillage (www.ivillage.com), while ads targeted to younger males may be more effective if placed in ESPN SportsZone (www.ESPN.SportsZone.com).

Banner ads are usually no larger than 468 × 60 pixels. That is about the same size as a typical classified ad. But animation and interactivity add greatly to the effectiveness of banner ads. Given the limited space, the content of the advertisement becomes all important. There's usually one chance to make a good impression and elicit a response from the viewer. That makes the job of the advertising agency all the more challenging.

Banner ads, just like television commercials, tend to wear out after a while. Click-through rates decline with successive exposures. After four exposures banners ads seem to lose their effectiveness. That means new ads must replace the old periodically. A study by the Internet Advertising Bureau (IAB) showed that even a single exposure can increase brand awareness, knowledge of product attributes, and purchase intent.

The IAB conducted its Online Advertising Effectiveness study across twelve leading Web sites: CNN, CompuServe, ESPN SportsZone, Excite, Geocities, HotWired, Looksmart, Lycos, MacWorld, National Geographic Online, Pathfinder (Time-Warner), and Ziff-Davis. A sample of over 16,000 consumers participated in the study. Some key findings:

- Even if the viewer does not click on the banner ad, there is still value in exposure to the banner ad.
- Online ads are more likely to be noticed than television advertising.
- Consumer acceptance of online advertising is comparable to that of traditional media.

These findings should be a source of great comfort to advertising agencies as well as to advertisers who have already made the Internet a part of their promotional mix. But advertisers must realize that Internet advertising cannot work in isolation. It has to be an integral part of the promotional mix and the overall marketing plan. If the Internet ad reinforces something the consumer saw on television, or vice versa, the results are bound to be more significant. There are exceptions to this rule. A marketer may want to target a different audience on the Internet and may want to keep the banner ads distinct from ads in the other media. The important point, however, is that one must understand the role of the Internet in the promotional mix before investing in Internet advertising.

Source: This is one of a series of Internet Insites prepared in April 1998 by Dr. Ramesh Venkat of Saint Mary's University for *Basic Marketing,* Ninth Canadian Edition.

pictures, videos, sound, text, a product database, order entry procedures, and much more.

Content on a Web site is very different from traditional advertising. The advertiser can put up a great deal more information and allow viewers to self-direct to those pages which interest them the most. The Web site can also provide links to other outside sources of information. Or it can invite the viewer to e-mail for more detailed information on a particular topic. It can even offer a sign-up for a weekly newsletter. The viewer may not buy right away, and may not "bookmark" the Web site to come back to later. But if the viewer subscribes to the e-mail newsletter, all is not lost and a sale will likely happen one day.

We talked about this sort of interactive communication in detail in Chapter 14. Now let's take a look at how Internet ads reach a target audience in the first place.

Some Web sites generate more exposure

Some advertisers are primarily interested in placing ads on Web sites that will give their ads a lot of exposure—almost without regard to the content of the Web site or who visits it. Although there are millions of Web sites on the Internet, a small subset account for a large percent of the potential "audience." For example, many people see the Netscape, Microsoft, or Yahoo Web site every time they use the Internet. Often that's because the software ("browser") they use to view Internet information starts at these Web sites. Some people refer to such Web sites as *portals* because they act like doorways to the Internet.

Some observers predict that a few portal Web sites will become for the Internet what the networks once were for television: *the* places where advertisers are willing to pay high rates because they are uniquely able to reach a very large, broad market. For example, Dell may want its computer ads on such a Web site so that they will be viewed by the large number of computer-user visitors. But what makes sense for Dell in that situation may not make sense for a different firm with a different target market and marketing mix. As with traditional media, getting lots of exposure for an Internet ad doesn't help if viewers are not in the firm's target market. Some advertisers don't see this and have just transferred their old, untargeted shotgun approach to this new medium. That's especially wasteful on the Internet!

Some Web sites are better for reaching target customers

Bristol-Myers Squibb's experiment with Web advertising is typical of what many firms are trying to do—place ads on Web sites that attract the desired target market. In the middle of income tax season, Bristol-Myers Squibb ran ads on financial Web sites extolling Excedrin as "the tax headache medicine." The ads offered a free sample of Excedrin. Within a month, more than 30,000 people clicked on the ad and typed their names into the firm's customer database. The cost of obtaining those names was half that of traditional methods. Now the firm can follow up the Excedrin samples with other database-directed promotions.

Context advertising links ad to content being viewed

The Excedrin ads were quite targeted, but targeting on the Internet can be even more precise. For example, ads for Fragrance Counter, a cosmetics retailer, pop up when the Internet user does a search on a term such as *perfume* or *Estee Lauder.* This approach is called *context advertising*—monitoring the content a net surfer is viewing and then serving up related ads. For example, if a consumer visits a Web site with information about cars, an ad for Amazon Books may appear with a note that that company carries books on buying a new car. When the consumer clicks on the Amazon ad, a list of relevant books appears on screen. More detailed information on each title is another click away.

In another variation noncompeting firms with similar target markets are able to post ads on each other's Web sites. The Web site for Maytag's Neptune high-efficiency washing machine has a link to P&G's Web site for Tide HE, a new detergent designed for use in washers like the Neptune.

Pointcasting determines which customers see an ad

Another approach that offers more precise targeting is pointcasting. Pointcasting involves displaying ads *only* to individuals who meet certain qualifications. For instance, a person may have previously expressed direct interest in the topic of the advertising. A pointcasting ad is usually included with other information that the customer wants and that a pointcasting service provides for free. An example shows how this works. A woman who is interested in financial planning might sign up with a pointcasting service and request that it routinely send her newly published articles on registered retirement savings plans. When the pointcaster sends her that information over the Internet, it may include an ad from a mutual fund company. The pointcasting service matches ads to customer interests. Many advertisers like this concept, but worry that pointcasting may overwhelm the recipient with too much clutter.

Over time, it may turn out that sending ads directly to target customers via e-mail is a simpler approach. A limitation of e-mail is that each person's e-mail software reformats messages in a different way. In the future, that is likely to change. However, a separate problem will continue: most people resent being "spammed" with a lot of unsolicited e-mail.

Some viewers get benefits if they agree to look at ads

Some Web sites offer people a benefit—like free e-mail or a chance to enter a contest—in return for providing information about themselves and agreeing to view ads selected to match their interests. A look at Juno, a firm that offers a free e-mail service, shows how this works. When people sign up for e-mail accounts, they also provide detailed information for a database. The information may include demographics as well as interests, what products they use, where they shop, and where they live. Then, when a person checks for e-mail messages, ads are displayed. Each ad is selected specifically for that person based on characteristics in the database. For example, a cosmetics firm might specify that its ads only be shown to women who are 16 or older and who routinely wear nail polish.

At some Web sites, ads are free if they don't get results

While the number of firms interested in putting ads on Web sites is growing, the number of Web sites that are chasing their ad dollars is growing even faster. Many Web sites charge advertisers a fee based on how frequently or how long their ads are shown. But it is still difficult to measure accurately how many people are exposed to an ad, or pay any attention if they are exposed. Many firms are springing up that rate Web site traffic. But their ratings often don't agree.

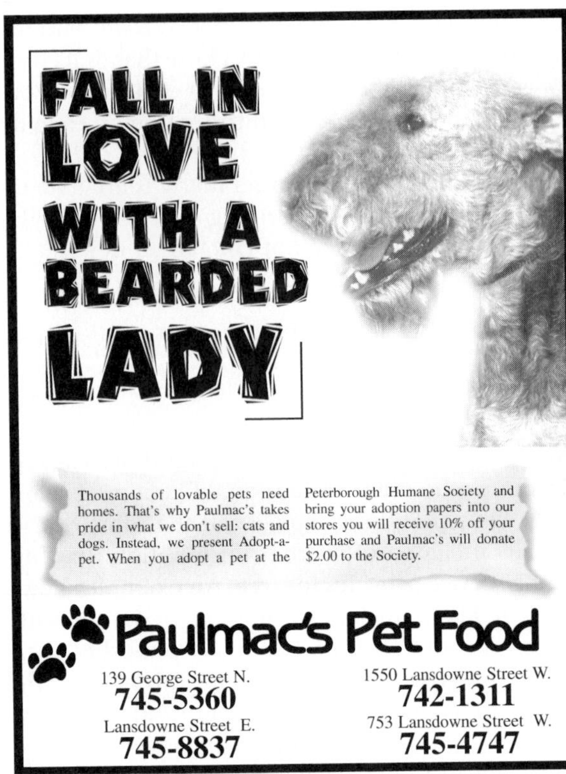

FALL IN LOVE WITH A BEARDED LADY
Thousands of lovable pets need homes. That's why Paulmac's takes pride in what we don't sell: cats and dogs. Instead, we present Adopt-a-pet. When you adopt a pet at the Peterborough Humane Society and bring your adoption papers into our stores you will receive 10% off your purchase and Paulmac's will donate $2.00 to the Society.
Paulmac's Pet Food
139 George Street N.
745-5360
1550 Lansdowne Street W.
742-1311
Lansdowne Street E.
745-8837
753 Lansdowne Street W.
745-4747

Did the copy thrust of this ad get your attention?

This problem, and the competition for advertisers, have pressed many Web sites to take a more novel approach. Some Web sites will display an ad for free, and charge a fee only if the ad gets results. For example, the fee the advertiser pays is sometimes based on "click-through"—the number of people who actually click on the ad and link to the advertiser's Web site. Some Web sites set fees based on actual sales that result from the click-through. This is efficient for advertisers, and variations on this approach are likely to become more common. This is a big shift from traditional media. Generally, firms have to pay for their TV and print ads whether they work or not. A lot more firms will put ads on Web sites if a direct relationship can be shown between costs and results. And Web sites will then have more incentive to attract those viewers that specific advertisers want to reach.

Internet advertising is still feeling its way

Innovations like these make it clear that Internet advertising holds great promise. On the other hand, this form of advertising is not yet able to provide the precise, laser beam targeting that would be ideal. As with other innovations, refinements to Internet advertising will take time. No one can yet be certain what it will be when it grows up—but it *is* growing.[12]

Planning the "best" message—what to communicate

Once you decide *how* the messages will reach the target audience, you have to decide on the **copy thrust**—what the words and illustrations should communicate.

Deciding upon the copy thrust is the job of advertising specialists. But the advertising manager and the marketing manager need to understand the process in order to ensure that the job is done well.

Let AIDA help guide message planning

Basically, the overall marketing strategy should determine *what* the message should say. Then management judgment—perhaps aided by marketing research—can help decide how to encode this content so that it will be decoded as intended.

As a guide to message planning, we can use the AIDA concept: getting Attention, holding Interest, arousing Desire, and obtaining Action.

Getting attention

Getting attention is an ad's first job. If an ad doesn't get attention, it doesn't matter how many people see or hear it. Many readers leaf through magazines and newspapers without paying attention to any of the ads. Many listeners or viewers do chores—or get snacks—during radio and TV commercials. When watching a program on videotape, they may zap past the commercial with a flick of the fast-forward button.

Many attention-getting devices are available. A large headline, newsy or shocking statements, attractive models, babies, animals, special effects—anything different or eye-catching—may do the trick. However, the attention-getting device can't detract from—and hopefully should lead to—the next step, which is holding interest.

Holding interest

Holding interest is more difficult. A humorous ad, an unusual video effect, or a sexy model may get your attention—but once you've seen it, then what? If there is no relationship between what got your attention and the marketing mix, you'll move on. To hold interest, the tone and language of the ad must fit with the experiences and attitudes of the target customers—and their reference groups. This is why many advertisers develop ads that relate to specific emotions. They hope that the good feeling about the ad will stick, even if its details are forgotten.

To hold interest, informative ads need to speak the target customer's language. Persuasive ads must provide evidence that convinces the customer. Celebrity endorsements may help. TV ads often demonstrate a product's benefits. Layouts for print ads should look right to the customer. Print illustrations and copy should be arranged to encourage the eye to move smoothly through the ad—perhaps from a headline that starts in the upper left-hand corner to the illustration or body copy in the middle and finally to the company or brand name ("signature") at the lower right-hand corner.[13]

Arousing desire

Arousing desire to buy a particular product is one of an ad's most difficult jobs. The ad must convince customers that the product can meet their needs. Testimonials may persuade a consumer that other people with similar needs have liked the product. Product comparisons may highlight the advantages of a particular brand.

Some experts feel that an ad should focus on one *unique selling proposition* that aims at an important unsatisfied need. This can help set the brand apart, and position it as especially effective in meeting the needs of the target market. For example, consumers who wear dentures are especially concerned about dentures not coming loose. Thus, print ads for Seabond denture fixative use a humorous approach and pictures to focus on Seabond's holding power.

Although products may satisfy certain emotional needs, many consumers find it necessary to justify their purchases on some logical basis. Snickers candy bar ads helped ease the guilt of calorie-conscious snackers by assuring them that "Snickers satisfies you when you need an afternoon energy break."

Obtaining action

Getting action is the final requirement—and not an easy one. From communication research, we now know that prospective customers must be led beyond considering how the product *might* fit into their lives, to actually trying it.

Direct-response ads can sometimes help promote action by encouraging interested consumers to do *something* that is less risky or demanding than actually making a purchase. For example, an ad that includes a toll-free telephone number might prompt some consumers who are not yet ready to buy to at least call for more information. Then follow-up brochures or a telephone salesperson can provide additional information and attempt to prompt another action—perhaps a visit to a store or a "satisfaction guaranteed" trial period. This approach seeks to get action one step at a time; the first action suggested provides a "foot in the door" for subsequent communication efforts.

To communicate more effectively, ads may emphasize strongly felt customer needs. Careful research on attitudes in the target market may help uncover such strongly felt *unsatisfied* needs. Appealing to important needs can get more action—and also provide the kind of information that buyers need to confirm their decisions. Some customers seem to read more advertising *after* a purchase than before. The ad may reassure them about the correctness of their decision.

Can global messages work?

Many international consumer products firms try to use one global advertising message all around the world. Of course, they translate the message and make other minor adjustments, but the focus is one global copy thrust. Some do this to cut the cost of developing different ads for each country. Others feel that their customers' basic needs are the same, even in different countries. Some just do it because it is fashionable to "go global."

This approach works for some firms. Coca-Cola and Gillette, for example, feel that the needs their products serve are very similar for all consumers. They focus on the similarities among consumers who make up their target market rather than on the differences. However, most firms who use this approach experience terrible results. They may save money by developing fewer ads, but they lose sales because they don't develop advertising messages—and entire marketing mixes—aimed at specific target markets. They're just trying to appeal to a global "mass market."

Combining smaller market segments into a single, large target market makes sense when the different segments can be served with a single marketing mix. But when that is not the case, the marketing manager should treat those segments as different target markets—and develop different marketing mixes for each.[14]

Advertising agencies often do the work

An advertising manager manages a company's advertising effort. Many advertising managers—especially those working for large retailers—have their own advertising departments that plan specific advertising campaigns and carry out the details. Others turn over much of the advertising work to specialists—the advertising agencies.

Ad agencies are specialists

Advertising agencies are specialists in planning and handling mass-selling details for advertisers. Agencies play a useful role, because they are independent of the advertiser and have an outsiders' point of view. Because they work for many other clients, they bring experience to an individual client's problems. As specialists, they can often do the job more economically than a company's own department. And an advertiser who is not satisfied can end the relationship and switch to a new agency.

Some full-service agencies handle any activities related to advertising. They may even handle overall strategic market planning as well as marketing research, product and package development, and sales promotion.

The biggest agencies handle much of the advertising

The vast majority of advertising agencies are small, with ten or fewer employees. But the largest agencies account for most of the billings.

Some big agencies have merged, creating mega-agencies with worldwide networks. Before the mergers, marketers in one country often had difficulty finding a capable, full-service agency in another country where they wanted to advertise. A mega-agency can offer varied services wherever in the world a marketing manager needs them. This may be especially important for managers in large corporations—like Toyota, Renault, Unilever, NEC, Phillips, Procter & Gamble, Nestlé, and Coca-Cola—which advertise worldwide.[15]

Smaller agencies will continue to play an important role. The really big agencies are less interested in smaller accounts. Smaller agencies will continue to appeal to customers who want more personal attention and a close relationship that is more attuned to their marketing needs.

Agencies usually get a commission on media costs

Most advertising agencies are paid a commission of about 15 percent on media and production costs. This arrangement evolved because media usually have two prices: one for national advertisers and a lower rate for local advertisers, such as local retailers. The advertising agency gets a 15 percent commission on national rates but not on local rates. This makes it worthwhile for producers and intermediaries selling across Canada to use agencies. National advertisers have to pay the full media rate anyway, so it makes sense to let the agency experts do the work—and earn their commission. Local retailers—who are allowed the lower media rate—seldom use agencies.

Are they paid too much?

There is growing resistance to the idea of paying agencies the same way regardless of the work performed or *the results achieved.* The commission approach also makes it hard for agencies to be completely objective about inexpensive media—or about promotion campaigns that use little space or time. Not all agencies are satisfied with the present arrangement either. Some would like to charge additional fees as their costs rise and as advertisers demand more services.

Firms that need a lot of service but spend relatively little on media—including most producers of business products—favour a fixed commission system.

Fee-for-service commonly used

Canadian advertising budgets are, on the average, much smaller than American ones. And the rates charged by Canadian media reaching a more limited audience are, on a per page or per minute basis, far lower than American rates. On the other hand, the work Canadian agencies must do when planning campaigns and preparing effective advertisements isn't much different or less demanding, and the salaries they must pay aren't much lower. Because of these factors, the fee-for-service basis for agency compensation is well established and widely used in Canada.

Some firms pay the agency based on results

A number of advertisers now "grade" the work done by their agencies—and the agencies' pay depends on the grade. For example, General Foods lowered its basic commission to about 13 percent. However, the company pays the agency a bonus of about 3 percent on campaigns that earn an A rating. If the agency only earns a B, it loses the bonus. If it earns a C, it must improve fast, or GF removes the account. Variations on this approach are becoming common.[16]

Measuring advertising effectiveness is not easy

It would be convenient if we could measure the results of advertising by looking at sales. Certainly some breakthrough ads do have a very direct effect on a company's sales—and the advertising literature is filled with success stories which "prove" that advertising increases sales. Similarly, market research can sometimes compare sales levels before and after the period of an ad campaign. That being said, we usually can't measure advertising success just by looking at sales. The total marketing mix—not just advertising—is responsible for the sales result. And sales results are also affected by what competitors do and by other changes in the external marketing environment. Only with direct-response advertising can a company make a direct link between advertising and sales results.

Ethical Dimensions

Confidential Information

Ad agencies usually work closely with their clients, and they often have access to confidential information. This can create ethical conflicts if an agency is working with two or more competing clients. Most agencies are very sensitive to the potential problems and keep people and information from competing accounts separated. But many advertisers don't think that's enough. They refuse to work with an agency that handles any competing accounts, even when they're handled in different offices. For example, a top executive for the Budweiser brand ended a 79-year relationship with an agency when one of the agency's subsidiaries accepted an assignment to buy media space for a competing brand of beer.

This potential conflict of interest in handling competing products has been a problem for the big international mega-agencies. Saatchi & Saatchi, for example, gained over $300 million in billings through its mergers but then quickly lost $462 million in billings when old clients departed because Saatchi's new clients—at one of its offices around the world—included competitors.[17]

Research and testing can improve the odds

Ideally, advertisers should pretest advertising before it runs, rather than relying solely on their own guesses about how good an ad will be. The judgment of creative people or advertising experts may not help much. They often judge only on the basis of the originality—or cleverness—of the copy and illustrations.

Many progressive advertisers now demand laboratory or market tests to evaluate an ad's effectiveness. For example, American Express used interviews to get reactions to a series of possible TV ads. The agency prepared picture boards presenting different approaches as well as specific copy. The one idea that seemed to be most effective became the basis for an ad that was tested again before being launched on TV.[18]

Split runs on cable TV systems in test markets are proving to be an important approach for testing ads in a normal viewing environment. Scanner sales data from retailers in those test markets can provide an estimate of how an ad is likely to affect sales. This approach will become even more powerful in the future as more cable systems and telephone companies add new interactive technologies that allow viewers to provide immediate feedback to an ad as it appears on the TV.

Hindsight may lead to foresight

After ads run, researchers may try to measure how much consumers recall about specific products or ads. Inquiries from customers may be used to measure the effectiveness of particular ads. The response to radio or television commercials—or magazine readership—can be estimated using various survey methods to check the size and composition of audiences (the Nielsen and Starch reports are examples).[19]

Various media audiences are measured by three major services in Canada: the Bureau of Broadcast Measurement (BBM) for radio and TV, Nielsen for TV, and the Print Measurement Bureau (PMB) for major consumer magazines and newspaper weekend supplements. In addition, the Canadian Outdoor Measurement Bureau (COMB) measures the total traffic passing by all outdoor advertising.

How to avoid unfair advertising

In most countries, the government takes an active role in deciding what kinds of advertising are allowable, fair, and appropriate. For example, France and Japan limit the use of cartoon characters in advertising to children, and Sweden and the province of Quebec ban *any* advertising targeted directly at children. In Switzerland, an advertiser cannot use an actor to represent a con-

Marketing Demo 16-3

The Competition Act—Misleading Advertising Provisions

The following description of some of the misleading advertising provisions of the *Competition Act* is provided by the Bureau of Competition Policy, Industry Canada, for information purposes only and should not be taken to be a complete statement of the law. Provisions of the Competition Act more closely related to price, product, or place are discussed in other chapters of this text.

Section 52(1)(*a*): All representations, in any form whatever, that are false or misleading in a material respect are prohibited. This general provision prohibits all misleading representations not specifically prohibited elsewhere.

Section 52(1)(*b*): Any representation in the form of a statement, warranty, or guarantee of the performance, efficacy, or length of life of a product, not based on an adequate and proper test, is prohibited. The onus is on the one making the claim to prove that it is based on an adequate and proper test.

Section 52(1)(*c*): This paragraph covers any representation that purports to be a warranty or guarantee of a product, or a promise to replace, maintain, or repair an article, or any part of an article. Such representations are prohibited where their form is materially misleading or where there is no reasonable prospect that the warranty, guarantee, or promise will be carried out.

Section 52(1)(*d*): Any materially misleading representation as to the price at which a product is ordinarily sold is prohibited. Here, price means the price that the product ordinarily sells for in the market area, unless specified to be the advertiser's own selling price.

Section 57: Advertising a product at a bargain price that the advertiser does not have available for sale in reasonable quantities is prohibited. Liability will be avoided where the advertiser can establish that the nonavailability of the product was due to circumstances beyond its control, the quantity of the product obtained was reasonable, or the customer was offered a rain check when supplies were exhausted.

Section 58: The supply of any product at a price higher than the price currently being advertised is prohibited. This section does not apply where the price advertised was erroneous and immediately corrected, or where the seller is not a person engaged in the business of dealing in that product.

Section 59: Any contest that does not disclose the number and approximate value of prizes or important information relating to the chances of winning in the contest, that does not select participants or distribute prizes on the basis of skill or on a random basis, or in which the distribution of prizes is unduly delayed, is prohibited.

Source: Marketing Practices Branch, Bureau of Competition Policy, Industry Canada, "Misleading Advertising Bulletin," April 1–June 30, 1994, p. 21.

---

sumer. New Zealand and Switzerland limit political ads on TV. In the United States, print ads must be identified so that they aren't confused with editorial matter. In other countries, ads and editorial copy can be intermixed.

What is seen as positioning in one country may be viewed as unfair or deceptive in another. For example, in many countries Pepsi advertised its cola as "the choice of the new generation." Japan's Fair Trade Committee didn't allow it—because Pepsi was not "the choice."[20]

Differences in rules mean that a marketing manager may face very specific limits in different countries. Local experts may have to be consulted to ensure that a firm doesn't waste money developing ads that will never be shown—or that consumers will think are deceptive.

Advertising abuses have been a favourite target of Canadian consumer activists. Their efforts, along with those of Consumer and Corporate Affairs Canada (now amalgamated with Industry Canada), have led to new legislation and to stricter enforcement of existing laws. Marketing Demo 16–3 provides a useful summary of the Competition Act provisions designed to prevent misleading advertising. For up-to-date information on enforcement efforts, go to the Competition Bureau's Web page (http://strategis.ic.gc.ca/sc_mrksv/competit/).

The stricter federal controls on advertising have their provincial counterparts. Such regulation is an especially prominent feature of the trade practices laws that have been passed by many Canadian provinces. Conflicting provincial legislation

Ethical Dimensions

Unfair or Deceptive Advertising

What constitutes unfair and deceptive advertising is a difficult question and one that marketing managers will have to wrestle with for years to come. Sometimes the law provides guidelines, but in most situations the marketing manager must make personal judgments as well. The social and political environment is changing worldwide. Practices considered acceptable some years ago are now being questioned. Saying or even implying that your product is best may be viewed as deceptive.

can make it impossible for national advertisers to use the same campaign across Canada. Provincial differences are greatest in the advertising of liquor, beer, and wine. Some provinces ban such ads outright, while others place restrictions on what can be said, and still others limit the advertiser to specific media. Complying with all this legislation is no easy task.

The Canadian Radio-television and Telecommunications Commission (CRTC) controls the content of all radio and television commercials. The CRTC lets the Health Protection Branch of Health Canada regulate TV and radio advertising of drugs, cosmetics, and other health-related products. Similarly, the CRTC allows food commercials to be regulated by Agriculture Canada.

These government agencies don't have the same kind of advance veto power over print advertising. However, they can and do insist that print advertisements that violate existing regulations be corrected. Also, both advertisers and their agencies have been brought to court for violating the false advertising provisions of the Competition Act or comparable provincial legislation.

Additional forms of regulation are imposed by the media themselves and by industry associations. The CBC and CTV television networks have their own codes of advertising acceptability. Advertising Standards Canada, in a process involving public representatives, administers a Code of Advertising Standards. More specific ASC codes govern advertisements directed toward children, the advertising of specific categories of products, and the use of potentially controversial practices such as comparative advertising. Guidelines to prevent advertising stereotyping also exist. As a way of adding teeth to its efforts at self-regulation, Advertising Standards Canada began in 1998 to make public the results of its investigations (see Marketing Demo 16–4).

Despite such efforts at self-regulation, critics of the mass media continue to find much that they consider offensive both in advertisements and the accompanying editorial or program content. That there is no effective way to control "spillover" American advertising obviously complicates Canadian efforts at self-regulation.

Sales promotion: do something different to stimulate change

Sales promotion refers to those promotion activities—other than advertising, publicity, and personal selling—that stimulate interest, trial, or purchase by final customers or by others in the channel. Exhibit 14–2 shows examples of typical sales promotions targeted at final customers, channel members, and a firm's own employees.

Advertising campaigns and sales force strategy decisions tend to have longer-term effects; in contrast, a particular sales promotion activity usually lasts for only a limited time. Sales promotion can often be implemented quickly, and get sales results sooner than advertising. Sales promotion objectives usually focus on prompting short-term action. For an intermediary, such an action might be a decision to stock a product, provide a special display, or give extra sales emphasis. For a consumer, the

Marketing Demo 16-4

Visible and Accountable

When Advertising Standards Canada released its 1997 Ad Complaints Report, it was the first time the ad industry's self-regulating body provided details of some of the consumer complaints sustained under the Canadian Code of Advertising Standards (Code) or the Gender Portrayal Guidelines (Guidelines). In their opening remarks in this Report, ASC chair Peter Elwood and ASC president and CEO Linda Nagel commented that "Until now, details about sustained complaints were treated as confidential and, therefore, not reported. This lack of disclosure precluded industry from gaining important insights about issues of concern to consumers."

Elwood and Nagel also indicated that the aim of "a more open complaints reporting system" is: "First—to enhance industry and public confidence in the advertising self-regulatory process; and second—to provide advertisers with information about issues of concern to the public."

Names and full details are released only in cases where the complaints are sustained and the advertisers did not drop or modify the offending ad before the ASC ruling. The following are selected verbatim Sustained Complaints rulings from the 1997 ASC Ad Complaints Report for the period Sept. 1–Dec. 31, 1997:

Canadian Code of Advertising Standards:
Clause 1 (Accuracy, Clarity)
Advertiser: A-Plus Software
Region: Ontario
Media: Newspaper
Complaints: 1
Description: In a newspaper advertisement, the Advertiser offered low prices and various rebates on software and computer accessories.
Complaint: That this advertisement omitted to state important conditions concerning the rebates.
Decision: Council found that to qualify for a mail-in-rebate, customers were required to purchase a computer accessory for an additional charge. Council found that this and other pertinent details dealing with the amount and method by which actual savings could be realized were omitted from the advertisement, contrary to Clause 1(c) of the Code. Council also found the advertisement contained an inaccurate and deceptive claim regarding the price of the products, contrary to Clause 1(a) of the Code.

Clause 10 (Safety)
Advertiser: Bell Mobility
Region: National (English) & Quebec (French)
Media: Television
Complaints: 12
Description: In a TV commercial for a cellular phone service, an adult man, who is re-living a childhood dare, licks a frozen pole in an outdoor setting. The result is that his tongue sticks to the pole.
Complaint: That the commercial might influence children to emulate the man's actions.
Decision: Council concluded the commercial violated Clause 10 of the Code by depicting a situation that might encourage unsafe or dangerous practices.

Gender Portrayal Guidelines:
Clause 3 (Sexuality)
Advertiser: Arnold Churgin Shoes Ltd.
Region: Alberta
Media: Newspaper
Complaints: 2
Description: In a newspaper advertisement, this shoe retailer featured a female model, posing behind a large cowboy hat and wearing only a pair of cowboy boots.
Complaint: That it was offensive to feature the sexualized image of a woman in order to sell footwear.
Decision: Panel concluded it was sexually exploitative and contrary to Clause 3(iv) of the Guidelines to show a woman wearing nothing but cowboy boots in order to sell a product (footwear) that was unrelated to sexuality.

Source: Abridged from "Visible and Accountable," *Marketing Magazine*, February 23, 1998, pp. 10–12.

desired action might be to try a new product, switch from another brand, or buy more of a product. The desired action by an employee might be a special effort to satisfy customers.

Sales promotion spending is growing

Sales promotion involves so many different types of activities that it is difficult to estimate accurately how much is spent in total. There is general consensus, however, that total spending on sales promotion exceeds spending on advertising.

Spending on sales promotion has grown rapidly. Companies that sell frequently purchased consumer products account for much of that increase. One reason is that they are often competing in mature markets. There's only so much soap, cereal, and deodorant that consumers want to buy, regardless of how many brands are vying for their dollars. There's also limited shelf space that retailers can allocate to a particular product category.[21]

The competitive situation is intensified by the growth of large, powerful retail chains. They have put more emphasis on their own dealer brands and are also demanding more sales promotion support for the manufacturer brands they do carry.

Perhaps in part because of this competition, many consumers have become more price sensitive. Many sales promotions, such as coupons, have the effect of lowering the prices consumers pay. So sales promotion helps overcome consumer price resistance.

Changes in technology have also made sales promotion more efficient. For example, with scanners at retail checkout counters, it's possible to pinpoint instantly a customer who is the target for a particular coupon. If a customer buys a bottle of Kraft salad dressing, Kraft can have the retailer's computerized cash register print out a coupon—on the spot—to encourage the customer to buy Kraft again the next time.

The growth of sales promotion has also been fostered by the availability of more agencies and specialists who help plan and implement sales promotion programs. Of course, the basic reason for the growth of spending on sales promotion is that it can be very effective if it is properly done. But there are problems in the sales promotion area.

Problems in managing sales promotion

Some experts think that marketing managers—especially those who deal with consumer packaged goods—put too much emphasis on sales promotions. They argue that the effect of most sales promotions is temporary and that money spent on advertising and personal selling helps the firm more over the long term. Their view is that most sales promotions don't help develop close relationships with consumers, but instead erode brand loyalty.

There *is* heavy use of sales promotion in mature markets where competition is fierce. When the market is not growing, sales promotions may simply encourage "deal-prone" customers (and intermediaries) to switch back and forth among brands. Here, all the expense of the sales promotions simply contributes to lower profits. Ultimately, it also increases the prices that consumers pay, by increasing selling costs.

However, once a marketing manager is in this situation there may be little choice but to continue. In a mature market, frequent sales promotions may be needed simply to offset the effects of competitors' promotions. The only escape from this rat race is for the marketing manager to seek new opportunities—with a strategy that doesn't rely solely on short-term sales promotions for competitive advantage.

There are alternatives

Procter & Gamble is a company that has changed its strategy, and promotion blend, to decrease its reliance on trade promotion. P&G has dramatically reduced its use of sales promotion targeted at intermediaries. Instead, it is offering them lower prices on many of its products and supporting those products with more advertising and promotion to final consumers. P&G believes that this approach will build its brand equity, serve consumers better, and lead to smoother-running relationships in its channels. Not all retailers are happy with P&G's changes. However, given the serious concerns about the impact of trade promotion on brand loyalty, many other producers are likely to follow P&G's lead.

Firms are also experimenting with other approaches. For example, some reimburse intermediaries for promotion effort in proportion to their sales to final consumers.[22]

Sales promotion is hard to manage

Another problem in the sales promotion area is that it is easy to make big, costly mistakes. Because sales promotion includes a wide variety of activities, each of which may be custom-designed and used only once, it's difficult for the typical company to develop skill in this area. Mistakes caused by lack of experience can be very costly as well. One promotion sponsored jointly by Polaroid and Trans World Airlines (TWA) proved to be a disaster. The promotion offered a coupon worth 25 percent off the price of any TWA ticket with the purchase of a $20 Polaroid camera. The companies intended to appeal to vacationers who take pictures when they travel. Instead, travel agents bought up many of the cameras. For the price of the $20 camera, they made an extra 25 percent on every TWA ticket they sold. And big companies bought thousands of the cameras to save on overseas travel expenses. This is not an isolated example. Such problems are common.[23]

Not a sideline for amateurs

Sales promotion mistakes are likely to be worse when a company has no sales promotion manager. When the personal selling or advertising managers are responsible for sales promotion, they often treat it as a "stepchild." They allocate money to sales promotion if there is any "left over"—or if a crisis develops.

Making sales promotion work is a learned skill, not a sideline for amateurs. That's why specialists in sales promotion have developed, both inside larger firms and as outside consultants. Some of these people are real experts. Even so, it's the marketing manager's responsibility to set sales promotion objectives and policies that will fit in with the rest of each marketing strategy.[24]

Different types of sales promotion for different targets

Much of the sales promotion aimed at final consumers or users tries to increase demand—perhaps temporarily—or speed up the time of purchase. Such promotion may involve developing materials to be displayed in retailers' stores—banners, sample packages, calendars, point-of-purchase materials, and so on. The sales promotion people also may develop special displays for supermarkets. They may be responsible for "sweepstakes" contests as well as for coupons designed to get customers to buy a product by a certain date.

All of these sales promotion efforts are aimed at specific objectives. For example, if customers already have a favourite brand, it may be hard to get them to try anything new. A free trial-size bottle of mouthwash may be just what it takes to get cautious consumers to try—and like—the new product. Sales of the new product may jump and then continue at the higher level after the promotion if satisfied customers make repeat purchases. In this situation, the cost of the sales promotion can be viewed as a long-term investment.

Once a product has been established, consumer sales promotion usually focuses on a short-term sales increase. For example, after a price-off coupon for a soft drink is distributed, sales may temporarily pick up as customers take advantage of buying at a lower price. However, once the coupon period is over, sales will probably return to the original level. Sales may even decline for a while if customers use the coupon to "stock up" on a product at the low price. Then it takes them longer than usual to buy the product again.

When the promotion is focused primarily on producing a short-term increase in sales, it's sensible for the marketing manager to evaluate the cost of the promotion relative to the extra sales expected. If the increase in sales won't at least cover the cost of the promotion, it probably doesn't make sense to do it. Otherwise, the firm is "buying sales" at the cost of reduced profit.

Sales promotion directed at industrial customers often uses the same kinds of ideas. In addition, the sales promotion people may set up and staff trade show exhibits. Here, attractive models are often used to encourage buyers to look at a firm's product—especially when it is displayed near other similar products in a circuslike atmosphere.[25]

Sales promotion for intermediaries

Sales promotion aimed at intermediaries—sometimes called *trade promotion*—stresses price-related matters. The objective may be to encourage intermediaries to stock new items, buy in larger quantity, buy early, or stress a product in their own promotion efforts.

The tools used here include merchandise allowances, promotion allowances, and perhaps sales contests to encourage retailers or wholesalers to sell specific items—or the company's whole line. Offering to send contest winners to Hawaii, for example, may increase sales.

About half of the sales promotion spending targeted at intermediaries has the effect of reducing the prices they pay for merchandise. In the next chapter, we'll go into more detail on the different types of trade discounts and allowances.[26]

Sales promotion for employees

Sales promotions aimed at the company's own sales force may try to encourage getting new customers, selling a new product, or selling the company's entire line. Depending on the objectives, the tools may be contests, bonuses on sales or number of new accounts, or holding sales meetings at fancy resorts to raise everyone's spirits.

Ongoing sales promotion work may also be aimed at the sales force, to help sales management. Sales promotion specialists may be responsible for preparing sales portfolios, videotapes on new products, displays, and other sales aids. They may also develop the sales training materials that the sales force uses in working with channel members, as well as special displays that the sales rep places with retailers.

Service-oriented firms, such as hotels and restaurants, now use sales promotions targeted at their employees. For example, some give a monthly cash prize for the employee who provides the "best service." And the employee's picture is displayed to give recognition.[27]

Questions and Problems

1. Identify the strategy decisions a marketing manager must make in the advertising area.
2. Discuss the relationship between advertising objectives and strategic market planning, and the kinds of advertising actually needed. Illustrate.
3. List several media that might be effective for reaching consumers in a developing nation with low per capita income and a high level of illiteracy. Briefly discuss the limitations and advantages of each medium you suggest.
4. Give three examples where advertising to intermediaries might be necessary. What are the objective(s) of such advertising?
5. What does it mean to say that "money is invested in advertising"? Is all advertising an investment? Illustrate.
6. Find advertisements to final consumers that illustrate the following types of advertising: (*a*) institutional, (*b*) pioneering, (*c*) competitive, and (*d*) reminder. What objectives does each of these ads have? List the needs each ad appeals to.
7. Describe the type of media that might be most suitable for promoting: (*a*) tomato soup, (*b*) greeting cards, (*c*) a business component material, and (*d*) playground equipment. Specify any assumptions necessary to obtain a definite answer.
8. Discuss the use of testimonials in advertising. Which of the four AIDA steps might testimonials accomplish? Are they suitable for all types of products? If not, for which types are they most suitable?
9. Find a magazine ad that you think does a particularly good job of communicating to the target audience. Would the ad communicate well to an audience in another country? Explain your thinking.
10. Johnson & Johnson sells its baby shampoo in many different countries. Do you think baby shampoo would be a good product for Johnson & Johnson to advertise with a single global message? Explain your thinking.
11. Discuss the future of smaller advertising agencies now that many of the largest have merged to form mega-agencies.
12. Does advertising cost too much? How can this be measured?
13. How would your local newspaper be affected if local supermarkets switched their weekly advertising and instead used a service that delivered weekly, free-standing ads directly to each home?
14. Is it unfair to advertise to children? Is it unfair to advertise to less-educated or less-experienced people of any age? Is it unfair to advertise for "unnecessary" products? Is it unfair to criticize a competitor's product in an ad?
15. Discuss the factors that have resulted in increased spending on sales promotion by consumer packaged goods firms during the past decade.
16. Discuss some ways that a firm can link its sales promotion activities to its advertising and personal selling efforts, so that all of its promotion efforts result in an integrated effort.
17. Indicate the type of sales promotion that a producer might use in each of the following situations and briefly explain your reasoning:
    a. A firm has developed an improved razor blade and obtained distribution, but customers are not motivated to buy it.
    b. A competitor is about to do a test market for a new brand and wants to track sales in test market areas to fine tune its marketing mix.
    c. A big grocery chain won't stock a firm's new popcorn-based snack product because it doesn't think there will be much consumer demand.
18. Why wouldn't a producer of shampoo just lower the price of its product rather than offer consumers a price-off coupon?
19. If sales promotion spending continues to grow—often at the expense of media advertising—how do you think this might affect the rates charged by mass media for advertising time or space? How do you think it might affect advertising agencies?

Suggested cases

1	Marketing a Web Site	23	Ontario Rutabaga Council
7	Naturally Yours	27	Lever, Ltd.

Computer-aided problem

Sales Promotion

As a community service, disc jockeys from radio station WMKT formed a basketball team to help raise money for local nonprofit organizations. The host organization finds or fields a competing team and charges $5 admission to the game. Money from ticket sales goes to the nonprofit organization.

Ticket sales were disappointing at recent games—averaging only about 300 people per game. When WMKT's marketing manager, Bruce Miller, heard about the problem, he suggested using sales promotion to improve ticket sales. The PTA for the local high school—the sponsor for the next game—is interested in the idea but is concerned that its budget doesn't include any promotion money. Miller tries to help them by reviewing his idea in more detail.

Specifically, he proposes that the PTA give a free T-shirt (printed with the school name and date of the game) to the first 500 ticket buyers. He thinks the T-shirt giveaway will create a lot of interest. In fact, he says he is almost certain the promotion would help the PTA sell 600 tickets—double the usual number. He speculates that the PTA might even have a sellout of all 900 seats in the school gym. Further, he notes that the T-shirts will more than pay for themselves if the PTA sells 600 tickets.

A local firm that specializes in sales promotion items agrees to supply the shirts and do the printing for $2.40 a shirt—if the PTA places an order for at least 400 shirts. The PTA thinks the idea is interesting but wants to look at it more closely, to see what will happen if the promotion doesn't increase ticket sales. To help the PTA evaluate the alternatives, Miller sets up a spreadsheet with the relevant information.

a. Based on the data from the initial spreadsheet, does the T-shirt promotion look like a good idea? Explain your thinking.
b. The PTA treasurer worries about the up-front cost of printing the T-shirts and wants to know where they would stand if they ordered the T-shirts and still sold only 300 tickets. He suggests it might be safer to order the minimum number of T-shirts (400). Evaluate his suggestion.
c. The president of the PTA thinks the T-shirt promotion will increase sales but wonders if it wouldn't be better just to lower the price. She suggests $2.60 a ticket, which she arrives at by subtracting the $2.40 T-shirt cost from the usual $5.00 ticket price. How many tickets would the PTA have to sell at the lower price to match the money it would make if it used the T-shirt promotion and actually sold 600 tickets? (Hint: Change the selling price in the spreadsheet and then vary the quantity using the What If analysis.)

For additional questions related to this problem, see Exercise 16–3 in the *Learning Aid for Use with Basic Marketing,* Ninth Canadian Edition.

When you finish this chapter, you should:

- Understand how pricing objectives should guide strategic planning for pricing decisions.
- Understand choices the marketing manager must make about price flexibility and price levels over the product life cycle.
- Understand the many possible variations of a price structure, including discounts, allowances, and who pays transportation costs.
- Understand some of the legal issues affecting pricing policies.
- Understand the important new terms (shown in orange).

Chapter seventeen

Pricing Objectives and Policies

BID BUMPER TO BUMPER BON VOYAGE.

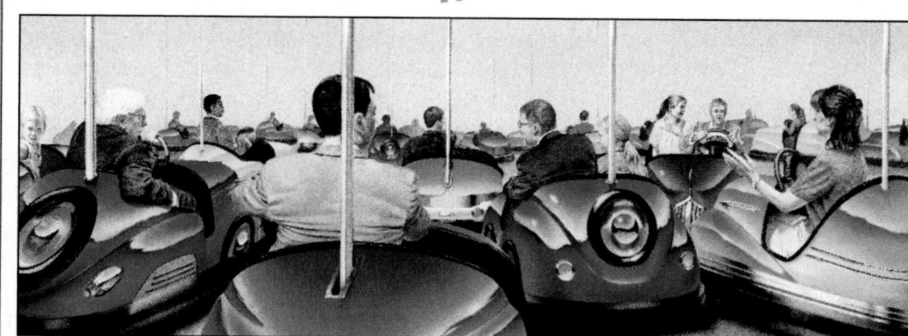

Say hello to the new Highway 407, Canada's first all electronic toll highway. It's fast. It's convenient. It's the new way to zip across town.

For more information, zip across the information highway and exit at www.407etr.com. Or contact us at 200 King Street West, Suite 2001, Box 80, Toronto, Ontario M5H 3T4, (416) 326-6606, or fax (416) 326-6460/9164.

407 ETR
ZIP ACROSS TOWN

Freeways are becoming an oxymoron. Toll highways are the roads of the future, and they're popping up all over North America.

The Highway 104 Western Alignment project in northern Nova Scotia, which opened Dec. 1, is Canada's second major toll road project. The $113-million, 45-kilometer superhighway connects Masstown in Colchester County and Thomson Station, Cumberland County, shaving 11 km off the old 104 circuit.

As a partnership venture between the provincial government and the private sector, building the road was easy. The tough part is convincing motorists toll roads are the way to go.

"The marketing challenge is not just like promoting a better mousetrap, but introducing consumers to a totally new type of mousetrap," says Mitch Patten, vice-president of communications and public affairs for Canadian Highways International Corporation. "Creating awareness of the benefits of toll routes is the first step."

Contracted to build Canada's first mega-highway toll roads, CHIC (a consortium of engineering and construction companies), assumes all construction risks, with tolls as its sole revenue source. The consortium constructed the $1.4-billion Highway 407 Express Toll Route (ETR) across Toronto—the world's first all-electronic toll road. The innovative technology includes transponders—a small electronic device, attached to a car's interior windshield, that communicates each entry and exit to the ETR via cameras located on overhead gantries.

CHIC is applying the lessons it learned with ETR to its marketing approach in Nova Scotia. CHIC overcame a number of challenges by the time ETR started charging tolls last Oct. 14. Among them: questions about the safe design of the road and a missed March 31, 1997, deadline for charging tolls. Drivers were able to use the ETR for free for three months, but once they had to start paying, traffic immediately dropped to 100,000 trips per day from 300,000 trips during the "free" period. Pamela Wing, vice-president of marketing for the Ontario Transportation Capital Corporation, the provincial government's agent in the ETR project, looks on the bright side: "At 100,000 trips per day, it's twice the volume we predicted."

"Marketing (in Ontario) hinges on changing people's attitudes towards tolling and getting them to alter their driving habits," Wing adds. "As with any new product, you have to build consumer confidence."

The three-month "free" period provided an opportunity to compare the 407's efficiency against other local commuter highways. That was crucial in building a customer base.

"As part of our strategy, we attended auto shows and conducted mall tours throughout the Greater Toronto Area. We partnered with the TD Bank, Petro-Canada, Home Hardware and Frontier Duty Shops in distributing our informational brochures, including transponder application forms," says Wing.

Ad agency Weaver Tanner Miller of Kitchener, Ont., focused the ETR's $3-million marketing campaign on print, outdoor billboards and radio. It produced a series of amusing ads featuring the traffic jams and snail's pace of "free" highways.

In contrast, marketing for Highway 104 is heavily information-based. The focus, says CHIC's Patten, is on the use of the credit card-sized transponder, called an E-Pass. About 30,000 flyers with E-Pass applications have been distributed to households throughout northern Nova Scotia, the main customers . . . "Ongoing marketing will concentrate on the E-Pass and the advantages of the highway," says Patten.

"Due to the success of the free period on the ETR, we also decided to run a two-week free tryout," Patten adds. "The differences in marketing strategies between the two projects stem from the very distinct uses of the roads—one is an urban commuter highway, the other a rural corridor for less frequent travellers. How well our marketing generates loyal customers is being closely watched by other provinces and countries, who see toll roads as a cost effective model for their own infrastructure plans."

Pamela Wing of the OTCC has found the challenge of promoting a toll route to be quite heady: "It's pioneering work, literally blazing new marketing paths. The process is exhilarating. But we've not invented a new wheel here—it is, after all, still only a highway." ●

Source: Abridged from Jack Kohane, "A Toll Order," *Marketing Magazine*, February 9, 1998, p. 17.

Price has many strategic dimensions

Price is one of the four major variables that a marketing manager controls. Price level decisions are especially important because they affect both the number of sales a firm makes and how much money it earns. As our opening discussion suggests, this is true for all kinds of products, even toll roads.

Guided by the company's objectives, marketing managers must develop a set of pricing objectives and policies. They must spell out what price situations the firm will face and how it will handle them. These policies should explain (1) how flexible prices will be, (2) at what level they will be set over the product life cycle, (3) to whom and when discounts and allowances will be given, and (4) how transportation costs will be handled. See Exhibit 17–1. These Price-related strategic decision areas

Exhibit 17–1 Strategic Planning for Price

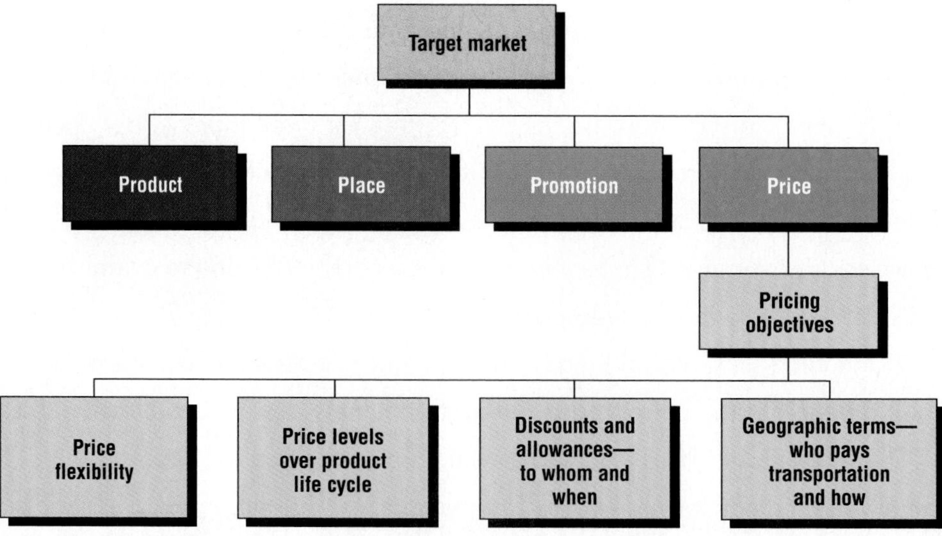

Exhibit 17-2 Price as Seen by Consumers or Users

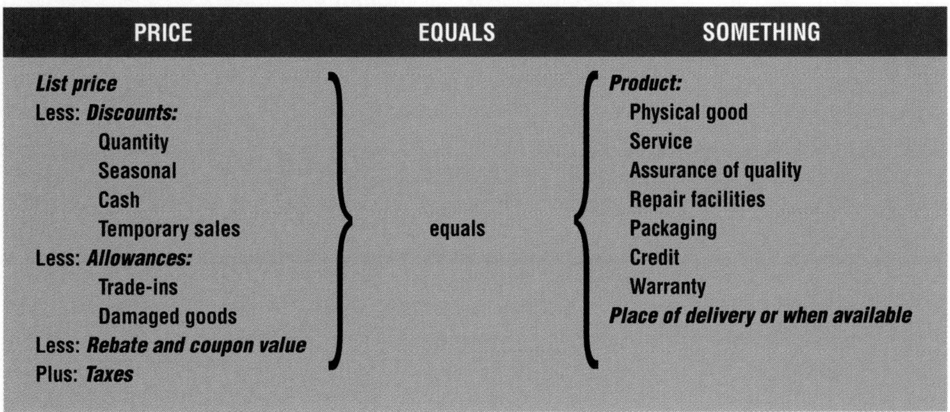

PRICE	EQUALS	SOMETHING
List price		***Product:***
Less: ***Discounts:***		Physical good
Quantity		Service
Seasonal		Assurance of quality
Cash		Repair facilities
Temporary sales	equals	Packaging
Less: ***Allowances:***		Credit
Trade-ins		Warranty
Damaged goods		***Place of delivery or when available***
Less: ***Rebate and coupon value***		
Plus: ***Taxes***		

are the focus of this chapter. In the next chapter, we will discuss how specific prices are set, consistent with the whole marketing strategy.

It's not easy to define price in real-life situations because prices reflect many factors. People who don't realize this can make big mistakes.

Suppose you've been saving to buy a new car and you see in an ad that the base price for the new-year model has been dropped to $19,500—5 percent lower than the previous year. At first this may seem like a real bargain. However, your view of this deal may change if you find out you also have to pay an extra $960 for an extended service warranty. The price may look even less attractive if you discover that the options you want cost $1,200 more than in the previous year. The transportation charge may come as an unpleasant surprise too. Further, how will you feel if you buy the car anyway and then learn that a friend who just bought the exact same model negotiated a much lower price?[1]

The price equation: price equals something

This example emphasizes that when a seller quotes a price, it is related to *some* assortment of goods and services. So **Price** is what is charged for "something." Of course, price may be called different things in different settings. Universities charge tuition. Landlords collect rent. Motels post a room rate. Banks ask for interest when they loan money. Transportation companies have fares, and mega-highways charge tolls. Doctors, lawyers, and consultants set fees. Employees want a wage. People may call it different things, but *any business transaction in our modern economy can be thought of as an exchange of money—the money being the Price—for something.*

The something can be a physical product in various stages of completion, with or without supporting services, with or without quality guarantees, and so on. Or it can be a pure service—dry cleaning, a lawyer's advice, or insurance on your car.

The nature and extent of this something determines the amount of money exchanged. Some customers pay list price. Others obtain large discounts or allowances because something is *not* provided. Exhibit 17–2 summarizes some possible variations for consumers or users, and Exhibit 17–3 does the same for channel members. These variations are discussed more fully later.

Objectives should guide strategic planning for price

Pricing objectives should flow from, and fit in with, company-level and marketing objectives. Pricing objectives should be *explicitly stated* because they have a direct effect on pricing policies as well as on the methods used to set prices.

Exhibit 17–4 shows the various types of pricing objectives we'll discuss.

Exhibit 17-3 Price as Seen by Channel Members

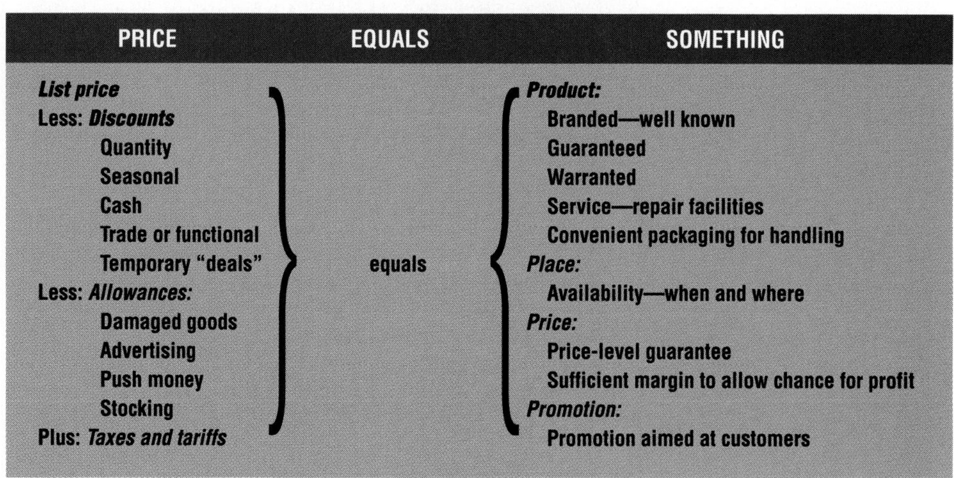
PRICE	EQUALS	SOMETHING
List price Less: *Discounts* Quantity Seasonal Cash Trade or functional Temporary "deals" Less: *Allowances:* Damaged goods Advertising Push money Stocking Plus: *Taxes and tariffs*	equals	*Product:* Branded—well known Guaranteed Warranted Service—repair facilities Convenient packaging for handling *Place:* Availability—when and where *Price:* Price-level guarantee Sufficient margin to allow chance for profit *Promotion:* Promotion aimed at customers

Exhibit 17-4 Possible Pricing Objectives

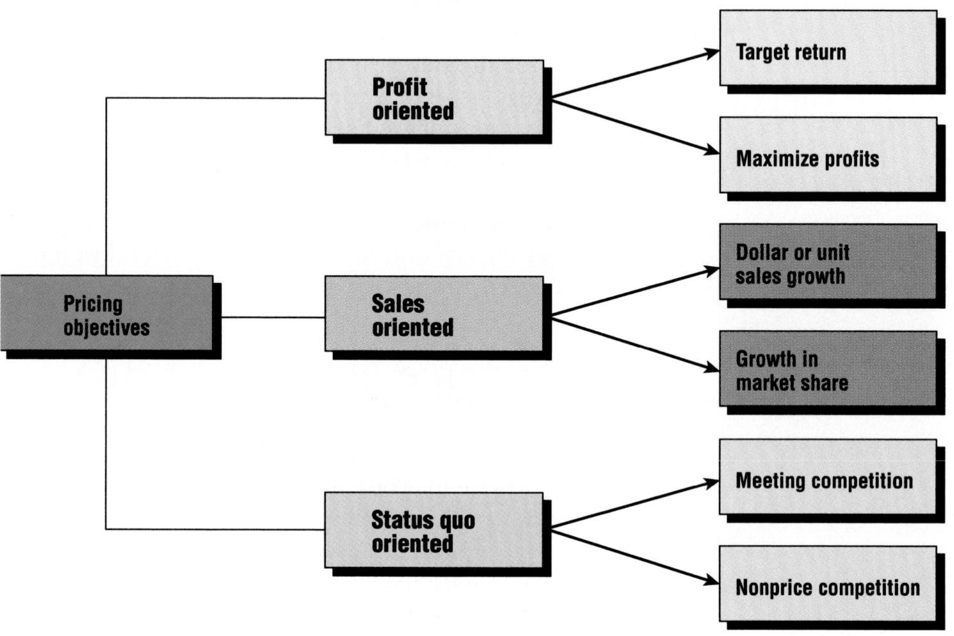

Profit-oriented objectives

A **target return objective** sets a specific level of profit as an objective. Often this amount is stated as a percentage of sales or of capital investment. A large manufacturer like Motorola might aim for a 15 percent return on investment. The target for Safeway and other grocery chains might be a 1 percent return on sales.

In a large company, a target return objective has administrative advantages. Performance can be compared against the target. Some companies eliminate divisions—or drop products—that aren't yielding the target rate of return. For example, General Electric sold its small appliance division to Black & Decker because it felt it could earn higher returns in other product-markets.

Some just want satisfactory profits

Some managers aim for merely satisfactory returns. They just want returns that ensure the firm's survival and convince shareholders they're doing a good job. Similarly, some small, family-run businesses aim for a profit that will provide a comfortable lifestyle.[2]

Companies that are industry leaders—like Alcoa and Du Pont of Canada—sometimes pursue only satisfactory long-run profits. Both the public and government officials expect them to set prices that are in the public interest. Similarly, firms that provide public services—including many utility and insurance companies and transportation firms—face government agencies that review and approve prices.[3]

Profit maximization can expand the market

A **profit maximization objective** seeks to get as much profit as possible, and might be stated as a desire to earn a rapid return on investment—or, more bluntly, to charge all the traffic will bear.

Some people believe that anyone seeking a profit maximization objective will charge high prices—prices that are not in the public interest. However, pricing to achieve profit maximization doesn't always lead to high prices. Low prices may expand the size of the market and result in greater sales and profits. For example, when prices of VCRs were very high, only innovators and wealthy people bought them. When Sony and its competitors lowered prices, nearly everyone bought a VCR.

When a firm is earning a very large profit, other firms will enter the market. Frequently, this leads to lower prices. IBM sold its original personal computer for about $4,500 in 1981. As Compaq, Dell, and other competitors started to copy IBM, all the firms in the industry added more power and features and cut prices.[4]

Sales-oriented objectives

A **sales-oriented objective** seeks some level of unit sales, dollar sales, or share of market, *without referring to profit.*

Sales growth doesn't always mean big profits

Some managers are more concerned about sales growth than profits. They think sales growth always leads to more profits. This kind of thinking causes problems when a firm's costs are growing faster than sales, or when managers don't keep track of their costs. Sometimes, major corporations have declining profits in spite of growth in sales. At the extreme, International Harvester kept cutting prices on its tractors—trying to reach its target sales levels in a weak economy—until it had to sell that part of its business. Generally, however, business managers now pay more attention to profits, not just sales.[5]

Market share objectives are usually used

Many firms seek to gain a specified share (percentage) of a market. One benefit of a market share objective is that it forces a manager to pay attention to what competitors are doing in the market. In addition, it's usually easier to measure a firm's market share than to determine whether profits are being maximized. Large consumer packaged goods firms such as Procter & Gamble, Coca-Cola, and General Foods often use market share objectives.

Aggressive companies often aim to increase market share or even to control a market. Sometimes this makes sense. A company that has a large market share may enjoy better economies of scale than its competitors. Then, if it sells at about the same price as its competitors, it will get more profit from each sale. Or lower costs may allow it to sell at a lower price and still make a profit.

A company with a longer-run view may decide that increasing market share is a sensible objective when the overall market is growing. The hope is that larger future volume will justify sacrificing some profit in the short run. Companies as diverse as 3M, Coca-Cola, and IBM looked at opportunities in Eastern Europe in this way. Of course, objectives aimed at increasing market share have the same limitations as straight sales growth objectives. A larger market share, if gained at too low a price, may lead to profitless "success."

The key point regarding sales-oriented objectives is this: larger sales volume, by itself, doesn't necessarily lead to higher profits.

Status quo pricing objectives

Managers satisfied with their current market share and profits sometimes adopt **status quo objectives**—that is, don't-rock-the-*pricing*-boat objectives. Managers may want to stabilize prices, or meet competition, or even avoid competition. This don't-rock-the-boat thinking is most common when the total market is not growing.

Or stress nonprice competition instead

A status quo pricing objective may be part of an aggressive overall marketing strategy focusing on **nonprice competition**—aggressive action on one or more of the Ps other than Price. For many years, fast-food chains such as McDonald's, Wendy's, and Burger King experienced very profitable growth by sticking to nonprice competition. However, when Taco Bell and others started to take away customers with price-cutting, the other chains also turned to price competition.[6]

Most firms set specific pricing policies—to reach objectives

Price policies usually lead to **administered prices**—that is, consciously set prices. In other words, instead of letting daily market forces decide their prices, most firms (including *all* of those in monopolistic competition) set their own prices.

If a firm doesn't sell directly to final customers, it usually wants to administer both the price it receives from intermediaries and the price final customers pay. After all, the price customers pay will ultimately affect its sales. But it is often difficult to administer prices throughout the channel. Other channel members may also wish to administer prices to achieve their own objectives.

Some firms don't even try to administer prices. They just meet competition—or worse, mark up their costs with little thought of demand. They act as if they have no choice in selecting a price policy.

Remember that Price has many dimensions. Managers *do* have many choices. They *should* administer their prices. And they should do it carefully because, ultimately, customers must be willing to pay these prices if the entire marketing mix is to succeed. In the rest of this chapter, we'll talk about policies a marketing manager must set in order to do an effective job of administering Price.[7]

Price flexibility policies

One of the first decisions a marketing manager has to make is about price flexibility. Should the firm use a one-price or a flexible-price policy?

One-price policy—the same price for everyone

A **one-price policy** means offering the same price to all customers who purchase products under essentially the same conditions and in the same quantities. The majority of Canadian firms use a one-price policy, mainly for administrative convenience and to maintain good will among customers.

A one-price policy makes pricing easier. But a marketing manager must be careful to avoid a rigid one-price policy. This can amount to broadcasting a price that competitors can then undercut—especially if the price is somewhat high. One reason for the growth of mass merchandisers is that conventional retailers rigidly applied traditional margins, and stuck to them.

Flexible-price policy—different prices for different customers

A **flexible-price policy** means offering the same product and quantities to different customers at different prices. When computers are used to implement flexible pricing, the decisions focus more on what type of customer will get a price break.

Pricing databases make flexible pricing easier

Various forms of flexible pricing are more common now that most prices are maintained in a computer database. Frequent changes are easier. You see this when grocery chains give frequent-shopper club members reduced prices on weekly specials. They simply change the database in the central office. The checkout scanner reads the code on the package, and then the computer assigns either the club price or the regular price depending on whether a club card has been scanned.

Another twist on this is more recent. Some marketing managers have set up relationships with Internet companies whose ads invite customers to "set your own price." For example, Priceline operates a Web site at www.priceline.com. Visitors to the Web site specify the desired schedule for an airline flight and what price they're willing to pay. Priceline electronically forwards the information to airlines, and if one accepts the offer the consumer is quickly notified. There is no auction or back-and-forth haggling. Priceline has a similar service for new cars and other products that is still in the planning stage.

It may appear that these marketing managers have given up on administering prices. Just the opposite is true: they are carefully administering a flexible price. Most airlines, for example, set a very high list price. Not many people pay it. Travellers who plan ahead or who accept nonpeak flights get a discount. Business travellers who want high-demand flights on short notice pay the higher prices. However, it doesn't make sense to stick to a high price and fly the plane half empty. So, the airline continuously adjusts what offered price from Priceline is high enough based on how many seats are left to fill. Other firms, especially service businesses, use this approach when they have excess capacity.

Salespeople can adjust prices to the situation

Flexible pricing is most common in the channels, in direct sales of business products, and at retail for expensive items and homogeneous shopping products. Retail shopkeepers in less-developed economies typically use flexible pricing. These situations usually involve personal selling, not mass selling. The advantage of flexible pricing is that the salesperson can make price adjustments, having considered the prices charged by competitors, the relationship with the customer, and the customer's bargaining ability. Flexible-price policies often specify a range in which the actual price charged must fall.[8]

Most auto dealers use flexible pricing. The producer suggests a list price, but the dealers bargain for what they can get. Their salespeople negotiate prices every day. Inexperienced consumers who are reluctant to bargain often pay hundreds of dollars more than the dealer is willing to accept. In contrast, Saturn dealers have earned high customer-satisfaction ratings by offering haggle-weary consumers a one-price policy.

Flexible pricing does have disadvantages. A customer who finds that others paid lower prices for the same marketing mix will be unhappy. This can cause real conflict in channels. Internet Insite 17–1 suggests that the Web will significantly contribute to price flexibility.

When buyers learn that negotiating can be in their interest, the time needed for bargaining increases. This can increase selling costs and reduce profits.

Too much price cutting erodes profits

Some sales reps let price cutting become a habit. This reduces the role of price as a competitive tool, and leads to a lower price level. It can also have a major effect on

Internet Insite 17-1

Flexi-pricing on the Web

When you shop at your local shopping mall, as a consumer you have no say in the price of the product. In theory, price is determined by the interaction between demand and supply. In practice, the supplier—or in this case the retailer in the mall—tends to dictate the price.

Does "one price fits all" make sense? Some argue that it does not. What if a product is in short supply? Shouldn't the supplier expect a higher price? Or consider a situation where a supplier has excess inventory. Rather than marking down the entire inventory by 50%, what if the supplier had the ability to solicit bids from prospective buyers and could then get the highest possible price?

On the Web, adjusting prices according to demand and supply is already in vogue. Practitioners of flexi-pricing, such as Sameer Dholarka of Trilogy Systems, argue that *sticker prices* or *list prices* are "basically irrelevant."[1] The Internet is a virtual marketspace that brings together suppliers and consumers from around the world. There is always someone looking to buy or sell something. Why not bring the sellers and buyers together and let the market determine the price?

This is precisely what is happening in "online auctions." There are now literally hundreds of online auction houses on the Internet. Online shoppers can bid on computer hardware, home electronics, clothing, collectibles and antiques, home appliances, used cars, tools and equipment, and so on. Some online auction houses deal in a wide range of product categories—for example, Surplus Auction (www.surplusauction.com), Onsale (www.onsale.com), and AuctionWare (www.auctionware.com). Others tend to specialize in products such as rare wines (www.auctionvine.com), sporting goods (www.sportingauction.com), and even old maps and medieval manuscripts (www.eworldauction.com). It is not just surplus or obsolete inventory that is sold on the Internet.

The Web has significantly lowered the costs of interaction. This has prompted Stuart I. Feldman, Director of IBM's Institute for Advanced Commerce, to say that "there's no pragmatic reason not to have competitive bidding on everything."[2] Early indications are that online auctions are a big hit.[3] Internet Shopping Network (www.isn.com) is auctioning about $1.5 million worth of goods each month, and this figure is expected to double within the year.[4] Onsale has had more than 4 million bids in three years, and has reported total sales of $115 million for 1997.[5] Experts predict that the popularity of online auctions will continue to grow. Consumers are lured to these sites by the low prices, variety, and convenience.

Auction sites provide descriptions of products and starting bid values. You can often inspect pictures of the product. Then bidders have to state the price they are willing to pay as well as provide credit card and other information. At some sites you have to open an account by filling out an online form. You can see the current bid values. The item is sold to the highest bidder by the bid closing time.

Some auction sites adopt a "reverse auction" format. For instance, at TravelBids, a traveller can state the desired trip, and travel agents then bid against each other for the business.[6] At Priceline (www.priceline.com) you can name your own price for airline tickets and let airlines pick the flights where they have empty seats.

The Web allows consumers to engage in comparison-shopping with great ease and at little cost. That means that even a strong brand name may not be able to demand the premium it once could. Does this mean all products will be reduced to commodities? "There's a commoditization at the top level of brands," according to Jay Walker, CEO of Priceline.[7]

Some big companies fear that prices will decline and that the value of their brands may be eroded. Clearly, branding strategy will have to be taken into consideration before a decision is made to engage in flexi-pricing. Airlines, which invest heavily in branding, also have a perishable commodity (i.e., airline seats). Selling the empty seats to the highest bidder makes sense. But in other product categories, flexi-pricing may dilute the brand image. Those who see flexi-pricing as the way of the future, including IBM's Feldman, argue that marketers have to be inventive in this price-competitive world.[8] For marketers, distinguishing products and maintaining consumer loyalty will not be easy. So far, it is consumers who seem to be the beneficiaries of flexi-pricing.

From the consumers' standpoint, how trustworthy are these auction sites? Doug Salot, who started Haggle Online, recommends against revealing credit card information on unfamiliar sites and suggests COD purchase.[9] Also, some intelligence gathering beforehand may reveal the manufacturer's price. Another piece of advice is to buy things where you know what to expect, where physical inspection is not required.

The Internet has changed the economics of haggling, and reduced the cost of transactions. In doing so, it has given the consumer greater power. But the good old saying, "let the buyer beware" still holds!

1. "Good Bye to Fixed Pricing?" *Business Week*, May 4, 1998, pp. 71–84.
2. Ibid.
3. Ibid.
4. Julia Pitta, "Competitive Shopping," *Forbes Magazine*, February 9, 1998 (www.forbes.com).
5. *Business Week*, *op. cit.*
6. "BN 6/19, Thrills, Prices Lure Many to Online Auctions: Money on the Net," *Bloomberg Online*, October 9, 1997 (www.bloomberg.com)
7. *Business Week op. cit*
8. Ibid.
9. *Bloomberg Online*, *Op. cit.*

Source: This is one of a series of Internet Insites prepared in April 1998 by Dr. Ramesh Venkat of Saint Mary's University for *Basic Marketing*, Ninth Canadian Edition.

profits. A small price cut may not seem like much; but keep in mind that all of the revenue that is lost is foregone profit. Say that a producer usually earns profits equal to 15 percent of sales; if that firm's salespeople cut prices by an average of about 5 percent, profits will drop by one-third!

Price level policies—over the product life cycle

When marketing managers administer prices—as most do—they must consciously set a price level policy. As they enter the market, they have to set introductory prices, which may have long-run effects. They must consider where in the life cycle their product is, and how fast it's moving. And they must decide if their prices should be above, below, or somewhere in between relative to the market.

Let's look for a moment at a new product in the market introduction stage of its product life cycle. The price level decision should focus first on the nature of market demand. There are few (or no) direct substitute marketing mixes. And considering the demand curve for this product, a high price may lead to higher profit from each sale, but also to fewer units sold. A lower price might appeal to more potential customers. With this in mind, should the firm set a high or low price?

Skim pricing—feeling out demand with a high price

A **skimming price policy** tries to sell the top (skim the cream) of a market—the top of the demand curve—at a high price before aiming at more price-sensitive customers. A skimming policy is more attractive if demand is quite inelastic—at least at the upper price ranges.

Skimming may maximize profits in the market introduction stage for an innovation, especially if there is little competition. Competitor analysis may help clarify whether barriers will prevent or discourage competitors from entering.

Price moves down the demand curve

A skimming policy usually involves a slow reduction in price over time (see Exhibit 17–5). Note that as price is reduced, new target markets are probably being sought. So as the price level steps down the demand curve, new Place, Product, and Promotion policies may be needed as well.

When Hewlett-Packard (HP) introduced its laser printer for personal computers, it initially set a high price—around $4,000. HP had a good headstart on competitors, and no close substitute was available. HP sold the high-priced printers mainly to computer professionals and to business users with serious desktop publishing needs, and distributed them through a select group of authorized HP computer dealers whose salespeople could explain the printer. When other firms entered the market

Ethical Dimensions

Criticisms of Skimming

Some critics argue that for new products that have important social consequences, firms should not try to maximize profits by using a skimming policy. A patent-protected, life-saving drug, or a genetic technique that increases crop yields, is likely to have an inelastic demand curve. Yet many of those who need the product may not have the money to buy it. This is a serious concern. However, it's also a serious problem if firms don't have any incentive to take the risks required to develop breakthroughs in the first place.[9]

Exhibit 17-5 Alternative Introductory Pricing Policies

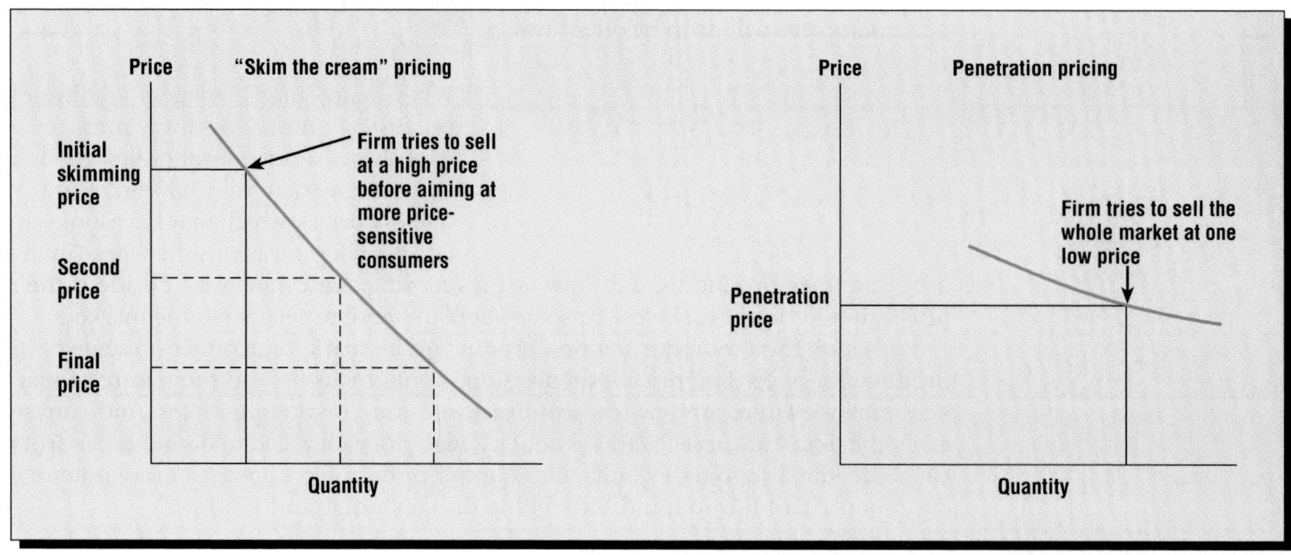

with similar printers, HP added features and lowered its price. It also did more advertising and added mail-order intermediaries to reach new target markets. Then, just as competitors were entering the market to go after budget-oriented buyers, HP introduced a new model at a lower price and added office-supply warehouse stores, like Office Depot, to the distribution channel. This is very typical of skimming, which involves dropping prices through a series of marketing strategy changes over the course of the product life cycle.

Penetration pricing—get volume at a low price

A **penetration pricing policy** tries to sell the whole market at one low price. Such an approach may be wise when the élite market—those willing to pay a high price—is small. This is the case when the entire demand curve is fairly elastic (see Exhibit 17–5).

A penetration policy is even more attractive when selling larger quantities results in lower costs because of economies of scale. Penetration pricing may be wise if the firm expects strong competition very soon after introduction. It discourages competitors from entering the market. For example, when personal computers became popular, Borland International came out with a complete programming language—including a textbook—for under $50. By the time competitors finally matched Borland's price, its large base of customers weren't interested in switching.

Introductory price dealing—temporary price cuts

Price cuts do attract customers. Therefore, marketers often use **introductory price dealing**—temporary price cuts—to speed new products into a market. However, don't confuse these *temporary* price cuts with low penetration prices. The plan here is to raise prices as soon as the introductory offer is over. Established competitors often choose not to meet introductory price dealing, as long as the introductory period is not too long or too successful.

Meeting competition may be necessary

Regardless of their introductory pricing policy, most firms face competition sooner or later in the product life cycle. When that happens, how high or low a price is may be relative not only to the market's demand curve but also to the prices charged by competitors.

Meeting competitors' prices may also be the practical choice in mature markets that are moving toward pure competition. Here, firms typically face downward pressure on both prices and profits. Profit margins are already thin—and for many firms they would disappear or turn into losses at a lower price. A higher price would simply prompt competitors to promote their price advantage.

Similarly, there is little choice in oligopoly situations. Pricing at the market—that is, meeting competition—may be the only sensible policy. Raising prices might lead to a large loss in sales, unless competitors adopt the higher price, too. And cutting prices would probably lead to similar reductions by competitors, thereby decreasing revenue for the industry and probably for each firm. The major North American airlines face these problems regularly.

To avoid these problems, each oligopolist may choose a status quo pricing objective and set its price at the competitive level. Some critics call this pricing behaviour conscious parallel action, implying it is unethical and the same as intentional conspiracy among firms. As a practical matter, however, that criticism seems overly harsh. It isn't sensible for firms to ignore their competitors.

There are alternatives in monopolistic competition

In monopolistic competition, there are more pricing options. At one extreme, some firms are clearly above-the-market—they may even brag about it. Tiffany's is well known as one of the most expensive jewellery stores in the world. Other firms emphasize below-the-market prices in their marketing mixes. Prices offered by discounters and mass merchandisers, such as Wal-Mart, illustrate this approach. Such firms may even promote their pricing policy with catchy slogans like "guaranteed lowest prices" or "we'll beat any advertised price."

Above or below which market?

Do these various strategies promote prices that are above or below the market—or do they actually result in different prices for different target markets or different marketing mixes? In setting price level policies, it is important to define clearly the *relevant target market* and *competitors* when making price comparisons.

Consider Wal-Mart prices again from this view. Wal-Mart may have lower camera prices than conventional camera retailers, but it offers less help in the store, and less selection, and it won't take old cameras in trade. Wal-Mart may have a strong appeal for budget-oriented shoppers who compare prices among different mass merchandisers. A specialty camera store, because it appeals to different customers, may not be a direct competitor! Thus, it may be better to think of Wal-Mart's price as part of a different marketing mix for a different target market—not as a below-the-market price.

It follows that a camera producer might develop different strategies for the Wal-Mart channel and the specialty store channel. In particular, the producer might offer the specialty store one or more models that are not available to Wal-Mart, to ensure that customers don't view the two stores as direct competitors with price the only difference.

Price level policies for the channel

When a product is sold to channel members instead of final consumers, the price should be set so that the channel members can cover costs and make a profit. For example, a producer of a slightly better product might set a price level that is low relative to competitors when selling to retailers, while suggesting an above-the-market retail price. This will encourage retailers to carry the product—and to emphasize it in their marketing mix—because it yields higher profits.

The price of money may affect the price level

We've been talking about the price level of a firm's product. But a nation's money also has a price level—what it is worth in some other currency. For example, in mid-May of 1998, 1 Canadian dollar was worth .812 German marks. In other words, the exchange rate for the German mark against the Canadian dollar was .812. Internet Illustration 17–1 highlights one of the online services that provides up-to-the-minute exchange rate information. Exchange rates change over time, and sometimes the changes are significant. For example, during 1993, a U.S. dollar was worth, on average, 1.65 German marks; in 1985, the average was 2.94 German marks.

Internet Illustration 17–1 The Universal Currency Converter™ (www.xe.net/currency/)

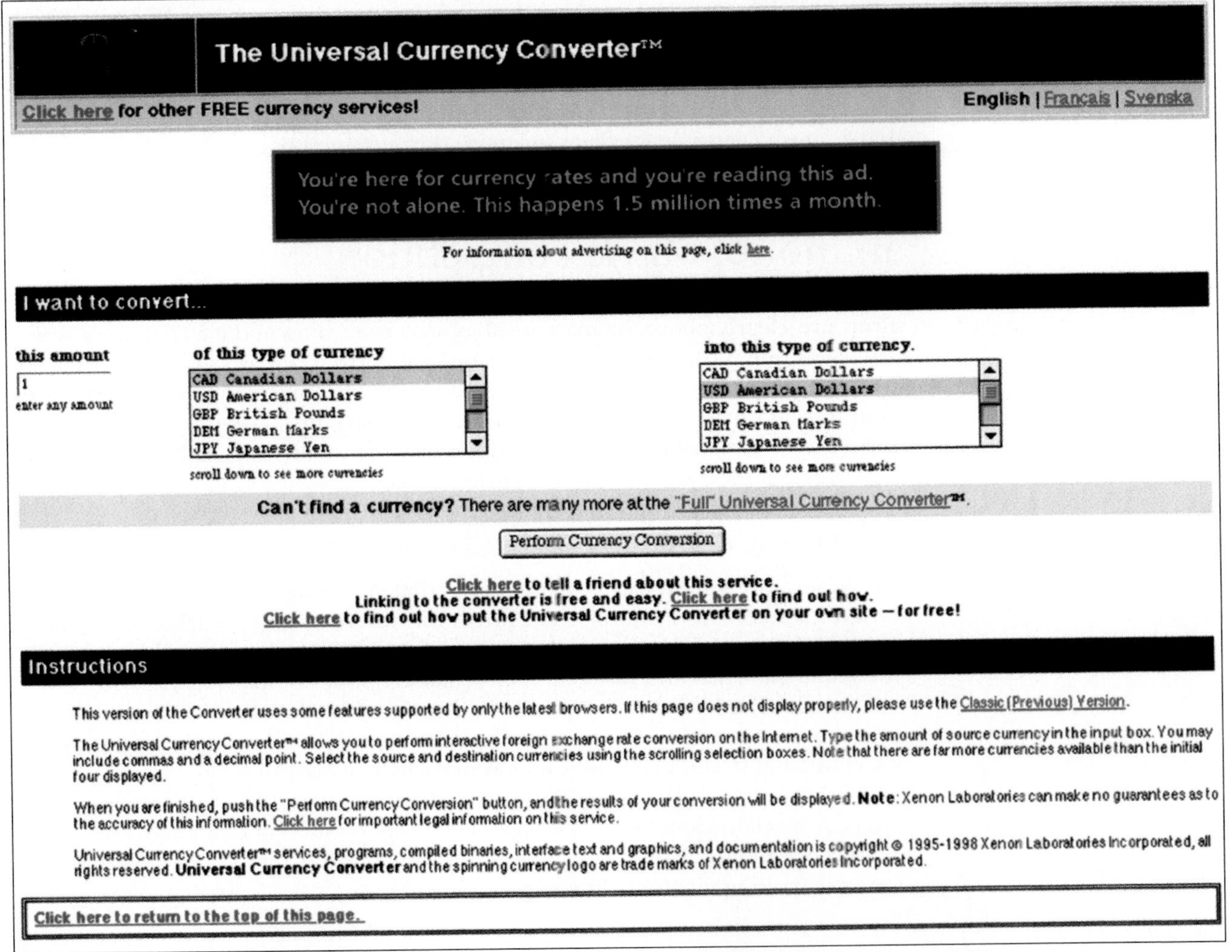

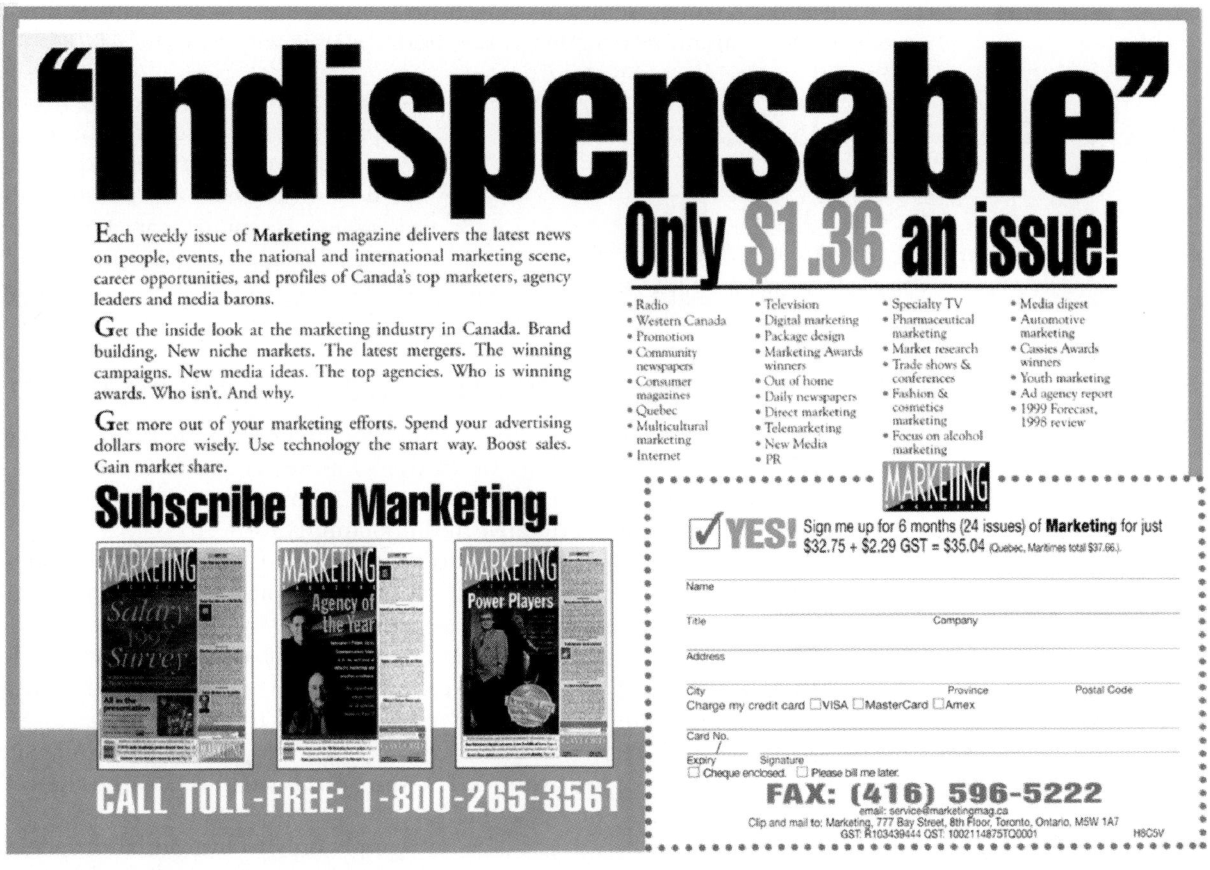

Magazine subscription rates offer quantity discounts.

Exchange rate changes can have a significant impact on the results of pricing decisions. As the following example shows, this can be true even for a small firm that sells only in its own local market.

In 1993, the marketing manager for ColorFast—a small firm that mixes and sells special dyes used by textile producers—set a meeting-competition wholesale price at about US$100 for a barrel of dye. The wholesalers who distributed her dyes also carried a competing product produced by a German firm. Its wholesale price was also US$100, which meant that the German firm got about DM165 (US$100 multiplied times DM1.65 per dollar) per barrel. However, when the exchange rate for the mark against the US dollar fell from DM1.65 to DM1.38, the German producer got 27 fewer marks for each US$100 barrel of dye (DM165 − DM138 = DM27).

Because Colorfast's marketing manager was selling dye only to local customers, she didn't pay any attention to the drop in the exchange rate—at first. However, she did pay attention when the German producer decided to raise its wholesale price to US$115 a barrel. At the US$115 price, the German firm got about DM159 per barrel (US$115 × DM1.38 per dollar)—less than it was getting before the exchange rate change. Colorfast's sales increased substantially—at the German competitor's expense—because of the lower Colorfast price. Colorfast's marketing manager concluded that it would probably take a while for the German firm to lower its price, even if the exchange rate went up again. So she decided that she could safely raise her price level by 10 percent—up to US$110—and still have a price advantage over the German supplier.[10]

Most price structures are built around list prices

Most price structures are built around a base price schedule or price list. **Basic list prices** are the prices final customers or users are normally asked to pay for products. In this book, unless noted otherwise, list price refers to basic list price.

In the next chapter, we discuss how firms set these list prices. For now, however, we'll consider variations from list price—and why they are made.

Discount policies—reductions from list prices

Discounts are reductions from list price given by a seller to buyers, who either give up some marketing function or provide the function themselves. Discounts can be useful in strategic market planning. In the following discussion, think about what function the buyers are giving up—or providing—when they get each of these discounts.

Quantity discounts encourage volume buying

Quantity discounts are discounts offered to encourage customers to buy in larger amounts. This lets a seller get more of a buyer's business, or shifts some of the storing function to the buyer, or reduces shipping and selling costs—or all of these. Such discounts are of two kinds: cumulative and noncumulative.

Cumulative quantity discounts apply to purchases over a given period, such as a year. The discount usually increases as the amount purchased increases. Cumulative discounts are intended to encourage *repeat* buying by a single customer by reducing the customer's cost for additional purchases. This is a way to develop closer, ongoing relationships with customers. For example, Beaver Lumber might give a cumulative quantity discount to a building contractor who is not able to buy all of the needed materials at once. Beaver Lumber wants to reward the contractor's patronage and discourage shopping around. The discount is small relative to the cost of constantly trying to attract new customers.

Noncumulative quantity discounts apply only to individual orders. Such discounts encourage larger orders but do not tie a buyer to the seller after that one purchase. Revy Home Centres may sell insulation products made by several competing producers. Owens/Corning might try to encourage Revy to stock larger quantities of its insulation products by offering a noncumulative quantity discount.

Cargill uses a seasonal discount to encourage buyers to stock products earlier than present demand requires.

While quantity discounts are usually given as price cuts, sometimes they are given as free or bonus products. Airline frequent flier programs use this approach.

Quantity discounts can be a very useful tool for the marketing manager. Some customers are eager to get them. But marketing managers must use quantity discounts carefully. In business markets, to avoid price discrimination, they must offer such discounts to all customers on equal terms.

Noncumulative discounts sometimes produce unexpected results. If the discount is too big, wholesalers or retailers may buy more than they can possibly sell to their own customers, to get the low price. Then they sell the excess at a low price to whoever will buy it, as long as the buyer doesn't compete in the same market area. These "grey market" channels often take customers away from regular channel members, perhaps with a retail price even lower than what most channel members pay. To avoid these problems, a marketing manager must consider the effect of discounts on the whole strategy—not just the effect on sales to a given intermediary.

Seasonal discounts—buy sooner

Seasonal discounts are discounts offered to encourage buyers to buy earlier than present demand requires. If used by producers, this discount tends to shift the storing function farther along in the channel. It also tends to even out sales over the year. For example, the manufacturer of garden tillers offers wholesalers a lower price on the tillers if they buy in the fall, when sales are slow. The wholesalers can then offer a seasonal discount to retailers, who may try to sell the tillers during a special fall sale.

Service firms that face irregular demand or capacity constraints often use seasonal discounts. For example, some telephone companies offer a discount for nighttime calls when the load of business calls is low. Some tourist attractions, such as ski resorts, offer lower weekday rates when attendance would otherwise be down.

Payment terms and cash discounts

Most sales to businesses are made on credit. The seller sends a bill (invoice), and the buyer's accounting department processes it for payment. Some firms depend on their suppliers for temporary working capital (credit). It is very important for both sides to state clearly the terms of payment—including the availability of cash discounts—and to understand the commonly used payment terms.

Net means that payment for the face value of the invoice is due immediately. These terms are sometimes changed to net 10 or net 30—which means that payment is due within 10 or 30 days of the date on the invoice.

Cash discounts are reductions in price to encourage buyers to pay their bills quickly. The terms for a cash discount usually modify the net terms.

2/10, net 30 means the buyer can take a 2 percent discount off the face value of the invoice if the invoice is paid within 10 days. Otherwise, the full face value is due within 30 days. And it usually is stated or understood that an interest charge will be added after the 30-day free-credit period.

Why cash discounts are given—and evaluated

Smart buyers carefully evaluate cash discounts. A discount of 2/10, net 30 may not look like much at first. But [illegible] buyer earns a 2 percent discount for paying the invoice just 20 days sooner than it should be paid anyway. By not taking the discount, the company, in effect, is borrowing at an annual rate of 36 percent. That is, assuming a 360-day year and dividing by 20 days, there are 18 periods during which the company could earn 2 percent—and 18 times 2 equals 36 percent a year.

Consumers say "charge it"

Credit sales are also important to retailers. Most retailers use credit card services, such as Visa or MasterCard, and pay a percentage of the revenue from each credit sale for this service. For this reason, some retailers offer discounts to consumers who pay cash.

Many consumers like the convenience of credit card buying. But some critics argue that the cards make it too easy for consumers to buy things they really can't afford. Further, because of high interest charges, credit card buying can increase the total costs to consumers.[11]

Trade discounts to channel members

A **trade (functional) discount** is a list price reduction given to channel members for the job they are going to do.

For example, a manufacturer might allow retailers a 30 percent trade discount from the suggested retail list price to cover the cost of the retailing function and their profit. Similarly, the manufacturer might allow wholesalers a *chain* discount of 30 percent and 10 percent off the suggested retail price. Here, the wholesalers would be expected to pass the 30 percent discount on to retailers.

Note that a violation of the price discrimination provisions of Canada's Competition Act can occur, for example, if a wholesaler is given a larger discount than a retailer purchasing the same qualtity and quantity of merchandise, if the wholesaler and retailer are competitors and if the larger discount is granted to the wholesaler as part of a practice of discrimination.[12]

Special sales reduce list prices—temporarily

A **sale price** is a temporary discount from the list price. Sale price discounts encourage immediate buying. In other words, to get the sale price, customers give up the convenience of buying when they want to buy, and instead buy when the seller wants to sell.

Special sales provide a marketing manager with a quick way to respond to changing market conditions, without changing the basic marketing strategy. For example, a retailer might use a sale to help clear extra inventory. Or a producer might offer an intermediary a special deal that makes it more profitable for the intermediary to push the product.

Sale prices and deals occur frequently. At first it may seem that consumers benefit from them. But prices that change constantly may confuse customers and increase selling costs.

To avoid these problems, some firms that sell consumer convenience products offer **everyday low pricing**—that is, they set a low list price instead of relying on frequent discounts or allowances from a high list price. Zellers has an everyday low pricing policy, and many supermarkets use this approach. Some producers, including P&G, use it for some product lines.

Sale prices should be used carefully, consistent with well-thought-out pricing objectives and policies. A marketing manager who constantly uses temporary sales to adjust the price level probably has not done a good job of setting the normal price.[13]

Allowance policies—off list prices

Allowances, like discounts, are given to final consumers, customers, or channel members for doing something or accepting less of something.

Advertising allowances—something for something

Advertising allowances are price reductions given to firms in the channel to encourage them to advertise or otherwise promote the supplier's products locally. For example, General Electric gave an allowance (1.5 percent of sales) to its wholesalers of housewares and radios. They, in turn, were expected to spend the allowance on local advertising.

Stocking allowances—get attention and shelf space

Stocking allowances—sometimes called slotting allowances—are given to an intermediary to get shelf space ("slots") for a product. For example, a producer might offer a retailer cash or free merchandise to stock a new item. Stocking allowances are a fairly recent development. So far, they're used mainly to prompt supermarket chains to handle new products. Supermarkets don't have enough slots on their shelves to handle all of the available new products. They're more willing to give space to a new product if the supplier will offset their handling costs and risk.

PMs—push for cash

Push money (or prize money) allowances—sometimes called PMs or spiffs—are given to retailers by manufacturers or wholesalers to pass on to the retailers' salesclerks for aggressively selling certain items. PM allowances are used for

Ethical Dimensions

Stocking Allowances

There is much controversy about stocking allowances. Critics say that retailer demands for big stocking allowances slow new product introductions, and make it hard for small producers to compete. Some producers feel that retailers' demands are unethical—a form of extortion. Retailers respond by pointing out that the fees protect them from producers that simply want to push more and more me-too products onto their shelves. Perhaps the best way for a producer to cope with the problem is to develop new products that offer consumers a real comparative advantage. Then it will benefit everyone in the channel—including retailers—to get the products to the target market.[14]

new items, slower-moving items, or higher-margin items. They are often used for pushing furniture, clothing, consumer electronics, and cosmetics. A salesclerk, for example, might earn an additional $5 for each item sold.

Bring in the old, ring up the new—with trade-ins

A **trade-in allowance** is a price reduction given for used products when similar new products are bought.

Trade-ins give the marketing manager an easy way to lower the effective price without reducing list price. Proper handling of trade-ins is important when selling durable products.

Some customers get extra somethings

Many producers and retailers offer discounts (or free items) through coupons distributed in packages, mailings, or print ads, or at the store. By presenting a coupon to a retailer, the consumer is given a discount off list price. This is especially common in the consumer packaged goods business, but the use of price-off coupons is growing in other lines of business as well.

Retailers are willing to redeem producers' coupons because it increases their sales, and because they usually are paid for the trouble of handling the coupons. For example, a retailer who redeems a 50 cents off coupon might be repaid 75 cents. In effect, the coupon increases the functional discount and makes it more attractive to sell the couponed product.

Couponing is so common that firms have been set up to help repay retailers for redeeming manufacturers' coupons. The total dollar amounts involved are so large that crime has become a big problem. Some dishonest retailers have gone to jail for collecting on coupons they redeemed without requiring customers to buy the products.

Cash rebates when you buy

Some producers offer **rebates**—refunds paid to consumers after a purchase. Rebates are sometimes very large. Some automakers offer rebates of $500 to $2,500 to promote sales of slow-moving models. Rebates are also used on lower-price items, ranging from Duracell batteries to Paul Masson wines.

Rebates give the producer a way to be certain that final consumers actually get the price reduction. If the rebate amount were simply taken off the price charged to intermediaries, they might not pass the savings along to consumers. Also, many consumers buy because the price looks lower with the rebate—but then they don't request the refund.[15]

List price may depend on geographic pricing policies

Retail list prices sometimes include free delivery. Or free delivery may be offered to some customers as an aid to closing the sale. But deciding who pays the freight charge is more important on sales to business customers than on sales to final consumers because more money is involved. Usually purchase orders specify place, time, method of delivery, freight costs, insurance, handling, and other charges. There are many possible variations for an imaginative marketing manager, and some specialized terms have developed.

F.O.B. pricing is easy

A commonly used transportation term is **F.O.B.**, which means free on board some vehicle at some place. Typically, F.O.B. pricing names a place—often the location of the seller's factory or warehouse, as in F.O.B. Taiwan or F.O.B. mill. This means that the seller pays the cost of loading the products onto some vehicle, then title to the products passes to the buyer. The buyer pays the freight and takes responsibility for damage in transit.

If a firm wants to pay the freight for the convenience of customers, it can use F.O.B. delivered or F.O.B. buyer's factory. Here, title does not pass until the products are delivered. If the seller wants title to pass immediately but is willing to prepay freight (and then include it in the invoice), F.O.B. seller's factory–freight prepaid can be used.

F.O.B. shipping point pricing simplifies the seller's pricing, but may also narrow the market. Since the delivered cost varies with the buyer's location, a distant customer must pay more and may buy from closer suppliers.

Zone pricing smooths delivered prices

Zone pricing means making an average freight charge to all buyers within specific geographic areas. The seller pays the actual freight charges and bills each customer for an average charge. For example, a company in Canada might divide the United States into seven zones, and then bill all customers in the same zone the same amount for freight even though actual shipping costs varied.

Uniform delivered pricing—one price to all

Uniform delivered pricing means making an average freight charge to all buyers. It is a kind of zone pricing—an entire country may be considered as one zone—that includes the average cost of delivery in the price. Uniform delivered pricing is most often used when (1) transportation costs are relatively low and (2) the seller wishes to sell in all geographic areas at one price—perhaps a nationally advertised price.

Freight-absorption pricing

When all firms in an industry use F.O.B. shipping point pricing, a firm usually competes well near its shipping point but not farther away. As sales reps look for business farther away, delivered prices rise and the firm finds itself priced out of the market.

This problem can be reduced with **freight absorption pricing**, which involves absorbing the freight cost so that a firm's delivered price meets the nearest competitor's. This amounts to cutting list price to appeal to new market segments.

With freight absorption pricing, the only limit on the size of a firm's territory is the amount of freight cost it is willing to absorb. These absorbed costs cut net return on each sale—but the new business may raise total profit. Some small firms look at international markets this way; they just figure that any profit from export sales is a bonus.

Pricing policies combine to impact customer value

We've discussed the details of pricing policies separately so far to emphasize that a manager should make *intentional* decisions in each of the areas of pricing policy. Overlooking any of them can be serious because ultimately they all combine to impact customer value and whether the firm has a competitive advantage.

Ever since Chapter 1, we've emphasized that customer value is based on the benefits that a customer sees in a firm's marketing mix and all of the costs. This value is relative to competitors' ways of meeting a need. Ideally, a target customer will be impressed that the specific strategy decisions that a marketing manager makes with respect to Product, Place, and Promotion offer a benefit. Perhaps if the decisions are not on target a customer will view them as a cost. For example, a consumer might view a producer's decision to use exclusive distribution as a negative if a product is harder to find, or if its "exclusive" image is a turn-off to friends. Even so, from the customer's view, Price is usually the main contributor to the cost part of the value equation.

That means that when we talk about Price we are really talking about the whole set of price policies that define the real price level. It's important to keep firmly in mind that superior value isn't just based on having a lower price than some competitor, but rather on the whole marketing mix.

Value pricing leads to superior customer value

Smart marketers look for the combination of Price decisions that results in value pricing. **Value pricing** means setting a fair price level for a marketing mix that really gives the target market superior customer value.

Value pricing doesn't necessarily mean cheap if cheap means bare-bones, or low-grade. It doesn't mean high prestige either if the prestige is not accompanied by the right quality goods and services. Rather the focus is on the customer's requirements—and how the whole marketing mix meets those needs.

Toyota is a good example of a firm that has been effective with value pricing. It has different marketing mixes for different target markets. But from the low-price Tercel to the $40,000 Avalon, the Japanese automaker consistently offers better quality and lower prices than its competitors. Marketing Demo 17–1 shows that Toyota is considering a move away from traditional car dealer bargaining to the one-price policy that Saturn first introduced. Among discount retailers, Wal-Mart is a value pricing leader. Its motto, "the low price on the brands you trust," says it all.

These companies deliver on their promises. They try to give the consumer pleasant surprises—like an unexpected service—because it increases value and builds customer loyalty. They return the price if the customer isn't completely satisfied. They avoid unrealistic price levels—prices that are high only because consumers already know the brand name. They build relationships so that customers will come back time and again.

Value pricing fits with market-oriented strategic planning

There are times when the marketing manager's hands are tied and there is little way to differentiate the marketing mix. However, most marketing managers do have choices—many choices—because they can vary strategy decisions with respect to all of the marketing mix variables—not just Price—to offer target customers superior value. And when a marketer's hands are really tied, it's time to look for new opportunities that offer more promise.

So, when you stop to think about it, value pricing is simply the best pricing approach for the type of market-oriented strategic planning we've been discussing throughout this whole text. To build profits and customer satisfaction, the whole marketing mix— including the price level—must meet target customers' needs and offer superior value.[16]

Marketing Demo 17-1

When the Action Gets Hot on the Lot

Vancouver businessman Peter Wong recently went shopping for a new Toyota Corolla. He walked into Downtown Toyota and asked salesman Adam Sumel, who had sold him a car in the past, if he could beat the price quoted by another dealer.

Mr. Sumel knocked $120 off that price of about $16,000. Is that all? Mr. Wong said, "Take off your glasses, look me in the eye and tell me it's the best you can do." The price came down another $60, not "a very, very good deal," Mr. Wong said later, but probably better than anywhere else.

He bought—and he's not alone.

"Whatever the price, people want to pay less," said Kevin Smith, whose family owns the dealership. "It's a nerve-racking thing. You have to do a lot of work to get the customer to the place where we can do business."

And now Toyota Canada Inc. is thinking of changing the way its business is done. Last week the company made a surprise announcement: It may restructure its dealer network, and, following the lead of General Motors' Saturn Corp, go to haggle-free sales by next year.

As things stand, a good salesman at Downtown Toyota sells about 100 vehicles a year; a top performer, with extra skill, hard work and a little luck, may top that by 30 or so. Their home turf is a showroom crammed with shiny specimens of Toyota technology, ranging from a sporty silver Celica (sticker price $38,663) and an outdoorsy 4-wheel-drive RAV4 ($29,851) to a functional white Tercel ($15,665).

High-pressure tactics are not obvious. "I want you to be happy," one salesman assures an elderly couple, while another tells a customer that "we want to show we appreciate your business."

According to Mr. Smith, good salesmen are born, and their instincts are developed with on-the-job experience. Those with the best skills can "read people," and know how to make a customer feel comfortable. And finally, they know how to close a deal.

Here is how Mr. Sumel says he does his job. When people walk into the showroom, he asks himself: "What do I have to do to make them my customers?" Which is a riddle he has solved about 1,400 times since he started selling cars in 1988.

As he chats up customers, he begins trying to figure out which vehicle is right for them, which one best fits their need. In the process, he tries to assess whether they are comfortable with him.

"It's not always just a matter of price," he said after selling the Corolla to Mr. Wong. "I think it's just as important for the customer to like the sales person. The customer has to trust me and feel that I'm treating him in the way he wants to be treated."

There is one question he always asks just before both sides sharpen their pencils: "If we can agree on a price, is there anything to stop the deal?" He'd rather not haggle for nothing. "Before I give a final price, I want to feel confident about the chances of closing."

In response to this commitment, he is prepared to hear out a customer on such questions as colour, the price of a trade-in, financing, an insurance payout or the need to have a spouse's approval.

He also realizes that many people do not hesitate to tell little white lies in an attempt to save money. They may try to mislead him about a price quoted by another dealer, the trade-in value of their current car or the size of their bank balance. On occasion, some go even further. They make a deposit on a car, drive straight to another dealer and negotiate a better price. Then they cancel the cheque on the first deal and try to walk away from it.

In most cases, though, once people decide on a car they are ready to work out a deal in good faith—either by asking Mr. Sumel to meet a certain price or by asking straight out what is the best he can do for them.

Some customers are happy if he can give them a discount below the list price. That's all they want. Others want to feel they have done the best they could to beat down the price; otherwise "they probably would feel like they were paying too much. Everyone wants a deal."

How much room a salesman has to manoeuvre depends on the price of the car. The markup on entry-level Corollas is around 8 per cent, with the profit margin rising on more expensive vehicles.

Mr. Sumel, who started out washing cars at Downtown Toyota in 1985, carries a pager and encourages customers to call him if they have problems with their cars. He clearly enjoys his job, and that includes the way he is paid: a commission based on the price he can fetch. "If I was on a salary, I would probably not give the same service—no incentive."

Nevertheless, as well as introducing no-dicker stickers, Toyota is thinking of eliminating commissions and relying on "personal account managers" to handle sales, arrange financing and maintain after-sales contact with customers.

Kevin Smith's father, Erwen Smith, has run Downtown Toyota for 27 years and has sold cars in Greater Vancouver for 45. He says he'd welcome a shift to full retail pricing; his balance sheet over the past five years shows a profit of less than 2 per cent.

"We sell below retail because customers demand it. If I thought I could get full retail, it would make my job a lot easier."

On the other hand, he doesn't think his sales staff is alone in preferring the current system. Like Mr. Sumel, he is certain that the customers like to bargain.

Source: Abridged from Robert Matas, "When the Action Gets Hot on the Lot," *The Globe and Mail*, September 22, 1997, A2. Reprinted with permission from *The Globe and Mail*.

Legal issues affecting pricing policies[17]

The Competition Act provides a framework for business conduct in Canada and encourages competition. Among its purposes are to ensure that small and medium sized enterprises have an equitable opportunity to participate in the Canadian economy and to provide consumers with competitive prices and product choices. Some pricing policies are subject to the rules of the Competition Act, and you should be aware of these rules.

Price fixing is illegal—you can go to jail!

Except in the case of prices charged in regulated industries, the prices firms charge in Canada don't need government approval. Businesses can charge what they want—even outrageously high prices—provided these prices are not fixed with competitors. Difficulties with pricing, and violations of the Competition Act, usually occur when competing marketing mixes are quite similar. When the success of an entire marketing strategy depends on price, there's pressure (and temptation) to make agreements (conspire) with competitors. **Price fixing**—competitors getting together to raise, lower, or stabilize prices—is relatively easy. *But it is also completely illegal.* To discourage price fixing, the Competition Act provides that both companies and individual managers can be held responsible. Companies can be fined penalties, and individual managers can be fined penalties, sentenced to jail, or both.

Bid-rigging, which is a form of price fixing, is also illegal in Canada. See Marketing Demo 17–2, which describes how the provisions of the Competition Act applied in a bid-rigging case.

Price discrimination

We have already discussed how trade or functional discounts can contravene the price discrimination provisions of the Competition Act. These provisions have to be considered whenever price differentials, such as discounts, rebates, allowances, price concessions, or other advantages, occur. But price discrimination on the basis of the quantities of goods purchased is legal in Canada. For example, a manufacturer can legally use a quantity discount structure that favours large customers.

Promotional allowances—that is, price reductions granted by sellers as payment for promotional services performed by buyers—are also subject to the price discrimination provisions of the Competition Act. Section 51 of the Act requires that promotional allowances be granted proportionately to all competing customers. For example, a small customer purchasing half as much as a larger competitor must receive a promotional allowance equal to half of what was offered to the larger firm. The term "allowance" is defined by section 51(1) to mean "any discount, rebate, price concession or other advantage that is or purports to be offered or granted for advertising or display purposes and is collateral to a sale or sales of products [goods and services] but is not applied directly to the selling price. . . ."

Predatory pricing

To give you an example of predatory pricing, imagine that a dominant firm charges low prices over a long enough period of time so as to drive a competitor from the market, or to deter others from entering the market, or both, and then the dominant firm raises its prices to recoup its losses. Section 50(1)(c) of the Competition Act provides:

> Every one engaged in a business who . . . engages in a policy of selling products [goods and services] at prices unreasonably low, having the effect or tendency of substantially lessening competition or eliminating a competitor, or designed to have such effect, is guilty of an indictable offence and is liable to imprisonment for two years.

Marketing Demo 17-2

Electrical Contractors Plead Guilty to Bid-rigging and Pay Fines of $2.55 Million

The following is a News Release issued by the Competition Bureau on December 19, 1997.

Konrad von Finckenstein, Q.C., Director of Investigation and Research under the *Competition Act,* announced today that four Toronto electrical contractors, 948099 Ontario Inc. (carrying on business as Plan Electric Co.), Ainsworth Inc., Guild Electric Limited, and The State Group Limited, pled guilty in the General Division of the Ontario Court, in Toronto, to bid-rigging, contrary to section 47 of the Act, and must pay fines totaling $2.55 million.

The charges relate to the period from 1988 to 1993 and are the result of an extensive criminal investigation conducted by the Competition Bureau into a scheme designed to create the illusion of competitive pricing.

Although the majority of the tenders which the companies were convicted of rigging affected electrical contracts for the renovation of commercial space, including certain leasehold improvements at Pearson Airport's Terminal III, some of the companies were also convicted of rigging tenders related to major new construction projects, including the SkyDome Hotel and BCE Place—Phase 2.

"Businesses go to great lengths to ensure they are obtaining the best possible price by using a tendering system," Mr. von Finckenstein stated. "Substantial penalties are necessary to deter those who seek to corrupt the competitive tendering process through illegal agreements."

Plan was convicted on 13 counts and was fined $750,000. Ainsworth was convicted on seven counts and was fined $750,000, Guild was convicted on six counts and was fined $300,000, and State was convicted on 13 counts and was fined $750,000. These parties have received favourable treatment for entering early guilty pleas. Ainsworth and Plan also received additional consideration as a result of having cooperated with the investigation.

The four companies have each taken steps to institute internal compliance programs designed to ensure compliance with the Act.

The Bureau's investigation into allegations of bid-rigging by other electrical contractors, and related conduct by a general contractor, in the Metropolitan Toronto area continues. The Director anticipates making recommendations concerning these other parties to the Attorney General of Canada in the near future.

The Competition Bureau offers an education program to assist companies that utilize the tendering process to detect and prevent bid-rigging, and also to educate bidders to ensure they comply with the Act. In addition, the Bureau has a program by which anyone, including those wishing to remain anonymous, can bring forward information concerning possible violations of the Act.

Resale price maintenance

Some manufacturers would like to control the resale prices that retailers charge for their products. However, resale price maintenance has been illegal in Canada since 1951. Section 50 of the Competition Act prohibits a manufacturer or supplier from requiring or inducing a retailer to sell a product [goods and services] at a particular price or not below a particular price. A "suggested retail price" is allowed under the rules of section 50 only if it is made clear to the retailer that the retailer can sell below the suggested price and that the retailer will not be discriminated against in any way if the product [goods and services] is sold at a lower price. The resale price maintenance provisions of the Competition Act give retailers the freedom to sell goods and services at whatever prices the retailers deem appropriate.

Questions and Problems

1. Identify the strategy decisions a marketing manager must make in the Price area. Illustrate your answer for a local retailer.
2. How should the acceptance of a profit-oriented, a sales-oriented, or a status quo–oriented pricing objective affect the development of a company's marketing strategy? Illustrate for each.
3. Distinguish between one-price and flexible-price policies. Which is most appropriate for a hardware store? Why?
4. How would differences in exchange rates between different countries affect a firm's decisions concerning the use of flexible-price policies in different foreign markets?
5. Cite two examples of continuously selling above the market price. Describe the situations.
6. Explain the types of competitive situations that might lead to a meeting-competition pricing policy.
7. What pricing objective(s) is a skimming pricing policy most likely implementing? Is the same true for a penetration pricing policy? Which policy is probably most appropriate for each of the following products? (*a*) a new type of home lawn-sprinkling system, (*b*) a new skin patch drug to help smokers quit, (*c*) a videotape of a best-selling movie, and (*d*) a new children's toy.
8. Would consumers be better off if all nations dropped their antidumping laws? Explain your thinking.
9. How would our marketing system change if manufacturers were required to set fixed prices on *all* products sold at retail and *all* retailers were required to use these prices? Would a manufacturer's marketing mix be easier to develop? What kind of an operation would retailing be in this situation? Would consumers receive more or less service?
10. Is price discrimination involved if a large oil company sells gasoline to taxicab associations for resale to individual taxicab operators for 2 1/2 cents a gallon less than the price charged to retail service stations? What happens if the cab associations resell gasoline not only to taxicab operators but to the general public as well?
11. Do stocking allowances increase or reduce conflict in a channel of distribution? Explain your thinking.
12. Are seasonal discounts appropriate in agricultural businesses (which are certainly seasonal)?
13. What are the effective annual interest rates for the following cash discount terms: (*a*) 1/10, net 20; (*b*) 1/5, net 10; and (*c*) net 25?
14. Why would a manufacturer offer a rebate instead of lowering the suggested list price?
15. How can a marketing manager change her F.O.B. terms to make an otherwise competitive marketing mix more attractive?
16. What type of geographic pricing policy is most appropriate for the following products (specify any assumptions necessary to obtain a definite answer)? (*a*) a chemical by-product, (*b*) nationally advertised candy bars, (*c*) rebuilt auto parts, and (d) tricycles.
17. How would a ban on freight absorption (that is, requiring F.O.B factory pricing) affect a producer with substantial economies of scale in production?

Suggested cases

22 Kelman Mfg., Inc.

24 Fraser Company

25 Lee Steel Supply and Service

Computer-aided problem

Cash Discounts

Joe Tulkin owns Tulkin Wholesale Co. He sells paper, tape, file folders, and other office supplies to about 120 retailers in nearby cities. His average retailer customer spends about $900 a month. When Tulkin started business in 1991, competing wholesalers were giving retailers invoice terms of 3/10, net 30. Tulkin never gave the issue much thought—he just used the same invoice terms when he billed customers. At that time, about half of his customers took the discount. Recently, he noticed a change in the way his customers pay their bills. Checking his records, he found that 90 percent of the retailers are taking the cash discount. With so many retailers taking the cash discount, it seems to have become a price reduction. In addition, Tulkin learned that other wholesalers are changing their invoice terms.

Tulkin decides he should rethink his invoice terms. He knows he could change the percent rate on the cash discount, the number of days the discount is offered, or the number of days before the face amount is due. Changing any of these—or any combination—will change the interest rate at which a buyer is, in effect, borrowing money if he does not take the discount. Tulkin decides that it will be easier to evaluate the effect of different invoice terms if he sets up a spreadsheet to let him change the terms and quickly see the effective interest rate for each change.

a. With 90 percent of Tulkin's customers now taking the discount, what is the total monthly cash discount amount?
b. If Tulkin changes his invoice terms to 1/5, net 20, what interest rate is each buyer paying by not taking the cash discount? With these terms, would fewer buyers be likely to take the discount? Why?
c. Tulkin thinks 10 customers will switch to other wholesalers if he changes his invoice terms to 2/10, net 30, while 60 percent of the remaining customers will take the discount. What interest rate does a buyer pay by not taking this cash discount? For this situation, what will the total gross sales (total invoice) amount be? The total cash discount? The total net sales receipts after the total cash discount? Compare Tulkin's current situation with what will happen if he changes his invoice terms to 2/10, net 30.

For additional questions related to this problem, see Exercise 17–3 in the *Learning Aid for Use with Basic Marketing*, Ninth Canadian Edition.

When you finish this chapter, you should

- Understand how most wholesalers and retailers set their prices using markups.
- Understand why turnover is so important in pricing.
- Understand the advantages and disadvantages of average-cost pricing.
- Know how to use break-even analysis to evaluate possible prices.
- Know the many ways that price setters use demand estimates in their pricing.
- Understand the important new terms (shown in orange).

Chapter eighteen

Price Setting in the Business World

Why is Nike jacking up the prices of its athletic shoes by as much as a whopping 20%? Because it can.

The Beaverton, Oregon-based athletic-apparel retailer claims it can do it because the technology its shoes sport justifies it. But analysts are quick to point out Nike can just do it because the market—a large component of which is youth with lots of discretionary dollars—will bear it. Nike boasts a brand-name and swoosh logo equity so strong that it has little fear a price increase would compromise its US$6 billion in annual worldwide sales.

NIKE Canada Ltd. of Thornhill, Ont., says its average increase in athletic shoe prices reflects the industry norm of 10%, but in its high-end shoes, the story's different. At a suggested retail price of $179.95, Air Equilibrium, the shoe that replaces last year's Air Structure II ($149.95), reflects a 20% increase. The Air Max, Nike's highest-priced shoe, climbed 10.5% from $189.95 to $209.95, making it the first athletic shoe in Canada to cross the $200 line.

Enlisting the support of an impressionable consumer with money to burn is part of the Nike success story, says Toronto retail analyst Anthony Stokan of Anthony Russell and Associates. "It's one of the few markets that offers very little price resistance. It's a group that desperately needs to belong to a trend or fad of the moment, so money is no object."

Roy Agostino, formerly in marketing communications at NIKE Canada and recently hired as its U.S.-based global public relations manager, talks about Nike's brand as having a "shared set of common values that are intrinsically linked with the athletic experience, and which are about performance and innovation." These values cut across all markets but are translated locally so they have relevance in specific regions. Colors and designs of shoes are selected for each market—in Canada, there are some 700 stock-keeping units. There are sponsorships with local NBA players, and tie-ins with regional athletic events.

The company's penchant for creating and building on a local mythology, which is then linked to its shoes and to the Nike name and logo, is expressed in starkly different executions. Two years ago, Nike splashed Toronto with transit and outdoor posters celebrating local heroes—people in the Toronto area who "Just Do It." More recently, a multimedia campaign featuring talent pretending they're NHL has-beens bested by pro-hockey players wearing Nike equipment appealed to the strong hockey heritage felt in Toronto and Montreal.

Agostino says that part of developing campaigns for markets means asking "an ongoing benchmark series of questions, more at the gut level of a brand." That "gut level" reading has as much to do with spirit as with the science of making a better shoe. "Sport is all about youthful energy and that's what fuels us," says Agostino.

Source: Abridged from James Pollock, "Bulletproof Brand Nike Has No Fear of Dramatic Price Increases," *Marketing Magazine*, April 7, 1997, p. 5.

Exhibit 18–1 Key Factors that Influence Price Setting

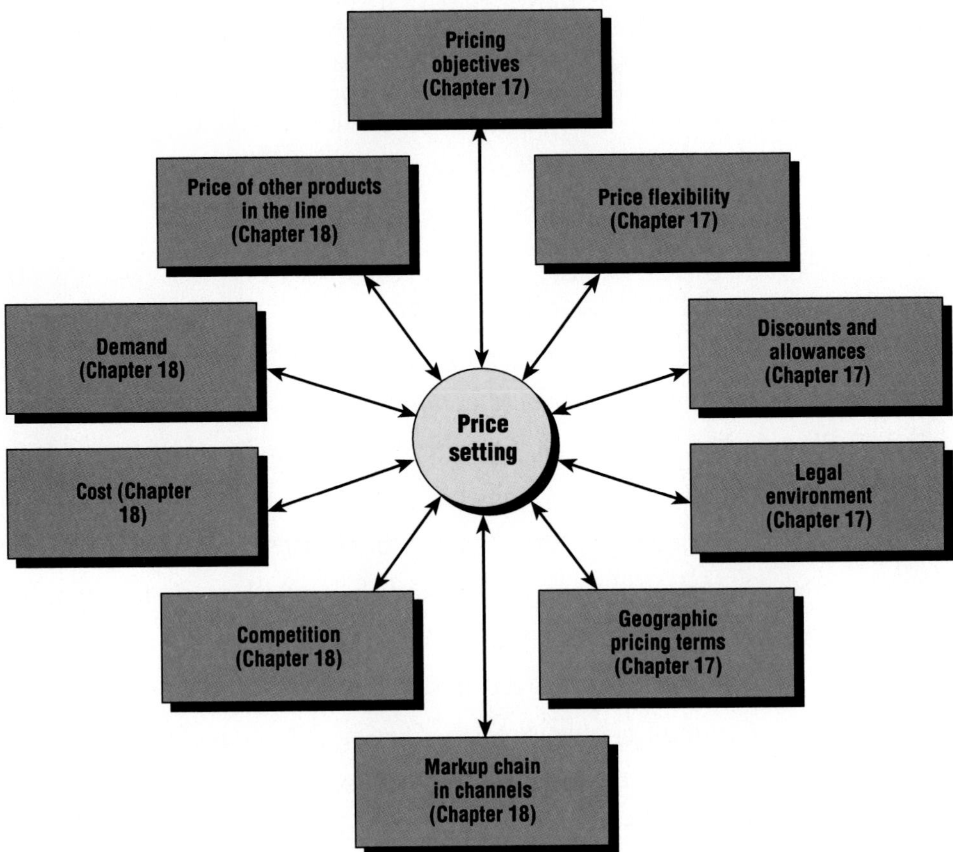

Price setting is a key strategic decision

In the last chapter, we discussed the idea that pricing objectives and policies should guide pricing decisions. We accepted the idea of a list price and went on to discuss variations from list. Now we'll see how the basic list price is set in the first place, based on information about costs, demand, and profit margins. See Exhibit 18–1.

Many firms set a price by just adding a standard markup to the average cost of the products they sell. But this is changing. More managers are realizing that they should set prices by evaluating the effect of a price decision not only on the profit margin for a given item but also on demand and, therefore, on sales volume and costs. For example, we have just seen that Nike can charge a premium price for a marketing mix that offers customers something unique. In very competitive markets, on the other hand, firms follow a low-price policy that is expected both to increase profits and at the same time reduce customers' costs.

There are many ways to set list prices. For simplicity, they can be reduced to two basic approaches: *cost-oriented* and *demand-oriented* price setting. We will discuss cost-oriented approaches first because they are most common. Also, understanding the problems of relying only on a cost-oriented approach will show why a marketing manager must also consider demand to make good price decisions. Let's begin by looking at how most retailers and wholesalers set cost-oriented prices.

Some firms just use markups

Some firms, including most retailers and wholesalers, set prices by using a **markup**—a dollar amount added to the cost of products to get the selling price. For example, suppose that a Pharmasave drugstore buys a bottle of Prell shampoo for $1. To make a profit, the drugstore obviously must sell the shampoo for more than $1. If it adds

50 cents to cover operating expenses and provide a profit, we say that the store is marking up the item 50 cents.

Markups, however, usually are stated as percentages rather than as dollar amounts. And this is where confusion sometimes arises. Is a markup of 50 cents on a cost of $1 a markup of 50 percent? Or should the markup be figured as a percentage of the selling price—$1.50—and therefore as 33⅓ percent? A clear definition is necessary.

Markup percent is based on selling price

Unless otherwise stated, **markup (percent)** means the percentage of selling price that is added to the cost to get the selling price. So the 50-cent markup on the $1.50 selling price is a markup of 33⅓ percent. Markups are related to selling price for convenience. There's nothing wrong with the idea of markup on cost. However, to avoid confusion, it's important to state clearly which markup percent you're using.

Managers often want to change a markup on cost to one based on selling price—or vice versa. The calculations used to do this are simple (see the section on markup conversion in Appendix B on marketing arithmetic).

Many use a "standard" markup percent

Many intermediaries select a standard markup percent and then apply it to all their products. This makes pricing easier. When you think of the large number of items the average retailer and wholesaler carry—and the small sales volume of any one item—this approach may make sense. Spending the time to find the best price to charge on every item in stock (day to day or week to week) might not pay.

Moreover, different companies in the same line of business often use the same markup percent. There is a reason for this: Their operating expenses are usually similar. So a standard markup is acceptable as long as it's large enough to cover the firm's operating expenses and provide a reasonable profit.

Markups are related to gross margins

How does a manager decide on a standard markup in the first place? A standard markup is often set close to the firm's *gross margin.* Managers regularly see gross margins on their operating (profit and loss) statements. The gross margin is the

Many drugstores carry gardening supplies, such as Ortho insecticides. Because the turnover on these products is likely to be lower than for many other drugstore items, the drugstore is likely to use a higher markup.

amount left, after subtracting the cost of sales (cost of goods sold) from net sales, to cover the expenses of selling products and operating the business. (See Appendix B on marketing arithmetic if you are unfamiliar with these ideas.) Our Pharmasave manager knows that there won't be any profit if the gross margin is not large enough. For this reason, Pharmasave might set a markup percent on Prell shampoo that is close to the store's usual gross margin percent.

Smart producers pay attention to the gross margins and standard markups of intermediaries in their channel. They usually allow trade (functional) discounts similar to the standard markups these intermediaries expect.

Markup chain may be used in channel pricing

Different firms in a channel often use different markups. A **markup chain**—the sequence of markups firms use at different levels in a channel—determines the price structure in the whole channel. The markup is figured on the *selling price* at each level of the channel.

For example, Black & Decker's selling price for an electric drill becomes the cost the Home Hardware wholesaler pays. The wholesaler's selling price becomes the hardware retailer's cost. And this cost plus a retail markup becomes the retail selling price. Each markup should cover the costs of running the business—and leave a profit.

Exhibit 18–2 illustrates the markup chain for an electric drill at each level of the channel system. The production (factory) cost of the drill is $21.60. In this case, the producer takes a 10 percent markup and sells the product for $24. The markup is 10 percent of $24 or $2.40. The producer's selling price now becomes the wholesaler's cost—$24. If the wholesaler is used to taking a 20 percent markup on selling price, the markup is $6—and the wholesaler's selling price becomes $30. $30 now becomes the cost for the hardware retailer. And a retailer who is used to a 40 percent markup adds $20, and the retail selling price becomes $50.

High markups don't always mean big profits

Some people, including many traditional retailers, think that high markups mean big profits. Often, this isn't true. A high markup may result in a price that's too high—a price at which few customers will buy. And you can't earn much if you don't sell much, no matter how high your markup. But many retailers and wholesalers seem more concerned with the size of their markup on a single item than with their total profit. And their high markups may lead to low profits—or even losses.

Lower markups can speed turnover—and the stockturn rate

Some retailers and wholesalers try to speed turnover to increase profit, even if this means reducing their markups. They realize that a business runs up costs over time.

Exhibit 18–2 Example of a Markup Chain and Channel Pricing

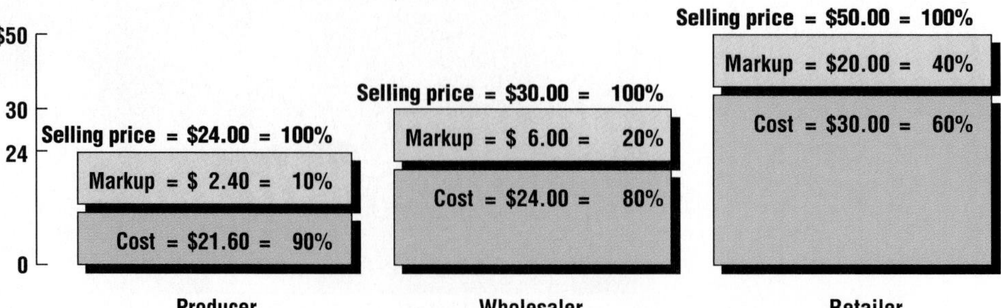

If they can sell a much greater amount in the same time period, they may be able to take a lower markup—and still earn higher profits at the end of the period.

An important idea here is the **stockturn rate**—the number of times the average inventory is sold in a year. Various methods of calculating stockturn rates can be used (see the section "Computing the Stockturn Rate" in Appendix B). A low stockturn rate may be bad for profits.

At the very least, a low stockturn increases inventory carrying cost and ties up working capital. If a firm with a stockturn of 1 (once per year) sells products that cost it $100,000, it has that much tied up in inventory all the time. But a stockturn of 5 requires only $20,000 worth of inventory ($100,000 cost ÷ 5 turnovers a year).

Whether a stockturn rate is high or low depends on the industry and on the product involved. A NAPA auto parts wholesaler may expect an annual rate of 1, while an A&P store may expect 10 to 12 stockturns for soaps and detergents and 50 to 60 stockturns for fresh fruits and vegetables.

Mass-merchandisers run in fast company

Some intermediaries use the same standard markup percent on all their products, but this policy ignores the importance of fast turnover. Mass merchandisers know this. They put low markups on fast-selling items and higher markups on items that sell less frequently. For example, Wal-Mart may put a small markup on fast-selling health and beauty aids (such as toothpaste or shampoo) but higher markups on appliances and clothing. Similarly, supermarket operators put low markups on fast-selling items like milk, eggs, and detergents. The markup on these items may be less than half the average markup for all grocery items, but this doesn't mean they're unprofitable. Rather, the store earns the small profit per unit more often.

Where does the markup chain start?

Some markups eventually become standard in a trade. Most channel members tend to follow a similar process, adding a certain percentage to the previous price. But who sets price in the first place?

The firm that brands a product is usually the one that sets its basic list price. It may be a large retailer, a large wholesaler, or, most often, the producer.

Wal-Mart may put a small markup on fast-selling items and higher markups on items that sell less frequently.

Some producers just start with a cost per unit figure and add a markup—perhaps a standard markup—to obtain their selling price. Or they may use some rule-of-thumb formula such as:

Selling price = Average production cost per unit × 3

A producer who uses this approach might develop rules and markups related to its own costs and objectives. Yet even the first step—selecting the appropriate cost per unit on which to build—isn't easy. Let's discuss several approaches to see how cost-oriented price setting really works.

Average-cost pricing is common and can be dangerous

Average-cost pricing means adding a reasonable markup to the average cost of a product. A manager usually finds the average cost per unit by studying past records. Dividing the total cost for the last year by all the units produced and sold in that period gives an estimate of the average cost per unit for the next year. If the cost was $32,000 for all labour and materials and $30,000 for fixed overhead expenses such as selling expenses, rent, and manager salaries, then the total cost is $62,000. If the company produced 40,000 items in that time period, the average cost is $62,000 divided by 40,000 units, or $1.55 per unit. To get the price, the producer decides how much profit per unit to add to the average cost per unit. If the company considers 45 cents a reasonable profit for each unit, it sets the new price at $2.00. Exhibit 18–3A shows that this approach produces the desired profit—if the company sells 40,000 units.

It does not allow for cost variations as output changes

Average-cost pricing is simple. But it can also be dangerous. It's easy to lose money with average-cost pricing. To see why, let's follow this example further.

Exhibit 18-3 Results of Average-Cost Pricing

A. CALCULATION OF PLANNED PROFIT IF 40,000 ITEMS ARE SOLD		B. CALCULATION OF ACTUAL PROFIT IF ONLY 20,000 ITEMS ARE SOLD	
Calculation of costs:		**Calculation of costs:**	
Fixed overhead expenses	$30,000	Fixed overhead expenses	$30,000
Labour and materials ($.80 a unit)	32,000	Labour and materials ($.80 a unit)	16,000
Total costs	$62,000	Total costs	$46,000
"Planned" profit	18,000		
Total costs and planned profit	$80,000		
Calculation of profit (or loss):		**Calculation of profit (or loss):**	
Actual unit sales × price ($2.00*)	$80,000	Actual unit sales × price ($2.00*)	$40,000
Minus: total costs	62,000	Minus: total costs	46,000
Profit (loss)	$18,000	Profit (loss)	($6,000)

Result:
Planned profit of $18,000 is earned if 40,000 items are sold at $2.00 each.

Result:
Planned profit of $18,000 is not earned. Instead, $6,000 loss results if 20,000 items are sold at $2.00 each.

*Calculation of "reasonable price": $\frac{\text{Expected total costs and planned profit}}{\text{Planned number of items to be sold}} = \frac{\$80,000}{40,000} = \$2.00$

First, remember that the average cost of $2.00 per unit was based on output of 40,000 units. But if the firm is only able to produce and sell 20,000 units in the next year, it may be in trouble. Twenty thousand units sold at $2.00 each ($1.55 cost plus 45 cents for expected profit) yield a total revenue of only $40,000. The overhead is still fixed at $30,000, and the variable material and labour cost drops by half to $16,000, for a total cost of $46,000. This results in a loss of $6,000, or 30 cents a unit. The method that was supposed to allow a profit of 45 cents a unit actually causes a loss of 30 cents a unit! See Exhibit 18–3B.

The basic problem with the average-cost approach is that it doesn't consider cost variations at different levels of output. In a typical situation, costs are high with low output, and then economies of scale set in—the average cost per unit drops as the quantity produced increases. This is why mass production and mass distribution often make sense. It's also why it's important to develop a better understanding of the different types of costs a marketing manager should consider when setting a price.

Marketing manager must consider various kinds of costs

Average-cost pricing may lead to losses because there are a variety of costs, and each changes in a *different* way as output changes. Any pricing method that uses cost must consider these changes. To understand why, we need to define six types of costs.

There are three kinds of total cost

1. **Total fixed cost** is the sum of those costs that are fixed in total, no matter how much is produced. Among these fixed costs are rent, depreciation, managers' salaries, property taxes, and insurance. Such costs stay the same even if production stops temporarily.
2. **Total variable cost,** on the other hand, is the sum of those changing expenses that are closely related to output—expenses for parts, wages, packaging materials, outgoing freight, and sales commissions.

   At zero output, total variable cost is zero. As output increases, so do variable costs. If Wrangler doubles its output of jeans in a year, its total cost for denim cloth also (roughly) doubles.
3. **Total cost** is the sum of total fixed and total variable costs. Changes in total cost depend on variations in total variable cost, since total fixed cost stays the same.

There are three kinds of average cost

The pricing manager usually is more interested in cost per unit than in total cost because prices are usually quoted per unit.

1. **Average cost** (per unit) is obtained by dividing total cost by the related quantity (that is, the total quantity that causes the total cost).
2. **Average fixed cost** (per unit) is obtained by dividing total fixed cost by the related quantity.
3. **Average variable cost** (per unit) is obtained by dividing total variable cost by the related quantity.

An example shows cost relations

A good way to get a feel for these different types of costs is to extend our average-cost pricing example (Exhibit 18–3A). Exhibit 18–4 shows the six types of cost and how they vary at different levels of output. The line for 40,000 units is highlighted because that was the expected level of sales in our average-cost pricing example. For

Exhibit 18–4 Cost Structure of a Firm

QUANTITY (Q)	COSTS (TFC)	AVERAGE FIXED COSTS (AFC)	AVERAGE VARIABLE COSTS (AVC)	TOTAL VARIABLE COSTS (TVC)	TOTAL COST (TC)	AVERAGE COST (AC)
0	$30,000	—	—	—	$30,000	—
10,000	30,000	$3.00	$0.80	$8,000	38,000	$3.80
20,000	30,000	1.50	0.80	16,000	46,000	2.30
30,000	30,000	1.00	0.80	24,000	54,000	1.80
40,000	30,000	0.75	0.80	32,000	62,000	1.55
50,000	30,000	0.60	0.80	40,000	70,000	1.40
60,000	30,000	0.50	0.80	48,000	78,000	1.30
70,000	30,000	0.43	0.80	56,000	86,000	1.23
80,000	30,000	0.38	0.80	64,000	94,000	1.18
90,000	30,000	0.33	0.80	72,000	102,000	1.13
100,000	30,000	0.30	0.80	80,000	110,000	1.10

[110,000 (TC) − 80,000 (TVC) = 30,000 (TVD)]

0.30 (AFC) = (Q)100,000) 30,000 (TFC)

0.80 (AVC)

[100,000 (Q) × 0.80 (AVC) = 80,000 (TVC)]

[30,000 (TFC) + 80,000 (TVC) = 110,000 (TC)]

1.10(AC) = (Q)100,000) 110,000 (TC)

Exhibit 18–5 Typical Shape of Cost (per unit) Curves When AVC Is Assumed Constant per Unit

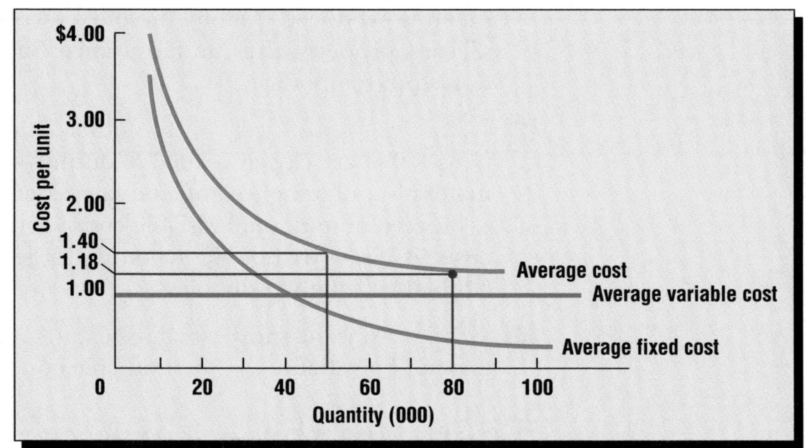

simplicity, we assume that average variable cost is the same for each unit. Notice, however, that total variable cost increases when quantity increases.

Exhibit 18–5 shows the three average cost curves from Exhibit 18–4. Notice that average fixed cost goes down steadily as the quantity increases. Although the average variable cost remains the same, average cost decreases continually, too. This is because average fixed cost is decreasing. With these relationships in mind, let's reconsider the problem with average-cost pricing.

Ignoring demand is the major weakness

Average-cost pricing works well if the firm actually sells the quantity it used to set the average-cost price. Losses may result, however, *if actual sales are much lower than expected.* On the other hand, if sales are much higher than expected, then profits may be very good. But this will only happen by luck—because the firm's demand is much larger than expected.

Exhibit 18-6 Evaluation of Various Prices Along a Firm's Demand Curve

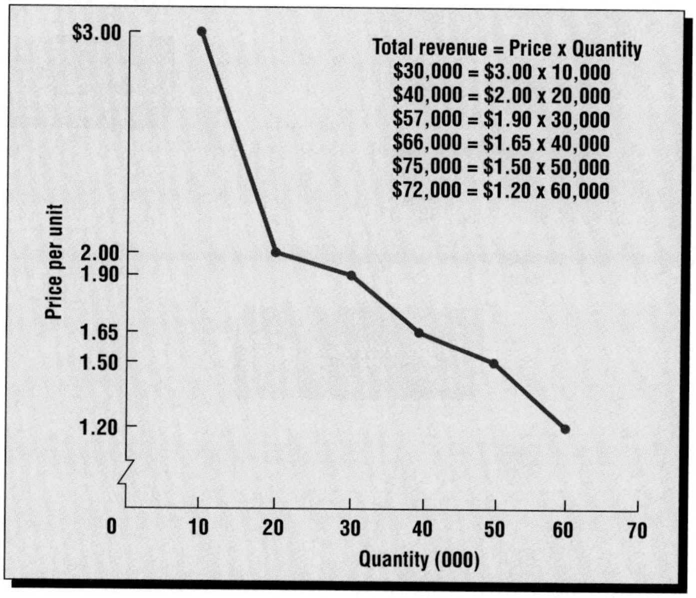

To use average-cost pricing, a marketing manager must make *some* estimate of the quantity to be sold in the coming period. Without a quantity estimate, it isn't possible to compute average cost. But unless this quantity is related to price—that is, unless the firm's demand curve is considered—the marketing manager may set a price that doesn't even cover a firm's total cost! You saw this happen in Exhibit 18–3B, when the firm's price of $2.00 resulted in demand for only 20,000 units—and a loss of $6,000.

The demand curve is still important even if management doesn't take time to think about it. For example, Exhibit 18–6 shows the demand curve for the firm we're discussing. This demand curve shows *why* the firm lost money when it tried to use average-cost pricing. At the $2.00 price, quantity demanded is only 20,000. With this demand curve and the costs in Exhibit 18–4, the firm will incur a loss whether management sets the price at a high $3 or a low $1.20. At $3, the firm will sell only 10,000 units for a total revenue of $30,000. But total cost will be $38,000—for a loss of $8,000. At the $1.20 price, it will sell 60,000 units—at a loss of $6,000. However, the curve suggests that at a price of $1.65 consumers will demand about 40,000 units, producing a profit of about $4,000.

In short, average-cost pricing is simple in theory—but often fails in practice. In stable situations, prices set by this method may yield profits—but not necessarily *maximum* profits. And note that such cost-based prices may be higher than a price that would be more profitable for the firm—as shown in Exhibit 18–6. When demand conditions are changing, average-cost pricing is even more risky.

Exhibit 18–7 summarizes the relationships discussed above. Cost-oriented pricing requires an estimate of the total number of units to be sold. That estimate determines the *average* fixed cost per unit and thus the average total cost. Then the firm adds the desired profit per unit to the average total cost to get the cost-oriented selling price. How customers react to that price determines the actual quantity the firm will be able to sell. But that quantity may not be the quantity used to compute the average cost! Further, the quantity the firm actually sells (times price) determines total revenue (and total profit or loss). A decision made in one area affects each of the others, directly or indirectly. Average-cost pricing does not consider these effects.[1] A manager who forgets this can make serious pricing mistakes.

Experience curve pricing is even riskier

In recent years, some aggressive firms have used a variation of average-cost pricing called experience curve pricing. **Experience curve pricing** is average-cost pricing using an estimate of *future* average costs. This approach is based on the

Exhibit 18-7 Summary of Relationships Among Quantity, Cost, and Price Using Cost-Oriented Pricing

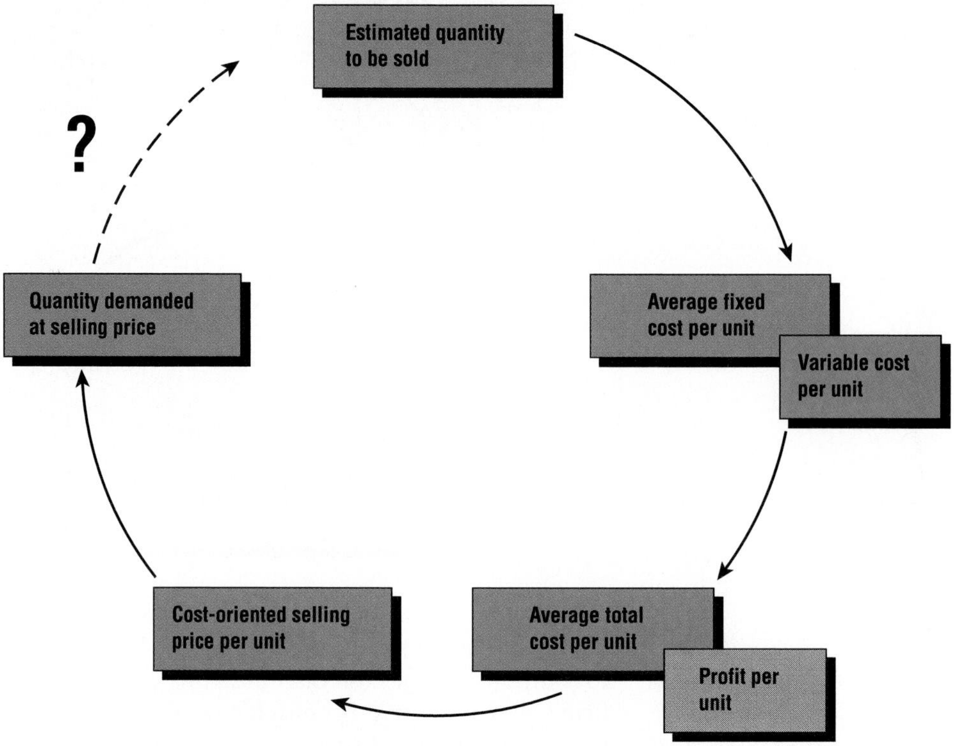

Estimated quantity to be sold

Average fixed cost per unit

Variable cost per unit

Average total cost per unit

Profit per unit

Cost-oriented selling price per unit

Quantity demanded at selling price

?

observation that over time, as an industry gains experience in certain kinds of production, managers learn new ways to reduce costs. The effect of such learning on costs varies in different businesses. Studies suggest that costs decrease about 15 to 20 percent each time cumulative production volume (experience) doubles—at least in some industries. So some firms set average-cost prices where they expect costs to be when products are sold in the future—not where costs actually are when the strategy is set. This approach is more common in rapidly growing markets (such as in the electronics business) because cumulative production volume (experience) grows faster.

If costs drop as expected, this approach can work fairly well. But it carries the same risks as regular average-cost pricing—unless demand is included in the price setting. This means that the price setter has to estimate what quantity will be sold in order to be able to read the right price from the experience-based average-cost curve.[2]

Don't ignore competitors' costs

Another danger of average-cost pricing is that it ignores competitors' costs and prices. Just as the price of a firm's own product influences demand, the price of available substitutes may have an impact on demand. By finding ways to cut costs, Wal-Mart is able to offer prices lower than competitors' and still make an attractive profit. Given a choice between Wal-Mart's low prices and higher prices for similar products at nearby stores, many consumers buy from Wal-Mart.

Some firms add a target return to cost

Target return pricing—adding a target return to the cost of a product—has become popular in recent years. With this approach, the price setter seeks to earn (1) a percentage return (say, 10 percent per year) on the investment or (2) a specific total dollar return.

This method is a variation of the average-cost method since the desired target return is added into total cost. As a simple example, if a company had $180,000 invested and wanted to make a 10 percent return on investment, it would add $18,000 to its annual total costs in setting prices.

This approach has the same weakness as other average-cost pricing methods. If the quantity actually sold is less than the quantity used to set the price, then the company doesn't earn its target return—even though the target return seems to be part of the price structure. We already saw this in Exhibit 18–3. Remember that we added $18,000 as an expected profit, or target return. But the return was much lower when the expected quantity was not sold. (It could be higher, too—but only if the quantity sold is much larger than expected.) Clearly, target return pricing does not guarantee that a firm will hit the target.

Hitting the target in the long run

In some larger firms, managers who want to achieve a long-run target return objective use another cost-oriented pricing approach—**long-run target return pricing**, which adds a long-run average target return to the cost of a product. Instead of estimating the quantity they expect to produce in any one year, they assume that during several years' time their plants will produce at, say, 80 percent of capacity. They use this quantity when setting their prices.

Companies that take this longer-run view assume that there will be recession years when sales drop below 80 percent of capacity. For example, Owens/Corning Fiberglas sells insulation. In years when there is little construction, output is low and the firm does not earn the target return. But the company also has good years when it sells more insulation and exceeds the target return. Over the long run, Owens/Corning managers expect to achieve the target return. And sometimes they're right, depending on how accurately they estimate demand.

Break-even analysis can evaluate possible prices

Some price setters use break-even analysis in their pricing. **Break-even analysis** evaluates whether the firm will be able to break even—that is, cover all its costs—with a particular price. This is important because a firm must cover all costs in the long run or there is not much point being in business. This method focuses on the **break-even point (BEP)**—the quantity where the firm's total cost will just equal its total revenue.

Break-even charts help find the BEP

To help understand how break-even analysis works, look at Exhibit 18–8, an example of a typical break-even chart. *The chart is based on a particular selling price*—in this case, $1.20 a unit. The chart has lines that show total costs (total variable plus total fixed costs) and total revenues at different levels of production. The break-even point on the chart is at 75,000 units, which is where the total cost and total revenue lines intersect. At that production level, total cost and total revenue are the same—$90,000.

This chart also shows some of the typical assumptions that are made to simplify break-even analysis. Note that the total revenue curve is assumed to be a straight line. This means that each extra unit sold adds the same amount to total revenue. Stated differently, this assumes that *any quantity can be sold at the same price.* For this chart, we are assuming a selling price of $1.20 a unit. You can see that if the firm sells the break-even quantity of 75,000 at $1.20 each, it will earn a total revenue of $90,000.

The total cost curve in the chart is also assumed to be a straight line. This means that average variable cost (AVC) is the same at different levels of output. For Exhibit 18–8, the AVC is 80 cents per unit.

The difference between the total revenue and the total cost at a given quantity is the profit—or loss! The chart shows that below the break-even point, total cost is

Exhibit 18-8 Break-Even Chart for a Particular Situation

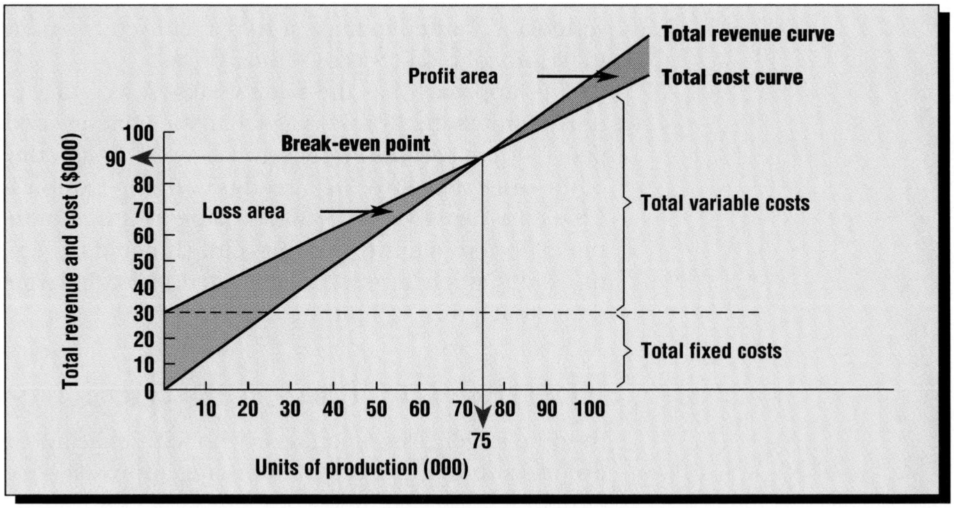

higher than total revenue—and the firm incurs a loss. The firm will make a profit above the break-even point. However, the firm will only reach the break-even point, or get beyond it into the profit area, *if* it can sell at least 75,000 units at the $1.20 price.

Break-even analysis can be very helpful if used properly, so let's look at this approach more closely.

How to compute a break-even point

A break-even chart is an easy-to-understand visual aid, but it's also useful to be able to compute the break-even point.

The BEP, in units, can be found by dividing total fixed costs (TFC) by the **fixed-cost (FC) contribution per unit**—the assumed selling price per unit less the variable cost per unit. This can be stated as a simple formula:

$$\text{BEP (in units)} = \frac{\text{Total fixed cost}}{\text{Fixed-cost contribution per unit}}$$

This formula makes sense when we think about it. To break even, we must cover total fixed costs. Therefore, we must calculate the contribution each unit will make to covering the total fixed costs (after paying for the variable costs to produce the item). When we divide this per unit contribution into the total fixed costs that must be covered, we have the BEP (in units).

To illustrate the formula, let's use the cost and price information in Exhibit 18–8. The price per unit is $1.20. The average variable cost per unit is 80 cents. So the FC contribution per unit is 40 cents ($1.20 − 80 cents). The total fixed cost is $30,000 (see Exhibit 18–8). Substituting in the formula:

$$\text{BEP} = \frac{\$30{,}000}{.40} = 75{,}000 \text{ units}$$

From this you can see that if this firm sells 75,000 units, it will exactly cover all its fixed and variable costs. If it sells even one more unit, it will begin to show a profit—in this situation, 40 cents per unit. Note that once the fixed costs are covered, the part of revenue formerly going to cover fixed costs is now *all profit.*

BEP can be stated in dollars too

The BEP can also be figured in dollars. The easiest way is to compute the BEP in units and then multiply by the assumed per unit price. If you multiply the selling price ($1.20) by the BEP in units (75,000), you get $90,000—the BEP in dollars.

Each possible price has its own break-even point

Often, it's useful to compute the break-even point for each of several possible prices and then compare the BEP for each price to likely demand at that price. The marketing manager can quickly reject some price possibilities when the expected quantity demanded at a given price is way below the break-even point for that price.

A target profit can be included

So far in our discussion of BEP we've focused on the quantity at which total revenue equals total cost—where profit is zero. We can vary this approach to see what quantity is required to earn a certain level of profit. The analysis is the same as described above for the break-even point in units, but the amount of target profit is added to the total fixed cost. Then, when we divide the total fixed cost plus profit figure by the contribution from each unit, we get the quantity that will earn the target profit.

Break-even analysis shows the effect of cutting costs

Break-even analysis makes it clear why managers must constantly look for effective new ways to get jobs done at lower costs. For example, if a manager can reduce the firm's total fixed costs—perhaps by using computer systems to cut out excess inventory carrying costs—the break-even point will be lower and profits will start to build sooner. Similarly, if the variable cost to produce and sell an item can be reduced, the fixed-cost contribution per unit increases; that too lowers the break-even point and profit accumulates faster for each product sold beyond the break-even point.

Break-even analysis is helpful—but not a pricing solution

Break-even analysis is helpful for evaluating alternatives. It is also popular because it's easy to use. Yet break-even analysis is too often misunderstood. Beyond the BEP, profits seem to be growing continually. And the graph—with its straight-line total revenue curve—makes it seem that any quantity can be sold at the assumed price. But this usually isn't true. It is the same as assuming a perfectly horizontal demand curve at that price. In fact, most managers face down-sloping demand situations. And their total revenue curves do *not* keep going up.

The firm and costs we discussed in the average-cost pricing example earlier in this chapter illustrate this point. You can confirm from Exhibit 18–4 that the total fixed cost ($30,000) and average variable cost (80 cents) for that firm are the same ones shown in the break-even chart (Exhibit 18–8). So this break-even chart is the one we would draw for that firm assuming a price of $1.20 a unit. But the demand curve for that case showed that the firm could only sell 60,000 units at a price of $1.20. So that firm would never reach the 75,000 unit break-even point at a $1.20 price. It would sell only 60,000 units, and it would lose $6,000! A firm with a different demand curve—say, one where the firm could sell 80,000 units at a price of $1.20—would in fact break even at 75,000 units.

Break-even analysis is a useful tool for analyzing costs. But it is a cost-oriented approach and suffers the same limitations as other cost-oriented approaches. Specifically, it does not consider the effect of price on the quantity that consumers will want—that is, the demand curve.[3]

Finding the most profitable price and quantity to produce

Marketing managers must choose only one price (for a time period). The problem is which price to choose. The price, of course, sets the quantity customers will buy.

To maximize profit, marketing managers should choose the price that will lead to the greatest difference between total revenue and total cost. To find the best price and quantity, they need to estimate the firm's demand curve. A practical approach here is to list a wide range of possible prices. Then, for each price, they estimate the quantity that might be sold. You can think of this as a summary of the answers to a series of what-if questions—*what* quantity will be sold *if* a particular price is selected? By multiplying each price by its related quantity, marketing managers can find the total revenue for that price. Then they estimate the firm's likely costs at each of the quantities. Finally, they get the profit for each price and quantity by subtracting the related total cost from the total revenue. See Exhibit 18–9 for an example.

In Exhibit 18–10, which graphs the data from Exhibit 18–9, you can see that the best price is the one where there is the greatest distance between the total revenue and total cost curves. In this example, the best price is $79. At that price, the related quantity is 6 units, and profit would be $106.

A profit range is reassuring

Estimating the quantity a firm might sell at each price isn't easy. But we need some estimate of the demand in order to set prices. This is just one of the tough jobs a marketing manager faces. Ignoring demand curves doesn't make them go away! So some estimates must be made.

Note that demand estimates don't have to be exact. Exhibit 18–11 shows that there is a range of profitable prices. The price that would result in the highest profit is $79, but this strategy would be profitable from a price of $53 all the way up to $117.

Exhibit 18-9 Revenue, Cost, and Profit for an Individual Firm

(1) PRICE P	(2) QUANTITY Q	(3) TOTAL REVENUE TR	(4) TOTAL COST TC	(5) PROFIT (TR – TC)
$150	0	$ 0	$200	$–200
140	1	140	296	–156
130	2	260	316	–56
117	3	351	331	+20
105	4	420	344	+76
92	5	460	355	+105
79	6	474	368	+106
66	7	462	383	+79
53	8	424	423	+1
42	9	378	507	–129
31	10	310	710	–400

Exhibit 18-10 Graphic Determination of the Price Giving the Greatest Total Profit for a Firm

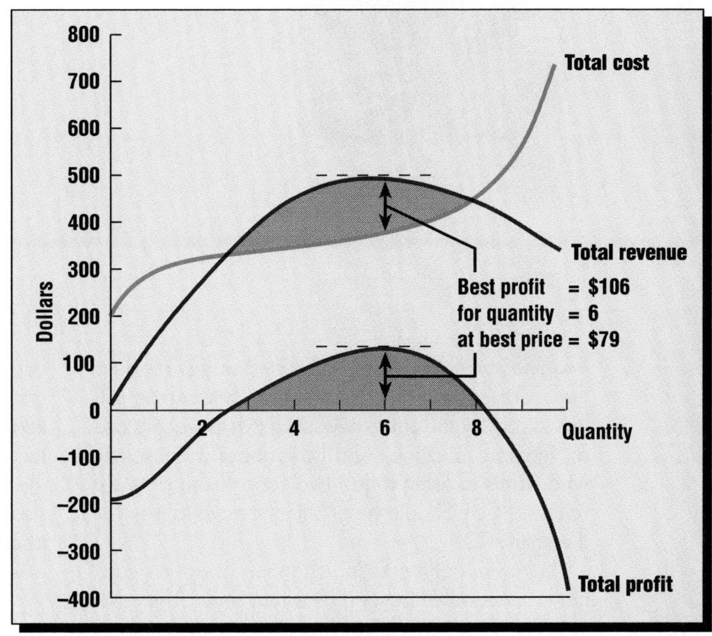

Exhibit 18-11 Range of Profitable Prices for Illustrative Data in Exhibits 18-9 and 18-10

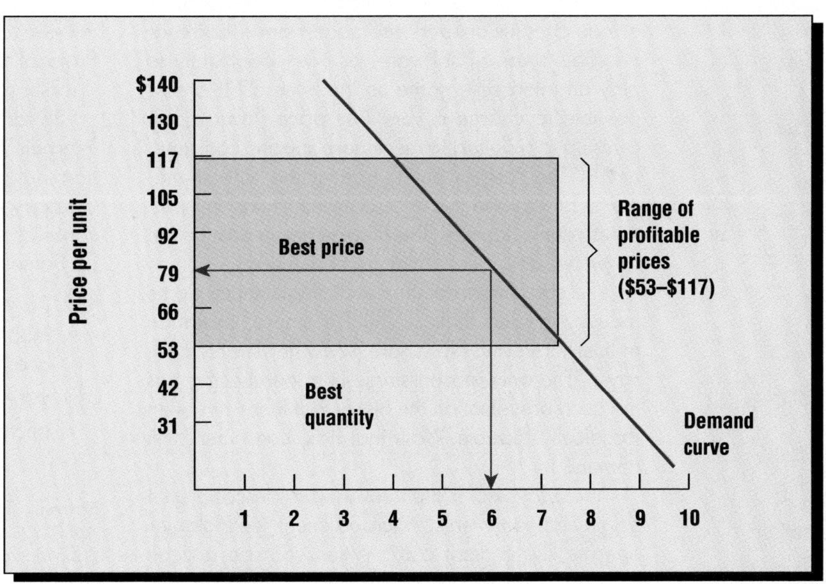

The marketing manager should try to estimate the best price—the one that earns the highest profit. But a slight miss doesn't mean failure. The effort of trying to estimate demand will probably lead to the firm being some place in the profit range. In contrast, mechanical use of average-cost pricing could lead to a price that is much too high—or much too low. This is why estimating demand isn't just desirable—it's essential.[4] It will become even more so when Web-based micropayment systems allow for the purchase of only part of a product rather than the entire item. See Internet Insite 18–1.

Internet Insite 18-1

Micropayment: Big Profits in Small Change?

Imagine someone who is interested in just reading the sports section of a newspaper. That person still has to pay for the entire newspaper at the local store or vending machine. And how about a consumer who wants to listen to just two songs from a newly released CD? Should he or she still have to pay for the entire CD?

In traditional marketing channels, products cannot be unbundled beyond a certain point. The costs of processing transactions (handling queries, taking the order, taking credit card information) make doing so difficult and uneconomical. Internet technology allows for purchasing and selling things that have a very low or transient value.

What about one news article from a newspaper, or one chapter or even one page from a book, or one hour's use of software, or one opportunity to play an interactive game on the Internet? It is now possible to charge a very low price (from a few cents up to a dollar) to meet these specific consumer needs. The costs of online transactions are significantly lower than the costs of transactions in traditional retail channels. This allows certain products to be priced on a per item or a per use basis.

Will consumers demand such single items? Some industry insiders think so. Bill Densmore, chairman of Internet startup Newshare (www.newshare.com), says, "The only reason single-item purchasing has not been prevalent on the Net is that it has not been technically feasible. Now that it is, consumers will demand it."

Micropayment is the term used to describe such single-item payments. Micropayment technologies operate like a debit card. When you use a debit card, the amount is subtracted from your bank balance. Consumers can buy micromoney or digital tokens, and each time they buy an item they can use the digital tokens at participating Web sites. Since the money has been preapproved, there are no hassles in processing the transaction. As with prepaid phone cards, you can buy micromoney, or digital tokens, and use them whenever you like.

Several companies are offering micropayment systems. Cybercash's CyberCoin (www.cybercash.com), a front-runner in this area, is promoted as a "cost effective way to offer electronic goods and services for prices ranging from $0.25 to $10.00 and up." Among the micropayment systems now being tested are Digital Equipment's Millicent (www.millicent.digital.com), IBM's Internet Keyed Payment Protocol or iKP (www.ibm.com), and Newshare's Clickshare (www.clickshare.com).

So far a lot of information has been free on the Internet. Web sites could start charging for information that is in demand. It is likely that a whole new category of information products will emerge because of micropayment technology.

Some questions to ponder:

1. Do you think consumers will accept micropayment on the Internet the way they have accepted debit cards?
2. What products and services can benefit from micropayment technology?

Source: This is one of a series of Internet Insites prepared in April 1998 by Dr. Ramesh Venkat of Saint Mary's University for *Basic Marketing*, Ninth Canadian Edition.

Demand-oriented approaches for setting prices

A manager who knows what influences target customers' price sensitivity can do a better job estimating the demand curve that the firm faces. Marketing researchers have identified a number of factors that influence price sensitivity across many different market situations.

The first factor is the most basic. When customers have *substitute ways* of meeting a need, they are likely to be more price sensitive. A cook who wants a cappuccino maker in order to be able to serve something distinctive to guests at a dinner party may be willing to pay a high price. However, if different machines are available and our cook sees them as quite similar, price sensitivity will be greater. It's important not to ignore dissimilar alternatives if the customer sees them as substitutes. If a machine for espresso were much less expensive than one for cappuccino, our cook might decide that an expresso machine would meet her needs just as well.

The impact of substitutes on price sensitivity is greatest when it is easy for customers to *compare prices*. For example, unit prices make it easier for our cook to compare the prices of espresso and cappuccino grinds on the grocery store shelf. Many people believe that the ease of comparing prices on the Internet will increase price sensitivity and–ultimately–bring down prices. If nothing else, it may make sellers more aware of competing prices.

People tend to be less price sensitive when someone else pays the bill or *shares the cost*. Perhaps this is just human nature. Casualty insurance companies, however, think that consumers would reject high home repair bills if they were paying all of their own bills. And executives might plan longer in advance to get better discounts on airline flights if their companies weren't footing the bills.

Customers tend to be more price sensitive the greater the *total expenditure*. Sometimes a big expenditure can be broken into smaller pieces. Mercedes knows this. When its ads focused on the cost of a monthly lease, rather than the total price of the car, more consumers became interested in trying a Mercedes.

Customers are less price sensitive the greater the *significance of the end benefit* of the purchase. Computer makers will pay more to get Intel processors if they believe that having an "Intel inside" sells more machines. Positioning efforts often focus on the emotional benefits of a purchase. For example, L'Oreal's ads for Preference, a hair colour, show closeups of beautiful hair while popular endorsers such as Cybil Shepherd tell women, "Don't be shy about it, say I'm worth it." A consumer who cares about the price of a bottle of hair colour might still believe that she's worth the difference in price.

Customers are sometimes less price sensitive if they already have a *sunk investment* that is related to the purchase. This is especially relevant with business customers. For example, once managers of a firm have invested to train employees to use Microsoft Excel, they are less likely to resist the high price of a new version of that software.

These factors apply in many different purchase situations, so it makes sense for marketing managers to consider each of them in refining their estimates of how customers will respond at different prices.[5]

Value-in-use pricing—how much will the customer save?

Organizational buyers think about how a purchase will affect their total costs. Many marketers who aim at business markets keep this in mind when estimating demand and setting prices. They use **value-in-use pricing,** which involves setting prices that will capture some of what customers will save by substituting the firm's product for the one currently being used.

For example, a producer of computer-controlled machines used to assemble cars knows that those machines don't just replace standard machines. They also reduce labour costs, quality control costs, and—after the car is sold—costs of warranty repairs. The potential savings (value in use) may be different for different customers, because those customers have different operations and costs. However, the marketer can estimate what each auto producer will save by using the machines—and then set a price that makes it less expensive for the auto producer to buy them than to stick with the old methods. The number of customers at different levels of potential savings also provides some idea about the shape of the demand curve.

Producing a "better product" that could save customers money in the long run isn't any guarantee that customers will be willing to pay a higher price. To capture the value created, the seller must convince buyers of the savings—and some buyers are likely to be sceptical. A salesperson needs to be able to prove the claims.[6]

Auctions are coming online fast

Auctions have always been a way to determine exactly what some group of potential customers will pay—or not pay—for a product. However, as we discussed in Chapter 13, auctions were traditionally used for specific types of products and drew only local buyers. That has changed dramatically with the development of online auctions on the Internet. New firms are setting up auctions that specialize in products ranging from vacation trips to electric energy. Some firms are setting up their own auctions—especially for products in short supply.

Customers may have reference prices

Some people don't devote much thought to what they pay for the products they buy—including some frequently purchased goods and services. But most consumers have a **reference price**—a price they expect to pay—for many of the products they purchase. And different customers may have different reference prices for the same basic type of purchase. For example, a person who really enjoys reading may have a higher reference price for a popular paperback book than another person who is only an occasional reader. Marketing research can sometimes identify different segments with different reference prices.[7] Advanced research techniques such as the one discussed in Marketing Demo 18–1 provide additional pricing guidance.

If a firm's price is lower than a customer's reference price, customers may view the product as a better value and demand may increase (see Exhibit 18–12). Sometimes a firm will try to position its product in such a way that consumers will compare it with a product that has a higher reference price. PBS TV stations do this when they ask viewers to make donations that match what they pay for "just one month of cable service." Insurance companies frame the price of premiums for homeowners' coverage in terms of the price to repair flood damage—and advertising makes the damage very vivid. Some retailers want consumers to use the manufacturer's list price as the reference price, even if no one anywhere actually pays that list price.

Leader pricing—make it low to attract customers

Leader pricing means setting some very low prices—real bargains—to get customers into retail stores. The idea is not to sell large quantities of the leader items but to get customers into the store to buy other products.[8] Certain products are picked for their promotion value and priced low—but above cost. In food stores, the leader prices are the "specials" that are advertised regularly to give an image of low prices. Leader items are usually well-known, widely used items that cus-

Marketing Demo 18-1

Software Swami

Visionary Shopper may sound like the moniker for a clairvoyant consumer, but it's actually a groundbreaking software program that lets marketers do simulated tests of various price and promotional variables. In Canada, it is available through Canada Market Research Ltd. of Toronto.

Consumers are typically recruited at malls for these tests. After a few basic instructions, they sit in front of a 17-inch color monitor that depicts simulated sections of supermarket or drugstore shelves. A trackball lets the user stroll through virtual store aisles. Products ranging from granola bars to laundry detergent are portrayed as three-dimensional images—complete with prices—and the consumer is asked to "shop" the shelves and "buy" products he or she actually uses or needs by touching an icon of a shopping cart.

Hugh Grant, CMR's executive VP, says the Visionary Shopper software accurately duplicates the shopping experience without burdening the manufacturer with the expense and/or headaches of a real-life shelf test: "A company might be thinking about introducing a couple of line extensions and wants to know if those line extensions, once placed in the store, will increase sales or if they are just going to steal business from the company's existing lines."

Visionary Shopper allows researchers to test "what if . . . ?" questions. For example, they can gauge the response to a rise or fall in the price of their product line, or even that of a competitor; what kind of promotions work best; and the best way to position products on the shelves. "Visionary Shopper is not an attitude measure, it's a behavior measure," says Grant.

Due to confidentiality agreements, the results of these tests—and even the names of the 33 companies that have used the software—remain closely guarded secrets. The only firm on record as being a client is Goodyear Tire & Rubber Co. of Akron, Ohio, which in 1993 used Visionary Shopper to measure its brand equity and the effectiveness of its warranties.

Ron Conlin, Goodyear's manager of market research and planning, told *Chain Store Age Executive* that Visionary Shopper "brings us closer to maximizing the control over what the consumer sees, thus enhancing the validity of the data." As well, he noted that prior to the advent of Visionary Shopper, "our tests were more laboratory-ish and less realistic."

Source: Abridged from David Menzies, "Retail and High-Tech: Software Swami," *Marketing Magazine,* August 5, 1996, p. 13.

Exhibit 18-12 **How Customer's Reference Price Influences Perceived Value (for a marketing mix with a given set of benefits and costs)**

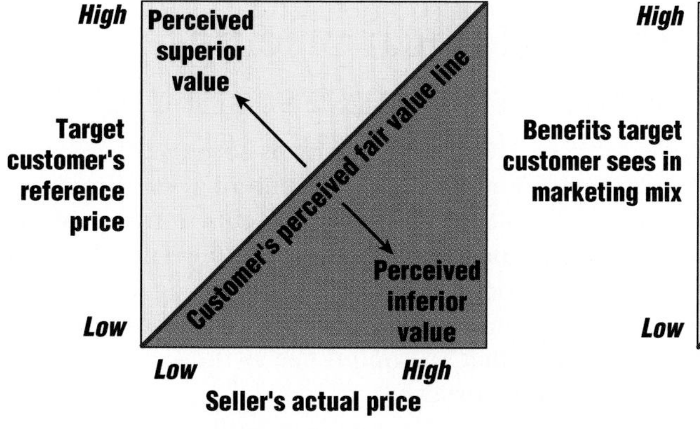

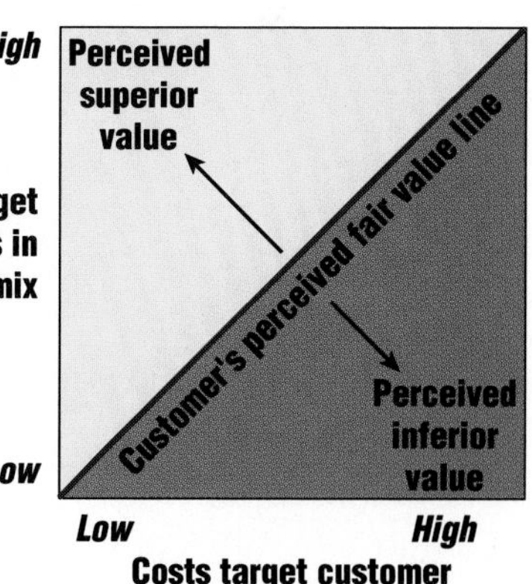

tomers don't stock heavily—milk, butter, eggs, or coffee—but on which they will recognize a real price cut. In other words, leader pricing is normally used with products for which consumers do have a specific reference price.

Leader pricing may try to appeal to customers who normally shop elsewhere. But it can backfire if customers buy only the low-price leaders. To avoid hurting profits, managers often select leader items that aren't directly competitive with major lines—as when bargain-priced recording tape is the leader for a stereo equipment store.

AT $79 IT'S SEXY.
AT $320 IT'S OBSCENE.
Designer clothing 40-70% off, every day. 5th Ave. & 18th St., Madison Ave. & 44th St.
DAFFY'S
CLOTHES THAT WILL MAKE YOU, NOT BREAK YOU.

If the price of a product is set higher than the target market's reference price, there is not likely to be much demand.

Bait pricing—offer a steal, but sell under protest

Bait pricing involves setting some very low prices to attract customers, but then trying to sell more expensive models or brands once the customer is in the store. For example, a furniture store may advertise a colour TV for $199. But once bargain hunters come to the store, salesclerks point out the disadvantages of the low-price TV and try to convince them to trade up to a better (and more expensive) set. Bait pricing is something like leader pricing. But here the seller *doesn't* plan to sell many at the low price.

If bait pricing is successful, the demand for higher-quality products expands. This approach may be a sensible part of a strategy to trade-up customers. And customers may be well-served if, once in the store, they find that a higher-priced product offers better value, perhaps because its features are better suited to their needs. But bait pricing is generally viewed as unethical, and in Canada it can contravene the misleading advertising rules of the Competition Act.

Psychological pricing—some prices just seem right

Psychological pricing means setting prices that have special appeal to target customers. Some people think there are entire ranges of prices that potential customers see as the same. So price cuts in these ranges do not increase the quantity sold. But just below this range, customers may buy more. Then, at even lower prices, the quantity demanded stays the same again—and so on. Exhibit 18–13 shows the kind of demand curve that leads to psychological pricing. Vertical drops mark the price ranges that customers see as the same. Pricing research shows that there *are* such demand curves.[9]

Odd–even pricing involves setting prices that end in certain numbers. For example, products selling below $50 often end in the number 5 or the number 9—for example, 49 cents or $24.95. Prices for higher-priced products are often $1 or $2 below the next even dollar figure—for example, $99 rather than $100.

Some marketers use odd–even pricing because they think consumers react better to these prices—perhaps seeing them as "substantially" lower than the next-highest even price. Marketers using these prices seem to assume that they have a rather jagged demand curve—that slightly higher prices will substantially reduce the quantity demanded. Long ago, some retailers used odd–even prices to force their clerks to make change. Then the clerks had to record the sale and could not pocket the money. Today, however, it's not always clear why firms use these prices—or whether they really work. Perhaps it's done simply because everyone else does it.[10]

Exhibit 18-13
Demand Curve When Psychological Pricing Is Appropriate

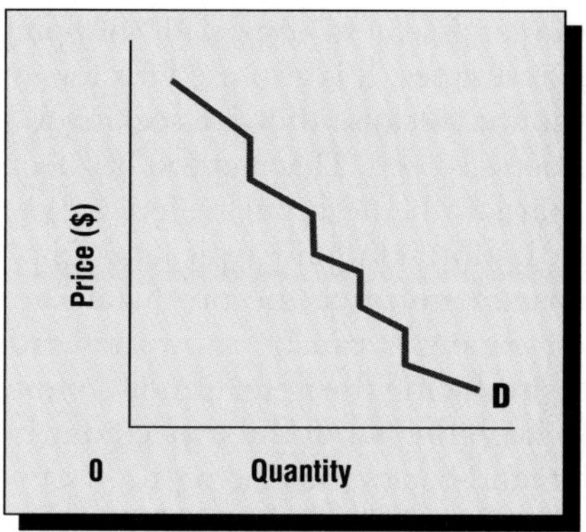

Exhibit 18-14
Demand Curve Showing a Prestige Pricing Situation

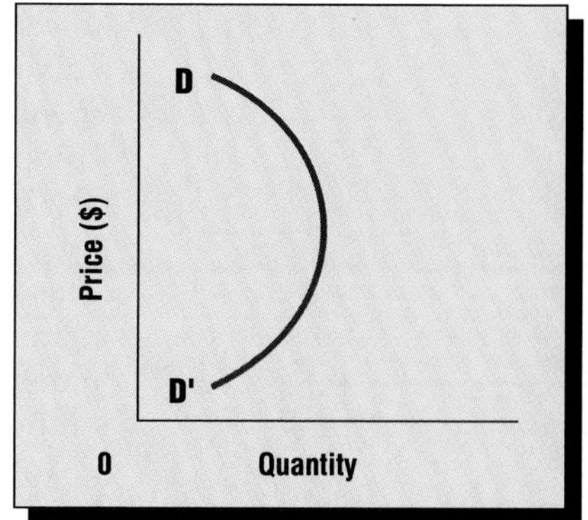

Prestige pricing indicates quality

With **prestige pricing** a rather high price is set to suggest high quality or high status. Some target customers want the best, so they will buy at a high price. If the price seems low, they worry about quality and don't buy.[11] Prestige pricing is most common for luxury products such as jewellery, leather goods, German cameras, and Swiss watches.

Prestige pricing is also common in service industries, where the customer can't see the product in advance and relies on price to judge its quality. Target customers who respond to prestige pricing give the marketing manager an unusual demand curve. Instead of a normal down-sloping curve, the curve goes down for a while and then bends back to the left again. See Exhibit 18–14.

Prestige pricing is most common for luxury products such as jewellery, perfume, and leather goods.

Price lining—a few prices cover the field

Price lining involves setting a few price levels for a product line and then marking all items at these prices. This approach assumes that customers have a certain reference price in mind that they expect to pay for a product. For example, most neckties are priced between \$10 and \$40. In price lining, there are only a few prices within this range. Ties will not be priced at \$10.00, \$10.50, \$11.00, and so on. They might be priced at four levels—\$10, \$20, \$30, and \$40.

Price lining has advantages other than just matching prices to what consumers expect to pay. The main advantage is simplicity, for both clerks and customers. It is less confusing than having many prices. Some customers may consider items in only one price class. Their big decision, then, is which item(s) to choose at that price.

For retailers, price lining has several advantages. Sales may increase because (1) they can offer a bigger variety in each price class and (2) it's easier to get customers to make decisions within one price class. Stock planning is simpler because demand is larger at the relatively few prices. Price lining can also reduce costs because inventory needs are lower.

Demand-backward pricing

Demand-backward pricing involves setting an acceptable final consumer price and working backward to what a producer can charge. It is commonly used by producers of final consumer products—especially shopping products such as women's and children's clothing and shoes. It is also used for toys or gifts, for which customers will spend a specific amount, because they are seeking a $5 or a $10 gift. Here, a reverse cost-plus pricing process is used. This method has been called market-minus pricing.

The producer starts with the retail (reference) price for a particular item and then works backward, subtracting the typical margins that channel members expect. This gives the approximate price the producer can charge. Then the average or planned marketing expenses can be subtracted from this price to arrive at how much can be spent producing the item. Candy companies do this. They alter the size of the candy bar to keep the bar at the expected price.

In order for demand-backward pricing to be successful, demand estimates are needed. The quantity that will be demanded affects production costs—that is, where the firm will be on its average cost curve. Also, since competitors can be expected to make the best product possible, it is important to know customer needs in order to set the best amount to spend on manufacturing costs. By increasing costs a little, the firm may so improve its product in consumers' eyes that it will sell many more units. But if consumers only want novelty, additional quality may not increase the quantity demanded—and shouldn't be offered.

Green pricing

Another method being discussed in various circles is "green" pricing. This pricing method takes into consideration the environmental costs of production and waste disposal.

Pricing a full line

Our emphasis has been—and will continue to be—on the problem of pricing an individual product, mainly because this makes our discussion clearer. But most marketing managers are responsible for more than one product. In fact, their "product" may be the company's entire line! So we'll discuss this matter briefly.

Full-line pricing—market- or firm-oriented?

Full-line pricing involves setting prices for a whole line of products. How this should be done depends on which of two basic situations a firm is facing.

In one situation, all products in the company's line are aimed at the same general target market, which makes it important for all prices to be related. For example, a producer of TV sets can offer several price and quality levels to give its target customers some choice. The different prices should seem reasonable when the target customers are evaluating them.

In the other situation, the different products in the line are aimed at entirely different target markets so there doesn't have to be any relationship between the various prices. For example, a chemical producer of a wide variety of products with several target markets probably should price each product separately.

Costs are complicated in full-line pricing

The marketing manager must try to recover all costs on the entire line—perhaps by pricing quite low on competitive items and much higher on less competitive items. Estimating costs for each product is a big problem because there is no single right way to assign a company's fixed costs to each of the products. Further, if any cost-oriented pricing method is carried through without demand being considered, it can lead to very unrealistic prices. To avoid mistakes, the marketing manager should judge demand for the entire line as well as demand for each individual product in each target market.

As an aid to full-line pricing, marketing managers can assemble directly variable costs on the many items in the line to calculate a price floor. To this floor they can add a reasonable markup based on the quality of the product, the strength of the demand for the product, and the degree of competition. But finally, the image projected by the full line must be evaluated.

Complementary product pricing

With **complementary product pricing,** prices are set on several products as a group. This may lead to one product being priced very low so that the profits from another product will increase—and increase the product group's total profits. A new Gillette shaver, for example, may be priced low to sell the blades, which must be replaced regularly.

Complementary product pricing differs from full-line pricing in that different production facilities may be involved—so there's no cost allocation problem. The real challenge is to understand the target market and the demand curves for each of the complementary products. Then, various combinations of prices can be tried to see which set will be best for reaching the company's pricing objectives.

Product-bundle pricing

A firm that offers its target market several different products may use **product-bundle pricing**—setting one price for a set of products. Firms that use product-bundle pricing usually set the overall price so that it's cheaper for the customer to buy the products at the same time rather than separately. Drugstores sometimes bundle the cost of a roll of film and the cost of the processing. A bank may offer a product-bundle price for a safe-deposit box, travellers cheques, and a savings account. Bundling encourages customers to spend more and buy products that they might not otherwise buy—because the "added cost" of the extras is not as high as it would normally be.

Most firms that use product-bundle pricing also set individual prices for the unbundled products. This may increase demand by attracting customers who want one item in a product assortment but don't want the extras. Many firms treat services this way. A software company may have a product-bundle price for its software and access to a toll-free telephone assistance service. However, customers who don't need help can pay a lower price and get just the software.[12]

Bid pricing and negotiated pricing depend heavily on costs

Bid pricing means offering a specific price for each possible job rather than setting a price that applies for all customers. Building contractors, for example, must bid on possible projects. And many companies selling services (like architects and engineers) must submit bids for jobs they would like to have.

The big problem in bid pricing is estimating all the costs that will apply to each job. This may sound easy, but a complicated bid may involve thousands of cost components. Further, management must include an overhead charge and a charge for profit.

Sometimes it isn't even possible to figure out costs in advance. This may lead to a contract where the customer agrees to pay the supplier's total cost plus an agreed-on profit figure (say, 10 percent of costs or a dollar amount) after the job is finished.

Demand must be considered too

Competition must be considered when adding in overhead and profit for a bid price. Usually, the customer will get several bids and accept the lowest one. So unthinking addition of typical overhead and profit rates should be avoided. Some bidders use the

Ethical Dimensions

Cost-plus Bid Pricing

Some unethical sellers give bid prices based on cost-plus contracts a bad reputation by faking their records to make costs seem higher than they really are. In other situations, there may be honest debate about which costs should be allowed.

same overhead and profit rates on all jobs, regardless of competition—and then are surprised when they don't get some jobs.

Because bidding can be expensive, marketing managers may want to be selective about which jobs to bid on, and choose those where they feel they have the greatest chance of success. Firms can spend thousands or even millions of dollars just developing bids for large business or government customers.[13]

Sometimes bids are negotiated

Some buying situations (including much government buying) require the use of bids, and the purchasing agent must take the lowest bid. In other situations, the customer asks for bids and then singles out the company that submits the *most attractive* bid—not necessarily the lowest—for further bargaining.

What will a specific customer pay?

The list price or bidding price the seller would like to charge is sometimes only the *starting point* for discussions with individual customers. What a customer will buy—if the customer buys at all—depends on the **negotiated price,** a price set based on bargaining between the buyer and seller.

As with simple bid pricing, negotiated pricing is most common in situations where the marketing mix is adjusted for each customer. This means that bargaining may involve the entire marketing mix, not just the price level. For example, a firm that produces machine tools used by other manufacturers to make their products might use this approach. Each customer may need custom-designed machines and different types of installation service. Through the bargaining process, the seller tries to determine which aspects of the marketing mix are most important to the customer. For one customer, selling price may be most important. There, the seller might try to find ways to reduce costs of other elements of the marketing mix—consistent with the customer's needs—in order to earn a profit. Another customer might want more of some other element of the marketing mix—perhaps more technical help after the sale—and be less sensitive to price.

Sellers must know their costs in order to negotiate prices effectively. However, negotiated pricing *is* a demand-oriented approach. Here, the seller is very carefully analyzing a particular customer's position on a demand curve—or on different possible demand curves based on different offerings—rather than the overall demand curve for a group of customers. This is a challenging job, the details of which are beyond the scope of this book. However, the techniques for supply and demand analysis we've been discussing apply here as they do with other price-setting approaches.

Questions and Problems

1. Why do many department stores seek a markup of about 40 percent when some discount houses operate on a 20 percent markup?

2. A producer distributed its riding lawn mowers through wholesalers and retailers. The retail selling price was $800, and the manufacturing cost to the company was $312. The retail markup was 35 percent and the wholesale markup 20 percent. (a) What was the cost to the wholesaler? To the retailer? (b) What percentage markup did the producer take?

3. Relate the concept of stock turnover to the growth of mass merchandising. Use a simple example in your answer.

4. If total fixed costs are $200,000 and total variable costs are $100,000 at the output of 20,000 units, what are the probable total fixed costs and total variable costs at an output of 10,000 units? What are the average fixed costs, average variable costs, and average costs at these two output levels? Explain what additional information you would want to determine which price should be charged.

5. Explain how experience curve pricing differs from average-cost pricing.

6. Construct an example showing that mechanical use of a very large or a very small markup might still lead to unprofitable operation while some intermediate price would be profitable. Draw a graph and show the break-even point(s).

7. The Davis Company's fixed costs for the year are estimated at $200,000. Its product sells for $250. The variable cost per unit is $200. Sales for the coming year are expected to reach $1,250,000. What is the break-even point? The expected profit? If sales are forecast at only $875,000, should the Davis Company shut down operations? Explain.

8. Discuss the idea of drawing separate demand curves for different market segments. It seems logical because each target market should have its own marketing mix. But won't this lead to many demand curves and possible prices? And what will this mean with respect to functional discounts and varying prices in the marketplace? Will it be legal? Will it be practical?

9. How does a prestige pricing policy fit into a marketing mix? Would exclusive distribution be necessary?

10. Cite a local example of odd–even pricing and evaluate whether it makes sense.

11. Cite a local example of psychological pricing and evaluate whether it makes sense.

12. Distinguish between leader pricing and bait pricing. What do they have in common? How can their use affect a marketing mix?

13. Is a full-line pricing policy available only to producers? Cite local examples of full-line pricing. Why is full-line pricing important?

Suggested cases

24 Fraser Company

25 Lee Steel Supply and Service

35 Chalaga Mussel Farms

Computer-aided problem

Break-Even/Profit Analysis

This problem lets you see the dynamics of break-even analysis. The starting values (costs, revenues, etc.) for this problem are from the break-even analysis example in this chapter (see Exhibit 18–8).

The first column computes a break-even point. You can change costs and prices to calculate new break-even points (in units and dollars). The second column goes further. There, you can specify target profit level, and the unit and dollar sales needed to achieve your target profit level will be computed. You can also estimate possible sales quantities and the program will compute costs, sales, and profits. Use this spreadsheet to answer the following questions.

a. Vary the selling price between $1.00 and $1.40. Prepare a table showing how the break-even point (in units and dollars) changes at the different price levels.

b. If you hope to earn a target profit of $15,000, how many units would you have to sell? What would total cost be? Total sales dollars? (Note: Use the right-hand ["profit analysis"] column in the spreadsheet.)

c. Using the "profit analysis" column (column 2), allow your estimate of the sale quantity to vary between 64,000 and 96,000. Prepare a table that shows, for each quantity level, what happens to total cost, average cost per unit, and profit. Explain why average cost changes as it does over the different quantity values.

For additional questions related to this problem, see Exercise 18–5 in the *Learning Aid for Use with Basic Marketing*, Ninth Canadian Edition.

When you finish this chapter, you should:

- Know the content of and differences among strategies, marketing plans, and a marketing program.
- Know how to use S.W.O.T. analysis and other planning approaches to zero in on a marketing strategy that fits the firm's objectives and resources and meets customers' needs.
- Understand why the product classes and typical mixes are a good starting point for planning.
- Understand the basic forecasting approaches and why they are used to evaluate the profitability of potential strategies.
- Know what is involved in preparing a marketing plan, including estimates of costs and revenue and specification of other time-related details.
- Understand the different ways a firm can plan to become involved in international marketing.
- Understand the important new terms (shown in orange).

Chap nineteen

Developing Innovative Marketing Plans

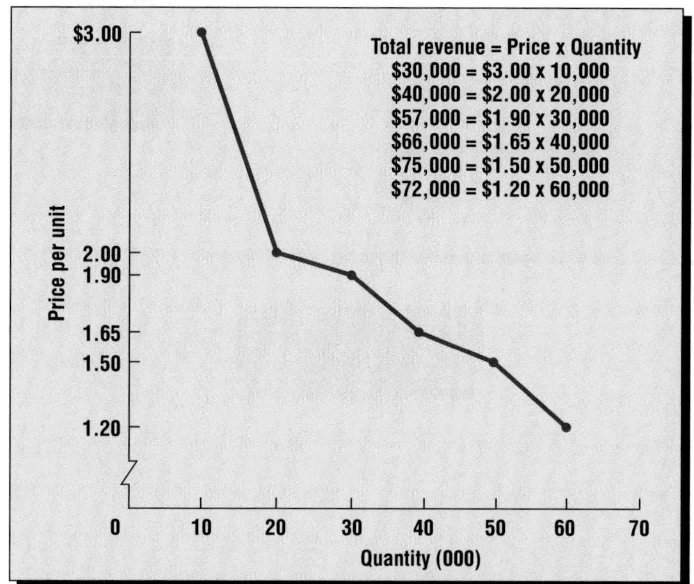

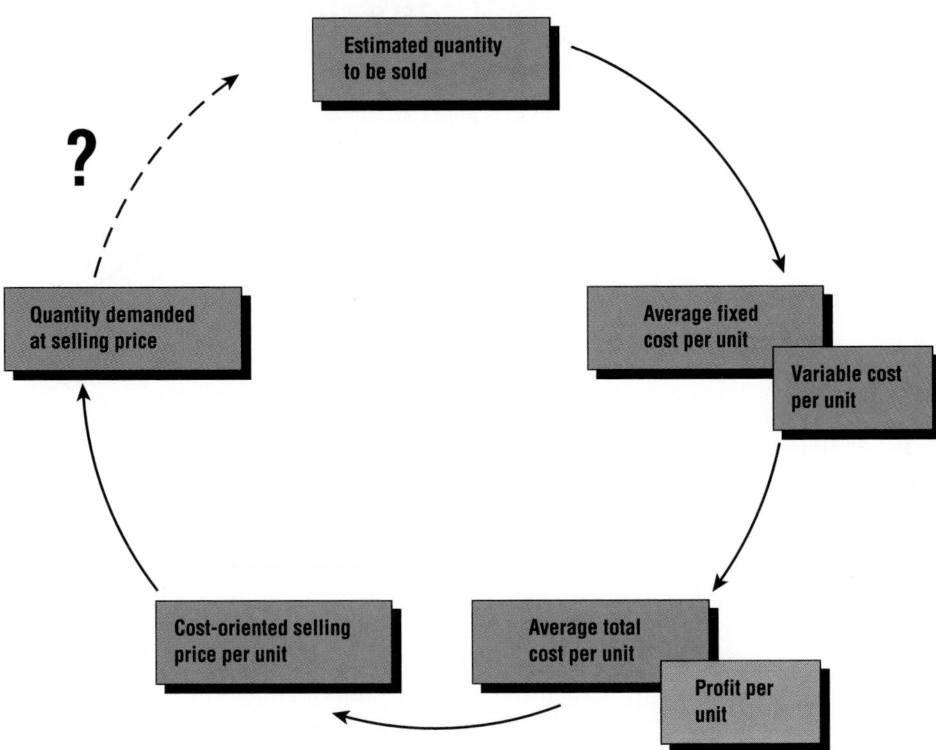

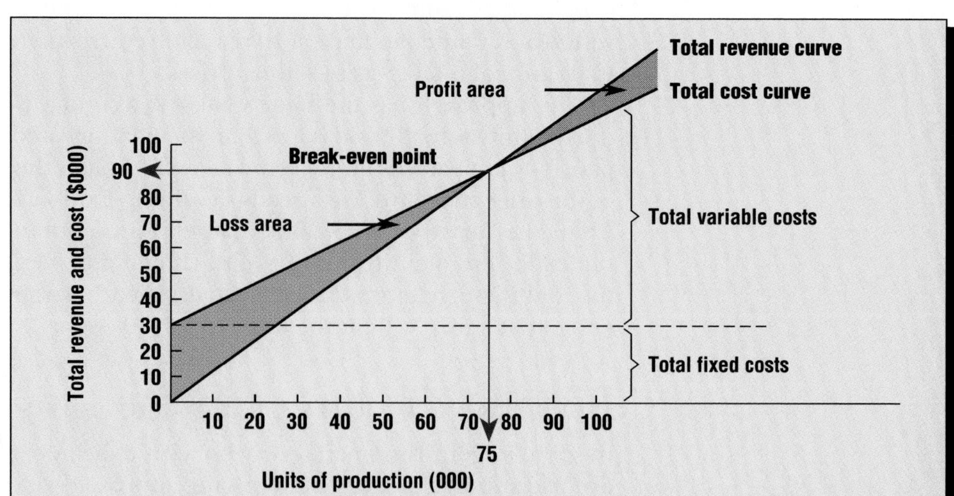

When Kellogg Canada introduced Nutri-Grain three years ago, it was more than just a product launch. It marked the creation of an entire category, cereal bars. And, despite stiff competition, Kellogg has sustained a lead in this fast-growing category.

The cereal bar category is now worth more than $61.5 million, up 6% from 1996, according to ACNeilsen of Markham, Ont. Nutri-Grain's Canadian success has inspired its recent launch in the U.K., and it is also being considered in France.

The fastest growth in this category, a whopping 56% increase, came in 1996, with the debut of copycats like Sun Ups and SnackWell's cereal bars by Christie Brown & Co. of Toronto. "Nutri-Grain drew attention to the category," says Christine Lowry, Kellogg's director of nutrition and corporate affairs.

But it was the "hectic morning" TV and outdoor ads by Leo Burnett Co. of Toronto that helped "build a relationship between the Nutri-Grain brand and the consumer," says Lowry. Ads asking rueful questions like "Spending more time on your hair than on breakfast?" or "Hitting the snooze button too often?" struck a familiar chord with the 90s working consumer.

Well, not everyone. "It's not for the person who gets up at six in the morning," says Burnett account director Chris Pastirik. He commends Kellogg for taking the risk of targeting Nutri-Grain to a specific group. With this group in mind, Kellogg saw an opportunity to market Nutri-Grain as a convenient and portable breakfast on the go. It made sense to place ads in subway cars, transit stations and on billboards.

The ads were part of a comprehensive marketing launch strategy that goes back to June 1994. This strategy also included a consumer survey and massive sampling.

The survey, done during morning rush hour, asked 6,630 people in Vancouver, Calgary, Toronto, Ottawa and Montreal whether they'd had breakfast that morning. Fifty-three percent said no, because they had no time. Samples of Nutri-Grain were offered to those busy yet hungry respondents.

Kellogg's Lowry says the survey served as good PR for Nutri-Grain because newspapers and radio stations picked up on the story.

And what kind of marketing would be complete without free samples of the new product—but 10 million within the first year? Kellogg distributed this huge number through partnerships with Air Canada and Petro-Canada, which handed out Nutri-Grain bars to their customers. More samples were included in morning issues of *The Globe and Mail.*

A marketing program of this size is nothing new to Kellogg. But, says Pastirik, when the company launches a new product, especially a new category, it goes all out.

Source: Elizabeth Adams, "Eating Up A Brand New Category," *Marketing Magazine,* December 22/29, 1997, p. 7.

Marketing planning process is more than assembling the four Ps

The Kellogg Canada Nutri-Grain™ case shows that developing a successful marketing strategy is a creative process. But it is also a logical process. And the logic that leads to a sound strategy may need to change as the market environment and target customers change.

Strategic planning is guided by basic principles. The marketing concept emphasizes that all of a firm's activities should focus on its target markets. A firm should try to find a competitive advantage in meeting the needs of some target market(s) that it can satisfy very well. The target market(s) should be large enough to support the firm's efforts and yield a profit. And ideally, the strategy should take advantage of trends in the external market, rather than buck them.

As we explained in Chapter 2, a marketing *strategy* consists of a target market and a marketing mix; it is a "big picture" of what a firm will do in some target market. A marketing *plan* includes the time-related details—including expected costs and revenues—for that strategy. In most firms, the marketing manager must ultimately combine the different marketing plans into an overall marketing *program*.

In this chapter, we'll develop these ideas further. We'll start with a review of the many variables that must be considered in the strategic market planning process, and we'll highlight some of the key ways a marketing manager can identify the right blend of the marketing mix for an innovative strategy. Then we'll discuss how these ideas come together in a marketing plan.

We'll also discuss ways to forecast target market potential and sales, which is important not only in evaluating opportunities but also in developing the time-related details for a plan. Of course, plans must ultimately be blended into an overall program, and we'll suggest ways to approach that task. Planning strategies for international markets presents some special challenges, so we'll end the chapter by describing the different ways a marketer can address these challenges.

Strategic market planning provides focus and direction

Developing a good marketing strategy and turning that strategy into a marketing plan requires blending the ideas we've discussed throughout this text. Exhibit 19–1 provides a broad overview of the major areas we've been talking about. Now we must integrate ideas about these different areas to narrow down to logical marketing mixes, marketing strategies, and marketing plans—and a marketing program.

As suggested in Exhibit 19–1, the process of developing an effective marketing strategy involves narrowing down to a specific target market and marketing mix that represents a real opportunity. This process requires a thorough understanding of the market. That understanding is enhanced by careful analysis of customers' needs, current or prospective competitors, and the firm's own objectives and resources. Similarly, favourable or unfavourable factors and trends in the external market environment may make a potential opportunity more or less attractive.

There are usually more different possible strategies than a firm can pursue. Each possible strategy usually has a number of different potential advantages and disadvantages. This can make it difficult to zero in on the best target market and marketing mix. However, as we discussed in Chapter 2, developing a set of specific qualitative and quantitative screening criteria—to define in what business and markets the firm wants to compete—can help eliminate potential strategies that are not well suited for the firm.

Exhibit 19-1 Overview of Strategic Market Planning Process

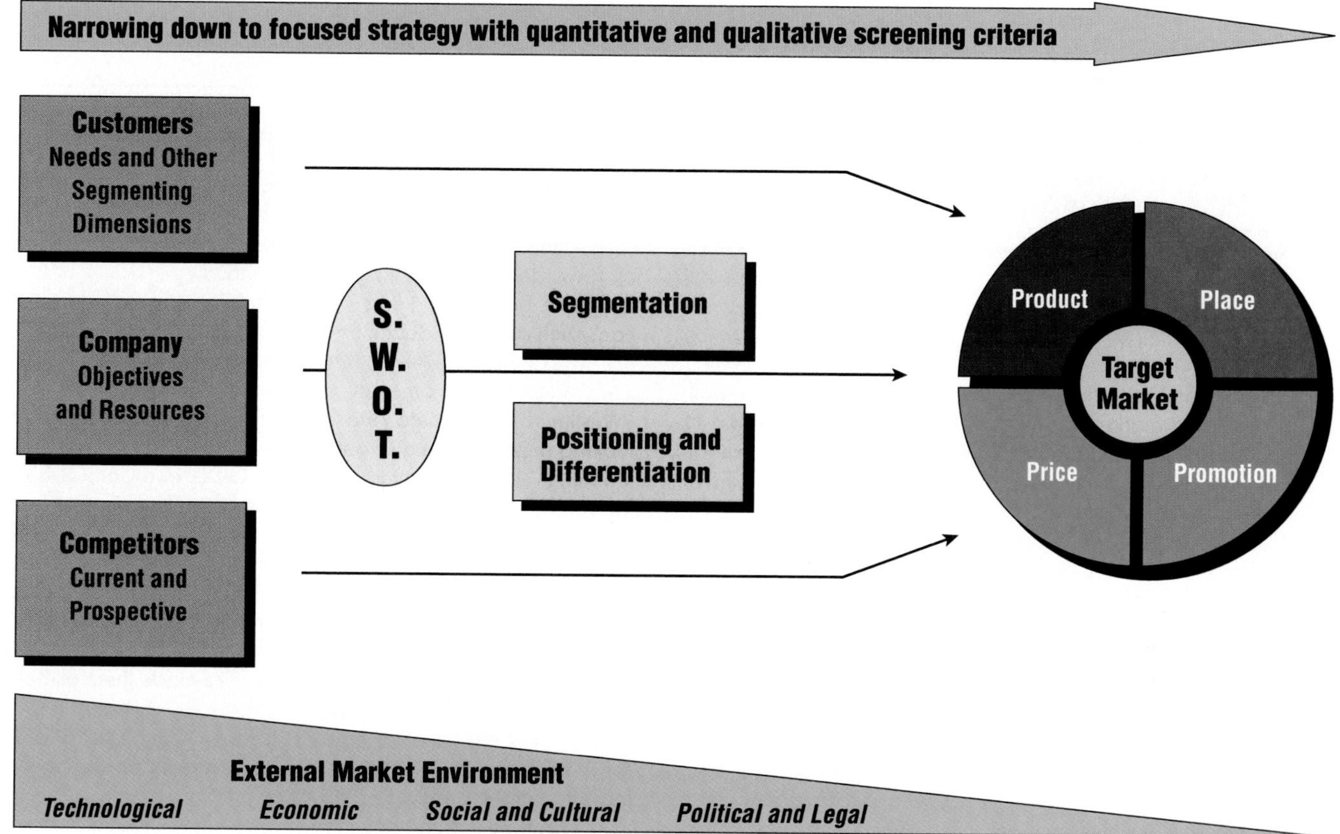

Another useful aid for zeroing in on a feasible strategy is *S.W.O.T. analysis,* which identifies and lists the firm's strengths and weaknesses and its opportunities and threats. S.W.O.T. is simply an abbreviation for the first letters of the words *s*trengths, *w*eaknesses, *o*pportunities, and *t*hreats. A good S.W.O.T. analysis helps the manager focus on a strategy that will take advantage of the firm's opportunities and strengths while avoiding its weaknesses and threats to its success. These can be compared with the pros and cons of strategies that are considered. For example, if a firm is considering a strategy that focuses on a target market that is already being served by several strong competitors, success will usually hinge on some sort of competitive advantage. Such a competitive advantage might be based on a better marketing mix—perhaps an innovative new product, improved distribution, more effective promotion, or a better price. Just offering a marketing mix that is like what is available from competitors usually doesn't provide a competitive advantage—or any real basis for the firm to position or differentiate its marketing mix as better for customers.

Marketing mix flows from target market dimensions

Ideally, the ingredients of a good marketing mix flow logically from all the relevant dimensions of a target market. The market definition and segmenting approaches we discussed in Chapter 8 help the marketing manager identify which dimensions are qualifying and which are determining in customers' choices.

Product benefits must match needs. How customers search for information helps define the promotion blend. Demographic dimensions reveal where customers are located and whether they have the income to buy. Where customers shop for or buy products helps define channel alternatives. The value of the entire marketing mix and the urgency of customer needs, combined with an understanding of what customers

Marketing Demo 19-1

Golf Island PEI

It wasn't that long ago that visitors to Prince Edward Island only thought about beaches, Anne of Green Gables and lobster. While those three staples are still part of the province's tourism attraction, golf can now be safely added to the mix.

And that hasn't happened by accident; it's been a well-co-ordinated marketing strategy that has taken the Island to the forefront of the Canadian golf tourism industry. It's a strategy that a number of other Canadian destination areas have adopted all in hope of attracting the travelling golfer.

"Four or five years ago, we were a non-entity," said Tourism PEI's Ron McNeill. "But we've made a lot of noise since then and our golf traffic has almost doubled."

What PEI did, and others are doing, is to form a consortium of the golf properties. Instead of 12 courses each trying to attract golfers on their own, they have banded together along with government cooperation, to form Golf Island PEI, figuring there is strength in numbers.

The group pooled money for advertising and marketing, hired some professionals to help with direction and then watched the [courses] jam up with golfers looking for a holiday within their own country.

"All the courses began to realize that if you bring a golfer to the Island, everyone benefits," McNeill says. "No one comes here to just play one course. They want to play three or four or more."

In other words, PEI went from being a province where there are a dozen courses, to a golf destination.

And the spin-offs were plentiful. In addition to the courses, the accompanying amenities also benefited. Restaurants, resorts, attractions, hotels, rental car companies and more were all rewarded by the golfing group's efforts . . .

While golf consortiums are old hat in U.S. golf destinations such as Myrtle Beach and Florida, PEI's was virtually the first in Canada. However, it has been joined by many more since. In fact, there are now marketing groups in Vancouver, Whistler, B.C., Toronto and Nova Scotia, with more areas looking at jumping in and getting a share of the booming golf market. A study conducted by SCORE GOLF and ComQUEST Research in December, 1996 indicated that Canada has just over five million golfers or 24 per cent of the adult population. That number provides huge potential for locations such as PEI and Vancouver . . .

In PEI, the level of standards is continually being raised as none of the courses wants to be left behind. "They all want to be as good as the best," McNeil says. "It's made them all better and the overall product better."

To further enhance the golf, PEI is looking at a centralized reservation system for all the courses, and even on-line booking for computer users . . .

"I can't see it doing anything but growing," McNeill adds. "Every community on the Island wants a course so they can get on board and we've barely even scratched markets like the U.S. or Japan."

Source: Abridged from Bob Weeks, "Teeing Off," *The Globe and Mail,* April 21, 1997, D6. Reprinted with permission from Bob Weeks.

see as substitute ways of meeting needs, help companies estimate price sensitivity. The Golf Island PEI product launch discussed in Marketing Demo 19–1 shows what can be accomplished through careful strategic planning.

It would seem that if we fully understand the needs and attitudes of a target market, then combining the four Ps should be easy. Yet there are three important gaps in this line of reasoning: (1) We don't always know as much as we would like to about the needs and attitudes of our target markets. (2) Competitors are also trying to satisfy these or similar needs—and their efforts may force a firm to shift its marketing mix. (3) The other dimensions of the marketing environment may be changing—which may require more changes in marketing mixes. These points warrant further consideration.

Product classes suggest typical marketing mixes

Even if you don't or can't know all you would like to about a potential target market, you usually know enough to decide whether the product is a consumer product or a business product, and which product class is most relevant (see Exhibit 9–3, which summarizes the product classes).

Identifying the proper product class helps because it suggests how a typical product should be distributed and promoted. So if you don't know as much as you'd like about potential customers' needs and attitudes, at least knowing how *they* would view the company's product can give you a head start on developing a marketing mix. A convenience product, for example, usually needs more intensive distribution, and the producer usually takes on more responsibility for promotion. A specialty product needs a clear brand identity, and this may require a positioning effort. A new unsought product will need a mix that leads customers through the adoption process.

It's reassuring to see that product classes do summarize some of what you would like to know about target markets and what marketing mixes are relevant. After all, what others have done in similar situations must have satisfied someone, and that can serve as a guide. Beyond this, you need judgment or perhaps some marketing research. In this way, you can use past experience—while not relying on that experience blindly.

Typical is not necessarily right

The typical marketing mix for a given product class is not necessarily right for all situations. Some very profitable marketing mixes depart from the typical in order to satisfy some target markets better.

A marketing manager may have to develop a mix that is *not* typical because of various market realities, including special characteristics of the product or target market, the competitive environment, and each firm's capabilities and limitations. In fact, it is often by differentiating the firm's product and/or other elements of the marketing mix that the marketing manager can offer target customers unique value.

Superior mixes may be breakthrough opportunities

When marketing managers fully understand their target markets, they may be able to develop marketing mixes that are superior to competitors' mixes. Such understanding may provide breakthrough opportunities. Taking advantage of these opportunities can lead to large sales and profitable growth. This is why we stress the importance of looking for breakthrough opportunities rather than just trying to imitate competitors' offerings.

NutraSweet built its original success on an innovative product that met consumers' needs. But the strategy that NutraSweet's marketing managers planned involved more than a good product. The typical marketing strategy for firms supplying ingredients to food and soft-drink companies emphasized personal selling to producers. In contrast, NutraSweet's marketing managers used mass selling to promote their brand name and red swirl logo directly to consumers.

They also persuaded producers who used the ingredient to feature the NutraSweet brand name prominently on containers and in ads. In addition, because there was little direct competition initially, they used a profitable skimming approach to pricing—and charged different producer-customers different prices, depending on the value that NutraSweet added to their product.[1]

Inferior mixes are easy to reject

Just as some mixes are superior, some mixes are clearly inferior or unsuitable. For example, a national TV advertising campaign might make sense for a large company, but it might be completely out of the question for a small manufacturer that only has the resources to start offering a new product in a limited geographic area.

Marketing manager must blend the four Ps

Exhibit 19–2 reviews the major marketing strategy decision areas organized by the four Ps. Each of these requires careful decision making. Yet, marketing planning involves much more than just independent decisions and assembling the parts into a marketing mix. The four Ps must be creatively *blended* so that the firm develops the best mix for its target market. In other words, each decision must fit well as part of a logical whole if it is to work well with all of the others.

Throughout the text, we've given the job of integrating the four Ps strategy decisions to the marketing manager. Now you should see the need for this integrating role. It is easy for specialists to focus on their own areas and expect the rest of the company to work for or around them. This is especially true in larger firms—where specialists are needed—simply because the size of the entire marketing job is too big for one person. Yet the ideas of the product manager, advertising manager, sales manager, and physical distribution manager may have to be adjusted to improve the whole mix. It's critical that each marketing mix decision work well with all of the others. A breakdown in any one decision area may doom the entire strategy to failure.

Exhibit 19–2 Strategic Decision Areas Organized by the Four Ps

Product	Place	Promotion	Price

Physical good
Service
Features
Quality level
Accessories
Installation
Instructions
Warranty
Product lines
Packaging
Branding
	Objectives
	Channel type
	Market exposure
	Kinds of intermediaries
	Kinds and locations of stores
	How to handle transporting and storing
	Service levels
	Recruiting intermediaries
	Managing channels
		Objectives
		Promotion blend
		Salespeople
		  Kind
		  Number
		  Selection
		  Training
		  Motivation
		Advertising
		  Targets
		  Kinds of ads
		  Media type
		  Copy thrust
		  Prepared by whom
		Sales promotion
		Publicity
			Objectives
			Flexibility
			Level over product life cycle
			Geographic terms
			Discounts
			Allowances

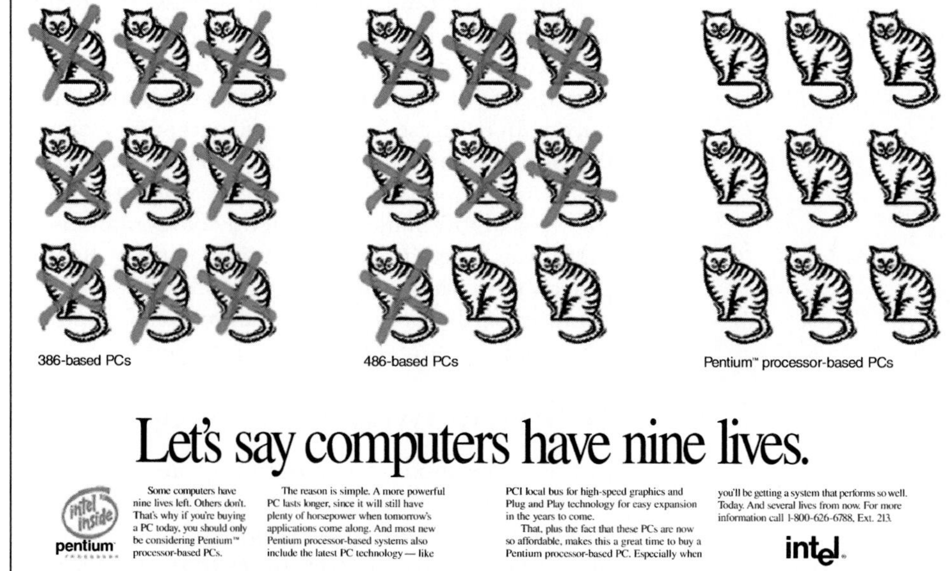

386-based PCs
486-based PCs
Pentium™ processor-based PCs
Let's say computers have nine lives.
intel inside pentium
Some computers have nine lives left. Others don't. That's why if you're buying a PC today, you should only be considering Pentium™ processor-based PCs.
The reason is simple. A more powerful PC lasts longer, since it will still have plenty of horsepower when tomorrow's applications come along. And most new Pentium processor-based systems also include the latest PC technology — like PCI local bus for high-speed graphics and Plug and Play technology for easy expansion in the years to come.
That, plus the fact that these PCs are now so affordable, makes this a great time to buy a Pentium processor-based PC. Especially when you'll be getting a system that performs so well. Today. And several lives from now. For more information call 1-800-626-6788, Ext. 213.
intel.

Intel could plan a marketing strategy—and forecast likely sales—for its Pentium processors based on the stage in the product life cycle and the experience it had with its earlier 386 and 486 processors.

Product life cycle guides planning

Careful consideration of where a firm's offering fits in the product life cycle can also be a big help in evaluating the best marketing mix. Exhibit 19–3 summarizes how marketing mix variables typically change over the product life cycle. This exhibit is a good review of many topics we've discussed throughout the text. Certainly, the pioneering effort required for a really new product concept is different from the job of taking market share away from an established competitor late in the market growth stage. See Marketing Demo 19–2 for a discussion of how BC TEL Interactive used life-cycle thinking and other key concepts when it launched its Sympatico™ Internet service.

When you're thinking about the product life cycle, don't forget that markets change continually. This means you must plan strategies that can adjust to changing conditions. The original marketing plan for a new marketing strategy may even include details about what adjustments in the marketing mix or target market will be required as the nature of competition and the adoption process evolve.[2]

Exhibit 19–3 Typical Changes in Marketing Variables over the Product Life Cycle

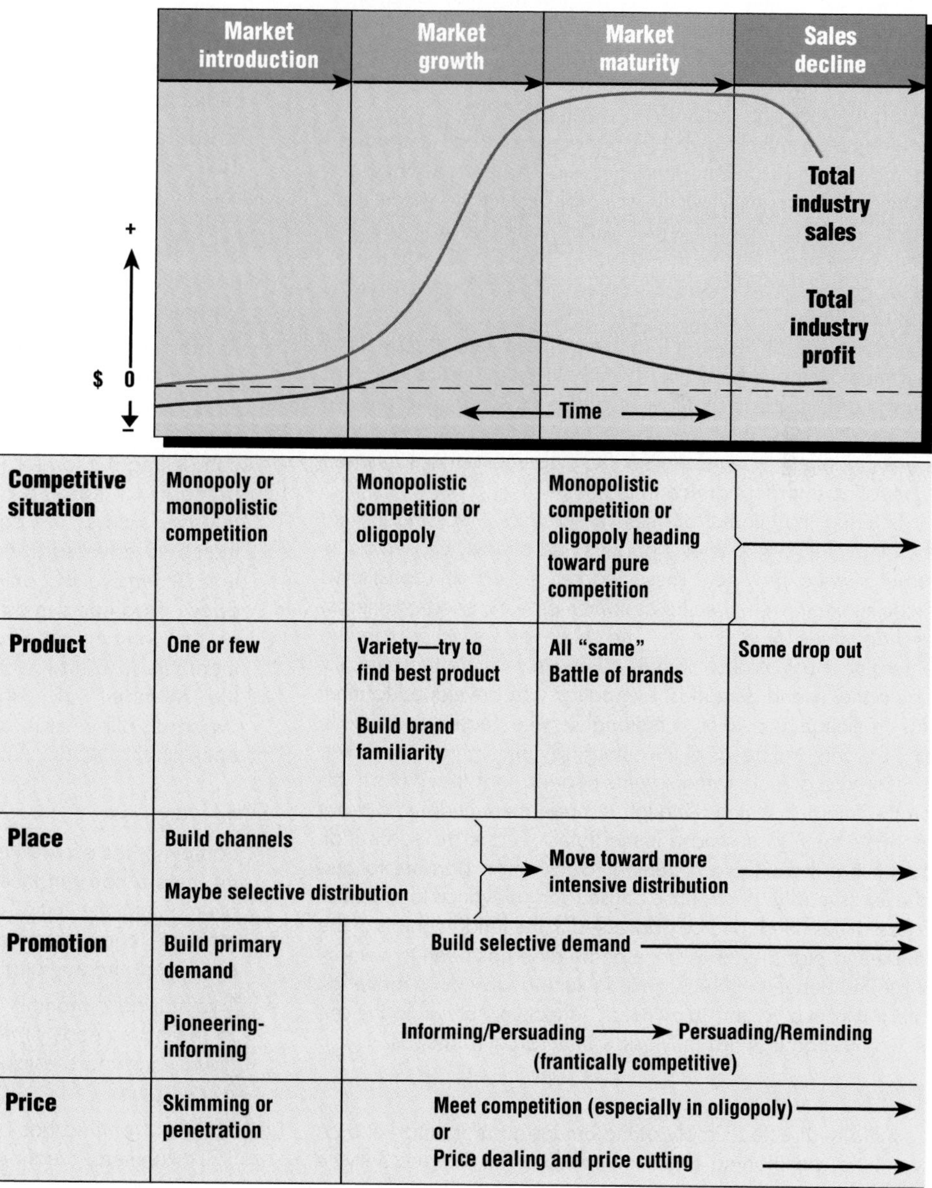

	Market introduction	Market growth	Market maturity	Sales decline
Competitive situation	Monopoly or monopolistic competition	Monopolistic competition or oligopoly	Monopolistic competition or oligopoly heading toward pure competition	→
Product	One or few	Variety—try to find best product Build brand familiarity	All "same" Battle of brands	Some drop out
Place	Build channels Maybe selective distribution	→ Move toward more intensive distribution →		
Promotion	Build primary demand Pioneering-informing	Build selective demand → Informing/Persuading → Persuading/Reminding (frantically competitive)		
Price	Skimming or penetration	Meet competition (especially in oligopoly) → or Price dealing and price cutting →		

Marketing Demo 19-2

Introducing the Internet as a New Consumer Product

Although the Internet has been around in academic, scientific, and government circles for over a quarter of a century, the Internet as a revolutionary new consumer service is a very recent phenomenon.

In fact, just two years ago BC TEL Interactive, the interactive multimedia division of BC TELECOM, was not in the Internet business at all. Today, its Sympatico™ Internet Service is the largest Internet Service Provider (ISP) in BC and, through MediaLinx Interactive and its telecommunications partners across the country, the biggest in Canada. Sympatico's expansion program means that the service is now available to over 85% of the population of BC and the service enjoys the highest market share of any ISP in the province. Year over year growth in 1997 exceeded 85%.

Sympatico has received high marks from consumers and the industry alike, culminating in a wide range of awards, including the People's Choice Award for Best World Wide Web Site at the 1997 International Digital Media Awards, the Best New Consumer Online Product of 1996, Top Canadian Internet Service Award and a host of web site-related awards and accolades.

Early research showed that there was a very high level of consumer demand for a user-friendly Internet service and that the majority of consumers were particularly eager to receive this service from their telephone companies. As a result of these findings, in early 1996 BC TEL Interactive launched Sympatico Internet Service in BC.

Entering the Internet business in the mid-1990s meant that the innovators and earliest adopters had already chosen an Internet service provider. These markets essentially constituted niche markets with specific customer profiles, usage patterns, and demands for the service. The challenge was to capture the emerging mass market, with its completely different profile, usage patterns and demands. Sympatico was developed to meet this challenge, providing a national service geared specifically to the wants and needs of the emerging mass consumer market.

Increasingly, consumers were hearing that they "must" be on the Internet, which although it made them curious, did not motivate them to purchase immediately. Further research indicated that there were a number of common barriers to purchase, primarily: price, ease of use, and relevance to their life. These issues needed to be addressed in the fundamentals of the marketing plan. A cornerstone of the plan has been to demonstrate the benefits of the service in such a way as to move the Internet from a "want" to a "need", effectively boosting the service's position upward in Maslow's hierarchy of needs.

Positioning

- Initially directed simply at the emerging mass market as a whole, positioning has evolved from The Internet Service for Everyone to focus more closely on individuals, leveraging the benefits of this very personalizable service.
- In addition, positioning leverages a key point of differentiation in this highly competitive market: The BC TEL brand, with BC TEL's well-known reputation for trust and reliability.

Product

- The product is constantly changing as both the Internet and the market continue to evolve. Today the consumer dial-up service includes: software, e-mail and Internet access, personal web pages, local and regional online communities (including interactive areas for news, sports, entertainment, financial and learning resources, and areas of specific interest to Chinese and Indo-Canadians), customer service and technical support. Success in the consumer dial-up market has also enabled the launch of a high-speed dedicated-access service and a business dial-up service.
- To address the "ease of use" issue, the Sympatico web site itself was designed to be analogous to a friendly community—where you can easily find whatever you're looking for and never hesitate to ask your neighbour for help. A simplified installation process, sufficient access ports to meet peak demand periods, and technical support 24 hours a day, 7 days a week were also essential.
- To address the question "how is this relevant to my life", the product is continually evolved with additional features, resources and services. While up-to-the-minute financial or sports information may be one person's compelling reason for joining, another may be interested primarily in learning and research, or in e-mailing their relatives across the country or across the globe. Since members have said that they need more local information, extensive BC online communities are being developed. Traditional media such as an introductory video and a members magazine have helped introduce novice members to a new world they can use in their everyday life. Member web pages and an easy-to-use web page "wizard" allow even beginners to create their own presence on the World Wide Web.

Pricing

- Sampling has allowed consumers to see for themselves how the Internet can enhance their lifestyle, while at the same time overcoming the initial Price barrier. However, rather than random "carpet-bombing", targeted distribution has been employed, thereby qualifying sales and reducing costs.
- Two standard monthly usage plans have been developed to meet the needs of new users, who expect to use fewer hours, and more established users, who tell us they need more hours.
- Preferred pricing has been developed to reward loyal BC TEL customers, creating special service packages such as

Internet and long distance; Internet and Call Answer; and Internet, E-mail Paging and Paging.

- Preferred pricing has also been developed for selected external partners, in exchange for their commitment to promote Sympatico to their customers and members.

Distribution

- Distribution continues to evolve new channels. Today these include two retail options (a high-value Starter Kit and a convenient in-store online activation program) as well as BC TEL channels, and external partner channels (distributing free introductory software).
- In addition, a member referral program rewards existing members for encouraging their friends to use the service, as research indicates that word of mouth is an exceptionally strong acquisition tool in this category.

Promotion

- Promoting a new product in the early stages of its life cycle, co-branded by a well-known regional company and a new national partner has necessitated the combined use of the "inform", "persuade" and "remind" strategies. Promotional messages have been crafted to address each of the barriers to entry. National and regional campaigns have employed all traditional mass market vehicles including television, newspaper, magazine, outdoor, and radio. Success has also been achieved with direct-response promotion, telemarketing, couponing, contests, sampling and co-marketing with a wide range of manufacturers from packaged goods to electronic goods. Innovative service packages have proven to be a particularly strong promotional tool.

Looking Forward

For all the growth to date, the Internet is still in the early stages of its product life cycle, with extremely high growth potential in all forecasts. The BC market currently boasts personal computer penetration of over 65%, Internet penetration of 30% and an Internet intender market of over 30%. Continuing to increase share in these early stages remains a priority.

Today, high-potential areas for growth include: online advertising, electronic commerce and smart cards, high-speed services, pay per use services, online applications, IP telephony, and alternative Internet access devices (such as telephones, televisions, game players, and mobile peripherals).

As you read this, keep in mind that the Internet is growing and changing at an amazing pace. Changes that have taken years in other high-growth industries are occurring in a matter of months and weeks in this industry. As a result, even medium-term predictions for this category will be out of date before this book goes to print. The challenges are great but the opportunities are limitless as we look toward harnessing a wide range of existing and emerging technologies, to address consumers' evolving wants and needs for communication, information, entertainment—and beyond.

Source: Marketing Demo 19–2 was written by Debra Hamilton, Marketing Communications Manager, BC TEL Interactive, for inclusion in *Basic Marketing*, Ninth Canadian Edition. Courtesy of BC TEL Interactive.

Forecasting Target Market Potential and Sales

Planning an effective strategy and developing a marketing plan require that future sales, costs, and profits be estimated. Without such information, it's hard to know if a strategy is potentially profitable.

The marketing manager's estimates of sales, costs, and profits are usually based on a forecast (estimate) of target **market potential** (what a whole market segment might buy) and a **sales forecast** (an estimate of how much an industry or firm hopes to sell to a market segment). Usually, we must try to judge market potential before we can estimate what share a particular firm may be able to win with its particular marketing mix.

Three levels of forecast are useful

We're interested in forecasting the potential in specific market segments. To do this, it helps to make three levels of forecasts.

Some economic conditions affect the entire global economy. Others may influence only one country or a particular industry. And still others may affect only one company or one product's sales potential. For this reason, a common approach to forecasting is as follows:

1. Develop a *national income forecast* (for each country in which the firm operates) and use this to—
2. Develop an *industry sales forecast,* which then is used to—
3. Develop *specific company* and *product forecasts.*

Generally, a marketing manager doesn't have to make forecasts for a national economy or the broad industry. This kind of forecasting—basically, trend projecting—is a specialty in itself. Such forecasts are available in business and government publications, and large companies often have their own technical specialists. Managers can use just one source's forecast or combine several. Unfortunately, the more targeted the marketing manager's earlier segmenting efforts have been, the less likely it is that industry forecasts will match the firm's product-markets. So managers have to move directly to estimating potential for their own companies—and for their specific products.

Two approaches to forecasting

Many methods are used to forecast market potential and sales, but they can all be grouped into two basic approaches: (1) extending past behaviour, and (2) predicting future behaviour. The large number of methods may seem confusing at first, but this variety has an advantage. Forecasts are so important that managers often develop forecasts in two or three different ways and then compare the differences before preparing a final forecast.

Extending past behaviour can miss important turning points

When we forecast for existing products, we usually have some past data to go on. The basic approach, called **trend extension,** extends past experience into the future. With existing products, for example, the past trend of actual sales may be extended into the future. See Exhibit 19–4.

Ideally, when extending past sales behaviour, we should determine why sales vary. This is the difficult and time-consuming part of sales forecasting. Usually we can gather a lot of data about the product or market, or about changes in the marketing environment. But unless we know the *reason* for past sales variations, it's hard to predict in what direction—and by how much—sales will move. Statistical techniques, including correlation and regression analysis, can be useful here. (These techniques are beyond our scope and are discussed in beginning statistics courses.)

Once we know why sales vary, we can usually develop a specific forecast. Sales may be moving directly up as population grows, for example. So we can just estimate how population is expected to grow, and then project the impact on sales.

The weakness of the trend extension method is that it assumes past conditions will continue unchanged into the future. In fact, the future isn't always like the past. For example, for years the trend in sales of disposable diapers moved closely with the number of new births. However, as the number of women in the workforce increased

Exhibit 19–4 Straight-Line Trend Projection—Extends Past Sales into the Future

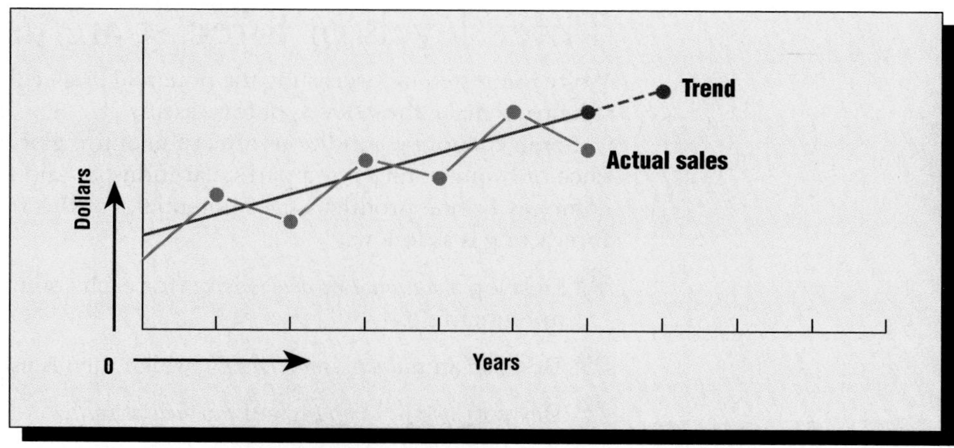

and as more women returned to jobs after babies were born, use of disposable diapers increased and the trend changed. As in this example, trend extension estimates will be wrong whenever big changes occur. For this reason—although they may extend past behaviour for one estimate—most managers look for other ways to forecast sharp market changes.

Predicting future behaviour takes judgment

When we try to predict what will happen in the future (instead of just extending the past), we have to use other methods and add a bit more judgment. Some of these methods (to be discussed later) include juries of executive opinion, salespeople's estimates, surveys, panels, and market tests.

Forecasting company and product sales by extending past behaviour

At the very least, a marketing manager ought to know what the firm's present markets look like and what it has sold to them in the past. A detailed sales analysis for products and geographic areas helps project future results.

Just extending past sales into the future may not seem like much of a forecasting method. But it's better than just assuming that next year's total sales will be the same as this year's.

Factor method includes more than time

A simple extension of past sales gives one forecast. But it's usually desirable to tie future sales to something more than the passage of time.

The factor method tries to do this. The **factor method** tries to forecast sales by finding a relationship between the company's sales and some other factor (or factors). The basic formula is as follows: something (past sales, industry sales, etc.) *times* some factor *equals* sales forecast. A **factor** is a variable that shows the relationship of some other variable to the item being forecast. For instance, in our example above, both the birthrate and the number of working mothers were factors related to sales of disposable diapers.

A bread producer example

The following example about a bread producer shows how firms can make forecasts for many geographic market segments using the factor method and available data. This general approach can be useful for any firm—producer, wholesaler, or retailer.

Analysis of past sales relationships showed that the bread manufacturer regularly sold 0.5 percent (0.005) of the total retail food sales in its various target markets. This is a single factor. By using this single factor, estimates of the manufacturer's sales for the coming period could be obtained by multiplying a forecast of expected retail food sales by 0.005.

Let's carry this bread example further, using data for Victoria, British Columbia. Let's assume that Victoria's food sales were $400,000,000 for the previous year. Start by simply accepting last year's food sales as an estimate of current year's sales. Then multiply the food sales estimate for Victoria by the 0.005 factor (the firm's usual share in such markets). The manager now has an estimate of the current year's bread sales in Victoria. That is, last year's food sales estimate ($400,000,000) times 0.005 equals this year's bread sales estimate of $2,000,000.

Going further, let's assume that the marketing manager expects that an especially aggressive promotion campaign would increase the firm's share by 10 percent. The single factor is increased from 0.005 to 0.0055 and then multiplied by the food sales estimate for Victoria to obtain an estimate for the firm's Victoria bread sales.

The factor method isn't limited to the use of just one factor. Two or more factors can be used together. The most widely used source of information about market size and importance is *Canadian Markets*, published annually by *The Financial Post*. In its 1996 report, *Canadian Markets* revealed that 2.83 percent of all Canadian households were to be found within Calgary. However, the retail market in Calgary, an area of higher-than-average incomes, accounted for 3.61 percent of total retail sales in Canada.[3] Suppose we wished to construct an index giving equal weight to the number of households and the percent of total retail sales. So we add 2.83 and 3.61 (= 6.44), and then divide by 2 (i.e., we weight the two factors equally). This leaves Calgary with a weighted value of 3.22.

We could, of course, easily adjust our weights for luxury products—giving, for example, Calgary's percentage of total retail sales a weight of 2 and its number of households a weight of 1. Doing this would leave Calgary with a weighted value of 3.35 (3.61 + 3.61 + 2.83 = 10.05/3 = 3.35) for this type of product. For every million dollars of **industry** sales throughout Canada of luxury products, we would expect $33,500 (3.35 percent) to be made in Calgary. Assuming that the company's marketing effort was as effective in Calgary as it was, on average, across the country, then 3.35 percent of company sales should be made in Calgary. If actual company sales are either higher or lower, the reasons why this is so should be determined.

The factor method, using either a single or multiple factors, can also be used to estimate the sales potential of a new product. Let's assume that a retailer is interested in estimating the potential for sets of novelty beer mugs in the Winnipeg area. If about 5 percent of the target market could be expected to buy a $25 set within a one-year period, and if that target consisted of just about every household, the appropriate numbers could be multiplied to get the following forecast. The example shows that 13,125 buying households, each spending $25, would generate a total sales potential of $328,125.

Households in Winnipeg	262,500
× Share of market (5%)	.05
	13,125
× Price of product ($25)	25
Total Sales Potential	$328,125

Producers of business products can also use several factors

Exhibit 19–5 shows how one manufacturer estimated the market for fibre boxes for a particular CMA. This approach could be used in each CMA to estimate the potential in many geographic target markets.

Here, SIC code data are used. This is common in the industrial sector because SIC code data are readily available and often very relevant. In this case, the value of box shipments by SIC code was collected by a trade association, but the rest of the data were available from government sources.

Basically, the approach involves calculating national consumption per employee for each SIC industry group and then multiplying by the number of employees in the particular CMA to estimate market potential for that group. Then the sum of these estimates becomes the total market potential in that CMA. A firm thinking of going into that market would need to estimate the share it could get with its own marketing mix.

Note that this approach can also aid management's control job. If the firm were already in this industry, it could compare its actual sales (by SIC code) with the potential and see how it's doing. If its typical market share is 10 percent of the market and it's obtaining only 2 to 5 percent of the market in various SIC submarkets, then some marketing mix changes may be in order.

Exhibit 19-5 Estimated Market for Corrugated Boxes and Cartons (by industry groups for a target CMA)

	(1)	(2)	(3)	(4) A TARGET CMA	(5)
INDUSTRY	VALUE OF BOX SHIPMENTS (BY END USE) ($000)	PRODUCTION WORKERS (BY INDUSTRY GROUP)	CONSUMPTION PER WORKER (1) ÷ (2) (DOLLARS)	PRODUCTION WORKERS (BY INDUSTRY GROUP)	ESTIMATED SIZE OF THE MARKET (3) × (4) ($000)
Food and beverage	$316,752	159,703	$1,983	24,343	$48,272
Tobacco products	6,100	5,606	1,088	—	—
Rubber and plastics products	35,375	45,681	774	12,546	9,711
Leather	6,450	22,577	286	3,986	1,140
Textile	19,504	53,073	367	7,195	2,641
Knitting mills	3,140	17,851	179	3,288	589
Clothing	10,670	83,418	128	13,467	1,724
Wood	4,694	94,328	48	3,499	168
Furniture and fixtures	30,968	44,328	699	13,780	9,632
Paper	51,785	99,491	520	12,824	6,668
Printing and publishing	9,492	63,964	148	19,020	2,815
Primary metal	2,916	92,337	32	—	—
Metal fabricating	38,895	120,450	323	30,024	9,698
Machinery	9,883	70,784	140	14,238	1,993
Transportation equipment	11,905	136,102	87	25,899	2,253
Electrical products	40,856	84,282	485	26,834	13,014
Nonmetallic mineral products	40,294	40,145	1,004	5,919	5,943
Petroleum and coal products	3,800	8,457	449	—	—
Chemical and chemical products	50,176	46,398	1,081	11,600	12,540
Miscellaneous manufacturing	25,292	48,354	523	19,263	10,075
TOTAL	$718,947				$138,876

Estimating a fluctuating future

Not all past economic or sales behaviour can be neatly extended with a straight line or some manipulation. Economic activity has its ups and downs. To cope with such variation, statisticians have developed *time series* analysis techniques. **Time series** are historical records of the fluctuations in economic variables. We can't go into a detailed discussion of these techniques here, but note that there are techniques to handle daily, weekly, monthly, seasonal, and annual variations.[4]

The dream of all forecasters is to find an accurate **leading series** (a time series that changes in the same direction *but ahead of* the series to be forecasted). For example, if an index of electrical power consumption always went up three months before a company's own sales of products that have some logical relation to electric power consumption (it's important that there be some logical relation!), then the managers might watch this "leading" series very carefully when forecasting monthly sales of its products.

No single series has yet been found that leads GNP or other important quantities. Lacking such a series, forecasters develop **indices** (statistical combinations of several time series) in an effort to find some time series that will lead the series they're attempting to forecast. The Bank of Canada, the Conference Board of Canada, and the chartered banks offer statistical information in their monthly reviews. The Conference Board also provides detailed information on many generally accepted measures of economic activity. And business magazines such as *Canadian Business* publish their own series and predictions.

Predicting future behaviour calls for more judgment and some opinions

These past-extending methods use quantitative data, projecting past experience into the future and assuming that the future will be like the past. But this is risky in competitive markets. Usually, it's desirable to add some judgment to other forecasts before making the final forecast for yourself.

Jury of executive opinion adds judgment

One of the oldest and simplest methods of forecasting, the **jury of executive opinion,** combines the opinions of experienced executives—perhaps from marketing, production, finance, purchasing, and top management. Each executive estimates market potential and sales for the *coming years.* Then they try to work out a consensus.

The main advantage of the jury approach is that it can be done quickly and easily. On the other hand, the results may not be very good. There may be too much extending of the past. Some of the executives may have little contact with outside market influences. But their estimates could point to major shifts in customer demand or competition.

Estimates from salespeople can help too

Using salespeople's estimates to forecast is like the jury approach. But salespeople are more likely than home office managers to be familiar with customer reactions and with what competitors are doing. Their estimates are especially useful in some business markets where the few customers may be well known to the salespeople. But this approach may be useful in any type of market. Good retail clerks have a feel for their markets, and their opinions shouldn't be ignored.

However, managers who use estimates from salespeople should be aware of the limitations. For example, new salespeople may not know much about their markets. Even experienced salespeople may not be aware of possible changes in the economic climate or the firm's other environments. And if salespeople think the manager is going to use the estimates to set sales quotas, the estimates may be low!

Surveys, panels, and market tests

Special surveys of final buyers, retailers, and/or wholesalers can show what's happening in different market segments. Some firms use panels of stores—or final consumers—to keep track of buying behaviour and to decide when just extending past behaviour isn't enough.

Surveys are sometimes combined with market tests when the company wants to estimate customers' reactions to possible changes in its marketing mix. A market test might show that a product increased its share of the market by 10 percent when its price was dropped 1 cent below competition. But even more business might be quickly lost if the price were increased 1 cent *above* competition. Such market experiments help the marketing manager make good estimates of future sales when one or more of the four Ps are changed.

The outcome depends on the marketing mix

Forecasting can help a marketing manager estimate the size of possible market opportunities. But the accuracy of any sales forecast depends on whether the firm selects and implements a marketing mix that turns these opportunities into sales and profits.[5]

Analysis of costs and sales can guide planning

Once a manager has narrowed down to a few reasonable marketing mixes (and the relevant forecasts), comparing the sales, costs, and profitability of the different alternatives helps in selecting the marketing mix the firm will implement.

Estimate the cost of each activity

Estimating the costs of marketing activities for a strategy may be easy or hard depending on the situation. Sometimes the accounting department can provide information about what average costs for similar activities have been in the past. Sometimes estimates of competitors' costs—perhaps pulled out of annual reports—can provide some guidance. But in general, the best approach for estimating costs is to use the task method. We recommended this approach in Chapter 14, where we focused on promotion costs and budgets. However, the same ideas apply to any area of marketing activity. The estimated cost and budget for each activity is based on the job to be done—perhaps the number of salespeople needed to call on new customers, or the amount of inventory required to provide some distribution customer service level. The costs of these individual tasks are totalled to determine how much should be budgeted for the overall plan. With this detailed approach, the firm can then assemble its overall marketing budget directly from individual plans, instead of relying on historical patterns or ratios.

Compare the profitability of alternative strategies

Once costs and revenue for possible strategies are estimated, it makes sense to compare them with respect to overall profitability. Exhibit 19–6 shows such a comparison for a product currently selling for $15—Mix A in the example. Here, the marketing manager simply estimates the costs and likely results of four reasonable alternatives. And, assuming that profit is the objective *and* that there are adequate resources to consider each of the alternatives, marketing Mix C is obviously the best alternative.

Spreadsheet analysis speeds up and simplifies calculations

Comparing the alternatives in Exhibit 19–6 is quite simple. But sometimes marketing managers need much more detail to evaluate a plan. Hundreds of calculations may be necessary to see how specific marketing resources relate to expected outcomes such as total costs, expected sales, and profit. To speed up and simplify that part of the planning job, marketing managers often use spreadsheet analysis. With **spreadsheet analysis,** costs, sales, and other information related to a problem

Exhibit 19-6 Comparing the Estimated Sales, Costs, and Profits of Four "Reasonable" Alternative Marketing Mixes*

MARKETING MIX	PRICE	SELLING COST	ADVERTISING COST	TOTAL UNITS	SALES	TOTAL COST	TOTAL PROFIT
A	$15	$20,000	$ 5,000	5,000	$ 75,000	$ 70,000	$ 5,000
B	15	20,000	20,000	7,000	105,000	95,000	10,000
C	20	30,000	30,000	7,000	140,000	115,000	25,000
D	25	40,000	40,000	5,000	125,000	125,000	0

*For the same target market, assuming product costs per unit are $5 and fixed (overhead) costs are $20,000.

Exhibit 19-7 A Spreadsheet Analysis Showing How a Change in Price Affects Sales and Profit (based on Marketing Mix C from Exhibit 19-6)

PRICE	SELLING COST	ADVERTISING COST	TOTAL UNITS	SALES	TOTAL COST	TOTAL PROFIT
$19.80	$30,000	$30,000	7,000	$138,600	$115,000	$23,600
19.90	30,000	30,000	7,000	139,300	115,000	24,300
20.00	30,000	30,000	7,000	140,000	115,000	25,000
20.10	30,000	30,000	7,000	140,700	115,000	25,700
20.20	30,000	30,000	7,000	141,400	115,000	26,400

are organized into a data table—a spreadsheet—to show how changing the value of one or more of the numbers affects the other numbers. This is possible because the relationships among the variables are programmed in the computer software. If you have used Lotus 1–2–3 or Excel or if you have been doing the computer-aided problems in this book, you're already familiar with spreadsheet analysis. Even if you haven't, the basic idea is not complicated.

A spreadsheet also answers "what if" questions

Spreadsheet analysis allows the marketing manager to evaluate what-if type questions. For example, a marketing manager might be interested in this question: "What if I charge a higher price and the number of units sold stays the same? What will happen to profit?" To look at how a spreadsheet program might be used to help answer this question, let's take a closer look at Mix C in Exhibit 19–6.

The table involves a number of relationships. For example, price times total units equals sales; and total cost equals selling cost plus advertising cost plus overhead cost plus total product costs (7,000 units × $5 per unit). If these relationships are programmed in the spreadsheet, a marketing manager can ask questions like "What if I raise the price to $20.20 and still sell 7,000 units? What will happen to profit?" To get the answer, all the manager needs to do is type the new price into the spreadsheet; the program then computes the new profit—$26,400.

The manager may also want to do many what-if analyses—for example, to see how sales and profits change over a range of prices. Computerized spreadsheet analysis does this quickly and easily. For example, if the manager wants to see what happens to total revenue as the price varies between some minimum (say, $19.80) and a maximum (say, $20.20), the program can show the total revenue and profit for a number of price levels in the range from $19.80 to $20.20. See Exhibit 19–7.

In a problem like this, the marketing manager might be able to do the same calculations quickly by hand. But with more complicated problems a spreadsheet program can be a big help, by making it very convenient to analyze different alternatives more carefully.

The marketing plan brings all the details together

Once the manager has selected the target market, decided on the (integrated) marketing mix to meet that target market's needs, and developed estimates of the costs and revenue for that strategy, it's time to put it all together in the marketing plan. The plan basically serves as a "blueprint" for what the firm will do.

Exhibit 19–8, provides a summary outline of the different sections of a complete marketing plan. You can see that this outline is basically an abridged overview of the topics we've covered throughout the text, and highlighted in this chapter. You can "flesh out" your thinking for any portion of a marketing plan by reviewing the section of the book where that topic is discussed in more detail.

Exhibit 19-8 Summary Outline of Different Sections of Marketing Plan

Name of Product-Market
Major screening criteria relevant to product-market opportunity selected
- Quantitative (ROI, profitability, risk level, etc.)
- Qualitative (nature of business preferred, social responsibility, etc.)
- Major constraints

Customer Analysis (organizational or final consumer)
Possible segmenting dimensions (customer needs, other characteristics)
- Identification of qualifying dimensions and determining dimensions

Identification of target market(s) (one or more specific segments)
- Operational characteristics (demographics, geographic locations, etc.)
- Potential size (number of people, dollar purchase potential, etc.) and likely growth

Key psychological and social influences on buying purchase
Type of buying situation
Nature of relationship with customers

Competitor Analysis
Nature of current/likely competition
Current and prospective competitors (and/or rivals)
- Current strategies and likely responses to plan

Competitive barriers to overcome and sources of potential competitive advantage

Analysis of Other Aspects of External Market Environment (favourable and unfavourable factors and trends)
Economic environment
Technological environment
Political and legal environment
Cultural and social environment

Company Analysis
Company objectives and overall marketing objectives
Company resources
S.W.O.T.: Identification of major *S*trengths, *W*eaknesses, *O*pportunities, and *T*hreats (based on above analyses of company resources, customers, competitors, and other aspects of external market environment)

Marketing Information Requirements
Marketing research needs (with respect to customers, marketing mix effectiveness, external environment, etc.)
Secondary data and primary data needs
Marketing information system needs

Product
Product class (type of consumer or business product)
Current product life-cycle stage
New-product development requirements (people, dollars, time, etc.)
- Product liability, safety, and social responsibility considerations

Specification of core physical good and/or service
- Features, quality, etc.

Supporting customer service(s) needed
Warranty (what is covered, timing, who will support, etc.)
Branding (manufacturer versus dealer, family brand versus individual brand, etc.)
Packaging
- Promotion needs
- Protection needs

Cultural sensitivity of product
Fit with product line

Place
Objectives
- Degree of market exposure required
- Distribution customer service level required

Type of channel (direct, indirect)
- Other channel members and/or facilitators required
  - Type and number of wholesalers (agent, merchant, etc.)
  - Type and number of retailers

Continued

Exhibit 19-8 Concluded

How discrepancies and separations will be handled
How marketing functions are to be shared
Coordination needed in channel
Information requirements (EDI, etc.)
Transportation requirements
Inventory requirements
Facilities required (warehousing, distribution centres, etc.)
Reverse channels (for returns, recalls, etc.)

Promotion
Objectives
Major message theme(s) for integrated marketing communications (desired "positioning")
Promotion blend
Advertising (type, media, copy thrust, etc.)
Personal selling (type and number of salespeople, how compensated, how effort will be allocated, etc.)
Sales promotion (for channel members, customers, employees)
Publicity
Mix of push and pull required

Price
Nature of demand (price sensitivity, elasticity)
Demand and cost analyses
Markup chain in channel
Price flexibility
Price level(s) (under what conditions)
Adjustments to list price (geographic terms, discounts, and allowances, etc.)

Special Implementation Problems to Be Overcome
People required
Other resources required

Control
Marketing information system needs
Criterion measures comparison with objectives (customer satisfaction, sales, cost, performance analysis, etc.)

Forecasts and Estimates
Costs (all elements in plan, over time)
Sales (by market, over time, etc.)
Estimated operating statement (*pro forma*)

Timing
Specific sequence of activities and events, etc.
Likely changes over the product life cycle

Marketing plan spells out the timing of the strategy

Some time schedule is implicit in any strategy. A marketing plan simply spells out this time period and the time-related details. Usually, we think in terms of some reasonable length of time—six months, a year, or a few years. But it might be only a month or two in some situations, especially when rapid changes in fashion or technology are important. Or a strategy might be implemented over several years—perhaps the length of a product life cycle or at least the early stages of the product's life.

Although the outline in Exhibit 19–8 does not explicitly show a place for the time frame for the plan or the specific costs for each decision area, these should be included in the plan—along with expected estimates of sales and profits—so that the plan can be compared with *actual performance* in the future. In other words, the plan not only makes it clear to everyone what is to be accomplished and how, but also provides a basis for the control process after the plan is implemented.

Flowcharts help set time-related details for the plan

Figuring out and planning the time-related details and schedules for all of the activities in the marketing plan can be a challenge, especially if the plan involves a big start-from-scratch effort. To do a better job in this area, many managers have turned to flowcharting techniques such as CPM (critical path method) or PERT (program evaluation and review technique). These methods were originally developed as part of the U.S. space program to ensure that the various contractors and subcontractors stayed on schedule and reached their goals as planned. PERT, CPM, and other similar project management approaches are even more popular now since inexpensive programs for personal computers make them easier and faster to use. Updating is easier, too.

The computer programs develop detailed flowcharts to show which marketing activities must be done in sequence and which can be done concurrently. These charts also show the time needed for various activities. Totalling the time allotments along the various chart paths shows the most critical (the longest) path, as well as the best starting and ending dates for the various activities.

Flowcharting is not really complicated. Basically, it requires that all the activities—which have to be performed anyway—be identified ahead of time and their probable duration and sequence shown on one diagram. It uses nothing more than addition and subtraction. Working with such information should be part of the planning function anyway. The chart can later be used to guide implementation and control.[6]

A complete plan spells out the reasons for decisions

The plan outline shown in Exhibit 19–8 is quite complete. It doesn't just provide information about marketing mix decisions—it also includes information about customers (including segmenting dimensions), competitors' strategies, other aspects of the marketing environment, and the company's objectives and resources. This material provides important background that is relevant to the "why" of the marketing mix and to target market decisions. Too often, managers do not include this information: Their plans just lay out the details of the target market and the marketing mix strategy decisions. This shortcut approach is more common when the plan is really just an update of a strategy that has been in place for some time. However, that approach can be risky.

Managers often make the mistake of casually updating plans in minor ways—perhaps just changing some costs or sales forecasts—but otherwise just sticking with what was done in the past. A big problem with this approach is that it's easy to lose sight of why those strategic decisions were made in the first place. When the market situation changes, the original reasons may no longer apply. Yet if the logic for those strategic decisions is not retained, it's easy to miss changes taking place that should result in the plan being reconsidered. For example, a plan that was established in the growth stage of the product life cycle may have been very successful for a number of years. But a marketing manager can't be complacent and assume that success will continue forever. When market maturity hits, the firm may be in for big trouble unless the basic strategy and plan are modified. If a plan spells out the details of the market analysis and logic for the marketing mix and target market selected, then it is a simple matter to routinely check and update it. Remember: The idea is for all of the analysis and strategy decisions to fit together as an integrated whole. As some of the elements of the plan or marketing environment change, the entire plan may need a fresh approach.

Companies plan and implement entire marketing programs

Most companies implement more than one marketing plan at the same time. A *marketing program* blends all a firm's marketing plans into one big plan.

When the various plans in the company's program are different, managers may be less concerned about how well the plans fit together—except as they compete for the firm's usually limited financial resources.

When the plans are more similar, however, the same sales force may be expected to carry out several plans. Or the firm's advertising department may develop the publicity and advertising for several plans. In these situations, product managers try to get enough of the common resources—say, salespeople's time—for their own plans.

Since a company's resources are usually limited, the marketing manager must make hard choices. You can't launch plans to pursue every promising opportunity. Instead, limited resources force you to choose among alternative plans—while you develop the program.

Finding the best program requires judgment

How do you find the best program? There is no one best way to compare various plans. Managers usually rely on evaluation tools such as those discussed in Chapter 2. Even so, much management judgment is usually required. Some calculations are helpful, too. If a five-year planning horizon seems realistic for the firm's markets, managers can compare expected profits over the five-year period for each plan.

Assuming the company has a profit-oriented objective, managers can evaluate the more profitable plans first, in terms of both potential profit and resources required. They also need to evaluate a plan's impact on the entire program. One profitable-looking alternative might be a poor first choice if it eats up all the company's resources and sidetracks several plans that together would be more profitable and spread the risks.

Some juggling among the various plans—comparing profitability to resources needed and available—moves the company toward the most profitable program. This is another area where spreadsheet analysis can help the manager evaluate a large number of alternatives.[7]

Planning for involvement in international marketing

When developing a plan for international markets, marketing managers must decide how involved the firm will be. We will discuss six basic kinds of involvement: exporting, licensing, contract manufacturing, management contracting, joint venturing, and wholly owned subsidiaries.

Exporting often comes first

Some companies get into international marketing just by **exporting**—selling some of what the firm produces to foreign markets. Some firms start exporting just to get rid of surplus output. For others, exporting comes from a real effort to look for new opportunities.

Some firms try exporting without doing much planning. As a result, some early efforts are not very satisfying, to buyers *or* sellers. When Toyota first exported cars to the United States, the effort was a failure. Americans just weren't interested in the Toyota model that sold well in Japan. Toyota tried again three years later with a new design and a new marketing mix. Obviously, Toyota's second effort was a real success.[8]

SPECIALISTS CAN HELP DEVELOP THE PLAN Exporting does require knowledge about the foreign market. But managers who don't have enough knowledge to plan the details of a program can often get expert help from intermediary specialists. As we discussed in Chapter 13, export agents can handle the paperwork as products are shipped outside the country. Then agents or merchant wholesalers can handle the importing details. Even large producers with many foreign operations turn to international intermediaries for some products or markets. Such intermediaries know how to handle the sometimes confusing formalities and specialized functions. A manager trying to develop a plan alone can make a small mistake that ties products up at national borders for days—or months.[9]

Exporting doesn't have to involve permanent relationships. Of course, channel relationships take time to build and shouldn't be treated lightly—sales reps' contacts in foreign countries are investments.

Some firms, on the other hand, plan more formal and permanent relationships with nationals in foreign countries. The relationships may involve licensing, contract manufacturing, management contracting, and joint venturing.

Licensing is an easy way

Licensing is a relatively easy way to enter foreign markets. **Licensing** means selling the right to use some process, trademark, patent, or other right for a fee or royalty. The licensee takes most of the risk because it must invest some capital to use the right. Further, the licensee usually does most of the planning for the markets it is licensed to serve. If good partners are available, this can be an effective way to enter a market. Gerber entered the Japanese baby food market this way.[10]

Contract manufacturing

Contract manufacturing means turning over production to others while retaining the marketing process. Sears used this approach when it opened stores in Latin America and Spain. This approach doesn't make it any easier to plan the marketing program, but it may make it a lot easier to implement.

WHEREVER YOU DO BUSINESS AROUND THE WORLD, WE'RE PART OF THE LOCAL FABRIC. At the AIG Companies, our business takes us from the canyons of Wall Street to the marketplaces of East Asia to the bazaars of the Middle East. But there's more to being global providers of insurance than just being a long way from home. AIG traces its roots to Shanghai in 1919, and today our network stretches across 130 countries and jurisdictions. We hire local managers who understand the business practices and needs of their own markets. If you're a multinational company doing business in today's fast-changing world, you need our unique global reach and global experience.
AIG
American International Group, Inc., Dept. A, 70 Pine Street, New York, NY 10270.

AIG, an international financial services firm, relies on local managers who understand their own markets to develop marketing plans that meet the needs of local clients.

For example, this approach can be especially desirable where labour relations are difficult or where there are problems obtaining supplies or government cooperation.

Management contracting sells know-how

Management contracting means the seller provides only management skills—others own the production and distribution facilities. Some mines and oil refineries are operated this way, and Hilton operates hotels all over the world for local owners. This is a relatively low-risk approach to international marketing. The company makes no commitment to fixed facilities, which can be taken over or damaged in riots or wars.

Joint venturing is more involved

Joint venturing involves a domestic firm entering into a partnership with a foreign firm. As with any partnership, there can be honest disagreements over objectives (e.g., how much profit is desired and how fast it should be paid out) as well as operating policies. Where a close working relationship can be developed, perhaps based on one firm's technical and marketing know-how and the foreign partner's knowledge of the market and political connections, this approach can be very attractive to both parties.

In some situations, a joint venture is the only type of involvement possible. For example, in the 1980s IBM wanted to increase its 2 percent share of the $1 billion a year that business customers in Brazil were spending on data processing services. But a Brazilian law severely limited expansion by foreign computer companies. To grow, IBM had to develop a joint venture with a Brazilian firm. Because of Brazilian laws, IBM could own only a 30 percent interest in the joint venture. But IBM decided it was better to have a 30 percent share of a business—and be able to pursue new market opportunities—than to stand by and watch competitors take the market.[11]

A joint venture usually requires a big commitment from both parties—and they both must agree on a joint plan. When the relationship doesn't work out well, the ensuing nightmare can make the manager wish the venture had been planned as a wholly owned operation. But the terms of the joint venture may block this for years.[12]

Wholly owned subsidiaries give more control

When a firm thinks a foreign market looks really promising, it may want to take the final step. A **wholly owned subsidiary** is a separate firm owned by a parent company. This gives the firm complete control of the marketing plan and operations, and also helps the foreign subsidiary work more easily with the rest of the company. For example, if a firm has too much capacity in a country with low production costs, it can move some production there from other plants and then export to countries with higher production costs.

Multinational corporations evolve to meet the challenge

As firms become more involved in international marketing, some begin to see themselves as worldwide businesses that transcend national boundaries. These **multinational corporations** have a direct investment in several countries and run their businesses according to the choices available anywhere in the world. Well-known North American–based multinational firms include Alcan, Coca-Cola, Eastman Kodak, Nortel, Warner-Lambert, Pfizer, Anaconda, Goodyear, Ford, IBM, and ITT. They regularly earn over one-third of their total sales or profits abroad. And well-known foreign-based multinationals, such as Nestlé, Shell (Royal Dutch Shell), Unilever, Sony, and Honda, have well-accepted brands all around the world.

These multinational operations no longer just export or import. They hire local workers and build local plants. They have relationships with local businesses and politicians. These powerful organizations learn to plan marketing strategies that deal with nationalistic feelings and typical border barriers, treating these simply as part of the marketing environment. We don't yet have one world politically—but business is moving in that direction.

Planning for international markets

Usually, marketing managers must plan the firm's overall marketing program so that it's adaptable to different countries. When the differences are significant, top management should delegate a great deal of responsibility for strategic planning to local managers (or even intermediaries). Often, it's not possible to develop a detailed plan without a "local feel." In extreme cases, local managers may not even be able to fully explain some parts of their plans because they're based on subtle cultural differences. In these situations, plans must be judged only by their results. The organizational setup should give these managers a great deal of freedom in their planning, but extend tight control over the plans they have developed. Top management can simply insist that managers stick to their budgets and meet the plans they themselves have created. When a firm reaches this stage, it is being managed like a well-organized domestic corporation, which insists that its managers (of divisions and territories) meet their own plans so that the whole company's program works as intended.[13]

Questions and Problems

1. Distinguish clearly between a marketing strategy, a marketing plan, and a marketing program.
2. Discuss how a marketing manager could go about choosing among several possible marketing plans, given that choices must be made because of limited resources. Would the job be easier in the consumer product or in the business product area? Explain.
3. Explain how understanding the product classes can help a marketing manager develop a marketing strategy for a really new product that is unlike anything currently available.
4. Distinguish between competitive marketing mixes and superior mixes that lead to breakthrough opportunities.
5. Explain the difference between a forecast of market potential and a sales forecast.
6. Suggest a plausible explanation for sales fluctuations for (a) bicycles, (b) ice cream, (c) lawn mowers, (d) tennis rackets, (e) oats, (f) disposable diapers, and (g) latex for rubber-based paint.
7. Explain the factor method of forecasting. Illustrate your answer.
8. Why is spreadsheet analysis a popular tool for strategic market planning?
9. In your own words, explain how a flowcharting technique such as PERT or CPM can help a marketing manager develop a better marketing plan.
10. Why should a complete marketing plan include details concerning the reasons for the marketing strategy decisions and not just the marketing activities central to the four Ps?
11. Consider how the marketing manager's job becomes more complex when it's necessary to develop and plan *several* strategies as part of a marketing program. Be sure to discuss how the manager might have to handle different strategies at different stages in the product life cycle. To make your discussion more concrete, consider the job of a marketing manager for a sporting goods manufacturer.
12. How would marketing planning be different for a firm that has entered foreign markets with a joint venture and a firm that has set up a wholly owned subsidiary?
13. How can a firm set the details of its marketing plan when it has little information about a foreign market it wants to enter?

Suggested Cases

34 Rocky Mountain House Co-op

35 Chalaga Mussel Farms

36 Argon Carpet Cleaning Company

37 Columbia Chrome

Computer-aided problem

Comparing Marketing Mixes

Amna Rao is a marketing manager who is looking for new market opportunities that use her firm's current resources. Her firm has been making plastic packages for producers of CDs, panty hose, and other products—but sales have dropped because these customers are switching away from plastic packages. She is considering the possibility of producing and marketing a new consumer product—sunglasses that float. Consumers in focus group interviews say they might be interested in buying floating sunglasses for when they're at the pool, on a boat, fishing, or otherwise near the water. So Rao is doing some rough comparisons of the likely costs and profitability of possible marketing mixes to reach her target market.

She is considering the likely outcomes with two possible marketing mixes. One marketing mix (Mix A) involves selling the sunglasses through discount stores. This mix would involve a plain frame with a simple finish, and the unit production cost would be $5.00. She knows she will have to pay for some consumer advertising to stimulate interest in the product. But personal selling costs would probably be quite low since she would need only one salesperson to call on some retail chains that would make large orders.

An alternative approach (Mix B) would focus on selling the glasses as an impulse product through snack bars at swimming pools and the beach. Selling to the large number of small snack bars would require more personal selling expense. The personal selling would need to be supported with direct-mail advertising to the snack-shop owners. However, the direct-mail ads would be less expensive than advertising to final consumers. To support a higher impulse purchase price in this channel, she would use a more stylish (and somewhat more costly to produce) finish on the sunglasses. She thinks she would sell a smaller quantity through this channel but the snack bars would be willing to pay a higher wholesale price.

To get a better idea of the likely profit and break-even levels for the two different mixes, Rao has developed a spreadsheet based on her estimates of likely sales and costs. She wants to make the biggest profit possible from this new product, but at present she does face one basic limitation: The owner of the company is not willing to invest in new equipment, and with the present equipment the firm cannot produce more than 300,000 pairs of glasses a year.

a. After considering the initial spreadsheet, for both marketing mixes, evaluate the effects of sales volume being 10 percent less than expected. Discuss the implications of your analysis.

b. Rao thinks her sales estimates are realistic for the two marketing mixes, but she is not certain what the implications would be if demand is greater than she expects. Discuss this issue and illustrate your conclusions with a specific analysis of your choice based on the spreadsheet.

c. Rao feels that the more costly finish for glasses in Mix B would be attractive to impulse buyers, but she also thinks that many of these prospects would buy the product even if the firm offered the lower-cost finish she is considering for Mix A. In that case, the unit production cost for Mix B would be the same as for Mix A. How high would sales have to be with Mix B and the lower unit production cost to make a profit of at least $107,000? If the lower-cost marketing mix was as likely to achieve this level of sales as the original plan for Mix B was to achieve sales of 50,000 units, which of the two variations would you recommend? Give your reasons.

For additional questions related to this problem, see Exercise 19–3 in the *Learning Aid for Use with Basic Marketing*, Ninth Canadian Edition.

Chapter twenty

Implementing and Controlling Marketing Plans

When you finish this chapter, you should

- Understand how information technology is speeding up feedback for better implementation and control.
- Know why effective implementation is critical to customer satisfaction and profits.
- Know how total quality management can improve implementation—including implementation of service quality.
- Understand how sales analysis can aid strategic market planning.
- Understand the differences in sales analysis and performance analysis using performance indexes.
- Understand the difference between the full-cost approach and the contribution-margin approach.
- Understand how planning and control can be combined to improve the marketing management process.
- Understand what a marketing audit is—and when and where it should be used.
- Understand the important new terms (shown in orange).

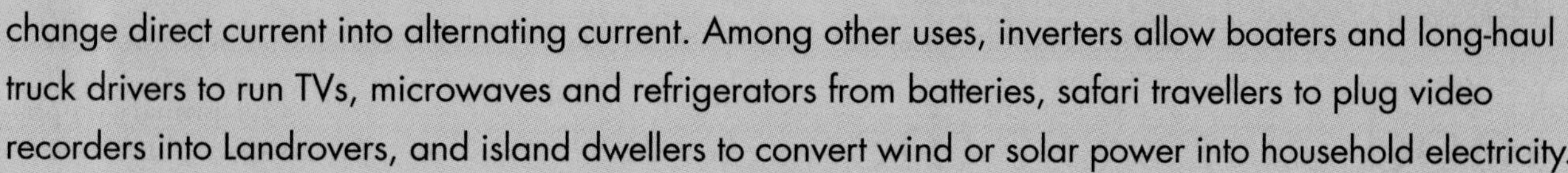

Statpower Technologies makes a device that allows children to watch television in the family car, because that's what the market wants.

"We're changing the culture from being very product- and technology-oriented to much more marketing- and customer-oriented, and we're not through yet," says Bart Tichelman, who joined the Burnaby company as president and CEO a year ago. "It's tough trying to get people to change their perspectives."

Statpower makes inverters, which electronically change direct current into alternating current. Among other uses, inverters allow boaters and long-haul truck drivers to run TVs, microwaves and refrigerators from batteries, safari travellers to plug video recorders into Landrovers, and island dwellers to convert wind or solar power into household electricity.

Other companies make similar products, but Statpower has seized the lead in turning inverters into a consumer product. Less than one-third the weight and one-half the size of their older industrial cousins, they look at home in a retail-store blister pack.

Statpower revenues have jumped dramatically from $4.7 million five years ago to $23 million this year. It is the second-largest player in the world in power-conversion products for household, recreational and light industrial use. Despite this success, it has been going through rapid change since Tichelman came on board.

A chemist and former president of food producer Cott Corp.'s eastern U.S. unit, Tichelman has brought in a marketing consultant, done some selective hiring and is coaching employees on the new philosophy.

The change is one of approach, not money, he says: Statpower still spends about 12 per cent of gross revenue on research and development, and 12 per cent on sales and marketing.

Like many young technology firms before it, Statpower initially developed a product, then tried to find a market.

As president, co-founder Konrad Mauch pursued many outlets. As a result, Statpower products are sold under such labels as Compaq, Hewlett Packard and Magnavox, and retailed under their own name at Radio Shack and Canadian Tire.

When Tichelman took over, he segmented the market and started seeking unique strategies for each segment. An exclusive deal with giant California retailer West Marine provided access to the store's extensive market research.

"Looking at how people are actually using your product lets you enhance to your core product," Tichelman said. "[For example], things that go into boats should be kind of white with a blue stripe on it. There are inexpensive ways of doing things that will make your product more closely fit what your customer is looking for."

Statpower has also taken full advantage of global opportunities to grow its business. Manufacturing is subcontracted to China, and product is shipped from Blaine, Wash., for the convenience of U.S. customers, who account for 60 per cent of the company's sales.

Today, Tichelman believes Statpower, which employs 100 people, has tremendous room for growth, noting it has tapped into less than five per cent of the marine market alone.

Customer-oriented products under consideration include a backup power system for markets in developing countries in which household power supply is inconsistent; a system to manage power load distribution in RVs, since the air-conditioning unit, fridge and microwave can't run all at the same time; a gauge to tell boaters how much power is left on their batteries; and battery-chargers with built-in microcomputers so boaters could connect a battery charger and leave their boats for long periods without fear of overcharging.

Tichelman's market-focused approach, while a difficult transition, was the obvious next step for Statpower's continued maturity and growth, says technology industry management consultant Burke Corbet.

Customer orientation "is something a lot of our tech companies must learn if they want to be successful," Corbet says.

Source: Abridged from Jenny Lee, "Tech Firm Adapting to Its Market," *The Vancouver Sun,* March 16, 1998, D1, D2.

Good plans set the framework for implementation and control

Our primary emphasis in this book is on the strategic planning part of the marketing manager's job. There's a good reason for this focus. The "one-time" strategy decisions—those which decide what business the company is in and the strategies it will follow—set the firm on a course either toward profitable opportunities or, alternatively, toward costly failure. If a marketing manager makes an error with these basic decisions, there may never be a second chance to set things straight. In contrast, if good strategies and plans are developed, the marketing manager—and everyone else in the organization—knows *what* needs to be done. Good marketing plans set the framework for effective implementation and control.

Implementation and control

Developing a potentially profitable plan does not ensure either satisfied customers or profit for the firm. Achieving the outcomes envisioned in the plan requires that the whole marketing management process work well. As you learned in Chapter 2, the marketing management process includes not only strategic market planning but also implementation and control (see Exhibit 2–1). In today's highly competitive markets, customer satisfaction often hinges on skilful implementation. Further, the ongoing success of the firm is often dependent on **control**—the feedback process that helps the marketing manager learn (1) how ongoing plans and implementation are working and (2) how to plan for the future. Our opening discussion shows that Statpower Technologies is now doing effective market planning. But that alone does not guarantee success. Statpower must be certain that its efforts at implementation and control are also first-rate.

We discussed some specific opportunities and challenges with respect to implementation and control as we introduced each of the marketing strategy decision areas. In this chapter, we'll go into more depth on concepts and on how-to approaches for making implementation and control more effective. We'll start with a discussion of how dramatic improvements in information technology are resulting in changes in implementation and control—and in the whole strategic planning process. For many firms, these changes are critically important. They offer revolutionary new ways to meet customer needs. After that, we'll highlight some of the new approaches, including total quality management, that are improving marketing implementation. Then we'll explain how marketing managers use control-related tools—such as sales and performance analysis—to improve the quality of planning and implementation decisions. We'll conclude with a discussion of what a marketing audit is, and why it is sometimes necessary.

Speed up information for better implementation and control

Not long ago, marketing managers planned their strategies and put them into action—but then it was usually a long time before they got feedback to learn whether the strategy and its implementation were really working as intended. For example, a marketing manager might not have much feedback on what was happening with sales, expenses, and profits until financial summaries were available—and that sometimes took months or even longer. Summary data weren't very useful in pinpointing which specific aspects of the plan were working and which weren't. In that environment, the feedback was so general and took so long that there often wasn't anything the manager could do about a problem except start over.

That situation has now changed dramatically in many types of business. In Chapter 4, we discussed how firms use marketing information systems to track sales and cost details day by day and week by week. Throughout the book you've seen examples of how marketers get more information faster and use it quickly to improve a strategy or its implementation. For example, scanner data from a consumer panel can provide a marketing manager with almost immediate feedback on whether a new consumer product is selling at the expected level in each specific store and whether it is actually selling to the intended target market rather than some other group.

Fast feedback can be a competitive advantage

Marketing managers who get faster feedback on their decisions can often use that feedback to develop a competitive advantage. They can quickly fine-tune a smooth-running implementation to make it work even better. If there are potential problems, they can often spot them early—and keep them from turning into big problems.

For example, a manager who gets detailed daily reports that compare actual sales results in different cities with sales forecasts in the plan is able to see very quickly if there is a problem in a specific city. Then the manager can track down the cause of the problem. If sales are going slowly because the new salesperson in that city is inexperienced, then the sales manager might immediately spend more time working with that rep. On the other hand, if the problem is that a chain of retail stores in that particular city isn't willing to allocate much shelf space for the firm's product, then the salesperson might need to develop a special analysis to show the buyers for that specific chain how the product could improve the chain's profit.

When information is slow coming in and there is less detail, making implementation changes is usually more difficult. By the time the need for a change is obvious, a bigger change is required for it to have any effect.

The basic strategic planning concepts we've emphasized throughout the text are enduring and will always be at the heart of marketing. Yet, the fast pace that is now possible in getting information for control is resulting in fundamental changes in how many managers work, make decisions, plan, and implement their plans. Managers who can quickly adjust the details of their efforts to better solve customer problems or respond to changes in the market can do a better job for their firms—because they can make certain that their plans are really performing as expected.

The marketing manager must take charge

Fast feedback can improve implementation and control. And computers now take the drudgery out of analyzing data. But this kind of analysis is not possible unless the data is in machine-processible form, so that it can be sorted and analyzed quickly. Here, creative marketing managers play a crucial role by insisting that the necessary data be collected. If the data they want to analyze are not captured as they come in, information will be difficult—if not impossible—to get later. A marketing manager may need many different types of information to improve implementation efforts or develop new strategies.

New information technologies offer speed and detail

New approaches to electronic communication help solve these problems. For example, many companies are using fibre-optic telephone lines or satellite transmission systems to *immediately* transfer data from a computer at one location to another. A sales manager with a portable computer can use a regular telephone to pull data off the firm's mainframe computer. And marketing managers working at different locations on different aspects of a strategy can use e-mail to communicate through networks. The Internet makes it possible for a manager to work at a computer on the other side of the world just as if he or she were at the head office.

Electronic pipelines like these make data available instantly. A report—such as one that summarizes sales by product, salesperson, or type of customer—that in the past was done once a month now might be done weekly or even daily. The computer software can even be programmed to search for and "flag" results that indicate a problem of some sort. Then the manager can allocate more time to resolving that particular problem.[1]

Effective implementation means that plans work as intended

Once a marketing manager has developed a good marketing plan, the challenge of implementing it often involves hundreds or even thousands of operational decisions and activities. In a small company, these may all be handled by a few people, or even by a single person. In a large corporation, literally hundreds of different people may be involved in implementation. That may require a massive amount of careful coordination and communication. Either way, when operational decisions and activities are executed well, customers get what is intended. And if the original plan is good, customers will be satisfied and come back again the next time the need arises. At the same time, even a great plan can leave customers unhappy—and switching to someone else's offering—if implementation is poor.

Building relationships with customers

Implementation is especially critical in mature and highly competitive markets. When several firms are all following basically the same strategy, and quickly imitating competitors' ideas, customers are often won or lost based on differences in the quality of implementation. Consider the rental car business. Hertz has a strategy that targets business travellers with a choice of quality cars, convenient reservations, fast pick-up and drop-off, availability at most major airports, and a premium price. Hertz is extremely successful with that strategy even though there is little to prevent other companies from trying the same approach. But a major part of Hertz's success is due to implementation. Customers keep coming back because the Hertz service is both reliable and pain-free.

When a Hertz "Gold" customer calls to make a reservation, the company already has the standard information about that customer in a computer database. At the airport, the customer skips over the line at the Hertz counter and instead just picks up an already-completed rental contract and goes straight to the Hertz bus. The driver gets the customer's name and radios ahead to have someone start the specific car that customer will drive. That way the air conditioner or heater is already doing its job when the bus driver delivers the customer right to the parking slot for his or her car. Customers are certain they're at the right place because there's an electronic sign beside each car with the customer's name on it. Making all of this work—day in and day out, customer after customer—isn't easy. But Hertz has set up systems to make it all easier because that's what it takes to implement its plan—and to keep customers loyal.[2] What Hertz is doing is what Marketing Demo 20–1 proposes—getting intimate with customers.

Marketing Demo 20-1

Getting Intimate with Customers

How To Gain an Edge Amid Today's Brutal Competition

In today's increasingly competitive business environment, it is becoming harder and harder to differentiate your business from that of your competitors.

Companies that used to derive a competitive advantage from their products and services are finding that their competition is quickly learning to replicate their technology and, in some cases, improve upon it by learning from their mistakes. Similarly, companies that used to focus on being the most efficient, low-cost producer are being beaten by competitors who simply outsource production to low-cost manufacturers.

Entire industries are becoming "commoditized" as technological and operational advantages become increasingly short-lived. Nowhere is this becoming more of a reality than in the telecommunications equipment and services market. Challenges faced by Canadian telecom companies are a sign of things to come for most industries that face growing competition for a limited number of customers.

The only way for most companies to gain a sustainable competitive advantage is to develop a relationship with their customers that the competition cannot break. If all you can do is sell the same product at the same price to the same customers as your competition, you better have a rock-solid relationship with those customers. This is often referred to as "customer intimacy": knowing your customers' needs better than the competition does.

But what exactly is a customer-intimacy strategy? A simple marketing tactic, a panacea or just a great-sounding vision statement? Marketers have known the value of customer intimacy for years. Direct marketing, target marketing, marketing research, affinity programs, customer retention and loyalty and direct-response advertising are just a few of the manifestations of a customer-intimacy strategy.

However, customer intimacy must go far beyond the walls of the marketing department. It must involve dramatic changes to the way a company sells, organizes itself, measures its success, manages information and creates a winning culture. And it is up to the CEO and all senior officers to champion the cause for a truly customer-intimate organization.

Information Systems: the Enabler

Advances in information technology have enabled customer intimacy. Technologies such as smart cards, swipe cards and the Internet allow us to capture more point-of-sale and customer data than ever before, and also allow the customer more choice in how to interface with suppliers.

Computing power allows vast amounts of customer information to be manipulated on a desktop in the marketing department, rather than on a mainframe in the basement. Data mining, sifting through historical transaction records for nuggets of useful information, is an important customer-intimacy tool because it helps us gain insight into the subtle behaviors of our customers. Once captured and manipulated, networking technology has brought customer data, information and knowledge to the front lines, providing a vital input into the customer-intimacy strategy.

Marketing: Increased Customer Knowledge

All this great new information opens up new doors for marketing. Once customer transaction data is available for analysis within the marketing department, detailed segmentation strategies can become a reality.

Some telecommunications companies, for example, can now segment based on more than 100 criteria, from calling patterns to promotional response, from number of employees to industry type. Since detailed information is available on all customers and segments, annual forecasting has been transformed from a top-down to a bottom-up process.

With all this customer knowledge available, marketing can cease to be a matter of selling one product to a group of people in an effort to gain market share. Instead, it can become a matter of selling a number of products to each customer in an effort to gain a greater share of each customer's total expenditure.

Nowhere is this more relevant than in telecommunications, where companies are aiming to bundle different services such as cable, cellular and long distance together to win over all of our communications expenditures.

Sales: Focusing on Target Accounts

Customer intimacy means that the sales department (and other channels) must focus on core accounts and customer segments. Sales must win a bigger proportion of the possible business at a smaller number of accounts—in many cases actually *reducing* the total number of customers.

The sales department must view its clients as a suite of relationships, not just a list of projects. It must become a business partner, not just another supplier to these accounts. Of course, this all sounds like motherhood, but a properly focused sales strategy is the linchpin to a successful customer-intimacy strategy.

Organizational Structure: New Non-traditional Roles

Perhaps the most dramatic impact of a customer-intimacy strategy is in the way customer-intimate organizations structure themselves. No longer are product managers the only ones responsible for managing the customer base.

Some retail and telecommunications companies have created new positions with titles such as "manager of student segment" or " VP of financial services clients," which shadow the traditional product-management roles. They have divided their organizations into "customer-facing" roles (such as a segment manager) and "content experts" (such as advertising).

Now it is the segment managers, not the product managers, who make the final decision on price, promotion, product and placement. This is because they are focused solely on understanding and meeting the specific needs of the target audience.

Financial Control: New Measurement Techniques

A new organizational structure requires a new form of financial reporting. In some cases, P&Ls have been developed for "the student segment" or "financial services clients." These financial statements show profit and loss on a market-segment basis, rather than a line-of-business or product basis.

P&Ls of this sort can even be used to drive strategic and capital allocation decisions. They can be a powerful management accounting tool, even though traditional financial accounting rules still require line-of-business reporting.

A customer-intimacy strategy can also require Finance to take a good hard look at how it valuates its customer base and treats its acquisition and development costs. Customer Lifetime Value is a key measure for companies that have ongoing relationships with their customers. CLV can often be the best way to translate the conceptual world of customer intimacy into the concrete world of asset and firm value.

Culture Change: Creating a 'Customer-Facing' Culture

Such dramatic organizational change requires an equally dramatic culture shift. A customer-intimate organization pushes decision-making to the front lines, where the customers are.

Sales, Customer Service and Collections staff must understand that in the customer's eyes they *are* the company. They must be sensitized to the subtle cues given by customers, and feel empowered to act in a way that creates a lasting relationship with each customer.

Conclusion

Our experience at Ernst & Young has shown that customer intimacy is more than a marketing tactic. It is a full-scale reorientation of a company's information, sales and marketing strategy, organizational structure, financial controls and corporate culture. It is a future state that can take a number of years to achieve.

Often, external consultants can facilitate this transition, but it must be driven internally. Leaders of organizations have the responsibility to begin the transformation of their companies into truly customer-intimate organizations. This may be the only way to gain a sustainable advantage in today's brutally competitive environment.

Source: Doug McCuaig and Christopher Holt, Ernst & Young, "Getting Intimate with Customers," *Marketing Magazine,* July 27, 1997. p. 16.

Dealing with internal or external matters

As the Hertz example illustrates, marketing implementation usually involves decisions and activities related to both internal and external matters. Figuring out how the correct car will end up in the right parking slot, how the Hertz bus driver will contact the office, and who will coordinate getting the message to the person who starts the car are all internal matters. They are invisible to the customer—as long as they work as planned. On the other hand, some implementation issues are external and involve the customer. For example, the contract must be completed correctly and be in the right spot when the rental customer comes to pick it up, and someone needs to have filled the car with gas and cleaned it.

Implementation has its own objectives

Whether implementation decisions and activities are internal or external, they all must be consistent with the objectives of the overall strategy and with the other details of the plan. That being said, there are three general objectives that apply to *all* implementation efforts. Other things being equal, the manager wants to get each implementation job done:

Better, so customers really get superior value as planned.

Faster, to avoid delays that cause customers problems.

At lower cost, that is, without wasting money on things that don't add value for the customer.

The ideal of doing things better, faster, and at lower cost is easy to accept. But in practice, implementation is often complicated by trade-offs among the three objectives. For example, doing a job better may take longer or cost more.

So, a marketing manager should constantly look for new strategic opportunities, but must also be creative in looking for better solutions to implementation problems. That may require finding ways to better coordinate the efforts of the different people involved, and setting up standard operating procedures to deal with recur-

Exhibit 20-1 Examples of Approaches to Overcome Specific Marketing Implementation Problems

MARKETING MIX DECISION AREA	OPERATIONAL PROBLEM	IMPLEMENTATION APPROACH
Product	Develop design of a new product as rapidly as possible without errors	Use 3-D computer-aided design software
	Pretest consumer response to different versions of a label	Prepare sample labels with desktop publishing software
Place	Coordinate inventory levels with intermediaries to avoid stock-outs	Use a bar code scanner and computerized reorder system
	Get franchisee's inputs and cooperation on a new program	Set up a televideo conference
Promotion	Quickly distribute TV ads to local stations in many different markets	Distribute final video version of the ad via satellite link
	Answer final consumers' questions about how to use a product	Put a toll-free telephone number on product label
Price	Identify frequent customers for a quantity discount	Create a "favoured customer" club with an ID card
	Figure out if price sensitivity affects demand for a product; make it easier for customers to compare prices	Show unit prices (for example, per oz.) on the shelf markers

ring problems, as well as juggling priorities to deal with the unexpected. When the Hertz bus driver is sick, someone still has to be there to pick up the customers and deliver them to their cars.

Implementation requires innovation too

Sometimes the implementation effort can be improved by approaching the task in a new or different way. Exhibit 20–1 shows some of the ways that firms are using information technology to improve specific implementation jobs. Note that some of the examples in Exhibit 20–1 focus on internal matters and some on external, customer-oriented matters.

While finding new approaches helps with some implementation problems, getting better implementation often depends on being vigilant in improving what the firm and its people are already doing. So let's take a closer look at some important ways that managers can improve the quality of their implementation efforts.[3]

Building quality into the implementation effort

As we've seen throughout this book, even people with the best intentions sometimes lapse into a production orientation. When the pressure's on to get a job done, they forget about satisfying the customer—let alone working together! When the product manager is screaming for a budget report, the accountant may view a customer's concerns about a billing error as something a salesperson can smooth over—alone.

TQM meets customer requirements

There are many different ways to improve implementation in each of the four Ps decision areas, but here we will focus on total quality management, which you can use to improve *any* implementation effort. With **total quality management (TQM),** everyone in the organization is concerned about quality, throughout all of the firm's activities, to better serve customer needs.

In Chapter 9, we explained that product quality means the ability of a product to satisfy a customer's needs or requirements. Now we'll expand that idea and think about the quality of the whole marketing mix, and how that mix is implemented to meet customer requirements.

Total quality management is not just for factories

Most of the early attention in quality management focused on reducing defects in goods produced in factories. Reliable goods are important, but there's usually a lot more to marketing implementation than that. Yet if we start by considering product defects, you'll see how the total quality management idea has evolved and how it applies to implementing a marketing program.

At one time, most firms assumed that defects were an inevitable part of mass production. They assumed that the cost of replacing defective parts or goods was just a cost of doing business—an insignificant one compared to the advantages of mass production. However, many firms were forced to rethink this assumption when Japanese producers of cars, electronics, and cameras showed that defects weren't inevitable. And their success in taking customers away from established competitors made it clear that the cost of defects wasn't just the cost of replacement!

Having dissatisfied customers is costly

From the customer's point of view, getting a defective product and having to complain about it is a big headache. The customer can't use the defective product and suffers the inconvenience of waiting for someone to fix the problem—if *someone* gets around to it. That erodes good will and leaves customers dissatisfied. The big cost of poor quality is the cost of lost customers.

Much to the surprise of some production-oriented managers, the Japanese experience showed that it is less expensive to do something right the first time than to pay to do it poorly and *then* pay again to fix problems. And quality wasn't just a matter of adding more assembly-line inspections. Products had to be designed from the start to meet customer needs. One defective part in 10,000 may not seem like much, but if that part keeps a completed car from cranking at the end of the automaker's production line, finding the problem is a costly nightmare.

Firms that adopted TQM methods to reduce manufacturing defects soon used the same approaches to overcome many other implementation problems. Their success brought attention to what is possible with TQM—whether the implementation problem concerns unreliable delivery schedules, poor customer service, advertising that appears on the wrong TV show, or salespeople who can't answer customers' questions.

Doing things right—the first time

The idea of doing things right the first time seems obvious, but it's easier said than done. Problems always come up, and it's not always clear what isn't being done as well as it could be. Most people tend to ignore problems that don't pose an immediate crisis. But firms that adopt TQM are always looking for ways to improve implementation through **continuous improvement**—a commitment to constantly make things better one step at a time. Once you accept the idea that there *may* be a better way to do something, and you look for it, you may just find it! The place to start is to clearly define "defects" in the implementation process—from the customers' point of view.

Things gone right and things gone wrong

Managers who use the TQM approach think of quality improvement as a sorting process—a sorting out of things gone right and things gone wrong. The sorting process calls for detailed measurements related to a problem. Then managers use a set of statistical tools to analyze the measurements and identify the problem areas that are the best candidates for fixing. The statistical details are beyond our scope here, but it's useful to get a feel for how managers use the tools.

Starting with customer needs

Let's consider a restaurant that does well during the evening hours but wants to improve its lunch business. The restaurant develops a strategy that targets local businesspeople with an attractive luncheon buffet. The restaurant decides on a buffet because research shows that target customers want a choice of good, healthy food and are willing to pay reasonable prices for it—as long as they can eat quickly and get back to work on time.

As the restaurant implements its new strategy, the manager wants a measure of how things are going. So she encourages customers to fill out comment cards that ask, "How did we do today?" As the manager reads the comment cards, she divides the ones with complaints into categories. She then counts the number of complaints in each category.

Slay the dragons first

Then the manager creates a graph showing a frequency distribution for the different types of complaints. Quality people call this a **Pareto chart**—a graph that shows the number of times a problem cause occurs, with problem causes ordered from most frequent to least frequent. The manager's Pareto chart, shown in Exhibit 20–2, reveals that customers complain most frequently that they have to wait for a seat. There were other common complaints—the buffet was not well organized, the table was not clean, and so on. However, the first complaint is much more common than the next most frequent.

This type of pattern is typical. The worst problems often arise over and over again. This focuses the manager's attention on which implementation problem to fix first. A rule of quality management is to slay the dragons first—which simply means start with the biggest problem. After removing that problem, the battle moves on to the next most frequent problem. If you do this *continuously*, you solve a lot of problems—and you don't just satisfy customers, you delight them!

Figure out why things go wrong

So far, our manager has only *identified* the problem. To *solve* it, she creates a **fishbone diagram**—a visual aid that helps organize cause-and-effect relationships for "things gone wrong."

Our restaurant manager, for example, discovers that customers must wait to be seated because tables aren't being cleared soon enough. In fact, the Pareto chart

Exhibit 20-2 Pareto Chart Showing Frequency of Different Complaints

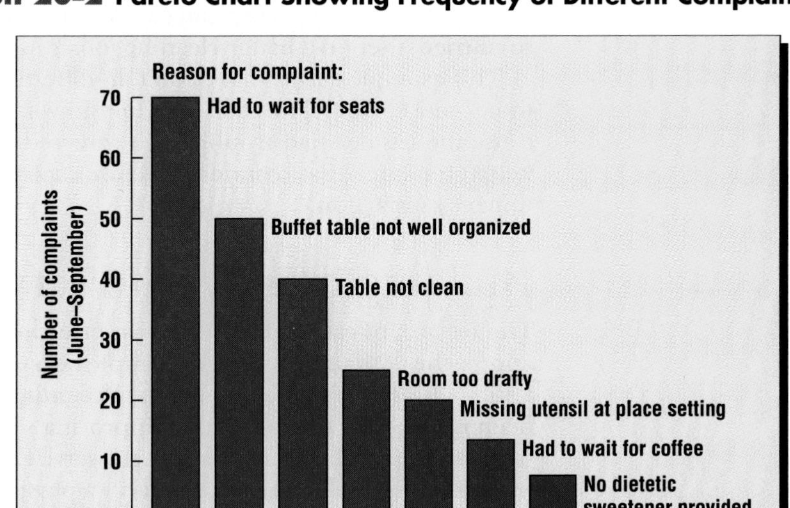

Exhibit 20–3 Fishbone Diagram Showing Cause and Effect for "Why Tables Are Not Cleared Quickly"

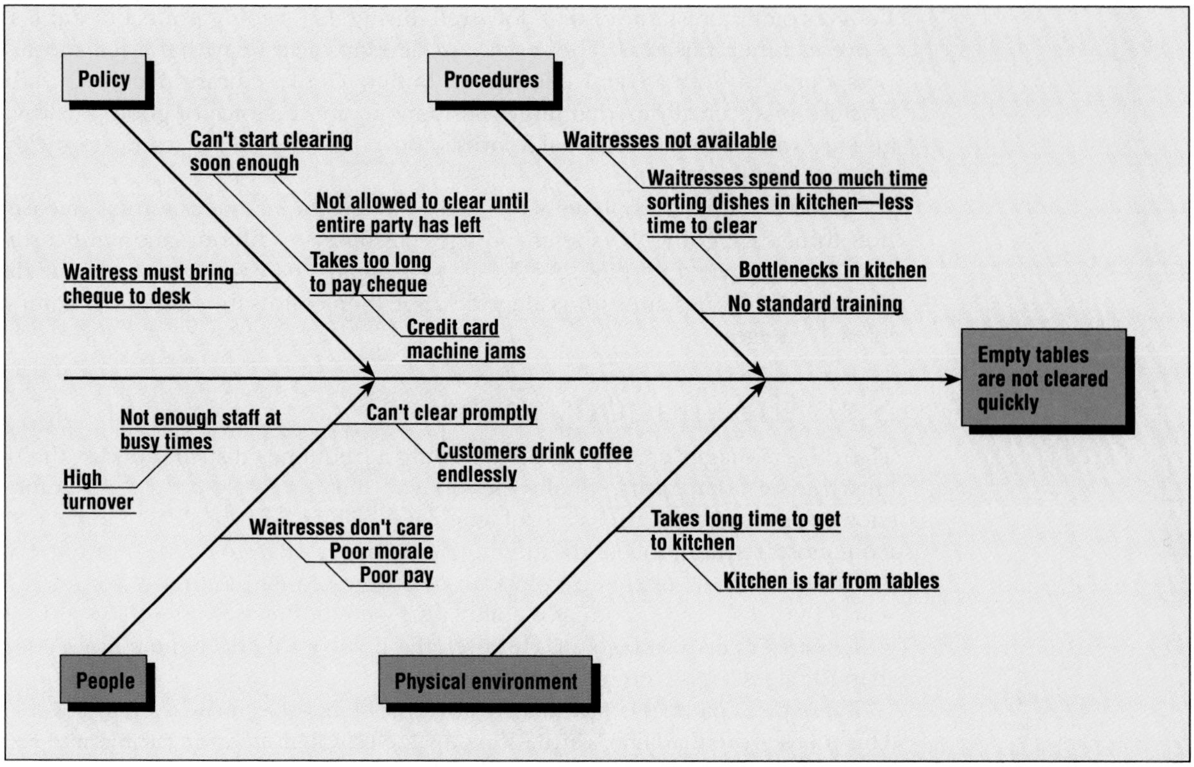

(Exhibit 20–2) shows that customers also complain frequently about tables not being clean. So the two implementation problems may be related.

The manager's fishbone diagram (Exhibit 20–3) summarizes the various causes for tables not being cleaned quickly. There are different basic categories of causes—restaurant policy, procedures, people problems, and the physical environment. Using this overview of different ways that the service operation is going wrong, the manager can decide what to fix. She establishes different formal measures. For example, she counts how frequently different causes delay customers from being seated. She finds that the cashier's faulty credit card machine is holding up cheque processing. The fishbone diagram shows that restaurant policy is to clear the table after the entire party leaves. But customers have to wait at their tables while the staff deal with the jammed credit card machine, and cleaning is delayed. With the credit card machine replaced, the staff can clear the tables sooner—and because they're not so hurried, they do a better cleaning job. Two dragons are on the way to being slain!

This example shows that people in different areas of an organization affect customer satisfaction. The staff couldn't do what was needed to satisfy customers because the cashier had trouble with the credit card machine. The TQM approach helps everyone see and understand how each job affects all the others —and the customer's satisfaction.[4]

Building quality into services

The restaurant case illustrates how a firm can improve implementation with TQM approaches. We used a service example because providing customer service is often a difficult area of implementation. Recently, marketers in service businesses have been paying a lot of attention to improving service quality.

Almost every firm must implement service quality as part of its plan, whether its product is primarily a service, primarily a physical good, or a blend of both. For example, a manufacturer of ball bearings isn't just providing wholesalers or producers with

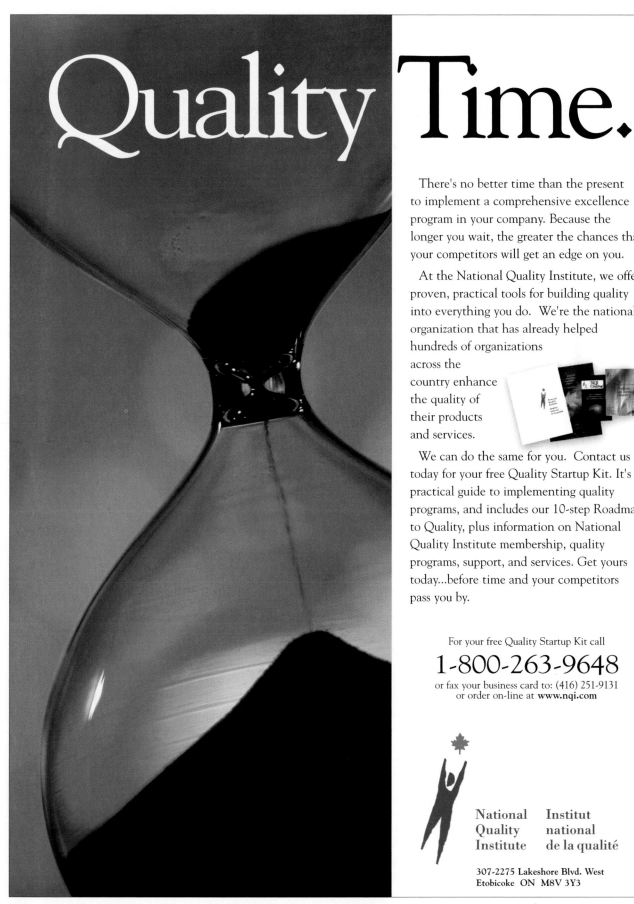

round pieces of steel. Customers need information about deliveries, they need orders filled properly, and they may have questions to ask the firm's accountant, receptionist, or engineers. Because almost every firm must manage the service it provides customers, let's focus on some of the special concerns of implementing quality service.

Train people and empower them to serve

Quality gurus like to say that the firm has only one job: to give customers exactly what they want, when they want it, and where they want it. Marketing managers have been saying that for some time, too. But customer service is hard to implement because the server is inseparable from the service. A person doing a specific service job may perform one specific task correctly but still annoy the customer in a host of other ways. Customers will not be satisfied if employees are rude or inattentive—even if they "solve the customer's problem." There are two keys to improving how people implement quality service: (1) training and (2) empowerment.

Firms that commit to customer satisfaction realize that all employees who have any contact with customers need training—many firms see 40 hours a year of training as a minimum. Simply showing customer-contact employees around the rest of the business—so that they learn how their contribution fits into the total effort—can be very effective. Good training usually includes role-playing on handling different types of customer requests and problems. This is not just sales training! A rental car attendant who is rude when a customer is trying to turn in a car may leave the customer dissatisfied, even if the rental car was perfect. How employees treat a customer is as important as whether they perform the task correctly.

Companies can't afford an army of managers to inspect how each employee implements a strategy—and such a system usually doesn't work anyway. Quality cannot be "inspected in." It must come from the people who do the service jobs. So firms that commit to service quality empower employees to satisfy customers' needs. **Empowerment** means giving employees the authority to correct a problem without first checking with management. At a Guest Quarters hotel, an empowered room-service employee knows it's OK to run across the street to buy the specific mineral water a guest requests. In the new Saturn car manufacturing plant, employees can stop the assembly line to correct a problem rather than passing it down the line.

Manage expectations—with good communication

The implementation effort sometimes leaves customers dissatisfied because they expect much more than it is possible for the firm to deliver. Some firms react to this by shrugging their shoulders and faulting customers for being unreasonable. Research in the service quality area, however, suggests that the problems often go away if marketers clearly communicate what they are offering. Customers are satisfied when the service matches their expectations, and careful communication leads to reasonable expectations.

Customers often tolerate a delay and remain satisfied with the service when they are given a full explanation. Most airline passengers seethe at the announcement of a takeoff delay but are happy to wait if they know the delay is caused by a thunderstorm high over the airport.

Separate the routine and plan for the special

Implementation usually involves some routine services and some that require special attention. Customer satisfaction increases when the two types of service encounters are separated. For example, banks set up special windows for commercial deposits, and supermarkets have cash-only lines. In developing the marketing plan, it's important to analyze the types of service customers will need and plan for both types of situations. In some cases, completely different strategies may be required.

Increasingly, firms try to use computers and other equipment to handle routine services. ATMs are quick and convenient for dispensing cash. Airline telephone systems allow customers to check fares, schedules, and arrival times without the need for an operator.

Firms that study special service requests can use training so that even unusual customer requests become routine to the staff. Every day, hotel guests lose their keys, bank customers run out of cheques, and supermarket shoppers leave their wallets at home. A well-run service operation anticipates these special events so that service providers can respond in ways that satisfy customers' needs.

Managers lead the quality effort

Quality implementation—whether in a service activity or in another activity—doesn't just happen by itself. Managers must show that they are committed to doing things right to satisfy customers—and that quality is everyone's job. Without top-level support, some people won't get beyond their business as usual attitude, and TQM won't work. The top executive at American Express had his board of directors give him the title Chief Quality Officer so that everyone in the company would know he was personally involved in the TQM effort.

Specify jobs and benchmark performance

Firms that are successful with quality programs usually make the effort to clearly specify and write out exactly what tasks need to be done, how, and by whom. This may seem unnecessary. After all, most people know, in general terms, what they're supposed to do. However, when the tasks are clearly specified, it's easier to see what criteria should be used to measure performance.

Criteria having been established, there needs to be some basis on which to evaluate the job being done. In our restaurant example, one part of the job specification for the cashier is to process credit card payments. In that case, relevant criteria might include the amount of time that it takes and the number of people waiting in line to pay. If the restaurant manager had seen a record of how long it was taking to process credit cards, she would have known that for many customers it was taking too long. Without the measure, the precise nature of the problem was hidden.

That takes us to the issue of **benchmarking**—picking a basis of comparison for evaluating how well a job is being done. For example, consider a situation in which a firm asks its customers to rate their satisfaction with the sales rep with whom they work. The company might then benchmark each sales rep against the others on the sales force based on average customer satisfaction. But if the firm's sales reps as a group are weak, that isn't a sensible approach. Thus, many firms try to benchmark against some external standard. For example, a sales manager might want to benchmark against competitors' sales reps. Or better, the manager might identify firms in which sales reps earn superlative customer satisfaction ratings—regardless of their industry—and benchmark against them. That approach can also reveal job specifications—things that should be done—that the sales manager had not considered or measured in the first place. For example, salespeople at Saturn dealers earn very high customer satisfaction ratings. IBM doesn't sell cars, but it might decide to benchmark against Saturn's sales reps to find ways to improve its sales effort.

Getting a return on quality is important

While the cost of poor quality is lost customers, keep in mind that the type of quality efforts we've been discussing also result in costs. It takes time and energy to keep records, analyze the details of implementation efforts, and search for ways to reduce whatever type of defects may appear. It's important to find the right balance between quality in the implementation effort and what it costs to achieve.

Marketing managers who lose sight of that balance have often created quality programs that cost more than they're worth. It's easy to fall into the trap of running up *unnecessary costs* trying to improve some facet of implementation that really isn't that important to customers, customer satisfaction, or customer retention. When that happens, customers may still be satisfied, but the firm can't make a profit because of the extra costs. In other words, there isn't a financial return on the money spent to improve the quality of the implementation effort. Remember that getting everyone to work together to satisfy customers should be the route to profits. If the firm is spending money on quality efforts that don't really contribute to customer satisfaction—or that cost more to provide than customers will ultimately be willing to pay—then someone has lost sight of the marketing concept.

TQM is not a cure-all. It is not the only method for improving marketing implementation, but it is an important approach. Some firms don't yet use TQM, and they may be missing an opportunity. Other firms apply some quality methods, but act like they are the private property of a handful of "quality specialists" who want to control things. That's not good either. Everyone must own a TQM effort—and keep a balanced view of how it improves customer satisfaction and what it costs.

As more marketing managers see the benefits of TQM, it will become a more important part of marketing thinking, especially marketing implementation. When managers really understand implementation, they can do a better job developing strategies and plans in the first place.[5]

Control provides feedback to improve plans and implementation

Computers and other types of information technology are speeding up the flow of feedback and allowing managers to improve plans and implementation quickly and continuously. On the other hand, the basic questions that a modern marketing manager wants to answer in order to make better implementation and strategy decisions are pretty similar to what they've always been.

A good manager wants to know which products' sales are highest and why, which products are profitable, what is selling where, and how much the marketing process is costing. Managers need to know what's happening—in detail—in order to improve the bottom line.

Traditional accounting reports are usually too general to be much help in answering these questions. A company may be showing a profit, while 80 percent of its business comes from only 20 percent of its products—or customers. The other 80 percent may be unprofitable. But without special analyses, managers won't know it. This 80/20 relationship is fairly common and is often referred to as *the 80/20 rule.*

It *is* possible for marketing managers to get detailed information about how marketing plans are working—but only if they ask for and help develop the necessary data. In this section we'll discuss the kinds of information that can be available and how to use it. The techniques are not really complicated. They basically require only simple arithmetic—and, of course, a computer can quickly and easily take care of that when a large volume of sorting, adding, and subtracting is required.

Sales analysis shows what's happening

Sales analysis—a detailed breakdown of a company's sales records—can be very informative. Detailed data can keep marketing executives in touch with what's happening in the market. In addition, routine sales analyses prepared each week, month, or year may show trends, and allow managers to check their hypotheses and assumptions.[6]

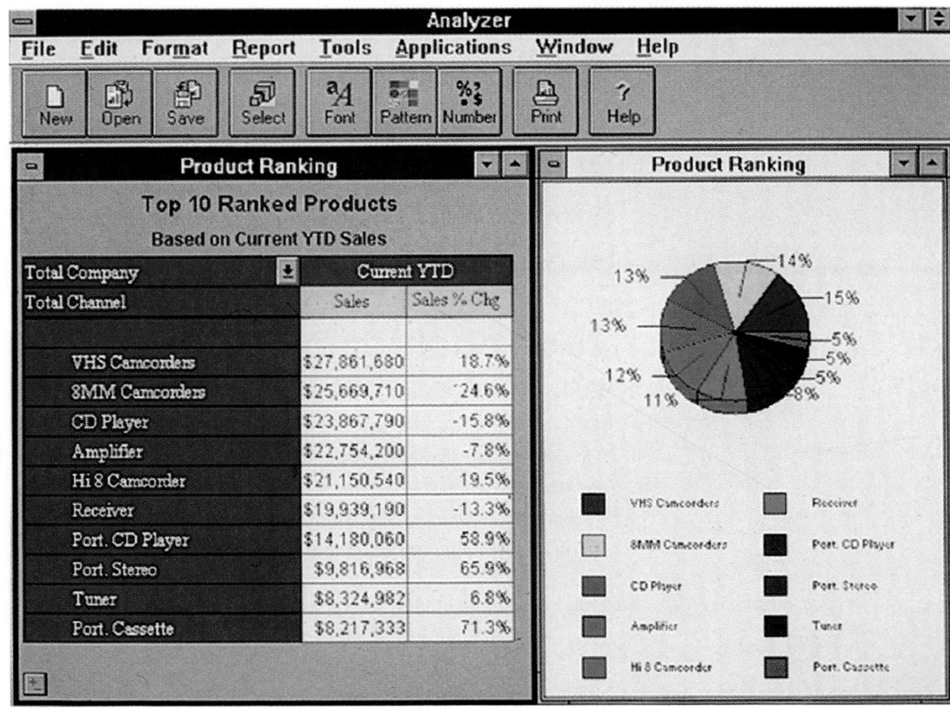

Total Company	Current YTD	
Total Channel	Sales	Sales % Chg
VHS Camcorders	$27,861,680	18.7%
8MM Camcorders	$25,669,710	24.6%
CD Player	$23,867,790	-15.8%
Amplifier	$22,754,200	-7.8%
Hi 8 Camcorder	$21,150,540	19.5%
Receiver	$19,939,190	-13.3%
Port. CD Player	$14,180,060	58.9%
Port. Stereo	$9,816,968	65.9%
Tuner	$8,324,982	6.8%
Port. Cassette	$8,217,333	71.3%

Information Resources, Inc., developed the Data Server Analyzer Software, illustrated here, to make it easy to do sales analysis. This program makes it easy to "see" patterns which might otherwise have been hidden in a table of numbers.

Today's profit is no guarantee that you'll make money tomorrow. In fact, ignoring sales analysis can lead not only to poor sales forecasting but to poor decisions in general. One manufacturer did much national advertising on the assumption that the firm was selling all over the country. But a simple sales analysis showed that most present customers were located within a 250-mile radius of the factory! In other words, the firm didn't know who or where its customers were—and it wasted most of the money it spent on national advertising.

But a marketing manager must ask for it

Detailed sales analysis is only possible if a manager asks for the data. Valuable sales information is often buried, perhaps on sales invoices or in billing records in a computer. Today, with computers and organized marketing information systems, effective sales analysis can be done easily and relatively inexpensively—if marketing managers decide they want it done. In fact, the desired information can be obtained as a by-product of basic billing and accounts receivable procedures. The manager need simply make sure that the company captures identifying information—on important dimensions such as territory and sales reps. Then computers can easily run sales analyses and simple trend projections.

What to ask for varies

There is no one best way to analyze sales data. Several breakdowns may be useful, depending on the nature of the company and product and what dimensions are relevant. Typical breakdowns include the following:

1. Geographic region—country, province, county, city, sales rep's territory.
2. Product, package size, grade, or colour.
3. Customer size.

4. Customer type or class of trade.
5. Price or discount class.
6. Method of sale—mail, telephone, or direct sales.
7. Financial arrangement—cash or charge.
8. Size of order.
9. Commission class.

Too much data can drown a manager

While some sales analysis is better than none—and better than getting data too late for action—sales breakdowns that are too detailed can drown a manager in reports. So wise managers only ask for breakdowns that will help them make decisions. They use computer programs that draw graphs and figures to make it easy to see patterns. To avoid coping with mountains of data, much of which may be irrelevant, most managers move on to *performance analysis.*

Performance analysis looks for differences

Performance analysis looks for exceptions or variations from planned performance. In simple sales analysis, the figures are merely listed or graphed—they aren't compared against standards. In performance analysis, managers make comparisons. They might compare one territory against another, against the same territory's performance last year, or against expected performance.

The purpose of performance analysis is to improve operations. The salesperson, territory, or other factor showing poor performance can be identified—and singled out for detailed analysis and corrective action. Or outstanding performances can be analyzed to see if they can be explained and made the general rule.

Performance analysis doesn't have to be limited to sales. Other data can be analyzed, too—for example, kilometres travelled, number of calls made, number of orders, and the cost of various tasks.

A performance analysis can be quite revealing, as shown in the following example.

Straight performance analysis—an illustration

A manufacturer of business products sells to wholesalers through five sales reps, each serving a separate territory. Total net sales for the year amount to $2,386,000. Sales force compensation and expenses come to $198,000, yielding a direct-selling expense ratio of 8.3 percent—that is, $198,000 ÷ $2,386,000 × 100.

This information, taken from a profit and loss statement, is interesting, but it doesn't explain what's happening from one territory to another. To get a clearer picture, the manager compares the sales results with other data *from each territory.* See Exhibits 20–4 and 20–5. Keep in mind that exhibits like these and others that follow in this chapter are now very easy to generate. Computer programs like Lotus 1 - 2 - 3 and dBASE IV make it easy to apply the ideas discussed here, even on inexpensive desktop computers.

The reps in sales areas D and E aren't doing well. Sales are low and marketing costs are high. Perhaps more aggressive sales reps could do a better job, but the number of customers suggests that sales potential may be low. Perhaps the entire plan needs revision.

The figures themselves, of course, don't provide the answers. But they do reveal the areas that need improvement. This is the main value of performance analysis. It's up to management to find the remedy—to either revise or change the marketing plan.

Exhibit 20-4 Comparative Performance of Sales Reps

SALES AREA	TOTAL CALLS	TOTAL ORDERS	ORDER CALL RATIO	SALES BY SALES REP	AVERAGE SALES REP ORDER	TOTAL CUSTOMERS
A	1,900	1,140	60.0%	$ 912,000	$800	195
B	1,500	1,000	66.7	720,000	720	160
C	1,400	700	50.0	560,000	800	140
D	1,030	279	27.1	132,000	478	60
E	820	165	20.1	62,000	374	50
Total	6,650	3,284	49.3%	$2,386,000	$634	605

Exhibit 20-5 Comparative Cost of Sales Reps

SALES AREA	ANNUAL COMPENSATION	EXPENSE PAYMENTS	TOTAL SALES REP COST	SALES PRODUCED	COST-SALES RATIO
A	$ 22,800	$11,200	$ 34,000	$ 912,000	3.7%
B	21,600	14,400	36,000	720,000	5.0
C	20,400	11,600	32,000	560,000	5.7
D	19,200	24,800	44,000	132,000	33.3
E	20,000	32,000	52,000	62,000	83.8
Total	$104,000	$94,000	$198,000	$2,386,000	8.3%

Performance indexes simplify human analysis

With a straight performance analysis, the marketing manager can evaluate the variations among sales reps to try to explain the "why." But this takes time. And poor performances are sometimes due to problems that sales figures alone don't reveal. Some uncontrollable factors in a particular territory—tougher competitors or ineffective intermediaries—may lower the sales potential. Or a territory just may not have much potential.

To get a better check on performance effectiveness, the marketing manager compares what did happen with what ought to have happened. This involves the use of performance indexes.

A performance index is like a batting average

When a manager sets standards (i.e., quantitative measures of what ought to happen), it's relatively simple to compute a **performance index**—a number like a baseball batting average that shows the relationship between two values.

Baseball batting averages are computed by dividing the actual number of hits by the number of times at bat (the possible number of times the batter could have had a hit) and then multiplying the result by 100 to get rid of decimal points. A sales performance index is computed the same way—by dividing actual sales by expected sales for the area (or sales rep, product, etc.) and then multiplying by 100. If a sales rep is batting 82 percent, the index is 82.

A simple example shows where the problem is

The computation of a performance index is shown in the following example, which assumes that population is an effective measure of sales potential.

Exhibit 20–6 Development of a Measure of Sales Performance by Region

REGIONS	(1) POPULATION AS PERCENTAGE OF CANADA—1997	(2) EXPECTED DISTRIBUTION OF SALES BASED ON POPULATION	(3) ACTUAL SALES	(4) PERFORMANCE INDEX
Atlantic	7.8%	78,000	75,000	96
Quebec	24.5	245,000	250,000	102
Ontario	37.8	378,000	390,000	103
Prairies	16.6	166,000	180,000	108
British Columbia, Yukon, and N.W.T.	13.3	133,000	105,000	79
Total	100%	$1,000,000	$1,000,000	

Source: Statistics Canada, adapted from "Quarterly Demographic Statistics, 1997," Catalogue No. 91-002, Volume 11, Number 2, page 15.

Exhibit 20–6 breaks down Canada's population by regions as a percentage of the total population. The regions are the Atlantic Provinces, Quebec, Ontario, the Prairies, and British Columbia, the Yukon, and the Northwest Territories.

Let's assume that a firm with $1 million in sales now wants to evaluate performance in each region. Column 2 shows the actual sales of $1 million broken down in proportion to the population in the five regions. This is what sales *should* have been if population were a good measure of future performance. Column 3 in Exhibit 20–6 shows the actual sales for the year for each region. Column 4 shows measures of performance (performance indexes): column 3 ÷ column 2 × 100.

The B.C., Yukon, and N.W.T. region isn't doing as well as expected. It has 13.3 percent of the total population, and expected sales (based on population) are $133,000. Actual sales, however, are only $105,000. This means that this region's performance index is only 79, calculated as (105,000 ÷ 133,000) × 100, because actual sales are much lower than expected on the basis of population. If population is a good basis for measuring expected sales (an important *if*), poor sales performance should be analyzed further. Perhaps sales reps in the B.C., Yukon, and N.W.T. region aren't working as hard as they should. Perhaps promotion there isn't as effective as elsewhere. Or competitive products may have entered the market.

Whatever the cause, it's clear that performance analysis doesn't solve problems. It only points out potential problems. and it does this well.

A series of performance analyses may find the real problem

Performance analysis helps a marketing manager see if the firm's marketing plans are working properly. If they aren't, it can lead to solutions to the problems. But this may require a series of performance analyses, as the following example shows. To get a feel for how performance analysis can be part of a problem-solving process, follow this example carefully, one exhibit at a time. Try to anticipate the marketing manager's decision.

The case of Stereo, Inc.

Stereo's sales manager found that sales for the Ontario region were $130,000 below the quota of $14,500,000 (that is, actual sales were $14,370,000) for the January to June period. The quota was based on forecast sales of the various types of stereo equipment the company sells. Specifically, the quota was based on forecasts for each product type in each store in each sales rep's territory.

Exhibit 20-7 Sales Performance, Ontario Region, January–June (in thousands of dollars)

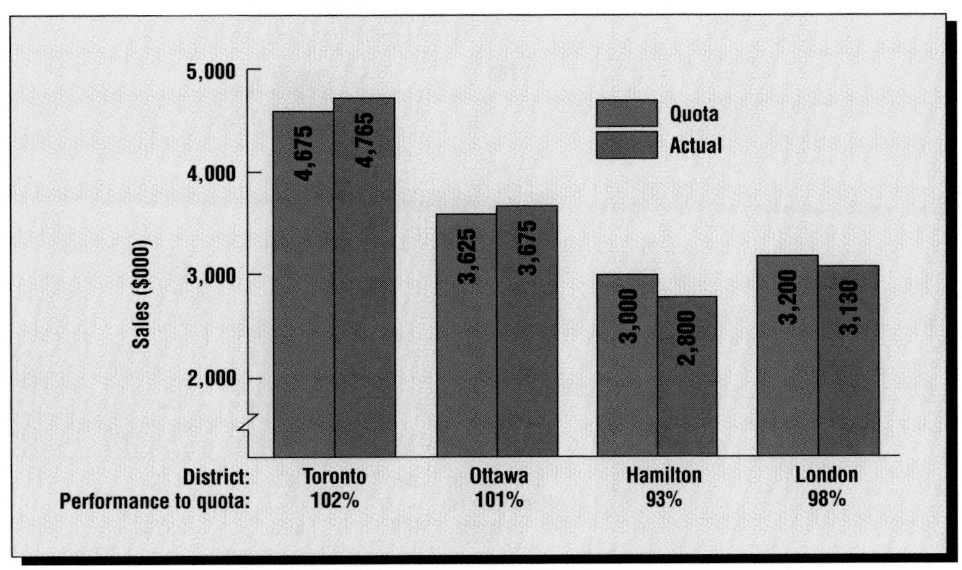

Exhibit 20-8 Sales Performance, Hamilton District, January–June (in thousands of dollars)

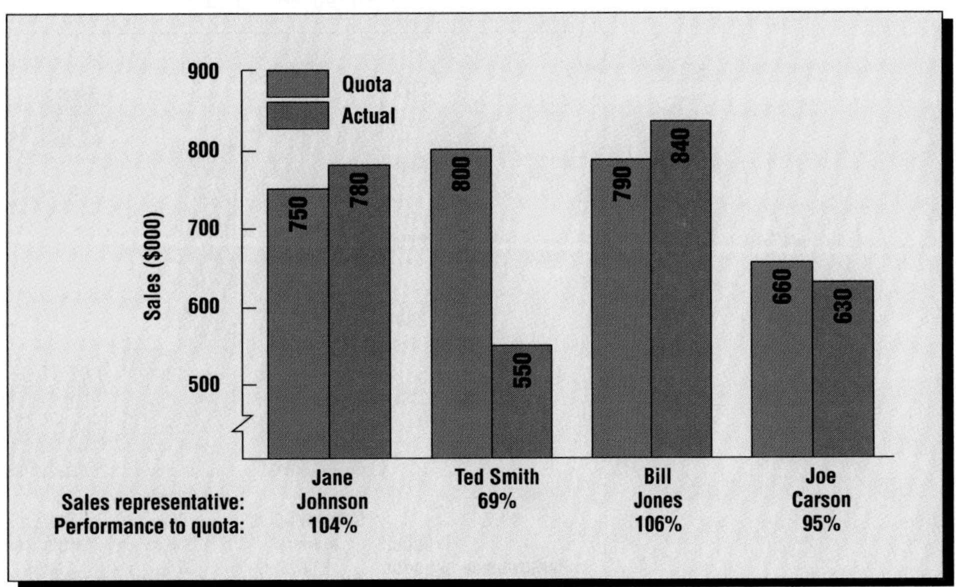

Pam Dexter, the sales manager, felt that this difference was not too large (1.52 percent) and was inclined to forget the matter, especially since forecasts are usually in error to some extent. But she thought about e-mailing a letter to all sales reps and district supervisors in the region—a letter aimed at stimulating sales effort.

Exhibit 20–7 shows the overall story of what is happening to Stereo's sales in Ontario. What do you think the manager should do?

The Hamilton district had the poorest performance, but it wasn't too bad. Before sending a "let's get with it" letter to Hamilton and then relaxing, the sales manager decided to analyze the performance of the four sales reps in the Hamilton district. Exhibit 20–8 breaks down Hamilton's figures by sales rep. What conclusion or action do you suggest now?

Since Ted Smith previously had been top sales rep, the sales manager wondered if Smith was having trouble with some of his larger customers. Before making a drastic

Exhibit 20–9 Sales Performance, Selected Stores of Ted Smith in Hamilton District, January–June (in thousands of dollars)

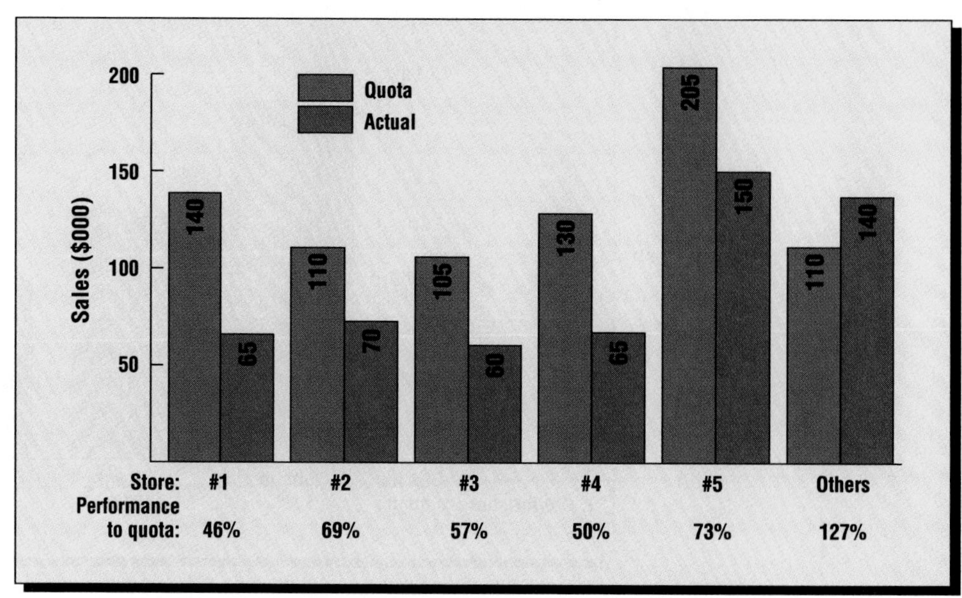

Exhibit 20–10 Sales Performance by Product for Ted Smith in Hamilton District, January–June (in thousands of dollars)

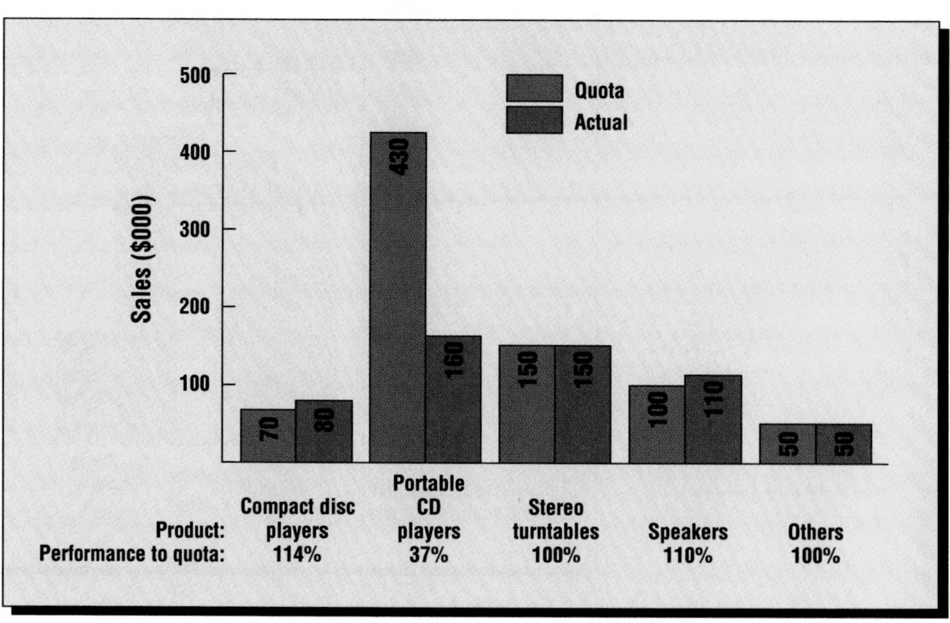

move, she obtained an analysis of Smith's sales to the five largest customers (see Exhibit 20–9). What action could the sales manager take now? Should Smith be fired?

Smith's sales in all the large stores were down significantly, although his sales in many small stores were holding up well. Smith's problem seemed to be general. Perhaps he just wasn't working. Before calling him, the sales manager decided to look at Smith's sales of the four major products, as Exhibit 20–10 shows. What action is indicated now?

Smith is having real trouble with portable CD players. Is the problem Smith or the players?

Further analysis by product for the entire region showed that everyone in Ontario was having trouble with portable CD players because a regional competitor was cutting prices. But higher sales on other products had hidden this fact. Since portable

CD player sales had been doing all right nationally, the problem was only now showing up. You can see that this is the *major* problem.

Since overall company sales were going fairly well, many sales managers wouldn't have bothered with this analysis. They might merely have traced the problem to Smith. And without detailed sales records and performance analysis, the natural human reaction for Smith would have been to blame business conditions or aggressive competition, or make some other handy excuse.

Stay home and use the computer

This case shows that total figures can be deceiving. Marketing managers should not jump on the first plane or reach for the phone until they have all the facts. Even worse than rushing to the scene would be a rash judgment based on incomplete information. Some students want to fire Smith after they see the store-by-store data in Exhibit 20–9.

The home office should have the records and facilities to isolate problem areas, and then rely on the field staff for explanations and help in identifying the specific problem. Continuing detailed analysis usually gives better insights into problems, as this case shows. With computers, this can be done routinely and in great detail *provided marketing managers ask for it.*

The iceberg principle—90 percent below the surface

One of the most interesting conclusions to be drawn from the Stereo illustration is the **iceberg principle**—much good information is hidden in summary data. Icebergs show only about 10 percent of their mass above the water level. The other 90 percent is below the water level—and not directly below, either. The submerged portion almost seems to seek out ships that come too near.

The same is true of much business and marketing data. Since total sales may be large and company activities varied, problems in one area may hide below the surface. Everything looks calm and peaceful. But closer analysis may reveal jagged edges that can severely damage or even sink the business. The 90:10 ratio—and the 80/20 rule we mentioned earlier—must not be ignored. It is helpful to average and summarize data, but be sure that summaries don't hide more than they reveal.

Marketing cost analysis—controlling costs too

So far, we've emphasized sales analysis. But sales come at a cost. And costs can and should be analyzed and controlled, too. You can see why in the case of Watanake Packaging, Ltd. (WPL). WPL developed a new strategy to target the packaging needs of producers of high-tech electronic equipment. WPL designed unique Styrofoam inserts to protect electronic equipment during shipping. It assigned order getters to develop new accounts and recruited agent intermediaries to develop overseas markets. The entire marketing mix was well received, and the firm's skimming price led to good profits. But over time, competing suppliers entered the market. When marketing managers at WPL analyzed costs, they realized that their once-successful strategy was slipping. Personal selling expense as a percentage of sales had doubled because it took longer to find and sell new accounts. It was costly to design special products for the many customers who purchased only small quantities. Profit margins were falling too, because of increased price competition. In contrast, the analysis showed that sales of ordinary cardboard shipping boxes for agricultural products were very profitable. So WPL stopped calling on *small* electronics firms, and developed a new plan to build the firm's share of the less glamorous but more profitable cardboard box business.

Marketing costs have a purpose

Detailed cost analysis is very useful in understanding production costs, but much less is done with *marketing cost analysis.*[7] One reason is that some accountants show little interest in their firm's marketing process—or they don't understand the different marketing activities. They just treat marketing as overhead and forget about it.

In the next chapter, when we discuss the relationship between marketing and accounting in more detail, we'll explain how some accountants and marketing managers are working together to address this problem. For now, however, you should be aware that careful analysis of most marketing costs shows that the money is spent for a specific purpose—for example, to develop or promote a particular product or to serve particular customers.

Let's reconsider Exhibit 20–5 from this perspective. It shows that the company's spending on sales compensation and sales expenses varies by salesperson and market area. By breaking out and comparing the costs of different sales reps, the marketing manager gains a much better idea of what it is costing to implement the strategy in each sales area. In this example, it's clear not only that the sales reps in sales areas D and especially E are falling short in sales but also that their costs are high relative to other reps who are getting more results. The table shows that the difference isn't due to annual compensation—which is lower. Rather, these reps have expenses that are two or three times the average. The smaller number of total customers in these sales areas (Exhibit 20–4) may explain the lower levels of sales, but it probably doesn't explain the higher expenses. Perhaps the customers are more spread out and require more travel to reach. Here again, the cost analysis doesn't explain *why* the results are as they are—but it does direct the manager's attention to a specific area that needs attention. A more detailed breakdown of costs may help pinpoint the specific cause.

Allocate costs to specific customers and products

Because marketing costs have a purpose, it usually makes sense to allocate costs to specific market segments (or customers) or to specific products. In some situations, companies allocate costs directly to the various geographical market segments they serve. This may let managers directly analyze the profitability of the firm's target markets. In other situations, companies allocate costs to specific customers or specific products—and then add these costs for market segments, depending on how much of which products each customer buys.

Should all costs be allocated?

So far, we've discussed general principles. But allocating costs is tricky. Some costs are likely to be fixed for the near future, regardless of what decision is made. And some costs are likely to be *common* to several products or customers, making allocation difficult.

Two basic approaches to handling this allocating problem are possible: the full-cost approach, and the contribution-margin approach.

Full-costing—allocate everything

In the **full-cost approach,** all costs are allocated to products, customers, or other categories. Even fixed costs and common costs are allocated in some way. Because all costs are allocated, we can subtract costs from sales and find the profitability of various customers, products, and so on. This *is* of interest to some managers.

The full-cost approach requires that difficult-to-allocate costs be split on some basis. Here, the managers assume that the work done for those costs is equally beneficial to customers, to products, or to whatever group they are allocated. Sometimes this allocation is done mechanically. But often logic can support the allocation—if we accept the idea that marketing costs are incurred for a purpose. For example, advertising costs not directly related to specific customers or products might be allocated to *all* customers based on their purchases, on the theory that advertising helps bring in the sales. We'll go into more detail on allocating costs in the next chapter.

The alternative—allocate only variable costs

When we use the **contribution-margin approach,** all costs are not allocated in *all* situations. Why?

When we compare various alternatives, it may be more meaningful to consider only those costs which are directly related to specific alternatives. Variable costs are relevant here.

The contribution-margin approach focuses attention on variable costs rather than on total costs. Total costs may include some fixed costs that do not change in the short run and can safely be ignored, or some common costs that are more difficult to allocate.[8]

Two approaches, different decisions

The difference between the full-cost approach and the contribution-margin approach is important. The two approaches may suggest different decisions, as we'll see in the following example.

FULL-COST EXAMPLE Exhibit 20–11 shows a profit and loss statement, using the full-cost approach, for a department store with three operating departments. (These could be market segments or customers or products.)

The administrative expenses, which here are the only fixed costs, have been allocated to departments based on the sales volume of each department. This is a typical method of allocation. In this situation, some managers argued that Department 1 was clearly unprofitable—and should be eliminated—because it showed a net loss of $500. Were they right?

To find out, see Exhibit 20–12, which shows what would happen if Department 1 were eliminated.

Several facts become clear right away. The overall profit of the store would be reduced if Department 1 were dropped. Fixed costs of $3,000—now being charged to Department 1—would have to be allocated to the other departments. This would reduce net profit by $2,500, since Department 1 previously covered $2,500 of the $3,000 in fixed costs. Such shifting of costs would then make Department 2 unprofitable!

Exhibit 20-11 Profit and Loss Statement by Department

	TOTALS	DEPT. 1	DEPT. 2	DEPT. 3
Sales	$100,000	$50,000	$30,000	$20,000
Cost of sales	80,000	45,000	25,000	10,000
Gross margin	20,000	5,000	5,000	10,000
Other expenses:				
Selling expenses	5,000	2,500	1,500	1,000
Administrative expenses	6,000	3,000	1,800	1,200
Total other expenses	11,000	5,500	3,300	2,200
Net profit or (loss)	$ 9,000	$ (500)	$ 1,700	$ 7,800

Exhibit 20-12 Profit and Loss Statement by Department if Department 1 Were Eliminated

	TOTALS	DEPT. 2	DEPT. 3
Sales	$50,000	$30,000	$20,000
Cost of sales	35,000	25,000	10,000
Gross margin	15,000	5,000	10,000
Other expenses:			
Selling expenses	2,500	1,500	1,000
Administrative expenses	6,000	3,600	2,400
Total other expenses	8,500	5,100	3,400
Net profit or (loss)	$ 6,500	$ (100)	$ 6,600

Exhibit 20-13 Contribution-Margin Statement by Departments

	TOTALS	DEPT. 1	DEPT. 2	DEPT. 3
Sales	$100,000	$50,000	$30,000	$20,000
Variable costs:				
Cost of sales	80,000	45,000	25,000	10,000
Selling expenses	5,000	2,500	1,500	1,000
Total variable costs	85,000	47,500	26,500	11,000
Contribution margin	15,000	$ 2,500	$ 3,500	$ 9,000
Fixed costs:				
Administrative expenses	6,000			
Net profit	$ 9,000			

CONTRIBUTION-MARGIN EXAMPLE Exhibit 20–13 shows a contribution-margin income statement for the same department store. Note that each department has a positive contribution margin. Here, the Department 1 contribution of $2,500 stands out better. This actually is the amount that would be lost if Department 1 were dropped. (Our example assumes that the fixed administrative expenses are *truly* fixed—that none of them would be eliminated if this department were dropped.)

A contribution-margin income statement shows the contribution of each department more clearly—including its contribution to both fixed costs and profit. As long as a department has some contribution margin—and as long as there is no better use for the resources it uses—that department should be retained.

Contribution-margin versus full-cost

Using the full-cost approach often leads to arguments within a company. Any method of allocation can make some products or customers appear less profitable.

For example, it's logical to assign all common advertising costs to customers based on their purchases. But this approach can be criticized on the grounds that it may make large-volume customers appear less profitable than they really are—especially if the marketing mix aimed at the larger customers emphasizes price more than advertising.

Those in the company who want the smaller customers to look more profitable usually argue *for* this allocation method on the grounds that general advertising helps build good customers through its impact on the overall image of the company and its products.

Arguments over allocation methods can be deadly serious. The method used may reflect on the performance of various managers—and it may affect their salaries and bonuses. Product managers, for example, are especially interested in how the various fixed and common costs are allocated to their products. Each may want to see costs shifted to others' products.

Arbitrary allocation of costs also may have a direct impact on sales reps' morale. If they see their variable costs loaded with additional common or fixed costs over which they have no control, they may ask, What's the use?

To avoid these problems, firms often use the contribution-margin approach, which is especially useful for evaluating alternatives—and for showing operating managers and salespeople how they're doing. The contribution-margin approach shows what they've actually contributed to covering general overhead and profit.

Top management, on the other hand, often finds full-cost analysis more useful. In the long run, some products, departments, or customers must pay for the fixed costs. So full-cost analysis has its place, too.

Planning and control combined

We've been treating sales and cost analyses separately up to this point. But management often combines them to keep a running check on its activities (i.e., to be sure its plans are working), and to see when and where new strategies are needed.

Sales + Costs + Everybody helps = $163,000

Let's see how this works at Cindy's Fashions, a typical retailer.

This firm netted $155,000 last year. Cindy Reve, the owner, expects no basic change in competition and slightly better local business conditions. So she sets this year's profit objective at $163,000—an increase of about 5 percent.

Next, she develops tentative plans to show how she can make this higher profit. She estimates the sales volumes, gross margins, and expenses—broken down by months and by departments in her store—that she would need to net $163,000.

Exhibit 20–14 is a planning and control chart that Reve has developed to show the contribution each department should make each month. At the bottom of Exhibit 20–14, the plan for the year is summarized. Note that space is provided to insert the actual performance and a measure of variation. So this chart can be used to do both planning and control.

Exhibit 20–14 shows that Reve is focusing on the monthly contribution to overhead and profit by each department. The purpose of monthly estimates is to get more frequent feedback and allow faster adjustment of plans. Generally, the shorter the planning and control period, the easier it is to correct problems before they become emergencies.

In this example, Reve has used a modified contribution-margin approach—some of the fixed costs can be allocated logically to particular departments. On this chart, the balance left after direct fixed and variable costs are charged to departments is called Contribution to Store. The idea is that each department will contribute to covering *general* store expenses—such as top management salaries and holiday decorations—and to net profits.

In Exhibit 20–14, we see that the whole operation is brought together when Reve computes the monthly operating profit. She totals the contribution from each of the four departments, and then subtracts general store expenses to obtain the operating profit for each month.

As time passes, Reve can compare actual sales with what's projected. If actual sales are less than projected, corrective action can take either of two courses: improving implementation efforts, or developing new, more realistic strategies.

The Marketing Audit

The analyses we've discussed so far are designed to help a firm plan and control its operations. They can help a marketing manager do a better job. Often, however, the control process tends to look at only a few critical elements—such as sales variations by product in different territories. It misses such things as the effectiveness of present and possible marketing strategies and mixes.

Exhibit 20-14 Planning and Control Chart for Cindy's Fashions

	CONTRIBUTION TO STORE							
	DEPT. A	DEPT. B	DEPT. C	DEPT. D*	TOTAL	STORE EXPENSE	OPERATING PROFIT	CUMULATIVE OPERATING PROFIT
January								
Planned	27,000	9,000	4,000	−1,000	39,000	24,000	15,000	15,000
Actual								
Variation								
February								
Planned	20,000	6,500	2,500	−1,000	28,000	24,000	4,000	19,000
Actual								
Variation								
November								
Planned	32,000	7,500	2,500	0	42,000	24,000	18,000	106,500
Actual								
Variation								
December								
Planned	63,000	12,500	4,000	9,000	88,500	32,000	56,500	163,000
Actual								
Variation								
Total								
Planned	316,000	70,000	69,000	−4,000	453,000	288,000	163,000	163,000
Actual								
Variation								

*The objective of minus $4,000 for this department was established on the same basis as the objectives for the other departments—that is, it represents the same percentage gain over last year, when Department D's loss was $4,200. Plans call for discontinuance of the department unless it shows marked improvement by the end of the year.

The marketing manager usually is responsible for day-to-day implementing as well as for planning and control, and may not have the time to evaluate the effectiveness of the firm's efforts. Sometimes, crises pop up in several places at the same time. Attention must focus on adjusting marketing mixes, or on shifting strategies in the short run.

To make sure that the whole marketing program is evaluated *regularly,* not just in times of crisis, marketing specialists have developed the marketing audit. A marketing audit is similar to an accounting audit or a personnel audit, which businesses have used for some time.

A **marketing audit** is a systematic, critical, and unbiased review and appraisal of the basic objectives and policies of the marketing function—and of the organization, methods, procedures, and people employed to implement the policies.[9]

A marketing audit requires a detailed look at the company's current marketing plans to see if they are still the best plans the firm can offer. Customers' needs and attitudes change, and competitors continually develop new and better plans. Plans more than a year or two old may be out of date or even obsolete. Sometimes, marketing managers are so close to the trees that they can't see the forest. An outsider can help the firm see whether it is really focusing on some unsatisfied needs and offering appropriate marketing mixes. Basically, the auditor uses our strategic planning framework. But instead of developing plans, the auditor works backward and evaluates the plans being implemented. The auditor also evaluates the quality of the effort, looking at who is doing what and how well. This means interviewing customers, competitors, channel members, and employees. A marketing audit can be a big job. But if it helps ensure that the company's strategies are on the right track and being implemented properly, it can be well worth the effort.

An audit shouldn't be necessary—but often it is

A marketing audit takes a big view of the business and evaluates the whole marketing program. It might be done by a separate department within the company—perhaps by a marketing controller. But to get both expert and objective evaluation, it's probably better to use an outside organization such as a marketing consulting firm.

Ideally, a marketing audit should not be necessary. Good managers do their very best in planning, implementing, and control, and should continually evaluate the effectiveness of the operation.

In practice, however, managers often become identified with certain strategies, and pursue them blindly when other strategies might be more effective. Since an outside view can give needed perspective, marketing audits may be more common in the future.

Questions and Problems

1. Give an example of how a firm has used information technology to improve its marketing implementation and do a better job of meeting your needs.
2. Should marketing managers leave it to the computer experts to develop reports that the marketing manager will use to improve implementation and control? Explain.
3. Give an example of a firm that has a competitive advantage because of the excellent job it does with implementation activities that have a direct impact on customer satisfaction. Explain why you think your example is a good one.
4. What are the major advantages of total quality management as an approach for improving implementation of marketing plans? What limitations can you think of?
5. Various breakdowns can be used for sales analysis depending on the nature of the company and its products. Describe a situation (one for each) where each of the following breakdowns would yield useful information. Explain why.
   a. By geographic region.
   b. By product.
   c. By customer.
   d. By size of order.
   e. By size of sales rep commission on each product or product group.
6. Distinguish between a sales analysis and a performance analysis.
7. Carefully explain what the iceberg principle should mean to the marketing manager.
8. Explain the meaning of the comparative performance and comparative cost data in Exhibits 20–4 and 20–5. Why does it appear that eliminating sales areas D and E would be profitable?
9. Most sales forecasting is subject to some error (perhaps 5 to 10 percent). Should we then expect variations in sales performance of 5 to 10 percent above or below quota? If so, how should we treat such variations in evaluating performance?
10. Why is there controversy between the advocates of the full-cost and the contribution-margin approaches to cost analysis?
11. The June profit and loss statement for the Browning Company is shown below. If competitive conditions make price increases impossible, and management has cut costs as much as possible, should the Browning Company stop selling to hospitals and schools? Explain.
12. Explain why a marketing audit might be desirable, even in a well-run company. Who or what kind of an organization would be best to conduct a marketing audit? Would a marketing research firm be good? Would the present CA firm be most suitable? Explain.

Browning Company Statement

	RETAILERS	HOSPITALS AND SCHOOLS	TOTAL
Sales			
80,000 units at $0.70	$56,000		$56,000
20,000 units at $0.60		$12,000	12,000
Total	56,000	12,000	68,000
Cost of sales	40,000	10,000	50,000
Gross margin	16,000	2,000	18,000
Sales and administrative expenses:			
Variable	6,000	1,500	7,500
Fixed	5,600	900	6,500
Total	11,600	2,400	14,000
Net profit (loss)	$ 4,400	$ (400)	$ 4,000

Suggested cases

17 Huntoon & Balbiera

19 KASTORS, Inc.

28 Imperial Lumber Limited

Computer-aided problem

Marketing Cost Analysis

This problem emphasizes the differences between the full-cost approach and contribution-margin approach to marketing cost analysis.

Tapco, Inc., currently sells two products. Sales commissions and unit costs vary with the quantity of each product sold. With the full-cost approach, Tapco's administrative and advertising costs are allocated to each product based on its share of total sales dollars. Details of Tapco's costs and other data are given in the spreadsheet. The first column shows a cost analysis based on the full-cost approach. The second column shows an analysis based on the contribution-margin approach.

a. If the number of product A units sold were to increase by 1,000 units, what would happen to the allocated administrative expense for product A? How would the change in sales of product A affect the allocated administrative expense for product B? Briefly discuss why the changes you observe might cause conflict between the product managers of the two different products.

b. What would happen to total profits if Tapco stopped selling product A but continued to sell 4,000 units of product B? What happens to total profits if the firm stops selling product B but continues to sell 5,000 units of product A? (Hint: To stop selling a product means that the quantity sold would be zero.)

c. If the firm dropped product B and increased the price of product A by $2.00, what quantity of product A would it have to sell to earn a total profit as large as it was originally earning with both products? (Hint: Change values in the spreadsheet to reflect the changes the firm is considering, and then use the What If analysis to vary the quantity of product A sold and display what happens to total profit.)

For additional questions related to this problem, see Exercise 20–3 in the *Learning Aid for Use with Basic Marketing,* Ninth Canadian Edition.

When you finish this chapter, you should:

- Understand why turning a marketing plan into a profitable business requires money, information, people, and a way to get or produce goods and services.
- Understand the ways that marketing strategy decisions may need to be adjusted in light of available financing.
- Understand how a firm can implement and expand a marketing plan using internally generated cash flow.
- Understand how different aspects of production capacity and flexibility should be coordinated with strategic market planning.
- Understand the ways that the location and cost of production affect strategic market planning.
- Know that marketing managers and accountants should work together to improve analysis of the costs and profitability of specific products and customers.
- Be aware of some of the human resource issues that a marketer should consider when planning a strategy and implementing a plan.
- Understand the important new terms (shown in orange).

Chapter twenty-one

Managing Marketing's Link with Other Functional Areas

'My commitment is to make our customers and our Company successful.'

James F. Shepard CHAIRMAN AND CHIEF EXECUTIVE OFFICER

to our shareholders

I am pleased to report that Finning International Inc. produced record results in 1997 for the fourth consecutive year. Revenue increased 24% to $2.3 billion and net income improved 18% to $104 million. The Company's return on shareholders' equity was 16.2% in 1997 – the third year in a row the Company earned a return above its 15% target.

This strong performance could not have been achieved without the commitment of our Finning employees around the world. By applying their expertise to individual customer needs they are consistently providing the best solutions – made possible by the fact that Finning sells and services the best equipment in its class, namely Caterpillar. Reliability, productivity and quality of design, manufacture and support are the key ingredients in Caterpillar's record of success.

Finning's record performance in 1997 can also be credited to our corporate strategy. We remained committed to our core business while stepping further out on the international stage. Earlier this decade, the Company embarked on a plan that would see Finning increase its diversification outside of Western Canada. In 1993, we acquired the Caterpillar dealership in Chile at a time when that economy was beginning to accelerate. On October 1, 1997, we completed the acquisition of H. Leverton Limited, the other Cat dealership in Britain, making our Finning (UK) Ltd. operation the sole British Cat dealership. Management is currently integrating the best practices of those two companies to create a stronger and more efficient dealership. The equipment industry in Britain remains highly competitive but we are expecting steady improvement in Finning (UK)'s market share and operating margins over the next three to four years.

PAGE 2

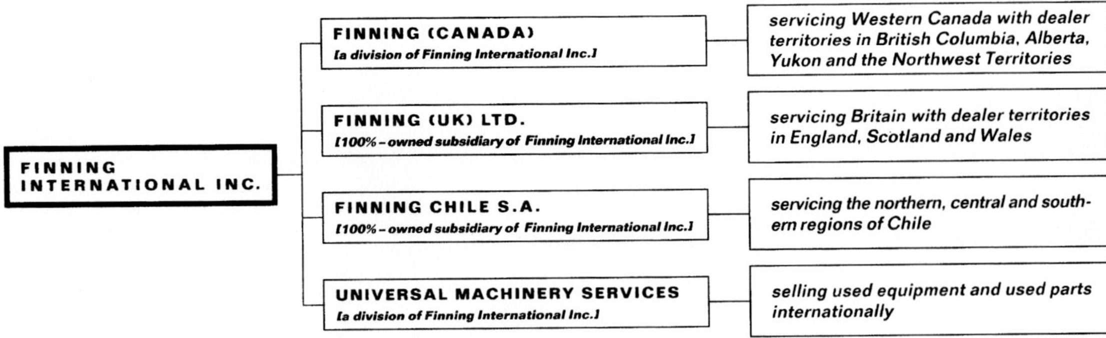

Because of our diversification, Finning now generates more than half of its revenue from activities outside of Canada. We serve an expanded customer base spread over three continents and operating in unique industries and separate economies. This diversification reduces our exposure to market cyclicality in any one sector of an economy, allowing our Company to focus on building long-term value. For example, even though the coastal forestry industry in British Columbia experienced weakness in 1997, double-digit growth in Alberta and Chile allowed us to achieve record results.

To further our international diversification, we are also committing more people and resources to our Universal Machinery Services division ("UMS"), previously called International Sales. UMS sells used equipment and used parts to end-users and other dealers around the world. In the last five years, the division has tripled its sales to $100 million in 1997 and is now expanding its marketing efforts in the areas of pipeline equipment and cranes.

While diversification has been a key to Finning's successful growth, so too has been the forward-looking and expansive product introduction program of Caterpillar. Since 1992, Caterpillar has introduced more than 244 new or improved products and this past year Cat completed a series of acquisitions and joint ventures to further expand its product line. In the agriculture sector, Cat has joined hands with German-based Claas KgaA to introduce a new line of Lexion combine harvesters that will be available in North America in 1999. Caterpillar also acquired Skogsjan AB and Perkins Engines (a division of LucasVarity plc) to expand their forest and power systems lines, respectively. In the second quarter of 1998, Cat will launch its new series of compact construction equipment at an industry trade show in Germany. The commitment to product leadership by Caterpillar provides Finning with expanded opportunities to sell and service new and existing equipment in all its dealer territories.

While Finning has grown in size significantly and enhanced its strategic position over this past decade, it is clear that we cannot stand still in a changing business environment. We must be ever vigilant to the opportunities and threats that are sure to appear in tomorrow's markets. Competition remains tough in each of our dealer territories and we are making the necessary internal changes to stay one step ahead. We recognize that our success in the past has been due to our ability to control costs and reposition our resources to best serve our customers. And we are continuing this approach. In our British operations, substantial relocation and restructuring efforts are underway as Finning (UK) and H. Leverton are being combined to maximize productivity. And in Canada, we have made the decision to relocate 220 positions from our Canadian head office on Great Northern Way in Vancouver to our renovated three-storey office building in Edmonton, Alberta. Edmonton, centrally located to our oil, gas, mining and agricultural customers, is also the gateway to the Northwest Territories which offers a promising future in the mining sector, especially diamonds. Finning (Canada) must be close to its customers in Alberta and the Northwest Territories where expansion opportunities in all key sectors will be the biggest source of our Canadian growth in the next decade. To provide state-of-the-art service support for customers in the Lower Mainland, a new $15 million branch facility is under construction in Surrey, B.C.

PAGE 4

In our continuing efforts to improve efficiency and customer service, Finning made a significant corporate-wide commitment to upgrading its information systems in 1997. Both Finning (Canada) and Finning (UK) successfully launched version 2.0 of the Dealer Business System (DBS) in the third quarter of 1997. DBS is customized software that improves support services for Finning's customers, and links the Company's database with Finning's operating units, the Caterpillar network and other Cat dealers worldwide. Finning Chile will be upgraded from an earlier version of DBS in the fourth quarter of 1998.

Finning also continues to benefit from the business acumen and informed governance of its Board of Directors. In this regard, the Board appointed two additional members in 1997 – Jim Dinning of Calgary, Alberta and Timothy Howden of Marlow, England. We look forward to the valued contribution of these two new members.

Looking forward, Finning's performance will continue to improve as each of the operating units capitalizes on its unrealized potential. Now that Finning (UK) is the national Caterpillar dealer in Britain, there is an opportunity to begin growing our market share in that territory and improving cost competitiveness over time. In Chile, increasing activity in construction and infrastructure projects will offset the decline in the growth rate of mining expected in that territory in 1998. And in Canada, continued activity in the petroleum industry, expansion of the oil sands, and new diamond mining projects in the Northwest Territories provide on-going growth opportunities.

By focusing on core strengths which enhance our "customer solutions" approach to business, the Company will continue to build long-term value. Through the dedication and commitment of all our employees, we will continue to be the leaders in the markets that we serve.

James F. Shepard CHAIRMAN AND CHIEF EXECUTIVE OFFICER

Source: Finning International Inc. 1997 Annual Report, pp. 1–4.

Marketing in the broader context

The marketing concept says that everyone in a firm should work together to satisfy customer needs at a profit. Once a marketing strategy has been developed, and turned into a marketing plan, the blueprint for what needs to be done is in place. So throughout the text we've developed concepts and how-to approaches relevant to strategic market planning, implementation, and control.

From the outset, we've emphasized that whether a marketing strategy is good or not depends on how it fits with the specific firm and its market environment. In Chapters 2 and 3 we discussed how a firm's resources and objectives might allow it to pursue some opportunities but not others.

Now that you have a better idea about how the marketing decisions fit together into an integrated strategy, we'll take a closer look at some of the most important ways that marketing links to other functional areas. As illustrated by the Chairman and CEO's Report to the Shareholders in the Finning International Inc. 1997 Annual Report, turning a strategy into a profitable business requires more than a marketing plan—it also requires money, people, and other resources, such as production capacity. Finning, working together with Caterpillar, whose products it sells and services, has blended all of these components together in a way that generated record results in 1997.

Cross-functional links affect strategic planning

In this chapter, we will continue to look at management issues from the point of view of a marketing manager. The emphasis is not on the technical details of other functional areas but rather on the most important ways that relationships with other areas affect choices among the strategic decisions we've discussed throughout the text. Learning about these cross-functional linkages will improve your ability to develop marketing strategies and plans that really work.

Implementing a marketing plan usually requires a financial investment, so we'll start with a discussion of financial issues. We'll consider both the funds required to start up a new plan and the funds that may be needed to meet ongoing expenses. Then we'll look at production and operations. We've already explained how marketing can make economies of scale in production possible, but here we'll go into more detail on how available production capacity, production flexibility, and operating issues affect marketing planning. We'll also take a closer look at how accounting people and marketing managers work together to get a better handle on marketing costs. Marketers sometimes get so focused on sales that they forget that profits depend on both revenues and costs. We'll conclude with a discussion of human resource issues—because it's people who put plans into action. New marketing strategies often upset the standard ways of doing things, and without everyone's wholehearted cooperation, change is difficult.

How important the linkages with production, finance, accounting, and human resources are for the marketing manager depends on the situation. In an entrepreneurial startup, the same person may be making all of the decisions and handling everything. In a small but established company that is trying to expand, the challenges may be different. And in a big company with many different specialists, the linkages may be much more complicated.

Cross-functional challenges are greatest with new efforts

Our emphasis will be on new efforts. When a new strategy involves only a slight modification to a plan that the firm is already implementing successfully, specialists in different areas usually have a pretty good idea of how their activities link to other areas. However, when a potential strategy involves a more significant change—perhaps the development and introduction of a totally new product idea, or a big reorganization of the firm's sales force or channel systems—understanding the links between the different functional areas is usually much more critical.

You can't expand, add new capabilities, or bring on people to handle new marketing activities if you can't pay the cost. You can't market a product you can't get or produce. And you can't implement your plan if there are not enough people with the right skills available.

The finance function: Money to implement marketing plans

Bright marketing ideas for new ways to satisfy customer needs don't go very far if there isn't enough money to put a plan into operation. Finding and allocating **capital**—the money invested in a firm—is usually handled by a firm's chief financial officer. Entrepreneurs and others who own their own companies may handle this job themselves, or they may get help from outside financial specialists and consultants. In most firms, however, there is a separate manager who handles financial matters and who works with the chief executive to make major finance decisions.

Good communication between a marketing manager and the firm's finance manager is critical. They must work together to ensure that marketing plans are realistic and that the firm can successfully implement them with the money that is or will be available. Further, a successful strategy should ultimately generate profit. The financial manager needs to know how much money to expect—and when to expect it—to be able to plan for how it will be used.

Opportunities compete for capital and budgets

Within an organization, different possible opportunities compete for capital. There's usually not enough money to do everything, so strategies that are inconsistent with the firm's financial objectives and resources are not likely to be funded. It's often best for the marketing manager to use relevant financial measures as quantitative screening criteria when evaluating various alternatives in the first place.

Marketing plans that *are* funded usually must work within a budget constraint. Ideally, the marketing manager should help determine the size of that budget. It isn't practical to develop a plan and budget that require money that simply isn't available.

This means that at least some important strategic marketing decisions may need to be adjusted, either in the short or long term, to work within the available budget. For example, a marketing manager might prefer to have control over the selling effort for a new product by hiring new people for a separate sales force. However, if there isn't enough money available for additional salaries and benefits as well as for travel and other selling expenses, then the best alternative might be to start with manufacturers' agents. These agents work for a commission and aren't paid until after they generate some sales—and some sales revenue. Later, as the market develops and the plan becomes profitable, there may be both the money and a good reason—perhaps lower cost or better control—to expand the firm's own sales force.

Working capital pays for short-term expenses

Finance managers usually think in terms of two different uses of capital. First, capital may be required to pay for investments in facilities, equipment, and other fixed assets. These installations are usually purchased and then used, and depreciated, over a number of years. In addition, a firm needs **working capital**—money to pay for short-term expenses such as employee salaries, advertising, marketing research, inventory storing costs, and what the firm owes suppliers. A firm usually must pay these ongoing expenses as they arise—and often that's before it gets revenue for the goods and services it sells. As a result, there is usually a continuing need for working capital.

It's useful for a marketing manager who is developing a plan to think about likely capital needs in this same way. In general, the more ambitious the plan, the greater the amount of capital that is needed. Capital is usually a critical resource when a plan calls for rapid growth, especially if that growth calls for expensive new facilities. Clearly, a plan to build a chain of 15 hotels requires more money for buildings and equipment—as well as more money for salaries, food, and supplies—than a plan for a single hotel. Such a plan might require that the firm borrow money from a commercial lender. In contrast, a plan that simply calls for improving the service at an existing hotel—perhaps by adding several people to handle room service—would require much less money. Here, increased food sales from room service might quickly generate more than enough earnings to pay for the added people.

Capital comes from internal or external sources

As these examples indicate, there are a number of different possible sources of capital. It's useful to boil them down to two categories: *external sources* such as loans, or sales of stocks or bonds, and *internal sources* such as cash accumulated from the firm's profits. A firm usually seeks outside funding in advance of when it is needed to invest

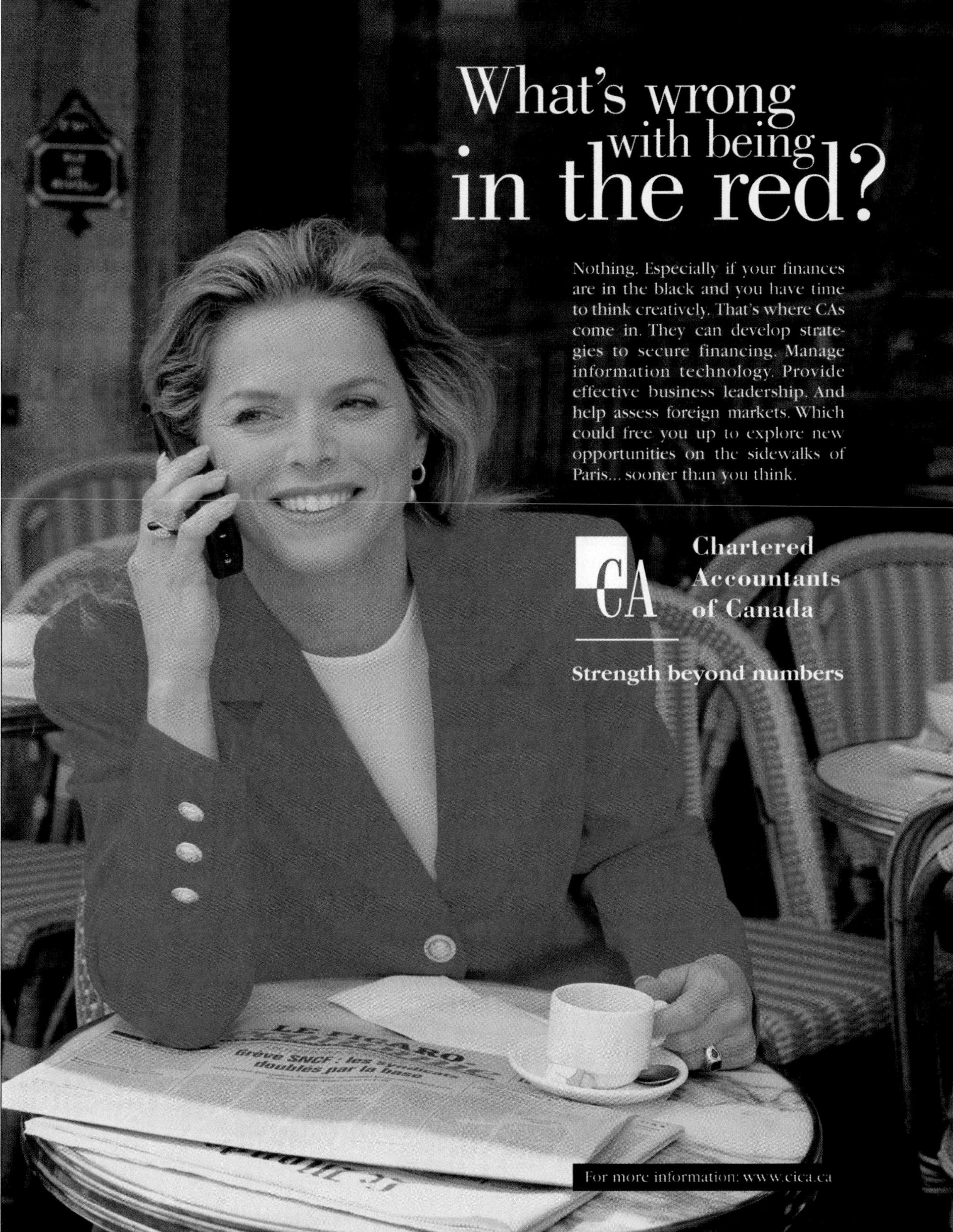
What's wrong with being in the red?
Nothing. Especially if your finances are in the black and you have time to think creatively. That's where CAs come in. They can develop strategies to secure financing. Manage information technology. Provide effective business leadership. And help assess foreign markets. Which could free you up to explore new opportunities on the sidewalks of Paris... sooner than you think.
CA
Chartered Accountants of Canada
Strength beyond numbers
For more information: www.cica.ca
LE FIGARO
Grève SNCF : les syndicats doublés par la base

in a new strategy. Internally generated profits may be accumulated and used in the same way, but often internal money is used as it becomes available. In other words, with internally generated funding a firm's marketing program may be expected to "pay its own way."

The timing of financing has an important effect on strategic market planning, so we'll look at this topic in more detail. We'll start by looking at external sources of funds.

External funding—investors expect a return

A firm might prefer to fund its marketing program from rapid growth in its own profits, but this is not always possible. New companies often don't have enough money to start that way. An established company with some capital may not have as much as it needs to make long-term investments in factories or other facilities and still have enough working capital for the routine expenses of implementing a plan. Also, getting started may involve losses—perhaps for several years—before earnings come in. In these circumstances, the firm may need to turn to one of several sources of external capital.

A firm may be able to raise money by selling stock—a share in the ownership of a company. Stock sales may be public or private, and the buyers may be individuals (including a firm's own employees) or institutional investors (such as a pension fund or venture capital firm).

People who own stock in a firm want a good return on their investment. That can happen if the company pays owners of its stock a regular dividend. It also happens if the value of the stock goes up over time. Neither is likely to occur if the firm isn't consistently earning profits. The value of a firm's stock typically doesn't increase unless its profits are *growing*. This is one reason why marketing managers are always looking for profitable new growth opportunities. Profits can also improve by being more efficient—getting the marketing jobs done at lower cost, doing a better job holding on to customers, and the like—but continued growth in profits usually requires that a firm pursue new market opportunities. Ultimately, a firm that doesn't have a successful (or at least promising) marketing strategy can't attract and keep investors.

Investors' time horizon is important

The time horizon for profit and growth that investors have in mind can be very important to the marketing manager. If investors are willing to wait for a new strategy to become profitable, a marketing manager may have the luxury of developing a plan that will be very profitable in the long run even if it racks up short-term losses. Many Japanese firms take this approach. However, most marketing managers face intense pressure to develop plans that will generate profits quickly. There's more risk for investors if potential profits are off in the future.

It isn't always possible to develop a plan that produces profit in the short term and also positions the firm for long-run success. For example, a low penetration price for a new product may help both to prevent competition and to build a large, loyal base of customers who will be repeat purchasers long into the future. Yet a skimming price may be better for profits in the short term. The marketing manager's plans and program must take the investors' time horizon into consideration. Unhappy investors can and often do demand new management, or they put their money somewhere else. A firm—or a marketing manager—that fails in the short run may find out that there *is* no long run!

Debt financing involves an interest cost

Rather than sell stock, some firms prefer **debt financing**—borrowing money based on a promise to repay, usually within a fixed time period and with a specific interest charge. This might involve a loan from a commercial bank or the use of corporate bonds. People or institutions that loan the money typically do not get an ownership share in the company, and they are usually even less willing to take a risk than are investors who buy stock.

Most commercial banks are conservative. There's an element of truth in the old adage that "a bank is only likely to make a loan to a company that really doesn't need one." That leaves out many firms—including most new ones—that don't have some valuable assets to put up as a guarantee that the lender will get its money. Investors who buy a firm's bonds are also very concerned about security. In general, the greater the risk that the borrower takes on to provide the loan, the greater the interest rate charge will be.

Interest expense may have an impact on prices

When a firm needs to borrow a large amount of money to fund its plans, the cost of borrowing the money can be a real financial burden—especially if the money is to be repaid over time rather than in a lump sum after a plan is already profitable. Just as a firm's selling price must cover all of the marketing expenses and the other costs of doing business before profits begin to accumulate, it must also cover the interest charge on borrowed money. The impact of interest charges on prices can be significant. For example, the spread between the prices charged by fast-growing, efficient supermarket chains and individual grocery stores would be even greater if the chains weren't paying big interest charges on loans to fund new facilities.

While the cost of borrowing money can be high, it may still make sense to use debt financing if the borrowed money is used to implement a marketing plan that earns an even greater return. In that way, the firm "leverages" the borrowed money to make a profit. Even so, there are often advantages if a firm can pay for its plans with internally generated capital.[1]

Winning strategies generate capital

A company with a successful marketing strategy has its own internal source of funds—profits that become cash in the bank! Reinvesting cash generated from operations is usually less expensive than borrowing money because no interest expense is involved. So internal financing often helps a firm earn more profit than a competitor that is operating on borrowed money—even if the internally financed company is selling at a lower price.

Expanding profits may support expanded plan

Firms that don't want the expense of borrowed money or that can't get external funding often start with a less costly strategy and a plan to expand it as quickly as is allowed by earnings. Consider the case of Sorrell Ridge, a small company that wanted to compete with the jams and jellies of big competitors like Welches and Smuckers. Sorrell Ridge started small with a strategy that focused on a better product—"spreadable fruit" with no sugar added—that was targeted at health-conscious consumers. After paying to update its production facilities, Sorrell Ridge didn't have much working capital to pay for promotion and other marketing expenses. So it turned to health food wholesalers and retailers to give the product a promotion push in the channel. As profits from the health food channel started to grow, Sorrell Ridge used some of the money for local TV and print ads in big cities in the Northeastern United States. The ads increased consumer demand for Sorrell Ridge's spreads and helped get shelf space from supermarkets in that region. Success from selling through supermarkets in the Northeast generated more volume and profit, which provided Sorrell Ridge with the financial base to enter the big California market. The big supermarket chains there wouldn't consider carrying a new fruit spread without a lot of trade promotion—including hefty stocking allowances. Sorrell Ridge had the money to pay for a coupon program to stimulate consumer trial, but that didn't leave enough money for the stocking allowance. However, the marketing manager had a creative idea that involved giving retailers the stocking allowance in the form of a credit against future purchases rather than cash "up front." With a plan for that blend of trade and consumer promotion in place, one of the best food brokers in California agreed to take on the line. And the expansion into the new large market resulted in fast and profitable growth.[2]

As the Sorrell Ridge case shows, a firm with limited resources can sometimes develop a plan that allows for growth through internally generated money. On the other hand, a company with a mature product that has limited growth potential can invest the earnings from that product in developing a new opportunity that is more profitable. Lotus Development, the software company, is a good example. It used profits from its Lotus 1 - 2 - 3 spreadsheet, which faced tough competition from Microsoft's Excel, to fund the development of Lotus Notes, an innovative product for the fast-growing segment of computer users who want an easy way to communicate with other members of their work group.

Cash flow looks at when money will be available

A marketing manager who wants to plan strategies based on the expected flow of internal funding needs a good idea of how much cash will be available. A **cash flow statement** is a financial report that forecasts how much cash will be available after paying expenses. The amount that's available isn't always just the "bottom line" or net profit figure shown on the firm's operating statement. Some expenses, such as depreciation of facilities and equipment, are subtracted from revenues for tax and accounting purposes but do not actually involve writing a cheque. In other words, depreciation is a "noncash" expense. So in determining cash flow, marketing managers and their finance manager colleagues often look at a company's earnings *before* these expenses are subtracted.[3]

Adjusting the strategy to money that's available

Most firms rely on a combination of internal and external capital. An adequate overall amount of capital makes it possible to expand more rapidly or to implement a more ambitious plan from the outset. However, when a marketing manager must rely at least in part on internally generated funds to make a strategy self-supporting, that may need to be considered in selecting between alternative strategies or in specific marketing mix decisions for a given strategy.

Improve return of current investment

When finances are tight, it's sensible to look for strategic alternatives that help get a better return on money that's already invested. A firm that sells diagnostic equipment to hospitals might look for another related product for its current salespeople to sell while calling on the same customers. Similarly, a firm that has a successful domestic product might look for new international markets where little or no modification of the product would be required. A firm that is constantly fighting to rewin customers might be better off with a program that offers loyal customers a discount. The increase in the number of customers served might more than offset the lost revenue per sale. Any increase in revenue and profit contribution that the strategy generates—without increasing fixed costs and capital invested—increases profit and the firm's return on investment.

Market mix decisions affect capital needed

Strategic decisions within each of the marketing mix areas often have significantly different capital requirements. In the product area, for example, new product development for a product that is closely related to a firm's existing line is usually less costly than venturing into a totally new area. And a brand extension or a product that uses a family brand name may require less up-front advertising and promotion expense to establish consumer awareness. But offering more models, package sizes, flavours, or colours of a product will almost certainly increase front-end capital needs and increase costs.

Place decisions often have significant financial implications, depending on how responsibilities are shifted and shared in the channel. Indirect distribution usually requires less investment capital than direct approaches. Merchant wholesalers and retailers who pay for products when they purchase them—and who pay the costs of carrying inventory—help a producer's cash flow. Similarly, agent intermediaries may take on much of the selling effort with a lower investment than would be required were the firm to do it alone. Working with intermediaries and facilitators—such as public warehousers and transportation firms—may help reduce the capital requirements for logistics facilities. Expanding into new market areas that can be served from an existing distribution centre may result in greater economies of scale without increased investment.

Similarly, capital requirements are less when intermediaries take on much of the responsibility for promotion in the channel. Wholesalers and retailers have less incentive to do promotion when the firm uses intensive distribution. Intensive distribution is also likely to require a bigger front-end investment in personal selling.

Promotion blends that focus on stimulating consumer pull usually require a big front-end investment in advertising and consumer promotions. For example, it's not unusual for a consumer packaged goods producer to spend half of a new product's first-year sales revenue on advertising. It may be less risky for a firm with limited capital to put more emphasis on a strategy that relies on push rather than pull.

Of course, when a marketing manager is looking at how different strategic decisions relate to the firm's financial situation, those decisions can't be considered separately. It's the financial impact of the entire strategy that must be considered. A strategy with the potential to produce the greatest profit or the fastest return on investment may not be best—or even sensible—if it isn't feasible given the firm's financial situation.

Production must be coordinated with the marketing plan

You know that being able to produce a product doesn't necessarily mean there's a market for it—or that you can sell it at a profit. On the other hand, if a firm is going to sell a product—whether it's a good or a service or a combination of the two—*somebody* has to be able to produce it. So in screening product-market opportunities, a marketing manager needs to have a realistic understanding of what is involved in turning a product concept into something the firm can actually deliver. If a firm is going to pursue an opportunity, it's also critical that there be effective coordination between marketing planning and **production capacity**, which is the ability to produce a certain quantity and quality of specific goods or services.

Different aspects of production capacity may be important in different situations. A firm may have the ability to easily or quickly produce some types of products but not others. For those it can currently produce, it may only be able to handle limited quantities without a major investment in new facilities, equipment, or people. Alternatively, it may have—and be paying for—more capacity than it can use. It may be able to produce only one product at a time—or it may be able to produce many different products. We'll consider these variations in more depth, because different aspects of production capacity have different impacts on marketing planning.[4]

Use excess capacity to improve profits

If a firm has unused production capacity, it's sensible for a marketing manager to try to identify new markets or new products that make more effective use of that investment. For example, a company that produces rubber floor mats for automobiles might be able to add a similar line of floor mats for pickup trucks. Because of economies of scale, expanded production might result in lower costs and better profits for the mats the firm was already producing. In addition, revenue and profit contribution from the new products could improve the return on the investment the firm had already made.

If a firm's production capacity is flexible, many different marketing opportunities may be possible. For example, in light of growing consumer interest in fancy pickup trucks, the marketing manager for the firm just mentioned might see even better profit potential in rubber pickup-truck bed liners than in floor mats. Opportunities further away from current markets may also be relevant. For example, there may be better growth and profits in static-electricity-free mats for computer and telecommunications equipment than there are for auto accessories.

Excess capacity may be a safety net

While excess capacity can be costly, it can also serve as a safety net if demand suddenly picks up. For example, many firms that make products for the construction industry faced costly excess capacity during the late 1980s and early 1990s. However, many of those firms were glad they had that capacity when residential construction subsequently started to boom. Whether excess capacity is a wasteful cost or a safety net for handling unexpected demand depends on the opportunity costs and likelihood of the two situations.

Or it may be a signal of problems

While it makes sense for a marketing manager to understand the firm's current production capacity, there's a hazard in too quickly screening out any other opportunities. Excess capacity may exist because the market for what a firm can produce never really materialized or has moved into long-term decline. Excess capacity may also indicate that there's too much competition, with many other firms all fighting for the same fixed demand. In situations like these, rather than struggling to find minor improvements in capacity use, it might be better for the marketing manager to lead the firm toward other, more profitable alternatives.

We're sorry if you can't find our new cereal.
NEW
Kellogg's
RICE KRISPIES TREATS CEREAL
Wholesome crispy clusters.
But we're sure you'll find it's worth the wait.
We at Kellogg's admit we just haven't been able to keep up with the demand for Kellogg's Rice Krispies Treats Cereal. It's just that so many people ran out to buy our new cereal that we couldn't make it fast enough. It's not your grocer's fault. It's ours. Please accept our apologies. And rest assured, we're doing all we can to make more.
Kellogg's

When Kellogg's introduced Rice Krispies Treats Cereal, production couldn't keep up with the unexpectedly high demand. So, Kellogg's used advertising to tell consumers and retailers about the shortages and to ask them to be patient.

Slow adjustments result in stock-outs

Another aspect of flexibility relates to how quickly and easily a firm can adjust the quantity of a product it produces. This can be an important consideration when demand is uncertain, as is often the case when the marketing manager is planning a new strategy. If a new marketing mix is more successful than expected, demand can quickly outstrip supply. This happened to RJR Nabisco when it developed fat-free Snackwell chocolate cookies. Health-conscious "chocoholics" responded so enthusiastically to promotion that the cookies were quickly out of stock at most supermarkets. Because the cookies required a special production line, it was a long time before stock-outs could be routinely replenished.[5]

Scarce supply wastes marketing effort

This kind of problem can be serious. Carefully planned promotion spending is wasted if advertising and other promotions can't be put on hold until supply catches up to demand. Consumers and channel members may quickly become frustrated by stock-outs. More nimble competitors may get a window of opportunity to introduce an imitation product. By the time the original innovator is able to increase production, consumers may already be loyal to the other brand.

Staged distribution may match capacity

Problems of matching supply and demand are likely to be greatest when a marketing plan calls for quick expansion into many different market areas all at once. That's one reason why many marketing managers plan a regional rollout of new product innovations. Similarly, initial distribution may focus on certain types of channels—say, drugstores alone rather than drugstores and supermarkets. Experience with the early stages of implementation efforts can help the marketing manager determine how much promotion effort is required to keep distribution channels full, and not stocked out. Conversely, if sales from these initial efforts are developing more slowly than expected, it may be possible to speed up the move into other market areas or new types of channels.

Virtual corporations may not make anything at all

Just because a firm doesn't have the capability to produce a product itself doesn't mean that a potential opportunity should be ignored. A profitable concept may justify investment in new production capabilities. Alternatively, an increasing number of firms have found that they can satisfy customers and build profits without doing any production "in house." Instead, they look for capable suppliers to produce a product that meets the specs laid out in the firm's marketing plan. At the extreme, a firm may even act like a **virtual corporation.** Such a corporation is primarily a coordinator—with a good marketing concept. See Internet Insite 21–1 for more information on Net-based organizations of this type.

Consider the case of Calvin Klein fashions. At one time, Calvin Klein was a large manufacturer of underwear and jeans. However, the company was better at analyzing markets, designing fashions, and marketing them than it was at production. So the firm sold its factories and arranged for other companies to make the products that carry the Calvin Klein brand.[6]

While out-sourcing production may increase a firm's flexibility in some ways, it often has disadvantages. Costs are often higher, and it may be difficult or even impossible to control quality. Similarly, product availability may be unpredictable. If several firms are involved in producing the final product, coordination and logistics problems may arise.

A company with a line of accessories for bicyclists faced this problem when it decided to introduce a plastic water bottle. Its other products were metal, so it turned to outside suppliers to produce the bottles. However, getting the job done required three suppliers. One made the plastic bottles, another printed the colourful designs on them, and the third attached a clip to hold the bottle to a bike.

Moving the product from one specialist to another added costs, and whenever one supplier hit a snag, all of the others were affected. The firm was constantly struggling to fill orders on time, and too often was losing the battle. As soon as the bottle proved to be profitable, the firm decided to invest in its own production facilities. By doing its own production, it could be faster and more flexible in responding to special requests from the large retailers who were handling its products.[7]

Design flexibility into operations

Because production flexibility can give a firm a competitive advantage in meeting a target market's needs better or faster, many firms are trying to design more flexibility into their operations. In fact, without flexible production systems, it may not be possible for a firm to provide business customers with the just-in-time delivery

Internet Insite 21-1

Virtual and Internetworked Organizations

In traditional organizations, different functional areas such as marketing, human resources, and production/operations often exist in functional "silos." Such organizations are slow to respond to external changes, in major part due to their internal structures, which do not facilitate efficient communication and information flow within the organization. The result is often a delayed response to a competitive threat or a new market opportunity. Many such organizations have had to endure costly *business process re-engineering* (BPR), an exercise that is supposed to realign the organization and improve the effectiveness of its business processes, thereby creating greater customer value as well as profits. However, failure rates in such re-engineering exercises are very high.[1] Critics argue that BPR is often a band-aid solution when the patient actually needs radical surgery.[2]

Those who advocate radical surgery think that the organizations of tomorrow are likely to bear very little resemblance to what we see today. The *silos* will be broken down. The relationship between marketing and other functional areas will have to be redefined. Don Tapscott describes this new organization as the "internetworked organization," one in which internal networks (i.e., Intranets) will eliminate duplication and facilitate free information flow within the organization. Further, interenterprise computing and information sharing through the Internet will become ubiquitous (i.e., Extranets).[3] Companies will share information in "real time" with suppliers and consumers, leading to lower order-processing costs and inventory carrying costs. Companies will no longer need to invest heavily in private networks that connect them with suppliers or customers (i.e., Electronic Data Interchange or EDI).[4] More significant than these cost savings will be the ability to create greater customer value by internetworking with strategic partners. Each partner will bring a unique core competency. Rather than one organization being the designer, fabricator, and marketer, there may be strategic partners, possibly from different countries or continents, playing each of these specialized roles.

James Martin shares a similar vision and prophesizes that we are soon likely to see a *cybercorp economy,* in which corporations will be "designed for real-time interaction over the information superhighways" and these organizations will be an "interlaced mesh of virtual operations."[5] In this cybereconomy, there will be very few national boundaries, and capital, management, skills, and resources will flow freely across the globe.[6]

From a micro-perspective, how will the internetworking of businesses change the way different functional tasks are performed within an organization? Here are some possibilities:

- **Production.** Prosumption will replace Production.[7] Consumers will become active participants in the design and production of products. Companies such as Dell (www.dell.com), which allows consumers to customize products, have already bridged the gap between production and consumption. Flexible manufacturing and mass customization will be the way of the future.[8] On the Internet, publishing companies are beginning to customize their product through push technologies and pointcasting.
- **Human Resources.** We are already beginning to see outsourcing of labour. In the Internetworked organizations, this will become easier. There will be companies that specialize in clerical and administrative support through the Internet. Flexible work schemes will become popular. Telecommuting, where employees work at home by logging into the company's computer, will be commonplace as businesses seek to gain a competitive edge. As organizations focus on "value streams," much of the work will become team-based and compensation will be linked to performance. Corporate Intranets (or internal networks) will play a big part in training employees, with much of the learning happening without a teacher.[9]
- **Finance.** In the cyber-economy, paper currency will be replaced by smart cards and e-cash. Virtual banks will facilitate electronic commerce. Several Internet banks are in existence now. The flow of money will be seamless and will be done electronically.
- **Accounting.** Internetworked organizations with global strategic partners will pose some new challenges to the accounting profession. The Canadian Institute of Chartered Accountants has already created a set of standards and principles for Electronic Commerce called WebTrust™ (www.cica.ca). Due to the electronic nature of the

cybereconomy, accounting costs are likely to diminish. At the same time, micro-transactions (i.e., transactions using infinitesimally divisible quantities of digital money) will come into vogue.[10]

- **Marketing.** The management of customer relations will become the focus of businesses. The Internet allows for the tracking and studying of consumer behaviour at a level that was inconceivable a few years ago. Real-time intelligence gathering on the Internet will make the internetworked organizations more agile. Instantaneous feedback from and to customers will be the norm. Customized marketing, online distribution, virtual distributors (cybermediaries), and innovative pricing policies (e.g., micropayments and online auctions) will become commonplace. Marketing on the Internet will be an integral part of the internetworked organizations.

1 See Archives of the Business Process Redesign and Reengineering (BPR-L), E-Mail Discussion List (http://ursus.jun.alaska.edu/archives/bpr/).
2 James Martin, *Cybercorp: The New Business Revolution,* AMACOM, 1996.
3 Don Tapscott, *Digital Economy,* McGraw-Hill, 1996.
4 For a more complete discussion of Electronic Data Interchange or EDI, see *Electronic Commerce* by Ravi Kalakota and Andrew B. Whinston, Addison-Wesley, 1996.
5 Martin, *Cybercorp.*
6 Ibid.
7 Tapscott, *Digital Economy.*
8 B. Joseph Pine, *Mass Customization: The New Frontier in Business Competition,* Harvard Business Press, 1992.
9 James Martin, *Cybercorp.*
10 Daniel C. Lynch and Leslie Lundquist, *Digital Money: The New Era of Internet Commerce,* John Wiley & Sons Inc., 1996.

Source: This is one of a series of Internet Insites prepared in April 1998 by Dr. Ramesh Venkat of Saint Mary's University for *Basic Marketing,* Ninth Canadian Edition.

service or rapid response replenishment of inventories that they want and expect. A firm that uses EDI or some other type of computerized reorder system may not be able to take advantage of the information if it can't do anything about it until weeks or months later.

Producing to order requires flexibility too

By contrast, flexible manufacturing systems may make it possible for a firm to respond more rapidly to customer needs. This was an advantage of Dell Computer's telephone order approach. Most other computer firms produced large quantities of standard models of computers and then shipped them to dealers for resale. If the dealer didn't have the right model in stock, it needed time to get it. Dell's approach was different. It allowed customers to order whatever computer configuration they wanted, and the parts were then assembled to match the order. For a small fee, Dell would even install software packages that the customer bought with the computer. This approach reduced the costs of finished goods inventories, constantly matched output to customer needs, and kept everyone at Dell focused on satisfying each and every customer.[8]

Mass customization—serves individual needs

Of course, automobile companies, producers of specialized machine tools, and other types of manufacturers—as well as many service firms—have been creating products based on specific orders from individual customers for a long time. However, a wide variety of companies are now looking for innovative ways to serve smaller segments of customers by using **mass customization**—tailoring the principles of mass production to meet the unique needs of individual customers.

Note that using the principles of mass production is not the same thing as trying to appeal to everyone in some mass market. With the mass-customization approach, a firm may still focus on certain market segments within a broad product market. However, in serving individuals within those target segments, it tries to gain a competitive advantage by finding low-cost ways to give each customer more or better choices.

The changes that are coming with mass customization are illustrated by Levi's Personal Pair personalized jeans program for women. With this program, a woman goes to a participating retail store and is carefully measured by a trained fit consultant. These measurements are entered into a computer, which directs the production of a

This woman is being measured by a fit consultant at a Levi's retail store; the Levi's factory will use the measurements to custom produce a personal pair of jeans for her.

prototype trial jean with these measurements. The customer tries on that prototype for fit. If necessary, other prototypes or modifications of measurements may be tried. When the customer is satisfied, the customer's measurements are sent via computer to the Levi's factory, where sewing operators construct the jeans. In about three weeks, the jeans are ready at the store, or they can be shipped directly to the customer via express mail. The customer's measurements are kept in a database to make it easy to place future orders—perhaps in a different colour, finish, or style.

Of course, not every firm will be able to adjust its offering to each individual customer, but advances in communications and computer-controlled production offer a host of possibilities for marketing managers—and firms—who are looking for better ways to meet the unique needs of individual customers.[9]

Batched production requires inventories

If it is expensive for a firm to switch production from one product (or product line) to another, it may have no alternative but to produce in large batches and maintain large inventories. Then it can supply demand from inventory while it is producing some other product. However, this approach requires careful planning of where in the channel inventories will be held. A firm that must pay the costs of carrying extra inventory to avoid stock-outs may not be able to compete with a firm that has more flexible production.

Where products are produced matters

A marketing manager also needs to consider carefully the marketing implications of *where* products are produced. It often does make sense for a firm to produce where it can produce most economically, if the cost of transporting and storing products to match demand doesn't offset the savings. On the other hand, production in areas distant from customers can make the distribution job much more complicated.

Offshore operations may complicate marketing

As an interesting example, consider the marketing implications of Hanes's decision to use offshore production for many of its men's underwear products. Hanes sells more underwear through big mass-merchandiser chains—such as Wal-Mart, Target, and Kmart—than through any other type of retail outlet. Buyers for these chains are constantly putting pressure on Hanes to find ways to cut prices. One key to cutting prices without killing profit margins is to cut production costs. Because labour costs are a large part of Hanes's cost of goods sold, it has little alternative but to move production to countries where hourly labour costs are much lower than in North America. That's why much of the sewing work on Hanes underwear is done in facilities throughout the Caribbean.

However, the only practical way to transport the bulky and inexpensive finished products back to North America is by boat. Boats are slow, and clearing customs can add further delays. In fact, Hanes had to beef up security at its facilities to prevent drug smugglers from gaining access to its bulk shipping cases.

At the port, the bulk cases of underwear must be handled again and broken down into quantities and assortments for shipping to the retailers' distribution centres. And at the distribution centres the cases need to be grouped with other products going to a specific store. All of these steps are necessary to meet customers' needs at the final point of consumption, but they also make it difficult to adjust supply quickly when there is an unexpected shift in demand.

Hanes's offshore production also makes other aspects of its marketing plan more difficult to implement. For example, as part of a special promotion to spark Christmas gift giving, a Hanes product manager wanted to put three-packs of underwear in a special gift box. However, there were delays getting the special packaging to the distant factories, and when the underwear was packaged in the boxes, the bulk shipping cases wouldn't hold the standard quantity of underwear.

Of course, any changes in operational routines required to implement a firm's marketing plan can result in unexpected surprises. When overseas production is involved, the ripple effect of any such problems is likely to be bigger.[10]

Service firms may transfer some tasks

Firms that produce services often must locate near their customers. However, some service firms are finding ways to reduce the cost of some of their production work with **task transfer**—using computers and telecommunications to move service operations to places where there are pools of skilled workers.

On the other hand, sometimes the decision to expand into a distant market requires moving production closer to that location. For example, import or export tariffs and quotas may make it impossible for an internationally oriented firm to compete if it doesn't have local production facilities. Similarly, some products are very expensive to ship long distances. That may give local firms a big advantage in cost and price.

Price must cover production costs

In Chapter 18, we discussed how cost curves and demand curves fit into the pricing puzzle. Production costs are usually an important component of the overall costs that must be considered in pricing. So a marketing manager needs to have a reasonable understanding of the costs associated with production, especially when product features called for in the marketing plan drive costs.

Cut costs that don't add value for customers

A marketing manager who is well informed in this area can play an important role in working with production people, to decide which costs are necessary in

Ethical Dimensions

Overseas Production

Marketing managers must be aware of and sensitive to criticisms that may arise concerning overseas production. Some of these concerns relate to nationalism. But other issues are sometimes at stake.

While low-cost overseas labour may reduce costs and prices for domestic consumers, some critics argue that the costs are only lower because the work is handled in countries with lower workplace safety standards and fewer employee protections.

Marketing managers can't ignore such concerns. Just as a firm has a social responsibility in the country where it sells products, it also has a social responsibility to the people who produce its products. However, it makes sense to consider the standard of living in that country. Pay or safety standards that seem low by the standards of developed nations may make it possible for workers in a less developed nation to have a better, healthier life.[11]

order to add value that meets customer needs, and which are just added expense with little real benefit. For example, a software firm was providing a very detailed instruction book along with the disks in its distribution package. The book was running up costs and causing delays because it needed to be changed and reprinted every time the firm came out with a new version of its software. The marketing manager realized that most of the detail in the book wasn't necessary. When users of the software had a problem, they didn't want to search for the book but instead wanted the information on the computer screen. Providing the updated information on the disk was faster and cheaper than printing the books. Packaging costs were lower without the book. And as icing on the cake, customers were more satisfied with the online help than they had been with the book.

In a situation like this, it is easy to identify specific costs associated with the production job. However, often it's difficult to get a good handle on all of the costs associated with a product (or customer) without help from the firm's accountants.

Accounting data can help in understanding costs and profit

Accounting data that help managers track where costs and profits are coming from is an important aid for strategic decisions. However, accounting statements that are prepared for tax purposes and for outside investors often aren't helpful for managers who need to make decisions about marketing strategy.

To understand profitability, managers must be able to identify the specific costs of different goods and services. You saw this in the last chapter when two basic approaches to handling costs—the full-cost approach and the contribution-margin approach—resulted in different views of profitability. At that point, however, we didn't go into any detail about how marketing managers and accountants can work together to get a better understanding of costs—especially how to allocate costs that seem to be *common* to several products or customers. In recent years, some accountants have devoted more attention to "activity-based accounting." Though this term is new, the basic ideas behind marketing cost analysis were developed years ago by a marketing specialist.[12]

Marketing cost analysis usually requires a new way of classifying accounting data. Instead of using the type of accounts typically used for financial analysis, we have to use functional accounts.

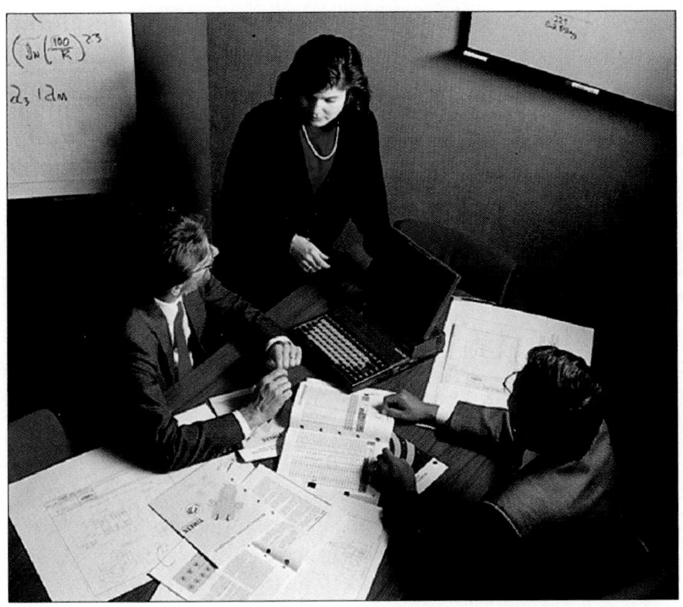

When top executives at Timken Company decided to streamline administrative procedures and reduce operating costs, teams of managers from different functional areas worked to identify the costs of specific activities and how they could be reduced.

Natural versus functional accounts

Natural accounts are the categories to which various costs are charged in the normal financial accounting cycle. These accounts include salaries, wages, Social Insurance, taxes, supplies, raw materials, auto, gas and oil expenses, advertising, and so on. These accounts are called *natural* because they have the names of their expense categories.

However, factories don't use this approach to cost analysis—and it's not the one we will use. In the factory, **functional accounts** show the *purpose* for which expenditures are made. Factory functional accounts include shearing, milling, grinding, floor cleaning, maintenance, and so on. Factory cost accounting records are organized so that managers can determine the cost of particular products or jobs and their likely contribution to profit.

Marketing jobs are done for specific purposes, too. With some planning, the costs of marketing can also be assigned to specific categories, such as customers and products. Then their profitability can be calculated.

First, get costs into functional accounts

The first step in marketing cost analysis is to reclassify all the dollar cost entries in the natural accounts into functional cost accounts. For example, the many cost items in the natural *salary* account may be allocated to functional accounts with the following names: storing, inventory control, order assembly, packing and shipping, transporting, selling, advertising, order entry, billing, credit extension, and accounts receivable. The same can be done for rent, depreciation, heat, light, power, and other natural accounts.

The best way of allocating natural account amounts to functional accounts depends on how the firm operates. Time studies, space measurements, actual counts, and managers' estimates may all be required.

Evaluating profitability of profit centres

The next step is to reallocate the functional costs to those items—or customers or market segments—for which the amounts were spent. The most common reallocation of functional costs is to products and customers. After these costs are reallocated, the detailed totals can be combined in any way desired—for example, by product, or customer class, or region.

The costs allocated to the functional accounts equal, in total, those in the natural accounts. They're just organized differently. But instead of being used only to show *total* company profits, the costs can now be used to calculate the profitability of territories, products, customers, salespeople, price classes, order sizes, distribution methods, sales methods, or any other breakdown desired. Each unit can be treated as a profit centre.

Cost analysis is not performance analysis

A cost analysis is not a performance analysis, of course. If the marketing manager budgeted costs to various jobs, it would be possible to extend this analysis to a performance analysis. This would be logical—and desirable—but many companies have not yet moved in this direction.

Now that more accounting and marketing information is routinely available on computers—and software to analyze it is easier to use—many managers are seizing the opportunity to do marketing cost and performance analysis, in the same way that factory cost accounting systems develop detailed cost estimates for products. These changes also mean that more managers are able to compare marketing cost and performance figures with "expected" figures to evaluate and control their marketing plans.

People put plans into action

The best marketing strategy in the world may fail if the right people aren't available to implement the plan. Large firms usually have a separate human resources department staffed by specialists who work with others in the firm to ensure that good people are available to do jobs that need to be done. A small firm may not have a separate department, but somebody (perhaps the owner or other managers) must deal with people management matters, such as recruiting and hiring new employees, deciding how people will be compensated, and deciding what to do when a job is not being performed well or is no longer necessary. Human resource issues are often critically important, both in a marketing manager's choices among different possible marketing opportunities and in the actual implementation of marketing plans.

You've already learned about some of the human resource issues that are important to a marketing manager. For example, in Chapter 15, when we reviewed strategy decisions in the personal selling area, we discussed a number of sales management issues, including selection, training, supervision, motivation, and compensation. Similarly, when we discussed total quality management in Chapter 20, we discussed why training and empowerment for service providers are often critical to achieving service quality and to satisfying customers.

In this section, we'll briefly reconsider these issues, but from a broader perspective: how and why they need to be considered in planning new strategies and implementing plans—especially plans that involve change. For example, change is likely to occur when a firm's sales are growing, and when it is expanding its marketing efforts to go after new markets or to introduce and promote new products.

New strategies usually require people changes

New strategies often involve new and different ways of doing things. Even if such changes are required to ensure that the firm will survive and make a profit, changes often upset the status quo and the long-established vested interests of current employees. A production manager who has spent a career becoming an expert in producing fine wood furniture may not like the idea of switching to an assemble-it-yourself line—even if that's what customers want. A senior sales rep with a well-established territory may not want to work hard at developing new accounts for a new product. When the market maturity stage of the product life cycle hits, a finance manager who looked like a hero during the profitable growth stage may not see that the picnic is over—and that profit growth will resume only if the firm takes some risk and invests in a new product concept.

As these examples suggest, many of the people affected by a new strategy may not be under the control of the marketing manager. And acting alone, the marketing manager may not be the "change agent" who can instantly turn everyone in the organization into an enthusiastic supporter of the plan. However, if the marketing manager doesn't think about how a new strategy will affect people—and how what people do will affect the success of the strategy—even the best strategy may fail.

Communication helps promote change

Communication is an important consideration here. The marketing manager must find ways to communicate with others in the organization to explain the new strategy, what needs to happen, and why. You can't expect people to pull together in an organizationwide effort if they don't know what's going on. Such communication might be handled in meetings, memos, casual discussions, internal newsletters, or any number of other ways, depending on the situation. However, the communication should occur. At a minimum, the marketing manager needs to have clear communication with the human resources manager, as well as with any other managers who will be participating in preparing the firm's personnel for a change.

Rapid growth strains human resources

When zeroing in on a marketing strategy or developing a marketing plan, a pragmatic marketing manager will take a realistic look at how quickly the firm's personnel can get geared up for the plan—or whether it will be possible to get people who can. Sometimes, a firm simply can't change or grow as fast from a people standpoint as the market might require.

Firms that are expecting or experiencing rapid growth face special challenges in getting enough qualified people to do what needs to be done. A fast-growing retail chain like Home Depot that opens many new stores doesn't just need money for new land and buildings and inventory. It also needs new store managers, assistant managers, sales clerks, customer service people, advertising managers, computer operators, and even maintenance people. Not all of these jobs are likely to be filled by internal promotions, so at least some of the "new blood" must learn about the culture of the company, its customers, and its products at the same time that they are learning the nuts and bolts of performing their jobs well. Hiring people and getting them up to speed takes time and energy.

Allow time for training and other changes

Training may be especially important in situations like this. But training, like other organizational changes, takes time. A marketing manager who wants to reorganize the firm's sales force so that salespeople are assigned to specific customers rather than by specific product lines may have a great idea, but it can't be implemented overnight. A salesperson who is supposed to be a specialist in meeting the needs of a certain customer won't be able to do a very good job if all he or she knows about is the specific product that was previously the focus. Even if nothing else were involved, the plan would need to include time for the training to take place.

Each change may result in several others

That may sound simple, but keep in mind that the changes may not stop there. A change in how sales territories and assignments are structured is likely to require changes in compensation. Someone needs to figure out the specifics of the new compensation system, and time is required to adjust computer programs to make certain that the salespeople actually get paid. Similarly, the changes in the sales force are likely to require changes in the structure of sales management assignments.

Our objective with this example is not simply to list all of the specific changes that may be required for this specific strategic decision, but rather to highlight this more general point: changing people usually takes time, and only so much change can be absorbed effectively in a limited period.

Plan time for changes from the outset

A marketing manager who ignores the "ripple effects" of a change in strategy may later expect everyone else in the organization to bend over backwards, work overtime, and otherwise do everything possible to meet a schedule that was put together with little or no forethought. Certainly there are cases of heroic efforts by people in organizations to turn someone's vision into a reality. Yet, it's more typical for such a plan to fall behind schedule, run up unnecessary costs, or just plain fail. Marketing managers who work that way are likely to be criticized for "not having the time to do it right the first time, but having the time to do it over again."

Cutbacks need human resource plans too

Decisions to *drop* products, channels of distribution, or certain types of customers can be even more traumatic. In these situations, people always worry that *someone* will lose his or her job.

Planning for dropping products, or for making other changes that will result in a cutback on people doing certain jobs, must be done very carefully, and with a good dose of humanity. To the extent possible, it's important to have a phase-out period so that people can make other plans. During the last decade, too many firms downsized (or, as some people call it, "rightsized") so rapidly that long-time loyal employees who had made valuable contributions to the firm and its customers were fired. If a phase-out is planned carefully, and considers not only the implications for production facilities and contracts with outside firms, but also the people inside, it may be possible to develop strategies that will create exciting new jobs for those who would otherwise be displaced.[13]

Marketing pumps life into an organization

This line of thinking highlights again that marketing is the heart that pumps the lifeblood through an organization. Marketing managers who create profitable marketing strategies and implement them well create a need for a firm's production workers, accountants, finance managers, lawyers, and—yes—even its human resources people. In this chapter, we've talked about marketing's links with those other functions, but when you get down to brass tacks, organizations and the various departments within them consist of *individuals*. When the marketing manager makes good strategic decisions—ones that lead to satisfied customers and to profits—each of the individuals in the organization has a chance to prosper and grow.

Questions and Problems

1. Identify some of the ways that a firm can raise money to support a new marketing plan. Give the advantages and limitations—from a marketing manager's perspective—of each approach.

2. An entrepreneur who started a chain of auto service centres to do fast oil changes wants to expand quickly by building new facilities in new markets, but doesn't have enough capital. His financial adviser suggested that he might be able to get around the financial constraint—and still grow rapidly—if he franchised his idea. That way, the franchisees would invest to build their own centres, but fees from the franchise agreement would also provide cash flow to build more company-owned outlets. Do you think this is a good idea? Explain.

3. Explain, in your own words, why investors in a firm's stock might be interested in a firm's marketing manager developing a new growth-oriented strategy. Would it be just as good, from the investors' standpoint, for the manager to just maintain the same level of profits? Explain.

4. A woman with extensive experience in home health care and a good marketing plan approaches a bank for a loan, most of which, she explains, she intends to "invest in advertising designed to recruit part-time nurses and to attract home-care patients for her firm's services." Other than the furniture in her leased office space, she has few assets. Is the bank likely to loan her the money? Explain.

5. Could the idea of mass customization be used by a publisher of college and university textbooks to allow different instructors to order customized teaching materials—perhaps even unique books made up of chapters from a number of different existing books? What do you think would be the major advantages and disadvantages of this approach?

6. Give examples of two different ways that a firm's production capacity might influence a marketing manager's choice of a marketing strategy.

7. Is a small company's flexibility increased or decreased by turning to outside suppliers to produce the products it sells? Explain.

8. Explain how a marketing manager's sales forecast for a new marketing plan might be used by:
   a. A financial manager.
   b. An accountant.
   c. A production manager.
   d. A human resources manager.

9. Explain the difference between natural accounts and functional accounts.

10. What types of human resource issues does a marketing manager face when planning to expand sales operations from a branch office in a new overseas market? Are the problems any different than they would be in a new domestic market?

Suggested cases

7 Naturally Yours

13 New North Media

30 Le Clair Chemical Company

36 Argon Carpet Cleaning Company

When you finish this chapter, you should:

- Understand why marketing must be evaluated differently at the micro and macro levels.
- Understand why the text argues that micro-marketing costs too much.
- Understand why the text argues that macro-marketing does not cost too much.
- Know some of the challenges marketers face as they work to develop ethical marketing strategies that serve consumers' needs.

Chapter twenty-two

Ethical Marketing in a Consumer-Oriented World: Appraisal and Challenges

You may already have heard something about the term "sustainable development," but could you define it? The first time the business world really woke up to sustainable development was in 1987. Many business leaders found a copy of *Our Common Future* in their in-trays. Produced by the *World Commission on Environment and Development,* chaired by Norwegian Prime Minister Gro Harlem Brundtland, the book reframed the environmental debate. The key sentence was this: "Humanity has the ability to make development sustainable—to ensure that it meets the needs of the present without compromising the ability of future generations to meet their own needs."

The report went on to make it clear that:

—Sustainable development is a *total concept* providing an agenda, though not a blueprint, for action;
—It is a *process* of harmonizing resource use, investment, technological development, and institutional change;
—The shift to sustainable development must be powered by a continuing flow of *wealth* from industry;
—But future wealth creation will need to be much less environmentally damaging, more just and more secure.[1]

Sustainable development is in many respects a revolutionary idea with far-reaching implications. That being so, it's surprising how quickly the concept gained a considerable degree of corporate acceptance. The World Business Council for Sustainable Development (WBCSD) is a coalition of 125 international companies united by a shared commitment to the environment and to the principles of economic growth and sustainable development. Its members are drawn from 35 countries and more than 20 major industrial sectors. Its Canadian members include Avenor, Noranda, Ontario Hydro, Suncor Energy, and Transalta. The WBCSD operates in conjunction with a global network of national and regional business councils and partner organizations.

The WBCSD was formed in January 1995 through a merger between the Business Council for Sustainable Development in Geneva and the World Industry Council for the Environment (WICE), which was an initiative of the Paris-based International Chamber of Commerce. Those two parent bodies had been at the forefront of business's response to the challenges arising from the Earth Summit in Rio de Janeiro in 1992. Today, the WBCSD has become the pre-eminent business voice on sustainable development. You can learn more about that organization by visiting its Web site (www.wbcsd.ch)

Sustainable development is such an all-encompassing concept that even sympathetic corporations may not know how to proceed. Fortunately, the WBCSD and a number of organizations sharing similar concerns can provide a great deal of assistance. Some of these organizations are Canadian-based. The National Round Table on the Environment and the Economy plays an important facilitating role by bringing together environmental groups, industry, government, and academia in a search for mutually acceptable, "win-win" environmental solutions.

The International Institute for Sustainable Development has an office in Calgary that provides "how to" information to corporations exploring what it means to become sustainability-driven. Its Web site (iisd1.iisd.ca/business) will lead you to a wide variety of special studies with further links to many other valuable sources of information. As a useful starting point, sustainable development is operationally defined from a business perspective:

> For the business enterprise, sustainable development means adopting business strategies and activities that meet the needs of the enterprise and its stockholders today while protecting, sustaining, and enhancing the human and natural resources that will be needed in the future.

Such a definition obviously has far-reaching implications for marketing managers. On the producer side, it goes well beyond "green marketing," by also addressing the environmental implications of the firm's production and waste disposal procedures. Sustainable consumption is an even more far-reaching concept. It suggests that "more is not necessarily better" and leads some to conclude that a *conserver society* must inevitably replace our society's current emphasis on consumption. Sustainable consumption thus raises a fundamental challenge to the consumer sovereignty and market economy concepts discussed in the remainder of this chapter.

Sustainable development is almost certain to grow in both social and managerial importance. Students who wish to learn more about the concept have a unique opportunity not only to do so but also to earn a certificate attesting to this fact. For more information on the Sustainable Development Challenge Brief and its associated on-line exam, visit (http://challenge.bi.no/sbc).[2]

How economies function

All societies must provide for the needs of their members. Therefore, every society needs some sort of **economic system**, which is defined as the way an economy organizes to use scarce resources to produce goods and services and distribute them for consumption by various people and groups in the society.

How an economic system operates depends on a society's objectives and the nature of its political institutions.[3] But regardless of what form these take, all economic systems must develop some method—along with appropriate economic institutions—to decide what and how much is to be produced and distributed by whom, when, to whom, and why. How these decisions are made may vary from nation to nation. But the macro-level objectives are basically similar: to create goods and services and make them available when and where they are needed, in order to maintain or improve each nation's standard of living or other socially defined objective.

There are two basic kinds of economic systems: planned systems and market-directed systems. Actually, no economy is entirely planned or entirely market-directed. Most are a mixture of the two extremes.

Government planners may make the decisions

In a **planned economic system,** government planners decide what and how much is to be produced and distributed by whom, when, to whom, and why. Producers generally have little choice about what goods and services to produce. Their main task is to meet their assigned production quotas. Prices are set by government planners and tend to be very rigid—not changing according to supply and demand. Consumers usually have some freedom of choice—it's impossible to control every single detail! But the assortment of goods and services may be quite limited. Activities such as market research, branding, and advertising usually are neglected. Sometimes they aren't done at all.

Government planning may work fairly well as long as an economy is simple and the variety of goods and services is small. It may even be necessary under certain conditions—during wartime, drought, or political instability, for example. However, as economies become more complex, government planning becomes more difficult. It may even break down. Planners may be overwhelmed by too many complex decisions. And consumers may lose patience if the planners don't respond to their needs.

The collapse of communism in Eastern Europe dramatically illustrates this. Citizens of the former Soviet Union were not satisfied with the government's plan, because products consumers wanted and needed were not available. To try to reduce consumer dissatisfaction, government planners tried to put more emphasis on making consumer goods available, but they were not able to produce the results consumers wanted. In short, it was consumer dissatisfaction with decisions made by government planners that brought about a revolution—one that is leading to the development of market-directed economies in the new, independent republics of Eastern Europe.[4]

A market-directed economy adjusts itself

In a **market-directed economic system,** the individual decisions of the many producers and consumers make the macro-level decisions for the whole economy. In a pure market-directed economy, consumers make a society's production decisions when they make their choices in the marketplace. Through their dollar "votes," they decide what is to be produced and by whom.

PRICE IS A MEASURE OF VALUE Prices in the marketplace are a rough measure of how society values particular goods and services. If consumers are willing to pay the market prices, then apparently they feel they are getting at least their money's worth. Similarly, the costs of labour and materials are a rough measure of the value of the resources used in the production of goods and services to meet these needs. New consumer needs that can be served profitably—not just the needs of the majority—will probably be met by some profit-minded businesses.

In summary, in a market-directed economic system, the prices in both the production sector (for resources) and the consumption sector (for goods and services) vary to allocate resources and distribute incomes according to consumer preferences. Over time, the result is a balance of supply and demand and the coordination of the economic activity of many individuals and institutions.

GREATER FREEDOM OF CHOICE Consumers in a market-directed economy enjoy great freedom of choice. They are not forced to buy any goods or services, except those which must be provided for the good of society—things such as national defence, schools, police and fire protection, highway systems, and public health services. These are provided by the community—and citizens are taxed to pay for them.

Similarly, producers are free to do whatever they wish, provided that they stay within the rules of the game set by government *and* receive enough dollar votes from consumers. If they do their job well, they earn a profit and stay in business. But profit, survival, and growth are not guaranteed.

CONFLICTS CAN RESULT When producers and consumers make free choices, conflicts and difficulties can arise. This is called the **micro-macro dilemma:** What is "good" for some producers and consumers may not be good for society as a whole.

Consider for a moment problems related to the sale of alcohol. Each year, thousands of people die or are hospitalized as an indirect or direct result of liquor consumption. The cost to society is high, yet the sale of alcohol is not banned. Alcohol consumption is an accepted practice in Canada, and producers profit by selling it. Should society limit its availability to certain segments of the population, or should society allow it to be freely available to anyone who wants to purchase it, regardless of social cost?

Many Canadians want the convenience of disposable products and products in easy-to-use, small-serving packages. But these same "convenient" products and packages often lead to pollution of the environment and inefficient use of natural resources. Should future generations be left to pay for the consequences of pollution that is the result of free choice by today's consumers? Alternatively, should all of us alive today endorse the Declaration of Interdependence of the David Suzuki Foundation (see Marketing Demo 22–1)?

Marketing Demo 22-1

Declaration of Interdependence

DECLARATION OF INTERDEPENDENCE

THIS WE KNOW

We are the earth, through the plants and animals that nourish us.
We are the rains and the oceans that flow through our veins.
We are the breath of the forests of the land, and the plants of the sea.
We are human animals, related to all other life as descendants of the firstborn cell.
We share with these kin a common history, written in our genes.
We share a common present, filled with uncertainty.
And we share a common future, as yet untold.

We humans are but one of thirty million species
weaving the thin layer of life enveloping the world.
The stability of communities of living things depends upon this diversity.
Linked in that web, we are interconnected -
using, cleansing, sharing and replenishing the fundamental elements of life.
Our home, planet Earth, is finite; all life shares its resources and the energy from the sun,
and therefore has limits to growth.
For the first time, we have touched those limits.
When we compromise the air, the water, the soil and the variety of life,
we steal from the endless future to serve the fleeting present.

THIS WE BELIEVE

Humans have become so numerous and our tools so powerful
that we have driven fellow creatures to extinction, dammed the great rivers,
torn down ancient forests, poisoned the earth, rain and wind, and ripped holes in the sky.
Our science has brought pain as well as joy; our comfort is paid for by the suffering of millions.
We are learning from our mistakes, we are mourning our vanished kin,
and we now build a new politics of hope.
We respect and uphold the absolute need for clean air, water and soil.
We see that economic activities that benefit the few while shrinking the inheritance of many are wrong.
And since environmental degradation erodes biological capital forever,
full ecological and social cost must enter all equations of development.
We are one brief generation in the long march of time; the future is not ours to erase.
So where knowledge is limited, we will remember all those who will walk after us,
and err on the side of caution.

THIS WE RESOLVE

All this that we know and believe must now become the foundation of the way we live.

At this turning point in our relationship with Earth,
we work for an evolution: from dominance to partnership;
from fragmentation to connection; from insecurity,
to interdependence.

THE DAVID SUZUKI FOUNDATION
Suite 219, 2211 West 4th Avenue, Vancouver, B.C., Canada V6K 4S2 • Telephone: (604) 732-4228 • Fax: (604) 732-0752

Questions like these are not easy to answer. The basic reason is that many different people may have a stake in the outcomes—and social consequences—of the choices made by individual managers *and* consumers in a market-directed system. Having read this book and learned more about marketing, you will also have learned more about social responsibility in marketing—and why it must be taken seriously.

THE ROLE OF GOVERNMENT The Canadian economy and most other Western economies are mainly market-directed—but not completely. Society assigns supervision of the system to the government. For example, besides setting and enforcing the "rules of the game," government agencies control interest rates and the supply of money. They also regulate radio and TV broadcasting, set import and export rules that affect international competition, sometimes control wages and prices, and so on. Government also tries to ensure that property is protected, contracts are enforced, individuals are not exploited, no group unfairly monopolizes markets, and producers deliver the kinds and quality of goods and services they claim to be offering.

How well does our macro-marketing system work?

A macro-marketing system does more than just deliver goods and services to consumers—it allows mass production with its economies of scale. Also, mass communication and mass transportation allow products to be shipped where they're needed. Coconuts from the tropics can be found in Canadian stores almost year-round, and electronic parts from Taiwan are used in making products all over the world.[5]

It encourages growth and new ideas

In addition to making mass production possible, a market-directed, macro-marketing system encourages **innovation**—the development and spread of new ideas and products. Competition for consumers' money forces firms to think of new and better ways to satisfy consumer needs.

It has its critics

In explaining marketing's role in society, we described some of the benefits of a market-directed, macro-marketing system. We can see this in Canada's macro-marketing system. That system provides—at least in material terms—one of the highest standards of living in the world. It seems to be effective and fair in many ways.

We must admit, however, that marketing, as it exists in Canada and other developed societies, has many critics. Marketing activity is especially open to criticism because it is the part of business most visible to the public. There is nothing like a pocketbook issue for getting consumers excited!

Typical complaints about marketing include these:

- Advertising is too often annoying, misleading, and wasteful.
- Products are not safe, or the quality is poor.
- Marketing makes people too materialistic and motivates them toward "things" instead of social needs.
- Easy consumer credit makes people buy things they don't need and really can't afford.
- Packaging and labelling are often confusing and deceptive.
- Intermediaries add to the cost of distribution, and raise prices without providing anything in return.
- Marketing creates interest in products that pollute the environment.

- Too many unnecessary products are offered.
- Marketing serves the rich and exploits the poor.

Such complaints cannot and should not be taken lightly. They show that many people aren't happy with some parts of the marketing system. Certainly, the strong public support for consumer protection laws proves that not all consumers feel that they are being treated like royalty.

We must evaluate at two levels

As you consider the various criticisms of marketing, keep in mind that some of them deal with the marketing practices of specific firms and are micro-marketing oriented. Others are really criticisms of the entire macro-marketing system. This is an important distinction. Some critics of specific ads, for example, probably wouldn't be satisfied with *any* advertising. When evaluating marketing, we must treat these two levels separately.

Consumer satisfaction is the objective in Canada

An earlier section of this text emphasized that *the basic objective of our market-directed economic system has been to satisfy consumer needs as they—the consumers—see them.* This objective implies that political freedom and economic freedom go hand in hand, and that citizens in a free society have the right to live as they choose. The majority of consumers in Canada and the United States would be unwilling to give up the freedom of choice they now enjoy. The same can be said of consumers in Great Britain and most other countries in the European Community. However, for focus, we will concentrate on marketing as it exists in North American society.

Can consumer satisfaction be measured?

Since consumer satisfaction is our objective, marketing's effectiveness must be measured by *how well* it satisfies consumers. Unfortunately, consumer satisfaction is hard to define—and even harder to measure.

Satisfaction depends on individual aspirations

There have been various efforts to measure overall consumer satisfaction, not only in Canada but also in other countries. However, measuring consumer satisfaction is difficult because satisfaction depends on consumers' levels of aspiration or expectation. Less prosperous consumers begin to expect more out of an economy as they see the higher living standards of others. Also, aspiration levels tend to rise with repeated successes—and fall with failures. Products considered satisfactory one day may not be satisfactory the next day, and vice versa. A few years ago, most of us were more than satisfied with a 19-inch colour TV that pulled in three or four channels. But once you've watched one of the newer large-screen models and enjoyed all the options possible with a cable hook-up or satellite, that old TV is never the same again. And once high-definition TVs become readily available, today's most satisfying units won't seem quite so acceptable. So consumer satisfaction is a highly personal concept—and looking at the "average" satisfaction of a whole society does not provide a reliable standard for evaluating macro-marketing effectiveness.[6]

Measuring macro-marketing must be subjective

If the objective of macro-marketing is to maximize consumer satisfaction, then we must measure total satisfaction—of everyone. But there's no good way to measure aggregate consumer satisfaction. Some consumers will always be more satisfied than others. So our evaluation of macro-marketing effectiveness can only be subjective.

Probably the supreme test is whether the macro-marketing system satisfies enough individual consumer-citizens that they vote—at the ballot box—to keep it running. So far, we've done so in North America.

Measuring micro-marketing can be less subjective

Measuring micro-marketing effectiveness is also difficult, but it can be done. Individual business firms can and should try to measure how well their marketing mixes satisfy their customers (or why they fail). In fact, most large firms now make some type of ongoing effort to determine whether they're satisfying their target markets. Many large and small firms measure customer satisfaction with attitude research studies. For example, the J. D. Power marketing research firm is well known for its studies of consumer satisfaction with different makes of automobiles and computers. Other widely used approaches involve unsolicited consumer responses (usually complaints), opinions of intermediaries and salespeople, market test results, and profits. Of course, customers may be very satisfied about some aspects of what a firm is doing but dissatisfied about other dimensions of performance.[7]

In our market-directed system, it's up to each customer to decide how effectively an individual firm satisfies his or her needs. Usually, customers will buy more of the products that satisfy them—and they'll do it repeatedly. That's why firms that develop really satisfying marketing mixes are able to develop profitable long-term relationships with the customers they serve. Because efficient marketing plans can increase profits, profitability can be used as a rough measure of a firm's efficiency in satisfying customers. Nonprofit organizations have a different bottom line, but they too will fail if they don't satisfy supporters and get the resources they need to continue to operate.

Evaluating marketing effectiveness—difficult but not impossible

Because it's hard to measure consumer satisfaction—and, therefore, the effectiveness of micro- and macro-marketing—it's easy to see why opinions differ. But if the objective of the economy is defined clearly, and the argument is stripped of emotion, the big questions about marketing effectiveness probably *can* be answered.

In this chapter, we argue that micro-marketing (how individual firms and channels operate) frequently *does* cost too much but that macro-marketing (how the whole marketing system operates) *does not* cost too much, *given the present objective of the Canadian economy—consumer satisfaction.* Accept this position not as *the* answer, but rather as a point of view. In the end, you'll have to make your own judgment.[8]

Micro-marketing often *does* cost too much

Throughout the text, we've explored what marketing managers can or should do to help their firms do a better job of satisfying customers. Many firms implement highly successful marketing programs; others are still too production-oriented and inefficient. For customers of these latter firms, micro-marketing often does cost too much.

Research shows that many consumers are not satisfied. But you know that already. All of us have had experiences when we weren't satisfied—when some firm didn't deliver on its promises. And the problem is much bigger than some marketers want to believe. Research suggests that the majority of consumer complaints are never reported. Worse, many complaints that *are* reported never get fully resolved.

The failure rate is high

Further evidence that too many firms are too production-oriented—and not nearly as efficient as they could be—is the fact that so many new products fail. New and old businesses, even ones that in the past were leaders in their markets, also regularly fail.

Marketing inefficiencies are due to one or more of the following three reasons:

1. Lack of interest in—or understanding of—the sometimes fickle customer.
2. Improper blending of the four Ps, caused in part by overemphasis on internal problems.
3. Lack of understanding of, or adjustment to, the marketing environment—especially what competitors do.

The high cost of poor marketing mixes

Perhaps lack of concern for the customer is most noticeable in the ways the four Ps are sometimes combined—or forced—into a marketing mix.

Too many firms develop a new product to satisfy some manager's pet idea, not to meet the needs of certain target customers. Or they see another company with a successful product and try to jump into the market with another me-too imitation—without even thinking about the competition they'll encounter. Often, they don't worry about quality. In fact, until very recently most North American manufacturers lacked *any* quality control procedures, even in the production of goods and services. The idea of using total quality management to implement marketing plans to meet customers' requirements was foreign to them.

Some marketing managers don't pay attention to getting needed support from intermediaries. Too many producers don't even consider the possibility that a big retail chain may see better value for its customers—and greater profit potential—in someone else's product.

Firms often ignore demand and set prices on a cost-plus basis. While margins are fairly definite, managers can only predict volume. So they choose high margins—which may lead to high prices and reduced volume.

If a product is poorly designed, if a firm uses inadequate channels, or if pricing isn't competitive, it's easy to see why promotion may be costly. Aggressive spending on promotion doesn't make up for other types of mistakes.

Top-management decisions on company objectives may increase the cost of marketing unnecessarily. Seeking sales growth for growth's sake, for example, often leads to too much spending for promotion and poor profits on what is sold.

Another sign of failure is the inability of firms to identify new target markets and new opportunities. A new marketing mix that isn't offered doesn't fail—but the lost opportunity can be significant both for a firm and for society. Too many managers seize on whatever strategy seems easiest instead of seeking really new ways to satisfy customers.

Micro-marketing costs too much, but things are changing

For reasons like these, marketing does cost too much in many firms. Despite all the lip service, the marketing concept is not really being applied.

But not all firms and marketers deserve criticism. More of them *are* becoming customer-oriented. And many are paying more attention to market-oriented planning to carry out the marketing concept more effectively. Throughout the text, we've highlighted firms and strategies that are making a difference. The successes of innovative firms—which include Wal-Mart, 3M, Toys "Я" Us, and Rubbermaid—do not go unnoticed. Yes, they make some mistakes. That's human—and marketing is a human enterprise. But they have also benefitted from the results that strategic market planning can produce.

Another encouraging sign is the end of the idea that anybody can run a business successfully. This never was true. Businesses are growing more complex and require many different types of professionals—not only business managers but also computer and communications specialists, psychologists, statisticians, and economists.

Managers who adopt the marketing concept as a way of business life do a better job. They look for target market opportunities and carefully blend the elements of the marketing mix to meet their customers' needs. As more of these managers rise in business, we can look forward to much lower micro-marketing costs—and strategies that do a better job of satisfying customer needs.

Macro-marketing does *not* cost too much

Many critics of marketing take aim at the macro-marketing system. In their view, (1) promotion in any form is socially undesirable, and (2) the macro-marketing system causes poor use of resources, limits income and employment, and leads to an unfair distribution of income. Most of these complaints imply that some micro-marketing activities should not be permitted, and that because they are, our macro-marketing system does a poor job. Let's look at some of these positions to help you form your own opinion.

Micro-efforts help the economy grow

Some critics feel that marketing helps create monopolies or at least monopolistic competition. Further, they think this leads to higher prices, restricted output, and reduction in national income and employment.

It's true that firms in a market-directed economy try to carve out separate monopolistic markets for themselves with new products. But consumers do have a choice. They don't *have* to buy the new product unless they think it's a better value. The old products are still available. In fact, to meet the new competition, prices of the old products usually drop. And that makes them even more available.

Over several years, the innovator's profits may rise—but rising profits encourage further innovation by competitors. This leads to new investments, which contribute to economic growth and higher levels of national income and employment. Around the world, many countries with centrally planned systems failed to achieve their potential for economic growth because this type of profit incentive didn't exist.

Increased profits also attract competition. Profits then begin to drop as new competitors enter the market and begin producing somewhat similar products. (Recall the rise and fall of industry profit during the product life cycle.)

Is advertising a waste of resources?

Advertising is the most criticized of all micro-marketing activities. Indeed, many ads *are* annoying, insulting, misleading, and downright ineffective. This is one reason why micro-marketing often does cost too much. However, advertising can also make both micro- and macro-marketing work better.

Advertising is an economical way to inform large numbers of potential customers about a firm's products. Provided that a product satisfies customer needs, advertising can increase demand for the product and foster economies of scale in manufacturing, distribution, and sales. Because these economies may more than offset advertising costs, advertising can actually *lower* prices to the consumer.[9]

At the macro level, the increased demand that advertising creates gives producers a faster return on their investment. This, in turn, stimulates further investment, encourages innovation, creates jobs, raises personal incomes, and generates economic growth.

Does marketing make people buy things they don't need?

From our discussion so far, it seems that micro-marketing activities aimed at satisfying consumer needs do *not* lead to improper use of resources. Giving individuals what they want, after all, is the purpose of our market-directed economic system. However, some critics feel that most firms—especially large corporations—don't really cater to the needs and wants of the consumer. They think that such firms use clever ads to persuade consumers to buy whatever the firms want to sell.

Historian Arnold Toynbee, for example, felt that North American firms manipulated consumers into buying products that aren't necessary to satisfy "the minimum material requirements of life." Toynbee saw American firms as mainly trying to fulfil "unwanted demand"—demand created by advertising—rather than "genuine wants." He defined genuine wants as "wants that we become aware of spontaneously, without having to be told by Madison Avenue that we want something that we should never have thought of wanting if we had been left in peace to find out our wants for ourselves."[10]

WHAT ARE THE MINIMUM REQUIREMENTS OF LIFE? One problem raised by this line of reasoning is this: How do we determine the minimum material requirements of life? Should people go back to living in caves or log cabins? Which products consumed today are unnecessary and should not be produced?

Obviously, we have to make some value judgments in order to answer such questions—and few of us share the same values. One critic suggested that Americans could and should do without such items as pets, newspaper comic strips, second family cars, motorcycles, snowmobiles, campers, recreational boats and planes, aerosol products, pop and beer cans, and hats.[11] You may agree with some of these. But who should determine the minimum material requirements of life—consumers or critics?

CONSUMERS ARE NOT PUPPETS The idea that firms can manipulate consumers to buy anything the company chooses to produce simply isn't true. A consumer who buys a soft drink that tastes terrible won't buy another can of that brand, regardless of how much it's advertised. In fact, many new products fail the test of the market. Not even large corporations are assured of success every time they launch a new product. Consider, for example, the dismal fate of products such as Ford's Edsel, Du Pont's Corfam, Campbell's Red Kettle Soups, and RCA's computers. And if powerful corporations know some way to get people to buy products against their will, would General Motors not so long ago have tallied the biggest loss in history?

NEEDS AND WANTS CHANGE Consumer needs and wants change constantly. Few of us would care to live the way our grandparents lived when they were our age—

Should consumers in China be allowed to decide what needs are important and what products should be available—or should those decisions be made by government planners?

let alone like the pioneers who travelled to unknown destinations in covered wagons. Marketing's job is not just to satisfy consumer wants as they exist at any particular point in time. Rather, marketing must keep looking for new—and better—ways to serve consumers.

Does marketing make people materialistic?

There is no doubt that marketing caters to materialistic values. However, people disagree as to whether marketing creates these values or simply appeals to values already there.

Even in the most primitive societies, people want to accumulate possessions. In fact, in some tribal villages social status is measured by how many goats or sheep a person owns. Further, the tendency for ancient pharaohs and kings to surround themselves with wealth and treasures can hardly be attributed to the persuasive powers of advertising agencies!

The idea that marketers create and serve "false tastes"—as defined by individual critics—was answered by a well-known economist:

> The marketplace responds to the tastes of consumers with the goods and services that are salable, whether the tastes are elevated or depraved. It is unfair to criticize the marketplace for fulfilling these desires . . . it is like blaming waiters in restaurants for obesity.[12]

MARKETING REFLECTS OUR OWN VALUES Experts who study materialism seem to agree that in the short run, marketing reflects social values, while in the long run, it enhances and reinforces them. One expert pointed out that consumers vote for what they want in the marketplace and in the polling place. To say that what they choose is wrong, he said, is to criticize the basic idea of free choice and democracy.[13]

PRODUCTS DO IMPROVE THE QUALITY OF LIFE More is not always better. The quality of life can't be measured just in terms of quantities of material goods. But when we view products as the means to an end rather than the end itself, they *do* make it possible to satisfy higher-level needs. For example, microwave ovens greatly reduce the amount of time people spend preparing meals, and this frees them to pursue other interests. And more dependable cars expand people's geographic horizons, affecting where they live, work, and play. The Internet empowers people with information in ways that could not have been imagined just a few years ago.

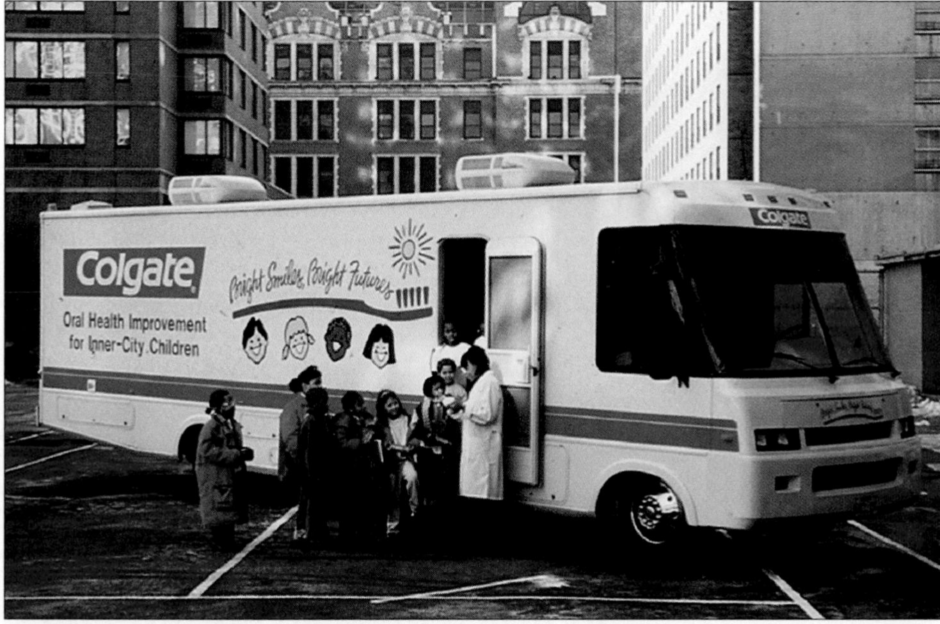

Colgate is concerned not only with profit but also with social responsibility; its dental vans offer free dental screenings to children in inner-city communities.

Consumers ask for it, consumers pay for it

The monopolistic competition typical of our economy results from customer preferences—*not* manipulation of markets by business. Monopolistic competition may seem costly at times when we look at micro-level situations. But if the role of the marketing system is to serve consumers, then the cost of whatever goods and services they demand cannot be considered too high. It's just the cost of serving consumers the way they want to be served.

Not all needs are met

Some critics argue that our macro-marketing system is flawed because it does not provide solutions to important problems, such as questions about how to help the homeless, the uneducated, dependent children, minorities who have suffered discrimination, the elderly poor, and the sick. Many of these people do live in dire circumstances. But is that the result of a market-directed system?

There is no doubt that many firms focus their efforts on people who can pay for what they have to offer. But as the forces of competition drive down prices, more people are able to afford more of what they need. And the matching of supply and demand stimulates economic growth, creates jobs, and spreads income among more people. In other words, a market-directed economy makes efficient use of resources. However, it can't guarantee that government aid programs will be effective. It doesn't ensure that all voters and politicians will agree on which problems should be solved first—or how taxes should be set and allocated. It can't eliminate the possibility that a child will be ignored.

These are important societal issues. But they are not the result of a market-directed system. Citizen-consumers in a democratic society assign some responsibilities to business and some to government. Most people in business share the concern that government too often does not do an effective job of addressing these problems. Many firms are working to identify and contribute solutions. But ultimately, consumer-citizens vote at the ballot box for how to deal with these concerns—just as they vote with their dollars for which firms to support. As more managers in the public sector understand and apply marketing concepts, we should be able to do a better job of meeting the needs of all people.

Challenges facing marketers

We've said that our macro-marketing system does *not* cost too much, given the present objective of our economy. But we admit that the performance of many business firms leaves a lot to be desired. This presents a challenge to serious-minded students and marketers. What needs to be done—if anything?

We need better performance at the micro level

Some business executives seem to feel that they should be completely free in a market-directed economy. They don't understand that ours is a market-directed system, and that they must serve the needs of consumer-citizens. Instead, they focus on their own internal problems—and don't satisfy consumers very well.

WE NEED BETTER MARKET-ORIENTED PLANNING Many firms are still production-oriented. Some hardly plan at all, while others simply extend one year's plans into the next. Progressive firms are beginning to realize that this doesn't work in our fast-changing markets. Strategic market planning is becoming more important in many companies. Firms are paying more attention to changes in the market—including trends in the marketing environment—and to how marketing strategies need to be adapted to consider these changes.

WE NEED CONTINUOUS IMPROVEMENT Good strategic market planning needs to focus on a specific target market and a marketing mix to meet its needs. The basic frameworks and ideas about how to do that haven't changed all that much over the years. At the same time, thinking about all these changes highlights the fact that marketing is dynamic. Marketing managers must constantly evaluate their strategies to be sure they're not being left in the dust by competitors who see new and better ways of doing things.

It's crazy for a marketing manager to constantly change a strategy that's working well. But too many managers fail to see or plan for *needed* changes. They're afraid to do anything different, and adhere to the idea that "if it ain't broke, don't fix it." But a firm can't always wait until a problem becomes completely obvious to do something about it. When customers move on and profits disappear, it may be too late to fix the problem. Marketing managers who take the lead in finding innovative new markets and approaches gain a competitive advantage.

Recent social and technological changes are having a positive effect on how marketers serve society. Whether it's because marketers are applying new technologies to solve old marketing problems or applying classic marketing concepts to new kinds of opportunities, consumers are better off. And this ongoing improvement is self-directing. As consumers shift their support to firms that do meet their needs, laggard businesses are forced to either improve or get out of the way.

We need to welcome international competition

Increasingly, marketing managers are facing global competition. Some managers hate that thought. Worldwide competition creates even more pressure on marketing managers to figure out what it takes to gain a competitive advantage, both at home and in foreign markets. But with the challenges come opportunities. The forces of competition in and among market-directed economies will help speed the diffusion of marketing advances to consumers everywhere. As macro-marketing systems improve worldwide, more consumers will have the income to buy products, from wherever in the world the products come.

Marketers can't afford to bury their heads in the sand and hope that international competition will go away. Rather, they must realize that it is part of today's marketing environment—and they must do strategic market planning that rises to the challenges it poses.

May need more social responsibility

Good business managers put themselves in the consumer's position. A useful rule to follow might be this: Do unto others as you would have others do unto you. In practice, this means developing satisfying marketing mixes for specific target markets. It may mean building in more quality or more safety. The consumer's long-run satisfaction should be considered, too. How will the product hold up in use? What about service guarantees? While trying to serve the needs of some target market, does the marketing strategy disregard the rights and needs of other consumers, or create problems that will be left for future generations?

Short-sighted, production-oriented approaches undoubtedly won't work in the future. Tougher competition, from companies at home and abroad, may force old-style, production-oriented business managers to change their thinking just to survive.

The environment is everyone's need

Marketers need to work harder and smarter at finding ways to satisfy consumer needs without sacrificing the current or future environment. All consumers need the environment whether they realize it yet or not. We are only beginning to understand the consequences of the environmental damage that's already been done. Acid rain, depletion of the ozone layer, and toxic waste in water supplies—to mention but a few current environmental problems—have catastrophic effects. Many top executives now say that preserving and protecting the environment will be one of the major challenges—if not *the* major challenge—of business firms in the next decade. This chapter opened with a discussion of sustainable development. The marketing management implications of this concept are elaborated upon in Marketing Demo 22–2.

Marketing Demo 22-2

What Sustainability Means to Consumer Product Marketers

In the environmental marketing world, it's no longer enough to be "green." Businesses and products must be "sustainable."

Sustainability is defined as meeting the needs of the present without compromising the ability of future generations to meet their needs. This means balancing the seemingly contradictory tasks of improving standards of living worldwide while cutting down on fossil fuels, cutting out pollution, and conserving natural resources.

To achieve global sustainability, some experts such as those at Germany's Wuppertal Institute believe that we will need to reduce our use of resources by as much as 10 times by 2040! With reductions such as these, consumer products and marketing as we know them won't survive. However, this doesn't necessarily mean lost business. Sustainability actually can be good for business.

Today, smart businesspeople embrace greening because it can pay off in more efficient processes and products and hence, reduce costs. (I like to say, "An environmentalist is an efficiency expert in a green cloak.") In the future, as it becomes important to use resources as sparingly as possible, the market will shift toward those companies and industries who align their products and services most closely with the needs of their customers (I call this, "Zero Waste equals 100% Customer Satisfaction"). This means companies who eliminate all the bells and whistles customers don't want in the first place (Gateway makes every computer it sells according to individual customer specs). Companies that eliminate the packaging that makes consumers feel guilty to throw away. Companies that cut down on the energy costs that make a product expensive to run. Look for the biggest opportunities to be created in the areas of energy efficiency and renewable resource management, pesticide-free agriculture, information management, alternative transportation, recycling and recovery, and ecotourism.

Forward-looking industrialists now prepare their companies and redesign or invent new products to compete in a sustainable economy. Here are some of the strategies they pursue:

Replace Material Products with "Dematerialized" Services. If you think about it, people don't need products per se. They just need the functional benefits the products provide. Oftentimes, services can do the job better than products, saving a lot of material and energy along the way. According to the United Nations Working Group on Sustainable Product Development, services can take several forms:

1. Product extension services such as repair and maintenance.
2. Services like car leasing or launderettes that allow some products to be shared. (In the Netherlands, a "green-wheels" service allows consumers to "time share" rather than own or lease cars. Our Atlanta-based client, Interface, has introduced an Evergreen Lease Program, which allows customers to lease carpeting and ancillary maintenance services; used carpeting is taken back for re-use or recycling).
3. Intangible services or "de-materialized" products that substitute services for products, for example, electronic voice mail replacing answering machines, and automated bill-paying services.
4. "Result services" designed with the aim of reducing the use of material products, e.g., pedestrian access rather than need for cars, integrated pest management versus pesticides.

New "R's" of Reuse and Remanufacturing—Move over Recycling. Businesses are learning how to lay claim to product residual value by adding re-use and remanufacturing to their materials-use arsenal. Grow Biz International has generated a $100 million business selling used equipment through its retail chains that include Play It Again Sports, Once Upon a Child, Computer Renaissance, Music Go Round, and Disc Go Round.

Control Population Growth. The biggest environmental problem may not be air or water pollution but population growth—too many people fighting for finite resources. Residents in developing countries need access to information on AIDS and birth control. Conventional radios are not always the answer because in these countries, batteries are not always available, and power supply is inconsistent. So, a British businessman invented the "Freeplay" radio, which operates using a clockwork mechanism powered by a carbon steel spring. Running on human power, it takes 25 seconds to wind up, and yields 25 minutes of play. Manufactured in Cape Town, South Africa, by 200 disabled workers, the radio has already sold 150,000 units.

Reduce Resource Use. 80% of the environmental impacts of washing machines occur during use. Hoover doubled its market share in the environmentally-conscious German market with its "New Wave" horizontal axis washing machine. The fully recyclable washing machine not only reduces water, energy, and detergent consumption, it creates less pollution and waste during production and distribution. Procter and Gamble is now test marketing Dryel, a technology that allows consumers to dry clean products at home.

Source: Abridged from Jacquelyn A. Ottman, "What Sustainability Means to Consumer Product Marketers," The Ottman Report on Environmental Marketing and Innovation, Vol. 5, No. 1 (1998) (http://www.greenmarketing.com/articles/ Ottman_Report.html).

In the past, most firms didn't pass the cost of environmental damage on to consumers in the prices that they paid. Pollution was a hidden and unmeasured cost for most companies. That is changing rapidly. Firms are already spending billions of dollars to correct problems—including problems created years ago. The government isn't accepting the excuse that "nobody knew it was a big problem." Consider yourself warned: Businesspeople who fail to anticipate the public backlash on this issue put their careers and businesses at risk!

May need attention to consumer privacy

While focusing on consumers' needs, marketers also must be sensitive to other consumer concerns. Today, sophisticated marketing research methods and new technologies make it easier to abuse consumers' rights to privacy. For example, credit card records—which reveal much about consumers' purchases and private lives—are routinely computerized and sold to anybody who pays for the list.

Most consumers don't realize how much data about their personal lives—some of it incorrect but treated as fact—is collected and available. A simple computer billing error may land consumers on a computer bad-credit list—without their knowledge. Marketing managers should use technology responsibly to improve the quality of life—not disrupt it. See Internet Insite 22–1 for a discussion of the ethical issues associated with this new breakthrough technology.

Need to rethink some present laws

One of the advantages of a market-directed economic system is that it operates automatically. But in our version of this system, consumer-citizens provide certain constraints (laws), which can be modified at any time. Managers who ignore consumer attitudes must realize that their actions may lead to new restraints.

Before piling on too many new rules, however, we should review the ones we have. Some of them may need to be changed, and others may need to be enforced more carefully. Antitrust laws, for example, are often applied to protect competitors from one another, when they were really intended to *encourage* competition.

Socially responsible marketing managers are concerned about the environmental impact of their products. Ford, for example, assembles cars with parts that can be recycled. The toy in this German ad was made from recycled auto parts. The headline says, "I was a car."

Internet Insite 22-1

Social Implications of Electronic Marketspace

In the previous chapters, the Internet Insites focused on how the Digital Revolution and Electronic Commerce can benefit the consumer and the marketer. But is the emergence of an electronic or virtual marketspace good for the society as a whole, or will it just benefit the privileged few? Will it simply lead to more wasteful materialism, or will it improve the quality of life for everyone? Several prominent authors have weighed in on these questions.

Don Tapscott, author of *Digital Economy,* suggests that in the knowledge-based digital world, "internetworked enterprises" connected to suppliers and customers will emerge.[1] As businesses "internetwork" and as manufacturers connect directly with customers, new business processes and models will emerge. One consequence will be "disintermediation"—the elimination or diminishing of intermediaries in the marketing channel. Many workers may be displaced, and most will have to retrain to succeed in the new economy.

Mitchell Kapor, founder of software company Lotus Development, is deeply concerned about the negative social effects of the Digital Revolution and the marginalization of a vast segment of the population. Mr. Kapor has founded the Electronic Frontier Foundation, a public interest organization dedicated to realizing the democratic potential of new computer and communications media. He argues that cyberspace is so far staying true to Jeffersonian ideals of liberty, commitment to pluralism, diversity, and community.[2] But he also seems to favour a role for the government and is encouraging public debate on the subject of the social implications of cyberspace.

Cybercommunities and chat groups are, to some, manifestations of grassroots democracy at work. Techno-idealists like George Gilder[3] and Don Tapscott foresee massive social changes, mostly positive, and greater economic prosperity resulting from the Digital Revolution. Others are far more cynical and fear that technology may dominate our lives in an Orwellian sense. Scholar and media critic Neal Postman, for instance, fears a "technopoly"[4]—a hegemony of technology where technological tools are not integrated into the culture, but instead *attack* that culture.

Technology will not cure all existing social problems. Some wonder if we will end up creating millions of information have-nots, who are marginalized, or if we will have the political will to harness the technology and use it for broad-based social and economic resurgence.[5] The Internet has a culture of its own. Some think it is Americanized and fear that other cultures could become Americanized. The Internet can be chaotic, with a high signal-to-noise ratio. It offers anonymity, which is misused by some.

Neal Postman rightly blames humanity, not technology itself, for some of the negatives. Take cyberporn, for example. The most frequently searched word on the Internet is "sex," according to a study by Reuters.[6] Some of the sites peddling digital erotica are generating a lot of traffic and advertising revenue. The Net also serves as a meeting place for those engaging in racist and hateful activities. Software tools such as Net Nanny® allow parents to monitor, screen, and block access to any inappropriate information, thus protecting children. Abuse of the technology, however, cannot be completely eliminated.

On the positive side, consumers now have greater access to information than ever before. Small businesses have access to newer markets. Nonprofit organizations such as MADD (www.madd.org) have a very effective channel for reaching the younger generation. Larger organizations communicate with suppliers and customers more effectively. Online communities are thriving. Distance is no longer an issue. The world has, in some ways, truly become a global village.

The generation following, called the Net Generation (N-Gen) will, according to Tapscott, think, learn, work, play, and communicate in fundamentally different ways from their parents.[7] The N-Gen is used to the "interactive" and nonlinear hypermedium. They will be at ease with chat rooms and e-mail. They will learn and consume through the Net.

The Internet has much to offer marketers and consumers. However, we need to be vigilant against abuses. In the long run, the impact of the technology is likely to be determined by the choices we make, both as individuals and collectively as a society.

[1]Don Tapscott, *Digital Economy: Promise and Peril of Networked Intelligence,* McGraw-Hill, 1995.
[2]Mitchell Kapor, "Where is the Digital Highway Really Heading?" in *Wired Magazine* (www.wired.com/wired/1.3/features/kapor.on.nii.html).
[3]George Gilder, "Washington's Bogeyman," *Forbes ASAP,* June 4, 1994.
[4]Neal Postman, *Technopoly: The Surrender of Culture to Technology,* Alfred A. Knopf, New York, 1992.
[5]Daniel Burnstein and David Kline, *Road Warriors: Dreams and Nightmares Along the Information Highway,* Dutton, 1995.
[6]CyberAtlas (www.cyberatlas.com/segments/retail/market_segments.html).
[7]Don Tapscott, *Growing Up Digital,* McGraw-Hill, 1998.

Source: This is one of a series of Internet Insites prepared in April 1998 by Dr. Ramesh Venkat of Saint Mary's University for *Basic Marketing,* Ninth Canadian Edition.

Canadian antitrust laws were originally developed with the idea that all firms competing in a market would be on a level playing field. That is no longer always true. For example, in many markets, individual North American firms compete with foreign firms whose governments urge them to cooperate with one another. Such foreign firms don't see one another as competitors; rather, they see firms from other countries—as a group—as their competition.

Laws should affect top managers

Strict enforcement of present laws could have far-reaching results if more price fixers, fraudulent or deceptive advertisers, and others who violate existing laws—thus affecting the performance of the macro-marketing system—were sent to jail or given heavy fines. A quick change in attitudes might occur if unethical top managers—those who plan strategy—were prosecuted, instead of the salespeople or product managers expected to deliver on weak or undifferentiated strategies.

In other words, if the government made it clear that it was serious about improving the performance of our economic system, much could be achieved within the present system—*without* adding new constraints.

Laws merely define minimal ethical standards

In our discussions of ethical issues in marketing, we have emphasized that a marketing manager doesn't face an ethical dilemma about complying with laws and regulations. Whether a marketer is operating in his or her own country or in a foreign nation, the legal environment sets the *minimum* standards of ethical behaviour as defined by a society. In addition, the American Marketing Association's Code of Ethics (Exhibit 1–5) provides a checklist of basic guidelines that a marketing manager should observe. But marketing managers constantly face ethical issues where there are no clearly defined answers. Every marketing manager should be aware of this and make a personal commitment to carefully evaluate the ethical consequences of strategic marketing decisions.

On the other hand, our marketing system is designed to encourage firms to compete aggressively as long as they do it fairly. New and better ways of serving customers and society give a firm a competitive advantage—at least for some period of time. This is how we move forward as a society. Innovative new marketing strategies *do* sometimes cause problems for those who have a vested interest in the old ways. Some people try to portray anything that disrupts their own personal interest as unethical. But protecting the status quo is not in itself an appropriate ethical standard. On the contrary, our society's most basic ethical charge to marketers is to find new and better ways to serve society's needs.

Need socially responsible consumers

We've stressed that marketers should act responsibly—but consumers have responsibilities, too.[14] Some consumers abuse policies about returning goods, change price tags in self-service stores, and expect attractive surroundings and courteous, well-trained

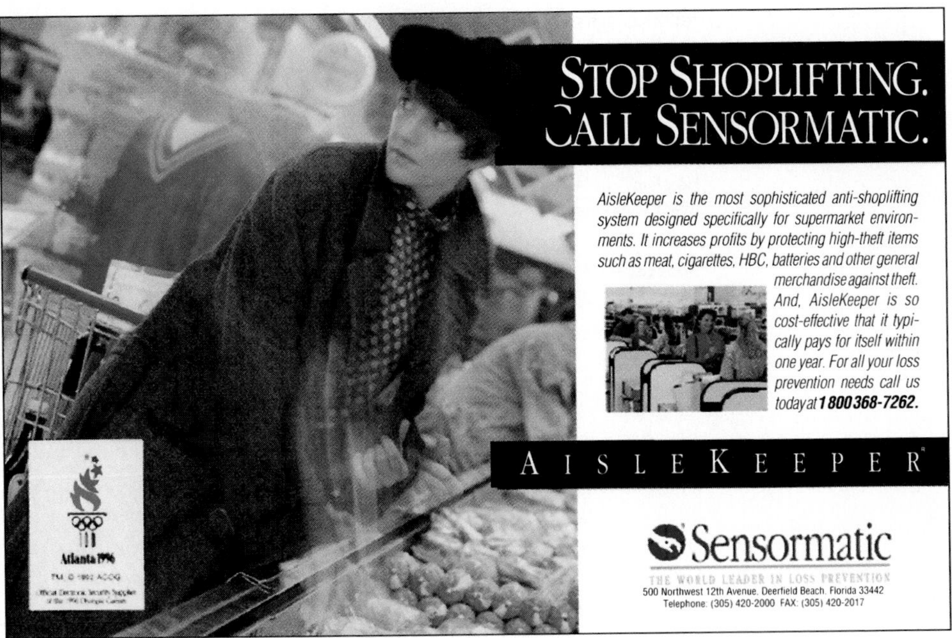

Consumers have social responsibilities, too.

sales and service people—*and* want discount prices. Some are downright abusive to salespeople. Others think nothing of ripping off businesses because "they're rich." Shoplifting is a major problem for most retailers, and honest consumers pay for the cost of shoplifting in higher prices.

Canadians tend to play their dual role of consumer-citizens with a split personality. We often behave one way as consumers, and then take the opposite position at the ballot box. For example, we cover our beaches and parks with garbage and litter, while urging our legislators to take stiff action to curb pollution. We protest sex and violence in the media, and then flock to see the latest R- or X-rated movies. Parents complain about advertising aimed at children, and then use TV as a Saturday morning babysitter.

Consumers share the responsibility for preserving an effective macro-marketing system. And they should take this responsibility seriously.

Let's face it, there's a wealth of information already available to aid consumer decision making. The consumerism movement has encouraged nutrition labelling, open dating, unit pricing, truth-in-lending, plain-language contracts and warranties, and so on. And government agencies publish many consumer buying guides, as do organizations such as Consumers Union. Yet the majority of consumers continue to ignore most of this information.

How far should the marketing concept go?

Our macro-marketing system is built on the assumption that we are trying to satisfy consumers. But how far should the marketing concept be allowed to go?

Consumers' freedom of choice

Achieving a better macro-marketing system is certainly a desirable objective. But what part should a marketer play in deciding what products to offer?

This is extremely important, because some marketing managers—especially those in large corporations—can have an impact far larger than they do in their roles as consumer-citizens. For example, should they refuse to produce hazardous products—such as skis or motorcycles—even though such products are in strong demand? Should they install safety devices that increase costs—and that customers don't want?

These are difficult questions to answer. Some things marketing managers do clearly benefit both the firm and consumers, in that they lower costs and/or improve consumers' options. But other choices may actually reduce consumer choice, and conflict with a desire to improve the effectiveness of our macro-marketing system.

Consumer-citizens should vote on the changes

It seems fair to suggest, therefore, that marketing managers should be expected to improve and expand the range of goods and services they make available to consumers—always trying to better satisfy their needs and preferences. This is the job we've assigned to business.

If pursuing this objective makes excessive demands on scarce resources—or has an unacceptable ecological effect—then consumer-citizens have the responsibility to vote for laws restricting individual firms that are trying to satisfy consumers' needs. This is the role that we, as consumers, have assigned to the government—to ensure that the macro-marketing system works effectively.

It is important to recognize that some *seemingly minor* modifications in our present system *might* result in very big, unintended problems. Allowing some government agency to prohibit the sale of products for seemingly good reasons could lead to major changes we never expected. (Bicycles, for example, are a very hazardous consumer product. Should they continue to be sold?) Clearly, such government actions could seriously reduce consumers' present rights to freedom of choice—including "bad" choices.[15]

We, as consumer-citizens, should be careful to distinguish between proposed changes designed simply to *modify* our system and those designed to *change* it—perhaps drastically. In either case, we should have the opportunity to make the decision (through elected representatives). This decision should not be left in the hands of a few well-placed managers or government planners.

Marketing—even more necessary in the future?

Regardless of the changes consumer-citizens may enact, we will need some kind of a marketing system in the future. Further, if satisfying more subtle needs—such as for the good life—becomes our objective, it could be even more important to have market-oriented firms. We may have to define not only an individual's needs, but also society's needs—perhaps for a better neighbourhood, and more enriching social experiences, and so on. As we move beyond tangible physical goods toward more sophisticated need-satisfying blends of goods and services, the trial-and-error approach of the typical production-oriented manager will become even less acceptable.

Questions and Problems

1. Explain why marketing must be evaluated at two levels. What criteria should be used to evaluate each level of marketing? Defend your answer. Explain why your criteria are better than alternative criteria.
2. Discuss the merits of various economic system objectives. Is the objective of the Canadian economic system sensible? Could it achieve more consumer satisfaction if sociologists—or public officials—determined how to satisfy the needs of lower-income or less-educated consumers? If so, what education or income level should be required before an individual is granted free choice?
3. Should the objective of our economy be maximum efficiency? If your answer is yes, efficiency in what? If not, what should the objective be?
4. Discuss the conflicts of interests among production, finance, accounting, and marketing executives. How does this conflict affect the operation of an individual firm? The economic system? Why does this conflict exist?
5. Why does adoption of the marketing concept encourage a firm to operate more efficiently? Be specific about the impact of the marketing concept on the various departments of a firm.
6. In the short run, competition sometimes leads to inefficiency in the operation of our economic system. Many people argue for monopoly in order to eliminate this inefficiency. Discuss this solution.
7. How would officially granted monopolies affect the operation of our economic system? Consider the effect on allocation of resources, the level of income and employment, and the distribution of income. Is the effect any different if a firm obtains a monopoly by winning out in a competitive market?
8. Comment on the following statement: "Ultimately, the high cost of marketing is due only to consumers."
9. How far should the marketing concept go? How should we decide this issue?
10. Should marketing managers, or business managers in general, refrain from producing profitable products that some target customers want but that may not be in their long-run interest? Should firms be expected to produce "good" but less profitable products? What if such products break even? What if they are unprofitable but the company makes other profitable products—so on balance it still makes some profit? What criteria are you using for each of your answers?
11. Should a marketing manager or a business refuse to produce an "energy-gobbling" appliance that some consumers are demanding? Should a firm install an expensive safety device that will increase costs but that customers don't want? Are the same principles involved in both these questions? Explain.
12. Discuss how slower economic growth or no economic growth would affect your college or university community—in particular, its marketing institutions.

Suggested Cases

- 21 Honda Hit • Run • Throw
- 31 The Parks Canada Dilemma
- 38 Ecolad Incorporated

Appendix A

Economics Fundamentals

When you finish this appendix, you should:

1. Understand the law of diminishing demand.
2. Understand demand and supply curves, and how they set the size of a market and its price level.
3. Know about elasticity of demand and supply.
4. Know why demand elasticity can be affected by availability of substitutes.
5. Know the different kinds of competitive situations and understand why they are important to marketing managers.
6. Recognize the important new terms (shown in orange).

A good marketing manager should be an expert on markets—and the nature of competition in markets. The economist's traditional analysis of demand and supply is a useful tool for analyzing markets. In particular, you should master the concepts of a demand curve and demand elasticity. A firm's demand curve shows how the target customers view the firm's product—really its whole marketing mix. And the interaction of demand and supply curves helps set the size of a market—and the market price. The interaction of supply and demand also determines the nature of the competitive environment, which has an important effect on strategic planning. These ideas are discussed more fully in the following sections.

Products and markets as seen by customers and potential customers

Economists provide useful insights

How potential customers (not the firm) see a firm's product (marketing mix) affects how much they are willing to pay for it, where it should be made available, and how eager they are for it—if they want it at all. In other words, their view has a very direct bearing on strategic market planning.

Economists have been concerned with market behaviour for years. Their analytical tools can be quite helpful in summarizing how customers view products and how markets behave.

Individual customers choose among alternatives

Economics is sometimes called the dismal science because it says that most customers have a limited income and simply cannot buy everything they want. They must balance their needs and the prices of various products.

Economists usually assume that customers have a fairly definite set of preferences, and that they evaluate alternatives in terms of whether the alternatives will make them feel better (or worse) or in some way improve (or change) their situation.

But what exactly is the nature of a customer's desire for a particular product?

Usually, economists answer this question in terms of the extra utility the customer can obtain by buying more of a particular product, or how much utility would be lost if the customer had less of the product. (Students who wish further discussion of this approach should refer to indifference curve analysis in any standard economics text.)

It is easier to understand the idea of utility if we look at what happens when the price of one of the customer's usual purchases changes.

The law of diminishing demand

Suppose that consumers buy potatoes in 4.5 kilogram (10-pound) bags at the same time they buy other foods such as bread and rice. If the consumers are mainly interested in buying a certain amount of food and the price of the potatoes drops, it seems reasonable to expect that they will switch some of their food money to potatoes and away from some other foods. But if the price of potatoes rises, you expect our consumers to buy fewer potatoes and more of other foods.

The general relationship between price and quantity demanded illustrated by this food example is called the **law of diminishing demand,** which says that if the price of a product is raised, a smaller quantity will be demanded and if the price of a product is lowered, a greater quantity will be demanded. Experience supports this relationship between prices and total demand in a market, especially for broad product categories or commodities such as potatoes.

Exhibit A–1 Demand Schedule for Potatoes (4.5-kilogram [10-pound] bags)

POINT	(1) PRICE OF POTATOES PER BAG (P)	(2) QUANTITY DEMANDED (BAGS PER MONTH) (Q)	(3) TOTAL REVENUE PER MONTH (P × Q = TR)
A	$1.60	8,000,000	$ 12,800,000
B	1.30	9,000,000	________
C	1.00	11,000,000	11,000,000
D	0.70	14,000,000	________
E	0.40	19,000,000	________

Exhibit A–2 Demand Curve for Potatoes (4.5-kilogram [10-pound] bags)

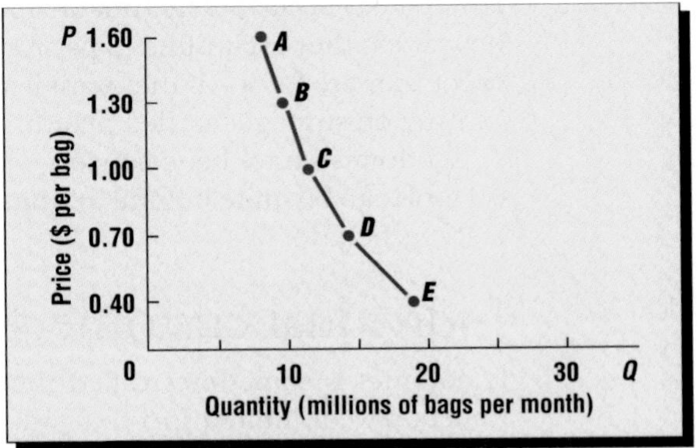

The relationship between price and quantity demanded in a market is what economists call a *demand schedule.* An example is shown in Exhibit A–1. For each row in the table, column 2 shows the quantity consumers will want (demand) if they have to pay the price given in column 1. The third column shows that the total revenue (sales) in the potato market is equal to the quantity demanded at a given price times that price. Note that as prices drop, the total *unit* quantity increases, yet the total *revenue* decreases. Fill in the blank lines in the third column and observe the behaviour of total revenue—an important number for the marketing manager. We will explain what you should have noticed—and why—a little later.

The demand curve—usually downsloping

If your only interest is seeing at which price the company will earn the greatest total revenue, the demand schedule may be adequate. But a demand curve shows more. A **demand curve** is a graph of the relationship between price and quantity demanded in a market, assuming that all other things stay the same. Exhibit A–2 shows the demand curve for potatoes—really just a plotting of the demand schedule in Exhibit A–1. It shows how many potatoes potential customers will demand at various possible prices. This is a *downsloping demand curve.*

Most demand curves are downsloping. This just means that if prices are decreased, the quantity customers demand will increase.

Demand curves always show the price on the vertical axis and the quantity demanded on the horizontal axis. In Exhibit A–2, we have shown the price in dollars. For consistency, we will use dollars in other examples. However, keep in mind that these same ideas hold regardless of what money unit (dollars, yen, francs,

Exhibit A-3 Demand Schedule for Microwave Ovens

POINT	(1) PRICE PER MICROWAVE OVEN (P)	(2) QUANTITY DEMANDED PER YEAR (Q)	(3) TOTAL REVENUE PER YEAR (P × Q = TR)
A	$300	20,000	$ 6,000,000
B	250	70,000	15,500,000
C	200	130,000	26,000,000
D	150	210,000	31,500,000
E	100	310,000	31,000,000

pounds) is used to represent price. Even at this early point, you should keep in mind that markets are not necessarily limited by national boundaries, or by one type of money.

Note that the demand curve shows only how customers will react to various possible prices. In a market, we see only one price at a time—not all of these prices. The curve, however, shows what quantities will be demanded, depending on what price is set.

You probably think that most businesspeople would like to set a price that would result in a large sales revenue. Before discussing this, however, we should consider the demand schedule and curve for another product to get a more complete picture of demand curve analysis.

Microwave oven demand curve looks different

A different demand schedule is the one for standard microwave ovens shown in Exhibit A–3. Column (3) shows the total revenue that will be obtained at various possible prices and quantities. Again, as the price goes down, the quantity demanded goes up. But here, unlike in the potato example, total revenue increases as prices go down—at least until the price drops to $100.

Demand curves and time periods

These general demand relationships are typical for all products. But each product has its own demand schedule and curve in each potential market, no matter how small the market. In other words, a particular demand curve has meaning only for a particular market. We can think of demand curves for individuals, groups of individuals who form a target market, regions, or even countries. And the time period covered really should be specified, although this is often neglected because we usually think of monthly or yearly periods.

The difference between elastic and inelastic

The demand curve for microwave ovens (see Exhibit A–4) is down-sloping, but note that it is flatter than the curve for potatoes. It is important to understand what this flatness means.

We will consider the flatness in terms of total revenue, since this is what interests business managers.*

When you filled in the total revenue column for potatoes, you should have noticed that total revenue drops continually as the price is reduced. This looks undesirable for sellers, and illustrates inelastic demand. **Inelastic demand** means that although the

*Strictly speaking, two curves should not be compared for flatness if the graph scales are different, but for our purposes now, we will do so to illustrate the idea of elasticity of demand. Actually, it would be more correct to compare two curves for one product on the same graph. Then both the shape of the demand curve and its position on the graph would be important.

Exhibit A-4 Demand Curve for 1-Cubic-Foot Microwave Oven

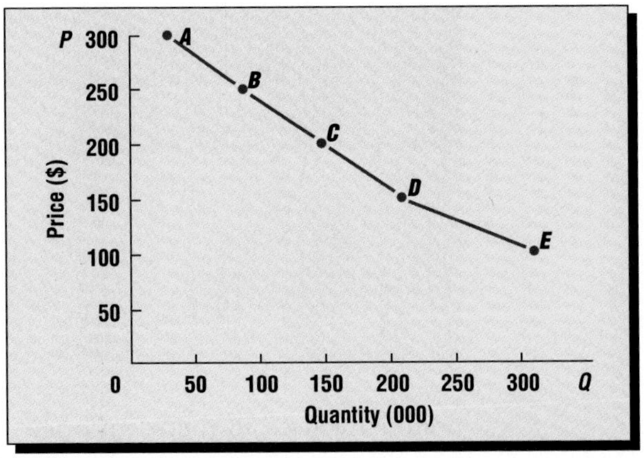

P 300
250
200
150
100
50
0
Price ($)
A
B
C
D
E
50 100 150 200 250 300 Q
Quantity (000)

quantity demanded increases as the price is decreased, the quantity demanded will not "stretch" enough—that is, it is not elastic enough—to avoid a decrease in total revenue.

In contrast, **elastic demand** means that as prices are dropped, the quantity demanded will stretch (increase) enough to increase total revenue. The upper part of the microwave oven demand curve is an example of elastic demand.

But note that if the microwave oven price is dropped from $150 to $100, total revenue will decrease. We can say, therefore, that between $150 to $100, demand is inelastic—that is, total revenue will decrease if price is lowered from $150 to $100.

Thus, elasticity can be defined in terms of changes in total revenue. *If total revenue will increase if price is lowered, then demand is elastic. If total revenue will decrease if price is lowered, then demand is inelastic.* (Note: A special situation known as *unitary elasticity of demand* occurs if total revenue stays the same when prices change.)

Total revenue may increase if price is raised

A point often missed in discussions of demand relates to what happens when prices are raised instead of lowered. With elastic demand, total revenue will *decrease* if the price is *raised.* With inelastic demand, however, total revenue will *increase* if the price is *raised.*

The possibility of raising price and increasing dollar sales (total revenue) at the same time is attractive to managers. This only occurs when the demand curve is inelastic. Here, total revenue will increase if price is raised, but total costs probably will not increase—and may actually go down—with smaller quantities. Keep in mind that profit is equal to total revenue less total costs. So when demand is inelastic, profit will increase as price is increased!

The ways total revenue changes as prices are raised are shown in Exhibit A–5. Here, total revenue is the rectangular area formed by a price and its related quantity. The larger the rectangular area, the greater the total revenue.

P_1 is the original price here, and the total potential revenue with this original price is shown by the area with blue shading. The area with red shading shows the total revenue with the new price, P_2. There is some overlap in the total revenue areas, so the important areas are those with only one colour. Note that in the left-hand figure—where demand is elastic—the revenue added (the red-only area) when the price is increased is less than the revenue lost (the blue-only area). Now, let's contrast this to the right-hand figure, where demand is inelastic. Only a small blue revenue area is given up for a much larger (red) one when price is raised.

An entire curve is not elastic or inelastic

It is important to see that it is *wrong to refer to a whole demand curve as elastic or inelastic.* Rather, elasticity for a particular demand curve refers to the change in total revenue between two points on the curve—not along the whole curve. You saw the change

Exhibit A–5 Changes in Total Revenue as Prices Increase

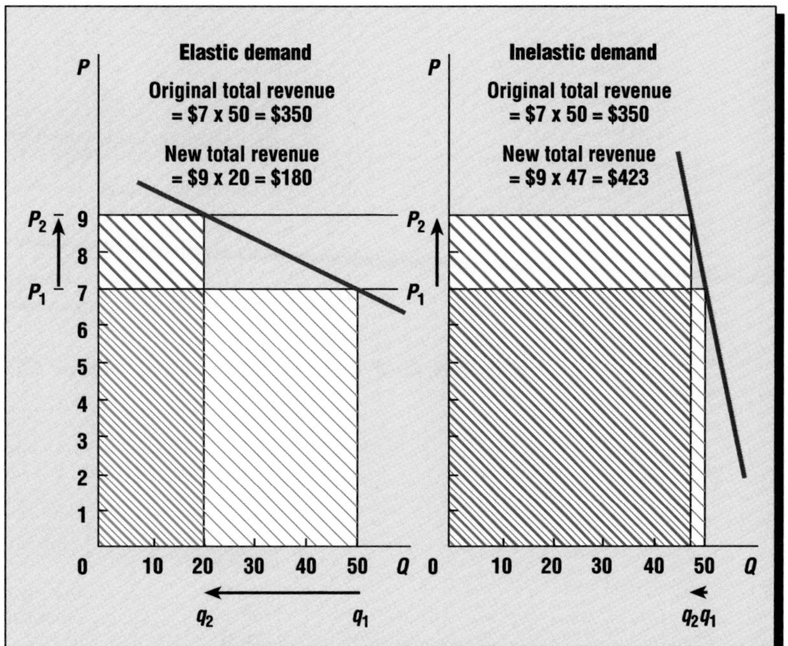

from elastic to inelastic in the microwave oven example. Generally, however, nearby points are either elastic or inelastic, so it is common to refer to a whole curve by the degree of elasticity in the price range that normally is of interest—the *relevant range.*

Elasticity and the availability of substitutes

At first, it may be difficult to see why one product has an elastic demand and another an inelastic demand. Many factors affect elasticity, such as the availability of substitutes, the importance of the item in the customer's budget, and the urgency of the customer's need and its relationship to other needs. By looking more closely at one of these factors—the availability of substitutes—you will better understand why demand elasticities vary.

Substitutes are products that offer the buyer a choice. For example, many consumers see grapefruit as a substitute for oranges and hot dogs as a substitute for hamburgers. The greater the number of "good" substitutes available, the greater will be the elasticity of demand. From the consumer's perspective, products are good substitutes if they are very similar (homogeneous). If consumers see products as extremely different—or heterogeneous—then a particular need cannot easily be satisfied by substitutes. And the demand for the most satisfactory product may be quite inelastic.

As an example, if the price of hamburger is lowered (and other prices stay the same), the quantity demanded will increase a lot, as will total revenue. The reason is that not only will regular hamburger users buy more hamburger, but some consumers who formerly bought hot dogs or steaks probably will buy hamburger too. But if the price of hamburger is raised, the quantity demanded will decrease—perhaps sharply. Still, consumers will buy some hamburger, depending on how much the price has risen, their individual tastes, and what their guests expect (see Exhibit A–6).

In contrast to a product with many substitutes, such as hamburger, consider a product with few or no substitutes. Its demand curve will tend to be inelastic. Motor oil is a good example. Motor oil is needed to keep cars running. Yet no one person or family uses great quantities of motor oil. So it is not likely that the quantity of motor oil purchased will change much as long as price changes are *within a reasonable*

Exhibit A-6 Demand Curve for Hamburger (a product with many substitutes)

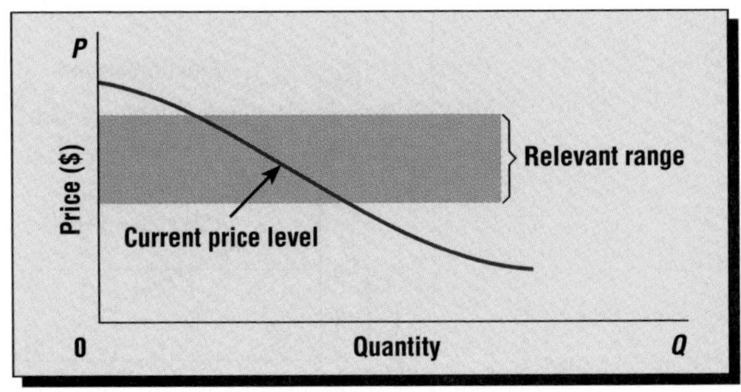

Exhibit A-7 Demand Curve for Motor Oil (a product with few substitutes)

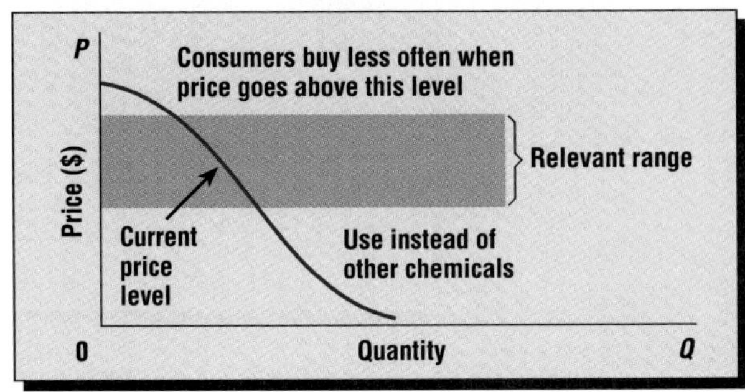

range. Of course, if the price is raised to a staggering figure, many people will buy less oil (change their oil less frequently). If the price is dropped to an extremely low level, manufacturers may buy more—say, as a lower-cost substitute for other chemicals typically used in making plastic (Exhibit A–7). But these extremes are outside the relevant range.

Demand curves are introduced here because the degree of elasticity of demand shows how potential customers feel about a product—and especially whether they see substitutes for the product. But to get a better understanding of markets, we must extend this economic analysis.

Markets as seen by suppliers

Customers may want some product, but if suppliers are not willing to supply it, then there is no market. So we'll study the economist's analysis of supply. Then we'll bring supply and demand together for a more complete understanding of markets.

Economists often use the kind of analysis we are discussing here to explain pricing in the marketplace. But that is not our intention. Here we are interested in how and why markets work, and in the interaction of customers and potential suppliers. Later in this appendix we will review how competition affects prices. Our full discussion of how individual firms set prices—or should set prices—was covered in Chapters 17 and 18.

Supply curves reflect supplier thinking

Generally speaking, suppliers' costs affect the quantity of products they are willing to offer in a market during any period. In other words, their costs affect their supply schedules and supply curves. While a demand curve shows the quantity of products customers will be willing to buy at various prices, a **supply curve** shows the quantity of products that will be supplied at various possible prices. Eventually, only one quantity will be offered and purchased. So a supply curve is really a hypothetical (what-if) description of what will be offered at various prices. It is, however, a very important curve. When combined with a demand curve, it summarizes the attitudes and probable behaviour of buyers and sellers regarding a particular product in a particular market—that is, in a product-market.

Some supply curves are vertical

We usually assume that supply curves tend to slope upward—that is, suppliers will be willing to offer greater quantities at higher prices. If a product's market price is very high, it seems only reasonable that producers will be anxious to produce more of the product, putting workers on overtime or perhaps hiring more workers to increase the quantity they can offer. Going further, it seems likely that producers of other products will switch their resources (farms, factories, labour, or retail facilities) to the product that is in great demand.

On the other hand, if consumers are willing to pay only a very low price for a particular product, it's reasonable to expect that producers will switch to other products, thus reducing supply. The supply schedule (Exhibit A–8) and supply curve (Exhibit A–9) for potatoes illustrate these ideas. This supply curve shows how many potatoes would be produced and offered for sale at each possible market price in a given month.

In the very short run (say, over a few hours, a day, or a week), a supplier may not be able to change the supply at all. In this situation, we would see a vertical supply curve. This situation is often relevant in the market for fresh produce. Fresh strawberries, for example, continue to ripen, and a supplier wants to sell them quickly—preferably at a higher price. But in any case, they must be sold.

If the product is a service, it may not be easy to expand the supply in the short run. Additional barbers or medical doctors are not quickly trained and licensed, and they only have so much time to give each day. Furthermore, the prospect of much higher prices in the near future cannot easily expand the supply of many services. For example, a hit play or an "in" restaurant or nightclub is limited in the amount of "product" it can offer at a particular time.

Exhibit A-8 Supply Schedule for Potatoes (4.5-kilogram [10-pound] bags)

POINT	POSSIBLE MARKET PRICE PER BAG	NUMBER OF BAGS SELLERS WILL SUPPLY PER MONTH AT EACH POSSIBLE MARKET PRICE
A	$1.60	17,000,000
B	1.30	14,000,000
C	1.00	11,000,000
D	0.70	8,000,000
E	0.40	3,000,000

Note: This supply curve is for a month, to emphasize that farmers may have some control over when they deliver their potatoes. There would be a different curve for each month.

Exhibit A-9 Supply Curve for Potatoes (4.5-kilogram [10-pound] bags)

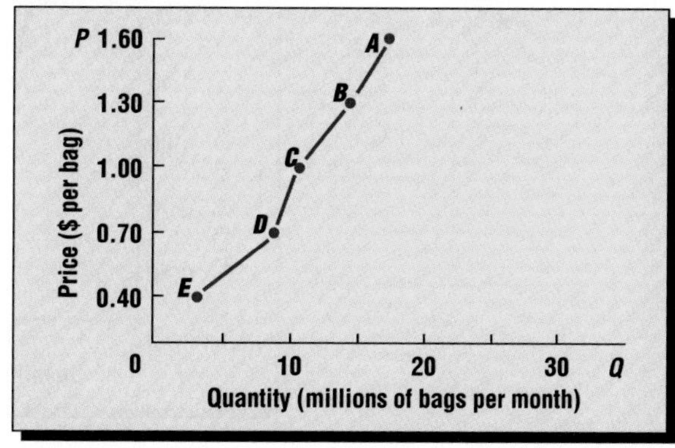

Elasticity of supply

The term *elasticity* also is used to describe supply curves. An extremely steep or almost vertical supply curve, often found in the short run, is called **inelastic supply** because the quantity supplied does not stretch much (if at all) if the price is raised. A flatter curve is called **elastic supply** because the quantity supplied does stretch more if the price is raised. A slightly upsloping supply curve is typical in longer-run market situations. Given more time, suppliers have a chance to adjust their offerings, and competitors may enter or leave the market.

Demand and supply interact to determine the size of the market and price level

We have treated market demand and supply forces separately. Now we must bring them together to show their interaction. The *intersection* of these two forces determines the size of the market and the market price—at which point (price and quantity) the market is said to be in *equilibrium*.

The intersection of demand and supply is shown for the potato data discussed above. In Exhibit A–10, the demand curve for potatoes is now graphed against the supply curve in Exhibit A–9.

In this potato market, demand is inelastic—the total revenue of all the potato producers would be greater at higher prices. But the market price is at the **equilibrium point,** where the quantity supplied and the price sellers are willing to accept are equal to the quantity demanded and the price buyers are willing to offer. The $1 equilibrium price for potatoes yields a smaller *total revenue* to potato producers than a higher price would. This lower equilibrium price comes about because the many producers are willing to supply enough potatoes at the lower price. *Demand is not the only determiner of price level. Cost also must be considered—via the supply curve.*

Some consumers get a surplus

Presumably, a sale takes place only if both buyer and seller feel they will be better off after the sale. But sometimes the price consumers pay in a sales transaction is less than what they would be willing to pay.

The reason for this is that demand curves are typically down-sloping, and some of the demand curve is above the equilibrium price. This is simply another way of showing that some customers would have been willing to pay more than the equilibrium price if necessary. In effect, some of them are getting a bargain by being able to buy

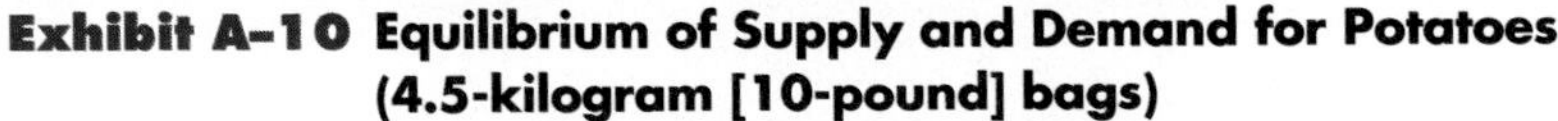
Exhibit A-10 Equilibrium of Supply and Demand for Potatoes (4.5-kilogram [10-pound] bags)

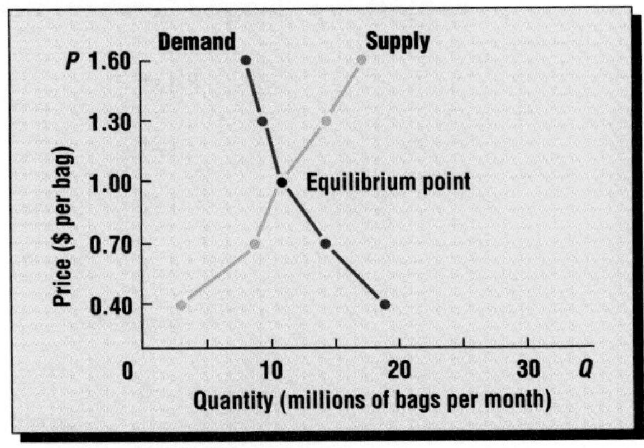

at the equilibrium price. Economists have traditionally called these bargains the **consumer surplus**—that is, the difference to consumers between the value of a purchase and the price they pay.

Some business critics assume that consumers do badly in any business transaction. In fact, sales take place only if consumers feel they are at least getting their money's worth. As we can see here, some are willing to pay much more than the market price.

Demand and supply help us understand the nature of competition

The elasticity of demand and supply curves—and their interaction—helps predict the nature of competition a marketing manager is likely to face. For example, an extremely inelastic demand curve means that the manager will have much choice in strategic planning and especially price setting. Apparently, customers like the product and see few substitutes. They are willing to pay higher prices before cutting back much on their purchases.

Clearly, the elasticity of a firm's demand curves makes a big difference in strategic planning. But other factors also affect the nature of competition. Among these are the number and size of competitors and the uniqueness of each firm's marketing mix. Understanding these market situations is important because the freedom of a marketing manager—especially control over price—is greatly reduced in some situations.

A marketing manager operates in one of four kinds of market situations. We'll discuss three kinds: pure competition, oligopoly, and monopolistic competition. The fourth kind, monopoly, isn't found very often and is usually subject to regulation. The important dimensions of these situations are shown in Exhibit A–11.

When competition is pure

When competition is pure, many competitors offer about the same thing. **Pure competition** is a market situation that develops when a market has:

1. Homogeneous (similar) products.
2. Many buyers and sellers who have full knowledge of the market.
3. Ease of entry for buyers and sellers—that is, new firms have little difficulty starting in business, and new customers can easily come into the market.

Exhibit A-11 Some Important Dimensions Regarding Market Situations

Important dimensions	Types of situations			
	Pure competition	Oligopoly	Monopolistic competition	Monopoly
Uniqueness of each firm's product	None	None	Some	Unique
Number of competitors	Many	Few	Few to many	None
Size of competitors (compared to size of market)	Small	Large	Large to small	None
Elasticity of demand facing firm	Completely elastic	Kinked demand curve (elastic and inelastic)	Either	Either
Elasticity of industry demand	Either	Inelastic	Either	Either
Control of price by firm	None (with care)	Some	Some	Complete

Exhibit A-12 Interaction of Demand and Supply in the Potato Industry and the Resulting Demand Curve Facing Individual Potato Producers

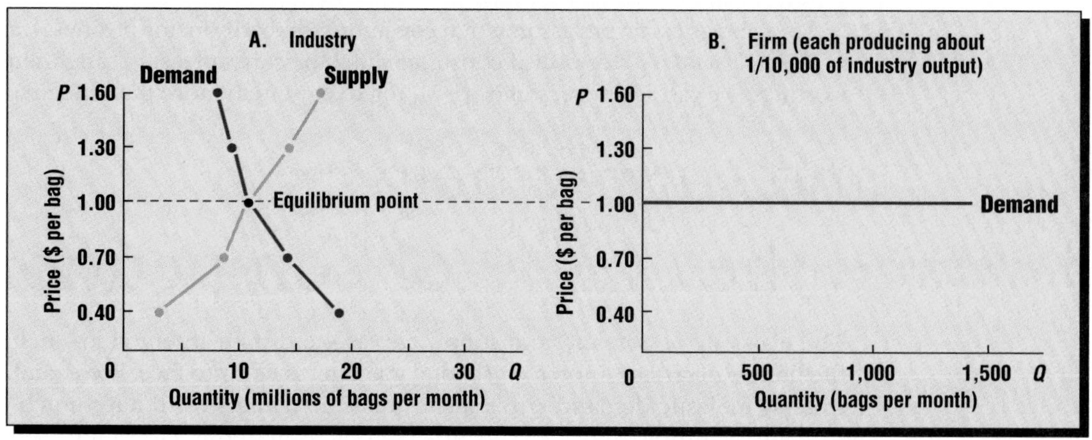

More or less pure competition is found in many agricultural markets. In the potato market, for example, there are thousands of small producers, and they are in pure competition. Let's look more closely at these producers.

Although the potato market as a whole has a downsloping demand curve, each of the many small producers in the industry is in pure competition, and each of them faces a flat demand curve at the equilibrium price. This is shown in Exhibit A–12.

As shown at the right of Exhibit A–12, an individual producer can sell as many bags of potatoes as he chooses at $1, the market equilibrium price. The equilibrium price is determined by the quantity that all producers choose to sell, given the demand curve they face.

But a small producer has little effect on overall supply (or on the equilibrium price). For example, if an individual farmer raises 1/10,000th of the quantity offered in the market, there will be little effect if that farmer goes out of business—or doubles production.

The reason why an individual producer's demand curve is flat is that the farmer probably couldn't sell any potatoes above the market price. And there is no point in selling below the market price! So, in effect, the individual producer has no control over price.

Markets tend to become more competitive

Not many markets are *purely* competitive. But many are close enough that we can talk about "almost" pure competition situations—those in which the marketing manager has to accept the going price.

Such highly competitive situations aren't limited to agriculture. Wherever *many* competitors sell *homogeneous* products—such as textiles, lumber, coal, printing, and laundry services—the demand curve seen by *each producer* tends to be flat.

Markets tend to become more competitive, moving toward pure competition (except in oligopolies—see below). On the way to pure competition, prices and profits are pushed down until some competitors are forced out of business. Eventually, in long-run equilibrium, the price level is only high enough to keep the survivors in business. Firms do not make any profit—they just cover costs. It's tough to be a marketing manager in this situation!

When competition is oligopolistic

In oligopoly, a few competitors offer similar things. Not all markets move toward pure competition. Some become oligopolies. **Oligopoly** situations are special market situations that develop when a market has:

Exhibit A-13 Oligopoly—Kinked Demand Curve—Situation

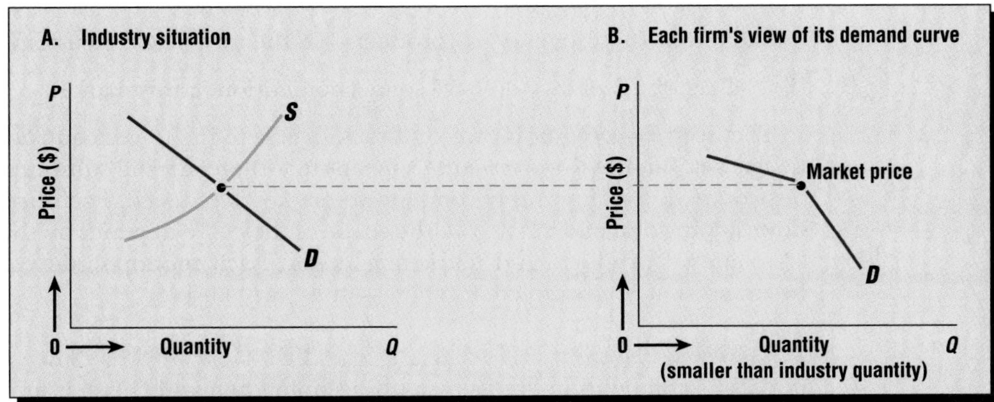

1 Essentially homogeneous products, such as basic industrial chemicals and gasoline.

2 Relatively few sellers, or a few large firms and many smaller ones who follow the lead of the larger ones.

3 Fairly inelastic industry demand curves.

The demand curve facing each firm is unusual in an oligopoly situation. Although the industry demand curve is inelastic throughout the relevant range, the demand curve facing each competitor looks "kinked." See Exhibit A–13. The current market price is at the kink.

There is a market price because the competing firms watch each other carefully—and know it's wise to be at the kink. Each firm must expect that raising its own price above the market price will cause a big loss in sales. Few, if any, competitors will follow the price increase. So the firm's demand curve is relatively flat above the market price. When the firm lowers its price, it must expect competitors to follow. Given inelastic industry demand, the firm's own demand curve is inelastic at lower prices—assuming it keeps "its share" of this market at lower prices. Since lowering prices along such a curve will drop total revenue, the firm should leave its price at the kink—the market price.

Actually, there *are* price fluctuations in oligopolistic markets. Sometimes they are caused by firms that don't understand the market situation and cut their prices to get business. In other situations, big increases in demand or supply can change the basic nature of the market and lead to price-cutting. Price cuts can be drastic, such as Du Pont's price cut of 25 percent for Dacron. This happened when Du Pont decided that industry production capacity already exceeded demand, and more plants were due to start production.

It's important to bear in mind that oligopoly situations don't just apply to entire industries and national markets. Competitors who are focusing on the same local target market often face oligopoly situations. A suburban community may have several gas stations, all of which provide essentially the same product. In this situation, the "industry" consists of the gas stations competing with each other in the local product-market.

As in pure competition, oligopolists face a long-run trend toward an equilibrium level, with profits driven toward zero. This may not happen immediately, and a marketing manager may try to delay price competition by relying more on other elements in the marketing mix.

When competition is monopolistic

Under monopolistic competition, a price must be set. You can see why marketing managers want to avoid pure competition or oligopoly situations. They prefer a market in which they have more control. **Monopolistic competition** is a market situation that develops when a market has:

1. Different (heterogeneous) products—in the eyes of some customers.
2. Sellers who feel they do have some competition in this market.

The word *monopolistic* means that each firm is trying to get control in its own little market. But the word *competition* means that there are still substitutes. The vigorous competition of a purely competitive market is reduced. Each firm has its own downsloping demand curve. But the shape of the curve depends on the similarity of competitors' products and marketing mixes. Each monopolistic competitor has freedom—but not complete freedom—in its own market.

JUDGING ELASTICITY WILL HELP SET THE PRICE Since a firm in monopolistic competition has its own downsloping demand curve, it must make a decision about price level as part of its strategic market planning. Here, estimating the elasticity of the firm's own demand curve is helpful. If it is highly inelastic, the firm may decide to raise prices to increase total revenue. But if demand is highly elastic, this may mean there are many competitors with acceptable substitutes. Then the price may have to be set near that of the competition. And the marketing manager probably should try to develop a better marketing mix.

Questions and Problems

1. Explain in your own words how economists look at markets and arrive at the law of diminishing demand.
2. Explain what a demand curve is and why it is usually downsloping. Then give an example of a product for which the demand curve might not be downsloping over some possible price ranges. Explain the reason for your choice.
3. What is the length of life of the typical demand curve? Illustrate your answer.
4. If the general market demand for men's shoes is fairly elastic, how does the demand for men's dress shoes compare to it? How does the demand curve for women's shoes compare to the demand curve for men's shoes?
5. If the demand for perfume is inelastic above and below the present price, should the price be raised? Explain.
6. If the demand for shrimp is highly elastic below the present price, should the price be lowered?
7. Discuss what factors lead to inelastic demand and supply curves. Are they likely to be found together in the same situation?
8. Why would a marketing manager prefer to sell a product that has no close substitutes? Are high profits almost guaranteed?
9. If a manufacturer's well-known product is sold at the same price by many retailers in the same community, is this an example of pure competition? When a community has many small grocery stores, are they in pure competition? What characteristics are needed to have a purely competitive market?
10. List three products that are sold in purely competitive markets and three that are sold in monopolistically competitive markets. Do any of these products have anything in common? Can any generalizations be made about competitive situations and marketing mix planning?
11. Cite a local example of an oligopoly, explaining why it is an oligopoly.

Appendix B
Marketing Arithmetic

When you finish this appendix, you should:

1. Understand the components of an operating statement (profit and loss statement).
2. Know how to compute the stockturn rate.
3. Understand how operating ratios can help analyze a business.
4. Understand how to calculate markups and markdowns.
5. Understand how to calculate return on investment (ROI) and return on assets (ROA).
6. Understand the important new terms (shown in orange).

Marketing students must become familiar with the essentials of the language of business. Business people commonly use accounting terms when talking about costs, prices, and profit. And using accounting data is a practical tool in analyzing marketing problems.

The operating statement

An **operating statement** is a simple summary of the financial results of a company's operations over a specified period of time. Some beginning students may feel that the operating statement is complex, but as we'll soon see, this really isn't true. *The main purpose of the operating statement is to determine the net profit figure—and present data to support that figure.* This is why the operating statement is often referred to as the *profit and loss statement.*

Exhibit B–1 shows an operating statement for a wholesale or retail business. The statement is complete and detailed so that you will see the framework throughout the discussion, but the amount of detail on an operating statement is *not* standardized. Many companies use financial statements with much less detail than this one. They emphasize clarity and readability rather than detail. To really understand an operating statement, however, you must understand its components.

Only three basic components

The basic components of an operating statement are *sales,* which come from the sale of goods and services; *costs,* which come from the making and selling process; and the balance, called *profit or loss,* which is just the difference between sales and costs. So there are only three basic components in the statement: sales, costs, and profit or loss. Other items on an operating statement are there only to provide supporting details.

Time period covered may vary

There is no one time period an operating statement covers. Rather, statements are prepared to satisfy the needs of a particular business. This may be at the end of each day or at the end of each week. Usually, however, an operating statement summarizes results for one month, three months, six months, or a full year. Since the time period does vary, this information is included in the heading of the statement as follows:

SMITH COMPANY
Operating Statement
For the (Period) Ended (Date)

Also, see Exhibit B–1.

Management uses of operating statements

Before going on to a more detailed discussion of the components of our operating statement, let's consider some of the uses for such a statement. As Exhibit B–1 shows, it presents a lot of information in a clear and concise manner. With this information, a manager can easily find the relationship between net sales and the cost of sales, the gross margin, expenses, and net profit. Opening and closing inventory figures are available—as is the amount spent during the period for the purchase of goods for resale. Total expenses are listed to make it easier to compare them with those listed on previous statements—and to help control these expenses.

All this information is important to a company's managers. Assume that a particular company prepares monthly operating statements. A series of these statements is a valuable tool for directing and controlling the business. By comparing results from one month to the next, managers can uncover unfavourable trends in the sales, costs, or profit areas of the business—and take any needed action.

Exhibit B–1 An Operating Statement (profit and loss statement)

SMITH COMPANY
OPERATING STATEMENT
FOR THE YEAR ENDED DECEMBER 31, 199X

Gross sales			$540,000
Less: Returns and allowances			40,000
Net sales			$500,000
Cost of sales:			
Beginning inventory at cost		$ 80,000	
Purchases at billed cost	$310,000		
Less: Purchase discounts	40,000		
Purchases at net cost	$270,000		
Plus freight-in	20,000		
Net cost of delivered purchases		$290,000	
Cost of products available for sale		$370,000	
Less: Ending inventory at cost		70,000	
Cost of sales			$300,000
Gross margin (gross profit)			$200,000
Expenses:			
Selling expenses:			
Sales salaries	$ 60,000		
Advertising expense	20,000		
Delivery expense	20,000		
Total selling expense		$100,000	
Administrative expense:			
Office salaries	$ 30,000		
Office supplies	10,000		
Miscellaneous administrative expense	5,000		
Total administrative expense		$ 45,000	
General expense:			
Rent expense	$ 10,000		
Miscellaneous general expenses	5,000		
Total general expense		$ 15,000	
Total expenses			$160,000
Net profit from operation			$ 40,000

A skeleton statement—essential details

Let's refer to Exhibit B–1 and begin to analyze this seemingly detailed statement to get first-hand knowledge of the components of the operating statement.

As a first step, suppose we take all the items that have dollar amounts extended to the third, or right-hand, column. When we focus on these items only, the operating statement looks like this:

Gross sales	$540,000
Less: Returns and allowances	40,000
Net sales	500,000
Less: Cost of sales	300,000
Gross margin	200,000
Less: Total expenses	160,000
Net profit (loss)	$40,000

Is this a complete operating statement? The answer is *yes*. This skeleton statement differs from Exhibit B–1 only in supporting detail. All the basic components are included. In fact, the only items we must list to have a complete operating statement are:

Net sales	$500,000
Less: Costs	460,000
Net profit (loss)	$ 40,000

These three items are the essentials of an operating statement. All other subdivisions or details are just useful additions.

Meaning of sales

Now let's define the terms in the skeleton statement.

The first item is sales. What do we mean by sales? The term **gross sales** is the total amount charged to all customers during some time period. However, there is always some customer dissatisfaction, or just plain errors in ordering and shipping goods. This results in returns and allowances, which reduce gross sales.

A **return** occurs when a customer sends back purchased products. The company either refunds the purchase price or allows the customer dollar credit on other purchases.

An **allowance** occurs when a customer is not satisfied with a purchase for some reason. The company gives a price reduction on the original invoice (bill), but the customer keeps the goods and services.

These refunds and price reductions must be considered when the firm computes its net sales figure for the period. Really, we're only interested in the revenue the company manages to keep. This is **net sales**—the actual sales dollars the company receives. All reductions, refunds, cancellations, and so forth made because of returns and allowances are deducted from the original total (gross sales) to get net sales. This is shown below:

Gross sales	$540,000
Less: Returns and allowances	40,000
Net sales	$500,000

Meaning of cost of sales

The next item in the operating statement—**cost of sales**—is the total value (at cost) of the sales during the period. We'll discuss this computation later. Meanwhile, note that after we obtain the cost of sales figure, we subtract it from the net sales figure to get the gross margin.

Meaning of gross margin and expenses

Gross margin (gross profit) is the money left to cover the expenses of selling the products and operating the business. Firms hope that a profit will be left after these expenses are subtracted.

Selling expense is commonly the major expense below the gross margin. Note that in Exhibit B–1, **expenses** are all the remaining costs subtracted from the gross margin to get the net profit. The expenses here are the selling, administrative, and general expenses. (Note that the cost of purchases and cost of sales are not included in this total expense figure—they were subtracted from net sales earlier to get the gross margin. Note, also, that some accountants refer to cost of sales as cost of goods sold.)

Net profit—at the bottom of the statement—is what the company earned from its operations during a particular period. It is the amount left after the cost of sales and the expenses are subtracted from net sales. *Net sales and net profit are not the same.* Many firms have large sales and no profits—they may even have losses! That's why understanding costs—and controlling them—is important.

Detailed analysis of sections of the operating statement

The cost of sales section includes details that are used to find the cost of sales ($300,000 in our example).

In Exhibit B–1, you can see that beginning and ending inventory, purchases, purchase discounts, and freight-in are all necessary to calculate costs of sales. The cost of sales section of the operating statement looks like this:

Cost of sales:			
Beginning inventory at cost		$ 80,000	
Purchases at billed cost	$310,000		
Less: Purchase discounts	40,000		
Purchases at net cost	270,000		
Plus: Freight-in	20,000		
Net cost of delivered purchases		290,000	
Cost of goods available for sale		370,000	
Less: Ending inventory at cost		70,000	
Cost of sales			$300,000

Cost of sales is the cost value of what is *sold*—not the cost of goods on hand at any given time.

Inventory figures merely show the cost of goods on hand at the beginning and end of the period the statement covers. These figures may be obtained by physically counting goods on hand on these dates, or they may be estimated from perpetual inventory records that show the inventory balance at any given time. The methods used to determine the inventory should be as accurate as possible, because these figures affect the cost of sales during the period—and net profit.

The net cost of delivered purchases must include freight charges and purchase discounts received, since these items affect the money actually spent to buy goods and bring them to the place of business. A **purchase discount** is a reduction of the original invoice amount for some business reason. For example, a cash discount may be given for prompt payment of the amount due. We subtract the total of such discounts from the original invoice cost of purchases to get the *net* cost of purchases. To this figure we add the freight charges for bringing the goods to the place of business. This gives the net cost of *delivered* purchases. When we add the net cost of delivered purchases to the beginning inventory at cost, we have the total cost of goods available for sale during the period. If we now subtract the ending inventory at cost from the cost of the goods available for sale, we get the cost of sales.

One important point should be noted about cost of sales. The way the value of inventory is calculated varies from one company to another—and can cause big differences in the cost of sales and the operating statement. (See any basic accounting textbook for how the various inventory valuation methods work.)

Cost of sales for a manufacturer

Exhibit B–1 shows how the managers of a wholesale or retail business arrive at their cost of sales. Such a business *purchases* finished products and resells them. In a manufacturing company, the purchases section of this operating statement is replaced by a section

Exhibit B–2 Cost of Sales Section of an Operating Statement for a Manufacturing Firm

Cost of sales:			
Finished products inventory (beginning)		$ 20,000	
Cost of production (Schedule 1)		100,000	
Total cost of finished products available for sale		$120,000	
Less: Finished products inventory (ending)		30,000	
Cost of sales			$ 90,000
Schedule 1, Schedule of Cost of Production			
Beginning work in process inventory			$ 15,000
Raw materials:			
Beginning raw materials inventory		$ 10,000	
Net cost of delivered purchases		80,000	
Total cost of materials available for use		$ 90,000	
Less: Ending raw materials inventory		15,000	
Cost of materials placed in production		$ 75,000	
Direct labour		20,000	
Manufacturing expenses:			
Indirect labour	$4,000		
Maintenance and repairs	3,000		
Factory supplies	1,000		
Heat, light, and power	2,000		
Total manufacturing expenses		$ 10,000	
Total manufacturing costs			$105,000
Total work in process during period			$120,000
Less: Ending work in process inventory			20,000
Cost of production			$100,000

called cost of production. This section includes purchases of raw materials and parts, direct and indirect labour costs, and factory overhead charges (such as heat, light, and power) that are necessary to produce finished products. The cost of production is added to the beginning finished products inventory to arrive at the cost of products available for sale. Often, a separate cost of production statement is prepared, and only the total cost of production is shown in the operating statement. See Exhibit B–2 for an illustration of the cost of sales section of an operating statement for a manufacturing company.

Expenses

Expenses go below the gross margin. They usually include the costs of selling and the costs of administering the business. They do not include the cost of sales—either purchased or produced.

There is no right method for classifying the expense accounts or arranging them on the operating statement. They can just as easily be arranged alphabetically or according to amount, with the largest placed at the top and so on down the line. In a business of any size, though, it is clearer to group the expenses in some way and use subtotals by groups for analysis and control purposes. This was done in Exhibit B–1.

Operating statements vary in detail

The statement presented in Exhibit B–1 contains all the major categories in an operating statement, together with a normal amount of supporting detail. Further detail can be added to the statement under any of the major categories without changing the nature of the statement. The amount of detail normally is determined by how the statement will be used. A shareholder may be given a sketchy operating statement; whereas the one prepared for internal company use may have a lot of detail.

Computing the stockturn rate

A detailed operating statement can provide the data needed to compute the **stockturn rate**—a measure of the number of times the average inventory is sold during a year. Note that the stockturn rate is related to the *turnover during a year*—not the length of time covered by a particular operating statement.

The stockturn rate is a very important measure because it shows how rapidly the firm's inventory is moving. Some businesses typically have slower turnover than others. But a drop in turnover in a particular business can be very alarming. It may mean that the firm's assortment of products is no longer as attractive as it was. Also, it may mean that the firm will need more working capital to handle the same volume of sales. Most businesses pay a lot of attention to the stockturn rate in an effort to get faster turnover (and lower inventory costs).

Three methods, all basically similar, can be used to compute the stockturn rate. Which method is used depends on the data available. These three methods—which usually give approximately the same results—are shown next.*

$$(1) \quad \frac{\text{Cost of sales}}{\text{Average inventory at cost}}$$

$$(2) \quad \frac{\text{Net sales}}{\text{Average inventory at selling price}}$$

$$(3) \quad \frac{\text{Sales in units}}{\text{Average inventory in units}}$$

Computing the stockturn rate will be illustrated only for Formula 1, since all are similar. The only difference is that the cost figures used in Formula 1 are changed to a selling price or numerical count basis in Formulas 2 and 3. Note: Regardless of the method used, you must have both the numerator and the denominator of the formula in the same terms.

If the inventory level varies a lot during the year, you may need detailed information about the inventory level at different times in order to compute the average inventory. If it stays at about the same level during the year, however, it's easy to get an estimate. For example, using Formula 1, the average inventory at cost is computed by adding the beginning and ending inventories at cost and dividing by 2. This average inventory figure is then divided into the cost of sales (in cost terms) to get the stockturn rate.

For example, suppose that the cost of sales for one year was $1,000,000. Beginning inventory was $250,000 and ending inventory $150,000. Adding the two inventory figures and dividing by 2, we get an average inventory of $200,000. We next divide the cost of sales by the average inventory ($1,000,000 ÷ $200,000) and get a stockturn rate of 5. The stockturn rate was covered further in Chapter 18.

Operating ratios analyze the business

Many businesspeople use the operating statement to calculate **operating ratios**—the ratio of items on the operating statement to net sales—and compare these ratios from one time period to another. They can also compare their own operating ratios with those of competitors. Such competitive data are often available through trade associations. Each firm may report its results to a trade association, which then distributes summary results to its members. These ratios help managers control their

*Differences occur because of varied markups and nonhomogeneous product assortments. In an assortment of tires, for example, those with low markups might have sold much better than those with high markups. But with Formula 3, all tires would be treated equally.

operations. If some expense ratios are rising, for example, those particular costs are singled out for special attention.

Operating ratios are computed by dividing net sales into the various operating statement items that appear below the net sales level in the operating statement. The net sales is used as the denominator in the operating ratio because it shows the sales the firm actually won.

We can see the relationship between operating ratios and the operating statement if we think of there being another column to the right of the dollar figures in an operating statement. This column contains percentage figures—using net sales as 100 percent. This approach can be seen in the following table.

Gross sales	$540,000	
Less: Returns and allowances	40,000	
Net sales	500,000	100%
Cost of sales	300,000	60
Gross margin	200,000	40
Expenses	160,000	32
Net profit	$ 40,000	8%

The 40 percent ratio of gross margin to net sales in the above example shows that 40 percent of net sales dollars are available to cover sales expenses and administer the business—and provide a profit. Note that the ratio of expenses to sales added to the ratio of profit to sales equals the 40 percent gross margin ratio. The net profit ratio of 8 percent shows that 8 percent of the net sales dollar is left for profit.

The value of percentage ratios should be obvious. The percentages are easily figured, and much easier to compare than large dollar figures.

Note that because these operating statement categories are interrelated, only a few pieces of information are needed in order to calculate the others. In this case, for example, knowing the gross margin percent and net profit percent makes it possible to figure the expenses and cost of sales percentages. Furthermore, knowing just one dollar amount and the percentages lets you calculate all the other dollar amounts.

Markups

A **markup** is the dollar amount added to the cost of sales to get the selling price. The markup usually is similar to the firm's gross margin because the markup amount added onto the unit cost of a product by a retailer or wholesaler is expected to cover the selling and administrative expenses—and to provide a profit.

The markup approach to pricing was presented in Chapter 18, so it will not be discussed at length here. But a simple example illustrates the idea. If the owners of a retail store buy an article that costs $1 when delivered to their store, they must sell it for more than this cost if they hope to make a profit. So they might add 50 cents onto the cost of the article to cover their selling and other costs and, hopefully, to provide a profit. The 50 cents is the markup.

The 50 cents is also the gross margin or gross profit from that item *if* it is sold. But note that it is *not* the net profit. Selling expenses may amount to 35 cents, 45 cents, or even 55 cents. In other words, there is no guarantee that the markup will cover costs. Furthermore, there is no guarantee that customers will buy at the marked up price. This may require markdowns, which are discussed later in this appendix.

Markup conversions

Often it is convenient to use markups as percentages instead of focusing on the actual dollar amounts. But markups can be figured as a percentage of cost *or* selling price. To have some agreement, *markup (percent)* will mean percentage of selling price unless stated otherwise. So the 50-cent markup on the $1.50 selling price is a markup of 33⅓ percent. On the other hand, the 50-cent markup is a 50 percent markup on cost.

Some retailers and wholesalers use markup conversion tables or spreadsheets to easily convert from cost to selling price, depending on the markup on selling price they want. To see the interrelationship, look at the two formulas below. They can be used to convert either type of markup to the other.

$$\text{(4)} \qquad \frac{\text{Percent markup}}{\text{on selling price}} = \frac{\text{Percent markup on cost}}{100\% + \text{Percent markup on cost}}$$

$$\text{(5)} \qquad \frac{\text{Percent markup}}{\text{on cost}} = \frac{\text{Percent markup on selling price}}{100\% - \text{Percent markup on selling price}}$$

In the previous example, we had a cost of $1, a markup of 50 cents, and a selling price of $1.50. The markup on selling price was 33⅓ percent, and on cost, it was 50 percent. Let's substitute these percentage figures, using Formulas 4 and 5, to see how to convert from one basis to the other. Assume, first of all, that we only know the markup on selling price and want to convert to markup on cost. Using Formula 5, we get:

$$\text{Percent markup on cost} = \frac{33\tfrac{1}{3}\%}{100\% - 33\tfrac{1}{3}\%} = \frac{33\tfrac{1}{3}\%}{66\tfrac{2}{3}\%} = 50\%$$

On the other hand, if we know only the percent markup on cost, we can convert to markup on selling price as follows:

$$\text{Percent markup on selling price} = \frac{50\%}{100\% + 50\%} = \frac{50\%}{150\%} = 33\tfrac{1}{3}\%$$

These results can be proved and summarized as follows:

Markup $0.50	= 50% of cost, or 33⅓% of selling price
+ Cost $1.00	= 100% of cost, or 66⅔% of selling price
Selling price $1.50	= 150% of cost, or 100% of selling price

It is important to see that only the percentage figures change while the money amounts of cost, markup, and selling price stay the same. Note, too, that when selling price is the base for the calculation (100 percent), then the cost percentage plus the markup percentage equal 100 percent. But when the cost of the product is used as the base figure (100 percent), the selling price percentage must be greater than 100 percent by the markup on cost.

Markdown ratios help control retail operations

The ratios we discussed above were concerned with figures on the operating statement. Another important ratio—the **markdown ratio**—is a tool many retailers use to measure the efficiency of various departments and their whole business. But note that it is *not directly related to the operating statement.* It requires special calculations.

A **markdown** is a retail price reduction required because customers won't buy some item at the originally marked up price. This refusal to buy may be for a variety of reasons—soiling, style changes, fading, damage caused by handling, or an original price that was too high. To get rid of these products, the retailer offers them at a lower price.

Though markdowns are generally considered to be due to business errors—such as poor buying practices, and original markups that are too high—some retailers use markdowns as a way of doing business rather than as a way to correct errors. For example, a store that buys out overstocked fashions from other retailers may start by marking each item with a high price and then reduce the price each week until it sells. Regardless of the reason, markdowns are reductions in the original price—and they are important to managers who want to measure the effectiveness of their operations.

Markdowns are similar to allowances in that price reductions are made. Thus, in computing a markdown ratio, markdowns and allowances are usually added together and then divided by net sales. The markdown ratio is computed as follows:

$$\text{Markdown \%} = \frac{\$ \text{ Markdowns} + \$ \text{ Allowances}}{\$ \text{ Net sales}} \times 100$$

The 100 is multiplied by the fraction to get rid of decimal points.

Returns are *not* included when figuring the markdown ratio. Returns are treated as consumer errors, not business errors, and therefore are not included in this measure of business efficiency.

Retailers who use markdown ratios usually keep a record of the amount of markdowns and allowances in each department and then divide the total by the net sales in each department. Over a period of time, these ratios give management one measure of the efficiency of buyers and salespeople in various departments.

It should be stressed again that the markdown ratio is not calculated directly from data on the operating statement since the markdowns take place before the products are sold. In fact, some products may be marked down and still not sold. Even if the marked down items are not sold, the markdowns—that is, the reevaluations of their value—are included in the calculations in the time period when they are taken.

The markdown ratio is calculated for a whole department (or profit centre)—*not* for individual items. What we are seeking is a measure of the effectiveness of a whole department—not how well the department did on individual items.

Return on investment (ROI) reflects asset use

Another off-the-operating-statement ratio is **return on investment (ROI)**—the ratio of net profit (after taxes) to the investment used to make the net profit, multiplied by 100 to get rid of decimals. Investment is not shown on the operating statement. But it is on the **balance sheet** (statement of financial condition), another accounting statement, which shows a company's assets, liabilities, and net worth. It may take some digging or special analysis, however, to find the right investment number.

Investment means the dollar resources the firm has invested in a project or business. For example, a new product may require $4 million in new money—for inventory, accounts receivable, promotion, and so on—and its attractiveness may be judged by its likely ROI. If the net profit (after taxes) for this new product is expected to be $1 million in the first year, then the ROI is 25 percent—that is, ($1 million ÷ $4 million) × 100.

There are two ways to figure ROI. The *direct* way is:

$$\text{ROI (in \%)} = \frac{\text{Net profit (after taxes)}}{\text{Investment}} \times 100$$

The *indirect* way is:

$$\text{ROI (in \%)} = \frac{\text{Net profit (after taxes)}}{\text{Sales}} \times \frac{\text{Sales}}{\text{Investment}} \times 100$$

This way is concerned with net profit margin and turnover—that is:

$$\text{ROI (in \%)} = \text{Net profit margin} \times \text{Turnover} \times 100$$

This indirect way makes it clearer how to *increase* ROI. There are three ways:

1. Increase profit margin (with lower costs or a higher price).
2. Increase sales.
3. Decrease investment.

Effective strategic market planning and implementation can increase profit margins and/or sales. And careful asset management can decrease investment.

ROI is a revealing measure of how well managers are doing. Most companies have alternative uses for their funds. If the returns in a business aren't at least as high as outside uses, then the money probably should be shifted to more profitable uses.

Some firms borrow more than others to make investments. In other words, they invest less of their own money to acquire assets—what we called *investments*. If ROI calculations use only the firm's own investment, this gives higher ROI figures to those who borrow a lot—which is called *leveraging*. To adjust for different borrowing proportions—to make comparisons among projects, departments, divisions, and companies easier—another ratio has come into use. **Return on assets (ROA)** is the ratio of net profit (after taxes) to the assets used to make the net profit, times 100. Both ROI and ROA measures are trying to get at the same thing—how effectively the company is using resources. These measures became increasingly popular as profit rates dropped and it became more obvious that increasing sales volume doesn't necessarily lead to higher profits—or ROI or ROA. Inflation and higher costs for borrowed funds also force more concern for ROI and ROA. Marketers must include these measures in their thinking or top managers are likely to ignore their plans—and their requests for financial resources.

Questions and Problems

1. Distinguish between the following pairs of items that appear on operating statements: (a) gross sales and net sales, and (b) purchases at billed cost and purchases at net cost.
2. How does gross margin differ from gross profit? From net profit?
3. Explain the similarity between markups and gross margin. What connection do markdowns have with the operating statement?
4. Compute the net profit for a company with the following data:

Beginning inventory (cost)	$ 150,000
Purchases at billed cost	330,000
Sales returns and allowances	250,000
Rent	60,000
Salaries	400,000
Heat and light	180,000
Ending inventory (cost)	250,000
Freight cost (inbound)	80,000
Gross sales	1,300,000

5. Construct an operating statement from the following data:

Returns and allowances	$ 150,000
Expenses	20%
Closing inventory at cost	600,000
Markdowns	2%
Inward transportation	30,000
Purchases	1,000,000
Net profit (5%)	300,000

6. Compute net sales and percent of markdowns for the data given below:

Markdowns	$ 40,000
Gross sales	400,000
Returns	32,000
Allowances	48,000

7. (a) What percentage markups on cost are equivalent to the following percentage markups on selling price? 20, 37½, 50, and 66⅔. (b) What percentage markups on selling price are equivalent to the following percentage markups on cost? 33⅓, 20, 40, and 50.
8. What net sales volume is required to obtain a stockturn rate of 20 times a year on an average inventory at cost of $100,000 with a gross margin of 25 percent?
9. Explain how the general managers of a department store might use the markdown ratios computed for their various departments. Is this a fair measure? Of what?
10. Compare and contrast return on investment (ROI) and return on assets (ROA) measures. Which would be best for a retailer with no bank borrowing or other outside sources of funds—that is, for a retailer who has put up all the money that the business needs?

When you finish this appendix, you should:

1. Understand the process of preparing a personal marketing plan.
2. Know how to identify personal payoffs and values, establish priorities, and construct a personal mission statement.
3. Know how to develop and write specific career goals.
4. Know how to prepare a personal and industry situation (SWOT) analysis.
5. Know how to identify and evaluate alternative career strategies.
6. Know how to prepare an action plan.

Appendix C

Marketing "YOU INC."—Preparing a Personal Marketing Plan*

*This material was prepared by Deborah Lawton of The University College of the Cariboo for *Basic Marketing*, Ninth Canadian Edition.

"Can people find satisfaction and happiness in a job?"

This is one of the big questions both young and not so young job seekers ask. Sal Divita, in an article in *Marketing News,* answers: "Absolutely. Both are achieved when the individual's personality profile is consistent with the demands of the job".[1]

Determining consistency in job fit is not a task taken lightly and can lead to unanticipated conclusions. Take this statement from a student who recently prepared a Personal Marketing Plan as a course requirement for an Introductory Marketing class.

This paper turned out a lot different than I had originally thought that it would have. I started out with the idea of starting life with a comfortable salary to feed my family in Canada, and after I had evaluated all of the above, I then realized that many opportunities awaited me in Australia also. I wanted to finish my Bachelors Degree here in Kamloops . . ., and then perhaps get a job with a public relations firm. By writing this paper, it has made me re-evaluate my life, and the choices I will be facing in the very immediate future.[2]

Why a personal marketing plan?

All marketing has the single purpose of helping companies and individuals address and manage change. Companies plan their marketing strategies but, unfortunately, many individuals have no plan at all. Yet nothing is more important than a plan for managing the inevitable changes that life brings.

A Personal Marketing Plan is vital if we are to harness and manage change. This textbook teaches the fundamentals of marketing: how to market goods and services and develop an effective marketing plan for a business organization. Many of the tools and techniques presented in the text have been proven to improve business profits, efficiency, and effectiveness. These principles can be adapted to market the most important product in your life: You. They are equally effective for an individual embarking on a career or a person in mid-life dealing with any inevitable job change.

In a complex world of changing technology, uncertain economic conditions, increasing competition, and information overload, change is constant. Employees no longer have the luxury of counting on the "golden handshake" after a lifetime of dedication to one company. Today, the average worker can expect to change careers at least three times. Most will work for more than six companies throughout their career.

Understanding the personal marketing planning process

This is the first time I have ever had to seriously delve into the uncharted waters of myself, and actually try and figure out what motivates me and what is important as well. . . . I preferred to swim happily along, oblivious to such information. I have (now) discovered . . . a great deal about my wants, needs, values and behaviour . . . Needless to say that in addition to completing a requirement of this course, I have also learned a lot about myself.[3]

The most important investment you can make in yourself

Think of yourself as a business: "YOU INC." To achieve career success, you must market yourself by offering your unique selling proposition and competitive advantage to the right target employer, at the right income or price, with the right blend of tools to promote your individual skills, education, and experience.

A planning framework provides direction and focus

This appendix is designed to help you write a personal marketing plan for "YOU INC." Exhibit C–1 summarizes the process. It presents a framework of marketing principles and outlines a series of independent but interrelated steps to follow in developing your own personal marketing plan. The process incorporates a systematic approach to making key life and career decisions. A planned approach to developing a personal marketing strategy will help you review progress and make revisions for effective execution.

Exhibit C–1 A Personal Marketing Planning Framework

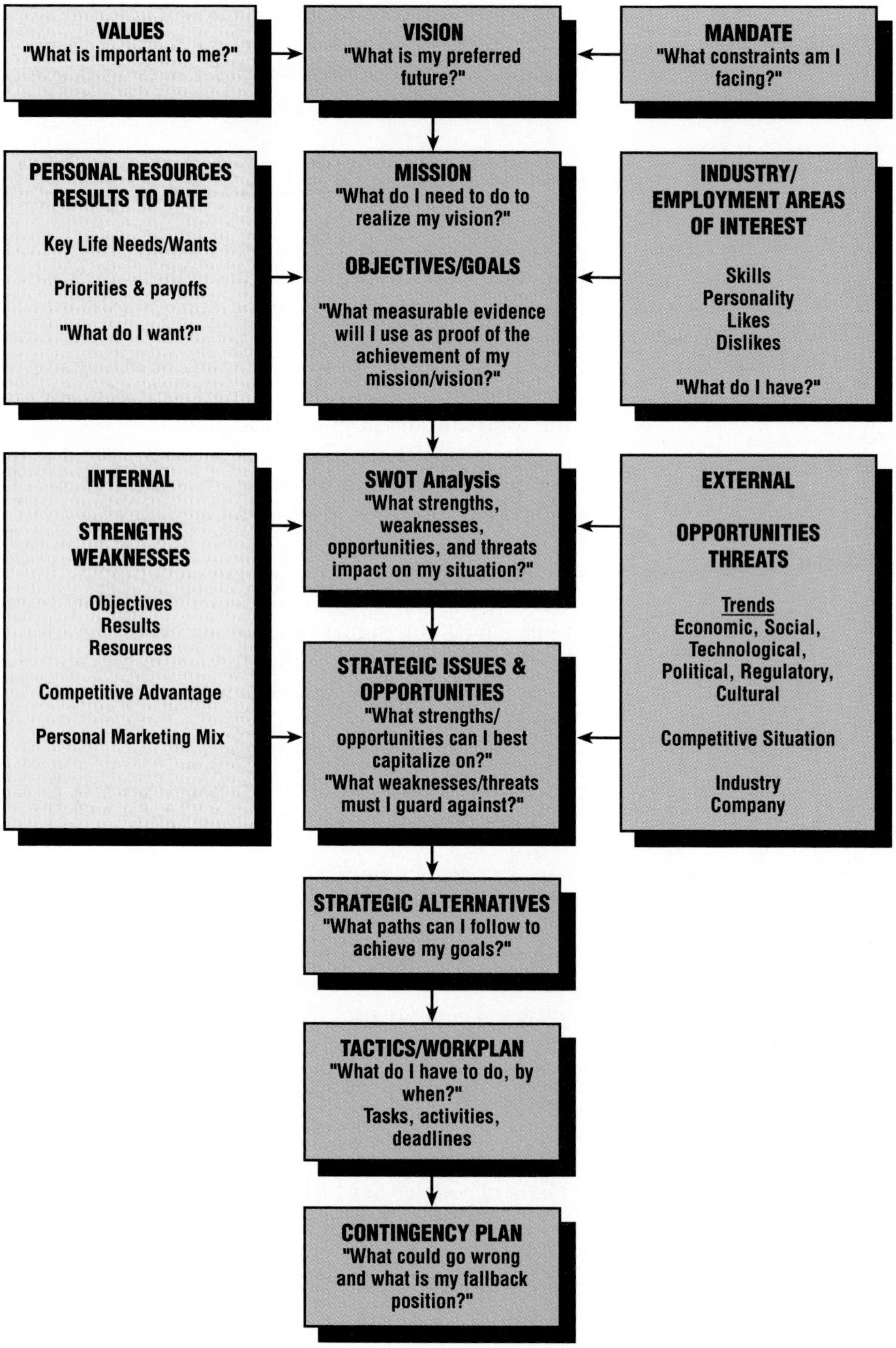

Establishing an overall career direction

To achieve a fulfilling career, we all must identify and define our own measure of success. This involves an honest self-appraisal, which includes the following:

1. Identifying your own wants, needs, values, dreams, strengths, and weaknesses.
2. Judging the "fit" of your unique skills and resources against the often uncontrollable environmental variables.
3. Establishing and keeping focused on your most critical life priorities.

Priorities keep us focused

We face many choices in life. We may naturally gravitate to one choice or another, but sometimes we need to make hard decisions. Our resources are limited. As options increase, we find it more difficult to allocate our resources. Setting priorities helps us sort out choices and keeps us focused on our most valuable payoffs.

A highly developed sense of priorities is an important planning skill and often marks the difference between an effective and an ineffective manager. A clear concept of priorities helps guard against a treadmill-like life. Exhibit C–2 illustrates a priority grid.[4] This tool helps sort out alternatives and identify the one with which to begin. The table is designed to rank ten items, but can be expanded.

Values underlie our concept of success

Values are attitudes and beliefs that form the foundation of our personal ethics. They are often culturally determined, having been passed down from generation to generation. They determine our choices and actions, and ultimately, our concept of success. They influence all we say and do.

Exhibit C–2 Prioritizing Grid Worksheet

Make a list of items and number them. Start with the top line of the grid. Compare items 1 and 2 on your list. Which one is more important to you? Ask yourself, "*Of all the things I could do with my time, which would bring me the best overall payoff?*" Circle your choice, then compare the other pairs.

1 2								
1 3	2 3							
1 4	2 4	3 4						
1 5	2 5	3 5	4 5					
1 6	2 6	3 6	4 6	5 6				
1 7	2 7	3 7	4 7	5 7	6 7			
1 8	2 8	3 8	4 8	5 8	6 8	7 8		
1 9	2 9	3 9	4 9	5 9	6 9	7 9	8 9	
1 10	2 10	3 10	4 10	5 10	6 10	7 10	8 10	9 10

Total times each number got circled.

1___ 2___ 3___ 4___ 5___ 6___ 7___ 8___ 9___ 10___

Priority order—highest # of circles = highest priority etc.

1___ 2___ 3___ 4___ 5___ 6___ 7___ 8___ 9___ 10___

Rewrite your list beginning with the item that got the most circles. This is your prioritized list.

Note: In the case of a tie, look back to see what you circled when you compared those two numbers. This should break the tie.

Source: Adapted from R.N. Bolles, *What Color is Your Parachute*, Ten Speed Press.

Values relate to both preferred consequences—what you want to happen—and modes of conduct—how you will behave to accomplish what you want. They influence our vision and guide our actions to realize it. To ensure career fulfilment we must be conscious of the most important values in our life, as compromising them will lead to personal tension. Awareness of our values enables us to make informed and satisfying career decisions.

For example, if you identify your core values as independence, creativity, equality, honesty, and ambition, you need to find an industry and company that reflects these values if you are to experience personal integrity. As Sal Divita says, "The value systems between employees and employers . . . must be compatible in order to form a 'perfect job.' "[5]

Your core values are reflected in your dreams and vision

Exhibit C–3 provides a framework for considering your values. To identify your core values, select the ten most important from the examples in Exhibit C–3. Add/reword any until they feel comfortable. Then rank them using the priority grid in Exhibit C–2. Write out your list. Your list should reflect your most cherished values.

Your core values are the basis of your dreams and goals. Living a life according to your personal values is critical to achieving an overall sense of well-being and fulfilment.

Clarifying vision—creating a picture of your preferred future

Once you have prioritized your values, you will have a clear understanding of the beliefs and attitudes that drive your actions and behaviours. Now you need to have a clear picture or vision of your values in action.

Entrepreneurs have a vision of the company they want to create. Artists have a picture in mind of their finished product. Their respective visions guide their decisions and actions. So too, each individual must have a vision of a personal future. Initially, the vision may be hazy and incomplete, but knowledge of personal values helps one to refine and clarify it. Visualizing your values in action will help you clarify the future you want to create for yourself.

Vision gives life meaning and purpose

Vision acts as a catalyst giving life meaning and purpose. Vision keeps us from just going through the motions. It gives meaning to everyday activities. A comfortable home, a happy family, challenging work, and public recognition may be the ultimate payoffs of your vision. But to realize these, you must fashion your daily activities—going to school, completing assignments, working in a less than satisfying job—as steps designed to take you to where you want to go. When you see how your daily activities link to your vision, you will have the motivation to get through the tough and tedious steps.

What you see in life is what you get, so construct an appropriate vision of your preferred future and plan the steps to make it come true.

Constructing a personal mission statement

Businesses express their values and vision in the form of mission statements designed to guide the development of operational plans. They guide what a company will do and how they will accomplish it. Mission statements act as context for objectives, strategies, and tactics.

Every organization/person has a mission or purpose, although some may not have written down their mission statement or intentionally developed a strategy to execute their vision.

Exhibit C-3 Instrumental and Terminal Values

INSTRUMENTAL/BEING VALUES (PREFERRED MODES OF CONDUCT)	TERMINAL/END STATE VALUES (PREFERRED END STATES)
Personal	**Physical**
Ambitious	Attractive
Analytical	Healthy
Courageous	Strong
Creative	Well-groomed
Decisive	
Flexible	**Security**
Imaginative	At peace
Independent	Comfortable
Organized	Free
Practical	Safe
Realistic	
Self-reliant	**Belonging**
Traditional	Loved, loving, intimate
	True friendship
Interpersonal	
Caring	**Self-esteem**
Cheerful	Accomplished
Compassionate	Contented
Courteous	Equal
Empathetic	Happy
Forgiving	Integrated
Helpful	Recognized
Honest	Self-respecting
Objective	Sense of accomplishment
Outgoing	
Principled	**Self-Actualization**
Reliable	Beauty (nature and arts)
Reserved	Inner harmony
Respectful	Spiritual peace
Responsible	Understanding
Self-controlled	Wisdom
Sincere	
Sympathetic	

A mission statement creates boundaries on what is done. It also sets the tone for the overall direction and coordination of efforts and resources. Like businesses, individuals need a mission statement to guide what they want to be and how they will make it happen.

Mission statements reflect vision and values

A personal mission statement expresses both your vision and your values. It suggests how you will take action on them. As Exhibit C–4 shows, a mission statement should address your values, your vision, and key markets, as well as how you will use your competitive advantage to benefit important areas of society.

For example, a marketer's mission statement may be:

I am an intelligent, ambitious person who takes pride in integrity, responsibility, personal growth and lifelong learning. I will fulfil my vision and dreams by creating exceptional results for a medium to large sized marketing oriented company. I will embrace challenge and pursue excellence throughout a career in consumer goods marketing.

Exhibit C-4 Characteristics of a Personal Mission Statement

1. It communicates your overall values and vision.
2. It expresses a picture of your preferred future—what you want to accomplish and for whom.
3. It clearly identifies the resources and skills you can provide.
4. It clearly identifies the industry/occupation you are interested in.
5. It briefly identifies your target market.

Mission statements are not cast in stone

Strategic decision making does not necessarily follow an orderly pattern. There is no one formula that can be applied in every situation. Business strategy is often formulated using a fluid process of identifying past success patterns and using them as a basis for creating new strategies.

Writing a personal mission statement may feel awkward. This feeling is normal. Companies often struggle with developing a mission statement and routinely take their senior executives "off site" for a few days to develop or reaffirm their mission.

Constructing a mission statement is not an exercise done once. People as well as businesses evolve and grow. A mission statement should be reviewed at regular intervals (once per year minimum) or whenever significant change occurs.

Setting goals—making your vision come true

Values and vision are the guiding principles expressed in your mission statement. Goals and objectives are the specific results needed to keep you on track to ensure that your values are preserved and that your visions are realized.

Goal setting acts as a framework for making your vision a reality. How you conceptualize your vision influences the goals you set and the strategies you implement. Goals help outline problems, clarify opportunities, and understand threats.

Goals are the practical side, the individual stepping stones of visions. A goal is a conscious decision based on logical analysis of the circumstances leading to your vision or dream. Goals give focus and direction, while vision provides purpose and energy.

Goals are the practical side of vision

For example, your mission statement may reflect a long-term dream of self-employment. On the other hand, your goals will lay out the specific results you will achieve as personal evidence of your vision in action. These may vary from saving a specific amount of money, to writing a business plan by a certain date or maintaining an A+ credit rating.

A goal must be written, as writing reflects commitment and makes the goal visible. It must have a deadline reinforcing the commitment.

Making goals "SMART"

Goals must be
Specific
Measurable
Attainable
Realistic
True

The techniques for ensuring that goals turn into results can be summed up by the acronym SMART. For a goal to be truly actionable, it must be Specific, Measurable, Attainable, Realistic, and True. Exhibit C–5 summarizes the meaning of each letter.

To ensure that your goal is *specific,* you must state unambiguously what you want to accomplish—the results you are striving to achieve. Your goal must express results in terms of specific and concrete evidence of accomplishment. For example, many of us want to be "better organized." This, however, is not clear or specific enough to be a goal. Furthermore, getting organized is highly subjective. To one person, being organized may mean maintaining an up-to-date personal calendar. To another, it may mean having a clean desktop and all papers filed. Thus, a goal must suggest a clear course of action and specify the results that will be used as proof of its successful completion.

Exhibit C-5 Making Goals "SMART"

In order to turn a problem or opportunity into a goal, the end condition or result of solving the problem must be clearly identified.

EVERY TIME YOU SET A GOAL, CHECK THAT IT IS "SMART."

S–SPECIFIC	WHAT IS TO BE ACHIEVED? Focus on specific, unambiguous, concrete key result areas or performance conditions. The goal must suggest action and leave no doubt as to its attainment.
M–MEASURABLE	HOW WILL YOU MEASURE IT? i.e., know it is achieved? Put goals into numbers—how many, how big, how often, how much, when. Set specific, quantitative conditions. Set a deadline.
A–ACHIEVABLE	DO YOU REALLY BELIEVE YOU CAN ACHIEVE IT? Compared to other situations/conditions and with the resources on hand at this time.
R–REALISTIC	DO YOU FEEL YOU HAVE A 60 TO 85 PERCENT CHANCE OF SUCCESS? Can you do it during this time, with the resources you have if nothing else changes? Have you ever done this before? Is there any room for error or obstacles? What is the minimum you need to accomplish? The ideal?
T–TRUE	WILL THIS UNQUESTIONABLY DELIVER A PERSONAL PAYOFF? Does this represent an important change of routine, solution, or opportunity to you? Is it really worthwhile? Is it of value to you, to the people it will impact? How will you feel if it isn't achieved? Is it worth the time, effort, and money to reach this goal? Is there an easier way that will give the same feeling of success?

Besides identifying the specific evidence of accomplishment, a goal must be *measurable.* A goal must include specific quantitative measures and deadlines—actual dates and timing. This reinforces and seals commitment.

Attaining goals should be a challenge, but routine

To make goals *attainable and realistic,* think of them in terms of the likelihood of accomplishment. What is the probability of achieving a goal if current circumstances, resources, and skills remain the same? Achieving goals should be the norm. Some might suggest setting a very challenging goal, with a low probability of success. They see this as motivation for people to reach beyond their means. But setting overly difficult goals can set up a situation of failure and disappointment. Evaluate your likelihood of success. To be attainable and realistic, while providing motivation or "stretch," goals should reflect a success probability of between 60 and 85 percent. Anything less than 60 percent courts failure, and thus can be discouraging and demotivating. On the other hand, anything above 85 percent does not have enough challenge. Such a goal is too easy to accomplish. Create a goal that stretches you to accomplish something you may not normally achieve without extra effort. If necessary, revise the goal until it reflects a challenging but realistic probability of success.

Finally, ensure that your goals are *true.* They must be important enough to warrant focus and unquestionably deliver a positive, personal payoff for you. Confirm that they are worth the time and effort to achieve.

Establishing goal hierarchies and time frames

The time frame of goals can vary depending on the clarity of your long-term mission. Short-term goals are set to support longer-term visions. Daily, weekly, or monthly goals keep your everyday activities focused and on track to realizing annual or longer-term objectives. Goals are directional to keep you focused. They should be reviewed and, if necessary, revised frequently. Continually ask yourself, does this goal keep me moving in the right direction?

Goals should be viewed within the context of your mission in terms of both complexity and time. The more complex the vision and the longer the time frame, the more difficult it is to make the goal "SMART." To ensure that it is may involve constructing a goal hierarchy, often through trial and error. It is important to always keep your long-term vision in mind.

Set goals using a "top down" or "bottom up" planning approach

You can set goals using a "top-down approach" by breaking your long-term vision into more manageable steps. Or you can use a "bottom-up approach" by executing small steps to explore your long-term dream.

For example, you may know you want to be a chartered accountant. A short-term goal of a high grade-point average in a finance course would support your longer-term vision. On the other hand, you may be unsure of what specific career you want but know that you like mathematics. In this situation, a more general goal, such as taking an accounting course, may be set as your first step. As you accomplish a sequence of goals, you will sort through your capabilities and specific interests and set more specific goals to support a longer-term vision.

Avoiding the pitfalls in goal setting

Goal setting requires precision of thought, forecasting ability, and the fortitude to make commitments. Goal execution requires discipline and a concerted effort to avoid being thrown off course. Three key principles regarding goal setting should be kept in mind:

1. *Define and clarify your payoffs.* Payoffs (especially internal, subjective ones) must be clearly thought through. Hasty identification of payoffs can result in a loss of interest in a goal. The motivational power of the payoff must be strong enough to maintain the activities necessary to ensure success. Clarifying payoffs requires concerted self-examination.

2. *Prioritize to avoid goal conflicts.* Sometimes two goals work against each other. For example, we often attempt to accomplish two goals simultaneously, such as:
   1. To get an "A" in a particular semester, and
   2. To earn $5,000 from part-time work during the semester.

   Unless you have above-average skills and resources, the probability of achieving both at the same time is low. That is why it is important to establish priorities and focus your goal-setting efforts on your highest priority. Be willing to compromise on your lower priorities.

3. *Review your goals often.* Sticking to goals is difficult. Many uncontrollable variables in the external environment can distract and throw us off track. Be aware of distractions, review your goals daily, and resolve to accomplish small steps on a regular basis.

Conducting a career-oriented situation analysis

A *SWOT analysis* is a technique designed to identify strengths, weaknesses, opportunities, and threats and ensure that internal and external variables are consistent. Think of strengths and weaknesses in terms of internal or personal aspects, and opportunities and threats in terms of external, environmental conditions. Naturally, we have more control over the former than the latter. Exhibit C–6 outlines questions you need to ask yourself when conducting a SWOT analysis.

Exhibit C-6 Conducting a SWOT Appraisal

Internal Appraisal

Strengths
- What is my present position?
- What am I good at?
- What major resources/expertise do I have?

Weaknesses
- What is my present position?
- What are the major problems I face?
- What am I poor at doing?
- What major resources/expertise deficiencies do I have?

External Appraisal

Opportunities
- What favourable environmental trends exist?
- How is my industry of choice developing?
- In what areas could I achieve success?

Threats
- What unfortunate environmental trends exist?
- How are my competitors developing?
- Where is my performance likely to suffer?

Identifying external opportunities and threats

As with any corporate marketing plan, a thorough analysis of uncontrollable variables is necessary in order to identify opportunities and threats in the external environment. This step ensures that your vision and mission are viable. Use the framework in Exhibit C–7 as a checklist for your external analysis. Plan to conduct research as if preparing a situation analysis for a company.

Conducting an environmental analysis

Research your career interests and analyze the external or environmental trends that influence your chosen career or employment area. Consider current and forecasted economic conditions. Examine legal, professional, and regulatory issues. What are the key technological, social, and cultural trends affecting your chosen area? Are there any location or mobility issues or opportunities? What external resources are available to assist you?

Choosing an occupation/employment area/industry

Your written mission statement should give you a sense of career direction to help you identify potential industries and/or employment areas.

If you have minimal experience in the workforce, choosing an industry may be difficult. Begin by considering areas of interest. Ask yourself what kinds of jobs are

Exhibit C-7 Conducting a Personal Marketing Plan Situation (SWOT) Analysis For YOU INC.: A Marketing Framework

EXTERNAL (ENVIRONMENTAL) ANALYSIS—OPPORTUNITIES AND THREATS

Environment Checklist	Industry/Target Market Checklist	Competitive Checklist
Economic conditions/trends	Industry size and growth	Intensity
Industry overview/considerations	Industry/life cycle position	Skills
Legal/regulatory/professional issues	Geographic scope	Strengths/weaknesses
Resource trends	Seasonality	Location
Societal & cultural issues/trends	Industry structure/segmentation	Contact modes
Technological trends	Employment rate/factors	Objectives
Economic trends	Segments, size, and accessability	Resources
Location/mobility trends	Target market(s)	
	Industries	Implications
Implications	Companies	Opportunities
Opportunities	Hiring practices	Threats
Threats	Decision makers, influencers, buyers, users	
	Needs/benefits/Information wanted	
	Mobility/promotion issues/opportunities	
	Implications	
	Opportunities	
	Threats	

available in these areas. If you have numerous areas of interest, use the priority grid to rank them. If you are considering starting your own business, you may first need to identify a market for investment sources, business advisors, and mentors. Begin with your highest-priority area, and gather information on your chosen career area.

Segmenting and identifying target markets

Once you have narrowed your choice to a key industry, segment the industry and define potential target markets. For the industry and key market segments, collect data to assess market size, life cycle, growth trends, seasonality, and any other factors important to your identification of opportunities.

Conducting a company analysis

Choose a target market with the best potential of employment, and then research individual companies to establish a contact list for your job search. Research employment trends, turnover, and promotion opportunities. How would you describe the climate and culture of your listed companies?

Constantly evaluate the fit of your findings against your mission statement and goals. Do not be discouraged if your research results in a false start or causes you to change direction. A trial-and-error approach is a natural part of the process. As long as you keep in mind your mission statement and values you will find yourself selecting the appropriate tools for a successful job search.

If you continue to experience positive signals, research the key decision makers. Determine the needs and the benefits they expect when employing a person with your skills and experience. Sal Divita recommends, "When competition is intense, you have to provide the prospective employer with compelling evidence and rationale supporting your claim that you're the best candidate for the position." He further describes that compelling evidence as "something that clearly and logically demonstrates that you offer the best solution to a need . . ., it's what you can do for the employer."[6]

Assessing competition

Research your competition. Consider graduation rates in your academic program or specialty, and labour market conditions, as well as the skills, resources, strategies, strengths, and weaknesses of other people vying for the same positions. How will you differentiate yourself? As Philip Kitchen comments, "in a world of competitive job rivalry, differentiation and focus seem to be the best strategies to deploy."[7] Identify your competitive advantage and unique selling proposition.

Summarizing opportunities and threats

Summarize your key findings and the implications they have for your career path. Prioritize the best opportunities and relevant threats. What overall strategic direction does your analysis suggest for the next two to five years? Product development? . . . Market development? . . . Market penetration? . . . or Diversification?

Conducting an internal or personal analysis

A SWOT analysis must also address internal or personal variables. A thorough self-analysis will help develop an effective personal marketing plan for YOU INC. As Sal Divita explains, "It's entirely possible that someone will hold the right job, but be unhappy with the work. This happens when the dominant personality of the company does not mesh with that of the person."[8]

Personal success demands that we lead from strengths and minimize weaknesses. A self-analysis enables you to do this by examining past and current objectives, resources, and results. Avoid any self-deception when conducting a personal analysis.

You can organize your self-analysis into three areas:

1. What you want.
2. What you have.
3. The results you have achieved to date.

Exhibit C–8 provides a framework to assist in your self-analysis.

Exhibit C–8 Conducting a Personal Marketing Plan Situation (SWOT) Analysis For YOU INC.: A Marketing Framework

1. INTERNAL (PERSONAL) ANALYSIS—STRENGTHS AND WEAKNESSES		
Objectives Checklist	**Resources Checklist**	**Results Checklist**
Dreams	Personality	Milestones/life happenings
Values	Social style	Successes/disappointments
Likes/dislikes	Support network	Growth potential
Industries/jobs of interest	Contacts	Strategies/tactics
Decision criteria/priorities	Reference/peer groups	Product positioning
Wants/needs/goals	Financial	Product
Key life categories	Education	Price
Priorities	Assets	Place
	Energy level	Promotion
	Health	Competitive advantage
	Experience	Unique selling proposition (USP)
	Skills	Opportunities lost
		Costs
		Obstacles
		Risks
		Payoffs
		Lessons learned

Assessing objectives: "What you want"

A clear definition of your values, a statement of mission, a review of wants and needs in all key life categories, and a clear sense of priorities will help clarify what you want. Any career decision will affect multiple areas of your life, so it is important to consider your career in the context of other areas of your life.

Exhibit C–9 presents a model for your "dream list"—eight life categories that interact with one another. Completing this exercise can help capture your wants and dreams as they relate to family, career, home, social, financial, educational, health, and personal development interests. Record your dreams and wants in each category that is relevant.

Prioritize your wants and needs from your "dream list." Confirm or adjust them based on the information you have collected regarding your potential employment area. Regularly review progress in each of the life areas to ensure that career goals support other important life goals.

Assessing resources: "What you have"

What you have is your own unique personal attributes and experiences. Your "tools" for self-analysis include your prioritized values list, an unbiased assessment of your strengths and weaknesses, and information regarding your interests, likes, and dislikes. In addition, consider such factors as health and energy level as well as education and experience.

Understanding your assets and liabilities will help you prepare a personal profile indicating how you will compete in the marketplace. To identify your personal resources

Exhibit C–9 Dream List—Key Life Categories: Worksheet

Brainstorm your wants and needs for each of the categories below. Let your imagination soar. Do not edit your reactions, trust your instincts. Prioritize when completed.

FAMILY	SOCIAL
____________	____________
____________	____________
____________	____________
____________	____________
CAREER/WORK	**FINANCIAL**
____________	____________
____________	____________
____________	____________
____________	____________
HOME/LIVING/LOCATION	**EDUCATIONAL**
____________	____________
____________	____________
____________	____________
____________	____________
PERSONAL DEVELOPMENT/SPIRITUAL	**PHYSICAL**
____________	____________
____________	____________
____________	____________
____________	____________

and limitations, develop a list of your strengths and weaknesses, skills, interests, likes, and dislikes. Many analytical tools exist to help organize a personal profile. Be ready and willing to use personality tests such as Myers-Briggs, management/leadership profiles, skills inventories, and school and employment records. Career counsellors, friends, and relatives may contribute to your analysis. Include support networks and mentors. As with all tools, the better they are, the better the results will be.

Be tough and honest to present a realistic picture. The future is the culmination of what you do today. An honest self-appraisal will help clarify and refine your vision.

Assessing results: "What you have done"

A self-analysis involves reviewing life "happenings." Each milestone in your personal history has contributed to your present position in life. Think in terms of life successes and disappointments rather than failures. Adopt the perspective that "failure" is simply a learning experience to get you back on track. A helpful exercise follows.

Draw a line representing your life. On the appropriate spots, mark the date you were born and the current date. In the area to the left of the current date indicate key successes, disappointments, and life happenings that reflect milestones in your life and that have contributed to where you are today.

Then, in the area to the right of the current date, fill in some of the dreams and visions you have of your future. With what will you fill the remaining space in your "cup of life"? A personal lifeline will help put your life into perspective.

Documenting "lessons learned"

Look at the strategies and tactics you have implemented and the results you have achieved to date. How would you describe your past activities? Have they been successful? If not, what needs to change?

Evaluate your results and your level of satisfaction with them. What lessons have you learned? In what direction do these lessons point?

When you have completed your situation analysis, you need to make sure your marketing mix reflects your career and personal priorities, will deliver high payoffs, and is consistent with the industry or employment area you have selected.

Developing strategies—generating broad marketing alternatives

In business, as well as in your personal life, there are many ways of allocating resources—that is, the time, energy, and money needed to accomplish goals. Brainstorm various strategies for effectively using your resources.

For example, if your goal is to earn your Chartered Accountant designation by December 2006, you must acquire certain education and experience. This suggests an overall "product development" strategy, but the method and order of accomplishing it may vary depending on your strengths and weaknesses and on the marketing mix area that is most important to plan. If your strengths lie in achieving high grades—the product area—you may select an "educational" product strategy. If, however, your key resources lie in work experience, you may focus on an "employment" place strategy, supplemented by night courses over time to fulfil the CA requirements.

When brainstorming strategies, keep your goal clearly in mind. Once you have generated a number of alternative ways to reach your goals, check to make sure that all alternatives will deliver a high, positive payoff. This will ensure equal motivation to execute each option.

Establishing your personal marketing mix

As with any business, whether by choice or chance you are still making marketing and transaction decisions for YOU INC. In order to ensure the best match between your personal resources and objectives and the external environment, you need to plan and execute a personal marketing mix.

Target market

Your target market is an industry or employment area and those companies which you want your marketing mix to appeal to. This includes the people who have the power to hire you.

You may have identified a single, specific target market or a number of attractive segments. Thus you may develop marketing strategies to appeal to one narrow market. On the other hand, you may be considering a broader, combined market or multiple target markets. Whatever approach you choose, a clear concept of your target markets will help you determine the best ways to appeal to each one.

Exhibit C–10 shows how you might adapt the traditional "4 Ps" of marketing to reflect your personal marketing plan. For each element of the marketing mix, you will need to develop objectives, strategies, and tactics.

Product

The product is YOU INC.: your personal goals, resources, strategies, and results. As quoted in a recent news story on personal marketing planning, Tom Peters wrote, "To be in business today, our most important job is to be head marketer for the brand called You."[9]

Write a concise and objective statement of product strategy outlining your features and benefits, key competitive advantage, and the image you want to project.

Place

Place is your preferred working location. As with any element of the marketing mix, you need to set objectives to guide your strategy. Assess what YOU, the product, needs in terms of your work, home, and leisure environments. Identify your preferred geographic location. Include other potential influences such as company culture, pre-

Exhibit C–10 Personal Marketing Mix—Strategy Decision Areas

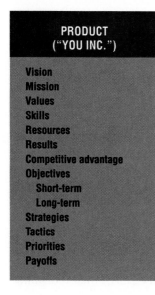

PRODUCT ("YOU INC.")	PLACE (DESIRED LOCATION)	PROMOTION (CONTACT STRATEGY)	PRICE (INCOME)
Vision	Objectives	Objectives	Objectives
Mission	Strategies	Inform, persuade, remind	Expectations
Values	Environment	Strategies	Short-term
Skills	Work	USP	Long-term
Resources	Living	Features/benefits	Type of compensation
Results	Leisure	Positioning	Benefits
Competitive advantage	Relocation	Tactics	Constraints
Objectives	Tactics	Résumé	Strategies
Short-term	Priorities	Networking	Flexibility
Long-term		Contact plan	Tactics
Strategies		Interview plan	
Tactics			
Priorities			
Payoffs			

ferred working environment, and mobility factors. Will you implement an extensive, selective, or exclusive distribution strategy? Do you require "intermediaries" to assist you?

Price

Price is the income you want to receive. Again, objectives set the tone for your short- and long-term expectations. Are you profit, sales, or status quo oriented? How flexible can you be? Will you price yourself higher, or lower, or equal to the competition? What type of compensation plan is most appropriate for you? What benefits do you expect?

Promotion

Promotion is how you communicate your benefits to the target market. Should you strive to inform, persuade, remind? Is your goal to attract attention, arouse interest, create desire, or achieve action? Which promotion area will be your priority—Mass Selling? Personal Selling?

Your promotion strategy should outline the broad "how" of creating your message and reaching your target. How will you position yourself relative to your competition? How best can you communicate your competitive advantage? How will you best reach your target audience? What blend of tactics will you use—résumés, networking, interviews, direct mail, cold calling?

Evaluating alternatives

The alternative you should first take action on should be the one that is the easiest to implement in terms of avoiding obstacles and minimizing costs and risks. Your text outlines a number of ways to evaluate and select the best alternative.

One quick and simple method, the *CORP method,* outlines key decision criteria and enables you to objectively evaluate each alternative.

Costs reflect your resources and values. Costs fall into three categories—time, money, and energy or emotional costs. Consider each alternative in terms of the level of resources needed.

Obstacles represent the barriers you are likely to encounter while implementing the strategy. These can be internal or external. For example, your strategy may require you to change a habit in order to reach your goal. Or there may be external problems, such as high local unemployment rates or strong competition, to be overcome. Often, identifying obstacles leads to the development of sub-steps that must be executed before or simultaneously with your main strategy.

Risks are the opportunities foregone by focusing on one particular strategy. Risk assessment makes it easier for you to consider the implications of taking an unproductive or dead end route.

Finally, assessment of the *payoffs* for each option enables us to focus on the relative rewards of each strategy. For maximum motivational power, every alternative should carry a high payoff. If your first assessment does not result in a high payoff, rework the strategy until it does, or alternatively, abandon it and replace it with a higher-payoff alternative.

Applying CORP criteria

Exhibit C–11 provides a framework for choosing the easiest yet highest-payoff strategy. When you apply CORP criteria to strategies, you consider both positive and negative implications. For each criterion, specify whether the expected outcome is high, medium, or low.

When first choosing outcomes, trust your instincts. An intuitive reaction results in better "truth." Often the "computer" of your mind can process complex data more efficiently than a conscious, calculated approach, so trust your initial instincts. As with any kind of screening method, both qualitative and quantitative criteria are valuable.

Exhibit C–11 The "CORP" Evaluation—Worksheet

ALTERNATIVE 1	High	Medium	Low
Net Cost (Time, $, Energy)	________	________	________
Key Obstacles	________	________	________
Risk Potential	________	________	________
Payoff Potential	________	________	________

ALTERNATIVE 2	High	Medium	Low
Net Cost (Time, $, Energy)	________	________	________
Key Obstacles	________	________	________
Risk Potential	________	________	________
Payoff Potential	________	________	________

ALTERNATIVE 3	High	Medium	Low
Net Cost (Time, $, Energy)	________	________	________
Key Obstacles	________	________	________
Risk Potential	________	________	________
Payoff Potential	________	________	________

SELECTION: (LOWEST COST, OBSTACLES, RISK, HIGHEST PAYOFF)

____

RESOURCES:

Available ________________________________

Required ________________________________

Putting it all together—preparing an action plan

Action plans are the heart of accomplishing your goals and ultimately your vision. Exhibit C–12 provides a format for summarizing the necessary information into a plan of action.

Tactics are specific action steps

Tactics are the specific and detailed steps needed to carry out your strategy. They must be clear and in chronological order. Deadlines should be set for each activity. This process helps reaffirm the appropriateness of your overall deadline by scheduling the steps needed. Your "Plan of Action" is really a series of short-term goals (daily or weekly) to keep you on track.

Schedule your tactics

Consider the elements in your personal marketing mix to develop your plan of action. What do you have to do to define and access your target market? What prod-

Exhibit C-12 PLAN OF ACTION—Worksheet

DATE: ____________________

"SMART" GOAL:
(Change of Routine, Problem, or Opportunity)

____

____

____

PROBABILITY:
Of Accomplishment with Current Resources? ______%

PAYOFFS:
(Concrete & Personal)
1. ____________________
2. ____________________
3. ____________________

ALTERNATIVES
Must Accomplish the Goal and Deliver Payoffs
1. ____________________
2. ____________________
3. ____________________

ACTION STEPS	EST. HOURS	DEADLINE

KEY PERFORMANCE MEASUREMENT	SOURCE	REVIEW

Date to Begin ____________________ Date Completed ____________________

Signed ____________________ Partner ____________________

uct actions are necessary to accomplish your goals? What place, price, and promotion activities have to be coordinated to bring all the pieces together? As with any marketing mix, the individual elements must work in tandem.

Marketing Demo C–1 contains an executive summary from a personal marketing plan prepared by a student taking an introductory marketing course. It shows how one person, with a vision of becoming a marketing manager for a large retail chain, integrated the steps in the personal marketing plan process to produce a personal marketing plan.

Staying on track—planning contingencies

Before you rush off to implement your personal marketing plan, one last step in the process must be taken—the preparation of a contingency plan. This plan examines the "what ifs"—the key assumptions that underpin your career plan. Contingency planning also helps you develop broad strategies for revising your plan in the event that your assumptions do not materialize.

For example, you may have assumed that the economy would continue to strengthen and that opportunities for your chosen industry would open up. What if this assumption is incorrect? What if the economy plunges back into a recession? What is your fall-back plan? Marketing mix assumptions must also be scrutinized and

Marketing Demo C-1

Personal Marketing Plan Executive Summary

The purpose of this report is to write a clear, concise plan for my career. My external analysis focused on evaluating the Canadian economic, social and cultural climate as well as technological trends affecting the retail clothing industry. More specifically, I looked at the opportunities and threats that large retail clothing chain stores face in Canada. I chose this field as my area of career interest because of my past experience working in retail sales and my desire to continue working in this field after graduation.

My external analysis discovered a growing, but changing retail sector due to advances in technology, a weak economic climate and penetration of U.S. retailers into many Canadian markets. This analysis pointed to some strong opportunities for a career in the retail sector, especially with large established retailers.

I also conducted an internal analysis of my strengths and weaknesses, prioritized my values and formulated a personal mission statement in order to best judge the fit of my own personal resources with the retail clothing environment. I found my key strengths are my outgoing, "Expressive" social style and my ability to juggle part-time work and school demands while still realizing respectable grades. My weaknesses are my inconsistent organization skills and my tendency to procrastinate.

My analysis of some individual retail chains resulted in my awareness that there is a strong need for educated and experienced individuals to be groomed for top marketing positions within large retail firms. However, I also discovered that many companies prefer advanced degrees (MBA's), particularly with merchandising and marketing concentrations. I concluded that my biggest strategic issue was the need for education beyond a general business degree. Thus, the implication is that a continued "Product Development" strategy would be my best course of action for the next five years.

The goal I set for myself is to receive my MBA by June, 2005. The key threats to this are the lack of financial resources and the strong competition I face to get accepted into a good MBA program. With this in mind, I came up with three alternatives that I felt would best help me achieve my goal. They are:

1. Reduce my current working hours and apply for a student loan to help finance my undergraduate education and ultimately my MBA.
2. Reduce my current working hours and focus my efforts on getting high grades to attract a scholarship.
3. Take two years off school when I finish my BBA and work to save enough money to finance post graduate education.

By applying the CORP evaluation criteria, I discovered that Alternative 2 would provide me with the highest payoff (no debt), with the least cost, obstacles and risks.

Some steps I will take to implement my plan are:

1. Research scholarship opportunities.
2. Discuss workload and career possibilities with my store supervisor.
3. Develop a study schedule and stick to it!

Receiving my MBA would be a major accomplishment for me and would significantly improve my chances of securing a good retail marketing position.

---

backed up. You may have based your plan on passing a critical test or relocating easily to a new location. However, life circumstances change, and the more we consider and embrace potential change, the better prepared we are to adapt.

A contingency plan acknowledges that no forecast is 100 percent accurate. It prepares you to be aware of and adjust to early warning signals that things may be moving off course.

Making it happen

Now that your plan is researched, written, and ready to execute, take a deep breath—the fun is just beginning. Now it is time to get out there and make things happen.

In an article in *Marketing News,* Sal Divita says that "there are four major problems" facing a job searcher,[10]

1. Not knowing how and where to start.
2. Lacking in direction and focus.

3. Imagining personal barriers [and allowing them] to contribute to a low sense of self-worth.

4. Lack of confidence in managing the future.

The preparation of a personal marketing plan will go a long way toward alleviating these problems. As Mr. Divita proclaims, "Is there a perfect job for you? You bet."[11] Effective self-marketing helps you identify it. A propensity for action ensures that you will find it.

---

1. Sal Divita, "Perfect Job Awaits If Your Personality Is Right," *Marketing News*, 4/24/95, p. 10.
2. P. Kolesnichenko, *Personal Marketing Plan Report*, University College of the Cariboo, BBUS 343 Course, 3/10/98, p. 11.
3. *Personal Marketing Plan Report*, University College of the Cariboo, BBUS 343 Course.
4. R.N. Bolles, *What Color Is Your Parachute?* Ten Speed Press.
5. Sal Divita, "Perfect Job Awaits If Your Personality Is Right," *Marketing News*, 4/24/95, p. 10.
6. Sal Divita, "How You Define Product Makes A Big Difference," *Marketing News*, 3/28/94, p. 10.
7. P. Kitchen, "Self-Marketing Is Easily Taught, But Hard to Learn," *Marketing News*, 8/29/94, p. 4.
8. Sal Divita, "Perfect Job Awaits If Your Personality Is Right," *Marketing News*, 4/24/95, p. 10.
9. Tom Peters, *You and Co*, as quoted in *The Vancouver Sun*, Saturday, 11/1/97.
10. Sal Divita, "Getting Started Is The Toughest Part of the Job," *Marketing News*, 8/28/95, p. 10.
11. Sal Divita, "Perfect Job Awaits If Your Personality Is Right," *Marketing News*, 4/24/95, p. 10.

Video Cases

Guide to the Use of These Cases

Basic Marketing includes two different types of marketing cases: the six special video cases in this section and the 38 traditional cases in the next section. All of the cases offer you the opportunity to evaluate marketing concepts at work in a variety of real-world situations. However, the video cases add a multimedia dimension in that we have produced a special video to accompany each of the written cases. The full-length videos are available to professors who adopt *Basic Marketing* for use in their course. (These case-based videos are in addition to 18 other video segments we have custom produced and made available to instructors for possible use with other parts of the text).

The videos bring to life many of the issues considered in each case. However, you can read and analyze the written case descriptions even if there is no time or opportunity to view the video. Either way, you'll find the cases interesting—and closely tied to the important concepts you've studied in the text.

The set of questions at the end of each case will get you started in thinking about the marketing issues in the case. Further, we provide instructors with a number of suggestions on using the video cases, for group discussion in class or for individual assignments. Thus, as is also true with the traditional cases in the next section, the video cases can be used in many different ways and sequences. You can analyze all of the cases or only a subset. In fact, the same case can be analyzed several times for different purposes. As your understanding of marketing deepens throughout the course, you'll "see" many more of the marketing issues considered in each case.

1 Volkswagen New Beetle*

Volkswagen's management was very surprised at the reaction to their latest design study, the Concept 1. Unveiled in Detroit at the North American International Auto Show in January 1994, the car was an instant hit with the public. Throngs of people crowded around the viewing stand to get a close look at what VW designers had created—a nineties version of the much loved "Beetle." The original Beetle had been sold in the United States from 1948 to 1981, and is still sold in some countries, such as Mexico and Brazil.

Automotive design studies are used to gauge public reaction to styling and design ideas. The overwhelming response to the Concept 1, which closely resembled the looks of the original Beetle, prompted VW to study what was behind the strong consumer response. They wanted to know if the favourable response was because of the uniquely identifiable profile of the Beetle, the fond memories of the millions of American Beetle owners, or simple nostalgia—a desire to be carried back to a "different" time.

It was clear that the Concept 1 touched the buying public at the auto show. The number of phone calls and letters to Volkswagen's U.S. headquarters was so overwhelming that VW management promptly put a product development team into action. The charge was to create a thoroughly modern version of the beloved Beetle—a car that would utilize the latest cutting edge technologies housed in the uniquely identifiable shape of the most widely produced car in history.

Since the original idea for the car was shown to the German government in 1934 by Dr. Ferdinand Porsche, 21 million original Beetles have been built. Porsche's dream was to build a simple, high-quality car for the masses—a car that even the average owner could learn to care for and maintain with minimal expense. That was the formula that had worked so well in the United States when Henry Ford introduced the Model T and put America on wheels.

Porsche's dream for the "people's car" (or Volkswagen) would not become a commercial reality until after World War II, though some prototypes and early production units had reached the public prior to the war's outbreak. By 1948, the war-damaged factory had been rebuilt and the Beetle was being produced in full scale in Europe. It was also in that year that the "Beetle" was shown to the American public at the New York Auto Show. By the late 1950s, the Beetle was the leading imported car in America and hundreds of thousands of Americans were driving the small cars with air-cooled engines. Many people loved the simplicity and economy of the car, and the quality was very high. The car represented very good value for the consumer's money.

*This case and the accompanying video script were prepared by Professor Jim Burley.

Japanese auto manufacturers took notice of Volkswagen's success in the United States and designed their own competing models of small, economical cars. But they were different in character than the Beetle. The Japanese-produced small cars were more like "shrunken" versions of full-size cars. They had big car styling and incorporated many features that American car buyers of the 1960s wanted, including power-assisted steering, power windows, and automatic transmissions. The small cars introduced by Toyota, Nissan, and Honda quickly cut into Volkswagen's sales volume. Although sales in the small-car category grew rapidly, increased competition left smaller sales volume for the previously dominant Beetle.

VW management held steadfastly to their "simple is beautiful" positioning, which was carefully reinforced in the Beetle's advertising campaign. Advertisements with headlines such as "Ugly Is Only Skin Deep" reminded customers that the real beauty of the VW was its simplicity and reliability, as well as the economical ownership experience it produced. Despite this message, many people in the market were attracted to the larger choice of options and features found on the Japanese entries. The Beetle's American sales peaked at 423,000 units in 1968, and then began to decline.

Volkswagen responded to the market changes that were taking place by introducing the Rabbit, a small European hatchback that was refined to incorporate many of the features Americans wanted. The Rabbit was an immediate hit. It did not have the instant recognizability of the Beetle, but it benefited from the Beetle's reputation.

The decline of the Beetle in the United States was complete in 1981, when VW management removed it from sale in the American market. However, VW continued to produce and sell the car in Mexico and South America. These were strong markets for the car because the Beetle was ideally suited to developing economies, where simple and reliable transportation was more important than a long list of fancy accessories.

Although the original Beetle was a simple car, the New Beetle is not. As VW marketers began to develop the concept for the "New Beetle," they realized that affluent American consumers expected features such as air conditioning, stereo systems, and security features—as well as government-mandated safety items such as airbags and 5 mph bumpers. Clearly, the New Beetle would require a degree of complexity and sophistication that Dr. Porsche could never have imagined.

The product development process incorporated customers' reactions from auto shows around the world. The reaction to the Concept 1 was nearly uniform worldwide, so VW management knew they would have a winner if they could build a street vehicle that incorporated the looks of the Concept 1 with an affordable platform. They found that platform in the one they were developing for the Golf, Europe's most popular car. With a few modifications, a New Beetle body could be built over a Golf chassis. This eliminated much of the time and expense of developing a completely new automobile. The use of the Golf platform also made it possible for VW to bring the New Beetle to market more quickly.

Just four years after first showing the Concept 1, VW management unveiled the New Beetle at the 1998 North American International Auto Show. The response to the "real" car was overwhelming. During much of the show it wasn't even possible to get near the car because of the crowds.

Executives from competing auto producers were astonished at consumers' reaction to the car, and were even more concerned when they learned more about VW's marketing strategy. Pre-introduction guesses by the automotive media had suggested a price of $18,000 for the base car, but VW management priced the New Beetle at a low $15,200. This price included airbags, air-conditioning, power door locks, a multispeaker stereo system, tilt and telescoping steering, and many other attractive features. The automotive press in attendance at the unveiling applauded loudly when the price was announced.

Volkswagen marketers had crafted a very desirable new product that their dealers and customers were anxious to have. A promotional strategy was created to build enthusiasm for the car's official arrival in showrooms in the spring of 1998. Dealers were shown the car at a special party at Disney World in Orlando, Florida. There they not only got to drive the car, but also to participate in "Disney" style clinics on the attitudes and expectations of the New Beetle target market. Nostalgia was an important component of the target customers' feelings toward the car, but testing also revealed a broad demographic and psychographic appeal that included many young buyers who had never owned an older-style Beetle. The dealers thought that the 50,000 units scheduled for production the first year would not be enough to satisfy the demand, but they were hopeful that some of the visitors to their showrooms could be switched to other VW products. VW's product line included cars that were either more economical or more spacious depending on the customers' needs. Jeff Williams, a VW dealer, explained the problems and the excitement associated with the new car: "I'm sure we'll have trouble meeting the demand that seems to be in the market. The car is really exciting customers. I have one customer who's ordered one for his 19-year-old daughter. He hopes she can have as much fun with her car as he did with his Beetle 30 years ago."

1. How can VW use the popularity of the New Beetle to increase showroom traffic for its dealers?
2. What type of advertising would be most effective for the "nostalgia" segment?
3. What are the risks of only targeting the "nostalgia" segment?
4. What advertising strategies would be most effective with Generation Xers?
5. If consumers in North America want all the New Beetles that VW can produce, what global strategies might VW management use? Keep in mind the success that is predicted worldwide.

2 Royal Appliance Manufacturing Company: Dirt Devil*

"You've just arrived on campus for the fall semester at college. Whether you're in a dorm room, apartment, or a rented home, in no time at all the place is sure to be a mess. And, looking at your current roommate situation, you probably won't get much help with the cleaning. You can either live with the disorder or get a new roommate—the Dirt Devil RoomMate. This new, lightweight upright vacuum may very well be the best companion a college student could ever have."

So begins an August 1997 press release from Dirt Devil, a subsidiary of Royal Appliance Manufacturing Company. The once staid and boring vacuum cleaner industry now sees college and university students as an interesting, vital target market.

The Dirt Devil brand has been responsible, in large part, for this new-found excitement. New product introductions and a groundbreaking advertising campaign are the latest chapters in the story of arguably the oldest vacuum cleaner manufacturing company in the world.

The first Royal vacuum cleaners were made by the P.A. Geier Company of Cleveland, Ohio, in 1905. As was the case with home computer companies in the 1970s and 1980s, Royal has its roots in a backyard garage. The company grew quickly and moved from the garage to a large, four-story structure, where it produced vacuum cleaners, mixers, hair dryers, and washing machine units.

The core business of the P.A. Geier Company, however, continued to be vacuum cleaners. The industry's first hand-held vacuum, the Royal Prince, was introduced in 1937. The Geier company maintained its position in the vacuum cleaner industry until the firm was acquired in 1953 and renamed the Royal Appliance Manufacturing Company. The newly named organization was purchased by a group of employees in 1954 and moved to Highland Heights, Ohio, in 1969.

In 1984, Royal Appliance introduced another innovative product, the Dirt Devil Hand Vac, which was touted as a cleaner for couch cushions, stairs, and other hard-to-reach places. Between 1984 and 1997, its light weight, low price, and attractive red plastic body combined to create total sales of over 17 million units, making it the largest-selling hand vac in the world. Royal now claims over 95 percent brand name awareness of the Dirt Devil name (up from 4 percent in 1990 and 21

*This case and accompanying video script were prepared by Professor Douglas Hausknecht. He expresses appreciation to Thomas F. Sherer, who assisted in developing the case.

percent in 1992), and it now commands 42 percent of the American market for hand-held vacuums.

Of course, there have been some stumbles along the way. In 1990, Royal began to market Dirt Devil products throughout Europe and Great Britain. However, the European market did not take to the new products as well as Royal had hoped. And on the domestic front, expensive promotion did not deliver a focused, unified message to American consumers. For example, dispersed promotion efforts in the United States in 1991 included advertising on Paul Harvey's radio program and sponsorship of race cars on the Indy Car and NASCAR circuits. Because of problems such as these, performance began to dip. By 1995, mounting financial losses necessitated a change in company management and the sale of Royal's European operations. Royal's stock price at the end of 1995 was $2.50 per share, but it rebounded to $9 per share by the end of 1996—a year that saw $286 million in sales and $9.4 million in profit.

A revitalized Royal states its mission on its Web site: "The company's mission is to bring innovative household products to the marketplace and thrill customers. It strives to recognize the needs of its customers and supply them with quality products that solve their cleaning problems . . . The success of the company depends upon the continued introduction and promotion of new, innovative, high quality products" (www.dirtdevil.com).

This mission is associated with the Dirt Devil name, which is now used on virtually all of the company's consumer goods. The Royal brand name is reserved for high end, heavy-duty, mostly industrial products. Most manufacturing is contracted out, leaving only some assembly to be done at corporate-owned facilities. This structure allows for the versatility and flexibility needed to introduce and manage innovative products.

One of these new, innovative products is the Broom Vac. Launched in 1996, the Broom Vac was seen to be as creative as the original Royal Prince was at its debut. It also represented the type of newsworthy breakthrough that the Dirt Devil group needed. The Dirt Devil Broom Vac is a cordless, rechargeable broom that has a vacuum in the centre of the unit's bristles to suck up dirt and dust in seconds. It does a better job of sweeping, and the user needs only to empty the filter and dirt compartment when full instead of bending over a dustpan.

Traditionally, the vacuum industry's products are classified as canister, upright, stick, or extractor cleaners. Hoover, which is recognized as the industry leader, emphasizes middle- and upper-end canisters, uprights, and sticks, and has an overall American market share of 27 percent; Eureka is in second place at 22 percent. Royal's strategy of innovative designs and distribution through mass merchandisers has earned the company third place in the market and an 18 percent share.

But the industry doesn't know how to classify the Broom Vac. It is usually categorized as a stick vacuum by retailers and in industry sales figures, but it does not really fit in that market sector.

The development team at Dirt Devil was also concerned about how consumers would view the product. Would they perceive sufficient advantage over the usual broom and dustpan to pay a premium price? How much of a premium would they be willing to pay? Where would they want to purchase the product? How should the product be promoted? What should be the message?

In the past, Royal has distributed its products through independent vacuum cleaner dealers, regional retail chains, mass merchants, and electronic and discount stores. However, none of these was considered to be completely adequate for introducing a high-volume product that would require demonstration of its advantages.

The decision was made to introduce the Broom Vac using direct-response television advertising. This enabled Dirt Devil to control the demonstrations that were seen by prospective purchasers and to experiment with marketing variables. In test markets, variables such as price, shipping cost, and payment options were manipulated. A $50 price point was selected for the direct-response introduction. As the product moved into regular retail channels, this price was expected to be retained throughout the first year of sales.

In order to demonstrate the product fully, a two-minute infomercial was developed. The longer format allowed for a more complete explanation of the features and advantages. Dirt Devil and its advertising agency took pains to produce a high-quality infomercial to counter consumers' possible negative stereotypes of this advertising form. The infomercials concluded with toll-free telephone numbers and shipping information.

Most of the infomercials aired during lower-cost daytime and late-night hours. This provided added cost efficiency in the media purchase. Later, 15-second lifts (excerpts) from the infomercial were aired during prime time for the retail launch of the product.

At first, retailers were concerned that direct-response TV ads would just compete for their customers, but that did not happen. Dirt Devil's retailers found that customers came in looking for the product that they had seen on television. This exposed consumers to the Dirt Devil displays, which featured bright, colourful packaging and plenty of product information. Retailers found that sales volumes were enhanced and that customers required less "selling effort."

Retailers were also encouraged to use special shelf or floor displays of the product. Additionally, some retailers used newspaper inserts or other retail advertising in which Dirt Devil participated on a cooperative advertising basis. Eventually, as the original Broom Vac diffused throughout the market, retailers discounted the product from its original $50 price point.

As 1996 drew to a close, Dirt Devil was poised to once again agitate the industry. This time the shock would come not from a product innovation, but rather from attention-getting communication. The grungy, boring, mature vacuum cleaner industry was to be represented in the showcase of American advertising—the Super Bowl.

On January 26, 1997, Dirt Devil aired three 15-second spots during the Super Bowl. Each spot highlighted a different product: the Broom Vac, the Ultra Hand Vac, and the Ultra MVP upright vacuum. This was the first Super Bowl exposure not only for Royal, but for any vacuum cleaner.

The commercials featured these products acting as "dance partners" with the late Fred Astaire. The ad campaign, designed by Cleveland advertising agency Meldrum and Fewsmith, achieved several technical breakthroughs in its execution.

Although requested many times in the past, Fred Astaire's image had never been licensed to market any product. An agreement was reached with Astaire's widow based, in part, on the fact that actual dance footage would be used and that Mr. Astaire would not be seen as verbally endorsing any product. In fact, he does not speak in any of the commercials.

Why use Fred Astaire? In his films, Astaire often danced with props. Atomic Films SME of Los Angeles created the movie magic that substituted Dirt Devil products for the props originally used in the films *Royal Wedding* (1951) and *Easter Parade* (1948). The message to be communicated was that using Dirt Devil products could make cleaning seem effortless, even fun!

Royal Appliance and its ad agency felt that the campaign needed to be both attention-getting and entertaining in order to be successful. Happily, it was both! Independent tests immediately following the Super Bowl credited the Dirt Devil commercials with achieving good brand name recall (fifth overall among Super Bowl advertisers) and excellent recall of celebrity/brand-name pairing (second among the advertisers using this technique). Separate research found the Astaire commercials finishing number one for correct sponsor identification and celebrity association with the brand. The performance was particularly notable since the Dirt Devil brand had relatively little exposure time (45 total seconds) compared to the other advertisers with higher-ranked recall scores (ranging from one to four minute on-air times). The Bruzzone Research Company, which has extensively studied Super Bowl advertising since 1992, concluded that the Dirt Devil spots were "noticed by more people per dollar investment in airtime than anything we've seen in the past six years."

The commercials were also well received by the broadcasting and advertising industries. *Advertising Age* and other trade outlets gave favourable exposure and reviews. In addition to the 130 million plus Super Bowl viewers, the commercials were shown and/or described on *Entertainment Tonight, CBS Evening News, NBC Today Show, Good Morning America* (ABC), and *Dateline NBC,* and in over 200 additional television stories and 1,100 newspaper and magazine articles.

Concurrently, retail insert advertising was increased. Mr. Astaire was featured in the print advertising as well as in retail display materials and on product packaging. Retailers were given advance notice of the campaign so that they could be prepared with adequate stock and have the option to participate in cooperative advertising. In most states, a Dirt Devil free-standing insert (FSI) also promoted a sweepstakes with a $1 million grand prize. Finally, positive publicity was generated when Mrs. Astaire announced that the campaign was the first outcome of a joint effort by the Astaire estate and Dirt Devil to sponsor the Arthritis Foundation. The "ease of use" benefit delivered by Dirt Devil's products was a natural linkage to the cause (arthritis). Royal executives, for their part, promised a redoubled effort to be responsive to the needs of consumers with arthritis in the design of new and modified products.

During 1997, some of these new products were tested and launched. The Mop Vac was introduced in April as a natural extension of the Broom Vac. With the Mop Vac, consumers could clean up by releasing a cleaning solution where needed from a container on the mop handle, scrubbing, then vacuuming the fluid through a squeegee to leave a clean, dry, streak-free floor. This new household tool was also introduced using direct-response advertising, at a $100 price point. The retail roll-out was to follow in time for Christmas shopping in the fall.

Other products flesh out the Dirt Devil line, ranging from two old-fashioned carpet sweepers (using only rollers and brushes, no electricity required) to a new Broom Vac Extra (more suction and more dirt capacity than the original). Two wet/dry vacuums also are available, both featuring a detachable leaf blower (when the suction motor detaches from the storage "tank"). This foray into the outdoors was followed late in 1997 with the Dirt Devil Pick-up. This is a plastic wheelbarrow that was test marketed via direct-response television. Its unique feature is a lift-and-load wheel mechanism that allows the container to be flush to the ground for loading and unloading, then lift up to 400 pounds. The pick-up also includes a front trap door that makes the wheelbarrow easy to empty. Another non-vacuum product that was tested, this time without advertising, was a rug cleaner spray. Dirt Devil Carpet Stain Remover was marketed in Wal-Mart stores without manufacturer advertising beyond point of sale.

With all of these products and more on the way, it is no wonder that the Royal Appliance Manufacturing Company's well-known tagline boasts, "Nothing escapes the power of a Dirt Devil!"

1. Describe Dirt Devil's pricing strategy for its recent product introductions.
2. Explain how Dirt Devil integrated its marketing mix in the introduction of the Broom Vac.
3. Was the use of Fred Astaire in television commercials a good idea?

4. What kinds of products might Dirt Devil introduce next?
5. What problems might arise with retailers if Dirt Devil continues to expand its product line beyond basic floor care?

3 Marketing in the Hardwood Industry*

Logs cut from hardwood forests are an important raw material used by many domestic and foreign producers. Unlike pine and other softwoods, which are used mostly for general construction, the demand for oak, black walnut, black cherry, white ash, maple, and other hardwoods derives from consumer demand for high-value products such as hardwood furniture, cabinets, flooring, millwork, and moldings. When properly finished, hardwoods offer a finish that is both durable and beautiful. The wood is also very strong, so even pieces that do not have a perfect appearance are well suited for making frames of chairs, sofas, and other furniture that are covered with various upholstery materials.

Hardwood forests cover many of the rural areas of the eastern United States—areas where there is often little other industry. Thus, the forest products industry is important to economic development, and to the employment and quality of life of people who live and work in these areas.

Unfortunately, that potential for economic development is not always achieved. A key reason for this is that many of the firms that harvest logs do not focus on any particular target market or specific customers. Rather, they just see the market opportunity in terms of the products they have always produced: hardwood logs or perhaps "green" roughsawn lumber cut from the logs. As a result, they sell a commodity product to distant customers who view logs from one supplier as like all of the others on the market and simply purchase logs at the lowest price.

Under this production-oriented, commodity approach, the hardwood produced in rural regions of the United States has usually been shipped to other regions—including foreign countries—before the wood is processed into intermediate and finished products. But when the wood is sold and shipped out of the region as an unfinished commodity, the profit opportunities—and associated employment—relevant to the secondary processing are exported as well.

Historically, in this commodity-market environment, successful producers were those who could operate with the lowest total cost. The major cost areas are raw material (lumber), labour, any processing that is done, transportation, and, of course, any marketing-related expenses. Small- and medium-sized producers are at an inherent disadvantage in this competitive, cost-oriented environment. They cannot achieve economies of scale because they can't spread their overhead expenses over a large number of units produced. As a result, there is little way for them to obtain a competitive advantage in production or distribution.

Some hardwood producers, including some smaller ones, were able to improve sales and profits—in both the United States and international markets—by differentiating their offerings with higher-quality products and service. For example, firms that worked to keep lumber dry and clean were better able to meet the needs of some customers. Further, some customers appreciated supplier firms that did a good job of sorting and grading different types of woods. And some suppliers focused on supplying species of wood that were desirable but less readily available.

In spite of such efforts, in the past most hardwood from American producers was just sold as a commodity in a very competitive market. However, some people in the hardwood industry are applying marketing concepts to help change this situation. They are focusing attention on ways to expand the market for existing hardwood products. They are also trying to identify markets with specific needs so that they can increase the value added to the hardwood lumber—by producing finished or semiprocessed products—before it is shipped out of the region where the trees are cut.

These efforts are having an effect. Some companies have found markets for hardwood-based composite materials for use as beams, columns, or rafters in building construction. Traditional materials for structural framing include softwood lumber and nonrenewable resources such as steel and aluminum. These structural hardwood composites are manufactured by breaking lower-quality hardwood logs into small pieces such as strands, flakes, or thin sheets of wood (veneer) and reforming the pieces into large members with names like "parallel-strand lumber" or "laminated veneer lumber" for the construction market. By finding market opportunities for structural hardwood composites, companies add value by using small or poorly formed logs, less desirable hardwood species, and sometimes even the hardwood waste from other industrial processes. Development of value-added markets for structural hardwood composites also has resulted in job creation and economic development in rural, forested areas.

However, producing structural hardwood composites is just one way to meet customer needs that were not previously being satisfied. An increasing number of customers want to buy kiln-dried boards rather than green lumber that isn't immediately ready to use for their own production purposes. So, many firms that cut and sell hardwood are taking the step of adding value to their product by doing the kiln-drying process. But numerous other opportunities to add value still exist. To uncover them, American hardwood suppliers are asking basic

*This case and the script for the accompanying video were prepared by Thomas G. Ponzurick and James P. Armstrong.

questions like: What are the needs of different customers in the broad product-market for hardwood? Who are these customers and where are they located? What kind of hardwood products—beyond the commodity lumber we've sold in the past—do they want? What are the opportunities to differentiate what we sell and add more value to our product through additional processing that meets the needs of specific target segments? How do we go about finding the answers to these questions?

One opportunity for expanding both the market and value-added product opportunities lies in the area of international exports. Prior to 1980, many firms that supplied hardwood ignored the export market. Domestic demand was sufficiently large to sustain growth and profitability. However, as domestic demand softened and competition grew more intense, American suppliers began to rethink entry into the international marketplace. In the last decade, efforts to market hardwood products to foreign markets have expanded significantly and the value of exported hardwood products has increased substantially.

Despite some recent success, there is still a vital need for more American suppliers to adopt the marketing concept, especially in targeting the export marketplace. Currently, international buyers are focusing most of their attention on the higher-grade hardwood products. But growth of sales and profits from exporting will depend on the American industry's ability to find markets for more of their available product inventory—including lower grades and species of hardwood. In fact, finding markets for value-added products may be the best way to improve sales of the lower grades and species. This would not only result in more efficient and profitable use of hardwood resources, but also could reduce costs by improving economies of scale in production.

However, the question that should be uppermost in marketers' minds is this: What do these customers want in the way of hardwood products? To answer this question, one must first determine the needs of these international buyers. In the case of American hardwood suppliers, Canadian buyers are currently the largest market for these products.

Most of the Canadian firms that import American hardwood to Canada are concentrated in a few geographic areas: over 75 percent are located in either Ontario or Quebec. Much of the imported lumber is purchased by Canadian manufacturers, who use it to produce their own products, including furniture, cabinets, hardwood flooring, and molding and millwork for the construction industry. However, these customers account for only about 31 percent of American imports. Canadian wholesalers, especially brokers and agents, account for more than half of the Canadian hardwood lumber purchased from American sources. Many of these intermediaries specialize in international sales. In fact, nearly 20 percent of all American hardwood lumber imported by Canada is subsequently resold and exported to Europe—usually after some value-adding activities such as grading, sorting, repackaging, and additional product processing.

Red oak, hard maple, and white oak are the principal hardwood species that Canadian customers import from the United States. However, there are also markets for some species of lesser value, including soft maple and yellow poplar.

All types of lumber are graded according to quality, and this grading is important to Canadian buyers, who have different hardwood needs. About 70 percent of the total volume of hardwood lumber purchased by Canadian firms is the higher-quality Number 1 Common grade or better. The other 30 percent of lumber imported is graded as Number 2 Common or lower. Firms that purchase the lower grades of lumber are mostly flooring manufacturers, furniture manufacturers, and brokers.

Marketing research studies indicate that Canadian hardwood lumber buyers are *relatively* satisfied with the quality of products and services now being provided by American suppliers. However, the research reveals that suppliers could enhance customer satisfaction and their competitive advantage by improving their product quality through more accurate grading and reporting of moisture content as well as by providing cleaner and straighter lumber. Buyers would also like to see better distribution customer service from American suppliers. This includes improving the reliability of lumber supplies and reducing order cycle time—that is, the time from when a customer orders lumber until it is delivered. And of course, organizational buyers are always interested in competitive pricing.

Importantly, the research also shows that over one-third of the firms that import hardwood lumber from the United States are potentially interested in purchasing finished hardwood parts from American suppliers. Examples in the area of finished hardwood parts include parts for making furniture, doors, stairways, and railings. Organizations showing an interest in these finished products include importers, export brokers, and manufacturers of various hardwood products. These results indicate that there may be a good opportunity for American suppliers of hardwood products to custom produce such parts for specific customers. Yet it is still unknown how substantial this opportunity may be—how eager Canadian buyers may be to purchase value-added finished hardwood products, and at what prices. To begin to answer these questions, American suppliers need to determine the types and specifications of the finished hardwood products desired by individual buyers. This will require that supplier firms do more marketing research or have more direct personal selling contact with buyers for specific firms than has been typical in the past. Alternatively, working with these customers may require closer relationships—partnerships—with intermediaries who can help producers with some of the required marketing functions.

It appears that American hardwood firms face a variety of possible opportunities to expand sales and improve profits. Export markets, including Canada, appear to offer greater potential than has been captured. Further, some of the opportunities are ones that focus on the value-added products that have the potential to foster economic development in rural areas of the United States, where such activities have in the past been limited. However, just having access to hardwood forests alone isn't enough to turn these opportunities into profitable business. Developing international markets for value-added hardwood products requires that individual supplier firms adapt their marketing strategies to marketplace needs. Producers need to identify specific target markets and understand the unique needs and buying behaviour of these markets. They also need to get beyond production-oriented thinking and develop whole marketing mixes to serve their target customers. That means figuring out what type of products and services to offer. It also means making decisions about how to price specific offerings, because a firm that is doing something unique for its customers won't just face perfect competition and a price that is set by the market. A firm that does a good job with this marketing strategy planning has the potential to satisfy some target customers very well—and in the process gain a sustainable competitive advantage. And, of course, as more firms do that they will not only make better profits, but also contribute to the economic development of the areas in which they operate.

1. Why is it important for firms that produce and supply hardwood to adopt the marketing concept?
2. What are some of the ways hardwood products can be adapted to meet value-added market needs?
3. In what ways is the marketing strategy different for hardwood suppliers who focus on a specific target market than for firms that just sell roughsawn logs or green lumber in the commodity market?
4. What are some of the potential target markets for American hardwood suppliers selling to the Canadian market? Which marketing mix variables are likely to be most important to the target markets you have identified?

4 Harley-Davidson Motor Company*

Somewhat like the mythical Phoenix, which arose from its own ashes, Harley-Davidson has staged a remarkable business comeback, from the brink of bankruptcy in 1981 to more worldwide demand than it can satisfy in the 1990s.

It all began in 1903 when Bill Harley and the three Davidson brothers started the company because they thought there was a market for a motor-driven bicycle. Their first model featured a 3.9 horsepower engine and a single-belt drive. They sold only three of those cycles. However, by 1908, when they introduced a 7 horsepower, 45-degree V-twin engine—the first of its kind—sales were up to 150 units.

Harley continued to prosper and grow until 1933, when the Depression cut sales to 6,000 units. However, during World War II Harley kept busy supplying bikes for the troops, and then after the war the company introduced its classic Hydra-Glide model. When the Indian Motorcycle Company went out of business in 1953, Harley was left as the sole manufacturer of motorcycles in the United States.

Throughout the 1960s the only serious competition that Harley faced came from imported British bikes with brandnames like BSA, Triumph, and Norton. But by the 1970s the competitive environment had changed. Japanese producers entered the American market and quickly built a following for their light and medium-weight cycles—the weak point in Harley's product line. Honda's ad campaign, with its "You meet the nicest people on a Honda" slogan, attacked Harley's bad-boy image and helped expand the market as it pulled in a new type of motorcycle rider.

In 1969, AMF (American Machine and Foundry) acquired Harley Davidson, hoping to take advantage of the growing market. And AMF's timing was good. By 1974, total American motorcycle sales had soared to 1.1 million as the key owner group—14 to 24 year olds—rose from 27 to 41 million. Eager buyers gave Harley a 78 percent share of the heavy-weight market.

Yet as AMF nearly tripled the output of Harleys in the 1970s, the founding families lost control of product quality. Harley's reputation suffered as its bikes became less dependable and more prone to oil leaks and breakdowns. And sales slipped fast as Japanese competitors stole Harley's customers by introducing heavy-weight cycles that were more reliable and technically sophisticated.

By 1980, Harley's share of the market for heavy-weight cycles had dwindled to only 30 percent, and the company was facing financial ruin. A 1981 leveraged buyout of the firm by a group of Harley executives marked a turning point—and the beginning of a new strategy and multifaceted comeback plan.

First they attacked the quality problems that had resulted in lost customers. With a loan of $100 million, they improved Harley's facilities and production processes. They also adopted statistical controls and employee involvement programs to improve quality. And they designed quality into their product line by creating cycles powered with a new V-twin engine developed for improved reliability. At the same time, management brought costs under control by downsizing the organization, cutting executive salaries and perks, and developing closer relationships and contracts with fewer suppliers. They also cut inventory expense by copying their Japanese competitors' just-in-time delivery approach.

Harley also worked to strengthen its relationships in the distribution channel and the quality of its dealers. For example, the company worked with dealers to modernize their showrooms and service facilities and to improve sales training.

*This case and the script for the accompanying video were prepared by Phillip B. Niffenegger.

In 1983, Harley charged its Japanese competitors with dumping cycles at predatory prices. And in response to a request from Harley's management, the U.S. government imposed a five-year tariff of 49 percent on imported motorcycles. The tariffs gave Harley a significant price advantage over Japanese producers.

Harley's sales improved quickly as all of these changes took effect. By 1987, its share of the big bike segment was up to 45 percent. In fact, Harley was strong enough that it asked the government to drop the protective tariffs a year early.

To build closer relationships with customers, Harley executives started a Harley Owners Group (HOG). Local HOG clubs across the United States have proved to be very popular. The company keeps HOG members involved with a *Harley* magazine and by sponsoring weekend rallies around the country, often coupled with free concerts featuring groups like ZZ Top. To stay in closer touch with their customers, Harley executives circulate among bikers at the rallies and solicit their suggestions and complaints.

The local HOGs now have over 250,000 owner-members. Harley's marketing research shows that a typical Harley owner is 38 years old and has a household income of $53,000. Sixty percent are married, about 30 percent have a college or university degree, and most (95 percent) are male. A surprising number are affluent professionals—doctors, lawyers, and the like. The Harley owners in this segment are nicknamed "Rubbies"—short for rich urban bikers. The Rubbies view their Harleys and the weekend HOG events as a way to express their individuality and as an escape from weekday pressures. To reinforce these attitudes, Harley advertising focuses not just on its' cycles but on the whole Harley lifestyle.

Harley has also been aggressive in expanding overseas, especially in the big Japanese and European markets. In fact, about 30 percent of Harley's total production is exported. To promote export growth, the company encourages overseas HOGs, publishes *Harley* magazine in foreign languages, and stages beer and band fests that are adapted to the local culture.

With all of these changes in marketing strategy, Harley's sales rose steadily, and by 1992 it had a 63 percent share of the superheavy-weight category. However, in 1993 and 1994 there was more demand than Harley could supply and Harley's share actually dropped slightly (to 56 percent). Even now, most dealers sell out their allocation of cycles by six months into the year. As a result, customers face a waiting list to buy one of the pricey bikes, which sell in the $6,000 to $19,000 range in the American market.

Despite pressure from dealers to increase the number of Harleys available to sell, Richard Teerlink—Harley-Davidson's CEO—has allowed only modest production increases at the two American plants, and he has refused to open overseas plants. He maintains that limited production is necessary to keep quality high, and he is determined that Harley not repeat the mistakes of the late 1970s when the company got sloppy with success and allowed quality and customer satisfaction to slip. Further, some observers think that the deliberate shortage of Harleys helps to maintain their exclusive image and high prices. It may also make buying a bike a better investment for customers; if an owner keeps a bike long enough, its resale value is often greater than the original price.

The combination of eager customers and high prices helps explain why Harley continues to rack up successive years of double-digit increases in sales and profits. In 1994, sales of 95,800 units resulted in profits of $163 million—a far cry from Harley's brush with bankruptcy in 1980.

Harley and its dealers are now putting more emphasis on sales of parts and accessories, because many owners want to express their individuality by customizing their bikes. These lines represent over 20 percent of the motorcycle division revenues. Part of the revenue comes from Harley's MotorClothes apparel line. Each year the firm sells millions of garments bearing the famous Harley trademark—and non-bikers make nearly 70 percent of those purchases.

1. How has Harley adjusted its marketing mix to meet the needs of its target customers? Be specific and consider both the nature of the target market and Harley's strategy decisions with respect to each of the 4Ps.
2. How have various aspects of the external market environment affected Harley's strategic planning over the years?
3. Japanese motorcycle companies still lead in sales of motorcycles in the light and medium-weight category. Should Harley develop a new strategy—concurrent with what it's already doing—to compete better in that market? Explain your logic.
4. What challenges do you think Harley faces as it moves to increase sales in international markets? How can it best address these challenges?
5. Should Harley increase its production capacity so that it can supply its dealers with more 'cycles and reduce the time customers must wait to get a new cycle? Explain.

5 Briggs & Stratton Corporation*

Briggs & Stratton is the world's largest producer of air-cooled gasoline engines for outdoor power equipment, mainly for lawn mowers. The company designs, manufactures, markets, and services these products, which are sold as components to original equipment manufacturers (OEMs) in 85 countries.

Steve Briggs and Harry Stratton started the company in 1909 to produce a six-cylinder, two-cycle engine similar to one Briggs had developed a few years earlier as an

*This case and the script for the accompanying video were prepared by Roger C. Shoenfeldt.

engineering student in college. The engine turned out to be too expensive to mass produce, so the partners turned their attention to designing and producing electrical parts for automobiles—including switches, starters, and regulators.

Later, B&S acquired the patent for the Motor Wheel—a gasoline engine designed to fit on a bicycle. It was a market success, and ultimately proved to be a good way to power several other types of vehicles. In some parts of Asia it was even used on rickshas.

To build on the success of the Motor Wheel, B&S looked for new markets for engines. Its search led to the development of a stationary utility engine for use on such products as garden cultivators and reel-type mowers. Before utility companies brought electricity to rural parts of the United States, these B&S engines even powered refrigerators, milking machines, and elevators.

After World War II, the booming American economy, the shift of population to the suburbs, and the growth of leisure time prompted new consumer interest in lawn and garden equipment. B&S saw this growth opportunity and shifted its focus to producing motors for the lawn mower manufacturers who served that market. But B&S didn't just try to push engines it was already producing.

At that time, most power mowers used two-cycle engines; their light weight made mowers easy to push. However, two-cycles weren't reliable and needed a mix of gas and oil, which was inconvenient for consumers. Four-cycle engines like the ones B&S produced were very reliable, but they were made from cast iron and very heavy. Marketing people at B&S realized that consumers wanted *both* reliability and light weight, so the firm designed a new lawn mower engine from aluminum alloy.

Over time, the Briggs & Stratton name has become almost synonymous with the lawn mower. Top producers such as Toro, Snapper, and John Deere proudly proclaim in their ads that their mowers are powered by Briggs & Stratton engines. In fact, Briggs & Stratton is often the most prominent brand name on the mower, even though the engine is just a component. The Briggs & Stratton name helps sell the mowers because it means quality, reliability, and performance to consumers. Because of this reputation—and consumer demand—many retailers won't sell a mower unless it uses a Briggs & Stratton motor.

Early in the 1980s, B&S faced a serious competitive threat. A shift in international exchange rates made Japanese products less expensive in the United States and other parts of the world. This gave Japanese motorcycle producers a pricing edge to expand into the market for small engines. Because B&S was the leading producer of small engines, any competitive inroads would be at its expense.

Marketers at B&S realized that in order to keep competitors from carving up its market, they would need to fine-tune the firm's offerings for specific market segments. A starting point for that effort was to develop new product lines—actually, whole marketing strategies—for each type of need rather than just trying to get economies of scale by serving bigger, but heterogeneous, product-markets. B&S invested $250 million to develop carefully targeted new products, build new plants, and develop new processes to improve quality and reduce costs.

B&S's new-product development effort for specific segments cut short the Japanese invasion, and increased customer satisfaction and brand loyalty. That put B&S in a better position to deal with another change—a big shift in the channel of distribution for lawn mowers. In the past, most consumers bought lawn mowers from independent lawn and garden equipment dealers. However, over time, mass merchandisers have taken away almost all of that business. In fact, five of the largest retail chains now account for half of all the lawn mowers sold in the United States, and about 80 percent of B&S's lawn and garden equipment sales are through mass merchandisers.

This concentration of purchasing power has given the big retail chains new clout in the channel of distribution. Retail buyers pressure lawn mower producers to keep costs and prices low; and the producers in turn expect B&S to keep its prices in check. While this has probably reduced the price premium that the B&S brand commands, it hasn't eliminated it. Retailers know that consumers want lawn mowers with B&S engines. So brand loyalty by final consumers gives B&S an advantage in negotiations with its producer-customers. Even so, the squeeze on profit margins throughout the channel—and intense competition—means that B&S must continue to find better ways to meet customers' needs if it is to maximize market share and earn attractive profits. And for B&S, developing innovative new products has long been the key to meeting needs better. Its skill in this arena is illustrated by its success in developing a 4 horsepower motor to fill a gap in its product line.

In 1993 B&S had four main lines of lawn mower engines. B&S's Classic 3.5 horsepower engine was at the low end of the price range, and it was found on mowers priced at about $99. As the name implies, this reliable model has been popular for many years. If a customer wanted a bit more power and a mower that took less pulling effort to start, B&S's 3.75 hp Sprint engine was available on mowers selling for about $119. For consumers who wanted an easy-starting engine that quietly conquered even the thickest grass, the Quantum 5.0 hp Plus line was the choice, on a mower that cost from $160 up to $500. Finally, B&S offered a top-of-the-line Diamond Plus model with about 6.0 hp, unique European styling, and all the "bells and whistles." A customer who had to ask how much it cost probably couldn't afford it.

In spite of multiple models in each of these lines, B&S did not have a good 4 hp mower engine. Yet, there was a clear market for one. B&S's main competitor, Tecumseh, proved that. Its 4 hp engine was a market leader. And B&S needed to develop a new engine if it wanted to compete for the segment of customers who wanted a 4.0 hp engine. To take customers away from Tecumseh, B&S marketers knew they needed to develop a cost-effective engine that was better than the Tecumseh model on all operating and performance criteria. Research also showed that styling was becoming an important purchase criteria for many customers—perhaps because that was the one difference in engines that consumers could see while shopping.

Although they had a clear idea of what the market wanted, marketing managers at B&S faced a real challenge. Creating a superior new engine wouldn't do much good if lawn mower producers and retailers didn't know about it, and *the* time and place to introduce an important new lawn and garden product was at a big, national trade show that was less than a year away. If they missed that date, they'd effectively lose a year. So getting the new product to market fast—without making costly mistakes—was critical.

To speed up development and also reduce costs, B&S designers created a contemporary, aerodynamic look with a computer-aided design (CAD) system; the tooling of the parts—direct from the computer drawings—was very fast. Further, B&S engineers used standard parts from other B&S engines when they could. This helped to control costs, reduce development time, and cut inventory requirements. And later it would make after-the-sale service easier and faster. As a result of efforts like these, the new product went from the concept stage to production in about nine months, in time for the trade-show deadline.

While the new product team was developing the engine, B&S's marketing people had other work to do. To emphasize the new engine's distinct identity, they used an individual brand name, Quattro. They also developed promotional materials to use at the trade show, and started work on ads and other cooperative promotional materials so they would be ready for producers and retailers to use when the Quattro started to appear on lawn mowers in retail stores.

The B&S salespeople also started to call on their top OEM customers. Besides explaining the advantages of the new Quattro motor and answering questions, they provided hundreds of sample motors. That made it possible for the producers to get a head start in creating prototypes of new mowers to show their retailer-customers. And, since the retailers have a big influence on the producer's purchase decisions, B&S salespeople also promoted the features of the new motor—and the pull appeal of the Briggs & Stratton name—to retail buyers.

The salespeople also explained the benefits of the B&S cooperative advertising arrangements and how they work. B&S provides co-op advertising allowances and materials to all of its OEM customers and to the retailers who sell B&S products.

As a result of all this front-end planning, the Quattro got off to a very successful start. In fact, customer reaction to the new engine's sleek appearance, power, and reliability were so strong that demand was double what B&S had forecast. By mid-1995, the company was hard pressed to keep up with demand.

That's one reason why during the first year B&S decided to focus its marketing for the Quattro primarily on the American market. It didn't make sense to spend money promoting the product in foreign markets if supply would be limited. However, exports account for 21 percent of all B&S engine and parts sales, and the Quattro isn't likely to be an exception to that pattern. When the time comes for the Quattro's international roll-out, some changes in the domestic marketing strategies may be required. For example, while lawn and garden equipment is important in nations with developed economies, in less-developed countries the Quattro is likely to be used for other types of applications—in agricultural, marine, and other commercial markets.

1. Are there any disadvantages to Briggs & Stratton's decision to hold off introducing its new Quattro engine in international markets? Explain.
2. What are the marketing implications for Briggs & Stratton of the fact that the American market for lawn mowers is in the market maturity stage?
3. Given that engines are such an important component in manufacturing lawn mowers, would it make sense for Briggs & Stratton to develop and market its own line of mowers? Explain.
4. Given B&S's ability to compete well with Japanese motorcycle producers when they tried to take market share away from its small engines, would it make sense for Briggs & Stratton to produce a small motorcycle—or perhaps a motorscooter—to market in India and in other countries where incomes are low but demand for personal transportation is increasing? Explain.

6 Papa John's International, Inc.*

From humble beginnings in a converted broom closet in the back of a Jeffersonville, Indiana, tavern in 1984, Papa John's has become America's fastest growing pizza chain.

Founder John Schnatter was just 21 years old in early 1984 when he began his first pizza venture. As a teenager, he had learned much about the art of creating a good pie through various jobs at a number of pizzerias. After graduating from Ball State University, John managed Mick's Lounge, a bar co-owned by his father in their hometown of Jeffersonville, Indiana. The bar was on the brink of bankruptcy. John implemented several pricing and marketing changes and began offering fresh pizza as an additional source of revenue.

"One night, I got a sledge hammer and tore down the closet to make an 8-by-10 foot kitchen, basically just enough for an oven," recalls Schnatter. The new product addition worked well. With an initial investment of

*This case and the script for the accompanying video were prepared by Phillip B. Niffenegger.

$1,600 for equipment and ingredients, he pounded out enough pizzas to save the lounge.

With bigger profits in mind, John leased a nearby storefront in 1985, which became the first Papa John's. By the following year, he had sold the first franchise.

Then, as now, the goal was to offer a high-quality pizza, priced to be an excellent value.

CEO John and his brother Chuck (senior vice-president) are of German-Irish descent and they like their pizza "with a sweeter sauce than most, I guess," says Chuck. They feel the most important element of a good pizza is the crust, so theirs is made with "a thinner, rather than a bready crust." And the pizzas are made with fresh dough, real mozzarella cheese, and sauce from fresh tomatoes, not concentrate.

To keep its profits up, Papa John's also follows a number of cost-containment approaches. Through its wholly owned commissionary system (PJ Food Service), Papa John's supplies fresh pizza dough, as well as food and paper products, to each restaurant twice weekly. Besides enabling the company to closely monitor and control product quality and consistency, Papa John's benefits from volume purchase discounts on the food and paper products. The four regional commissaries now in place will allow Papa John's to serve a total of 1,200 restaurants in the 20 states in which the company and its franchisees now operate.

A focused menu also allows Papa John's to maintain quality and control costs. It's limited to pizza, bread sticks, cheese sticks, and canned soft drinks. However, Papa John's provides a buttery "special garlic sauce"—for dipping pizza crust—and two pepperoncini peppers with each pie to heighten the perception of added value. Unlike its major competitors, who have added items like buffalo wings and new types of pizza, Papa John's is determined to continue its simplified menu. Says CEO Schnatter, "We will not be adding more menu items. We feel that if we do what we do better—and better than anyone else—then we will maximize profits." Adds the company president, J. Daniel Holland: "We've learned that if you're willing to do it right and do it consistently right and not lose your focus, you can be successful, no matter how many players are in a particular market."

Another cost-containment effort involves minimizing site costs. Most new Papa John's restaurants are built into existing buildings (in retail strip developments, for example) rather than in new, free-standing structures. And by emphasizing delivery and take-out sales rather than sit-down dining, the average size is kept down to 1,200 to 1,500 square feet (no dough-making machines required). "Pull In, Pull Out" is the norm in Papa John's. The red, green, and white decor emphasizes cleanliness more than coziness; there is no enticement to linger.

Both the company and its franchisees purchase equipment packages from the company's J-Town Equipment Division—which provides a cost-effective means of opening a restaurant. As a result, a new Papa John's restaurant can be capitalized for $125,000 to $150,000, which makes it easier to earn an attractive return on investment.

Finally, the employee training and incentive programs are structured to exemplify the Japanese-like principle of continuous improvement. All store managers and supervisors are required to complete a two-week training program at one of eight regional training centres. Store managers are trained and certified at every store position: order-taking, dough-slapping, pizza-topping, routing, and delivery. The company provides an on-site training crew three days before and after the opening of a franchisee's first two restaurants, and on-going supervision through company-employed franchise consultants. An employee stock purchase plan is also in place; employees who have been with the company for a year are awarded options to buy shares of the company's common stock. The company policy states: "We feel there is no limit to what can be accomplished when the right people are put in the right environment. We are dedicated to constant and never-ending improvement." Adds Schnatter: "It's like playing sports: Do you want an occasional excellent game, or a game of excellence every day? We strive for excellence every day."

Papa John's is headquartered in Louisville, a 15-minute drive from its broom closet beginnings. Its growth strategy is to cluster company-owned restaurants in regional markets, from Louisville to Orlando and Atlanta, which allows it to take advantage of distribution efficiencies from its commissaries in those areas. Targeted regional ad campaigns are run to maximize consumer awareness. Expansion takes place to fill in the circles surrounding the core markets while avoiding cannibalization of existing restaurant sales.

So far the strategy has worked well. In 1994, sales were up 81 percent to $89.2 million, with profits increasing 77 percent over 1993 to $7.2 million. Sales in the 133 company-owned restaurants were up to $670,000 (from $653,000 in 1993), about $200,000 above the average for Domino's and 10 percent over Pizza Hut's. The company and its franchisees have aggressive plans to open 525 new restaurants during 1995 and 1996. Meanwhile, Domino's profits for 1994 were up by 15 percent (to $31 million) while Pizza Hut's fell by 21 percent for the year.

Nonetheless, Schnatter is determined to avoid the pitfalls of overexpansion: "We'll build them one at a time; and as long as we can do them and do them well, we'll continue to grow. And if we can't, then we'll stop at that point and make sure we're building the company properly."

1. What factors account for Papa John's strong growth rate?
2. What are the potential advantages and disadvantages of Papa John's working with both company-owned restaurants and franchisees?
3. Should Papa John's follow the lead of Pizza Hut and Domino's and expand its menu as a way of attracting additional customers? Explain.

Cases

Guide to the Use of These Cases

Cases can be used in many ways. And the same case can be analyzed several times for different purposes.

"Suggested cases" are listed at the end of most chapters, but these cases can also be used later in the text. The main criterion for the order of these cases is the amount of technical vocabulary—or text principles—needed to read the case meaningfully. The first cases are "easiest" in this regard. This is why an early case can easily be used two or three times—with different emphasis. Some early cases might require some consideration of Product and Price, for example, and might be used twice, perhaps regarding product planning and, later, pricing. In contrast, later cases, which focus more on Price, might be treated more effectively *after* the Price chapters are covered.

In some of the cases, we have disguised certain information—such as names or proprietary financial data—at the request of the people or firms involved in the case. However, such changes do not alter the basic substantive problems you will be analyzing in a case.

1 Marketing a Web Site*

Designing commercial Web sites is a relatively simple business to enter with few competitive barriers preventing newcomers from giving it a try. After all, designers only really need a good computer, a proper software package, and a place to work. However, artistically and creatively motivated designers may find it somewhat difficult to find clients. For some potential clients, the issue may be whether they can afford the services; others may prefer to do the work internally rather than deal with an outside company.

Sandra MacDonald recently graduated with a degree in marketing after studying part-time for several years at a local university. This fitted well with her plans to be at home to raise her children, and now she was looking for ways to combine her interests in Internet Web site design and marketing. Recently she thought she had come across an ideal opportunity for starting up her own service.

While planning their children's summer activities, Sandra and her husband Tom began poring through the catalogues they had received from children's day and sleep-away camps. This was an annual ritual that involved their two children, David (11) and Nicole (14), as well as Sandra and Tom. Sandra would keep an eye open for pamphlets and newspaper advertising inserts that advertised camps, and she would buy a magazine or two that usually ran articles about camps and how to go about selecting one.

Her kids were experienced campers, having attended sleep-away camps since they were eight. Although they loved camp, their interests were changing and they wanted to consider a new choice for this year that offered more water sports. In particular, Nicole had become quite comfortable with water activities such as kayaking, boating, canoeing, windsurfing, and so forth.

It was while trying to identify and get more information about these sorts of camps that Sandra realized how useful a Web site with this camp information would be. She searched the Internet looking for camp directories, using search engines such as www.yahoo.com, but found it difficult to get local geographic information that was useful to her family. She noticed that many of the larger camps had their own Web sites and that some magazine-style Web sites which wrote about camps and family recreation sold advertising space on each Web page. This obviously provided a source of revenue for the Web managers, in addition to whatever they would charge the individual camps that were listed in their directories.

After investigating the cost of "renting" a large Web site space from a local Internet service provider, Sandra estimated that she would have to pay on average $100 per year for each camp listing. To get started, she would have to prepay $5,000 to the provider, for a volume discount on the site and her own Web name, which she decided would be www.canadian-children's-camps.com. All of her design work could be uploaded from her home to the service provider's computer, and users would be able to access the site from anywhere in the world at any time of day by entering the name she chose.

Now all she had to do was figure out how to design the Web site so that it would be an attractive and informative site for consumers to visit. She considered a magazine approach that would include articles about camping and follow a similar format that printed magazines used, as well as a "database" orientation that would allow users to enter criteria for searching camps they wanted more detailed information about quickly. In either case, revenue could be earned from the camps that would be profiled on the site as well as from advertisers who wanted to reach this particular target audience.

1. Develop a marketing plan that you would recommend to Sandra for launching the camp Web site to both camp advertisers and consumers who would use the service.
2. Create a sketch of the first page that users would find after arriving at Sandra's Web site.
3. What content would you provide about the camps, and how would you price your services? (Hint: How much does newspaper advertising cost? the Yellow Pages?)

*This case was written by Dr. Brahm Canzer, who at the time of its preparation was associated with John Abbott College and Concordia University.

2 Disco Jet Canada*

Keith Williams and Don Eisner were elated. They had recently returned from Davis, California, where they had acquired the Canadian rights to the VTOL (Vertical Take-Off and Landing) craft developed by Paul Moller. The aircraft promised to revolutionize amateur flying in the country. Powered by eight rotary Wankel engines, the nine-foot diameter disc looked like a flying saucer, which in fact it was.

Their preliminary calculations suggested a market potential of 14,000 units, based on the number of trained pilots in Canada. This number was increasing at a rate of 8 percent each year. Using these figures, they estimated sales of 1,120 units per year at $25,000 per unit for an annual volume of $28 million. On this reckoning, they expected to recover the $100,000 that it cost to acquire the Canadian rights to the product within one year. But as they talked to their consultant they were alarmed to hear him say that it might be some time before the project would take off.

*This case was written by Dr. Ken Blawatt, who at the time of its preparation was associated with Simon Fraser University as an Adjunct Professor at the University College of the Cariboo.

PRODUCT INFORMATION: THE DISCOJET

The Discojet is a vertical take-off and landing (VTOL) vehicle designed to combine the most attractive features of the helicopter and the light airplane. Successful flights of earlier test prototypes—together with wind tunnel tests, extensive computer-aided studies, and test bed data—have resulted in the design of a practical VTOL aircraft with low initial cost, ease of operation, inherent operator safety, and economical performance.

DISCOJET SPECIFICATIONS	
Cruise speed	165 mph
Top speed	200 mph
Rate of climb	2375 fpm
Hover ceiling	5000 ft. (OGE)
Absolute ceiling	15,500 ft.
mpg	16.5
Payload	425 lbs.
Gross take-off weight	1100 lbs.
Diameter	9′3″
Height	3′4″
Profile drag coefficient	.13
Fan loading	50 lb./ft.^{2}
Range	325 mi.
External noise level	82 dbA
Installed power	205 hp
Baggage volume	9.7 ft.^{2}

The performance data for the Discojet production prototype are derived from design studies and wind tunnel tests. Final performance data will be available only after the flight test program has been completed by mid 1999.

COST

Constructed 90 percent of lightweight Fibreglas (similar to the body of Chevrolet's Corvette), the Discojet incorporates a unique stability and control system. Eight identical self-contained thrust modules power the unit, which is made of a two-piece, inexpensive monocoque airframe. The engines used in the thrust modules are Wankel snowmobile engines, a model that has been certified for aircraft use by the German government. The combination of a moderately expensive computerized control and stabilization system, low-cost engines, and very inexpensive airframe results in an aircraft priced competitively with light aircraft sold on the market. Current cost projections indicate a retail price under $25,000 when production reaches 5,000 units.

EASE OF OPERATION

Pitch and roll control are the two degrees of freedom that are most difficult for the relatively untrained pilot to handle. The Discojet uses a highly redundant stabilization system that provides automatic pitch and roll control when used in conjunction with the thrust module design. Manual override is available in case of emergency. Normal pilot control is over the rectilinear motion (up–down, forward–backward, and sideways). Simulator studies have shown that controlling only this aspect of flight is relatively simple. Engine starting and operation is nearly identical to that of an automobile.

SAFETY

Any widely used VTOL aircraft must be able to deal easily and safely with engine failure. The Discojet uses multiple engines started and operated together, which are fed from a central redundant carburetor system. Failure of one engine or even two nonadjacent engines can be dealt with safely from any altitude. In addition, successful tests indicate that a backup system (parachute) can be provided to allow safe descent even if all engines fail.

ECONOMY

Because of their complexity, all previous VTOL aircraft have proven exorbitantly expensive to maintain. In addition, previous VTOLs have had high fuel consumption in cruise due to high drag, and in the hovering mode due to high fan loading. The Discojet, with its moderate fan loading and low drag coefficient, is able to attain an efficient balance between hover and cruise performance. It combines the cruising speed of the light plane with the hovering ability of the helicopter. Compared on the basis of the performance criteria—payload times speed/power required—the Discojet outperforms the helicopter above 80 mph and the light plane above 140 mph. The Discojet's simple mechanics, with its corresponding low maintenance, means that overall operating costs will be 70 percent less than the cost of operating a two-place helicopter with comparable performance.

COMPANY HISTORY

Discojet Corporation is the result of extensive research into a number of aspects of aerodynamics. The products have evolved as solutions to design problems encountered in a search for a practical VTOL aircraft.

Design work had been initiated on this aircraft as an extension of an earlier study at McGill University on a radial diffuser. Following extensive test-bed experiments and model work, construction of a full-size prototype was begun in Davis, California, in 1983.

The first test flight of Prototype I took place in the spring of 1985. Flights continued for two years, with many design changes and a complete engine retrofit. Prototype I, although bulky and expensive to build, provided invaluable data on ground effect, aerodynamic stability, and vehicle control. This prototype was capable of flying free of ground effect.

During the flight test phase of Prototype I, development work was started on a new design to surmount the size and construction complications of the first vehicle. In addition, an engine fail-safe characteristic was incorporated.

Prototype II flew successfully in mid-1980s. Even though limited engine power (60 hp) prevented flights free of ground effect, the tests did establish the feasibility of a compact, multiengine, stable VTOL aircraft. Prototype II was not ideal for mass production, however, because its rotor system was expensive and the airframe somewhat complicated.

FACILITIES

During the past three years, Discojet has grown into 10,000 square feet of floor space. But present facilities are not suitable for the long and sensitive FAA certification period that lies ahead. For that reason, the company has recently concluded leasing arrangements for space at an airport six miles from Davis. A new, 25,000-square-foot building is being designed, and the company expects to move into it by March 1999. It will include complete test facilities for the production prototype Discojet, with land and water take-off pads.

1. Outline the steps that are required in a market opportunity analysis for the Discojet in Canada.
2. What would the student suggest in the way of a research design?
3. Environmental factors are important in assessing the value of this opportunity. What are these? Comment on their impact on the venture.
4. What are the estimates for success of the new undertaking?

3 Blue Metropolis Magazine*

After working for *Saturday Night* in a senior managerial position and for several specialized magazines in the Canadian market, Sarah Kramer felt that she understood the publishing business as well as anyone. However, she was not completely sure that her decision to launch a new Canadian general-interest magazine fashioned after the internationally popular *New Yorker* was a correct one.

Blue Metropolis would publish articles on the arts, film, entertainment, politics, and business from a Montreal base and target sophisticated, urban business and professional people in households across Canada. These, she knew, were the consumers that most advertisers of cars, airline tickets, alcoholic beverages, non-alcoholic beverages, financial services, hotels, restaurants, theatres, films, cosmetics, and so on were interested in. Sarah felt that if she could put her creative talents to work along with the network of writers and producers she knew were available, she would be able to produce an attractive magazine of interest to this target audience.

Nonetheless, Sarah was still unclear about many business questions and decided to invest in some marketing research before going any further. This afternoon she was meeting with Matthew Braxton, a market researcher who specialized in media consulting. His general report on the publishing industry, which Sarah had purchased last month as part of the consulting contract, revealed the following:

- There were few competitors for this sort of magazine.
- People got most of their lifestyle news from TV, newspapers, and general magazines such as *Time* and *Macleans.*
- The closest competitor, *Saturday Night,* had a direct circulation of 60,000 plus another 250,000 through newspaper inserts in selected cities across Canada.
- Advertisers paid $5,000 per full-colour page in *Saturday Night,* and a 100-page issue generally contained 25 pages of advertising.
- More women than men were interested in this sort of magazine.
- The market was more likely to be made up of people over 35 years of age.
- Economies-of-scale studies showed that printing costs levelled off at $1/unit after 30,000 copies and that mailing costs were also $1/unit.

Sarah knew that many readers would be open to a new magazine, but was not confident that a Montreal-oriented magazine would work for readers in, say, Vancouver. She asked Matthew Braxton to research this point along with a more basic question of what sort of product content readers across Canada would be motivated to buy. Should the magazine contain local listings of cultural events or only do so through advertisements? She even considered the idea of a bilingual magazine that could attract both language markets across Canada, but wondered whether either or both markets might be "turned off" by that sort of presentation.

In addition, she needed to know whether the magazine should be published monthly or quarterly, what the newsstand price should be, and how she should go about building up distribution for subscribers.

Should she risk offending some readers by accepting tobacco and alcoholic beverage advertising, or jump right into the rising popularity of smoking—as demonstrated by the success of the American publication *Cigar Magazine*—by creating a special section of the magazine devoted to this lifestyle?

Matthew Braxton anticipated Sarah's concerns and presented her with a list of content items he intended to use during focus group interviews with potential consumers. If Sarah approved, he would be able to report

*This case was written by Dr. Brahm Canzer, who at the time of its preparation was associated with John Abbott College and Concordia University.

back to her on just what sort of magazine she should produce. Sarah was impressed with the detail of the survey and approved the plan.

1. Assume the role of Matthew Braxton and prepare a full marketing report for Sarah that addresses all of the questions discussed in the case. Conduct your own student focus-group research answering the questions presented in the case. You may also choose to ask other people outside your university.
2. Prepare a plan showing what you expect revenues and expenses to be as *Blue Metropolis* attempts to reach its targets for subscriptions and retail purchases for its first operating year. Present your plan in quarterly (three-month) segments and explain what marketing activities will be undertaken in each period. Remember, publishers generally try to cover production and distribution costs through subscription and retail sales, and to earn their profit from advertising revenue. Use this rule of thumb as a guide for estimating reasonable targets.

4 Starbucks Pouring Hot in Canada*

The battle in the Canadian specialty coffee market is heating up. The strength of this industry can be seen in the proliferation of coffee shops in recent years. Although only 4 percent of adult Canadians drank specialty coffees in 1994, this percentage doubled within a year, and the popularity of these premium-priced beverages remains quite strong. One of the new kids on the block is Seattle-based Starbucks. Since its entry into Canada in 1987, Starbucks has aggressively sought to increase its market share in large urban centres. Initially, Starbucks confined its operations to Vancouver; its success there motivated entry into other Canadian cities. In 1996, when the company planned its entry into the Toronto market, it stirred up considerable controversy when it attempted to acquire prime locations for its corporate-owned stores adjacent to existing Second Cup franchises. The casualties in this confrontation were neighbourhood cafes, and this resulted in considerable negative press for Starbucks. Nevertheless, the company has continued its penetration of the Canadian market by opening stores in Edmonton and Calgary. Observers are questioning whether this success will continue. What is it that sets Starbucks apart from the competition? Are such differences sustainable, or are they merely part of some fad?

How is it that Starbucks has been able to penetrate a market served by such well-known brands as Tim Hortons, Second Cup, A.L. Van Houtte, and Timothy's Coffees of the World? The specialty coffee shops in Canada differentiate themselves according to various aspects of coffee drinking. Tim Hortons' president, Paul House, identifies his company as being in the "snack occasion" business and adds that the growth segments are lunches and bagels. The focus of Second Cup is on street-level stores—takeout coffee bars in commuter stations, hospitals, and shopping malls. Van Houtte, primarily a wholesale distributor to supermarkets and a supplier of coffee machines in offices and institutions, operates a number of retail outlets. Paul-Andre Guillotte, president of A.L. Van Houtte, says that his establishment caters to 18–25-year-olds who are increasingly using coffee shops as meeting places. Van Houtte's customers view its coffee shops as young, hip places serving high-quality coffee. The focus for Timothy's Coffees of the World is on the standard cup of fresh-brewed coffee. While Starbucks offers espresso-based products such as caffe latte, caffe mocha, and cappuccino, some would argue that Starbucks' success is attributable to its ability to offer customers a total brand experience that extends beyond the consumption of a beverage. This process has involved a positioning of the company—its ideals and image—with various stakeholder groups: the community, its employees, and its customers.

Starbucks' ability to transform coffee into a lifestyle choice flows from its mission statement, which directs the company to a role of environmental leadership in all facets of its business. These words have been transformed into a variety of socially responsible actions, including sale of a reusable coffee tumbler designed to commemorate the 100th anniversary in 1997 of the YWCA in Vancouver. In 1996, Starbucks and the Hospital for Sick Children in Toronto forged a long-term partnership that resulted in Starbucks making an annual contribution to the hospital foundation and opening a Starbucks location in the hospital's lobby. Starbucks actively supports organizations that benefit children's welfare, AIDS outreach, and environmental awareness; is involved in a variety of community cultural events; and supports a variety of programs in Guatemala, Indonesia, Kenya, and Ethiopia—all coffee-growing countries. This protection of the environment can be seen within the individual stores, where "everything" that can be recycled is: from the cardboard butter patties to the used coffee grounds. Stale-dated coffee is donated to charitable organizations such as women's shelters.

The positive press that the company receives from such community involvement extends to its internal marketing efforts. Despite the recent unionization of workers at some Canadian locations, Starbucks is known for its progressive personnel policies and generous compensation packages. In a proactive move, Starbucks offered all employees, or "partners," the same wages regardless of whether they were unionized. The company's claim that it is in the "people development" business as much as the coffee business is evidenced by its training programs, in which partners are encouraged

*This case was prepared by Judith A. Cumby, Assistant Professor, Faculty of Business Administration, Memorial University of Newfoundland, as a basis for class discussion and is not intended to reflect either an effective or an ineffective handling of management problems.

to share their feelings about selling, about coffee, and about working for Starbucks. They are also encouraged to take personal responsibility for all aspects of their work, including the production of beverages to exact specifications and the encouragement of recycling and conservation wherever possible. Partners devote special attention to educating consumers about the explanations for Starbucks' Italian drink names, the necessity to buy new beans weekly, and the requirement to never let coffee stand for more than twenty minutes. The relationship marketing efforts between Starbucks and its partners have translated into annual staff, or "barista," turnover of 60 percent, compared with 140 percent for hourly workers in the fast-food business.

This affinity toward Starbucks is also felt by customers, 10 percent of whom visit the store twice a day; the average customer visits 18 times a month. The strength of such customer loyalty has provided the company with the luxury of using very little traditional advertising. Instead, the company has concentrated on creating an experience that customers are happy to promote. Starbucks devotees feel that the brand is defined as much by attitude as by products. It is Starbucks' treatment of its employees, the community, and the environment that has earned it respect with customers. This positive image is backed by premium products, including traditional specialty coffees and the new *Frappuccino,* a frozen coffee drink that is tremendously popular during the summer. Customers can buy Starbucks ice cream and bottled drinks in the supermarket. Some argue that the proliferation of brand extensions could serve to dilute the core concept.

What have other coffee companies been doing in the wake of Starbucks' aggressive marketing campaigns? Distribution is critical and has been extended beyond traditional retail outlets. There are Second Cup kiosks in all Borders bookstores in Canada, while Starbucks has opened outlets in Chapters bookshops. Second Cup coffee is served on all Air Canada flights, an alliance that accounts for 10 percent of the company's coffee sales in Canada. Second Cup and Tim Hortons operate franchises in hospitals. Tim Hortons coffee is available at over 1,100 company and franchise restaurants, many in rural locations, and through some Esso gas stations, and is promoted with the theme of "You've always got time for Tim Hortons." This is supplemented by the use of an emotional appeal in recent advertising campaigns in which the focus is on the unique role of Tim Hortons stores in the community. Lillian, age 86, is shown walking through Lunenburg, Nova Scotia, on her way to enjoying her daily cup of Tim Hortons coffee. Customers have found Lillian to be warm and charming—just the image that the advertising creators were looking for. Another advertisement includes a spot on Sammi, a dog from Saint John, New Brunswick, who picks up her master's coffee from the local drive-through window. The use of such true stories is quite popular with customers in Atlantic Canada.

There are those who question whether the specialty coffee market will continue to grow or whether it is just a fad. Supporters maintain that the proliferation of coffee houses reflects changes in social views, particularly with young adults. Both Starbucks and Second Cup hope to capitalize on the profitability associated with catering to the time-strapped boomer by producing, selling, and playing CDs designed to attract people to the stores. Starbucks even maintains designers and architects in-house who adapt the mellow urban look to a given site and customer demographics. The creation of such a comfortable environment to complement the eclectic product offerings and corporate image is proving to be quite popular with Canadians in urban centres. Will this success continue in other parts of the country? Is it even sustainable over the long run in existing centres? What changes will be necessary over the next few years?

1. Who are the target markets for Starbucks? How do they differ from those of other coffee shops?
2. What is Starbucks' competitive advantage? Is it sustainable?
3. How is the company positioned? Illustrate this with a positioning map that reflects the major players in the coffee market.
4. Does the proliferation of Starbucks' brand extension dilute the core concept and negatively affect the company's positioning and competitive advantage?

5 Parker's Classics*

Philip Parker is the proprietor of Parker's Classics, a men's wear store with three branches in Vancouver. During the last few years Parker's Classics had been experiencing a slight decline in sales. Philip felt that this was attributable to a high level of competition in the Vancouver market. In addition, Holt Renfrew and other upscale stores in the suburbs of Vancouver, together with Eaton's and the upscale Bay in downtown Vancouver, presented a major challenge.

Philip had over 20 years of experience in the men's wear market, having worked in some of Canada's leading department stores for several years. He had also had a two-year stint with a French designer of men's wear. In 1985, at the age of 46, he decided to be his own boss and opened the first of the Parker's Classics stores in the west end of Vancouver. Within four years he had three more stores: one in Vancouver, one in West Vancouver, and one in Coquitlam, a Vancouver suburb.

Parker's Classics quickly established a name for itself in upscale men's wear. Philip prided himself on being

*This case was prepared by Dr. Ramesh Venkat of Saint Mary's University as a basis for classroom discussion and is not meant to illustrate either effective or ineffective marketing techniques. Copyright 1995. Used with permission.

able to completely dress an upscale man. Parker's carried a wide range of clothing from casual to semi-formal and formal wear. In addition, the stores had a large selection of male accessories and colognes. Parker's carried such well-known names as Hugo Boss and Armani, as well as its own Parker's Classic suits, specially designed by a New York-based designer.

Growing competition and a slowing economy in the early 1990s had put a stop to the frenzied growth that Parker's experienced in the late 1980s. Sales and profits continued to show a steady decline in 1994 and 1995. Philip knew that he had to do something to reverse this trend. In mid-July 1995 Philip, together with his 27-year-old son Jonathon, who has an MBA degree, and Christine Delaney, the manager of the downtown Vancouver store for the last eight years, met to review the second quarter and devise a strategy for the firm's future.

During the course of the meeting, Christine remarked that she had come to know some of the regular clients well, and that she was surprised to find out that many of them were gay. Philip knew that many of his clients were leading lawyers, bankers, businessmen, and doctors. He too was surprised by this revelation and found it somewhat disconcerting. He expressed his discomfort and asked Jonathon and Christine how this might affect the firm.

Jonathon had some gay friends and immediately saw a business opportunity. His view was that Parker's Classics, in specific locations such as the west end of Vancouver, should openly target gay consumers. Jonathon felt that such a market niching strategy would ensure continued growth for the company. The major competitors, he felt, would be unwilling to go after this market segment. Jonathon asked Christine if she knew what percentage of the customers in her store were gay. Christine did not have a definite answer, but she thought it would be less than 20 percent.

Philip was uncomfortable with his son's idea. He felt that as more gay customers came into his stores he was, perhaps, losing many of his heterosexual clientele and maybe this was the reason for the declining performance in the stores. Philip was of the view that openly targeting gay consumers would antagonize other customers. Furthermore, he was not comfortable with the idea of associating Parker's Classics' image with gay consumers.

Jonathon felt that "upscale" was not a homogenous market and that there were several subsegments. Christine agreed that going after one smaller segment, the gay market, would give Parker's the edge over its more traditional rivals. Jonathon and Christine felt that the stores that currently attracted gay consumers could specifically target gays without antagonizing other customers. The other stores in the suburbs would not have any specific promotions targeted to the gay market and would continue to go after a broader clientele. Philip disagreed. After a heated exchange of views, all three agreed that further market research was required to determine the percentage of gay customers, as well as social attitudes and possible competitive reaction which might affect such a market niching strategy.

That same evening, Jonathon arranged a meeting with David Gower, a management consultant with considerable experience in lifestyle-based market segmentation. The next day Philip, Jonathon, and Christine had a lunch meeting with David Gower. First, Gower asked Philip if he had considered opening stores in smaller markets in the east as a growth strategy. Philip replied that he wanted to be based on the west coast and did not want to be national at this stage. Philip then voiced his concern over his son's proposal and asked Gower what he knew about the gay market.

Gower then gave a lengthy discourse on how marketers were dealing with the gay market. He pointed out that members of the gay community were often young, well-educated, in high paying jobs, and had a taste for fine living. Gower talked about how consumer product giants like Procter & Gamble and Toyota were seeking detailed demographic information on the gay community. Gower thought that it was only a matter of time before such companies had specific brands and promotions targeted to the gay market. In fact, Toyota had recently placed an ad in an Australian gay magazine.

Philip, still not convinced, asked Gower if there were any companies specifically targeting the gay market, and if so, how they were performing. Gower readily provided some examples. For instance, the Nordstrom department store chain had placed ads in *Washington Blade,* a gay newspaper, and Calvin Klein had run several ads with nude or partially clothed men. Other clothing stores like Banana Republic and The Gap had run ads featuring well-known gay people. In Canada, Gower said, IKEA, the Swedish furniture manufacturer, had run television ads featuring gay consumers. Gower also mentioned that more information was now available on the gay market, through market research firms such as the Chicago-based Overlooked Opinions, who were specializing in this market.

Philip, as well as Jonathon and Christine, were surprised that some of the leading clothing stores were openly targeting gay consumers. Based on in-store customer surveys, Philip had determined that his clientele was mostly in the 24 to 45 age group and he felt that the older of these consumers might be more conservative in their views. He was still worried about a possible backlash from these people. He probed Gower further about problems and failures associated with targeting the gay market.

Gower narrated the experiences of California-based Levi Strauss, which is considered to be a gay friendly company. Levi Strauss had to face a boycott, as well as a lot of unwanted publicity, when the Family Research Council, a Washington-based conservative advocacy group, joined boycotts of gay-supportive companies. Other companies, like Kmart, pulled an ad featuring two men after only a few airings, because some people believed it portrayed a gay couple and protested. Gower then said, "I'm not sure if such protests have any long-term implications. I don't think the average heterosexual consumer cares if a company sells its products to gay people. There seems to be a growing tolerance and acceptance."

After mulling over this comment for a few minutes, Philip asked how big the gay market was in Vancouver and the rest of Canada. Philip pointed out that from what Gower had indicated, it appeared that it was only large companies who were taking the risk of going after that particular market. He wanted to know if a small company like his could withstand any negative publicity or protest as a result of targeting the gay market.

Gower said that he would have to do some secondary research and conduct some focus groups to be able to provide answers to such questions. Gower went on to say that the gay market was a growing segment, to which not many companies had paid any attention, and that it was a segment with few dependents. Consequently, this segment had more disposable income to spend on items such as expensive clothes. As the meeting concluded, Jonathon and Christine were convinced that there was tremendous potential in the gay market. Philip still had lingering doubts, but he agreed to commission a market research study.

1. Do you think that Parker's Classics should target the gay market? Alternatively, should they pursue other growth opportunities? Elaborate.
2. Is the purchase behaviour of the gay consumer different from that of other consumers? Substantiate your answer.
3. Identify promotional themes/messages for the gay market that Parker's Classics might use. What are the potential problems in designing promotional messages for this market?
4. Can Parker's Classics target the gay market without alienating other consumers?
5. In general, what opportunities and problems do you see arising from marketers paying greater attention to the gay market?

6 The Hand Guard*

Alice Dicks was pondering the success of the hand guard that she had developed a number of years ago. As a nurse working for the Canadian Red Cross, she realized there was a need for a device to protect the hands of health care workers responsible for transferring blood between syringes. Alice experimented with several prototypes of a hand guard before progressing to field trials. She hired patent lawyers in Ottawa to ensure that her trademark was legal. With assistance from the National Research Council, an injection mould was developed to produce a hand shield, which was imprinted with the product and corporate names. In response to an invitation, Alice displayed her hand shields at the Medi-Tech trade show in London, Ontario, and lined up a Canadian distributor. So far, Alice had "done everything by the book" and was quite encouraged by the headway she was making in Canada. She decided to attend another medical trade show, this time in Florida. That was when all the trouble started.

In the 1980s, Alice Dicks, RN, had been working at the Canadian Red Cross blood donor clinic in Grand Falls–Windsor, Newfoundland. In order to collect blood from donors, a 16-gauge needle is used. After collection, three samples must be transferred from the thick needle into 7-millilitre test tubes, each of which has rubber on the top. This process requires the health care professional to hold the three test tubes in one hand and the 16-gauge needle in the other. The reason for the transfer to the test tubes is to allow the testing of donated blood for viruses and infections. The transfer to the three test tubes must be made relatively quickly and consecutively. This requires considerable precision and caution by the health care worker so as not to jab oneself in the process. With no protective guard between the 16-gauge needle and the tops of the three test tubes, workers tended to prick themselves with the needle on occasion. Alice did this three times; the most recent stab was caused when she turned suddenly as she heard a donor yell out just before fainting!

Although the opportunity for infection associated with transferring blood had existed for many years, the consequences had suddenly become quite extreme. The prevalence of the HIV virus in the 1980s meant that such accidents could become a death sentence for those who had jabbed themselves with a donor's blood. Now that Alice had stabbed herself with a needle carrying someone else's blood, she had to undergo twelve months of testing to ensure that she had not been infected. In order to be considered safe, three months of negative HIV readings were required, and eventually they were received. During the testing process, Alice was quite worried about her health. She also kept thinking about the fact that there had to be some product out there that would prevent a reoccurrence.

Alice knew that in the blood bank setting in North America, there were thousands of needle pricks happening each year. She searched extensively and found only one apparatus designed to guard against such injuries. It was a very expensive intravenous (IV) line, which would necessitate a change to the clinic's entire blood collection system. Each IV line would have to be discarded after use, thus increasing the operating costs of the blood donor clinics and contributing to the problem of medical waste.

Alice was interested in a lightweight, economical device that she and other workers could carry in their

*This case was written by Judith A. Cumby, Assistant Professor, Faculty of Business Administration, Memorial University of Newfoundland, as a basis for class discussion and is not intended to reflect either an effective or an ineffective handling of a management problem. The author wishes to thank Alice Dicks for her support and assistance in the preparation of this case.

pockets. Such a device should be simple to use, relatively inexpensive, and capable of being reused. That the protective unit should not be disposable was important to Alice, who felt that there is far too much damage being done to the environment through disposal of many items used in the health care sector. She felt it was important that the hand shield be made of a material that could be sterilized after use. Other factors that influenced the product design included the fact that the guard needed to be transparent so that the person transferring the blood could see the test tubes below the protective shield. The material used in the guard needed to be impervious to needle scratches and cuts.

In the beginning, the hand shield was made from solid, opaque plastic. However, Alice soon realized that the guard had to be transparent and somewhat flexible. Initially, she worked with a local company that had designed a shield made from Plexiglas that did not have any rolled edges. However, it was quickly discovered that if you score Plexiglas with a needle, it can slip and puncture your wrist or crack the Plexiglas. Alice knew that there was a definite need for a hand guard, but was at a loss as to how to design a functional and safe product. She called the National Research Council and talked with a petroleum engineer and a specialist in Autocad design. Together, they developed a prototype for the hand guard, which Alice decided to call a Hema-Shield (the word *hema* means blood).

Field trials of the new product were conducted. Alice felt that this was a critical step to the development of any viable product because the actual users will offer suggestions for improvement. Through information obtained from the field trials and consultation with medical specialists, the Hema-Shield was altered again. The plastic was melted in order to provide rolled edges for the product. These edges would prevent the needle from sliding off the shield during use.

Supported by funding from the Industrial Research Assistance Program of the National Research Council, Alice had a firm in Ontario develop an injection mould that would be used to manufacture the hand guards. The manufacturers suggested a more pliable resin, which was ultimately used in the manufacture of the Hema-Shields. It took six months working with the manufacturers to finalize the design. The mould was imprinted with the product and corporate names, Hema-Shield: Med Search Corp, and these names then appeared on 10,000 hand shields. Alice said that she did not have to do any marketing research. She knew that the demand was there; there was an unfilled niche in the market. What was needed was a suitable product and a means by which to get it to the customers.

Alice hired patent lawyers in Ottawa to register her trademark, Hema-Shield, so that she would be protected from patent infringement. Her lawyers told her that there was no other product registered with the Patent Office of the federal government in Ottawa. She accepted an invitation to display her product at the Medi-Tech show in London, Ontario. Dicks also had brochures developed and displayed at the trade show. There she was approached by a lot of people who wanted to distribute the Hema-Shield. Eventually, she reached an agreement with a distributor in Etobicoke that would receive a commission based on the selling price of between $5.00 and $5.50 per shield.

Alice proceeded to Florida for a medical trade show, where her display generated considerable interest. Shortly after returning to Newfoundland, Alice received a letter from a company in New Jersey that said that she was being sued for patent infringement. The people in New Jersey had developed a silicon patch or graft that was used internally to repair aneurysms and veins. Many years ago, the company had applied to the Canadian government for a patent, but it was not registered in the patent database. As such, the Hema-Shield developed in the United States did not show when an initial patent search was done. Alice explained to the people in New Jersey that her Hema-Shield did not infringe on their product because the two shields served totally different functions. Alice hired new lawyers and was eventually convinced that she would have to change the name of her product. She feels that this infringement of the name was done through no fault of her own; it was the fault of the patent office and the lawyers. Still, Alice was the one incurring more costs and inconvenience.

Alice renamed her product the Med Search Hand Guard. However, with many of the original 10,000 products still in inventory and with the original Hema-Shield name imprinted in the manufacturing mould, Alice had to manually score through the original name before the products could be shipped.

Those who use the product find it quite convenient, almost too convenient from a business perspective. The reorders for the product have been slow because the health care professionals are getting over a year's use from one hand guard. All health care workers at the Canadian Red Cross have to use Alice's product; it is now part of the standard operating procedure in the organization's manual. Her hand guard is also being used by all of the American Red Cross clinics that do not use the expensive and disposable IV line systems. Alice feels that she benefits from word-of-mouth promotion among health care workers. However, she feels that the distributors are not even scratching the market for her hand guard. She says that there are many other markets where blood work is done and the hand guard should be used, such as veterinary clinics and police laboratories.

She realizes that the durable design of her product is not conducive to making a lot of money through repeat orders. However, Alice, a talented artist, is adamant that the environmental damage associated with more medical waste should be stopped. In retrospect, she feels that patents are a waste of money; there is nothing that cannot be copied. There are many examples of copycat products that sell quite well: CDs, Rolex watches, and Fendi bags. What is important, Alice feels, is developing a product that can serve a niche and sell for an attractive price. It is important to get one's trademark known. She feels that advertising is a waste of money in this regard; what is important is direct selling and making contacts through relationship marketing. There are still orders coming in for Alice's hand guard. As well, she is in the process of developing a digitized machine to be used for mixing red blood cells with anticoagulants. Still, Alice wonders what, if anything, she should be doing to increase sales of her hand guard.

1. Would formalized market research prior to the development of the hand guard have helped Alice in any way?
2. Evaluate Alice's decision to use distributors in Ontario in light of her feeling that there are many markets that have not yet been reached.
3. What could Alice have done differently to increase sales?
4. How have Alice's personal values and ethics influenced her business decisions?

7 Naturally Yours*

For the past decade, Naturally Yours has been the only company specializing in the distribution of organic produce in western Canada. By 1996, annual sales were over $5 million annually, profits were steady, dividends to members were significant and growing, and the Naturally Yours name was well known and respected in the food business in western Canada.

Naturally Yours has developed its market based on the production of organically grown (chemical-free) produce that appeals to health-conscious and environmentally conscious consumers. The organization is structured as a co-operative. The co-op buys produce from organic farmers, distributes it, and ploughs the profits back into the business. As a result, all members are committed to making the co-operative successful and realize the importance of producing good-quality produce. Naturally Yours has excellent relations with its suppliers, a good client list, and considerable credibility.

Organic farms in Canada tend to be small, are subject to stringent government regulation, and enjoy a relatively short growing season because of the length of the Canadian winter. Recently in Canada, the market for fresh fruit in general has been growing at the rate of about 12 percent per year. To date, all organic produce has been supplied by Canadian producers, although there are no regulations preventing the import of such produce from the United States. There is little branding of organic foods in the Canadian market. Organically grown produce does not always have the "eye-appeal" that conventionally grown produce does. Some segments of the produce market see this difference as cosmetic only and are willing to pay more for produce that is healthier than the conventionally grown equivalent. The results of market research involving surveys of grocery shoppers in the greater Vancouver area indicated that 25 percent would be very or somewhat likely to buy organic produce. Ninety percent of those surveyed indicated that they were unhappy about the current pesticide and chemical practices of traditional producers.

Oregon Organics was a well established distributor of organically grown fruits and vegetables in Oregon, Washington, and northern California. When Oregon Organics started producing organic apple juice, the members of Naturally Yours considered doing the same. Oregon Organics was generous in providing Naturally Yours with market information because the two organizations were not direct competitors.

Oregon Organics had tried both high prices and low prices, as well as high and low levels of advertising and promotion. They found that market shares varied, depending on the combination of price and advertising and promotion (see the table below).

Given the similarities of the produce markets in western Canada and the western United States, it is thought that these market shares would probably be about the same in Canada. Based on Statistics Canada data, Naturally Yours estimated the size of the apple juice market in western Canada to be 520,000 cases annually. The contribution per case would be $3.50 at the low price and $5.10 at the high price.

Oregon Organics had used only point-of-purchase materials in some areas; in others, it had supplemented point-of-purchase materials with personalized direct mail to a mailing list of known purchasers of organic produce. If Naturally Yours were to use similar advertising and promotion materials, point-of-purchase alone would cost approximately $5,000, while the mailing would cost $8,000. In addition, Naturally Yours would have to hire a part-time sales person to support the new apple juice. The sales person's compensation and expenses would

MARKET SHARES(%)

	LOW PRICE	HIGH PRICE
Low advertising and promotion	1.2	0.8
High advertising and promotion	2.0	1.0

*This case was prepared by Judith A. Cumby, Assistant Professor, Faculty of Business Administration, Memorial University of Newfoundland. The facts of this case are based on the *Wild West Organic Harvest Co-operative* case, written by Dr. Katherine Gallagher of Memorial University.

amount to $15,000 annually. Product development costs would be minimal, mostly related to package design. They would total $5,000 in the first year only.

Some of the co-op members were hesitant to go ahead with the manufacture and distribution of apple juice. They thought it was too risky to get into manufacturing. In a meeting, the members of the co-op decided that they would only go ahead if there was a reasonable chance that the new product would produce a profit by the end of its first year.

1. Provide a financial analysis to support a decision regarding whether Naturally Yours should enter the apple juice market. Indicate clearly whether the numbers support entering the market and, if so, at what price and what level of promotion/advertising.
2. State your recommendation about whether Naturally Yours should introduce organic apple juice. What factors other than the quantitative ones in question 1 influenced your decision? Support your recommendation.
3. Suggest an advertising campaign for Naturally Yours. As part of your answer, identify the target audience, the advertising goals, and an advertising message and execution approach you would use.

8 Diego's*

Dr. Albert Collins, a Montreal physician, faced a difficult decision as to whether or not to invest in a new fast-food franchise concept specializing in Mexican food. Dr. Collins had made several good business investments, and while he thought this was a great opportunity, he recognized that there was a chance it wouldn't succeed. He decided to discuss the concept with his friend Jack Timlin, a marketing consultant, who had advised him on a number of earlier ventures. Dr. Collins arranged a meeting and presented the following information to Timlin.

THE CONCEPT

About six months ago, Dr. Collins had read an article in a major U.S. magazine about a relatively new but already successful fast-food franchiser based in Phoenix, Arizona. In operation for less than five years, this franchiser had opened 55 locations (some franchised, some corporately owned) in Arizona and several other southwest states, had sold (to one firm) the franchise rights for 80 locations in Florida, and had sold many other, soon to be built, franchises in the midwestern states.

Although Mexican food is very popular in the southern United States, this firm, in all of its advertising and store signs, always uses the phrase "We serve marinated charbroiled chicken and Mexican food" to indicate that it offers a choice of items so that people who don't like Mexican food can also patronize the chain.

On the door of each location is a sticker stating that this restaurant is approved by the American Heart Association as a healthy place to eat away from home. Dr. Collins believed that this endorsement was obtained because of the manner in which the chicken is prepared. First it is marinated in a secret recipe of natural fruit juices and herbs and then it is charbroiled so that the fat drips out of the meat. Chicken prepared this way is lower in cholesterol than fried chicken and is juicier than barbeque (BBQ) chicken. To further enhance its healthy image, the chain does not serve french fries but does offer baked potatoes and an assortment of salads.

A quote from the article provided a very strong endorsement from at least one customer: "I do not have a great deal of experience in eating Mexican food, but the dishes were different than what I expected. The chicken was tender and juicy and had a subtle flavour—for my taste it was better than BBQ chicken. The other dishes were very tasty and definitely not spicy. If this is what Mexican food is like, I am a convert."

Dr. Collins investigated further and found out that the recipes could not be protected by patent or copyright. In fact, he learned that the Arizona chain found out how a California chain of chicken restaurants marinated their chicken and then they used the recipe themselves. Dr. Collins then purchased some of the American marinated chicken, had it analyzed by a laboratory, and then had a food technologist develop and test the formula and the correct procedures to cook the chicken.

He gathered a group of investors (primarily friends and acquaintances) who liked the concept and were willing to put up most of the money required to open up one or two locations to show that the concept would be successful in Canada. The plan was to sell franchises across the country.

For each location, franchisees would be charged an initial fee plus an ongoing 5 percent royalty on the gross sales of the franchises. In return for these fees, the franchisee would have the right to use the trade name, which the investors decided would be Diego's. The franchisee's staff would be trained to prepare the food as per set procedures and the franchisee would purchase the chicken marinade from the franchiser. The franchisee would be assisted in site selection, construction of the restaurant, and purchasing of the required equipment, and would receive ongoing managerial assistance. In addition, the franchisee would benefit from a co-op advertising program to be funded by a charge of 4 percent of gross sales levied on each location—franchised or corporately owned.

*This case was written by Maurice Borts, who at the time of its preparation was associated with McGill University. The author acknowledges the assistance of David Roy and Michel Seguin of Statistics Canada in providing the relevant data.

PRELIMINARY RESEARCH

Dr. Collins met with the investment group several times, and although nothing was formalized, a considerable amount of preliminary research had been conducted. A location was found for the first Diego's restaurant in a relatively new suburban residential area where most of the homes have been built in the last 10 years. New homes were still being built in the area, and there was enough vacant land to more than double the population of the area. Most of the homes sold for $150,000 to $225,000 (compared to the current Montreal average price of $89,500 per home). Census data suggested that the typical home owner in this area was raising a young family and had a managerial job or was a professional with a practice that had not yet developed fully.

Studies have shown that most people will travel about 2.5 to 3.5 km (5 minutes) to go to a fast-food restaurant. Since Diego's would be very distinctive, the first few locations probably would draw customers from a slightly larger trading area. Information was obtained from recent census data for the census tracts that would likely constitute the trading area (Exhibit 1).

INVESTOR GROUP MEETING

After the information was collected, the investors held a meeting where a lively debate took place about the proposed image of Diego's, the target market, and other matters.

The investment group couldn't agree on what image Diego's should have and what types of customers they should concentrate on satisfying. Some of the members wanted to concentrate their efforts on attracting and satisfying families with young children (e.g., offering free magic shows on selected evenings and on weekends, offering children free balloons, and perhaps offering a special children's menu of items that will appeal to children).

One investor argued that this market segment appeared to be important. A recent newspaper article reported the results of an American study that, in 85 percent of the cases when parents go out to eat with their young children, the children make the final decision on which restaurant the family will go to.

Some of the group argued that children are known as very finicky eaters and maybe they wouldn't like Diego's food. They suggested that Diego's should go after the teenage market or possibly should concentrate on the adult fast-food market.

One member of the investment group had conducted an analysis of the competition in the trading area. He noted that at least two competitors in the trading area, McDonald's and Chi Chi's, had special strategies for attracting children. Two other successful restaurants, St. Hubert B.B.Q. and Swiss Chalet (both specialize in BBQ chicken), have outlets in the area. Another group member provided some data prepared by Statistics Canada that dealt with food purchased from restaurants (Exhibit 2).

One of the members of the investor group was a practising accountant. He estimated that if the average bill at a restaurant of this type was $4.50 (excluding tax) and the actual cost of the food and the packaging was 30 percent of the selling price, the restaurant would need to serve 225,000 meals a year to break even.

Information on traffic flows was also collected. One Thursday, Dr. Collins went to the proposed site and between 12:00 noon and 1:00 PM counted 2,000 cars moving in the four directions at the intersection. Between 5:00 PM and 6:30 PM, the street heading north in front of the site became a "parking lot" as people headed home. He felt that this was a positive sign in that people could stop on the same side of the street as they were already travelling (and not have to cut across traffic), pick up food for supper, and then continue home.

Related to the decision as to which target market(s) to appeal to, some members wondered if people would be confused if the restaurant was simultaneously pro-

Exhibit 1 Trading Area Demographic Data

Total population	118,043
Private households	40,358
Total families	32,087
With 1 child at home	8,132
With 2 children at home	10,199
With 3 or more children at home	4,575
No children at home	9,178
Ages of children	
0 to 4 years	8,295
5 to 9 years	8,888
10 to 14 years	9,000
15 to 19 years	8,817

Source: Statistics Canada Statistical Reference Centre 1996 Census—Montreal CMA

Exhibit 2 Weekly Food Purchases from Restaurants per Family (Canada 1992)

	FOOD PURCHASE	INCOME
Average	$33.30	$43,825
1st quintile	12.88	11,171
2nd quintile	22.51	23,807
3rd quintile	31.29	37,561
4th quintile	39.03	54,504
5th quintile	50.48	92,082

Note: The average weekly food purchase from restaurants in the Montreal Metropolitan Area was $34.87.

Source: Statistics Canada, Family Food Expenditures in Canada—17 Metropolitan Areas, Cat. 62-554.

moted as a chicken restaurant and as a Mexican food restaurant. That is, would potential customers perceive the chicken as a Mexican dish or would they consider the chicken to be a suitable alternative to BBQ chicken or fried chicken?

Various members of the investment group then raised the following questions and issues:

- Will consumers recognize the fact that Diego's is really two different restaurants in one, and even if a person does not like Mexican food (or is afraid to try it), he or she can order a very tasty chicken? Or will some stay away because they view Diego's as a Mexican restaurant? Perhaps Diego's is too strong a Mexican name for what we would like to achieve?
- Both images should be positive. Diego's proposed first location is not far from Chi Chi's, which exposed the consumer to and expanded the market for Mexican food. According to comparisons made by some of the group, Diego's Mexican dishes taste better and will cost less than the same items at Chi Chi's.
- On the other hand, for many years chicken has been more popular in Quebec than in other parts of the country. It may be due to cultural differences or may be the result of the success of the St. Hubert B.B.Q. chain, which started in Quebec (Exhibit 3).
- In addition, over the last three or four years the consumption of chicken across Canada has increased significantly as people switched away from red meats, which are higher in cholesterol than chicken. This ties in very nicely with the emphasis that the American chain places on the health aspect of its chicken meals.

Some of the investors debated whether legally they could use an approach similar to the one Americans use and were not convinced that the "healthy" image will be a unique selling proposition that will cause people to pick their restaurant over the competition. They argued that the Canadian laws concerning food advertising were different and more restrictive than the U.S. laws.

Exhibit 3 Estimated per Capita Regional Differences in Food Consumption

NATIONAL AVERAGE = 100 PERCENT	CHICKEN	ITALIAN	CHINESE	GREEK
National	100%	100%	100%	100%
Quebec	125	120	145	130
Ontario	90	75	85	80
Prairies	90	165	35	25
B.C.	90	120	100	85
Atlantic provinces	175	80	55	45

In Canada, the advertising of the cholesterol content of food (with the exception of vegetable oils such as Mazola) is prohibited. In addition, it appears that, even if it wanted to, the Canadian Heart Association would be unable, given the present legal environment, to endorse the restaurant. As well, they argued that many Quebecers are not especially health conscious when it comes to food.

One person had obtained a copy of a research study conducted in Montreal about bakery products. This study concluded that French-speaking respondents were less concerned with food additives than the English-speaking segment of the population. It was also found that older people were less concerned with this issue than the younger generation. Quebecers consumed large amounts of especially greasy french fries and poutine (French fries, sauce, and melted cheese). In other parts of Canada, the preference was for crispier, less oily french fries.

Some research conducted in the Montreal area by one of the group indicated that more than half of the respondents want french fries with their BBQ chicken. Consumers like and expect the combination, and that is what the chicken restaurants offer with their meals.

In spite of this information, other investors would like to follow the lead of the American firm and not serve french fries but instead offer a choice of baked potatoes or Mexican rice.

One person pointed out that Quebecers love fine food and are receptive to ethnic foods. However, for some reason, Mexican food has not caught on in Quebec. Taco Bell, a large U.S. Mexican fast-food chain that has opened in Ontario, does not, at this time, have any Quebec locations. In Montreal proper, several small Mexican restaurants have opened. None of them appears to be especially successful.

In addition, one of the investment team visited about a dozen supermarkets (some in the area of the proposed location, others in various parts of Montreal and other suburbs). Each store has a small section of packaged Mexican foods. The managers of these stores described the sales of Mexican foods as "slow but steady."

Because there is a lot of money at stake, the investors paid for some basic research. They conducted focus groups in a restaurant setting similar to what is being considered and the respondents had the chance to taste the food. (Exhibit 4 provides a summary of the comments.) The results of the research were interesting in that in two cases, the findings went against what the investors thought the consumer might want or accept.

First, it was planned to prepare the food out in the front of the restaurant where it could be seen by people inside and outside. This was intended to show that Diego's had nothing to hide and that the food was prepared under hygienic conditions. In addition, it was hoped that seeing the golden brown chicken on the grill and the aroma of cooking chicken would encour-

Exhibit 4 Focus Group Comments

Positive Comments

- The food is delicious.
- Great food.
- I never tasted Mexican food before; it is really good and not at all spicy.
- I am happy that you don't serve french fries. My seven-year-old son just ate nutritious food, not the junk food that he prefers.
- I enjoyed the food. The chicken was moist but not greasy.
- I liked it. I would come back again.
- I hope it opens soon. I am bored and fed up with the traditional fast foods.

Negative Comments

- The chicken looks yellow. What's wrong with it? Is it cheaper quality chicken?
- I don't think French Canadians are ready to eat BBQ chicken on paper plates using plastic cutlery.
- I don't want to see the chicken being cooked. I don't want to know that it was once a living thing.
- The chickens were brought to the grill in a pail. Do they use the same pail to wash the floors?
- For me BBQ chicken and french fries go together. Something is missing and the meal is not enjoyable without french fries.

age people to order. According to the focus groups, some people viewed this as a strong negative.

Secondly, while travelling through New England, Dr. Collins came across a very successful chain of seafood restaurants that, in order to keep prices low, serves on paper plates and provides plastic cutlery. This makes sense because Harvey's and other fast-food chains also use disposables. Again, based on the results of the focus groups, there seems to be resistance in Montreal to eating chicken in this way.

Another research finding was of special interest and requires more study. When respondents were offered a choice between traditional BBQ sauce and salsa, a Mexican sauce, the vast majority opted for the BBQ sauce. Was it because it was something unknown? Was it the fear of something spicy? Or, perhaps, it was just a habit.

THE DECISION

Dr. Collins concluded the presentation to Timlin with the following comments: "As you can see, there is a lot of information to consider. In fact, I am confused as to what I should do. I know that the concept is successful in Arizona but I have also obtained a great deal of information, some of which is not positive, about duplicating this concept in Canada and particularly in Quebec.

"I don't know if I should invest in this project or not. If it succeeds, it will be the chance of a lifetime to make a lot of money. Should I go into it, or not? What, if anything, can be done to improve the concept so that the risk of failure will be reduced?"

What would you recommend that Dr. Collins do? Why?

9 Doug Hanson Buys a Car*

Shortly after Doug Hanson started his new job at The Family Health Club in the spring of 1990, he realized that his 1980 Toyota Celica, which he had bought from the original owner in 1982, was no longer the sporty new car it once was. Each day that Doug drove to work, his need for a new car became more and more apparent. Every morning before starting his car, he said a quick prayer before turning the key in the ignition. When he actually made it into the parking lot at work, he let out a sigh of relief. He was thankful that his Celica, which had almost 330,000 kilometres on it, had survived another 10 kilometre journey.

Doug, who was born and raised in Pembroke, Ontario, had recently obtained his BA degree from the University of Ottawa. He selected this university because it offered good academics and was close to home. On graduating, Doug decided to move to Vancouver, British Columbia. Vancouver not only offered him an alternative to the harsh weather of the East, but also provided him an affordable graduate education. Doug planned to go to Simon Fraser University for an MBA degree.

Doug's trek to the West Coast was an adventure, to say the least. The Celica broke down once while passing through Saskatchewan and had a tough time making it through the Rockies. When Doug finally arrived in Vancouver, he knew he had pushed the Celica to its limit. He realized that before long he would have to retire the ten-year-old car.

In the spring of 1991, Doug began to work part time on his MBA. This meant driving more kilometres each week to get to the SFU campus. Clearly, his need for a new car was becoming more obvious. Unfortunately, he was not making enough money to afford a new car.

In the fall of 1992, Doug was promoted to manager of his department, and his salary increased significantly. He was now in a position to seriously consider replacing his car.

Coincidentally, Doug's 73-year-old landlady, Edna Johnson, informed him that she was getting ready to trade in her 1986 Buick LaSabre. A friend of hers at the bridge club had just purchased a 1993 Toyota Camry. Mrs. Johnson was so impressed with the manoeuvrability and ease of handling of the Camry that she made up her mind to buy one of her own.

Mrs. Johnson's Buick was in mint condition. She always kept the car in the garage, so the car never saw dust, let alone a scratch. In addition, the car had only been driven 48 000 kilometres, and all parts appeared to be in perfect shape. The Toyota dealership offered to give her $3,000 for the Buick as a trade-in. Her car was in such good condition that she felt as though she would be giving it away at this price. However, she did

*This case was written by Barbara Schneider and Doug Henkel under the supervision of David S. Litvack. Copyright 1993. Faculty of Administration, University of Ottawa.

not want the hassle of trying to sell it on the open market, so she was left with no other alternative.

As she saw Doug out in the street tinkering with his car once again, the thought crossed her mind to offer it to him before she traded it in. She told Doug that he could have the car for the same price that the dealer had offered her. In addition, because Doug was such a reliable tenant, she would allow him to pay it off over six months.

Clearly this was a golden opportunity for Doug to solve his transportation problems. He knew the Buick was in excellent shape, and he could get at least $500 for his car! On top of that, she was willing to take payments! Doug told her that he would think it over. He had two days to make his decision before Mrs. Johnson would go for her new Toyota.

Doug knew that he could not pass up such a good deal, yet he felt he would not be entirely happy with the Buick. The idea of driving a Buick was not particularly appealing to him. Every day, when Doug pulled into the parking lot at work, he admired the latest sports cars driven by his co-workers and clientele. Additionally, his girlfriend had recently bought a 1992 Acura Integra. Doug had hoped to purchase a car similar to hers.

The next morning, while paging through the *Vancouver Sun,* Doug noticed an ad offering a "lease special" for 1993 Acura Integras. The ad stated that one could lease this vehicle for only $250 a month. Doug's first impression was how affordable driving a brand new Acura could be. He called the telephone number listed in an effort to get more information. He knew that his girlfriend had purchased her car for approximately $17,000. She had made a $7,000 down payment and was paying $200 a month on a $10,000 loan. Doug knew that he could not afford a $7,000 down payment, but $250 a month was no problem.

Leasing a car is certainly different from owning one. After the lease term, you have to give the car back. In addition, the dealership usually limits the number of kilometres that can be driven each year. Doug considered these factors but felt that if he could drive an Acura for $250 a month without having to come up with a down payment, he would be satisfied. He planned to visit the dealership the following weekend to inquire about the lease.

When he arrived home from work one day, he saw his neighbor, Jay Smith, polishing his 1969 Corvette. The Corvette was one of three high-performance vehicles that Jay, an avid race enthusiast, owned. Jay would often help Doug when he was having trouble with the Celica. He had known Jay for a couple of years, and always enjoyed talking to him about the latest sports cars on the market. He decided to run the idea of purchasing Mrs. Johnson's car by Jay for some feedback. "Buick does make a decent car, but I have never been too impressed by their styling or performance," Jay responded. "I have always classified them as family cars. What you need is a sports car. There are a lot of new models out this year. For someone your age, shopping for a sports car should be like taking a kid into a candy store!"

"I only wish that I could afford something sporty," returned Doug. "What do you mean," Jay replied. "In my latest issue of *Car and Driver,* I saw a handful of new sporty models available for under $18,000. You just got a nice raise, and I'm sure you could afford the payments! Why don't you wait here and I'll go inside and get the magazine for you." "Maybe Jay is right," Doug thought to himself as Jay ran inside. "Perhaps I need something sporty."

With all the ideas about cars floating around in his head, he decided to get some additional information. Later that evening he decided to give his Uncle Barry a call. Barry, who lived back in Ontario, had been a mechanic for many years. He had helped Doug fix his car a few times, and even helped him put in a new clutch before he left for B.C. Doug respected his opinion very much.

After telling Barry his problem, his uncle suggested that he look into the Chevy Cavalier. "Yeah, if I were in your shoes, I might consider the Cavalier. It has a good four cylinder and antilock brakes all around. It even has a decent stereo in it." "Sounds interesting, do you know what they're going for?" asked Doug. "I think they're somewhere in the $12,000 range." "That's cheap," said Doug. "Oh, and I read somewhere that they come standard with a four-year 80 000 kilometre warranty," added Barry. Doug's uncle also reminded him that he should "Buy Canadian." "Speaking of Canadian cars," said Doug, "Let me tell you about the deal my landlady offered me on her 1986 Buick." Doug told his uncle about Mrs. Johnson's offer. "Gee, that sounds like a great deal," said Barry. "I wish I lived in Vancouver. I'd snap that one up in a second."

Doug woke up early the following Saturday morning excited to begin his search for a car. He figured he would spend the entire day test-driving new cars. His first stop was the Acura dealership. He soon learned that since he had never had a previous car loan, he was not qualified for the lease program. This was not mentioned in the newspaper ad or during the course of his telephone conversation with the dealership. Regardless, the salesman tried to encourage Doug to buy an Acura, but they started at the high end of his price range. It became apparent to Doug that the ad was just a "come on." He was annoyed with the misleading sales tactics and decided to look elsewhere.

His next stop was the Toyota dealership where he had always taken his Celica for servicing. Doug had a great deal of confidence in Toyota, considering his Celica had served him well the past ten years.

As he was browsing through the lot, he was approached by a salesman. He soon discovered that the only Toyota besides the Celica that potentially suited him was the MR2. Doug did not want to buy another Celica because he was not impressed with the new body design. The MR2 was Toyota's four-cylinder sports model. He had seen one on the freeway and admired its sleek design. A major drawback with the MR2 was the fact that it was a small two-seater. Furthermore, it started at over $20,000.

His next stop was the Dodge dealer. He had seen the new Lancer model pictured in the *Car and Driver* magazine and was impressed with its looks. It came in three versions. The base model had a four-cylinder engine that had very little horsepower. The midrange version also had four cylinders, but its multivalve engine design gave it 50 percent more horsepower than the base model. As for the top of the line version, this car had the most powerful engine due to its turbo design. The base model started at around $14,000, the midrange sold for approximately $17,000, and the highest priced Lancer sold for close to $20,000. Despite the different engines, all three models had the same body design.

Doug test-drove the base model first. It drove smoothly; however, it had very little pickup. The midrange version was priced at the upper limits of his range, but he decided to test-drive it anyway. He was extremely pleased with the overall performance of this car. The turbo model was priced beyond his range, not to mention the fact that the insurance would be almost double that of the other two models.

Doug really liked the midrange Lancer and decided to negotiate a deal. The asking price for the car he was interested in was $18,300. It had all of the extras Doug wanted. Furthermore, it was the only one on the lot that came in the colour he wanted. After haggling with the sales manager, the two agreed on a selling price of $17,300. In addition, the dealership gave Doug $1,000 for his Celica as a trade-in. He even qualified for the special first-time buyer interest rate for his car loan. Doug went with his gut feeling and decided to buy the car.

After signing the necessary papers, Doug was given the keys to his first brand-new car. He felt somewhat numb at this point. Doug was about to drive his car off the lot when the salesman ran after him yelling, "Stop, wait just a minute!" "What's the matter?!" asked Doug. The salesman replied, "Just give me a minute—you look so good next to that car I want to take a picture." The salesman pulled out his camera and snapped the picture. Doug was flabbergasted, but managed to crack a big smile anyway.

As he pulled his new car into the driveway, Doug was greeted by Mrs. Johnson and his neighbor Jay. They both admired his Lancer. Doug couldn't help but feel proud. He gave them both a spin and told them all about the great deal he got.

In the following weeks, Doug continued to enjoy his new car. He especially liked knowing that it would get him to work on time without fail. One day, while going through his mail, he noticed a large envelope from the dealership. "I wonder what this is," he thought to himself. He opened it and found a calendar with a picture of him standing beside his new car. There were also valuable coupons inside for discounts on an oil change, a tune-up, and other services. Doug set the items aside and reminisced about the day he purchased his car, knowing that he made the right choice.

1. Show how Doug Hanson's behaviour relates to the consumer problem-solving process outlined in Chapter 6 of this text.
2. Summarize Doug's evaluation process as it relates to each of the cars he considered.

10 Crankcase Transmission*

Bill Hartley was worried. He and his family were travelling on vacation to Western Canada when his recreational vehicle, a Ford truck camper, began acting up. Thinking a transmission adjustment might be necessary, he dropped the camper off that morning at a franchised transmission centre in Sault Ste. Marie, Ontario, for diagnosis and took his family to a nearby shopping mall. Now, some four hours later, he was told that he would require a rebuilt transmission, a new torque converter, an external cooler, and other items that would cost twice the few hundred dollars he had expected to pay out. He was running short on time and had to decide within the next hour what he should do.

THE COMPANY

Crankcase Transmission is a Canadian franchise organization. It began operations in the 1960s. Based on a business strategy that simply states WE ONLY DO TRANSMISSIONS, the organization grew to its present size as a major servicer of automotive transmissions in the country. Part of its success has been due to an excellent selection of reputable franchisees who are supported by the franchiser in terms of national advertising, operations support, financing, and even real estate development. Its network of over 200 centres permits a nationwide warranty program, and its fleet account program provides franchisee access to over 250,000 motor vehicles.

The company actively promotes its franchise network through radio and television ads. As a result of its promotional campaign and recognized service, most people trust and accept the merits of Crankcase Transmission.

A CONSUMER PROBLEM

In July, Bill Hartley and his wife and young daughter loaded up their truck camper and began a four-week holiday that would take them from Toronto to the Canadian Rockies and beyond. Bill sensed that the transmission should be looked at since the odometer on the ten-year-old Ford XLT F250 was approaching the 100,000 kilometre mark. The motor, a powerful 460 (only a few months old), was in perfect working order,

*This case was written by Dr. Ken Blawatt, who at the time of its preparation was associated with Simon Fraser University as an Adjunct Professor at the University College of the Cariboo.

but he felt a bit of slippage from time to time when reversing the vehicle. He also noted a bit of transmission oil leakage and found that he had to add a pint of fluid every few weeks.

On the third day, while travelling between Sudbury and Sault Ste. Marie, Bill noticed that the vehicle was beginning to generate a low growl from what he perceived to be the transmission area whenever he attempted to exceed 100 kilometres an hour. Worried about the noise and concerned about the transmission, he decided to stop in Sault Ste. Marie early the next day to have the unit checked out. A fellow camper who happened to be a mechanic recommended Crankcase Transmission in the city.

THE INITIAL EXAMINATION

The initial contact with Crankcase Transmission personnel was reassuring. The manager was very helpful, and Randy, the serviceman assigned to check out Hartley's truck, was friendly and confident. He drove the camper a few blocks in the city, revving the engine and using the vehicle's low gears to check for slippage. As they returned to the centre, Randy told Hartley that there appeared to be some slippage, and that they should remove the bottom pan and inspect the transmission.

He stated that at worst the repair would cost $700. The good news was that they could do it that day by 5 P.M. and that Bill and his family could then continue on their way.

Bill considered the situation with his wife. Since they were a bit pressed for time, they decided to allow Randy to proceed, at least with the inspection. They barely had $700 in reserve, and his wife was worried about being caught short on the trip.

They returned to the centre's office, where Hartley was asked whether he could take the camper off the truck or if he would prefer to leave it on. If he were to leave it on the truck, it would have to be worked on at a second franchise centre in another part of town, apparently owned by the same operator. At 9:30 A.M., the manager of the second centre cheerfully drove the Hartley family to a nearby large shopping mall so that they could browse and keep themselves entertained while the inspection and possible reconditioning took place.

"What we normally do," said Leonard Pissey, "is remove the pan, inspect the seals, ports, and gaskets, and replace whatever is worn out. It's really quite simple. Give me a call in an hour and I'll tell you how we're doing." At 10:30 A.M., Bill called Pissey, who was unable to take the call. At 11:30 Bill called again. This time Pissey said they were just removing the pan and asked Hartley to call back. After lunch, at 12:30, Bill called Pissey again.

THE PROBLEM

Pissey: Well, we've checked over your unit. I'm afraid it's going to cost a bit more than we thought.

Hartley: (becoming concerned): How much?

Pissey: You need a new torque converter, a C6 unit and . . .

Hartley: Wait a minute, Leonard. Aren't those things all a part of the transmission?

Pissey: Yes they are, but you see yours is . . .

Hartley: Leonard, your people quoted me $700 at the worse possible condition. Now what is this all about?

Pissey: Mr. Hartley, if you want your unit repaired the best possible way, you need this work done!

Bill pauses, becoming angry now. He doesn't understand mechanical things but he feels there is something amiss. Nevertheless, he knows his anger will not gain anything at this point.

Hartley: How much, Leonard?

Pissey: Counting the new external cooler you need for your transmission, it'll be about 1,500 dollars.

Hartley: Hold on! Why an external cooler? I've driven that truck and camper for 100,000 kilometres over a period of thirteen years in weather hot and cold and never had a problem! Without an external cooler!

Pissey: Well, Mr. Hartley, if you want the company to give you a twelve-month warranty, you have to have the cooler! Now if you lived in town here we would guarantee our work, but if you want another centre in Toronto or Winnipeg to honour the job, you need the cooler. That's company policy!

Hartley: I'll call you back in half an hour!

Bill goes to discuss the problem with his family.

1. How does the company's reputation assist or hinder in Bill Hartley's deliberations?
2. Are all franchisees the same, and are they consistent with the company's image of service, and so on?
3. What should Hartley do?
4. What are the marketing implications from the case?

11 Ralph the Optician*

"The new glasses that you selected yesterday are ready. Try them on and I will make the final adjustments. Now look at yourself in the mirror—these new glasses help convey your image of success and good taste.

*This case was written by Maurice Borts, who at the time of its preparation was associated with McGill University. The author acknowledges the cooperation and assistance of Denise Villeneuve and Greta Auerbach.

"Maurice, now that I looked after you as my customer, I want to become your client. I need some advice about a threat that my business is facing. If you have some time we could have a coffee in my office and I will tell you about my dilemma."

I agreed. Ralph poured two cups of freshly brewed Blue Mountain coffee and closed the door to his office so that we would not be disturbed.

"Maurice, I have been an optician for almost 30 years and over time, with hard work, I built a successful business and I now earn a good income. I take pride in the fact that over the years I was able to successfully adjust to the major changes in my business. For example, there have been technical changes such as the introduction of contact lenses, shatterproof lenses, and graduated bifocals. My staff and I periodically attend seminars and courses so that we are knowledgeable about the latest innovations.

"Other kinds of changes have been more difficult for me. Over time, major optical firms such as Lens Crafters and Sears started to operate in Canada. These chains tend to place great emphasis on heavy promotion and low price. In addition, Lens Crafters offers the convenience that your new lenses will be ready in about an hour.

"In fact, the share of the market held by independent opticians such as me is declining as the price-sensitive segment of the market grows. In spite of reduced market share, my sales are growing because the market is now growing quickly thanks to aging baby boomers. As people age, usually starting in their 40s they tend to need reading glasses or glasses for distance. Even people who wear contact lens often require reading glasses for close work. There is also evidence that as some people age, they are less likely to wear contacts for long periods of time.

"What did I do to protect my business against my large, price-oriented competitors?

"First, I upgraded the type of frames that I carry. Instead of carrying a large selection of low and medium price frames by unknown manufacturers, we have upgraded and place the emphasis on well-known, quality designs such as Fendi, Gucci, Hugo Boss, Alfred Sung, and Givenchy. It is not uncommon for a person to pay between 300 and 450 dollars for a new pair of glasses at my store. This is very different from the chains, where I think the average price would probably be between 100 and 150 a pair.

"Secondly, my staff and I are very careful to give the customer as much time as needed for choosing the proper frames, to fully answer questions, and to explain any technical differences between the options. We never rush a decision. In fact, many of our customers have been dealing with us for years, and if possible we try to greet them by name and acknowledge the fact that we recognize and appreciate their ongoing business. Based on statistics, the average pair of glasses lasts two years. However, some of my customers are fashion conscious and buy new frames more often.

"Third, I implemented a print and radio advertising program. Although my budget is modest compared to the major chains, I make an impact by concentrating my promotion in periodic short bursts when I feature a special item or a sale.

"Although all opticians sell products which enhance sight, my product is different in that I help clients not only see better but also look better and convey the image that they want. A frame makes a statement on your face, and the statement changes from style to style. To support the fashion orientation of my business, I purchased a camera and TV device that allows a person to more objectively see how he or she looks in the frame. In addition, I subscribe to magazines such as *Vogue* and *Elle* to see what frames are being shown to the fashion leaders.

"Everybody who sells glasses is basically in competition with everybody else. However, some of us are licensed as opticians and others are optometrists. Opticians specialize in selling glasses; optometrists are permitted to sell glasses but they are also trained to diagnose eye disease and to prescribe corrective lenses. Ophthalmologists, on the other hand, are medical doctors who specialize in eye diseases. They prescribe corrective lenses, but most do not sell glasses or contact lenses.

"Because I don't prescribe lenses, it is important to me to be located close to ophthalmologists' offices and to hospitals with eye clinics, so that it is convenient for clients to enter my store after they receive a new vision prescription. As you know, the location of my store is excellent in that I am close to a large number of busy ophthalmologists and two major hospitals.

"The aggressive chains sell their products on different variations of price. For example, Price Club charges substantially less than you might expect to pay for contact lenses and bifocals. Their prices on frames also tend to be good value. However, because Price Club does volume business, their customer service is not as good as mine. In addition, their selection of frames is oriented toward more popular price points, and although the frames tend to be reasonably fashionable, they are designed for the mass market. They do not sell the same frames that I do. Price Club does not advertise or run promotions. Their promotion is mainly through word-of-mouth advertising and a large membership who appreciate the Price Club philosophy of low markup, low or no-frills service.

"Another pricing technique used by some competitors is the famous two-for-one sale. Some of these two-for-one sales offer really good value to the shopper. Because of the high markup on frames and glasses, the retailer can actually make some money on a true two-for-one sale. However, some two-for-one sales are designed to offer you a deal on part of the purchase, but you must pay full price on the rest. For example, the sale may be two-for-one for the lenses, but you pay full price for the frames (or vice versa). Sometimes, any additional features that you select, such as scratchproof or UV coating, are charged at full price for both pairs.

"Because of the multitude of brand names and styles, it is very difficult for most of us to know what is a fair price for a pair of frames and lenses. Because we lack the expertise, we have to take the seller's word for quality and price. The sale boils down to which seller(s) does the buyer trust.

"Maurice, I apologize for being so long-winded to get to my problem. I read in yesterday's newspaper that Price Club is planning to open a new outlet about eight kilometres from my store. I need to know what kinds of changes I should make to my operation (I think you call it a marketing mix), so that I will not lose a lot of business to my new competitor.

"About three months ago, I participated in an omnibus marketing research study and asked people why they prefer to do business with a specific source of eyewear. This is a sample of the type of responses given [see appendix]."

APPENDIX

Respondent Quotations—Omnibus Study

RALPH'S

I spend thousands of dollars each season on designer clothes. Why should I risk hurting my appearance by wearing inexpensive glasses or glasses that are not in fashion?

I want distinctive frames. I do not want to see many people wearing the same style of frames.

The first thing that people notice is your face. If I have to wear glasses, they should help to convey a very positive first impression of who I am.

I trust Ralph and his staff. The frames and the lenses that they have recommended have always been excellent.

I like their service, never rushed, always helpful. One thing that I especially like in today's impersonal world—they greet me by name.

A friend told me how satisfied she was with Ralph's selection of frames and his service. She was right. In the last six years, I bought five pairs of glasses from Ralph's.

PRICE CLUB

My insurance company allows me to spend up to $100 for a pair of glasses. I try to find a deal so that I do not have to pay anything out of my pocket.

I usually wear contacts. I need an inexpensive pair of glasses for the occasional time when I can't wear my contact lenses.

I am on a tight budget. If I can save money and still get a quality product, I am especially happy.

I have been shopping at Price Club for many years. I trust their pricing. In addition, I like being able to shop for eyewear at the same time I shop for other things.

When I go to another optician, a member of the staff wants to help me select my frames and gives me an opinion of how he or she thinks I look in the frames. I prefer to browse and make up my own mind as to how I look. At Price Club, there is no pressure to buy.

Glasses are glasses.

12 Sleepy-Inn Motel

Jack Roth is trying to decide whether he should make some minor changes in the way he operates his Sleepy-Inn Motel or if he should join either the Days Inn or Holiday Inn motel chains. Some decision must be made soon because his present operation is losing money. But joining either of the chains will require fairly substantial changes, including new capital investment if he goes with Holiday Inn.

Jack bought the recently completed 60-room motel two years ago after leaving a successful career as a production manager for a large producer of industrial machinery. He was looking for an interesting opportunity that would be less demanding than the production manager job. The Sleepy-Inn is located at the edge of a very small town near a rapidly expanding resort area and about one-half mile off an interstate highway. It is 10 miles from the tourist area, with several nationally franchised full-service resort motels suitable for "destination" vacations. There are a Best Western, a Ramada Inn, and a Hilton Inn, as well as many "mom and pop" and limited service–lower price motels in the tourist area. The interstate highway near the Sleepy-Inn carries a great deal of traffic since the resort area is between several major metropolitan areas. No development has taken place around the turnoff from the interstate highway. The only promotion for the tourist area along the interstate highway is two large signs near the turnoffs. They show the popular name for the area and that the area is only 10 miles to the west. These signs are maintained by the tourist area's Tourist Bureau. In addition, the state transportation department maintains several small signs showing (by symbols) that near this turnoff one can find gas, food, and lodging. Jack does not have any signs advertising Sleepy-Inn except the two on his property. He has been relying on people finding his motel as they go toward the resort area.

Initially, Jack was very pleased with his purchase. He had travelled a lot himself and stayed in many different hotels and motels, so he had some definite ideas about what travellers wanted. He felt that a relatively plain but modern room with a comfortable bed, standard bath facilities, and free cable TV would appeal to most customers. Furthermore, Jack thought a swimming pool or any other non-revenue-producing additions were not necessary. And he felt a restaurant would be a greater management problem than the benefits it would offer. However, after many customers commented about the lack of convenient breakfast facilities, Jack served a free continental breakfast of coffee, juice, and rolls in a room next to the registration desk.

Day-to-day operations went fairly smoothly in the first two years, in part because Jack and his wife handled registration and office duties—as well as general management. During the first year of operation, occupancy began to stabilize around 55 percent of capacity. But according to industry figures, this was far below the average of 68 percent for his classification—motels without restaurants.

After two years of operation, Jack was concerned because his occupancy rates continued to be below average. He decided to look for ways to increase both occupancy rate and profitability and still maintain his independence.

Jack wanted to avoid direct competition with the full-service resort motels. He stressed a price appeal in his signs and brochures—and was quite proud of the fact that he had been able to avoid all the "unnecessary expenses" of the full-service resort motels. As a result, Jack was able to offer lodging at a very modest price—about 40 percent below the full-service hotels and comparable to the lowest-priced resort area motels. The customers who stayed at Sleepy-Inn said they found it quite acceptable. But he was troubled by what seemed to be a large number of people driving into his parking lot, looking around, and not coming in to register.

Jack was particularly interested in the results of a recent study by the regional tourist bureau. This study revealed the following information about area vacationers:

1. 68 percent of the visitors to the area are young couples and older couples without children.
2. 40 percent of the visitors plan their vacations and reserve rooms more than 60 days in advance.
3. 66 percent of the visitors stay more than three days in the area and at the same location.
4. 78 percent of the visitors indicated that recreational facilities were important in their choice of accommodations.
5. 13 percent of the visitors had family incomes of less than $20,000 per year.
6. 38 percent of the visitors indicated that it was their first visit to the area.

After much thought, Jack began to seriously consider affiliating with a national motel chain in hopes of attracting more customers and maybe protecting his motel from the increasing competition. There were constant rumors that more motels were being planned for the area. After some investigating, he focused on two national chain possibilities: Days Inn and Holiday Inn. Neither had affiliates in the area.

Days Inn of America, Inc., is an Atlanta-based chain of economy lodgings. It has been growing rapidly and is willing to take on new franchisees. A major advantage of Days Inn is that it would not require a major capital investment by Jack. The firm is targeting people interested in lower-priced motels—in particular, senior citizens, the military, school sports teams, educators, and business travellers. In contrast, Holiday Inn would probably require Jack to upgrade some of his facilities, including adding a swimming pool. The total new capital investment would be between $300,000 and $500,000, depending on how fancy he got. But then Jack would be able to charge higher prices—perhaps $70 per day on the average, rather than the $40 per day per room he's charging now.

The major advantages of going with either of these national chains would be their central reservation systems—and their national names. Both companies offer toll-free reservation lines nationwide, which produce about 40 percent of all bookings in affiliated motels.

A major difference between the two national chains is their method of promotion. Days Inn uses little TV advertising and less print advertising than Holiday Inn. Instead, Days Inn emphasizes sales promotions. In a recent campaign, for example, Blue Bonnet margarine users could exchange proof-of-purchase seals for a free night at a Days Inn. This tie-in led to the Days Inn system *selling* an additional 10,000 rooms. Further, Days Inn operates a September Days Club for over 300,000 senior citizens who receive such benefits as discount rates and a quarterly travel magazine. This club accounts for about 10 percent of the chain's room revenues.

Both firms charge 8 percent of gross room revenues for belonging to their chain—to cover the costs of the reservation service and national promotion. This amount is payable monthly. In addition, franchise members must agree to maintain their facilities—and make repairs and improvements as required. Failure to maintain facilities can result in losing the franchise. Periodic inspections are conducted as part of supervising the whole chain and helping the members operate more effectively.

1. Evaluate Jack Roth's present strategy.
2. What should he do? Explain.

13 New North Media*

Late one afternoon in 1993, Chris Keevill burst into the cubicle of David Alston. He announced that a new business concept had been given the first green light by their employer, NBTel. He had two days to produce promotional material for a trade show he would be attending. With David's Mac, some copy writing, and a photograph of a child's building blocks and a toy telephone, Chris and David produced the first brochure for what would become New North Media.

New North Media's initial business partners were the New Brunswick Telephone Company Limited (NBTel) and Nortel (Northern Telecom), a major hardware and software provider for communications networks. Nortel had been a longtime partner with the small, innovative New Brunswick telco. In fact, the two companies had

*This case was written by Mark Henderson, who at the time of its preparation was associated with the Electronic Commerce Centre of the University of New Brunswick at Saint John. Based on interviews with David Alston, New North Media conducted 16 and 29 July 1997.

made such a highly advanced telecommunications network available to the province's 759,000 residents that New Brunswick had earned a reputation for being the industry's *LivingLAB*™.[1] New North's job would be to show New Brunswick and the world that the same telephone system that allowed people to call one another could be used to transport other kinds of useful data into the consumer's home.

The services that New North offers to consumers have been built for use on a specific telephone technology. New North's mandate is to create services that require the use of the Vista 350, a Nortel telephone that has a small liquid crystal display screen and several programming buttons in addition to the usual buttons available on touch-tone phones. The 350 possesses a computer chip with limited memory and communicates with a server on New North's network. The telephone and the network behind it allow users to interact with a variety of services made possible by New North technological innovations.

Menus appearing on the 350's screen allow the user access to telco features, banking services, and CallMall. The most popular telco feature is caller ID, which displays the origin of an incoming call on the screen when the phone is ringing and during the call itself. Banking services allow customers to move funds between their own accounts or to make electronic payments to utilities or other organizations set up to receive payments over the network. CallMall allows the user to select what kind of information he or she wishes to see and hear, from weather and horoscope updates to consumer product promotions.

Providing these applications and developing new ones are instrumental to New North's business model. Revenue is generated by getting businesses to sponsor one of the services; in return, an audio or text message will promote sponsoring businesses while the service is in operation.

Alternatively, businesses may sponsor their own customized application to offer service to their customers, as is the case with banks and telcos. To distribute New North's services to consumers, telcos marketing the Vista 350 are assisted in the development of their business case to further market penetration. David has dubbed this business model "the chicken or the egg" model: which comes first, securing the value of your product to the consumer, the telco, or the sponsor? To succeed in winning the confidence of one, you must first win the confidence of the other two.

NBTel's local telephone service monopoly was New North's first test and implementation site. New Brunswickers earn on average less than $50,000 per household, and as a group have limited first-hand experience with advanced technology. Nevertheless, 16 percent of NBTel subscribers rent the Vista 350 and use New North applications. Up to 80 percent of New North business is now generated outside of New Brunswick in markets such as Ontario, and Bell Canada recently purchased controlling interest in the company. The organization that once employed six now employs a hundred. Chris is general manager, and David leads the design team for New North's interactive services. David has the privilege of coordinating the activities of a highly creative technical and marketing team to produce applications of high value to consumers.

David believes that New North has won market acceptance in part by offering access to an advanced electronic information network in the form of a user-friendly, familiar telephone. The 350 is far less expensive than a personal computer and less expensive than most other interactive screen phones in the world market. Users do not have to know that when they push a button, the Vista 350 is dialing up a server for information, and sometimes even supporting transactions between the user and an organization's Web pages. As far as the user is concerned, he or she has used the phone and not computer technology with Internet access.

To provide services, New North Media invested a great deal in technological development. The protocol[2] underlying the Vista 350's network environment is ADSI. New North employees developed ADSI tools that continue to allow New North to develop new products for distribution over the 350.

Almost one year ago, Nortel and Sun Microsystems received international attention when they announced plans for the Java phone. Sun has made its mark by holding 60 percent of the market share of servers that support the Internet. Java is a framework of applications that enable network communications and is reputed to allow "any machines with microchips" to communicate with one another over networks, regardless of computer language differences. This generation of "high-end" screen phone promises to bring the interactivity of the Internet to the telephone, and companies that stand to be affected are trying to understand the significance of this promise.

What the Vista 350 and Java phone share is their promise of network interactivity with a phone set as user interface. Both can offer messages designed to be seen or heard. In contrast, Java phone applications can be designed and built quickly from the many Java "applets" available; ADSI typically requires new system architecture and construction for each new application it must access. The Vista 350 offers a two-dimensional, black text on a monochrome background, but proven Java ap-

[1] *LivingLAB* is a trademark of NBTel.

[2] If computers joined by a network of wires and electronic devices can be said to communicate with one another, a protocol is the language a computer uses to communicate. The easier the language is to interpret, the more useful it will be in communicating with other computers on the network, which might not be using the same language. In this context, applications such as New North services are messages written in ADSI sent back and forth across a telephone network between New North's server and consumers' screen phones. Occasionally, the server, exchanging the messages of many users, will have to send and receive messages from other organizations' servers in order to complete transactions for consumers.

plications have enabled 3D images, video clips and other pyrotechnical displays. For consumers, however, the present Vista 350 should be only a fraction of the cost of the Java phone.

The Java phone will be test marketed in the coming months and will likely be available to targeted markets in 1998. Judging by public excitement surrounding the Internet and all things new, should New North embrace the Java phone to give consumers and businesses the latest technology? David is concerned about the Java phone's impact, but he believes that New North's acceptance by consumers has been based on the value of services, not on the technology that supports those services. Should New North forfeit the sweat equity it has in ADSI in favour of Java? David is not convinced that New North's market will respond better to the latest and greatest technology, especially if the result is a more expensive user interface that may intimidate the non-computer user. Besides, the 350 will continue to offer more access to Internet applications without changing the user interface. David is confident that his co-workers will also insist on retaining the Vista 350, but he knows that New North should evaluate whether the Java phone is an opportunity or a threat. As a safeguard, New North must decide on a strategy and implementation plan that anticipates the introduction of the Java phone.

1. Will the new phone cause further segmentation in the current screen phone market?
2. Should market niches be defined for the Vista 350 to co-exist with the Java phone?
3. Can the market support niche marketing or segmentation?

14 Dalton Olds, Inc.

Bob Dalton owns Dalton Olds, Inc., an Oldsmobile-Nissan dealership in Richmond, British Columbia. Bob is seriously considering moving into a proposed auto mall—a large display and selling area for 10 to 15 auto dealers, none handling the same car brands. This mall will be a few miles away from his current location but easily available to his present customers and quite convenient to many more potential customers. He can consider moving now because the lease on his current location will be up in one year. He is sure he can renew the lease for another five years, but he feels the building owner is likely to want to raise the lease terms, so his total fixed costs will be about $100,000 more per year than his current fixed costs of $650,000 per year. Moving to the new mall will probably increase his total fixed costs to about $1.1 million per year. Further, fixed costs—wherever he is—will probably continue to rise with inflation. But he doesn't see this as a major problem. Car prices tend to rise at about the same rate as inflation, so these rising revenues and costs tend to offset each other.

Bob Dalton is considering moving to an auto mall because he feels this is the future trend. Malls do seem to increase sales per dealership. Some dealers in auto malls have reported sales increases of as much as 30 percent over what they were doing in their former locations outside the mall. The auto mall concept seems to be a continuing evolution from isolated car dealerships to car dealer strips along major traffic arteries to more customer-oriented clusters of dealerships that make it easier for customers to shop.

Bob is considering moving to a mall because of the growing number of competing brands and the desire of some consumers to shop more conveniently. Instead of just the Big Three, now over 30 different brands of cars and 15 brands of trucks compete in the North American market—not including specialty cars such as Lamborghini and Rolls-Royce. Increasing competition is already taking its toll on some domestic and foreign car dealers as they have to take less profit on each sale. For example, even owners of luxury car franchises such as Porsche, Audi, and Acura are having troubles, and some have moved into malls. Dealer ranks have thinned considerably, too. Failures are reported all the time. Recently, some dealers tried to become "megadealers" operating in several markets, but this did not work too well because they could not achieve economies of scale. Now owners of multiple dealerships seem to be going to malls to reduce their overhead and promotion costs. And if customers begin to go to these malls, then this may be *the* place to be—even for a dealer with only one or two auto franchises. That's the position that Bob Dalton is in with his Oldsmobile and Nissan franchises. And he wonders if he should become well positioned in a mall before it is too late.

Bob Dalton's dealership is now selling between 550 and 700 new and used cars per year, at an average price of about $11,000. With careful management, he is grossing about $1,000 per car. This $1,000 is not all net profit, however. It must go toward covering his fixed costs of about $650,000 per year. So if he sells more than 650 cars he will more than cover his fixed costs and make a profit. Obviously, the more cars he sells beyond 650, the bigger the profit—assuming he controls his costs. So he is thinking that moving to a mall might increase his sales and therefore lead to a larger profit. A major question is whether he is likely to sell enough extra cars in a mall to help pay for the increase in fixed costs. He is also concerned about how his Oldsmobile products will stand up against all of the other cars when consumers can more easily shop around and compare. Right now, Bob has some loyal customers who regularly buy from him because of his seasoned, helpful sales force *and* his dependable repair shop. But he worries that making it easy for these customers to compare other cars might lead to brand switching or put greater pressure on price to keep some of his "loyal" customers.

Another of Bob's concerns is whether the Big Three car manufacturers will discourage dealers from going into auto malls. Now these auto manufacturers do not encourage dealers to go into a supermarket setting. Instead, they prefer their dealers to devote their full energies to one brand in a freestanding location. But as real estate prices rise, it becomes more and more difficult to insist on freestanding dealerships in all markets and still have profitable dealerships. The rising number of bankruptcies of dealerships in financial difficulties has caused the manufacturers to be more relaxed about insisting on freestanding locations.

1. Evaluate Bob Dalton's present and possible new strategy.
2. What should Bob Dalton do? Why?

15 Lucas Foods*

Harold Riley was marketing manager of Lucas Foods, a diversified food manufacturing and wholesaling company based in Calgary. The company had recently had some success with a new product, Gold Medal Crumpettes. Jerry Lucas, the president of Lucas Foods, asked his marketing manager to recommend an appropriate strategy for the new product, which would best capture the available opportunity and support the mission of the company.

THE INDUSTRY

Lucas Foods was in the food manufacturing and wholesaling business, marketing a broad product line that included frozen egg products, shortening, flour, baking mixes, spices, and bulk ingredients. Its primary customers were the five major national food wholesalers, with smaller regional wholesalers and independent grocery stores accounting for a smaller portion of its sales.

Gold Medal Crumpettes was a recent entry in Lucas Foods' bakery products group. It fell into the class commonly known as biscuits. Competitive products in this class included crumpets, scones, English muffins, and tea biscuits. Competition also came from a variety of substitute items such as toast, doughnuts, and muffins. Biscuit producers included such prominent names as Weston Bakeries and McGavin Foods Ltd. domestically, as well as the American firm of S.B. Thomas, which concentrated on English muffins and dominated that market.

Lucas Foods estimated that the product life cycle for specialty bakery goods was from five to seven years. Generally, if a new product was going to be successful, it enjoyed quick acceptance in the marketplace. Introduced in 1984, Gold Medal Crumpettes had had limited distribution. They had been sold in Alberta and Saskatchewan and had been recently introduced in Manitoba, Montana, and Minnesota. Safeway was the only major chain to carry the item in Canada, but sales growth had been steady to date.

HISTORY OF LUCAS FOODS

The company was originally formed under another name over 50 years ago. It specialized in frozen egg products and later diversified into cabbage rolls and frozen meat products. The company was purchased by a major brewery in 1972, but the frozen egg portion of the business was sold back to the original owners six years later. They sold the business to Jerry Lucas in 1979. Since then, sales have doubled to their present annual level of $12 million.

The company followed a "portfolio approach" to its product line, regularly adding or deleting items according to established criteria with respect to the marketing cycle. With the single exception of frozen egg products, no specific product or product family dominated its overall product offering. (An exception was made for frozen egg products because of their unique life cycle and recession-proof qualities.)

In its statement of business mission, Lucas Foods indicated a desire to grow to an annual sales level of $50 million and to become a major national food manufacturer and wholesaler, as well as an exporter. Its major competitive weapons were believed to be its excellent reputation, product knowledge, marketing expertise, and level of customer service.

MARKETING GOLD MEDAL CRUMPETTES

Lucas Foods believed that the consumption of biscuit items was uniform across age groups, seasons, and geographic locations. It is a mature market. The merchandise itself was targeted toward the "upscale buyer." Package design, pricing policy, and product ingredients positioned Gold Medal as high priced and high quality relative to the competition. Therefore, the primary variables for segmenting the market were socioeconomic: Gold Medal Crumpettes were a luxury item.

The Crumpettes were designed to incorporate the taste and texture of scones, English muffins, and biscuits, and could be eaten with or without butter, either toasted or untoasted. They were available in four flavours—plain, raisin, cheese, and onion—and the company had plans to add three more flavours, including pizza. The product could be stored frozen. The name Gold Medal Crumpettes was specifically selected to imply quality.

Since wholesale food distribution in Canada was dominated by relatively few firms, management felt that it had little choice in the distribution of its products. Lucas Foods did not own a large warehouse to store its finished baked goods but manufactured Gold Medal Crumpettes to order. The merchandise was then transported by common carrier to various customers under net-30-days credit terms.

The goal of the company's promotional efforts was to stimulate and encourage consumer trial of the product. There was some radio advertising when the item was first

*This case was written by John Fallows under the supervision of Dr. Walter S. Good, who at the time of this case's preparation was associated with the University of Manitoba.

Exhibit 1 Total Potential Market for Gold Medal Crumpettes

	YEARLY SALES	
	CASES	VOLUME
Alberta	43,000	$ 520,000
Canada	960,000	$ 11,500,000
United States	9,600,000	$115,000,000

introduced. Although Lucas suggested the retail price, the distributor, especially in the case of Safeway, did most of the promotion. Typical promotions included:

- Hostesses distributing free samples in supermarkets.
- Crossover coupon promotions with jam companies.
- Mailout coupons to consumers.
- Free products to stores.
- Temporary price reductions for distributors.

So far, $50,000 had been spent on the promotion of Gold Medal Crumpettes. To complement these promotional efforts, Lucas Foods had three salespeople who, along with the marketing manager, regularly called on all major accounts.

Gold Medal's high price was consistent with its positioning and was arrived at after evaluating consumer surveys and the company's production costs. The expected price sensitivity of the market was also considered. A package of eight biscuits retailed for $1.89. The product was sold to supermarket chains in cases of 12 packages, with a factory price of $12 per case. Manufacturing costs, including allocated overhead, were $8.40 per case. This provided a contribution margin of $3.60 per case, or 30 percent. Production capacity was available for up to 16,000 cases per month.

CAPTURING THE OPPORTUNITY

For an estimate of the potential market for Gold Medal Crumpettes, see Exhibit 1. Harold Riley judged that Lucas Foods held a 16 percent share of the Alberta market.

The Alberta consumer had been very receptive to the product, but outside Alberta the company had only a limited reputation and was not well known as a wholesale food supplier. This lack of awareness made it more difficult for the item to obtain the acceptance of retailers. Also, the company faced an almost total lack of consumer awareness outside the province.

If Gold Medal succeeded in obtaining quick acceptance in new markets, competitors might view the development of a similar product as an attractive proposition. This could be particularly distressing if the competitor taking such an action was a major producer with an existing broad distribution system. Therefore, the speed with which Gold Medal Crumpettes could be introduced and developed into a dominant market position was very important to the long-term survival and profitability of the item. There was also the question of whether or not the degree of consumer acceptance the product had achieved in Alberta could be repeated in other areas.

Pricing research conducted by the company indicated that consumers were not prepared to cross the $2 price level at retail. If production costs were to rise and force an increase in selling price, sales might decline. Also, while the current exchange rate allowed Lucas to be quite competitive in the American market, a strengthening of the Canadian dollar could damage the company's export position.

SELECTING A STRATEGY

Harold Riley had to propose a marketing strategy to Jerry Lucas that he considered would best take advantage of the opportunity available to Gold Medal Crumpettes. He was considering three alternatives:

1. Maintenance of the product's existing market coverage and strategy. This implied limiting distribution and focusing the company's efforts on the Prairie provinces and the states of Montana and Minnesota.
2. Phased expansion. This would involve expanding across Canada, region by region, to become a major force in the Canadian biscuit market and begin selective entry into the American market.
3. Rapid expansion. This approach would involve an attempt to expand rapidly in both countries, to precede and preferably preempt competitive products in all markets, and to seek a dominant position in the North American biscuit market.

During their early discussions, Jerry had pointed out that the company had the financial capacity to undertake any of these options. It was a question of how to best focus the available resources.

Before evaluating his alternatives, Harold drew up the following criteria to guide him in coming to an appropriate decision:

- The alternative should be feasible.
- The alternative should be profitable.
- The market opportunity should be exploited as far as possible while still meeting the first two criteria.
- The alternative should fit into the activities of the company.
- The alternative should be consistent with the mission of the company.
- The alternative should be consistent with Lucas Foods' portfolio management approach concerning return, risk, and diversity.
- There should be early evidence to support the alternative.

1. Which of the three possible strategies should Lucas Foods follow?
2. Why is the strategy chosen a better choice than the other two possibilities?

16 Runners World

Tamara Lang, owner of the Runners World, is trying to decide what she should do with her retail store and how committed she should be to her current target market.

Tamara is 36 years old, and she started her Runners World retail store in 1984 when she was only 24 years old. She was a nationally ranked runner herself, and felt that the growing interest in jogging offered real potential for a store that provided serious runners with the shoes and advice they needed. The jogging boom helped to quickly turn Runners World into a profitable business, and Tamara made a very good return on her investment for the first five or six years. However, sales flattened out as more and more people found that jogging was hard work—and hard on the body, especially the knees. For the past three years, sales have slowly declined and Tamara has dabbled in various changes to try to recover her lost profitability.

From 1984 until 1990, Tamara emphasized Nike shoes, which were well accepted and seen as top quality. At that time, Nike's aggressive promotion and quality shoes resulted in a positive image that made it possible to get a $5 to $7 per pair premium for Nike shoes. Good volume and good margins resulted in attractive profits for Tamara Lang.

Committing so heavily to Nike seemed like a good idea when its quality was up and the name was good. But in the late 1980s Nike quality began to slip. It hurt not only Nike but retailers such as Tamara who were heavily committed to the Nike line. Now Nike has gotten its house in order again, and it has worked hard at developing other kinds of athletic shoes, including walking shoes, shoes for aerobic exercise, basketball shoes, tennis shoes, and cross-trainers.

While Nike was making these changes and emphasizing engineering function, a number of other firms started to focus on fashion and style in their shoe lines. In addition, with this shift more and more consumers—including many who don't really do any serious exercise—were just buying running shoes as their day-to-day casual shoes. As a result, many department stores, discount stores, and regular shoe stores put more emphasis on athletic shoes in their product assortment.

All of this change has forced Tamara to reconsider the emphasis in her store and to question what she should do. As growth in sales of running shoes started to flatten out, Tamara was initially able to keep profits up by adding a line of running accessories for both men and women. Her current customers seemed to be a ready market for a carefully selected line of ankle weights, warm-up suits, athletic bras, T-shirts, and water bottles. These items offered good margins and helped with profits. However, as the number of serious runners declined, sales of these items dropped off as well, and Tamara and her salespeople found that they were "pushing" products that other customers didn't want. Further, many of the sporting goods stores in the Runners World market area started to offer similar items—often at lower prices.

Tamara also tried adding specialized shoes for other types of athletic activities—such as shoes for serious walkers and for aerobic exercise. She was hopeful that some of the past runners would be interested in high-quality shoes designed specifically for walking or other types of exercise. However, demand for these shoes hasn't been strong, and keeping a varied line in stock—without fast turnover—is an expensive proposition.

For the past few years traffic in the store has continued to drop. In addition, an increasing number of the customers who come in the store to browse do only that—and leave without buying anything. From discussions with many of these shoppers, Tamara is pretty certain that they're more interested in style, fashion, and economy than in the high-quality shoes designed for specific athletic activities that she carries. For example, a number of customers who came in looking for "walking shoes" left quickly when they realized that Tamara's walking shoes were in the $60 and up range.

Part of the problem is that a number of retail chains offer lower-cost and lower-quality versions of similar shoes as well as related fashion apparel. Even Wal-Mart has expanded its assortment of athletic shoes—and it offers rock-bottom prices. Other chains, like Lady Foot Locker, have focused their promotion and product lines on specific target markets.

Tamara is not certain what to do. Although sales have dropped, she is still making a reasonable profit and has a relatively good base of repeat customers—primarily serious runners. She worries that she'll lose their loyalty if she shifts the store further away from her running "niche" toward fashion and casual wear. Even a change in the name of the store—to pull in more customers who are not runners—might have a serious impact on her current customers.

An important question that Tamara is debating is whether there really is a big enough market in her area for serious athletic shoes. Furthermore, is there a market for the Nike version of these shoes that tends to emphasize function over fashion? She has already added shoes from other companies to provide customers with more choices, including some lower-priced ones. She is trying to decide if there is anything else she can do to better promote her current store and product line, or if she should think about changing her strategy in a more dramatic way. At a minimum, that would involve retraining her current salespeople and perhaps hiring more fashion-oriented salespeople.

She thinks that a small shift in emphasis probably won't make much of a difference. Actually, that's what she's tried already. But a real shift in emphasis would require that Tamara make some hard decisions about her target market and her whole marketing mix. She's got some flexibility—it's not like she's a manufacturer of shoes with a big investment in a factory that can't be changed. On the other hand, she's not certain she's ready for a big change—especially a change that would mean starting over again from scratch. She started Runners World because she was interested in running and felt that she had something special to offer. Now, she worries that she's just clutching at straws without a real sense of purpose—or any obvious competitive advantage. She also knows that she is already much more successful than she ever dreamed when she started her business—and in her heart she wonders if she wasn't just spoiled by growth that came fast and easy at the start.

1. Evaluate Tamara Lang's present strategy. Evaluate the alternative strategies she is considering.
2. What should she do? Why?

17 Huntoon & Balbiera

The partners of Huntoon & Balbiera are having a serious discussion about what the firm should do in the near future.

Huntoon & Balbiera is a large regional chartered accounting firm based in Calgary, Alberta, with branch offices in Edmonton and Saskatoon. Huntoon & Balbiera has nine partners and a professional staff of approximately 105 accountants. Gross service billings for the fiscal year ending June 30, 1995, were $6.9 million. Financial data for 1993, 1994, and 1995 are presented in Exhibit 1.

H&B's professional services include auditing, tax preparation, and bookkeeping. Its client base includes municipal governments (cities, villages, and townships), manufacturing companies, professional organizations (lawyers, doctors, and dentists), and various other small businesses. A good share of revenue comes from the firm's municipal practice. Exhibit 1 gives H&B's gross revenue by service area and client industry for 1993, 1994, and 1995.

Exhibit 1 Fiscal Year Ending June 30

	1995	1994	1993
Gross billings	$6,900,000	$6,400,000	$5,800,000
Gross billings by service area:			
Auditing	3,100,000	3,200,000	2,750,000
Tax preparation	1,990,000	1,830,000	1,780,000
Bookkeeping	1,090,000	745,000	660,000
Other	720,000	625,000	610,000
Gross billings by client industry			
Municipal	3,214,000	3,300,000	2,908,000
Manufacturing	2,089,000	1,880,000	1,706,000
Professional	1,355,000	1,140,000	1,108,000
Other	242,000	80,000	78,000

At the monthly partners' meeting held in July, Pat Hogan, the firm's managing partner (CEO), expressed concern about the future of the firm's municipal practice. Hogan's presentation to his partners appears below:

> Although our firm is considered to be a leader in municipal auditing in our geographic area, I am concerned that as municipals attempt to cut their operating costs, they will solicit competitive bids from other accounting firms to perform their annual audits. Due to the fact that the local offices of most of the Big Six firms* in our area concentrate their practice in the manufacturing industry—which typically has December 31 fiscal year-ends—they have "available" staff during the summer months.
>
> Therefore, they can afford to low-ball competitive bids to keep their staffs busy and benefit from on-the-job training provided by municipal clientele. I am concerned that we may begin to lose clients in our most established and profitable practice area.†

Ann Yost, a senior partner in the firm and the partner in charge of the firm's municipal practice, was the first to respond to Pat Hogan's concern.

> Pat, we all recognize the potential threat of being underbid for our municipal work by our Big Six competitors. However, H&B is a recognized leader in municipal auditing in Alberta, and we have much more local experience than our competitors. Furthermore, it is a fact that we offer a superior level of service to our clients—which goes beyond the services normally expected during an audit to include consulting on financial and other operating issues. Many of our less sophisticated clients depend on our nonaudit consulting assistance. Therefore, I believe, we have been successful in differentiating our services from our competitors'. In many recent situations, H&B was selected over a field of as many as 10 competitors even though our proposed prices were much higher than those of our competitors.

The partners at the meeting agreed with Ann Yost's comments. However, even though H&B had many

*The "Big Six" firms are a group of the six largest chartered accounting firms in Canada. They maintain offices in almost every major Canadian city. Until recently, these firms were known as the "Big Eight," but after several mergers they have come to be known as the "Big Six." After a forthcoming merger, they will become the "Big Five."

†Organizations with December fiscal year ends require audit work to be performed during the fall and in January and February. Those with June 30 fiscal year ends require auditing during the summer months.

success stories regarding its ability to retain its municipal clients—despite being underbid—it had lost three large municipal clients during the past year. Ann Yost was asked to comment on the loss of those clients. She explained that the lost clients were larger municipalities with a lot of in-house financial expertise—and therefore less dependent on H&B's consulting assistance. As a result, H&B's service differentiation went largely unnoticed. Ann explained that the larger, more sophisticated municipals regard audits as a necessary evil and usually select the low-cost reputable bidder.

Pat Hogan then requested ideas and discussion from the other partners at the meeting. One partner, Joe Reid, suggested that H&B should protect itself by diversifying. Specifically, he felt that a substantial practice development effort should be directed toward manufacturing. He reasoned that since manufacturing work would occur during H&B's off-season, H&B could afford to price very low to gain new manufacturing clients. This strategy would also help to counter (and possibly discourage) Big Six competitors' low-ball pricing for municipals.

Another partner, Bob LaMott, suggested that "if we have consulting skills, we ought to promote them more, instead of hoping that the clients will notice and come to appreciate us. Furthermore, maybe we ought to be more aggressive in calling on smaller potential clients."

Another partner, John Smith, agreed with LaMott but wanted to go further. He suggested that they recognize that there are at least two types of municipal customers and that two (at least) different strategies be implemented, including lower prices for auditing only for larger municipal customers and/or higher prices for smaller customers who are buying consulting, too. This caused a big uproar from some who said this would lead to price-cutting of professional services and that H&B didn't want to be price cutters: "One price for all is the professional way."

However, another partner, Megan Cullen, agreed with John Smith and suggested they go even further—pricing consulting services separately. In fact, she suggested that the partners consider setting up a separate department for consulting—like the Big Six have done. This can be very profitable business. But it is a different kind of business and eventually may require different kinds of people and a different organization. For now, however, it may be desirable to appoint a manager for consulting services—with a budget—to be sure it gets proper attention. This suggestion too caused serious disagreement. Some of the partners knew that having a separate consulting arm had led to major conflicts in some firms. The main problem seemed to be that the consultants brought in more profit than the auditors, but the auditors controlled the partnership and did not properly reward the successful consultants—at least as they saw it!

Pat Hogan thanked everyone for their comments and charged them with thinking hard about the firm's future before coming to a one-day retreat (in two weeks) to continue this discussion and come to some conclusions.

1. Evaluate Huntoon & Balbiera's situation.
2. What strategy(ies) should the partners select? Why?

18 Blackburn Company

Frank Blackburn, owner of Blackburn Company, feels his business is threatened by a tough new competitor. And now Frank must decide quickly about an offer that may save his business.

Frank Blackburn has been a sales rep for lumber mills for about 20 years. He started selling in a clothing store but gave it up after two years to work in a lumberyard because the future looked much better in the building materials industry. After drifting from one job to another, Frank finally settled down and worked his way up to manager of a large wholesale building materials distribution warehouse in Hamilton, Ontario. In 1975, he formed Blackburn Company and went into business for himself, selling carload lots of lumber to lumberyards in the Niagara Peninsula area.

Frank works with five large lumber mills on the West Coast. They notify him when a carload of lumber is available to be shipped, specifying the grade, condition, and number of each size board in the shipment. Frank isn't the only person selling for these mills—but he is the only one in his area. He isn't required to take any particular number of carloads per month—but once he tells a mill he wants a particular shipment, title passes to him and he has to sell it to someone. Frank's main function is to find a buyer, buy the lumber from the mill as it's being shipped, and have the railway divert the car to the buyer.

Having been in this business for 20 years, Frank knows all of the lumberyard buyers in his area very well, and is on good working terms with them. He does most of his business over the telephone from his small office, but he tries to see each of the buyers about once a month. He has been marking up the lumber between 4 and 6 percent—the standard markup, depending on the grades and mix in each car—and has been able to make a good living for himself and his family. The going prices are widely publicized in trade publications, so the buyers can easily check to be sure Frank's prices are competitive.

In the last few years, a number of Frank's lumberyard customers have gone out of business, and others have lost sales. The problem is competition from several national home-improvement chains that have moved into Frank's market area. These chains buy lumber in large quantities direct from a mill, and their low prices are taking some customers away from the traditional lumberyards. Some customers think the quality of the lumber is not quite as good at the big chains, and some stick with the lumberyards out of loyalty. However, if it weren't for a boom in the construction market—helping to make up for lost market share—Frank's profits would have taken an even bigger hit.

Six months ago, things got worse. An aggressive young salesman set up in the same business, covering about the same area but representing different lumber mills. This new salesman charges about the same prices as Frank but undersells him once or twice a week in order to get the sale. Many lumber buyers—feeling the price competition from the big chains and realizing that they are dealing with a homogeneous product—seem to be willing to buy from the lowest-cost source. This has hurt Frank financially and personally—because even some of his old friends are willing to buy from the new competitor if the price is lower. The near-term outlook seems dark, since Frank doubts that there is enough business to support two firms like his, especially if the markup gets shaved any closer. Now they seem to be splitting the shrinking business about equally, as the newcomer keeps shaving his markup.

A week ago, Frank was called on by Mr. Talbott of Bear Mfg. Co., a large manufacturer of windows and accessories. Bear doesn't sell to the big chains; instead, it distributes its line only through independent lumberyards. Talbott knows that Frank is well acquainted with the local lumberyards and wants him to become Bear's exclusive distributor (sales rep) of residential windows and accessories in his area. Talbott gave Frank several brochures on the Bear product lines. He also explained Bear's new support program, which will help train and support Frank and interested lumberyards on how to sell the higher markup accessories. Talbott explained that this program will help Frank and interested lumberyards differentiate themselves in this very competitive market.

Most residential windows of specified grades are basically "commodities" that are sold on the basis of price and availability, although some premium and very low-end windows are sold also. The national home-improvement chains usually stock and sell only the standard sizes. Most independent lumberyards do not stock windows because there are so many possible sizes. Instead, the lumberyards custom order from the stock sizes each factory offers. Stock sizes are not set by industry standards; they vary from factory to factory, and some offer more sizes. Most factories can deliver these custom orders in two to six weeks, which is usually adequate to satisfy contractors, who buy and install them according to architectural plans. This part of the residential window business is well established, and most lumberyards buy from several different window manufacturers in order to ensure sources of supply in case of strikes, plant fires, and so on. How the business is split depends on price and the personality and persuasiveness of the sales reps. And given that prices are usually similar, the sales rep–customer relationship can be quite important.

Bear Mfg. Co. gives more choice than just about any supplier. It offers many variations in ⅛-inch increments, to cater to remodellers who must adjust to many situations. Talbott has approached Frank Blackburn in part because of Frank's many years in the business. Another reason is that Bear is aggressively trying to expand, relying on its made-to-order windows, a full line of accessories, and a newly developed factory support system to help differentiate it from the many other window manufacturers.

To give Frank a quick big picture of the opportunity he is offering, Talbott explained the window market as follows:

1. For commercial construction, the usual building code ventilation requirements are satisfied with mechanical ventilation. So the windows do not have to operate to permit natural ventilation. They are usually made with heavy-grade aluminum framing. Typically, a distributor furnishes and installs the windows. As part of its service, the distributor provides considerable technical support, including engineered drawings and diagrams, to the owners, architects, and/or contractors.
2. For residential construction, on the other hand, windows must be operable to provide ventilation. Residential windows are usually made of wood, frequently with light-gauge aluminum or vinyl on the exterior. The national chains get some volume with standard size windows, but lumberyards are the most common source of supply for contractors in Frank's area. These lumberyards do not provide any technical support or engineered drawings. A few residential window manufacturers do have their own sales centres in selected geographic areas, which provide a full range of support and engineering services, but none are anywhere near Frank's area.

Bear Mfg. Co. feels that a big opportunity exists in the commercial building repair and rehabilitation market—sometimes called the retrofit market—for a crossover of residential windows to commercial applications, and it has designed some accessories and a factory support program to help lumberyards get this "commercial" business. For applications such as nursing homes and dormitories (which must meet commercial codes), the wood interior of a residential window is desired, but the owners and architects are accustomed to commercial grades and building systems. And in some older facilities, the windows may have to provide supplemental ventilation for a deficient mechanical system. So what is needed is a combination of the residential *operable* window with a heavy-gauge commercial exterior "frame" that is easy to specify and install. And this is what Bear Mfg. Co. is offering with a combination of its basic windows and easily adjustable accessory frames. Two other residential window manufacturers offer a similar solution, but neither has pushed its products aggressively and neither offers technical support to lumberyards or trains sales reps like Frank to do the necessary job. Talbott feels this could be a unique opportunity for Frank.

The sales commission on residential windows would be about 5 percent of sales. Bear Mfg. Co. would do the billing and collecting. By getting just 20 to 30 percent of his lumberyards' residential window business, Frank could earn about half of his current income. But the real upside would come from increasing his residential window share. To do this, Frank would have to help the lumberyards get a lot more (and more profitable) business by invading the commercial market with residential windows and the bigger-markup accessories needed for this market. Frank would also earn a 20 percent commission on the accessories—adding to his profit potential.

Frank is somewhat excited about the opportunity because the retrofit market is growing. And owners and architects are seeking ways to reduce costs (which Bear's approach does—over usual commercial approaches). But he is also concerned that a lot of sales effort will be needed to introduce this new idea. He is not afraid of work, but he is concerned about his financial survival.

Frank thinks he has three choices:

1. Take Talbott's offer and sell both products.
2. Take the offer and drop lumber sales.
3. Stay strictly with lumber and forget the offer.

Talbott is expecting an answer within one week, so Frank has to decide soon.

1. Evaluate Frank Blackburn's current strategy and how the present offer fits in.
2. What should he do now? Why?

19 KASTORS, Inc.

Rick Moore, marketing manager for KASTORS, Inc., is trying to figure out how to explain to his boss why a proposed new product line doesn't make sense for them. Rick is sure it's wrong for KASTORS, Inc., but isn't able to explain why.

KASTORS, Inc., is a producer of malleable iron castings for automobile and aircraft manufacturers, as well as a variety of other users of castings. Last year's sales of castings amounted to over $70 million.

KASTORS also produces about 30 percent of all the original equipment bumper jacks installed in new American-made automobiles each year. This is a very price-competitive business, but KASTORS has been able to obtain its large market share through frequent personal contact between the company's executives and its customers—supported by very close cooperation between the company's engineering department and its customers' buyers. This has been extremely important because the wide variety of models and model changes often requires alterations in the specifications of the bumper jacks. All of KASTORS's bumper jacks are sold directly to the automobile manufacturers. No attempt has been made to sell bumper jacks to final consumers through hardware and automotive channels, although they are available through the manufacturers' automobile dealers.

Tim Owen, KASTORS's production manager, now wants to begin producing hydraulic garage jacks for sale through automobile-parts wholesalers to retail auto parts stores. Owen saw a variety of hydraulic garage jacks at a recent automotive show and knew immediately that his plant could produce these products. This especially interested him, because of the possibility of using excess capacity, now that auto sales are down. Furthermore, he says, "jacks are jacks," and the company would merely be broadening its product line by introducing hydraulic garage jacks. (Note: Hydraulic garage jacks are larger than bumper jacks and are intended for use in or around a garage. They are too big to carry in a car's trunk.)

As Tim Owen became more enthusiastic about the idea, he found that KASTORS's engineering department already had a design that appeared to be at least comparable to the products now offered on the market. None of these products have any patent protection. Furthermore, Owen says that the company would be able to produce a product that is better made than the competitive products (i.e., smoother castings, and so forth)—although he agrees that most customers probably wouldn't notice the difference. The production department estimates that the cost of producing a hydraulic garage jack comparable to those currently offered by competitors would be about $48 per unit.

Rick Moore, the marketing manager, has just received a memo from Bill Borne, the company president, explaining the production department's enthusiasm for broadening KASTORS's present jack line into hydraulic jacks. Bill Borne seems enthusiastic about the idea, too, noting that it would be a way to make fuller use of the company's resources and increase its sales. Borne's memo asks for Rick's reaction, but Bill Borne already seems sold on the idea.

Given Borne's enthusiasm, Rick Moore isn't sure how to respond. He's trying to develop a good explanation of why he isn't excited about the proposal. He knows he's already overworked and couldn't possibly promote this new line himself—and he's the only sales rep the company has. So it would be necessary to hire someone to promote the line. And this sales manager would probably have to recruit manufacturers' agents (who probably will want 10 to 15 percent commission on sales) to sell to automotive wholesalers who would stock the jack and sell to the auto parts retailers. The wholesalers will probably expect trade discounts of about 20 percent, trade show exhibits, some national advertising, and sales promotion help (catalogue sheets, mailers, and point-of-purchase displays). Furthermore, Rick Moore sees that KASTORS's billing and collection system will have to be expanded because many more customers will be involved. It will also be necessary to keep track of agent commissions and accounts receivable.

Auto parts retailers are currently selling similar hydraulic garage jacks for about $99. Rick Moore has learned that such retailers typically expect a trade discount of about 35 percent off the suggested list price for their auto parts.

All things considered, Rick Moore feels that the proposed hydraulic jack line is not very closely related to the company's present emphasis. He has already indicated his lack of enthusiasm to Tim Owen, but this made little difference in Tim's thinking. Now it's clear that Rick will have to convince the president or he will soon be responsible for selling hydraulic jacks.

1. Contrast KASTORS's, Inc.'s current strategy with the proposed strategy.
2. What should Rick Moore say to Bill Borne to persuade him to change his mind? Or should he just plan to sell hydraulic jacks? Explain.

20 Bemis Cable, Inc.

Jack Meister, vice president of marketing for Bemis Cable, Inc., is deciding how to organize and train his sales force—and what to do about Tom Brogs.

At its Pittsburgh and Montreal plants, Bemis Cable, Inc., produces wire cable ranging from .5 inch to 4 inches in diameter. Bemis sells across the United States and Canada. Customers include firms that use cranes and various other overhead lifts in their own operations—ski resorts and amusement parks, for example. The company's main customers, however, are cement plants, railway and boat yards, heavy-equipment manufacturers, mining operations, construction companies, and steel manufacturers.

Bemis employs its own sales specialists to call on and try to sell the buyers of potential users. All of Bemis's sales reps are engineers who go through an extensive training program covering the different applications, product strengths, and other technical details concerning wire rope and cable. Then they are assigned their own district—the size depending on the number of potential customers. They are paid a good salary plus generous travel expenses, with small bonuses and prizes to reward special efforts.

Tom Brogs went to work for Bemis in 1981, immediately after receiving a civil engineering degree from McGill University. After going through the training program, he took over as the only company rep in the Quebec district. His job was to call on and give technical help to present customers of wire cable. He was also expected to call on new customers, especially when inquiries came in. But his main activities were to (1) service present customers and supply the technical assistance needed to use cable in the most efficient and safe manner, (2) handle complaints, and (3) provide evaluation reports to customers' management regarding their use of cabling.

Tom Brogs soon became Bemis's outstanding representative. His exceptional ability to handle customer complaints and provide technical assistance was noted by many of the firm's customers. This helped Tom bring in more sales dollars per customer and more in total from present customers than any other rep. He also brought in many new customers—mostly heavy equipment manufacturers in Quebec. Over the years, his sales have been about twice the sales rep average, and always at least 20 percent higher than the next best rep—even though each district is supposed to have about the same sales potential.

Tom's success established Quebec as Bemis's largest-volume district. Although the company's sales in Quebec have not continued to grow as fast in the last few years because Tom seems to have found most of the possible applications and won a good share for Bemis, the replacement market has been steady and profitable. This fact is mainly due to Tom Brogs. As one of the purchasing agents for a large machinery manufacturer mentioned, "When Tom makes a recommendation regarding use of our equipment and cabling, even if it is a competitor's cable we are using, we are sure it's for the best for our company. Last week, for example, a cable of one of his competitors broke, and we were going to give him a contract. He told us it was not a defective cable that caused the break but rather the way we were using it. He told us how it should be used and what we needed to do to correct our operation. We took his advice and gave him the contract as well!"

Four years ago, Bemis introduced a unique and newly patented wire sling device for holding cable groupings together. The sling makes operations around the cable much safer, and its use could reduce hospital and lost-time costs due to accidents. The slings are expensive, and the profit margin is high. Bemis urged all its representatives to push the sling, but the only sales rep to sell the sling with any success was Tom Brogs. Eighty percent of his customers are currently using the wire sling. In other areas, sling sales are disappointing.

As a result of Tom's success, Jack Meister is now considering forming a separate department for sling sales and putting Tom Brogs in charge. His duties would include travelling to the various sales districts and training other representatives to sell the sling. The Quebec district would be handled by a new rep.

1. Evaluate Jack Meister's strategy(ies).
2. What should he do about Tom Brogs—and his sales force? Explain.

21 Honda Hit•Run•Throw*

Greg and Todd were a little nervous just before the Year-end Honda Hit•Run•Throw (HHRT) Meeting with Honda Canada. They felt that they had done a good job in staging the national final at SkyDome the week before, particularly in light of the fact that both men had been newly hired by Baseball Canada. But this was a new domain.

Greg White, a graduate student in human kinetics at the University of Ottawa, had started with the

*This case was written by Gregory B. White under the supervision of David S. Litvack, Faculty of Administration, University of Ottawa, Ottawa.

organization as a student intern some four months earlier. But at that time he had done PR work with the national junior team and was not really acquainted with the HHRT program. When Lee Ann Lalonde resigned her HHRT national coordinator position for another job less than a month before the national final, Greg was appointed to the position on an interim basis. He knew that this was a great career opportunity, but also felt that it would be a tremendous challenge.

Todd Wallin's tenure with Baseball Canada was even more abbreviated. He had been hired as manager of events and marketing for the organization just a few weeks prior. Although he had accumulated a significant amount of sport marketing experience through previous positions with the Ottawa Rough Riders and Synchro Canada, he was still familiarizing himself with his new surroundings.

As if staging the national final of HHRT within such a short period had not been enough, the two were then required to quickly gather the annual data (in concert with the ten provincial coordinators) in order to piece together a final summary report, which was presented to Honda Canada. It had truly been a "baptism by fire" for the new recruits!

"I want to congratulate you both on an excellent event last week," said Richard Pendrill, marketing manager for Honda Canada, as he took his seat at the far end of the board room in the Toronto Blue Jays front office at SkyDome. "I also think that you've done a fine job with the Final Report."

The kind words were quite comforting to the two Baseball Canada representatives. But just as they began to feel that the pressure was lifting, Mr. Pendrill turned the heat up once more. "I'm going to cut to the chase . . . what happened to our numbers in Ontario this year?"

Mr. Pendrill was referring to the low number of participants in Ontario—the largest market in Canada, and the most highly targeted province for the title sponsor. Despite attracting more than 36,000 children between the ages of 7 and 13 to the program Canada-wide, Ontario had only managed to register 4,500 participants—a failure by any yardstick.

Following a somewhat passionate debate between the various partners, the meeting was adjourned. The participants agreed that Baseball Canada would conduct market research among local baseball coordinators across the province to get their feedback pertaining to the program. The following factors, among others, would be surveyed: awareness level, strengths, weaknesses, why they did or did not participate, whether they would again in the following year, and suggestions. This information was to be used to produce a brief marketing strategy to be implemented for HHRT in the province of Ontario in the following year. Just when the two thought they could relax, it was back to the drawing board.

It was an onerous task attempting to contact these individuals on such short notice. Often the contact names that were available to them were presidents of the organizations, not the minor baseball coordinators themselves. In other cases, there were no contact names or numbers at all, just the address of the organization (which was of little use given the time constraints). In the end, about 40 coordinators were contacted—a response rate of 15 to 20 percent. (Some of the key points of the survey are summarized in Exhibit 2.)

A few days after completing the survey, Todd and Greg met to discuss the program results over the past year, the recent Ontario survey, and the marketing strategy that they would create and implement in response to this data.

AN OVERVIEW OF HHRT IN 1997

In 1997 Honda Canada, the Toronto Blue Jays, Major League Baseball Canada, and Baseball Canada joined forces for the third consecutive year to present Honda Hit•Run•Throw on a national basis. The program also received generous support from Easton Sports Canada, Irvin Sports (Cooper), All Sport Insurance Marketing, Gatorade, and Heritage/Sport Canada. The program was delivered in Ontario by Baseball Canada, the Ontario Baseball Association, and the Toronto Blue Jays, with the first-named organization taking the leadership role.

Honda Hit•Run•Throw is a grass roots baseball skills competition for kids aged 7 to 13. There are currently four categories, which are based on age and gender. The first three age groups—Pre-Rookie, Rookie, and Mosquito—are co-ed; the last, Pee Wee, is gender exclusive (i.e., there are separate categories for boys and girls). Events are held at the local level, with winners advancing to regional, provincial, and, finally, national competitions. It is very easy to implement—all that is required is a limited amount of equipment and any open field. It is volunteer driven, which keeps costs down, but also creates some problems.

Overall, Honda Hit•Run•Throw was a success in 1997. Despite disappointments in individual provinces, it achieved 110.5 percent of the estimated participation for the year, surpassing the previous year's participation (+8.1 percent) and site (+8.2 percent) numbers by a healthy margin. The media coverage allotted to the program also expanded, realizing a 13.2 percent increase in newsprint coverage over 1996 (see Exhibit 1).

Honda Hit•Run•Throw was not, however, free of setbacks in 1997. Poor weather, staff turnover, problematic supplier deals, and declining registration in baseball nationwide were obstacles for the program (sports such as soccer and softball are cutting into baseball registration). Despite such difficulties, the program continued to grow and expand, entrenching itself as a rite of spring in communities across Canada. The most glaring exception was Ontario.

Baseball Canada's provincial affiliates had varying financial results in 1997. About half of the provinces announced a small profit from the program; others suffered losses, which sometimes reached $5,000. Despite some adverse results, the provinces are steadfast in their support of the program.

In contrast to 1996, Baseball Canada was unable to administer the program at a break-even level. Over the

Exhibit 1 Some Key Statistics

	1996 LEVEL	1997 ESTIMATE	1997 ACTUAL	% OF '97 ESTIMATE	% CHANGE FROM '96
Participation	34,101	33,350	36,856	110.5	+8.1
Sites	305	305	330	108.2	+8.2
Media coverage	5,374,521	—	6,082,009	—	+13.2

past year, Baseball Canada invested some $40,000 into HHRT. The problems associated with new suppliers and excess shipping costs accounted for some of the loss. Nevertheless, it was agreed that in order to continue administering the program at the current level, the bottom line would have to be improved through the introduction of new revenues and/or cost-cutting measures.

THE TASK AHEAD

"Given that Honda's goal for Ontario in 1997 was 8,000 participants, I think that we really need to knock their socks off in 1998," said Todd. "To do that we need to enrol 9,000 to 10,000 kids. That won't be easy, given the political situation."

"You know, I don't understand why there has been such a problem with participation," said Greg, scratching his head. "The OBA alone has approximately 100,000 kids enrolled who are eligible to participate in HHRT." Greg was referring to the Ontario Baseball Association, the dominant body for baseball in the province, and Baseball Canada's affiliate in Ontario. "Why wouldn't baseball people be interested in a program that is fun and exciting, and is an excellent way to introduce newcomers to the sport?" he continued rhetorically.

"I agree, it *is* hard to understand," remarked Todd. "I think it's a lack of communication through the volunteer hierarchy, coupled with an already busy summer schedule. Even if local organizers want to run an HHRT event, they don't know who to contact, or they don't have time to do it by the time they do find out about it. Events simply have to be decided earlier. We can't tell people in the spring and expect a positive response in that short a time frame."

Greg nodded in agreement. "Then there's the matter of Little League. Many of the eligible participants for HHRT are Little League members." Little League, an American-based organization that rivals the OBA, boasted an estimated 20,000 members in Ontario, most of them in the Ottawa and Windsor areas. "It is frustrating when you have two groups that basically have the same wants and needs but are separated by politics. It sure would be great if we could secure their support, but if we want to bring them on board, they will surely want a slice of the pie. I think we could give their organization some publicity through the program but we certainly don't have the resources to give them any monetary compensation."

"From what I understand, the OBA has invited some Little League organizers to their upcoming convention," Todd suddenly remembered. "That would be a great chance to promote the program among both OBA and Little League, and kill two birds with one stone!"

"With the Baseball Canada and OBA conventions coming up in a few weeks, it would be great if we could announce that the program will be full speed ahead for 1998," said Greg. "That would give our people plenty of notice to execute the proper planning for the year ahead."

"But it's not just Little League that makes things tricky," replied Todd with a sigh. "The situation isn't made any easier by the rift between some members of the OBA and the Blue Jays. These problems will make it difficult to increase our numbers. If we can't get beyond the politicking and lack of communication, we may have to move beyond the traditional market of baseball associations, and target other organizations with kids in those age groups."

"It would also be good to encourage more female participation," said Greg. "The competition is open to both genders, but only the Pee Wee category is gender exclusive—the rest are co-ed. Adding an extra category would cost us more, but it could really spark female participation."

"You're absolutely right," said Todd enthusiastically. "Girls' participation is on the rise, and we need to capitalize on that. If we could, it might open the door for more sponsorship opportunities."

"The survey also indicated that there are other areas we could exploit, like tournaments," said Greg. "We need to go to where the kids already are, and tournaments offer that opportunity. Also, the volunteer structure is already in place, so it wouldn't be difficult to stage. I think it would add value to the tournament . . . it could be used like an all-star competition. And what about summer camps and schools? We've had some camps involved in the past. If we could penetrate these two markets, the possibilities would be staggering."

"I agree, but we have to be careful not to bite off more than we can chew," said Todd. "The financial and human resources that are currently available to the HHRT program are very limited. It might be best to solidify our position in our more traditional markets before we jump into foreign territory. That said, I don't think we should rule out the idea altogether. Maybe we could do some test marketing in these areas."

"I guess you're right, it *is* difficult to manoeuvre when you're operating with such limited resources,"

Exhibit 2 Some Key Points from Ontario Survey

Awareness

- Most organizations are aware of program. Many of the contacted had hosted in past.
- It was difficult getting contacts' numbers for organizations that have not hosted.
- Politics between rival organizations was a factor. Little League, for instance, is a separate entity and will not share its contacts with Baseball Canada.
- There is no clear channel by which local organizations become aware of HHRT.
  - Ontario Baseball Association (OBA: provincial)
  - Honda
  - Little League (rival)
  - Baseball Canada (national)

Strengths

- Most organizations felt that HHRT was a competitive yet fun day for kids and parents and that it was a valuable program.
- Good value in kits; lots of goodies for kids.
  - Autographed Blue Jays Baseball
  - Sizzler (baseball) cards
  - Scorecards
  - Hot dogs/Gatorade
  - Poster

Suggested Improvements

- Place, time, and date of regionals should be established early (it would help improve coordination of dates for local events).
- Timely delivery of site kits is critical.
- Some events run long.
- Need national hot dog sponsor for picnic.
- Additional promotional support would be welcomed.
- New, gender-exclusive categories would encourage girls' participation.

Honda Dealer Involvement

- Mostly supportive. In some situations, however, the support was little more than verbal.
- Often, local coordinators expected more support.
- Need to reinforce perception that Honda is primary backer of program.

Why Organizations Didn't Host

- Some local organizations didn't have volunteer capacity.
- Short season and many other baseball events.
- Lack of awareness in Metro Toronto.

Registration

- Most registration begins early in year with mail-out; this is often followed by sit-down registration in March/April.
- Most organizations were positive about including HHRT literature at registration.

HHRT Regional Meetings

- Most coordinators indicated that they would attend a regional coordinator meeting.
- Little League presidents' meetings are held on a monthly basis.

Support for 1998

- Most organizations said they would host again.
- Of those who have not previously hosted, most were interested in doing so.

Comments

- Organizations have to book their fields early.
- Improve promotional vehicles.
- Set regional events early.

Recommendations

- Need to solidify sponsorship deal early in order to move ahead with certainty.
- Kiosk and presentation at Baseball Canada and OBA conventions only one of several promotional opportunities with target market.
- Little League officials in Ottawa districts will attend OBA convention; this will be a good opportunity to get more associations on board.
- Make presentations at Little League presidents' meetings.
- Continuous communication is key.
- Use a mail-out as an initial approach to organizations in December or before.
- Host regional HHRT meetings with local coordinators (January/February).
- Make some promotional literature available for organizations at registration time (early in year, in some cases as early as December of the current year).
- Add incentives for local coordinators to host (Blue Jay tickets, etc.).
- For associations that are reluctant to host due to small volunteer base (or whatever), offer support in the first year. After that they may become more accommodating.
- Must get Sudbury to host local and regional event for Northern Ontario. This is a key for maintaining a presence in that region.
- Must raise awareness nationally.
- Build the event around a larger event (tournament) or Photo Day.
- Must keep value in kits; this is particularly salient in generating excitement at new sites.

said Greg. "One thing is for sure—it's great to work with first-class organizations like the Blue Jays and Major League Baseball. They believe the program is very important for developing baseball awareness in the community. They also give us a lot of marketing support, not to mention that potential sponsors are attracted by the opportunity to affiliate themselves not just with amateur but also with big-league baseball."

"You know, there was some talk that we could promote the program through the Blue Jays Caravan," said Todd, referring to the promotional event that visits major Canadian cities each winter in anticipation of the new baseball season. "It would be an excellent way to highlight our relationship with the Blue Jays and Major League Baseball, and would give HHRT a promotional shot in the arm!"

"We should also exploit our connections at TSN [The Sports Network]," added Greg. "The CRTC [Canadian Radio-television and Telecommunications Commission] has made it clear that an important part of TSN's operational mandate is to help promote amateur sport in Canada. They [TSN] have said they are willing to give us some public service spots to help promote our programs."

After talking things over, they agreed that the program still had much potential. They also felt that despite shortcomings in Ontario in 1997, the program was a success. After a mere three years of operation on a national basis, HHRT boasted more than 36,000 competitors at more than 300 sites across Canada. The work would be hard for the two newcomers, but both felt assured about the value of the program and their ability to move it to the next level.

1. What are the alternatives open to Baseball Canada?
2. Which of these alternatives should be chosen? Explain.

22 Kelman Mfg., Inc.

Al Kelman, the marketing manager of Kelman Mfg., Inc., wants to increase sales by adding sales reps rather than playing with price, which is how Al describes what Henry Kelman, his father and Kelman's president, is suggesting. Henry is not sure what to do, either. But he does want to increase sales, so something new is needed.

Kelman Mfg., Inc., is a leading producer in the plastic forming machinery industry. It has patents covering over 200 variations, but Kelman's customers seldom buy more than 30 different types in a year. The machines are sold to plastic forming manufacturers to increase production capacity or replace old equipment.

Established in 1952, the company has enjoyed a steady growth to its present position, with annual sales of $50 million.

Some six firms compete in the Canadian plastic forming machinery market. Several Japanese, German, and Swedish firms compete in the global market, but the Kelmans have not seen them in western Canada. Apparently, the foreign firms rely on manufacturers' agents who have not provided an ongoing presence. They don't follow up on inquiries, and their record for service on the few sales they have made is not good. So the Kelmans are not worried about them right now.

Each of the Canadian competitors is about the same size and manufactures basically similar machinery. Each has tended to specialize in its own geographic area. None has exported much because of high labour costs in Canada. Four of the competitors are located in the east, and two—including Kelman—are in the west. The other western Canadian firm is in Calgary, Alberta. All of the competitors offer similar prices and sell F.O.B. their factories. Demand has been fairly strong in recent years. As a result, all of the competitors have been satisfied to sell in their geographic areas and avoid price-cutting. In fact, price-cutting is not a popular idea in this industry. About 20 years ago, one firm tried to win more business and found that others immediately met the price cut—but industry sales (in units) did not increase at all. Within a few years, prices returned to their earlier level, and since then competition has tended to focus on promotion, avoiding price.

Kelman's promotion depends mainly on six company sales reps, who cover British Columbia and the Prairies. In total, these reps cost about $660,000 per year, including salary, bonuses, supervision, travel, and entertaining. When the sales reps are close to making a sale, they are supported by two sales engineers, at a cost of about $120,000 per year per engineer. Kelman does some advertising in trade journals—less than $50,000—and occasionally uses direct mailings. But the main promotion emphasis is on personal selling. Any personal contact outside the western market is handled by manufacturers' agents, who are paid 4 percent on sales—but sales are very infrequent. Henry Kelman is not satisfied with the present situation. Industry sales have levelled off and so have Kelman's sales, although the firm continues to hold its share of the market. Henry would like to find a way to compete more effectively in the other regions because he sees great potential outside of western Canada.

Competitors and buyers agree that Kelman is the top-quality producer in the industry. Its machines have generally been somewhat superior to others in terms of reliability, durability, and productive capacity. The difference, however, usually has not been great enough to justify a higher price (because the others are able to do the necessary job) unless a Kelman sales rep convinces the customer that the extra quality will improve the customer's product and lead to fewer production line breakdowns. The sales rep also tries to sell Kelman's better sales engineers and technical service people—and sometimes is successful. But if a buyer is only interested in comparing delivered prices for basic machines—the usual situation—Kelman's price must be competitive in order for it to get the business. In short, if such a buyer has a choice between Kelman's and another machine *at the same price,* Kelman will usually win the business in its part of the western market. But it's clear that Kelman's price has to be at least competitive in such situations.

The average plastic forming machine sells for about $220,000, F.O.B. shipping point. Shipping costs within each major region average about $4,000—but another $3,000 to $6,000 must be added on shipments from western Canada to Ontario or Quebec (and vice versa).

Henry Kelman is thinking about expanding sales by absorbing the extra $3,000 to $6,000 in freight cost that arises if a customer in eastern Canada buys from his western Canadian location. By doing this, he would not be cutting price in those markets but rather reducing his net return. He thinks that his competitors would not see this as price competition—and therefore would not resort to cutting prices themselves.

Al Kelman, the marketing manager, disagrees. Al thinks that the proposed freight absorption plan would stimulate price competition in the eastern markets and perhaps in western Canada as well. He proposes instead that Kelman hire some sales reps to work the eastern markets, selling quality rather than relying on the manufacturers' agents. He argues that two additional sales reps in each of these regions would not increase costs too much, and might greatly increase the sales from these markets over those brought in by the agents. With this plan, there would be no need to absorb the freight and risk disrupting the status quo. Adding more of Kelman's own sales reps is especially important, he argues, because competition in the east is somewhat hotter than in the west, due to the number of competitors (including foreign competitors) in the region. A lot of expensive entertaining, for example, seems to be required just to be considered as a potential supplier. In contrast, the situation has been rather quiet in the west because only two firms are sharing this market and each is working harder near its home base. The eastern competitors don't send any sales reps to western Canada, and if they have any manufacturers' agents, they haven't gotten any business in recent years.

Henry Kelman agrees that his son has a point, but industry sales are levelling off and Henry wants to increase sales. Furthermore, he thinks the competitive situation may change drastically in the near future anyway, as global competitors get more aggressive and some possible new production methods and machines become more competitive with existing ones. He would rather be a leader in anything that is likely to happen rather than a follower. But he is impressed with Al's comments about the greater competitiveness in the other markets and therefore is unsure about what to do.

1. Evaluate Kelman's current strategies.
2. Given Henry Kelman's sales objective, what should Kelman Mfg. do? Explain.

23 Ontario Rutabaga Council*

In June 1996, Smithfield Communications was retained by the Ontario Rutabaga Council (ORC) to develop a new promotional campaign for Ontario rutabagas. This was a fairly unusual account for the medium-sized agency, which specialized in agriculture. The average Smithfield client had a promotional budget of $4 million. The firm's clients included a number of organizations in the fertilizer, chemical, feed, and seed industries. They also handled a few industrial accounts, the largest of which was the $6 million Warren ("Windows to the World") Window account.

The agency was established in 1972 by Simon Smithfield, a former sales representative for Massey Ferguson. Smithfield had started by working with equipment accounts, but as the business prospered and the staff expanded, the firm moved into other areas of agribusiness and industrial products. The agency remained fairly conservative in its approach. Smithfield's own specialty was slogans, but the agency's real emphasis was on "quality" promotion designed to inform customers. Though Smithfield himself had no formal marketing training, he was a great believer in hiring account executives with a marketing background because he recognized that ad executives couldn't work in a vacuum.

"We have to work on behalf of the client! We have to look at their strategy or help them develop one. Otherwise they may as well toss their money down a rat hole for all the good a flashy ad campaign will do! What's more, we gotta have the guts to tell them their ideas stink! We owe them that honesty!"

This philosophy was still at work at Smithfield, though Simon had retired. Every junior account man was thoroughly versed in the philosophy and history of the company.

Though the agency dealt mainly with agribusiness accounts, Smithfield had never been in favour of hiring only those with an agricultural background. As Simon often said, "Too narrow-minded! If he grew up on a hog farm in Simcoe, then basically he thinks he has the last word on hogs! In this business you need a wide range of experience and a quick, open mind."

Most of Smithfield's junior ad people came right out of university. One of the latest additions was Ted Banner, a graduate of the Ontario Agricultural College. Ted had been with Smithfield for two years. He learned fast and was quite ambitious. To date, his greatest success had been the brochure for Farnum Feed. On the basis of his past performance, Smithfield executives felt that he was ready to take on the ORC account.

*This case was prepared by Thomas Funk and Jane Funk of the Ontario Agricultural College at the University of Guelph, Guelph, Ontario. It is intended as a basis for classroom discussion and is not designed to present either correct or incorrect handling of administrative problems. Some data in the case have been disguised to protect confidentiality.

Ted realized that this was his big chance. The ORC account was expected to increase to around $300,000 for 1996–97, and he planned to make the campaign a real landmark. However, he knew he must do his homework first, so he began studying all the background material he had collected on the ORC.

RUTABAGA INDUSTRY IN CANADA

Canadian rutabagas were originally used as feed for sheep that were bound for New England markets in the mid-1800s. In those days, rutabagas were called turnips. The sheep buyers themselves tried the vegetable and ordered more for their own consumption. These early turnips were a far cry from the sweeter-tasting turnip developed in the 1930s and known as the Laurentian. This variety became known officially as rutabaga in 1967. The rutabaga is large and globular in shape, with yellow flesh and a purple top. Usually it is waxed to preserve it during shipping and storage. Rutabagas vary in size from one to three pounds and cost anywhere from 25 to 30 cents a pound.

Ontario is the centre for Canadian rutabaga production, though some Canadian competition comes from Quebec and P.E.I. The Ontario industry supports 130 growers and a number of shippers and packers. In 1988, the farm value of rutabagas in Ontario was $5.9 million, making it the eighth-highest for vegetables grown in Ontario. Rutabagas reach the consumer by way of the following channel: Farmer→Packer→Shipper→Wholesaler→ Supermarkets and Fruit and Vegetable Stores.

A large percentage of the Ontario rutabaga crop is shipped to the United States; in fact, rutabagas account for approximately 15 to 20 percent of the value of all fresh and processed vegetables exported to the United States from Canada. Rutabagas are also grown in the United States, but Ontario rutabagas are considered superior. Since there is no tariff on rutabagas, Canadian rutabagas compete effectively in price with American-grown ones.

PAST PROMOTIONAL EFFORTS

Although the ORC had coordinated promotional programs on behalf of rutabaga producers for many years, its efforts were hampered by small budgets, which often varied significantly from year to year. For example, last year the ORC had a $60,000 promotional budget, while the year before it was over $100,000. This budget was used, mainly in the United States, to promote rutabagas to housewives as a unique and different vegetable. In the United States, most rutabagas are consumed south of the Mason Dixon Line and east of the Mississippi River, and the ORC felt that the main competition in this area was white turnips and turnip greens; hence, their program of differentiating the rutabaga.

To formulate their promotional program, the ORC hired the advertising agency J.B. Cruikshank Ltd. This agency prepared a promotion mix consisting of magazine ads, press releases for radio, a TV video, and a video for high school family science teachers. All of this was developed around the persona of "June Conway," the fictional resident home economist for the ORC.

The magazine ads appeared in *Woman's Day* and *Family Circle* magazines during the months of November (the beginning of the holiday season in the United States, which is the peak period of rutabaga consumption) and April (the end of the turnip season in the United States). These full-page ads stressed new uses and recipe ideas, and featured a sample recipe and picture. They mentioned but did not stress nutrition, and they included a free write-in offer of a rutabaga recipe book. The agency reported that this phase of the program received "a reasonable response" of 1,000 requests per month.

Other aspects of this promotional program included press releases for radio and a short TV video. The agency hoped the radio releases would be aired in the late morning or early afternoon on women's shows. The television video, produced at a cost of $28,000 and titled "Everything You Wanted to Know About Rutabagas—But Didn't Know Who to Ask," was distributed upon request to cable TV channels for use at their convenience. The agency felt that "this scheduling gave the video excellent exposure without requiring the ORC to pay for air time." The film highlighted the growing of rutabagas and their nutritional value, and included attractive recipe ideas. In addition to this, a new video, "The Ontario Rutabaga in the Kitchen," was distributed to high school family science teachers.

The TV video, like the magazine ads, included a write-in address for recipes, but response here was not as high as for the magazines. Mr. Cruikshank explained, "This doesn't indicate less interest, but rather that TV viewers are less likely to copy an address down and mail for more information than those who see advertisements in a magazine or newspaper." Mr. Cruikshank further reported that "by use, the video appears successful. All ten prints are booked well in advance." He encouraged the ORC to increase the number of video copies and increase the number of high school videos available. Board member Fred Hunsberger supported this idea—especially increasing the number of high school videos available. He felt that "we have to let those kids know what a good value tur—uh, rutabagas are. If we get them early on, we've got them for life."

CURRENT SITUATION

The ORC's president, Clyde Carson, was not as excited as Fred about Cruikshank's suggestion. He had recently seen a publication titled "Report on the New England Market for Canadian Rutabagas," which documented a decline in rutabaga consumption in that area. Further research revealed that per capita, rutabaga consumption had been declining for the past twenty years, and that growers were reducing their acreage or leaving the industry altogether. Clyde presented these depressing statistics to the ORC and suggested a new "marketing strategy" such as that discussed at a seminar he had recently attended. As expected, Clyde ran into heavy opposition from other board members, who did not understand what a marketing strategy was and who were more interested in increasing their production levels. Fred Hunsberger had been particularly adamant about keeping their current promotional program:

"Clyde, we're already telling 'em about all the vitamins and offering free recipes. Now what woman wouldn't jump at a free recipe? And that June Conway is a mighty fine woman! The way she talks about those rutabagas just makes my mouth water. And the kids are sure to like the video. I sure would have been pleased to see videos when I was in school! That TV cable film is doing the job too. Booked solid all last year. It looks real classy to have our own TV film. Just a fluke that consumption is down. People don't know when they're well off these days. You wait! The old values will come back soon and people will see that turnips—uh, rutabagas—are good solid food!"

Clyde persevered, and finally got the board to agree to a large-scale study of the North American rutabaga market. This project was funded mainly by the Ontario Ministry of Agriculture and involved two stages. The first stage was to obtain rutabaga awareness and consumption information from 2,000 Canadian and 6,000 American households. More detailed information was obtained in the second stage on consumption, attitudes, and preferences from 300 households in Canada and 800 in the United States. Based on this report, Clyde was able to convince the ORC that a drastic overhaul was needed. The first thing they did was find a replacement for J.B. Cruikshank Ltd., the ad agency responsible for "Everything You Always Wanted to Know About . . ." Fred Hunsberger had insisted that Smithfield Communications be hired as a replacement: "That's a classy outfit! I knew old Sim when he was with Massey and I'll never forget his big 'Keep Pace With Case' campaign. That's what we need. A catchy slogan! It will turn the tide in a few weeks. Look at the milk people. My grandkids won't stop singing 'Drink Milk, Love Life.' Drives me crazy but they say it sells the milk. Why not tur—uh, rutabagas too? Of course, we'll keep June Conway."

Clyde didn't argue with Fred, though he privately felt that perhaps Smithfield Communications was not the best choice and questioned the usefulness of a slogan. Fred, on the other hand, thought that Smithfield Communications' familiarity with agriculture would be an asset. The two men planned a meeting with Ted Banner, the Smithfield Communications manager assigned to the ORC account.

RESEARCH PROJECT RESULTS

Ted Banner sat at his desk at the offices of Smithfield Communications. In front of him were various documents and folders containing background and past promotional programs of the ORC. On top of the pile was a manuscript, "Consumer Analysis of the North American Rutabaga Market," the report that presented the results of the large-scale survey done in 1990. Ted knew that this report had to form the basis of his recommendations to the ORC. In preparation for his initial meeting with Clyde Carson and Fred Hunsberger, Ted looked through the report and summarized the main points.

Common product names

The report revealed that the product is called by many different names, including rutabaga, swede, swede turnip, and turnip. In the United States, 78 percent of consumers referred to the product as a rutabaga, compared to only 20 percent in Canada.

Awareness and frequency of use

Consumers were placed in one of six categories depending on their awareness and frequency of rutabaga use. These results are shown in Exhibit 1.

The first category is relatively small and includes people who are not aware of rutabagas. The second category includes people who are aware of rutabagas but have never purchased one. This group is relatively small in Canada but large in the United States. The third group includes people who have not purchased a rutabaga in the last twelve months. These are probably "lapsed users" who have discontinued use of the product. This is a relatively small group.

The last three groups are classified as current rutabaga users and account for 64 percent of Canadian consumers and 31 percent of American consumers. The heavy-user segment accounts for 16 percent of Canadian consumers and only 3 percent of American consumers.

User and non-user profiles

Analysis of the above groups in terms of demographic characteristics revealed some distinct profiles. In Canada, rutabaga usage tends to be highest among older consumers, consumers who live in rural areas and small communities, French-speaking Canadians, families whose female head is either a homemaker or retired, and families whose male and female head have less education. American results are very similar, with rutabaga usage being highest among older consumers, lower-income families, families whose male and female heads have less education, single-person households, and blacks.

Vegetable purchase criteria

Consumers in the study were asked to rank six possible purchase criteria. The highest-ranking criteria were quality, nutritional value, and taste preference. Price and the time needed to prepare the vegetable were of some but lesser importance. Rutabaga users consistently ranked price higher than taste preference. Non-users ranked taste preference ahead of price.

Consumers in both countries responded to a series of statements designed to measure attitudes toward a

Exhibit 1 Rutabaga Market Segments, United States and Canada

MARKET SEGMENTS	PERCENT OF CANADIAN HOUSEHOLDS	PERCENT OF UNITED STATES HOUSEHOLDS
Non-user, not aware	11	14
Non-user, aware	16	40
Lapsed user (not used in past year)	8	14
Light user (less than 4 times a year)	23	19
Medium user (5 to 12 times a year)	25	9
Heavy user (more than 12 times a year)	16	3

number of issues related to vegetable and rutabaga usage. The following attitudes emerged:

- Consumers feel they are eating about the right quantity and variety of vegetables, but a sizable group think they should eat more and a greater variety. This is particularly true for the non-user segment.
- Rutabagas are not considered expensive relative to other vegetables, but consumers stated that large price increases could cause some reduction in consumption.
- A large percentage of consumers increased their purchases of rutabagas when they were on special. Most consumers felt that rutabagas were seldom "featured" items at their stores.
- Most consumers felt that rutabagas are neither conveniently located nor attractively displayed at their stores. Also, they often aren't available at all.
- A large percentage of consumers felt that rutabagas are generally too large for the size of their household. They indicated an interest in pre-sliced, ready-to-cook rutabagas or, especially in the United States, ready-to-serve rutabaga casseroles.
- Most consumers judge product quality by external appearance, and many felt that the rough, black or brown spots on the exterior of the rutabaga indicated inferior quality.
- Many consumers commented on the difficulty of preparing a rutabaga.
- Most consumers have little information on the nutritional value of rutabagas and would like more.

Reasons for non and lapsed users

Both non-users and lapsed users listed not liking the taste as the main reason for non-use. The second-most-frequent reply given by non-users was that they didn't know how to cook or prepare them. Lapsed users listed several secondary reasons: too much trouble to prepare, too hard to cut, poor quality, and prefer more nutritious vegetables.

Purchase and use

Rutabaga users were asked about their purchase and use of the product. Their responses indicated the following:

- Approximately one-half of all users decide to purchase the product after entering a store.
- Almost all purchases were made in supermarkets.
- The most popular methods of preparation are boiled and mashed.
- Less than 30 percent of all users serve the vegetable raw.
- The vegetables that consumers consider close substitutes for rutabagas are carrots and squash.
- Most consumers consider the rutabaga as an ordinary everyday dish.
- Over 80 percent of all current users indicated that they were using rutabagas just as often or more often than five years ago.
- Most consumers obtain recipe ideas from magazines and newspapers.

TED'S REACTION

After thoroughly studying the background information and the research report, Ted knew that the problem he faced was far more complex than he imagined. His telephone conversations with Clyde Carson indicated that Carson was aware of the severity and complexity of the problem, but Carson hinted that other council members expected a "magic cure-all" along the lines of the famous "Keep Pace With Case" campaign of a few years ago. Ted knew he would need to call on all his tact as well as his past marketing background in order to come up with a promotional campaign for the ORC. His first task, however, would be to develop a set of marketing strategy recommendations based on the research report he had just read.

1. What is the current situation at the Ontario Rutabaga Council? Why is consumption declining?
2. Evaluate the current promotional program. What recommendations should Ted have for the board?
3. Outline a promotional program based on the above recommendations.

24 Fraser Company*

Alice Howell, president of the Columbia Plastics Division of the Fraser Co., leaned forward at her desk in her bright, sunlit office and said, "In brief, our two options are either to price at a level that just covers our costs or we face losing market leadership to those upstart Canadians at Vancouver Light. Are there no other options?" Tamara Chu, Columbia's marketing manager, and Sam Carney, the production manager, had no immediate reply.

Columbia Plastics, based in Seattle, Washington, had been the area's leading manufacturer of plastic moulded skylights for use in houses and offices for almost 15 years. However, two years earlier, Vancouver Light, whose main plant was located in Vancouver, British Columbia, Canada, 150 miles to the north of Seattle, had opened a sales office in the city and sought to gain business by pricing aggressively. Vancouver Light began by offering skylights at 20 percent below Columbia's price for large orders. Now, Vancouver Light had just announced a further price cut of 10 percent.

COMPANY BACKGROUND

The primary business of the Fraser Co., which had recently celebrated the 50th anniversary of its existence, was the supply of metal and plastic fabricated parts for its well-known Seattle neighbour, Boeing Aircraft. Until the 1960s, Boeing had accounted for more than 80 percent of Fraser's volume, but Fraser then decided to diversify in order to protect itself against the boom-and-bust cycle that seemed to characterize the aircraft industry. Even now, Boeing still accounted for nearly half of Fraser's $50 million[†] in annual sales.

Columbia Plastics had been established to apply Fraser's plastic moulding skills in the construction industry. Its first products, which still accounted for nearly 30 percent of its sales, included plastic garage doors, plastic gutters, and plastic covers for outdoor lights, all of which had proved to be popular among Seattle home builders. In 1968, Columbia began production of what was to be its most successful product, skylights for homes and offices. Skylights now accounted for 70 percent of Columbia's sales.

THE SKYLIGHT MARKET

Although skylights varied greatly in size, a typical one measured 3 feet by 3 feet and would be installed in the ceiling of a kitchen, bathroom, or living room. It was made primarily of moulded plastic with an aluminum frame. Skylights were usually installed by homebuilders upon initial construction of a home, or by professional contractors as part of a remodelling job. Because of the need to cut through the roof to install a skylight and to then seal the joint between the roof and skylight so that water would not leak through, only the most talented of "do-it-yourselfers" would tackle this job on their own. At present, 70 percent of the market was in home and office buildings, 25 percent in professional remodelling, and 5 percent in the do-it-yourself market.

Skylights had become very popular. Homeowners found the natural light they brought to a room quite attractive and perceived skylights to be energy conserving. Although opinion was divided on whether the heat loss from a skylight was more important to consumers than the light gained, the general perception was quite favourable. Homebuilders found that featuring a skylight in a kitchen or other room was an important plus in attracting buyers, and they often included at least one skylight as a standard feature in a home. Condominium builders had also found that their customers liked the openness that a skylight seemed to provide. Skylights were also a popular feature of the second homes that many people owned on Washington's lakes or in ski areas throughout the northwest.

In Columbia Plastics' primary market area of Washington, Oregon, Idaho, and Montana, sales of skylights had levelled off in recent years at about 45,000 units per year. Although Columbia would occasionally sell a large order to California homebuilders, such sales were made only to fill slack in the plant and, after including the cost of transportation, were only break-even propositions at best.

Four homebuilders accounted for half the sales of skylights in the Pacific Northwest. Another five bought an average of 1,000 each, and the remaining sales were split among more than 100 independent builders and remodellers. Some repackaged the product under their own brand name; many purchased only a few dozen or less.

Columbia would ship directly only to builders who ordered at least 500 units per year, although it would subdivide the orders into sections of one gross (144) for shipping. Most builders and remodellers bought their skylights from building supply dealers, hardware stores, and lumberyards. Columbia sold and shipped directly to these dealers, who typically marked up the product by 50 percent. Columbia's average factory price was $200 when Vancouver Light first entered the market.

Columbia maintained a sales force of three for making contact with builders, remodellers, and retail outlets. The sales force was responsible for Columbia's complete line of products, which generally went through the same channels of distribution. The cost of maintaining the sales force, including necessary selling support and travel expense, was $90,000 annually.

Until the advent of Vancouver Light, there had been no significant local competition for Columbia. Several California manufacturers had small shares of the market, but Columbia had held a 70 percent market share until two years ago.

*This case was written by Dr. Charles Weinberg, who at the time of its preparation was associated with the University of British Columbia.

[†]All prices and costs are in U.S. dollars.

Vancouver Light's entry

Vancouver Light was founded in the early 1970s by Jennifer McLaren, an engineer, and Carl Garner, an architect, and several of their business associates, in order to manufacture skylights. They believed that there was a growing demand for skylights, but there was no ready source of supply available in western Canada. Their assessment proved correct, and their business was successful.

Two years ago, the Canadian company had announced the opening of a sales office in Seattle. McLaren came to this office two days a week and devoted her attention to selling skylights only to the large-volume builders. Vancouver Light announced a price 20 percent below Columbia's, with a minimum order size of 1,000 units to be shipped all at one time. It quickly gained all the business of one large builder, True Homes, a Canadian-owned company. In the previous year, that builder had ordered 6,000 skylights from Columbia.

A year later, one of Columbia's sales representatives was told by the purchasing manager of Chieftain Homes, a northwest builder who had installed 7,000 skylights the previous year, that Chieftain would switch to Vancouver Light for most of its skylights unless Columbia was prepared to match Vancouver's price. Columbia then matched that price for orders above 2,500 units, guessing that smaller customers would value highly the local service that Columbia could provide. Chieftain then ordered 40 percent of its needs from Vancouver Light. Two small builders had since switched to Vancouver Light as well. Before Vancouver's latest price cut had been reported, Tamara Chu, Columbia's marketing manager, projected that Vancouver Light would sell about 11,000 units this year, compared to the 24,000 that Columbia was now selling. Columbia's volume represented a decline of 1,000 units per year in each of the last two years, following the initial loss of the True Homes account.

Columbia had asked its lawyers to investigate whether Vancouver Light's sales could be halted on charges of export dumping—that is, selling below cost in a foreign market—but a quick investigation revealed that Vancouver Light's specialized production facility provided a 25 percent savings on variable cost, although one-third of that was lost due to the additional costs involved in importing and transporting the skylights across the border.

THE IMMEDIATE CRISIS

Alice Howell and her two colleagues had reviewed the situation carefully. Sam Carney, the production manager, had presented the cost accounting data, which showed a total unit cost of $135 for Columbia's most popular skylight. Vancouver Light, he said, was selling a closely similar model at $144. The cost of $135 included $15 in manufacturing overheads, directly attributable to skylights, but not the cost of the sales force or the salaries, benefits, and overheads associated with the three executives in the room. General overheads, including the sales force and executives, amounted to $390,000 per year at present for Columbia as a whole.

Tamara Chu was becoming quite heated about Vancouver Light by this time. "Let's cut the price a further 10 percent to $130 and drive those Canadians right out of the market! That Jennifer McLaren started with those big builders and now she's after the whole market. We'll show her what competition really is!"

But Carney was shocked: "You mean we'll drive her *and* us out of business at the same time! We'll both lose money on every unit we sell. What has that sales force of yours, Tamara, been doing all these years if not building customer loyalty for our product?"

"We may lose most of our sales to the big builders," cut in Howell, "but surely most customers wouldn't be willing to rely on shipments from Canada? Maybe we should let Vancouver Light have the customers who want to buy on the basis of price. We can then make a tidy profit from customers who value service, need immediate supply, and have dealt with our company for years."

1. Should the Fraser Company match Vancouver Light's prices, undercut that firm, or continue its current pricing policy?
2. Why is your choice superior to the other two courses of action?

25 Lee Steel Supply and Service*

Lee Steel Supply and Service (LSSS) is a medium-sized processor and distributor of rolled steel and aluminum products. The company was originally established as a dealer in scrap iron products in 1946. The initial facility in Buffalo, New York, has been expanded to include an 80,000-square-foot manufacturing plant, warehouse, and sales office. The total New York market is covered from this location. In 1957, a 30,000-square-foot warehouse and sales office was set up in Mississauga, Ontario, to service the nearby Canadian market. The company's present sales volume is $45 million, with 65 percent in New York and the remainder in Ontario.

THE PRODUCT MIX

The LSSS product line is classified into three basic categories:

1. Standard finished products: These include such items as cold-rolled slit coil, sheared-to-size blanks (which manufacturers employ directly in their production processes), and standard-size steel sheets.
2. Items preprocessed for inventory: Examples of products in this category are 28-gauge 36-inch by 98-inch galvanized sheets and 60-inch by 120-inch

14-gauge hot-rolled sheet, as used in the manufacture of oil tanks.

3. Custom job processing orders: Recent custom orders have included 100,000 pounds of customer-supplied 43-inch, 22-gauge, cold-rolled coil to be slit into 8½-inch widths, and 50,000 pounds of customer-supplied galvanized satin coat 32-inch, 24-gauge coil to be slit into 1½-inch widths. Although relatively insignificant in dollar volume, the custom operation accounts for almost 30 percent by weight of the metal processed by LSSS.

TECHNOLOGY AND PRODUCTION METHODS

The production process consists of three major operations: shearing, slitting, and cutting to length. Each of these job centres consists of a number of machines. This production flow presents scheduling difficulties because of the varied number of products and operations performed. Although machinery obsolescence is very low, monthly maintenance costs are high due to the need to keep equipment in working order. Generally, there is a conscious attempt by LSSS management to purchase unusual, specialized equipment to produce specialized products. In this way, competition can be effectively eliminated for a number of products, which allows LSSS considerable flexibility in price setting.

CUSTOMER PROFILE

No major customers account for a large portion of volume. In fact, LSSS's largest customer represents only 4 percent of total dollar sales. Likewise, no single product contributes significantly to the firm's total revenue.

Most of LSSS's customers are located in the Buffalo and Toronto–Montreal areas. Typically, product requirements for these two major markets differ considerably. Thus, separate sales strategies have been developed.

PRESENT INDUSTRY SITUATION

Early in 1991, Brian Matthews, general manager of LSSS, was somewhat pessimistic about future business prospects. The economy was almost one year into a recessionary period. Government action designed to tone down inflation had resulted in an unprecedented level of unemployment. As a result, 1990 dollar sales were down almost 8 percent below 1989, and 1991 expectations were poor.

At present, inventories and production are high throughout the industry, causing price deterioration in most product lines. Matthews believed that the possible Canadian steel strike, expected in mid-1991, would remedy this situation by increasing Canadian demand for LSSS's products. But if the strike failed to materialize, conditions would deteriorate, after the summer peak period, back to where they were at present.

GENERAL PRICING GUIDELINES

Essentially, LSSS uses a cost-plus basis in determining selling prices. A base processing cost is established for each order, consisting of labour-machine costs (electricity, maintenance, and other variable costs). This figure is added to material and scrap freight costs and subtracted from the estimated selling price to set the gross margin for that particular order. The net margin is obtained by subtracting the fixed costs allocated to each order (plant overhead, marketing, paperwork, and administration).

To determine the cost of production for each order, the cost at each phase of production is calculated. Using a two-shift basis, the base processing costs of each machine are calculated per hour. These costs are revised monthly.

The various overhead costs are determined weekly and allocated to each order. To calculate these costs, the total plant production in hours is determined and each order receives a percentage of these costs in relation to its percentage of the total weekly production.

Price lists are accordingly established for the standard items produced. The production cost estimates are checked each month, but in each order-cost determination, changes are made only when long-term trends would justify them.

To facilitate this cost-plus basis of pricing, LSSS has a computerized recordkeeping system. Administration, sales, delivery, and other such costs are reported weekly. Each cost centre within the plant reports its costs to the administrative department on a daily basis, and monthly production reports are subsequently prepared. The reports produced show breakdowns by customer, total order cost, total order price, and total gross margin.

The ultimate responsibility for pricing rests with Brian Matthews. Three people working in the administrative department report directly to him. In theory, the two people in administration at Mississauga report directly to him as well. In practice, these people nearly always act independently, since the Ontario market is distinct from that of New York.

ACTUAL PRICING

The pricing guidelines referred to above are often modified considerably in actual practice. The major factor affecting final price is the particular demand–supply situation existing at the time of sale.

Gross margins on orders to different customers vary widely—from 5 to 60 percent on standard items and up to 100 percent on custom orders. Generally, as the demand for a product rises, prices are increased for all except the best customers. Irregular or occasional customers are charged the highest price obtainable.

In general, the high-margin products are characterized by low turnover. They include small custom orders and sophisticated products that require specialized equipment. Low-margin products are high-turnover items and are produced in large quantities for two or three customers. Competitive pressure on these quantity products is the major reason for the lower margins. There is very little relationship, however, between gross margin and order regularity, customer size, and so forth.

Other criteria, although infrequently used, influence the pricing process. For example, prices may be lowered to obtain orders that will employ unused capacity, to fill delivery trucks, or to obtain very large orders.

The high dollar value of inventories, combined with handling costs, obsolescence, and spoilage (rust), results in extremely high inventory carrying costs. As a result, "stress pricing," or selling at less than cost, will occasionally be undertaken to get rid of very-slow-moving items. Also, LSSS will sell a product as a "loss leader" to pick up sales of a higher-margin product.

Matthews frequently revises his price lists and sends them to all salespeople as the lower limit on which to base their quotations. One of the key factors by which he evaluates the performance of his salespeople is the price above this "lower limit" that the salespeople can obtain for their products.

Situation 1

LSSS has been requested by the New York State government to submit a quotation on work for a very large construction project. Although he is not certain of the exact figures, Brian Matthews thinks this could represent a sizable revenue, based on his present method of pricing. To his knowledge, four other firms have been asked to bid. Alternatively, Matthews knows that if the Canadian steel strike should materialize, LSSS will not have the capacity to handle both the contract and the expected heavy Canadian demand for his firm's products. In this situation, he would prefer to forgo the New York government contract, because the Canadian strike would generate large profits due to the short supply of metal. However, if LSSS does not win the contract and the Canadian strike does not occur, LSSS will most certainly operate only at a marginal profit level. Furthermore, if he wants to be certain of winning the contract, Matthews will have to submit a very low bid to the state, and this would result in quite low profits.

Situation 2

In an effort to expand market share significantly, Superior Steel, the major competitor of LSSS, has lowered the price of its rolled-steel products to a level below the cost price of similar products carried by LSSS. In pursuing this strategy, Superior Steel hopes to lower its fixed costs per order enough to permit it to undercut LSSS substantially in the long run.

Situation 3

Early in 1991, Brian Matthews was concerned about the discrepancy between LSSS's formal pricing policy and the company's actual pricing practices. He believed that the formal policy should be updated to conform more closely with current market conditions.

In May, Matthews hired a second-year MBA student, Bill Witzel, to work on this problem as a summer project.

1. Evaluate the pros and cons of each alternative in Situation 1. What pricing strategy should Brian Matthews employ in Situation 1?
2. Evaluate the alternatives available to LSSS in Situation 2 and design a suitable strategy in response to the Superior Steel move.
3. Provide a "business school" impression of LSSS's actual pricing practice in Situation 3 and suggest how the company can improve its pricing policy.

26 Cutters, Inc.

Tony Kenny, president and marketing manager of Cutters, Inc., is deciding what strategy—or strategies—to pursue.

Cutters, Inc., is a manufacturer of industrial cutting tools. These tools include such items as lathe blades, drill press bits, and various other cutting edges used in the operation of large metal cutting, boring, or stamping machines. Tony Kenny takes great pride in the fact that his company, whose $5.2 million sales in 1991 is small by industry standards, is recognized as a producer of a top-quality line of cutting tools.

Competition in the cutting-tool industry is intense. Cutters competes not only with the original machine manufacturers but also with many other larger domestic and foreign manufacturers that offer cutting tools as one of their many different product lines. This has had the effect, over the years, of standardizing the price, the specifications, and, in turn, the quality of the competing products of all manufacturers. It has also led to fairly low prices on standard items.

About a year ago, Tony was tiring of the financial pressure of competing with larger companies enjoying economies of scale. At the same time, he noted that more and more potential cutting-tool customers were turning to small tool and die shops because of specialized needs that could not be met by the mass production firms. Tony thought that perhaps he should consider some basic strategy changes. Although he was unwilling to become strictly a custom producer, he thought that the recent trend toward buying customized cutting edges suggested that new markets might be developing—markets too small for the large, multiproduct-line companies to serve profitably but large enough to earn a good profit for a flexible company of Cutters's size.

Tony hired a marketing research company, Holl Associates, to study the feasibility of serving these markets. The initial results were encouraging. It was estimated that Cutters might increase sales by 65 percent and profits by 90 percent by serving the emerging markets. This research showed that there are many large users of standard cutting tools that buy directly from large cutting-tool manufacturers (domestic or foreign) or from wholesalers that represent these manufacturers. This is the bulk of the cutting-tool business (in terms of units sold and sales dollars). But there are also many smaller users all over North America who buy in small but regular quantities. And some of these needs are becoming more specialized. That is, a special cutting tool may make a machine and/or worker much more productive, perhaps eliminating several steps with time-consuming setups. This is the area that the research company sees as potentially attractive.

Next, Tony had the sales manager hire two technically oriented market researchers (at a total cost of $60,000 each per year, including travel expenses) to maintain continuous contact with potential cutting-tool customers. The researchers were supposed to identify any present or future needs that might exist in enough cases to make it possible to profitably produce a specialized product. The researchers were not to take orders or sell Cutters's products to the potential customers. Tony felt that only through this policy could these researchers talk to the right people.

The initial feedback from the market researchers was most encouraging. Many firms (large and small) had special needs—although it often was necessary to talk to the shop supervisor or individual machine operators to find these needs. Most operators were making do with the tools available. Either they didn't know that customizing was possible or they doubted that their supervisors would do anything about it if they suggested that a more specialized tool would increase productivity. But these operators were encouraging because they said that it would be easier to persuade supervisors to order specialized tools if the tools were already produced and in stock than if they had to be custom made. So Tony decided to continually add high-quality products to meet the ever-changing, specialized needs of users of cutting tools and edges.

Cutters's potential customers for specialized tools are located all over North America. The average sale per customer is likely to be less than $500, but the sale will be repeated several times within a year. Because of the widespread market and the small order size, Tony doesn't think that selling direct, as is done by small custom shops, is practical. At the present time, Cutters sells 90 percent of its regular output through a large industrial wholesaler, National Mill Supplies, Inc., which serves the entire area east of the Manitoba–Ontario border and carries a very complete line of industrial supplies (to "meet every industrial need"). Each of National's sales reps sells over 10,000 items from a 910-page catalogue. National Mill Supplies, although very large and well known, is having trouble moving cutting tools. National is losing sales of cutting tools in some cities to newer wholesalers specializing in the cutting-tool industry. The new wholesalers are able to give more technical help to potential customers and therefore better service. National's president is convinced that the newer, less-experienced firms either will realize that they can't maintain a substantial profit margin along with their aggressive strategies, or will eventually go broke trying to overspecialize.

From Tony's standpoint, the present wholesaler has a good reputation and has served Cutters well in the past. National Mill Supplies has been of great help in holding down Tony's inventory costs by increasing the inventory in National's 35 branch locations. Tony has received several complaints about the lack of technical assistance given by National's sales reps, as well as their lack of knowledge about Cutters's new special products, but he feels that the present wholesaler is providing the best service it can. All its sales reps have been told about the new products at a special training session, and a new page has been added to the catalogue they carry with them. Tony dismisses the complaints as "the usual things you hear when you're in business."

Tony thinks there are more urgent problems than a few complaints. Profits are declining, and sales of the new cutting tools are not nearly as high as forecast, even though all research reports indicate that the company's new products meet the intended markets' needs perfectly. The high costs involved in producing small quantities of special products and in adding the market research team, together with lower-than-expected sales, have significantly reduced Cutters's profits. Tony is wondering whether it is wise to continue to try to cater to the needs of many specific target markets when the results are this discouraging. He also is considering increasing advertising expenditures in the hope that customers will pull the new products through the channel.

1. Evaluate Cutters's situation and Tony Kenny's present strategy.
2. What should he do now?

27 Lever, Ltd.*

Joe Hall is product manager for Guard Deodorant Soap. He was just transferred to Lever, Ltd., a Canadian subsidiary of Lever Group, Inc., from world headquarters in New York. Joe is anxious to make a good impression because he is hoping to transfer to Lever's London office. He is working on developing and securing management approval of next year's marketing plan for Guard. His first job is submitting a draft marketing plan to Sarah Long, his recently appointed group product manager, who is responsible for several such plans from product managers like Joe.

*Adapted from a case prepared by Daniel Aronchick, who at the time of its preparation was marketing manager at Thomas J. Lipton, Limited.

Exhibit 1 Past 12-Month Share of Bar Soap Market (percent)

	MARITIMES	QUEBEC	ONTARIO	MANITOBA/SASKATCHEWAN	ALBERTA	BRITISH COLUMBIA
Deodorant segment						
Zest	21.3%	14.2%	24.5%	31.2%	30.4%	25.5%
Dial	10.4	5.1	12.8	16.1	17.2	14.3
Lifebuoy	4.2	3.1	1.2	6.4	5.8	4.2
Guard	2.1	5.6	1.0	4.2	4.2	2.1
Beauty bar segment						
Camay	6.2	12.3	7.0	4.1	4.0	5.1
Lux	6.1	11.2	7.7	5.0	6.9	5.0
Dove	5.5	8.0	6.6	6.3	6.2	4.2
Lower-priced bars						
Ivory	11.2	6.5	12.4	5.3	5.2	9.0
Sunlight	6.1	3.2	8.2	4.2	4.1	8.0
All others (including stores' own brands)	26.9	30.8	18.6	17.2	16.0	22.6
Total bar soap market	100.0%	100.0%	100.0%	100.0%	100.0%	100.0%

Exhibit 2 Standard Cases of 3-Ounce Bars Consumed per 1,000 People in 12 Months

	MARITIMES	QUEBEC	ONTARIO	MANITOBA/SASKATCHEWAN	ALBERTA	BRITISH COLUMBIA
Guard	4.1	10.9	1.9	8.1	4.1	6.2
Sales index	66	175	31	131	131	100

Joe's marketing plan is the single most important document he will produce on this assignment. This annual marketing plan does three main things:

1. It reviews the brand's performance in the past year, assesses the competitive situation, and highlights problems and opportunities for the brand.
2. It spells out marketing strategies and the plan for the coming year.
3. Finally, and most importantly, the marketing plan sets out the brand's sales objectives and advertising/promotion budget requirements.

In preparing this marketing plan, Joe gathered the information in Exhibit 1.

Joe was somewhat surprised at the significant regional differences in the bar soap market.

1. The underdevelopment of the deodorant bar segment in Quebec with a corresponding overdevelopment of the beauty bar segment. But some past research suggested that this is due to cultural factors—English-speaking people have been more interested than others in cleaning, deodorizing, and disinfecting. A similar pattern is seen in most European countries, where the adoption of deodorant soaps has been slower than in North America. For similar reasons, the perfumed soap share is highest in French-speaking Quebec.
2. The overdevelopment of synthetic bars in the Prairies. These bars, primarily in the deodorant segment, lather better in the hard water of the Prairies. Nonsynthetic bars lather very poorly in hard-water areas—and leave a soap film.
3. The overdevelopment of the "all other" segment in Quebec. This segment, consisting of smaller brands, fares better in Quebec, where 43 percent of the grocery trade is done by independent stores. Conversely, large chain grocery stores dominate in Ontario and the Prairies.

Joe's brand, Guard, is a highly perfumed deodorant bar. His business is relatively weak in the key Ontario market. To confirm this share data, Joe calculated consumption of Guard per thousand people in each region. See Exhibit 2.

These differences are especially interesting since per capita sales of all bar soap products are roughly equal in all provinces.

A consumer attitude and usage research study was conducted approximately a year ago. This study revealed that consumer "top-of-mind" awareness of the Guard brand differed greatly across Canada. This was true despite the even expenditure (by population) of advertising funds in past years. Also, trial of Guard was low in the Maritimes, Ontario, and British Columbia. See Exhibit 3.

The attitude portion of the research revealed that consumers who had heard of Guard were aware that its deodorant protection came mainly from a high fragrance level. This was the main selling point in the copy, and it was well communicated by Guard's advertising. The other important finding was that consumers who had tried Guard were satisfied with the product. About 70 percent of those trying Guard had repurchased the product at least twice.

Joe has also discovered that bar soap competition is especially intense in Ontario. It is Canada's largest market, and many competitors seem to want a share of it. The chain stores are also quite aggressive in promotion and pricing, offering specials, in-store coupons, and so on. They want to move goods. And because of this, two key Ontario chains have put Guard on their pending delisting sheets. These chains, which control about half the grocery volume in Ontario, are dissatisfied with how slowly Guard is moving off the shelves.

Now Joe feels he is ready to set a key part of the brand's marketing plan for next year: how to allocate the advertising/sales promotion budget by region.

Guard's present advertising/sales promotion budget is 20 percent of sales. With forecast sales of $4 million, this would amount to an $800,000 expenditure. Traditionally such funds have been allocated in proportion to population. See Exhibit 4.

Joe feels he should spend more heavily in Ontario, where the grocery chain delisting problem exists. Last year, 36 percent of Guard's budget was allocated to Ontario, which accounted for only 12 percent of Guard's sales. Joe wants to increase Ontario spending to 48 percent of the total budget by taking funds proportionately from all other areas. Joe expects this will increase business in the key Ontario market, which has over one-third of Canada's population, because it is a big increase and will help Guard "out-shout" the many other companies who are promoting heavily.

Joe presented this idea to Sarah, his newly appointed group product manager. Sarah strongly disagrees. She has also been reviewing Guard's business and feels that promotion funds have historically been misallocated. It is her strong belief that, to use her words, "a brand should spend where its business is." Sarah believes that the first priority in allocating funds regionally is to support the areas of strength. She suggested to Joe that there may be more business to be had in the brand's strong areas, Quebec and the Prairies, than in chasing sales in Ontario. The needs and attitudes toward Guard, as well as competitive pressures, may vary a lot among the provinces. Therefore, Sarah suggested that spending for Guard in the coming year be proportional to the brand's sales by region rather than to regional population.

Joe is convinced this is wrong, particularly in light of the Ontario situation. He asked Sarah how the Ontario market should be handled. Sarah said that the conservative way to build business in Ontario is to invest incremental promotion funds. However, before these incremental funds are invested, a test of this Ontario investment proposition should be conducted. Sarah recommended that some of the Ontario money should be used to conduct an investment-spending market test in a small area or town in Ontario for 12 months. This will enable Joe to see if the incremental spending results in higher sales and profits—profits large enough to justify higher spending. In other words, an investment payout should be assured before any extra money is spent in Ontario. Similarly, Sarah would do the same kind of test in Quebec, to see if more money should go there.

Joe feels this approach would be a waste of time and unduly cautious, given the importance of the Ontario market and the likely delistings in two key chains.

1. Evaluate the present strategy for Guard and Joe's and Sarah's proposed strategies.
2. How should the promotion money be allocated? Should investment-spending market tests be run first? Why? Explain.

Exhibit 3 Usage Results (in percent)

	MARITIMES	QUEBEC	ONTARIO	MANITOBA/SASKATCHEWAN	ALBERTA	BRITISH COLUMBIA
Respondents aware of Guard	20%	58%	28%	30%	32%	16%
Respondents ever trying Guard	3	18	2	8	6	4

Exhibit 4 Allocation of Advertising/Sales Promotion Budget, by Population

	MARITIMES	QUEBEC	ONTARIO	MANITOBA/ SASKATCHEWAN	ALBERTA	BRITISH COLUMBIA	CANADA
Percent of population	10%	27%	36%	8%	8%	11%	100%
Possible allocation of budget based on population (in 000s)	$80	$216	$288	$64	$64	$88	$800
Percent of Guard business at present	7%	51%	12%	11%	11%	8%	100%

28 Imperial Lumber Limited*

Imperial Lumber is a large forest products company based in Vancouver, British Columbia. Major product divisions include plywood, panelling, pulp, and lumber. The company is fully integrated. Operations include everything from logging camps and manufacturing plants to approximately 25 retail branches located coast-to-coast in Canada.

Susan McKay, central division manager for Imperial, had to make training and remuneration decisions regarding her sales reps (see Exhibit 1). The decisions were complicated by a number of factors:

1. Head office had indicated that due to the downturn in 1999, a maximum of four reps could be recommended for maximum salary increments based on performance.
2. Two of the branches in her division were showing signs of atypical performance. Windsor's sales and gross profits were down substantially because of that district's reliance on the automobile industry, which was no longer a major customer. On the other hand, Ottawa, a new branch, was experiencing rapid growth. One of the central division objectives for 2000 and 2001 was to penetrate this market as rapidly as possible in an attempt to capture a large share of the residential construction contractors' business.
3. McKay knew that sales volume figures for reps could be misleading to the extent that much of Imperial's product mix (approximately 85 lines) generated substantially different gross profits. Just because a representative produced a substantial sales volume did not automatically imply an associated large gross profit. Furthermore, the price a representative might obtain for the company's products was, within limits, a function of how well he or she could negotiate terms with the customer.

The Ottawa sales force was doing well for relative "newcomers" to the company (see Exhibit 2, "Basis Month Average" column). Their gross profit/sales ratios were above average (Brumec, 10.3; Kyle, 13.2; and Blackman,

*This case was prepared by Professor Lindsay Meredith, who at the time of its preparation was associated with Simon Fraser University.

Exhibit 1

TO: S. McKay, Central Division Manager
FROM: L. Meredith, Sales Analyst II
DATE: February 1, 2000

Attached [Exhibit 2] is the sales and gross profit analysis for our representatives in the Central Division. I hope this will be of some use in your efforts to determine:

(a) Which of the employees from Central Division you wish to send to the annual training program in order to improve sales performance.

(b) Those employees you wish to recommend for maximum salary increments due to outstanding performance in the previous year.

The representatives have been ranked according to sales achievement for 1999.

Exhibit 2 Analysis of Sales Staff Ranked According to Average Sales Dollars per Month and Average Gross Profit per Month as at December 31

BASIS MONTH AVERAGE	NAME	LOCATION	SALES RANK	AVERAGE SALES PER MONTH	G.P. RANK	AVERAGE G.P. PER MONTH	OTHER DUTIES
12	S. Richards	Toronto	1	312,510	2	34,915	
12	R. McCain	Toronto	2	301,950	3	34,134	
7	N. Walker	Hamilton	3	299,420	6	28,560	
10	G. Pedersen	Kingston	4	295,650	1	35,478	
12	L. Nielson	Hamilton	5	287,777	4	29,842	
12	J. Morrison	Thunder Bay	6	284,920	9	25,643	
8	B. Brumec	Ottawa	7	280,000	5	28,840	
12	G. Andrews	Thunder Bay	8	273,255	11	18,581	
12	E. Davis	Kingston	9	268,125	10	17,696	
12	F. Gordon	Hamilton	10	230,122	12	14,958	
12	F. Scott	Thunder Bay	11	228,500	13	14,853	SSR*
6	J. Kyle	Ottawa	12	214,752	8	28,400	
12	M. Fisk	Kingston	13	204,912	14	13,319	SSR
4	R. Blackman	Ottawa	14	193,155	7	28,520	ASR†
12	A. Hobson	Windsor	15	181,122	16	9,056	
12	A. McDonald	Toronto	16	150,110	15	9,757	
12	P. Greenway	Windsor	17	115,055	17	5,753	
12	E. Fleischer	Windsor	18	92,110	18	4,606	

14.8). Consideration of their sales volumes (which fell in the middle to lower end of the distribution) had to be tempered by the fact that Ottawa was a new branch and that these salespeople were still developing new accounts. Andrews, Davis, Gordon, and McDonald all had gross profit/sales ratios below average (6.8, 6.6, 6.5, and 6.5, respectively). They all had at least one year's experience with Imperial. They all came from branches where their colleagues were able to substantially "outperform" them. Finally these people all fell in the middle to lower range of the sales volume ranking.

McKay, after careful consideration of the data, recommended:

- Richards, McCain, and Pedersen receive maximum salary increments.
- Andrews, Davis, Gordon, and McDonald receive further training in order to upgrade their sales skills.

1. Given the wide range of possible recommendations, why did Susan McKay select these people?
2. Give your justification for her decision.

29 Parker Instruments Ltd.*

Parker Instruments Ltd. (PI) is a British firm that operates as a manufacturer and an importer/distributor. Its field is electronic instruments, and the imported products account for about 75 percent of sales. One of the companies Parker Instruments represents in the United Kingdom is Electro Industries (EI), a Canadian precision instrument firm. PI and EL have been working together for about 10 years. The relationship between the two companies was good for a number of years. Then things started to go wrong, and this was accentuated by an accident a year ago that robbed EI of its top two executives. George Parker feels strong ties to EI but is increasingly worried by the Canadian company's seeming indifference to its international operations in general and to the relationship with PI in particular.

George Parker locked the door of his car and walked across the parking lot toward the station entrance. Although it was a sunny spring morning and the daffodils and tulips provided welcome colour after the grayness of winter, Parker hardly noticed. Within a few minutes, the train from London would be arriving with Bruce MacDonald, the export sales manager for Electro Industries. Parker would be spending the day with MacDonald, and he wondered what the outcome of their discussions would be.

PARKER INSTRUMENTS LTD.

George Parker was managing director of Parker Instruments Ltd., part of a small, family-owned U.K. group of companies. The company gained its first sales agency in 1923 (from an American manufacturer), which made it one of the most well-established international trading firms in electronic instruments. PI sales were the equivalent of about $1 million, with 75 percent coming from imported distributed items and 25 percent from sales of its own manufactured items. The company had a total of 15 employees.

PI was the British distributor for 15 manufacturers located in the United States, Canada, Switzerland, and Japan. Like many firms, it found that the 80/20 rule held true: About 80 percent of its import sales of $750,000 were generated by 20 percent of the distributorships it held. With current sales of $165,000, the Electro Industries distributorship was an important one.

ELECTRO INDUSTRIES

Electro Industries was a younger and larger organization than its U.K. distributor. Located in southern Ontario, it was founded in the mid-1950s and had current sales of $4 million and a workforce of 90 employees. EI had developed a strong reputation over the years for its high-precision instrumentation and testing equipment, and this led to considerable market expansion. The company had moved in a number of new product directions. The original products were very precise devices for use in standards laboratories. From this base it had more recently established a presence in the oceanographic and electric power fields.

As a result of this expansion, 80 percent of its sales were now made outside Canada, split evenly between the United States and offshore markets. In the United States, the company had its own direct-sales organization, whereas indirect methods were used elsewhere. In the "best" 15 offshore markets, EI had exclusive distributors; in 30 other markets, it relied on commission agents.

WORKING TOGETHER

EI and PI first made contact in New York City, and the two companies agreed to work together. George Parker was on a business trip in the United States when he received a cable from his brother saying that a representative of EI wanted to get in touch with him. Parker and his wife met the senior executive in their hotel room and, after initial introductions, settled down to exchange information. At some point, Parker, who had had a hectic day, fell asleep. He awoke to find that PI was now more or less EI's U.K. distributor, his wife having kept the discussion rolling while he slept.

The two firms soon began to prosper together, The distributorship gave PI a product line to complement those it already carried. Furthermore, the EI instruments were regarded as the "Cadillacs" of the industry. This ensured entry to the customer's premises and an interest in the rest of the PI product line. As far as EI was concerned, it could hardly have chosen a more suitable partner: PI's staff was technically competent, facilities existed for product servicing, and customer contacts were good. Moreover, as time passed, George Parker's

*This case was prepared by Professor Philip Rosson of Dalhousie University, Halifax, Nova Scotia.

long experience and international connections proved invaluable to EI. He was often asked for an opinion prior to some new move by the Canadian producer. Parker preferred to have a close working relationship with the firms he represented, so he was happy to provide advice. In this way, PI did an effective job of representing EI in the United Kingdom and helped with market expansion elsewhere.

As might be expected, the senior executives of the companies got along well together. The president and vice president of marketing—EI's "international ambassadors"—and George Parker progressed from being business partners to becoming close personal friends. Then, after nine successful years, a tragedy occurred: the two EI executives were killed in an airplane crash on their way home from a sales trip.

The tragic accident created a management succession crisis within EI. During this period, international operations were left dangling while other priorities were attended to. Nobody was able to take charge of the exporting activities that had generated such good sales for the company. Although there was an export sales manager, Bruce MacDonald, he was a relative newcomer, having been in training at the time of the accident. He was also a middle-level executive, whereas his international predecessors were the company's most senior personnel.

From Parker's point of view, things were still not right a year later. The void in EI's international operations had not been properly filled. Bruce MacDonald had proved to be a competent manager, but he lacked support because a new vice president of marketing had yet to be appointed. A new president headed the company, but he was the previous vice president of engineering and preferred to deal with technical rather than business issues. So despite the fact that MacDonald had a lot of ideas about what should be done internationally (most of which were similar to George Parker's ideas), he lacked both the position and the support of a superior to bring about the necessary changes.

While the airplane accident precipitated the current problems in the two companies' relationship, Parker realized that things had been going sour for a couple of years. At the outset of the relationship, EI executives had welcomed the close association with PI. Over time, however, as the manufacturer grew in size and new personnel came along, it seemed to Parker that his input was increasingly resented. This was unfortunate, because Parker believed that EI could become a more sophisticated international competitor if it considered advice given by informed distributors. In the past, EI had been open to advice and had benefited considerably from it. Yet there were still areas where EI could effect improvements. For example, its product literature was of poor quality and was often inaccurate or outdated. Prices were also worrisome. EI seemed unable to hold its costs, and its competitors now offered better value-for-money alternatives. Other marketing practices needed attention, also.

THE OCEANOGRAPHIC MARKET

One area where EI and PI were in disagreement was the move into the oceanographic field. George Parker was pleased to see EI moving into new fields, but wondered if EI truly appreciated how "new" the field was. In a way, he believed the company had been led by the technology into the new field rather than having considered the fit between its capabilities and success criteria for the new field. For example, the customer fit did not seem even close. The traditional buyers of EI products for use in standards laboratories were scientists, some of whom were employed by government, some by industry, and some by universities. By and large, they were academic types, used to getting their equipment when the budget permitted. As a result, selling was "gentlemanly," and follow-up visits were required to maintain contacts. Patience was often required, since purchasing cycles could be relatively long. Service needs were not extensive, for the instruments were used very carefully.

In contrast, the oceanographic products were used in the very demanding sea environment. Service needs were acute, due not just to the harsh operating environment but also to the cost associated with having inoperable equipment. For example, ocean research costs were already high but became even higher if faults in shipboard equipment prevented taking sea measurements. In such a situation, the customer demanded service today or tomorrow, wherever the faulty equipment was located. The oceanographic customer was also a difficult type—still technically trained but concerned about getting the job done as quickly as possible. Purchasing budgets were much less of a worry; if the equipment was good, reliable, and with proven back-up, chances were it could be sold. But selling required more of a push than the laboratory equipment.

When EI entered the oceanographic field, a separate distributor was appointed in the United Kingdom. However, the arrangement did not work out. EI then asked George Parker to carry the line, and with great reluctance he agreed. The lack of enthusiasm was due to Parker's perception that his company was not capable of functioning well in this new arena. Because PI was ill equipped to service the oceanographic customer, it was thought that there could even be repercussions in its more traditional field. Parker was unwilling to risk the company's established reputation in this way. However, while he preferred not to represent EI in the oceanographic field, he worried about a "one market, one distributor" mentality at EI.

THE CURRENT VISIT

George Parker had strong personal sentiments for EI as a company. In his opinion, however, some concrete action was required if the business relationship was to survive, let alone prosper.

Parker recognized the good sales of EI products, but also took note of shrinking profit margins over the last few years due to the increased costs PI faced with the EI product line. Since EI was slow to respond to service and other problems, PI had been putting things right and absorbing the associated costs more and more frequently. However, these costs could not be absorbed forever. Parker had been willing to help tide EI over the last difficult year but expected a more positive response in the future.

George Parker hoped that Bruce MacDonald would bring good news from Canada. Ideally, he hoped to drop the oceanographic line and rebuild the "bridges" that used to exist between his firm and the manufacturer. A return to the close and helpful relationship that once existed would be welcomed. However, he wondered if EI's management wanted to operate in a more formal and distant "buy and sell" manner. If this were the case, George Parker would have to give more serious thought to the EI distributorship.

1. Discuss the role of overseas distributors and the value they contribute. What benefits can be realized using overseas distributors compared to other methods?
2. What is meant by "commitment to international marketing"? What is meant by "lip service to marketing"?
3. What should be done in the situation described in the case?

30 LeClair Chemical Company*

"What the heck was I thinking . . . What did I get myself into . . . Joe Foster wondered to himself as he prepared for the long drive from Montreal to Toronto. This was a trip that Joe was destined to become very familiar with.

Six weeks ago, Joe decided that his marketing career was stuck in the proverbial rut. He'd spent almost 25 years in the medical products industry. He'd begun as a salesman, and worked his way up to Eastern Division Sales and Marketing Manager for the Canadian branch of a large British firm. Joe had built strong relationships with the organizations of some of the largest hospitals from southern Ontario to St. John's, Newfoundland. He had built a solid reputation of being truly focused on his customers' needs. It was that reputation that led to the offer from LeClair.

LeClair Chemicals is a global chemicals company. Its Canadian headquarters are Toronto, Ontario. LeClair manufactures a well-known polymer known as "Plaston." Stanley Easterbrook, the business manager of LeClair's Plaston Division, was looking for ways to pull his "production-oriented" department into the 90s with more of a customer orientation. Through time, the Plaston division had developed the mindset that the only way to make money in the chemical industry was to concentrate on reducing manufacturing costs by continuously improving technology and keeping a sharp eye on fixed costs. Unfortunately, this led to a kind of "marketing myopia" that saw the division completely losing sight of the fact that it even had customers.

Stanley had heard of Joe's reputation through a golfing buddy, and decided to make Joe an offer to join his team. This would be the first step in Stanley's refocusing strategy. Financially, the offer looked quite attractive to Joe. But more importantly, it was a chance to try something completely different—almost like a new lease on life!

THE BUSINESS OF BY-PRODUCTS

"Joe, I think I have the perfect opportunity for you to demonstrate to our organization the power of the customer-oriented approach. And let me tell you something else, this is a tough problem that we really need to get resolved. So there are a couple of good reasons for getting you involved as soon as possible.

"You know, although Plaston has been around for many years, it is still widely used and the market is growing as new applications continue to be found. However, the growth is not rapid and Plaston is viewed as being well into the maturity phase of its life cycle."

Joe became more excited as Stanley finally began to get to the meat of his new adventure.

"There is a by-product in the manufacture of Plaston. It is a weak organic acid known in the industry as 'Triple A.' For many years, Triple A was treated as a waste product, and burned as fuel or simply disposed of in water sources. Several years ago, it was discovered that with minimal processing, Triple A could be converted into a useful product known as 'Solvent E.' Over these past few years, demand for Solvent E has grown rapidly, and LeClair now converts every pound of Triple A to Solvent E. There is an excellent margin on Solvent E, even higher than those received on the sale of Plaston.

"LeClair has enjoyed a position as the only manufacturer of Solvent E in North America. The European market for Solvent E is saturated by LeClair's Plaston competitors, and LeClair holds a small fraction of that market; the Asia-Pacific market is in its infancy. Now, one of LeClair's Plaston competitors in N.A. has announced that it will begin converting its Triple A to Solvent E and introduce it to the market. We expect that we will lose a significant amount of market share, and that there will also be an erosion in price.

"It has also been discovered that with no processing, Triple A can be sold directly for a rapidly growing environmental application. The margin on Triple A at this point is significantly lower than on Solvent E, but the market is growing rapidly.

"Due to the growth in concern for protection of the environment, simply burning or disposing of Triple A is not desirable—heck, it may not even be acceptable! You

*© 1996. Faculty of Administration, University of Ottawa. This case was prepared by Joe Menchefski under the supervision of Dr. David S. Litvack, who at the time of its preparation was associated with the University of Ottawa.

know, burning the stuff makes carbon dioxide which contributes to the greenhouse affect; and treating it means using lots of energy and still ending up with a final product to dispose of! So, Joe, I want you to spend some time at our manufacturing facility in Montreal. All of our production and R&D folks are located there. They're good people—their focus is just oriented towards finding better ways to make Plaston and Solvent E. Work with them, Joe, make them part of the solution."

Highway 20 was now turning into the 401 just outside of Cornwall as Joe Foster's mind began to reflect on more recent events: his first meeting with the Plaston by-products team, the experts in the technology and production of Triple A and Solvent E.

THE PRODUCTION TEAM

Joe had started the meeting: "Guys, I've pulled this meeting together for a few reasons. First of all, I wanted to meet all of you face to face. We'll all be working together for a while, so a voice on the telephone or a name at the bottom of an e-mail is just not enough to build a relationship on—not in my books. Second, I wanted to gather together all of the information on the market situation around Solvent E and Triple A. I think we all have little pieces of the puzzle, and hopefully, today, we can pull it together. And finally, I'd like to talk about some potential strategies for proceeding. . . ."

"Well, I'll tell you what, you want some pieces in the puzzle, I'll give you a couple of the biggest ones," said Jim Pankhurst, the Solvent E production manager. "No matter what Easterbrook may have told you, the boys in Toronto don't give a fiddler's diddly about Triple A or Solvent E. LeClair's whole world revolves around Plaston. All of the company's energies are focused on Plaston. And every penny that's spent in Montreal is spent on improving the way we make Plaston. Triple A is an unfortunate necessity, and Solvent E is an opportunity for some publicity to make the environmentalists happy. We pulled together the Triple E manufacturing facility on a shoestring budget, and we haven't put a nickel into it since it was built."

"Don't let Jim scare you, Joe. He only talks that way because manufacturing managers are supposed to be rough and tough and most of all, grumpy!" There was a chuckle from the crowd as Linda Dubinski broke some of the tension created by Pankhurst. Linda was the technical specialist assigned to the Triple E unit. She had a great relationship with Jim and the rest of the team, so she could get away with a remark like that. "The reason that the Triple E plant was built on a shoestring budget is that it's quite simple to produce. I'm sure I could make it in my backyard with old oil tanks and some moonshine stills. As a matter of fact, the tollers who make 50 percent of Canada's Triple E product and all of the American product are basically 'Mom and Pop' chemical companies who do it in their backyards with second-hand equipment and dirt cheap labour."

"Yeah, there's a couple of key points in what you just said, Linda," responded Joe. "First, 90 percent of North America Plaston production is done by tollers. These companies take the Triple A and convert it to Solvent E at an agreed upon cost per pound. Even though it's sold as 'LeClair's Solvent E,' it was produced by the tollers. The second key point is that the barriers to entry into Triple E production are almost nil!"

"Well, that second point isn't exactly correct, Joe," said Ron Wu, R&D specialist for Solvent E and Triple A applications. "Although anybody could make Solvent E, they need to have Triple A to start with. And the only people who have Triple A are the other Plaston producers. There isn't a snowball's chance in hell of new companies entering the Plaston business now—the economies of scale are much too large and the technology is much too complex. One other thing, Joe, is that I don't think we should too quickly disregard Jim's comments about the way Toronto looks at these by-products businesses."

MARKET SIZE AND PRODUCTION CAPACITY

"Thanks for the clarification, Ron," said Joe. "Can you give us a little more info on the production of Triple A and Solvent E that would help in our decision-making process?"

"Sure, Joe. I hate to steal any marketing thunder away from you, but some of the market numbers are key in understanding why the technical points are so critical."

"Seems to me that Ron just wants to show off his newly acquired MBA, don't you Ron?" joked Linda.

"Of course, Linda. I need to make sure that Jim knows about it when he starts handing out the raises in the spring!"

Jim half-smiled, as he knew that Ron was only half-joking.

"Anyway, let me continue. The global market for Plaston is about 500 million pounds a year. LeClair presently holds approximately 200 million pounds a year of that total market share. For every pound of Plaston produced, .01 pounds of Triple A are produced. So the global capacity for producing Triple A is 5 million pounds a year. Each pound of Triple A produced can be converted to 1 pound of Solvent E, so the global availability of raw material for producing Solvent E translates to 5 million pounds a year of potential Solvent E production." You could see Ron bursting with pride as he displayed his business knowledge.

"That's good information, Ron," said Foster. "Now let me add some info that I got from Stanley this week. The existing global market for Solvent E is approximately 1.5 million pounds. 0.5 million is in Europe and is being satisfied by European producers. LeClair has a production facility in Europe which is serving a small portion of the European market. The Asian Pacific market is approximately 0.25 million pounds. One of LeClair's Plaston competitors is serving approximately 0.10 million pounds of that market, and LeClair expects to have over 0.20 million pounds of production capacity in the Far East within the next two years."

"I wouldn't hold my breath on that Far East production capacity, Joe," said Jim Pankhurst, now trying to play down his "grumpy" image. "That's the Indonesia Plaston project, which is in the process of being one of the biggest screw-ups in LeClair history . . . Then again, I don't think that matters a whole lot. I was always of the impression that the North American market was kind of independent."

"That's right, Jim," added Ron, "and the North American market for Solvent E is 0.75 million pounds and is presently served entirely by LeClair. LeClair's N.A. competitor is introducing almost 0.25 million pounds of Solvent E into the market this year."

"Well, I don't have an MBA," said Linda, "but I do know something about what's out there in terms of competitors: globally, there is about 5 million pounds a year of available Triple A, which translates into 5 million pounds of potential Solvent E production. All of the Plaston producers are under the same pressure from environmentalists to find more environmentally friendly ways to deal with their Triple A, so the market for Solvent E and the potential market for Triple A both look as if they will become extremely competitive in the next few years."

"Ron, is there any way to differentiate our Triple A and Solvent E?" asked Joe.

"Well, not significantly. We can make minor reductions in the levels of impurities in both products, but I don't know if our customers would see any value in it."

THE CUSTOMERS

Joe saw his opportunity at this point to shift the conversation toward the customers. "You know, as we've been talking, we've looked at the size of the market, and we've even alluded to some of the applications for these products, but we haven't really talked about our customers. What do we know about them?"

"Joe" said Linda, "I have had several opportunities to deal with Solvent E customers in resolving quality issues. I think I could give you a little insight into their wants and needs."

"Go ahead, Linda," said Joe.

"Well, nobody uses Solvent E in the kind of volumes we make. We have many, many customers who use small amounts of Solvent E. We sell the solvent in bulk loads to three or four distributors, who then put it into drums and bottles to be sold to the final users. The distributors do all the sales. We simply provide them with technical data and they try to match the product with the user—as well as giving the sales pitch about Solvent E's 'environmental superiority.' "

"And who are the final users?" asked Joe.

"Well, it's the same people who buy any kind of organic solvent—you know, companies who paint or coat things. The last one I visited put plastic coatings on clothes hangers. When you visit these places, you can smell all the other coatings they use—the acetone, methyl-ethyl ketone, iso-propyl alcohol—it's kind of gross, actually."

"That's the best thing about Solvent E, Linda," interrupted Ron. "It has similar solvent properties to those other chemicals you mentioned, but it doesn't evaporate as easily. This reduces the amount of volatile organic compounds—VOCs—that make their way into the atmosphere."

"Was that what you were referring to, Jim, when you mentioned that LeClair got good publicity out of Solvent E?" asked Joe.

"That's right, Joe. The Solvent E goes a long way to providing the coaters with some good enviro publicity, but the bottom line is still the bottom line. We've lost customers before when we've driven the price too high—just remember that there are plenty of low-cost alternatives out there. They'll pay an environmental premium, but only to a certain point!"

"Good point, Jim—those industries are really competitive and margins are really tight," said Joe, excited to see the team shifting their focus toward their customers. "That will be extremely important when competitors start driving their Solvent E into the market. Now, what do you guys know about Triple A?"

"I've been involved with some of the applications research for Triple A, Joe," said Ron. "It's a weak organic acid, so industries use it to control the pH in the water used to scrub contaminated air before it leaves their plants. It's the heavy industries like steel making and copper and nickel smelting that use it to scrub their effluent gases."

"So, what added value does Triple A bring to these industries," asked Joe.

"Well actually, not a heck of a lot. There are many, many low-cost alternatives out there that will do the same job. That's why the margins are so much lower than what we see in Solvent E. However, the total volume of organic acids used in these industries is incredible. If we could make Triple A the acid of choice," added Ron, "we could easily sell every drop of it."

"Do we also sell Triple A through distributors?" asked Joe.

"No," said Pankhurst. "At least I don't think so. We're not really selling any of it right now, but for the trial runs, we shipped in tank trucks directly from our plant. Remember, they use tons of this stuff. The guy you replaced, Jack Burns, set it all up with the two steel mills where we ran the tests."

STRATEGIC OPTIONS

"OK guys, I'm starting to get the picture now. What do you think are some of our options?" asked Joe. "Ron, you already talked about trying to sell all of the Triple A to the industrial scrubbing market. What else can we do?"

"Well," said Linda, "if this company really wants to show what it's made of, I would suggest we invest in our own manufacturing facilities. We could reduce our variable costs by eliminating the fees we pay to tollers, and it wouldn't increase our fixed costs. The lower production costs would allow us to go head to head with our competitors and hold on to a big share of the Solvent E market." Linda was always a risk taker. "You know what else bugs me, is that we let distributors sell our Solvent E. These guys are also selling all of the alternative solvents that compete with Solvent E. We need to spend some money on promotion, Joe."

"Another option is to put some money into finding new applications for one or both products, so that we can expand the total market," added Ron. "Or along that same line we could see if we could find ways to process Triple A so that it's differentiated from all the other organic acids out there".

"All of those things cost money, guys," said Jim. "Joe, let me tell you what you've got to do, first and foremost: you've got to get Easterbrook to define exactly how LeClair is going to look at by-products. If we're a waste-processing division, then we can take low margins, or even stand to lose a few bucks. Our strategy would be quite different than if we were a real SBU, with profit objectives and all that stuff! I have a feeling that the strategy will come down to deciding on the mix of Solvent E and Triple A to make in order to minimize the amount we have to burn. By the way, we have to pay a penny a pound to burn Triple A, so the environmentalists are not our only concern here."

"What about lobbying for legislation to reduce VOCs so that coating industries will be forced to use more Solvent E?" asked Ron. "I saw this kind of strategy in a case study in a marketing course I just completed."

"That's not a bad thought," answered Joe. "But it sounds kind of risky—we're going to ask the government to force our customers to increase their operating costs. If I were them, I'd be sending LeClair a very clear message by buying any Solvent E I needed from somebody else!

"Guys, I've got to get back to Toronto tonight. Let me bring your ideas back to Easterbrook to see how he reacts, and we'll have another go at this next week. Thanks a lot for your help, and it's been great meeting all of you."

Joe had to stop for gas in Belleville, where he started mulling over all the information he received from the production team that day. "The team had some great ideas, I really must tell Stanley that these guys are a lot further along than he believes. I need to know if anyone will be willing to spend the kind of money those guys were talking about. I wonder if we can reduce our costs enough to keep our competitors out of the Solvent E market and let them fight over the 'Triple A scraps' ? What about playing 'wait and see,' and responding to our competitor's moves . . . or what about some market research to see if we can differentiate ourselves through customer service . . . LeClair's got some good experience in coatings . . . I think . . . man . . . all of a sudden, I'm longing for the smell of hospital hallways!"

1. Should LeClair invest in facilities to manufacture their own Solvent E?
2. Should there be any changes in promotional activities or channels of distribution?
3. Should there be an increase in R&D expenditure to find new applications or new users for Triple A and Solvent E to expand their total market?
4. Is differentiation for this type of product a possibility?

31 The Parks Canada Dilemma*

Jennie Sparkes, the national visitor-risk management specialist, was in her office trying to develop her recommendations for the future course of public safety communications at Parks Canada. A client-oriented approach required identification of which segment(s) of the population should be targeted and the types of message themes which would be most effective in creating awareness and encouraging changed behaviours in the segment(s) leading to fewer occasions requiring the intervention of Parks Canada Public Safety Specialists.

After reviewing the many reports on her desk, Jennie understood the meaning of being stuck between a rock and a hard place.

It is estimated that more than 25 million person visits are made annually to Canada's 38 national parks, 4 national marine conservation areas, 129 national historic sites and 9 historic canals. It is expected that the number of visitors will almost double over the next ten years. Part of the increase will be due to the opening of new national parks, bringing the total to more than 50 covering more than 2 percent of Canada's land. These new parks are, for the most part, located in wilderness area away from communications and Parks Canada resources. The balance of the increase in visits will come from the aging population, who will spend more on recreation, and from federal government initiatives to encourage domestic and foreign tourists to visit Canada's heritage areas.

In spite of the projected increase in visitor activity, Parks Canada has experienced significant reductions in funding and personnel. Additional cuts will occur over the next few years.

In 1986, Parks Canada adopted a policy whereby responsibility for public safety is shared between visitors and Parks Canada. This policy does not negate any legal responsibility that the government may have but actively solicits the visitor's participation in the safety

*This case was written by Maurice Borts and Jim Mintz. The authors acknowledge the advice and encouragement of Per Nilsen, Head Appropriate Activity, Assessment and Risk Management, Department of Canadian Heritage. At the time of the case's preparation, Maurice Borts was associated with McGill University, and Jim Mintz was Director, Marketing and Partnership Division, Health Canada.

process (see Exhibit I for a generic example). Parks Canada recognizes that a generic safety message may only be accepted by some people, and may not be recognized and acted on by those people who can benefit the most from the information.

Risk management is a science that takes into consideration many factors including:

- The frequency of the incident occurring.
- The extent of the potential loss (consequences).
- The costs of search and rescue efforts.
- The costs of activities to prevent or reduce the occurrence of the risk. Some types of risks can be eliminated or significantly reduced by education, training and the use of suitable equipment. However some incidents are completely unpredictable and are considered acts of God (see Exhibit 2 for examples of incidents that may be reduced).

Since Parks Canada does not have the resources to address all possible risk situations, the risk management factors need to be included in the decision as to which market segment(s) to concentrate on. That cost–benefit analysis is a key factor in prioritizing potential risk reduction strategies.

As the result of effective risk management activities, benefits should accrue to both visitors and Parks Canada.

(a) Increased visitor satisfaction because of fewer incidents of loss or physical injury and an increased sense of personal control or management over the activities pursued.

(b) Reduced costs to Parks Canada in mounting search and rescue efforts and less need to provide physical barriers to protect visitors. That is, increased visitors' responsibility will translate into reduced visitors' loss incidents and therefore into reduced search and rescue costs.

(c) Reduced risk of lawsuits.

One might think that presenting messages that relate to shared responsibility for personal safety would not have any competition. This is far from the truth.

One frequently featured type of competing media message promotes risk as glamorous and sexy. This type of message is often implied in lifestyle advertising (e.g., beer and car advertisers frequently target youth with messages that risk is attractive and sexy). Similar messages often appear in movie and TV program situations, where the risk takers almost always succeed and in addition gain the admiration of others, especially attractive people of the opposite sex.

A second type of conflicting message is based on promoting risk as part of the total product experience. Adventure vacations such as white-water rafting and wilderness treks often feature risk. Not only is the type of message often in conflict with safety messages, but the use of expert guides and special equipment tends to mask the danger of these activities for those who are not as skilled or well equipped.

Similarly, some marketers of outdoor gear portray their products as a means to control personal risk. That is, the products represent a "quick" means of obtaining an experience that once required the development of an extensive skill set.

Finally, competition comes from other organizations which also promote safety. The multitude of safety-related messages may impact in two negative ways. First, the multitude of safety messages may produce wear-out of all safety messages (i.e., people will ignore the existence of all safety messages). Second, different and sometimes conflicting messages may produce confusion and interfere with people adopting the desired behaviour. For example, the Parks Canada message that you are responsible for avoiding trouble is very different in meaning and implication from messages from other organizations, which proudly proclaim that we are there to help you if you get into trouble.

Over the years, Parks Canada has looked at many possible ways to segment the visitor market. Although marketing research studies have profiled some possible market segments, Parks Canada has not, at this time, commissioned a specific definitive segmentation project for a public safety communications strategy.

The following section outlines some of the possible segments considered by Parks Canada:

(a) **Male/Female**
Statistics indicate that although the types of incidents vary by sex, the sexes appear almost equally in the list of Parks Canada interventions.

(b) **Age**
Older people, say over 40 years of age, tend to participate in less risky and less strenuous activities. However, aging baby boomers are now in this life cycle stage and will constitute the largest single market segment. Park wardens are already reporting an increased number of rescues involving knee problems (associated with aging). In addition, mountain bikes allow the general public to access areas previously visited only by people in top physical condition.

Young people 16 to 24 years of age have the highest rate of accidents per 1,000 visitors to Parks Canada. This is consistent with other research findings by the Smart Risk Foundation and the Canadian Red Cross (Drowning Reports). These people often feel immortal—death happens to older people—and take unadvisable risks. As a group, this age category tends to resent authority and is less likely to read and follow safety information.

(c) **Type of Experience Sought and Activity**
In general terms, there appears to be five types of visitors:

- **Extreme Recreational Adventurist**
These individuals seek a high degree of risk as an element of their experience and tend to participate in activities requiring physical fitness, preparedness, skill and ability. Typical activities include mountain climbing, ice climbing, and ski mountaineering.
- **Active Recreational Adventurist**
Individuals in this category expect various degrees of risk in their activities and are often experienced and well-prepared for personal challenges. Participants in this category engage in moderate risk activities, such as rock climbing, back country hiking, and skiing.
- **Recreationalist**
Recreationalists tend to favour high-use activities where facilities are provided and where a sense of security is evident. Seeking educational, discovery, and personal growth experiences, these visitors participate in less adventurous activities, such as boating, swimming, and back-country hiking and camping.

Exhibit 1 Examples of Situations Involving Parks Canada Personnel

Peer Pressure Leads to Tragedy
Maligne Canyon at Jasper National Park is rugged, steep, and deep. At places, the edges of the canyon narrow and are very close together. At one spot in particular, young thrill seekers have been known to dare one another to jump across. Some visitors dared a 12-year-old boy to jump. He jumped, slipped, and fell to his death.

A Tense Night in the Woods
A mother and her two children were hiking by the ocean at Long Beach. When they tried to return to their campsite, they missed the signs indicating the trail and became lost in the dense bush. When the hikers did not return, Parks Canada launched a search with a helicopter and searchers on the ground. The three lost hikers were found the next day cold but alive, after spending the night huddled together in a rainstorm.

Unforgiving Lake
Lake Superior is well known for its treacherous conditions, as demonstrated by the experience of four canoeists. In two canoes, they rounded a headland on a late August afternoon and encountered large waves. By the time they realized the conditions outmatched their expertise, both canoes were swamped and capsized. Fortunately, the visitors were outfitted with PFDs and good floatation gear and were able to withstand the cold water long enough to be rescued by Park Wardens.

Diswasher Dies
In the spring of 1993, three young men attempted to climb a steep slope west of the waterfall on Cascade Mountain. The three friends, employees of a nearby hotel, climbed through the thinning forest toward the base of a large cliff, led by the one with the most scrambling experience. The two inexperienced scramblers fell behind and the group was eventually separated. One straggler slipped on the shale and tumbled 130 m to his death.

Swept Away
In 1992, a family from Great Britain was visiting Pacific Rim National Park. The father and his two sons, unaware of the power of the ocean, went down onto the rocks to get a better look at the monstrous waves that were pounding the beach. They had worked themselves out onto a dangerous and exposed area when a large wave swept the three out to sea. Luckily, the father and the younger son were tossed back onto the rocks on the next wave. They then had 10 to 15 seconds to scramble to safety before another wave hit. Unfortunately, the man's other teenage son was not as lucky. He was pulled out to sea. Despite an intensive multi-agency SAR comprising Parks Canada, the Coast Guard, and the RCMP, the boy was never found.

The $50,000 Search
A woman hiking in the Rainbow Lakes trail area of Wood Buffalo National Park became lost and failed to return to her car. An intensive search was launched involving park personnel, the RCMP, GNWT Renewable Territorial Five Centre personnel, GNWT Department of Highways workers, and local volunteers. The search involved a helicopter outfitted with an infrared scanner, ground search teams, and specially trained search dogs. In order to increase the chances of locating the woman, search coordinators used the Mattson Consensus technique to plot the most likely search areas. The woman was found alive and in good condition, after a 75-hour search that cost $50,000.

Broken Ankle
A woman hiking in the vicinity of Edith Pass broke her ankle after slipping on an exposed tree root. Several hours passed before friends notified the Warden Office. The subsequent rescue required wardens to transport her several hundred metres by stretcher and then by heli-sling to the highway and a waiting ambulance.

A Needless Death
A 19-year-old Quebec man stumbled over a cliff and fell more than 60 metres to his death in Banff National park while trying to retrieve his diary. The man was part of a group who were descending the steep back side of Tunnel Mountain. Somehow the person's pack, including the diary, went over the edge. He started to scramble down to look for it and slid over a steep edge and was killed.

According to a Public Safety Warden, people hike up Tunnel Mountain every day without mishap. But a growing number of adventure-seeking hikers, usually young men, stray off the well-travelled path and venture onto the exceedingly steep, forested slope.

Source: Visitor Risk Management Handbook, 1994, Parks Canada

Exhibit 2 Self-Reliant Message Example (responsibility of park users)

You are responsible for your own safety

We expect that you:

- are aware of the natural hazards
- are properly equipped and provisioned
- have the adequate knowledge, skill and fitness level
- are prepared for emergencies

Do you need information?
We'd like to help you with:

- hazards information
- back country trip planning
- route information and advice
- voluntary safety registration for high risk activities

Source: Parks Canada Posters

- **Passive Recreationalist**
  These visitors participate in leisure activities in scenic nature or interesting cultural settings. Seeking relaxation, fun, and entertainment, this group tends to rely on information and Park facilities in predominantly high visitor use areas.
- **Touring Recreationalist**
  These visitors seek the company of others, security, convenience, and facilities in low-risk activities where little preparation is required. Activities typical of this group include bus tours, educational group hikes, pleasure driving, and special events.

(d) **By Education Level**
It might be reasonable to assume that the higher a person's level of education (and IQ) the more likely is the individual to be risk adverse. This is not true. A disproportionately large number of people who visit heritage areas are highly educated. Because they are not really mentally challenged at school and work, they seek out physical challenges sometimes resulting in injury and death.

At the other end of the scale, there is an education/skill category referred to as "the Pot Scrubber" by Parks Wardens. This describes a young person, often a school drop-out with no skills, who gets a job in or near a Park (often doing dishes in a restaurant) so that he/she can do exciting activities in the Park. The lack of skills and education make him/her a prime candidate to become a statistic.

After reviewing the segments, it became apparent that these segments are not mutually exclusive and perhaps there are other possible segmentation bases which may be relevant.

Exhibit 3 Socio-Cultural Profile of Young People (15–24 years)

Key descriptions include:

- take risks for the thrill of risks
- interested in the novel/unusual
- free to act as an adult
- accepting of violence
- adaptable to complex challenges/difficulties
- hedonistic
- sexually permissive
- confident in technology, business, and advertising
- more influenced by emotion than by reason

Issues of no interest include:

- health
- mortality
- fear
- family
- financial concerns

Source: Selected Marketing Research Results from Parks Canada Studies

Jennie looked out of her office window and saw the sun shining on the tree-lined Ottawa River and, in the background, on the House of Commons. She realized that she could not leave work today without reaching a decision on which segment(s) to concentrate on, and why.

1. Which market segments are in most danger?
2. What are the possibilities of changing the behaviour in each market segment? Which segments should be targeted and why?
3. What type of message themes are most appropriate for each such segment? Why do you say this?

32 Sure-Grow Fertilizers*

It was a cool, rainy day in November 1996, and Len Dow, manager of Sure-Grow Fertilizers, was sitting in his office looking over the past season's records. Volume in 1996 was 10 000 tonnes (see Exhibit 1) and the profit margin was approximately 6%. In spite of this good performance, Len was not completely satisfied; he wanted to increase the volume and profitability of the outlet, but was not sure what direction he should take.

THE COMPANY

Sure-Grow Fertilizers is located in Goodland, a town in the middle of a major corn and potato producing area of Ontario. Sure-Grow does most of its business within

*This case was prepared by Thomas Funk of the Ontario Agricultural College at the University of Guelph, Guelph, Ontario. It is intended as a basis for classroom discussion and is not designed to present either correct or incorrect handling of administrative problems. Some data in the case has been disguised to protect confidentiality.

Exhibit 1 Sure Grow Fertilizer Sales

YEAR	LIQUID AND DRY FERTILIZERS (TONNES)	MICRONUTRIENTS (TONNES)
1992	10 000	—
1993	10 000	—
1994	7 000	—
1995	8 400	10
1996	10 000	100

Exhibit 2 Sure-Grow Fertilizer Sales By Farm Type

FARM TYPE	PERCENTAGE OF DRY FERTILIZER SALES	PERCENT OF ACRES SERVED
Potato and vegetable	60%	35%
Corn and cereals	33%	60%
Sod	7%	5%

a five-mile radius of Goodland (60%); however, it does have some sales and distribution extending 20 miles from its plant (35%), and a very small wholesale market over 100 miles away in Northern Ontario (5%). At the present time, Sure-Grow is involved only in the sale of fertilizers and related services. Dry bulk blends and bagged blends make up the majority of Sure-Grow's fertilizer volume (9000 tonnes) with 28% liquid nitrogen making up a much smaller portion (1000 tonnes). Potato and vegetable farmers purchase almost 60% of Sure-Grow's production, corn and cereal farmers account for 33%, and sod farmers purchase the remaining 7% (see Exhibit 2). Sure-Grow's dry fertilizer plant has a peak season capacity of approximately 10000 tonnes under ideal conditions.

Sure-Grow sells a custom application service for bulk fertilizers and rents application equipment to farmers who wish to apply their own fertilizer. Since Len purchased the organization, he has cut the full-time staff from seven to five including himself. One of his newest employees is a young agricultural university graduate who spends most of his time in a sales capacity calling on present and potential customers in the area. Len also spends some of his time making farm calls. Of Sure-Grow's 85 local customers in 1996, five are merchant dealers who resell to farmers. These five dealers account for 2000 tonnes of Sure-Grow's business and range in volume from 100 to 1000 tonnes each. For the most part these dealers are located on the fringes of Sure-Grow's 20-mile trading area. Of the remaining 80 local customers, Len's records show that 70 are within five miles of the Goodland plant and ten are at a greater distance. Almost all of these customers are large farmers who purchase more than 50 tonnes of fertilizer a year from Sure-Grow.

Sure-Grow sold 10 tonnes of micronutrients in 1995 and over 100 tonnes in 1996. Micronutrients are basic elements that a plant requires in relatively small amounts, compared to the larger amounts of nitrogen, phosphorus, and potassium found in most regular, blended fertilizers. Micronutrients have been proven by university and industry research in the U.S. to improve the quality and yield of crops. Commercial trials carried out in Ontario have indicated similar positive results.

THE MARKET AND COMPETITION

The total market for fertilizer in Sure-Grow's trading area has been remarkably stable at approximately 50 000 tonnes for the past several years. This is not expected to change significantly in the future although some shifts in types used are possible. Within five miles of Goodland there are four major fertilizer outlets competing with Sure-Grow for approximately 25 000 tonnes of fertilizer business, and within 20 miles there are an additional three fertilizer outlets competing for the remaining 25 000 tonnes. Len estimates that there are approximately 550 farmers within a five-mile radius of Goodland.

Although the market for fertilizer is very competitive, Len feels that he has been able to better his competition by offering excellent service, by remaining open extended hours, by offering advice and timely delivery to his customers, and by knowing how to deal with the large farmer. Len quickly came to realize that farmers place service ahead of price when deciding where to buy fertilizer as long as the price is close to that of the competition. Len feels that by offering a superior service, he has nurtured a high level of dealer loyalty in his customers which has resulted in a lower turnover relative to his competition.

GROWTH OPPORTUNITIES

Although the business has been doing well, Len realizes that growth is essential to future success. He therefore has been giving this matter considerable thought the past couple of months. So far, he has been able to identify several avenues of growth; now his problem is to evaluate each and arrive at a plan for 1997 and beyond.

Liquid nitrogen

Len has been toying with the idea of getting into 28% liquid nitrogen in a bigger way. He estimates that a total of 4000 tonnes of 28% liquid nitrogen were sold in his 20-mile trading area in 1996, of which Sure-Grow sold 1000 tonnes to three large corn farmers. Because of its ease of handling, liquid nitrogen is of particular interest to larger farmers.

Although the price per tonne of liquid nitrogen is usually less than the price per tonne of nitrogen in a

Exhibit 3 Fertilizer Prices and Margins

	DRY FERTILIZER $/TONNE	%	LN WINTER $/TONNE	%	LN SPRING $/TONNE	%	MICRONUTRIENTS $/TONNE	%
Selling price	$248	100	$138	100	$170	100	$700	100
Cost of sales	$203	82	$131	95	$136	80	$595	85
Margin	$45	18	$7	5	$34	20	$105	15
Fixed costs	$260,000			$15,000			$5,000	

granular form such as urea, comparisons between the two can be made only after adjusting for the percentage of actual nitrogen in each form. Because liquid nitrogen contains 28% actual nitrogen and urea contains 45% actual nitrogen, a farmer would need to purchase a greater volume of liquid nitrogen than urea to reach the same level of actual nitrogen applied to his crop.

Liquid nitrogen is very corrosive, which means that the farmer must purchase a stainless steel sprayer costing about $2,000 if he is to use 28% liquid nitrogen. This relatively high initial capital outlay is another factor restricting use to fairly large farmers. Of the 400 corn farmers in his trading area, approximately 200 have sufficient acreage to be possible 28% liquid nitrogen users, and Len estimates that about 20 farmers were using 28% liquid nitrogen in 1996. Price is the major purchase criterion since the product is a commodity and little service is involved. Len felt that well over half of the 28% liquid nitrogen in the Goodland area is sold in December for delivery in the spring (see Exhibit 3 for prices, costs, and margins).

Sure-Grow's current holding capacity for liquid nitrogen is 10,000 gallons or 50 tonnes. If output is increased, additional storage and nurse tanks would have to be purchased, as well as another pumping system. A pumping system costs $4,000, storage tanks cost 15 cents per gallon, and a 1,400 gallon nurse tank costs $1,000. Len feels that one additional pumping system, one more 10,000 gallon storage tank, and two more nurse tanks should be sufficient to allow for a large increase in sales.

No matter what Len decides to do, he wants to stay ahead of his competition by at least two years. Because he feels that 28% liquid nitrogen could be a big thing in the future, he is excited about this possibility. Recently, he saw a new type of potato planter which required only liquid fertilizer. If this type of planter became popular, the potential for liquid fertilizer could increase dramatically.

Despite these positive feelings about this market, Len was concerned about the relatively low liquid nitrogen margins and the slow growth of this market in the past.

Micronutrients

Another opportunity confronting Len was to try to expand micronutrient sales in a major way. Currently, Sure-Grow is a dealer for the Taylor Chemical Company, which produces and sells a complete line of micronutrients. Included in their line are manganese, zinc, iron, copper, molybdenum, boron, calcium, and sulfur. These materials are sold separately or in various combinations designed to treat specific crops. An example of the latter is the company's vegetable mix, which contains magnesium, sulfur, copper, iron, manganese, and zinc in fixed proportions. The individual materials and mixes are sold in two forms: (1) dry for mixing by the dealer with other fertilizer products, and (2) liquid for spray application by the farmer on the foliage of the growing crop. Although foliar application is more bother for the farmer, and may result in some leaf burning, some farmers prefer it because they can postpone micronutrient application until visible signs of deficiencies are present. Also, there is some research which indicates that micronutrients can be most effective if absorbed through the leaves at the peak growth period of the plant. Despite the apparent advantages of foliar application, Len has not sold any micronutrients in this form during his first two years in this business. If properly applied, he feels that liquid micronutrients offer the most value to his customers, yet he has noticed some reluctance and scepticism on the part of even the most progressive farmers in his area to try this product form.

Sales of dry, mixed micronutrients have grown considerably over the past year, and it appears that the product offers real value to customers. One of Len's customers applied micronutrients to half of a large potato field, and none to the other half. The treated portion yielded 327 hundredweight of potatoes compared to only 304 hundredweight on the untreated portion. This 23 hundredweight gain resulted in a $111.55 per acre revenue increase for the farmer when computed at the current $4.85 per hundredweight price for potatoes. Unfortunately, the University of Guelph, which many farmers look to for technical information, is not promoting or even recommending the use of micronutrients (see Exhibit 4). Their soil testing service, which analyzes soil samples and makes fertilizer use recommendations, doesn't even include an analysis for micronutrients. Len feels that competitors do not want to get involved in this business unless there is a very high demand and not being involved starts to affect their other fertilizer business.

Exhibit 4 No Substitutes for Rotation

This past year there has been a lot of interest in Perth and Huron counties about micronutrients. There are numerous plots out this year with different formulations and mixes and ways of application, both on corn and beans. We are sure there will be a lot of discussion this winter about the subject.

Some things are becoming evident about micronutrients, at least we think they are. The first is that you cannot expect dramatic yield increases with individual nutrients on small areas.

Secondly, none of the micronutrient sales staff has been able to explain to us the problem of over-applying micronutrients. They suggest if you put on too much potash you may tie up magnesium. If you put on too much phosphorus, you may need to put on more zinc and manganese. We believe, with our variable soils, in some fields you can put on too much zinc and manganese.

Finally, these micronutrients seem to be most attractive to growers with poor crop rotations. Some of your neighbors have gone to poor crop rotations and their yields have dropped. (You know they are the ones that think Pioneer corn followed by Cargill corn is crop rotation.) Now they are searching for something to pull their yield back to former highs. Micronutrients appear to them to be an answer.

What puzzles us is why some of you are willing to spend large sums of money on products you are not sure will work: shotgun micro-nutrients. We both know what the problem is. You have to get more crops into the rotation, especially perennial forages. I suppose the bottom line is when you hear your neighbor talking about all the micronutrients he is using. That's just a polite way for him to tell you he has a terrible crop rotation.

Exhibit 5 Micronutrient Sales By Crop, 1996

CROP	TONNES SOLD	ACRES	APPLICATION RATE	COST/ACRE
Potatoes	75	3,500	50#/acre	$15.90
Corn	15	1,300	25#/acre	$ 8.00
Vegetables	10	400	50#/acre	$15.90

Of the 100 tonnes sold in 1996, 75 went to six large potato farmers representing 3,500 acres, 10 tonnes went to vegetable farmers, and 15 tonnes went to corn farmers (see Exhibit 5 for rates and costs per acre). Len has been receiving excellent service and advice from the company distributing the micronutrients. He feels that the use of micronutrients is becoming accepted by the farmers using them, and that sales should rise in the future. Len chuckled to himself as he recalled the day two very large potato farmers who were brothers were sitting in his office and the subject of micronutrients came up. One of the brothers, Jack, asked the Taylor sales rep if he thought they should be using micronutrients. The sales rep related all of the advantages of using micronutrients to them, whereupon Jack turned to his brother Peter and asked, "Well, what do you think?" Peter replied, "Yes, I think we should be using them." With that Len landed a micronutrients order worth several thousand dollars.

Len was convinced that micronutrients had potential in his area. His major concern was how he could convince farmers to spend an additional $10 to $15 per acre on a product for which there was no objective basis for determining need.

Northern Ontario

Len also was considering expanding sales in Northern Ontario. Currently he has three dealers selling bagged fertilizer for Sure-Grow in Sault Ste. Marie, Thunder Bay, and Sudbury. Sure-Grow's current volume in Northern Ontario is approximately 500 tonnes of bagged fertilizer only. Several Co-op outlets have most of the market in this area. Prices are very competitive and there appears to be some farmer loyalty to the Co-ops. There are many small farms in the region with 75 to 100 acres of workable land per farm. The crop types in the area are mixed grain, barley, hay, and a few hundred acres of potatoes near Sudbury. On the average, farmers in Northern Ontario who use fertilizer purchase 2 to 3 tonnes of bagged fertilizer per year and do their purchasing in the winter months. Because the retail price of fertilizer in Northern Ontario is similar to that around Goodland, the margins to Sure-Grow are reduced by about $17 a tonne, the sum of the $12 dealer commission and the $5 freight cost. The lower margins are offset to some extent by lower personal selling costs, since dealers are used. Although the growing season in Northern Ontario is only two to three weeks behind that of Goodland, because most sales occur in the winter months, Sure-Grow's ability to service the Goodland area in the spring is not affected by what they do in Northern Ontario.

In addition to the lower margins earned on sales in Northern Ontario, Len is also concerned about possible credit problems, particularly because the cost of collection could run very high due to the distance involved. On the more positive side, Len is quite optimistic about the long-run potential growth of this market. He feels that there is a total industry potential in this market of 60 000 tonnes of dry fertilizer, of which less than 20% has been developed at the present time.

Agricultural chemicals

So far, Sure-Grow's product line consists only of fertilizers. Len observed, however, that all of his competitors were carrying insecticides, herbicides, and fungicides as well. Although he always believed that concentrating on one line was the way to go, lately he has wondered if he shouldn't be getting into the agricultural chemical business. By doing this, he would be able to better meet the needs of some customers who prefer to purchase more products from the same supplier. It could also be a way for Len to attract new customers that he could sell fertilizer to as well as agricultural chemicals. In the past, Len sized up his customers as not wanting to buy everything from one dealer, so he was satisfied to receive all or most of their fertilizer business and to leave agricultural chemicals to other dealers. Increasingly, he has wondered if this assessment was correct.

Agricultural chemicals are very competitively priced, leaving small margins in the neighbourhood of 5% to 10% for the dealer. The set-up costs for carrying chemicals would be approximately $20,000 for warehouse upgrading. No other direct costs would be attributable to the chemical line, but Len knew that servicing the line would take valuable time away from servicing and selling the fertilizer line, which could possibly result in lower sales and profits. Len estimated that the average farmer in his trading area spent $3,000 to $5,000 per year on agricultural chemicals.

Dry fertilizers

An alternative Len thought particularly attractive was to expand dry fertilizer sales in his local trading area. Although he had a substantial share of this market already, he felt it would be possible to pick up additional business through aggressive marketing. As part of his strategy to do this, he was thinking about adding another person to his staff who would act as a second salesperson and develop and offer a comprehensive crop management service to interested farmers. He was also considering the possibility of developing a local advertising program aimed at developing more awareness and interest among farmers outside his immediate 5 mile concentrated area. The total cost of the new sales specialist would be about $35,000 per year, and the local advertising would cost about $10,000 per year. Since he was near capacity now, expanding dry fertilizer sales would require an addition to his plant that would cost approximately $60,000.

The decision

Len knew he would have to make a decision soon if he were to make some changes for 1997. Although he had identified what he thought were several good opportunities for future growth, he knew he could not pursue all of them right away and that he would therefore have to establish some priorities. To help in this assessment, he recently wrote away to the University of Guelph and received a publication entitled *Farmer Purchasing and Use of Fertilizers in Ontario* (see Exhibit 6 for a summary of this study). With this new information, plus his own size-up of the situation, Len began the process of planning for 1997 and beyond.

1. Which of the possible opportunities should Len pursue? Which should not be followed up?
2. On what are you basing your decisions?

Exhibit 6 Results Of Fertilizer Marketing Research Study

1. **Only 7 percent of total crop acreage in southern Ontario is not fertilized at the present time. This acreage is almost entirely in soybeans, pasture, and forages.**
2. **The average fertilizer application rate for southern Ontario farmers is 384 pounds per acre. Most farmers use soil test recommendations from the University of Guelph to determine the application rate. There is some tendency for farmers to apply more fertilizer than recommended by their soil tests.**
3. **The major types of fertilizer used by southern Ontario farmers are dry bulk blends and liquid nitrogen. Of lesser importance are dry bagged fertilizers, anhydrous ammonia, and liquid mixes (N-P-K). Liquid nitrogen fertilizers are almost exclusively used by very large farmers.**
4. **Most farmers find the quality and availability of fertilizers to be very good.**
5. **In southern Ontario as a whole, a relatively small percentage of farmers purchase a large percentage of the fertilizer products sold. The breakdown is as follows:**

SIZE CATEGORIES	% OF FARMERS	% OF PURCHASES
Under 25 tonnes	30%	10%
26–50 tonnes	35	25
51–100 tonnes	20	20
Over 100 tonnes	15	45

Exhibit 6 Results Of Fertilizer Marketing Research Study (continued)

6. About two-thirds of all dry fertilizers are sold to farmers in April and May. Only one-third of liquid fertilizers are sold in the spring.
7. Thirty percent of Ontario farmers use dealer custom application services, while 70 percent apply the fertilizer themselves using rented dealer application equipment. There is some tendency for larger farmers to be more inclined to want custom application services.
8. In the course of a year, farmers discuss their fertilizer program with a number of parties to get information and advice on various aspects of fertilizer use and dealer selection. The influence groups most widely consulted are the local fertilizer dealer, other farmers, and family members. In addition to these influence groups, fertilizer company representatives, agricultural extension officials, and university scientists are consulted by some farmers. In the case of company representatives and university scientists, proportionately more larger farmers visit these people than smaller farmers.
9. Farmers also obtain fertilizer information from soil test results, various government publications, company-sponsored farmer meetings, dealer demonstration plots, and company and dealer displays at farm shows and fairs.
10. Over 60% of all farmers contact more than one fertilizer dealer before making a purchase. Larger farmers have a tendency to contact more dealers than smaller farmers.
11. Over 50% of all farmers reported receiving an on-farm call by a fertilizer dealer in the last year. Larger farmers reported receiving more dealer calls than smaller farmers.
12. In addition to fertilizers, southern Ontario farmers purchase, on the average, more than three other products from their fertilizer supplier. Of these, the most common are herbicides, insecticides, general farm supplies, and seeds. Large farmers are more likely to purchase herbicides and insecticides from their fertilizer supplier than small farmers.
13. Six dealer services were identified as being essential to all but a very small proportion of farmers: application equipment that is available when needed and in good repair; custom application services; custom fertilizer blending; fertilizer information through a well-informed staff, brochures, newsletters, and farmer meetings; soil testing; and demonstrations.
14. Other dealer services that were reported as being important to smaller groups of farmers were crop management assistance, help in securing expert assistance with problems, and custom herbicide application.
15. Dealer location, price, and availability of product when needed are the major factors farmers consider when selecting a fertilizer dealer. In general, dealer location and availability of product when needed are more important to smaller farmers, while price is more important to larger farmers.
16. Over 45% of all farmers purchase fertilizer from their nearest dealer. On the average, farmers purchase from dealers located less than five miles from their farms.
17. Thirty percent of all farmers purchase from more than one dealer. Larger farmers have a greater tendency to spread their purchases over more dealers than do small farmers.
18. Analysis of dealer switching showed that one-third of the farmers made no dealer changes in the past five years, one-third made only one change, and the remaining one-third made two or more changes. Those farmers making several dealer changes are the larger, younger farmers.

33 New Brunswick Telephone Company Limited*

Rising above the 130,000 residents of greater Saint John, New Brunswick, is an office tower decked in satellite dishes. The roof is illuminated by the brilliant blue logo of NBTel, the New Brunswick Telephone Company Limited. When Eleanor Austin arrived at NBTel in the summer of 1996, she found that her cubicle was located on the nineteenth floor. The location had an air of mystery, since the elevator buttons indicated that the eighteenth floor was the highest floor in the building. As NBTel's first and only behavioural research specialist, Eleanor would be working in the Planning and Marketing Department. And while the department's location would later be explained as an underestimation of the growing company's need for space, the secretive nineteenth floor would add to the mystique of the élite team of which Eleanor was to become a member.

*This case was written by Mark Henderson, who at the time of its preparation was associated with the Electronic Commerce Centre of the University of New Brunswick at Saint John. Based on interviews with Eleanor Austin, NBTel, conducted 7 August and 5 September, 1997.

NBTEL AND THE CHANGING IT INDUSTRY

In recent years, the history of the telecommunications industry has been a history of realignment, and telephone companies (telcos) have often found themselves at the eye of a storm. In 1984, the American telco giant, AT&T, was ordered to break up to curtail monopolization. Less than ten years later, telcos were realigning not through conglomerate breakup but through small business acquisition. In Canada, business diversification and technological convergence were bringing their own share of threats and opportunities. The Radio-television and Telecommunications Commission (CRTC) was dealing with cross-competition between telcos and cable companies and with the invasion of communications services via satellite. Adding to the uncertainty of CRTC policy revision and changing markets was the explosion of Internet services into the public imagination.

NBTel executives have decided to take advantage of converging technologies by discarding the telco's image as a telephone service provider and re-envisioning it as an electronic services integrator. A new vision is only a beginning. Executives share the widely held belief that the public is losing patience with the sheer amount of information being broadcast toward it through communications technologies. Members of the public want particular information to help them do the things they want to do. They want useless, time-consuming information screened out of their information sources. NBTel's new commitment is to buy when possible, create when necessary, the applications that will help its customers find desired information packaged in a way that makes it ready for use.

NBTel is the keystone company in the telecommunications group owned by Bruncor. To further its renewed commitment to service provision, NBTel has formed and has cooperated in forming several small businesses that fall beneath the Bruncor umbrella. These businesses develop and provide products and services, which NBTel in turn makes available to its customers. Businesses are responsible for developing and implementing business plans to make them self-sufficient, plans which include selling products and services to other telecommunications service providers in other markets.

The new corporate vision is part and parcel of a process that began years earlier. As a traditional telco directly employing over 2,000 New Brunswickers across the province, NBTel had developed and maintained highly structured departments and processes that fit their respective functions. However, executives have responded to the growing argument for a matrix structure of teams by applying new team concepts to the top-down, management-by-function structure of the old organization. On Eleanor's arrival, NBTel's organizational structure appeared to be a network of cross-functional teams stretched across a framework of departments divided by function, a hybrid of the old and the new. Organizational change was evident, but she did not know how the changes would affect her position and her position's relationship to teams and team members.

The Planning and Marketing Department has necessarily changed, as well. At the birth of the information technology (IT) industry, the new-product-development process tended to follow a model common across industrial sectors. A generalized, seven-step, linear model consists of (1) a new product development strategy, (2) idea generation, (3) screening and evaluation, (4) business analysis, (5) development, (6) market testing, and (7) commercialization. A post-purchase evaluation often follows to identify gaps between consumer expectations and experience with the aim of improving product quality based on gap analysis results.[1] The department has moved away from this model to keep pace with the IT industry and to support application development for business transactions over computer-moderated networks, which are being referred to increasingly and generically as electronic commerce (EC). Planning and Marketing works closely in product development with other Bruncor companies and with Future Services, which is the department charged with the in-house development of new products.

Eleanor's new position is symptomatic of a major shift in regard to how market research is incorporated into an EC application's development. As recently as ten years ago, engineers across technological industry sectors would have been familiar with the process whereby they developed new products, which marketers then tested with focus groups until they found a marketable use for the product. In general, major development and marketing decisions took place *before* the product was introduced to its market. This generalization is useful to show why the behavioural research specialist's challenge is unique and entirely new.

The new method of application development requires the technical developer and the marketer to work side by side. Major application development and marketing decisions are often made *after* the product has been introduced into the market. If the old model could be described as a process spiralling upward toward the development of a marketable application, in the new model the spiral has been compressed, with development, marketing, and market reaction feeding off one another to speed application development. In the new model, the seven traditional steps are followed, but less time is afforded them. However, commercialization becomes a new process in itself. Initial commercialization is followed by an analysis of market reaction. Based on this new information, the product is developed further. Dramatic changes to the product lead to another commercialization process. These steps are repeated until the product manager determines that there is no longer value in continuing them.

THE POSITION

Planning and Marketing management has decided that a new model calls for a new kind of researcher to help NBTel get the most out of the new processes. Eleanor has come to NBTel with no formal business education or traditional business experience. She was hired in part because of her fourteen years of journalistic experience, much of it in radio, where research, interviews, and new program development were major responsibilities. By conducting in-depth interviews with customers, Eleanor would acquire knowledge that would be put back into the product development process.

The position of behavioural research specialist was created to help NBTel's marketers and planners learn what their customers want to do and how they want to do it. This information will enable the department to recommend the purchase or creation of products that are most likely to increase use of NBTel integration services. The department has directed Eleanor to share research findings and her expertise with application developers working within or for NBTel. Eleanor describes the sense of adventure and trepidation that comes with her position as that of being asked to find the best way through "a field of tall grain through which no one has cut a path before."

The first "field of tall grain" to which Eleanor has been assigned is the customer base of the Vista 350 and its applications. The 350 is a telephone equipped with a

[1]Crane, F.G., Grant, E.S., & Hartley, S.W. (1997), *Marketing Canadian Insights and Applications*, Toronto: McGraw-Hill, pp. 218, 472–3.

small liquid crystal display screen and several buttons added to a standard touch-tone keypad. The visual display and recorded, structured audio messages enable users to access telco applications such as caller identification and a callers' log; "window-shop" from a menu of advertisers that they create themselves; electronically transfer bank funds into other accounts or pay utilities; and entertain themselves by listening to horoscopes or by checking winning lottery ticket numbers. Nortel produces the Vista line of screen phones, and applications are developed by New North Media, a young company originally supported by Nortel and NBTel to develop the business case for Vista 350 rentals and services.

NBTel marketers already know which functions are used, and how much, through quantitative research based on company records. What they do not know is why some functions are used and others not, and what things their customers might like to do with the 350 if it were possible. They do not know what customers *need*—the gap between what customers want and what NBTel currently offers. Eleanor's job is to create the process through which to discover this information, execute the process, record and interpret research results, and disseminate this information in a way that ensures it will be incorporated into future application purchase or development.

THE VISTA 350 RESEARCH PROJECT

Eleanor's position evolved naturally out of the environment that NBTel has built in New Brunswick. The province's population of 759,000 has grown accustomed to their province's reputation as a *LivingLAB*™[2] for telecommunications network applications. Time to market is reduced because the small population's access to a state-of-the-art network makes New Brunswick both a test market and an implementation site, supporting the compressed model for application development. The province's demographics are typical of the age, gender, income, and urbanization mix throughout Canada and many parts of the United States. The Vista 350 and its applications had been first implemented in New Brunswick and had achieved 16 percent market penetration. At the time of Eleanor's project, 80 percent of Vista 350 application business was being generated outside of New Brunswick, supporting the theory that what is implemented in New Brunswick can be marketed for export quickly.

Eleanor began her project by phrasing a simple question that she wanted her research to answer. The classic technology/business question is, "Will people buy what I build?" She modified the question to match the new environment: What do people want to buy that I can build?" Since she was asking this question about applications already on the market, she chose to go to the people using the products to gather her information. Which applications did they choose to use, choose not to use, and why? What would make them want to use applications more? What would they like to be able to do with their phone, and how would they like to be able to do it? And to get underneath people's understanding of themselves and to discover deeper motivations of which they might be unaware, Eleanor asked other, less direct questions. How is the phone used in the home? What other objects are located near the phone? How do users feel about the phone? And of particular significance, how does the phone make them feel?

[2] *LivingLAB* is a trademark of NBTel.

Eleanor determined that 36 subjects would represent a significant sample and that twelve interviews from each of three targeted segments would reveal themes consistent for each segment's population. This qualitative information would be quantified and statistically tested to ensure that the results were significant. In Saint John, twelve respondents were chosen, aged 55 and over, to represent the growing "grey market" of ageing people who have, as a group, significant disposable income. Another twelve people, aged 34 to 54, were chosen to represent the most significant current demographic group, the baby boomers. To test her findings in Saint John, Eleanor selected twelve more random users in Fredericton, one of the three largest cities in the province.

Groups of potential Saint John respondents were targeted for selection, but individuals ultimately self-selected. Eleanor attended community meetings to let Vista 350 users know about her project and made some preliminary telephone interviews as determined by telephone number prefixes. Prefixes tend to be a reliable indicator of whether telephones in greater Saint John are located in urban, suburban, or rural areas, so Eleanor was able to keep her sample representative of where users live. Selection for the major interviews was based on how well individuals demonstrated their willingness to share information about themselves.

The major interview took place in the user's home and began with an explanation of the project. Eleanor asked respondents to show her how they operated 350 applications. If a respondent so desired, Eleanor demonstrated how to operate unused functions. Respondents were then asked questions about their family, friends, and lifestyle. These questions led to others about how they perceived the role the 350 played in their lives, the sorts of things they would like to be able to do but couldn't, and whether the 350 could somehow be used to help them do what they wanted to do. Interviews lasted an average of two hours. Eleanor later mailed letters to respondents to inform them that they had received long-distance gift certificates for their cooperation. The final contact, Eleanor believed, caused respondents to see the gift as a reward instead of a bribe to cooperate, and she used occasional calls as an opportunity to follow up any issues arising out of the interviews. For instance, she learned that use of previously unused functions increased after she showed respondents how to operate them.

THE RESULTS

"The results of this study have reinforced two truths for me," says Eleanor. "First, behind any marketing statistics are living, breathing human beings engaged in very active relationships with other human beings, using our technology in ways we hadn't imagined. Second, the lure of technology has been the same since the invention of the wheel: people want control over their environment, and technology is a tool for control." Throughout the interview process, Eleanor was struck by the openness of respondents to share their life experiences with her, the delight in walking another person through their daily routines, and the thoughtfulness of their responses. Most respondents felt that Vista 350 technology brought them control: control in deciding whether and how to answer the phone, control in knowing who was calling and why, and control in choosing access only to those information or financial services which were useful to them. The elderly and parents of young children, for example, saw the telephone as a home security device that gave them the ability to monitor who was calling their home, whether or not they were at home at the time the call was made.

Respondents were particularly aware of the messages they sent to others by the *way* they used technology. If you return a call that was made to your number in your absence, hasn't the caller received the message that you are aware of what goes on around your home even when you are not there? If you abruptly interrupt a telephone conversation to talk to a second caller on another line, haven't you been rude to the first caller? If an information service helps you find information valuable to your friends and family, do they not see you as a knowledgeable, helpful person? Users indicated that the kind of technology they choose and how they choose to use it impart a whole set of character traits—a public persona that influences how others see them.

TRANSLATING RESULTS INTO ACTION

Eleanor's confidence in her research methods has been supported by market researchers with whom she has attended conferences. Other researchers representing major players in the IT industry, have envied the level of intimacy she has achieved with customers in the small-town, "down home" atmosphere of New Brunswick. Eleanor understands her organization's market in ways that would be impossible for organizations in major centres across North America. This level of intimacy and understanding outweighs any concerns about scientific weaknesses in the sampling process.[3]

Eleanor has been able to put the knowledge gained from her project to use for the Planning and Marketing Department. She has contributed to the decision-making process for the purchase of a new customer service, and she has provided advice and written copy for the telemarketing of telco products. Her research has also been used in positioning the Vista 350 in new markets. But before she prepares for her next research assignment, she wants to ensure that NBTel and its application development partners take full advantage of her research results.

Application development teams acknowledge the flattened development spiral that requires ongoing product development, but their reward systems tend to focus on the development of new applications. Team members are typically rewarded for developing new concepts, for turning those new concepts into usable applications, and for the profit the new applications reap for the company. Development teams are a particular challenge for Eleanor, not because they fail to cooperate but because she does not yet see how her role fits into the processes they follow. Current practices do not give her an opportunity to measure her effectiveness in, and contribution to, product development and improvement.

1. To ensure that the telco and its technology partners benefit from the full value of the behavioural research specialist's position, should structural changes be made to current new product development processes?
2. How can new marketing information be integrated back into the development spiral when application development teams are already working on the development of new applications?
3. How can research results be put to best use?
4. How can the product development process be assisted and the impact of new information be measured?

[3]A perennial battle between quantitative and qualitative researchers is whether the sampling methods and subsequent sample sizes of qualitative research meet the rigors enforced by quantitative research. Qualitative researchers respond to questions of reliability by arguing the validity of their sample size and the robustness of the quality of responses gleaned from smaller samples.

34 Rocky Mountain House Co-op*

Frank Gallagher, general manager of Rocky Mountain House Co-op (RMHC), was sitting in his office reviewing the performance of his organization when Milt Zirk, petroleum manager of the company, hurried into the room. "Frank, I'm afraid I've got some bad news," exclaimed Milt. "The word is out that United Farmers of Alberta (UFA) is planning to open a new petroleum outlet in Rocky Mountain House. The petroleum end of our business has been going fairly well for us over the past couple of years. This could really mess things up! You know they are very aggressive marketers, and because they are a co-op like us, they could really eat into our market share. Frank, I'm worried! We're going to have to make sure we're ready for them. We've got to develop a plan to minimize their impact on our sales and profits."

*This case was prepared by Thomas Funk of the Ontario Agricultural College, University of Guelph, Guelph, Ontario, Canada. It is intended as a basis for classroom discussion and is not intended to represent either correct or incorrect handling of administrative problems. Much of the data in the case has been disguised to protect confidentiality.

Exhibit 1 Product Line Breakdown

	HOME CENTRE	SHOPPING CENTRE	PETROLEUM
Sales	$4,620,000	$11,044,000	$2,550,000
Less: cost of good sold	$3,536,000	$8,418,000	$2,294,000
Gross margin	$1,084,000	$2,626,000	$256,000
Less: operating expenses	$931,000	$2,106,000	$189,000
Contribution	$153,000	$520,000	$67,000

ROCKY MOUNTAIN HOUSE CO-OP

Rocky Mountain House Co-op is a retail outlet located in Rocky Mountain House, Alberta, approximately 80 km west of Red Deer, on Highway 11. Rocky Mountain House is a community of approximately 6,000 people with both an agricultural and a commercial economic base. The area is characterized by mixed farming, with most farms being relatively small and having at least some livestock. Industry in the area includes general business, trucking, construction, oil exploration, and logging.

The trading area served by RMHC is much larger than Rocky Mountain House itself and contains the following communities: Alder Flats, Alhambra, Caroline, Condor, Leslieville, Nordegg, Rocky Mountain House, and Stauffer. The trading area has an approximate population of 16,000 people and a radius of 50 km, although the trading area on the west extends nearly 100 km to the Rocky Mountains.

RMHC is a co-operative type business. Co-operatives are like regular businesses except that they are owned by their users, who purchase shares in the business. Instead of earning "profits," co-operatives earn "savings," which can be returned to members through "patronage dividends." RMHC is owned by 7,332 active members. For the most part, these "owners" are people in the trading area who have become members by purchasing shares in the organization. Each share is valued at $1.00, and a minimum of five shares must be purchased to become a member. The main reason for being a member is to share in the savings of the business through patronage dividends. Patronage dividends are based on the amount of business a member does each year and have amounted to about 5 percent of purchases at RMHC over the past several years. In addition, members have a voice in the affairs of the co-op through their right to elect a board of directors to represent their views.

RMHC is involved in a number of retail businesses, which they classify under three divisions: Home Centre, Shopping Centre, and Petroleum. The Home Centre consists of building materials, hardware, animal health products, livestock feed, livestock equipment, and twine; the Shopping Centre consists of food, hardware, clothing, and a cafeteria; and the Petroleum Division consists of bulk fuels, propane, oil/lubes, cardlock, and a gas bar. Despite the fact that Rocky Mountain House is in a significant grain-producing area of the province, RMHC has elected so far not to sell crop supplies. Sales, cost of goods sold, and gross margins for each division for 1995 are shown in Exhibit 1. Exhibit 2 shows the operating statement of RMHC for the same year.

Exhibit 2 Operating Statement

Sales	$18,214,000
Less: cost of goods sold	$14,248,000
Gross margin	$3,966,000
Less: operating expenses	$3,226,000
Contribution	$740,000
Less: indirect interest expense	($96,000)
Less: general overhead	$432,000
Savings	$404,000
Patronage dividends from federated co-ops	$683,000
Retained savings	$1,087,000

In 1995, RMHC received patronage dividends of $683,000 from Federated Co-operatives Limited in Saskatoon, the large wholesaling co-operative, which is owned by several hundred local co-ops like RMHC across western Canada. Like most other local co-ops, RMHC used Federated Co-op as their main source of supply for all products they sold. The patronage dividend they received from Federated was based on a percentage of purchases. In the same year, RMHC allocated $614,000 in patronage dividends to local owners. This, together with current savings, left RMHC with retained savings of slightly more than $1 million. This represented funds the organization could use for future expansion.

PETROLEUM DIVISION

The petroleum division of RMHC has always been a tough business. Margins in the petroleum division are much lower than in other areas of the company, largely due to intense competition and the commodity-type products being sold. In the Rocky Mountain House trading area alone there are six major oil companies competing for a total fuel market of approximately 26.9 million litres. Exhibit 3 lists the major petroleum companies with facilities in Rocky Mountain House and their approximate fuel sales.

Most of the 26.9 million liters of petroleum sold in the Rocky Mountain House trading area went to commercial

Exhibit 3 Competitive Petroleum Suppliers

	Estimated Litres
Co-op	5,900,000
Esso	7,500,000
Shell	4,000,000
Petro-Canada	3,500,000
Turbo	3,500,000
Husky	2,500,000
	26,900,000

Exhibit 4 Approximate Market Shares by Type of Account

	FARM	COMMERCIAL	CONSUMER	TOTAL
Co-op	34%	17%	30%	23%
Esso	31%	27%	27%	28%
Shell	13%	15%	16%	15%
Petro Canada	6%	17%	4%	13%
Turbo	12%	13%	13%	13%
Husky	4%	11%	10%	9%
	100%	100%	100%	100%

Exhibit 6 Petroleum Department Expenses

Depreciation	$5,600
Utilities	$500
Insurance	$4,900
Repairs & maintenance	$9,000
Taxes & licences	$4,600
Total standby costs	$24,600
Employee benefits	$18,000
Staff discounts	$1,600
Training	$1,800
Salaries & wages	$99,000
Uniforms	$1,500
Total staff costs	$121,900
Advertising & promotion	$5,600
Delivery trucks	$29,000
Other expenses	$7,900
Total operating costs	$189,000
Contribution	**$67,000**

Exhibit 5 Financial Summary for Petroleum Products

	FUELS	PROPANE	OIL/LUBES	GAS BAR	TOTAL
Sales	$2,016,000	$41,000	$126,000	$367,000	$2,550,000
Cost of goods	$1,829,000	$34,000	$106,000	$325,000	$2,294,000
Gross margin	$187,000	$7,000	$20,000	$42,000	$256,000

accounts. Commercial accounts purchased 18.3 million litres in 1995 compared to 6.1 million litres to farm accounts and 2.5 million litres to consumers. Although precise market shares were not known, Milt estimated that Co-op and Esso were the major petroleum suppliers in the area, followed by Shell, Petro-Canada, Turbo, and Husky. Exhibit 4 shows approximate market shares for each company by type of account.

RMHC currently sells four product lines in petroleum: bulk fuels, propane, oil/lubes, and gas bar (self-service pumps at the Shopping Centre). Sales, cost of goods sold, and gross margins for these products in 1995 are shown in Exhibit 5. Exhibit 6 shows the petroleum department expenses for the same year.

Like most petroleum suppliers in the area, RMHC sells five types of petroleum products: premium gasoline, regular gasoline, clear diesel, marked gasoline, and marked diesel. Exhibit 7 shows 1995 sales of the five products in each of the major markets, while Exhibit 8 shows current pricing for each product in each major market. Marked gasoline and marked diesel are dyed a purple colour to distinguish them from clear product. This is done to identify these products as tax exempt because they are used for off-road purposes and not subject to normal fuel taxes. At the moment, marked fuels sell for approximately $0.09 per litre less than clear fuels, which are intended for on-road use and subject to a road tax. The prices established by RMHC are very similar to those of other petroleum suppliers in the area. Only Turbo and Husky sell petroleum at lower prices than other companies in the area, and in both cases, the differences are very small.

Margins on petroleum products do not vary by type of product, but do vary by type of customer. Current margins in the farm market are $0.049 per litre; in the commercial market, $0.034 per litre; and in the consumer market, $0.063 per litre.

In the petroleum end of the business, RMHC deals with three main types of customers: farms accounts, commercial accounts, and consumers.

At the moment, RMHC has about 350 farm accounts, which purchase 2,086,000 million litres of fuel. Although the average farm account purchases about 6,000 litres of fuel each year, some purchase much larger

Exhibit 7 Petroleum Sales by Market

	FARM	COMMERCIAL	CONSUMER	TOTAL
Premium gasoline			16,500	16,500
Regular gasoline	200,000	1,173,000	666,500	2,039,500
Clear diesel		1,154,000	63,000	1,217,000
Marked gasoline	949,000	50,000		999,000
Marked diesel	937,000	736,000		1,673,000
	2,086,000	3,113,000	746,000	5,945,000

Exhibit 8 Petroleum Prices by Market

	FARM	COMMERCIAL	CONSUMER
Premium gasoline			$0.540
Regular gasoline	$0.495	$0.480	0.500
Clear diesel		0.390	0.420
Marked gasoline	0.403	0.390	
Marked diesel	0.300	0.300	

Exhibit 9 Types of Commercial Accounts

TYPE OF ACCOUNT	PERCENT
General business	29%
Loggers	11
Truckers	18
Construction	17
Oil company contractors	22
Institutional	3

amounts and many purchase much smaller amounts. The largest RMHC farm account purchases nearly 20,000 litres of fuel a year. Farms in the RMHC trading area are somewhat smaller than typical Alberta farms. A very high proportion of these farms have livestock as their principle operation.

Commercial accounts represent the major proportion of RMHC petroleum business. At the moment, RMHC has 175 commercial accounts, which together purchase approximately 3,113,000 litres of fuel and range in size from 5,000 litres per year to as much as 300,000 litres per year. The average commercial account buys 18,000 litres. Exhibit 9 provides a breakdown of commercial accounts into various types of businesses.

The final category of customer is individual consumers, who currently purchase 746,000 litres of fuel. About 80 percent of consumer sales are through the gas bar at the Shopping Centre, and the remaining 20 percent are through the cardlock system described below.

Although all three types of accounts (farm, commercial, and consumer) can use the cardlock system, it is very popular among commercial accounts. The cardlock system allows approved buyers to have 24-hour access to bulk fuels at the main RMHC petroleum outlet. To obtain fuel, the buyer inserts a card into a metering device, which then pumps the requested amount of a certain type of fuel into the user's tank. The user's name and the amount of the purchase are recorded electronically for future billing. Use of this system is growing very rapidly among farm and commercial accounts because of convenience and cost savings. The price of fuel purchased through the cardlock is generally $0.008 per litre less than bulk delivery. Although RMHC has a good, very clean cardlock operation, there are two problems that make it less than ideal. One problem is that currently it does not sell marked gasoline and does not have the capability of adding this product into the existing system. This undoubtedly prevents some potential customers from using the RMHC cardlock. Another problem with the cardlock is that access to the facility is a little more difficult than some customers would like.

At the moment, the marketing program used by RMHC is fairly similar to that used by other petroleum suppliers in the area. In 1995, less than $6,000 per year was being spent on advertising petroleum products. Most of this was for ads placed in local papers highlighting special deals on oils and lubricants. In addition to advertising, a substantial amount of selling is done by Milt on the farm, at the offices of commercial accounts, and on the phone. Milt maintains contact at least four times a year with most customers, and more often with larger customers. Some very large customers are contacted on a weekly basis. In addition, he spends a considerable amount of time calling on prospective customers. Milt's philosophy is that regular contact with prospects will put him in contention for their business if there is ever a reason for a customer to switch. History shows this to be a good strategy, as RMHC has picked up a number of new customers each year when they became dissatisfied with their present supplier. Customer loyalty in petroleum, however is very high. Milt figures that less than 10 percent of customers change suppliers each year. Milt also follows the practice of driving the delivery truck himself on occasion so that he can have more contact with customers.

Frank and Milt have long thought that the success of RMHC in the petroleum business was due to a number of factors:

- The company provides excellent service. All people working for RMHC are topnotch individuals committed to providing good service. In addition, the company prides itself on clean, modern facilities and prompt attention to detail. Any customer who needs fuel can expect to receive it the same day an order is placed. RMHC currently spends more than its competitors on staff training.
- Co-op products are quality products that are produced under strict quality control measures.
- Patronage refunds provide customers with "cash back" at the end of the year based on their volume of business. For many customers this is a real incentive to do business with a co-op.
- The company has an excellent highway location in Rocky Mountain House. This provides excellent visibility in the community.
- RMHC offers a very wide range of products, making "one stop shopping" possible for customers.

UNITED FARMERS OF ALBERTA

United Farmers of Alberta (UFA), like RMHC, is a member-owned co-operative. UFA has approximately 30 outlets in Alberta in which they sell petroleum and a complete line of farm supplies. In addition, they operate approximately 90 outlets in which only petroleum products are sold, through bulk plants, cardlocks, and gas bars. UFA has shown considerable growth in recent years through very aggressive marketing. This growth has come both from an increase in the number of retail distribution points and from an increase in the volume sold through existing outlets.

Recently, UFA was granted a development permit to build a farm supply facility in Rocky Mountain House. The permit allows UFA to construct a facility that contains the following: a 2,200 square foot building, a bulk petroleum plant, a gas bar, a cardlock, and a farm supply distribution facility. It is expected that UFA will sell a complete line of both crop and livestock farm supplies through this facility. It is also expected that UFA will construct a cardlock facility that is larger than any other in the area and will sell a complete line of fuels.

The entry of UFA into this market has the potential of causing significant problems for RMHC, for a number of reasons:

- UFA is a co-op like RMHC and therefore very similar in structure and philosophy. As a result, they may be considered a good alternative by many current RMHC customers.
- The fact that they are building a complete farm supply outlet may be attractive to many current RMHC customers who would like to purchase crop supplies where they buy petroleum.
- UFA's facility will be much newer than that of RMHC. This is of particular concern for the cardlock.
- UFA currently has a number of commercial accounts on the fringes of the RMHC trading area. This gives them a foothold into the market.
- In similar situations, UFA has demonstrated a willingness to enter new markets in a very aggressive manner. Often this entails aggressive pricing, introductory advertising in local media, a direct mail campaign targeted to larger potential customers, and special introductory deals.
- UFA traditionally supports its marketing efforts with a high level of excellent service. This includes the availability of skilled technical experts who can answer questions and help customers make informed buying decisions, attention to detail in all aspects of the business, and frequent sales calls (either phone or in person) with key customers.

DECISION

Although at first Frank was not overly concerned about the situation, as he considered it in more detail, he began to worry about the potential effects it might have. RMHC had worked hard over the last ten years to build a strong customer base and some of this investment in time and marketing dollars appeared to be at risk. To determine the seriousness of the situation, and to develop some plans to counteract it, Frank called a meeting with Milt for early next week.

The meeting began with Frank raising the issue of what impacts the entry of UFA might have on RMHC. After some discussion, the two men agreed that if RMHC did nothing to soften the impact, it was conceivable they could lose a significant portion of both their farm and their commercial business, especially the larger accounts that were more price sensitive. Although it was hard to come up with specific numbers, they felt that up to a quarter of their present volume might be at risk. What was even more alarming was the fact that RMHC had three very large commercial customers who each purchased 300 000 litres of fuel a year. Losing these people alone would result in a very large sales decline. Although these large commercial accounts had been with RMHC for a number of years, and Milt provided a high level of personal service through almost weekly contact, it was conceivable they could switch allegiance if they perceived greater value in an alternative supplier.

Given the seriousness of the situation, they then began to discuss alternative courses of action they might pursue to counteract the problem. A number of possibilities were identified and briefly discussed.

1. The first idea that came to mind was to pursue a pre-emptive pricing strategy. Under this strategy, RMHC

would begin immediately cutting prices and margins to existing customers. The idea behind this strategy, of course, was to solidify business relationships with customers to the point that it would be very difficult for UFA to be successful in taking customers from RMHC.

2. A second strategy they discussed was to match UFA's promotional programs dollar for dollar and engage in a substantial amount of local advertising and direct marketing themselves. Although neither Frank nor Milt had a precise idea of what UFA would spend entering the Rocky Mountain House market, they felt that $30,000 was not an unrealistic amount. They considered stressing two main points in the promotion: their excellent staff, and their outstanding record of providing patronage dividends. Frank envisioned ads and direct mail pieces with pictures and human interest stories about the staff, as well as charts showing the steady growth in patronage dividends over the past few years.
3. Another idea they considered was to develop a program in which the rate of patronage dividends would vary by department. Under such a scheme it would be possible for the petroleum division, for example, to announce a patronage dividend of 8 percent where some other division's dividend might decline to 3 percent. They felt this might be particularly effective in the short run to meet a competitive challenge.
4. Yet another alternative they were considering was to get into the fertilizer and ag chemical business. On the assumption that some RMHC customers might be attracted to UFA because they had a complete line of crop and livestock supplies, this might provide existing customers with enough reason to stay with RMHC. It would, however, be a major investment for RMHC in a business they knew little about. Frank estimated it would require an investment of approximately $600,000 in facilities and working capital. In addition, two new full-time people would be required to run the business and work with farm customers. An additional five seasonal employees would be needed for a couple of months each year to help during peak sales seasons. Total additional labour costs would amount to approximately $150,000 plus another $50,000 in administrative costs. Margins on fertilizer were typically in the 15 to 20 percent range on product that sold for an average price of $250 per ton. Although an average farmer in the Rocky Mountain House trading area currently used only 25 to 30 tons of fertilizer a year, use appeared to be growing fairly rapidly as more farmers were starting to use fertilizer and those already using fertilizer were increasing application rates. Ag chemicals were not widely used in the Rocky Mountain House trading area, so this would be considered a break-even business that simply provided a complementary service to farmers who purchased fertilizer. Presently there are three fertilizer suppliers serving the 1,200 farmers in the Rocky Mountain House trading area. One of these suppliers is a large, independent farm supply outlet specializing in crop inputs; the other two are smaller operations, one of which is the local Esso dealer.
5. The final alternative Frank identified was to move up construction of a new bulk petroleum facility. The current facility was old and starting to show its age. Of particular concern was the fact that the cardlock system had reached its capacity and could not add a tank and pumping system for marked gasoline. Frank knew that the new UFA facility would be "state of the art" and have ample capacity for the present and for future expansion. Although Frank had hoped to get another five years out of the present facility, he felt that one option was to invest immediately in new facilities so that they would be ready at least by the time the UFA facility was built. A new facility that would include a new bulk plant, an expanded sales area, and a new and expanded cardlock would cost $300,000 to construct.

Frank and Milt concluded the meeting wondering what to do. They agreed to consider the options more fully and do some real thinking about the consequences of each option and then meet again in a week to make a decision.

1. How serious is the threat posed by the imminent entry of UFA? What impact could this have on RMHC sales and profits?
2. Carefully analyze each of the options Frank and Milt have outlined, and any others you can identify, in terms of their pros, cons, and financial implications.
3. What should Frank and Milt do? What will be the likely outcome of such a decision?

35 Chalaga Mussel Farms*

In July 1994, mussel farmer Malcolm Wilson was examining the mussel industry in Atlantic Canada. As a mussel farmer, he was concerned about competition from two areas. One was the United States, particularly Maine, since it appeared to control the low end of the market. The other was Prince Edward Island, where "Island Blue" mussels were positioned at the high end of the market. Wilson was searching for an appropriate strategy that would make Chalaga Mussel Farms more competitive.

*This case was prepared by Dr. Christopher Vaughan and Dr. Julia Sagebien of Saint Mary's University as a basis for classroom discussion and is not meant to illustrate either effective or ineffective marketing management. The case is based on material gathered by Ian McLeod for his master's research project at Saint Mary's University, together with material from a case previously published by Dr. Julia Sagebien and copyright by the Atlantic Entrepreneurial Institute. Used with permission from the authors.

MALCOLM WILSON'S BACKGROUND IN MUSSEL FARMING

In the late 1980s, while attending the Marine Institute in St. John's, Newfoundland, Malcolm Wilson worked part time for a small mussel farming operation. He quickly saw potential for the mussel industry and conducted some secondary research on the industry. His findings indicated that there was a future in owning and operating a mussel farm. However, he realized that several marketing issues needed careful attention. For example, Wilson felt that Newfoundland was not a viable location since there were difficulties with respect to distribution that, in turn, affected marketability. Wilson particularly wanted to enter the Minneapolis market since a previous visit to that region had been very encouraging.

In January 1992, he relocated to Halifax, Nova Scotia, and he and a partner, who had some previous entrepreneurial experience, bought some mussels and equipment and started Chalaga Mussel Farms on the eastern shore of Nova Scotia.

Chalaga Mussel Farms was a small operation, and the two partners realized that they needed an increased sales volume in order to survive in an increasingly competitive marketplace. They felt that a steady supply of good-quality mussels was necessary for survival and to enhance market share. However, distribution posed a problem. One way to improve profit margins would be for them to own their own processing plant to clean, grade, and bag mussels, since this would permit them to market directly instead of being required to sell to others who had the ability to process.

The growing cycle of mussels requires approximately two years before the product can go to market, and Chalaga Mussel Farms needed to develop appropriate inventory and distribution channels in order to be competitive. By June 1993, Chalaga Mussel Farms had begun production on a larger scale and was also examining distribution and pricing strategies. Chalaga Mussel Farms bought the appropriate equipment and set up a processing plant.

By late 1993, Chalaga Mussel Farms had sold 175,000 pounds of mussels directly to supermarkets, local brokers, and brokers in Quebec City, Montreal, and Toronto. The operation began to show a small profit, and plans were made to increase production by 15 to 25 percent a year for the next three years.

Wilson was convinced that he would continue working in the mussel farm business, and he felt that having the right products in the right markets was the key to success. He then began to seek out more information on the mussel industry in Canada and the United States.

RESEARCH ON THE MUSSEL INDUSTRY

Wilson obtained several consulting reports, book and magazine articles on the mussel industry, and information from the Department of Fisheries and Oceans and *Canadian Aquaculture Magazine.* To supplement his secondary research, Wilson conducted several interviews with mussel growers, brokers, and retailers in Canada and the United States. He also set up focus groups comprised of individuals from Newfoundland, Nova Scotia, and Prince Edward Island who were knowledgeable about the mussel industry.

Data concerning mussel meat yield varied, but Wilson came up with an average percentage: whole mussel meats (16 percent recoverable yield) and broken meats (2 percent recoverable yield). Broken meats are often thrown away, but Wilson felt that they could be used for chowders and soups in the food service or institutional markets. From his research, Wilson decided that priority should be given to the development and expansion of Chalaga Mussel Farms' product line. For example, whole meats could be individually quick frozen (IQF) or sold in one-pound block form; a mussel salad could be developed to compete with other mussel salads currently on the market, such as Limfjord and Marina; smoked mussels could also be considered to compete with M'Lord brand; a yogurt pairing campaign might be undertaken (in Europe, cream-based and yogurt-based mussel salads are common) and recipes developed that paired mussel salad with yogurt.

The information Wilson gathered generally segmented the mussel market in three ways: geographically (American and Canadian cities, Europe); by product type (wild, long-line cultured, and bottom-cultivated); and by sector (institutional or food service and restaurants versus consumer or retail); overall, 75 percent of fresh mussel product goes to the food service sector and 25 percent to the retail sector.

The volume consumed by the food service sector versus that consumed by the retail sector varied considerably by city. According to one of the studies that Wilson had reviewed, markets with a large retail sector volume offered good opportunities to long-line mussel growers because the retail sector catered to sophisticated consumers who could distinguish between the different types of mussels.

Another study suggested that the growth in North American demand for mussels in the 1980s could in part be traced to the dietary preferences of yuppies: mussels were high in protein, low in calories and cholesterol, and considered chic to eat. Mussel consumption was clustered around large North American cities (see Exhibits 1 and 2). Growth was anticipated in the restaurant sector of these cities because mussels were trendy and their high markup, particularly of bottom-cultivated mussels, made them attractive to restaurant managers. The retail trade was expected to have much slower growth.

The Canadian market, by industry sector, consisted of approximately 70 percent in the food service industry (mainly restaurants) and 30 percent in the retail trade (supermarkets, etc.). The retail trade was directed mainly at ethnic populations residing in large cities. The type of mussel consumed varied from city to city (see Exhibit 1).

Exhibit 1 1994 Canadian Market, Institutional and Retail Combined, Selected Cities (percent breakdown by city)

CITY	TONNAGE PER YEAR	WILD (%)	BOTTOM CULTIVATED (%)	LONG-LINE CULTURED (%)
Montreal	850	50%	15%	35%
Quebec City	300	40	20	40
Ottawa	220	25	50	25
Toronto	810	10	75	15
Vancouver	220	10	55	35
Total	2,400			

Source: Market Analysis Group (1994), Department of Fisheries and Oceans, and estimates.

Exhibit 2 1994 U.S. Market, Institutional and Retail Combined, Selected Cities (percent breakdown by city)

CITY	TONNAGE PER YEAR	WILD (%)	BOTTOM CULTIVATED (%)	LONG-LINE CULTURED (%)
New York	3,200	7%	83%	10%
Los Angeles	450	2	93	5
Chicago	450	8	88	4
Atlanta	240	6	81	3
Seattle	265	na	50	50
Total	4,605			

Source: Market Analysis Group (1994), Department of Fisheries and Oceans, and estimates.

Even though Quebec purchased a good deal of Prince Edward Island mussels, the "Buy Quebec" preferential purchase policies limited the market potential. Other market segments Wilson considered were value-added products and export markets. Even though transportation costs limited the potential of these markets, Wilson knew that Island Blues were already being flown to Los Angeles and other American cities. He had to find a way to distribute his product more economically. Government research indicated that Europe was a mature market with few prospects for export; however, Wilson felt that there was still potential in Europe, particularly in the Baltic States and the Moscow region of Russia.

MUSSEL PROCESSING

There are basically three types of mussels marketed: long-line cultured, bottom-cultivated, and wild. Since the marketing approach for each type of mussel varied, Wilson had to pay particular attention to the different growing methods.

Chalaga Mussel Farms used the long-line suspension method of growing cultured mussels. This method involves the suspension of mussel "seed"—small mussels from intertidal zones, stuffed in "socks" about three metres long. The socks are suspended on a line supported by buoys at the surface and attached to the bottom by weights. After harvesting, fresh whole mussels are brought to the processing plant, which often houses two separate processing areas in one building: primary processing (fresh product) and secondary processing (value-added product). Tote boxes are used to carry the mussels, with approximately 80 to 100 pounds per box.

The first stage of production includes declumping, grading, and debyssing (the mussel attaches itself to surfaces by means of tough filaments called *byssal threads*). The mussels are manually shovelled into a hopper that leads to the declumper, where they are drum-rotated to break up the clumps. Next, they are separated by use of a bar grader and carried by conveyor belt to the debysser, constantly being sprayed with water during this process. The mussels are then debyssed and are again put in tote boxes while awaiting further processing or packaging for the fresh market.

Secondary processing requires that the mussels be cooked in a large steam kettle. This takes place in a separate area of the plant. Approximately 80 to 100 pounds are steamed for about 15 minutes per kettle load. The cooked mussels are then dumped onto a shaker that vibrates rapidly, thereby separating the meat from the shell. Mussel meats are then collected and placed in a tub of salted water where the meats float and the shells and other debris sink to the bottom. Finally, the mussel meats can be either marinated for a retail mussel salad product or stored in a chill room for later processing.

Compared to other types of mussels, the long-line mussel is cleaner (no pearls or grit) and has a nicer shell and a higher meat yield. The market price for these mussels tends to be higher than the price for wild or bottom-cultivated mussels (see Exhibit 3).

In 1989, the Department of Fisheries and Oceans conducted some research on growing methods that Wilson considered very promising for long-line growers. New methods could improve growing yields and increase the industry margin of long-line cultured mussels between 30 and 35 percent at current wholesale prices.

Wild mussels were harvested from in-shore areas using bottom dredges. The mussels were then picked by hand from the dredged material. Like bottom-cultivated mussels, wild mussels had a reduced meat yield and a higher content of sand and pearls than long-line cultured mussels. Quebec consumed a high proportion of wild mussels. Once harvested, all mussel types had a shelf life of 7 to 14 days if properly stored. They had to be processed for market (cleaning, sorting, etc.) and handled carefully during transport. Mussels shipments usually constituted part of a mixed load of seafood products.

Exhibit 3 Price per Pound 1994

	WILD	BOTTOM CULTIVATED	LONG-LINE CULTURED PRINCE EDWARD ISLAND	LONG-LINE CULTURED NEWFOUNDLAND	LONG-LINE CULTURED NOVA SCOTIA
Wholesale	na	$.35	$1.20	$1.30	$.95
Retail	na	.49	1.49	1.92	1.29

All prices are in Canadian dollars. Prices were obtained from a survey of wholesalers and retailers. Seasonal price fluctuations were wide.

From his interviews with retailers, Wilson discovered that even though its shell was cleaner and the meat yield higher, to the average consumer, the long-line cultured mussel was difficult to distinguish from the wild mussel and the bottom-cultivated mussel whether in or out of the shell.

American markets

In 1993, the American food service sector accounted for 80 percent of mussel demand while the retail sector accounted for 20 percent. The type of mussel consumed also varied from city to city (see Exhibit 2).

CANADIAN SUPPLY

In 1993, Canada supplied only between 2 and 3 percent of the world's mussels. In 1993, 3,885 tonnes of mussels (mostly long-line mussels) were produced in Canada. Exports represented 20 percent or 777 tonnes. In addition, 800 tonnes were imported from the United States. Almost all of the imported mussels were bottom-cultivated mussels. Most of the Canadian supply of mussels came from Atlantic Canada, but there were problems with distribution and not only to Canadian destinations. Canadian west coast production still faced large technical difficulties.

Wilson had seen the mussel industry grow at a fast rate. He knew that the American and Canadian markets were large, but he also felt that he was missing out on many opportunities for export. A biologist's report mentioned that the environmental conditions in the Atlantic region could lead to a long-line cultured mussel capacity of 50,000 tonnes a year. This figure could double if bottom-cultivated methods were considered.

AMERICAN SUPPLY

Bottom-cultivated mussels grown by Maine companies dominated the American mussel market. Maine mussels also had a strong presence in the Canadian market. In 1993, American growers produced over 17,000 tonnes of mussels. Recent developments in the Maine industry concerned Wilson. Bottom-cultivating had been the prevalent growing method in the industry, but some growers were experimenting with long-line technology in anticipation of a more educated and demanding consumer. Most of the 20 American producers were on the east coast, and four major operations (three in Maine) dominated the industry.

THE MUSSEL SCARE

Since 1989, mussel farming has been an industry plagued by inconsistent quality standards, seasonal supply, environmental hazards, and problems of mussel toxicity. The efforts of most of the private growers and producers who Wilson knew were directed toward preventing a repeat of the crisis of December 1987, when two deaths and 134 cases of illness were attributed to toxic molluscs from Prince Edward Island. On the American east coast, the "Red Tide" (a marine condition that makes mussels toxic) had created havoc in the mollusc industry. Even though water temperature and other environmental conditions made the Red Tide a threat to Prince Edward Island waters but not to Nova Scotian waters, consumers assumed that all Atlantic products were at risk.

Industry self-regulation and government authorities had made improvements in quality control. The federal government had revamped its Shellfish Monitoring Program, which included testing of water quality by Environment Canada, testing of the product by the Department of Fisheries and Oceans, and policing of growing areas by various agencies in order to prevent harvesting in closed areas. Wilson was prepared to support these activities, but he also needed to make decisions concerning product line and what markets to pursue.

1. What type of products (growing methods) should be adopted by Chalaga Mussel Farms? What markets should be pursued?
2. What pricing strategy must be adopted, given the products and markets that are selected?

36 Argon Carpet Cleaning Company*

The company's fiscal year end on March 31 was six weeks away. Bill Sartoris, the founding owner/manager, and his wife, Bena, had worked day and night for over six years building the company. He now felt he was at a

*This case was written by Dr. Ken Blawatt, who at the time of its preparation was associated with Simon Fraser University as an Adjunct Professor at the University College of the Cariboo.

turning point in his life. He had just reached his 56th birthday and was still working 60 hours a week. But while his company was making a good profit, he believed that success was eluding him. At breakfast that morning, his wife raised the thought that perhaps he should sell the company and do something else.

INTRODUCTION

The company, Argon Carpet Cleaning Company Drapery & Upholstery Cleaners Limited, was founded in January, 1988 as a sole proprietorship. Starting with little more than a vacuum cleaner and a scrub bucket, Mr. Sartoris targeted building managers and apartment building owners as his primary customers. In order to set himself apart from the usual "mop and pail" operators in the industry, he offered extra free services, cleaning entranceways or common areas at no charge whenever he was called on to provide apartment cleaning services. Six years later he had become relatively successful with sales approaching $1 million.

THE CLEANING INDUSTRY

The company is in an industry that has enjoyed solid growth over the last decade. The building services sector, including office, plant, and apartment maintenance, renovations, and restoration, has grown at an average annual rate of 12 percent each year since 1986, with little indication of a decline.

Up until the late 1950s, most office, apartment, business, and manufacturing operations performed their own cleaning and maintenance with in-house staff. For example, Cadillac-Fairview during the early 1960s maintained a staff of 50 people to look after the apartment complexes it was developing in Toronto. By the mid-1970s, the cleaning and maintenance of rental housing (already approaching 10,000 rental units in the Toronto market) was causing at least one major property management company no end of problems in staffing, and it replaced its staff of over 200 full and part-time employees with outside contracting services. This started a trend toward using building service contractors in Canada.

Today the *services to buildings and dwellings* sector (SIC 9953) of the business services industry exceeds $2.5 billion in revenue and employs over 100,000 people in Canada. From 1986 to 1990 total revenues increased from $1.09 billion to $1.75 billion, a 61 percent increase over a five-year period, with almost 9,000 firms in 1990.

The average company does about $200,000 in annual sales. The more typical firms—that is to say those which earn less than $2 million in revenue—average only $123,000 per year in annual sales. These smaller companies make up 99 percent of the industry. In fact, there are fewer than 100 firms in Canada doing more than $2 million annually. The industry in British Columbia has also experienced considerable growth, most of it in the last few years. From 1986 to 1990 total revenue grew at an annual rate of 18 percent to $281 million, most of it in the greater Vancouver market, where it is estimated that the industry will reach $450 million for 1994 (see Exhibit 1).

Exhibit 1 Canadian Janitorial (Cleaning) Services, British Columbia

	REVENUE	NO. FIRMS
1986	$146.5 million	805
1987	$158.9 million	805
1988	$194.3 million	1,139
1989	$235.0 million	1,314
1990	$281.0 million	1,447
1994*	$415.0 million	1,901

*Estimate

Source: Statistics Canada, Cat. No. 63-232.

There are 1,900 companies competing in the B.C. market. Most of these are small operators. Only a few earn $6 million in sales.

THE BUILDING SERVICES MARKET

Most of the building services market in British Columbia is in the commercial or business sector, which accounts for 78 percent of all revenues. Government institutions—schools, offices, and other facilities—represent 18 percent while private households take up the balance.

Within the business sector there are seven segments:

MARKET CLEANING SEGMENTS	
Offices	2.95 million sq. ft.
Hotels	30,000 units
Retail	40 million sq. ft.
Restaurant	5 million sq. ft.
Shopping malls	8 million sq. ft.
Plants and warehouses	1 million sq. ft.
Rental apartments	110,000 units

Within these there are seven markets, which include:

- Drapery and blind services
- Window cleaning
- Walls and ceilings
- Carpet cleaning and service
- Floor cleaning and service
- Restoration (flood and fire)
- Other

Office cleaning

There are almost 3 million square feet of office space in the greater Vancouver area. The market is relatively competitive for cleaning services; prices range from $2.07 per square foot in the suburban areas to $1.26 for larger, downtown buildings. The costs for repair and maintenance range from $1.56 in the downtown area to $1.44 in the outlying areas. This indicates an annual sales volume of $8 to $10 million (based on BOMA statistics), with an additional $10 to $20 million from other office markets. The total potential is about $25 million annually.

Hotels

There is not a great deal of statistical information on cleaning services in the hotel and accommodation sector. There are an estimated 30,000 units in the Vancouver area, but many such establishments hire their own staff to service the rooms and do the cleaning. However, excluding cleaning services and using office costs as a guide, the potential for carpet repair services could reach $5 million a year.

Retail stores

There are roughly 40 million square feet of commercial retail space in Vancouver, with much of this contracted out to cleaning services. Here, approximately 15,000 stores are expected to spend $65 to $100 million for cleaning. The likely average is $80 million a year.

Restaurants

Most restaurants employ their own staff to clean the premises. However, taking into account repair and replacement for draperies, blinds, and so on, the estimated income potential runs about $5 million a year.

Shopping malls

Malls (including both stores and common areas) account for about 8 million square feet, or $20 million in revenue potential.

Plants and warehouses

There are few reliable sources of statistics for this market sector. Most production plants and warehouses use their own employees for cleaning, but specialized services such as cleaning and repairing draperies and blinds could result in sales between $3 million and $10 million.

Apartment rental units

There are 110,000 rental units in the greater Vancouver area (Refer to CMHC Published Statistics), representing over $20 million in cleaning services. This market has been growing significantly in the GVRD and is expected to double with the addition of condominium services in the next decade.

Exhibit 2 Revenue Sources

1. Offices	3 million sq. ft. (BOMA)	$8 to $30 million
2. Hotels	30,000 units	$5 to $10 million
3. Retail	40 million sq. ft.	$65 to $100 million
4. Restaurants	5 million sq. ft.	$5 to $10 million
5. Shopping malls	8 million sq. ft.	$15 to $25 million
6. Plants and warehouses		$3 to $10 million
7. Rental apartments		$8 to $20 million
8. Other		$30 to $50 million
Total		$139 to $255 million

SUMMARY MARKET POTENTIAL

Exhibit 2 sets out the potential for the greater Vancouver market.

Statistics Canada information (Exhibit 1) indicates a potential for this sector of $415 million in British Columbia. Assuming that the GVRD accounts for 60 percent of this value, the total revenue potential that is calculated using Exhibit 1 comes to $249 million, or close to the $255 million amount shown in Exhibit 2.

COMPETITION

There are five or six big players and a thousand "mop and pail" operators in Vancouver and the Lower Mainland. Statistics Canada listed 1,447 firms in 1990 and an estimated 1,901 in 1994. The top few account for 38 percent of the volume, while the balance (1,882 firms) have annual sales of $175 million, or about $93,000 each. Argon is expected to reach just under $1,000,000 for the 1993–94 period, making it one of the larger organizations in the market.

There are about 200 competitors listed in the Vancouver Yellow Pages that compete with Argon. However, taking into account the company's 14 percent annual growth, there is little reason why the firm should be concerned with competitors at this point, particularly since Argon Carpet Cleaning accounts for less than 1 percent of the market. However, there is a considerable amount of guerrilla warfare taking place in the market. A number of larger firms have expressed concern about the "mop and pail" competition. In one contract bid situation, a big company's $2,500/month bid for a government contract was given to a "mop and pail" for about $1,000/month, or the cost of labour.

ARGON'S COMPETITIVE ADVANTAGE

Most companies, mainly rental property managers, have a favourable attitude toward Argon. A typical observation is that managers actively seek out high-quality cleaning contractors. They rely on outside services for all carpet cleaning, drape and blind service, and renovations, and there are a number of important components that influence the buying decision.

1. Availability, regardless of the time.
2. Company personality—the ability to get along with tenants.
3. Reliability and consistency.
4. Value for price. In this respect the evaluation goes beyond quality of workmanship, which is an expectation.

Argon has been very sensitive to these elements and has incorporated them into their selling strategy. Consequently, the company has been able to develop a positive, professional reputation and is able to inspire confidence in tenants and managers alike.

Most managers prefer to establish a long-term relationship with their outside contractors. Argon already has a good customer base representing over 400 building complexes and managers, including some of the larger real-estate management firms such as North American Management, Viam Group, Bristol Management, Continental Realty, Nacel Properties, and Ranch Realty.

As it expands its operations and continues to provide that same sense of value, there is little reason why it should not expect good, solid growth.

HISTORY OF ARGON CARPET CLEANING COMPANY

From 1988 to 1991, Mr. Sartoris barely managed to break even as he learned the business and began to establish a network of customers and suppliers who could help him grow. In 1991 the cleaning side of the business began to earn a profit with sales of $286,000 and gross profit of $60,000, increasing to $630,000 in sales for the first ten months of 1993.

	ALLOCATION OF REVENUE SOURCES:
Cleaning services	56%
Drapery and blind sales	11
Flood and restoration	18
Carpet repair and installation	15
	100%

During the 1993–94 period (fiscal year end is March 31), the company operated as a mixed service organization and responded to whatever orders were called in by building managers. In one respect this is a positive aspect of the business. Their reputation as a reliable, consistently available cleaning company has offset the need for a sales force to generate orders.

The company operates from a 6,000 square foot plant in New Westminster, centrally located to serve its Lower Mainland market. The company has a lean administrative staff consisting of an administrative manager, a coordinator, a receptionist-dispatcher, and an accounts clerk.

The company originally started its business in cleaning carpets, flooring, and other areas of offices and apartments. Starting with a single van, the company progressed to ten truck vans and expects to add two in the coming year. Each vehicle is self-contained and has $5,000 worth of equipment, and each operator manages the vehicle as a small business. Argon Carpet assumes responsibility for the vehicle, its upkeep, operations, and supply of cleaning chemicals. The operator realizes a 26 percent commission.

The company schedules jobs for each of the ten cleaning operators, who are also required to perform other services. Typically, they pick up and deliver drapes and window blinds that have been cleaned, repaired, or newly supplied by Argon Carpet. They are encouraged to do other jobs at a site if approached by the building manager, and end each job by filling out a quality checklist that is used to assess the cleaning job and prospects for other cleaning and repair opportunities. The vans return each night to the plant, where the equipment and vehicles are serviced, and where supplies are restocked for the following day.

DRAPERY MANUFACTURING

The company supplies drapes and Venetian blinds to apartments and offices on an intermittent basis. It has recently moved into full-time production of these products in answer to a need by building managers for quick, consistent, and reliable service. The company has two people on sewing operations, including a supervisor, and is now producing 10 to 15 sets per week. The production department is located on the second floor of the plant in 1,000 square feet of space.

FLOOD AND RESTORATION

The company would like to expand this part of its business portfolio. The attraction to this market is the relatively high markup for providing fast, quality cleanup of homes and businesses following a flood or fire. Offsetting the good profitability is the 90 to 120 day aged receivable period, since the bills are paid out of insurance claims. However, Argon has factored these "hidden costs" into the selling price. The company uses its coordinators to look after these projects, which draw on one or more cleaners from the company's regular cleaning operation.

CARPET INSTALLATION

This is a very profitable part of the company. In the past this service was provided to customers as a courtesy. However, the business is now continuous and flows from Argon's cleaning service. The company maintains a list of reliable carpet layers, who are scheduled as the jobs come up. It purchases its own materials, usually based on a standard for the installation. The company's main inputs to this service are scheduling and purchasing. Labour is contracted to do the job.

DRY CLEANING OPERATIONS

Argon owns a soon-to-be-obsolete dry cleaning plant. This 1,200 square foot operation is separate from the main business, and after B.C. government regulations covering perchloride emissions are implemented at the end of 1994, it will be redundant. During the last fiscal year, this operation received approximately $5,000 worth of business monthly from Argon, in addition to doing $300 daily in walk-in trade. The plan is to consolidate this operation and to purchase an environmentally acceptable dry cleaning business.

COMPANY OPERATIONS

The company's past experience provides a solid basis for establishing the costs of future operations. Operating costs have been established as follows:

Operating Costs

ANNUAL ($)	
1. Rent and business taxes	42,000
2. Plant overhead: shop expense, training, equipment leases, misc.	13,600
3. Depreciation	15,000
4. Maintenance	6,900
5. Utilities	7,000
6. Vehicles: insurance, fuel, repairs	54,700 (10% increase)
7. Vehicle leasing	18,300 (20% increase)
8. Payroll (includes office)	333,400 (10% increase)
	490,900

Also, administration and marketing costs include accounting, advertising, bad debts, consulting, insurance, damage, office expense and supplies, telephone, travel, and entertainment. These costs are projected at $92,600 for 1994 and are expected to increase 20 percent annually.

Comparative Performance

	STATISTICS CANADA AVERAGE	ARGON CARPET CLEANING COMPANY
Cost of goods	3%	17%
Salaries, wages	61	43
Rent	1	3
Repair and maintenance	1	1
Advertising	1	2
Depreciation	1	2
Occupancy expense	3	3
Others	23	17
Profit margin	6	12
	100%	100%

Source: Stats Canada, Cat: 63-232

There is a considerable difference between the Argon Carpet operations and the average firm. First, the company is twice as profitable. Second, it generates more value-added content through its repair and replacement activities (high cost of goods sold). Part of the company in fact does manufacturing.

ORGANIZATION

Bill's son Fredericci looks after the company's accounting, while his wife Bena looks after the banking. The company payroll is managed by the bank. Fred doubles as a coordinator and project boss when floods and other emergency cleanup jobs come into the plant on weekends and evenings.

1. What marketing strategy would you employ to double the company's sales?
2. What are the some of the problems that will have to be addressed if the firm is to grow?
3. As a consultant to the company, what would be your *detailed* recommendations in regard to marketing and operations management?
4. Should Sartoris sell the company?

Argon Carpet Cleaning Company, Drapery & Upholstery Cleaners
Balance Sheet
January 31, 1994

ASSETS		
Current Assets		
Petty cash	0.58–	
Cash clearing	0.00	
Royal Bank	25,363.86–	
Bank of Montreal	1,406.39	
AAA Fuels	72,155.32	
Accounts receivable	155,505.75	
Advance receivable	455.00	
Receivables: net		204,158.02
Prepaid exp. and deposits		7,694.92
Prepaid vehicle insurance		5,842.20
Deferred finance charges		6,934.39
Total Current Assets		224,629.53
Fixed Assets		
Vehicles	98,368.94	
Trailer	12,758.00	
Accum deprec: vehicles	5,159.03–	
Vehicles: net		105,967.91
Cleaning equipment	135,735.62	
Office furniture & equip.	24,480.07	
Accum deprec.: furn & equip	16,518.90–	
Drapery-making equipment	5,782.31	
Shop equipment	32,292.69	
Furniture & equipment: net		181,771.79
Computer	14,579.40	
Accum. deprec.–computer	1,436.91–	
Computer: net		13,142.49
Dry cleaning equip.		8,056.00
Dry cleaning goodwill		12,000.00
Total Fixed Assets		320,938.19
Total Assets		545,567.72

LIABILITIES		
Current Liabilities		
Loan-line of credit		74,000.00
Accounts payable		2,206.03
Misc. accrued payables		4,153.37
Vacation payable		6,980.63
Corp. income taxes payable		292.65–
UIC payable	58.23–	
CPP payable	22.00–	
Federal income tax payable	63.59–	
Rec. gen payable: total		143.82–
Misc. deductions		13.25
WCB payable		5,834.12
Shareholder's loan		203,183.03
GST charged on sales	4,558.98	
GST paid on purchases	2,127.56–	
GST owing		2,431.42
PST payable		390.51
Total Current Liabilities		298,755.89
Long Term		
Cond. sale contract—11		20,837.89
Cond. sale contract—9		19,436.38
Royal Bank loan—vehicle		36,689.00
Drycleaning sale contract		6,900.00
Total Long Term		83,863.27
Total Liabilities		382,619.16
Equity		
Common shares		100.00
Total Share Capital		100.00
Retained Earnings		
Retained earnings		67,480.47
Current earnings		95,368.09
Total Retained Earnings		162,848.56
Total Equity		162,948.56
Liabilities and Equity		545,567.72

Argon Carpet Cleaning Company, Drapery & Upholstery Cleaners
Income
April 1, 1993, to January 31, 1994

REVENUE		
Service Revenue		
Dry cleaning		3,918.91
Area rug cleaning		1,325.51
Carpet cleaning		330,841.85
Blind cleaning		11,352.88
Flood/restoration		36,512.25
Scotchguard/deodorizer		5,560.12
Pressure washing		12,297.50
Drapery cleaning		35,991.01
Upholstery cleaning		5,254.56
Drapery sales		82,647.61
Blind sales		969.96
Carpet repair		13,386.39
Lino and carpet installation		93,379.60
Blind repair		334.31
Drapery repair		70.00
Pet odour control		1,024.00
Service call	6,043.69	
Labour on flood/rest.	40,985.26	
Equipment rental	36,815.00	
Underlay supplied	10,871.92	
Misc. material supplied	2,406.12	
Total flood/restoration		97,121.99
Miscellaneous revenue		1,233.50
Total Sales Revenue		733,221.95
Total Revenue		733,221.95

EXPENSE		
Cost of Goods		
Service equipment rental		842.84
Cleaning supplies		16,790.03
Dry cleaning supplies		4,317.05
Repair supplies		5,178.00
Carpet and underlay material		56,704.59
Drapery materials		36,013.45
Blind materials		2,271.20
Total Cost of Goods Sold		122,117.16
Operating Expenses		
Shop expense		2,637.14
Technician courses		1,382.37
Accounting		5,192.00
Advertising		11,308.10
Equipment repair and mainte.		5,761.40
Bad debts		215.00
Bank charges and interest		7,542.07
Consulting/legal fees		9,792.35
Insurance		3,770.72
Miscellaneous		1,139.51
Damaged goods or property		531.54
Office expense		12,858.34
Office supplies		5,174.65
Rent and taxes		35,097.17
Telephone		20,335.87
Travel and entertainment		4,246.76
Utilities		5,872.83
Shareholder's wages	41,800.00	
Wages	257,547.44	
UIC expense	9,379.40	
CPP expense	5,172.53	
WCB expense	5,732.77	
Payroll expense: total		319,632.14
Vehicle, gas and oil		20,536.57
Vehicle insurance		10,149.55
Vehicle, repairs and mainte.		14,908.59
Vehicle, lease payments		15,251.52
Equipment lease payments		2,440.51
Total Operating Expenses		515,736.70
Total Expense		637,853.86
Income		95,368.09

37 Columbia Chrome: A Joint Venture with India*

Columbia Chrome Industries Ltd. is engaged in repairing, rebuilding, and manufacturing of hydraulic and pneumatic components on various types of mechanical equipment. In their 40,000 square foot plant in Langley, British Columbia, the company offers fully integrated services with cutting edge technology in hard chroming, honing, grinding, machining, welding, and so on. Customer experience reveals that rebuilt rods, pins, and valves wear much longer than the originals; yet the cost is only one-third to one-half of the price of new ones, resulting in savings of hundreds of thousands of dollars on new equipment.

Columbia Chrome services machines used in a number of industries, but the main target market is mining companies that use various types of mining equipment. The strategy is to offer customers the best in quality control and fast service, at competitive prices. This strategy has enabled the company to outperform its rivals. Sales and profits have steadily increased over the years; current combined sales exceed $15 million.

The company has eight branches in western Canadian mining towns. Its head office and production plant are in Langley, B.C. In the United States it has expanded into the mining states of Colorado, Wyoming, Arizona, Nevada, and Washington.

The next natural expansion was to markets outside North America. Pursuing an aggressive international marketing program, Columbia Chrome set up joint ventures with Malaysia, Papua New Guinea, Australia, Thailand, and Indonesia in the Asia Pacific, and also made direct sales of turnkey plants to Columbia and Peru in South America.

Foreign expansion is a priority for the company, and the company's international marketing strategy is to *go global*—that is, go where the markets are. This strategy involves simultaneous entry in entirely different markets—and through different entry modes, if warranted. The latest expansion is a joint venture with India. Also, discussions are under way for joint ventures with three other countries—the People's Republic of China, Kuwait, and Ireland. To facilitate such expansion, an international subsidiary called Colco International Industries Ltd. has been created. President of the new division is Mr. John Jansen, who was previously president of Columbia Chrome. Mr. Jansen trots around the globe making new deals and overseeing projects in various stages of completion.

THE INDIA PARTNER

Colco's partner in India is an engineering firm, Concast India Ltd., which in reality is a holding company under the Concast name with head offices in Mumbai (formerly Bombay). The Concast group offers a variety of engineering services and products to the Indian market such as steel plant equipment manufacturing, continuous casting machines, and pollution control systems. The technology for some of these services and products has been acquired through foreign collaborations.

Concast is owned mostly by Mr. Narinder Nayar, the managing director, who started the business in 1973 and singlehandedly built the Concast group of companies. They employ 225 people, including project planning teams, technical consultants, marketing personnel, and service engineers. In spite of keen competition, sales have grown steadily to their present level of 400 million rupees, or about 16 million dollars. As local technology in hard chroming is outdated, Concast has been on the lookout for foreign collaborators for some time.

In 1995 an equity joint-venture agreement was signed between Concast and Colco. The new enterprise was named Columbia Chrome India Private Ltd. A private limited company incorporated in India has restrictions on the right of transfer of shares—it cannot have more than 50 shareholders or make public issue of its shares or debentures.

The primary objective of the joint venture is to obtain a competitive edge in the marketplace in high-precision technology applications in hard chroming and maintenance of hydraulic cylinders. The long-term plan is to use the experience gained from the first plant to build a chain of service facilities in key markets in India.

The main target market of Columbia Chrome India Pr. Ltd. is the mining companies. To this end, Goa, a seaport on the west coast of India about 500 kilometres south of Mumbai, has been selected as the location for the first plant. Goa (which was once a Portuguese colony) and the nearby states of Karnataka and Andhra Pradesh contain vast deposits of iron ore, copper, bauxite, and manganese, which are presently mined with old equipment and outdated technology. So there is immense scope not only for chroming technology, but also for the upgrading and optimizing of mining operations as a whole, to make them competitive in terms of quality and cost.

THE PATTERN OF NEGOTIATIONS

Initial contacts between Colco and Concast started in 1991, soon after the Indian government abandoned its old model of a "mixed economy" and opened up the country for large-scale foreign investment. A year after liberalization, Barton Biggs, chairman of Morgan Stanley Management, stated that "India is an interesting example for foreign investment because the overall economy will grow 5% to 6% a year even though the mass of the economy is the agricultural and government sectors . . . as we calculate it, the private sector's real GNP growth is about 10% a year. It is a dynamic story."

A study of 128 foreign companies operating in India in 1993 showed net profits before tax as a percentage of

*This case was written by Dr. George Jacob, who at the time of its preparation was associated with BCIT.

net worth and capital employed at 32.1 percent and 19.1 percent, respectively.

Concast initiated the venture through networking with the Canadian Trade Commissioner in India as well as the Canada-India Business Council. After an exchange of visits by senior executives of the two firms, a detailed feasibility study was undertaken. It showed excellent short-term as well as long-term potential for profit.

Concast is the major shareholder in the joint venture, with 60 percent of equity. Colco has 40 percent. Five directors are appointed, three from the Indian side and two from Canada. The project's implementation, day-to-day operations, and marketing will all be looked after by Concast personnel; no expatriates from Canada will be required. However, initially a group of technicians from India will go to Canada to acquire training of three to four weeks' duration in chroming technology. Their visit will be facilitated by the Canadian International Development Agency.

Between the initial stages of searching for a partner and the signing of the final agreement, four years elapsed. Both parties wanted to proceed faster with an agreement; however, the Indian bureaucracy turns its wheels slowly. Interestingly, in a poll conducted on governmental bureaucracy by Roper Starch Worldwide, the Indian government received low ratings. More than two-thirds of those polled said that the bureaucratic challenges of doing business in India were greater than in other developing countries.

Also contributing to the slow pace of negotiations was the variance in management styles between the two countries. In comparison to Canada, decision making in India, generally speaking, is slower, and once decisions are made, implementation also is slower. Besides, Indian managers work in an environment characterized by scarcity; many are not yet used to thinking in terms of efficiency, quality, core competency, and the like—the common parameters of a successful business in a competitive environment.

The joint venture is now at the implementation stage. Land has been acquired in Goa, and a project team from Concast is overseeing the plant construction. However, during the long negotiation period, some of the competing companies have acquired chroming technology with foreign collaboration; hence, Concast may have lost its competitive advantage. To be on the safe side, Concast and Colco are now contemplating a project with a smaller scope than originally envisaged.

1. Evaluate the economic, cultural, and political risks Columbia Chrome took in its decision to set up the joint venture in India. What are some of the typical problems investors encounter?
2. What opportunities does India offer to market North American products and services?

38 Ecolad Incorporated*

Ecolad Inc. is a family-owned business incorporated in 1986. The firm is located on Ouellette Avenue, the heart of the business district in Windsor, Ontario. The president of the firm is Gary Awad, and he works with his three brothers, who are actively engaged in the business. Ecolad employs a secretary and an artist.

A FAMILY BUSINESS

After the business was established in Windsor, Gary Awad was able to convince his brother, Tom, to join the new firm. Previously, Tom worked for twelve years with General Motors as an industrial engineer. He then set up his own firm and bought a custom framing shop, called Noon Day Graphics, in the same building occupied by Ecolad. Roger is also part of the family enterprise and was working for Chrysler Canada before joining the other family members. Roger Awad, the third brother, is now in Toronto trying to establish Ecolad's presence in Canada's largest city.

Finally, Richard Awad, a school teacher by training, will move shortly to London, Ontario, to manage the Ecolad franchise, which recently had been repurchased by the company. In the last few years, the London franchise had not done very well and it was in poor financial health. The family is now the main source of financing for Ecolad.

ECOLAD'S MISSION

Ecolad is primarily in the business of selling advertising space to any firm or organization wishing to advertise on the side of a litter container. The litter containers are located in high-traffic areas in those cities and shopping malls where Ecolad is able to obtain territorial exclusivity. For example, the greater Windsor area has over 120 litter containers owned and maintained by Ecolad.

Presently, Ecolad supplies free of charge the containers to any participating city or mall. In return, the company asks for a three to five year contract granting Ecolad the exclusive right to offer such a service in the area. It hopes to expand the number of available locations to include schools and university campuses, as well as recreational areas such as campgrounds, golf courses, sports clubs, and so forth. Ecolad feels that its litter containers are a service to the public at no cost to cities or firms that are willing to permit their display. According to Gary Awad, "Ecolad is also in the business of fostering good litter habits among consumers."

Understandably, most city administrators are very receptive to the arrangement proposed by Ecolad. Gary

*This case was written by Dr. Robert Tamilia, who at the time of its preparation was associated with UQAM (University of Québec at Montreal).

Awad, the president, and Tom, VP, are the family members most actively involved in seeking contractual permissions to locate the litter containers in approved locations. Once permission is granted, they and other commissioned sales representatives attempt to sell advertising space available on the four panels of the litter containers.

Ecolad's advertising media service is not a new idea, at least in the greater Windsor area. The idea of providing advertising space on litter containers was first introduced in the city in the late 1960s. Unfortunately, that original provider went bankrupt because the containers available then were of poor quality and were easily damaged. As a result, they had to be replaced too often and their high replacement cost led to the company's demise. In the United States, such a business venture was successful right at the beginning because the litter containers used were much heavier and sturdier, and did not have to be replaced as often.

Initially, Ecolad began importing American-made litter containers. Later on, Gary Awad secured an agreement with Alcan of Canada to make the containers. The aluminum is poured into a special mold that was developed in accordance with Ecolad's specific needs. As a result, these containers are now sturdy enough to take abuse and are resistant to oxidation. The top part of the container has a movable aluminum flap on which is inscribed "Waste Only." Each container cost Ecolad about $300. The potential advertising revenue per container varies between $50 and $100 per panel per month, depending on its location. Thus, a litter container can generate as much as $400 per month (assuming all four sides are used).

Ecolad feels that the service it provides accomplishes two functions. First, with its free containers, Ecolad provides a free waste management program to any city, mall, or other organization willing to participate. Second, this advertising medium is less costly compared to most other established media, including outdoor. Ecolad offers small and medium sized companies an affordable advertising medium.

The approximate size of each panel is 60 by 90 cm (or 2 by 3 feet). The artist produces all the panels according to customers' advertising specifications. Each panel is laminated to protect it from the elements. The actual cost of preparing each panel advertisement varies widely, from $50 to $400 or more, depending on what is to be done and the quality of the colour reproduction desired.

All maintenance of the litter containers is done by Ecolad. The firm cleans and washes the containers on a weekly basis. Ecolad repairs and replaces those containers as necessary. Such quick servicing is not available for billboards, for which repairs can take up to one month and which are cleaned only a couple of times a year. Ecolad gives advertisers free exposure time equivalent to the time lost while the container was out of use. As an added service, a new Ecolad advertiser is given up to one week of free advertising time on a company truck, which has space reserved for such a purpose—a service unmatched by any other outdoor media firm. However, emptying the containers is the responsibility of the city, the mall, or the organization under contract with Ecolad.

THE RICKY RECEPTACLE AWARENESS PROGRAM

Ecolad is now in the process of changing the moveable flaps on the containers to ones that have the inscription "Ricky Receptacle says Thank You." The containers are now only available in the Windsor area, but Ecolad hopes to expand the program to all other markets it serves. The reason for the change is to make the litter containers more user friendly—to give the containers human qualities. It is hoped that the new inscription on the flap will personalize the containers and help promote Ecolad's image of being an ecologically responsible firm.

Gary Awad is confident that the new Ricky Receptacle initiative will further enhance Ecolad's corporate image, especially in those cities which have yet to grant Ecolad's need for exclusive distribution rights. Ecolad is also hoping that the new Ricky Receptacle program will create goodwill among current advertising users. More importantly, Tom Awad is convinced that the new program will add credibility and goodwill to any business buying advertising space on Ecolad's containers.

Advertisers will want to associate themselves with a firm that has such a favourable image in the community. All the other Awad brothers expressed the same feeling that the Ricky Receptacle inscription on the litter containers will be a big boost to their business. Irrespective of this new initiative, Ecolad has always faced the drawback of trying to convince advertisers that a garbage container can be used to help promote their goods and services. Tom Awad prefers to call Ecolad's litter containers "pollution control devices" so as to minimize any negative connotations that advertisers or consumers associate with garbage cans.

The Ricky Receptacle program was launched in Windsor and was not only aimed at Ecolad's prime market but also at kids. An Ecolad spokesperson, taking the role of "Ricky Receptacle," visited kindergarten classes and other educational institutions and gave advice to kids on the benefits of litter control. Children were able to talk to Ricky and were able to ask him questions about pollution and the consequences of poor waste management habits. As part of this pollution awareness campaign, Ecolad made it possible for children to send letters to Ricky Receptacle, which were answered. It also sent questionnaires to parents to find out if their children's litter habits had changed as a result of Ecolad's efforts to promote sound litter habits. The educational litter awareness program aimed at kids was very successful in that it received wide media coverage with the CBC and the CTV networks. It also enjoyed much local press and radio coverage. This free publicity for Ecolad made the firm the talk of the town and had a favourable impact on Ecolad's business.

SOME PROBLEMS FOR ECOLAD

City administrators and mall operators request far more containers than Ecolad is willing or capable of supplying. Ecolad's distribution policy of litter containers is based on the amount of advertising space it can sell in the area, not on the number of litter containers needed by the city or a mall. For Ecolad, there is an optimum number of containers that can be distributed in a given area. This number is always lower than the total number of litter containers a city or mall needs.

Also, the Ricky Receptacle program is becoming far too costly for Ecolad to manage. Using Ecolad people to educate the public about litter issues was not the most efficient way for those people to generate sales for the company. Gary Awad thinks that the best way to solve this problem is to obtain municipal grants or some other form of government financial assistance to keep the litter educational awareness program going.

1. Is there any conflict of interest in Ecolad's mission of serving its own needs while at the same time attempting to serve the needs of the community?
2. What business is Ecolad in?
3. Is Ecolad's demand for exclusive distribution rights for litter containers appropriate?
4. Should the Ricky Receptacle program be extended to all Ecolad's markets?
5. To what extent will the new inscription on the container's flap affect consumers?
6. What should Gary Awad do with the Ricky Receptacle awareness program?
7. Can Ecolad change the litter habits of kids? What about adults? What about a community, or society in general?

Notes

Chapter 1

1. Christopher H. Lovelock and Charles B. Weinberg, *Marketing for Public and Nonprofit Managers* (New York: John Wiley & Sons, 1984); Ruby Roy Dholakia, "A Macromarketing Perspective on Social Marketing: The Case of Family Planning in India," *Journal of Macromarketing* 4, no. 1 (1984), pp. 53–61.
2. Gregory D. Upah and Richard E. Wokutch, "Assessing Social Impacts of New Products: An Attempt to Operationalize the Macro-Marketing Concept," *Journal of Public Policy and Marketing* 4 (1985), pp. 166–78.
3. See *Marketing News,* March 1, 1985, p. 1. See also Ernest F. Cooke, C. L. Abercrombie, and J. Michael Rayburn, "Problems with the AMA's New Definition of Marketing Offer Opportunity to Develop an Even Better Definition," *Marketing Educator,* Spring 1986, p. 1ff; O. C. Ferrell and George H. Lucas, Jr., "An Evaluation of Progress in the Development of a Definition of Marketing," *Journal of the Academy of Marketing Science,* Fall 1987, pp. 12–23.
4. Malcolm P. McNair, "Marketing and the Social Challenge of Our Times," in *A New Measure of Responsibility for Marketing,* ed. Keith Cox and Ben M. Enis (Chicago: American Marketing Association, 1968). John W. Barnes, "Marketing Exchange Relationships, Transactions, and Their Media," *Journal of the Academy of Marketing Science,* Winter 1996, pp. 79–80.
5. Northern Telecom, *1996 Annual Report.*
6. George Fisk, "Editor's Working Definition of Macromarketing," *Journal of Macromarketing* 2, no. 1 (1982), pp. 3–4; Shelby D. Hunt and John J. Burnett, "The Macromarketing/ Micromarketing Dichotomy: A Taxonomical Model," *Journal of Marketing,* Summer 1982, pp. 11–26.
7. Charles R. Weiser, "Championing the Customer," *Harvard Business Review,* November 1995–December 1995, pp. 113–16; Stanley F. Slater and John C. Narver, "Market Orientation and the Learning Organization," *Journal of Marketing,* July 1995, pp. 63–74; Regina F. Maruca, "Getting Marketing's Voice Heard," *Harvard Business Review,* January–February 1998, pp. 10–11; Francis J. Gouillart and Frederick D. Sturdivant, "Spend a Day in the Life of Your Customers," *Harvard Business Review,* January 1994–February 1994, pp. 116–20ff.; George S. Day, "The Capabilities of Market-Driven Organizations," *Journal of Marketing,* October 1994, pp. 37–52; R. W. Ruekert, "Developing a Market Orientation: An Organizational Strategy Perspective," *International Journal of Research in Marketing,* August 1992, pp. 225–46; J. David Lichtenthal and David T. Wilson, "Becoming Market Oriented," *Journal of Business Research,* May 1992, pp. 191–208; George J. Avlonitis and Spiros P. Gounaris, "Marketing Orientation and Company Performance: Industrial Vs. Consumer Goods Companies," *Industrial Marketing Management,* September 1997, pp. 385–402; Bernard J. Jaworski and Ajay K. Kohli, "Market Orientation: Antecedents and Consequences," *Journal of Marketing,* July 1993, pp. 53–70. See also "The Marketing Revolution at Procter & Gamble," *Business Week,* July 25, 1988, pp. 72–73ff.; Frederick E. Webster, Jr., "The Changing Role of Marketing in the Corporation," *Journal of Marketing,* October 1992, pp. 1–17; Franklin S. Houston, "The Marketing Concept: What It Is and What It Is Not," *Journal of Marketing,* April 1986, pp. 81–87; George S. Day, "The Capabilities of Market-Driven Organizations," *Journal of Marketing,* October 1994, pp. 37–52.
8. For more on the marketing concept in the banking industry, see "Little Banks Are Sprouting in the Shadow of Giants," *Business Week,* May 4, 1998, p. 44; "High Finance, Hard Sell," *American Demographics,* February 1998, pp. 43–47; "On the Road with a Rolling Bank Branch," *The Wall Street Journal,* November 6, 1997, p. B1ff.; "Have You Noticed All of Those ATMs Suddenly Appearing?" *The Wall Street Journal,* October 7, 1997, p. A1ff.; "Got a Bank? Industry Launches TV Ads," *The Wall Street Journal,* September 23, 1997, p. B8; Maria Sannella, "Dollars Through the Doors: A Pre-1930 History of Bank Marketing in America," *Journal of the Academy of Marketing Science,* Summer 1997, pp. 267–68.
9. Susan Noakes, "Learning the Marketing Ropes," *The Financial Post,* July 9, 1992, p. 16.
10. "Smart Managing: The Power of Reflection," *Fortune,* November 24, 1997, pp. 291–96; "Toyota's New Deal," *Brandweek,* October 20, 1997; pp. 34–44; "Home Depot: Beyond Do-It-Yourselfers," *Business Week,* June 30, 1997, pp. 86–88; "Why some Customers Are More Equal than Others," *Fortune,* September 19, 1994, pp. 215–24; Stanley F. Slater and John C. Narver, "Market Orientation, Customer Value, and Superior Performance," *Business Horizons,* March–April 1994, pp. 22–28; "How to Get Closer to Your Customers," *Business Week,* Enterprise 1993, pp. 42–45; "Companies That Serve You Best," *Fortune,* May 31, 1993, pp. 74–88; "Relationships: Six Steps to Success," *Sales & Marketing Management,* April 1992, pp. 50–58; Stanley F. Slater, "Developing a Customer Value-Based Theory of the Firm," *Journal of the Academy of Marketing Science,* Spring 1997, pp. 162–67; Sharon E. Beatty, "Keeping Customers," *Journal of Marketing,* April 1994, pp. 124–25; Thomas W. Gruen, "Relationship Marketing: The Route to Marketing Efficiency and Effectiveness," *Business Horizons,* November–December 1997, pp. 32–38; A. Parasuraman, "Reflections on Gaining Competitive Advantage Through Customer Value," *Journal of the Academy of Marketing Science,* Spring 1997, pp. 154–61; Alan W. H. Grant and Leonard A. Schlesinger, "Realize Your Customers' Full Profit Potential," *Harvard Business Review,* September 1995–October 1995, pp. 59–72; Diana L. Deadrick, R. B. McAfee, and Myron Glassman, " 'Customers for Life': Does It Fit Your Culture?" *Business Horizons,* July–August 1997, pp. 11–16; Robert B. Woodruff, "Customer Value: The Next Source for Competitive Advantage," *Journal of the Academy of Marketing Science,* Spring 1997, pp. 139–53; Robert M. Morgan, "Aftermarketing: How to Keep Customers for Life Through Relationship Marketing," *Journal of the Academy of Marketing Science,* Winter 1997, pp. 92–93; "Here's the Maine Store for the Great Outdoors," *The Blade,* (Toledo, Ohio), August 26, 1990; "L.L. Bean Scales Back Expansion Goals to Ensure Pride in Its Service Is Valid," *The Wall Street Journal,* July 31, 1989, p. B3; "Training at L.L. Bean," *TRAINING, The Magazine of Human Resources Development,* October 1988; "Using the Old (L.L.) Bean," *The Reader's Digest,* June 1986.
11. "This Exhibit Is Brought to You by . . .," *Business Week,* November 10, 1997, pp. 91–94; "Supermarket Solutions," *Newsweek,* August 11, 1997, p. 45; "In Funding Squeeze, PBS Cozies Up to Madison Avenue, 'Sponsors,' " *The Wall Street Journal,* July 3, 1996, p. B1ff.; "Non-Profits Get Market-Savvy," *Advertising Age,* May 29, 1995, p. 1ff.; "Finally, Human Rights for Motorists," *Business Week,* May 1, 1995, p. 45; William G. Bowen, "When a Business Leader Joins a Nonprofit Board," *Harvard Business Review,* September–October 1994, pp. 38–44; "Charities Draw Younger Donors with Hip Events and Door Prizes," *The Wall Street Journal,* April 25, 1994, p. B1; "Nonprofits Dig into Databases for Big Donors," *The Wall Street Journal,* September 8, 1992, p. B1ff.; William A. Sutton, "Sports Marketing: Competitive Business Strategies for Sports," *Journal of the Academy of Marketing Science,* Spring 1996, pp. 176–77; Russell W. Jones, Carolyn Marshall, and Thomas P. Bergman, "Can a Marketing Campaign Be Used to Achieve Public Policy Goals?" *Journal of Public Policy & Marketing,* Spring 1996, pp. 98–107; J. G. Dees, "Enterprising Nonprofits," *Harvard Business Review,* January–February 1998, pp. 55–67;

W. C. Kim and Renee Mauborgne, "Value Innovation: The Strategic Logic of High Growth," *Harvard Business Review,* January–February 1997, pp. 102–12; Gerald E. Smith and Paul D. Berger, "The Impact of Direct Marketing Appeals on Charitable Marketing Effectiveness," *Journal of the Academy of Marketing Science,* Summer 1996, pp. 219–31; Shohreh A. Kaynama, "Fundraising for Non-Profits," *Journal of the Academy of Marketing Science,* Spring 1997, p. 173; C. Scott Greene and Paul Miesing, "Public Policy, Technology, and Ethics: Marketing Decisions for NASA's Space Shuttle," *Journal of Marketing,* Summer 1984, pp. 56–67; Alan R. Andreasen, "Nonprofits: Check Your Attention to Customers," *Harvard Business Review,* May–June 1982, pp. 105–10.

12. Stanley J. Shapiro, "Ethical Decision Making in Marketing," *Journal of Public Policy & Marketing,* Fall 1996, pp. 321–23; Oswald A. Mascarenhas, "Exonerating Unethical Marketing Executive Behaviors: A Diagnostic Framework," *Journal of Marketing,* April 1995, pp. 43–57; Gina Vega, "Caveat Emptor: Ethical Chauvinism in the Global Economy," *Journal of Business Ethics,* September 1997, pp. 1353–62; George G. Brenkert, "Competing With Integrity in International Business," *Journal of Business Ethics,* January 1997, pp. 6, 22ff. For a discussion of some criticisms of advertising, see Banwari Mittal, "Public Assessment of TV Advertising: Faint Praise and Harsh Criticism," *Journal of Advertising Research,* January/February 1994, pp. 35–53. For a discussion of ethical issues in marketing, see Anusorn Singhapakdi et al., "The Perceived Importance of Ethics and Social Responsibility on Organizational Effectiveness: A Survey of Marketers," *Journal of the Academy of Marketing Science,* Spring 1995, pp. 49–56; Ishmael P. Akaah and Daulatram Lund, "The Influence of Personal and Organizational Values on Marketing Professionals' Ethical Behavior," *Journal of Business Ethics,* June 1994, pp. 417–30; Edward J. O'Boyle and Lyndon E. Dawson, Jr., "The American Marketing Association Code of Ethics: Instructions for Marketers," *Journal of Business Ethics,* December 1992, pp. 921–30; Ellen J. Kennedy and Leigh Lawton, "Ethics and Services Marketing," *Journal of Business Ethics,* October 1993, pp. 785–96; Michael R. Hyman, Robert Skipper, and Richard Tansey, "Ethical Codes Are Not Enough," *Business Horizons,* March–April, 1990, pp. 15–22; John Tsalikis and David J. Fritzsche, "Business Ethics: A Literature Review with a Focus on Marketing Ethics," *Journal of Business Ethics,* September, 1989, pp. 695–702; G.R. Laczniak, R.F. Lusch, and P.E. Murphy, "Social Marketing: Its Ethical Dimensions," *Journal of Marketing,* Spring 1979, pp. 29–36.

Chapter 2

1. Mary Anne Raymond and Hiram C. Barksdale, "Corporate Strategic Planning and Corporate Marketing: Toward an Interface," *Business Horizons,* September–October, 1989, pp. 41–48; George S. Day, "Marketing's Contribution to the Strategy Dialogue," *Journal of the Academy of Marketing Science,* Fall 1992, pp. 323–30; P. Rajan Varadarajan and Terry Clark, "Delineating the Scope of Corporate, Business, and Marketing Strategy," *Journal of Business Research,* October–November 1994, pp. 93–106.

2. "Broderbund: Identify a Need, Turn a Profit," *Fortune,* November 30, 1992, pp. 78–79.

11. "See the Doctor, Get a Toaster," *Business Week,* December 8, 1997, pp. 86–87; "Hospitals Use TV Spots to Boost Business," *The Wall Street Journal,* September 26, 1996, p. B10; "Rx: Thirty Minutes on the StairMaster Twice Weekly," *Newsweek,* March 17, 1997, p. 46; "Designing a New Hospital? Let Malls Be Your Muse," *The Wall Street Journal,* August 1, 1994, p. B1ff.; "Offering Aerobics, Karate, Aquatics, Hospitals Stress Business of 'Wellness,' " *The Wall Street Journal,* August 9, 1993, p. B1ff.

3. "A Place Called Home," *Royal Bank Reporter,* Fall 1990.

4. Orville C. Walker, Jr., and Robert W. Ruekert, "Marketing's Role in the Implementation of Business Strategies: A Critical Review and Conceptual Framework," *Journal of Marketing,* July 1987, pp. 15–33; Thomas V. Bonoma, "A Model of Marketing Implementation," *1984 AMA Educators' Proceedings* (Chicago: American Marketing Association, 1984), pp. 185–89; Kevin Romer and Doris C. Van Doren, "Implementing Marketing in a High-Tech Business," *Industrial Marketing Management,* August 1993, pp. 177–86.

5. *1993 Annual Report,* Gillette Company.

6. "Timex Puts 'Iron' into TV with $5M," *Brandweek,* September 22, 1997, p. 6; "Timex Lines Goes for Museum-Goers," *Brandweek,* July 21, 1997, p. 8; "Timex Back to Basics to Retro-fit Gen X," *Brandweek,* August 5, 1996, p. 3; "Sunglass Hut Plots to Shake Up Watch Biz," *Brandweek,* April 1, 1996, p. 1ff.; "Swatch Adds Metal Watch," *Advertising Age,* November 7, 1994, p. 60; Benetton Readies Watch Campaign," *Brandweek,* August 8, 1994, p. 5; "Indiglo Watch Lights Up Better Times for Timex," *Brandweek,* April 25, 1994, pp. 30–32; "Seiko Show the Way to Cocka-Doodle-Doo It," *Advertising Age,* April 25, 1994, p. 62; "High Time for Timex," *Adweek's Marketing Week,* July 29, 1991, p. 24; "Watchmakers Put Emphasis on Technology," *Advertising Age,* April 3, 1989, p. 28; "Timex, Swatch Push Fashion," *Advertising Age,* July 18, 1988, p. 4.

7. Mark B. Houston, "Competing for the Future: Breakthrough Strategies for Seizing Control of Your Industry and Creating the Markets of Tomorrow," *Journal of the Academy of Marketing Science,* Winter 1996, pp. 77–79; George S. Day and Robin Wensley, "Assessing Advantage: A Framework for Diagnosing Competitive Superiority," *Journal of Marketing,* April 1988, pp. 1–20; Kevin P. Coyne, "Sustainable Competitive Advantage—What It Is, What It Isn't," *Business Horizons,* January/February 1986, pp. 54–61; Michael E. Porter, *Competitive Advantage—Creating and Sustaining Superior Performance* (New York: Free Press, MacMillan, 1986).

8. For more on McDonald's, see "Fast-food Icon Wants Shine Restored to Golden Arches," *USA Today,* May 1, 1998, p. 1Bff.; "McD's Eyes Rollout of Loyalty Card," *Advertising Age,* April 27, 1998, p. 3; "Ronald McDonald, New Kids Character Share Center Stage," *Advertising Age,* March 2, 1998, p. 1ff.; "A Really Big Mac," *Newsweek,* November 17, 1997, pp. 56–58; "Why You Won't Find Any Egg McMuffins for Breakfast in Brazil," *The Wall Street Journal,* October 23, 1997, p. A1ff.; "Burger Wars Sizzle as McDonald's Clones the Whopper," *The Wall Street Journal,* September 17, 1997, p. B1ff.; "Toilet Paper and a Big Mac," *American Demographics,* July 1996, p. 15–16; "McDonald's Conquers the World," *Fortune,* October 17, 1994, pp. 103–16. For more on Microsoft, see Chapter 4, endnote 21. For more on ski resorts, see "Bikers Give Ski Resorts Summertime Lift," *The Wall Street Journal,* July 7, 1994, p. B1ff. For more on Coleman, see "Growing to Match Its Brand Name," *Fortune,* June 13, 1994, p. 114; "Coleman's Familiar Name Is Both Help and Hindrance," *The Wall Street Journal,* May 17, 1990, p. B2. For more on diversifications, see "Where P&G's Brawn Doesn't Help Much," *Business Week,* November 10, 1997, pp. 112–14; "Pepsi Has Had Its Fill of Pizza, Tacos, Chicken," *The Wall Street Journal,* January 24, 1997, p. B1ff; "Spinning Away," *Time,* August 26, 1996, pp. 30–31; "Kellogg Hopes to Put Bagels on Its Menu," *The Wall Street Journal,* November 19, 1996, p. B1ff.

9. Frank R. Bacon, Jr., and Thomas W. Butler, Jr., *Planned Innovation,* rev. ed. (Ann Arbor: Institute of Science and Technology, University of Michigan, 1980).

10. Paul F. Anderson, "Marketing, Strategic Planning and the Theory of the Firm," *Journal of Marketing,* Spring 1982, pp. 15–26; George S. Day, "Analytical Approaches to Strategic Market Planning," in *Review of Marketing 1981,* ed. Ben M. Enis and Kenneth J. Roering (Chicago: American Marketing Association, 1981), pp. 89–105; Ronnie Silverblatt and Pradeep Korgaonkar, "Strategic Market Planning in a Turbulent Business Environment," *Journal of Business Research,* August 1987, pp. 339–58.

11. Richard N. Cardozo and David K. Smith, Jr., "Applying Financial Portfolio Theory to Product Portfolio Decisions: An Empirical Study," *Journal of Marketing,* Spring 1983, pp. 110–19; Yoram Wind, Vijay Mahajan, and Donald J. Swire, "An Empirical Comparison of Standardized Portfolio Models," *Journal of Marketing,* Spring 1983, pp. 89–99; Philippe Haspeslagh, "Portfolio Planning: Uses and Limits," *Harvard Business Review,* January–February 1982, pp. 58–73.

12. Keith B. Murray and Edward T. Popper, "Competing under Regulatory Uncertainty: A U.S. Perspective on Advertising in the Emerging European Market," *Journal of Macromarketing,* Fall 1992, pp. 38–54; "Inside Russia—Business Most Unusual," *UPS International Update,* Spring 1994, p. 1ff.; "Freighted with Difficulties," *The Wall Street Journal,* December 10, 1993, p. R4; "The Trick to Selling in Europe," *Fortune,* September 20, 1993, p. 82; "Japan Begins to Open the Door to Foreigners, a Little," *Brandweek,* August 2, 1993, pp. 14–16; "Russia Snickers after Mars Invades," *The Wall Street Journal,* July 13, 1993, p. B1ff.; "Enticed by Visions of Enormous Numbers, More Western Marketers Move into China," *The Wall Street Journal,* July 12, 1993, p. B1ff.; Michael G. Harvey and James T. Rothe, "The Foreign Corrupt Practices Act: The Good, the Bad and the Future," in *1983 American Marketing Association Educators' Proceedings,* ed. P. E. Murphy et al. (Chicago: American Marketing Association, 1983), pp. 374–79.

13. "What Makes Italy Easier?" *Going Global—Italy (supplement to Inc.),* 1994; "Jean Cloning," *Brandweek,* May 30, 1994, pp. 15–22; "Double Entendre: The Life and the Life of Pepsi Max," *Brandweek,* April 18, 1994, p. 40; "Global Ad Campaigns, After Many Missteps, Finally Pay Dividends," *The Wall Street Journal,* August 27, 1992, p. A1ff.; Kamran Kashani, "Beware the Pitfalls of Global Marketing," *Harvard Business Review,* September–October 1989, pp. 91–98; "How to Go Global—and Why," *Fortune,* August 28, 1989, pp. 70–76; "Marketers Turn Sour on Global Sales Pitch Harvard Guru Makes," *The Wall Street Journal,* May 12, 1988, p. 1ff.

Chapter 3

1. Nuala Beck, *Shifting Gears, Thriving in the New Economy* (Toronto: HarperCollins, 1992).

2. Nuala Beck, *Excelerate: Growing in the New Economy* (Toronto: HarperCollins, 1996).

3. See Peter F. Drucker, *Management: Tasks, Responsibilities, Practices, and Plans* (New York: Harper & Row, 1973).

4. This point of view is discussed at much greater length in a classic article by T. Levitt, "Marketing Myopia," *Harvard Business Review,* September–October 1975, p. 1ff. See also David J. Morris, Jr., "The Railroad and Movie Industries: Were They Myopic?" *Journal of the Academy of Marketing Science,* Fall 1990, pp. 279–84.

5. "Reichhold Chemicals: Now the Emphasis Is on Profits Rather than Volume," *Business Week,* June 20, 1983, pp. 178–79; Carolyn Y. Woo, "Market-Share Leadership—Not Always So Good," *Harvard Business Review,* January–February 1984, pp. 50–55; Robert Jacobson and David A. Aaker, "Is Market Share All That It's Cracked Up to Be?" *Journal of Marketing,* Fall 1985, pp. 11–22.

6. "Harley-Davidson's U-Turn," *USA Today,* March 2, 1990, p. 1Bff.; "How Harley Beat Back the Japanese," *Fortune,* September 25, 1989, pp. 155–64.

7. Peter J. Williamson, "Asia's New Competitive Game," *Harvard Business Review,* September–

October 1997, pp. 55–67; David J. Collis and Cynthia A. Montgomery, "Competing on Resources: Strategy in the 1990s," *Harvard Business Review,* July–August 1995, pp. 118–28; "How Goodyear Forecast a Great Decade," *American Demographics,* March 1995, p. 39; "Firms Analyze Rivals to Help Fix Themselves," *The Wall Street Journal,* May 3, 1994, p. B1ff.; Thomas S. Gruca and D. Sudharshan, "A Framework for Entry Deterrence Strategy: The Competitive Environment, Choices, and Consequences," *Journal of Marketing,* July 1995, pp. 44–55; Venkatram Ramaswamy, Hubert Gatignon, and David J. Reibstein, "Competitive Marketing Behavior in Industrial Markets," *Journal of Marketing,* April 1994, pp. 45–55; Z. S. Deligonul and S. T. Cavusgil, "Does the Comparative Advantage Theory of Competition Really Replace the Neoclassical Theory of Perfect Competition?" *Journal of Marketing,* October 1997, pp. 65–73; J. S. Armstrong, "Co-Opetition," *Journal of Marketing,* April 1997, pp. 92–95; John L. Haverty and Myroslaw J. Kyj, "What Happens when New Competitors Enter an Industry," *Industrial Marketing Management* 20, no. 1 (1991), pp. 73–80; Arch G. Woodside and Elizabeth J. Wilson, "Diagnosing Customer Comparisons of Competitors' Marketing Mix Strategies," *Journal of Business Research,* October–November 1994, pp. 133–44; David W. Cravens and Shannon H. Shipp, "Market-Driven Strategies for Competitive Advantage," *Business Horizons,* January–February, 1991, pp. 53–61; William W. Keep, Glenn S. Omura, and Roger J. Calantone, "What Managers Should Know about Their Competitors' Patented Technologies," *Industrial Marketing Management,* July 1994, pp. 257–64.

8. *Kao* (Cambridge, MA: Harvard Business School Press, 1984).

9. "P&G Wins Lawsuit, Loses Market," *Advertising Age,* September 18, 1989, p. 72. For more on other cases, see "China's Spies Target Corporate America," *Fortune,* March 30, 1998, pp. 118–22; "In the Debris of a Failed Merger: Trade Secrets," *The Wall Street Journal,* March 10, 1998, p. B1ff.; "Ex-Kodak Manager Is Sentenced to Jail; Company Sues Scherer," *The Wall Street Journal,* November 17, 1997, p. B17; "How Safe Are Your Secrets?" *Fortune,* September 8, 1997, pp. 114–20; "High-Tech Tools Usher in Stolen-Information Age," *USA Today,* April 10, 1997, p. 1Bff.; Shaker A. Zahra, "Unethical Practices in Competitive Analysis: Patterns, Causes and Effects," *Journal of Business Ethics,* January 1994, pp. 53–62.

10. "Canada's Export Strategy," Supply and Services Canada, Cat. C2-226, 1995–1E.

11. Chad Rubel, "Canada, Mexico, Still Await the 'Best of NAFTA,' " *Marketing News,* February 13, 1995, p. 2.

12. For more on EU, see "Here's What You Need to Care about the Euro," *Newsweek,* May 4, 1998, p. 42; "Au Revoir, Malaise: Europe's Economies Are Back in Business," *The Wall Street Journal,* April 9, 1998, p. A1ff.; "The Case for the Euro–II," *The Wall Street Journal,* March 25, 1998, p. A22; "A Tale of Two Nations Shows Europe's Union Has Differing Sides," *The Wall Street Journal,* July 28, 1997, p. A1ff.; "No One Ever Said It Would Be Easy," *Time,* March 1, 1993, p. 32ff.; "Europe's Borders Fade and People and Goods Can Move More Freely," *The Wall Street Journal,* May 18, 1993, p. A1ff.; Valerie L. Vaccaro, "European Retailing's Vanishing Borders," *Journal of the Academy of Marketing Science,* Fall 1996, pp. 386–88; Alan Wolfe, "The Single European Market: National or Euro-Brands?" *International Journal of Advertising* 10, no. 1 (1991), pp. 49–58; Jack G. Kaikati, "Opportunities for Smaller U.S. Industrial Firms in Europe," *Industrial Marketing Management,* November, 1990, pp. 339–48. Available from World Wide Web: <http://www.nafta.org>. For more on NAFTA, see "Nafta Jam," *USA Today,* April 3, 1998, p. 1Bff.; "Stir Fry: Mexican Vegetables in U.S. Woks," *The Wall Street Journal,* March 5, 1998, p. A19; "Apparel Makers Move South," *Fortune,* November 24, 1997, p. 62; "NAFTA," *The Wall Street Journal,* October 28, 1994, pp. R1–13; Kent Jones, "NAFTA Chapter 19: Is There Hope for Bilateral Dispute Resolution of Unfair Trade Law Decisions?" *Journal of Public Policy & Marketing,* Fall 1994, pp. 300–6; Paul A. Dion and Peter M. Banting, "What Industrial Marketers Can Expect From U.S.-Canadian Free Trade," *Industrial Marketing Management,* February, 1990, pp. 77–80.

13. "Time for a Reality Check," *Business Week,* December 2, 1996, pp. 58–67; "Industry Covets Potential of Pacific Rim," *USA Today,* June 17, 1996, p. 1Bff.; Paul Coomes, "Recession Winners and Losers," *American Demographics,* October 1992, p. 62; "We're #1 and It Hurts," *Time,* October 24, 1994, pp. 50–56; "Biggest Show of Force in a Decade Halts Slide of the Dollar—for Now," *The Wall Street Journal,* May 5, 1994, p. A1ff.; "Price Index Overstates Inflation," *USA Today,* January 14, 1994, p. 1Bff.; "Demand for Wood Leads to Building Panic," *USA Today,* March 17, 1993, p. 1Bff.; "The Global Economy: Can You Compete?" (Special Report), *Business Week,* December 17, 1990, pp. 60–93.

14. "In HDTV Age, Successor to VCR Is a Long Way Off," *The Wall Street Journal,* April 8, 1998, p. B1ff.; "The Automakers' Big-Time Bet on Fuel Cells," *Fortune,* March 30, 1998, pp. 122C-P; "Take the Internet with You in a Phone, Watch or Shoe," *USA Today,* March 19, 1998, p. 1Bff.; "Detroit's Impossible Dream," *Business Week,* March 2, 1998, pp. 66–68; "Computer Industry Races to Conquer the Automobile," *The Wall Street Journal,* February 23, 1998, p. B1ff.; "Let's Talk: Speech Technology," *Business Week,* February 23, 1998, pp. 61–80; "Technology, Not Fashion, Now Seen as Crucial to Selling Athletic Shoes," *Brandweek,* February 16, 1998, p. 16; "The Power of Invention," *Newsweek Special Issue,* Winter 1997–98; "Envisioning the Era of the $500 PC," *The Wall Street Journal,* November 18, 1997, p. B1ff.; "Intel's New Chip Has Real Flash," *Business Week,* September 29, 1997, p. 40; "Waiting for HDTV? Don't Go Dumping Your Old Set Just Yet," *The Wall Street Journal,* September 12, 1997, p. A1ff.; "Scrambling for the Sky: Motorola Plan Could Spark Space Wars," *USA Today,* June 18, 1997, p. 1Bff.; "Shippers Pitch Power of Gizmos, Gadgets," *The Wall Street Journal,* June 2, 1997, p. B1; "The Ultimate Plastic," *Business Week,* May 19, 1997, pp. 119–22; "Crisp Picture as Easy as DVD," *USA Today,* April 15, 1997, p. 10D; "New Satellite Era Looms Just over the Horizon," *The Wall Street Journal,* March 18, 1997, p. B1ff.; "How Smart Sensors Keep Factories Humming," *Fortune,* March 17, 1997, pp. 144A–H; "In Digital Dorm, Click on Return for Soda," *The Wall Street Journal,* January 23, 1997, p. B1ff.; "Fliers Call Electronic Ticketing a Drag," *The Wall Street Journal,* January 17, 1997, p. B1ff. "TV Seminars and CD-Roms Train Workers," *The Wall Street Journal,* January 3, 1996, p. B1ff.; "The Digital Factory," *Fortune,* November 14, 1994, pp. 92–110; "Making Sense of the Internet," *Newsweek,* October 24, 1994, pp. 46–49; "Technology Has Travelers under Seige," *USA Today,* October 14, 1994, p. 1Bff.; "Video Conference Calls Change Business," *The Wall Street Journal,* October 12, 1994, p. B1ff.; "High-Tech Edge Gives U.S. Firms Global Lead in Computer Networks," *The Wall Street Journal,* September 9, 1994, p. A1ff.; "Battle for the Soul of the Internet," *Time,* July 25, 1994, pp. 50–56; "Waking Up to the New Economy," *Fortune,* June 17, 1994, pp. 36–46; "The Productivity Payoff Arrives," *Fortune,* June 27, 1994, pp. 79–84; Noel Capon and Rashi Glazer, "Marketing and Technology: A Strategic Coalignment," *Journal of Marketing,* July 1987, pp. 1–14.

15. "Made in Japan? Not for Home Team," *The Wall Street Journal,* February 18, 1998, p. A6; "U.S. Backpedals on Law that Hung 'Made in China' Tag on European Goods," *The Wall Street Journal,* August 8, 1997, p. A2; Gopalkrishnan R. Iyer, "Anticompetitive Practices in Japan: Their Impact on the Performance of Foreign Firms," *Journal of Marketing,* October 1997, pp. 97–99; Michael G. Harvey, "Buy American": Economic Concept or Political Slogan?" *Business Horizons,* May–June 1993, pp. 40–46; "Made in America Becomes a Boast in Europe," *The Wall Street Journal,* January 19, 1994, p. B1ff.; Terry Clark, "National Boundaries, Border Zones, and Marketing Strategy: A Conceptual Framework and Theoretical Model of Secondary Boundary Effects," *Journal of Marketing,* July 1994, pp. 67–80.

16. Brian Lyons, *Canadian Microeconomics: Problems and Policies* (Scarborough, Ont.: Prentice Hall, 1983) pp. 184–86.

17. Seymour Lipset, *Continental Divide: The Values and Institutions of the United States and Canada* (New York: Routledge, 1990).

18. "More Dads Raise Families without Mom," *The Wall Street Journal,* October 3, 1997, p. B1ff.; "Ads that Portray Women," *USA Today,* September 9, 1996, p. 4B; "In Fitful Pursuit of American Women," *Advertising Age,* January 8, 1996, P. S4ff.; "Imperfect Picture," *The Wall Street Journal,* April 24, 1995, p. R7; "Home Front," *Advertising Age,* September 19, 1994, p. 1ff.; "Narrowcast in Past, Women Earn Revised Role in Advertising," *Advertising Age,* October 4, 1993, p. S1ff.; "Stay-at-Home Moms Are Fashionable Again in Many Communities," *The Wall Street Journal,* July 23, 1993, p. A1ff.; Eric Panitz, "Marketing in a Multicultural World: Ethnicity, Nationalism and Cultural Identity," *Journal of the Academy of Marketing Science,* Spring 1997, pp. 169–71; Victoria D. Bush and Thomas Ingram, "Adapting to Diverse Customers: A Training Matrix for International Marketers," *Industrial Marketing Management,* September 1996, pp. 373–83.

Chapter 4

1. John T. Mentzer and Nimish Gandhi, "Expert Systems in Marketing: Guidelines for Development," *Journal of the Academy of Marketing Science,* Winter, 1992, pp. 73–80; William D. Perreault, Jr., "The Shifting Paradigm in Marketing Research," *Journal of the Academy of Marketing Science,* Fall 1992, pp. 367–76; J.M. McCann, W.G. Lahti, and J. Hill, "The Brand Manager's Assistant: A Knowledge-Based System Approach to Brand Management," *International Journal of Research in Marketing,* April, 1991, pp. 51–74.

2. Philip B. Evans and Thomas S. Wurster, "Strategy and the New Economics of Information," *Harvard Business Review,* September–October 1997, pp. 70–82; Deborah Utter, "Information-Driven Marketing Decisions: Development of Strategic Information Systems," *Journal of the Academy of Marketing Science,* Spring 1998, pp. 157–58; James M. Sinkula, "Market Information Processing and Organizational Learning," *Journal of Marketing,* January 1994, pp. 35–45; Lawrence B. Chonko, John F. Tanner, Jr., and Ellen Reid Smith, "The Sales Force's Role in International Marketing Research and Marketing Information Systems," *Journal of Personal Selling and Sales Management,* Winter, 1991, pp. 69–80; James C. Bondra and Tim R. V. Davis, "Marketing's Role in Cross-Functional Information Management," *Industrial Marketing Management,* May 1996, pp. 187–95; Alfred C. Holden, "How to Locate and Communicate with Overseas Customers," *Industrial Marketing Management* 20, no. 3 (1991), pp. 161–68.

3. "Focusing on Customers' Needs and Motivations," *Business Marketing,* March 1991, pp. 41–43; James M. Sinkula, "Perceived Characteristics, Organizational Factors, and the Utilization of External Market Research Suppliers," *Journal of Business Research,* August 1990, pp. 1–18; Earl Naumann and Douglas J. Lincoln, "Systems Theory Approach to

Conducting Industrial Marketing Research," *Journal of Business Research,* September 1989, p. 151; Bruce Stern and Scott Dawson, "How to Select a Market Research Firm," *American Demographics,* March 1989, p. 44.

4. For a discussion of ethical issues in marketing research, see "How 'Tactical Research' Muddied Diaper Debate: a Case," *The Wall Street Journal,* May 17, 1994, p. B1ff.; John R. Sparks and Shelby D. Hunt, "Marketing Researcher Ethical Sensitivity: Conceptualization, Measurement, and Exploratory Investigation," *Journal of Marketing,* April 1998, pp. 92–109; Naresh K. Malhotra and Gina L. Miller, "An Integrated Model for Ethical Decisions in Marketing Research," *Journal of Business Ethics,* February 1998, pp. 263–80; Stephen B. Castleberry, Warren French and Barbara A. Carlin, "The Ethical Framework of Advertising and Marketing Research Practitioners: A Moral Development Perspective," *Journal of Advertising,* June 1993, pp. 39–46; Ishmael P. Akaah, "Attitudes of Marketing Professionals toward Ethics in Marketing Research: A Cross-National Comparison," *Journal of Business Ethics,* January, 1990, pp. 45–54.

5. "Grandma Got Run Over by Bad Research," *Inc.,* January 1998, p. 27; "The 'Bloodbath' in Market Research," *Business Week,* February 11, 1991, pp. 72–74; Bickley Townsend, "Market Research That Matters," *American Demographics,* August 1992, p. 58.

6. An excellent review of commercially available secondary data may be found in William R. Dillon, Thomas J. Madden, and Neil H. Firtle, *Marketing Research in a Marketing Environment,* 3rd ed. (Burr Ridge, Ill.: Irwin/McGraw-Hill, 1993). For more on U.S. Census data, see "Census 2000: Math, Not Politics, Please," *Business Week,* September 22, 1997, p. 42; "Two Words and a Number," *American Demographics,* February 1997, pp. 10–15; "Preparing for 2000, Census Bureau Tests Carrots vs. Sticks," *The Wall Street Journal,* May 2, 1996, p. B1ff.; Jackson Morton, "Census on the Internet," *American Demographics,* March 1995, p. 52; "The Best 100 Sources for Marketing Information," *American Demographics,* January 1995, p. 21.

7. Available from World Wide Web: <http:www.burke.com/ice/online>; "Focus Groups Meeting in Cyberspace," *The Wall Street Journal,* February 4, 1994, p. B1; William J. McDonald, "Focus Group Research Dynamics and Reporting: An Examination of Research Objectives and Moderator Influences," *Journal of the Academy of Marketing Science,* Spring 1993, pp. 161; Thomas Kiely, "Wired Focus Groups," *Harvard Business Review,* January–February 1998, pp. 12–16; Joe L. Welch, "Researching Marketing Problems and Opportunities with Focus Groups," *Industrial Marketing Management,* November, 1985, pp. 245–54.

8. "Selling Sibelius Isn't Easy," *American Demographics,* The 1994 Directory, pp. 24–25; "Symphony Strikes a Note for Research as it Prepares to Launch a New Season," *Marketing News,* August 29, 1988, p. 12.

9. Available from World Wide Web: <http://www.sawtooth.com/pages/glossary> "Surprise! A Home Builder (Finally) Surveys Buyers," *The Wall Street Journal,* February 11, 1998, p. B1ff.; Christine M. Fox, K. L. Robinson, and Debra Boardley, "Cost-Effectiveness of Follow-Up Strategies in Improving the Response Rate of Mail Surveys," *Industrial Marketing Management,* March 1998, pp. 127–33; Kathy E. Green, "Sociodemographic Factors and Mail Survey Response," *Psychology & Marketing,* March 1996, pp. 171–84; Terry L. Childers and Steven J. Skinner, "Toward a Conceptualization of Mail Survey Response Behavior," *Psychology & Marketing,* March 1996, pp. 185–209; Frederick Wiseman and Maryann Billington, "Comment on a Standard Definition of Response Rates, *Journal of Marketing Research,* August 1984, pp. 336–38.

10. "The 'Bloodbath' in Market Research," pp. 72–74; Nicolaos E. Synodinos and Jerry M. Brennan, "Computer Interactive Interviewing in Survey Research," *Psychology & Marketing,* Summer 1988, pp. 117–38. A. Dianne Schmidley, "How to Overcome Bias in a Telephone Survey," *American Demographics,* November 1986, pp. 50–51.

11. "The Naked Truth," *Brandweek,* October 13, 1997, pp. 22–26; "Marketers Seek the 'Naked' Truth in Consumer Psyches," *The Wall Street Journal,* May 30, 1997, p. B1ff.; "Where You Really Need to Hear Consumers," *Brandweek,* January 20, 1997, p. 17; Stephen J. Grove and Raymond P. Fisk, "Observational Data Collection Methods for Services Marketing: An Overview," *Journal of the Academy of Marketing Science,* Summer 1992, pp. 217–24; "Coupon Clippers, Save Your Scissors," *Business Week,* June 20, 1994, pp. 164–66; Magid M. Abraham and Leonard M. Lodish, "An Implemented System for Improving Promotion Productivity Using Store Scanner Data," *Marketing Science,* Summer 1993, pp. 248–69; "The Nitty-Gritty of ECR Systems: How One Company Makes It Pay," *Advertising Age,* May 2, 1994, pp. S1ff.; Peter J. Danaher and Terence W. Beed, "A Coincidental Survey of People Meter Panelists: Comparing What People Say with What They Do," *Journal of Advertising Research,* January/February 1993, p. 86.

12. "Ads Awaken to Fathers' New Role in Family Life," *Advertising Age,* January 10, 1994, p. S8; "AT&T's Secret Multimedia Trials Offer Clues to Capturing Interactive Audiences," *The Wall Street Journal,* July 28, 1993, p. B1ff.; "Experimenting in the U.K.: Phone, Cable Deals Let U.S. Test Future," *USA Today,* June 28, 1993, p. 1Bff.; "America's Next Test Market? Singapore," *Adweek's Marketing Week,* February 4, 1991, p. 22; Raymond R. Burke, "Virtual Shopping: Breakthrough in Marketing Research," *Harvard Business Review,* March–April 1996, pp. 120–31; Glen L. Urban, Bruce D. Weinberg, and John R. Hauser, "Premarket Forecasting of Really-New Products," *Journal of Marketing,* January 1996, pp. 47–60; "Bar Wars: Hershey Bites Mars," *Fortune,* July 8, 1985, pp. 52–57.

13. For more detail on data analysis techniques, see William R. Dillon, Thomas J. Madden, and Neil H. Firtle, *Marketing Research in a Marketing Environment,* 3rd ed. (Burr Ridge, Ill.: Irwin/McGraw-Hill, 1993) or other current marketing research texts; see also Michael D. Johnson and Elania J. Hudson, "On the Perceived Usefulness of Scaling Techniques in Market Analysis," *Psychology & Marketing,* October 1996, pp. 653–75; Milton D. Rosenau, "Graphing Statistics and Data: Creating Better Charts," *Journal of Product Innovation Management,* March 1997, p. 144.

14. See John G. Keane, "Questionable Statistics," *American Demographics,* June 1985, pp. 18–21. Detailed treatment of confidence intervals is beyond the scope of this text, but it is covered in most marketing research texts, such as Donald R. Lehmann, *Analysis for Marketing Planning* 4th ed. (Burr Ridge, Ill.: Irwin/McGraw-Hill, 1997).

15. E. Jerome McCarthy et al., *Basic Marketing: A Managerial Approach,* 1st Australasian ed., (Richard D. Irwin: Burr Ridge, IL, 1994), pp. 128–29.

16. "GM Seeks Revival of Buick and Olds," *The Wall Street Journal,* April 12, 1988, p. 37.

17. Alan R. Andreasen, "Cost-Conscious Marketing Research," *Harvard Business Review,* July–August, 1983, pp. 74–81; A. Parasuraman, "Research's Place in the Marketing Budget," *Business Horizons,* March–April 1983, pp. 25–29; Jack J. Honomichl, "Point of View: Why Marketing Information Should Have Top Executive Status," *Journal of Advertising Research,* November/December 1994, pp. 61–66; Jim Bessen, "Riding the Marketing Information Wave," *Harvard Business Review,* September–October 1993, pp. 150–61.

Chapter 5

1. David K. Foot with Daniel Stoffman, *Boom, Bust & Echo: How to Profit from the Coming Demographic Shift* (Toronto: Macfarlane Walter & Ross, 1996).

2. Statistics Canada, *Dictionary of the 1971 Census Terms,* Cat. 12-540 (Ottawa: Information Canada, December 1972).

3. "Going Where the Grass Is Greener," *Brandweek,* August 22, 1994, pp. 20–21; "Census Finds Fewer People Are on the Move," *The Wall Street Journal,* November 17, 1992, p. A5; "Mobility of U.S. Society Turns Small Cities into Giants," *The Wall Street Journal,* February 8, 1991, p. B1ff.; "Americans on the Move," *American Demographics,* June 1990, pp. 46–49; James R. Lumpkin and James B. Hunt, "Mobility as an Influence on Retail Patronage Behavior of the Elderly: Testing Conventional Wisdom," *Journal of the Academy of Marketing Science,* Winter 1989, pp. 1–12.

4. The source of the statistical data in this section is Statistics Canada, *The Daily,* February 17, 1998, Catalogue 11–001 E.

5. The material in this section first appeared in James Pollock, "The Economies of Growing Communities," *Marketing,* July 3–10, 1995, p. 11.

6. This section is drawn, almost verbatim, from Jennifer Lynn, "Approaching Diversity," *Marketing,* July 3–10, 1995, p. 11.

7. The source of the statistical data in this section is Statistics Canada, *The Daily,* December 2, 1997, Catalogue 11-001 E.

8. P.C. Lefrancois and Giles Chatel, "The French-Canadian Consumer: Fact and Fancy," in *New Ideas for Successful Marketing, Proceedings of the 1966 World Congress,* ed. J. S. Wright and J. L. Goldstucker (Chicago: American Marketing Association, 1966), p. 706.

9. The source of the mother-tongue data on the Quebec and French-speaking markets is Statistics Canada, *The Daily,* December 2, 1997, Catalogue 11-001 E.

10. See Ron Boychuk, "The Impact of English Media on Francophones," *Marketing,* June 13, 1983, pp. 23–25.

11. Francois Vary, "Quebec Consumer Has Unique Buying Habits," *Marketing,* March 23, 1992, p. 28.

12. Print Measurement Bureau, PMB 94.

13. The source of the statistical data in this section is Statistics Canada, *The Daily,* October 14, 1997, Catalogue 11-001 E.

14. Statistics Canada, *Summary Vital Statistics Indicators, Canada, Provinces and Territories,* 1995, Catalogue 84-210, p. 4.

15. Statistics Canada, *Annual Demographic Statistics,* Catalogue 91-213, 1996, p. 73.

16. Anita Lahey, "Gluttons for media," *Marketing Online,* September 1, 1997; Anita Lahey, "Looking the Other Way," Marketing Online, September 1, 1997; Anita Lahey, "Looking Forward," *Marketing Online,* September 23, 1996; John Straiton, "Persuading the Skeptical Consumer," *Marketing Online,* September 23, 1996.

17. Statistics Canada, *Incomes in 1996,* Catalogue 13-207, pp. 17–18.

18. Statistics Canada, *Income Distribution by Size in Canada,* 1996, Catalogue 13-207, pp. 160–61.

19. Edward Alden, "Widening Gap Between Rich and Poor New for Canada," *The Vancouver Sun,* December 24, 1997, A1, A12.

20. The source of the "Low Income Cutoff" data in this section is Statistics Canada, *Low Income Cut-offs (1992 Base) 1980 to 1987,* Catalogue 13-55, January 1998, p. 18.

21. Christopher Sarlo, *Poverty in Canada,* 2nd ed. (Vancouver: The Fraser Institute, 1996).

22. Statistics Canada, Labour Force Statistics, *Canadian Economy Observer,* Catalogue 11-210, 1996, p. 97.

23. This description of lifestages is adapted from a presentation made to the British Columbia Chapter of the American Marketing Association by George Clements, International vice president

and national director of Strategic Planning and Research, J. Walter Thompson Canada, November 17, 1992.
24. Barbara Passmore, "Understanding the Game of Life," PMB '95, pp. 13–14.

Chapter 6

1. Kristina D. Frankenberger, "Consumer Psychology for Marketing," *Journal of the Academy of Marketing Science,* Summer 1996, pp. 279–81; K. H. Chung, *Motivational Theories and Practices* (Columbus, Ohio: Grid, 1977), pp. 40–43; A. H. Maslow, *Motivation and Personality* (New York: Harper & Row, 1970).
2. "What Works for One Works for All," *Business Week,* April 20, 1992, pp. 112–13.
3. Jennifer Gregan-Paxton and Deborah R. John, "Consumer Learning by Analogy: A Model of Internal Knowledge Transfer," *Journal of Consumer Research,* December 1997, pp. 266–84; M. C. Macklin, "Preschoolers' Learning of Brand Names From Visual Cues," *Journal of Consumer Research,* December 1996, pp. 251–61; Jaideep Sengupta, Ronald C. Goodstein, and David S. Boninger, "All Cues Are Not Created Equal: Obtaining Attitude Persistence Under Low-Involvement Conditions," *Journal of Consumer Research,* March 1997, pp. 351–61; John Kim, Jeen-Su Lim, and Mukesh Bhargava, "The Role of Affect in Attitude Formation: A Classical Conditioning Approach," *Journal of the Academy of Marketing Science,* Spring 1998, pp. 143–52; Paul S. Speck and Michael T. Elliott, "Predictors of Advertising Avoidance in Print and Broadcast Media," *Journal of Advertising,* Fall 1997, pp. 61–76; Frances K. McSweeney and Calvin Bierley, "Recent Developments in Classical Conditioning," *Journal of Consumer Research,* September 1984, pp. 619–31; Scott A. Hawkins and Stephen J. Hoch, "Low-Involvement Learning: Memory without Evaluation," *Journal of Consumer Research,* September 1992, pp. 212–25.
4. Vikas Mittal, William T. Ross, and Patrick M. Baldasare, "The Asymmetric Impact of Negative and Positive Attribute-Level Performance on Overall Satisfaction and Repurchase Intentions," *Journal of Marketing,* January 1998, pp. 33–47; Mary F. Luce, "Choosing to Avoid: Coping With Negatively Emotion-Laden Consumer Decisions," *Journal of Consumer Research,* March 1998, pp. 409–33; Calvin P. Duncan and Richard W. Olshavsky, "External Search: The Role of Consumer Beliefs," *Journal of Marketing Research,* February 1982, pp. 32–43; M. Joseph Sirgy, "Self-Concept in Consumer Behavior: A Critical Review," *Journal of Consumer Research,* December 1982, pp. 287–300.
5. "Living Larger," *USA Today,* March 16, 1998, p. 4D; "It's Not Easy Being Lean in Cairo Today, but Women Do Try," *The Wall Street Journal,* March 4, 1998, p. A1ff.; "If Fat-Free Pork Is Your Idea of Savory, It's a Bright Future," *The Wall Street Journal,* January 29, 1998, p. A1ff.; "Pork Is Tasty, Say National Ads that Shift Focus from Nutrition," August 13, 1997, p. B5; "Americans Develop More Discriminating Taste," *USA Today,* June 6, 1997, p. 1Bff.; "Hershey Craves Gumdrops, Hard Candy amid Fat Fear," *The Wall Street Journal,* October 23, 1996, p. B1ff.; "Three Diet Firms Settle False-Ad Case; Two Others Vow to Fight FTC Charges," *The Wall Street Journal,* October 1, 1993, p. B5.
6. For more on Van Heusen, see "Men Are Taking a Cotton to Wrinkle-Free Pants," *USA Today,* June 16, 1994, p. 5D; " 'Wrinkle-Free' Shirts Don't Live Up to the Name," *The Wall Street Journal,* May 11, 1994, p. B1ff. See also "Frozen Pizza's Popularity Rises," *USA Today,* January 14, 1998, p. 5B; A. Parasuraman, Valarie A. Zeithaml, and Leonard L. Berry, "Reassessment of Expectations As a Comparison Standard in Measuring Service Quality: Implications for Further Research," *Journal of Marketing,* January 1994, pp. 111–24; Alain Genestre and Paul Herbig, "Service Expectations and Perceptions Revisited: Adding Product Quality to SERVQUAL," *Journal of Marketing Theory & Practice,* Fall 1996, pp. 72–82; Valarie A. Zeithaml, Leonard L. Berry, and A. Parasuraman, "The Nature and Determinants of Customer Expectations of Service," *Journal of the Academy of Marketing Science,* Winter 1993, pp. 1–12.
7. Harold H. Kassarjian and Mary Jane Sheffet, "Personality and Consumer Behavior: An Update," in H. Kassarjian and T. Robertson, *Perspectives in Consumer Behavior* (Glenview, Ill.: Scott, Foresman, 1981), p. 160; Todd A. Mooradian and James M. Olver, " 'I Can't Get No Satisfaction:' The Impact of Personality and Emotion on Postpurchase Processes," *Psychology & Marketing,* July 1997, pp. 379–93.
8. For more on kids' influence in purchase decisions, see James U. McNeal, "Tapping the Three Kids' Markets," *American Demographics,* April 1998, pp. 37–41; "Software Firms Coddle a Growing Market: The Preschool Crowd," *The Wall Street Journal,* April 2, 1998, p. A1ff.; "Not All Approve of Barbie's MasterCard," *USA Today,* March 30, 1998, p. 6B; "More than Play Dough," *Brandweek,* November 24, 1997, pp. 18–19; "Kodak Focuses on Putting Kids behind a Camera," *The Wall Street Journal,* May 6, 1997, p. B8; "Cybergiants See the Future—and It's Jack and Jill," April 14, 1997, p. 44; "*Special Report: Reaching Kids,*" *Advertising Age,* February 10, 1997, pp. 25–28; "The Rise of the Net-Generation," *Advertising Age,* October 14, 1996, p. 31ff.; Sharon E. Beatty and Salil Talpade, "Adolescent Influence in Family Decision Making: A Replication with Extension," *Journal of Consumer Research,* September 1994, pp. 332–41. See also Ugur Yavas, Emin Babakus, and Nejdet Delener, "Family Purchasing Roles in Saudi Arabia: Perspectives from Saudi Wives," *Journal of Business Research,* September 1994, pp. 75–86; Rosemary Polegato and Judith L. Zaichkowsky, "Family Food Shopping: Strategies Used by Husbands and Wives," *Journal of Consumer Affairs,* Winter 1994, pp. 278–99; Eric H. Shaw and Stephen F. I. Pirog, "A Systems Model of Household Behavior," *Journal of Marketing Theory & Practice,* Summer 1997, pp. 17–30; Kay M. Palan and Robert E. Wilkes, "Adolescent-Parent Interaction in Family Decision Making," *Journal of Consumer Research,* September 1997, pp. 159–69; Mary C. Gilly, John L. Graham, Mary F. Wolfinbarger, and Laura J. Yale, "A Dyadic Study of Interpersonal Information Search," *Journal of the Academy of Marketing Science,* Spring 1998, pp. 83–100; Conway L. Lackman, David P. Hanson, and John M. Lanasa, "Social Relations in Culture and Marketing," *Journal of Marketing Theory & Practice,* Winter 1997, pp. 144–52; Ellen R. Foxman, Patriya S. Tansuhaj, and Karin M. Ekstrom, "Adolescents' Influence in Family Purchase Decisions: A Socialization Perspective," *Journal of Business Research,* March 1989, pp. 159–72; C. Lackman and J.M. Lanasa, "Family Decision-Making Theory: An Overview and Assessment," *Psychology & Marketing,* March/April 1993, pp. 81–94.
9. See Gurprit S. Kindra, Michel LaRoche, and Thomas C. Muller, *Consumer Behaviour in Canada* (Scarborough, Ont.: Nelson Canada, 1989), pp. 301–40.
10. "Geek Chic: Phone Lines as Status Symbols," *The Wall Street Journal,* April 17, 1998, p. W10; Rebecca Piirto Heath, "The New Working Class," *American Demographics,* January 1998, pp. 51–55; "Education Marks a Widening Income Divide," *The Wall Street Journal,* June 28, 1996, p. R2; "Class in America," *Fortune,* February 7, 1994, pp. 114–26; Basil G. Englis and Michael R. Solomon, "To Be and Not to Be: Lifestyle Imagery, Reference Groups, and the Clustering of America," *Journal of Advertising,* Spring 1995, pp. 13–28; Greg J. Duncan, Timothy M. Smeeding, and Willard Rodgers, "The Incredible Shrinking Middle Class," *American Demographics,* May 1992, pp. 34–38; Dennis L. Rosen and Richard W. Olshavsky, "The Dual Role of Informational Social Influence: Implications for Marketing Management," *Journal of Business Research,* April 1987, pp. 123–44; Terry L. Childers and Akshay R. Rao, "The Influence of Familial and Peer-based Reference Groups on Consumer Decisions," *Journal of Consumer Research,* September 1992, pp. 198–211; Basil G. Englis and Michael R. Solomon, "To Be and Not to Be: Lifestyle Imagery, Reference Groups, and The Clustering of America," *Journal of Advertising,* Spring 1995, pp. 13–28.
11. "Marketing Superstars: Aki Maita, Tamagotchi," *Advertising Age International,* December 1997, p. 10; James H. Myers and Thomas S. Robertson, "Dimensions of Opinion Leadership," *Journal of Marketing Research,* February 1972, pp. 41–46.
12. "After Early Stumbles, P&G Is Making Inroads Overseas," *The Wall Street Journal,* February 6, 1989, p. B1; Sydney Roslow, "International Consumer Behavior: Its Impact on Marketing Strategy Development," *Journal of the Academy of Marketing Science,* Summer 1996, pp. 278–79; R. Mead, "Where is the Culture of Thailand?," *International Journal of Research in Marketing,* September 1994, pp. 401–04.
13. John L. Graham, "How Culture Works," *Journal of Marketing,* April 1996, pp. 134–35; Gary D. Gregory and James M. Munch, "Cultural Values in International Advertising: An Examination of Familial Norms and Roles in Mexico," *Psychology & Marketing,* March 1997, pp. 99–119; Shiretta F. Ownbey and Patricia E. Horridge, "Acculturation Levels and Shopping Orientations of Asian-American Consumers," *Psychology & Marketing,* January 1997, pp. 1–18; Jennifer L. Aaker and Durairaj Maheswaran, "The Effect of Cultural Orientation on Persuasion," *Journal of Consumer Research,* December 1997, pp. 315–28; Grant McCracken, "Culture and Consumption: A Theoretical Account of the Structure and Movement of the Cultural Meaning of Consumer Goods," *Journal of Consumer Research,* June 1986, pp. 71–84.
14. This material on time has been condensed from the collected, copyrighted works of Dr. Paul M. Lane and Dr. Carol Felker Kaufman of Western Michigan University and Rutgers University, respectively. It includes works done with coauthors Dr. Jay D. Lindquist and Esther Page-Wood of Western Michigan University, and Gary M. Goscenski of Perspectives Consulting Group.
15. Charles S. Areni, Pamela Kiecker, and Kay M. Palan, "Is It Better to Give Than to Receive? Exploring Gender Differences in the Meaning of Memorable Gifts," *Psychology & Marketing,* January 1998, pp. 81–109; Russell W. Belk, "Situational Variables and Consumer Behavior," *Journal of Consumer Research* 2, 1975, pp. 157–64; John F. Sherry, Jr., "Gift Giving in Anthropological Perspective," *Journal of Consumer Research,* September 1983, pp. 157–68.
16. Adapted and updated from James H. Myers and William H. Reynolds, *Consumer Behavior and Marketing Management* (Boston: Houghton Mifflin, 1967), p. 49. See also Judith Lynne Zaichkowsky, "Consumer Behavior: Yesterday, Today, and Tomorrow," *Business Horizons,* May/June 1991, pp. 51–58.
17. Ravi Dhar and Steven J. Sherman, "The Effect of Common and Unique Features in Consumer Choice," *Journal of Consumer Research,* December 1996, pp. 193–203; Victor V. Cordell, "Consumer Knowledge Measures As Predictors in Product Evaluation," *Psychology & Marketing,* May 1997, pp. 241–60; John V. Petrof and Naoufel Daghfous, "Evoked Set: Myth or Reality?" *Business Horizons,* May–June 1996, pp. 72–77; Wayne D. Hoyer, "An Examination of Consumer Decision Making for a Common Repeat Purchase Product," *Journal of Consumer Research,* December 1984, pp. 822–29; James R. Bettman, *An Information Processing Theory of Consumer Choice*

(Reading, Mass.: Addison-Wesley Publishing, 1979); Richard W. Olshavsky and Donald H. Granbois, "Consumer Decision Making—Fact or Fiction?" *Journal of Consumer Research,* September 1979, pp. 93–100.
18. Cele Otnes, Tina M. Lowrey, and L. J. Shrum, "Toward an Understanding of Consumer Ambivalence," *Journal of Consumer Research,* June 1997, pp. 80–93; Ronald E. Goldsmith, "Consumer Involvement: Concepts and Research," *Journal of the Academy of Marketing Science,* Summer 1996, pp. 281–83; Jeffrey B. Schmidt and Richard A. Spreng, "A Proposed Model of External Consumer Information Search," *Journal of the Academy of Marketing Science,* Summer 1996, pp. 246–56; Judith L. Zaichkowsky, "The Personal Involvement Inventory: Reduction, Revision, and Application to Advertising," *Journal of Advertising,* December 1994, pp. 59–70; Raj Arora, "Consumer Involvement—What It Offers to Advertising Strategy," *International Journal of Advertising* 4, no. 2 (1985), pp. 119–30; J. Brock Smith and Julia M. Bristor, "Uncertainty Orientation: Explaining Differences in Purchase Involvement and External Search," *Psychology & Marketing,* November/December 1994, pp. 587–608; Don R. Rahtz and David L. Moore, "Product Class Involvement and Purchase Intent," *Psychology and Marketing,* Summer 1989, pp. 113–28.
19. Adapted from E. M. Rogers with F. Shoemaker, *Communication of Innovation: A Cross Cultural Approach* (New York: Free Press, 1968). For some sampling (trial examples, see "The Cookie Queen," *The Wall Street Journal,* March 30, 1998, p. 6; "Brand Builders: Progresso Warriors," *Brandweek,* June 23, 1997, pp. 20–22; "Read This. It's Free," *Brandweek,* June 16, 1997, p. 42.
20. "3M's Aggressive New Consumer Drive," *Business Week,* July 16, 1984, pp. 114–22.
21. William Cunnings and Mark Venkatesan, "Cognitive Dissonance and Consumer Behavior: A Review of the Evidence," *Journal of Marketing Research,* August 1976, pp. 303–8; Sarah Fisher Gardial et al., "Comparing Consumers' Recall of Prepurchase and Postpurchase Product Evaluation Experience," *Journal of Consumer Research,* March 1994, pp. 548–60.
22. Robert M. March, *The Honourable Customer: Marketing and Selling to the Japanese in the 1990s* (Melbourne, Vic.: Longman Professional, 1990); Robert Gottliebsen, "Japan's Stark Choices," *Business Review Weekly,* October 16, 1992.

Chapter 7

1. "Detroit to Suppliers: Quality or Else," *Fortune,* September 30, 1996, p. 134Cff.; G. M. Naidu, V. K. Prasad, and Arno Kleimenhagen, "Purchasing's Preparedness for ISO 9000 International Quality Standards," *International Journal of Purchasing & Materials Management,* Fall 1996, pp. 46–53; Wade Ferguson, "Impact of the ISO 9000 Series Standards on Industrial Marketing," *Industrial Marketing Management,* July 1996, pp. 305–10.
2. Larry C. Giunipero and Judith F. Vogt, "Empowering the Purchasing Function: Moving to Team Decisions," *International Journal of Purchasing & Materials Management,* Winter 1997, pp. 8–15; Jerome M. Katrichis, "Exploring Departmental Level Interaction Patterns in Organizational Purchasing Decisions," *Industrial Marketing Management,* March 1998, pp. 135–46; Robert D. McWilliams, Earl Naumann, and Stan Scott, "Determining Buying Center Size," *Industrial Marketing Management,* February 1992, pp. 43–50; Ajay Kohli, "Determinants of Influence in Organizational Buying: A Contingency Approach," *Journal of Marketing,* July 1989, pp. 50–65; Melvin R. Mattson, "How to Determine the Composition and Influence of a Buying Center," *Industrial Marketing Management,* August 1988, pp. 205–14.
3. W.E.I. Patton, "Use of Human Judgment Models in Industrial Buyers' Vendor Selection Decisions," *Industrial Marketing Management,* March 1996, pp. 135–49; Minette E. Drumwright, "Socially Responsible Organizational Buying: Environmental Concern As a Noneconomic Buying Criterion," *Journal of Marketing,* July 1994, pp. 1–19; Lisa M. Ellram, "A Structured Method for Applying Purchasing Cost Management Tools," *International Journal of Purchasing & Materials Management,* Winter 1996, pp. 11–19; Morgan P. Miles, Linda S. Munilla, and Gregory R. Russell, "Marketing and Environmental Registration/Certification: What Industrial Marketers Should Understand About ISO 14000," *Industrial Marketing Management,* July 1997, pp. 363–70; Morry Ghingold and Bruce Johnson, "Technical Knowledge As Value Added in Business Markets," *Industrial Marketing Management,* May 1997, pp. 271–80; Sime Curkovic and Robert Handfield, "Use of ISO 9000 and Baldrige Award Criteria in Supplier Quality Evaluation," *International Journal of Purchasing & Materials Management,* Spring 1996, pp. 2–11; M. Bixby Cooper, Cornelia Droge, and Patricia J. Daugherty, "How Buyers and Operations Personnel Evaluate Service," *Industrial Marketing Management* 20, no. 1 (1991), pp. 81–90.
4. Jeanette J. Arbuthnot, "Identifying Ethical Problems Confronting Small Retail Buyers During the Merchandise Buying Process," *Journal of Business Ethics,* May 1997, pp. 745–55; Gail K. McCracken and Thomas J. Callahan, "Is There Such a Thing As a Free Lunch?" *International Journal of Purchasing & Materials Management,* Winter 1996, pp. 44–50; Robert W. Cooper, Garry L. Frank, and Robert A. Kemp, "The Ethical Environment Facing the Profession of Purchasing and Materials Management," *International Journal of Purchasing & Materials Management,* Spring 1997, pp. 2–11; I. Frederick Trawick, John E. Swan, Gail W. McGee, and David R. Rink, "Influence of Buyer Ethics and Salesperson Behavior on Intention to Choose a Supplier," *Journal of the Academy of Marketing Science,* Winter 1991, pp. 17–24; Michael J. Dorsch and Scott W. Kelley, "An Investigation into the Intentions of Purchasing Executives to Reciprocate Vendor Gifts," *Journal of the Academy of Marketing Science,* Fall 1994, pp. 315–327; J. A. Badenhorst, "Unethical Behaviour in Procurement: A Perspective on Causes and Solutions," *Journal of Business Ethics,* September 1994, pp. 739–46.
5. H.L. Brossard, "Information Sources Used by an Organization During a Complex Decision Process: An Exploratory Study," *Industrial Marketing Management,* January 1998, pp. 41–50; Michele D. Bunn, "Taxonomy of Buying Decision Approaches," *Journal of Marketing,* January 1993, pp. 38–56; Patricia M. Doney and Gary M. Armstrong, "Effects of Accountability on Symbolic Information Search and Information Analysis by Organizational Buyers," *Journal of the Academy of Marketing Science,* Winter 1996, pp. 57–65; Thomas G. Ponzurick, "International Buyers Perspective Toward Trade Shows and Other Promotional Methods," *Journal of Marketing Theory & Practice,* Winter 1996, pp. 9–19; Mark A. Farrell and Bill Schroder, "Influence Strategies in Organizational Buying Decisions," *Industrial Marketing Management,* July 1996, pp. 293–303; R. Venkatesh, Ajay K. Kohli, and Gerald Zaltman, "Influence Strategies in Buying Centers," *Journal of Marketing,* October 1995, pp. 71–82; Richard G. Newman, "Monitoring Price Increases With Economic Data: A Practical Approach," *International Journal of Purchasing & Materials Management,* Fall 1997, pp. 35–40; Barbara Kline and Janet Wagner, "Information Sources and Retailer Buyer Decision-Making: The Effect of Product-Specific Buying Experience," *Journal of Retailing,* Spring 1994, p. 75; Ellen Day and Hiram C. Barksdale, Jr., "How Firms Select Professional Services," *Industrial Marketing Management,* May 1992, pp. 85–92; H. Michael Hayes and Steven W. Hartley, "How Buyers View Industrial Salespeople," *Industrial Marketing Management* 18, no. 2 (1989), pp. 73–80; Peter Banting et al., "Similarities in Industrial Procurement Across Four Countries," *Industrial Marketing Management,* May 1985, pp. 133–44; Edward F. Fern and James R. Brown, "The Industrial/Consumer Marketing Dichotomy: A Case of Insufficient Justification," *Journal of Marketing,* Spring 1984, pp. 68–77; Rowland T. Moriarty, Jr. and Robert E. Spekman, "An Empirical Investigation of the Information Sources Used During the Industrial Buying Process," *Journal of Marketing Research,* May 1984, pp. 137–47.
6. Richard E. Plank, et al., "The Impact of Computer Usage by Purchasing," *Industrial Marketing Management,* August 1992, pp. 243–48; John W. Henke, Jr., A. Richard Krachenberg, and Thomas F. Lyons, "Competing Against an In-House Supplier," *Industrial Marketing Management* 18, no. 3 (1989), pp. 147–54.
7. "Setting Standards for Corporate Purchasing on the Internet," *Fortune,* September 8, 1997, pp. 156–58; "Invoice? What's an Invoice?" *Business Week,* June 10, 1996, pp. 110–12; "On-Line Service Offers Fast Lane to Small Businesses," *The Wall Street Journal,* October 11, 1994, p. B2; Earl D. Honeycutt, Theresa B. Flaherty, and Ken Benassi, "Marketing Industrial Products on the Internet," *Industrial Marketing Management,* January 1998, pp. 63–72; A. C. Samli, James R. Wills, and Paul Herbig, "The Information Superhighway Goes International: Implications for Industrial Sales Transactions," *Industrial Marketing Management,* January 1997, pp. 51–58; Barbara C. Perdue, "The Size and Composition of the Buying Firm's Negotiation Team in Rebuys of Component Parts," *Journal of the Academy of Marketing Science,* Spring 1989, pp. 121–28.
8. "The New Golden Rule of Business," *Fortune,* February 21, 1994, pp. 60–64; Janet L. Hartley and Thomas Y. Choi, "Supplier Development: Customers As a Catalyst of Process Change," *Business Horizons,* July–August 1996, pp. 37–44; Theodore P. Stank, Margaret A. Emmelhainz, and Patricia J. Daugherty, "The Impact of Information on Supplier Performance," *Journal of Marketing Theory & Practice,* Fall 1996, pp. 94–105. "The Push to Streamline Supply Chains," *Fortune,* March 3, 1997, pp. 108C-R; "Push from Above," *The Wall Street Journal,* May 23, 1996, p. R24.
9. Much of the discussion in this section is based on research reported in Joseph P. Cannon and William D. Perreault, Jr., "Buyer-Seller Relationships in Business Markets," Working Paper, Colorado State University, June 1998; Alexandra J. Campbell, "What Affects Expectations of Mutuality in Business Relationships?" *Journal of Marketing Theory & Practice,* Fall 1997, pp. 1–11; James C. Anderson, Hakan Hakansson, and Jan Johanson, "Dyadic Business Relationships Within a Business Network Context," *Journal of Marketing,* October 1994, pp. 1–15; Patricia M. Doney and Joseph P. Cannon, "An Examination of the Nature of Trust in Buyer-Seller Relationships," *Journal of Marketing,* April 1997, pp. 35–51; James M. Comer and B.J. Zirger, "Building a Supplier-Customer Relationship Using Joint New Product Development," *Industrial Marketing Management,* March 1997, pp. 203–11; Arun Sharma and Jagdish N. Sheth, "Supplier Relationships: Emerging Issues and Challenges," *Industrial Marketing Management,* March 1997, pp. 91–100; William W. Keep, Stanley C. Hollander, and Roger Dickinson, "Forces Impinging on Long-Term Business-to-Business Relationships in the United States: An Historical Perspective," *Journal of Marketing,* April 1998, pp. 31–45.

10. "Purchasing's New Muscle," *Fortune,* February 20, 1995, pp. 75–83; Rosemary P. Ramsey and Ravipreet S. Sohi, "Listening to Your Customers: The Impact of Perceived Salesperson Listening Behavior on Relationship Outcomes," *Journal of the Academy of Marketing Science,* Spring 1997, pp. 127–37.
11."Firms Boost Suppliers' Speeds, Win Investors' Hearts," *The Wall Street Journal,* April 6, 1998, p. A20; "Stores' Demands Squeeze Apparel Companies," *The Wall Street Journal,* July 15, 1997, p. B1ff.; "New Saturn Is Heavy on Outsourcing," *USA Today,* July 5, 1996, p. 1Bff.; John Ramsay, "The Case Against Purchasing Partnerships," *International Journal of Purchasing & Materials Management,* Fall 1996, pp. 13–19; John V. Petrof, "Relationship Marketing—the Emperor in Used Clothes," *Business Horizons,* March–April 1998, pp. 79–82; Shankar Ganesan, "Determinants of Long-Term Orientation in Buyer-Seller Relationships," *Journal of Marketing,* April 1994, pp. 1–19; Brian K. H. Low, "Long-Term Relationship in Industrial Marketing: Reality or Rhetoric?" *Industrial Marketing Management,* January 1996, pp. 23–35; Allan J. Magrath and Kenneth G. Hardy, "Building Customer Partnerships," *Business Horizons,* January–February 1994, pp. 24–28; Paul Dion, Debbie Easterling, and Shirley Jo Miller, "What is Really Necessary in Successful Buyer/Seller Relationships?," *Industrial Marketing Management,* January 1995, pp. 1–10; "Hardball Is Still GM's Game," *Business Week,* August 8, 1994, p. 26; "Big Customers' Late Bills Choke Small Suppliers," *The Wall Street Journal,* June 22, 1994, p. B1; Marvin W. Tucker and David A. Davis, "Key Ingredients for Successful Implementation of Just-in-Time: A System for All Business Sizes," May–June 1993, pp. 59–65.
12. "Polaroid Corp. Is Selling Its Technique for Limiting Supplier Price Increases," *The Wall Street Journal,* February 13, 1985, p. 36. For other examples, see "Making Honda Parts, Ohio Company Finds, Can Be Road to Ruin," *The Wall Street Journal,* October 5, 1990, p. A1ff.; "Toshiba Official Finds Giving Work to Firms in U.S. Can Be Tricky," *The Wall Street Journal,* March 20, 1987, p. 1ff.
13. "Toyota's Fast Rebound after Fire at Supplier Shows Why It Is Tough," *The Wall Street Journal,* May 8, 1997, p. A1ff.; Larry R. Smeltzer and Sue P. Siferd, "Proactive Supply Management: The Management of Risk," *International Journal of Purchasing & Materials Management,* Winter 1998, pp. 38–45; Paul D. Larson and Jack D. Kulchitsky, "Single Sourcing and Supplier Certification: Performance and Relationship Implications," *Industrial Marketing Management,* January 1998, pp. 73–81; Rasmus F. Olsen and Lisa M. Ellram, "A Portfolio Approach to Supplier Relationships," *Industrial Marketing Management,* March 1997, pp. 101–13.; Cathy Owens Swift, "Preferences for Single Sourcing and Supplier Selection," *Journal of Business Research,* February 1995, pp. 105-12.
14. For more detail, see "SIC: The System Explained," *Sales & Marketing Management,* April 22, 1985, pp. 52–113; "Enhancement of SIC System Being Developed," *Marketing News Collegiate Edition,* May 1988, p. 4.
15. "Perfecting the Pitch," *The Wall Street Journal,* May 23, 1996, p. R26ff.; "The Future of Services," *American Demographics,* November 1995, pp. 30–47; *1996 Annual Report,* Canon; "Can Anyone Duplicate Canon's Personal Copiers' Success?" *Marketing and Media Decisions,* Special Issue, Spring 1985, pp. 97–101.
16. *1996 Annual Report,* Super Valu.
17. *1996 Annual Report, Safeway; 1996 Annual Report,* Food Lion; *1996 Annual Report,* Winn-Dixie; *1996 Annual Report,* A&P; Daulatram B. Lund, "Retail Scanner Checkout System: How Buying Committees Functioned," *Industrial Marketing Management* 18, no. 3 (1989), pp. 179–86; Janet Wagner, Richard Ettenson, and Jean Parrish, "Vendor Selection Among Retail Buyers: An Analysis by Merchandise Division," *Journal of Retailing,* Spring 1989, pp. 58–79.
18. "Create Open-to Buy Plans the Easy Way," *Retail Control,* December 1984, pp. 21–31.
19. Terry Bullick, "Rural Sophisticates", *Marketing Magazine,* February 19, 1996, pp. 10–11.
20. Brian Lyons, *Canadian Microeconomics: Policies and Problems* (Scarborough, Ont.; Prentice-Hall Canada Inc., 1983), pp. 277–290.
21. Rhéal Sequin, "Rules Must Apply to All, GATT Head tells Farmers," *The Globe and Mail,* June 2, 1992, p. B4.

Chapter 8

1. "American Greetings Thinks Time for 'Anytime' Is Now," *The Wall Street Journal,* March 24, 1998, p. B9; "American Greeting, Hallmark's Cards Will Send an Earful," *The Wall Street Journal,* November 5, 1993, p. B10B; "Old-Fashioned Sentiments Go High-Tech," *The Wall Street Journal,* November 9, 1992, p. B1ff.
2. Shelby D. Hunt and Robert M. Morgan, "Resource-Advantage Theory: A Snake Swallowing Its Tail or a General Theory of Competition?" *Journal of Marketing,* October 1997, pp. 74–82; Stavros P. Kalafatis and Vicki Cheston, "Normative Models and Practical Applications of Segmentation in Business Markets," *Industrial Marketing Management,* November 1997, pp. 519–30; Lisa R. Adam, "Nichecraft: Using Your Specialness to Focus Your Business, Corner Your Market, and Make Customers Seek You Out," *Journal of the Academy of Marketing Science,* Summer 1997, pp. 259–60; S. Ratneshwar, Cornelia Pechmann, and Allan D. Shocker, "Goal-Derived Categories and the Antecedents of Across-Category Consideration," *Journal of Consumer Research,* December 1996, pp. 240–50; George S. Day, A. D. Shocker, and R. K. Srivastava, "Customer-Oriented Approaches to Identifying Product-Markets," *Journal of Marketing,* Fall 1979, pp. 8–19; Rajendra K. Srivastava, Mark I. Alpert, and Allan D. Shocker, "A Customer-Oriented Approach for Determining Market Structures," *Journal of Marketing,* Spring 1984, pp. 32–45.
3. "The Riches in Market Niches," *Fortune,* April 27, 1987, pp. 227–30; Robert E. Linneman and John L. Stanton, Jr., "Mining for Niches," *Business Horizons,* May–June 1992, pp. 43–51; Michael E. Raynor, "The Pitfalls of Niche Marketing," *The Journal of Business Strategy,* March/April, 1992, pp. 29–32.
4. Terry Elrod and Russell S. Winer, "An Empirical Evaluation of Aggregation Approaches for Developing Market Segments," *Journal of Marketing,* Fall 1982, pp. 32–34; Frederick W. Winter, "A Cost-Benefit Approach to Market Segmentation," *Journal of Marketing,* Fall 1979, pp. 103–11; Andrew Hilton, "Mythology, Markets, and the Emerging Europe," *Harvard Business Review,* November–December 1992, pp. 50–127.
5. Hershey H. Friedman and Linda W. Friedman, "Reducing the 'Wait' in Waiting-Line Systems: Waiting Line Segmentation," *Business Horizons,* July–August 1997, pp. 54–58; Alex Chernev, "The Effect of Common Features on Brand Choice: Moderating Role of Attribute Importance," *Journal of Consumer Research,* March 1997, pp. 304–11; Dianne S.P. Cermak, Karen Maru File, and Russ Alan Prince, "A Benefit Segmentation of the Major Donor Market," *Journal of Business Research,* February 1994, pp. 121–30; Robert L. Armacost and Jamshid C. Hosseini, "Identification of Determinant Attributes Using the Analytic Hierarchy Process," *Journal of the Academy of Marketing Science,* Fall 1994, pp. 383–92; Joel S. Dubow, "Occasion-based vs. User-based Benefit Segmentation, A Case Study," *Journal of Advertising Research,* March/April 1992, pp. 11–19; Peter R. Dickson and James L. Ginter, "Market Segmentation, Product Differentiation, and Marketing Strategy," *Journal of Marketing,* April 1987, pp. 1–10; Russell I. Haley, "Benefit Segmentation—20 Years Later," *Journal of Consumer Marketing* 1, no. 2 (1984), pp. 5–14.
6. "How Big Liquor Takes Aim at Teens," *Business Week,* May 19, 1997, p. 92; "How 'Medicaid Moms' Became a Hot Market for Health Industry," *The Wall Street Journal,* May 1, 1997, p. A1ff.; Suzeanne Benet, Robert E. Pitts, and Michael LaTour, "The Appropriateness of Fear Appeal Use for Health Care Marketing to the Elderly: Is It OK to Scare Granny?," *Journal of Business Ethics,* January 1993, pp. 45–56; "New Converse Shoe Named Run 'N Gun Is Angering Critics," *The Wall Street Journal,* February 8, 1993, p. B5; " 'Black Death' Becomes 'Black Hat' so that Vodka Can Stay on Shelves," *The Wall Street Journal,* May 12, 1992, p. B6; "Malt Liquor Makers Find Lucrative Market in the Urban Young," *The Wall Street Journal,* March 9, 1992, p. A1ff.; Richard W. Pollay, S. Siddarth, Michael Siegel, Anne Haddix et al., "The Last Straw? Cigarette Advertising and Realized Market Shares Among Youths and Adults, 1979–1993," *Journal of Marketing,* April 1996, pp. 1–16; N. C. Smith and Elizabeth Cooper-Martin, "Ethics and Target Marketing: The Role of Product Harm and Consumer Vulnerability," *Journal of Marketing,* July 1997, pp. 1–20.
7. Berkowitz et al., *Marketing,* Third Canadian Edition (Toronto: McGraw-Hill Ryerson, 1998) p. 156.
8. Girish Punj and David W. Stewart, "Cluster Analysis in Marketing Research: Review and Suggestions for Application," *Journal of Marketing Research,* May 1983, pp. 134–48; Fernando Robles and Ravi Sarathy, "Segmenting the Computer Aircraft Market with Cluster Analysis," *Industrial Marketing Management,* February 1986, pp. 1–12.
9. David A. Aaker and J. Gary Shansby, "Positioning Your Product," *Business Horizons,* May/June, 1982, pp. 56–62; Al Ries and Jack Trout, *Positioning: The Battle for Your Mind* (New York: McGraw-Hill, 1981), p. 53. For some current examples of positioning, see "From the Horse's Mouth: Try a Little Hoof Fix on Your Nails," *The Wall Street Journal,* July 29, 1994, p. B1ff.; "Campbell's New Ad Campaign Is Stirring Up Dormant Soup Sales," *The Wall Street Journal,* March 17, 1994, p. B5; Hans Muhlbacher, Angelika Dreher, and Angelika Gabriel-Ritter, "MIPS-Managing Industrial Positioning Strategies," *Industrial Marketing Management,* October 1994, pp. 287–98; "Chew on This: Wrigley's Extra Tackles Tooth Decay," *Advertising Age,* December 21, 1992, p. 30; "Lure of a Lovelier Smile Prompts a Rush to Buy Do-It-Yourself Teeth Whiteners," *The Wall Street Journal,* July 6, 1992, pp. 13–14.

Chapter 9

1. Joseph M. Juran, "Made In U.S.A.: A Renaissance in Quality," *Harvard Business Review,* July–August 1993, pp. 42–53; "Measuring Quality Perception of America's Top Brands," *Brandweek,* April 4, 1994, pp. 24–26; Ajay Menon, Bernard J. Jaworski, and Ajay K. Kohli, "Product Quality: Impact of Interdepartmental Interactions," *Journal of the Academy of Marketing Science,* Summer 1997, pp. 187–200; Neil A. Morgan and Nigel F. Piercy, "Market-Led Quality," *Industrial Marketing Management,* May 1992, pp. 111–18; H. Michael Hayes, "ISO9000: The New Strategic Consideration," *Business Horizons,* May–June 1994, pp. 52–60.
2. *1996 Annual Report,* MCI; *1996 Annual Report,* Merrill Lynch; "Service Is Everybody's Business," *Fortune,* June 27, 1994, pp. 48–60; James Golleher, "Value-Added Customer Service," *Journal of Personal Selling & Sales Management,* Spring 1997, p. 71; James Reardon, Chip Miller, Ronald Hasty, and Blaise J. Waguespack, "A Comparison of Alternative Theories of Services Marketing," *Journal of Marketing Theory & Practice,* Fall 1996, pp. 61–71; Kirk Smith, "Service Aspects

of Industrial Products Lead to Future Product Purchase Intentions," *Industrial Marketing Management,* January 1998, pp. 83–93; James C. Anderson and James A. Narus, "Capturing the Value of Supplementary Services," *Harvard Business Review,* January 1995–February 1995, pp. 75–83; Banwari Mittal and Walfried M. Lassar, "The Role of Personalization in Service Encounters," *Journal of Retailing,* Spring 1996, pp. 95–109; Barry J. Babin and James S. Boles, "Employee Behavior in a Service Environment: A Model and Test of Potential Differences Between Men and Women," *Journal of Marketing,* April 1998, pp. 77–91; Mary Jo Bitner, Bernard H. Booms, and Lois A. Mohr, "Critical Service Encounters: The Employee's Viewpoint," *Journal of Marketing,* October 1994, pp. 95–106; Leonard L. Berry, A. Parasuraman, and Valarie A. Zeithaml, "The Service-Quality Puzzle," *Business Horizons,* September/October 1988, pp. 35–43; Leonard L. Berry, "Services Marketing Is Different," in Christopher H. Lovelock, *Services Marketing* (Englewood Cliffs, N.J.: Prentice-Hall, 1984), pp. 29–37.

3. *1996 Annual Report,* Sara Lee; *1996 Annual Report,* Enterprise; *1996 Annual Report,* 3M; Edward M. Tauber, "Why Do People Shop?" *Journal of Marketing,* October 1972, pp. 46–49; Christopher H. Lovelock, "Classifying Services to Gain Strategic Marketing Insights," *Journal of Marketing,* Summer 1983, pp. 9–20; Tom Boyt and Michael Harvey, "Classification of Industrial Services," *Industrial Marketing Management,* July 1997, pp. 291–300.

4. Dennis W. Rook, "The Buying Impulse," *Journal of Consumer Research,* September 1987, pp. 189–99; Cathy J. Cobb and Wayne D. Hoyer, "Planned Versus Impulse Purchase Behavior," *Journal of Retailing,* Winter 1986, pp. 384–409.

5. William S. Bishop, John L. Graham, and Michael H. Jones, "Volatility of Derived Demand in Industrial Markets and Its Management Implications," *Journal of Marketing,* Fall 1984, pp. 95–103.

6. William B. Wagner and Patricia K. Hall, "Equipment Lease Accounting in Industrial Marketing Strategy," *Industrial Marketing Management* 20, no. 4 (1991), pp. 305–10; Robert S. Eckley, "Caterpillar's Ordeal: Foreign Competition in Capital Goods," *Business Horizons,* March/April 1989, pp. 80–86; M. Manley, "To Buy or Not to Buy," *Inc.,* November 1987, pp. 189–90.

7. P. Matthyssens and W. Faes, "OEM Buying Process for New Components: Purchasing and Marketing Implications," *Industrial Marketing Management,* August 1985, pp. 145–57; Paul A. Herbig and Frederick Palumbo, "Serving the Aftermarket in Japan and the United States," *Industrial Marketing Management,* November 1993, pp. 339–46; Ralph W. Jackson and Philip D. Cooper, "Unique Aspects of Marketing Industrial Services," *Industrial Marketing Management,* May 1988, pp. 111–18; Timothy L. Wilson and Frank E. Smith, "Business Services 1982–1992: Growth, Industry Characteristics, Financial Performance," *Industrial Marketing Management,* March 1996, pp. 162–71.

8. Ruth H. Krieger and Jack R. Meredith, "Emergency and Routine MRO Part Buying," *Industrial Marketing Management,* November 1985, pp. 277–82; Warren A. French et al., "MRO Parts Service in the Machine Tool Industry," *Industrial Marketing Management,* November 1985, pp. 283–88.

9. For more on brand extensions, see "Clorox Tries Formula 409 for Carpets," *Advertising Age,* March 10, 1997, p. 6; "Can Betty Crocker Heat Up General Mills' Cereal Sales?" *The Wall Street Journal,* July 19, 1996, p. B1ff.; Elise K. Prosser, "Brand Marketing: Building Winning Brand Strategies That Deliver Value and Customer Satisfaction," *Journal of the Academy of Marketing Science,* Winter 1996, pp. 86–87; David A. Aaker, "Should You Take Your Brand to Where the Action Is?" *Harvard Business Review,* September–October 1997, pp. 135–43; Richard C. Leventhal, "Branding Strategy," *Business Horizons,* September–October 1996, pp. 17–23; Deborah R. John, Barbara Loken, and Christopher Joiner, "The Negative Impact of Extensions: Can Flagship Products Be Diluted?" *Journal of Marketing,* January 1998, pp. 19–32; Cathy J. Cobb-Walgren, Cynthia A. Ruble, and Naveen Donthu, "Brand Equity, Brand Preference, and Purchase Intent," *Journal of Advertising,* Fall 1995, pp. 25–40; Vijay Vishwanath and Jonathan Mark, "Your Brand's Best Strategy," *Harvard Business Review,* May–June 1997, pp. 123–29; Michael A. Kamins and Nancy A. Frost, "A 'Brand' New Language," *Journal of Marketing,* April 1994, pp. 129–30; John A. Quelch and David Kenny, "Extend Profits, Not Product Lines," *Harvard Business Review,* September 1994–October 1994, pp. 153–60; Linda B. Samuels and Jeffery M. Samuels, "Famous Marks Now Federally Protected Against Dilution," *Journal of Public Policy & Marketing,* Fall 1996, pp. 307–10; Pamela W. Henderson and Joseph A. Cote, "Guidelines for Selecting or Modifying Logos," *Journal of Marketing,* April 1998, pp. 14–30; Erich Joachimsthaler and David A. Aaker, "Building Brands Without Mass Media," *Harvard Business Review,* January–February 1997, pp. 39–50; "Nabisco to Bring Top Cookie Brands to Breakfast Line," *The Wall Street Journal,* February 23, 1994, p. B5; "Multiple Varieties of Established Brands Muddle Consumers, Make Retailers Mad," *The Wall Street Journal,* January 24, 1992, p. B1ff. See also "Brands Still Rule Supreme," *Advertising Age,* January 26, 1998, p. 26; "Brand Buddies," *Brandweek,* February 23, 1998, pp. 22–30; "Power Brands '97," *Discount Store News,* October 20, 1997, pp. 21–65; Kevin Lane Keller, "Conceptualizing, Measuring, and Managing Customer-Based Brand Equity," *Journal of Marketing,* January 1993, pp. 1–22.

10. "Global Products Require Name-Finders," *The Wall Street Journal,* April 11, 1996, p. B8; Martin S. Roth, "Effects of Global Market Conditions on Brand Image Customization and Brand Performance," *Journal of Advertising,* Winter 1995, pp. 55–75.

11. For a detailed discussion of a recent Canadian trademark controversy, see Eric Swetsky, "Wool-Mart Versus Wal-Mart," *Marketing Magazine* (June 24, 1996), p. 20; Brian Banks and David North "Ticked Off: Wal-Mart's Infuriating Ways," *Canadian Business* (January 1996), pp. 23–24.

12. Charles H. Schwepker, "Trademark Problems and How to Avoid Them," *Journal of the Academy of Marketing Science,* Winter 1997, pp. 89–90; Lee B. Burgunder, "Trademark Protection of Product Characteristics: A Predictive Model," *Journal of Public Policy & Marketing,* Fall 1997, pp. 277–88; Itamar Simonson, "Trademark Infringement from the Buyer Perspective: Conceptual Analysis and Measurement Implications," *Journal of Public Policy & Marketing,* Fall 1994, pp. 181–99; "Asian Trademark Litigation Continues," *The Wall Street Journal,* February 16, 1994, p. B8.

13. "China's CD Pirates Find a New Hangout," *Business Week,* December 15, 1997, p. 138F; "Busting Bogus Merchandise Peddlers with the Logo Cops," *The Wall Street Journal,* October 24, 1997, p. B1ff.; "Reebok Tussles with Venezuelan Company over Name, Designs," *Ad Age International,* September 1997, p. I38; "CD Piracy Flourishes in China, and West Supplies Equipment," *The Wall Street Journal,* April 24, 1997, p. A1ff.; "A Pirate under Every Rock," *Business Week,* June 17, 1996, pp. 50–51; "Hackers Put Pirated Software on Internet," *The Wall Street Journal,* October 31, 1994, p. B5; Janeen E. Olsen and Kent L. Granzin, "Using Channels Constructs to Explain Dealers' Willingness to Help Manufacturers Combat Counterfeiting," *Journal of Business Research,* June 1993, pp. 147–70; Ronald F. Bush, Peter H. Bloch, and Scott Dawson, "Remedies for Product Counterfeiting," *Business Horizons,* January–February 1989, pp. 59–65; Alexander Nill and Clifford J. Clifford J II, "The Scourge of Global Counterfeiting," *Business Horizons,* November–December 1996, pp. 37–42.

14. For more on licensing, see "Deals that Go Bump in the Night," *Business Week,* February 16, 1998, p. 84; "Brand Builders: Licensing, the Color of Money," *Brandweek,* September 15, 1997, pp. 22–23; "Toy Makers Offer the Moon for New 'Star Wars' Licenses," *The Wall Street Journal,* August 19, 1997, p. B1ff.; "Arm & Hammer's Owner Looks at Licensing to Freshen Results," *The Wall Street Journal,* August 6, 1997, p. B2; "Star TV Chefs Cook Up Big Licensing Deals," *The Wall Street Journal,* October 17, 1996, p. B1ff.; "A Week in Licensing," *Brandweek,* June 24, 1996, pp. 21–39.

15. "Brand Managing's New Accent," *Adweek's Marketing Week,* April 15, 1991, pp. 18–22; "Brand Managers: '90s Dinosaurs?" *Advertising Age,* December 19, 1988, p. 19; "The Marketing Revolution at Procter & Gamble," *Business Week,* July 25, 1988, pp. 72–76; Amitabh Mungale, "Managing Product Families," *Journal of Product Innovation Management,* January 1998, pp. 102–03; Gloria Barczak, "Product Management," *Journal of Product Innovation Management,* September 1997, pp. 425–26.

16. "Ten Years May Be Generic Lifetime," *Advertising Age,* March 23, 1987, p. 76; Brian F. Harris and Roger A. Strang, "Marketing Strategies in the Age of Generics," *Journal of Marketing,* Fall 1985, pp. 70–81.

17. "Dr. Pop and Frisk Help a Grocery Chain Grow," *The Wall Street Journal,* April 13, 1998, p. B1ff.; Marcia Mogelonsky, "When Stores Become Brands," *American Demographics,* February 1995, pp. 32–38; "Big Firms Come Out Fighting, Slow Sales of Private-Label Rivals," *The Wall Street Journal,* July 7, 1994, p. B8; "Exposing the Five Myths of Private Label Brands," *Brandweek,* June 20, 1994, p. 17; R. Sethuraman and J. Mittelstaedt, "Coupons and Private Labels: A Cross-Category Analysis of Grocery Products," *Psychology & Marketing,* November/December 1992, pp. 487–500; "Store-Brand Sales Have Their Ups and Downs as Buying Habits Shift," *The Wall Street Journal,* May 12, 1994, p. B6; John A. Quelch and David Harding, "Brands Versus Private Labels: Fighting to Win," *Harvard Business Review,* January–February 1996, pp. 99–109.

18. "Excedrin Is Upfront about New Package," *The Wall Street Journal,* April 8, 1998, p. B8; "Quaker, Coca-Cola Introduce Colorful Drink Contenders," *Advertising Age,* January 26, 1998, p. 52; "What's Foiling the Aluminum Can," *Business Week,* October 6, 1997, pp. 106–8; "Breakthrough Bottles," *Brandweek,* May 20, 1996, pp. 32–52; "If Your Brand's Number Two, Get with the Package Program," *Brandweek,* June 27, 1994, pp. 26–27; Brian Wansink, "Can Package Size Accelerate Usage Volume?" *Journal of Marketing,* July 1996, pp. 1–14.

19. Paula Fitzgerald, Bone Corey, and Robert J. Corey, "Ethical Dilemmas in Packaging: Beliefs of Packaging Professionals," *Journal of Macromarketing,* Spring 1992, pp. 45–54. For more on downsizing, see "Big Trend: Smaller Packaging," *USA Today,* April 1, 1993, p. 1Bff.; "State AGs Attack Downsized Brands," *Advertising Age,* February 18, 1991, p. 1ff.; "Critics Call Cuts in Package Size Deceptive Move," *The Wall Street Journal,* February 5, 1991, p. B1ff. For more discussion on disposable products, see "Disposing of the Green Myth," *Adweek's Marketing Week,* April 13, 1992, pp. 20–21; "The Waste Land," *Adweek,* November 11, 1991, p. 26; "Ridding the Nation of Polystyrene Peanuts," *Adweek's Marketing Week,* October 22, 1990, p. 17.

20. J.E. Russo, "The Value of Unit Price Information," *Journal of Marketing Research,* May 1977, pp. 193–201; David A. Aaker and Gary T. Ford, "Unit Pricing Ten Years Later: A Replication," *Journal of Marketing,* Winter 1983, pp. 118–22.

21. Sections 52(1)(b), 52(1)(c), and 52(1)(a) of the Competition Act.

22. For more on service guarantees, see "It's Service in a Box from Hewlett-Packard," *Advertising Age,* May 10, 1993, p. 5; "More Firms Pledge Guaranteed Service," *The Wall Street Journal,* July 17, 1991, p. B1ff. For more on warranties, see M. E. Blair and Daniel E. Innis, "The Effects of Product Knowledge on the Evaluation of Warranteed Brands," *Psychology & Marketing,* August 1996, pp. 445–56; Ellen M. Moore and F. Kelly Shuptrine, "Warranties: Continued Readability Problems After the 1975 Magnuson-Moss Warranty Act," *Journal of Consumer Affairs,* Summer 1993, pp. 23–36; M.A.J. Menezes and I.S. Currim, "An Approach for Determination of Warranty Length," *International Journal of Research in Marketing,* May 1992, pp. 177–96; "Service Dealers Complain about Warranty Business," *The Wall Street Journal,* February 20, 1992, p. B2.

Chapter 10

1. Robert W. Veryzer, "Key Factors Affecting Customer Evaluation of Discontinuous New Products," *Journal of Product Innovation Management,* March 1998, pp. 136–50; Laura Birou, Stanley E. Fawcett, and Gregory M. Magnan, "Integrating Product Life Cycle and Purchasing Strategies," *International Journal of Purchasing & Materials Management,* Winter 1997, pp. 23–31; Frank H. Alpert and Michael A. Kamins, "An Empirical Investigation of Consumer Memory, Attitude and Perceptions Toward Pioneer and Follower Brands," *Journal of Marketing,* October 1995, pp. 34–45; Neil A. Morgan, "Managing Imitation Strategies: How Later Entrants Seize Market Share From Pioneers," *Journal of Marketing,* October 1995, pp. 104–06; David M. Szymanski, Lisa C. Troy, and Sundar G. Bharadwaj, "Order of Entry and Business Performance: An Empirical Synthesis and Reexamination," *Journal of Marketing,* October 1995, pp. 17–33; George Day, "The Product Life Cycle: Analysis and Applications Issues," *Journal of Marketing,* Fall 1981, pp. 60–67; John E. Swan and David R. Rink, "Fitting Marketing Strategy to Varying Product Life Cycles," *Business Horizons,* January/February 1982, pp. 72–76; Igal Ayal, "International Product Life Cycle: A Reassessment and Product Policy Implications," *Journal of Marketing,* Fall 1981, pp. 91–96; Edward T. Popper and Bruce D. Buskirk, "Technology Life Cycles in Industrial Markets," *Industrial Marketing Management,* February 1992, pp. 23–32; Vijay Mahajan, Subhash Sharma, and Robert D. Buzzell, "Assessing the Impact of Competitive Entry on Market Expansion and Incumbent Sales," *Journal of Marketing,* July 1993, pp. 39–52; Mary Lambkin and George S. Day, "Evolutionary Processes in Competitive Markets: Beyond the Product Life Cycle," *Journal of Marketing,* July 1989, pp. 4–20.

2. Jorge Alberto Sousa De Vasconcellos, "Key Success Factors in Marketing Mature Products," *Industrial Marketing Management* 20, no. 4 (1991), pp. 263–78; Paul C.N. Michell, Peter Quinn, and Edward Percival, "Marketing Strategies for Mature Industrial Products," *Industrial Marketing Management* 20, no. 3 (1991), pp. 201–6; "Computers Become a Kind of Commodity, to Dismay of Makers," *The Wall Street Journal,* September 5, 1991, p. A1ff.; Peter N. Golder and Gerard J. Tellis, "Pioneer Advantage: Marketing Logic or Marketing Legend?" *Journal of Marketing Research,* May 1993, pp. 158–70; "As Once Bright Market for CAT Scanners Dims, Smaller Makers of the X-Ray Devices Fade Out," *The Wall Street Journal,* May 6, 1980, p. 40.

3. Jennifer Pitchburn, "Comforts of Home Are Getting More Elaborate," *The Vancouver Sun,* March 19, 1998, E14.

4. "Pepsi, Coke Say They're Loyal to NutraSweet," *The Wall Street Journal,* April 22, 1992, p. B1ff.; "A Sweet Case of the 'Blahs,'" *Advertising Age,* May 27, 1991, p. 3; "NutraSweet Launches New Ads," *Adweek's Marketing Week,* May 20, 1991, p. 6; "NutraSweet Tries Being More of a Sweetie," *Business Week,* April 8, 1991, p. 88; "NutraSweet Rivals Stirring," *Advertising Age,* June 26, 1989, p. 3ff.

5. "Rivals Square Off Toe to Toe," *USA Today,* August 24, 1993, p. 1Bff.; "The Patent Pirates Are Finally Walking the Plank," *Business Week,* February 17, 1992, pp. 125–27; "Is It Time to Reinvent the Patent System?" *Business Week,* December 2, 1991, pp. 110–15; C.C. Baughn, Michael Bixby, and L.S. Woods, "Patent Laws and the Public Good: IPR Protection in Japan and the United States," *Business Horizons,* July–August 1997, pp. 59–65; Karen Bronikowski, "Speeding New Products to Market," *The Journal of Business Strategy,* September/October 1990, pp. 34–37.

6. "Betamax Wars All Over Again," *Business Week,* September 29, 1997, pp. 35–36; "The Next Great Gadget," *Time,* January 20, 1997, p. 66; "Sony Isn't Mourning the 'Death' of Betamax," *Business Week,* January 25, 1988, p. 37; Sigvald J. Harryson, "How Canon and Sony Drive Product Innovation Through Networking and Application-Focused R&D," *Journal of Product Innovation Management,* July 1997, pp. 288–95; M. Lambkin, "Pioneering New Markets: A Comparison of Market Share Winners and Losers," *International Journal of Research in Marketing,* March 1992, pp. 5–22.

7. "Can the Limited Fix Itself?" *Fortune,* October 17, 1994, pp. 161–72; "Limited Puts 'Weiss Methodology' to Test," *The Wall Street Journal,* August 9, 1993, p. B1ff.; "The Winning Organization," *Fortune,* September 26, 1988, pp. 50–58.

8. "One More Face-Lift for Penney," *Business Week,* March 23, 1998, pp. 86–88; "Fidel Meets Naomi," *The Wall Street Journal,* March 2, 1998, p. B1ff.; "Updating a Classic: The Man in the Gray Spandex Suit," *The Wall Street Journal,* January 27, 1998, p. B1ff.; "Teletubbies Are Coming: Brit Hit Sets U.S. Invasion," *Advertising Age,* January 19, 1998, p. 12; "Rural Kids Like Hip Clothes, Too, Hot Chain Discovers," *The Wall Street Journal,* January 15, 1998, p. B1ff.; "A Grumpy Old Lady Becomes a Big Hit for Hallmark," *The Wall Street Journal,* December 24, 1997, p. B1ff.; "How Belgian Engineer Created a Global Backpack Trend," *The Wall Street Journal,* December 10, 1997, p. B1ff.; "Will Working Women Wear This Stuff?" *The Wall Street Journal,* October 8, 1997, p. B1ff.; "Virtual Pets Are Some Campers' Best Friends," *USA Today,* July 29, 1997, p. 1D; "They're Going Space Crazy," *Business Week,* July 28, 1997, pp. 89–92; "The Beanie Factor," *Brandweek,* June 16, 1997, pp. 22–27; "Tiger Striving to Nurture Giga Pets—on a Budget," *Advertising Age,* May 12, 1997, p. 24; "Toy Stores Bet 'Virtual Pets' Are Next Craze," *The Wall Street Journal,* May 2, 1997, p. B1ff.; "Chew on This: Crunch Is Latest Food Fad," *The Wall Street Journal,* April 2, 1997, p. B1ff.; "Desperately Seeking . . . a Fad," *Business Week,* November 18, 1996, p. 78; Martin G. Letscher, "How to Tell Fads from Trends," *American Demographics,* December 1994, pp. 38–45; R.E. Goldsmith, J.B. Freiden, and J.C. Kilsheimer, "Social Values and Female Fashion Leadership: A Cross-Cultural Study," *Psychology & Marketing,* September/October 1993, pp. 399–412; "Special Report: Fashion Marketing," *Advertising Age,* August 22, 1994, pp. 23–28; Craig J. Thompson and Diana L. Haytko, "Speaking of Fashion: Consumers' Uses of Fashion Discourses and the Appropriation of Countervailing Cultural Meanings," *Journal of Consumer Research,* June 1997, pp. 15–42.

9. *1997 Annual Report,* RJR Nabisco; "Oreo, Ritz Join Nabisco's Low-Fat Feast," *Advertising Age,* April 4, 1994, p. 3ff.; "They're Not Crying in Their Crackers at Nabisco," *Business Week,* August 30, 1993, p. 61; "Nabisco Unleashes a New Batch of Teddies," *Adweek's Marketing Week,* September 24, 1990, p. 18; *1997 Annual Report,* Procter & Gamble; "Boom in Liquid Detergents Has P&G Scrambling," *The Wall Street Journal,* September 25, 1997, p. B1ff.; "Ultra-Clean—Retail Cheers Still More P&G Concentrates," *Advertising Age,* August 22, 1994, p. 1ff.; "Detergent Industry Spins into New Cycle," *The Wall Street Journal,* January 5, 1993, p. B1ff.; "P&G Unleashes Flood of New Tide Products," *Advertising Age,* June 16, 1986, p. 3ff; "'Good Products Don't Die,' P&G Chairman Declares," *Advertising Age,* November 1, 1976, p. 8.

10. For more on rejuvenating mature products, see "Dawn Gets Grease Out of Traffic's Way after Tanker Truck Spill," *The Raleigh News & Observer,* May 6, 1998, p. 1Aff.; Brian Wansink, "Making Old Brands New," *American Demographics,* December 1997, pp. 53–58; "Classic Roller Skates Return as Safety Fears Dull Blades," *The Wall Street Journal,* October 24, 1997, p. B1ff.; "Dusting Off the *Britannica,*" *Business Week,* October 20, 1997, pp. 143–46; "Never Say 'Old and Lousy,'" *Fortune,* October 13, 1997, p. 40; "At Du Pont, Time to Both Sow and Reap," *Business Week,* September 29, 1997, pp. 107–8; "A Boring Brand Can Be Beautiful," *Fortune,* November 18, 1991, pp. 169–77; "Teflon Is 50 Years Old, but Du Pont Is Still Finding New Uses for Invention," *The Wall Street Journal,* April 7, 1988, p. 34; Stephen W. Miller, "Managing Imitation Strategies: How Later Entrants Seize Markets From Pioneers," *Journal of the Academy of Marketing Science,* Summer 1996, pp. 277–78; Richard E. Anderson, "Phased Product Development Friend or Foe?" *Business Horizons,* November–December 1996, pp. 30–36; Regina Fazio Maruca and Amy L. Halliday, "When New Products and Customer Loyalty Collide," *Harvard Business Review,* November–December 1993, pp. 22–36.

11. "Novel P&G Product Brings Dry Cleaning Home," *The Wall Street Journal,* November 19, 1997, p. B1ff.; "Colgate Places a Huge Bet on a Germ-Fighter," *The Wall Street Journal,* December 29, 1997, p. B1ff.; "Smart Toothbrush," *Fortune,* November 4, 1991, p. 168.

12. "Diaper Firms Fight to Stay on the Bottom," *The Wall Street Journal,* March 23, 1993, p. B1ff.; "Multiple Varieties of Established Brands Muddle Consumers, Make Retailers Mad," *The Wall Street Journal,* January 24, 1992, p. B1ff.; "Do Americans Have Too Many Brands?" *Adweek's Marketing Week,* December 9, 1991, pp. 14–15; "Kimberly-Clark Bets, Wins on Innovation," *The Wall Street Journal,* November 22, 1991, p. A5.

13. Mark Maremont, "A Large Investment in a Humble Product," *The Vancouver Sun,* April 16, 1998, D20.

14. "Special Report: New Products," *Ad Age International,* April 13, 1998, pp. 17–20; "The Ghastliest Product Launches," *Fortune,* March 16, 1998, p. 44; "New and Improved," *American Demographics,* March 1998, p. 32; "Seems the Only Problem with New Products Is That They're New," *Brandweek,* August 22, 1994, pp. 36–40; "Flops: Too Many New Products Fail. Here's Why—and How to Do Better," *Business Week,* August 16, 1993, pp. 76–82; Brian D. Ottum and William L. Moore, "The Role of Market Information in New Product Success/Failure," *Journal of Product Innovation Management,* July 1997, pp. 258–73.

15. "Makers of Chicken Tonight Find Many Cooks Say, 'Not Tonight,'" *The Wall Street Journal,* May 17, 1994, p. B1ff.; "Failure of Its Oven Lovin' Cookie Dough Shows Pillsbury Pitfalls of New Products," *The Wall Street Journal,* June 17, 1993, p. B1ff.; Sharad Sarin and Gour M. Kapur, "Lessons From New Product Failures: Five Case Studies," *Industrial Marketing Management,* November 1990, pp. 301–14.

16. "Fast-Selling Software that Hurries Products to Market," *Fortune,* April 29, 1996, p. 150Cff.; Joseph T. Vesey, "Time-to-Market: Put Speed in

Product Development," *Industrial Marketing Management,* May 1992, pp. 151–58; "Mattel's Wild Race to Market," *Business Week,* February 21, 1994, pp. 62–63; "How H-P Continues to Grow and Grow," *Fortune,* May 2, 1994, pp. 90–100; Marco Iansiti and Alan MacCormack, "Developing Product on Internet Time," *Harvard Business Review,* September–October 1997, pp. 108–17; Bryan Lilly and Rockney Walters, "Toward a Model of New Product Preannouncement Timing," *Journal of Product Innovation Management,* January 1997, pp. 4–20; Richard Bauhaus, "Developing Products in Half the Time," *Journal of Product Innovation Management,* January 1997, pp. 68–69; Kathleen M. Eisenhardt and Shona L. Brown, "Time Pacing: Competing in Markets That Won't Stand Still," *Harvard Business Review,* March–April 1998, pp. 59–69.

17. Robert Polk, Richard E. Plank, and David A. Reid, "Technical Risk and New Product Success: An Empirical Test in High Technology Business Markets," *Industrial Marketing Management,* November 1996, pp. 531–43; X.M. Song and Mark E. Parry, "A Cross-National Comparative Study of New Product Development Processes: Japan and the United States," *Journal of Marketing,* April 1997, pp. 1–18; Robert G. Cooper, "Overhauling the New Product Process," *Industrial Marketing Management,* November 1996, pp. 465–82; Jeffrey B. Schmidt and Roger J. Calantone, "Are Really New Product Development Projects Harder to Shut Down?" *Journal of Product Innovation Management,* March 1998, pp. 111–23; S. N. Wasti and Jeffrey K. Liker, "Risky Business or Competitive Power? Supplier Involvement in Japanese Product Design," *Journal of Product Innovation Management,* September 1997, pp. 337–55; Cheryl Nakata and K. Sivakumar, "National Culture and New Product Development: An Integrative Review," *Journal of Marketing,* January 1996, pp. 61–72; William H. Murphy and Linda Gorchels, "How to Improve Product Management Effectiveness," *Industrial Marketing Management,* January 1996, pp. 47–58; Gary S. Lynn, Joseph G. Morone, and Albert S. Paulson, "Marketing and Discontinuous Innovation: The Probe and Learn Process," *California Management Review,* Spring 1996, pp. 8–37; Dorothy Leonard and Jeffrey F. Rayport, "Spark Innovation Through Empathic Design," *Harvard Business Review,* November–December 1997, pp. 102–8ff.; Gary L. Ragatz, Robert B. Handfield, and Thomas V. Scannell, "Success Factors for Integrating Suppliers into New Product Development," *Journal of Product Innovation Management,* May 1997, pp. 190–202; X.M. Song and Mitzi M. Montoya-Weiss, "Critical Development Activities for Really New Versus Incremental Products," *Journal of Product Innovation Management,* March 1998, pp. 124–35.

18. "Where Great Ideas Come From," *Inc.,* April 1998, pp. 76–94; Ari-Pekka Hameri and Jukka Nihtila, "Distributed New Product Development Project Based on Internet and World-Wide Web: A Case Study," *Journal of Product Innovation Management,* March 1997, pp. 77–87; "Seeing the Future First," *Fortune,* September 5, 1994, pp. 64–70; "Detroit's New Strategy to Beat Back Japanese Is to Copy Their Ideas," *The Wall Street Journal,* October 1, 1992, p. A1ff.; "Getting Hot Ideas from Customers," *Fortune,* May 18, 1992, pp. 86–87; "How to Let Innovation Happen," *Industry Week,* March 16, 1992, p. 43.

19. Don R. Graber, "How to Manage a Global Product Development Process," *Industrial Marketing Management,* November 1996, pp. 483–89; "U.S. Companies Shop Abroad for Product Ideas," *The Wall Street Journal,* March 14, 1990, p. B1ff.

20. Eric von Hippel, *The Sources of Innovation* (New York: Oxford University Press, 1988).

21. "Why One Jury Dealt a Big Blow to Chrysler in Minivan-Latch Case," *The Wall Street Journal,* November 19, 1997, p. A1ff.; "Chinese Discover Product-Liability Suits," *The Wall Street Journal,* November 13, 1997, p. B1ff.; "How Many Fingers Is He Holding Up?" *Fortune,* October 13, 1997, p. 29; Paula Mergenhagen, "Product Liability: Who Sues?" *American Demographics,* June 1995, pp. 48–55; "How a Jury Decided that a Coffee Spill Is Worth $2.9 Million," *The Wall Street Journal,* September 1, 1994, p. A1ff.; Paul A. Herbig and James E. Golden, "Innovation and Product Liability," *Industrial Marketing Management,* July 1994, pp. 245–56; Robert N. Mayer and Debra L. Scammon, "Caution: Weak Product Warnings May Be Hazardous to Corporate Health," *Journal of Business Research,* June 1992, pp. 347–60; Thomas V. Greer, "Product Liability in the European Community: The Legislative History," *Journal of Consumer Affairs,* Summer 1992, pp. 159–76.

22. "Want Shelf Space at the Supermarket? Ante Up," *Business Week,* August 7, 1989, pp. 60–61; "Grocer 'Fee' Hampers New-Product Launches," *Advertising Age,* August 3, 1987, p. 1ff.; Frank H. Alpert, Michael A. Kamins, and John L. Graham, "An Examination of Reseller Buyer Attitudes Toward Order of Brand Entry," *Journal of Marketing,* July 1992, pp. 25–37.

23. Fred Langerak, Ed Peelen, and Harry Commandeur, "Organizing for Effective New Product Development," *Industrial Marketing Management,* May 1997, pp. 281–89; Keith Goffin, "Evaluating Customer Support During New Product Development—An Exploratory Study," *Journal of Product Innovation Management,* January 1998, pp. 42–56; Paul S. Adler, Avi Mandelbaum, Vien Nguyen, and Elizabeth Schwerer, "Getting the Most Out of Your Product Development Process," *Harvard Business Review,* March–April 1996, pp. 134–52; Frank R. Bacon, Jr., and Thomas W. Butler, Jr., *Planned Innovation,* rev. ed. (Ann Arbor: Institute of Science and Technology, University of Michigan, 1980); Christer Karlsson and Par Ahlstrom, "Perspective: Changing Product Development Strategy—A Managerial Challenge," *Journal of Product Innovation Management,* November 1997, pp. 473–84.

24. "Industry's Amazing New Instant Prototypes," *Fortune,* January 12, 1998, pp. 120E-L; "Secrets of Product Testing," *Fortune,* November 28, 1994, pp. 166–72; "A Smarter Way to Manufacture," *Business Week,* April 30, 1990, pp. 110–17; "Oops! Marketers Blunder Their Way through the 'Herb Decade,' " *Advertising Age,* February 13, 1989, p. 3ff.

25. "Oops! Marketers Blunder Their Way Through the 'Herb Decade,' " *Advertising Age,* February 13, 1989, p. 3ff.

26. "Test Market USA," *Brandweek,* May 8, 1995, pp. 40–43; "The Company Store: How to Test Market for Fun and Profit," *Inc.,* November 1989, pp. 153–55; John R. Dickinson and Carolyn P. Wilby, "Concept Testing With and Without Product Trial," *Journal of Product Innovation Management,* March 1997, pp. 117–25.

27. William E. Souder, David Buisson, and Tony Garrett, "Success Through Customer-Driven New Product Development: A Comparison of U.S. and New Zealand Small Entrepreneurial High Technology Firms," *Journal of Product Innovation Management,* November 1997, pp. 459–72; Artemis March, "Usability: The New Dimension of Product Design," *Harvard Business Review,* September 1994–October 1994, pp. 144–49; Peter H. Bloch, "Seeking the Ideal Form: Product Design and Consumer Response," *Journal of Marketing,* July 1995, pp. 16–29; Roger J. Calantone, "Engines of Innovation: U.S. Industrial Research at the End of an Era," *Journal of Product Innovation Management,* July 1997, pp. 315–17; George M. Chryssochoidis and Veronica Wong, "Rolling Out New Products Across Country Markets: An Empirical Study of Causes of Delays," *Journal of Product Innovation Management,* January 1998, pp. 16–41; Erik J. Hultink, Abbie Griffin, Susan Hart, and Henry S. Robben, "Industrial New Product Launch Strategies and Product Development Performance," *Journal of Product Innovation Management,* July 1997, pp. 243–57; Alan Flaschner, "Technology Fountainheads: The Management Challenge of R&D Consortia," *Journal of Product Innovation Management,* July 1997, pp. 309–12; William Q. Judge, Gerald E. Fryxell, and Robert S. Dooley, "The New Task of R&D Management: Creating Goal-Directed Communities for Innovation," *California Management Review,* Spring 1997, pp. 72–85; John P. Workman, Jr., "Marketing's Limited Role in New Product Development in One Computer Systems Firm," *Journal of Marketing Research,* November 1993, pp. 405–21.

28. "Brands at Work," *Brandweek,* April 13, 1998, pp. 27–35; "Special Report: Auto Marketing & Brand Management," *Advertising Age,* April 6, 1998, pp. S1–28; "Doubts on GM Brand System," *Advertising Age,* March 9, 1998, pp. 26–27; "P&G Redefines the Brand Manager," *Advertising Age,* October 13, 1997, p1ff.; "Brand Power," *Newsweek,* March 17, 1997, pp. 48–50; Don Frey, "Learning the Ropes: My Life as a Product Champion," *Harvard Business Review,* September/October 1991, pp. 46–57; "Brand Managing's New Accent," *Adweek's Marketing Week,* April 15, 1991, pp. 18–22; Stephen K. Markham, "New Products Management," *Journal of Product Innovation Management,* July 1997, pp. 312–14; Manfred F. Maute and William B. Locander, "Innovation as a Socio-Politial Process: An Empirical Analysis of Influence Behavior among New Product Managers," *Journal of Business Research,* June 1994, pp. 161–74.

29. Anita Lahey, "Brand Revolution," *Marketing,* January 26, 1998, 10–11; Anita Lahey, "Less Is More," *Marketing,* September 22, 1997, pp. 12–13; Esther Benzie, "An Introduction to Category Management," London, Ont.: Western Business School, Case #9–95–A005, 1995; David Lonsdale and Rudolph Struse, *Category Management,* Nielsen Marketing Research, Chicago: American Marketing Association, 1992.

Chapter 11

1. William Mcinnes, "A Conceptual Approach to Marketing," in *Theory in Marketing,* second series, ed. Reavis Cox, Wroe Alderson, and Stanley J. Shapiro (Homewood, IL: Richard D. Irwin, 1964), pp. 51–67.

2. For more on Coke and Pepsi's attempt to sell more in different locales in U.S., see "For Pepsi, a Battle to Capture Coke's Fountain Sales," *The Wall Street Journal,* May 11, 1998, p. B1ff.; "Pepsi Hits Coca-Cola with an Antitrust Lawsuit," *The Wall Street Journal,* May 8, 1998, p. A3ff.; "A Coke and a Perm? Soda Giant Is Pushing into Unusual Locales," *The Wall Street Journal,* May 8, 1997, p. A1ff. For a classic discussion of the discrepancy concepts, see Wroe Alderson, "Factors Governing the Development of Marketing Channels," in *Marketing Channels for Manufactured Goods,* ed. Richard M. Clewett (Homewood, IL: Richard D. Irwin, 1954), pp. 7–9.

3. For some examples on how channels change to adjust discrepancies, see "How Magazines Arrive on Shelves, and Why Some Soon May Not," *The Wall Street Journal,* February 26, 1998, p. A1ff.; "Blockbuster Seeks a New Deal with Hollywood," *The Wall Street Journal,* March 25, 1998, p. B1ff.; Robert A. Mittelstaedt and Robert E. Stassen, "Structural Changes in the Phonograph Record Industry and Its Channels of Distribution, 1946–1966," *Journal of Macromarketing,* Spring 1994, pp. 31–44; Arun Sharma and Luis V. Dominguez, "Channel Evolution: A Framework for Analysis," *Journal of the Academy of Marketing Science,* Winter 1992, pp. 1–16.

4. *1997 Annual Report,* Colgate-Palmolive; "It's Becoming a Dogfight for the $15 Billion Pet Supply Market," *The Raleigh News & Observer,* September 25, 1994, p. 5F; "Pet Superstores

Collar Customers from Supermarkets, Small Shops," *The Wall Street Journal,* November 18, 1993, p. B12; "Pet-Food Makers Are Trying to Entice Dog, Cat Owners with Healthier Fare," *The Wall Street Journal,* August 16, 1991, p. B4B; "New Pet Food Scrap in Supermarkets," *Advertising Age,* January 28, 1991, p. 3ff.

5. For a discussion of the advantages and disadvantages of direct channel systems, see "Jim Taylor, Gateway 2000," *Superbrands '98,* October 20, 1997, pp. 102–105; "Have Brands, Will Travel," *Brandweek,* October 6, 1997, pp. 22–26; also available from World Wide Web: <http://www.gateway.com>; "Motorola Bets Big on China," *Fortune,* May 27, 1996, pp. 116–24; "Direct Sellers Defy Odds, Making PC Books Winners, Too," *Advertising Age,* November 9, 1992, p. S2; Donald Bowersox and M. Bixby Cooper, *Strategic Marketing Channel Management,* 2nd ed. (Burr Ridge, IL: Irwin/McGraw-Hill, 1992). See also David Shipley, Colin Egan, and Scott Edgett, "Meeting Source Selection Criteria: Direct versus Distributor Channels," *Industrial Marketing Management* 20, no. 4 (1991), pp. 297–304; Thomas L. Powers, "Industrial Distribution Options: Trade-Offs to Consider," *Industrial Marketing Management* 18, no. 3 (1989), pp. 155–62.

6. For a discussion of indirect channel systems, see Richard Parker and G. R. Funkhouser, "The Consumer As an Active Member of the Channel: Implications for Relationship Marketing," *Journal of Marketing Theory & Practice,* Spring 1997, pp. 72–79; Gordon C. Bruner, "Cyberspace: The Marketing Frontier," *Journal of Marketing,* January 1997, pp. 112–13; Lou E. Pelton, David Strutton, and James R. Lumpkin, *Marketing Channels: A Relationship Management Approach* (Burr Ridge, IL: Irwin/McGraw-Hill, 1997). See also Bert Rosenbloom and Trina L. Larsen, "How Foreign Firms View Their U.S. Distributors," *Industrial Marketing Management,* May 1992, pp. 93–102; Frank Lynn, "The Changing Economics of Industrial Distribution," *Industrial Marketing Management,* November 1992, pp. 355–60. For more on middlemen intermediaries and their functions, see Richard Greene, "Wholesaling," *Forbes,* January 2, 1984, pp. 226–28; James D. Hlavacek and Tommy J. McCuistion, "Industrial Distributors—When, Who, and How?" *Harvard Business Review,* January–February 1983, pp. 96–101; Elizabeth J. Wilson and Arch G. Woodside, "Marketing New Products with Distributors," *Industrial Marketing Management,* February 1992, pp. 15–22; W. Benoy et al., "How Industrial Distributors View Distributor-Supplier Partnership Arrangements," *Industrial Marketing Management,* January 1995, pp. 27–36.

7. "What's Wrong with Selling Used CDs?" *Business Week,* July 26, 1993, p. 38; Jakki J. Mohr, Robert J. Fisher, and John R. Nevin, "Collaborative Communication in Interfirm Relationships: Moderating Effects of Integration and Control," *Journal of Marketing,* July 1996, pp. 103–15; Amy E. Cox and Orville C. Walker, "Reactions to Disappointing Performance in Manufacturer-Distributor Relationships: The Role of Escalation and Resource Commitments," *Psychology & Marketing,* December 1997, pp. 791–821; Rajiv P. Dant and Patrick L. Schul, "Conflict Resolution Processes in Contractual Channels of Distribution," *Journal of Marketing,* January 1992, pp. 38–54.

8. "Making the Middleman an Endangered Species," *Business Week,* June 6, 1994, pp. 114–15; Jule B. Gassenheimer et al., "Models of Channel Maintenance: What Is the Weaker Party to Do?" *Journal of Business Research,* July 1994, pp. 225–36; Gregory T. Gundlach, Ravi S. Achrol, and John T. Mentzer, "The Structure of Commitment in Exchange," *Journal of Marketing,* January 1995, pp. 78–92; Jan B. Heide, "Interorganizational Governance in Marketing Channels, *Journal of Marketing,* January 1994, pp. 71–85; Jean L. Johnson et al., "The Exercise of Interfirm Power and Its Repercussions in U.S.-Japanese Channel Relationships," *Journal of Marketing,* April 1993, pp. 1–10.

9. Ravi S. Achrol, "Changes in the Theory of Interorganizational Relations in Marketing: Toward a Network Paradigm," *Journal of the Academy of Marketing Science,* Winter 1997, pp. 56–71; Aric Rindfleisch and Jan B. Heide, "Transaction Cost Analysis: Past, Present, and Future Applications," *Journal of Marketing,* October 1997, pp. 30–54; Robert F. Lusch and James R. Brown, "Interdependency, Contracting, and Relational Behavior in Marketing Channels," *Journal of Marketing,* October 1996, pp. 19–38; Robert D. Buzzell, "Is Vertical Integration Profitable?" *Harvard Business Review,* January–February 1983, pp. 92–102; Michael Etgar and Aharon Valency, "Determinants of the Use of Contracts in Conventional Marketing Channels," *Journal of Retailing,* Winter 1983, pp. 81–92; Louis W. Stern and Torger Reve, "Distribution Channels as Political Economies: A Framework for Comparative Analysis," *Journal of Marketing,* Summer 1980, pp. 52–64.

10. "Esprit's Spirited Style Is Hot Seller," *USA Today,* March 25, 1986, p. B5; "Apparel Firm Makes Profits, Takes Risks by Flouting Tradition," *The Wall Street Journal,* June 11, 1985, p. 1ff.

11. *1997 Annual Report,* Reebok; "Reebok's Direct Sales Spark a Retail Revolt," *Adweek's Marketing Week,* December 2, 1991, p. 7. See also Saul Sands and Robert J. Posch, Jr., "A Checklist of Questions for Firms Considering a Vertical Territorial Distribution Plan," *Journal of Marketing,* Summer 1982, pp. 38–43; Debra L. Scammon and Mary Jane Sheffet, "Legal Issues in Channels Modification Decisions: The Question of Refusals to Deal," *Journal of Public Policy and Marketing* 5 (1986), pp. 82–96.

12. Gregory T. Gundlach and Patrick E. Murphy, "Ethical and Legal Foundations of Relational Marketing Exchanges," *Journal of Marketing,* October 1993, pp. 35–46; Craig B. Barkacs, "Multilevel Marketing and Antifraud Statutes: Legal Enterprises or Pyramid Schemes?" *Journal of the Academy of Marketing Science,* Spring 1997, pp. 176–77; Robert A. Robicheaux and James E. Coleman, "The Structure of Marketing Channel Relationships," *Journal of the Academy of Marketing Science,* Winter 1994, pp. 38–51; Brett A. Boyle and F. Robert Dwyer, "Power, Bureaucracy, Influence and Performance: Their Relationships in Industrial Distribution Channels," *Journal of Business Research,* March 1995, pp. 189–200.

13. See, for example, "P&G to Stores: Keep the Dented Crisco Cans," *The Wall Street Journal,* March 21, 1997, p. B1ff.; "Turning Trash into Cash," *Traffic Management,* October 1993, pp. 46–48; Harvey Alter, "Cost of Recycling Municipal Solid Waste With and Without a Concurrent Beverage Container Deposit Law," *Journal of Consumer Affairs,* Summer 1993, pp. 166–86.

Chapter 12

1. Available from World Wide Web: <http://www.fmi.org/media/bg/ecr1>; "Delivering the Goods," *Fortune,* November 28, 1994, pp. 64–78; "Making the Middleman an Endangered Species," *Business Week,* June 6, 1994, pp. 114–15; "The Nitty-Gritty of ECR Systems: How One Company Makes It Pay," *Advertising Age,* May 2, 1994, pp. S1ff.; "Behind the Tumult at P&G," *Fortune,* March 7, 1994, pp. 74–82.

2. "Compaq Stumbles as PCs Weather New Blow," *The Wall Street Journal,* March 9, 1998, p. B1ff.; "At What Profit Price?" *Brandweek,* June 23, 1997, pp. 24–28; "Delivering the Goods," *Fortune,* November 28, 1994, pp. 64–78; Brian F. O'Neil and Jon L. Iveson, "Strategically Managing the Logistics Function," *The Logistics and Transportation Review,* December 1991, pp. 359–78; Lloyd M. Rinehart, M. Bixby Cooper, and George D. Wagenheim, "Furthering the Integration of Marketing and Logistics Through Customer Service in the Channel," *Journal of the Academy of Marketing Science,* Winter 1989, pp. 63–72; Philip B. Schary, "A Concept of Customer Service," *The Logistics and Transportation Review,* December 1992, pp. 341–52; Edward A. Morash and John Ozment, "Toward Management of Transportation Service Quality," *The Logistics and Transportation Review,* June 1994, pp. 115–40; Michael H. Morris and Duane L. Davis, "Measuring and Managing Customer Service in Industrial Firms," *Industrial Marketing Management,* November 1992, pp. 343–54; Gary L. Frazier, Robert E. Spekman, and Charles R. O'Neal, "Just-In-Time Exchange Relationships in Industrial Markets," *Journal of Marketing,* October 1988, pp. 52–67; William D. Perreault, Jr., and Frederick A. Russ, "Physical Distribution Service in Industrial Purchase Decisions," *Journal of Marketing,* April 1976, pp. 3–10.

3. "Costs Too High? Bring in the Logistics Experts," *Fortune,* November 10, 1997, pp. 200C-T; "Ryder Sees the Logic of Logistics," *Business Week,* August 5, 1996, p. 56; Carol J. Emerson and Curtis M. Grimm, "The Relative Importance of Logistics and Marketing Customer Service: A Strategic Perspective," *Journal of Business Logistics,* 1998, pp. 17–32; Edward A. Morash, Cornelia L. M. Droge, and Shawnee K. Vickery, "Strategic Logistics Capabilities for Competitive Advantage and Firm Success," *Journal of Business Logistics,* 1996, pp. 1–22; John L. Kent and Daniel J. Flint, "Perspectives on the Evolution of Logistics Thought," *Journal of Business Logistics,* 1997, pp. 15–29; Jonathan W. Kohn and Michael A. McGinnis, "Logistics Strategy: A Longitudinal Study," *Journal of Business Logistics,* 1997, pp. 1–14; Steven R. Clinton and David J. Closs, "Logistics Strategy: Does It Exist?" *Journal of Business Logistics,* 1997, pp. 19–44; Prabir K. Bagchi and Helge Virum, "Logistical Alliances: Trends and Prospects in Integrated Europe," *Journal of Business Logistics,* 1998, pp. 191–213.

4. Forrest E. Harding, "Logistics Service Provider Quality: Private Measurement, Evaluation, and Improvement," *Journal of Business Logistics,* 1998, pp. 103–20; Carol C. Bienstock, John T. Mentzer, and Monroe M. Bird, "Measuring Physical Distribution Service Quality," *Journal of the Academy of Marketing Science,* Winter 1997, pp. 31–44; G. T. M. Hult, "Measuring Cycle Time of the Global Procurement Process," *Industrial Marketing Management,* September 1997, pp. 403–12; R. Mohan Pisharodi, "Preference for Supplier When Supplier and Customer Perceptions of Customer Service Levels Differ," *The Logistics and Transportation Review,* March 1994, pp. 31–54; Benson P. Shapiro, V.K. Rangan, and J.J. Sviokla, "Staple Yourself to an Order," *Harvard Business Review,* July–August, 1992, pp. 113–22; J.B. Fuller, J. O'Conor, and R. Rawlinson, "Tailored Logistics: The Next Advantage," *Harvard Business Review,* May–June 1993, pp. 87–98.

5. Lisa M. Ellram and Sue P. Siferd, "Total Cost of Ownership: A Key Concept in Strategic Cost Management Decisions," *Journal of Business Logistics,* 1998, pp. 55–84; Scott R. Swenseth and Michael R. Godfrey, "Estimating Freight Rates for Logistics Decisions," *Journal of Business Logistics,* 1996, pp. 213–31; Philip T. Evers, "The Impact of Transshipments on Safety Stock Requirements," *Journal of Business Logistics,* 1996, pp. 109–33.

6. *1997 Annual Report,* Tyson Foods; "Holly Farms' Marketing Error: The Chicken that Laid an Egg," *The Wall Street Journal,* February 9, 1988, p. 44.

7. Richard Germain, Cornelia Droge, and Nancy Spears, "The Implications of Just-in-Time for Logistics Organization Management and Performance," *Journal of Business Logistics,* 1996, pp. 19–34; Claudia H. Pragman, "JIT II: A Purchasing Concept for Reducing Lead Times in Time-Based Competition," *Business Horizons,* July–August 1996, pp. 54–58; Faye W. Gilbert,

Joyce A. Young, and Charles R. O'Neal, "Buyer-Seller Relationships in Just-in-Time Purchasing Environments," *Journal of Business Research,* February 1994, pp. 111–20; Steve McDaniel, Joseph G. Ormsby, and Alicia B. Gresham, "The Effect of JIT on Distributors," *Industrial Marketing Management,* May 1992, pp. 145–50; "Allen-Edmonds Shoe Tries 'Just-in-Time' Production," *The Wall Street Journal,* March 4, 1993, p. B2.

8. Available from World Wide Web: <http://silmaril.smeal.psu.edu/misc/supply_chain>; "The Push to Streamline Supply Chains," *Fortune,* March 3, 1997, pp. 108C-R; Chickery J. Kasouf and Kevin G. Celuch, "Interfirm Relationships in the Supply Chain: The Small Supplier's View," *Industrial Marketing Management,* November 1997, pp. 475–86; William H. Borghesani, Peter L. de la Cruz, and David B. Berry, "Controlling the Chain: Buyer Power, Distributive Control, and New Dynamics in Retailing," *Business Horizons,* July–August 1997, pp. 17–24; Jeffrey H. Dyer, Dong S. Cho, and Wujin Chu, "Strategic Supplier Segmentation: The Next 'Best Practice' in Supply Chain Management," *California Management Review,* Winter 1998, pp. 57–77; Noel P. Greis and John D. Kasarda, "Enterprise Logistics in the Information Era," *California Management Review,* Summer 1997, pp. 55–78; Craig R. Carter and Lisa M. Ellram, "Reverse Logistics: A Review of the Literature and Framework for Future Investigation," *Journal of Business Logistics,* 1998, pp. 85–102; Harry L. Sink and C.J. Langley, "A Managerial Framework for the Acquisition of Third-Party Logistics Services," *Journal of Business Logistics,* 1997, pp. 163–89; Robert C. Lieb and Hugh L. Randall, "A Comparison of the Use of Third-Party Logistics Services by Large American Manufacturers, 1991, 1994, and 1995," *Journal of Business Logistics,* 1996, pp. 305–20; B.C. Arntzen, G.C. Brown, T.P. Harrison et al., "Global Supply Chain Management at Digital Equipment Corporation," *Interfaces,* January–February, 1995.

9. "Who's Winning the Information Revolution," *Fortune,* November 30, 1992, pp. 110–17; "Circuit City's Wires Are Sizzling," *Business Week,* April 27, 1992, p. 76; "Earning More by Moving Faster," *Fortune,* October 7, 1991, pp. 89–94; Lisa R. Williams, Avril Nibbs, Dimples Irby, and Terence Finley, "Logistics Integration: The Effect of Information Technology, Team Composition, and Corporate Competitive Positioning," *Journal of Business Logistics,* 1997, pp. 31–41; Paul R. Murphy and James M. Daley, "International Freight Forwarder Perspectives on Electronic Data Interchange and Information Management Issues," *Journal of Business Logistics,* 1996, pp. 63–84; Kenneth B. Kahn and John T. Mentzer, "EDI and EDI Alliances: Implications for the Sales Forecasting Function," *Journal of Marketing Theory & Practice,* Spring 1996, pp. 72–78; Ira Lewis and Alexander Talalayevsky, "Logistics and Information Technology: A Coordination Perspective," *Journal of Business Logistics,* 1997, pp. 141–57.

10. "A Smart Cookie at Pepperidge," *Fortune,* December 22, 1986, pp. 67–74.

11. Douglas Lambert, James R. Stock, and Lisa M. Ellram, *Fundamentals of Logistics* (Burr Ridge, IL: Irwin/McGraw-Hill, 1998).

12. For more detail on deregulation of transportation, see Paul D. Larson, "Transportation Deregulation, JIT, and Inventory Levels," *The Logistics and Transportation Review,* June 1991, pp. 99–112; James C. Nelson, "Politics and Economics in Transport Regulation and Deregulation—A Century Perspective of the ICC's Role," *The Logistics and Transportation Review,* March, 1987, pp. 5–32; Karl M. Ruppentha, "U.S. Airline Deregulation-Winners and Losers," *The Logistics and Transportation Review,* March 1987, pp. 65–82.

13. For a more detailed comparison of mode characteristics, see Robert Dahlstrom, Kevin M. McNeilly, and Thomas W. Speh, "Buyer-Seller Relationships in the Procurement of Logistical Services," *Journal of the Academy of Marketing Science,* Spring 1996, pp. 110–24; Roger Dale Abshire and Shane R. Premeaux, "Motor Carriers' and Shippers' Perceptions of the Carrier Choice Decision," *The Logistics and Transportation Review,* December 1991, pp. 351–58; Brian J. Gibson, Harry L. Sink, and Ray A. Mundy, "Shipper-Carrier Relationships and Carrier Selection Criteria," *The Logistics and Transportation Review,* December 1993, pp. 371–82.

14. "Tired of Costs, Delays of Railroads, Firms Lay Their Own Tracks," *The Wall Street Journal,* February 6, 1998, p. A1ff.; "America's Railroads Struggle to Recapture Their Former Glory," *The Wall Street Journal,* December 5, 1997, p. A1ff.; "The Rails: Trouble Behind, Trouble Ahead," *Business Week,* November 24, 1997, pp. 40–42; "An Unsolved Mystery: Where Are Shippers' Rail Cars?" *The Wall Street Journal,* October 13, 1997, p. B1ff.; "Union Pacific Tie-Ups Reach across Economy," *The Wall Street Journal,* October 8, 1997, p. B1ff.; "The Great Train Game," *Fortune,* November 11, 1996, pp. 151–54; "High Tech Puts Them Back on Track," *USA Today,* November 2, 1994, p. 1Bff.

15. "Hauling Super Freight Takes Ingenuity and a Huge Rig," *The Wall Street Journal,* April 13, 1998, p. B1ff.; "Extra-Big Rigs Could Barrel Down More Roads," *The Wall Street Journal,* June 16, 1997, p. B1ff.; "More Trucks Shake Residential America," *The Wall Street Journal,* April 29, 1997, p. B1ff.; "Riding the Data Highway," *Newsweek,* March 21, 1994, p. 54–55; "Hauling It for Less," *Nation's Business,* January 1994, pp. 46–48.

16. Statistics Canada, Cats. 52-201, 57-205 (Ottawa: Ministry of Supply and Services Canada, December 31, 1983).

17. "Why FedEx Is Flying High," *Fortune,* November 10, 1997, pp. 155–60; "UPS Puts Its Back into It," *Business Week,* October 27, 1997, p. 50; "FedEx Hears International Opportunity Knocking," *USA Today,* October 7, 1997, p. 3B; "Federal Express, UPS Battle for a Foothold in Asia," *The Wall Street Journal,* January 22, 1997, p. B1ff.; "UPS, Feeling Boxed In, Stages Its Own Coming Out," *The Wall Street Journal,* September 17, 1996, p. B4; "Can Europe Deliver," *The Wall Street Journal,* September 30, 1994, p. R15ff.

18. K. Raguraman and Claire Chan, "The Development of Sea-Air Intermodal Transportation: An Assessment of Global Trends," *The Logistics and Transportation Review,* December 1994, p. 379; "Cargo that Phones Home," *Fortune,* November 15, 1993, p. 143; "Grain Processor Improvises to Stay Afloat," *The Wall Street Journal,* July 21, 1993, p. B1ff.

19. *1997 Annual Report,* Du Pont; *1997 Annual Report,* Matlack; *1997 Annual Report,* Shell; "Conservation Power," *Business Week,* September 16, 1991, pp. 86–91; "On the Road Again and Again and Again: Auto Makers Try to Build Recyclable Car," *The Wall Street Journal,* April 30, 1991, p. B1; "Clean-Air Proposal Eventually May Add as Much as $600 to Car Sticker Prices," *The Wall Street Journal,* October 11, 1990, p. B1ff.

20. Kant Rao, Richard R. Young, and Judith A. Novick, "Third Party Services in the Logistics of Global Firms," *The Logistics and Transportation Review,* December 1993, pp. 363–70; Judith A. Fuerst, "Sorting Out the Middlemen," *Handling and Shipping Management,* March 1985, pp. 46–50.

21. "You Make It, They Distribute It," *Nation's Business,* March 1994, pp. 46–48; C.H. White and R.B. Felder, "Turn Your Truck Fleet into a Profit Center," *Harvard Business Review,* May–June 1983, pp. 14–17.

22. "Hospital Cost Cutters Push Use of Scanners to Track Inventories," *The Wall Street Journal,* June 10, 1997, p. A1ff.; "Retired General Speeds Deliveries, Cuts Costs, Helps Sears Rebound," *The Wall Street Journal,* July 16, 1996, p. A1ff.; Paul Zinszer, "Supply Chain Strategies for Managing Excess Inventories," *Journal of Marketing Theory & Practice,* Spring 1996, pp. 55–60; Paul A. Dion, Loretta M. Hasey, Patrick C. Dorin, and Jean Lundin, "Consequences of Inventory Stockouts," *Industrial Marketing Management* 20, no. 1 (1991), pp. 23–28.

23. Anita Lahey, "Brand Revolution," from <http://www.fmi.org>.

24. "Compaq Borrows Wal-Mart's Idea to Boost Production," *The Wall Street Journal,* June 17, 1994, p. B4; Wade Ferguson, "Buying an Industrial Service Warehouse Space," *Industrial Marketing Management,* February 1983, pp. 63–66; Arnold B. Maltz, "Outsourcing the Warehousing Function: Economics and Strategic Considerations," *The Logistics and Transportation Review,* September 1994, pp. 245–66; Patricia J. Daugherty, Dale S. Rogers, and Theodore P. Stank, "Benchmarking: Strategic Implications for Warehousing Firms," *The Logistics and Transportation Review,* March 1994, pp. 55–72.

25. "Cotter DC Rides the Wave of Technology into the Future," *Hardware Age,* October 1995, p. 50ff.; "Scanning the Distribution Horizon," *Foodservice Equipment & Supplies Specialist,* June 1994, pp. 44–52.

26. "Distribution Center Doubles Output with Paperless System," *Modern Materials Handling/Scan Tech News,* September 1994, pp. S17–19; Maureen E. Lynch, Sharon J. Imada, and James H. Bookbinder, "The Future of Logistics in Canada: A Delphi-Based Forecast" *The Logistics and Transportation Review,* March 1994, p. 95.

Chapter 13

1. Joel R. Evans, Barry Berman, and William J. Wellington, *Marketing Essentials* (Scarborough, Ont.: Prentice Hall Canada, Inc., 1998) p. 272.

2. Ibid.

3. "Report on Retail," *Marketing,* August 1–8, 1994, pp. 17–21; "Retailers Look Ahead to the Year 2000," *Computing Canada.* December 21, 1994, p. 16; "Rating the Stores: The World of Retailing Has Changed Dramatically in the Past Decade," *Consumer Reports,* November 1994, pp. 712–21; "Change at the Checkout: A Survey of Retailing," *The Economist,* March 4–10, 1995, p. Survey 1–18.

4. "All in Stride for Brown's (the 32-Store Footwear Chain's Success Is the Result of Gutsy Buying, Smooth Merchandising and Careful Staffing)," *This Week in Business,* September 6, 1991, pp. C8–C9ff.; "Special Report: Premiums and Incentives; Retailers Are Getting into the Game," *Strategy,* April 17, 1995, pp. 31–34.

5. "Why Subway Is 'The Biggest Problem in Franchising,' " *Fortune,* March 16, 1998, pp. 126–34; "Fast-Food Fight," *Business Week,* June 2, 1997, pp. 34–36; "Rattling the Chains," *Brandweek,* April 21, 1997, pp. 28–40; "Lawsuit Spoils the Party at Tupperware," *The Wall Street Journal,* November 29, 1996, p. B1ff.; "Court Decides Franchisees Get Elbow Room," *The Wall Street Journal,* August 14, 1996, p. B1ff.; "Chicken and Burgers Create Hot New Class: Powerful Franchisees," *The Wall Street Journal,* May 21, 1996, p. A1ff.; "Some Franchisees Say Moves by McDonald's Hurt Their Operations," *The Wall Street Journal,* April 17, 1996, p. A1ff.; Robert Dahlstom, "Franchising: Contemporary Issues and Research," *Journal of Public Policy & Marketing,* Spring 1996, pp. 159–61; Surinder Tikoo, "Assessing the Franchise Option," *Business Horizons,* May–June 1996, pp. 78–82; Rajiv P. Dant, Audhesh K. Paswan, and Patrick J. Kaufman, "What We Know About Ownership Redirection in Franchising: A Meta-Analysis," *Journal of Retailing,* Winter 1996, pp. 429–44; Alessandro Baroncelli and Angelo Manaresi, "Franchising As a Form of Divestment: An Italian Study," *Industrial Marketing Management,* May 1997, pp. 223–35; Roger D. Blair and Jill B. Herndon, "Franchise Supply Agreements: Quality Control or Illegal Tying?" *Journal of the Academy of Marketing Science,* Spring 1997, pp. 177–78; Richard C. Hoffman and John F. Preble,

"Franchising into the Twenty-First Century," *Business Horizons,* November–December 1993, pp. 35–43; "Trouble in Franchise Nation," *Fortune,* March 6, 1995, pp. 115–29; Francine Lafontaine and Patrick J. Kaufmann, "The Evolution of Ownership Patterns in Franchise Systems," *Journal of Retailing,* Summer 1994, pp. 97–114; "The Franchise Hall of Fame," *Inc.,* April 1994, pp. 86–95.

6. "Push-Button Lover," *The Economist,* November 16, 1991, p. 88; "Machines Start New Fast-Food Era," *USA Today,* July 19, 1991, pp. 1B-2B; "High-Tech Vending Machines Cook Up a New Menu of Hot Fast-Food Entrees," *The Wall Street Journal,* May 13, 1991, p. B1ff.

7. "Is There a Future for the TV Mall?" *Brandweek,* March 25, 1996, pp. 24–26; "QVC Draws Wares from Everywhere," *USA Today,* November 1, 1994, p. 1Dff.; "Battling for Buck$," *Profiles,* November 1994, pp. 49–52; "MTV Home Shopping Picks Model Host," *The Wall Street Journal,* July 18, 1994, p. B5; "TV or Not TV," *Inc.,* June 1994, pp. 63–68; "Purchasing Power," *U.S. News & World Report,* January 31, 1994, pp. 56–59; "Home Shoppers to Be Given Yet Another Service," *The Wall Street Journal,* January 14, 1994, p. B1ff.

8. "Store Chains Put Squeeze on Suppliers," *Financial Post,* November 26–28, 1994, p. 13; "Suppliers Don't Like New Sears Policies," *Montreal Gazette,* December 6, 1994, pp. C1–C2; "Drugs in a Big Box (Will Mass Merchandisers Upset Quebec's Market?)" *Marketing,* April 10, 1995, p. 12; "West Meets East (Albert Cohen is Looking for Ways to Grow his Retail Empire)," *Marketing,* June 12, 1995, pp. 27–28.

9. "Career Choices: A Study of Career Choices among College and University Students in Ontario," John C. Williams Consultants, Limited, March 1995 (Ontario Retail Sector Strategy, Human Resources Group).

10. "Evolve to Survive Retailers Warned," *Toronto Star,* November 12, 1994, P. C1; "Measuring Up: Knowing Your Core Market and How to Find New Customers Key to Small Retailers," *Calgary Herald,* January 16, 1995, p. C1; "The Ladies Who Lunch Have All Gone to Florida (Ira Berg Store Changes with the Times)," *Toronto Life,* March 1995, pp. 68–70ff.

11. "Retail Council Fights Back: Forget the Past and Plan for the Future," *Canadian Footwear,* August 1994, p. 58; "Retailers Told to Focus on Satisfaction," *The Globe and Mail,* September 22, 1994, p. B16; Stanley N. Logan, "The Small Store—A Struggle to Survive," *Arthur Andersen Retailing Issues Letter,* January 1995.

12. "Survey Plumbs Where We Shop and Why We Buy," *Montreal Gazette,* February 18, 1995, P. D1.

13. "What's Your Favourite Colour? Make the Wrong Choice Decorating Your Store and You'll Lose Sales," *Calgary Herald,* February 13, 1995, p. C1.

14. Art Good, "Value, Value, Value, and Now—Situational Value," *Retail Today,* May 1995, pp. 1–2.

15. "Leaning on Language: Ro-Na Counts on Multi-Lingual Staff in St. Laurent Store," *Montreal Gazette,* August 25, 1994, pp. D1–2; "Ford Does Distance Learning by the Numbers," *Training,* October 1994, p. 97; "Canadian Retailer Invests in Education," *Apparel Manufacturer,* January 1995, p. 8; "Salesgirl Solidarity: the Sales Clerks at a Chain of Trendy Clothing Stores are Tired of Being Treated Like Disposable Mannequins," *This Magazine,* February 1995, pp. 12–19.

16. "How Did Sears Blow this Gasket?" *Business Week,* June 29, 1992, p. 38; "An Open Letter to Sears Customers," *USA Today,* June 25, 1992, p. 8A.

17. "Retailers Press Ottawa to Open Access to Interac," *Financial Post,* August 20–22, 1994, p. 6; "Debit Cards a Big Hit with Ontario Shoppers," *Toronto Star,* February 8, 1995, p. B3.

18. "Point-of-Sale: Future Arrives Now for Retailers," *Calgary Herald,* December 28, 1994, P. D1.

19. "Wal-Mart Strong and Getting Stronger, says New Kubas Study," *Marketing,* December 5, 1994, p. 4; "The Retail Way: Canada's Major Shopkeepers Take the Lead in Implementing EDI with Suppliers," *Materials Management and Distribution,* December 1994, p. 24.

20. "Beyond Mail Order: Catalogs Now Sell Image, Advice," *The Wall Street Journal,* July 29, 1997, p. B1ff.; "Catalogers Expand in Asia," *USA Today,* October 18, 1996, p. 4B; "Spiegel's Book Is a Real Page-Turner," *Business Week,* September 12, 1994, pp. 74–76; "U.S. Catalogers Test International Waters," *The Wall Street Journal,* April 19, 1994, p. B1; C.R. Jasper and P.N.R. Lan, "Apparel Catalog Patronage: Demographic, Lifestyle, and Motivational Factors," *Psychology & Marketing,* July/August 1992, pp. 275–96; "Shoppers Seem to Prefer Mail over Mall," *USA Today,* August 12, 1993, p. 4B.

21. Foo N. Ho, Beng S. Ong, and Seonsu Lee, "A Multicultural Comparison of Shopping Patterns Among Asian Consumers," *Journal of Marketing Theory & Practice,* Winter 1997, pp. 42–51.

22. Philip R. Cateora, *International Marketing,* 10th ed. (Burr Ridge, IL: Irwin/McGraw-Hill, 1999); Saeed Samiee, "Retailing and Channel Considerations in Developing Countries: A Review and Research Propositions," *Journal of Business Research,* June 1993, pp. 103–30; "In Guam, Shopping Sprees Are Replacing Tanning," *The Wall Street Journal,* August 23, 1996, p. B4; "How's This for a Cultural Revolution? Chinese Are Getting Home Shopping," *The Wall Street Journal,* January 4, 1996, p. A6; "Retailers Go Global," *Fortune,* February 20, 1995, pp. 102–8; "Russians Say 'Ja' to Swedish Shops," *Advertising Age,* November 7, 1994, p. 47; "A Different World," *The Wall Street Journal,* October 28, 1994, p. R6; "Wal-Mart Is Slowed by Problems of Price and Culture in Mexico," *The Wall Street Journal,* July 29, 1994, p. A1ff.; "A Bargain Basement Called Japan," *Business Week,* June 27, 1994, pp. 42–43; "From Men's Suits to Sake, Discounting Booms in Japan," *Advertising Age International,* March 21, 1994, p. I1ff.; "Europe's Smaller Food Shops Face Finis," *The Wall Street Journal,* May 12, 1993, p. B1ff.

23. Wendy Evans and Steven Cox, *Retail Border Wars III: Case Studies of International Retailers Operating in Canada,* CSCA Research Report #10, 1997 (Centre for the Study of Commercial Activity at Ryerson Polytechnic University).

24. Wendy Evans, *Retail Border Wars II: Canadian Cases in International Retailing,* CSCA Research Report #8, 1997 (Centre for the Study of Commercial Activity at Ryerson Polytechnic University).

25. For a detailed discussion of wholesaling within a channels context, see Louis W. Stern, Adel L. El-Ansary and James R. Brown, "Management in Marketing Channels" (Englewood Cliffs, N.J.: Prentice Hall, 1989).

26. "Why Manufacturers Are Doubling as Distributors," *Business Week,* January 17, 1983, p. 41. See also "Who Is Bob Kierlin—and Why Is He So Successful?" *Fortune,* December 8, 1997, pp. 245–48; Robert F. Lusch, Deborah S. Coykendall, and James M. Kenderdine, *Wholesaling in Transition: An Executive Chart Book* (Norman, OK: Distribution Research Program, University of Oklahoma, 1990).

27. Available from World Wide Web: <http://www.inmac.com>; "Special Report: Direct Marketing," *Advertising Age,* September 25, 1990, pp. S1–16.

28. "Fruit Fight: Independent Growers Challenge Agribusiness Giants," *Insight,* July 29, 1991, pp. 13–19.

29. For more on manufacturers' agents being squeezed, see "Wal-Mart Draws Fire: Reps, Brokers Protest Being Shut Out by New Policy," *Advertising Age,* January 13, 1992, p. 3ff.; Patrick R. Mehr, "Identifying Independent Reps," *Industrial Marketing Management,* November 1992, pp. 319–22; "Independent Sales Reps Are Squeezed by the Recession," *The Wall Street Journal,* December 27, 1991, p. B1. For more discussion on wholesaling abroad, see "Japan Rises to P&G's No. 3 Market," *Advertising Age,* December 10, 1990, p. 42; " 'Papa-Mama' Stores in Japan Wield Power to Hold Back Imports," *The Wall Street Journal,* November 14, 1988, p. 1ff.; Yoo S. Yang, Robert P. Leone, and Dana L. Alden, "A Market Expansion Ability Approach to Identify Potential Exporters," *Journal of Marketing,* January 1992, pp. 84–96; Daniel C. Bello and Ritu Lohtia, "The Export Channel Design: The Use of Foreign Distributors and Agents," *Journal of the Academy of Marketing Science,* Spring 1995, pp. 83–93; Jim Gibbons, "Selling Abroad with Manufacturers' Agents," *Sales & Marketing Management,* September 9, 1985, pp. 67–69; Evelyn A. Thomchick and Lisa Rosenbaum, "The Role of U.S. Export Trading Companies in International Logistics," *Journal of Business Logistics,* September 1984, pp. 85–105.

30. Statistics Canada, Catalogue 63-008XPB, *Wholesale Trade,* December 1997, p.v.

31. "Middlemen Find Ways to Survive Cyberspace Shopping," *The Wall Street Journal,* December 12, 1996, p. B6; "Invoice? What's an Invoice?" *Business Week,* June 10, 1996, pp. 110–12; "Computer Wholesalers Face Shakeout and Consolidation," *The Wall Street Journal,* August 26, 1994, p. B4; "Electric Power Brokers Create New Breed of Business," *The Wall Street Journal,* August 2, 1994, p. B4; "Cut Out the Middleman? Never," *Business Week,* January 10, 1994, p. 96; "Marketers Shouldn't Give Up on Wholesalers Just Yet," *Brandweek,* July 5, 1993, p. 13; Allan J. Magrath, "The Hidden Clout of Marketing Middlemen," *Journal of Business Strategy,* March/April 1990, pp. 38–41.

32. "Cold War: Amana Refrigeration Fights Tiny Distributor," *The Wall Street Journal,* February 26, 1992, p. B2. For another example, see "Quickie-Divorce Curbs Sought By Manufacturers' Distributors," *The Wall Street Journal,* July 13, 1987, p. 27; Merger of Two Bakers Teaches Distributors a Costly Lesson (3-parts)," *The Wall Street Journal,* September 14, 1987, p. 29; October 19, 1987, p. 35; November 11, 1987, p. 33.

33. "The Impact of Electronic Commerce on Marketing," *Harvard Business Review,* May–June 1996, p. 137; Raymond R. Burke, "Do You See What I See? The Future of Virtual Shopping," *Journal of the Academy of Marketing Science,* Fall 1997, pp. 352–60; Joseph Alba, John Lynch, Barton Weitz, Chris Janiszewski et al., "Interactive Home Shopping: Consumer, Retailer, and Manufacturer Incentives to Participate in Electronic Marketplaces," *Journal of Marketing,* July 1997, pp. 38–53; Birud Sindhav, "Net Gain: Expanding Markets Through Virtual Communities," *Journal of Marketing,* January 1998, pp. 120–21; "Doing Business in the Internet Age," *Business Week,* June 22, 1998, pp. 121–72; "Entrepreneurs Reap Riches from Net Niches," *USA Today,* April 20, 1998, p. 3B; "Cybershopping Becomes a 2-Way Street," *The Wall Street Journal,* March 26, 1998, p. B8; "Portal Combat Comes to the Net," *Business Week,* March 2, 1998, pp. 73–78; "Digitizing Dinner," *Brandweek,* February 16, 1998, pp. 38–40.

Chapter 14

1. "Cabbage Patch Campaigner Tells Secret," *The Chapel Hill Newspaper,* December 1, 1985, p. D1.

2. "Old-Fashioned PR Gives General Mills Advertising Bargains," *The Wall Street Journal,* March 20, 1997, p. A1ff.; "Name That Chintz! How Shelter Magazines Boost Brands," *The Wall Street Journal,* March 14, 1997, p. B1ff.; "Rosie and 'Friends' Make Drake's Cakes a Star," *The Wall Street Journal,* February 10, 1997, p. B1ff.; "Toy Story: How Shrewd Marketing Made Elmo a Hit," *The Wall Street Journal,* December 16, 1996, p. B1ff.; "PR Shouldn't Mean 'Poor Relations,' " *Industry Week,* February 3, 1992, p. 51; Siva K.

Balasubramanian, "Beyond Advertising and Publicity: Hybrid Messages and Public Policy Issues," *Journal of Advertising,* December 1994, pp. 29–46; Thomas H. Bivins, "Ethical Implications of the Relationship of Purpose to Role and Function in Public Relations," *Journal of Business Ethics,* January, 1989, pp. 65–74.

3. "Talbots Mounting Its Biggest Integrated Marketing Push," *Advertising Age,* August 11, 1997, p. 29; "Olds' Intrigue Stars in Web Game Based on NBC TV Show," *Advertising Age,* July 28, 1997, p. 16ff.; "Oldsmobile Ryder," *Advertising Age,* July 21, 1997, p. 18; "Product Program Flea Control," *Advertising Age,* Special Issue, 1997, p. E8; "Promotion Marketing," *Brandweek,* March 4, 1996, pp. 22–26; J.R. Shannon, "The New Promotions Mix: A Proposed Paradigm, Process, and Application," *Journal of Marketing Theory & Practice,* Winter 1996, pp. 56–68; Kathleen J. Kelly, "Integrated Marketing Communication: Putting It Together & Making It Work," *Journal of the Academy of Marketing Science,* Winter 1997, pp. 83–85; "Special Report: Integrated Marketing," *Advertising Age,* November 8, 1993, pp. S1–12.

4. "The Hottest Thing on Wheels," *The Vancouver Sun,* May 6, 1998, A18.

5. "High-Tech Branding: Pushing Digital PCS," *Brandweek,* August 4, 1997, pp. 30–34; "Brand Builders: Delivery Guy Chic," *Brandweek,* June 30, 1997, pp. 18–19; "Eye-Catching Logos All Too Often Leave Fuzzy Images in Minds of Consumers," *The Wall Street Journal,* December 5, 1991, p. B1ff.; David I. Gilliland and Wesley J. Johnston, "Toward a Model of Business-to-Business Marketing Communications Effects," *Industrial Marketing Management,* January 1997, pp. 15–29; Michel T. Pham and Gita V. Johar, "Contingent Processes of Source Identification," *Journal of Consumer Research,* December 1997, pp. 249–65; Louisa Ha and Barry R. Litman, "Does Advertising Clutter Have Diminishing and Negative Returns?" *Journal of Advertising,* Spring 1997, pp. 31–42; Barbara B. Stern, "A Revised Communication Model for Advertising: Multiple Dimensions of the Source, the Message, and the Recipient," *Journal of Advertising,* June 1994, pp. 5–15; Ronald E. Dulek, John S. Fielden, and John S. Hill, "International Communication: An Executive Primer," *Business Horizons,* January/February 1991, pp. 20–25; Kaylene C. Williams, Rosann L. Spiro, and Leslie M. Fine, "The Customer-Salesperson Dyad: An Interaction/Communication Model and Review," *Journal of Personal Selling and Sales Management,* Summer 1990, pp. 29–44; Susan Mitchell, "How to Talk to Young Adults," *American Demographics,* April 1993, p. 50; Richard F. Beltramini and Edwin R. Stafford, "Comprehension and Perceived Believability of Seals of Approval Information in Advertising," *Journal of Advertising,* September 1993, pp. 3–14; Jacob Jacoby and Wayne D. Hoyer, "The Comprehension/Miscomprehension of Print Communication: Selected Findings," *Journal of Consumer Research,* March 1989, pp. 434–43.

6. "Marketing in Which We Bash a Baby Seal," *Fortune,* September 8, 1997, p. 36ff; Jagdish Agrawal and Wagner A. Kamakura, "The Economic Worth of Celebrity Endorsers: An Event Study Analysis," *Journal of Marketing,* July 1995, pp. 56–62; David J. Moore, John C. Mowen, and Richard Reardon, "Multiple Sources in Advertising Appeals: When Product Endorsers Are Paid by the Advertising Sponsor," *Journal of the Academy of Marketing Science,* Summer 1994, pp. 234–43.

7. "Hey, #!@*% Amigo, Can You Translate the Word 'Gaffe'?" *The Wall Street Journal,* July 8, 1996, p. B2; "Lost in Translation: How to 'Empower Women' in Chinese," *The Wall Street Journal,* September 13, 1994, p. A1ff.; "In World Cup Games, Words Get Lost and Gained in Translation," *The Wall Street Journal,* July 14, 1994, p. B1ff.; "Too Many Computer Names Confuse Too Many Buyers," *The Wall Street Journal,* June 29, 1994, p. B1ff.; "Go Ask Alice," *Adweek,* January 17, 1994, p. 32.

8. "Collagen Corp.'s Video Uses News Format," *The Wall Street Journal,* March 29, 1994, p. B8; "*Totally Hidden Video," Inside PR,* August 1990, pp. 11–13; " 'News' Videos That Pitch Drugs Provoke Outcry for Regulations," *The Wall Street Journal,* February 8, 1990, p. B6; Thomas H. Bivins, "Public Relations, Professionalism, and the Public Interest," *Journal of Business Ethics,* February 1993, pp. 117–26; Siva K. Balasubramanian, "Beyond Advertising and Publicity: Hybrid Messages and Public Policy Issues," *Journal of Advertising,* December 1994, pp. 47–58.

9. "Ryder Redraws the Self-Move Map with Service, Convenience," *Brandweek,* January 25, 1993, pp. 34–35; *Mover's Advantage: The Complete Home Moving Guide & Planning Kit,* (Ryder System, October 1990); "At the Echo Awards, It's Not Just Junk Mail Anymore," *Adweek's Marketing Week,* October 29, 1990, pp. 20–21; Albert Schofield, "Alternative Reply Vehicles in Direct-Response Advertising," *Journal of Advertising Research,* September/October 1994, pp. 28–34. For an electronic direct mail example, see "Web Slice," *Brandweek,* May 26, 1997, pp. 22–23; Judy F. Davis, "Maintaining Customer Relationships Through Effective Database Marketing: A Perspective for Small Retailers," *Journal of Marketing Theory & Practice,* Spring 1997, pp. 31–42; Craig A. Conrad, "Response! The Complete Guide to Direct Marketing," *Journal of the Academy of Marketing Science,* Winter 1998, pp. 70–71; Kapil Bawa, "Influences on Consumer Response to Direct Mail Coupons: An Integrative Review," *Psychology & Marketing,* March 1996, pp. 129–56; William J. Carner, "Direct Marketing Through Broadcast Media: TV, Radio, Cable, Infomercials, Home Shopping, and More," *Journal of the Academy of Marketing Science,* Winter 1997, pp. 86–87.

10. Robert E. Thomas and Virginia G. Maurer, "Database Marketing Practice: Protecting Consumer Privacy," *Journal of Public Policy & Marketing,* Spring 1997, pp. 147–55; Marren J. Roy, "Regulation of Automatic Dialing and Announcing Devices Upheld," *Journal of the Academy of Marketing Science,* Summer 1997, pp. 269–70; "An Untapped Market of 11 Million Homes," *The Wall Street Journal,* September 7, 1994, p. B1; "For Charity Groups, 'Tis a Prime Season for Sending Lots of Direct-Mail Appeals," *The Wall Street Journal,* December 23, 1993, p. B1ff.; "Special Report: Direct Response," *Advertising Age,* July 12, 1993, pp. S1–8; Keith Fletcher, Colin Wheeler, and Julia Wright, "Database Marketing: a Channel, a Medium or a Strategic Approach?" *International Journal of Advertising* 10, no. 2 (1991), pp. 117–28; "Devising Mailing Lists for Every Marketer," *The Wall Street Journal,* May 7, 1991, p. B1; Rachel Kaplan, "Video on Demand," *American Demographics,* June 1992, pp. 38–45; Gordon Storholm and Hershey Friedman, "Perceived Common Myths and Unethical Practices Among Direct Marketing Professionals," *Journal of Business Ethics,* December 1989, pp. 975–80. For more on the privacy issue, see George R. Milne and Mary Ellen Gordon, "Direct Mail Privacy-Efficiency Trade-Offs Within an Implied Social Contract Framework," *Journal of Public Policy & Marketing,* Fall 1993, pp. 206–15; "Canadian Privacy Code Shows U.S. the Way," *American Demographics,* September 1993, p. 15.

11. Donna L. Hoffman and Thomas P. Novak, "Marketing in Hypermedia Computer-Mediated Environments: Conceptual Foundations," *Journal of Marketing,* July 1996, pp. 50–68; Gregory C. Mosier and James M. Jackman, "Personal Jurisdiction: Is Internet Presence Enough?" *Journal of the Academy of Marketing Science,* Spring 1998, p. 164; Pierre Berthon, Leyland Pitt, and Richard T. Watson, "Marketing Communication and the World Wide Web," *Business Horizons,* September–October 1996, pp. 24–32.

12. See, for example, "Campaign for Prozac Targets Consumers," *The Wall Street Journal,* July 1, 1997, p. B1ff.; "Branding Fever Strikes among Prescription Drugs," *Advertising Age,* November 22, 1993, p. 12; "New Contraceptive Targets the Pill," *USA Today,* November 15, 1993, p. 3B; "TV Ads Boost Nestle's Infant Formula," *The Wall Street Journal,* March 30, 1993, p. B1ff.; "Drug Ads: A Prescription for Controversy," *Business Week,* January 18, 1993, pp. 58–60; "Kellogg Shifts Strategy to Pull Consumers In," *The Wall Street Journal,* January 22, 1990, p. B1ff.; Steven W. Kopp and Mary J. Sheffet, "The Effect of Direct-to-Consumer Advertising of Prescription Drugs on Retail Gross Margins: Empirical Evidence and Public Policy Implications," *Journal of Public Policy & Marketing,* Fall 1997, pp. 270–76; Mary C. Gilly and Mary Wolfinbarger, "Advertising's Internal Audience," *Journal of Marketing,* January 1998, pp. 69–88; S.A. Erdem and L.J. Harrison-Walker, "Managing Channel Relationships: Toward an Identification of Effective Promotional Strategies in Vertical Marketing Systems," *Journal of Marketing Theory & Practice,* Spring 1997, pp. 80–87; Michael Levy, John Webster, and Roger Kerin, "Formulating Push Marketing Strategies: A Method and Application," *Journal of Marketing,* Winter 1983, pp. 25–34.

13. "Compensation and Expenses," *Sales & Marketing Management,* June 28, 1993, p. 65; "The Cost of Selling Is Going Up," *Boardroom Reports,* December 15, 1991, p. 15; "An In-House Sales School," *Inc.,* May 1991, pp. 85–86.

14. "Word of Mouth Makes Kansas Store a Star," *The Wall Street Journal,* November 7, 1997, p. B1ff.; "Why the Veterinarian Really Recommends that 'Designer' Chow," *The Wall Street Journal,* November 3, 1997, p. A1ff.; "Foot Soldiers Help Sell Street Chic," *USA Today,* June 16, 1997, p. 1Bff.; "Think Big," *The Wall Street Journal,* June 17, 1996, p. R27; Chip Walker, "Word of Mouth," *American Demographics,* July 1995, pp. 38–44; "Reaching Influential Buyers," *Inc.,* May 1991, p. 86–88; Jagdip Singh, "Voice, Exit, and Negative Word-of-Mouth Behaviors: An Investigation Across Three Service Categories," *Journal of the Academy of Marketing Science,* Winter 1990, pp. 1–16; Jeffrey G. Blodgett, Donald H. Granbois, and Rockney G. Walters, "The Effects of Perceived Justice on Complainants' Negative Word-of-Mouth Behavior and Repatronage Intentions," *Journal of Retailing,* Winter 1993, pp. 399–428; Paula Fitzgerald Bone, "Word-of-Mouth Effects on Short-term and Long-term Product Judgments," *Journal of Business Research,* March 1995, pp. 213–24; Bruce MacEvoy, "Change Leaders and the New Media," *American Demographics,* January 1994, pp. 42–49; Dale F. Duhan, Scott D. Johnson, James B. Wilcox, and Gilbert D. Harrell, "Influences on Consumer Use of Word-of-Mouth Recommendation Sources," *Journal of the Academy of Marketing Science,* Fall 1997, pp. 283–95; Russell N. Laczniak, Thomas E. DeCarlo, and Carol M. Motley, "Retail Equity Perceptions and Consumers' Processing of Negative Word-of-Mouth Communication," *Journal of Marketing Theory & Practice,* Fall 1996, pp. 37–48.

15. Meera P. Venkatraman, "Opinion Leaders, Adopters, and Communicative Adopters: A Role Analysis," *Psychology and Marketing,* Spring 1989, pp. 51–68; S. Ram and Hyung-Shik Jung, "Innovativeness in Product Usage: A Comparison of Early Adopters and Early Majority," *Psychology & Marketing,* January/February 1994, pp. 57–68; Robert J. Fisher and Linda L. Price, "An Investigation into the Social Context of Early Adoption Behavior," *Journal of Consumer Research,* December 1992, p. 477; Leisa R. Flynn, Ronald E. Goldsmith, and Jacqueline K. Eastman, "Opinion Leaders and Opinion Seekers: Two New Measurement Scales," *Journal of the Academy of Marketing Science,* Spring 1996, pp. 137–47; Everett M. Rogers and F. Floyd Shoemaker, *Communication of Innovations: A Cross-Cultural Approach* (New York: Free Press, 1971), pp. 203–9.

16. Kusum L. Ailawadi, Paul W. Farris and Mark

E. Parry, "Share and Growth Are Not Good Predictors of the Advertising and Promotion/Sales Ratio," *Journal of Marketing,* January 1994, pp. 86–97.
17. Kim P. Corfman and Donald R. Lehmann, "The Prisoner's Dilemma and the Role of Information in Setting Advertising Budgets," *Journal of Advertising,* June 1994, pp. 35–48; C.L. Hung and Douglas West, "Advertising Budgeting Methods in Canada, the UK and the USA," *International Journal of Advertising* 10, no. 3 (1991), pp. 239–50; Pierre Filiatrault and Jean-Charles Chebat, "How Service Firms Set Their Marketing Budgets," *Industrial Marketing Management,* February 1990, pp. 63–68; James E. Lynch and Graham J. Hooley, "Industrial Advertising Budget Approaches in the U.K.," *Industrial Marketing Management* 18, no. 4 (1989), pp. 265–70; "Beat the Budgeting Blues," *Business Marketing,* July 1989, pp. 48–57; Douglas J. Dalrymple and Hans B. Thorelli, "Sales Force Budgeting," *Business Horizons,* July/August 1984, pp. 31–36; Peter J. Danaher and Roland T. Rust, "Determining the Optimal Level of Media Spending," *Journal of Advertising Research,* January/February 1994, pp. 28–34.

Chapter 15

1. "The Seoul Answer to Selling," *Going Global (supplement to Inc.,* March 1994; "AIG Sells Insurance in Shanghai, Testing Service Firms' Role," *The Wall Street Journal,* July 21, 1993, p. A1ff.; "Hungarians Seeking to Find a New Way Find Instead Amway," *The Wall Street Journal,* January 15, 1993, p. A1ff.; "The Secret to Northern's Japanese Success: When in Tokyo . . .," *Business Week,* July 27, 1992, p. 57; "U.S. Companies in China Find Patience, Persistence and Salesmanship Pay Off," *The Wall Street Journal,* April 3, 1992, p. B1ff.; Paul A. Herbig and Hugh E. Kramer, "Do's and Don'ts of Cross-Cultural Negotiations," *Industrial Marketing Management,* November 1992, pp. 287–98; Alan J. Dubinsky et al., "Differences in Motivational Perceptions among U.S., Japanese, and Korean Sales Personnel," *Journal of Business Research,* June 1994, pp. 175–86; Carl R. Ruthstrom and Ken Matejka, "The Meanings of 'YES' in the Far East," *Industrial Marketing Management,* August 1990, pp. 191–92.
2. Joel R. Evans, Barry Berman, and William J. Wellington, *Marketing Essentials,* (Scarborough Ont.: Prentice Hall Canada, 1998) p. 326.
3. Tom Richman, "Seducing the Customer: Dale Ballard's Perfect Selling Machine," *Inc.,* April, 1988, pp. 96–104; *1987 Annual Report,* Ballard Medical Products.
4. Thomas R. Wotruba, "The Transformation of Industrial Selling: Causes and Consequences," *Industrial Marketing Management,* September 1996, pp. 327–38; William M. Strahle, Rosann L. Spiro, and Frank Acito, "Marketing and Sales: Strategic Alignment and Functional Implementation," *Journal of Personal Selling & Sales Management,* Winter 1996, pp. 1–20; Paul Boughton, "Winning Customers, Building Accounts: Some Do It Better Than Others," *Journal of the Academy of Marketing Science,* Spring 1996, pp. 175–76; Jerome A. Colletti and Lawrence B. Chonko, "Change Management Initiatives: Moving Sales Organizations From Obsolescence to High Performance," *Journal of Personal Selling & Sales Management,* Spring 1997, pp. 1–30; Marvin A. Jolson, "Broadening the Scope of Relationship Selling," *Journal of Personal Selling & Sales Management,* Fall 1997, pp. 75–88; Douglas M. Lambert, Howard Marmorstein, and Arun Sharma, "Industrial Salespeople as a Source of Market Information," *Industrial Marketing Management,* May 1990, pp. 141–48.
5. Mark A. Moon and Susan F. Gupta, "Examining the Formation of Selling Centers: A Conceptual Framework," *Journal of Personal Selling & Sales Management,* Spring 1997, pp. 31–41; S. Joe Puri and Pradeep Korgaonkar, "Couple the Buying and Selling Teams," *Industrial Marketing Management* 20, no. 4 (1991), pp. 311–18; "P&G Rolls Out Retailer Sales Teams," *Advertising Age,* May 21, 1990, p. 18.
6. Dan C. Weilbaker and William A. Weeks, "The Evolution of National Account Management: A Literature Perspective," *Journal of Personal Selling & Sales Management,* Fall 1997, pp. 49–59; C.J. Lambe and Robert E. Spekman, "National Account Management: Large Account Selling or Buyer-Supplier Alliance?" *Journal of Personal Selling & Sales Management,* Fall 1997, pp. 61–74; Catherine Pardo, "Key Account Management in the Business to Business Field: The Key Account's Point of View," *Journal of Personal Selling & Sales Management,* Fall 1997, pp. 17–26; Sanjit Sengupta, Robert E. Krapfel, and Michael A. Pusateri, "Switching Costs in Key Account Relationships," *Journal of Personal Selling & Sales Management,* Fall 1997, pp. 9–16; Paul Dishman and Philip S. Nitse, "National Accounts Revisited: New Lessons From Recent Investigations," *Industrial Marketing Management,* January 1998, pp. 1–9; "Telephone Sales Reps Do Unrewarding Jobs that Few Can Abide," *The Wall Street Journal,* September 9, 1993, p. A1ff.; Brett A. Boyle, "The Importance of the Industrial Inside Sales Force: A Case Study," *Industrial Marketing Management,* September 1996, pp. 339–48; "How to Unite Field and Phone Sales," *Inc.,* July 1992, p. 115; "Telemarketers Take Root in the Country," *The Wall Street Journal,* February 2, 1989, p. B1; "FCC Adopts Rules to Curb Telemarketing," *The Wall Street Journal,* September 18, 1992, p. B1; "Congress' 'Cure' for Junk Calls Faces a Skeptical FCC," *The Wall Street Journal,* May 19, 1992, B6.
7. "How to Remake Your Sales Force," *Fortune,* May 4, 1992, pp. 98–103; "What Flexible Workers Can Do," *Fortune,* February 13, 1989, pp. 62–64; "Apparel Makers Play Bigger Part on Sales Floor," *The Wall Street Journal,* March 2, 1988, p. 31; Ravipreet S. Sohi, Daniel C. Smith, and Neil M. Ford, "How Does Sharing a Sales Force Between Multiple Divisions Affect Salespeople?" *Journal of the Academy of Marketing Science,* Summer 1996, pp. 195–207; David W. Cravens and Raymond W. LaForge, "Salesforce Deployment Analysis," *Industrial Marketing Management,* July 1983, pp. 179–92; Michael S. Herschel, "Effective Sales Territory Development," *Journal of Marketing,* April 1977, pp. 39–43.
8. Available from World Wide Web: <http://www.achievement.com/sales>; Ellen B. Pullins, Leslie M. Fine, and Wendy L. Warren, "Identifying Peer Mentors in the Sales Force: An Exploratory Investigation of Willingness and Ability," *Journal of the Academy of Marketing Science,* Spring 1996, pp. 125–36; Alan J. Dubinsky, "Some Assumptions About the Effectiveness of Sales Training," *Journal of Personal Selling & Sales Management,* Summer 1996, pp. 67–76; Earl D. Honeycutt, Ashraf M. Attia, and Angela R. D. Auria, "Sales Certification Programs," *Journal of Personal Selling & Sales Management,* Summer 1996, pp. 59–65; "Systematizing Salesperson Selection," *Sales and Marketing Management,* February 1992, pp. 65–68; "The Faxable International Sales-Rep Application," *Inc.,* November 1993, pp. 95–97; Patrick L. Schul and Brent M. Wren, "The Emerging Role of Women in Industrial Selling: A Decade of Change," *Journal of Marketing,* July 1992, pp. 38–54; William A. Weeks and Carl G. Stevens, "National Account Management Sales Training and Directions for Improvement: A Focus on Skills/Abilities," *Industrial Marketing Management,* September 1997, pp. 423–31; Earl D. Honeycutt, Jr., John B. Ford, and John F. Tanner, Jr., "Who Trains Salespeople? The Role of Sales Trainers and Sales Managers," *Industrial Marketing Management,* February 1994, pp. 65–70; Jeffrey K. Sager, "Recruiting and Retaining Committed Salespeople," *Industrial Marketing Management* 20, no. 2 (1991), pp. 99–104; S. Joe Puri, "Where Industrial Sales Training is Weak," *Industrial Marketing Management,* May 1993, pp. 101–8.
9. Douglas M. Lambert, Arun Sharma, and Michael Levy, "What Information Can Relationship Marketers Obtain From Customer Evaluations of Salespeople?" *Industrial Marketing Management,* March 1997, pp. 177–87; Erin Anderson and Thomas S. Robertson, "Inducing Multiline Salespeople to Adopt House Brands," *Journal of Marketing,* April 1995, pp. 16–31; Stephen B. Knouse and David Strutton, "Molding a Total Quality Salesforce Through Managing Empowerment, Evaluation, and Reward and Recognition Processes," *Journal of Marketing Theory & Practice,* Summer 1996, pp. 24–35; Ajay K. Kolhi and Bernard J. Jaworksi, "The Influence of Coworker Feedback on Salespeople," *Journal of Marketing,* October 1994, pp. 82–94; "Fire Up Your Sales Force," *Business Marketing,* July 1990, pp. 52–55; William L. Cron, Alan J. Dubinsky, and Ronald E. Michaels, "The Influence of Career Stages on Components of Salesperson Motivation," *Journal of Marketing,* January 1988, pp. 78–92.
10. Rene Y. Darmon, "Selecting Appropriate Sales Quota Plan Structures and Quota-Setting Procedures," *Journal of Personal Selling & Sales Management,* Winter 1997, pp. 1–16; Thomas E. Tice, "Managing Compensation Caps in Key Accounts," *Journal of Personal Selling & Sales Management,* Fall 1997, pp. 41–47; Kissan Joseph and Manohar U. Kalwani, "The Role of Bonus Pay in Salesforce Compensation Plans," *Industrial Marketing Management,* March 1998, pp. 147–59; Russell Abratt and Michael R. Smythe, "A Survey of Sales Incentive Programs," *Industrial Marketing Management,* August 1989, pp. 209–14; "Incentive Pay Isn't Good for Your Company," *Inc.,* September 1994, pp. 23–24; "The Few, the True, the Blue," *Business Week,* May 30, 1994, pp. 124–26; Arun Sharma, "Customer Satisfaction-Based Incentive Systems: Some Managerial and Salesperson Considerations," *Journal of Personal Selling & Sales Management,* Spring 1997, pp. 61–70; William Strahle and Rosann L. Spiro, "Linking Market Share Strategies to Salesforce Objectives, Activities, and Compensation Policies," *Journal of Personal Selling and Sales Management,* August 1986, pp. 11–18.
11. "Companies Sold on the Latest Technology for the Sales Force," *Chicago Tribune,* November 8, 1992, Sect. 19, p. 5; "New Software Is Helping Reps Fill Custom Orders without Glitches," *The Wall Street Journal,* August 11, 1992, p. B6; "Salespeople on Road Use Laptops to Keep in Touch," *The Wall Street Journal,* April 25, 1991, p. B1.
12. Richard L. Oliver and Erin Anderson, "An Empirical Test of the Consequences of Behavior- and Outcome-Based Sales Control Systems," *Journal of Marketing,* October 1994, pp. 53–67; Susan K. DelVecchio, "The Salesperson's Operating Freedom: A Matter of Perception," *Industrial Marketing Management,* January 1998, pp. 31–40; Vlasis Stathakopoulos, "Sales Force Control: A Synthesis of Three Theories," *Journal of Personal Selling & Sales Management,* Spring 1996, pp. 1–12; Gregory A. Rich, "The Constructs of Sales Coaching: Supervisory Feedback, Role Modeling and Trust," *Journal of Personal Selling & Sales Management,* Winter 1998, pp. 53–63; Goutam N. Challagalla and Tasadduq A. Shervani, "Dimensions and Types of Supervisory Control: Effects on Salesperson Performance and Satisfaction," *Journal of Marketing,* January 1996, pp. 89–105; Steven P. Brown and Robert A. Peterson, "The Effect of Effort on Sales Performance and Job Satisfaction," *Journal of Marketing,* April 1994, pp. 70–80; Paul A. Dion, Debbie Easterling, and Raj Javalgi, "Women in the Business-to-Business Salesforce: Some Differences in Performance Factors," *Industrial Marketing Management,* September 1997, pp. 447–57;

Frederick A. Russ, Kevin M. McNeilly, and James M. Comer, "Leadership, Decision Making and Performance of Sales Managers: A Multi-Level Approach," *Journal of Personal Selling & Sales Management,* Summer 1996, pp. 1–15; Jhinuk Chowdhury, "The Motivational Impact of Sales Quotas on Effort," *Journal of Marketing Research,* February 1993, pp. 28–41; Alan J. Dubinsky, Francis J. Yammarino, and Marvin A. Jolson, "Closeness of Supervision and Salesperson Work Outcomes: An Alternate Perspective," *Journal of Business Research,* March 1994, pp. 225–38; David W. Cravens et al., "Behavior-Based and Outcome-Based Salesforce Control Systems," *Journal of Marketing,* October 1993, pp. 47–59; Daniel A. Sauers, James B. Hunt, and Ken Bass, "Behavioral Self-Management as a Supplement to External Sales Force Controls," *Journal of Personal Selling and Sales Management,* Summer 1990, pp. 17–28; Douglas N. Behrman and William D. Perreault, Jr., "A Role Stress Model of the Performance and Satisfaction of Industrial Salespersons," *Journal of Marketing,* Fall 1984, pp. 9–21; Richard T. Hise and Edward L. Reid, "Improving the Performance of the Industrial Sales Force in the 1990s," *Industrial Marketing Management,* October 1994, pp. 273–80.

13. William C. Moncrief, et al., "Examining the Roles of Telemarketing in Selling Strategy," *Journal of Personal Selling and Sales Management,* Fall 1989, pp. 1–12; J. David Lichtenthal, Saameer Sikri, and Karl Folk, "Teleprospecting: An Approach for Qualifying Accounts," *Industrial Marketing Management,* February 1989, pp. 11–18.

14. "When Should I Give Up on a Sales Prospect?" *Inc.,* May 1998, p. 129; "Downloading Their Dream Cars," *Business Week,* March 9, 1998, pp. 93–94; "The New Wave of Sales Automation," *Business Marketing,* June 1991, pp. 12–16; L. Brent Manssen, "Using PCs to Automate and Innovate Marketing Activities," *Industrial Marketing Management,* August 1990, pp. 209–14; Doris C. Van Doren and Thomas A. Stickney, "How to Develop a Database for Sales Leads," *Industrial Marketing Management,* August 1990, pp. 201–8.

15. For more on sales presentation approaches, see "The 60-Second Sales Pitch," *Inc.,* October 1994, pp. 87–89; Jon M. Hawes, James T. Strong, and Bernard S. Winick, "Do Closing Techniques Diminish Prospect Trust?" *Industrial Marketing Management,* September 1996, pp. 349–60; Stephen B. Castleberry and C. David Shepherd, "Effective Interpersonal Listening and Personal Selling," *Journal of Personal Selling & Sales Management,* Winter 1993, pp. 35–50; Morgan P. Miles, Danny R. Arnold, and Henry W. Nash, "Adaptive Communication: The Adaption of the Seller's Interpersonal Style to the Stage of the Dyad's Relationship and the Buyer's Communication Style," *Journal of Personal Selling and Sales Management,* Winter 1990, pp. 21–28; Harish Sujan, Barton A. Weitz, and Nirmalya Kumar, "Learning Orientation, Working Smart, and Effective Selling," *Journal of Marketing,* July 1994, pp. 39–52.

16. For more on selling tactics, see "In Marketing of Drugs, Genentech Tests Limits of What Is Acceptable," *The Wall Street Journal,* January 10, 1995, p. A1ff.; "Pharmacy Chain's Successful Sales Pitch Dismays Some Doctors and Drug Firms," *The Wall Street Journal,* February 26, 1993, p. B1ff. "Did Sears Take Other Customers for a Ride?" *Business Week,* August 3, 1992, pp. 24–25. See also Bulent Menguc, "Organizational Consequences, Marketing Ethics and Salesforce Supervision: Further Empirical Evidence," *Journal of Business Ethics,* March 1998, pp. 333–52; David Strutton, J.B.I. Hamilton, and James R. Lumpkin, "An Essay on When to Fully Disclose in Sales Relationships: Applying Two Practical Guidelines for Addressing Truth-Telling Problems," *Journal of Business Ethics,* April 1997, pp. 545–60; Lawrence B. Chonko, John F. Tanner, and William A. Weeks, "Ethics in Salesperson Decision Making: A Synthesis of Research Approaches and an Extension of the Scenario Method," *Journal of Personal Selling & Sales Management,* Winter 1996, pp. 35–52; Alan J. Dubinsky, Marvin A. Jolson, Masaaki Kotabe, and Chae Un Lim, "A Cross-National Investigation of Industrial Salespeople's Ethical Perceptions," *Journal of International Business Studies,* Winter 1991, pp. 651–70.

Chapter 16

1. "Special Report: U.S. Multinationals," *Ad Age International,* January 1998, pp. 17–26; "Colgate-Palmolive Is Really Cleaning Up in Poland," *Business Week,* March 15, 1993, pp. 54–56; Charles R. Taylor, Gordon E. Miracle, and R. D. Wilson, "The Impact of Information Level on the Effectiveness of U.S. and Korean Television Commercials," *Journal of Advertising,* Spring 1997, pp. 1–18; Ann M. Barry, "Advertising and Culture: Theoretical Perspectives," *Journal of the Academy of Marketing Science,* Winter 1998, pp. 67–68; Siew M. Leong, Sween H. Ang, and Leng L. Tham, "Increasing Brand Name Recall in Print Advertising Among Asian Consumers," *Journal of Advertising,* Summer 1996, pp. 65–81; Ronald E. Taylor, Mariea G. Hoy, and Eric Haley, "How French Advertising Professionals Develop Creative Strategy," *Journal of Advertising,* Spring 1996, pp. 1–14; Nan Zhou and Mervin Y. T. Chen, "A Content Analysis of Men and Women in Canadian Consumer Magazine Advertising: Today's Portrayal, Yesterday's Image?" *Journal of Business Ethics,* April 1997, pp. 485–95; Johny K. Johansson, "The Sense of 'Nonsense': Japanese TV Advertising," *Journal of Advertising,* March 1994, pp. 17–26; Yong Zhang and Betsy D. Gelb, "Matching Advertising Appeals to Culture: The Influence of Products' Use Conditions," *Journal of Advertising,* Fall 1996, pp. 29–46; John L. Graham, Michael A. Kamins and Djoko S. Oetomo, "Content Analysis of German and Japanese Advertising in Print Media from Indonesia, Spain, and the United States," *Journal of Advertising,* June 1993, pp. 5–16; Bob D. Cutler and Rajshekhar G. Javalgi, "A Cross-Cultural Analysis of the Visual Components of Print Advertising: The United States and the European Community," *Journal of Advertising Research,* January/February 1992, p. 71; Terence Nevett, "Differences Between American and British Television Advertising: Explanations and Implications," *Journal of Advertising,* December 1992, pp. 61–72; Bob D. Cutler and Rajshekhar G. Javalgi, "Comparison of Business-to-Business Advertising: The United States and the United Kingdom," *Industrial Marketing Management,* April 1994, pp. 117–24.

2. Estimate provided by the Canadian Advertising Advisory Board.

3. "Survey: Comparative Ads Can Dent Car's Credibility," *Advertising Age,* May 4, 1998, p. 26; "Rivals Take the Gloves Off as Taste-Test Wars Heat Up," *The Wall Street Journal,* March 30, 1998, p. B10; "Industry Panel Refers FedEx Case to FTC," *The Wall Street Journal,* April 11, 1997, p. B6; Diana L. Haytko, "Great Advertising Campaigns: Goals and Accomplishments," *Journal of Marketing,* April 1995, pp. 113–15; Carolyn Tripp, "Services Advertising: An Overview and Summary of Research, 1980-1995," *Journal of Advertising,* Winter 1997, pp. 21–38; Dhruv Grewal, Sukumar Kavanoor, Edward F. Fern, Carolyn Costley, and James Barnes, "Comparative Versus Noncomparative Advertising: A Meta-Analysis," *Journal of Marketing,* October 1997, pp. 1–15; Marla R. Stafford and Ellen Day, "Retail Services Advertising: The Effects of Appeal, Medium, and Service," *Journal of Advertising,* Spring 1995, pp. 57–71.

4. For other examples of comparative advertising, see "Allergy Drugs Wage a Bitter War of the Noses," *The Wall Street Journal,* May 23, 1996, p. B1ff.; "New Drug Ads Give Doctors Heartburn," *The Wall Street Journal,* April 25, 1996, p. B9; "Bitter Ads to Swallow," *Time,* April 1, 1996, pp. 48–49; "More Heartburn Relief Unsettles Market," *The Wall Street Journal,* February 7, 1996, p. B6; "New Ammo for Comparative Ads," *Advertising Age,* February 14, 1994, p. 26; Thomas E. Barry, "Comparative Advertising: What Have We Learned in Two Decades?," *Journal of Advertising Research,* March/April 1993, pp. 19–29; Naveen Donthu, "Comparative Advertising Intensity," *Journal of Advertising Research,* November/December 1992, pp. 53–58.

5. "Brawl Erupts Over Do-Good Advertising," *The Wall Street Journal,* September 29, 1997, p. B1ff.; "Cause and Effects Marketing," *Brandweek,* April 22, 1996, pp. 38–40; "Are Good Causes Good Marketing?" *Business Week,* March 21, 1994, pp. 64–66; "Chemical Firms Press Campaigns to Dispel Their 'Bad Guy' Image," *The Wall Street Journal,* September 20, 1988, p. 1ff.; "Spiffing up the Corporate Image," *Fortune,* July 21, 1986, pp. 68–72; Minette E. Drumwright, "Company Advertising With a Social Dimension: The Role of Noneconomic Criteria," *Journal of Marketing,* October 1996, pp. 71–87; Eric Haley, "Exploring the Construct of Organization As Source: Consumer's Understandings of Organizational Sponsorship of Advocacy Advertising," *Journal of Advertising,* Summer 1996, pp. 19–35; John K. Ross III, Larry T. Patterson, and Mary Ann Stutts, "Consumer Perceptions of Organizations That Use Cause-Related Marketing," *Journal of the Academy of Marketing Science,* Winter 1992, pp. 93–98.

6. "Store Owners Rip into Benetton," *Advertising Age,* February 6, 1995, p. 1; "Benetton, German Retailers Squabble," *Advertising Age,* February 6, 1995, p. 46; "Benetton Brouhaha," *Advertising Age,* February 17, 1992, p. 62.
"Intel Will Help Pay Costs of PC Makers' Web Ads," *USA Today,* August 5, 1997, p. 1B; "Changes to Intel's Co-Op Program Could Boost Web Advertising 40%," *The Wall Street Journal,* August 5, 1997, p. B7; "Intel Co-op Could Bring $150 Million to the Web," *Advertising Age,* July 28, 1997, p. 16; "How Strong Is the Case Against Intel?" *Business Week,* June 22, 1998, p. 42; "Intel Proposal Is Angering Web Publishers," *The Wall Street Journal,* January 16, 1998, p. B1ff.; "Trade Bait," *Brandweek,* December 1, 1997, pp. 36–44; "Intel's Amazing Profit Machine," *Fortune,* February 17, 1997, pp. 60–72.

7. For more on co-op ads, see "Retailers Open Doors Wide for Co-op," *Advertising Age,* August 1, 1994, p. 30; John P. Murry and Jan B. Heide, "Managing Promotion Program Participation Within Manufacturer-Retailer Relationships," *Journal of Marketing,* January 1998, pp. 58–68; For more on joint promotions, see "Joint Marketing with Retailers Spreads," *The Wall Street Journal,* October 24, 1996, p. B6; "Joint Promotions Spawn Data Swap," *Advertising Age,* October 7, 1991, p. 44; "H&R Block, Excedrin Discover Joint Promotions Can Be Painless," *The Wall Street Journal,* February 28, 1991, p. B3.

8. *Standard Rate and Data,* 1997. For more on the Yellow Pages medium, see "The Truth About Yellow Pages: Making Them Work for You," *Journal of the Academy of Marketing Science,* Winter 1998, pp. 71–72; " 'Sleeping Giant,' the Yellow Pages, Tries to Waken Madison Avenue," *The Wall Street Journal,* August 19, 1993, p. B6. For more on videotapes medium, see "Are Spots on Home Video Badvertising?" *Brandweek,* January 29, 1996, p. 40; "Special Report: Direct Marketing," *Advertising Age,* October 28, 1996, pp. S1–6; "Direct Marketers Press Fast-Forward on Videotape Use," *The Wall Street Journal,* October 31, 1994, p. B8B. For more on the outdoor medium, see "Dynamic Year, New Prosperity," *Advertising Age,* July 21, 1997; Charles R. Taylor and John C. Taylor, "Regulatory Issues in Outdoor Advertising: A Content Analysis of Billboards," *Journal of Public Policy & Marketing,* Spring 1994, pp. 97–107; "More Firms Turn to Skies as New Medium," *The Wall Street Journal,* January 5, 1995, p. B6; "Special Report: Out-of-Home," *Advertising Age,* August 1, 1994, pp. 27–30. For more on the radio medium, see "Radio's New Spin on an Oldie: Pay-for-Play," *The*

Wall Street Journal, March 16, 1998, p. B1ff.; "Radio Ad Sales Rise amid Consolidation," *The Wall Street Journal,* June 20, 1997, p. B7; Darryl W. Miller and Lawrence J. Marks, "Mental Imagery and Sound Effects in Radio Commercials," *Journal of Advertising,* December 1992, pp. 83–94; "Special Report: Radio," *Advertising Age,* September 14, 1992, pp. 41–43. For more on the newspaper medium, see "Newspapers," *Advertising Age,* April 20, 1998, pp. S1–22; "Newspapers," *Advertising Age,* April 28, 1997, pp. S1–15; Lawrence C. Soley and Robert L. Craig, "Advertising Pressures on Newspapers: A Survey," *Journal of Advertising,* December 1992, pp. 1–10; "Bound to the Printed Word," *Newsweek,* June 20, 1994, pp. 52–53; Srini S. Srinivasan, Robert P. Leone, and Francis J. Mulhern, "The Advertising Exposure Effect of Free Standing Inserts," *Journal of Advertising,* Spring 1995, pp. 29–40; Karen W. King, Leonard N. Reid, and Margaret Morrison, "Large-Agency Media Specialists' Opinions on Newspaper Advertising for National Accounts," *Journal of Advertising,* Summer 1997, pp. 1–17. For more on the magazine medium, see "Magazines," *Advertising Age,* October 27, 1997, pp. S1–32; "Magazines," *Advertising Age,* October 14, 1996, pp. S1–14. For more on the television and cable medium, see "Cable TV," *Advertising Age,* April 13, 1998, pp. S1–24; "TV's Upfront," *Advertising Age,* May 12, 1997, pp. S1–36; "Infomercial '97" (Special Supplement), *Adweek,* 1997. See also Jean L. Rogers, "Mail Advertising and Consumer Behavior," *Psychology & Marketing,* March 1996, pp. 211–33; Elizabeth C. Hirschman and Craig J. Thompson, "Why Media Matter: Toward a Richer Understanding of Consumers' Relationships With Advertising and Mass Media," *Journal of Advertising,* Spring 1997, pp. 43–60; Richard J. Fox and Gary L. Geissler, "Crisis in Advertising?" *Journal of Advertising,* December 1994, pp. 79–84; Roland T. Rust and Richard W. Oliver, "The Death of Advertising," *Journal of Advertising,* December 1994, pp. 71–77.

9. "U.S. Admakers Cover It Up; Others Don't Give a Fig Leaf," *USA Today,* June 27, 1997, p. 1Bff.; "Mars Inc. Dips into Sex to Lure Consumers into Arms of M&M's," *The Wall Street Journal,* January 21, 1997, p. B9; "Underwear Ads Caught in Bind over Sex Appeal," *Advertising Age,* July 8, 1996, p. 27; "No Sexy Sales Ads, Please—We're Brits and Swedes," *Fortune,* October 21, 1991, p. 13.

10. "Looking for Mr. Plumber," *MediaWeek,* June 27, 1994, p. 7ff.; "Those Really Big Shows Are Often Disappointing to Those Who Advertise," *The Wall Street Journal,* June 14, 1994, p. B1ff; "Yech and Yada in 'Seinfeld' Ads," *Advertising Age,* May 18, 1998, p. 63; " 'Seinfeld' Finale Advertisers Put on Game Faces," *USA Today,* April 29, 1998, p. 1B; "NBC May Get Only $1.5 Million for Ad Spots on 'Seinfeld' Finale," *The Wall Street Journal,* March 4, 1998, p. B6; "Gardenburger's Ad May Help Its Rival," *The Wall Street Journal,* May 20, 1998, p. B8; "Gardenburger Bets the (Soybean) Farm on the Last 'Seinfeld,' " *The Wall Street Journal,* April 13, 1998, p. A1ff.

11. "ATMs Are Latest Place-Based Medium," *Advertising Age,* November 24, 1997, p. 1ff.; "Bright Idea Has Business Looking Up for Ad Blimps," *The Wall Street Journal,* October 14, 1997, p. B1ff.; "Saturday Night at the Ads," *Business Week,* September 15, 1997, pp. 63–64; "Speed Sells," *Business Week,* August 11, 1997, pp. 86–90; "Firm Gets A Handle on Customers . . . Even as They Shop," *The Wall Street Journal,* February 5, 1997, p. B4; "Jocks Don Pay Apparel," *USA Today,* January 3, 1997, p. 1Bff.; "New Marketing Spin: the PR 'Experience,' " *Advertising Age,* August 5, 1996, p. 33; "The New Hucksterism," *Business Week,* July 1, 1996, pp. 76–84; "New Breed of Sponsors Race to NASCAR," *USA Today,* April 5, 1996, p. 1Bff.; "The Writing on the Bathroom Wall," *Business Week,* October 31, 1994, p. 8; "Technology Has Travelers under Seige," *USA Today,* October 14, 1994, p. 1Bff.; Alan J. Greco and Linda E. Swayne, "Sales Response of Elderly Consumers to Point-of-Purchase Advertising," *Journal of Advertising Research,* September/October 1992, pp. 43–53.

12. "Internet Ad Sales Approach $1 Billion," *Advertising Age,* April 6, 1998, pp. 32–34; "The Internet Is Mr. Case's Neighborhood," *Fortune,* March 30, 1998, pp. 69–80; "On-Line Ads Beginning to Click," *USA Today,* February 24, 1998, p. 6B; "The New Ratings Game," *Business Week,* April 27, 1998, pp. 73–78; "Online Media Strategies for Advertising," (Special Supplement) *Advertising Age,* Spring 1998; "Web Ads Start to Click," *Business Week,* October 6, 1997, pp. 128–38; "Web Sites Say: Your Ad Sells or It's on Us," *The Wall Street Journal,* June 27, 1997, p. B9; "How Net Is Becoming More Like Television to Draw Advertisers," *The Wall Street Journal,* December 13, 1996, p. A1ff.; "Wired Up or Beamed In, It's Coming Cheaper, Faster," *USA Today,* June 11, 1996, p. 1Bff.; "Don't Surf to Us, We'll Surf to You," *Business Week,* September 9, 1996, pp. 108–109; "Old-Fashioned Ethic of Separating Ads Is Lost in Cyberspace," *The Wall Street Journal,* July 25, 1996, p. B1; "Purists Beware: Ads Have Invaded On-Line Services," *The Wall Street Journal,* August 23, 1994, p. B1ff.; "Advertisers Anticipate Interactive Media as Ingenious Means to Court Consumers," *The Wall Street Journal,* August 17, 1994, p. B1ff.; Richard T. Watson, Sigmund Akselsen, and Leyland F. Pitt, "Attractors: Building Mountains in the Flat Landscape of the World Wide Web," *California Management Review,* Winter 1998, pp. 36–56; W. W. Kassaye, "Global Advertising and the World Wide Web," *Business Horizons,* May–June 1997, pp. 33–42.

13. "NBA Bravely Plans for Post-Jordan Era," *The Wall Street Journal,* February 6, 1998, p. B1ff.; "Falling Stars," *Brandweek,* February 2, 1998, pp. 22–27; "Honda Hopes Mr. Clean Helps to Make Its Image Sparkle," *The Wall Street Journal,* September 26, 1997, p. B20; "Madison Avenue Picks an Average Joe as '90s Pitchman," *The Wall Street Journal,* September 11, 1996, p. B1ff.; "Gap Ad Shows Perils of Using Pols in Pitches," *The Wall Street Journal,* April 9, 1996, p. B1ff.; Erik L. Olson, "How Magazine Articles Portrayed Advertising From 1900 to 1940," *Journal of Advertising,* Fall 1995, pp. 41–54; Audhesh K. Paswan, "Marketing to the Mind: Right Brain Strategies for Advertising and Marketing," *Journal of the Academy of Marketing Science,* Winter 1998, pp. 68–69; Avery M. Abernethy and George R. Franke, "The Information Content of Advertising: A Meta-Analysis," *Journal of Advertising,* Summer 1996, pp. 1–17; James H. Leigh, "The Use of Figures of Speech in Print Ad Headlines," *Journal of Advertising,* June 1994, pp. 17–33; Bruce A. Huhmann and Timothy P. Brotherton, "A Content Analysis of Guilt Appeals in Popular Magazine Advertisements," *Journal of Advertising,* Summer 1997, pp. 35–45; Margaret F. Callcott and Wei-Na Lee, "A Content Analysis of Animation and Animated Spokes-Characters in Television Commercials," *Journal of Advertising,* December 1994, pp. 1–12; Alan J. Bush and Victoria D. Bush, "The Narrative Paradigm As a Perspective for Improving Ethical Evaluations of Advertisements," *Journal of Advertising,* September 1994, pp. 31–41; L. W. Turley and Scott W. Kelley, "A Comparison of Advertising Content: Business to Business Versus Consumer Services," *Journal of Advertising,* Winter 1997, pp. 39–48; Eleonora Curlo and Robert Chamblee, "Ad Processing and Persuasion: The Role of Brand Identification," *Psychology & Marketing,* May 1998, pp. 279–99; V. C. Broach, Thomas J. Page, and R. D. Wilson, "Television Programming and Its Influence on Viewers' Perceptions of Commercials: The Role of Program Arousal and Pleasantness," *Journal of Advertising,* Winter 1995, pp. 45–54; Laurie A. Babin and Alvin C. Burns, "Effects of Print Ad Pictures and Copy Containing Instructions to Imagine on Mental Imagery That Mediates Attitudes," *Journal of Advertising,* Fall 1997, pp. 33–44; Noel M. Murray and Sandra B. Murray, "Music and Lyrics in Commercials: A Cross-Cultural Comparison Between Commercials Run in the Dominican Republic and in the United States," *Journal of Advertising,* Summer 1996, pp. 51–63; Barbara B. Stern, "Advertising Intimacy: Relationship Marketing and the Services Consumer," *Journal of Advertising,* Winter 1997, pp. 7–19; Baba Shiv, Julie A. Edell, and John W. Payne, "Factors Affecting the Impact of Negatively and Positively Framed Ad Messages," *Journal of Consumer Research,* December 1997, pp. 285–94; Harlan E. Spotts, Marc G. Weinberger, and Amy L. Parsons, "Assessing the Use and Impact of Humor on Advertising Effectiveness: A Contingency Approach," *Journal of Advertising,* Fall 1997, pp. 17–32; Martha Rogers and Kirk H. Smith, "Public Perceptions of Subliminal Advertising: Why Practitioners Shouldn't Ignore This Issue," *Journal of Advertising Research,* March/April 1993, pp. 10–18; Kathryn T. Theus, "Subliminal Advertising and the Psychology of Processing Unconscious Stimuli: A Review of Research," *Psychology & Marketing,* May/June 1994, pp. 271–90; Carolyn A. Lin, "Cultural Differences in Message Strategies: A Comparison between American and Japanese TV Commercials," *Journal of Advertising Research,* July/August 1993, pp. 40–49; Robert Chamblee and Dennis M. Sandler, "Business-to-Business Advertising: Which Layout Style Works Best?," *Journal of Advertising Research,* November/December 1992, pp. 39–46.

14. "McCann Finds Global a Tough Sell in Japan," *The Wall Street Journal,* June 19, 1997, p. B2; "Microsoft Global Image Campaign Is Dizzying without a Hard Sell," *The Wall Street Journal,* November 11, 1994, p. B7; Fred Zandpour et al., "Global Reach and Local Touch: Achieving Cultural Fitness in TV Advertising," *Journal of Advertising Research,* September/October 1994, pp. 35–63; Michael G. Harvey, "A Model to Determine Standardization of the Advertising Process in International Markets," *Journal of Advertising Research,* July/August 1993, pp. 57–64; Barbara Mueller, "Standardization vs. Specialization: An Examination of Westernization in Japanese Advertising," *Journal of Advertising Research,* January/February 1992, pp. 15–24; Dana L. Alden, Wayne D. Hoyer, and Chol Lee, "Identifying Global and Culture-Specific Dimensions of Humor in Advertising: A Multinational Analysis," *Journal of Marketing,* April 1993, pp. 64–75; "International Special Report: Global Media," *Advertising Age International,* July 18, 1994, pp. I11–16; Ali Kanso, "International Advertising Strategies: Global Commitment to Local Vision," *Journal of Advertising Research,* January/February 1992, pp. 10–14; "Professor Stands by His Theory on Global Advertising," *The Wall Street Journal,* October 13, 1992, p. B10; Theodore Levitt, "The Globalization of Markets," *Harvard Business Review,* May–June 1983, pp. 92–102; Kamran Kashani, "Beware the Pitfalls of Global Marketing," *Harvard Business Review,* September/October 1989, pp. 91–98; Ludmilla G. Wells, "Western Concepts, Russian Perspectives: Meanings of Advertising in the Former Soviet Union," *Journal of Advertising,* March 1994, pp. 83–95; William L. Shanklin and David A. Griffith, "Crafting Strategies for Global Marketing in the New Millennium," *Business Horizons,* September-October 1996, pp. 11–16.

15. "Regional Agency Rankings," *Advertising Age,* June 8, 1998, pp. 17–22; "The Best Agencies," *Advertising Age,* April 30, 1998, pp. S1–22; "Agency Report," *Advertising Age,* April 27, 1998, pp. S1–42; "World Brands," *Advertising Age International,* September 1997, pp. I1–11; "Superbrands '98" (Special Issue) *Brandweek,* October 20, 1997; "Top 25 Global Ad Organizations," *Advertising Age,* May 12, 1997, pp. 52–53; M. Louise Ripley, "Why Industrial Advertising Is Often Done in House," *Industrial*

Marketing Management, November 1992, pp. 331–34; Murray Young and Charles Steilen, "Strategy-Based Advertising Agency Selection: An Alternative to 'Spec' Presentations," *Business Horizons,* November–December 1996, pp. 77–80; Douglas C. West, "Purchasing Professional Services: The Case of Advertising Agencies," *International Journal of Purchasing & Materials Management,* Summer 1997, pp. 2–9; Douglas W. LaBahn and Chiranjeev Kohli, "Maintaining Client Commitment in Advertising Agency-Client Relationships," *Industrial Marketing Management,* November 1997, pp. 497–508; Alan T. Shao and John S. Hill, "Executing Transnational Advertising Campaigns: Do U.S. Agencies Have the Overseas Talent?," *Journal of Advertising Research,* January/February 1992, pp. 49–58.

16. "Becoming Strategic Partners in the 1990s," *Advertising Age,* June 8, 1998, p. 28; "P&G Poised to Rewrite Ad Agency Pay Policies," *Advertising Age,* February 16, 1998, p. 1ff.; "Blame-the-Messenger Mentality Leaves Scars on Madison Avenue," *The Wall Street Journal,* November 20, 1991, p. B4; R. Susan Ellis and Lester W. Johnson, "Agency Theory as a Framework for Advertising Agency Compensation Decisions," *Journal of Advertising Research,* September/October 1993, p. 76; Thorolf Helgesen, "Advertising Awards and Advertising Agency Performance Criteria," *Journal of Advertising Research,* July/August 1994, pp. 43–53.

17. "Bowl Postmortem: Tadpoles, Ad Polls," *Advertising Age,* February 6, 1995, p. 44; "Why A-B Bounced Bud," *Advertising Age,* November 21, 1994, p. 1ff.; "Ties that Bind Agency, Client Unravel," *The Wall Street Journal,* November 16, 1994, p. B9; Paul C.N. Mitchell, Harold Cataquet, and Stephen Hague, "Establishing the Causes of Disaffection in Agency-Client Relations," *Journal of Advertising Research,* March/April 1992, pp. 41–48.

18. "Behind the Scenes at an American Express Commercial," *Business Week,* May 20, 1985, pp. 84–88.

19. "When Ads Get Creative, Some Click, Some Bomb," *USA Today,* December 15, 1997, p. 1Bff.; "Creative Differences," *Advertising Age,* November 17, 1997, p. 1ff.; Gerald J. Tellis and Doyle L. Weiss, "Does TV Advertising Really Affect Sales? The Role of Measures, Models, and Data Aggregation," *Journal of Advertising,* Fall 1995, pp. 1–12; John H. Holmes, "When Ads Work," *Journal of the Academy of Marketing Science,* Winter 1997, pp. 88–89; Karen Whitehill King, John D. Pehrson, and Leonard N. Reid, "Pretesting TV Commercials: Methods, Measures, and Changing Agency Roles," *Journal of Advertising,* September 1993, p. 85; "Researchers Probe Ad Effectiveness Globally," *Marketing News,* August 29, 1994, pp. 6–7; "New David Ogilvy Award Takes Research Out of Hiding," *The Wall Street Journal,* April 13, 1994, p. B8; Mukesh Bhargava, Naveen Donthu, and Rosanne Caron, "Improving the Effectiveness of Outdoor Advertising: Lessons from a Study of 282 Campaigns," *Journal of Advertising Research,* March/April 1994, pp. 46–55; Erik du Plessis, "Recognition versus Recall," *Journal of Advertising Research,* May/June 1994, pp. 75–91; Russell I. Haley, James Staffarone, and Arthur Fox, "The Missing Measures of Copy Testing," *Journal of Advertising Research,* May/June 1994, pp. 46–61; John R. Rossiter and Geoff Eagleson, "Conclusions from the ARF Copy Research Validity Project," *Journal of Advertising Research,* May/June 1994, pp. 19–32.

20. "Vietnamese Police Raid Bates' Ho Chi Minh Office," *Advertising Age,* May 4, 1998, p. 6; "Pakistan Cracks Whip," *Ad Age International,* February 9, 1998, p. 26; "Indian Court Tells Lever to Clean Up Ad Claims," *Ad Age International,* January 1998, p. 32; "PepsiCo's Pitch in Japan Has New Twist," *The Wall Street Journal,* May 23, 1997, p. B10; "Infomercials in Asia Turn as American as Apple Pie," *The Wall Street Journal,* June 25, 1996, p. B9; Alexander Simonson, "The Impact of Advertising Law on Business and Public Policy," *Journal of Marketing,* October 1994, pp. 123–25; Ross D. Petty, "Advertising Law in the United States and European Union," *Journal of Public Policy & Marketing,* Spring 1997, pp. 2–13; Steve Lysonski and Michael F. Duffy, "The New Zealand Fair Trading Act of 1986: Deceptive Advertising," *Journal of Consumer Affairs,* Summer 1992, pp. 177–99; "Drop That Remote! In Britain, Watching TV Can Be a Crime," *The Wall Street Journal,* September 27, 1993, p. A1ff.; "East Europeans Adjust to Western Ads; Information after Years of Propaganda," *The Wall Street Journal,* July 17, 1993, p. A5B; Albert Schofield, "International Differences in Advertising Practices: Britain Compared with Other Countries," *International Journal of Advertising* 10, no. 4 (1991), pp. 299–308.

21. "Events & Promotions," *Advertising Age,* March 17, 1997, pp. S1–6; "Special Report: Promotional Marketing," *Advertising Age,* March 21, 1994, pp. S1–14; "Special Report: Sales Promotion," *Advertising Age,* May 4, 1992, pp. 29–36; "More Marketers Leaving a (Prepaid) Calling Card," *The Wall Street Journal,* July 25, 1994, p. B1; "Beyond the Plastic Swizzle Stick," *Adweek's Marketing Week,* May 13, 1991, p. 20; K. Sivakumar, "Tradeoff Between Frequency and Depth of Price Promotions: Implications for High- and Low-Priced Brands," *Journal of Marketing Theory & Practice,* Winter 1996, pp. 1–8.

22. "Make It Simple," *Business Week,* September 9, 1996, pp. 96–104; "Pay for Performance Picking Up Speed," *Advertising Age,* August 9, 1993, p. 19; Donald R. Lichtenstein, Scot Burton, and Richard G. Netemeyer, "An Examination of Deal Proneness Across Sales Promotion Types: A Consumer Segmentation Perspective," *Journal of Retailing,* Summer 1997, pp. 283–97; Donald R. Glover, "Distributor Attitudes Toward Manufacturer-Sponsored Promotions," *Industrial Marketing Management* 20, no. 3 (1991), pp. 241–50; A.S.C. Ehrenberg, Kathy Hammond, and G.J. Goodhardt, "The After-Effects of Price-related Consumer Promotions," *Journal of Advertising Research,* July/August 1994, pp. 11–21; Jean J. Boddewyn and Monica Leardi, "Sales Promotions: Practice, Regulation and Self-Regulation Around the World," *International Journal of Advertising* 8, no. 4 (1989), pp. 363–74.

23. P. Rajan Varadarajan, "Horizontal Cooperative Sales Promotion: A Framework for Classification and Additional Perspectives," *Journal of Marketing,* April, 1986, pp. 61–73.

24. J.F. Engel, M. R. Warshaw, and T. C. Kinnear, *Promotional Strategy* (Homewood, Ill.: Richard D. Irwin, 1988).

25. Marnik G. Dekimpe, Pierre Francois, Srinath Gopalakrishna, Gary L. Lilien, and Christophe Van den Bulte, "Generalizing About Trade Show Effectiveness: A Cross-National Comparison," *Journal of Marketing,* October 1997, pp. 55–64; Scott Barlass, "How to Get the Most Out of Trade Shows," *Journal of Product Innovation Management,* September 1997, pp. 423–24; Srinath Gopalakrishna, Gary L. Lilien, Jerome D. Williams, and Ian K. Sequeira, "Do Trade Shows Pay Off?" *Journal of Marketing,* July 1995, pp. 75–83; Ronald C. Curhan and Robert J. Kopp, "Obtaining Retailer Support for Trade Deals: Key Success Factors," *Journal of Advertising Research,* December 1987–January 1988, pp. 51–60; Donald W. Jackson, Janet E. Keith, and Richard K. Burdick, "The Relative Importance of Various Promotional Elements in Different Industrial Purchase Situations," *Journal of Advertising* 16, no. 4 (1987), pp. 25–33.

26. "Getting Tough on Trade," *Adweek,* April 13, 1992, pp. 20–30; "A Shift in Direction?" *Adweek's Marketing Week,* April 13, 1992, pp. 26–27; Mary A. Raymond and Jong W. Lim, "Promotion and Trade Mix Considerations for Entering and Competing in the Korean Market," *Journal of Marketing Theory & Practice,* Winter 1996, pp. 44–55; Sunil Gupta, "Impact of Sales Promotions on When, What, and How Much to Buy," *Journal of Marketing Research,* November 1988, pp. 342–55.

27. "3M Distributors Go for the Gold," *Business Marketing,* May 1991, p. 49; "Chain Finds Incentives a Hard Sell," *The Wall Street Journal,* July 5, 1990, p. B1ff.; "Rewards for Good Work," *USA Today,* April 8, 1988, p. B1; Joanne Y. Cleaver, "Employee Incentives Rising to Top of Industry," *Advertising Age,* May 5, 1986, p. S1ff.

Chapter 17

1. "Adding Options Helps Car Firms Increase Prices," *The Wall Street Journal,* December 27, 1993, p. 9ff.; "Car Makers Seek to Mask Price Increases," *The Wall Street Journal,* August 16, 1989, p. B1.

2. Alfred Rappaport, "Executive Incentives versus Corporate Growth," *Harvard Business Review,* July–August 1978, pp. 81–88; David M. Szymanski, Sundar G. Bharadwaj, and P. Rajan Varadarajan, "An Analysis of the Market Share-Profitability Relationship," *Journal of Marketing,* July 1993, pp. 1–18.

3. Pricing "in the public interest" is often an issue in pricing government services; for an interesting example, see "Price Policy on Space Shuttle's Commercial Use Could Launch—or Ground—NASA's Rockets," *The Wall Street Journal,* March 21, 1985, p. 64.

4. "Cheap PCs," *Business Week,* March 23, 1998, pp. 28–32; "Good-Quality Laptops Are Starting to Get a Little Less Expensive," *The Wall Street Journal,* March 26, 1998, p. B1; "Crashing Prices," "Five Easy PCs," *Fortune,* November 10, 1997, pp. 311–12; "I'm Not Going to Pay a Lot for This Aptiva," *Business Week,* October 13, 1997, p. 59; "Now PC Buyers Are Getting More for Even Less," *The Wall Street Journal,* June 18, 1996, p. B1ff.; "PC Price War May Break Out, Starting in Fall," *The Wall Street Journal,* July 22, 1994, p. B1ff.; "Computer Chaos," *U.S. News & World Report,* July 26, 1993, pp. 46–49; "U.S. Computer Firms, Extending PC Wars, Charge into Japan," *The Wall Street Journal,* March 31, 1993, p. A1ff.; "PC Land's Little Guys Get Slaughtered," *Business Week,* February 15, 1993, pp. 105–6; "Here's a PC for Peanuts," *Newsweek,* January 25, 1993, p. 63.

5. "Harvester Sells Many Trucks below Cost, Citing Need to Maintain Dealer Network," *The Wall Street Journal,* April 19, 1983, p. 8.

6. "What Are Price Wars Good For? Absolutely Nothing," *Fortune,* May 12, 1997, p. 156; "Price Wars," *Adweek's Marketing Week,* June 8, 1992, pp. 18–22; "A Remarkable Gamble in an Industry Slump Pays Off Fast for Agco," *The Wall Street Journal,* August 19, 1997, p. A1ff.; "Why the Price Wars Never End," *Fortune,* March 23, 1992, pp. 68–78; "Avis, Sidestepping Price Wars, Focuses on the Drive Itself," *Adweek's Marketing Week,* February 12, 1990, p. 24.

7. Michael V. Marn and Robert L. Rosiello, "Managing Price, Gaining Profit," *Harvard Business Review,* September–October 1992, pp. 84–94; Subhash C. Jain and Michael B. Laric, "A Framework for Strategic Industrial Pricing," *Industrial Marketing Management* 8 (1979), pp. 75–80; Peter R. Dickson and Joel E. Urbany, "Retailer Reactions to Competitive Price Changes," *Journal of Retailing,* Spring 1994, pp. 1–22; Mary Karr, "The Case of the Pricing Predicament," *Harvard Business Review,* March–April, 1988, pp. 10–23; Saeed Samiee, "Pricing in Marketing Strategies of U.S. and Foreign-Based Companies," *Journal of Business Research,* February 1987, pp. 17–30; Gerard J. Tellis, "Beyond the Many Faces of Price: An Integration of Pricing Strategies," *Journal of Marketing,* October 1986, pp. 146–60.

8. "Good-Bye to Fixed Pricing," *Business Week,* May 4, 1998, pp. 71–84; "One-Price Deals Save Time, Hassles, but Not Money," *USA Today,* March 11, 1998, p. 1Bff; "Airlines Raise Their Class Consciousness," *Business Week,* February 23, 1998,

p. 40; "Haggling in Cyberspace Transforms Car Sales," *The Wall Street Journal,* December 30, 1997, p. B1ff.; "Car Hagglers May Still Drive Best Car Deals," *The Wall Street Journal,* October 12, 1994, p. B1ff.; "Flexible Pricing," *Business Week,* December 12, 1977, pp. 78–88; Ronald C. Goodstein, "UPC Scanner Pricing Systems: Are They Accurate?" *Journal of Marketing,* April 1994, pp. 20–30; Eric Matson, "Customizing Prices," *Harvard Business Review,* November–December 1995, pp. 13–14; Sanjay K. Dhar and Stephen J. Hoch, "Price Discrimination Using in-Store Merchandising," *Journal of Marketing,* January 1996, pp. 17–30; Michael H. Morris, "Separate Prices as a Marketing Tool," *Industrial Marketing Management,* May 1987, pp. 79–86; P. Ronald Stephenson, William L. Cron, and Gary L. Frazier, "Delegating Pricing Authority to the Sales Force: The Effects on Sales and Profit Performance," *Journal of Marketing,* Spring 1979, pp. 21–24.

9. "AZT Price Cut for Third World Mothers-to-Be," *The Wall Street Journal,* March 5, 1998, p. B1ff.; "Breakthrough in Birth Control May Elude Poor," *The Wall Street Journal,* March 4, 1991, p. B1ff; "Burroughs Wellcome Reaps Profits, Outrage from Its AIDS Drug," *The Wall Street Journal,* September 15, 1989, p. A1ff.; Richard A. Spinello, "Ethics, Pricing and the Pharmaceutical Industry," *Journal of Business Ethics,* August 1992, pp. 617–26; Dhruv Grewal and Larry D. Compeau, "Comparative Price Advertising: Informative or Deceptive?" *Journal of Public Policy & Marketing,* Spring 1992, pp. 52–62.

10. For up-to-date information on exchange rates, see The Universal Currency Converter™ (www.xe.net/currency1) or current issues of *The Financial Post.*

11. "Printer Wars: Toner Discount Incites Rivals," *The Wall Street Journal,* April 10, 1998, p. B1ff.; "Snaring Cheap Fares on the Internet," *The Wall Street Journal,* October 10, 1997, p. B10; "Ask and It Shall Be Discounted," *Business Week,* October 6, 1997, pp. 116–18; "The Latest Weapon in the Price Wars," *Fortune,* July 7, 1997, p. 200; "Owens Corning: Back from the Dead," *Fortune,* May 26, 1997, pp. 118–26; "Travelers Take Internet Route for Discounts," *USA Today,* January 13, 1997, p. 3B; Douglas D. Davis and Charles A. Holt, "List Prices and Discounts: The Interrelationship Between Consumer Shopping Patterns and Profitable Marketing Strategies," *Psychology & Marketing,* July 1996, pp. 341–63; David W. Arnesen, C.P. Fleenor, and Rex S. Toh, "The Ethical Dimensions of Airline Frequent Flier Programs," *Business Horizons,* January–February 1997, pp. 47–56; K.J. Blois, "Discounts in Business Marketing Management," *Industrial Marketing Management,* April 1994, pp. 93–100; James B. Wilcox et al., "Price Quantity Discounts: Some Implications for Buyers and Sellers," *Journal of Marketing,* July 1987, pp. 60–70; Mark T. Spriggs and John R. Nevin, "The Legal Status of Trade and Functional Price Discounts," *Journal of Public Policy & Marketing,* Spring 1994, pp. 61–75; Judith Waldrop, "The Seasons of Business," *American Demographics,* May 1992, pp. 40–45; "Cash Discounts," *Electrical Wholesaling,* May 1989, pp. 90–96.

12. Competition Act, R.S.C. 1985, c. C-34.

13. For more on P&G's everyday low pricing, see "P&G, Others Try New Uses for Coupon-Heavy Media," *Advertising Age,* September 22, 1997, p. 20; "Move to Drop Coupons Puts Procter & Gamble in Sticky PR Situation," *The Wall Street Journal,* April 17, 1997, p. A1ff.; "Zeroing In on Zero Coupons," *Brandweek,* June 3, 1996, pp. 30–36; "Company Makes Big Cuts to Stay Fit," *USA Today,* July 16, 1993, p. 1Bff.; "P&G Plays Pied Piper on Pricing," *Advertising Age,* March 9, 1992, p. 6; Stephen J. Hoch, Xavier Dreze, and Mary E. Purk, "EDLP, Hi-Lo, and Margin Arithmetic," *Journal of Marketing,* October 1994, pp. 16–27; George S. Bobinski, Dena Cox, and Anthony Cox, "Retail 'Sale' Advertising, Perceived Retailer Credibility, and Price Rationale," *Journal of Retailing,* Fall 1996, pp. 291–306; Francis J. Mulhern and Daniel T. Padgett, "The Relationship Between Retail Price Promotions and Regular Price Purchases," *Journal of Marketing,* October 1995, pp. 83–90.

14. "Beer Makers Frothing over Plan to Charge for Retail Shelf Space," *The Wall Street Journal,* April 22, 1994, p. B1ff.; "Getting Around Slotting Fees," *Food Business,* June 17, 1991, p. 12; "Want Shelf Space at the Supermarket? Ante Up," *Business Week,* August 7, 1989, pp. 60–61.

15. William D. Diamond, "Just What Is a "Dollar's Worth"? Consumer Reactions to Price Discounts vs. Extra Product Promotions," *Journal of Retailing,* Fall 1992, pp. 254–70; Kenneth A. Hunt and Susan M. Keaveney, "A Process Model of the Effects of Price Promotions on Brand Image," *Psychology & Marketing,* November/December 1994, pp. 511–32; "Coupon Scams Are Clipping Companies," *Business Week,* June 15, 1992, pp. 110–11; "Rebates' Secret Appeal to Manufacturers: Few Consumers Actually Redeem Them," *The Wall Street Journal,* February 10, 1998, p. B1ff.; Peter K. Tat, "Rebate Usage: A Motivational Perspective," *Psychology & Marketing,* January/February 1994, pp. 15–26; Abdul Ali, Marvin A. Jolson, and Rene Y. Darmon, "A Model for Optimizing the Refund Value in Rebate Promotions," *Journal of Business Research,* March 1994, pp. 239–46.

16. "Two-Tier Marketing," *Business Week,* March 17, 1997, pp. 82–90; "Makeup Ads Downplay Glamour for Value," *The Wall Street Journal,* June 20, 1994, p. B5; "Value Pricing Kicks off Model Year," *USA Today,* October 1, 1993, p. 1Bff.; "Value Pricing Comes to Funerals," *USA Today,* July 14, 1993, p. 5B; "Tide, Cheer Join P&G 'Value Pricing' Plan," *Advertising Age,* February 15, 1993, p. 3ff.; "More Stores Switch from Sales to 'Everyday Low Prices,'" *The Wall Street Journal,* November 12, 1992, p. B1ff.; "Value Marketing," *Business Week,* November 11, 1991, pp. 132–40; Louis J. De Rose, "Meet Today's Buying Influences with Value Selling," *Industrial Marketing Management* 20, no. 2 (1991), pp. 87–90.

17. Based on the Competition Act, R.S.C. 1985, c. C-34.

Chapter 18

1. Mary L. Hatten, "Don't Get Caught with Your Prices Down: Pricing in Inflationary Times," *Business Horizons,* March 1982, pp. 23–28; Douglas G. Brooks, "Cost Oriented Pricing: A Realistic Solution to a Complicated Problem," *Journal of Marketing,* April 1975, pp. 72–74.

2. William W. Alberts, "The Experience Curve Doctrine Reconsidered," *Journal of Marketing,* July 1989, pp. 36–49; G. Dean Kortge et al., "Linking Experience, Product Life Cycle, and Learning Curves: Calculating the Perceived Value Price Range," *Industrial Marketing Management,* July 1994, pp. 221–28.

3. G. Dean Kortge, "Inverted Breakeven Analysis for Profitable Marketing Decisions," *Industrial Marketing Management,* October 1984, pp. 219–24; Thomas L. Powers, "Breakeven Analysis with Semifixed Costs," *Industrial Marketing Management,* February 1987, pp. 35–42.

4. Approaches for estimating price-quantity relationships are reviewed in Kent B. Monroe, *Pricing: Making Profitable Decisions* (New York: McGraw-Hill, 1979). For a specific example see Frank D. Jones, "A Survey Technique to Measure Demand under Various Pricing Strategies," *Journal of Marketing,* July 1975, pp. 75–77; or Gordon A. Wyner, Lois H. Benedetti, and Bart M. Trapp, "Measuring the Quantity and Mix of Product Demand," *Journal of Marketing,* Winter 1984, pp. 101–9. See also Michael H. Morris and Mary L. Joyce, "How Marketers Evaluate Price Sensitivity," *Industrial Marketing Management,* May, 1988, pp. 169–76; David E. Griffith and Roland T. Rust, "The Price of Competitiveness in Competitive Pricing," *Journal of the Academy of Marketing Science,* Spring 1997, pp. 109–16; Robert J. Dolan, "How Do You Know When the Price Is Right?" *Harvard Business Review,* September–October 1995, pp. 174–83; S. C. Choi, "Price Competition in a Duopoly Common Retailer Channel," *Journal of Retailing,* Summer 1996, pp. 117–35.

5. Dhruv Grewal, Kent B. Monroe, and R. Krishnan, "The Effects of Price-Comparison Advertising on Buyers' Perceptions of Acquisition Value, Transaction Value, and Behavioral Intentions," *Journal of Marketing,* April 1998, pp. 46–59; John T. Gourville, "Pennies-a-Day: The Effect of Temporal Reframing on Transaction Evaluation," *Journal of Consumer Research,* March 1998, pp. 395–408; Joel E. Urbany, Rosemary Kalapurakal, and Peter R. Dickson, "Price Search in the Retail Grocery Market," *Journal of Marketing,* April 1996, pp. 91–104; Venkatesh Shankar and Lakshman Krishnamurthi, "Relating Price Sensitivity to Retailer Promotional Variables and Pricing Policy: An Empirical Analysis," *Journal of Retailing,* Fall 1996, pp. 249–72; Chakravarthi Narasimhan, Scott A. Neslin, and Subrata K. Sen, "Promotional Elasticities and Category Characteristics," *Journal of Marketing,* April 1996, pp. 17–30; K. Sivakumar and S.P. Raj, "Quality Tier Competition: How Price Change Influences Brand Choice and Category Choice," *Journal of Marketing,* July 1997, pp. 71–84.

6. "New Long-Life Bulbs May Lose Brilliance in a Crowded Market," *The Wall Street Journal,* June 2, 1992, p. B4; Benson P. Shapiro and Barbara P. Jackson, "Industrial Pricing to Meet Customer Needs," *Harvard Business Review,* November–December 1978, pp. 119–27; "The Race to the $10 Light Bulb," *Business Week,* May 19, 1980, p. 124; see also Michael H. Morris and Donald A. Fuller, "Pricing an Industrial Service," *Industrial Marketing Management,* May 1989, pp. 139–46.

7. Thomas T. Nagle, *The Strategy and Tactics of Pricing* (Englewood Cliffs, NJ: Prentice-Hall, 1987), pp. 249–55; Richard A. Briesch, Lakshman Krishnamurthi, Tridib Mazumdar, and S.P. Raj, "A Comparative Analysis of Reference Price Models," *Journal of Consumer Research,* September 1997, pp. 202–14; Tracy A. Suter and Scot Burton, "Believability and Consumer Perceptions of Implausible Reference Prices in Retail Advertisements," *Psychology & Marketing,* January 1996, pp. 37–54; K. N. Rajendran and Gerard J. Tellis, "Contextual and Temporal Components of Reference Price," *Journal of Marketing,* January 1994, pp. 22–34; Abhijit Biswas, Elizabeth J. Wilson, and Jane W. Licata, "Reference Pricing Studies in Marketing: A Synthesis of Research Results," *Journal of Business Research,* July 1993, pp. 239–56; Daniel S. Putler, "Incorporating Reference Price Effects into a Theory of Consumer Choice," *Marketing Science,* Summer 1992, pp. 287–309; Kristina D. Frankenberger and Ruiming Liu, "Does Consumer Knowledge Affect Consumer Responses to Advertised Reference Price Claims?," *Psychology & Marketing,* May/June 1994, pp. 235–52; Tridib Mazumdar and Kent B. Monroe, "Effects of Inter-store and In-store Price Comparison on Price Recall Accuracy and Confidence," *Journal of Retailing,* Spring 1992, pp. 66–89.

8. For an example applied to a high-price item, see "Sale of Mink Coats Strays a Fur Piece from the Expected," *The Wall Street Journal,* March 21, 1980, p. 30.

9. Noel M. Noel and Nessim Hanna, "Benchmarking Consumer Perceptions of Product Quality With Price: An Exploration," *Psychology & Marketing,* September 1996, pp. 591–604; Niraj Dawar and Philip Parker, "Marketing Universals: Consumers' Use of Brand Name, Price, Physical Appearance, and Retailer Reputation As Signals of Product Quality," *Journal of Marketing,* April 1994, pp. 81–95; Tung-Zong Chang and Albert R. Wildt, "Impact of Product Information on the Use of Price As a Quality Cue," *Psychology & Marketing,* January 1996, pp. 55–75; B.P. Shapiro, "The

Psychology of Pricing," *Harvard Business Review*, July–August 1968, pp. 14–24.
10. Robert M. Schindler and Patrick N. Kirby, "Patterns of Rightmost Digits Used in Advertised Prices: Implications for Nine-Ending Effects," *Journal of Consumer Research*, September 1997, pp. 192–201; Mark Stiving and Russell S. Winer, "An Empirical Analysis of Price Endings With Scanner Data," *Journal of Consumer Research*, June 1997, pp. 57–67; Robert M. Schindler and Alan R. Wiman, "Effects of Odd Pricing on Price Recall," *Journal of Business Research*, November 1989, pp. 165–78.
11. Rebecca Piirto Heath, "Life on Easy Street," *American Demographics*, April 1997, pp. 33–38; "Perhaps It's Time to Look Again at Your Watch," *USA Today*, January 7, 1997, p. 6D; "The '80s Are Gone, but Caviar Is Back," *The Wall Street Journal*, September 6, 1996, p. B1ff.; "Luxury's Gaudy Times," *Time*, March 25, 1996, p. 48; "Special Report: Marketing to the Affluent," *Advertising Age*, October 19, 1987, pp. S1–32; K. M. Monroe and S. Petroshius, "Buyers' Subjective Perceptions of Price: An Update of the Evidence," in *Perspectives in Consumer Behavior*, ed. T. Robertson and H. Kassarjian (Glenview, IL: Scott Foresman, 1981), pp. 43–55; G. Dean Kortge and Patrick A. Okonkwo, "Perceived Value Approach to Pricing," *Industrial Marketing Management*, May 1993, pp. 133–40; Valarie A. Zeithaml, "Consumer Perceptions of Price, Quality, And Value: A Means-End Model and Synthesis of Evidence," *Journal of Marketing*, July 1988, pp. 2–22.
12. Andrea Ovans, "Make a Bundle Bundling," *Harvard Business Review*, November–December 1997, pp. 18–20; Preyas S. Desai and Kannan Srinivasan, "Aggregate Versus Product-Specific Pricing: Implications for Franchise and Traditional Channels," *Journal of Retailing*, Winter 1996, pp. 357–82; Manjit S. Yadav and Kent B. Monroe, "How Buyers Perceive Savings in a Bundle Price: An Examination of a Bundle's Transaction Value," *Journal of Marketing Research*, August 1993, pp. 350–58; Dorothy Paun, "When to Bundle or Unbundle Products," *Industrial Marketing Management*, February 1993, pp. 29–34.
13. Peter E. Connor and Robert K. Hopkins, "Cost Plus What? The Importance of Accurate Profit Calculations in Cost-Plus Agreements," *International Journal of Purchasing & Materials Management*, Spring 1997, pp. 35–40; Daniel T. Ostas, "Ethics of Contract Pricing," *Journal of Business Ethics*, February 1992, pp. 137–46; J. Steve Davis, "Ethical Problems in Competitive Bidding: The Paradyne Case," *Business and Professional Ethics Journal*, 7, no. 2 (1988), pp. 3–26; David T. Levy, "Guaranteed Pricing in Industrial Purchases: Making Use of Markets in Contractual Relations," *Industrial Marketing Management*, October 1994, pp. 307–14; Akintola Akintoye and Martin Skitmore, "Pricing Approaches in the Construction Industry," *Industrial Marketing Management*, November 1992, pp. 311–18.

Chapter 19

1. Monsanto, 1993 *Annual Report;* "Monsanto Touts New Sugar Substitute as Sweetest Yet," *The Wall Street Journal*, March 29, 1991, p. B1; "NutraSweet Rivals Stirring," *Advertising Age*, June 26, 1989, p. 3ff.; "New Sweeteners Head for the Sugar Bowl," *The Wall Street Journal*, February 6, 1989, p. B1.
2. John E. Smallwood, "The Product Life Cycle: A Key to Strategic Marketing Planning," *MSU Business Topics*, Winter 1973, pp. 29–35; Richard F. Savach and Laurence A. Thompson, "Resource Allocation within the Product Life Cycle," *MSU Business Topics*, Autumn 1978, pp. 35–44; Peter F. Kaminski and David R. Rink, "PLC: The Missing Link between Physical Distribution and Marketing Planning," *International Journal of Physical Distribution and Materials Management* 14, no. 6 (1984), pp. 77–92.
3. *1996 Canadian Markets* published by *The Financial Post.* Estimated population and retail spending. Reproduced in *Media Digest 1997-98.* Prepared by the Canadian Media Directors' Council and published by *Marketing Magazine.*
4. See most basic statistics textbooks under time series analysis.
5. Checking the accuracy of forecasts is a difficult subject. See John B. Mahaffie, "Why Forecasts Fail," *American Demographics*, March 1995, pp. 34–40; "Don't Be Trapped By Past Success," *Nation's Business*, March 1992, pp. 52–54; Margaret K. Ambry, "States of the Future," *American Demographics*, October 1994, pp. 36–45; Marcus O Connor, William Remus, and Ken Griggs, "Going Up-Going Down: How Good Are People at Forecasting Trends and Changes in Trends?" *Journal of Forecasting*, May 1997, pp. 165–76; Marshall L. Fisher, Janice H. Hammond, Walter R. Obermeyer, and Ananth Raman, "Making Supply Meet Demand in an Uncertain World," *Harvard Business Review*, May–June 1994, pp. 83–89; Craig S. Galbraith and Gregory B. Merrill, "The Politics of Forecasting: Managing the Truth," *California Management Review*, Winter 1996, pp. 29–43; Larry D. Compeau, "Forecasting and Market Analysis Techniques: A Practical Approach," *Journal of the Academy of Marketing Science*, Spring 1996, pp. 181–83; Richard H. Evans, "Analyzing the Potential of a New Market," *Industrial Marketing Management*, February 1993, pp. 35–40; Shelby H. McIntyre, Dale D. Achabal, and Christopher M. Miller, "Applying Case-Based Reasoning to Forecasting Retail Sales," *Journal of Retailing*, Winter 1993, pp. 372–98; Paul A. Berbig, John Milewicz, and James E. Golden, "The Do's and Don'ts of Sales Forecasting," *Industrial Marketing Management*, February 1993, pp. 49–58; David L. Kendall and Michael T. French, "Forecasting the Potential for New Industrial Products," *Industrial Marketing Management* 20, no. 3 (1991), pp. 177–84; F. William Barnett, "Four Steps to Forecast Total Market Demand," *Harvard Business Review*, July–August 1988, pp. 28–40; D. M. Georgoff and R. G. Murdick, "Manager's Guide to Forecasting," *Harvard Business Review*, January–February 1986, pp. 110–20. See also "1997 Survey of Buying Power," (Supplement) *Sales & Marketing Management*, 1997, and available from World Wide Web: <http://www.sbponline.com>.
6. Gloria Barczak, "Analysis for Marketing Planning," *Journal of Product Innovation Management*, September 1997, pp. 424–25; William A. Sahlman, "How to Write a Great Business Plan," *Harvard Business Review*, July–August 1997, pp. 98–108; Paul Boughton, "The 1-Day Marketing Plan: Organizing and Completing the Plan That Works," *Journal of the Academy of Marketing Science*, Summer 1996, pp. 275–76; William Sandy, "Avoid the Breakdowns Between Planning and Implementation," *The Journal of Business Strategy*, September/October 1991, pp. 30–33; Michael MacInnis and Louise A. Heslop, "Market Planning in a High-Tech Environment," *Industrial Marketing Management*, May 1990, pp. 107–16; David Strutton, "Marketing Strategies: New Approaches, New Techniques," *Journal of the Academy of Marketing Science*, Summer 1997, pp. 261–62; Rita G. McGrath and Ian C. MacMillan, "Discovery-Driven Planning," *Harvard Business Review*, July–August 1995, pp. 44–54; Jeffrey Elton and Justin Roe, "Bringing Discipline to Project Management," *Harvard Business Review*, March–April 1998, pp. 153–58; Tridib Mazumdar, K. Sivakumar, and David Wilemon, "Launching New Products With Cannibalization Potential: An Optimal Timing Framework," *Journal of Marketing Theory & Practice*, Fall 1996, pp. 83–93; Andrew Campbell and Marcus Alexander, "What's Wrong With Strategy?" *Harvard Business Review*, November–December 1997, pp. 42–51; "Marketing Software Review: Project Management Made Easy," *Business Marketing*, February 1989, pp. 20–27.
7. For further discussion on evaluating and selecting alternative plans, see Francis Buttle, "The Marketing Strategy Worksheet—A Practical Planning Tool," *Long Range Planning*, August 1985, pp. 80–88; Douglas A. Schellinck, "Effect of Time on a Marketing Strategy," *Industrial Marketing Management*, April 1983, pp. 83–88; George S. Day and Liam Fahey, "Valuing Market Strategies," *Journal of Marketing*, July 1988, pp. 45–57.
8. Sam C. Okoroafo, "Modes of Entering Foreign Markets," *Industrial Marketing Management* 20, no. 4 (1991), pp. 341–46; Mike Van Horn, "Market-Entry Approaches for the Pacific Rim," *The Journal of Business Strategy*, March/April 1990, pp. 14–19; Refik Culpan, "Export Behavior of Firms: Relevance of Firm Size," *Journal of Business Research*, May, 1989, pp. 207–18; Anthony C. Koh and Robert A. Robicheaux, "Variations in Export Performance Due to Differences in Export Marketing Strategy: Implications for Industrial Marketers," *Journal of Business Research*, November 1988, pp. 249–58; S. Tamer Cavusgil, Shaoming Zou, and G.M. Naidu, "Product and Promotion Adaptation in Export Ventures: An Empirical Investigation," *Journal of International Business Studies*, Third Quarter 1993, pp. 479–506; Camille P. Schuster and Charles D. Bodkin, "Market Segmentation Practices of Exporting Companies," *Industrial Marketing Management*, May 1987, pp. 95–102.
9. "For U.S. Marketers, the Russian Front Is No Bowl of 'Vishnyas,' " *Adweek's Marketing Week*, March 5, 1990; "Learning the Exporting Ropes," *Business Marketing*, May 1989, pp. 80–85; " 'Papa-Mama' Stores in Japan Wield Power to Hold Back Imports," *The Wall Street Journal*, November 14, 1988, p. A1ff.; Jerry Haar and Marta Ortiz-Buonafina, "The Internationalization Process and Marketing Activities: The Case of Brazilian Export Firms," *Journal of Business Research*, February 1995, pp. 175–82; "U.S. Concerns Trying to Do Business in Japan Face Government, Market, Cultural Barriers," *The Wall Street Journal*, July 8, 1985, p. 16; Robert E. Morgan and Constantine S. Katsikeas, "Exporting Problems of Industrial Manufacturers," *Industrial Marketing Management*, March 1998, pp. 161–76.
10. Masaaki Kotabe, Arvind Sahay, and Preet S. Aulakh, "Emerging Role of Technology Licensing in the Development of Global Product Strategy: Conceptual Framework and Research Propositions," *Journal of Marketing*, January 1996, pp. 73–88; John A. Quelch, "How to Build a Product Licensing Program," *Harvard Business Review*, May–June 1985, p. 186ff.
11. "The Steel Deal That Could Boost Big Blue in Brazil," *Business Week*, May 19, 1986, p. 66. See also Robert Porter Lynch, "Building Alliances to Penetrate European Markets," *The Journal of Business Strategy*, March/April 1990, pp. 4–9; D. Robert Webster, "International Joint Ventures with Pacific Rim Partners," *Business Horizons*, March–April 1989, pp. 65–71; Kenichi Ohmae, "The Global Logic of Strategic Alliances," *Harvard Business Review*, March–April 1989, pp. 143–54.
12. "Top U.S. Companies Move into Russia," *Fortune*, July 31, 1989, pp. 165–71; "When U.S. Joint Ventures with Japan Go Sour," *Business Week*, July 24, 1989, pp. 30–31; Ashish Nanda and Peter J. Williamson, "Use Joint Ventures to Ease the Pain of Restructuring," *Harvard Business Review*, November–December 1995, pp. 119–28; Paul Lawrence and Charalambos Vlachoutsicos, "Joint Ventures in Russia: Put the Locals in Charge," *Harvard Business Review*, January–February 1993, pp. 44–55; F. Kingston Berlew, "The Joint Venture—A Way into Foreign Markets," *Harvard Business Review*, July–August 1984, pp. 48–55.
13. "Young Managers Learn Global Skills," *The Wall Street Journal*, March 31, 1992, p. B1; "As Costs of Overseas Assignments Climb, Firms

Select Expatriates More Carefully," *The Wall Street Journal,* January 9, 1992, p. B1ff.; Regina F. Maruca, "The Right Way to Go Global: An Interview With Whirlpool CEO David Whitwam," *Harvard Business Review,* March–April 1994, pp. 134–45; Tevfik Dalgic, "Multinational Companies in United States International Trade: A Statistical and Analytical Sourcebook," *Journal of the Academy of Marketing Science,* Spring 1997, pp. 172–73; Keith Cerny, "Making Local Knowledge Global," *Harvard Business Review,* May–June 1996, pp. 22–26; Chi-fai Chan and Neil B. Holbert, "Whose Empire Is This, Anyway? Reflections on the Empire State of Multi-National Corporations," *Business Horizons,* July–August 1994, pp. 51–54; Syed H. Akhter and Yusuf A. Choudhry, "Forced Withdrawal from a Country Market: Managing Political Risk," *Business Horizons,* May–June 1993, pp. 47–54; M. Krishna Erramilli and C.P. Rao, "Service Firms' International Entry-Mode Choice: A Modified Transaction-Cost Analysis Approach," *Journal of Marketing,* July 1993, pp. 19–38.

Chapter 20

1. Kevin Rollins, "Using Information to Speed Execution," *Harvard Business Review,* March–April 1998, p. 81; Clayton M. Christensen, "Making Strategy: Learning by Doing," *Harvard Business Review,* November–December 1997, pp. 141–56; Ram Charan, "How Networks Reshape Organizations—For Results," *Harvard Business Review,* September–October 1991, pp. 104–15; William J. Bruns, Jr., and W. Warren McFarlan, "Information Technology Puts Power in Control Systems," *Harvard Business Review,* September–October, 1987, pp. 89–94.

2. Available from World Wide Web: <http://www.hertz.com>; "How Market Leaders Keep Their Edge," *Fortune,* February 6, 1995, pp. 88–98.

3. Thomas M. Hout and John C. Carter, "Getting It Done: New Roles for Senior Executives," *Harvard Business Review,* November 1995–December 1995, pp. 133–41ff.; Hemant C. Sashittal and David Wilemon, "Marketing Implementation in Small and Midsized Industrial Firms: An Exploratory Study," *Industrial Marketing Management,* January 1996, pp. 67–78; Hemant C. Sashittal and Clint Tankersley, "The Strategic Market Planning-Implementation Interface in Small and Midsized Industrial Firms: An Exploratory Study," *Journal of Marketing Theory & Practice,* Summer 1997, pp. 77–92; Thomas V. Bonoma, "Making Your Marketing Strategy Work," *Harvard Business Review,* March–April 1984, pp. 68–76; Barbara J. Coe, "Key Differentiating Factors and Problems Associated with Implementation of Strategic Market Planning," in *1985 American Marketing Association Educators' Proceedings,* ed. R. F. Lusch et al. (Chicago: American Marketing Association, 1985), pp. 275–81.

4. The restaurant case is adapted from Marie Gaudard, Roland Coates and Liz Freeman, "Accelerating Improvement," *Quality Progress,* October 1991, pp. 81–88. For more on quality management and control, see Roland T. Rust, Anthony J. Zahorik, and Timothy L. Keiningham, "Return on Quality (ROQ): Making Service Quality Financially Accountable," *Journal of Marketing,* April 1995, pp. 58–70; "TQM: More than a Dying Fad?" *Fortune,* October 18, 1993, pp. 66–72; "Quality Control from Mars," *The Wall Street Journal,* January 27, 1992, p. A12; William B. Locander and Daniel J. Goebel, "The Quality Train Is Leaving and Marketers Are Nodding Off in the Club Car," *Journal of Marketing Theory & Practice,* Summer 1996, pp. 1–10; William C. LaFief, "Total Quality Marketing: The Key to Regaining Market Shares," *Journal of the Academy of Marketing Science,* Fall 1996, pp. 377–78; David W. Finn, Julie Baker, Greg W. Marshall, and Roy Anderson, "Total Quality Management and Internal Customers: Measuring Internal Service Quality," *Journal of Marketing Theory & Practice,* Summer 1996, pp. 36–51; Robert F. Hurley, Melissa T. Gropper, and Gianpaolo Roma, "The Role of TQM in Advertising: A Conceptualization and a Framework for Application," *Journal of Marketing Theory & Practice,* Summer 1996, pp. 11–23; Teresa A. Swartz, "Why TQM Fails and What to Do About It," *Journal of the Academy of Marketing Science,* Fall 1996, pp. 380–81; Iris Mohr-Jackson, "Managing a Total Quality Orientation: Factors Affecting Customer Satisfaction," *Industrial Marketing Management,* March 1998, pp. 109–25; Cengiz Haksever, "Total Quality Management in the Small Business Environment," *Business Horizons,* March–April 1996, pp. 33–40; Michael P. Bigwood, "Total Quality Management at Work: Development of an Effective Competitive Analysis Process," *Industrial Marketing Management,* September 1997, pp. 459–66.

5. Roland T. Rust, Anthony J. Zahorik, and Timothy L. Keiningham, *Return on Quality* (Chicago: Probus, 1994); Warren S. Martin and Wendy K. Martin, "The Application of Benchmarking to Marketing," *Journal of Marketing Theory & Practice,* Summer 1996, pp. 52–59; J.J. Cronin and Steven A. Taylor, "SERVPERF Versus SERVQUAL: Reconciling Performance-Based and Perceptions-Minus-Expectations Measurement of Service Quality," *Journal of Marketing,* January 1994, pp. 125–31; Timothy C. Johnston and Molly A. Hewa, "Fixing Service Failures," *Industrial Marketing Management,* September 1997, pp. 467–73; Shirley Taylor, "Waiting for Service: The Relationship Between Delays and Evaluations of Service," *Journal of Marketing,* April 1994, pp. 56–69; Mary J. Bitner, Bernard H. Booms, and Lois A. Mohr, "Critical Service Encounters: The Employee's Viewpoint," *Journal of Marketing,* October 1994, pp. 95–106; G. T. M. Hult, "Service Quality: New Directions in Theory and Practice," *Journal of the Academy of Marketing Science,* Summer 1997, pp. 264–65; Scott W. Kelley, Timothy Longfellow, and Jack Malehorn, "Organizational Determinants of Service Employees' Exercise of Routine, Creative, and Deviant Discretion," *Journal of Retailing,* Summer 1996, pp. 135–57; Pierre Filiatrault, Jean Harvey, and Jean-Charles Chebat, "Service Quality and Service Productivity Management Practices," *Industrial Marketing Management,* May 1996, pp. 243–55; Joseph H. Foegen, "Are Managers Losing Control?" *Business Horizons,* March–April 1998, pp. 2–5; Robert Simons, "Control in an Age of Empowerment," *Harvard Business Review,* March 1995–April 1995, pp. 80–88; "Finding, Training & Keeping the Best Service Workers," *Fortune,* October 3, 1994, pp. 110–22; Timothy L. Keiningham, Roland T. Rust, and M. Marshall Weems, "The Bottom Line on Quality," *Financial Executive,* September/October 1994, pp. 50–52.

6. Ed Weymes, "A Different Approach to Retail Sales Analysis," *Business Horizons,* March/April 1982, pp. 66–74; Robert H. Collins, Regan F. Carey, and Rebecca F. Mauritson, "Microcomputer Applications: Maps on a Micro—Applications in Sales and Marketing Management," *Journal of Personal Selling and Sales Management,* November 1987, p. 83ff.

7. Robin Cooper and W. B. Chew, "Control Tomorrow's Costs Through Today's Designs," *Harvard Business Review,* January–February 1996, pp. 88–97; Robin Cooper and Robert S. Kaplan, "Profit Priorities From Activity-Based Costing," *Harvard Business Review,* May–June 1991, pp. 130–37; Douglas M. Lambert and Jay U. Sterling, "What Types of Profitability Reports Do Marketing Managers Receive?" *Industrial Marketing Management,* November, 1987, pp. 295–304; Nigel F. Piercy, "The Marketing Budgeting Process: Marketing Management Implications," *Journal of Marketing,* October 1987, pp. 45–59; Michael J. Sandretto, "What Kind of Cost System Do You Need?" *Harvard Business Review,* January–February 1985, pp. 110–18; Patrick M. Dunne and Harry I. Wolk, "Marketing Cost Analysis: A Modularized Contribution Approach," *Journal of Marketing,* July 1977, pp. 83–94.

8. Technically, a distinction should be made between variable and direct costs, but we will use these terms interchangeably. Similarly, not all costs that are common to several products are fixed costs, and vice versa. But the important point here is to recognize that some costs are fairly easy to allocate, and other costs are not. See Stewart A. Washburn, "Establishing Strategy and Determining Costs in the Pricing Decision," *Business Marketing,* July 1985, pp. 64–78.

9. James T. Rothe, Michael G. Harvey, and Candice E. Jackson, "The Marketing Audit: Five Decades Later," *Journal of Marketing Theory & Practice,* Summer 1997, pp. 1–16; Douglas Brownlie, "The Conduct of Marketing Audits," *Industrial Marketing Management,* January 1996, pp. 11–22; Leonard L. Berry, Jeffrey S. Conant, and A. Parasuraman, "A Framework for Conducting a Services Marketing Audit," *Journal of the Academy of Marketing Science,* Summer 1991, pp. 255–68; John F. Grashof, "Conducting and Using a Marketing Audit," in *Readings in Basic Marketing,* ed. E.J. McCarthy, J.J. Grashof, and A.A. Brogowicz (Homewood, Ill.: Richard D. Irwin, 1984).

Chapter 21

1. W. Keith Schilit, "The Globalization of Venture Capital," *Business Horizons,* January–February 1992, pp. 17–23; Nikolaos Tzokas, Michael Saren, and Douglas Brownlie, "Generating Marketing Resources by Means of R&D Activities in High Technology Firms," *Industrial Marketing Management,* July 1997, pp. 331–40; George S. Bobinski and Gabriel G. Ramirez, "Advertising to Investors: The Effect of Financial-Relations Advertising on Stock Volume and Price," *Journal of Advertising,* December 1994, pp. 13–28; Rajendra K. Srivastava, Tasadduq A. Shervani, and Liam Fahey, "Market-Based Assets and Shareholder Value: A Framework for Analysis," *Journal of Marketing,* January 1998, pp. 2–18; Gary Tighe, "From Experience: Securing Sponsors and Funding for New Product Development Projects—The Human Side of Enterprise," *Journal of Product Innovation Management,* January 1998, pp. 75–81; Robert C. Pozen, "Institutional Investors: The Reluctant Activists," *Harvard Business Review,* January–February 1994, p. 140; Michael E. Porter, "Capital Disadvantage: America's Failing Capital Investment System," *Harvard Business Review,* September–October 1992, pp. 65–83; Bill Parks, "Rate of Return—The Poison Apple?" *Business Horizons,* May–June 1993, pp. 55–58.

2. *Sorrell Ridge: Slotting Allowances* (Cambridge, MA: Harvard Business School Press, 1988).

3. Julie H. Hertenstein and Sharon M. McKinnon, "Solving the Puzzle of the Cash Flow Statement," *Business Horizons,* January–February 1997, pp. 69–76; Amar Bhide, "Bootstrap Finance: The Art of Start-Ups," *Harvard Business Review,* November–December 1992, pp. 109–17; Marv Rubinstein, "Effective Industrial Marketing with a Piggy Bank Budget," *Industrial Marketing Management,* August 1992, pp. 203–14; Amar Bhide, "How Entrepreneurs Craft Strategies That Work," *Harvard Business Review,* March–April 1994, pp. 150–63.

4. David M. Upton, "What Really Makes Factories Flexible?" *Harvard Business Review,* July 1995–August 1995, pp. 74–79ff.; John P. MacDuffie and Susan Helper, "Creating Lean Suppliers: Diffusing Lean Production Through the Supply Chain," *California Management Review,* Summer 1997, pp. 118–51; Robert J. Fisher, Elliot Maltz, and Bernard J. Jaworski, "Enhancing Communication Between Marketing and Engineering: The Moderating Role of Relative Functional Identification," *Journal of*

Marketing, July 1997, pp. 54–70; X. M. Song, Mitzi M. Montoya-Weiss, and Jeffrey B. Schmidt, "Antecedents and Consequences of Cross-Functional Cooperation: A Comparison of R&D, Manufacturing, and Marketing Perspectives," *Journal of Product Innovation Management,* January 1997, pp. 35–47; Roger G. Schroeder and Michael J. Pesch, "Focusing the Factory: Eight Lessons," *Business Horizons,* September–October 1994, pp. 76–81; Andrew D. Bartmess, "The Plant Location Puzzle," *Harvard Business Review,* March–April 1994, pp. 20–38; Robert H. Hayes and Gary P. Pisano, "Beyond World-Class: The New Manufacturing Strategy," *Harvard Business Review,* January–February 1994, pp. 77–87; Victoria L. Crittenden, Lorraine R. Gardiner, and Antonie Stam, "Reducing Conflict between Marketing and Manufacturing," *Industrial Marketing Management,* November 1993, pp. 299–310; Paul A. Konijnendijk, "Dependence and Conflict Between Production and Sales," *Industrial Marketing Management,* August 1993, pp. 161–68; Kenneth B. Kahn and John T. Mentzer, "Norms that Distinguish between Marketing and Manufacturing," *Journal of Business Research,* June 1994, pp. 111–18; William B. Wagner, "Establishing Supply Service Strategy for Shortage Situations," *Industrial Marketing Management,* December 1994, pp. 393–402; Roger W. Schmenner, "So You Want to Lower Costs?," *Business Horizons,* July–August 1992, pp. 24–28.

5. For more on Nabisco's Snackwell cookies, see "Man Walked on the Moon but Man Can't Make Enough Devil's Food Cookie Cakes," *The Wall Street Journal,* September 26, 1993, p. B1ff.; "They're Not Crying in Their Crackers at Nabisco," *Business Week,* August 30, 1993, p. 61. For more on Rice Krispies Treats cereal, see "Special Report: Brand in Demand," *Advertising Age,* February 7, 1994, pp. S1–10; "Kellogg to Consumers: Please Bear with Us," *Advertising Age,* March 29, 1993, p. 44; see also J. Mahajan et al., "An Exploratory Investigation of the Interdependence between Marketing and Operations Functions in Service Firms," *International Journal of Research in Marketing,* January 1994, pp. 1–16.

6. "Remember When Companies Made Things?" *The Wall Street Journal,* September 18, 1997, p. C1; " 'Virtual' Companies Leave the Manufacturing to Others," *The New York Times,* July 17, 1994, Sect. 3, p. 5; "Shaken by a Series of Business Setbacks, Calvin Klein is Redesigning Itself," *The Wall Street Journal,* March 21, 1994, p. B1; "Calvin Klein Inc.: Definitive Pact Is Reached on Sale of Jeans Division," *The Wall Street Journal,* July 15, 1994, p. B4; Ravi Venkatesan, "Strategic Sourcing: To Make or Not To Make," *Harvard Business Review,* November–December 1992, pp. 98–108.

7. L. Scott Flaig, "The 'Virtual Enterprise': Your New Model for Success," *Electronic Business,* March 30, 1992, pp. 153–55; William H. Davidow and Michael S. Malone, *The Virtual Corporation* (New York: Harper Collins, 1992).

8. Available from World Wide Web: <http://www.dell.com>; "Michael Dell Rocks," *Fortune,* May 11, 1998, pp. 58–70; "Dell No Longer Wants to Be Viewed as a Discounter," *The Wall Street Journal,* April 10, 1998, p. B5; "No Big Deal: Why Michael Dell Isn't Afraid of The New Compaq," *Fortune,* March 2, 1998, pp. 189–92; "The Once and Future King," *Time,* December 22, 1997, p. 16; "And Give Me an Extra-Fast Modem with That, Please," *Business Week,* September 29, 1997, p. 38; "Now Everyone in PCs Wants to Be like Mike," *Fortune,* September 8, 1997, pp. 91–92; "Michael Dell Turns the PC World Inside Out," *Fortune,* September 8, 1997, pp. 76–86; "Dell Fights PC Wars by Emphasizing Customer Service," *The Wall Street Journal,* August 15, 1997, p. B4; "Dell: Built-to-Order Success, Rivals Rush to Imitate Direct Sell," *USA Today,* June 30, 1997, p. 1Bff.; "Michael Dell's Plan for the Rest of the Decade," *Fortune,* June 9, 1997, p. 138.

9. "Sale of Modern Music Keyed to Customization," *Inc.,* May 1998, pp. 23–25; "Jeans Made in Heaven: Earthly Fit," *Inc.,* May 1988, p. 24; "Producing Unique Goods—and Headaches," *Inc.,* May 1998, pp. 24–25; "Mass Production Gives Way to Mass Customization," *USA Today,* February 16, 1998, p. 3B; "Give 'Em Exactly What They Want," *Fortune,* November 10, 1997, pp. 283–85; "Have It Your Way," *Inc. Tech,* No. 4, 1997, pp. 56–64. For more on Levi Strauss' custom-fit jeans for women, see "One Writer's Hunt for the Perfect Jeans," *Fortune,* April 17, 1995, p. 30; "Levi Strauss Sizes the Retail Scene," *Advertising Age,* January 23, 1995, p. 4; James H. Gilmore and B. Joseph Pine, "The Four Faces of Mass Customization," *Harvard Business Review,* January–February 1997, pp. 91–101; B. Joseph Pine, Bart Victor, and Andrew C. Boynton, "Making Mass Customization Work," *Harvard Business Review,* September–October 1993, pp. 108–21.

10. *Sara Lee: Rapid Response at Hanes Knitware* (Cambridge, MA: Harvard Business School Press, 1993); see also Richard Peisch, "When Outsourcing Goes Awry," *Harvard Business Review,* May–June 1995, pp. 24–37; "A Killing in the Caymans?" *Business Week,* May 11, 1998, pp. 50–54; Stanley E. Fawcett, Linda L. Stanley, and Sheldon R. Smith, "Developing a Logistics Capability to Improve the Performance of International Operations," *Journal of Business Logistics,* 1997, pp. 101–27; P. F. Johnson and Michiel R. Leenders, "Make-or-Buy Alternatives in Plant Disposition Strategies," *International Journal of Purchasing & Materials Management,* Spring 1997, pp. 20–26; Thomas Kiely, "Business Processes: Consider Outsourcing," *Harvard Business Review,* May–June 1997, pp. 11–12; Edward W. Davis, "Global Outsourcing: Have U.S. Managers Thrown the Baby Out with the Bath Water?," *Business Horizons,* July–August 1992, pp. 58–65.

11. For more on Levi Strauss hiring foreign labor, see "Managing by Values," *Business Week,* August 1, 1994, pp. 46–52; "Working for Mr. Clean Jeans," *U.S. News & World Report,* August 2, 1993, pp. 49–50; Martha Nichols, "Third-World Families at Work: Child Labor or Child Care?," *Harvard Business Review,* January–February 1993, pp. 12–23.

12. Joseph A. Ness and Thomas G. Cucuzza, "Tapping the Full Potential of ABC," *Harvard Business Review,* July 1995–August 1995, pp. 130–38; Jae K. Shim and Joel G. Siegel, *Modern Cost Management and Analysis* (Hauppauge, NY: Barrons, 1992); John K. Shank and Vijay Govindarajan, *Strategic Cost Management: The New Tool for Competitive Advantage* (New York: The Free Press, 1993); Robin Cooper and Robert S. Kaplan, "Profit Priorities From Activity-Based Costing," *Harvard Business Review,* May–June 1991, pp. 130–37; Douglas M. Lambert and Jay U. Sterling, "What Types of Profitability Reports Do Marketing Managers Receive?" *Industrial Marketing Management,* November, 1987, pp. 295–304.

13. "Low-Wage Lessons: How Marriott Keeps Good Help," *Business Week,* November 11, 1996, pp. 108–16; "Hiring Welfare People, Hotel Chain Finds, Is Tough but Rewarding," *The Wall Street Journal,* October 31, 1996, p. A1ff.; Randy Englund, "Human Resource Skills for the Project Manager: The Human Aspects of Project Management, Volume Two," *Journal of Product Innovation Management,* January 1998, pp. 99–100; Patricia W. Meyers, "Organizational Change and Redesign: Ideas and Insights for Improving Performance," *Journal of Product Innovation Management,* March 1997, pp. 144–45; Dave Ulrich, "A New Mandate for Human Resources," *Harvard Business Review,* January–February 1998, pp. 124–34; Vincent A. Mabert and Roger W. Schmenner, "Assessing the Roller Coaster of Downsizing," *Business Horizons,* July–August 1997, pp. 45–53; Myron Glassman and Bruce McAfee, "Integrating the Personnel and Marketing Functions: The Challenge of the 1990s," *Business Horizons,* May–June 1992, pp. 52–59; Madhubalan Viswanathan and Eric M. Olson, "The Implementation of Business Strategies: Implications for the Sales Function," *Journal of Personal Selling & Sales Management,* Winter 1992, pp. 45–58; Jeanie Daniel Duck, "Managing Change: The Art of Balancing," *Harvard Business Review,* November–December 1993, pp. 109–18.

Chapter 22

1. This material is drawn from the web site of the World Business Council for Sustainable Development (www.wbcsd.ch).

2. For more information on sustainability, visit the three web sites that were mentioned and the many others to which these three are "hotlinked."

3. For an historical review of this topic see Robert W. Nason and Phillip D. White, "The Visions of Charles C. Slater: Social Consequences of Marketing," *Journal of Macromarketing* 1, no. 2 (1981), pp. 4–18.

4. "Capitalism 101: U.S. Consultants Help Tiny Moldova Switch from Soviet Ways," *The Wall Street Journal,* July 25, 1997, p. A1ff.; "The Russians Are Here, the Russians Are Here," *Business Week,* July 7, 1997, pp. 94–95; "Russia's Robber Barons," *Fortune,* March 3, 1997, pp. 120–26; "Murder in Moscow," *Fortune,* March 3, 1997, pp. 128–34; "Special Report: Russia '96," *Time,* May 27, 1996, pp. 46–72; Stanislaw Gajewski, "Consumer Behavior in Economics of Shortage," *Journal of Business Research,* January 1992, pp. 5–10; Krystyna Iwinska-Knop, "Distribution as a Barrier to Application of Marketing in the Centrally Planned Economy (Case Study of Poland)," *Journal of Business Research,* January 1992, pp. 19–26; "Russia's New Capitalism," *Business Week,* October 10, 1994, pp. 68–80.

5. Reed Moyer, *Macro Marketing: A Social Perspective* (New York: John Wiley & Sons, 1972), pp. 3–5; see also Roger A. Layton, "Measures of Structural Change in Macromarketing Systems," *Journal of Macromarketing,* Spring 1989, pp. 5–15.

6. "Now Are You Satisfied? The 1998 American Customer Satisfaction Index," *Fortune,* February 16, 1998, pp. 161–68; Claes Fornell, Michael D. Johnson, Eugene W. Anderson, Jaesung Cha, and Barbara E. Bryant, "The American Customer Satisfaction Index: Nature, Purpose, and Findings," *Journal of Marketing,* October 1996, pp. 7–18; Eugene W. Anderson, Claes Fornell, and Donald R. Lehmann, "Customer Satisfaction, Market Share, and Profitability: Findings From Sweden," *Journal of Marketing,* July 1994, pp. 53–66; John F. Gaski and Michael J. Etzel, "The Index of Consumer Sentiment Toward Marketing," *Journal of Marketing,* July 1986, pp. 71–81; "The Limits of Customer Satisfaction," *Brandweek,* March 3, 1997, p. 17; Hiram C. Barksdale et al., "A Cross-National Survey of Consumer Attitudes Toward Marketing Practices, Consumerism, and Government Regulations," *Columbia Journal of World Business,* Summer 1982, pp. 71–86; Hiram C. Barksdale and William D. Perreault, Jr., "Can Consumers Be Satisfied?" *MSU Business Topics,* Spring 1980, pp. 19–30.

7. "A Satisfied Customer Isn't Enough," *Fortune,* July 21, 1997, pp. 112–13; Theodore P. Stank, Patricia J. Daugherty, and Alexander E. Ellinger, "Voice of the Customer: The Impact on Customer Satisfaction," *International Journal of Purchasing & Materials Management,* Fall 1997, pp. 2–9; Jeffrey G. Blodgett, Donna J. Hill, and Stephen S. Tax, "The Effects of Distributive, Procedural, and Interactional Justice on Postcomplaint Behavior," *Journal of Retailing,* Summer 1997, pp. 185–210; Thorsten Hennig-Thurau and Alexander Klee,

"The Impact of Customer Satisfaction and Relationship Quality on Customer Retention: A Critical Reassessment and Model Development," *Psychology & Marketing,* December 1997, pp. 737–64; Scott W. Hansen, Thomas L. Powers, and John E. Swan, "Modeling Industrial Buyer Complaints: Implications for Satisfying and Saving Customers," *Journal of Marketing Theory & Practice,* Fall 1997, pp. 12–22; Paul G. Patterson, Lester W. Johnson, and Richard A. Spreng, "Modeling the Determinants of Customer Satisfaction for Business-to-Business Professional Services," *Journal of the Academy of Marketing Science,* Winter 1997, pp. 4–17; Stanley F. Slater, Eric M. Olson, and Venkateshwar K. Reddy, "Strategy-Based Performance Measurement," *Business Horizons,* July–August 1997, pp. 37–44; Stephen S. Tax, Stephen W. Brown, and Murali Chandrashekaran, "Customer Evaluations of Service Complaint Experiences: Implications for Relationship Marketing," *Journal of Marketing,* April 1998, pp. 60–76; Sunder Narayanan, "Customer Satisfaction Measurement and Management," *Journal of the Academy of Marketing Science,* Summer 1996, pp. 276–77; Mary C. Gilly, William B. Stevenson, and Laura J. Yale, "Dynamics of Complaint Management in the Service Organization," *The Journal of Consumer Affairs,* Winter 1991, pp. 295–322; F. Gouillart and F. Sturdivant, "Spend a Day in the Life of Your Customers," *Harvard Business Review,* January–February 1994, pp. 116–27; Erdener Kaynak, Orsay Kucukemiroglu, and Yavuz Odabasi, "Consumer Complaint Handling in an Advanced Developing Economy: An Empirical Investigation," *Journal of Business Ethics,* November 1992, pp. 813–30; Jagdip Singh, "Industry Characteristics and Consumer Dissatisfaction," *The Journal of Consumer Affairs,* Summer 1991, pp. 19–56; A. Parasuraman, Valarie A. Zeithaml, and Leonard L. Berry, "SERVQUAL: A Multiple-Item Scale for Measuring Consumer Perceptions of Service Quality," *Journal of Retailing,* Spring 1988, pp. 12–40.

8. Kevin J. Clancy and Robert S. Shulman, *Marketing Myths That Are Killing Business: The Cure for Death Wish Marketing* (New York: McGraw-Hill, 1994); Regina E. Herzlinger, "Can Public Trust in Nonprofits and Governments Be Restored?" *Harvard Business Review,* March–April 1996, pp. 97–107; Michael S. Minor, "Relentless: The Japanese Way of Marketing," *Journal of the Academy of Marketing Science,* Spring 1998, pp. 160–61; Charles C. Snow, "Twenty-First-Century Organizations: Implications for a New Marketing Paradigm," *Journal of the Academy of Marketing Science,* Winter 1997, pp. 72–74; Frederick F. Reichheld, "Learning From Customer Defections," *Harvard Business Review,* March–April 1996, pp. 56–61ff. For a classic discussion of the problem and mechanics of measuring the efficiency of marketing, see Reavis Cox, *Distribution in a High-Level Economy* (Englewood Cliffs, N.J.: Prentice-Hall, 1965).

9. For more on criticisms of advertising, see Barbara J. Phillips, "In Defense of Advertising: A Social Perspective," *Journal of Business Ethics,* February 1997, pp. 109–18; Charles Trappey, "A Meta-Analysis of Consumer Choice and Subliminal Advertising," *Psychology & Marketing,* August 1996, pp. 517–30; Karl A. Boedecker, Fred W. Morgan, and Linda B. Wright, "The Evolution of First Amendment Protection for Commercial Speech," *Journal of Marketing,* January 1995, pp. 38–47; Thomas C. O'Guinn and L. J. Shrum, "The Role of Television in the Construction of Consumer Reality," *Journal of Consumer Research,* March 1997, pp. 278–94; see also Robert B. Archibald, Clyde A. Haulman, and Carlisle E. Moody, Jr., "Quality, Price, Advertising, and Published Quality Ratings," *Journal of Consumer Research,* March 1983, pp. 347–56.

10. Arnold J. Toynbee, *America and World Revolution* (New York: Oxford University Press, 1966), pp. 144–45; see also John Kenneth Galbraith, *Economics and the Public Purpose* (Boston: Houghton Mifflin, 1973), pp. 144–45.

11. Russell J. Tomsen, "Take It Away," *Newsweek,* October 7, 1974, p. 21.

12. Michael J. Barone, Randall L. Rose, Kenneth C. Manning, and Paul W. Miniard, "Another Look at the Impact of Reference Information on Consumer Impressions of Nutrition Information," *Journal of Public Policy & Marketing,* Spring 1996, pp. 55–62; Thomas A. Hemphill, "Legislating Corporate Social Responsibility," *Business Horizons,* March–April 1997, pp. 53–58; Priscilla A. La Barbera and Zeynep Gurhan, "The Role of Materialism, Religiosity, and Demographics in Subjective Well-Being," *Psychology & Marketing,* January 1997, pp. 71–97; Dennis J. Cahill, "Consumption and the World of Goods," *Journal of Marketing,* April 1994, pp. 131–32; Jacqueline K. Eastman, Bill Fredenberger, David Campbell, and Stephen Calvert, "The Relationship Between Status Consumption and Materialism: A Cross-Cultural Comparison of Chinese, Mexican and American Students," *Journal of Marketing Theory & Practice,* Winter 1997, pp. 52–66; James A. Muncy and Jacqueline K. Eastman, "Materialism and Consumer Ethics: An Exploratory Study," *Journal of Business Ethics,* January 1998, pp. 137–45; Donald P. Robin and R. Eric Reidenbach, "Identifying Critical Problems for Mutual Cooperation Between the Public and Private Sectors: A Marketing Perspective," *Journal of the Academy of Marketing Science,* Fall 1986, pp. 1–12.

13. Frederick Webster, *Social Aspects of Marketing* (Englewood Cliffs, N.J.: Prentice-Hall, 1974), p. 32; Terrence H. Witkowski, "The Early American Style: A History of Marketing and Consumer Values," *Psychology & Marketing,* March 1998, pp. 125–43. "This School Was Sponsored by . . .," *Parenting,* March 1998, p. 23; "Channel One Taps Principals as Promoters," *The Wall Street Journal,* September 15, 1997, p. B1ff.; "School's Back, and So Are the Marketers," *The Wall Street Journal,* September 15, 1997, p. B1ff.; "Hey Kid, Buy This!" *Business Week,* June 30, 1997, pp. 62–69; "This Class Brought to You by . . .," *USA Today,* January 3, 1997, p. 3A; "New Ad Vehicles: Police Car, School Bus, Garbage Truck," *The Wall Street Journal,* February 20, 1996, p. B1ff.; "A Lesson in Sample Arithmetic," *Advertising Age,* January 2, 1995, p. 22; "Companies Teach All Sorts of Lessons with Educational Tools They Give Away," *The Wall Street Journal,* April 19, 1994, p. B1ff.

14. William P. Cordeiro, "Suggested Management Responses to Ethical Issues Raised by Technological Change," *Journal of Business Ethics,* September 1997, pp. 1393–1400; W.P. Cunningham, "The Golden Rule As Universal Ethical Norm," *Journal of Business Ethics,* January 1998, pp. 105–09; Eli P. I. Cox, Michael S. Wogalter, Sara L. Stokes, and Elizabeth J.T. Murff, "Do Product Warnings Increase Safe Behavior? A Meta-Analysis," *Journal of Public Policy & Marketing,* Fall 1997, pp. 195–204; James A. Roberts, "Will the Real Socially Responsible Consumer Please Step Forward?" *Business Horizons,* January–February 1996, pp. 79–83; Paul N. Bloom, George R. Milne, and Robert Adler, "Avoiding Misuse of New Information Technologies: Legal and Societal Considerations," *Journal of Marketing,* January 1994, pp. 98–110; H. R. Dodge, Elizabeth A. Edwards, and Sam Fullerton, "Consumer Transgressions in the Marketplace: Consumers' Perspectives," *Psychology & Marketing,* December 1996, pp. 821–35; John Priddle, "Marketing Ethics, Macromarketing, and the Managerial Perspective Reconsidered," *Journal of Macromarketing,* Fall 1994, pp. 47–62; Bernard Avishai, "What Is Business's Social Compact?," *Harvard Business Review,* January–February 1994, pp. 38–49. For more on privacy, see "A Little Privacy, Please," *Business Week,* March 16, 1998, pp. 98–100; "Don't Expect Your Secrets to Get Kept on the Internet," *The Wall Street Journal,* February 6, 1998, p. B5; "No Solitude in Cyberspace," *USA Today,* June 9, 1997, p. 1Dff.; "No Privacy on the Web," *Time,* June 2, 1997, pp. 64–65; Ellen R. Foxman and Paula Kilcoyne, "Information Technology, Marketing Practice, and Consumer Privacy: Ethical Issues," *Journal of Public Policy & Marketing,* Spring 1993, pp. 106–19;. For more on shoplifting, see "Electronic Tags Are Beeping Everywhere," *The Wall Street Journal,* April 20, 1998, p. B1ff.; "A Time to Steal," *Brandweek,* February 16, 1998, p. 24; Scott Dawson, "Consumer Responses to Electronic Article Surveillance Alarms," *Journal of Retailing,* Fall 1993, pp. 353–62. For more on ethics, see " 'Ethnic Pricing' Means Unfair Air Fares," *The Wall Street Journal,* December 5, 1997, p. B1ff.; "On the Net, Anything Goes," *Newsweek,* July 7, 1997, pp. 28–30; "Levi's" As Ye Sew, So Shall Ye Reap," *Fortune,* May 12, 1997, pp. 104–16; "48% of Workers Admit to Unethical or Illegal Acts," *USA Today,* April 4, 1997, p. 1Aff.; "Ethics for Hire," *Business Week,* July 15, 1996, pp. 26–28; "How a Drug Firm Paid for University Study, Then Undermined It," *The Wall Street Journal,* April 25, 1996, p. A1ff.; James A. Muncy and Scott J. Vitell, "Consumer Ethics: An Investigation of the Ethical Beliefs of the Final Consumer," *Journal of Business Research,* June 1992, pp. 297–312; Gene R. Laczniak and Patrick E. Murphy, "Fostering Ethical Marketing Decisions," *Journal of Business Ethics,* April 1991, pp. 259–72.

15. "Diesel Vehicles, in Greener Mode, May Stage Comeback," *The Wall Street Journal,* April 9, 1998, p. B4; "As Old Pallets Pile Up, Critics Hammer Them as a New Eco-Menace," *The Wall Street Journal,* April 1, 1998, p. A1ff.; "A Maine Forest Firm Prospers by Earning Eco-Friendly Label," *The Wall Street Journal,* November 26, 1997, p. A1ff.; "When Green Begets Green," *Business Week,* November 10, 1997, pp. 98–104; "Is It Rainforest Crunch Time?" *Business Week,* July 15, 1996, pp. 70–71; Kent L. Granzin, Jeffrey D. Brazell, and John J. Painter, "An Examination of Influences Leading to Americans' Endorsement of the Policy of Free Trade," *Journal of Public Policy & Marketing,* Spring 1997, pp. 93–109; Anil Menon and Ajay Menon, "Enviropreneurial Marketing Strategy: The Emergence of Corporate Environmentalism As Market Strategy," *Journal of Marketing,* January 1997, pp. 51–67; William E. Kilbourne, "Green Advertising: Salvation or Oxymoron?" *Journal of Advertising,* Summer 1995, pp. 7–19; "Who Scores Best on the Environment?" *Fortune,* July 26, 1993, pp. 114–22.

Accessories short-lived capital items—tools and equipment used in production or office activities.

Accumulating collecting products from many small producers.

Administered channel systems various channel members informally agree to cooperate with one another.

Administered prices consciously set prices aimed at reaching the firm's objectives.

Adoption curve shows when different groups accept ideas.

Adoption process the steps individuals go through on the way to accepting or rejecting a new idea.

Advertising any *paid* form of nonpersonal presentation of ideas, goods, or services by an identified sponsor.

Advertising agencies specialists in planning and handling mass-selling details for advertisers.

Advertising allowances price reductions to firms in the channel to encourage them to advertise or otherwise promote the firm's products locally.

Advertising managers managers of their company's mass selling effort in television, newspapers, magazines, and other media.

Agent middlemen wholesalers who do not own (take title to) the products they sell.

Agribusiness a term used to describe the move toward bigger and more businesslike agricultural enterprises.

AIDA model consists of four promotion jobs—(1) to get *Attention,* (2) to hold *Interest,* (3) to arouse *Desire,* and (4) to obtain *Action.*

Allowance (accounting term) occurs when a customer is not satisfied with a purchase for some reason and the seller gives a price reduction on the original invoice (bill), but the customer keeps the goods or services.

Allowances reductions in price given to final consumers, customers, or channel members for doing something or accepting less of something.

Assorting putting together a variety of products to give a target market what it wants.

Attitude a person's point of view toward something.

Auction companies agent middlemen who provide a place where buyers and sellers can come together and complete a transaction.

Automatic vending selling and delivering products through vending machines.

Average cost (per unit) the total cost divided by the related quantity.

Average-cost pricing adding a reasonable markup to the average cost of a product.

Average fixed cost (per unit) the total fixed cost divided by the related quantity.

Average variable cost (per unit) the total variable cost divided by the related quantity.

Bait pricing setting some very low prices to attract customers but trying to sell more expensive models or brands once the customer is in the store.

Balance sheet an accounting statement that shows a company's assets, liabilities, and net worth.

Basic list prices the prices that final customers or users are normally asked to pay for products.

Basic sales tasks *order-getting, order-taking,* and *supporting.*

Battle of the brands the competition between dealer brands and manufacturer brands.

Belief a person's opinion about something.

Benchmarking picking a basis of comparison for evaluating how well a job is being done.

Bid pricing offering a specific price for each possible job rather than setting a price that applies for all customers.

Birthrate the number of babies per 1,000 people.

Brand equity the value of a brand's overall strength in the market.

Brand familiarity how well customers recognize and accept a company's brand.

Brand insistence customers insist on a firm's branded product and are willing to search for it.

Brand managers manage specific products, often taking over the jobs formerly handled by an advertising manager—sometimes called product managers.

Brand name a word, letter, or a group of words or letters.

Brand nonrecognition final customers don't recognize a brand at all—even though middlemen may use the brand name for identification and inventory control.

Brand preference target customers usually choose the brand over other brands, perhaps because of habit or favourable past experience.

Brand recognition customers remember the brand.

Brand rejection potential customers won't buy a brand, unless its image is changed.

Branding the use of a name, term, symbol, or design—or a combination of these—to identify a product.

Break-even analysis an approach to determine whether the firm will be able to break even—that is, cover all its costs—with a particular price.

Break-even point (BEP) the sales quantity where the firm's total cost will just equal its total revenue.

Glossary

Breakthrough opportunities opportunities that help innovators develop hard-to-copy marketing strategies that will be very profitable for a long time.

Brokers agent middlemen who specialize in bringing buyers and sellers together.

Bulk-breaking dividing larger quantities into smaller quantities as products get closer to the final market.

Business and organizational customers any buyers who buy for resale or to produce other goods and services.

Business products products meant for use in producing other products.

Buying centre all the people who participate in or influence a purchase.

Buying function looking for and evaluating goods and services.

Capital the money invested in a firm.

Capital item a long-lasting product that can be used and depreciated for many years.

Cash-and-carry wholesalers like service wholesalers, except that the customer must pay cash.

Cash discounts reductions in the price to encourage buyers to pay their bills quickly.

Cash flow statement a financial report that forecasts how much cash will be available after paying expenses.

Catalogue selling involves mailing catalogues describing products for sale to potential or previous customers with executed orders then being mailed back to the retailer to be filled. Both advertising and ordering can now be done via the Internet.

Catalogue showroom retailers stores that sell several lines out of a catalogue and display showroom with backup inventories.

Catalogue wholesalers sell out of catalogues that may be distributed widely to smaller industrial customers or retailers who might not be called on by other middlemen.

Census Metropolitan Area the "main labour market area" of a continuous built-up area having a population of 100,000 or more.

Central markets convenient place where buyers and sellers can meet one-on-one to exchange goods and services.

Chain of supply the complete set of firms and facilities and logistics activities that are involved in procuring materials, transforming them into intermediate and finished products, and distributing them to customers.

Channel captain a manager who helps direct the activities of a whole channel and tries to avoid—or solve—channel conflicts.

Channel of distribution any series of firms or individuals who participate in the flow of products from producer to final user or consumer.

Close the salesperson's request for an order.

Clustering techniques approaches used to try to find similar patterns within sets of data.

Combination export manager a blend of manufacturers' agent and selling agent, who handles the entire export function for several producers of similar but noncompeting lines.

Combined target market approach combining two or more submarkets into one larger target market as a basis for one strategy.

Combiners firms that try to increase the size of their target markets by combining two or more segments.

Commission merchants handle products shipped to them by sellers, complete the sale, and then send the money collected less their commission to the original producer. They are most commonly found serving agricultural markets.

Communication process a source trying to reach a receiver with a message.

Comparative advertising advertising that makes specific brand comparisons using actual product names.

Competitive advantage a firm has a marketing mix that the target market sees as better than a competitor's mix.

Competitive advertising advertising that tries to develop selective demand for a specific brand rather than a product category.

Competitive barriers the conditions that may make it difficult, or even impossible, for a firm to compete in a market.

Competitive bids terms of sale offered by different suppliers in response to the buyer's purchase specifications.

Competitive environment the number and types of competitors the marketing manager must face, and how they may behave.

Competitive rivals a firm's closest competitors.

Competitor analysis an organized approach for evaluating the strengths and weaknesses of current or potential competitors' marketing strategies.

Complementary product pricing setting prices on several related products as a group.

Components processed expense items that become part of a finished product.

Concept testing getting reactions from customers about how well a new product idea fits their needs.

Confidence intervals the range on either side of an estimate from a sample that is likely to contain the true value for the whole population.

Consignment selling is when the supplier, rather than the retailer, remains the owner of the product until it is sold. The Competition Tribunal can prohibit such action if it is used to fix prices at retail or to discriminate among resellers.

Consultative selling approach a type of sales presentation in which the salesperson develops a good understanding of the individual customer's needs before trying to close the sale.

Consumer Packaging and Labelling Act This Act calls for bilingual labels and for the standardization of package sizes and shapes.

Consumer panel a group of consumers who provide information on a continuing basis.

Consumer products products meant for the final consumer.

Consumer surplus the difference to consumers between the value of a purchase and the price they pay.

Consumerism a social movement that seeks to increase the rights and powers of consumers.

Containerization grouping individual items into an economical shipping quantity and sealing them in protective containers for transit to the final destination.

Continuous improvement a commitment to constantly make things better one step at a time.

Contract farming involves farmers obtaining supplies and working capital from local dealers or manufacturers who agree to purchase that farm's output.

Contract manufacturing turning over production to others while retaining the marketing process.

Contractual channel systems various channel members agree by contract to cooperate with one another.

Contribution-margin approach a cost analysis approach in which all costs are not allocated in *all* situations.

Control the feedback process that helps the marketing manager learn (1) how ongoing plans and implementation are working and (2) how to plan for the future.

Convenience (food) stores a convenience-oriented variation of the conventional limited-line food stores.

Convenience products products a consumer needs but isn't willing to spend much time or effort shopping for.

Cooperative advertising middlemen and producers sharing in the cost of ads.

Cooperative chains retailer-sponsored groups, formed by independent retailers, to run their own buying organizations and conduct joint promotion efforts.

Copy thrust what the words and illustrations of an ad should communicate.

Corporate chain a firm that owns and manages more than one store—and often it's many.

Corporate channel systems corporate ownership all along the channel.

Corrective advertising ads to correct deceptive advertising.

Cost of sales total value (at cost) of the sales during the period.

Countertrade a special type of bartering in which products from one country are traded for products from another country.

Cues products, signs, ads, and other stimuli in the environment.

Cultural and social environment affects how and why people live and behave as they do.

Culture the whole set of beliefs, attitudes, and ways of doing things of a reasonably homogeneous set of people.

Cumulative quantity discounts reductions in price for larger purchases over a given period, such as a year.

Customer satisfaction the extent to which a firm fulfils a consumer's needs, desires, and expectations.

Customer service level how rapidly and dependably a firm can deliver what customers want.

Customer value the difference between the benefits a customer sees from a market offering and the costs of obtaining those benefits.

Dealer brands brands created by middlemen—sometimes referred to as private brands.

Debt financing borrowing money based on a promise to repay the loan, usually within a fixed time period and with a specific interest charge.

Decision support system (DSS) a computer program that makes it easy for marketing managers to get and use information *as they are making decisions.*

Decoding the receiver in the communication process translating the message.

Demand-backward pricing setting an acceptable final consumer price and working backward to what a producer can charge.

Demand curve a graph of the relationship between price and quantity demanded in a market—assuming all other things stay the same.

Department stores larger stores that are organized into many separate departments and offer many product lines.

Derived demand demand for business products derives from the demand for final consumer products.

Description (specification) buying buying from a written (or verbal) description of the product.

Determining dimensions the dimensions that actually affect the customer's purchase of a *specific* product or brand in a *product-market.*

Differentiation the marketing mix is distinct from and better than what's available from a competitor.

Direct mail retailing involves approaching prospective purchasers either through addressed promotional pieces or flyers delivered to their homes.

Direct marketing direct communication between a seller and an individual customer using a promotion method other than face-to-face personal selling.

Direct type advertising competitive advertising that aims for immediate buying action.

Discount houses stores that sell hard goods (cameras, TVs, appliances) at substantial price cuts to customers who go to discounter's low-rent store, pay cash, and take care of any service or repair problems themselves.

Discounts reductions from list price given by a seller to buyers, who either give up some marketing function or provide the function themselves.

Discrepancy of assortment the difference between the lines a typical producer makes and the assortment final consumers or users want.

Discrepancy of quantity the difference between the quantity of products it is economical for a producer to make and the quantity final users or consumers normally want.

Discretionary income what is left of disposable income after paying for necessities.

Disposable income income that is left after taxes.

Dissonance tension caused by uncertainty about the rightness of a decision.

Distribution centre a special kind of warehouse designed to speed the flow of goods and avoid unnecessary storing costs.

Diversification moving into totally different lines of business—perhaps entirely unfamiliar products, markets, or even levels in the production/marketing system.

Diversion in transit allows redirection of railway carloads already in transit.

Door-to-door selling going directly to the consumer's home.

Drive a strong stimulus that encourages action to reduce a need.

Drop-shippers wholesalers who own (take title to) the products they sell, but do not actually handle, stock, or deliver them.

Dual distribution when a producer uses several competing channels to reach the same target market—perhaps using several middlemen in addition to selling directly.

Dumping pricing a product sold in a foreign market below the cost of producing it or at a price lower than in its domestic market.

Early adopters the second group in the adoption curve to adopt a new product; these people are usually well respected by their peers and often are opinion leaders.

Early majority a group in the adoption curve that avoids risk and waits to consider a new idea until many early adopters try it—and like it.

Economic and technological environment affects the way firms—and the whole economy—use resources.

Economic buyers people who know all the facts and logically compare choices in terms of cost and value received, to get the greatest satisfaction from spending their time and money.

Economic needs needs concerned with making the best use of a consumer's time and money, as the consumer judges it.

Economic system the way an economy organizes itself to use scarce resources to produce goods and services and distribute them for consumption by various people and groups in the society.

Economies of scale as a company produces larger numbers of a particular product, the cost for each of these products goes down.

Elastic demand if prices are dropped, the quantity demanded will stretch enough to increase total revenue.

Elastic supply the quantity supplied does stretch more if the price is raised.

Electronic commerce the exchange of valuable information, goods, and services. It includes but is not limited to the actual sale of merchandise.

Electronic data interchange (EDI) an approach that puts information in a standardized format easily shared between different computer systems.

Emergency products products that are purchased immediately when the need is great.

Empowerment giving employees the authority to correct a problem without first checking with management.

Empty nesters people whose children are grown and who are now able to spend their money in other ways.

Encoding the source in the communication process deciding what it wants to say and translating it into words or symbols that will have the same meaning to the receiver.

Equilibrium point the quantity and the price sellers are willing to offer are equal to the quantity and price that buyers are willing to accept.

Everyday low pricing setting a low list price rather than relying on a high list price that frequently changes with various discounts or allowances.

Exclusive distribution selling through only one middleman in a particular geographic area.

Expectation an outcome or event that a person anticipates or looks forward to.

Expense item a product whose total cost is treated as a business expense in the period it's purchased.

Expenses all the remaining costs that are subtracted from the gross margin to get the net profit.

Experience curve pricing average-cost pricing using an estimate of *future* average costs.

Experimental method a research approach in which researchers compare the responses of two or more groups that are similar except on the characteristic being tested.

Export agents manufacturers' agents who specialize in export trade.

Export brokers brokers who specialize in bringing together buyers and sellers from different countries.

Export commission houses represent relatively small Canadian producers in foreign markets in return for receiving a commission on each sale made.

Exporting selling some of what the firm produces to foreign markets.

Extensive problem solving the type of problem solving consumers use for a completely new or important need—when they put much effort into deciding how to satisfy it.

Facilitators firms that provide one or more of the marketing functions other than buying or selling.

Factor a variable that shows the relationship of some other variable to the item being forecast.

Factor method an approach to forecast sales by finding a relationship between the company's sales and some other factor (or factors).

Fad an idea that is fashionable only to certain groups who are enthusiastic about it—but these groups are so fickle that a fad is even more short-lived than a regular fashion.

Family brand a brand name that is used for several products.

Farm products products grown by farmers, such as oranges, wheat, sugar cane, cattle, poultry, eggs, and milk.

Fashion currently accepted or popular style.

Financing provides the necessary cash and credit to produce, transport, store, promote, sell, and buy products.

Fishbone diagram a visual aid that helps organize cause-and-effect relationships for "things gone wrong."

Fixed-cost (FC) contribution per unit the selling price per unit minus the variable cost per unit.

Flexible-price policy offering the same product and quantities to different customers at different prices.

F.O.B. a transportation term meaning free on board some vehicle at some point.

Focus group interview an interview of 6 to 10 people in an informal group setting.

Form utility provided when someone produces something tangible.

Franchise operation a franchisor develops a good marketing strategy, and the retail franchise holders carry out the strategy in their own units.

Freight absorption pricing absorbing freight cost so that a firm's delivered price meets the nearest competitor's.

Freight forwarders transportation wholesalers who combine the small shipments of many shippers into more economical shipping quantities.

Full-cost approach all costs are allocated to products, customers, or other categories.

Full-line pricing setting prices for a whole line of products.

Functional accounts the categories to which various costs are charged to show the *purpose* for which expenditures are made.

General Agreement on Tariffs and Trade (GATT) a set of rules governing restrictions on world trade, agreed to by most of the nations of the world.

General merchandise wholesalers service wholesalers who carry a wide variety of nonperishable items such as hardware, electrical supplies, plumbing supplies, furniture, drugs, cosmetics, and automobile equipment.

General stores early retailers who carried anything they could sell in reasonable volume.

Generic market a market with *broadly* similar needs—and sellers offering various and *often diverse* ways of satisfying those needs.

Generic products products that have no brand at all other than identification of their contents and the manufacturer or middleman.

Gross margin (gross profit) the money left to cover the expenses of selling the products and operating the business.

Gross national product (GNP) the total market value of goods and services produced in an economy in a year.

Gross sales the total amount charged to all customers during some time period.

Hazardous Products Act This Act gives Industry Canada the authority either to ban or to regulate the sale, distribution, and labelling of hazardous products.

Heterogeneous shopping products shopping products the customer sees as different—and wants to inspect for quality and suitability.

Homogeneous shopping products shopping products the customer sees as basically the same—and wants at the lowest price.

Hypermarkets very large stores that try to carry not only food and drug items but all goods and services that the consumer purchases *routinely* (also called supercentres).

Hypotheses educated guesses about the relationships between things or about what will happen in the future.

Iceberg principle much good information is hidden in summary data.

Ideal market exposure when a product is available widely enough to satisfy target customers' needs but not exceed them.

Implementation putting marketing plans into operation.

Import agents manufacturers' agents who specialize in import trade.

Import brokers brokers who specialize in bringing together buyers and sellers from different countries.

Import commission houses represent foreign producers in Canada in return for receiving a commission on each sale made.

Impulse products products that are bought quickly as *unplanned* purchases because of a strongly felt need.

Indices statistical combinations of several time series, used to find some time series that will lead the series to be forecast.

Indirect type advertising competitive advertising that points out product advantages in order to affect future buying decisions.

Individual brands separate brand names used for each product.

Individual product a particular product within a product line.

Inelastic demand although the quantity demanded increases if the price is decreased, the quantity demanded will not stretch enough to avoid a decrease in total revenue.

Inelastic supply the quantity supplied does not stretch much (if at all) if the price is raised.

Innovation the development and spread of new ideas and products.

Innovators the first group to adopt new products.

Inspection buying looking at every item.

Installations important capital items such as buildings, land rights, and major equipment.

Institutional advertising advertising that tries to promote an organization's image, reputation, or ideas, rather than a specific product.

Integrated marketing communications the intentional coordination of every communication from a firm to a target customer to convey a consistent and complete message.

Intensive distribution selling a product through all responsible and suitable wholesalers or retailers who will stock and/or sell the product.

Intermediary a middleman.

Internet a system for linking computers around the world.

Intranet a system for linking computers within a company.

Introductory price dealing temporary price cuts to speed new products into a market.

Inventory the amount of goods being stored.

ISO 9000 a way for a supplier to document its quality procedures according to internationally recognized standards.

Job description a written statement of what a salesperson is expected to do.

Joint venturing in international marketing, a domestic firm entering into a partnership with a foreign firm.

Jury of executive opinion forecasting by combining the opinions of experienced executives, perhaps from marketing, production, finance, purchasing, and top management.

Just-in-time delivery reliably getting products there *just* before the customer needs them.

Laggards prefer to do things the way they have been done in the past and are very suspicious of new ideas—sometimes called nonadopters (see *adoption curve*).

Late majority a group of adopters who are cautious about new ideas (see *adoption curve*).

Law of diminishing demand if the price of a product is raised, a smaller quantity will be demanded; and if the price of a product is lowered, a greater quantity will be demanded.

Leader pricing setting some very low prices—real bargains—to get customers into retail stores.

Leading series a time series that changes in the same direction *but ahead of* the series to be forecast.

Learning a change in a person's thought processes caused by prior experience.

Licensed brand a well-known brand that sellers pay a fee to use.

Licensing selling the right to use some process, trademark, patent, or other right for a fee or royalty.

Lifestages a classification that focuses on the very different stages that each person passes through from birth to death.

Lifestyle analysis the analysis of a person's day-to-day pattern of living as expressed in that person's *A*ctivities, *I*nterests, and *O*pinions—sometimes referred to as AIOs or psychographics.

Limited-function wholesalers merchant wholesalers who provide only *some* wholesaling functions.

Limited-line stores stores that specialize in certain lines of related products rather than a wide assortment—sometimes called single-line stores.

Limited problem solving when a consumer is willing to put *some* effort into deciding the best way to satisfy a need.

Logistics the transporting, storing, and handling of goods to match target customers' needs with a firm's marketing mix, both within individual firms and along a channel of distribution (i.e., another name for physical distribution).

Long-run target return pricing pricing to cover all costs and over the long run achieve an average target return.

Low-involvement purchases purchases that have little importance or relevance for the customer.

Macro-marketing a social process that directs an economy's flow of goods and services from producers to consumers in a way that effectively matches supply with demand and accomplishes the objectives of society.

Mail-order wholesalers sell out of catalogues that are distributed widely to smaller industrial customers or retailers unlikely to be called upon by other market intermediaries.

Major accounts sales force salespeople who sell directly to large accounts such as major retail chain stores.

Management contracting the seller provides only management skills—others own the production and distribution facilities.

Manufacturer brands brands created by producers.

Manufacturers' agents agent middlemen who sell similar products for several noncompeting producers for a commission on what is actually sold.

Manufacturers' sales branches separate warehouses that producers set up away from their factories.

Marginal analysis evaluating the change in total revenue and total cost from selling one more unit to find the most profitable price and quantity.

Marginal cost the change in total cost that results from producing one more unit.

Marginal profit profit on the last unit sold.

Marginal revenue the change in total revenue that results from the sale of one more unit of a product.

Markdown a retail price reduction that is required because customers won't buy some item at the originally marked up price.

Markdown ratio a tool used by many retailers to measure the efficiency of various departments and their whole business.

Market a group of potential customers with similar needs who are willing to exchange something of value with sellers offering various goods and/or services—that is, ways of satisfying those needs.

Market development trying to increase sales by selling present products in new markets.

Market-directed economic system the individual decisions of the many producers and consumers make the macro-level decisions for the whole economy.

Market growth a stage of the product life cycle when industry sales grow fast, and industry profits rise—but then start falling.

Market information function the collection, analysis, and distribution of all the information needed to plan, carry out, and control marketing activities.

Market introduction a stage of the product life cycle when sales are low as a new idea is first introduced to a market.

Market maturity a stage of the product life cycle when industry sales level off and competition gets tougher.

Market penetration trying to increase sales of a firm's present products in its present markets probably through a more aggressive marketing mix.

Market potential what a whole market segment might buy.

Market segment a relatively homogeneous group of customers who will respond to a marketing mix in a similar way.

Market segmentation a two-step process of: (1) *naming* broad product-markets and (2) *segmenting* these broad product-markets in order to select target markets and develop suitable marketing mixes.

Marketing audit a systematic, critical, and unbiased review and appraisal of the basic objectives and policies of the marketing function and of the organization, methods, procedures, and people employed to implement the policies.

Marketing boards are an important type of marketing institution for agricultural products. They differ in the powers they can exercise.

Marketing company era a time when, in addition to short-run marketing planning, marketing people develop long range plans—sometimes 10 or more years ahead—and the whole company effort is guided by the marketing concept.

Marketing concept the idea that an organization should aim *all* its efforts at satisfying its *customers*—at a *profit*.

Marketing department era a time when all marketing activities are brought under the control of one department to improve short-run policy planning and to try to integrate the firm's activities.

Marketing ethics the moral standards that guide marketing decisions and actions.

Marketing information system (MIS) an organized way of continually gathering, accessing, and analyzing information that marketing managers need in order to make decisions.

Marketing management process the process of (1) *planning* marketing activities, (2) directing the *implementation* of the plans, and (3) *controlling* these plans.

Marketing mix the controllable variables that the company puts together to satisfy a target group.

Marketing model a statement of relationships among marketing variables.

Marketing orientation trying to carry out the marketing concept.

Marketing plan a written statement of a marketing strategy *and* the time-related details for carrying out the strategy.

Marketing program blends all of the firm's marketing plans into one big plan.

Marketing research procedures to develop and analyze new information to help marketing managers make decisions.

Marketing research process a five-step application of the scientific method that includes (1) defining the problem, (2) analyzing the situation, (3) getting problem-specific data, (4) interpreting the data, and (5) solving the problem.

Marketing strategy specifies a target market and a related marketing mix.

Markup a dollar amount added to the cost of products to get the selling price.

Markup chain the sequence of markups firms use at different levels in a channel, which together determine the price structure in the whole channel.

Markup (percent) the percentage of selling price that is added to the cost to get the selling price.

Mass customization tailoring the principles of mass production to meet the unique needs of individual customers.

Mass marketing the typical production-oriented approach that aims vaguely at everyone with the same marketing mix.

Mass merchandisers large self-service stores with many departments that emphasize soft goods (housewares, clothing, and fabrics) and staples (like health and beauty aids), and that sell on lower margins to get faster turnover.

Mass-merchandising concept the idea that retailers should offer low prices to get faster turnover and greater sales volume by appealing to larger numbers.

Mass selling communicating with large numbers of potential customers at the same time.

Megalopolis a strip of land running approximately 750 miles from Quebec City in the east to Windsor in the west.

Merchant wholesalers wholesalers who own (take title to) the products they sell.

Message channel the carrier of the message.

Micro-macro dilemma what is good for some producers and consumers may not be good for society as a whole.

Micro-marketing the performance of activities that seek to accomplish an organization's objectives by anticipating customer or client needs and directing a flow of need-satisfying goods and services from producer to customer or client.

Middleman someone who specializes in trade rather than production, sometimes called an intermediary.

Mission statement sets out the organization's basic purpose for being.

Missionary salespeople supporting salespeople who work for producers by calling on their middlemen and their customers.

Modified rebuy the in-between process where some review of the buying situation is done—though not as much as in new-task buying or as little as in straight rebuys.

Monopolistic competition a market situation that develops when a market has (1) different (heterogeneous) products and (2) sellers who feel they do have some competition in this market.

Multinational corporations firms that have a direct investment in several countries and run their businesses depending on the choices available anywhere in the world.

Multiple buying influence several people share in making a purchase decision—perhaps even top management.

Multiple target market approach segmenting the market and choosing two or more segments, then treating each as a separate target market needing a different marketing mix.

Nationalism an emphasis on a country's interests before everything else.

Natural accounts the categories to which various costs are charged in the normal financial accounting cycle.

Natural products products that occur in nature, such as fish and game, timber and maple syrup, and copper, zinc, iron ore, oil, and coal.

Needs the basic forces that motivate a person to do something.

Negotiated contract buying agreeing to a contract that allows for changes in the purchase arrangements.

Negotiated price a price that is set based on bargaining between the buyer and seller.

Net an invoice term meaning that payment for the face value of the invoice is due immediately also see *cash discounts.*

Net profit what the company earns from its operations during a particular period.

Net sales the actual sales dollars the company receives.

New product a product that is new *in any way* for the company concerned.

New-task buying when an organization has a new need and the buyer wants a great deal of information.

New unsought products products offering really new ideas that potential customers don't know about yet.

Noise any distraction that reduces the effectiveness of the communication process.

Nonadopters prefer to do things the way they have been done in the past and are very suspicious of new ideas—sometimes called laggards (see *adoption curve*).

Noncumulative quantity discounts reductions in price when a customer purchases a larger quantity on an *individual order.*

Nonprice competition aggressive action on one or more of the Ps other than Price.

North American Free Trade Agreement (NAFTA) lays out a plan to reshape the rules of trade among the United States, Canada, and Mexico.

North American Industry Classification System (NAICS) codes codes used to identify groups of firms in similar lines of business.

Odd-even pricing setting prices that end in certain numbers.

Oligopoly a special market situation that develops when a market has (1) essentially homogeneous products, (2) relatively few sellers, and (3) fairly inelastic industry demand curves.

One-price policy offering the same price to all customers who purchase products under essentially the same conditions and in the same quantities.

Open to buy a buyer has budgeted funds that he can spend during the current time period.

Operating ratios ratios of items on the operating statement to net sales.

Operating statement a simple summary of the financial results of a company's operations over a specified period of time.

Operational decisions short-run decisions to help implement strategies.

Opinion leader a person who influences others.

Order getters salespeople concerned with establishing relationships with new customers and developing new business.

Order-getting seeking possible buyers with a well-organized sales presentation designed to sell a product, service, or idea.

Order takers salespeople who sell to the regular or established customers, complete most sales transactions, and maintain relationships with their customers.

Order-taking the routine completion of sales made regularly to the target customers.

Packaging promoting and protecting the product.

Pareto chart a graph that shows the number of times a problem cause occurs, with problem causes ordered from most frequent to least frequent.

Penetration pricing policy trying to sell the whole market at one low price.

Perception how we gather and interpret information from the world around us.

Performance analysis analysis that looks for exceptions or variations from planned performance.

Performance index a number that shows the relationship of one value to another.

Personal needs an individual's need for personal satisfaction unrelated to what others think or do.

Personal selling direct spoken communication between sellers and potential customers, usually in person but sometimes over the telephone.

Phony list prices misleading prices that customers are shown to suggest that the price they are to pay has been discounted from list.

Physical distribution (PD) the transporting, storing, and handling of goods to match target customers' needs with a firm's marketing mix—both within individual firms and along a channel of distribution.

Physical distribution (PD) concept all transporting, storing, and product-handling activities of a business and a whole channel system should be coordinated as one system that seeks to minimize the cost of distribution for a given customer service level.

Physiological needs biological needs such as the need for food, drink, rest, and sex.

Piggyback service loading truck trailers or flat-bed trailers carrying containers onto railcars to provide both speed and flexibility.

Pioneering advertising advertising that tries to develop primary demand for a product category rather than demand for a specific brand.

Place making goods and services available in the right quantities and locations, when customers want them.

Place utility having the product available *where* the customer wants it.

Planned economic system government planners decide what and how much is to be produced and distributed by whom, when, to whom, and why.

Pool car service allows groups of shippers to pool their shipments of like goods into a full railcar.

Population in marketing research, the total group you are interested in.

Portfolio management treats alternative products, divisions, or strategic business units (SBUs) as though they are stock investments to be bought and sold using financial criteria.

Positioning an approach that refers to how customers think about proposed and/or present brands in a market.

Possession utility obtaining a good or service and having the right to use or consume it.

Prepared sales presentation a memorized presentation that is not adapted to each individual customer.

Prestige pricing setting a rather high price to suggest high quality or high status.

Price the amount of money that is charged for "something" of value.

Price discrimination injuring competition by selling the same products to different buyers at different prices.

Price fixing competitors illegally getting together to raise, lower, or stabilize prices.

Price leader a seller who sets a price that all others in the industry follow.

Price lining setting a few price levels for a product line and then marking all items at these prices.

Primary data information specifically collected to solve a current problem.

Primary demand demand for the general product idea, not just the company's own brand.

Private brands brands created by middlemen—sometimes referred to as dealer brands.

Private warehouses storing facilities owned or leased by companies for their own use.

Producers' cooperatives operate essentially as full-service wholesalers with the profits going to the cooperative's customer-members. Sunkist, Sunmaid Raisin Growers Association, and B.C. Hothouse are examples of such organizations.

Product the need-satisfying offering of a firm.

Product advertising advertising that tries to sell a specific product.

Product assortment the set of all product lines and individual products that a firm sells.

Product-bundle pricing setting one price for a set of products.

Product development offering new or improved products for present markets.

Product liability the legal obligation of sellers to pay damages to individuals who are injured by defective or unsafe products.

Product life cycle the stages a new product idea goes through from beginning to end.

Product line a set of individual products that are closely related.

Product managers manage specific products, often taking over the jobs formerly handled by an advertising manager—sometimes called brand managers.

Product-market a market with *very* similar needs—and sellers offering various *close substitute* ways of satisfying those needs.

Production actually *making* goods or *performing* services.

Production capacity the ability to produce a certain quantity and quality of specific goods or services.

Production era a time when a company focuses on production of a few specific products—perhaps because few of these products are available in the market.

Production orientation making whatever products are easy to produce and *then* trying to sell them.

Professional services specialized services that support a firm's operations.

Profit maximization objective an objective to get as much profit as possible.

Promotion communicating information between seller and potential buyer or others in the channel to influence attitudes and behaviour.

Prospecting following all the leads in the target market to identify potential customers.

Psychographics the analysis of a person's day-to-day pattern of living as expressed in that persons's *A*ctivities, *I*nterests, and *O*pinions—sometimes referred to as AIOs or lifestyle analysis.

Psychological pricing setting prices that have special appeal to target customers.

Public relations communication with noncustomers, including labour, public interest groups, stockholders, and the government.

Public warehouses independent storing facilities.

Publicity any *unpaid* form of nonpersonal presentation of ideas, goods, or services.

Pulling using promotion to get consumers to ask middlemen for the product.

Purchase discount a reduction of the original invoice amount for some business reason.

Purchasing managers buying specialists for their employers.

Pure competition a market situation that develops when a market has (1) homogeneous (similar) products, (2) many buyers and sellers who have full knowledge of the market, and (3) ease of entry for buyers and sellers.

Pure subsistence economy each family unit produces everything it consumes.

Push money (or prize money) allowances allowances (sometimes called PMs or spiffs) given to retailers by manufacturers or wholesalers to pass on to the retailers' salesclerks for aggressively selling certain items.

Pushing using normal promotion effort—personal selling, advertising, and sales promotion—to help sell the whole marketing mix to possible channel members.

Qualifying dimensions the dimensions that are relevant to including a customer-type in a product-market.

Qualitative research seeks in-depth, open-ended responses, not yes or no answers.

Quality a product's ability to satisfy a customer's needs or requirements.

Quantitative research seeks structured responses that can be summarized in numbers (e.g., percentages, averages, or other statistics).

Quantity discounts discounts offered to encourage customers to buy in larger amounts.

Quotas the specific quantities of products that can move in or out of a country.

Rack jobbers merchant wholesalers who specialize in hard-to-handle assortments of products that a retailer doesn't want to manage—and who often display the products on their own wire racks.

Random sampling each member of the research population has the *same* chance of being included in the sample.

Raw materials unprocessed expense items—such as logs, iron ore, wheat, and cotton—that are moved to the next production process with little handling.

Rebates refunds to consumers after a purchase.

Receiver the target of a message in the communication process, usually a potential customer.

Reciprocity trading sales for sales—that is, "If you buy from me, I'll buy from you."

Reference group the people to whom an individual looks when forming attitudes about a particular topic.

Reference price the price a consumer expects to pay.

Refusal to supply when a buyer cannot obtain, on the usual terms, a product not generally in short supply. Under certain conditions, the Competition Tribunal can require sellers to provide the product.

Regrouping activities adjusting the quantities and/or assortments of products handled at each level in a channel of distribution.

Regularly unsought products products that stay unsought but not unbought forever.

Reinforcement occurs in the learning process when the consumer's response is followed by satisfaction—that is, reduction in the drive.

Reminder advertising advertising to keep the product's name before the public.

Requisition a request to buy something.

Research proposal a plan that specifies what marketing research information will be obtained and how.

Resident buyers independent buying agents who work in central markets for several retailer or wholesaler customers based in outlying areas or other countries.

Response an effort to satisfy a drive.

Response rate the percentage of people contacted in a research sample who complete the questionnaire.

Retailing all of the activities involved in the sale of products to final consumers.

Return when a customer sends back purchased products.

Return on assets (ROA) the ratio of net profit (after taxes) to the assets used to make the net profit, multiplied by 100 to get rid of decimals.

Return on investment (ROI) ratio of net profit (after taxes) to the investment used to make the net profit, multiplied by 100 to get rid of decimals.

Reverse channels channels used to retrieve products that customers no longer want.

Risk taking bearing the uncertainties that are part of the marketing process.

Routinized response behaviour when consumers regularly select a particular way of satisfying a need when it occurs.

Rule for maximizing profit the highest profit is earned at the price where marginal cost is just less than or equal to marginal revenue.

Safety needs needs concerned with protection and physical well-being.

Sale price a temporary discount from the list price.

Sales analysis a detailed breakdown of a company's sales records.

Sales decline a stage of the product life cycle when new products replace the old.

Sales era a time when a company emphasizes selling because of increased competition.

Sales forecast an estimate of how much an industry or firm hopes to sell to a market segment.

Sales managers managers concerned with managing personal selling.

Sales-oriented objective an objective to get some level of unit sales, dollar sales, or share of market, without referring to profit.

Sales presentation a salesperson's effort to make a sale or address a customer's problem.

Sales promotion those promotion activities, other than advertising, publicity, and personal selling, that stimulate interest, trial, or purchase by final customers or others in the channel.

Sales promotion managers managers of a company's sales promotion efforts.

Sales quota the specific sales or profit objective a salesperson is expected to achieve.

Sales territory a geographic area that is the responsibility of one salesperson or several working together.

Sample a part of the relevant population.

Sampling buying looking at only part of a potential purchase.

Scientific method a decision-making approach that focuses on being objective and orderly in *testing* ideas before accepting them.

Scrambled merchandising retailers carrying any product lines that they think they can sell profitably.

Search engine a computer program that helps a marketing manager find information that is needed.

Seasonal discounts discounts offered to encourage buyers to buy earlier than present demand requires.

Secondary data information that has been collected or published already.

Segmenters aim at one or more homogeneous segments and try to develop a different marketing mix for each segment.

Segmenting an aggregating process that clusters people with similar needs into a market segment.

Selective demand demand for a company's own brand rather than a product category.

Selective distribution selling through only those middlemen who will give the product special attention.

Selective exposure our eyes and minds seek out and notice only information that interests us.

Selective perception people screen out or modify ideas, messages, and information that conflict with previously learned attitudes and beliefs.

Selective retention people remember only what they want to remember.

Selling agents agent middlemen who take over the whole marketing job of producers, not just the selling function.

Selling formula approach a sales presentation that starts with a prepared presentation outline—much like the prepared approach—and leads the customer through some logical steps to a final close.

Selling function promoting the product.

Senior citizens people over 65.

Service a deed performed by one party for another.

Service mark those words, symbols, or marks that are legally registered for use by a single company to refer to a service offering.

Service wholesalers merchant wholesalers who provide all the wholesaling functions.

Shopping products products that a customer feels are worth the time and effort to compare with competing products.

Simple trade era a time when families traded or sold their surplus output to local middlemen, who then resold these goods to other consumers or distant middlemen.

Single-line (or general-line) wholesalers service wholesalers who carry a narrower line of merchandise than general merchandise wholesalers.

Single-line stores stores that specialize in certain lines of related products rather than a wide assortment—sometimes called limited-line stores.

Single target market approach segmenting the market and picking one of the homogeneous segments as the firm's target market.

Situation analysis an informal study of what information is already available in the problem area.

Skimming price policy trying to sell the top of the market—the top of the demand curve—at a high price before aiming at more price-sensitive customers.

Social class a group of people who have approximately equal social position as viewed by others in the society.

Social needs needs concerned with love, friendship, status, and esteem—things that involve a person's interaction with others.

Social responsibility a firm's obligation to increase its positive effects on society and reduce its negative effects.

Sorting separating products into grades and qualities desired by different target markets.

Source the sender of a message.

Specialty products consumer products that the customer really wants and makes a special effort to find.

Specialty shop a type of conventional limited-line store—usually small and with a distinct personality.

Specialty wholesalers service wholesalers who carry a very narrow range of products and offer more information and service than other service wholesalers.

Spreadsheet analysis organizing costs, sales, and other information into a data table to show how changing the value of one or more numbers affects the other numbers.

Standardization and grading sorting products according to size and quality.

Staples products that are bought often, routinely, and without much thought.

Statistical packages easy-to-use computer programs that analyze data.

Status quo objectives "don't-rock-the-*pricing*-boat" objectives.

Stock a share in the ownership of a company.

Stocking allowances allowances given to middlemen to get shelf space for a product—sometimes called slotting allowances.

Stockturn rate the number of times the average inventory is sold during a year.

Storing the marketing function of holding goods.

Storing function holding goods until customers need them.

Straight rebuy a routine repurchase that may have been made many times before.

Strategic business unit (SBU) an organizational unit (within a larger company) that focuses its efforts on some product-markets and is treated as a separate profit centre.

Strategic (management) planning the managerial process of developing and maintaining a match between an organization's resources and its market opportunities.

Substitutes products that offer the buyer a choice.

Supercentres very large stores that try to carry not only foods and drug items, but all goods and services that the consumer purchases *routinely* (also called hypermarkets).

Supermarkets large stores specializing in groceries, with self-service and wide assortments.

Supplies expense items that do not become part of a finished product.

Supply curve the quantity of products that will be supplied at various possible prices.

Supporting salespeople salespeople who help the order-oriented salespeople but don't try to get orders themselves.

S.W.O.T. analysis identifies and lists the firm's strengths and weaknesses and its opportunities and threats.

Syndicated data is collected by specialist firms and then sold on a shared cost basis to companies with the same type of data needs.

Target market a fairly homogeneous (similar) group of customers to whom a company wishes to appeal.

Target marketing a marketing mix is tailored to fit some specific target customers.

Target return objective a specific level of profit as an objective.

Target return pricing pricing to cover all costs and achieve a target return.

Tariffs taxes on imported products.

Task method an approach to developing a budget—basing the budget on the job to be done.

Task transfer using telecommunications to move service operations to places where there are pools of skilled workers.

Task utility provided when someone performs a task for someone else—for instance, when a bank handles financial transactions.

Team selling different sales reps working together on a specific account.

Technical specialists supporting salespeople who provide technical assistance to order-oriented salespeople.

Technology the application of science to convert an economy's resources to output.

Telemarketing using the telephone to call on customers or prospects.

Television retailing involves either the use on regular channels of commericals encouraging immediate purchase or the promotion of items over home shopping networks.

Telephone and direct-mail retailing allows consumers to shop at home, usually by placing orders by mail or a toll-free long-distance telephone call and charging the purchase to a credit card.

Time series historical records of the fluctuations in economic variables.

Time utility having the product available *when* the customer wants it.

Total cost the sum of total fixed and total variable costs.

Total cost approach evaluating each possible PD system and identifying *all* of the costs of each alternative.

Total fixed cost the sum of those costs that are fixed in total, no matter how much is produced.

Total quality management (TQM) a management approach in which everyone in the organization is concerned about quality, throughout all of the firm's activities, to better serve customer needs.

Total variable cost the sum of those changing expenses that are closely related to output, such as expenses for parts, wages, packaging materials, outgoing freight, and sales commissions.

Trade (functional) discount a list price reduction given to channel members for the job they are going to do.

Trade-in allowance a price reduction given for used products when similar new products are bought.

Trademark those words, symbols, or marks that are legally registered for use by a single company.

Trademarks Act when a trademark is registered under this Act, the registering firm is legally protected against any other company using a trademark that might be confused with its own.

Traditional channel systems a channel in which the various channel members make little or no effort to cooperate with each other.

Transporting the marketing function of moving goods.

Transporting function the movement of goods from one place to another.

Trend extension extends past experience to predict the future.

Truck wholesalers wholesalers who specialize in delivering products that they stock in their own trucks.

2/10, net 30 allows a 2 percent discount off the face value of the invoice if the invoice is paid within 10 days.

Unfair trade practice acts put a lower limit on prices, especially at the wholesale and retail levels.

Uniform delivered pricing making an average freight charge to all buyers.

Unit-pricing placing the price per ounce (or some other standard measure) on or near the product.

Universal functions of marketing buying, selling, transporting, storing, standardizing and grading, financing, risk taking, and market information.

Universal product code (UPC) special identifying marks for each product, readable by electronic scanners.

Unsought products products that potential customers don't yet want or know they can buy.

Utility the power to satisfy human needs.

Validity the extent to which data measures what it is intended to measure.

Value-in-use pricing setting prices that will capture some of what customers will save by substituting the firm's product for the one currently being used.

Value pricing setting a fair price level for a marketing mix that really gives the target market superior customer value.

Vendor analysis formal rating of suppliers on all relevant areas of performance.

Vertical integration acquiring firms at different levels of channel activity.

Vertical marketing systems channel systems in which the whole channel focuses on the same target market at the end of the channel.

Virtual corporation the firm is primarily a coordinator—with a good marketing concept—instead of a producer.

Voluntary chains wholesaler-sponsored groups that work with independent retailers.

Wants needs that are learned during a person's life.

Warranty what the seller promises about its product.

Wheel of retailing theory new types of retailers enter the market as low-status, low-margin, low-price operators and then—if successful—evolve into more conventional retailers offering more services with higher operating costs and higher prices.

Wholesalers firms whose main function is providing *wholesaling activities.*

Wholesaling the *activities* of those persons or establishments that sell to retailers and other merchants, and/or to industrial, institutional, and commercial users, but who do not sell in large amounts to final consumers.

Wholly owned subsidiary a separate firm owned by a parent company.

World Trade Organization (WTO) the only international body dealing with the rules of trade between nations.

Working capital money to pay for short-term expenses such as employee salaries, advertising, marketing research, inventory storing costs, and what the firm owes suppliers.

Zone pricing making an average freight charge to all buyers within specific geographic areas.

Illustration Credits

Chapter 1
Photos/ads: P.2, Limited Snowboards Inc. logo reproduced with permission. P.4, Photography by: Scott Serfas, © 1997. Rider: Etienne Tremblay, Limited Team Rider, at Blackcomb, B.C. P.7, Basketball Ontario ad used with permission. P.20, L.L. Bean catalogue cover used with permission. P.21, Courtesy of Geoffrey B. Roche & Partners.

Chapter 2
Photos/ads: P.29, Reproduced with permission of Bombardier Inc. P.40, Courtesy of Timex Corporation. P.42, Courtesy of W.K. Buckley Limited. Ads created by Bensimone/Byrne. P.44, Reprinted with permission: Andersen Consulting.

Chapter 3
Photos/ads: P.69, Courtesy of the International Institute for Management Development. P.78, © Province of British Columbia. Created and produced for the B.C. Ministry of Forests' Fire Protection Program, 1996, by BBDO, Vancouver, B.C.

Chapter 4
Photos/ads: P.87, Used with permission of Health Canada. P.109, Courtesy of Colgate-Palmolive Company. P.111, The Target System #1: courtesy of TVA Communication.

Chapter 5
Photos/ads: P.135, Reproduced by permission from Laurentian University.

Chapter 6
Photos/ads: P.149, Little Spice Girls photo by Greg Henkenhaf/Toronto Sun. P.152, Courtesy of Great Brands of Europe, Inc. P.161, Used with permission of General Motors of Canada Ltd.

Chapter 7
Photos/ads: P.173, Logo for Canada's 50 Best Managed Private Companies reproduced with permission from Arthur Andersen. P.176, Artwork provided by the Purchasing Management Association of Canada. P.178, Both photos © Roger Ball Photography. P.183, Courtesy of Canadian Airlines International Ltd. P.186, Courtesy of Rentway Ltd. P.191, Courtesy of Lukens Steel Company. P.195, Courtesy of Saskatchewan Wheat Pool and McKay Goettler Miley Communications. P.199, Courtesy of Contracts Canada.

Chapter 8
Photos/ads: P.206, © 1997 CALVIN KLEIN COSMETIC CORPORATION. CK ONE AND DESIGN is a registered trademark of Calvin Klein Trademark Trust, used under license. P.217, Courtesy of Vince the Mover.

Chapter 9
Photos/ads: P.231, Courtesy of Holt Renfrew. P.235, Both photos courtesy of Imasco Limited. P.239, Courtesy of Participaction. P.248, Courtesy of The Thomas Pigeon Design Group.

Chapter 10
Photos/ads: P.259, Used with permission of Nestlé Canada. P.262, Courtesy of Sony Corporation. P.269, Reprinted with permission of Kellogg Canada Inc. P.271, Both ads courtesy of 3M. P.273, © 1994 Louis Psihoyos/Matrix.

Chapter 11
Photos/ads: P.281, Courtesy of Lenore Spence. P.290, Photo by Caroline Parson/Liaison International/courtesy of GE. P.292, Courtesy of Bruno's. P.296, Both photos courtesy of Colgate-Palmolive Company.

Chapter 12
Photos/ads: P.305, Photo by Peter Battistoni/Vancouver Sun. P.318, Courtesy of Canadian Freightways Limited. P.319, Courtesy of Hyundai Motor America. P.321, Courtesy of Ryder System, Inc. P.325, © Ovak Arslanian.

Chapter 13
Photos/ads: P.331, Courtesy of Roots Canada Ltd. P.333, Courtesy of Ganges Village Market, Salt Spring Island, B.C. P.336, Courtesy of Tilley Endurables. P.343, Courtesy of IKEA North America Services, Inc. P.350, Courtesy of McLane Company, Inc.

Chapter 14
Photos/ads: P.363, Courtesy of Canadian Tire Corporation, Limited. P.366, Used with permission of Canada NewsWire Ltd. P.368, "The Tasting Race" by Giovannina Colalillo. Reprinted with permission from Giovannina Colalillo. P.371, Canon is a registered trademark of Canon Inc. Reprinted with the express written consent of Canon Computer Systems, Inc. All rights reserved. P.372, Courtesy of The National Federation of Coffee Growers of Colombia. P.382, Copyright © The McGraw-Hill Companies.

Chapter 15
Photos/ads: P.393, Courtesy of Mr. Vaughn Wyant, President, Jubilee Ford Sales Ltd., Saskatoon. P.396, Photograph (left) courtesy of Glaxo Holdings. Photograph (right) courtesy of ARAMARK. P.397, Photograph (left) courtesy of Bridgestone/Firestone. Photograph (right) provided by Maytag Corporation. Photographer: Arnold Zann. P.399, © 1998 Ted Goff www.tedgoff.com. P.402, Courtesy of Quebecor Printing. P.409, © 1998 Ted Goff www.tedgoff.com.

Chapter 16

Photos/ads: P.419, Courtesy of Molson Breweries. P.424, Courtesy of Pattison Outdoor, a Division of Jim Pattison Industries Limited. P.427, Courtesy of Mothers Against Drunk Driving, Art Director: Matt Whitfield. P.434, Courtesy of *Chatelaine* Magazine. P.435, Courtesy of Holt Renfrew. P.440, Courtesy of David Carmichael, Paulmac's Pet Food.

Chapter 17

Photos/ads: P.455, Marty Myers, Illustrator. P.466, "Universal Currency Converter" is a trademark of Xenon Laboratories Incorporated. Courtesy of Xenon Laboratories Incorporated. P.467, Courtesy of *Marketing Magazine.* P.468, Courtesy of Cargill, Inc.

Chapter 18

Photos/ads: P.481, Courtesy of Nike Inc. P.483, © 1994 John Harding. P.485, Courtesy of Wal-Mart. P.500, Courtesy of Devito/Verdi, New York. P.501, Courtesy of Gucci America, Inc.

Chapter 19

Photos/ads: P.509, Reprinted with permission and all rights reserved to Kellogg Canada Inc. P.514, © 1994 Intel Corporation. P.529, Courtesy of American International Group, Inc.

Chapter 20

Photos/ads: P.535, Photo by Bill Keay/Vancouver Sun. P.545, Courtesy of the National Quality Institute. Mediaplus Advertising, Ottawa, Canada. P.549, Courtesy of Information Resources Inc.

Chapter 21

Photos/ads: P.565 to 568, Courtesy of Finning International Inc. P.571, Printed with permission of The Canadian Institute of Chartered Accountants. P.576, ™ ® Kellogg Company © Kellogg Company. P.580, © E. Lee White. P.583, Courtesy of The Timken Company.

Chapter 22

Photos/ads: P.589, Courtesy of the World Business Council for Sustainable Development. P.592, Courtesy of The David Suzuki Foundation. P.598, Robin Moyer/Time Magazine. P.599, Courtesy of Colgate-Palmolive Company. P.603, Courtesy of Young & Rubicam Gmbh. P.606, Courtesy of Sensormatic Corporation: Agency Daniel & Roberts, Inc.

Author Index

A

B

L

M

N

O

P

Q

R

S

T

Subject Index

N

S

URL Index